D1629578

1000 CLASSIC

RECIPES

FOR EVERY COOK

1000 CLASSIC

RECIPES

FOR EVERY COOK

p

INTRODUCTION

This book contains 1000 classic recipes from all around the world. Each recipe contains the following information: nutritional calculations, preparation and cooking times and level of difficulty (one chef's hat means an easy recipe, rising to five chef's hats which is difficult).

Basic Recipes

The following recipes form the basis of many recipes in the book.

Cornflour (Cornstarch) Paste

Cornflour (cornstarch) paste is made by mixing 1 part cornflour (cornstarch) with about 1½ parts of cold water. Stir the mixture until smooth. The paste is used to thicken sauces.

Basic Pasta Dough

450 g/1 lb/4 cups durum wheat flour
4 eggs, lightly beaten
1 tbsp olive oil
salt

1 Lightly flour a work surface (counter). Sift the flour with a pinch of salt into a mound. Make a well in the centre and add the eggs and olive oil. Using a fork or your fingertips, gradually work the mixture until the ingredients are combined. Knead vigorously for 10-15 minutes

2 Set the dough aside to rest for 25 minutes, before rolling it out as thinly and evenly as possible.

Béchamel Sauce

600 m/1 pint/2½ cups
4 cloves
1 bay leaf
pinch of freshly grated nutmeg
25 g/1 oz/2 tbsp butter or margarine
25 g/1 oz/2 tbsp plain (all-purpose) flour
salt and pepper

1 Put the milk in a saucepan and add the coves, bay leaf and nutmeg. Gradually bring to the boil. Remove from the heat and leave for 15 minutes.

2 Melt the butter or margarine in another saucepan and stir in the flour to make a roux. Cook, stirring, for 1 minute. Remove the pan from the heat.

3 Strain the milk and gradually blend into the roux. Return the pan to the heat and bring to the boil, stirring, until the sauce thickens. Season with salt and pepper to taste and add any flavourings.

Basic Tomato Sauce

2 tbsp olive oil
1 small onion, chopped
1 garlic clove, chopped
400 g/14 oz can chopped tomatoes
2 tbsp chopped parsley
1 tsp dried oregano
2 bay leaves
2 tbsp tomato purée (paste)
1 tsp sugar
salt and pepper

1 Heat the oil in a pan over a medium heat and fry the onion for 2-3 minutes or until translucent. Add the garlic and fry for 1 minute. Stir in the chopped tomatoes, parsley, oregano, bay leaves, tomato purée (paste), sugar, and salt and pepper to taste.

2 Bring the sauce to the boil, then simmer, uncovered, for 15–20 minutes or until the sauce has reduced by half. Taste the sauce and adjust the seasoning if necessary. Discard the bay leaves just before serving.

Italian Red Wine Sauce

- 150 ml/¼ pint/⅝ cup Brown Stock (see page 8)
- 150 ml/¼ pint/⅔ cup Espagnole Sauce (see right)
- 125 ml/4 fl oz/½ cup red wine
- 2 tbsp red wine vinegar
- 4 tbsp shallots, chopped
- 1 bay leaf
- 1 thyme sprig
- pepper

1 First make a demi-glace sauce. Put the Brown Stock and Espagnole Sauce in a pan and heat for 10 minutes, stirring occasionally.

2 Meanwhile, put the red wine, red wine vinegar, shallots, bay leaf and thyme in a pan, bring to the boil and reduce by three-quarters.

3 Strain the demi-glace sauce and add to the pan containing the Red Wine Sauce and leave to simmer for 20 minutes, stirring occasionally. Season with pepper to taste and strain the sauce before using.

Espagnole Sauce

- 2 tbsp butter
- 25 g/1 oz/¼ cup plain (all-purpose) flour
- 1 tsp tomato purée (paste)
- 250 ml/9 fl oz/1⅛ cups hot veal stock
- 1 tbsp Madeira
- 1½ tsp white wine vinegar
- 2 tbsp olive oil
- 25 g/1 oz bacon, diced
- 25 g/1 oz carrot, diced
- 25 g/1 oz onion, diced
- 15 g/½ oz celery, diced
- 15 g/½ oz leek, diced
- 15 g/½ oz fennel, diced
- 1 fresh thyme sprig
- 1 bay leaf

1 Melt the butter in a pan, add the flour and cook, stirring, until lightly coloured. Add the tomato purée (paste), then stir in the hot veal stock, Madeira and white wine vinegar and cook for 2 minutes.

2 Heat the oil in a separate pan, add the bacon, carrot, onion, celery, leek, fennel, thyme sprig and bay leaf and fry until the vegetables have softened. Remove the vegetables from the pan with a slotted spoon and drain thoroughly. Add the vegetables to the sauce and leave to simmer for 4 hours, stirring occasionally. Strain the sauce before using.

Italian Cheese Sauce

- 2 tbsp butter
- 25 g/1 oz/¼ cup plain (all-purpose) flour
- 300 ml/½ pint/1¼ cups hot milk
- pinch of nutmeg
- pinch of dried thyme
- 2 tbsp white wine vinegar
- 3 tbsp double (heavy) cream
- 60 g/2 oz/½ cup grated Mozzarella cheese
- 60 g/2 oz/½ cup Parmesan cheese
- 1 tsp English mustard
- 2 tbsp soured cream
- salt and pepper

1 Melt the butter in a pan and stir in the flour. Cook, stirring, over a low heat until the roux is light in colour and crumbly in texture. Stir in the hot milk and cook, stirring, for 15 minutes until thick and smooth.

2 Add the nutmeg, thyme, white wine vinegar and season to taste. Stir in the cream and mix well.

3 Stir in the cheeses, mustard and cream and mix until the cheeses have melted and blended into the sauce.

Fresh Fish Stock

MAKES 1.75 LITRES/3 PINTS/7½ CUPS

1 head of a cod or salmon, etc, plus the trimmings, skin and bones or just the trimmings, skin and bones
1-2 onions, sliced
1 carrot, sliced
1-2 celery sticks, sliced
good squeeze of lemon juice
1 bouquet garni or 2 fresh or dried bay leaves

1 Wash the fish head and trimmings and place in a saucepan. Cover with water and bring to the boil.

2 Remove any scum with a perforated spoon, then add the remaining ingredients. Cover and simmer for about 30 minutes.

3 Strain and cool. Store in ther refrigerator and use within 2 days.

Brown Stock

Roast veal bones and shin of beef with dripping (drippings) in the oven for 40 minutes. Transfer the bones to a large pan and add sliced leeks, onion, celery and carrots, a bouquet garni, white wine vinegar and a thyme sprig and cover with cold water. Simmer over a very low heat for about 3 hours. Strain and blot the fat from the surface with kitchen paper.

Chinese Stock

This basic stock is used in Chinese cooking not only as the basis for soup-making, but also whenever liquid is required instead of plain water.

MAKES 2.5L/4½ PINTS/10 CUPS

750 g/1 lb 10 oz chicken pieces
750 g/1 lb 10 oz pork spare ribs
3.75 litres/6½ pints/15 cups cold water
3-4 pieces ginger root, crushed
3-4 spring onions (scallions), each tied into a knot
3-4 tbsp Chinese rice wine or dry sherry

1 Trim off any excess fat from the chicken and spare ribs; chop them into large pieces.

2 Place the chicken and pork in a large pan with the water; add the ginger and spring onion (scallion) knots.

3 Bring to the boil, and skim off the scum. Reduce the heat and simmer uncovered for at least 2-3 hours.

4 Strain the stock, discarding the chicken, pork, ginger and spring onions (scallions); add the wine and return to the boil, simmer for 2-3 minutes.

5 Refrigerate the stock when cool; it will keep for up to 4-5 days. Alternatively, it can be frozen in small containers and be defrosted as required.

Fresh Vegetable Stock

This can be kept chilled for up to three days or frozen for up to three months. Salt is not added when cooking the stock: it is better to season it according to the dish in which it its to be used.

MAKES 1.5 LITRES/2¾ PINTS/6¼ CUPS

250 g/9 oz shallots
1 large carrot, diced
1 celery stalk, chopped
½ fennel bulb
1 garlic clove
1 bay leaf
a few fresh parsley and tarragon sprigs
2 litres/ 3½ pints/8¾ cups water
pepper

1 Put all the ingredients in a large saucepan and bring to the boil.

2 Skim off the surface scum with a flat spoon and reduce to a gentle simmer. Partially cover and cook for 45 minutes. Leave to cool.

3 Line a sieve (strainer) with clean muslin (cheesecloth) and put over a large jug or bowl. Pour the stock through the sieve (strainer). Discard the herbs and vegetables.

4 Cover and store in small quantities in the refrigerator for up to three days.

Fresh Beef Stock

MAKES: 1.75 LITRES/3 PINTS/7½ CUPS

about 1 kg/2 lb 4 oz bones from a cooked joint or raw chopped beef
2 onions, studded with 6 cloves, or sliced or chopped coarsely
2 carrots, sliced
1 leek, sliced
1–2 celery sticks, sliced
1 bouquet garni
about 2.25 litres/4 pints/2 quarts water

1 Use chopped marrow bones with a few strips of shin of beef if possible. Put in a roasting tin (pan) and cook in a preheated oven at 230°C/450°F/Gas Mark 8 for 30–50 minutes until browned.

2 Transfer to a large saucepan with the other ingredients. Bring to the boil and remove any scum from the surface with a perforated spoon.

3 Cover and simmer gently for 3–4 hours. Strain the stock and leave to cool. Remove any fat from the surface and chill. If stored for more than 24 hours the stock must be boiled every day, cooled quickly and chilled again.

4 The stock may be frozen for up to 2 months; place in a large plastic bag and seal, leaving at least 2.5 cm/1 inch of headspace to allow for expansion.

Fresh Chicken Stock

MAKES 1.75 LITRES/3 PINTS/7½ CUPS

1 kg/2 lb 4 oz chicken, skinned
2 celery sticks
1 onion
2 carrots
1 garlic clove
few sprigs of fresh parsley
2 litres/3½ pints/9 cups water
salt and pepper

1 Put all the ingredients into a large saucepan.

2 Bring to the boil. Skim away surface scum using a large flat spoon. Reduce the heat to a gentle simmer, partially cover, and cook for 2 hours. Allow to cool.

3 Line a sieve (strainer) with clean muslin (cheesecloth) and place over a large jug or bowl. Pour the stock through the sieve (strainer). The cooked chicken can be used in another recipe. Discard the other solids. Cover the stock and chill.

4 Skim away any fat that forms before using. Store in the refrigerator for 3-4 days, until required, or freeze in small batches.

Fresh Lamb Stock

MAKES 1.75 LITRES/3 PINTS/7½ CUPS

about 1 kg/2 lb 4 oz bones from a cooked joint or raw chopped lamb bones
2 onions, studded with 6 cloves, or sliced or chopped coarsely
2 carrots, sliced
1 leek, sliced
1-2 celery sticks, sliced
1 bouquet garni
about 2.25 litres/4 pints/2 quarts water

1 Chop or break up the bones and place in a large saucepan with the other ingredients.

2 Bring to the boil and remove any scum from the surface with a perforated spoon. Cover and simmer gently for 3-4 hours. Strain the stock and leave to cool.

3 Remove any fat from the surface and chill. If stored for more than 24 hours the stock must be boiled every day, cooled quickly and chilled again. The stock may be frozen for up to 2 months; place in a large plastic bag and seal, leaving at least 2.5 cm/1 inch of headspace to allow for expansion.

Soups & Starters

The traditional way to begin a meal is with a soup or starter, carefully selected to complement the following courses. In this chapter you will find a range of delicious soups from around the world to suit any occasion, for example Spicy Dal & Carrot Soup which is a variation of Indian dal, Louisiana Seafood Gumbo from New Orleans or the classic French soup, Vichysoisse. A good piece of advice, although it takes a little longer, it is always worth making your own stock to form the basis of your soups; ready-made stock cubes or granules often contain large quantities of salt and flavourings. If you prefer something other than soup there is also a range of delicious starters in this chapter, such as Spinach & Ricotta Cheese Patties or Salsa & Tortilla Chips.

Chicken & Sweetcorn Soup

A hint of chilli and sherry flavour this soup while red (bell) pepper and tomato add colour.

NUTRITIONAL INFORMATION

Calories	199	Sugars	8g
Protein	12g	Fat	8g
Carbohydrate	19g	Saturates	1g

 5 MINS  20 MINS

SERVES 4

INGREDIENTS

- 1 skinless, boneless chicken breast, about 175 g/6 oz
- 2 tbsp sunflower oil
- 2–3 spring onions (scallions), thinly sliced diagonally
- 1 small or ½ large red (bell) pepper, thinly sliced
- 1 garlic clove, crushed
- 125 g/4½ oz baby sweetcorn (corn-on-the-cob), thinly sliced
- 1 litre/1¾ pints/4 cups chicken stock
- 200 g/7 oz can of sweetcorn niblets, well drained
- 2 tbsp sherry
- 2–3 tsp bottled sweet chilli sauce
- 2–3 tsp cornflour (cornstarch)
- 2 tomatoes, quartered and deseeded, then sliced
- salt and pepper
- chopped fresh coriander (cilantro) or parsley, to garnish

1 Cut the chicken breast into 4 strips lengthways, then cut each strip into narrow slices across the grain.

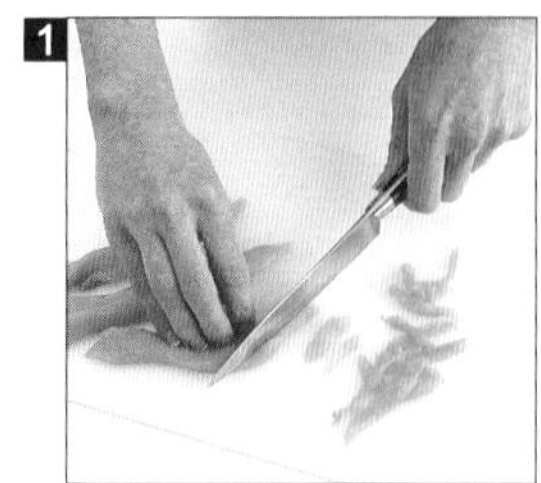

2 Heat the oil in a wok or frying pan (skillet), swirling it around until it is really hot.

3 Add the chicken and stir-fry for 3–4 minutes, moving it around the wok until it is well sealed all over and almost cooked through.

4 Add the spring onions (scallions), (bell) pepper and garlic, and stir-fry for 2–3 minutes. Add the sweetcorn and stock and bring to the boil.

5 Add the sweetcorn niblets, sherry, sweet chilli sauce and salt to taste, and simmer for 5 minutes, stirring from time to time.

6 Blend the cornflour (cornstarch) with a little cold water. Add to the soup and bring to the boil, stirring until the sauce is thickened. Add the tomato slices, season to taste and simmer for 1–2 minutes.

7 Serve the chicken and sweetcorn soup hot, sprinkled with chopped coriander (cilantro) or parsley.

Chicken Soup with Almonds

This soup can also be made using pheasant breasts. For a really gamy flavour, make game stock from the carcass and use in the soup.

NUTRITIONAL INFORMATION

Calories	219	Sugars	2g
Protein	18g	Fat	15g
Carbohydrate	2g	Saturates	2g

10 MINS

20 MINS

SERVES 4

INGREDIENTS

- 1 large or 2 small boneless skinned chicken breasts
- 1 tbsp sunflower oil
- 4 spring onions (scallions), thinly sliced diagonally
- 1 carrot, cut into julienne strips
- 700 ml/1¼ pints/3 cups chicken stock
- finely grated rind of ½ lemon
- 40 g/1½ oz/⅓ cup ground almonds
- 1 tbsp light soy sauce
- 1 tbsp lemon juice
- 25 g/1 oz/¼ cup flaked almonds, toasted
- salt and pepper

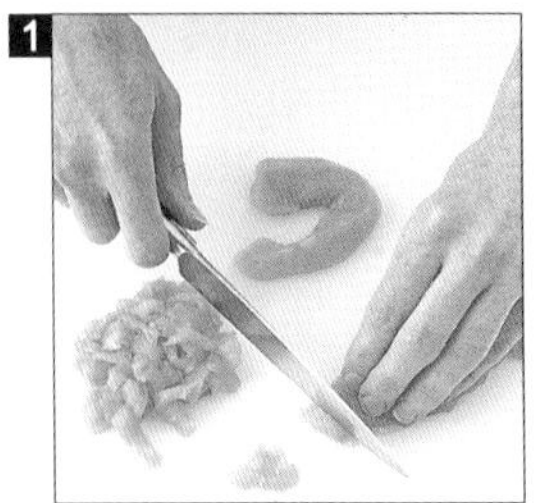
1

3

3

1 Cut each breast into 4 strips lengthways, then slice very thinly across the grain to give shreds of chicken.

2 Heat the oil in a wok, swirling it around until really hot.

3 Add the spring onions (scallions) and cook for 2 minutes, then add the chicken and toss it for 3-4 minutes until sealed and almost cooked through, stirring all the time. Add the carrot strips and stir.

4 Add the stock to the wok and bring to the boil. Add the lemon rind, ground almonds, soy sauce, lemon juice and plenty of seasoning. Bring back to the boil and simmer, uncovered, for 5 minutes, stirring from time to time.

5 Adjust the seasoning, add most of the toasted flaked almonds and continue to cook for a further 1-2 minutes.

6 Serve the soup very hot, in individual bowls, sprinkled with the remaining flaked almonds.

COOK'S TIP

To make game stock, break up a pheasant carcass and place in a pan with 2 litres/3½ pints/8 cups water. Bring to the boil slowly, skimming off any scum. Add 1 bouquet garni, 1 peeled onion and seasoning. Cover and simmer gently for 1½ hours. Strain, and skim any surface fat.

Lemon & Chicken Soup

This delicately flavoured summer soup is surprisingly easy to make, and tastes delicious.

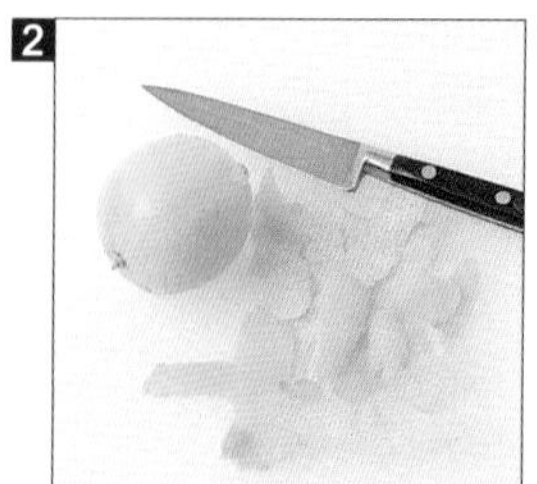

NUTRITIONAL INFORMATION

Calories	506	Sugars	4g
Protein	19g	Fat	31g
Carbohydrate	41g	Saturates	19g

 5-10 MINS  1¼ HOURS

SERVES 4

INGREDIENTS

- 60 g/2 oz/4 tbsp butter
- 8 shallots, thinly sliced
- 2 carrots, thinly sliced
- 2 celery sticks (stalks), thinly sliced
- 225 g/8 oz boned chicken breasts, finely chopped
- 3 lemons
- 1.2 litres/2 pints/5 cups chicken stock
- 225 g/8 oz dried spaghetti, broken into small pieces
- 150 ml/¼ pint/⅝ cup double (heavy) cream
- salt and white pepper

TO GARNISH

- fresh parsley sprig
- 3 lemon slices, halved

1 Melt the butter in a large saucepan. Add the shallots, carrots, celery and chicken and cook over a low heat, stirring occasionally, for 8 minutes.

2 Thinly pare the lemons and blanch the lemon rind in boiling water for 3 minutes. Squeeze the juice from the lemons.

3 Add the lemon rind and juice to the pan, together with the chicken stock. Bring slowly to the boil over a low heat and simmer for 40 minutes, stirring occasionally.

4 Add the spaghetti to the pan and cook for 15 minutes. Season to taste with salt and white pepper and add the cream. Heat through, but do not allow the soup to boil or it will curdle.

5 Pour the soup into a tureen or individual bowls, garnish with the parsley and half slices of lemon and serve immediately.

COOK'S TIP

You can prepare this soup up to the end of step 3 in advance, so that all you need do before serving is heat it through before adding the pasta and the finishing touches.

Chicken & Pasta Broth

This satisfying soup makes a good lunch or supper dish and you can use any vegetables you like. Children will love the tiny pasta shapes.

NUTRITIONAL INFORMATION

Calories	185	Sugars	5g
Protein	17g	Fat	5g
Carbohydrate	20g	Saturates	1g

 5 MINS  15-20 MINS

SERVES 6

INGREDIENTS

- 350 g/12 oz boneless chicken breasts
- 2 tbsp sunflower oil
- 1 medium onion, diced
- 250 g/9 oz/1 ½ cups carrots, diced
- 250 g/9 oz cauliflower florets
- 850 ml/1 ½ pints/3 ¾ cups chicken stock
- 2 tsp dried mixed herbs
- 125 g/4 ½ oz small pasta shapes
- salt and pepper
- Parmesan cheese (optional) and crusty bread, to serve

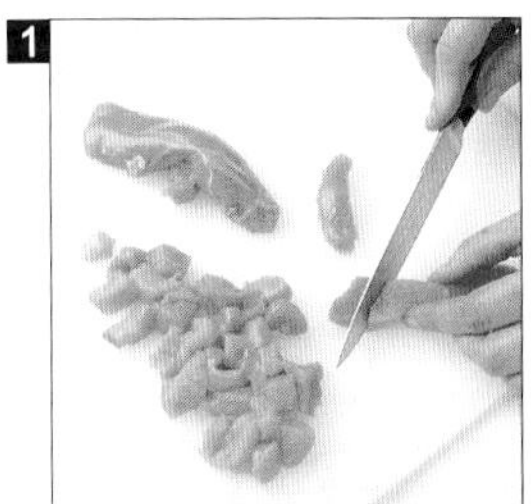

1 Using a sharp knife, finely dice the chicken, discarding any skin.

2 Heat the oil in a large saucepan and quickly sauté the chicken, onion, carrots and cauliflower until they are lightly coloured.

3 Stir in the chicken stock and dried mixed herbs and bring to the boil.

4 Add the pasta shapes to the pan and return to the boil. Cover the pan and leave the broth to simmer for 10 minutes, stirring occasionally to prevent the pasta shapes from sticking together.

5 Season the broth with salt and pepper to taste and sprinkle with Parmesan cheese, if using. Serve the broth with fresh crusty bread.

COOK'S TIP

You can use any small pasta shapes for this soup – try conchigliette or ditalini or even spaghetti broken up into small pieces. To make a fun soup for children you could add animal-shaped or alphabet pasta.

Clear Chicken & Egg Soup

This tasty chicken soup has the addition of poached eggs, making it both delicious and filling. Use fresh, home-made stock for a better flavour.

NUTRITIONAL INFORMATION

Calories	138	Sugars	1g
Protein	16g	Fat	7g
Carbohydrate	1g	Saturates	2g

 5 MINS  35 MINS

SERVES 4

INGREDIENTS

- 1 tsp salt
- 1 tbsp rice wine vinegar
- 4 eggs
- 850 ml/1½ pints/3¾ cups chicken stock
- 1 leek, sliced
- 125 g/4½ oz broccoli florets
- 125 g/4½ oz/1 cup shredded cooked chicken
- 2 open-cap mushrooms, sliced
- 1 tbsp dry sherry
- dash of chilli sauce
- chilli powder, to garnish

1 Bring a large saucepan of water to the boil and add the salt and rice wine vinegar.

2 Reduce the heat so that it is just simmering and carefully break the eggs into the water, one at a time. Poach the eggs for 1 minute.

3 Remove the poached eggs with a slotted spoon and set aside.

4 Bring the chicken stock to the boil in a separate pan and add the leek, broccoli, chicken, mushrooms and sherry and season with chilli sauce to taste. Cook for 10–15 minutes.

5 Add the poached eggs to the soup and cook for a further 2 minutes. Carefully transfer the soup and poached eggs to 4 soup bowls. Dust with a little chilli powder and serve immediately.

VARIATION

You could use 4 dried Chinese mushrooms, rehydrated according to the packet instructions, instead of the open-cap mushrooms, if you prefer.

Chinese Cabbage Soup

This is a piquant soup, which is slightly sweet-and-sour in flavour. It can be served as a hearty meal or appetizer.

NUTRITIONAL INFORMATION

Calories	65	Sugars	7g
Protein	3g	Fat	0.5g
Carbohydrate	11g	Saturates	0.1g

5 MINS 30 MINS

SERVES 4

INGREDIENTS

- 450 g/1 lb pak choi
- 600 ml/1 pint/2½ cups vegetable stock
- 1 tbsp rice wine vinegar
- 1 tbsp light soy sauce
- 1 tbsp caster (superfine) sugar
- 1 tbsp dry sherry
- 1 fresh red chilli, thinly sliced
- 1 tbsp cornflour (cornstarch)
- 2 tbsp water

1 Wash the pak choi thoroughly under cold running water, rinse and drain. Pat dry on kitchen paper (paper towels) .

2 Trim the stems of the pak choi and shred the leaves.

3 Heat the vegetable stock in a large saucepan. Add the pak choi and cook for 10–15 minutes.

4 Mix together the rice wine vinegar, soy sauce, caster (superfine) sugar and sherry in a small bowl. Add this mixture to the stock, together with the sliced chilli.

5 Bring to the boil, lower the heat and cook for 2–3 minutes.

6 Blend the cornflour (cornstarch) with the water to form a smooth paste.

7 Gradually stir the cornflour (cornstarch) mixture into the soup. Cook, stirring constantly, until it thickens. Cook for a further 4–5 minutes.

8 Ladle the Chinese cabbage soup into individual warm serving bowls and serve immediately.

COOKS TIP

Pak choi, also known as bok choi or spoon cabbage, has long, white leaf stalks and fleshy, spoon-shaped, shiny green leaves. There are a number of varieties available, which differ mainly in size rather than flavour.

Lamb & Rice Soup

This is a very filling soup, as it contains rice and tender pieces of lamb. Serve before a light main course.

NUTRITIONAL INFORMATION

Calories	116	Sugars	0.2g
Protein	9g	Fat	4g
Carbohydrate	12g	Saturates	2g

 5 MINS  35 MINS

SERVES 4

INGREDIENTS

- 150 g/5½ oz lean lamb
- 50 g/1¾ oz/¼ cup rice
- 850 ml/1½ pints/3¾ cups lamb stock
- 1 leek, sliced
- 1 garlic clove, thinly sliced
- 2 tsp light soy sauce
- 1 tsp rice wine vinegar
- 1 medium open-cap mushroom, thinly sliced
- salt

1 Using a sharp knife, trim any fat from the lamb and cut the meat into thin strips. Set aside until required.

2 Bring a large pan of lightly salted water to the boil and add the rice. Bring back to the boil, stir once, reduce the heat and cook for 10–15 minutes, until tender.

3 Drain the rice, rinse under cold running water, drain again and set aside until required.

4 Meanwhile, put the lamb stock in a large saucepan and bring to the boil.

5 Add the lamb strips, leek, garlic, soy sauce and rice wine vinegar to the stock in the pan. Reduce the heat, cover and leave to simmer for 10 minutes, or until the lamb is tender and cooked through.

6 Add the mushroom slices and the rice to the pan and cook for a further 2–3 minutes, or until the mushroom is completely cooked through.

7 Ladle the soup into 4 individual warmed soup bowls and serve immediately.

VARIATION

Use a few dried Chinese mushrooms, rehydrated according to the packet instructions and chopped, as an alternative to the open-cap mushroom. Add the Chinese mushrooms with the lamb in step 4.

Potato & Pesto Soup

Fresh pesto is a treat to the taste buds and very different in flavour from that available from supermarkets. Store fresh pesto in the refrigerator.

NUTRITIONAL INFORMATION

Calories	548	Sugars	0g
Protein	11g	Fat	52g
Carbohydrate	10g	Saturates	18g

 5–10 MINS 50 MINS

SERVES 4

INGREDIENTS

- 3 slices rindless, smoked, fatty bacon
- 450 g/1 lb floury potatoes
- 450 g/ 1 lb onions
- 2 tbsp olive oil
- 25 g/1 oz/2 tbsp butter
- 600 ml/1 pint/2 ½ cups chicken stock
- 600 ml/1 pint/2 ½ cups milk
- 100 g/3 ½ oz/ ¾ cup dried conchigliette
- 150 ml/ ¼ pint/ ⅝ cup double (heavy) cream
- chopped fresh parsley
- salt and pepper
- freshly grated Parmesan cheese and garlic bread, to serve

PESTO SAUCE

- 60 g/2 oz/1 cup finely chopped fresh parsley
- 2 garlic cloves, crushed
- 60 g/2 oz/ ⅔ cup pine nuts (kernels), crushed
- 2 tbsp chopped fresh basil leaves
- 60 g/2 oz/ ⅔ cup freshly grated Parmesan cheese
- white pepper
- 150 ml/ ¼ pint/ ⅝ cup olive oil

1 To make the pesto sauce, put all of the ingredients in a blender or food processor and process for 2 minutes, or blend by hand using a pestle and mortar.

2 Finely chop the bacon, potatoes and onions. Fry the bacon in a large pan over a medium heat for 4 minutes. Add the butter, potatoes and onions and cook for 12 minutes, stirring constantly.

3 Add the stock and milk to the pan, bring to the boil and simmer for 10 minutes. Add the conchigliette and simmer for a further 10-12 minutes.

4 Blend in the cream and simmer for 5 minutes. Add the parsley, salt and pepper and 2 tbsp pesto sauce. Transfer the soup to serving bowls and serve with Parmesan cheese and fresh garlic bread.

Indian Bean Soup

A thick and hearty soup, nourishing and substantial enough to serve as a main meal with wholemeal (whole wheat) bread.

NUTRITIONAL INFORMATION

Calories	237	Sugars	9g
Protein	9g	Fat	9g
Carbohydrate	33g	Saturates	1g

 20 MINS  50 MINS

SERVES 6

INGREDIENTS

- 4 tbsp vegetable ghee or vegetable oil
- 2 onions, peeled and chopped
- 225 g/8 oz/1½ cups potato, cut into chunks
- 225 g/8 oz/1½ cups parsnip, cut into chunks
- 225 g/8 oz/1½ cups turnip or swede (rutabaga), cut into chunks
- 2 celery sticks, sliced
- 2 courgettes (zucchini), sliced
- 1 green (bell) pepper, seeded and cut into 1 cm/½ inch pieces
- 2 garlic cloves, crushed
- 2 tsp ground coriander
- 1 tbsp paprika
- 1 tbsp mild curry paste
- 1.2 litres/2 pints/5 cups vegetable stock
- salt
- 400 g/14 oz can black-eye beans (peas), drained and rinsed
- chopped coriander (cilantro), to garnish (optional)

1 Heat the ghee or oil in a saucepan, add all the prepared vegetables, except the courgettes (zucchini) and green (bell) pepper, and cook over a moderate heat, stirring frequently, for 5 minutes. Add the garlic, ground coriander, paprika and curry paste and cook, stirring constantly, for 1 minute.

2 Stir in the stock and season with salt to taste. Bring to the boil, cover and simmer over a low heat, stirring occasionally, for 25 minutes.

3 Stir in the black-eye beans (peas), sliced courgettes (zucchini) and green (bell) pepper, cover and continue cooking for a further 15 minutes, or until all the vegetables are tender.

4 Process 300 ml/½ pint/1¼ cups of the soup mixture (about 2 ladlefuls) in a food processor or blender. Return the purééd mixture to the soup in the saucepan and reheat until piping hot. Sprinkle with chopped coriander (cilantro), if using and serve hot.

Veal & Ham Soup

Veal and ham is a classic combination, complemented here with the addition of sherry to create a richly-flavoured Italian soup.

NUTRITIONAL INFORMATION

Calories	501	Sugars	10g
Protein	38g	Fat	18g
Carbohydrate	28g	Saturates	10g

 5 MINS  3¼ HOURS

SERVES 4

INGREDIENTS

- 60 g/2 oz/4 tbsp butter
- 1 onion, diced
- 1 carrot, diced
- 1 celery stick (stalk), diced
- 450 g/1 lb veal, very thinly sliced
- 450 g/1 lb ham, thinly sliced
- 60 g/2 oz/½ cup plain (all-purpose) flour
- 1 litre/1¾ pints/4⅜ cups beef stock
- 1 bay leaf
- 8 black peppercorns
- pinch of salt
- 3 tbsp redcurrant jelly
- 150 ml/¼ pint/⅝ cup cream sherry
- 100 g/3½ oz/¾ cup dried vermicelli
- garlic croûtons (see Cook's Tip), to serve

1 Melt the butter in a large pan. Add the onions, carrot, celery, veal and ham and cook over a low heat for 6 minutes.

2 Sprinkle over the flour and cook, stirring constantly, for a further 2 minutes. Gradually stir in the stock, then add the bay leaf, peppercorns and salt. Bring to the boil and simmer for 1 hour.

3 Remove the pan from the heat and add the redcurrant jelly and cream sherry, stirring to combine. Set aside for about 4 hours.

4 Remove the bay leaf from the pan and discard. Reheat the soup over a very low heat until warmed through.

5 Meanwhile, cook the vermicelli in a saucepan of lightly salted boiling water for 10-12 minutes. Stir the vermicelli into the soup and transfer to soup bowls. Serve with garlic croûtons.

COOK'S TIP

To make garlic croûtons, remove the crusts from 3 slices of day-old white bread. Cut the bread into 5 mm/¼ inch cubes. Heat 3 tbsp oil over a low heat and stir-fry 1–2 chopped garlic cloves for 1–2 minutes. Remove the garlic and add the bread. Cook, stirring frequently, until golden. Remove with a slotted spoon and drain.

Chinese Potato & Pork Broth

In this recipe the pork is seasoned with traditional Chinese flavourings – soy sauce, rice wine vinegar and a dash of sesame oil.

NUTRITIONAL INFORMATION

Calories	166	Sugars	2g
Protein	10g	Fat	5g
Carbohydrate	26g	Saturates	1g

 5 MINS  20 MINS

SERVES 4

INGREDIENTS

- 1 litre/1¾ pints/4½ cups chicken stock
- 2 large potatoes, diced
- 2 tbsp rice wine vinegar
- 2 tbsp cornflour (cornstarch)
- 4 tbsp water
- 125 g/4½ oz pork fillet, sliced
- 1 tbsp light soy sauce
- 1 tsp sesame oil
- 1 carrot, cut into very thin strips
- 1 tsp ginger root, chopped
- 3 spring onions (scallions), sliced thinly
- 1 red (bell) pepper, sliced
- 225 g/8 oz can bamboo shoots, drained

4

5

5

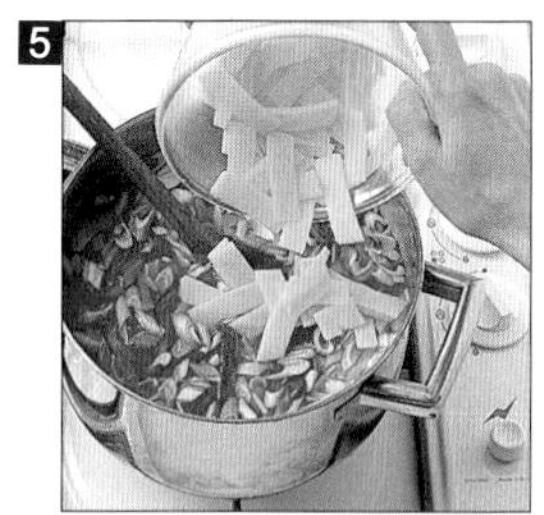

1 Add the chicken stock, diced potatoes and 1 tbsp of the rice wine vinegar to a saucepan and bring to the boil. Reduce the heat until the stock is just simmering.

2 Mix the cornflour (cornstarch) with the water then stir into the hot stock.

3 Bring the stock back to the boil, stirring until thickened, then reduce the heat until it is just simmering again.

4 Place the pork slices in a dish and season with the remaining rice wine vinegar, the soy sauce and sesame oil.

5 Add the pork slices, carrot strips and ginger to the stock and cook for 10 minutes. Stir in the spring onions (scallions), red (bell) pepper and bamboo shoots. Cook for a further 5 minutes. Pour the soup into warmed bowls and serve immediately.

VARIATION

For extra heat, add 1 chopped red chilli or 1 tsp of chilli powder to the soup in step 5.

Mussel & Potato Soup

This quick and easy soup would make a delicious summer lunch, served with fresh crusty bread.

NUTRITIONAL INFORMATION

Calories	804	Sugars	3g
Protein	17g	Fat	68g
Carbohydrate	32g	Saturates	38g

10 MINS 35 MINS

SERVES 4

INGREDIENTS

750 g/1 lb 10 oz mussels
2 tbsp olive oil
100 g/3½ oz/7 tbsp unsalted butter
2 slices rindless fatty bacon, chopped
1 onion, chopped
2 garlic cloves, crushed
60 g/2 oz/½ cup plain (all-purpose) flour
450 g/1 lb potatoes, thinly sliced
100 g/3½ oz/¾ cup dried conchigliette
300 ml/½ pint/1¼ cups double (heavy) cream
1 tbsp lemon juice
2 egg yolks
salt and pepper

TO GARNISH

2 tbsp finely chopped fresh parsley
lemon wedges

1 Debeard the mussels and scrub them under cold water for 5 minutes. Discard any mussels that do not close immediately when sharply tapped.

2 Bring a large pan of water to the boil, add the mussels, oil and a little pepper. Cook until the mussels open. (discard any mussels that remain closed.

3 Drain the mussels, reserving the cooking liquid. Remove the mussels from their shells.

4 Melt the butter in a large saucepan, add the bacon, onion and garlic and cook for 4 minutes. Carefully stir in the flour. Measure 1.2 litres/2 pints/5 cups of the reserved cooking liquid and stir it into the pan.

5 Add the potatoes to the pan and simmer for 5 minutes. Add the conchigliette and simmer for a further 10 minutes.

6 Add the cream and lemon juice, season to taste with salt and pepper, then add the mussels to the pan.

7 Blend the egg yolks with 1-2 tbsp of the remaining cooking liquid, stir into the pan and cook for 4 minutes.

8 Ladle the soup into 4 warm individual soup bowls, garnish with the chopped fresh parsley and lemon wedges and serve immediately.

2

3

6

Spicy Prawn (Shrimp) Soup

Lime leaves are used as a flavouring in this soup to add tartness.

NUTRITIONAL INFORMATION

Calories	217	Sugars	16g
Protein	16g	Fat	4g
Carbohydrate	31g	Saturates	1g

 10 MINS  20 MINS

SERVES 4

INGREDIENTS

- 2 tbsp tamarind paste
- 4 red chilies, very finely chopped
- 2 cloves garlic, crushed
- 2.5 cm/1 inch piece Thai ginger, peeled and very finely chopped
- 4 tbsp fish sauce
- 2 tbsp palm sugar or caster (superfine) sugar
- 1.2 litres/2 pints/5 cups fish stock
- 8 lime leaves
- 100 g/3½ oz carrots, very thinly sliced
- 350 g/12 oz sweet potato, diced
- 100 g/3½ oz/1 cup baby corn cobs, halved
- 3 tbsp fresh coriander (cilantro), roughly chopped
- 100g/3½ oz cherry tomatoes, halved
- 225 g/8 oz fan-tail prawns (shrimp)

1 Place the tamarind paste, red chillies, garlic, ginger, fish sauce, sugar and fish stock in a preheated wok or large, heavy frying pan (skillet). Roughly tear the lime leaves and add to the wok. Bring to the boil, stirring constantly to blend the flavours.

2 Reduce the heat and add the carrot, sweet potato and baby corn cobs to the mixture in the wok.

3 Leave the soup to simmer, uncovered, for about 10 minutes, or until the vegetables are just tender.

4 Stir the coriander (cilantro), cherry tomatoes and prawns (shrimp) into the soup and heat through for 5 minutes.

5 Transfer the soup to a warm soup tureen or individual serving bowls and serve hot.

COOK'S TIP

Thai ginger or galangal is a member of the ginger family, but it is yellow in colour with pink sprouts. The flavour is aromatic and less pungent than ginger.

1

2

4

Shrimp Dumpling Soup

These small dumplings filled with shrimp and pork may be made slightly larger and served as dim sum on their own, if you prefer.

NUTRITIONAL INFORMATION

Calories	311	Sugars	2g
Protein	18g	Fat	8g
Carbohydrate	41g	Saturates	2g

20 MINS

10 MINS

SERVES 4

INGREDIENTS

DUMPLINGS

- 150 g/5½ oz/1⅝ cups plain (all-purpose) flour
- 50 ml/2 fl oz/¼ cup boiling water
- 30 ml/1 fl oz/⅛ cup cold water
- 1½ tsp vegetable oil

FILLING

- 125 g/4½ oz minced (ground) pork
- 125 g/4½ oz cooked peeled shrimp, chopped
- 50 g/1¾ oz canned water chestnuts, drained, rinsed and chopped
- 1 celery stick, chopped
- 1 tsp cornflour (cornstarch)
- 1 tbsp sesame oil
- 1 tbsp light soy sauce

SOUP

- 850 ml/1½ pints/3¾ cups fish stock
- 50 g/1¾ oz cellophane noodles
- 1 tbsp dry sherry
- chopped chives, to garnish

1 To make the dumplings, mix together the flour, boiling water, cold water and oil in a bowl until a pliable dough is formed.

2 Knead the dough on a lightly floured surface for 5 minutes. Cut the dough into 16 equal sized pieces.

3 Roll the dough pieces into rounds about 7.5 cm/ 3 inches in diameter.

4 Mix the filling ingredients together in a large bowl.

5 Spoon a little of the filling mixture into the centre of each round. Bring the edges of the dough together, scrunching them up to form a 'moneybag' shape. Twist the gathered edges to seal.

6 Pour the fish stock into a large saucepan and bring to the boil.

7 Add the cellophane noodles, dumplings and dry sherry to the pan and cook for 4–5 minutes, until the noodles and dumplings are tender. Garnish with chopped chives and serve immediately.

3

5
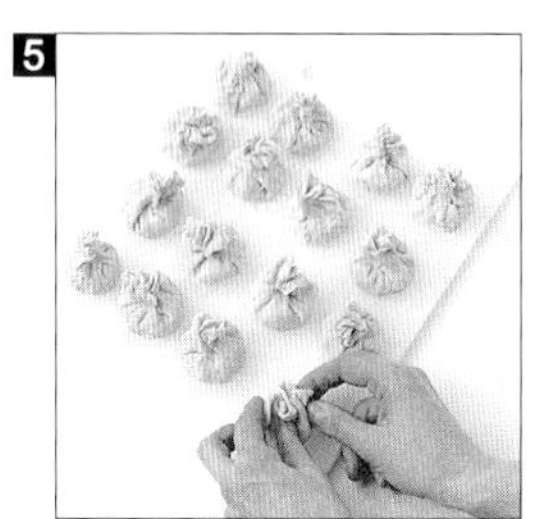

7

Louisiana Seafood Gumbo

Gumbo is a hearty, thick soup, almost a stew. This New Orleans classic must be served with a scoop of hot, fluffy, cooked rice.

NUTRITIONAL INFORMATION

Calories	267	Sugars	6g
Protein	27g	Fat	8g
Carbohydrate	24g	Saturates	1g

 5 MINS  35 MINS

SERVES 4

INGREDIENTS

- 1 tbsp plain flour
- 1 tsp paprika
- 350 g/12 oz monkfish fillets, cut into chunks
- 2 tbsp olive oil
- 1 onion, chopped
- 1 green (bell) pepper, cored, seeded and chopped
- 3 celery sticks, finely chopped
- 2 garlic cloves, crushed
- 175 g/6 oz okra, sliced
- 600 ml/1 pint/2½ cups vegetable stock
- 1 x 425 g/15 oz can chopped tomatoes
- 1 bouquet garni
- 125 g/4½ oz peeled prawns (shrimp)
- juice of 1 lemon
- dash of Tabasco
- 2 tsp Worcestershire sauce
- 175 g/6 oz/generous 1 cup cooked long-grain American rice

1 Mix the flour with the paprika. Add the monkfish chunks and toss to coat well.

2 Heat the olive oil in a large, heavy-based pan. Add the monkfish pieces and fry until browned on all sides. Remove from the pan with a slotted spoon and set aside.

3 Add the onion, green (bell) pepper, celery, garlic and okra and fry gently for 5 minutes until softened.

4 Add the stock, tomatoes and bouquet garni. Bring to the boil, reduce the heat and simmer for 15 minutes.

5 Return the monkfish to the pan with the prawns (shrimp), lemon juice, Tabasco and Worcestershire sauces. Simmer for a further 5 minutes.

6 To serve, place a mound of cooked rice in each warmed, serving bowl, then ladle over the seafood gumbo.

2

3

4

Tuscan Veal Broth

Veal plays an important role in Italian cuisine and there are dozens of recipes for all cuts of this meat.

NUTRITIONAL INFORMATION

Calories	420	Sugars	5g
Protein	54g	Fat	7g
Carbohydrate	37g	Saturates	2g

 2¼ HOURS  4¾ HOURS

SERVES 4

INGREDIENTS

- 60 g/2 oz/⅓ cup dried peas, soaked for 2 hours and drained
- 900 g/2 lb boned neck of veal, diced
- 1.2 litres/2 pints/5 cups beef or brown stock (see Cook's Tip)
- 600 ml/1 pint/2½ cups water
- 60 g/2 oz/⅓ cup barley, washed
- 1 large carrot, diced
- 1 small turnip (about 175 g/6 oz), diced
- 1 large leek, thinly sliced
- 1 red onion, finely chopped
- 100 g/3½ oz chopped tomatoes
- 1 fresh basil sprig
- 100 g/3½ oz/¾ cup dried vermicelli
- salt and white pepper

1 Put the peas, veal, stock and water into a large pan and bring to the boil over a low heat. Using a slotted spoon, skim off any scum that rises to the surface.

2 When all of the scum has been removed, add the barley and a pinch of salt to the mixture. Simmer gently over a low heat for 25 minutes.

3 Add the carrot, turnip, leek, onion, tomatoes and basil to the pan, and season with salt and pepper to taste. Leave to simmer for about 2 hours, skimming the surface from time to time to remove any scum. Remove the pan from the heat and set aside for 2 hours.

4 Set the pan over a medium heat and bring to the boil. Add the vermicelli and cook for 12 minutes. Season with salt and pepper to taste; remove and discard the basil. Ladle into soup bowls and serve immediately.

COOK'S TIP

The best brown stock is made with veal bones and shin of beef roasted with dripping (drippings) in the oven for 40 minutes. Transfer the bones to a pan and add sliced leeks, onion, celery and carrots, a bouquet garni, white wine vinegar and a thyme sprig and cover with cold water. Simmer over a very low heat for 3 hours; strain before use.

Seafood & Tofu Soup

Use prawn (shrimp), squid or scallops, or a combination of all three in this healthy soup.

NUTRITIONAL INFORMATION

Calories	97	Sugars	0g
Protein	17g	Fat	2g
Carbohydrate	3g	Saturates	0.4g

 3½ HOURS  10 MINS

SERVES 4

INGREDIENTS

- 250 g/9 oz seafood: peeled prawns (shrimp), squid, scallops, etc. defrosted if frozen
- ½ egg white, lightly beaten
- 1 tbsp cornflour (cornstarch) paste (see page 6)
- 1 cake tofu (bean curd)
- 700 ml/1¼ pints/3 cups Chinese Stock (see page 8)
- 1 tbsp light soy sauce
- salt and pepper
- fresh coriander (cilantro) leaves, to garnish (optional)

1 Small prawns (shrimp) can be left whole; larger ones should be cut into smaller pieces; cut the squid and scallops into small pieces.

2 If raw, mix the prawns (shrimp) and scallops with the egg white and cornflour (cornstarch) paste to prevent them from becoming tough when they are cooked. Cut the cake of tofu into about 24 small cubes.

3 Bring the stock to a rolling boil. Add the tofu and soy sauce, bring back to the boil and simmer for 1 minute.

4 Stir in the seafood, raw pieces first, pre-cooked ones last. Bring back to the boil and simmer for just 1 minute.

5 Adjust the seasoning to taste and serve, garnished with coriander, (cilantro) leaves, if liked.

COOK'S TIP

Tofu, also known as bean curd, is made from puréed yellow soya beans, which are very high in protein. Although almost tasteless, tofu absorbs the flavours of other ingredients. It is widely available in supermarkets, and Oriental and health-food stores.

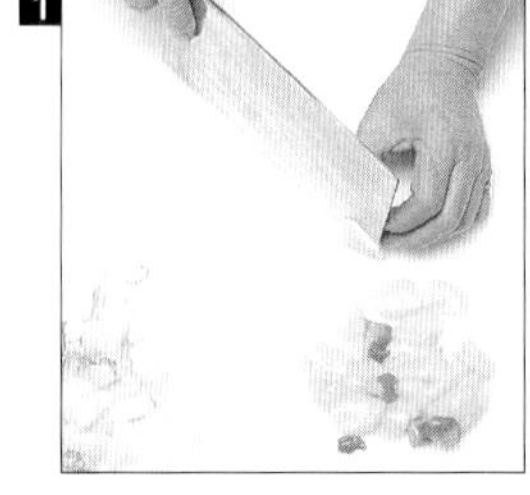

1

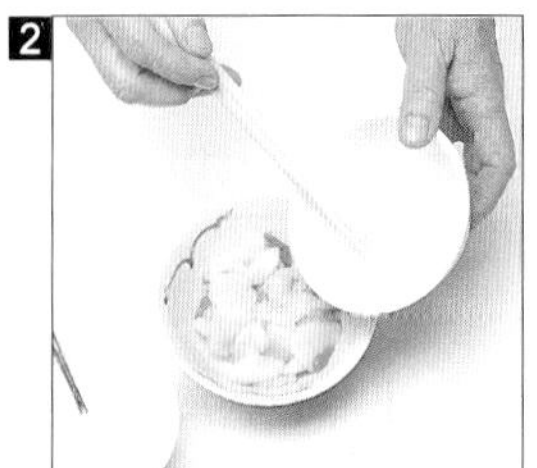

2

4

Minestrone

Minestrone translates as 'big soup' in Italian. It is made all over Italy, but this version comes from Livorno, a port on the western coast.

NUTRITIONAL INFORMATION

Calories	311	Sugars	8g
Protein	12g	Fat	19g
Carbohydrate	26g	Saturates	5g

10 MINS

30 MINS

SERVES 4

INGREDIENTS

- 1 tbsp olive oil
- 100 g/3½ oz pancetta ham, diced
- 2 medium onions, chopped
- 2 cloves garlic, crushed
- 1 potato, peeled and cut into 1 cm/½ inch cubes
- 1 carrot, peeled and cut into chunks
- 1 leek, sliced into rings
- ¼ green cabbage, shredded
- 1 stick celery, chopped
- 450 g/1 lb can chopped tomatoes
- 200 g/7 oz can flageolet (small navy) beans, drained and rinsed
- 600 ml/1 pint/2½ cups hot ham or chicken stock, diluted with 600 ml/1 pint/2½ cups boiling water
- bouquet garni (2 bay leaves, 2 sprigs rosemary and 2 sprigs thyme, tied together)
- salt and pepper
- freshly grated Parmesan cheese, to serve

1

2

3

1 Heat the olive oil in a large saucepan. Add the diced pancetta, chopped onions and garlic and fry for about 5 minutes, stirring, or until the onions are soft and golden.

2 Add the prepared potato, carrot, leek, cabbage and celery to the saucepan. Cook for a further 2 minutes, stirring frequently, to coat all of the vegetables in the oil.

3 Add the tomatoes, flageolet (small navy) beans, hot ham or chicken stock and bouquet garni to the pan, stirring to mix. Leave the soup to simmer, covered, for 15–20 minutes or until all of the vegetables are just tender.

4 Remove the bouquet garni, season with salt and pepper to taste and serve with plenty of freshly grated Parmesan cheese.

Crab & Ginger Soup

Two classic ingredients in Chinese cooking are blended together in this recipe for a special soup.

NUTRITIONAL INFORMATION

Calories	32	Sugars	1g
Protein	6g	Fat	0.4g
Carbohydrate	1g	Saturates	0g

 10 MINS  25 MINS

SERVES 4

INGREDIENTS

- 1 carrot
- 1 leek
- 1 bay leaf
- 850 ml/1½ pints/3¾ cups fish stock
- 2 medium-sized cooked crabs
- 2.5-cm/1-inch piece fresh root ginger (ginger root), grated
- 1 tsp light soy sauce
- ½ tsp ground star anise
- salt and pepper

1 Using a sharp knife, chop the carrot and leek into small pieces and place in a large saucepan with the bay leaf and fish stock.

2 Bring the mixture in the saucepan to the boil.

3 Reduce the heat, cover and leave to simmer for about 10 minutes, or until the vegetables are nearly tender.

4 Remove all of the meat from the cooked crabs. Break off and reserve the claws, break the joints and remove the meat, using a fork or skewer.

5 Add the crabmeat to the pan of fish stock, together with the ginger, soy sauce and star anise and bring to the boil. Leave to simmer for about 10 minutes, or until the vegetables are tender and the crab is heated through.

6 Season the soup then ladle into a warmed soup tureen or individual serving bowls and garnish with crab claws. Serve immediately.

1

4

5

VARIATION

If fresh crabmeat is unavailable, use drained canned crabmeat or thawed frozen crabmeat instead.

Sweetcorn & Crab Soup

Be sure to use proper creamed sweetcorn for this soup. It has a slightly mushy consistency making a deliciously thick, creamy soup.

NUTRITIONAL INFORMATION

Calories	133	Sugars	6g
Protein	10g	Fat	3g
Carbohydrate	19g	Saturates	0.4g

 3½ HOURS  10 MINS

SERVES 4

INGREDIENTS

- 125 g/4½ oz crab meat (or 1 chicken breast)
- ¼ tsp finely chopped ginger root
- 2 egg whites
- 2 tbsp milk
- 1 tbsp cornflour (cornstarch) paste (see page 6)
- 600 ml/1 pint/2½ cups Chinese Stock (see page 8)
- 1 x 250 g/9 oz can American-style creamed sweetcorn
- salt and pepper
- finely chopped spring onions (scallions), to garnish

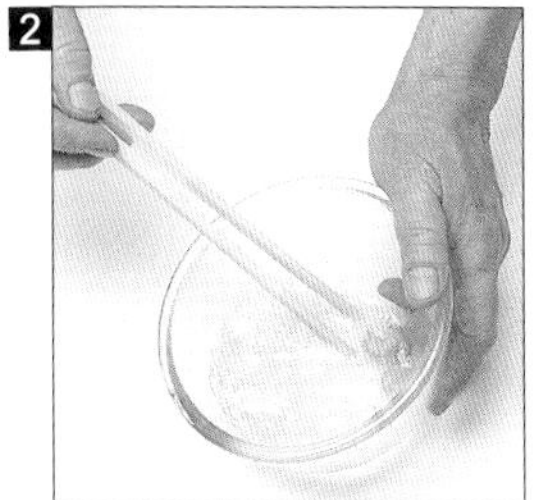

1 In a small bowl, flake the crab meat. Add the chopped ginger root and mix well. If using chicken breast, coarsely chop and mix with the ginger.

2 Beat the egg whites until frothy, add the milk and cornflour (cornstarch) paste and beat again until smooth.

3 Blend the crab meat or chicken into the egg-white mixture.

4 In a wok or large frying pan (skillet), bring the stock to the boil, add the sweetcorn and bring back to the boil, stirring gently.

5 Stir in the crab meat or chicken pieces and egg-white mixture.

6 Add salt and pepper to taste and stir the soup gently until the mixture is well blended.

7 Pour the soup into a warm tureen or individual serving bowls, garnish with chopped spring onions (scallions) and serve immediately.

COOK'S TIP

Always obtain the freshest possible crab, although frozen or canned will work in this recipe. The delicate, sweet flavour of crab diminishes very quickly which is why Chinese chefs tend to buy live crabs.

Tuscan Onion Soup

This soup is best made with white onions, which have a mild flavour. If you cannot get hold of them, try using large Spanish onions instead.

NUTRITIONAL INFORMATION

Calories	390	Sugars	0g
Protein	9g	Fat	33g
Carbohydrate	15g	Saturates	14g

 5–10 MINS  40–45 MINS

SERVES 4

INGREDIENTS

- 50 g/1¾ oz pancetta ham, diced
- 1 tbsp olive oil
- 4 large white onions, sliced thinly into rings
- 3 garlic cloves, chopped
- 850 ml/1½ pints/3½ cups hot chicken or ham stock
- 4 slices ciabatta or other Italian bread
- 50 g/1¾ oz/3 tbsp butter
- 75 g/2¾ oz Gruyère or Cheddar
- salt and pepper

1 Dry fry the pancetta in a large saucepan for 3–4 minutes until it begins to brown. Remove the pancetta from the pan and set aside until required.

2 Add the oil to the pan and cook the onions and garlic over a high heat for 4 minutes. Reduce the heat, cover and cook for 15 minutes or until the onions are lightly caramelized.

3 Add the stock to the saucepan and bring to the boil. Reduce the heat and leave the mixture to simmer, covered, for about 10 minutes.

4 Toast the slices of ciabatta on both sides, under a preheated grill (broiler), for 2–3 minutes or until golden. Spread the ciabatta with butter and top with the Gruyère or Cheddar cheese. Cut the bread into bite-size pieces.

5 Add the reserved pancetta to the soup and season with salt and pepper to taste.

6 Pour into 4 soup bowls and top with the toasted bread.

COOK'S TIP

Pancetta is similar to bacon, but it is air- and salt-cured for about 6 months. Pancetta is available from most delicatessens and some large supermarkets. If you cannot obtain pancetta use unsmoked bacon instead.

Gazpacho

This Spanish soup is full of chopped and grated vegetables with a puréed tomato base. It requires chilling, so prepare well in advance.

NUTRITIONAL INFORMATION

Calories	140	Sugars	12g
Protein	3g	Fat	9g
Carbohydrate	13g	Saturates	1g

 6½ HOURS  0 MINS

SERVES 4

INGREDIENTS

- ½ small cucumber
- ½ small green (bell) pepper, seeded and very finely chopped
- 500 g/1 lb 2 oz ripe tomatoes, peeled or 400 g/14 oz can chopped tomatoes
- ½ onion, coarsely chopped
- 2–3 garlic cloves, crushed
- 3 tbsp olive oil
- 2 tbsp white wine vinegar
- 1–2 tbsp lemon or lime juice
- 2 tbsp tomato purée (paste)
- 450 ml/16 fl oz/scant 2 cups tomato juice
- salt and pepper

TO SERVE

- chopped green (bell) pepper
- thinly sliced onion rings
- garlic croûtons

1 Coarsely grate the cucumber into a large bowl and add the chopped green (bell) pepper.

2 Process the tomatoes, onion and garlic in a food processor or blender, then add the oil, vinegar, lemon or lime juice and tomato purée (paste) and process until smooth. Alternatively, finely chop the tomatoes and finely grate the onion, then mix both with the garlic, oil, vinegar, lemon or lime juice and tomato purée (paste).

3 Add the tomato mixture to the bowl and mix well, then add the tomato juice and mix again.

4 Season to taste, cover the bowl with clear film (plastic wrap) and chill thoroughly – for at least 6 hours and preferably longer so that the flavours have time to meld together.

5 Prepare the side dishes of green (bell) pepper, onion rings and garlic croûtons, and arrange in individual serving bowls.

6 Ladle the soup into bowls, preferably from a soup tureen set on the table with the side dishes placed around it. Hand the dishes around to allow the guests to help themselves.

2

3

5

Creamy Tomato Soup

This quick and easy creamy soup has a lovely fresh tomato flavour. Basil leaves complement tomatoes perfectly.

NUTRITIONAL INFORMATION

Calories	218	Sugars	10g
Protein	3g	Fat	19g
Carbohydrate	10g	Saturates	11g

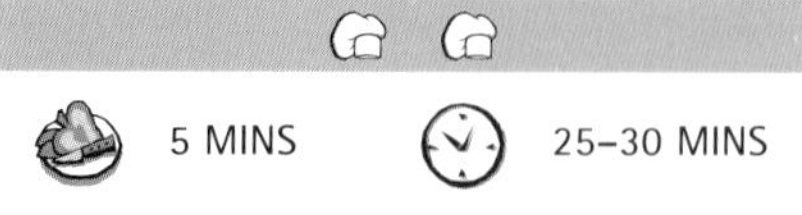

5 MINS 25–30 MINS

SERVES 4

INGREDIENTS

- 50 g/1 ¾ oz/3 tbsp butter
- 700 g/1 lb 9 oz ripe tomatoes, preferably plum, roughly chopped
- 850 ml/1 ½ pints/3 ¾ hot vegetable stock
- 50 g/1 ¾ oz/ ¼ cup ground almonds
- 150 ml/¼ pint/ ⅔ cup milk or single (light) cream
- 1 tsp sugar
- 2 tbsp shredded basil leaves
- salt and pepper

1 Melt the butter in a large saucepan. Add the tomatoes and cook for 5 minutes until the skins start to wrinkle. Season to taste with salt and pepper.

2 Add the stock to the pan, bring to the boil, cover and simmer for 10 minutes.

3 Meanwhile, under a preheated grill (broiler), lightly toast the ground almonds until they are golden-brown. This will take only 1-2 minutes, so watch them closely.

4 Remove the soup from the heat and place in a food processor and blend the mixture to form a smooth consistency. Alternatively, mash the soup with a potato masher until smooth.

5 Pass the soup through a sieve to remove any tomato skin or pips.

6 Place the soup in the pan and return to the heat. Stir in the milk or cream, toasted ground almonds and sugar. Warm the soup through and add the shredded basil leaves just before serving.

7 Transfer the creamy tomato soup to warm soup bowls and serve hot.

COOK'S TIP

Very fine breadcrumbs can be used instead of the ground almonds, if you prefer. Toast them in the same way as the almonds and add with the milk or cream in step 6.

Pumpkin & Orange Soup

This thick, creamy soup has a wonderful, warming golden colour. It is flavoured with orange and thyme.

NUTRITIONAL INFORMATION

Calories	111	Sugars	4g
Protein	2g	Fat	6g
Carbohydrate	5g	Saturates	2g

10 MINS

35–40 MINS

SERVES 4

INGREDIENTS

- 2 tbsp olive oil
- 2 medium onions, chopped
- 2 cloves garlic, chopped
- 900 g/2 lb pumpkin, peeled and cut into 2.5 cm/1 inch chunks
- 1.5 litres /2¾ pints/6¼ cups boiling vegetable or chicken stock
- finely grated rind and juice of 1 orange
- 3 tbsp fresh thyme, stalks removed
- 150 ml/¼ pint/⅔ cup milk
- salt and pepper
- crusty bread, to serve

1

2

5

1 Heat the olive oil in a large saucepan. Add the onions to the pan and cook for 3–4 minutes or until softened. Add the garlic and pumpkin and cook for a further 2 minutes, stirring well.

2 Add the boiling vegetable or chicken stock, orange rind and juice and 2 tablespoons of the thyme to the pan. Leave to simmer, covered, for 20 minutes or until the pumpkin is tender.

3 Place the mixture in a food processor and blend until smooth. Alternatively, mash the mixture with a potato masher until smooth. Season to taste.

4 Return the soup to the saucepan and add the milk. Reheat the soup for 3–4 minutes or until it is piping hot but not boiling.

5 Sprinkle with the remaining fresh thyme just before serving.

6 Divide the soup among 4 warm soup bowls and serve with lots of fresh crusty bread.

COOK'S TIP

Pumpkins are usually large vegetables. To make things a little easier, ask the greengrocer to cut a chunk off for you. Alternatively, make double the quantity and freeze the soup for up to 3 months.

Cream of Artichoke Soup

A creamy soup with the unique, subtle flavouring of Jerusalem artichokes and a garnish of grated carrots for extra crunch.

NUTRITIONAL INFORMATION

Calories	19	Sugars	0g
Protein	0.4g	Fat	2g
Carbohydrate	0.7g	Saturates	0.7g

10–15 MINS 55–60 MINS

SERVES 6

INGREDIENTS

- 750 g/1 lb 10 oz Jerusalem artichokes
- 1 lemon, sliced thickly
- 60 g/2 oz/¼ cup butter or margarine
- 2 onions, chopped
- 1 garlic clove, crushed
- 1.25 litres/2¼ pints/5½ cups chicken or vegetable stock
- 2 bay leaves
- ¼ tsp ground mace or ground nutmeg
- 1 tbsp lemon juice
- 150 ml/¼ pint/⅔ cup single (light) cream or natural fromage frais
- salt and pepper

TO GARNISH

- coarsely grated carrot
- chopped fresh parsley or coriander (cilantro)

1 Peel and slice the artichokes. Put into a bowl of water with the lemon slices.

2 Melt the butter or margarine in a large saucepan. Add the onions and garlic and fry gently for 3–4 minutes until soft but not coloured.

3 Drain the artichokes (discarding the lemon) and add to the pan. Mix well and cook gently for 2–3 minutes without allowing to colour.

4 Add the stock, seasoning, bay leaves, mace or nutmeg and lemon juice. Bring slowly to the boil, then cover and simmer gently for about 30 minutes until the vegetables are very tender.

5 Discard the bay leaves. Cool the soup slightly then press through a sieve (strainer) or blend in a food processor until smooth. If liked, a little of the soup may be only partially puréed and added to the rest of the puréed soup, to give extra texture.

6 Pour into a clean pan and bring to the boil. Adjust the seasoning and stir in the cream or fromage frais. Reheat gently without boiling. Garnish with grated carrot and chopped parsley or coriander (cilantro).

1

3

5

Indian Potato & Pea Soup

A slightly hot and spicy Indian flavour is given to this soup with the use of garam masala, chilli, cumin and coriander.

NUTRITIONAL INFORMATION

Calories	153	Sugars	6g
Protein	6g	Fat	6g
Carbohydrate	18g	Saturates	1g

 5 MINS

35 MINS

SERVES 4

INGREDIENTS

- 2 tbsp vegetable oil
- 225 g/8 oz floury (mealy) potatoes, diced
- 1 large onion, chopped
- 2 garlic cloves, crushed
- 1 tsp garam masala
- 1 tsp ground coriander
- 1 tsp ground cumin
- 900 ml/1½ pints/3¾ cups vegetable stock
- 1 red chilli, chopped
- 100 g/3½ oz frozen peas
- 4 tbsp low-fat natural yogurt
- salt and pepper
- chopped fresh coriander (cilantro), to garnish

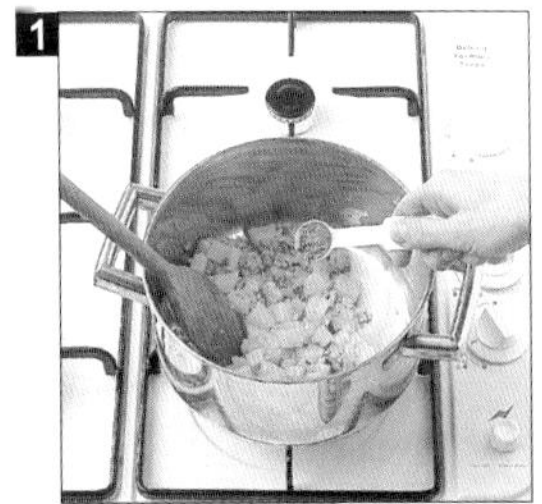

1 Heat the vegetable oil in a large saucepan and add the diced potatoes, onion and garlic. Sauté gently for about 5 minutes, stirring constantly. Add the ground spices and cook for 1 minute, stirring all the time.

2 Stir in the vegetable stock and chopped red chilli and bring the mixture to the boil. Reduce the heat, cover the pan and simmer for 20 minutes.

3 Add the peas and cook for a further 5 minutes. Stir in the yogurt and season to taste.

4 Pour the soup into warmed bowls, garnish with the chopped fresh coriander (cilantro) and serve hot with warm bread.

COOK'S TIP

For slightly less heat, deseed the chilli before adding it to the soup. Always wash your hands after handling chillies as they contain volatile oils that can irritate the skin and make your eyes burn if you touch your face.

Veal & Wild Mushroom Soup

Wild mushrooms are available commercially and an increasing range of cultivated varieties is now to be found in many supermarkets.

NUTRITIONAL INFORMATION

Calories	413	Sugars	3g
Protein	28g	Fat	22g
Carbohydrate	28g	Saturates	12g

5 MINS

3¼ HOURS

SERVES 4

INGREDIENTS

450 g/1 lb veal, thinly sliced
450 g/1 lb veal bones
1.2 litres/2 pints/5 cups water
1 small onion
6 peppercorns
1 tsp cloves
pinch of mace
140 g/5 oz oyster and shiitake mushrooms, roughly chopped
150 ml/¼ pint/⅔ cup double (heavy) cream
100 g/3½ oz/¾ cup dried vermicelli
1 tbsp cornflour (cornstarch)
3 tbsp milk
salt and pepper

1 Put the veal, bones and water into a large saucepan. Bring to the boil and lower the heat. Add the onion, peppercorns, cloves and mace and simmer for about 3 hours, until the veal stock is reduced by one-third.

2 Strain the stock, skim off any fat on the surface with a slotted spoon, and pour the stock into a clean saucepan. Add the veal meat to the pan.

3 Add the mushrooms and cream, bring to the boil over a low heat and then leave to simmer for 12 minutes, stirring occasionally.

4 Meanwhile, cook the vermicelli in lightly salted boiling water for 10 minutes or until tender, but still firm to the bite. Drain and keep warm.

5 Mix the cornflour (cornstarch) and milk to form a smooth paste. Stir into the soup to thicken. Season to taste with salt and pepper and just before serving, add the vermicelli. Transfer the soup to a warm tureen and serve immediately.

1

2

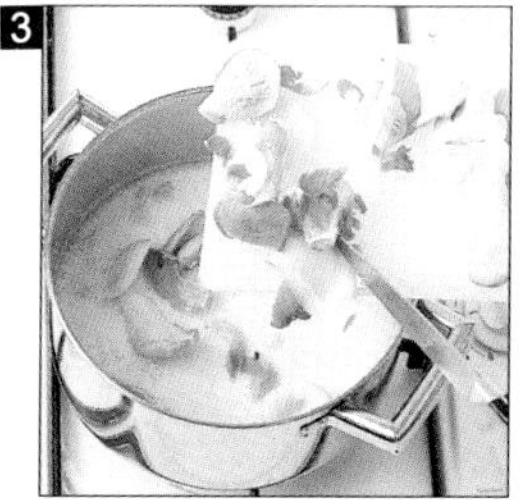
3

COOK'S TIP

You can make this soup with the more inexpensive cuts of veal, such as breast or neck slices. These are lean and the long cooking time ensures that the meat is really tender.

Curried Parsnip Soup

Parsnips make a delicious soup as they have a slightly sweet flavour. In this recipe, spices are added to complement this sweetness.

NUTRITIONAL INFORMATION

Calories	152	Sugars	7g
Protein	3g	Fat	8g
Carbohydrate	18g	Saturates	3g

 10 MINS  35 MINS

SERVES 4

INGREDIENTS

- 1 tbsp vegetable oil
- 15 g/½ oz/1 tbsp butter
- 1 red onion, chopped
- 3 parsnips, chopped
- 2 garlic cloves, crushed
- 2 tsp garam masala
- ½ tsp chilli powder
- 1 tbsp plain (all-purpose) flour
- 850 ml/1½ pints/3¾ cups vegetable stock
- grated rind and juice of 1 lemon
- salt and pepper
- lemon rind, to garnish

1

3

4

1 Heat the oil and butter in a large saucepan until the butter has melted. Add the onion, parsnips and garlic and sauté, stirring frequently, for about 5–7 minutes, until the vegetables have softened, but not coloured.

2 Add the garam masala and chilli powder and cook, stirring constantly, for 30 seconds. Sprinkle in the flour, mixing well and cook, stirring constantly, for a further 30 seconds.

3 Stir in the stock, lemon rind and juice and bring to the boil. Reduce the heat and simmer for 20 minutes.

4 Remove some of the vegetable pieces with a slotted spoon and reserve until required. Process the remaining soup and vegetables in a food processor or blender for about 1 minute, or until a smooth purée. Alternatively, press the vegetables through a strainer with the back of a wooden spoon.

5 Return the soup to a clean saucepan and stir in the reserved vegetables. Heat the soup through for 2 minutes until piping hot.

6 Season to taste with salt and pepper, then transfer to soup bowls, garnish with grated lemon rind and serve.

Chilli Fish Soup

Chinese mushrooms add an intense flavour to this soup which is unique. If they are unavailable, use open-cap mushrooms, sliced.

NUTRITIONAL INFORMATION

Calories	166	Sugars	1g
Protein	23g	Fat	7g
Carbohydrate	4g	Saturates	1g

 15 MINS  15 MINS

SERVES 4

INGREDIENTS

- 15 g/½ oz Chinese dried mushrooms
- 2 tbsp sunflower oil
- 1 onion, sliced
- 100 g/3½ oz/1½ cups mangetout (snow peas)
- 100 g/3½ oz/1½ cups bamboo shoots
- 3 tbsp sweet chilli sauce
- 1.2 litres/2 pints/5 cups fish or vegetable stock
- 3 tbsp light soy sauce
- 2 tbsp fresh coriander (cilantro), plus extra to garnish
- 450 g/1 lb cod fillet, skinned and cubed

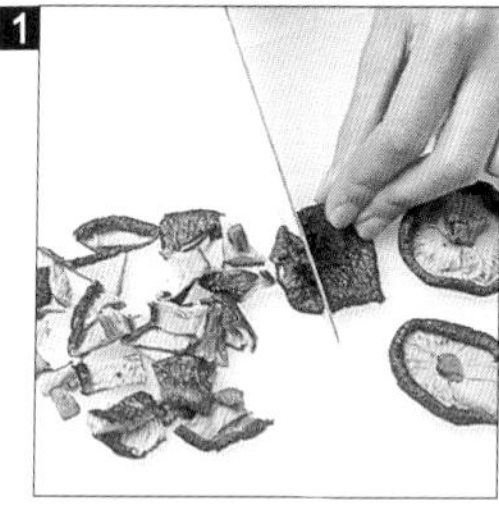
1

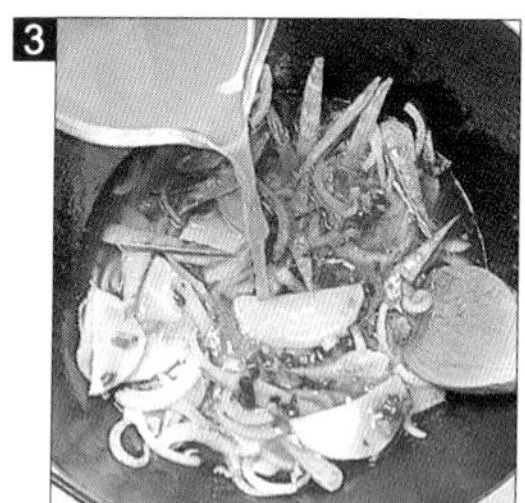
3

4

1 Place the mushrooms in a large bowl. Pour over enough boiling water to cover and leave to stand for 5 minutes. Drain the mushrooms thoroughly in a colander. Using a sharp knife, roughly chop the mushrooms.

2 Heat the sunflower oil in a preheated wok or large frying pan (skillet). Add the sliced onion to the wok and stir-fry for 5 minutes, or until softened.

3 Add the mangetout (snow peas), bamboo shoots, chilli sauce, stock and soy sauce to the wok and bring to the boil.

4 Add the coriander (cilantro) and cod and leave to simmer for 5 minutes or until the fish is cooked through.

5 Transfer the soup to warm bowls, garnish with extra coriander (cilantro), if wished, and serve hot.

COOK'S TIP

Cod is used in this recipe as it is a meaty white fish. For real luxury, use monkfish tail instead.

There are many different varieties of dried mushrooms, but shiitake are best. They are not cheap, but a small amount will go a long way.

Hot & Sour Soup

This is the favourite soup in Chinese restaurants throughout the world. Strain the soaking liquid and use in other soups, sauces and casseroles.

NUTRITIONAL INFORMATION

Calories	118	Sugar	0.3g
Protein	14g	Fats	4g
Carbohydrates	7g	Saturates	1g

 4¼ HOURS  10 MINS

SERVES 4

INGREDIENTS

- 4-6 dried Chinese mushrooms (Shiitake), soaked
- 125 g/4½ oz cooked lean pork or chicken
- 1 cake tofu (bean curd)
- 60 g/2 oz canned sliced bamboo shoots, drained
- 600 ml/1 pint/2½ cups Chinese Stock (see page 8) or water
- 1 tbsp Chinese rice wine or dry sherry
- 1 tbsp light soy sauce
- 2 tbsp rice vinegar
- 1 tbsp cornflour (cornstarch) paste (see page 6)
- salt, to taste
- ½ tsp ground white pepper
- 2-3 spring onions (scallions), thinly sliced, to serve

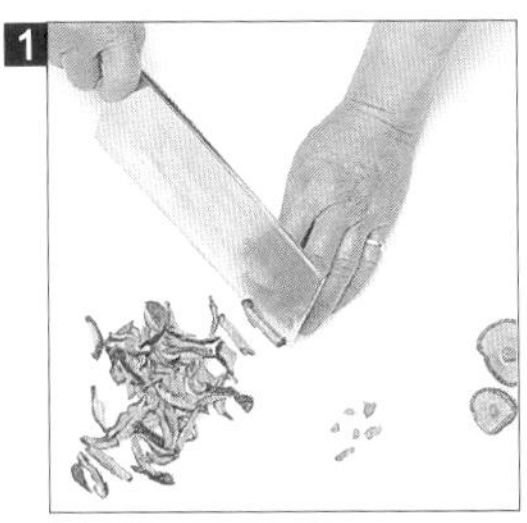
1

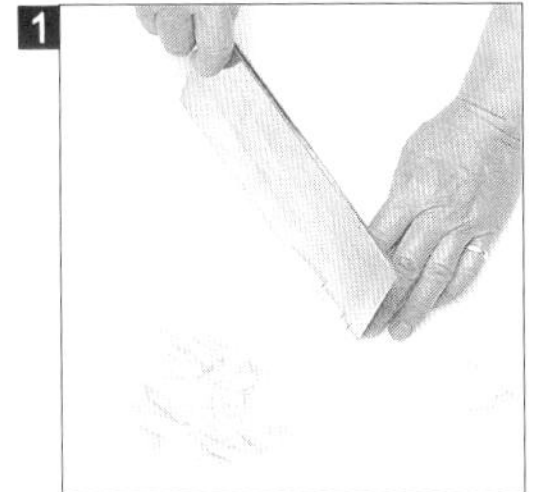
1

2

1 Drain the mushrooms, squeeze dry and discard the hard stalks. Thinly slice the mushrooms. Slice the meat, tofu and bamboo shoots into narrow shreds.

2 Bring the stock or water to a rolling boil in a wok or large pan and add all the ingredients. Bring back to the boil then simmer for about 1 minute.

3 Add the wine, soy sauce and vinegar to the wok or pan.

4 Bring back to the boil once more, and add the cornflour (cornstarch) paste to thicken the soup. Gently stir the soup while it is thickening. Serve the soup hot, sprinkled with the sliced spring onions (scallions).

COOK'S TIP

There are many varieties of dried mushrooms, which add a particular flavour to Chinese cooking. Shiitake mushrooms are one of the favourite kinds. Soak in hot water for 25-30 minutes before use and cut off the hard stems.

Chick-pea & Tomato Soup

A thick vegetable soup which is a delicious meal in itself. Serve with Parmesan cheese and warm sun-dried tomato bread.

NUTRITIONAL INFORMATION

Calories	285	Sugar	11g
Protein	16g	Fats	12g
Carbohydrates	29g	Saturates	3g

 5 MINS  15 MINS

SERVES 4

INGREDIENTS

2 tbsp olive oil

2 leeks, sliced

2 courgettes (zucchini), diced

2 garlic cloves, crushed

2 x 400 g/14 oz cans chopped tomatoes

1 tbsp tomato purée (paste)

1 fresh bay leaf

850 ml/1½ pints/3¾ cups chicken stock

400 g/14 oz can chick-peas (garbanzo beans), drained and rinsed

225 g/8 oz spinach

TO SERVE

Parmesan cheese, freshly-grated

sun-dried tomato bread

1 Heat the oil in a large saucepan, add the leeks and courgettes (zucchini) and cook briskly for 5 minutes, stirring constantly.

2 Add the garlic, tomatoes, tomato purée (paste), bay leaf, chicken stock and chick-peas (garbanzo beans).

3 Bring to the boil and simmer for 5 minutes.

4 Shred the spinach finely, add to the soup and cook for 2 minutes. Season to taste.

5 Discard the bay leaf. Serve the soup immediatly with freshly-grated Parmesan cheese and warm sun-dried tomato bread.

COOK'S TIP

Chick-peas (garbanzo beans) are used extensively in North African cuisine and are also found in Spanish, Middle Eastern and Indian cooking. They have a nutty flavour with a firm texture and are excellent canned.

1

2

3

Spicy Dal & Carrot Soup

This delicious, warming and nutritious soup includes a selection of spices to give it a 'kick'. It is simple to make and extremely good to eat.

NUTRITIONAL INFORMATION

Calories	173	Sugars	11g
Protein	9g	Fat	5g
Carbohydrate	24g	Saturates	1g

 10 MINS  50 MINS

SERVES 6

INGREDIENTS

- 125 g/4½ oz split red lentils
- 1.2 litres/2 pints/5 cups vegetable stock
- 350 g/12 oz carrots, peeled and sliced
- 2 onions, peeled and chopped
- 1 x 250 g/9 oz can chopped tomatoes
- 2 garlic cloves, peeled and chopped
- 2 tbsp vegetable ghee or oil
- 1 tsp ground cumin
- 1 tsp ground coriander
- 1 fresh green chilli, seeded and chopped, or use 1 tsp minced chilli (from a jar)
- ½ tsp ground turmeric
- 15 ml/1 tbsp lemon juice
- salt
- 300 ml/½ pint/1¼ cups skimmed milk
- 30 ml/2 tbsp chopped fresh coriander
- yogurt, to serve

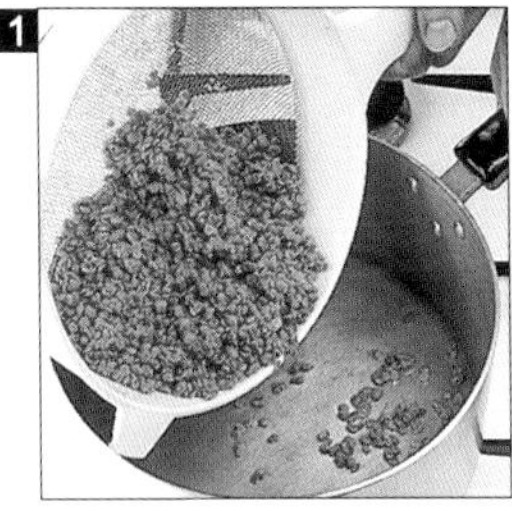
1

2

3

1 Place the lentils in a sieve and wash well under cold running water. Drain and place in a large saucepan with 850 ml/1½ pints/3½ cups of the stock, the carrots, onions, tomatoes and garlic. Bring the mixture to the boil, reduce the heat, cover and simmer for 30 minutes.

2 Meanwhile, heat the ghee or oil in a small pan, add the cumin, coriander, chilli and turmeric and fry gently for 1 minute.

3 Remove from the heat and stir in the lemon juice and salt to taste.

4 Purée the soup in batches in a blender or food processor. Return the soup to the saucepan, add the spice mixture and the remaining 300 ml/½ pint/1¼ cups stock or water and simmer for 10 minutes.

5 Add the milk to the soup, taste and adjust the seasoning according to taste.

6 Stir in the chopped coriander and reheat gently. Serve hot, with a swirl of yogurt.

Fish & Vegetable Soup

A chunky fish soup with strips of vegetables, all flavoured with ginger and lemon, makes a meal in itself.

NUTRITIONAL INFORMATION

Calories	88	Sugars	1g
Protein	12g	Fat	3g
Carbohydrate	3g	Saturates	0.5g

 40 MINS  20 MINS

SERVES 4

INGREDIENTS

- 250 g/9 oz white fish fillets (cod, halibut, haddock, sole etc)
- ½ tsp ground ginger
- ½ tsp salt
- 1 small leek, trimmed
- 2-4 crab sticks, defrosted if frozen (optional)
- 1 tbsp sunflower oil
- 1 large carrot, cut into julienne strips
- 8 canned water chestnuts, thinly sliced
- 1.2 litres/2 pints/5 cups fish or vegetable stock
- 1 tbsp lemon juice
- 1 tbsp light soy sauce
- 1 large courgette (zucchini), cut into julienne strips
- black pepper

1 Remove any skin from the fish and cut into cubes, about 2.5 cm/1 inch. Combine the ground ginger and salt and use to rub into the pieces of fish. Leave to marinate for at least 30 minutes.

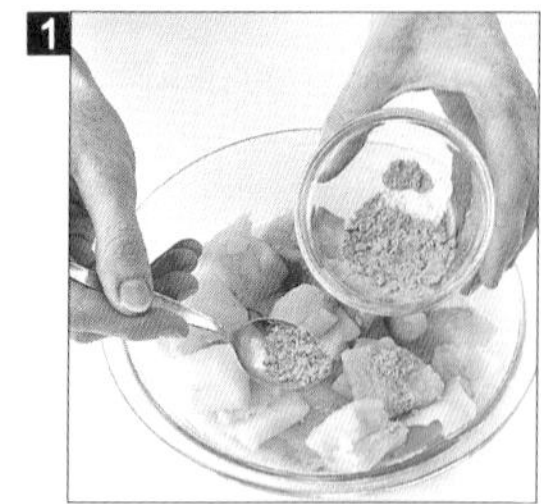

1

2 Meanwhile, divide the green and white parts of the leek. Cut each part into 2.5 cm/1 inch lengths and then into julienne strips down the length of each piece, keeping the two parts separate. Slice the crab sticks into 1 cm/½ inch pieces.

3 Heat the oil in the wok, swirling it around so it is really hot. Add the white part of the leek and stir-fry for a couple of minutes, then add the carrots and water chestnuts and continue to cook for 1-2 minutes, stirring thoroughly.

3

4 Add the stock and bring to the boil, then add the lemon juice and soy sauce and simmer for 2 minutes.

5 Add the fish and continue to cook for about 5 minutes until the fish begins to break up a little, then add the green part of the leek and the courgettes (zucchini) and simmer for about 1 minute. Add the sliced crab sticks, if using, and season to taste with black pepper. Simmer for a further minute or so and serve piping hot.

5

COOK'S TIP

To skin fish, place the fillet skin-side down and insert a sharp, flexible knife at one end between the flesh and the skin. Hold the skin tightly at the end and push the knife along, keeping the blade flat against the skin.

Calabrian Mushroom Soup

The Calabrian Mountains in southern Italy provide large amounts of wild mushrooms that are rich in flavour and colour.

NUTRITIONAL INFORMATION

Calories	452	Sugars	5g
Protein	15g	Fat	26g
Carbohydrate	42g	Saturates	12g

 5 MINS  25–30 MINS

SERVES 4

INGREDIENTS

- 2 tbsp olive oil
- 1 onion, chopped
- 450g/1 lb mixed mushrooms, such as ceps, oyster and button
- 300 ml/½ pint/1 ¼ cup milk
- 850 ml/1 ½ pints/3 ¾ cups hot vegetable stock
- 8 slices of rustic bread or French stick
- 2 garlic cloves, crushed
- 50 g/1 ¾ oz/3 tbsp butter, melted
- 75 g/2 ¾ oz Gruyère cheese, finely grated
- salt and pepper

1 Heat the oil in a large frying pan (skillet) and cook the onion for 3–4 minutes or until soft and golden.

2 Wipe each mushroom with a damp cloth and cut any large mushrooms into smaller, bite-size pieces.

3 Add the mushrooms to the pan, stirring quickly to coat them in the oil.

4 Add the milk to the pan, bring to the boil, cover and leave to simmer for about 5 minutes. Gradually stir in the hot vegetable stock and season with salt and pepper to taste.

5 Under a preheated grill (broiler), toast the bread on both sides until golden.

6 Mix together the garlic and butter and spoon generously over the toast.

7 Place the toast in the bottom of a large tureen or divide it among 4 individual serving bowls and pour over the hot soup. Top with the grated Gruyère cheese and serve at once.

COOK'S TIP

Mushrooms absorb liquid, which can lessen the flavour and affect cooking properties. Therefore, carefully wipe them with a damp cloth rather than rinsing them in water.

Vichyssoise

This is a classic creamy soup made from potatoes and leeks. To achieve the delicate pale colour, be sure to use only the white parts of the leeks.

NUTRITIONAL INFORMATION

Calories	208	Sugars	5g
Protein	5g	Fat	12g
Carbohydrate	20g	Saturates	6g

 10 MINS  40 MINS

SERVES 6

INGREDIENTS

- 3 large leeks
- 40 g/1½ oz/3 tbsp butter or margarine
- 1 onion, thinly sliced
- 500 g/1 lb 2 oz potatoes, chopped
- 850 ml/1½ pints/3½ cups vegetable stock
- 2 tsp lemon juice
- pinch of ground nutmeg
- ¼ tsp ground coriander
- 1 bay leaf
- 1 egg yolk
- 150 ml/¼ pint/⅔ cup single (light) cream
- salt and white pepper

TO GARNISH

- freshly snipped chives

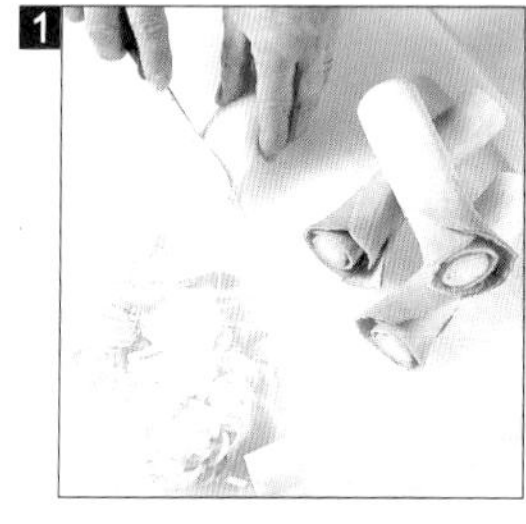

1

2

5

1 Trim the leeks and remove most of the green part. Slice the white part of the leeks very finely.

2 Melt the butter or margarine in a saucepan. Add the leeks and onion and fry, stirring occasionally, for about 5 minutes without browning.

3 Add the potatoes, vegetable stock, lemon juice, nutmeg, coriander and bay leaf to the pan, season to taste with salt and pepper and bring to the boil. Cover and simmer for about 30 minutes, until all the vegetables are very soft.

4 Cool the soup a little, remove and discard the bay leaf and then press through a strainer or process in a food processor or blender until smooth. Pour into a clean pan.

5 Blend the egg yolk into the cream, add a little of the soup to the mixture and then whisk it all back into the soup and reheat gently, without boiling. Adjust the seasoning to taste. Cool and then chill thoroughly in the refrigerator.

6 Serve the soup sprinkled with freshly snipped chives.

Pumpkin Soup

This is an American classic that has now become popular worldwide. When pumpkin is out of season use butternut squash in its place.

NUTRITIONAL INFORMATION

Calories	112	Sugars	7g
Protein	4g	Fat	7g
Carbohydrate	8g	Saturates	2g

 10 MINS  30 MINS

SERVES 6

INGREDIENTS

- about 1 kg/2 lb 4 oz pumpkin
- 40 g/1½ oz/3 tbsp butter or margarine
- 1 onion, sliced thinly
- 1 garlic clove, crushed
- 900 ml/1½ pints/3½ cups vegetable stock
- ½ tsp ground ginger
- 1 tbsp lemon juice
- 3–4 thinly pared strips of orange rind (optional)
- 1–2 bay leaves or 1 bouquet garni
- 300 ml/½ pint/1¼ cups milk
- salt and pepper

TO GARNISH

- 4–6 tablespoons single (light) or double (heavy) cream, natural yogurt or fromage frais
- snipped chives

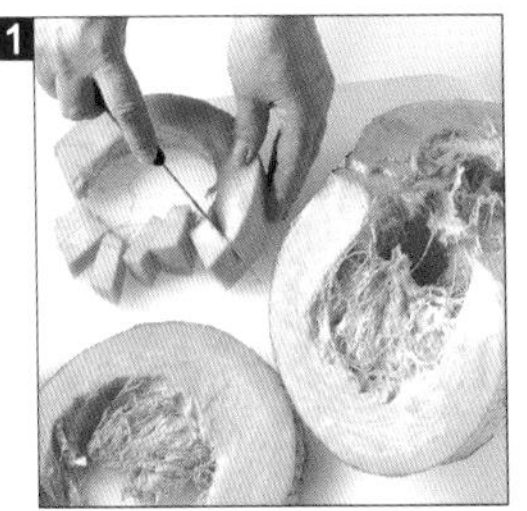

1 Peel the pumpkin, remove the seeds and then cut the flesh into 2.5 cm/1 inch cubes.

2 Melt the butter or margarine in a large, heavy-based saucepan. Add the onion and garlic and fry over a low heat until soft but not coloured.

3 Add the pumpkin and toss with the onion for 2–3 minutes.

4 Add the stock and bring to the boil over a medium heat. Season to taste with salt and pepper and add the ginger, lemon juice, strips of orange rind, if using, and bay leaves or bouquet garni. Cover and simmer over a low heat for about 20 minutes, until the pumpkin is tender.

5 Discard the orange rind, if using, and the bay leaves or bouquet garni. Cool the soup slightly, then press through a strainer or process in a food processor until smooth. Pour into a clean saucepan.

6 Add the milk and reheat gently. Adjust the seasoning. Garnish with a swirl of cream, natural yogurt or fromage frais and snipped chives, and serve.

Brown Lentil & Pasta Soup

In Italy, this soup is called *Minestrade Lentiche*. A *minestra* is a soup cooked with pasta; here, farfalline, a small bow-shaped variety, is used.

NUTRITIONAL INFORMATION

Calories	225	Sugars	1g
Protein	13g	Fat	8g
Carbohydrate	27g	Saturates	3g

 5 MINS  25 MINS

SERVES 4

INGREDIENTS

- 4 rashers streaky bacon, cut into small squares
- 1 onion, chopped
- 2 garlic cloves, crushed
- 2 sticks celery, chopped
- 50 g/1 ¾ oz/ ¼ cup farfalline or spaghetti, broken into small pieces
- 1 x 400 g/14 oz can brown lentils, drained
- 1.2 litres/2 pints/5 cups hot ham or vegetable stock
- 2 tbsp chopped, fresh mint

1 Place the bacon in a large frying pan (skillet) together with the onions, garlic and celery. Dry fry for 4–5 minutes, stirring, until the onion is tender and the bacon is just beginning to brown.

2 Add the pasta to the pan (skillet) and cook, stirring, for about 1 minute to coat the pasta in the oil.

3 Add the lentils and the stock and bring to the boil. Reduce the heat and leave to simmer for 12–15 minutes or until the pasta is tender.

4 Remove the pan (skillet) from the heat and stir in the chopped fresh mint.

5 Transfer the soup to warm soup bowls and serve immeditely.

COOK'S TIP

If you prefer to use dried lentils, add the stock before the pasta and cook for 1–1¼ hours until the lentils are tender. Add the pasta and cook for a further 12–15 minutes.

Tuscan Bean Soup

A thick and creamy soup that is based on a traditional Tuscan recipe. If you use dried beans, the preparation and cooking times will be longer.

NUTRITIONAL INFORMATION

Calories	250	Sugars	4g
Protein	13g	Fat	10g
Carbohydrate	29g	Saturates	2g

 2 MINS  10 MINS

SERVES 4

INGREDIENTS

- 225 g/8 oz dried butter beans, soaked overnight, or 2 x 400 g/14 oz can butter beans
- 1 tbsp olive oil
- 2 garlic cloves, crushed
- 1 vegetable or chicken stock cube, crumbled
- 150 ml/¼ pint/⅔ cup milk
- 2 tbsp chopped fresh oregano
- salt and pepper

1 If you are using dried beans that have been soaked overnight, drain them thoroughly. Bring a large pan of water to the boil, add the beans and boil for 10 minutes. Cover the pan and simmer for a further 30 minutes or until tender. Drain the beans, reserving the cooking liquid. If you are using canned beans, drain them thoroughly and reserve the liquid.

2 Heat the oil in a large frying pan (skillet) and fry the garlic for 2–3 minutes or until just beginning to brown.

3 Add the beans and 400 ml/14 fl oz/1⅔ cup of the reserved liquid to the pan (skillet), stirring. You may need to add a little water if there is insufficient liquid. Stir in the crumbled stock cube. Bring the mixture to the boil and then remove the pan from the heat.

4 Place the bean mixture in a food processor and blend to form a smooth purée. Alternatively, mash the bean mixture to a smooth consistency. Season to taste with salt and pepper and stir in the milk.

5 Pour the soup back into the pan and gently heat to just below boiling point. Stir in the chopped oregano just before serving.

Noodles in Soup

Noodles in soup are far more popular than fried noodles in China. You can use different ingredients for the dressing according to taste.

NUTRITIONAL INFORMATION

Calories	231	Sugars	1g
Protein	18g	Fat	11g
Carbohydrate	16g	Saturates	2g

 4 HOURS  15 MINS

SERVES 4

INGREDIENTS

- 250 g/9 oz chicken fillet, pork fillet, or any other ready-cooked meat
- 3-4 Chinese dried mushrooms, soaked
- 125 g/4½ oz canned sliced bamboo shoots, rinsed and drained
- 125 g/4½ oz spinach leaves, lettuce hearts, or Chinese leaves (cabbage), shredded
- 2 spring onions (scallions), finely shredded
- 250 g/9 oz egg noodles
- about 600 ml/1 pint/2½ cups Chinese Stock (see page 8)
- 2 tbsp light soy sauce
- 2 tbsp vegetable oil
- 1 tsp salt
- ½ tsp sugar
- 2 tsp Chinese rice wine or dry sherry
- a few drops sesame oil
- 1 tsp red chilli oil (optional)

1 Using a sharp knife or meat cleaver, cut the meat into thin shreds.

2 Squeeze dry the soaked Chinese mushrooms and discard the hard stalk.

3 Thinly shred the mushrooms, bamboo shoots, spinach leaves and spring onions (scallions).

4 Cook the noodles in boiling water according to the instructions on the packet, then drain and rinse under cold water. Place the noodles in a bowl.

5 Bring the Chinese stock to the boil, add about 1 tablespoon soy sauce and pour over the noodles. Keep warm.

6 Heat the vegetable oil in a preheated wok, add about half of the spring onions (scallions), the meat and the vegetables (mushrooms, bamboo shoots and greens). Stir-fry for about 2-3 minutes. Add all the seasonings and stir until well combined.

7 Pour the mixture in the wok over the noodles, garnish with the remaining spring onions (scallions) and serve immediately.

3

5

6

COOK'S TIP

Noodle soup is wonderfully satisfying and is ideal to serve on cold winter days.

Fish & Seafood Chowder

Served with warm crusty bread and a salad, this tasty soup makes a substantial lunch or supper dish.

NUTRITIONAL INFORMATION

Calories	286	Sugars	6g
Protein	30g	Fat	3g
Carbohydrate	31g	Saturates	1g

20 MINS 25 MINS

SERVES 4

INGREDIENTS

- 1 kg/2 lb 4 oz mussels in their shells
- 1 large onion, thinly sliced
- 2 garlic cloves, chopped
- 3 bay leaves
- a few stalks of parsley
- a few stalks of thyme
- 300 ml/½ pint/1¼ cups water
- 225 g/8 oz smoked haddock fillets
- 500 g/1 lb 2 oz potatoes, peeled and diced
- 4 celery stalks, thickly sliced
- 1 x 250 g/9 oz can sweetcorn kernels, drained and rinsed
- 150 ml/¼ pint/⅔ cup low-fat natural yogurt
- 1 tsp cornflour (cornstarch)
- 150 ml/¼ pint/⅔ cup dry white wine, or dry cider
- ½ tsp cayenne pepper, or to taste
- black pepper
- 2 tbsp chopped parsley

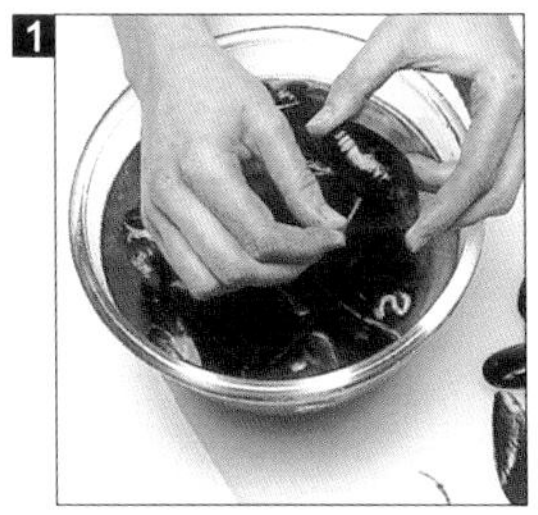
1

2

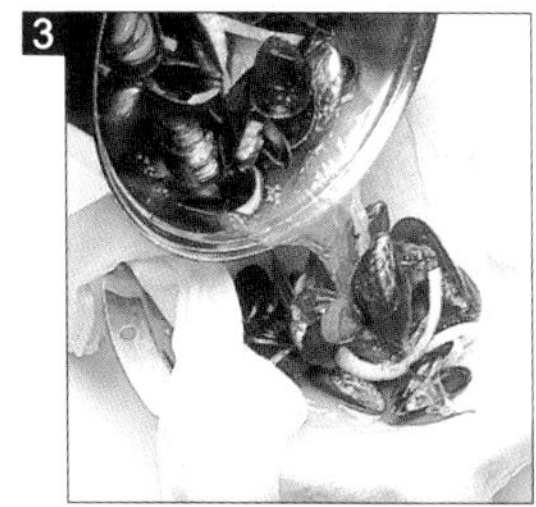
3

1 Scrub the mussels, pull off the 'beards' and rinse thoroughly. Discard any shells that remain open when tapped.

2 Put the onion, garlic, herbs, water and the mussels in a large pan. Cover and cook over high heat for 5 minutes, shaking the pan once or twice.

3 Line a colander with muslin or cheesecloth and strain the mussel liquor into a bowl. Shell the mussels. and discard the rest. Reserve the liquor.

4 Put the haddock and vegetables into a pan, add 600 ml/1 pint/2½ cups of cold water, cover and simmer for 10 minutes. Remove thc fish, and skin, bone and flake it. Strain the liquor into the seafood liquor. Reserve the vegetables.

5 Return the cooking liquor to the rinsed pan, add the sweetcorn and bring to the boil. Stir together the yogurt and cornflour (cornstarch). Stir in a little of the fish liquor, then pour it into the pan. Stir the yogurt in well, then add the reserved fish and vegetables. Add the white wine, season with cayenne and black pepper and heat the soup gently, without boiling. Season and transfer to a platter, and sprinkle with the parsley.

Chicken & Coconut Soup

This fragrant soup combines citrus flavours with coconut and a hint of piquancy from chillies.

NUTRITIONAL INFORMATION

Calories	345	Sugars	2g
Protein	28g	Fat	24g
Carbohydrate	5g	Saturates	18g

 $2^1/_4$ HOURS  15 MINS

SERVES 4

INGREDIENTS

- 350 g/12 oz/1¾ cups cooked, skinned chicken breast
- 125 g/4½ oz/1⅓ cups unsweetened desiccated coconut
- 500 ml/16 fl oz/2 cups boiling water
- 500 ml/18 fl oz/2 cups Fresh Chicken Stock (see page 9)
- 4 spring onions (scallions), white and green parts, sliced thinly
- 2 stalks lemon grass
- 1 lime
- 1 tsp grated ginger root
- 1 tbsp light soy sauce
- 2 tsp ground coriander
- 2 large fresh red chillies
- 1 tbsp chopped fresh coriander (cilantro)
- 1 tbsp cornflour (cornstarch) mixed with 2 tbsp cold water
- salt and white pepper
- chopped red chilli to garnish

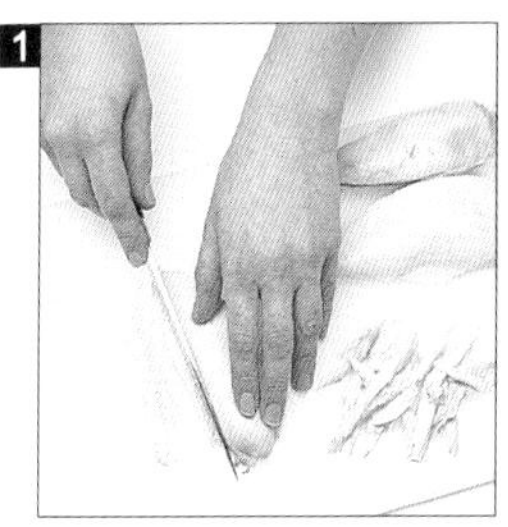

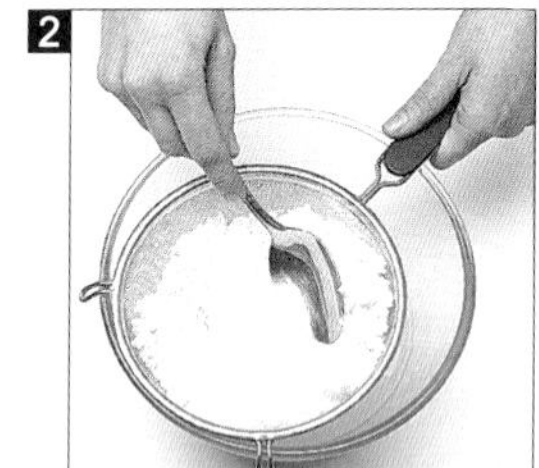

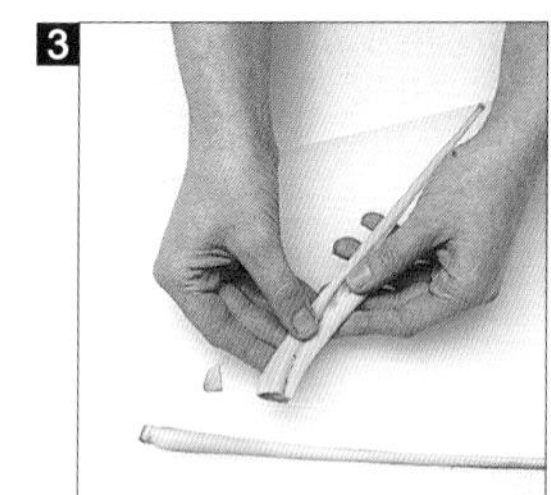

1 Using a sharp knife, slice the chicken into thin strips.

2 Place the coconut in a heatproof bowl and pour over the boiling water. Work the coconut mixture through a sieve (strainer). Pour the coconut water into a large saucepan and add the stock.

3 Add the spring onions (scallions) to the saucepan. Slice the base of each lemon grass and discard damaged leaves. Bruise the stalks and add to the saucepan.

4 Peel the rind from the lime in large strips. Extract the juice and add to the pan with the lime strips, ginger, soy sauce and coriander. Bruise the chillies with a fork then add to the pan. Heat the pan to just below boiling point.

5 Add the chicken and fresh coriander (cilantro) to the saucepan, bring to the boil, then simmer for 10 minutes.

6 Discard the lemon grass, lime rind and red chillies. Pour the blended cornflour (cornstarch) mixture into the saucepan and stir until slightly thickened. Season with salt and white pepper to taste and serve immediatley, garnished with chopped red chilli.

Spanish Tomato Soup

This Mediterranean tomato soup is thickened with bread, as is traditional in some parts of Spain, and served with garlic bread.

NUTRITIONAL INFORMATION

Calories	297	Sugars	7g
Protein	8g	Fat	13g
Carbohydrate	39g	Saturates	2g

 10 MINS  20 MINS

SERVES 4

INGREDIENTS

- 4 tbsp olive oil
- 1 onion, chopped
- 3 garlic cloves, crushed
- 1 green (bell) pepper, seeded and chopped
- ½ tsp chilli powder
- 500 g/1 lb 2 oz tomatoes, chopped
- 225 g/8 oz French or Italian bread, cubed
- 1 litre/1¾ pints/4 cups vegetable stock

GARLIC BREAD

- 4 slices ciabatta or French bread
- 4 tbsp olive oil
- 2 garlic cloves, crushed
- 25 g/1 oz/¼ cup grated Cheddar cheese
- chilli powder, to garnish

1 Heat the olive oil in a large frying pan (skillet). Add the onion, garlic and (bell) pepper and sauté over a low heat, stirring frequently, for 2–3 minutes, or until the onion has softened.

2 Add the chilli powder and tomatoes and cook over a medium heat until the mixture has thickened.

3 Stir in the bread cubes and stock and cook for 10–15 minutes, until the soup is thick and fairly smooth.

4 Meanwhile, make the garlic bread. Toast the bread slices under a medium grill (broiler). Drizzle the oil over the top of the bread, rub with the garlic, sprinkle with the cheese and return to the grill (broiler) for 2–3 minutes, until the cheese has melted. Sprinkle with chilli powder and serve with the soup.

VARIATION

Replace the green (bell) pepper with red or orange (bell) pepper, if you prefer.

Bacon, Bean & Garlic Soup

A mouth-wateringly healthy vegetable, bean and bacon soup with a garlic flavour. Serve with granary or wholemeal (whole wheat) bread.

NUTRITIONAL INFORMATION

Calories	261	Sugars	5g
Protein	23g	Fat	8g
Carbohydrate	25g	Saturates	2g

 5 MINS  20 MINS

SERVES 4

INGREDIENTS

- 225 g/8 oz smoked back lean bacon slices
- 1 carrot, sliced thinly
- 1 celery stick, sliced thinly
- 1 onion, chopped
- 1 tbsp oil
- 3 garlic cloves, sliced
- 700 ml/1¼ pints/3 cups hot vegetable stock
- 200 g/7 oz can chopped tomatoes
- 1 tbsp chopped fresh thyme
- about 400 g/14 oz can cannellini beans, drained
- 1 tbsp tomato purée (paste)
- salt and pepper
- grated Cheddar cheese to garnish

1

1
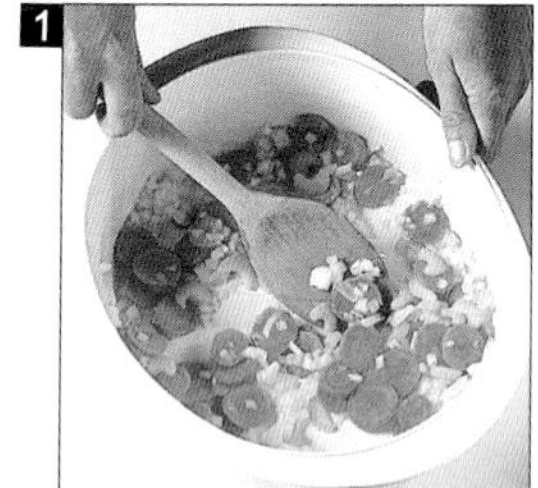

2

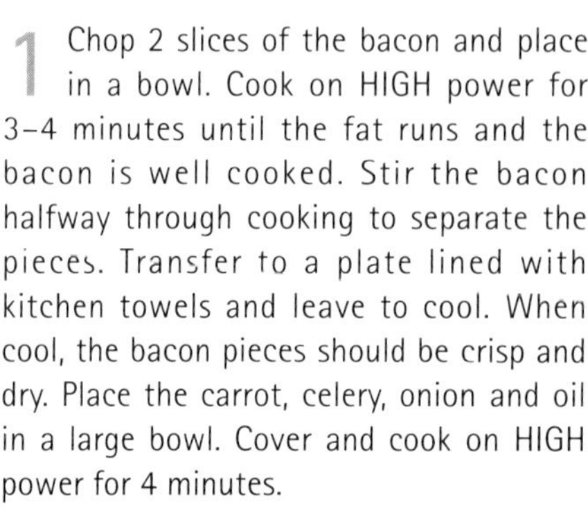

1 Chop 2 slices of the bacon and place in a bowl. Cook on HIGH power for 3–4 minutes until the fat runs and the bacon is well cooked. Stir the bacon halfway through cooking to separate the pieces. Transfer to a plate lined with kitchen towels and leave to cool. When cool, the bacon pieces should be crisp and dry. Place the carrot, celery, onion and oil in a large bowl. Cover and cook on HIGH power for 4 minutes.

2 Chop the remaining bacon and add to the bowl with the garlic. Cover and cook on HIGH power for 2 minutes.

3 Add the stock, the contents of the can of tomatoes, the thyme, beans and tomato purée (paste). Cover and cook on HIGH power for 8 minutes, stirring halfway through. Season to taste. Ladle the soup into warmed bowls and sprinkle with the crisp bacon and grated cheese.

COOK'S TIP

For a more substantial soup add 60 g/2 oz cup small pasta shapes or short lengths of spaghetti when you add the stock and tomatoes. You will also need to add an extra 150 ml/¼ pint/⅔ cup vegetable stock.

Mulligatawny Soup

This soup, based on Madras curry, became popular with army officers in India at the beginning of the century.

NUTRITIONAL INFORMATION

Calories	154	Sugars	6g
Protein	6g	Fat	7g
Carbohydrate	17g	Saturates	4g

 5½ HOURS  1 HOUR

SERVES 4–6

INGREDIENTS

- 45 g/1½ oz/3 tbsp butter or margarine
- 1 large onion, chopped
- 2 carrots, chopped
- 2–3 celery sticks, chopped
- 1 dessert apple, peeled, cored and chopped
- 1 tbsp plain (all-purpose) flour
- 1–2 tsp Madras curry powder
- 1–2 tsp curry paste
- ½ tsp ground coriander
- 1.25 litres/2¼ pints/5 cups Beef, Chicken or Vegetable Stock (see pages 8-9)
- 225 g/8 oz can chopped tomatoes
- 60 g/2 oz/½ cup cooked long grain rice (optional)
- 60–90 g/2–3 oz/⅓–½ cup cooked chicken, beef or lamb, chopped very finely
- salt and pepper
- poppadoms to serve (optional)

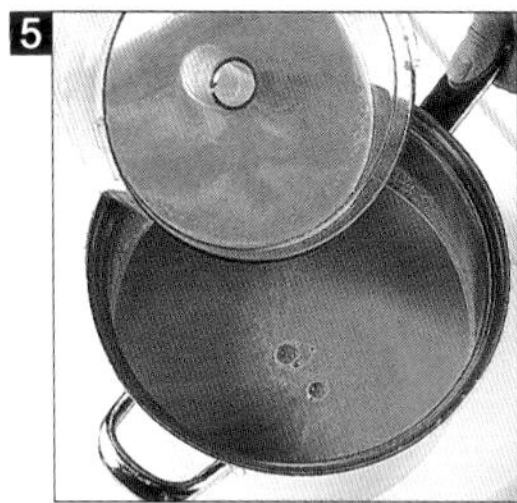

1 Melt the butter or margarine in a large saucepan and fry the onion, carrots, celery and apple, stirring occasionally, until just soft and lightly browned.

2 Stir in the flour, curry powder, curry paste and coriander and cook for a minute or so, stirring all the time.

3 Gradually add the stock and bring to the boil, stirring constantly.

4 Add the tomatoes and plenty of seasoning, cover the pan and simmer for about 45 minutes until the vegetables and apple are tender.

5 Cool the soup a little, then press through a sieve (strainer) or blend in a food processor or blender until smooth. Pour the soup into a clean pan.

6 Add the rice (if using) and the chicken or meat, adjust the seasoning and bring to the boil. Simmer gently for 5 minutes.

7 Serve the soup in warmed bowls, with poppadoms (if using).

Ravioli alla Parmigiana

This soup is traditionally served at Easter and Christmas in the province of Parma.

NUTRITIONAL INFORMATION

Calories	554	Sugars	3g
Protein	26g	Fat	24g
Carbohydrate	64g	Saturates	9g

4½–5 HOURS 25 MINS

SERVES 4

INGREDIENTS

285 g/10 oz Basic Pasta Dough (see page 6)

1.2 litres/2 pints/5 cups veal stock

freshly grated Parmesan cheese, to serve

FILLING

125 ml/4 fl oz/½ cup Espagnole Sauce (see page 7)

100 g/3½ oz/1 cup freshly grated Parmesan cheese

100 g/3½ oz/1⅔ cup fine white breadcrumbs

2 eggs

1 small onion, finely chopped

1 tsp freshly grated nutmeg

1 Make some pasta dough and the Espagnole Sauce (see page 7).

2 Carefully roll out 2 sheets of the pasta dough and cover with a damp tea towel (dish cloth) while you make the filling for the ravioli.

3 To make the filling, place the freshly grated Parmesan cheese, fine white breadcrumbs, eggs, Espagnole Sauce, finely chopped onion and the freshly grated nutmeg in a large mixing bowl, and mix together well.

4 Place spoonfuls of the filling at regular intervals on 1 sheet of pasta dough. Cover with the second sheet of pasta dough, then cut into squares and seal the edges.

5 Bring the veal stock to the boil in a large saucepan.

6 Add the ravioli to the pan and cook for about 15 minutes.

7 Transfer the soup and ravioli to warm serving bowls and serve, generously sprinkled with Parmesan cheese.

3

4

4

COOK'S TIP

It is advisable to prepare the Basic Pasta Dough (see page 6) and the Espagnole Sauce (see page 7) well in advance, or buy ready-made equivalents if you are short of time.

Consommé

A traditional clear soup made from beef bones and lean minced (ground) beef. Thin strips of vegetables provide a colourful garnish.

NUTRITIONAL INFORMATION

Calories	109	Sugars	6g
Protein	13g	Fat	3g
Carbohydrate	7g	Saturates	1g

$6^1/_4$ HOURS $1^1/_4$ HOURS

SERVES 4–6

INGREDIENTS

- 1.25 litres/2¼ pints/5 cups strong Beef Stock (see page 9)
- 225 g/8 oz/1 cup extra lean minced (ground) beef
- 2 tomatoes, skinned, seeded and chopped
- 2 large carrots, chopped
- 1 large onion, chopped
- 2 celery sticks, chopped
- 1 turnip, chopped (optional)
- 1 bouquet garni
- 2–3 egg whites
- shells of 2–4 eggs, crushed
- 1–2 tbsp sherry (optional)
- salt and pepper
- melba toast, to serve

TO GARNISH

- julienne strips of raw carrot, turnip, celery or celeriac (celery root) or a one-egg omelette, cut into julienne strips

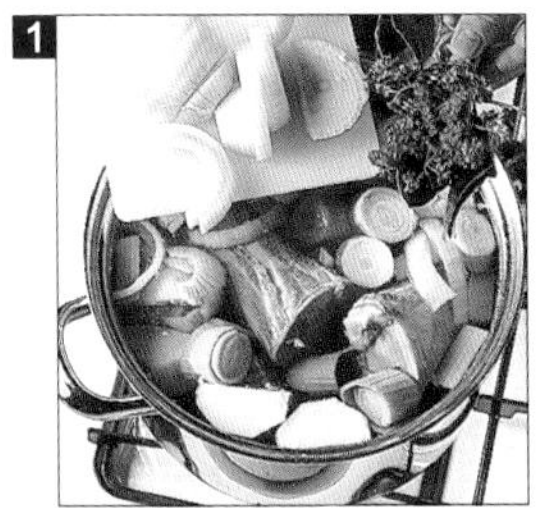
1

1

3

1 Put the stock and minced (ground) beef in a saucepan. Leave for 1 hour. Add the tomatoes, carrots, onion, celery, turnip (if using), bouquet garni, 2 of the egg whites, the crushed shells of 2 of the eggs and plenty of seasoning. Bring to almost boiling point, whisking hard all the time with a flat whisk.

2 Cover and simmer for 1 hour, taking care not to allow the layer of froth on top of the soup to break.

3 Pour the soup through a jelly bag or scalded fine cloth, keeping the froth back until the last, then pour the ingredients through the cloth again into a clean pan. The resulting liquid should be clear.

4 If the soup is not quite clear, return it to the pan with another egg white and the crushed shells of 2 more eggs. Repeat the whisking process as before and then boil for 10 minutes; strain again.

5 Add the sherry (if using) to the soup and reheat gently. Place the garnish in the warmed soup bowls and carefully pour in the soup. Serve with melba toast.

Mediterranean Fish Soup

Juicy chunks of fish and sumptuous shellfish are cooked in a flavoursome stock. Serve with toasted bread rubbed with garlic.

NUTRITIONAL INFORMATION

Calories	316	Sugar	4g
Protein	53g	Fats	7g
Carbohydrates	5g	Saturates	1g

 1 HOUR  15 MINS

SERVES 4

INGREDIENTS

- 1 tbsp olive oil
- 1 large onion, chopped
- 2 garlic cloves, finely chopped
- 425 ml/15 fl oz/1¾ cups Fresh Fish Stock (see page 8)
- 150 ml/5 fl oz/⅔ cup dry white wine
- 1 bay leaf
- 1 sprig each fresh thyme, rosemary and oregano
- 450 g/1 lb firm white fish fillets (such as cod, monkfish or halibut), skinned and cut into 2.5 cm/1 inch cubes
- 450 g/1 lb fresh mussels, prepared
- 400 g/14 oz can chopped tomatoes
- 225 g/8 oz peeled prawns (shrimp), thawed if frozen
- salt and pepper
- sprigs of thyme, to garnish

TO SERVE

- lemon wedges
- 4 slices toasted French bread, rubbed with cut garlic clove

1 Heat the olive oil in a large saucepan and gently fry the onion and garlic for 2–3 minutes until just softened.

2 Pour in the stock and wine and bring to the boil.

3 Tie the bay leaf and herbs together with clean string and add to the saucepan together with the fish and mussels. Stir well, cover and simmer for 5 minutes.

4 Stir in the tomatoes and prawns (shrimp) and continue to cook for a further 3–4 minutes until piping hot and the fish is cooked through.

5 Discard the herbs and any mussels that have not opened. Season to taste, then ladle into warm bowls.

6 Garnish with sprigs of fresh thyme and serve with lemon wedges and toasted bread.

1

2

3

Lettuce & Tofu Soup

This is a delicate, clear soup of shredded lettuce and small chunks of tofu (bean curd) with sliced carrot and spring onion (scallion).

NUTRITIONAL INFORMATION

Calories	113	Sugars	2g
Protein	5g	Fat	8g
Carbohydrate	3g	Saturates	1g

 5 MINS  15 MINS

SERVES 4

INGREDIENTS

- 200 g/7 oz tofu (bean curd)
- 2 tbsp vegetable oil
- 1 carrot, sliced thinly
- 1 cm/½ inch piece ginger root, cut into thin shreds
- 3 spring onions (scallions), sliced diagonally
- 1.2 litres/2 pints/5 cups vegetable stock
- 2 tbsp soy sauce
- 2 tbsp dry sherry
- 1 tsp sugar
- 125 g/4½ oz/1½ cups cos (romaine) lettuce, shredded
- salt and pepper

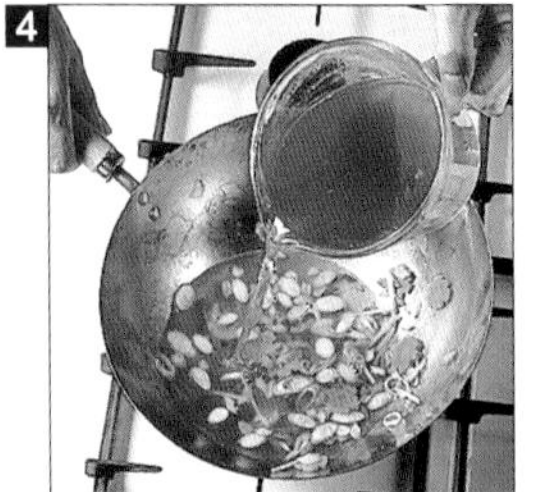

1 Using a sharp knife, cut the tofu (bean curd) into small cubes.

2 Heat the vegetable oil in a preheated wok or large saucepan, add the tofu (bean curd) and stir-fry until browned. Remove with a perforated spoon and drain on kitchen paper (paper towels).

3 Add the carrot, ginger root and spring onions (scallions) to the wok or saucepan and stir-fry for 2 minutes.

4 Add the vegetable stock, soy sauce, sherry and sugar. Stir well to mix all the ingredients. Bring to the boil and simmer for 1 minute.

5 Add the cos (romaine) lettuce to the wok or saucepan and stir until it has just wilted.

6 Return the tofu (bean curd) to the pan to reheat. Season with salt and pepper to taste and serve the soup immediately in warmed bowls.

COOK'S TIP

For a prettier effect, score grooves along the length of the carrot with a sharp knife before slicing. This will create a flower effect as the carrot is cut into rounds. You could also try slicing the carrot on the diagonal to make longer slices.

Chicken Noodle Soup

Quick to make, this hot and spicy soup is hearty and warming. If you like your food really fiery, add a chopped dried or fresh chilli with its seeds.

NUTRITIONAL INFORMATION

Calories	196	Sugars	4g
Protein	16g	Fat	11g
Carbohydrate	8g	Saturates	2g

10 MINS 25 MINS

SERVES 4-6

INGREDIENTS

- 1 sheet of dried egg noodles from a 250 g/9 oz pack
- 1 tbsp oil
- 4 skinless, boneless chicken thighs, diced
- 1 bunch spring onions (scallions), sliced
- 2 garlic cloves, chopped
- 2 cm/¾ inch piece fresh ginger root, finely chopped
- 850 ml/1½ pints/3¾ cups chicken stock
- 200 ml/7 fl oz/scant 1 cup coconut milk
- 3 tsp red curry paste
- 3 tbsp peanut butter
- 2 tbsp light soy sauce
- 1 small red (bell) pepper, chopped
- 60 g/2 oz/½ cup frozen peas
- salt and pepper

1. Put the noodles in a shallow dish and soak in boiling water as the pack directs.
2. Heat the oil in a large preheated saucepan or wok.
3. Add the diced chicken to the pan or wok and fry for 5 minutes, stirring until lightly browned.
4. Add the white part of the spring onions (scallions), the garlic and ginger and fry for 2 minutes, stirring.
5. Stir in the chicken stock, coconut milk, red curry paste, peanut butter and soy sauce.
6. Season with salt and pepper to taste. Bring to the boil, stirring, then simmer for 8 minutes, stirring occasionally.
7. Add the red (bell) pepper, peas and green spring onion tops and cook for 2 minutes.
8. Add the drained noodles and heat through. Spoon the chicken noodle soup into warmed bowls and serve with a spoon and fork.

VARIATION

Green curry paste can be used instead of red curry paste for a less fiery flavour.

Noodle & Mushroom Soup

This soup is very quickly and easily put together, and is cooked so that each ingredient can still be tasted in the finished dish.

NUTRITIONAL INFORMATION

Calories	74	Sugars	1g
Protein	13g	Fat	3g
Carbohydrate	9g	Saturates	0.4g

 4 HOURS  10 MINS

SERVES 4

INGREDIENTS

- 15 g/½ oz/¼ cup dried Chinese mushrooms or 125 g/4½ oz/1⅓ cups field or chestnut (crimini) mushrooms
- 1 litre/1¾ pints/4 cups hot Fresh Vegetable Stock (see page 8)
- 125 g/4½ oz thread egg noodles
- 2 tsp sunflower oil
- 3 garlic cloves, crushed
- 2.5 cm/1 inch piece ginger, shredded finely
- ½ tsp mushroom ketchup
- 1 tsp light soy sauce
- 125 g/4½ oz/2 cups bean sprouts
- coriander (cilantro) leaves, to garnish

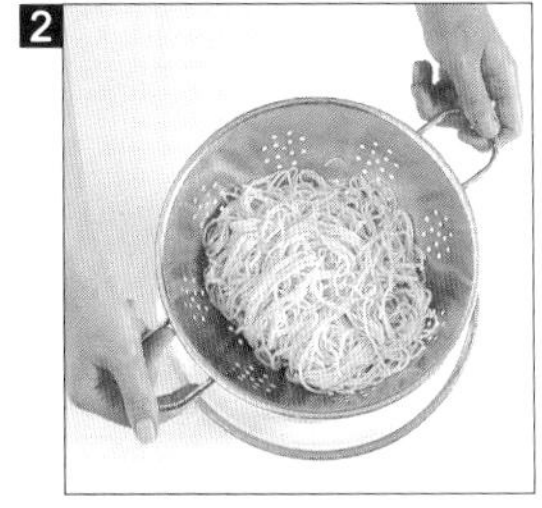
2

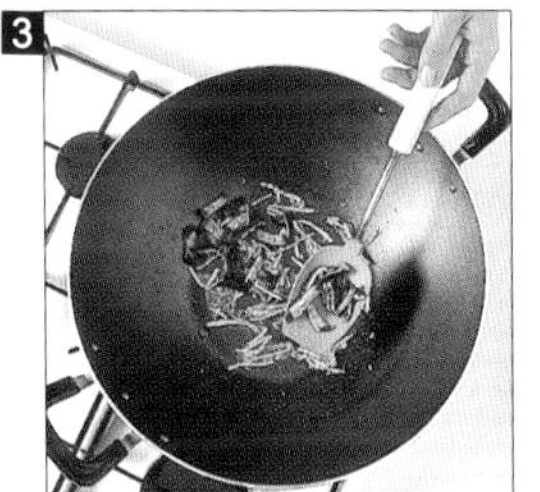
3

4

1 Soak the dried Chinese mushrooms, if using, for at least 30 minutes in 300 ml/½ pint/1¼ cups of the hot vegetable stock. Remove the stalks and discard, then slice the mushrooms. Reserve the stock.

2 Cook the noodles for 2–3 minutes in boiling water. Drain, rinse and set aside until required.

3 Heat the oil over a high heat in a wok or large, heavy frying pan (skillet). Add the garlic and ginger, stir and add the mushrooms. Stir over a high heat for 2 minutes.

4 Add the remaining vegetable stock with the reserved stock and bring to the boil. Add the mushroom ketchup and soy sauce and mix well.

5 Stir in the bean sprouts and cook until tender. Serve over the noodles, garnished with coriander (cilantro) leaves.

COOK'S TIP

Dried mushrooms are highly fragrant and add a special flavour to Chinese dishes. There are many different varieties but Shiitake are the best. Although not cheap, a small amount will go a long way and they will keep indefinitely in an airtight jar.

Vegetarian Hot & Sour Soup

This popular soup is easy to make and very filling. It can be eaten as a meal on its own or served as an appetizer before a light menu.

NUTRITIONAL INFORMATION

Calories	61	Sugars	1g
Protein	5g	Fat	2g
Carbohydrate	8g	Saturates	0.2g

 30 MINS  10 MINS

SERVES 4

INGREDIENTS

- 4 Chinese dried mushrooms (if unavailable, use open-cup mushrooms)
- 125 g/4½ oz firm tofu (bean curd)
- 60 g/2 oz/1 cup canned bamboo shoots
- 600 ml/1 pint/2½ cups vegetable stock or water
- 60 g/2 oz/⅓ cup peas
- 1 tbsp dark soy sauce
- 2 tbsp white wine vinegar
- 2 tbsp cornflour (cornstarch)
- salt and pepper
- sesame oil to serve

1 Place the Chinese dried mushrooms in a small bowl and cover with warm water. Leave to soak for about 20–25 minutes.

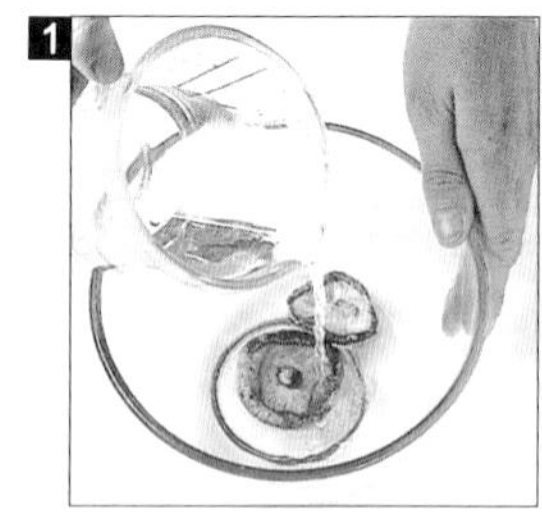

2 Drain the mushrooms and squeeze out the excess water, reserving this. Remove the tough centres and cut the mushrooms into thin shreds. Shred the tofu (bean curd) and bamboo shoots.

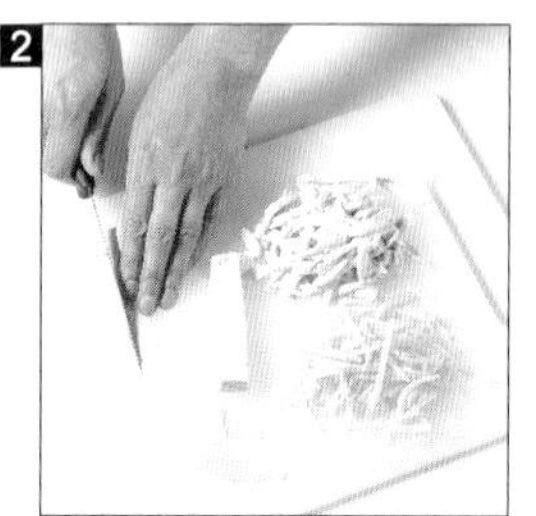

3 Bring the stock or water to the boil in a large saucepan. Add the mushrooms, tofu (bean curd), bamboo shoots and peas. Simmer for 2 minutes.

4 Mix together the soy sauce, vinegar and cornflour (cornstarch) with 2 tablespoons of the reserved mushroom liquid.

5 Stir the soy sauce and cornflour (cornstarch) mixture into the soup with the remaining mushroom liquid. Bring to the boil and season with salt and plenty of pepper. Simmer for 2 minutes.

6 Serve in warmed bowls with a few drops of sesame oil sprinkled over the top of each.

COOK'S TIP

If you use open-cup mushrooms instead of dried mushrooms, add an extra 150 ml/¼ pint/⅔ cup vegetable stock or water to the soup, as these mushrooms do not need soaking.

Minted Pea & Yogurt Soup

A deliciously refreshing soup that is full of goodness. It is also extremely tasty served chilled.

NUTRITIONAL INFORMATION

Calories	208	Sugars	9g
Protein	10g	Fat	7g
Carbohydrate	26g	Saturates	2g

 10 MINS  25 MINS

SERVES 4

INGREDIENTS

- 2 tbsp vegetable ghee or oil
- 2 onions, peeled and coarsely chopped
- 225 g/8 oz potato, peeled and coarsely chopped
- 2 garlic cloves, peeled
- 2.5 cm/1 inch ginger root, peeled and chopped
- 1 tsp ground coriander
- 1 tsp ground cumin
- 1 tbsp plain flour
- 850 ml/1½ pints/3½ cups vegetable stock
- 500 g/1 lb 2 oz frozen peas
- 2-3 tbsp chopped fresh mint, to taste
- salt and freshly ground black pepper
- 150 ml/¼ pint/⅔ cup low-fat natural yogurt
- ½ tsp cornflour (cornstarch)
- 300 ml/½ pint/¼ cups skimmed milk
- a little extra yogurt, for serving (optional)
- mint sprigs, to garnish

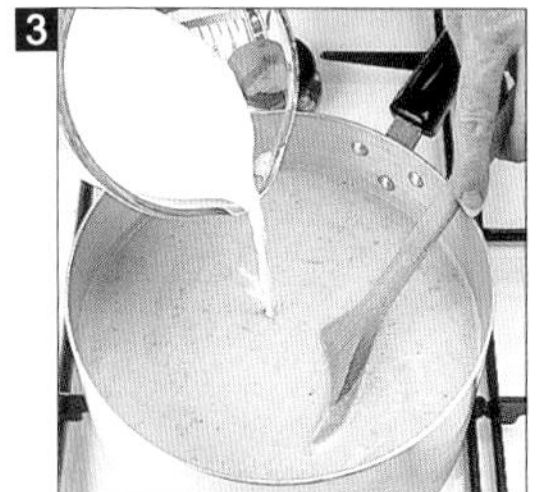

1 Heat the ghee or oil in a saucepan, add the onions and potato and cook gently for 3 minutes. Stir in the garlic, ginger, coriander, cumin and flour and cook for 1 minute, stirring. Add the stock, peas and half the mint and bring to the boil, stirring. Reduce the heat, cover and simmer gently for 15 minutes.

2 Purée the soup in a blender or food processor. Return the mixture to the pan and season with salt and pepper to taste. Blend the yogurt with the cornflour (cornstarch) and stir into the soup.

3 Add the milk and bring almost to the boil, stirring all the time. Cook very gently for 2 minutes. Serve hot, sprinkled with the remaining mint and a swirl of extra yogurt, if wished.

COOK'S TIP

The yogurt is mixed with a little cornflour (cornstarch) before being added to the hot soup – this helps to stabilize the yogurt and prevents it separating when heated.

Partan Bree

This traditional Scottish soup is thickened with a purée of rice and crab meat cooked in milk. Add soured cream, if liked, at the end of cooking.

NUTRITIONAL INFORMATION

Calories	112	Sugars	5g
Protein	7g	Fat	2g
Carbohydrate	18g	Saturates	0.3g

 1 HOUR  35 MINS

SERVES 6

INGREDIENTS

- 1 medium-sized boiled crab
- 90 g/3 oz/scant ½ cup long-grain rice
- 600 ml/1 pint/2½ cups skimmed milk
- 600 ml/1 pint/2½ cups Fish Stock (see page 8)
- 1 tbsp anchovy essence (paste)
- 2 tsp lime or lemon juice
- 1 tbsp chopped fresh parsley or l tsp chopped fresh thyme
- 3–4 tbsp soured cream (optional)
- salt and pepper
- snipped chives, to garnish

1 Remove and reserve all the brown and white meat from the crab, then crack the claws and remove and chop that meat; reserve the claw meat.

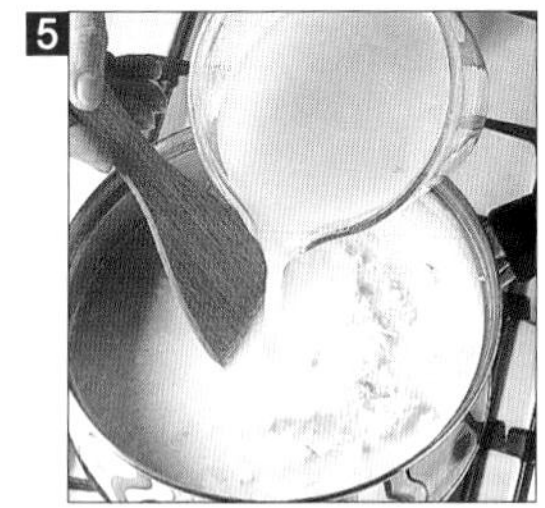

2 Put the rice and milk into a saucepan and bring slowly to the boil. Cover and simmer gently for about 20 minutes.

3 Add the reserved white and brown crab meat and seasoning and simmer for a further 5 minutes.

4 Cool a little, then press through a sieve (strainer), or blend in a food processor or blender until smooth.

5 Pour the soup into a clean saucepan and add the fish stock and the reserved claw meat. Bring slowly to the boil, then add the anchovy essence (paste) and lime or lemon juice and adjust the seasoning.

6 Simmer for a further 2–3 minutes. Stir in the parsley or thyme and then swirl soured cream (if using) through each serving. Garnish with snipped chives.

COOK'S TIP

If you are unable to buy a whole crab, use about 175 g/ 6 oz frozen crab meat and thaw thoroughly before use; or a 175 g/6 oz can of crab meat which just needs thorough draining.

Prawn (Shrimp) Gumbo

This soup is thick with onions, red (bell) peppers, rice, prawns (shrimp) and okra, which both adds flavour and acts as a thickening agent.

NUTRITIONAL INFORMATION

Calories	177	Sugar	5g
Protein	12g	Fats	8g
Carbohydrates	15g	Saturates	1g

 1 HOUR 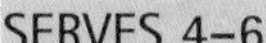 45 MINS

SERVES 4–6

INGREDIENTS

- 1 large onion, chopped finely
- 2 slices lean bacon, chopped finely (optional)
- 1–2 garlic cloves, crushed
- 2 tbsp olive oil
- 1 large or 2 small red (bell) peppers, chopped finely or minced coarsely
- 850 ml/1½ pints/3½ cups Fish or Vegetable Stock (see page 8)
- 1 fresh or dried bay leaf
- 1 blade mace
- good pinch of ground allspice
- 40 g/1½ oz/3 tbsp long-grain rice
- 1 tbsp white wine vinegar
- 125–175 g/4½–6 oz okra, trimmed and sliced very thinly
- 90–125 g/3–4½ oz/½–⅔ cup peeled prawns (shrimp)
- 1 tbsp anchovy essence (paste)
- 2 tsp tomato purée (paste)
- 1–2 tbsp chopped fresh parsley
- salt and pepper

TO GARNISH

- whole prawns (shrimp)
- sprigs of fresh parsley

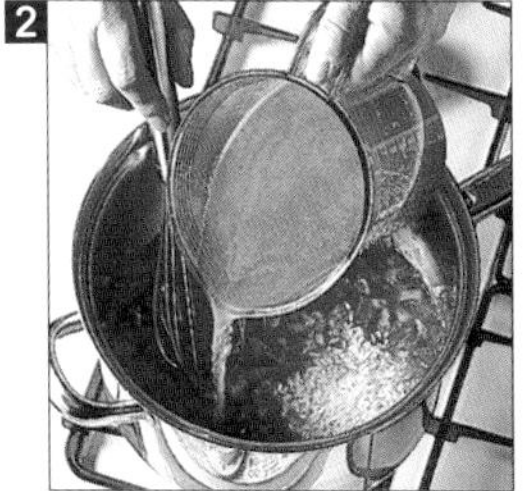

1 Gently fry the onion, bacon (if using) and garlic in the oil in a large saucepan for 4–5 minutes until soft. Add the (bell) peppers to the pan and continue to fry gently for a couple of minutes.

2 Add the stock, bay leaf, mace, allspice, rice, vinegar and seasoning and bring to the boil. Cover and simmer gently for about 20 minutes, giving an occasional stir, until the rice is just tender.

3 Add the okra, prawns (shrimp), anchovy essence (paste) and tomato purée (paste), cover and simmer gently for about 15 minutes until the okra is tender and the mixture slightly thickened.

4 Discard the bay leaf and mace from the soup and adjust the seasoning. Stir in the parsley and serve each portion garnished with a whole prawn (shrimp) and parsley sprigs.

Bean Soup

Beans feature widely in Mexican cooking, and here pinto beans are used to give an interesting texture. Pinto beans require soaking overnight.

NUTRITIONAL INFORMATION

Calories	188	Sugars	9g
Protein	13g	Fat	1g
Carbohydrate	33g	Saturates	0.3g

 20 MINS  3 HOURS

SERVES 4

INGREDIENTS

- 175 g/6 oz pinto beans
- 1.25 litres/2¼ pints water
- 175–225 g/6–8 oz carrots, finely chopped
- 1 large onion, finely chopped
- 2–3 garlic cloves, crushed
- ½–1 chilli, seeded and finely chopped
- 1 litre /1¾ pints vegetable stock
- 2 tomatoes, peeled and finely chopped
- 2 celery sticks, very thinly sliced
- salt and pepper
- 1 tbsp chopped coriander (cilantro) (optional)

CROUTONS

- 3 slices white bread, crusts removed
- oil, for deep-frying
- 1–2 garlic cloves, crushed

VARIATION

Pinto beans are widely available, but if you cannot find them or you wish to vary the recipe, you can use cannellini beans or black-eyed beans (peas) as an alternative.

1 Soak the beans overnight in cold water; drain and place in a pan with the water. Bring to the boil and boil vigorously for 10 minutes. Lower the heat, cover and simmer for 2 hours, or until the beans are tender.

2 Add the carrots, onion, garlic, chilli and stock and bring back to the boil. Cover and simmer for a further 30 minutes, until very tender.

3 Remove half the beans and vegetables with the cooking juices and press through a strainer or process in a food processor or blender until smooth.

4 Return the bean purée to the saucepan and add the tomatoes and celery. Simmer for 10–15 minutes, or until the celery is just tender, adding a little more stock or water if necessary.

5 Meanwhile, make the croûtons. Dice the bread. Heat the oil with the garlic in a small frying pan (skillet) and fry the croûtons until golden brown. Drain on kitchen paper (paper towels).

6 Season the soup and stir in the chopped coriander (cilantro), if using. Transfer to a warm tureen and serve immediately with the croûtons.

Jerusalem Artichoke Soup

Jerusalem artichokes are native to North America, but are also grown in Europe. They have a nutty flavour which combines well with orange.

NUTRITIONAL INFORMATION

Calories	211	Sugars	17g
Protein	7g	Fat	8g
Carbohydrate	29g	Saturates	4g

 10 MINS  30 MINS

SERVES 4

INGREDIENTS

- 675 g/1½ lb Jerusalem artichokes
- 5 tbsp orange juice
- 25 g/1 oz/2 tbsp butter
- 1 leek, chopped
- 1 garlic clove, crushed
- 300 ml/½ pint/1¼ cups vegetable stock
- 150 ml/¼ pint/⅔ cup milk
- 2 tbsp chopped coriander (cilantro)
- 150 ml/¼ pint/⅔ cup natural (unsweetened) yogurt
- grated orange rind, to garnish

1 Rinse the Jerusalem artichokes and place in a large saucepan with 2 tablespoons of the orange juice and enough water to cover. Bring to the boil, reduce the heat and cook for 20 minutes, or until the artichokes are tender.

2 Drain the artichokes, reserving 425 ml/¾ pint/ 2 cups of the cooking liquid. Leave the artichokes to cool, then peel and place in a large bowl. Mash the flesh with a potato masher.

3 Melt the butter in a large saucepan. Add the leek and garlic and fry over a low heat, stirring frequently, for 2–3 minutes, until the leek soft.

1

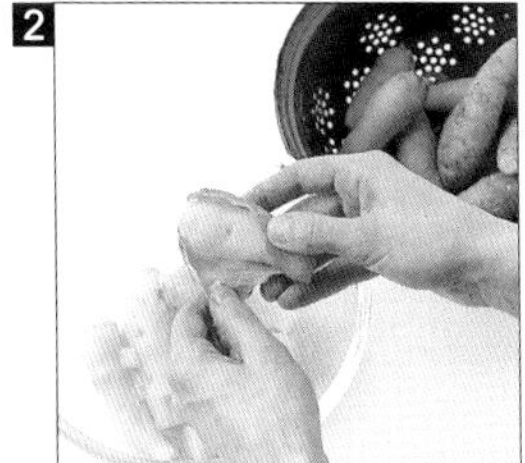
2

4

4 Stir in the mashed artichoke, stock, milk, remaining orange juice and reserved cooking water. Bring to the boil, then simmer for 2–3 minutes.

5 Remove a few pieces of leek with a slotted spoon and reserve. Process the remainder in a food processor for 1 minute until smooth. Alternatively, press through a strainer with the back of a spoon.

6 Return the soup to a clean saucepan and stir in the reserved leeks, coriander (cilantro) and yogurt and heat through. Transfer to individual soup bowls, garnish with orange rind and serve.

Mussels in White Wine

This soup of mussels, cooked in white wine with onions and cream, can be served as an appetizer or a main dish with plenty of crusty bread.

NUTRITIONAL INFORMATION

Calories	396	Sugars	2g
Protein	23g	Fat	24g
Carbohydrate	8g	Saturates	15g

 5–10 MINS  25 MINS

SERVES 4

INGREDIENTS

- about 3 litres/5¼ pints/12 cups fresh mussels
- 60 g/2 oz/¼ cup butter
- 1 large onion, chopped very finely
- 2–3 garlic cloves, crushed
- 350 ml/12 fl oz/1½ cups dry white wine
- 150 ml/¼ pint/⅔ cup water
- 2 tbsp lemon juice
- good pinch of finely grated lemon rind
- 1 bouquet garni sachet
- 1 tbsp plain (all-purpose) flour
- 4 tbsp single (light) or double (thick) cream
- 2–3 tbsp chopped fresh parsley
- salt and pepper
- warm crusty bread, to serve

1

3

5

1 Scrub the mussels in several changes of cold water to remove all mud, sand, barnacles, etc. Pull off all the 'beards'. All of the mussels must be tightly closed; if they don't close when given a sharp tap, they must be discarded.

2 Melt half the butter in a large saucepan. Add the onion and garlic, and fry gently until soft but not coloured.

3 Add the wine, water, lemon juice and rind, bouquet garni and plenty of seasoning. Bring to the boil then cover and simmer for 4–5 minutes.

4 Add the mussels to the pan, cover tightly and simmer for 5 minutes, shaking the pan frequently, until all the mussels have opened. Discard any mussels which have not opened. Remove the bouquet garni.

5 Remove the empty half shell from each mussel. Blend the remaining butter with the flour and whisk into the soup, a little at a time. Simmer gently for 2–3 minutes until slightly thickened.

6 Add the cream and half the parsley to the soup and reheat gently. Adjust the seasoning. Ladle the mussels and soup into warmed large soup bowls, sprinkle with the remaining parsley and serve with plenty of warm crusty bread.

Fiery Salsa

Make this Mexican-style salsa to perk up jaded palates. Its lively flavours really get the tastebuds going. Serve with hot tortilla chips.

NUTRITIONAL INFORMATION

Calories	328	Sugars	2g
Protein	4g	Fat	26g
Carbohydrate	21g	Saturates	5g

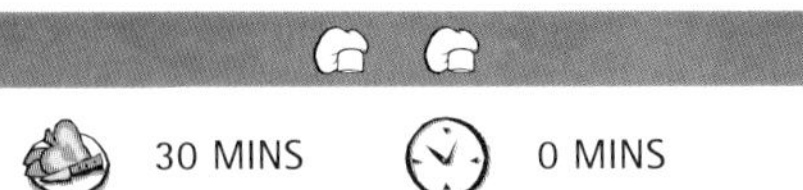

30 MINS 0 MINS

SERVES 4

INGREDIENTS

- 2 small fresh red chillies
- 1 tbsp lime or lemon juice
- 2 large ripe avocados
- 5 cm/2 inch piece of cucumber
- 2 tomatoes, peeled
- 1 small garlic clove, crushed
- few drops of Tabasco sauce
- salt and pepper
- lime or lemon slices, to garnish
- tortilla chips, to serve

1 Remove and discard the stem and seeds from 1 fresh red chilli. Chop the flesh very finely and place in a large mixing bowl.

2 To make a chilli 'flower' for garnish, using a small, sharp knife, slice the remaining chilli from the stem to the tip several times without removing the stem. Place in a bowl of iced water, so that the 'petals' open out.

3 Add the lime or lemon juice to the mixing bowl. Halve, stone (pit) and peel the avocados. Add the flesh to the mixing bowl and mash thoroughly with a fork. The salsa should be slightly chunky. (The lime or lemon juice prevents the avocado from turning brown.)

4 Chop the cucumber and tomatoes finely and add to the avocado mixture with the crushed garlic.

5 Stir in the Tabasco sauce and season with salt and pepper. Transfer the dip to a serving bowl. Garnish with slices of lime or lemon and the chilli flower.

6 Put the bowl on a large plate, surround with tortilla chips and serve. Do not keep this dip standing for long or it will discolour.

1

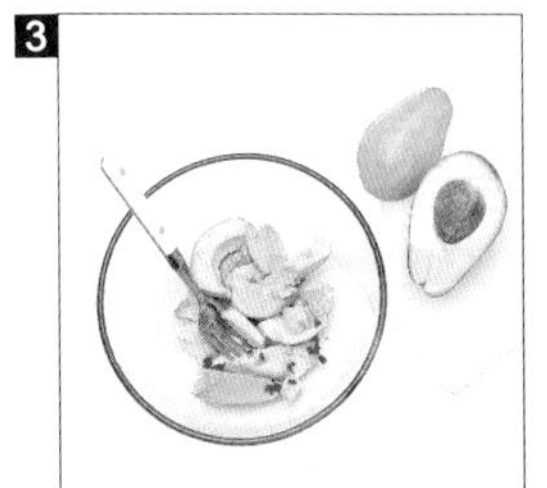
3

5

Figs & Parma Ham (Prosciutto)

This colourful fresh salad is delicious at any time of the year. Prosciutto di Parma is thought to be the best ham in the world.

NUTRITIONAL INFORMATION

Calories	121	Sugars	6g
Protein	1g	Fat	11g
Carbohydrate	6g	Saturates	2g

 15 MINS  5 MINS

SERVES 4

INGREDIENTS

- 40 g/1½ oz rocket (arugula)
- 4 fresh figs
- 4 slices Parma ham (prosciutto)
- 4 tbsp olive oil
- 1 tbsp fresh orange juice
- 1 tbsp clear honey
- 1 small red chilli

1 Tear the rocket (arugula) into more manageable pieces and arrange on 4 serving plates.

2 Using a sharp knife, cut each of the figs into quarters and place them on top of the rocket (arugula) leaves.

3 Using a sharp knife, cut the Parma ham (prosciutto) into strips and scatter over the rocket (arugula) and figs.

4 Place the oil, orange juice and honey in a screw-top jar. Shake the jar until the mixture emulsifies and forms a thick dressing. Transfer to a bowl.

5 Using a sharp knife, dice the chilli, remembering not to touch your face before you have washed your hands (see Cook's Tip, below). Add the chopped chilli to the dressing and mix well.

6 Drizzle the dressing over the Parma ham (prosciutto), rocket (arugula) and figs, tossing to mix well. Serve at once.

2
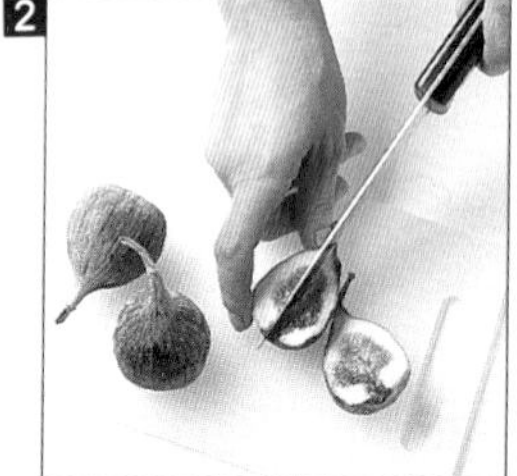

3
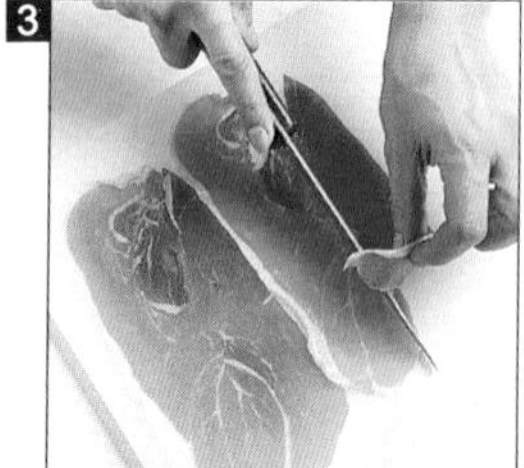

5

COOK'S TIP

Chillies can burn the skin for several hours after chopping, so it is advisable to wear gloves when you are handling the very hot varieties.

Preserved Meats (Salumi)

Mix an attractive selection of these preserved meats (salumi) with olives and marinated vegetables for extra colour and variety.

NUTRITIONAL INFORMATION

Calories	227	Sugars	5g
Protein	10g	Fat	19g
Carbohydrate	5g	Saturates	1g

 10 MINS  5–10 MINS

SERVES 4

INGREDIENTS

- 3 ripe tomatoes
- 3 ripe figs
- 1 small melon
- 60 g/2 oz Italian salami, sliced thinly
- 4 thin slices mortadella
- 6 slices Parma ham (prosciutto)
- 6 slices bresaola
- 4 fresh basil leaves, chopped
- olive oil
- 90 g/3 oz/½ cup marinated olives, pitted
- freshly ground black pepper, to serve

1 Slice the tomatoes thinly and cut the figs into quarters.

2 Halve the melon, scoop out the seeds, and cut the flesh into wedges.

3 Arange the meats on one half of a serving platter. Arrange the tomato slices in the centre and sprinkle with the basil leaves and oil.

4 Cover the rest of the platter with the figs and melon and scatter the olives over the meats.

5 Serve with a little extra olive oil to drizzle over the bresaola, and sprinkle with coarsely ground black pepper.

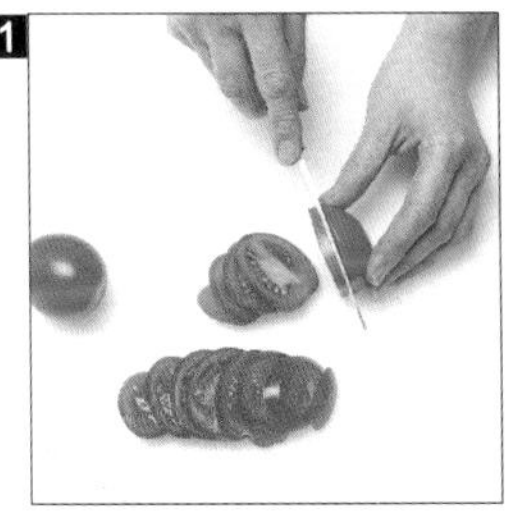
1

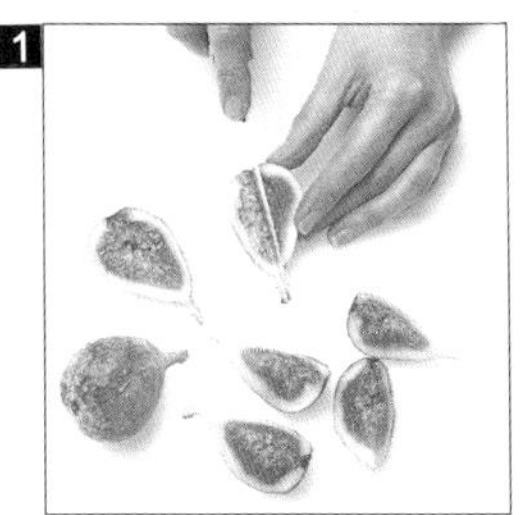
1

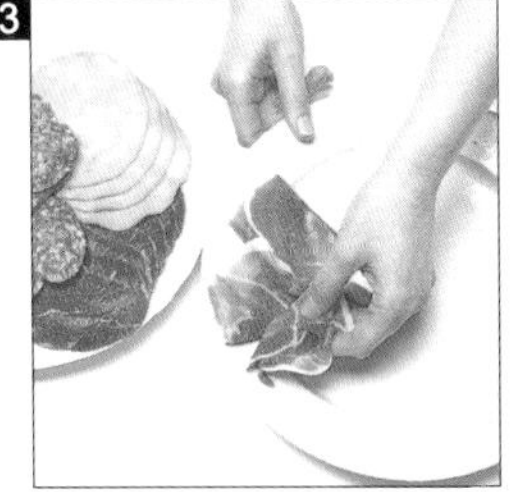
3

Prawn (Shrimp) Parcels

These small prawn (shrimp) bites are packed with the flavour of lime and coriander (cilantro) for a quick and tasty starter.

NUTRITIONAL INFORMATION

Calories	305	Sugars	2g
Protein	15g	Fat	21g
Carbohydrate	14g	Saturates	8g

 15 MINS  20 MINS

SERVES 4

INGREDIENTS

- 1 tbsp sunflower oil
- 1 red (bell) pepper, deseeded and very thinly sliced
- 75 g/2¾ oz/¾ cup beansprouts
- finely grated zest and juice of 1 lime
- 1 red chili, deseeded and very finely chopped
- 1 cm/½ inch piece of root ginger, peeled and grated
- 225 g/8 oz peeled prawns (shrimp)
- 1 tbsp fish sauce
- ½ tsp arrowroot
- 2 tbsp chopped fresh coriander (cilantro)
- 8 sheets filo pastry
- 25 g/1 oz/2 tbsp butter
- 2 tsp sesame oil
- oil, for frying
- spring onion (scallion) tassels, to garnish
- chilli sauce, to serve

1 Heat the sunflower oil in a large preheated wok. Add the red (bell) pepper and beansprouts and stir-fry for 2 minutes, or until the vegetables have softened.

2 Remove the wok from the heat and toss in the lime zest and juice, red chilli, ginger and prawns (shrimp), stirring well.

3 Mix the fish sauce with the arrowroot and stir the mixture into the wok juices. Return the wok to the heat and cook, stirring, for 2 minutes, or until the juices thicken. Toss in the coriander (cilantro) and mix well.

4 Lay the sheets of filo pastry out on a board. Melt the butter and sesame oil and brush each pastry sheet with the mixture.

5 Spoon a little of the prawn (shrimp) filling on to the top of each sheet, fold over each end, and roll up to enclose the filling.

6 Heat the oil in a large wok. Cook the parcels, in batches, for 2–3 minutes, or until crisp and golden. Garnish with spring onion (scallion) tassels and serve hot with a chilli dipping sauce.

4

5

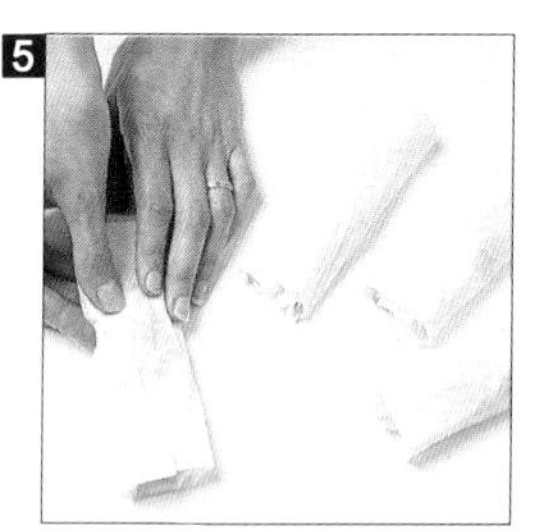

5

COOK'S TIP

If using cooked prawns (shrimp), cook for 1 minute only otherwise the prawns (shrimp) will toughen.

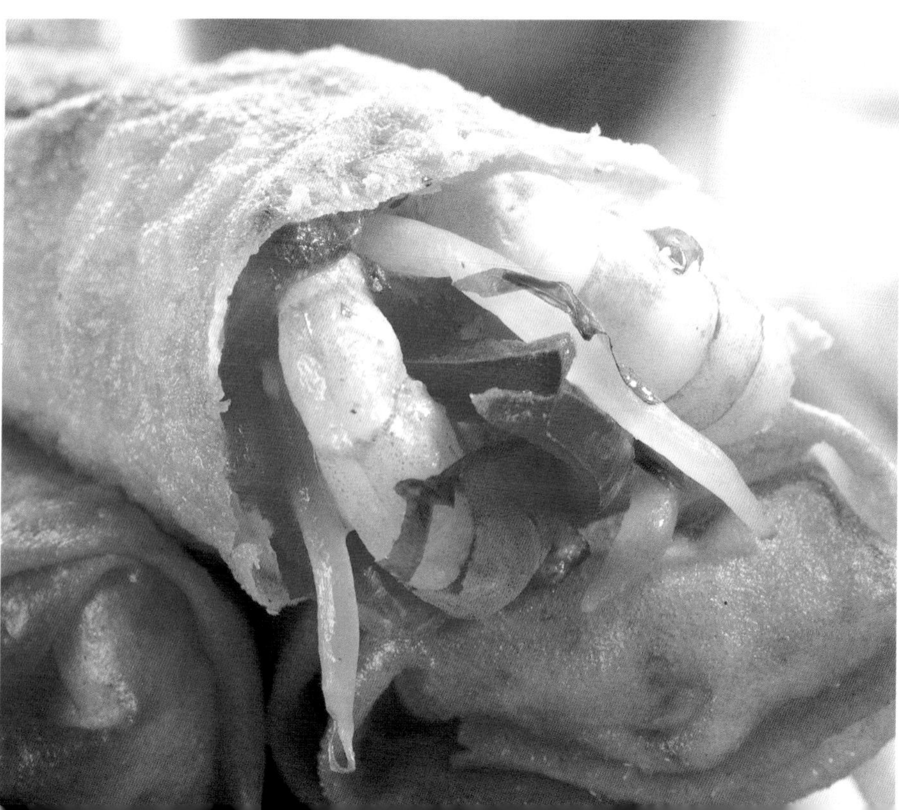

Spicy Sweetcorn Fritters

Cornmeal can be found in most supermarkets or health food shops. Yellow in colour, it acts as a binding agent in this recipe.

NUTRITIONAL INFORMATION

Calories	213	Sugars	6g
Protein	5g	Fat	8g
Carbohydrate	30g	Saturates	1g

 5 MINS  15 MINS

SERVES 4

INGREDIENTS

- 225 g/8 oz/¾ cup canned or frozen sweetcorn
- 2 red chillies, deseeded and very finely chopped
- 2 cloves garlic, crushed
- 10 lime leaves, very finely chopped
- 2 tbsp fresh coriander (cilantro), chopped
- 1 large egg
- 75 g/2¾ oz/½ cup cornmeal
- 100 g/3½ oz fine green beans, very finely sliced
- groundnut oil, for frying

1 Place the sweetcorn, chillies, garlic, lime leaves, coriander (cilantro), egg and cornmeal in a large mixing bowl, and stir to combine.

2 Add the green beans to the ingredients in the bowl and mix well, using a wooden spoon.

3 Divide the mixture into small, evenly sized balls. Flatten the balls of mixture between the palms of your hands to form rounds.

4 Heat a little groundnut oil in a preheated wok or large frying pan (skillet) until really hot. Cook the fritters, in batches, until brown and crispy on the outside, turning occasionally.

5 Leave the fritters to drain on absorbent kitchen paper (paper towels) while frying the remaining fritters.

6 Transfer the fritters to warm serving plates and serve immediately.

COOK'S TIP

Kaffir lime leaves are dark green, glossy leaves that have a lemony-lime flavour. They can be bought from specialist Asian stores either fresh or dried. Fresh leaves impart a delicious flavour.

Crudités with Shrimp Sauce

In this recipe, fruit and vegetable crudités are served with a spicy, garlicky shrimp sauce.

NUTRITIONAL INFORMATION

Calories	85	Sugars	11g
Protein	7g	Fat	1g
Carbohydrate	12g	Saturates	0.2g

 12¼ HOURS  0 MINS

SERVES 4

INGREDIENTS

about 750 g/1 lb10 oz prepared raw fruit and vegetables, such as broccoli, cauliflower, apple, pineapple, cucumber, celery, (bell) peppers and mushrooms

SAUCE

60 g/2 oz dried shrimps

1 cm/½ inch cube shrimp paste

3 garlic cloves, crushed

4 red chillies, seeded and chopped

6 stems fresh coriander (cilantro), coarsely chopped

juice of 2 limes

fish sauce, to taste

brown sugar, to taste

1. Soak the dried shrimps in warm water for 10 minutes.

2. To make the sauce, place the shrimp paste, drained shrimps, garlic, chillies and coriander (cilantro) in a food processor or blender and process until well chopped but not smooth.

3. Turn the sauce mixture into a bowl and add the lime juice, mixing well.

4. Add fish sauce and brown sugar to taste to the sauce. Mix well.

5. Cover the bowl tightly and chill the sauce in the refrigerator for at least 12 hours, or overnight.

6. To serve, arrange the fruit and vegetables attractively on a large serving plate. Place the prepared sauce in the centre for dipping.

COOK'S TIP

Hard-boiled quail's eggs are often added to this traditional fruit and vegetable platter and certainly would be offered on a special occasion.

1

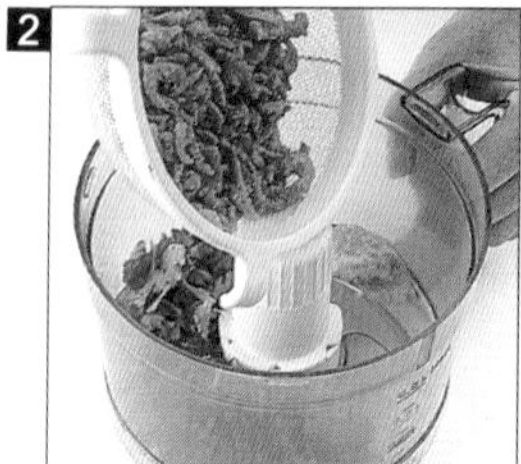
2

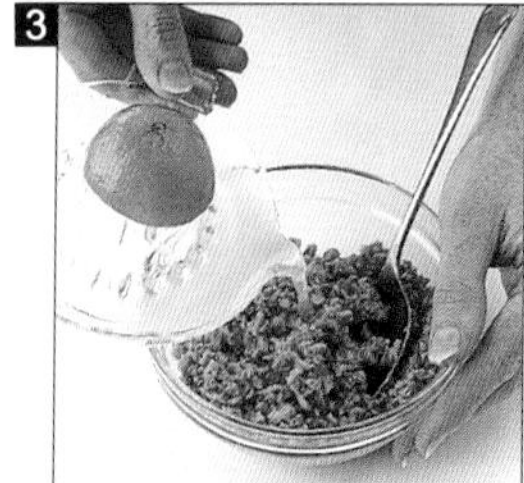
3

Crispy Crab Wontons

These delicious wontons are a superb appetizer. Deep-fried until crisp and golden, they are delicious with a chilli dipping sauce.

NUTRITIONAL INFORMATION

Calories	266	Sugars	0.4g
Protein	10g	Fat	17g
Carbohydrate	18g	Saturates	5g

10 MINS

15 MINS

SERVES 4

INGREDIENTS

- 175 g/6 oz white crabmeat, flaked
- 50 g/1¾ oz canned water chestnuts, drained, rinsed and chopped
- 1 small fresh red chilli, chopped
- 1 spring onion (scallion), chopped
- 1 tbsp cornflour (cornstarch)
- 1 tsp dry sherry
- 1 tsp light soy sauce
- ½ tsp lime juice
- 24 wonton wrappers
- vegetable oil, for deep-frying
- sliced lime, to garnish

1

3

4

1 To make the filling, mix together the crabmeat, water chestnuts, chilli, spring onion (scallion), cornflour (cornstarch), sherry, soy sauce and lime juice.

2 Spread out the wonton wrappers on a work surface (counter) and spoon one portion of the filling into the centre of each wonton wrapper.

3 Dampen the edges of the wonton wrappers with a little water and fold them in half to form triangles. Fold the two pointed ends in towards the centre, moisten with a little water to secure and then pinch together to seal.

4 Heat the oil for deep-frying in a wok or deep-fryer to 180°C–190°C/350°F–375°F, or until a cube of bread browns in 30 seconds. Fry the wontons, in batches, for 2–3 minutes, until golden brown and crisp. Remove the wontons from the oil and leave to drain on kitchen paper (paper towels).

5 Serve the wontons hot, garnished with slices of lime.

COOK'S TIP

Handle wonton wrappers carefully as they can be easily damaged. Make sure that the wontons are sealed well and secured before deep-frying to prevent the filling coming out and the wontons unwrapping.

Seven Spice Aubergines

This is a really simple dish which is perfect served with a chilli dip.

NUTRITIONAL INFORMATION

Calories	169	Sugars	2g
Protein	2g	Fat	12g
Carbohydrate	15g	Saturates	1g

 35 MINS  20 MINS

SERVES 4

INGREDIENTS

- 450 g/1 lb aubergines (eggplants), wiped
- 1 egg white
- 50 g/1¾ oz/3½ tbsp cornflour (cornstarch)
- 1 tsp salt
- 1 tbsp seven spice seasoning
- oil, for deep-frying

1 Using a sharp knife, thinly slice the aubergines (eggplants). Place the aubergine (eggplant) in a colander, sprinkle with salt and leave to stand for 30 minutes. This will remove all the bitter juices.

2 Rinse the aubergine (eggplant) thoroughly and pat dry with absorbent kitchen paper (paper towels).

3 Place the egg white in a small bowl and whip until light and foamy.

4 Using a spoon, mix together the cornflour (cornstarch), salt and seven spice powder on a large plate.

5 Heat the oil for deep-frying in a large preheated wok or heavy-based frying pan (skillet).

6 Dip the aubergines (eggplants) into the egg white, and then into the cornflour (cornstarch) and seven spice mixture to coat evenly.

7 Deep-fry the coated aubergine (eggplant) slices, in batches, for 5 minutes, or until pale golden and crispy.

8 Transfer the aubergines (eggplants) to absorbent kitchen paper (paper towels) and leave to drain. Transfer the seven spice aubergines (eggplants) to serving plates and serve hot.

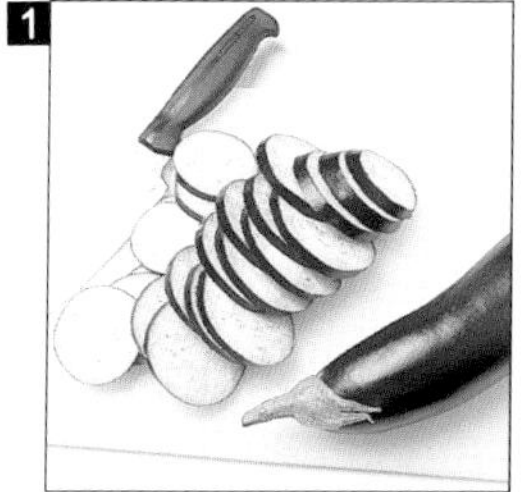

1

4

6

COOK'S TIP

The best oil to use for deep-frying is groundnut oil which has a high smoke point and mild flavour, so it will neither burn or taint the food. About 600 ml/1 pint oil is sufficient.

Bang-Bang Chicken

The cooked chicken meat is tenderized by being beaten with a rolling pin, hence the name for this very popular Szechuan dish.

NUTRITIONAL INFORMATION

Calories	82	Sugars	1g
Protein	13g	Fat	3g
Carbohydrate	2g	Saturates	1g

 $1^1/_4$ HOURS  40 MINS

SERVES 4

INGREDIENTS

- 1 litre/1¾ pints/4 cups water
- 2 chicken quarters (breast half and leg)
- 1 cucumber, cut into matchstick shreds

SAUCE

- 2 tbsp light soy sauce
- 1 tsp sugar
- 1 tbsp finely chopped spring onions (scallions), plus extra to garnish
- 1 tsp red chilli oil
- ¼ tsp pepper
- 1 tsp white sesame seeds
- 2 tbsp peanut butter, creamed with a little sesame oil, plus extra to garnish

1

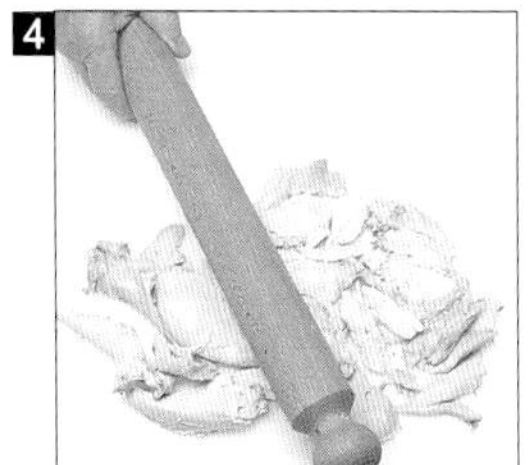

4

4

1 Bring the water to a rolling boil in a wok or a large saucepan. Add the chicken pieces, reduce the heat, cover and cook for 30-35 minutes.

2 Remove the chicken from the wok or pan and immerse in a bowl of cold water for at least 1 hour to cool it, ready for shredding.

3 Remove the chicken pieces, drain and dry on absorbent kitchen paper (paper towels). Take the meat off the bone.

4 On a flat surface, pound the chicken with a rolling pin, then tear the meat into shreds with 2 forks. Mix the chicken with the shredded cucumber and arrange in a serving dish.

5 To serve, mix together all the sauce ingredients until thoroughly combined and pour over the chicken and cucumber in the serving dish. Sprinkle some sesame seeds and chopped spring onions (scallions) over the sauce and serve.

COOK'S TIP

Take the time to tear the chicken meat into similar-sized shreds, to make an elegant-looking dish. You can do this quite efficiently with 2 forks, although Chinese cooks would do it with their fingers.

Butterfly Prawns (Shrimp)

Use unpeeled, raw king or tiger prawns (jumbo shrimp) which are about 7-10cm (3-4 inches) long.

NUTRITIONAL INFORMATION

Calories	157	Sugars	0.3g
Protein	8g	Fat	9g
Carbohydrate	11g	Saturates	2g

 25 MINS  10 MINS

SERVES 4

INGREDIENTS

- 12 raw tiger prawns (jumbo shrimp) in their shells
- 2 tbsp light soy sauce
- 1 tbsp Chinese rice wine or dry sherry
- 1 tbsp cornflour (cornstarch)
- vegetable oil, for deep-frying
- 2 eggs, lightly beaten
- 8-10 tbsp breadcrumbs
- salt and pepper
- shredded lettuce leaves, to serve
- chopped spring onions (scallions), either raw or soaked for about 30 seconds in hot oil, to garnish

1 Shell and devein the prawns (shrimp) leaving the tails on. Split them in half from the underbelly about halfway along, leaving the tails still firmly attached. Mix together the salt, pepper, soy sauce, wine and cornflour (cornstarch), add the prawns (shrimp) and turn to coat. Leave to marinate for 10-15 minutes.

2 Heat the oil in a preheated wok. Pick up each prawn (shrimp) by the tail, dip it in the beaten egg then roll it in the breadcrumbs to coat well.

3 Deep-fry the prawns (shrimp) in batches until golden brown. Remove them with a slotted spoon and drain on paper towels.

4 To serve, arrange the prawns (shrimp) neatly on a bed of lettuce leaves and garnish with spring onions (scallions).

COOK'S TIP

To devein prawns (shrimp), first remove the shell. Make a shallow cut about three-quarters of the way along the back of each prawn (shrimp), then pull out and discard the black intestinal vein.

1
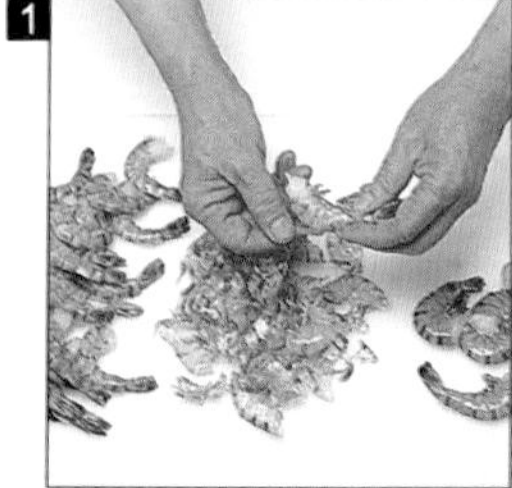

2

4

Pork Dim Sum

These small steamed parcels are traditionally served as an appetizer and are very adaptable to your favourite fillings.

NUTRITIONAL INFORMATION

Calories	478	Sugars	3g
Protein	33g	Fat	29g
Carbohydrate	21g	Saturates	9g

 10 MINS  15 MINS

SERVES 4

INGREDIENTS

- 400 g/14 oz minced (ground) pork
- 2 spring onions (scallions), chopped
- 50 g/1¾ oz canned bamboo shoots, drained, rinsed and chopped
- 1 tbsp light soy sauce
- 1 tbsp dry sherry
- 2 tsp sesame oil
- 2 tsp caster (superfine) sugar
- 1 egg white, lightly beaten
- 4½ tsp cornflour (cornstarch)
- 24 wonton wrappers

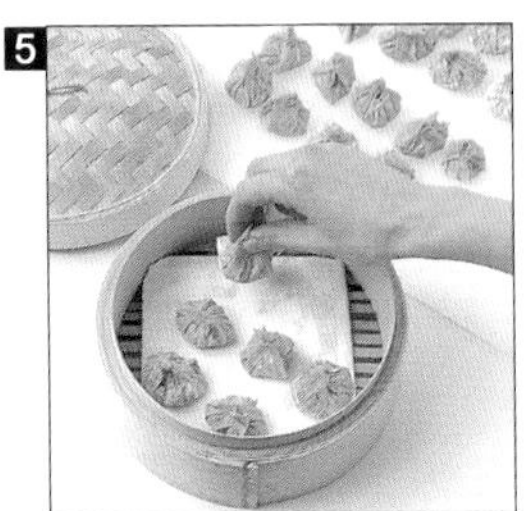

1 Place the minced (ground) pork, spring onions (scallions), bamboo shoots, soy sauce, dry sherry, sesame oil, caster (superfine) sugar and beaten egg white in a large mixing bowl and mix until all the ingredients are thoroughly combined.

2 Stir in the cornflour (cornstarch), mixing until thoroughly incorporated with the other ingredients.

3 Spread out the wonton wrappers on a work surface (counter). Place a spoonful of the pork and vegetable mixture in the centre of each wonton wrapper and lightly brush the edges of the wrappers with water.

4 Bring the sides of the wrappers together in the centre of the filling, pinching firmly together.

5 Line a steamer with a clean, damp tea towel (dish cloth) and arrange the wontons inside.

6 Cover and steam for 5–7 minutes, until the dim sum are cooked through. Serve immediately.

COOK'S TIP

Bamboo steamers are designed to rest on the sloping sides of a wok above the water. They are available in a range of sizes.

Salt & Pepper Prawns

Szechuan peppercorns are very hot, adding heat and a red colour to the prawns (shrimp). They are effectively offset by the sugar in this recipe.

NUTRITIONAL INFORMATION

Calories	174	Sugars	1g
Protein	25g	Fat	8g
Carbohydrate	1g	Saturates	1g

 5 MINS  10 MINS

SERVES 4

INGREDIENTS

- 2 tsp salt
- 1 tsp black pepper
- 2 tsp Szechuan peppercorns
- 1 tsp sugar
- 450 g/1 lb peeled raw tiger prawns (jumbo shrimp)
- 2 tbsp groundnut oil
- 1 red chilli, deseeded and finely chopped
- 1 tsp freshly grated ginger
- 3 cloves garlic, crushed
- spring onions (scallions), sliced, to garnish
- prawn (shrimp) crackers, to serve

1 Grind the salt, black pepper and Szechuan peppercorns in a pestle and mortar.

2 Mix the salt and pepper mixture with the sugar and set aside until required.

3 Rinse the tiger prawns (jumbo shrimp) under cold running water and pat dry with absorbent kitchen paper (paper towels).

4 Heat the oil in a preheated wok or large frying pan (skillet).

5 Add the prawns (shrimp), chopped red chilli, ginger and garlic to the wok or frying pan (skillet) and stir-fry for 4–5 minutes, or until the prawns (shrimp) are cooked through.

6 Add the salt and pepper mixture to the wok and stir-fry for 1 minute, stirring constantly so it does not burn on the base of the wok.

7 Transfer the prawns (shrimp) to warm serving bowls and garnish with spring onions (scallions). Serve hot with prawn (shrimp) crackers.

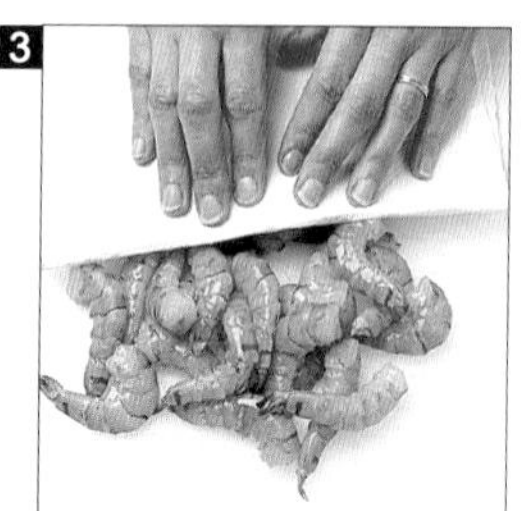

COOK'S TIP

Tiger prawns (jumbo shrimp) are widely available and have a lovely meaty texture. If using cooked tiger prawns (shrimp), add them with the salt and pepper mixture in step 5 – if the cooked prawns (shrimp) are added any earlier they will toughen up and be inedible.

Deep-fried Seafood

Deep-fried seafood is popular all around the Mediterranean, where fish of all kinds is fresh and abundant.

NUTRITIONAL INFORMATION

Calories	393	Sugars	0.2g
Protein	27g	Fat	26g
Carbohydrate	12g	Saturates	3g

 5 MINS  15 MINS

SERVES 4

INGREDIENTS

- 200 g/7 oz prepared squid
- 200 g/7 oz blue (raw) tiger prawns (shrimp), peeled
- 150 g/5 ½ oz whitebait
- oil, for deep-frying
- 50 g/1 ½ oz plain (all-purpose) flour
- 1 tsp dried basil
- salt and pepper

TO SERVE

- garlic mayonnaise
- lemon wedges

1 Carefully rinse the squid, prawns (shrimp) and whitebait under cold running water, completely removing any dirt or grit.

2 Using a sharp knife, slice the squid into rings, leaving the tentacles whole.

3 Heat the oil in a large saucepan to 180°–190°C/350°–375°F or until a cube of bread browns in 30 seconds.

4 Place the flour in a bowl, add the basil and season with salt and pepper to taste. Mix together well.

5 Roll the squid, prawns (shrimp) and whitebait in the seasoned flour until coated all over. Carefully shake off any excess flour.

6 Cook the seafood in the heated oil, in batches, for 2–3 minutes or until crispy and golden all over. Remove all of the seafood with a perforated spoon and leave to drain thoroughly on kitchen paper.

7 Transfer the deep-fried seafood to serving plates and serve with garlic mayonnaise (see page 30) and a few lemon wedges.

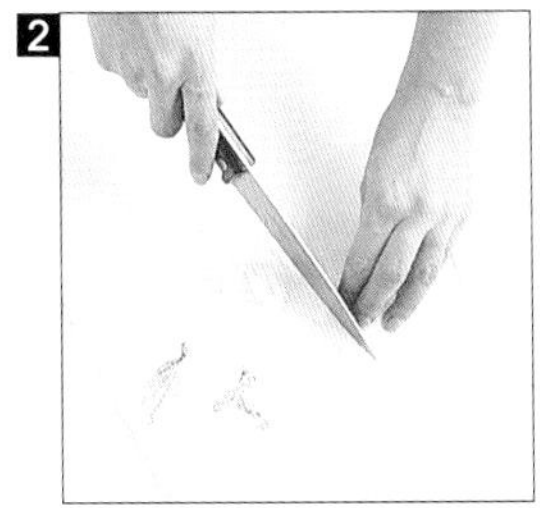

2

5

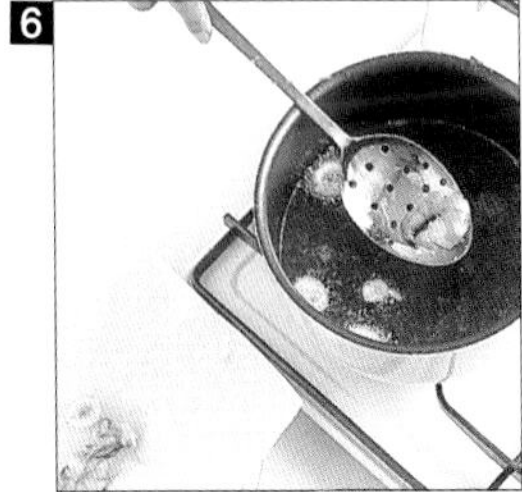

6

Rosy Melon & Strawberries

The combination of sweet melon and strawberries macerated in rosé wine and a hint of rose water is a delightful start to a special meal.

NUTRITIONAL INFORMATION

Calories	59	Sugars	8g
Protein	1g	Fat	0.1g
Carbohydrate	8g	Saturates	0g

 2½ HOURS  0 MINS

SERVES 4

INGREDIENTS

- ¼ honeydew melon
- ½ Charentais or Cantaloupe melon
- 150 ml/5 fl oz/⅔ cup rosé wine
- 2–3 tsp rose water
- 175 g/6 oz small strawberries, washed and hulled
- rose petals, to garnish

1 Scoop out the seeds from both melons with a spoon. Then carefully remove the skin, taking care not to remove too much flesh.

2 Cut the melon flesh into thin strips and place in a bowl. Pour over the wine and sufficient rose water to taste. Mix together gently, cover and leave to chill in the refrigerator for at least 2 hours.

3 Halve the strawberries and carefully mix into the melon.

4 Allow the melon and strawberries to stand at room temperature for about 15 minutes for the flavours to develop – if the melon is too cold, there will be little flavour.

5 Arrange on individual serving plates and serve sprinkled with a few rose petals.

COOK'S TIP

Rose water is generally available from large pharmacies and leading supermarkets as well as from more specialist food suppliers.

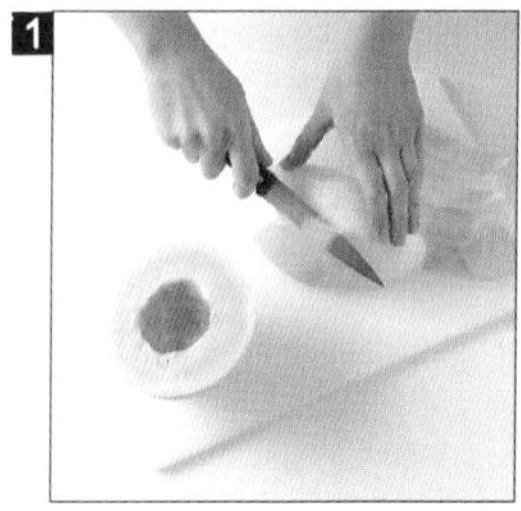

1

2

3

Crispy Wontons

Mushroom-filled crispy wontons are served on skewers with a dipping sauce flavoured with chillies.

NUTRITIONAL INFORMATION

Calories	302	Sugars	1g
Protein	3g	Fat	25
Carbohydrate	15g	Saturates	6g

45 MINS

20 MINS

SERVES 4

INGREDIENTS

- 8 wooden skewers, soaked in cold water for 30 minutes
- 1 tbsp vegetable oil
- 1 tbsp chopped onion
- 1 small garlic clove, chopped
- ½ tsp chopped ginger root
- 60 g/2 oz/½ cup flat mushrooms, chopped
- 16 wonton skins
- vegetable oil, for deep-frying
- salt

SAUCE

- 2 tbsp vegetable oil
- 2 spring onions (scallions), shredded thinly
- 1 red and 1 green chilli, deseeded and shredded thinly
- 3 tbsp light soy sauce
- 1 tbsp vinegar
- 1 tbsp dry sherry
- pinch of sugar

1 Heat the vegetable oil in a preheated wok or frying pan (skillet).

2 Add the onion, garlic and ginger root to the wok or pan and stir-fry for 2 minutes. Stir in the mushrooms and fry for a further 2 minutes. Season well with salt and leave to cool.

2

3 Place 1 teaspoon of the cooled mushroom filling in the centre of each wonton skin.

4 Bring two opposite corners of each wonton skin together to cover the mixture and pinch together to seal. Repeat with the remaining corners.

4

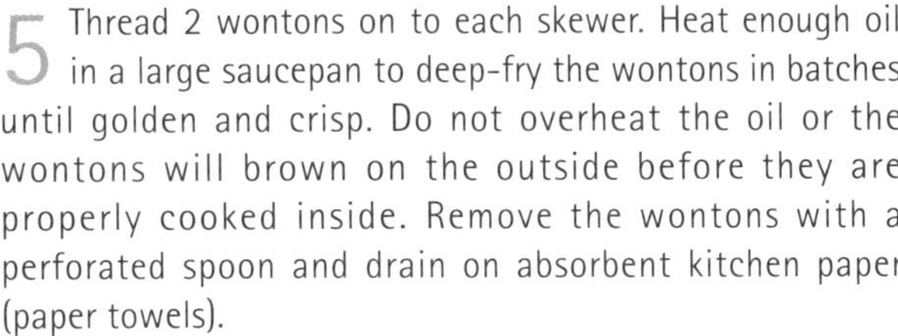
5 Thread 2 wontons on to each skewer. Heat enough oil in a large saucepan to deep-fry the wontons in batches until golden and crisp. Do not overheat the oil or the wontons will brown on the outside before they are properly cooked inside. Remove the wontons with a perforated spoon and drain on absorbent kitchen paper (paper towels).

5

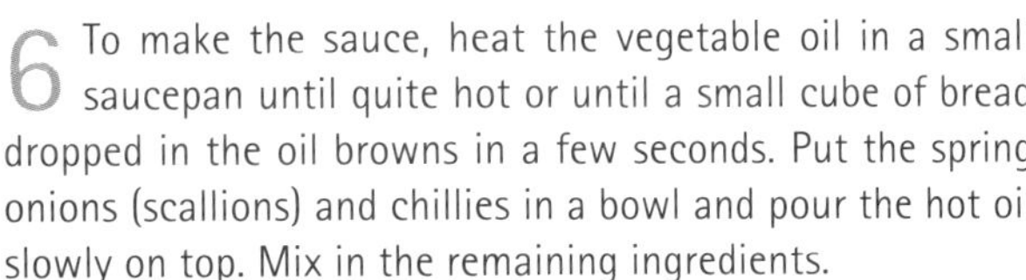
6 To make the sauce, heat the vegetable oil in a small saucepan until quite hot or until a small cube of bread dropped in the oil browns in a few seconds. Put the spring onions (scallions) and chillies in a bowl and pour the hot oil slowly on top. Mix in the remaining ingredients.

7 Transfer the crispy wontons to a serving dish and serve with the dipping sauce.

Roasted (Bell) Peppers

These (bell) peppers can be used as an *antipasto*, as a side dish or as a relish to accompany meat and fish.

NUTRITIONAL INFORMATION

Calories	98	Sugars	13g
Protein	3g	Fat	4g
Carbohydrate	15g	Saturates	1g

5 MINS 40 MINS

SERVES 4

INGREDIENTS

- 2 each, red, yellow and orange (bell) peppers
- 4 tomatoes, halved
- 1 tbsp olive oil
- 3 garlic cloves, chopped
- 1 onion, sliced in rings
- 2 tbsp fresh thyme
- salt and pepper

1 Halve and deseed the (bell) peppers. Place them, cut-side down, on a baking tray (cookie sheet) and cook under a preheated grill (broiler) for 10 minutes.

2 Add the tomatoes to the baking tray (cookie sheet) and grill (broil) for 5 minutes, until the skins of the (bell) peppers and tomatoes are charred.

3 Put the (bell) peppers into a polythene bag for 10 minutes to sweat, which will make the skin easier to peel.

4 Remove the tomato skins and chop the flesh. Peel the skins from the (bell) peppers and slice the flesh into strips.

5 Heat the oil in a large frying pan (skillet) and fry the garlic and onion, stirring occasionally, for 3–4 minutes or until softened.

6 Add the (bell) peppers and tomatoes to the frying pan (skillet) and cook for 5 minutes. Stir in the fresh thyme and season to taste with salt and pepper.

7 Transfer to serving bowls and serve warm or chilled.

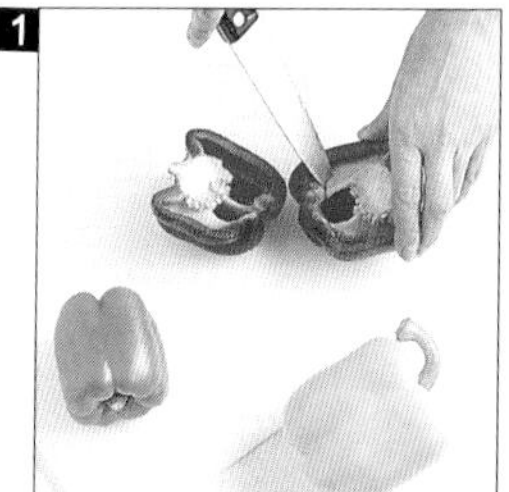
1

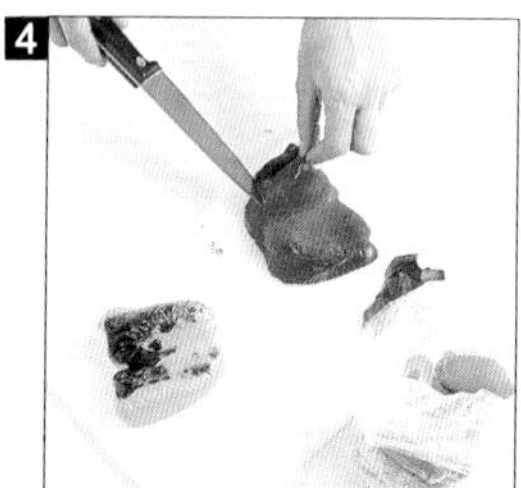
4

6

COOK'S TIP

Preserve (bell) peppers in the refrigerator by placing them in a sterilized jar and pouring olive oil over the top to seal. Or, heat 300 ml/½ pint/¼ cup white wine vinegar with a bay leaf and 4 juniper berries and bring to the boil. Pour over the (bell) peppers and set aside until cold. Pack into sterilized jars.

Vegetable Spring Rolls

There are many different versions of spring rolls throughout the Far East, a vegetable filling being the classic.

NUTRITIONAL INFORMATION

Calories	189	Sugars	4g
Protein	2g	Fat	16g
Carbohydrate	11g	Saturates	5g

10 MINS — 15 MINS

SERVES 4

INGREDIENTS

- 225 g/8 oz carrots
- 1 red (bell) pepper
- 1 tbsp sunflower oil, plus extra for frying
- 75 g/2¾ oz/¾ cup bean sprouts
- finely grated zest and juice of 1 lime
- 1 red chilli, deseeded and very finely chopped
- 1 tbsp soy sauce
- ½ tsp arrowroot
- 2 tbsp chopped fresh coriander (cilantro)
- 8 sheets filo pastry
- 25 g/1 oz butter
- 2 tsp sesame oil

TO SERVE

- chilli sauce
- spring onion (scallion) tassels

1

4

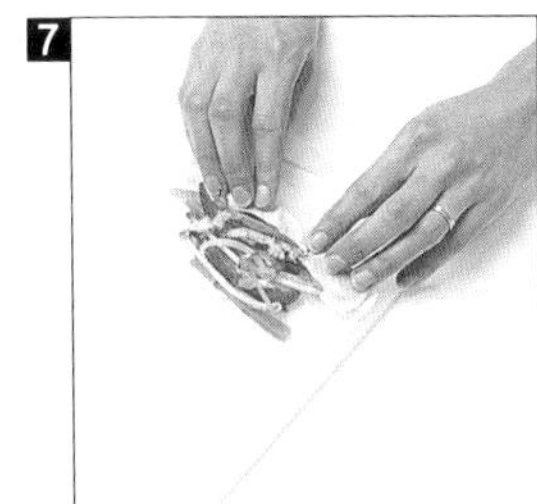

7

1 Using a sharp knife, cut the carrots into thin sticks. Deseed the (bell) pepper and cut into thin slices.

2 Heat the sunflower oil in a large preheated wok.

3 Add the carrot, red (bell) pepper and bean sprouts and cook, stirring, for 2 minutes, or until softened. Remove the wok from the heat and toss in the lime zest and juice, and the red chilli.

4 Mix the soy sauce with the arrowroot. Stir the mixture into the wok, return to the heat and cook for 2 minutes or until the juices thicken.

5 Add the chopped fresh coriander (cilantro) to the wok and mix well.

6 Lay the sheets of filo pastry out on a board. Melt the butter and sesame oil and brush each sheet with the mixture.

7 Spoon a little of the vegetable filling at the top of each sheet, fold over each long side, and roll up.

8 Add a little oil to the wok and cook the spring rolls in batches, for 2–3 minutes, or until crisp and golden.

9 Transfer the spring rolls to a serving dish, garnish and serve hot with chilli dipping sauce.

Black Olive Pâté

This pâté is delicious served as a starter on toasted triangles of bread. It can also be served as a cocktail snack on small rounds of fried bread.

NUTRITIONAL INFORMATION

Calories	149	Sugars	1g
Protein	2g	Fat	14g
Carbohydrate	4g	Saturates	6g

5 MINS 5 MINS

SERVES 4

INGREDIENTS

- 225 g/8 oz/1½ cups pitted juicy black olives
- 1 garlic clove, crushed
- finely grated rind of 1 lemon
- 4 tbsp lemon juice
- 25 g/1 oz/½ cup fresh breadcrumbs
- 60 g/2 oz/¼ cup full fat soft cheese
- salt and pepper
- lemon wedges, to garnish

TO SERVE

- thick slices of bread
- mixture of olive oil and butter

1 Roughly chop the olives and mix with the garlic, lemon rind and juice, breadcrumbs and soft cheese. Pound the mixture until smooth, or place in a food processor and work until fully blended. Season to taste with salt and freshly ground black pepper.

2 Store the pâté in a screw-top jar and chill for several hours before using – this allows the flavours to develop.

3 For a delicious cocktail snack, use a pastry cutter to cut out small rounds from a thickly sliced loaf.

4 Fry the bread rounds in a mixture of olive oil and butter until they are a light golden brown colour. Drain thoroughly on paper towels.

5 Top each round with a little of the pâté, garnish with lemon wedges and serve immediately. This pâté will keep chilled in an airtight jar for up to 2 weeks.

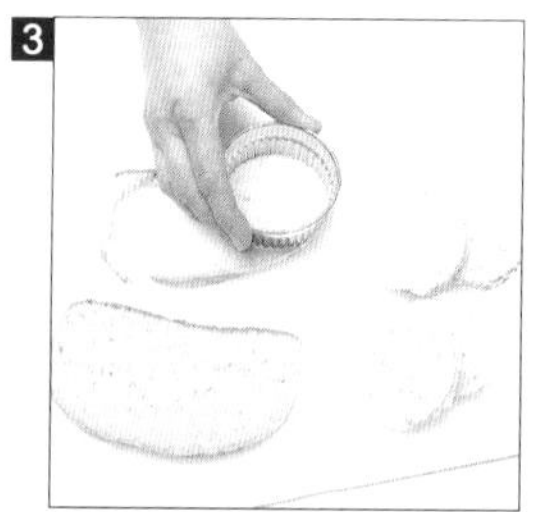

Sweet & Sour Baby Onions

This typical Sicilian dish combines honey and vinegar to give a sweet and sour flavour. Serve hot as an accompaniment or cold with cured meats.

NUTRITIONAL INFORMATION

Calories	131	Sugars	11g
Protein	2g	Fat	6g
Carbohydrate	19g	Saturates	1g

 2 MINS  15 MINS

SERVES 4

INGREDIENTS

- 350 g/12 oz baby or pickling onions
- 2 tbsp olive oil
- 2 fresh bay leaves, torn into strips
- thinly pared rind of 1 lemon
- 1 tbsp soft brown sugar
- 1 tbsp clear honey
- 4 tbsp red wine vinegar

1 Soak the onions in a bowl of boiling water – this will make them easier to peel. Using a sharp knife, peel and halve the onions.

2 Heat the oil in a large frying pan (skillet). Add the bay leaves and onions to the pan and cook for 5–6 minutes over a medium-high heat or until browned all over.

3 Cut the lemon rind into thin matchsticks. Add to the frying pan (skillet) with the sugar and honey. Cook for 2-3 minutes, stirring occasionally, until the onions are lightly caramelized.

4 Add the red wine vinegar to the frying pan (skillet), being careful because it will spit. Cook for about 5 minutes, stirring, or until the onions are tender and the liquid has all but disappeared.

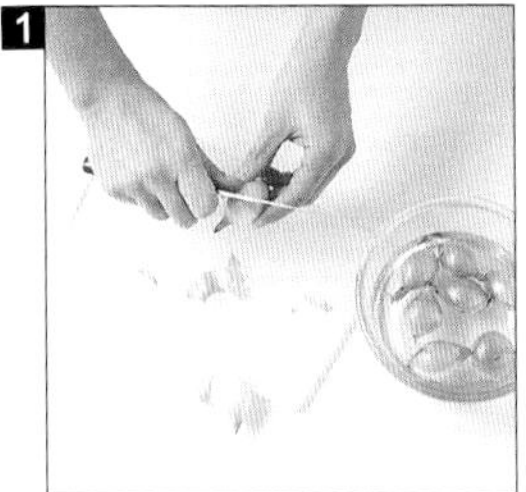
1

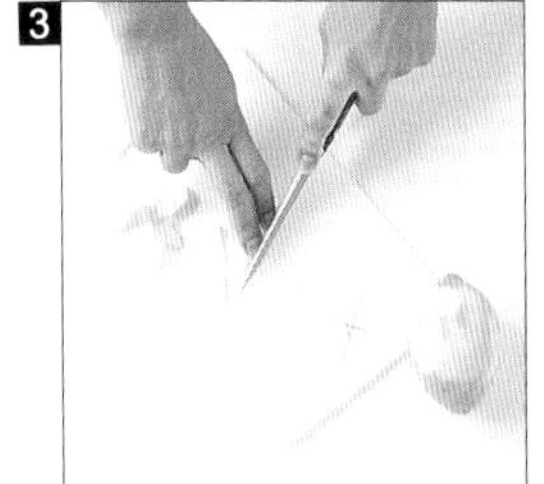
3

4

5 Transfer the onions to a serving dish and serve at once.

COOK'S TIP

Adjust the piquancy of this dish to your liking by adding extra sugar for a sweeter, more caramelized taste or extra red wine vinegar for a sharper, tarter flavour.

Chicken or Beef Satay

In this dish, strips of chicken or beef are threaded on to skewers, grilled (broiled) and served with a spicy peanut sauce.

NUTRITIONAL INFORMATION

Calories	314	Sugars	8g
Protein	32g	Fat	16g
Carbohydrate	10g	Saturates	4g

 2¼ HOURS  15 MINS

SERVES 6

INGREDIENTS

- 4 boneless, skinned chicken breasts or 750 g/1 lb 10 oz rump steak, trimmed

MARINADE

- 1 small onion, finely chopped
- 1 garlic clove, crushed
- 2.5 cm/1 inch piece ginger root, peeled and grated
- 2 tbsp dark soy sauce
- 2 tsp chilli powder
- 1 tsp ground coriander
- 2 tsp dark brown sugar
- 1 tbsp lemon or lime juice
- 1 tbsp vegetable oil

SAUCE

- 300 ml/½ pint/1¼ cups coconut milk
- 4 tbsp/⅓ cup crunchy peanut butter
- 1 tbsp fish sauce
- 1 tsp lemon or lime juice
- salt and pepper

1 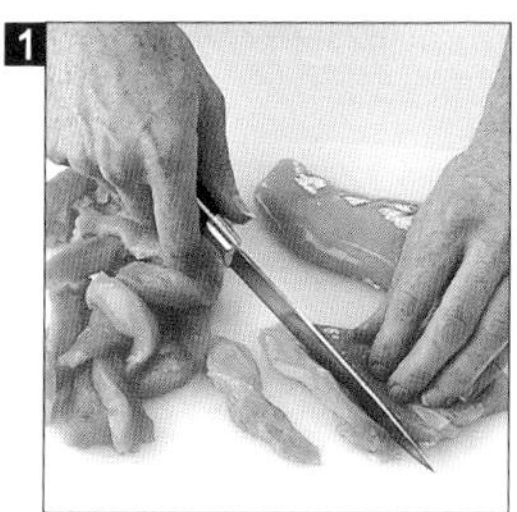

2 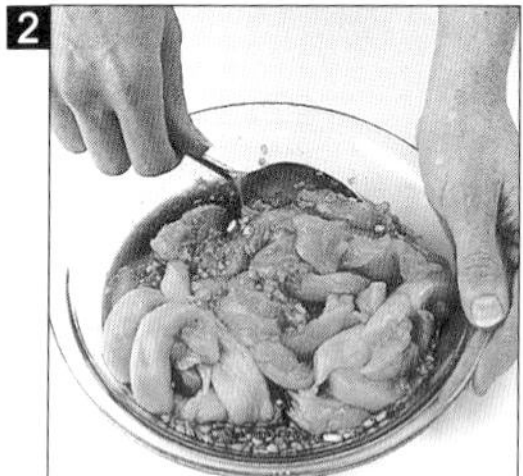

3 

1 Using a sharp knife, trim any fat from the chicken or beef then cut into thin strips, about 7 cm/3 inches long.

2 To make the marinade, place all the ingredients in a shallow dish and mix well. Add the chicken or beef strips and turn in the marinade until well coated. Cover with cling film (plastic wrap) and leave to marinate for 2 hours or stand overnight in the refrigerator.

3 Remove the meat from the marinade and thread the pieces, concertina style, on pre-soaked bamboo or thin wooden skewers.

4 Grill (broil) the chicken and beef satays for 8-10 minutes, turning and brushing occasionally with the marinade, until cooked through.

5 Meanwhile, to make the sauce, mix the coconut milk with the peanut butter, fish sauce and lemon or lime juice in a saucepan. Bring to the boil and cook for 3 minutes. Season to taste.

6 Transfer the sauce to a serving bowl and serve with the cooked satays.

Crostini alla Fiorentina

Serve as a starter, or simply spread on small pieces of crusty fried bread (crostini) as an appetizer with drinks.

NUTRITIONAL INFORMATION

Calories	393	Sugars	2g
Protein	17g	Fat	25g
Carbohydrate	19g	Saturates	9g

10 MINS 40–45 MINS

SERVES 4

INGREDIENTS

3 tbsp olive oil
1 onion, chopped
1 celery stalk, chopped
1 carrot, chopped
1–2 garlic cloves, crushed
125 g/4½ oz chicken livers
125 g/4½ oz calf's, lamb's or pig's liver
150 ml/¼ pint/⅔ cup red wine
1 tbsp tomato purée (paste)
2 tbsp chopped fresh parsley
3–4 canned anchovy fillets, chopped finely
2 tbsp stock or water
25–40 g/1–1½ oz/2–3 tbsp butter
1 tbsp capers
salt and pepper
small pieces of fried crusty bread, to serve
chopped parsley, to garnish

1 Heat the oil in a pan, add the onion, celery, carrot and garlic, and cook gently for 4–5 minutes or until the onion is soft, but not coloured.

2 Meanwhile, rinse and dry the chicken livers. Dry the calf's or other liver, and slice into strips. Add the liver to the pan and fry gently for a few minutes until the strips are well sealed on all sides.

3 Add half of the wine and cook until it has mostly evaporated. Then add the rest of the wine, tomato purée (paste), half of the parsley, the anchovy fillets, stock or water, a little salt and plenty of black pepper.

4 Cover the pan and leave to simmer, stirring occasionally, for 15–20 minutes or until tender and most of the liquid has been absorbed.

5 Leave the mixture to cool a little, then either coarsely mince or put into a food processor and process to a chunky purée.

6 Return to the pan and add the butter, capers and remaining parsley. Heat through gently until the butter melts. Adjust the seasoning and turn out into a bowl. Serve warm or cold spread on the slices of crusty bread and sprinkled with chopped parsley.

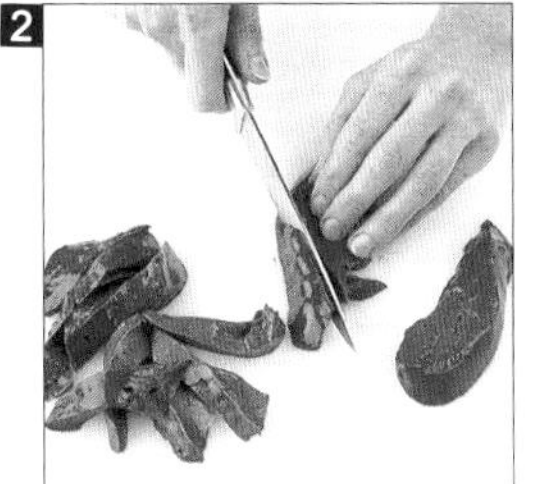

2

3

6

Cauliflower Roulade

A light-as-air mixture of eggs and vegetables produces a stylish vegetarian dish that can be enjoyed hot or cold.

NUTRITIONAL INFORMATION

Calories	271	Sugars	4g
Protein	15g	Fat	20g
Carbohydrate	7g	Saturates	11g

 30 MINS  40 MINS

SERVES 6

INGREDIENTS

- 1 small cauliflower, divided into florets
- 4 eggs, separated
- 90 g/3 oz/¾ cup grated Cheddar cheese
- 60 g/2 oz/¼ cup cottage cheese
- pinch of grated nutmeg
- ½ tsp mustard powder
- salt and pepper

FILLING

- 1 bunch watercress, trimmed
- 60 g/2 oz/¼ cup butter
- 25 g/1 oz/¼ cup flour
- 175 ml/6 fl oz/¾ cup natural (unsweetened) yogurt
- 25 g/1 oz/¼ cup grated Cheddar cheese
- 60 g/2 oz/¼ cup cottage cheese

1 Line a Swiss roll tin (jelly roll pan) with baking parchment.

2 Steam the cauliflower until just tender, then drain under cold water. Process the cauliflower in a food processor or chop and press through a strainer.

3 Beat the egg yolks, then stir in the cauliflower, 60 g/2 oz/½ cup of the Cheddar and the cottage cheese. Season with nutmeg, mustard, and salt and pepper. Whisk the egg whites until stiff but not dry, then fold them in.

4 Spread the mixture evenly in the tin (pan). Bake in a preheated oven, 190°C/375°F/Gas Mark 5, for about 20-25 minutes, until risen and golden.

5 Chop the watercress, reserving a few sprigs for garnish. Melt the butter in a small pan. Cook the watercress, stirring, for 3 minutes, until wilted. Blend in the flour, then stir in the yogurt and simmer for 2 minutes. Stir in the cheeses.

6 Turn out the roulade on to a damp tea towel (dish cloth) covered with baking parchment. Peel off the paper and leave for a minute to allow the steam to escape. Roll up the roulade, including a new sheet of paper, starting from one narrow end.

7 Unroll the roulade, spread the filling to within 2.5 cm/1 inch of the edges, and roll up. Transfer to a baking tray (cookie sheet), sprinkle with the remaining Cheddar and return to the oven for 5 minutes. Serve immediately if serving hot or allow to cool completely.

4

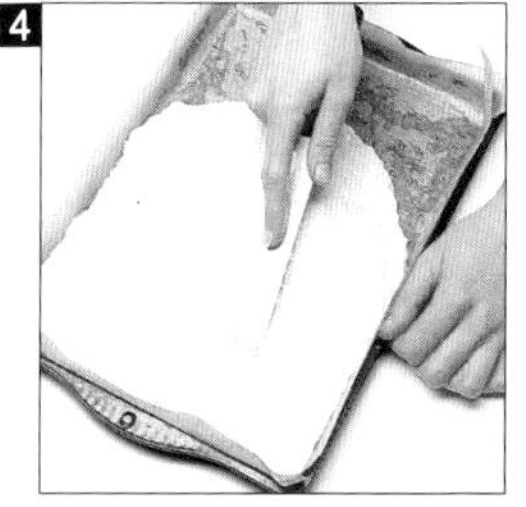

6

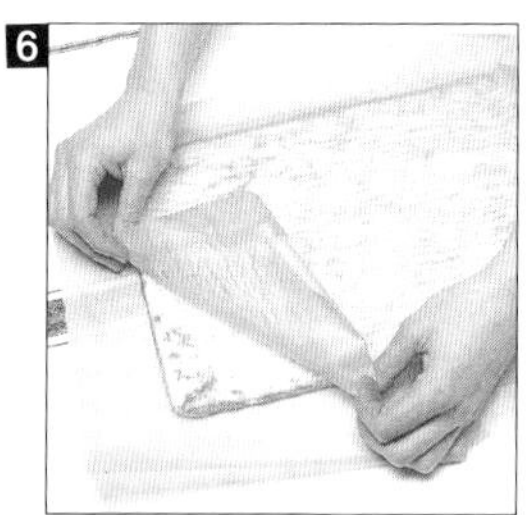

7

Spinach & Ricotta Patties

Nudo or naked is the word used to describe this mixture, which can also be made into thin pancakes or used as a filling for tortelloni.

NUTRITIONAL INFORMATION

Calories	374	Sugars	4g
Protein	16g	Fat	31g
Carbohydrate	9g	Saturates	19g

5 MINS 30 MINS

SERVES 4

INGREDIENTS

- 450 g/1 lb fresh spinach
- 250 g/9 oz ricotta cheese
- 1 egg, beaten
- 2 tsp fennel seeds, lightly crushed
- 50 g/1¾ oz pecorino or Parmesan cheese, finely grated, plus extra to garnish
- 25 g/1 oz plain (all-purpose) flour, mixed with 1 tsp dried thyme
- 75 g/2 ¾ oz/5 tbsp butter
- 2 garlic cloves, crushed
- salt and pepper
- tomato wedges, to serve

1 Wash the spinach and trim off any long stalks. Place in a pan, cover and cook for 4–5 minutes until wilted. This will probably have to be done in batches as the volume of spinach is quite large. Place in a colander and leave to drain and cool.

2 Mash the ricotta and beat in the egg and the fennel seeds. Season with plenty of salt and pepper, then stir in the pecorino or Parmesan cheese.

3 Squeeze as much excess water as possible from the spinach and finely chop the leaves. Stir the spinach into the cheese mixture.

4 Taking about 1 tablespoon of the spinach and cheese mixture, shape it into a ball and flatten it slightly to form a patty. Gently roll in the seasoned flour. Continue this process until all of the mixture has been used up.

5 Half-fill a large frying pan (skillet) with water and bring to the boil. Carefully add the patties and cook for 3–4 minutes or until they rise to the surface. Remove with a perforated spoon.

6 Melt the butter in a pan. Add the garlic and cook for 2–3 minutes. Pour the garlic butter over the patties, season with freshly ground black pepper and serve at once.

1

2

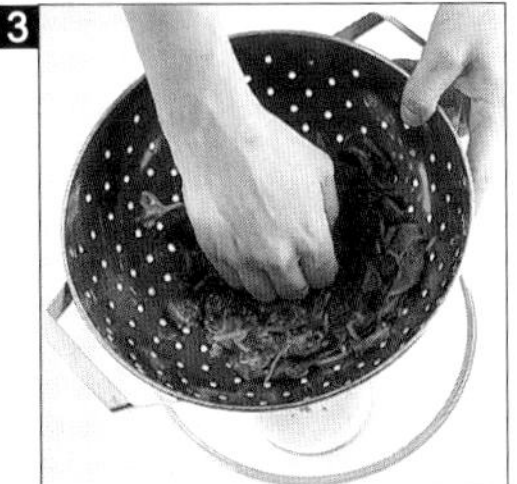
3

Little Golden Parcels

These little parcels will draw admiring gasps from your guests, but they are fairly simple to prepare.

NUTRITIONAL INFORMATION

Calories	320	Sugars	1g
Protein	6g	Fat	21g
Carbohydrate	28g	Saturates	5g

 35 MINS  35 MINS

SERVES 4

INGREDIENTS

- 1 garlic clove, crushed
- 1 tsp chopped coriander (cilantro) root
- 1 tsp pepper
- 250 g/9 oz/1 cup boiled mashed potato
- 175 g/6 oz/1 cup water chestnuts, chopped finely
- 1 tsp grated ginger root
- 2 tbsp ground roasted peanuts
- 2 tsp light soy sauce
- ½ tsp salt
- ½ tsp sugar
- 30 wonton sheets, defrosted
- 1 tsp cornflour (cornstarch), made into a paste with a little water
- vegetable oil for deep-frying
- fresh chives to garnish
- sweet chilli sauce, to serve

1 Mix together all the ingredients except the wonton sheets, cornflour (cornstarch) and oil.

2 Keeping the remainder of the wonton sheets covered with a damp cloth, lay 4 sheets out on a work surface (counter). Put a teaspoonful of the mixture on each. Make a line of the cornflour (cornstarch) paste around each sheet, about 1 cm/½ inch from the edge.

3 Bring all four corners to the centre and press together to form little bags. Repeat with all the wonton sheets.

4 Heat 5 cm/2 inches of the oil in a pan until a light haze appears on top and fry the parcels, in batches of 3, until golden brown. Remove and drain on paper towels. Tie a chive around the neck of each bag to garnish, and serve with a sweet chilli sauce for dipping.

2

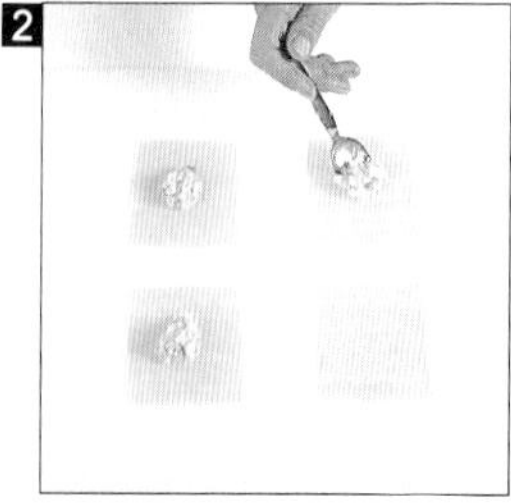

2

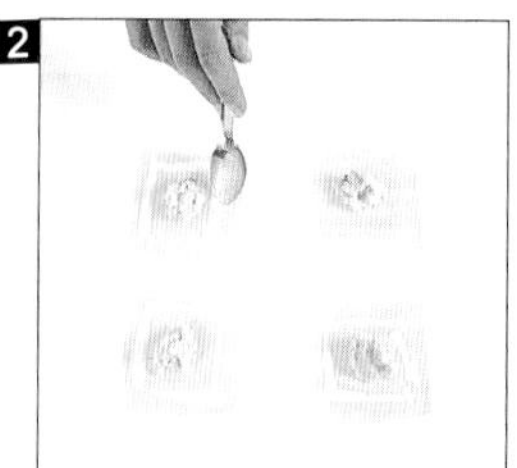

3

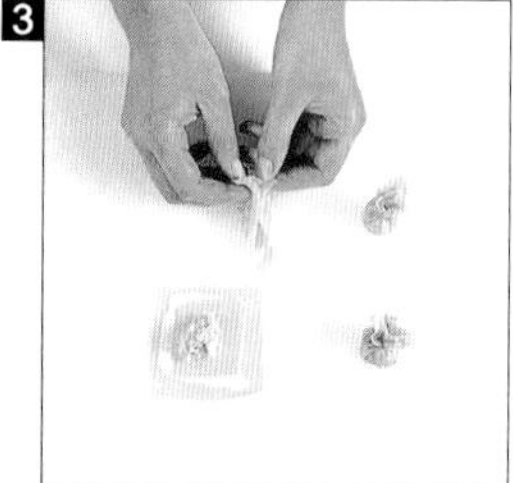

VARIATION

If wonton sheets are not available, use spring roll sheets or filo pastry, and cut the large squares down to about 10 cm/4 inches square.

Stewed Artichokes

This is a traditional Roman dish. The artichokes are stewed in olive oil with fresh herbs.

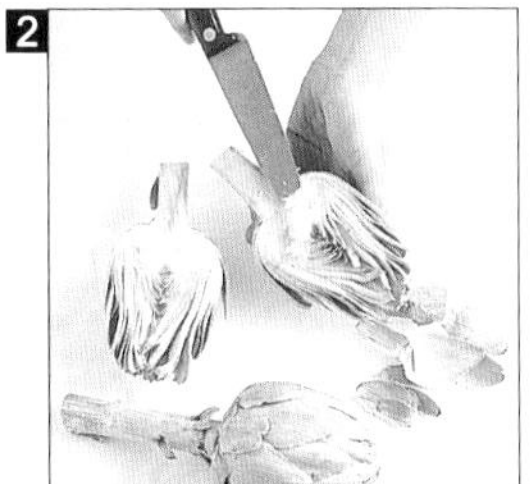
2

3

6

NUTRITIONAL INFORMATION

Calories	129	Sugars	0g
Protein	4g	Fat	8g
Carbohydrate	10g	Saturates	1g

 5 MINS  50 MINS

SERVES 4

INGREDIENTS

- 4 small globe artichokes
- olive oil
- 4 garlic cloves, peeled
- 2 bay leaves
- finely grated rind and juice of 1 lemon
- 2 tbsp fresh marjoram
- lemon wedges, to serve

1 Using a sharp knife, carefully peel away the tough outer leaves surrounding the artichokes. Trim the stems to about 2.5 cm/1 inch.

2 Using a knife, cut each artichoke in half and scoop out the choke (heart).

3 Place the artichokes in a large heavy-based pan. Pour over enough olive oil to half cover the artichokes in the pan.

4 Add the garlic cloves, bay leaves and half of the grated lemon rind.

5 Start to heat the artichokes gently, cover the pan and continue to cook over a low heat for about 40 minutes. It is important that the artichokes should be stewed in the oil, not fried.

6 Once the artichokes are tender, remove them with a perforated spoon and drain thoroughly. Remove the bay leaves and discard.

7 Transfer the artichokes to warm serving plates. Garnish the artichokes with the remaining grated lemon rind, fresh marjoram and a little lemon juice. Serve with lemon wedges.

COOK'S TIP

To prevent the artichokes from oxidizing and turning brown before cooking, brush them with a little lemon juice. In addition, use the oil used for cooking the artichokes for salad dressings – it will impart a lovely lemon and herb flavour.

Buttered Nut & Lentil Dip

This tasty dip is very easy to make. It is perfect to have at barbecues, as it gives your guests something to nibble while they are waiting.

NUTRITIONAL INFORMATION

Calories	395	Sugars	4g
Protein	12g	Fat	31g
Carbohydrate	18g	Saturates	10g

 5-10 MINS  40 MINS

SERVES 4

INGREDIENTS

- 60 g/2 oz/¼ cup butter
- 1 small onion, chopped
- 90 g/3 oz/⅓ cup red lentils
- 300 ml/½ pint/1¼ cups vegetable stock
- 60 g/2 oz/½ cup blanched almonds
- 60 g/2 oz/½ cup pine nuts
- ½ tsp ground coriander
- ½ tsp ground cumin
- ½ tsp grated root ginger
- 1 tsp chopped fresh coriander (cilantro)
- salt and pepper
- sprigs of fresh coriander (cilantro) to garnish

TO SERVE

- fresh vegetable crudités
- bread sticks

1 Melt half the butter in a saucepan and fry the onion over a medium heat, stirring frequently, until golden brown.

2 Add the lentils and vegetable stock. Bring to the boil, then reduce the heat and simmer gently, uncovered, for about 25–30 minutes, until the lentils are tender. Drain well.

3 Melt the remaining butter in a small frying pan (skillet). Add the almonds and pine nuts and fry them over a low heat, stirring frequently, until golden brown. Remove from the heat.

4 Put the lentils, almonds and pine nuts, with any remaining butter, into a food processor blender. Add the ground coriander, cumin, ginger and fresh coriander (cilantro). Process for about 15–20 seconds, until the mixture is smooth. Alternatively, press the lentils through a strainer to purée them and then mix with the finely chopped nuts, spices and herbs.

5 Season the dip with salt and pepper and garnish with sprigs of fresh coriander (cilantro). Serve with fresh vegetable crudités and bread sticks.

VARIATION

Green or brown lentils can be used, but they will take longer to cook than red lentils. If you wish, substitute peanuts for the almonds. Ground ginger can be used instead of fresh – substitute ½ teaspoon and add it with the other spices.

Filled Cucumber Cups

These attractive little cups would make an impressive appetizer at a dinner party.

NUTRITIONAL INFORMATION

Calories	256	Sugars	7g
Protein	10g	Fat	21g
Carbohydrate	8g	Saturates	4g

 10 MINS  0 MINS

SERVES 4

INGREDIENTS

- 1 cucumber
- 4 spring onions (scallions), chopped finely
- 4 tbsp lime juice
- 2 small red chillies, deseeded and chopped finely
- 3 tsp sugar
- 150 g/5½ oz/1¼ cups ground roasted peanuts
- ¼ tsp salt
- 3 shallots, sliced finely and deep-fried, to garnish

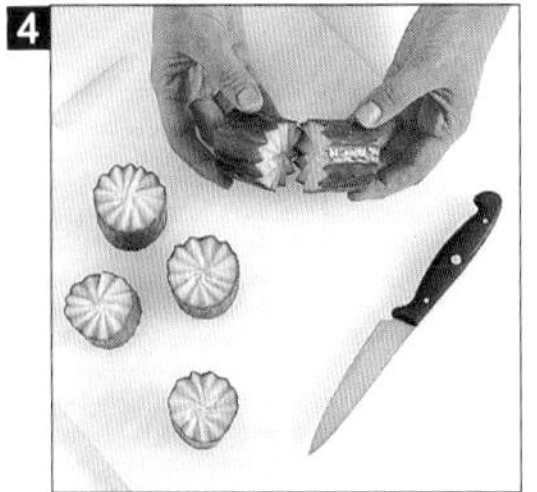

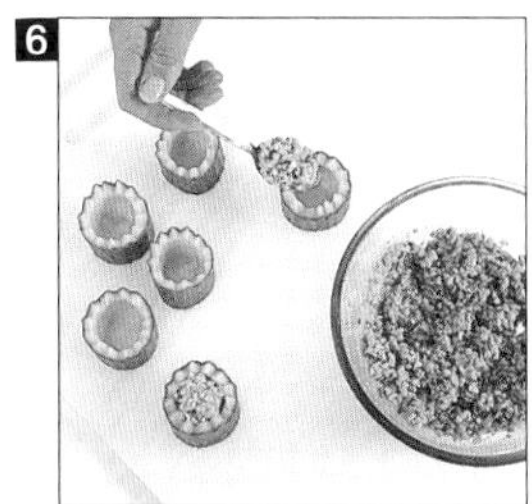

1 Wash the cucumber thoroughly and pat dry with absorbent kitchen paper (paper towels).

2 To make the cucumber cups, cut the ends off the cucumber, and divide it into 3 equal lengths. Mark a line around the centre of each one as a guide.

3 Make a zigzag cut all the way around the centre of each section, always pointing the knife towards the centre of the cucumber.

4 Pull apart the two halves. Scoop out the centre of each cup with a melon baller or teaspoon, leaving a base on the bottom of each cup.

5 Put the spring onions (scallions), lime juice, red chillies, sugar, ground roasted peanuts and salt in a bowl and mix well to combine.

6 Divide the filling evenly between the 6 cucumber cups and arrange on a serving plate.

7 Garnish the cucumber cups with the deep-fried shallots and serve.

COOK'S TIP

Cherry tomatoes can also be hollowed out very simply with a melon baller and filled with this mixture. The two look very pretty arranged together on a serving dish.

Steamed Cabbage Rolls

These small cabbage parcels are quick and easy to prepare and cook. They are ideal for a speedy starter.

NUTRITIONAL INFORMATION

Calories	162	Sugars	0.3g
Protein	24g	Fat	7g
Carbohydrates	2g	Saturates	1g

 5 MINS  20 MINS

SERVES 4

INGREDIENTS

- 8 cabbage leaves, trimmed
- 225 g/8 oz skinless, boneless chicken
- 175 g/6 oz peeled raw or cooked prawns (shrimp)
- 1 tsp cornflour (cornstarch)
- ½ tsp chilli powder
- 1 egg, lightly beaten
- 1 tbsp vegetable oil
- 1 leek, sliced
- 1 garlic clove, thinly sliced
- sliced fresh red chilli, to garnish

1 Blanch the cabbage for 2 minutes. Drain and pat dry with absorbent kitchen paper (paper towels).

2 Mince (grind) the chicken and prawns (shrimp) in a food processor. Place in a bowl with the cornflour (cornstarch), chilli powder and egg. Mix well to combine all the ingredients.

3 Place 2 tablespoons of the chicken and prawn (shrimp) mixture towards one end of each cabbage leaf. Fold the sides of the cabbage leaf around the filling and roll up.

4 Arrange the parcels, seam-side down, in a single layer on a heatproof plate and cook in a steamer for 10 minutes.

5 Meanwhile, sauté the leek and garlic in the oil for 1–2 minutes.

6 Transfer the cabbage parcels to warmed individual serving plates and garnish with red chilli slices. Serve with the leek and garlic sauté.

COOK'S TIP

Use Chinese leaves (cabbage) or Savoy cabbage for this recipe, choosing leaves of a similar size for the parcels.

1

3

3

Deep-fried Risotto Balls

The Italian name for this dish translates as 'telephone wires' which refers to the strings of melted Mozzarella cheese contained within the risotto balls.

NUTRITIONAL INFORMATION

Calories	280	Sugars	2g
Protein	5g	Fat	13g
Carbohydrate	35g	Saturates	3g

5 MINS

35–40 MINS

SERVES 4

INGREDIENTS

- 2 tbsp olive oil
- 1 medium onion, finely chopped
- 1 garlic clove, chopped
- ½ red (bell) pepper, diced
- 150 g/5½ oz/¾ cup arborio (risotto) rice, washed
- 1 tsp dried oregano
- 400 ml/14 fl oz/1⅔ cup hot vegetable or chicken stock
- 100 ml/3½ fl oz/½ scant cup dry white wine
- 75 g/2¾ oz Mozzarella cheese
- oil, for deep-frying
- fresh basil sprig, to garnish

1 Heat the oil in a frying pan (skillet) and cook the onion and garlic for 3–4 minutes or until just softened.

2 Add the (bell) pepper, arborio (risotto) rice and oregano to the pan. Cook for 2–3 minutes, stirring to coat the rice in the oil.

3 Mix the stock together with the wine and add to the pan a ladleful at a time, waiting for the liquid to be absorbed by the rice before you add the next ladleful of liquid.

4 Once all of the liquid has been absorbed and the rice is tender (it should take about 15 minutes in total), remove the pan from the heat and leave until the mixture is cool enough to handle.

5 Cut the cheese into 12 pieces. Taking about 1 tablespoon of risotto, shape the mixture around the cheese pieces to make 12 balls.

6 Heat the oil until a cube of bread browns in 30 seconds. Cook the risotto balls, in batches of 4, for 2 minutes or until golden.

7 Remove the risotto balls with a perforated spoon and drain thoroughly on absorbent kitchen paper. Garnish with a sprig of basil and serve the risotto balls hot.

Onion & Mozzarella Tarts

These individual tarts are delicious hot or cold and are great for lunchboxes or picnics.

NUTRITIONAL INFORMATION

Calories	327	Sugars	3g
Protein	5g	Fat	23g
Carbohydrate	25g	Saturates	9g

45 MINS

45 MINS

SERVES 4

INGREDIENTS

- 250g/9 oz packet puff pastry, defrosted if frozen
- 2 medium red onions
- 1 red (bell) pepper
- 8 cherry tomatoes, halved
- 100g/3½ oz Mozzarella cheese, cut into chunks
- 8 sprigs thyme

1 Roll out the pastry to make 4 x 7.5 cm/3 inch squares. Using a sharp knife, trim the edges of the pastry, reserving the trimmings. Leave the pastry to chill in the refrigerator for 30 minutes.

2 Place the pastry squares on a baking tray (cookie sheet). Brush a little water along each edge of the pastry squares and use the reserved pastry trimmings to make a rim around each tart.

3 Cut the red onions into thin wedges and halve and deseed the (bell) peppers.

4 Place the onions and (bell) pepper in a roasting tin (pan). Cook under a preheated grill (broiler) for 15 minutes or until charred.

5 Place the roasted (bell) pepper halves in a polythene bag and leave to sweat for 10 minutes. Peel off the skin from the (bell) peppers and cut the flesh into strips.

6 Line the pastry squares with squares of foil. Bake in a preheated oven at 200°C/400°F/Gas Mark 6 for 10 minutes. Remove the foil squares and bake for a further 5 minutes.

7 Place the onions, (bell) pepper strips, tomatoes and cheese in each tart and sprinkle with the fresh thyme.

8 Return to the oven for 15 minutes or until the pastry is golden. Serve hot.

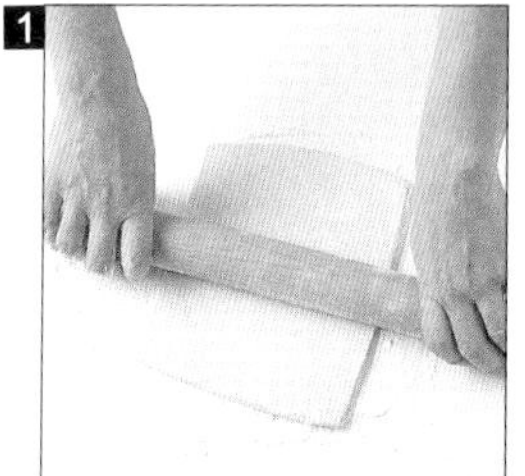
1

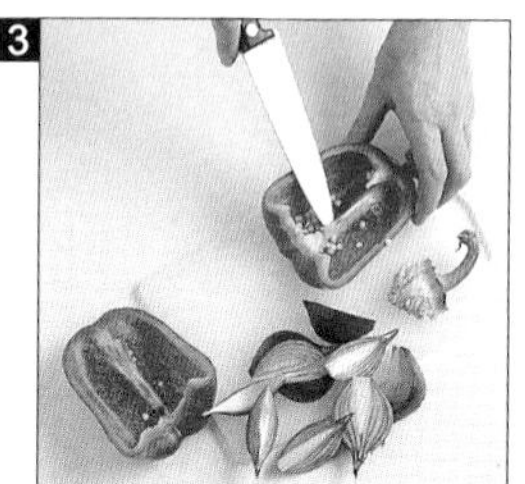
3

6

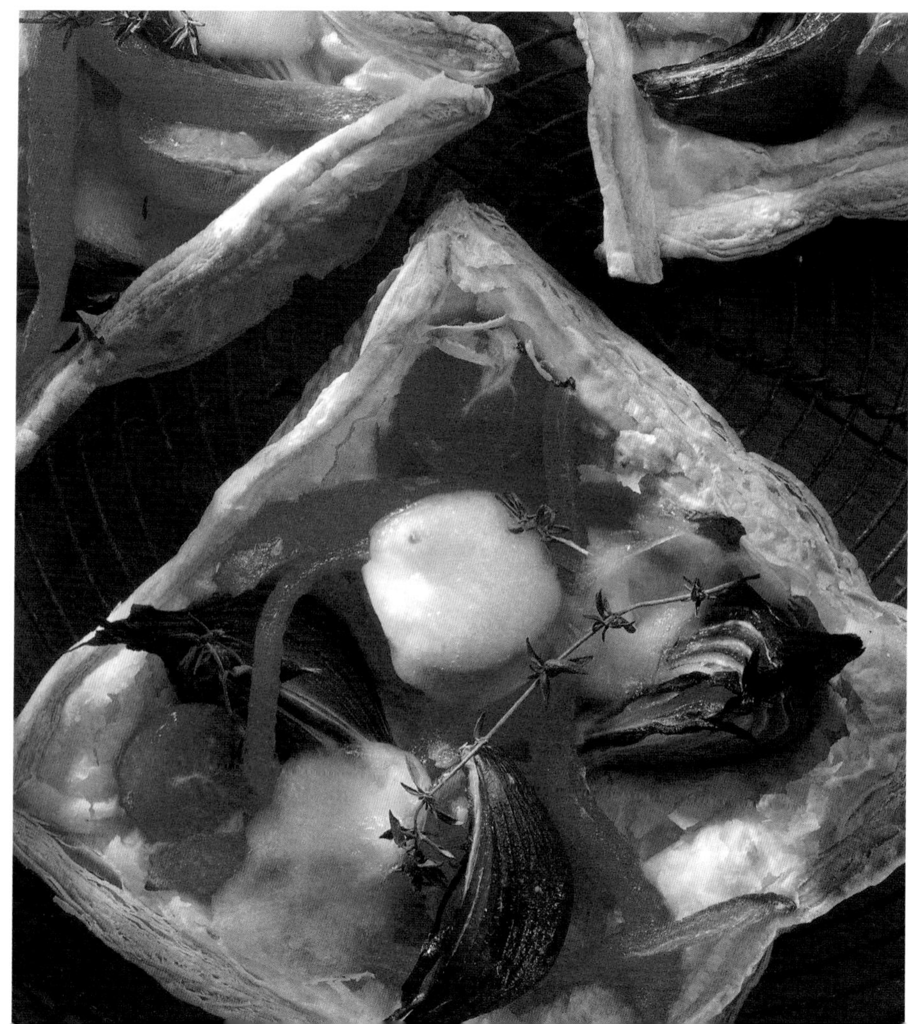

Onions à la Grecque

This is a well-known method of cooking vegetables and is perfect with shallots or onions, served with a crisp salad.

NUTRITIONAL INFORMATION

Calories	200	Sugars	26g
Protein	2g	Fat	9g
Carbohydrate	28g	Saturates	1g

 10 MINS  15 MINS

SERVES 4

INGREDIENTS

- 450 g/1 lb shallots
- 3 tbsp olive oil
- 3 tbsp clear honey
- 2 tbsp garlic wine vinegar
- 3 tbsp dry white wine
- 1 tbsp tomato purée (paste)
- 2 celery stalks, sliced
- 2 tomatoes, seeded and chopped
- salt and pepper
- chopped celery leaves, to garnish

1 Peel the shallots. Heat the oil in a large saucepan, add the shallots and cook, stirring, for 3–5 minutes, or until they begin to brown.

2 Add the honey and cook over a high heat for a further 30 seconds, then add the garlic wine vinegar and dry white wine, stirring well.

3 Stir in the tomato purée (paste), celery and tomatoes and bring the mixture to the boil. Cook over a high heat for 5–6 minutes. Season to taste and leave to cool slightly.

4 Garnish with chopped celery leaves and serve warm. Alternatively chill in the refrigerator before serving.

1

2

3

Courgette (Zucchini) Fritters

These tasty little fritters are great with Roasted (Bell) Peppers (see page 84) as a relish for a drinks party.

NUTRITIONAL INFORMATION

Calories	162	Sugars	2g
Protein	7g	Fat	6g
Carbohydrate	20g	Saturates	2g

 5-10 MINS  20 MINS

MAKES 16-30

INGREDIENTS

- 100 g/3½ oz self–raising flour
- 2 eggs, beaten
- 50 ml/2 fl oz milk
- 300 g/10½ oz courgettes (zucchini)
- 2 tbsp fresh thyme
- 1 tbsp oil
- salt and pepper

1 Sift the self-raising flour into a large bowl and make a well in the centre. Add the eggs to the well, and using a wooden spoon, gradually draw in the flour.

2 Slowly add the milk to the mixture, stirring constantly to form a thick batter.

3 Meanwhile, wash the courgettes (zucchini). Grate the courgettes (zucchini) over a sheet of kitchen paper placed in a bowl to absorb some of the juices.

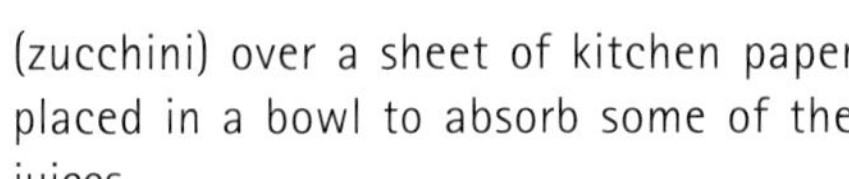

4 Add the courgettes (zucchini), thyme and salt and pepper to taste to the batter and mix thoroughly.

5 Heat the oil in a large, heavy-based frying pan (skillet). Taking a tablespoon of the batter for a medium-sized fritter or half a tablespoon of batter for a smaller-sized fritter, spoon the mixture into the hot oil and cook, in batches, for 3–4 minutes on each side.

6 Remove the fritters with a perforated spoon and drain thoroughly on absorbent kitchen paper. Keep each batch of fritters warm in the oven while making the rest. Transfer to serving plates and serve hot.

VARIATION

Try adding ½ teaspoon of dried, crushed chillies to the batter in step 4 for spicier tasting fritters.

Lentil Pâté

Red lentils are used in this spicy recipe for speed as they do not require pre-soaking. You can substitute other types of lentils, if preferred.

NUTRITIONAL INFORMATION

Calories	267	Sugars	12g
Protein	14g	Fat	8g
Carbohydrate	37g	Saturates	1g

 30 MINS  1¼ HOURS

SERVES 4

INGREDIENTS

- 1 tbsp vegetable oil, plus extra for greasing
- 1 onion, chopped
- 2 garlic cloves, crushed
- 1 tsp garam masala
- ½ tsp ground coriander
- 850 ml/1½ pints/3¾ cups vegetable stock
- 175 g/6 oz/¾ cup red lentils
- 1 small egg
- 2 tbsp milk
- 2 tbsp mango chutney
- 2 tbsp chopped parsley
- chopped parsley, to garnish
- salad leaves (greens) and toast, to serve

2

3

4

1 Heat the oil in a large saucepan and sauté the onion and garlic, stirring constantly, for 2–3 minutes. Add the spices and cook for a further 30 seconds.

2 Stir in the stock and lentils and bring the mixture to the boil. Reduce the heat and simmer for 20 minutes, until the lentils are cooked and softened. Remove the pan from the heat and drain off any excess moisture.

3 Put the mixture in a food processor and add the egg, milk, mango chutney and parsley. Process until smooth.

4 Grease and line the base of a 450 g/ 1 lb loaf tin (pan) and spoon in the mixture, levelling the surface. Cover and cook in a preheated oven, 200°C/400°F/ Gas Mark 6, for 40–45 minutes, or until firm to the touch.

5 Cool in the tin (pan) for 20 minutes, then transfer to the refrigerator.

6 Turn out the pâté on to a serving plate, slice and garnish with chopped parsley. Serve with salad leaves (greens) and toast.

VARIATION

Use other spices, such as chilli powder or Chinese five-spice powder, to flavour the pâté and add tomato relish or chilli relish instead of the mango chutney, if you prefer.

Red Curry Fishcakes

You can use almost any kind of fish fillets or seafood for these delicious fishcakes which can be eaten as an appetizer or a light meal.

NUTRITIONAL INFORMATION

Calories	203	Sugars	1g
Protein	32g	Fat	8g
Carbohydrate	1g	Saturates	1g

 15 MINS  15 MINS

SERVES 6

INGREDIENTS

- 1 kg/2 lb 4 oz fish fillets or prepared seafood, such as cod, haddock, prawns (shrimp), crab meat or lobster
- 1 egg, beaten
- 2 tbsp chopped fresh coriander (cilantro)
- Red Curry Paste (see page 218)
- 1 bunch spring onions (scallions), finely chopped
- vegetable oil, for deep-frying
- chilli flowers, to garnish

CUCUMBER SALAD

- 1 large cucumber, peeled and grated
- 2 shallots, peeled and grated
- 2 red chillies, seeded and very finely chopped
- 2 tbsp fish sauce
- 2 tbsp dried powdered shrimps
- 1½-2 tbsp lime juice

1 Place the fish in a blender or food processor with the egg, coriander (cilantro) and curry paste and purée until smooth and well blended.

2 Turn the mixture into a bowl, add the spring onions (scallions) and mix well to combine.

2

3 Taking 2 tablespoons of the fish mixture at a time, shape into balls, then flatten them slightly with your fingers to make fishcakes.

3

4 Heat the vegetable oil in a preheated wok or frying pan (skillet) until hot.

5 Add a few of the fishcakes to the wok or pan and deep-fry for a few minutes until brown and cooked through. Remove with a slotted spoon and drain on absorbent kitchen paper (paper towels). Keep warm while cooking the remaining fishcakes.

5

6 Meanwhile, to make the cucumber salad, mix the cucumber with the shallots, chillies, fish sauce, dried shrimps and lime juice.

7 Serve the cucumber salad immediately, with the warm fishcakes.

COOK'S TIP

When handling chillies bc very careful not to touch your face or eyes: chilli juice is a powerful irritant, and can be very painful on the skin. Always wash your hands after preparing chillies.

Aspagarus Parcels

These small parcels are ideal as part of a main meal and irresistible as a quick snack with extra plum sauce for dipping.

2

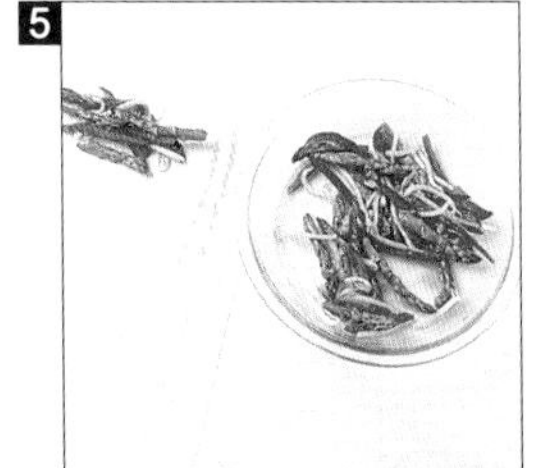
5

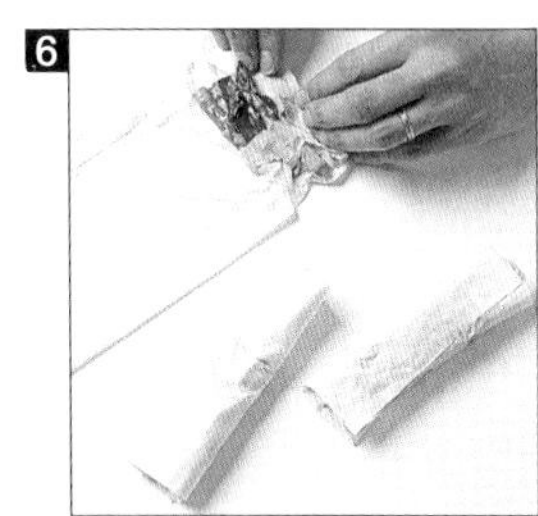
6

NUTRITIONAL INFORMATION

Calories	194	Sugars	2g
Protein	3g	Fat	16g
Carbohydrate	11g	Saturates	4g

 5 MINS  25 MINS

SERVES 4

INGREDIENTS

- 100 g/3½ oz fine tip asparagus
- 1 red (bell) pepper, deseeded and thinly sliced
- 50 g/1¾ oz/½ cup bean sprouts
- 2 tbsp plum sauce
- 1 egg yolk
- 8 sheets filo pastry
- oil, for deep-frying

1 Place the asparagus, (bell) pepper and beansprouts in a large mixing bowl.

2 Add the plum sauce to the vegetables and mix until well-combined.

3 Beat the egg yolk and set aside until required.

4 Lay the sheets of filo pastry out on to a clean work surface (counter).

5 Place a little of the asparagus and red (bell) pepper filling at the top end of each filo pastry sheet. Brush the edges of the filo pastry with a little of the beaten egg yolk.

6 Roll up the filo pastry, tucking in the ends and enclosing the filling like a spring roll. Repeat with the remaining filo sheets.

7 Heat the oil for deep-frying in a large preheated wok. Carefully cook the parcels, 2 at a time, in the hot oil for 4–5 minutes or until crispy.

8 Remove the parcels with a slotted spoon and leave to drain on absorbent kitchen paper (paper towels).

9 Transfer the parcels to warm serving plates and serve immediately.

COOK'S TIP

Be sure to use fine-tipped asparagus as it is more tender than the larger stems.

Hummus & Garlic Toasts

Hummus is a real favourite spread on these flavoursome garlic toasts for a delicious starter or snack.

NUTRITIONAL INFORMATION

Calories	731	Sugars	2g
Protein	22g	Fat	55g
Carbohydrate	39g	Saturates	8g

 20 MINS  3 MINS

SERVES 4

INGREDIENTS

HUMMUS

- 400 g/14 oz can chickpeas (garbanzo beans)
- juice of 1 large lemon
- 6 tbsp tahini (sesame seed paste)
- 2 tbsp olive oil
- 2 garlic cloves, crushed
- salt and pepper
- chopped coriander (cilantro) and black olives, to garnish

TOASTS

- 1 ciabatta loaf (Italian bread), sliced
- 2 garlic cloves, crushed
- 1 tbsp chopped coriander (cilantro)
- 4 tbsp olive oil

2

3

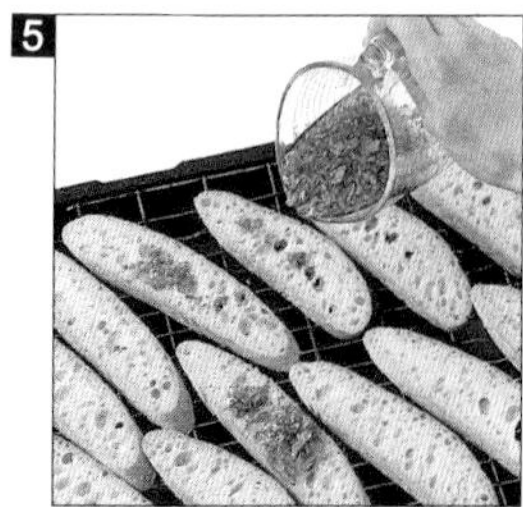

5

1 To make the hummus, firstly drain the chickpeas (garbanzo beans), reserving a little of the liquid. Put the chickpeas (garbanzo beans) and liquid in a food processor and process, gradually adding the reserved liquid and lemon juice. Blend well after each addition until smooth.

2 Stir in the tahini (sesame seed paste) and all but 1 teaspoon of the olive oil. Add the garlic, season to taste and blend again until smooth.

3 Spoon the hummus into a serving dish and smooth the top. Drizzle the remaining olive oil over the top, garnish with chopped coriander (cilantro) and olives. Set aside in the refrigerator to chill while you are preparing the toasts.

4 Place the slices of ciabatta (Italian bread) on a grill (broiler) rack in a single layer.

5 Mix the garlic, coriander (cilantro) and olive oil together and drizzle over the bread slices. Cook under a hot grill (broiler), turning once, for about 2–3 minutes, until golden brown. Serve the toasts immediately with the hummus.

COOK'S TIP

Make the hummus 1 day in advance, and chill, covered, in the refrigerator until required. Garnish and serve.

Spinach Meatballs

Balls of pork mixture are coated in spinach and steamed before being served with a sesame and soy sauce dip.

NUTRITIONAL INFORMATION

Calories	137	Sugars	2g
Protein	13g	Fat	7g
Carbohydrate	6g	Saturates	2g

 20 MINS  25 MINS

SERVES 4

INGREDIENTS

- 125 g/4½ oz pork
- 1 small egg
- 1-cm/½-inch piece fresh root ginger (ginger root), chopped
- 1 small onion, finely chopped
- 1 tbsp boiling water
- 25 g/1 oz canned bamboo shoots, drained, rinsed and chopped
- 2 slices smoked ham, chopped
- 2 tsp cornflour (cornstarch)
- 450 g/1 lb fresh spinach
- 2 tsp sesame seeds

SAUCE

- 150 ml/¼ pint/⅔ cup vegetable stock
- ½ tsp cornflour (cornstarch)
- 1 tsp cold water
- 1 tsp light soy sauce
- ½ tsp sesame oil
- 1 tbsp chopped chives

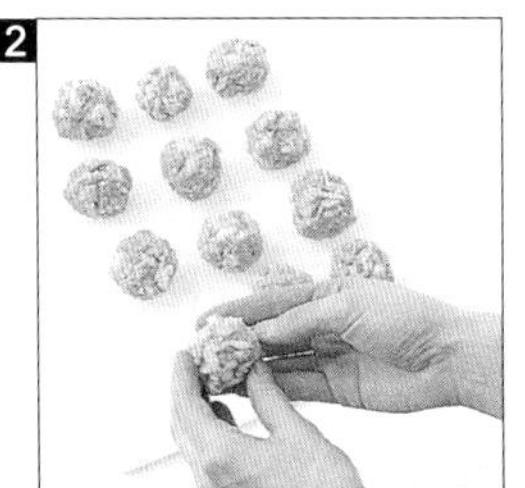

1 Mince (grind) the pork very finely in a food processor. Lightly beat the egg in a bowl and stir into the pork.

2 Put the ginger and onion in a separate bowl, add the boiling water and let stand for 5 minutes. Drain and add to the pork mixture with the bamboo shoots, ham and cornflour (cornstarch). Mix thoroughly and roll into 12 balls.

3 Wash the spinach and remove the stalks. Blanch in boiling water for 10 seconds, drain well then slice into very thin strips and mix with the sesame seeds. Roll the meatballs in the mixture to coat.

4 Place the meatballs on a heatproof plate in the base of a steamer. Cover and steam for 8–10 minutes, until cooked through and tender.

5 Meanwhile, make the sauce. Put the stock in a saucepan and bring to the boil. Mix together the cornflour (cornstarch) and water to a smooth paste and stir it into the stock. Stir in the soy sauce, sesame oil and chives. Transfer the cooked meatballs to a warm plate and serve with the sauce.

Mushroom & Garlic Soufflés

These individual soufflés are very impressive starters, but must be cooked just before serving to prevent them from sinking.

NUTRITIONAL INFORMATION

Calories	179	Sugars	3g
Protein	6g	Fat	14g
Carbohydrate	8g	Saturates	8g

10 MINS 20 MINS

SERVES 4

INGREDIENTS

- 50 g/1¾ oz/4 tbsp butter
- 75 g/2¾ oz/1 cup chopped flat mushrooms,
- 2 tsp lime juice
- 2 garlic cloves, crushed
- 2 tbsp chopped marjoram
- 25 g/1 oz/¼ cup plain (all-purpose) flour
- 225 ml/8 fl oz/1 cup milk
- salt and pepper
- 2 eggs, separated

1 Lightly grease the inside of four 150 ml/¼ pint/⅔ cup individual soufflé dishes with a little butter.

2 Melt 25 g/1 oz/2 tbsp of the butter in a frying pan (skillet). Add the mushrooms, lime juice and garlic and sauté for 2–3 minutes. Remove the mushroom mixture from the frying pan (skillet) with a slotted spoon and transfer to a mixing bowl. Stir in the marjoram.

2

3 Melt the remaining butter in a pan. Add the flour and cook for 1 minute, then remove from the heat. Stir in the milk and return to the heat. Bring to the boil, stirring until thickened.

4 Mix the sauce into the mushroom mixture and beat in the egg yolks.

4

5 Whisk the egg whites until they form peaks and fold into the mushroom mixture until fully incorporated.

5

6 Divide the mixture between the soufflé dishes. Place the dishes on a baking tray (cookie sheet) and cook in a preheated oven, 200°C/400°F/Gas Mark 6, for about 8–10 minutes, or until the soufflés have risen and are cooked through. Serve immediately.

COOK'S TIP

Insert a skewer into the centre of the soufflés to test if they are cooked through – it should come out clean. If not, cook for a few minutes longer, but do not overcook otherwise they will become rubbery.

Toasted Nibbles

These tiny cheese balls are rolled in fresh herbs, toasted nuts or paprika to make tasty nibbles for parties, buffets, or pre-dinner drinks.

NUTRITIONAL INFORMATION

Calories	310	Sugars	1g
Protein	15g	Fat	27g
Carbohydrate	1g	Saturates	12g

40 MINS 5 MINS

SERVES 4

INGREDIENTS

- 125 g/4½ oz/½ cup ricotta cheese
- 125 g/4½ oz/1 cup finely grated Double Gloucester (brick) cheese
- 2 tsp chopped parsley
- 60 g/2 oz/½ cup chopped mixed nuts
- 3 tbsp chopped herbs, such as parsley, chives, marjoram, lovage and chervil
- 2 tbsp mild paprika
- pepper
- herb sprigs, to garnish

1 Mix together the ricotta and Double Gloucester (brick) cheeses. Add the parsley and pepper and work together until thoroughly combined.

2 Form the mixture into small balls and place on a plate. Cover and chill in the refrigerator for about 20 minutes, until they are firm.

3 Scatter the chopped nuts on to a baking tray (cookie sheet) and place them under a preheated grill (broiler) until lightly browned. Take care as they can easily burn. Leave them to cool.

4 Sprinkle the nuts, herbs and paprika into 3 separate small bowls. Remove the cheese balls from the refrigerator and divide into 3 equal piles. Roll 1 quantity of the cheese balls in the nuts, 1 quantity in the herbs and 1 quantity in the paprika until they are all well coated.

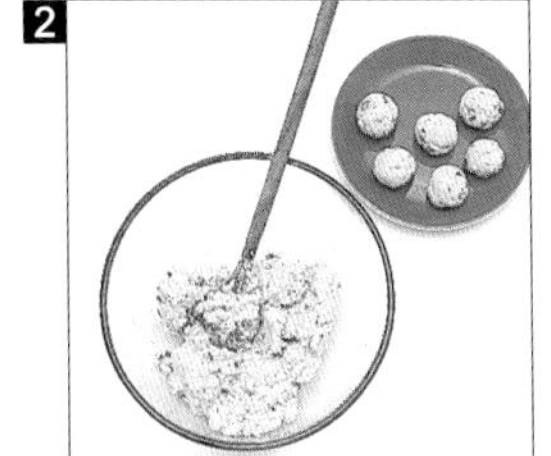

5 Arrange the coated cheese balls alternately on a large serving platter. Chill in the refrigerator until ready to serve and then garnish with sprigs of fresh herbs.

Mixed Bhajis

These small bhajis are often served as accompaniments to a main meal, but they are delicious as a starter with a small salad and yogurt sauce.

NUTRITIONAL INFORMATION

Calories	414	Sugars	7g
Protein	9g	Fat	26g
Carbohydrate	38g	Saturates	3g

25 MINS 30 MINS

SERVES 4

INGREDIENTS

BHAJIS

- 175 g/6 oz/1¼ cups gram flour
- 1 tsp bicarbonate of soda (baking soda)
- 2 tsp ground coriander
- 1 tsp garam masala
- 1½ tsp turmeric
- 1½ tsp chilli powder
- 2 tbsp chopped coriander (cilantro)
- 1 small onion, halved and sliced
- 1 small leek, sliced
- 100 g/3½ oz cooked cauliflower
- 9-12 tbsp cold water
- salt and pepper
- vegetable oil, for deep-frying

SAUCE

- 150 ml/¼ pint/⅔ cup natural (unsweetened) yogurt
- 2 tbsp chopped mint
- ½ tsp turmeric
- 1 garlic clove, crushed
- mint sprigs, to garnish

1 Sift the flour, bicarbonate of soda (baking soda) and salt to taste into a mixing bowl and add the spices and fresh coriander (cilantro). Mix thoroughly.

1

2

3

2 Divide the mixture into 3 and place in separate bowls. Stir the onion into one bowl, the leek into another and the cauliflower into the third bowl. Add 3–4 tbsp of water to each bowl and mix each to form a smooth paste.

3 Heat the oil for deep-frying in a deep fryer to 180°C/350°F or until a cube of bread browns in 30 seconds. Using 2 dessert spoons, form the mixture into rounds and cook each in the oil for 3–4 minutes, until browned. Remove with a slotted spoon and drain well on absorbent kitchen paper (paper towels). Keep the bhajis warm in the oven while cooking the remainder.

4 Mix all of the sauce ingredients together and pour into a small serving bowl. Garnish with mint sprigs and serve with the warm bhajis.

Minted Onion Bhajis

Gram flour (also known as besan flour) is a fine yellow flour made from chick peas and is available from supermarkets and Asian food shops.

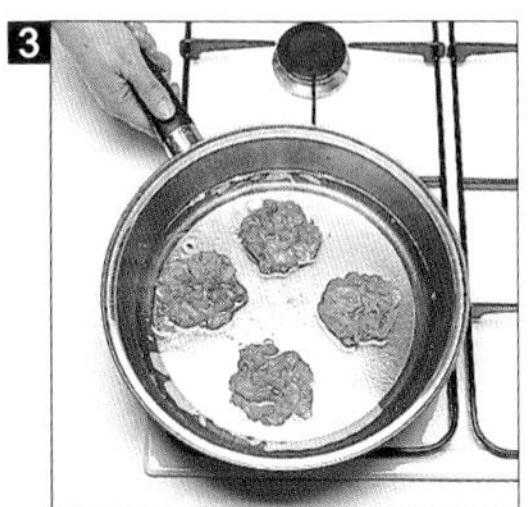

NUTRITIONAL INFORMATION

Calories	251	Sugars	7g
Protein	7g	Fat	8g
Carbohydrate	39g	Saturates	1g

 5 MINS  15 MINS

MAKES 12

INGREDIENTS

- 125 g/4½ oz/1 cup gram flour
- ¼ tsp cayenne pepper
- ¼–½ tsp ground coriander
- ¼–½ tsp ground cumin
- 1 tbsp chopped fresh mint
- 4 tbsp strained thick low-fat yogurt
- 65 ml/2½ fl oz/¼ cup cold water
- 1 large onion, quartered and thinly sliced
- vegetable oil, for frying
- salt and pepper
- sprigs of mint, to garnish

1 Put the gram flour into a bowl, add the cayenne pepper, coriander, cumin and mint and season with salt and pepper to taste. Stir in the yogurt, water and sliced onion and mix well together.

2 One-third fill a large, deep frying pan with oil and heat until very hot. Drop heaped spoonfuls of the mixture, a few at a time, into the hot oil and use two forks to neaten the mixture into rough ball-shapes.

3 Fry the bhajis until golden brown and cooked through, turning frequently.

4 Drain the bhajis on absorbent kitchen paper (paper towels) and keep warm while cooking the remainder in the same way.

5 Arrange the bhajis on a platter and garnish with sprigs of fresh mint. Serve hot or warm.

COOK'S TIP

Gram flour is excellent for making batter and is used in India in place of flour. It can be made from ground split peas as well as chick-peas (garbanzo beans).

Chinese Vegetable Pancakes

Chinese pancakes are made with hardly any fat – they are simply flattened white flour dough.

NUTRITIONAL INFORMATION

Calories	312	Sugars	5g
Protein	13g	Fat	19g
Carbohydrate	25g	Saturates	7g

 5 MINS

10 MINS

SERVES 4

INGREDIENTS

- 1 tbsp vegetable oil
- 1 garlic clove, crushed
- 2.5 cm/1 inch piece root (fresh) ginger, grated
- 1 bunch spring onions (scallions), trimmed and shredded lengthwise
- 100 g/3½ oz mangetout (snow peas), topped, tailed and shredded
- 225 g/8 oz tofu (bean curd), drained and cut into 1 cm/½ inch pieces
- 2 tbsp dark soy sauce, plus extra to serve
- 2 tbsp hoisin sauce, plus extra to serve
- 60 g/2 oz canned bamboo shoots, drained
- 60 g/2 oz canned water chestnuts, drained and sliced
- 100 g/3½ oz bean sprouts
- 1 small red chilli, deseeded and sliced thinly
- 1 small bunch fresh chives
- 12 soft Chinese pancakes

TO SERVE

- shredded Chinese leaves (cabbage)
- 1 cucumber, sliced
- strips of red chilli

2

3

5

1 Heat the oil in a non-stick wok or a large frying pan (skillet) and stir-fry the garlic and ginger for 1 minute.

2 Add the spring onions (scallions), mangetout (snow peas), tofu (bean curd), soy and hoisin sauces. Stir-fry for 2 minutes.

3 Add the bamboo shoots, water chestnuts, bean sprouts and sliced red chilli to the pan.

4 Stir-fry gently for a further 2 minutes until the vegetables are just tender.

5 Snip the chives into 2.5 cm/1 inch lengths and stir into the mixture.

6 Heat the pancakes according to the packet instructions and keep warm.

7 Divide the vegetables and tofu (bean curd) among the pancakes. Roll up and serve with the Chinese leaves (cabbage), cucumber, chilli and extra sauce for dipping.

Pork with Chilli & Garlic

Any leftovers from this dish can be used for a number of other dishes, for example Twice-cooked Pork (see page 383).

NUTRITIONAL INFORMATION

Calories	137	Sugars	0.1g
Protein	16g	Fat	8g
Carbohydrate	1g	Saturates	2g

 5 HOURS  35 MINS

SERVES 4

INGREDIENTS

500 g/1 lb 2 oz leg of pork, boned but not skinned

SAUCE

1 tsp finely chopped garlic

1 tsp finely chopped spring onions (scallions)

2 tbsp light soy sauce

1 tsp red chilli oil

½ tsp sesame oil

sprig of fresh coriander (cilantro), to garnish (optional)

1 Place the pork, tied together in one piece, in a large saucepan, add enough cold water to cover, and bring to a rolling boil over a medium heat.

2 Using a slotted spoon, skim off the scum that rises to the surface, cover the pan with a lid and simmer gently for 25-30 minutes.

3 Leave the meat in the liquid to cool, under cover, for at least 1-2 hours.

4 Lift out the meat with 2 slotted spoons and leave to cool completely, skin-side up, for 2-3 hours.

5 To serve, cut off the skin, leaving a very thin layer of fat on top like a ham joint. Cut the meat in small thin slices across the grain, and arrange on a plate in an overlapping pattern.

6 In a small bowl, mix together the sauce ingredients, and pour the sauce evenly over the pork.

7 Garnish the pork with a sprig of fresh coriander (cilantro), if wished, and serve at once.

COOK'S TIP

This is a very simple dish, but beautifully presented. Make sure you slice the meat as thinly and evenly as possible to make an elegantly arranged dish.

Garlic & Pine Nut Tarts

A crisp lining of bread is filled with garlic butter and pine nuts to make a delightful light meal.

NUTRITIONAL INFORMATION

Calories	435	Sugars	1g
Protein	6g	Fat	39g
Carbohydrate	17g	Saturates	20g

 20 MINS  15 MINS

SERVES 4

INGREDIENTS

- 4 slices wholemeal or granary bread
- 50 g/1¾ oz pine nuts
- 150 g/5½ oz/10 tbsp butter
- 5 garlic cloves, peeled and halved
- 2 tbsp fresh oregano, chopped, plus extra for garnish
- 4 black olives, halved
- oregano leaves, to garnish

1 Using a rolling pin, flatten the bread slightly. Using a pastry cutter, cut out 4 circles of bread to fit your individual tart tins (pans) – they should measure about 10 cm/4 inches across. Reserve the offcuts of bread and leave them in the refrigerator for 10 minutes or until required.

2 Meanwhile, place the pine nuts on a baking tray (cookie sheet). Toast the pine nuts under a preheated grill (broiler) for 2–3 minutes or until golden.

3 Put the bread offcuts, pine nuts, butter, garlic and oregano into a food processor and blend for about 20 seconds. Alternatively, pound the ingredients by hand in a mortar and pestle. The mixture should have a rough texture.

4 Spoon the pine nut butter mixture into the lined tin (pan) and top with the olives. Bake in a preheated oven at 200°C/400°F/Gas Mark 6 for 10–15 minutes or until golden.

5 Transfer the tarts to serving plates and serve warm, garnished with the fresh oregano leaves.

VARIATION

Puff pastry can be used for the tarts. Use 200 g/7oz puff pastry to line 4 tart tins (pans). Leave the pastry to chill for 20 minutes. Line the tins (pans) with the pastry and foil and bake blind for 10 minutes. Remove the foil and bake for 3–4 minutes or until the pastry is set. Cool, then continue from step 2, adding 2 tbsp breadcrumbs to the mixture.

Mozzarella in Carriages

These deep-fried Mozzarella sandwiches are a tasty snack at any time of the day, or serve smaller triangles as an antipasto with drinks.

NUTRITIONAL INFORMATION

Calories	379	Sugars	4g
Protein	20g	Fat	22g
Carbohydrate	28g	Saturates	5g

 20 MINS

5-10 MINS

SERVES 4

INGREDIENTS

- 8 slices bread, preferably slightly stale, crusts removed
- 100 g/3 ½ oz Mozzarella cheese, sliced thickly
- 50 g/1 ¾ oz black olives, chopped
- 8 canned anchovy fillets, drained and chopped
- 16 fresh basil leaves
- 4 eggs, beaten
- 150 ml/5 floz/⅔ cup milk
- oil, for deep-frying
- salt and pepper

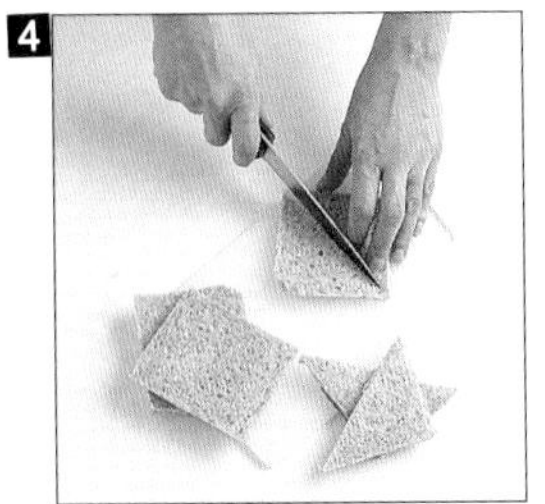

1 Cut each slice of bread into 2 triangles. Top 8 of the bread triangles with the Mozzarella slices, olives and chopped anchovies.

2 Place the basil leaves on top and season with salt and pepper to taste.

3 Lay the other 8 triangles of bread over the top and press down round the edges to seal.

4 Mix the eggs and milk and pour into an ovenproof dish. Add the sandwiches and leave to soak for about 5 minutes.

5 Heat the oil in a large saucepan to 180°-190°C/350°-375°F or until a cube of bread browns in 30 seconds.

6 Before cooking the sandwiches, squeeze the edges together again.

7 Carefully place the sandwiches in the oil and deep-fry for 2 minutes or until golden, turning once. Remove the sandwiches with a perforated spoon and drain on absorbent kitchen paper. Serve immediately while still hot.

Spanish Tortilla

This classic Spanish dish is often served as part of a tapas (appetizer) selection. A variety of cooked vegetables can be added to this recipe.

NUTRITIONAL INFORMATION

Calories	430	Sugars	6g
Protein	16g	Fat	20g
Carbohydrate	50g	Saturates	4g

 10 MINS  35 MINS

SERVES 4

INGREDIENTS

- 1 kg/2 lb 4 oz waxy potatoes, thinly sliced
- 4 tbsp vegetable oil
- 1 onion, sliced
- 2 garlic cloves, crushed
- 1 green (bell) pepper, seeded and diced
- 2 tomatoes, seeded and chopped
- 25 g/1 oz canned sweetcorn (corn), drained
- 6 large eggs, beaten
- 2 tbsp chopped parsley
- salt and pepper

1 Parboil the potatoes in a saucepan of lightly salted boiling water for 5 minutes. Drain well.

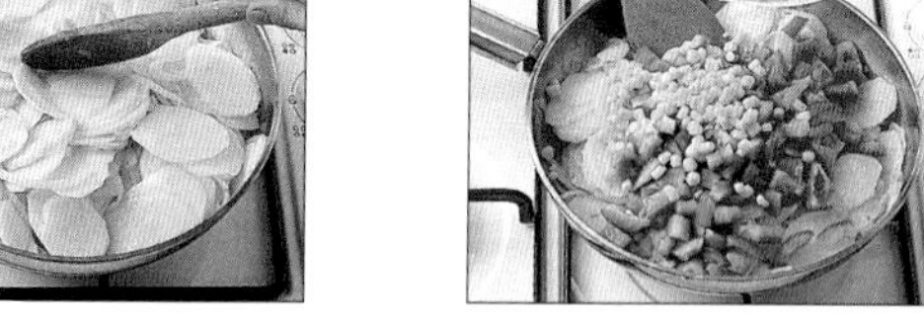

2 Heat the oil in a large frying pan (skillet), add the potato and onions and sauté over a low heat, stirring constantly, for 5 minutes, until the potatoes have browned.

3 Add the garlic, diced (bell) pepper, chopped tomatoes and sweetcorn (corn), mixing well.

4 Pour in the eggs and add the chopped parsley. Season well with salt and pepper. Cook for 10-12 minutes, until the underside is cooked through.

5 Remove the frying pan (skillet) from the heat and continue to cook the tortilla under a preheated medium grill (broiler) for 5-7 minutes, or until the tortilla is set and the top is golden brown.

6 Cut the tortilla into wedges or cubes, depending on your preference, and transfer to serving dishes. Serve with salad. In Spain tortillas are served hot, cold or warm.

COOK'S TIP

Ensure that the handle of your pan is heatproof before placing it under the grill (broiler) and be sure to use an oven glove when removing it as it will be very hot.

Cheese, Garlic & Herb Pâté

This wonderful soft cheese pâté is fragrant with the aroma of fresh herbs and garlic. Serve with triangles of Melba toast for a perfect starter.

NUTRITIONAL INFORMATION

Calories	392	Sugars	1g
Protein	17g	Fat	28g
Carbohydrate	18g	Saturates	18g

 20 MINS  10 MINS

SERVES 4

INGREDIENTS

- 15 g/½ oz/1 tbsp butter
- 1 garlic clove, crushed
- 3 spring onions (scallions), finely chopped
- 125 g/4½ oz/½ cup full-fat soft cheese
- 2 tbsp chopped mixed herbs, such as parsley, chives, marjoram, oregano and basil
- 175 g/6 oz/1½ cups finely grated mature (sharp) Cheddar cheese
- pepper
- 4–6 slices of white bread from a medium-cut sliced loaf
- mixed salad leaves (greens) and cherry tomatoes, to serve

TO GARNISH

- ground paprika
- herb sprigs

1 Melt the butter in a small frying pan (skillet) and gently fry the garlic and spring onions (scallions) together for 3–4 minutes, until softened. Allow to cool.

2 Beat the soft cheese in a large mixing bowl until smooth, then add the garlic and spring onions (scallions). Stir in the herbs, mixing well.

3 Add the Cheddar and work the mixture together to form a stiff paste. Cover and chill until ready to serve.

4 To make the Melba toast, toast the slices of bread on both sides, and then cut off the crusts. Using a sharp bread knife, cut through the slices horizontally to make very thin slices. Cut into triangles and then lightly grill (broil) the untoasted sides until golden.

5 Arrange the mixed salad leaves (greens) on 4 serving plates with the cherry tomatoes. Pile the cheese pâté on top and sprinkle with a little paprika. Garnish with sprigs of fresh herbs and serve with the Melba toast.

2

3

4

Crispy Seaweed

This tasty Chinese starter is not all that it seems – the 'seaweed' is in fact pak choi which is then fried, salted and tossed with pine kernels.

NUTRITIONAL INFORMATION

Calories	214	Sugars	14g
Protein	6g	Fat	15g
Carbohydrate	15g	Saturates	2g

 10 MINS  5 MINS

SERVES 4

INGREDIENTS

- 1 kg/2 lb 4 oz pak choi
- groundnut oil, for deep-frying (about 850 ml/1½ pints/3¾ cups)
- 1 tsp salt
- 1 tbsp caster (superfine) sugar
- 50 g/1¾ oz/2½ tbsp toasted pine kernels (nuts)

1 Rinse the pak choi leaves under cold running water and then pat dry thoroughly with absorbent kitchen paper (paper towels).

2 Discarding any tough outer leaves, roll each pak choi leaf up, then slice through thinly so that the leaves are finely shredded. Alternatively, use a food processor to shred the pak choi.

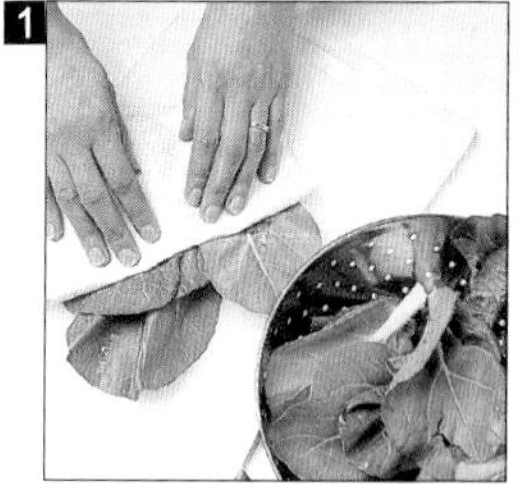
1

2

5

3 Heat the groundnut oil in a large wok or heavy based frying pan (skillet).

4 Carefully add the shredded pak choi leaves to the wok or frying pan (skillet) and fry for about 30 seconds or until they shrivel up and become crispy (you will probably need to do this in several batches, depending on the size of the wok).

5 Remove the crispy seaweed from the wok with a slotted spoon and drain on absorbent kitchen paper (paper towels).

6 Transfer the crispy seaweed to a large bowl and toss with the salt, sugar and pine kernels (nuts). Serve immediately.

COOK'S TIP

The tough, outer leaves of pak choi are discarded as these will spoil the overall taste and texture of the dish.

Use savoy cabbage instead of the pak choi if it is unavailable, drying the leaves thoroughly before frying.

Dumplings in Yogurt Sauce

Adding a baghaar (seasoned oil dressing) just before serving makes this a mouth-watering accompaniment to any meal.

NUTRITIONAL INFORMATION

Calories	719	Sugars	9g
Protein	9g	Fat	60g
Carbohydrate	38g	Saturates	7g

 35 MINS  35 MINS

SERVES 4

INGREDIENTS

DUMPLINGS

100 g/3½ oz/¾ cup gram flour
1 tsp chilli powder
½ tsp bicarbonate of soda (baking soda)
1 medium onion, finely chopped
2 green chillies
coriander (cilantro) leaves
150 ml/¼ pint/⅔ cup water
300 ml/½ pint/1¼ cups vegetable oil
salt

YOGURT SAUCE

300 ml/½ pint/1¼ cups natural (unsweetened) yogurt
3 tbsp gram flour
150 ml/¼ pint/⅔ cup water
1 tsp chopped root ginger
1 tsp crushed garlic
1½ tsp chilli powder
½ tsp turmeric
1 tsp ground coriander
1 tsp ground cumin

SEASONED DRESSING

150 ml/¼ pint/⅔ cup vegetable oil
1 tsp white cumin seeds
6 dried red chillies

1 To make the dumplings, sift the gram flour into a large bowl. Add the chilli powder, ½ teaspoon salt, bicarbonate of soda (baking soda), onion, green chillies and coriander (cilantro) and mix. Add the water and mix to form a thick paste. Heat the oil in a frying pan (skillet). Place teaspoonfuls of the paste in the oil and fry over a medium heat, turning once, until a crisp golden brown. Set aside.

2 To make the sauce, place the yogurt in a bowl and whisk with the gram flour and the water. Add all of the spices and 1½ teaspoons salt and mix well.

3 Press this mixture through a large strainer into a saucepan. Bring to a boil over a low heat, stirring constantly. If the yogurt sauce becomes too thick, add a little extra water.

4 Pour the sauce into a deep serving dish and arrange all the dumplings on top. Set aside and keep warm.

5 To make the dressing, heat the oil in a frying pan (skillet). Add the white cumin seeds and the dried red chillies and fry until darker in colour and giving off their aroma. Pour the dressing over the dumplings and serve hot.

1

1

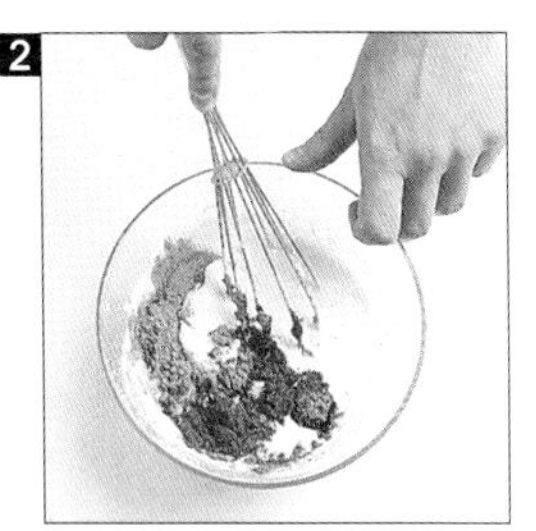
2

Vegetable & Nut Samosas

These delicious little fried pastries are really quite simple to make. Serve them hot or cold as a starter to an Indian meal.

NUTRITIONAL INFORMATION

Calories	343	Sugars	2g
Protein	5g	Fat	26g
Carbohydrate	24g	Saturates	5g

 30 MINS  40 MINS

MAKES 12

INGREDIENTS

- 350 g/12 oz potatoes, diced
- salt
- 125 g/4½ oz/1 cup frozen peas
- 3 tbsp vegetable oil
- 1 onion, chopped
- 2.5 cm/1 inch piece of root ginger, chopped
- 1 garlic clove, crushed
- 1 tsp garam masala
- 2 tsp mild curry paste
- ½ tsp cumin seeds
- 2 tsp lemon juice
- 60 g/2 oz/½ cup unsalted cashews, coarsely chopped
- vegetable oil, for shallow frying
- coriander (cilantro) sprigs, to garnish
- mango chutney, to serve

PASTRY

- 225 g/8 oz/2 cups plain (all-purpose) flour
- 60 g/2 oz/¼ cup butter
- 6 tbsp warm milk

1 Cook the potatoes in a saucepan of boiling, salted water for 5 minutes. Add the peas and cook for a further 4 minutes, or until the potatoes are tender. Drain well. Heat the oil in a frying pan (skillet) and fry the onion, potato and pea mixture, ginger, garlic and spices for 2 minutes. Stir in the lemon juice and cook gently, uncovered, for 2 minutes. Remove from the heat, slightly mash the potato and peas, then add the cashews, mix well and season with salt.

1

2 To make the pastry, put the flour in a bowl and rub in the butter. Mix in the milk to form a dough. Knead lightly and divide into 6 portions. Form each into a ball and roll out to an 18 cm/7 inch round. Cut each one in half.

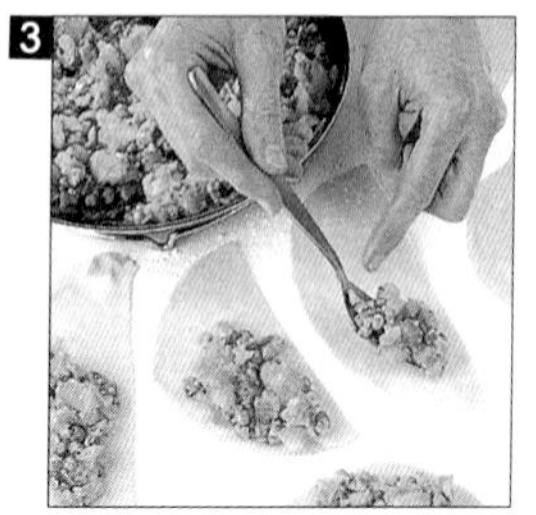

3

3 Divide the filling equally between the semi-circles of pastry, spreading it out to within 5 mm/¼ inch of the edges. Brush the edges of pastry all the way round with water and fold over to form triangular shapes, sealing the edges well together to enclose the filling completely.

4

4 Heat the vegetable oil in a frying pan (skillet) to 180°C/350°F or until a cube of bread browns in 30 seconds. Fry the samosas, a few at a time, turning frequently until golden brown and heated through. Drain on kitchen paper (paper towels) and keep warm while cooking the remainder. Garnish with coriander (cilantro) sprigs and serve hot.

Money Bags

These traditional steamed dumplings can be eaten on their own or dipped in a mixture of soy sauce, sherry and slivers of ginger root.

NUTRITIONAL INFORMATION

Calories	315	Sugars	3g
Protein	8g	Fat	8g
Carbohydrate	56g	Saturates	1g

 45 MINS  20 MINS

SERVES 4

INGREDIENTS

- 3 Chinese dried mushrooms (if unavailable, use thinly sliced open-cup mushrooms)
- 250 g/9 oz/2 cups plain (all-purpose) flour
- 1 egg, beaten
- 75 ml/3 fl oz/⅓ cup water
- 1 tsp baking powder
- ¾ tsp salt
- 2 tbsp vegetable oil
- 2 spring onions (scallions), chopped
- 90 g/3 oz/½ cup sweetcorn kernels
- ½ red chilli, deseeded and chopped
- 1 tbsp brown bean sauce

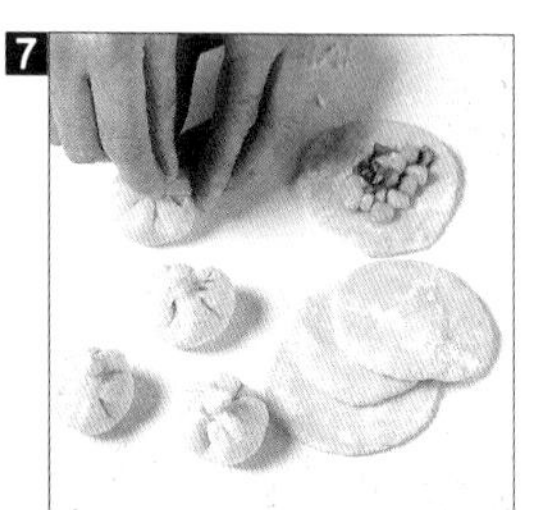

1 Place the dried mushrooms in a small bowl, cover with warm water and leave to soak for 20–25 minutes.

2 To make the wrappers, sift the plain (all-purpose) flour into a bowl. Add the beaten egg and mix in lightly. Stir in the water, baking powder and salt. Mix to make a soft dough.

3 Knead the dough lightly on a floured board. Cover with a damp tea towel (dish cloth) and set aside for 5–6 minutes. This allows the baking powder time to activate, so that the dumplings swell when steaming.

4 Drain the mushrooms, squeezing them dry. Remove the tough centres and chop the mushrooms.

5 Heat the vegetable oil in a wok or large frying pan (skillet) and stir-fry the mushrooms, spring onions (scallions), sweetcorn and chilli for 2 minutes.

6 Stir in the brown bean sauce and remove from the heat.

7 Roll the dough into a large sausage and cut into 24 even-sized pieces. Roll each piece out into a thin round and place a teaspoonful of the filling in the centre. Gather up the edges to a point, pinch together and twist to seal.

8 Stand the dumplings in an oiled steaming basket. Place over a saucepan of simmering water, cover and steam for 12–14 minutes before serving.

Fried Tofu with Peanut Sauce

This is a very sociable dish if put in the centre of the table where people can help themselves with cocktail sticks.

NUTRITIONAL INFORMATION

Calories	338	Sugars	9g
Protein	16g	Fat	22g
Carbohydrate	21g	Saturates	4g

5 MINS 20 MINS

SERVES 4

INGREDIENTS

- 500 g/1 lb 2 oz marinated or plain tofu (bean curd)
- 2 tbsp rice vinegar
- 2 tbsp sugar
- 1 tsp salt
- 3 tbsp smooth peanut butter
- ½ tsp chilli flakes
- 3 tbsp barbecue sauce
- 1 litre/1¾ pints/4 cups sunflower oil
- 2 tbsp sesame oil

BATTER

- 4 tbsp plain (all-purpose) flour
- 2 eggs, beaten
- 4 tbsp milk
- ½ tsp baking powder
- ½ tsp chilli powder

1 Cut the tofu (bean curd) into 2.5 cm/1 inch triangles. Set aside until required.

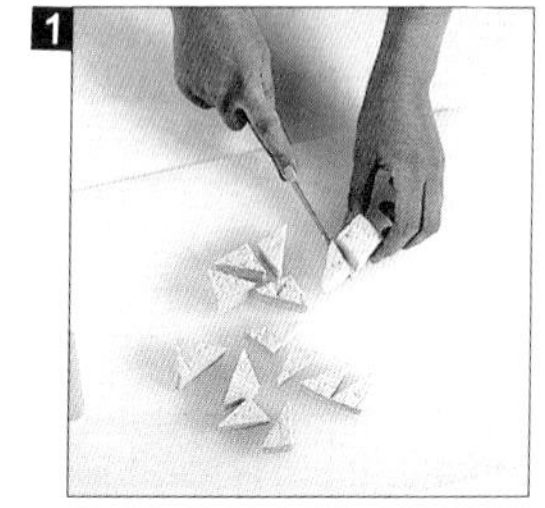

2 Combine the rice vinegar, sugar and salt in a saucepan. Bring to the boil and then simmer for 2 minutes.

3 Remove the sauce from the heat and add the smooth peanut butter, chilli flakes and barbecue sauce, stirring well until thoroughly blended.

4 To make the batter, sift the plain (all-purpose) flour into a bowl, make a well in the centre and add the eggs. Draw in the flour, adding the milk slowly. Stir in the baking powder and chilli powder.

5 Heat both the sunflower oil and sesame oil in a deep-fryer or large saucepan until a light haze appears on top.

6 Dip the tofu (bean curd) triangles into the batter and deep-fry until golden brown. You may need to do this in batches. Drain on absorbent kitchen paper (paper towels).

7 Transfer the tofu (bean curd) triangles to a serving dish and serve with the peanut sauce.

COOK'S TIP

Tofu (bean curd) is made from puréed soya beans. It is white, with a soft cheese-like texture, and is sold in blocks, either fresh or vacuum-packed. Although it has a bland flavour, it blends well with other ingredients, and absorbs the flavours of spices and sauces.

Barbecue Spare Ribs

This is a simplified version of the half saddle of pork ribs seen hanging in the windows of Cantonese restaurants.

NUTRITIONAL INFORMATION

Calories	271	Sugars	4g
Protein	13g	Fat	22g
Carbohydrate	5g	Saturates	8g

6½ HOURS 50 MINS

SERVES 4

INGREDIENTS

- 500 g/1 lb 2 oz pork finger spare ribs
- 1 tbsp sugar
- 1 tbsp light soy sauce
- 1 tbsp dark soy sauce
- 3 tbsp hoi-sin sauce
- 1 tbsp rice wine or dry sherry
- 4-5 tbsp water or Chinese Stock (see page 8)
- mild chilli sauce, to dip
- coriander (cilantro) leaves, to garnish

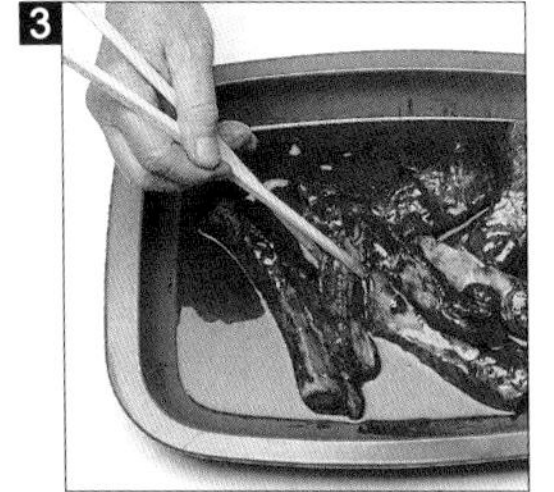

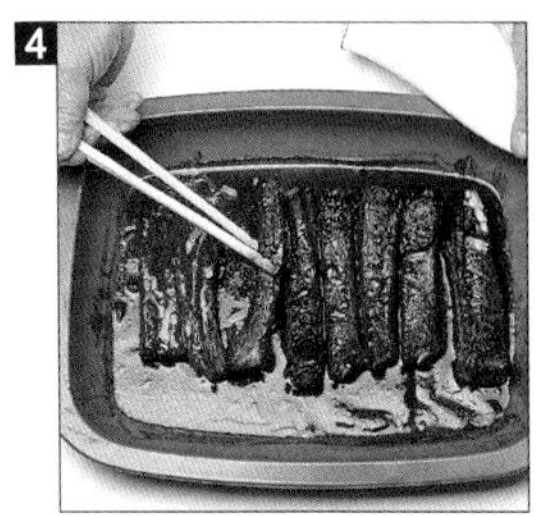

1 Using a sharp knife, trim off any excess fat from the spare ribs and cut into pieces. Place the ribs in a baking dish.

2 Mix together the sugar, light and dark soy sauce, hoi-sin sauce and wine. Pour over the ribs in the baking dish. Turn to coat the ribs thoroughly in the mixture and leave to marinate for about 2-3 hours.

3 Add the water or Chinese stock to the ribs and spread them out in the dish. Roast in a preheated hot oven for 15 minutes.

4 Turn the ribs over, lower the oven temperature and cook for 30-35 minutes longer.

5 To serve, chop each rib into 3-4 small, bite-sized pieces with a large knife or Chinese cleaver and arrange neatly on a serving dish.

6 Pour the sauce from the baking dish over the spare ribs and garnish with a few coriander (cilantro) leaves. Place some mild chilli sauce into a small dish and serve with the ribs as a dip. Serve immediately.

COOK'S TIP

Finger ribs are specially small, thin ribs. Ask your local butcher to cut some if you can't find the right size in the supermarket. Don't throw away any trimmings from the ribs – they can be used for soup or stock.

Son-in-Law Eggs

This recipe is supposedly so called because it is an easy dish for a son-in-law to cook to impress his new mother-in-law!

NUTRITIONAL INFORMATION

Calories	229	Sugars	8g
Protein	9g	Fat	18g
Carbohydrate	8g	Saturates	3g

15 MINS 15 MINS

SERVES 4

INGREDIENTS

- 6 eggs, hard-boiled (hard-cooked) and shelled
- 4 tbsp sunflower oil
- 1 onion, sliced thinly
- 2 fresh red chillies, sliced
- 2 tbsp sugar
- 1 tbsp water
- 2 tsp tamarind pulp
- 1 tbsp liquid seasoning, such as Maggi
- rice, to serve

1 Prick the hard-boiled (hard-cooked) eggs 2 or 3 times with a cocktail stick (toothpick).

2 Heat the sunflower oil in a wok and fry the eggs until crispy and golden. Drain on absorbent kitchen paper (paper towels).

3 Halve the eggs lengthways and put on a serving dish.

4 Reserve one tablespoon of the oil, pour off the rest, then heat the tablespoonful in the wok. Cook the onion and chillies over a high heat until golden and slightly crisp. Drain on kitchen paper (paper towels).

5 Heat the sugar, water, tamarind pulp and liquid seasoning in the wok and simmer for 5 minutes until thickened.

6 Pour the sauce over the eggs and spoon over the onion and chillies. Serve immediately with rice.

COOK'S TIP

Tamarind pulp is sold in oriental stores, and is quite sour. If it is not available, use twice the amount of lemon juice in its place.

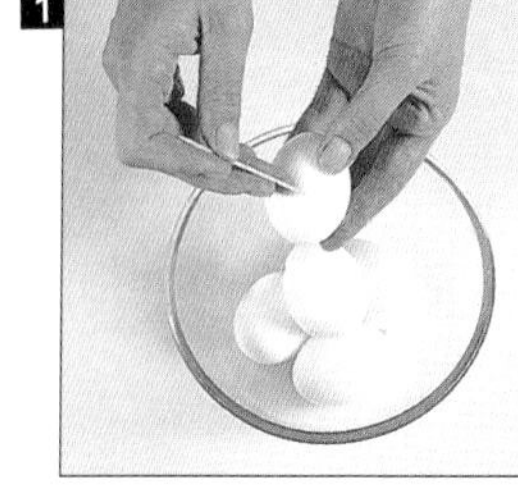

1

2

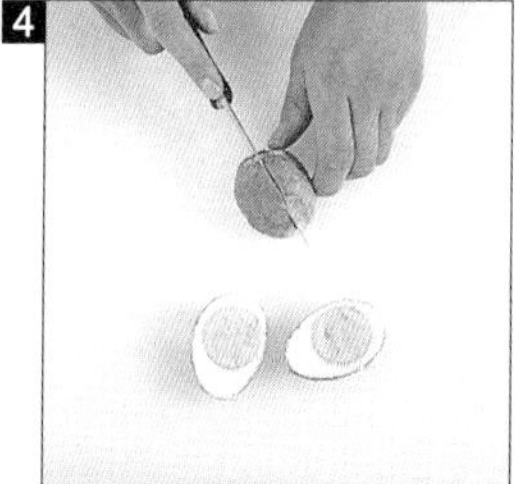

4

Vegetables with Tahini Dip

This tasty dip is great for livening-up simply-cooked vegetables. You can vary the vegetables according to the season.

NUTRITIONAL INFORMATION

Calories	126	Sugars	7g
Protein	11g	Fat	6g
Carbohydrate	8g	Saturates	1g

 5 MINS  20 MINS

SERVES 4

INGREDIENTS

- 225 g/8 oz small broccoli florets
- 225 g/8 oz small cauliflower florets
- 225 g/8 oz asparagus, sliced into 5 cm/ 2 inch lengths
- 2 small red onions, quartered
- 1 tbsp lime juice
- 2 tsp toasted sesame seeds
- 1 tbsp chopped fresh chives, to garnish

HOT TAHINI & GARLIC DIP

- 1 tsp sunflower oil
- 2 garlic cloves, crushed
- ½–1 tsp chilli powder
- 2 tsp tahini (sesame seed paste)
- 150 ml/¼ pint/⅔ cup low-fat natural fromage frais
- 2 tbsp chopped fresh chives
- salt and pepper

1

3

4

1 Line the base of a steamer with baking parchment and arrange the vegetables on top.

2 Bring a wok or large saucepan of water to the boil, and place the steamer on top. Sprinkle with lime juice and steam for 10 minutes.

3 To make the hot tahini & garlic dip, heat the sunflower oil in a small non-stick saucepan, add the garlic, chilli powder and seasoning to taste and fry gently for 2–3 minutes until the garlic is softened.

4 Remove the saucepan from the heat and stir in the tahini (sesame seed paste) and fromage frais. Return to the heat and cook gently for 1–2 minutes without boiling. Stir in the chives.

5 Remove the vegetables from the steamer and place on a warmed serving platter. Sprinkle with the sesame seeds and garnish with chopped chives. Serve with the hot dip.

Avocado Margherita

The colours of the tomatoes, basil and Mozzarella cheese in this patriotic recipe represent the colours of the Italian flag.

NUTRITIONAL INFORMATION

Calories	249	Sugars	2g
Protein	4g	Fat	24g
Carbohydrate	4g	Saturates	6g

5-10 MINS 10-15 MINS

SERVES 4

INGREDIENTS

- 1 small red onion, sliced
- 1 garlic clove, crushed
- 1 tbsp olive oil
- 2 small tomatoes
- 2 avocados, halved and pitted
- 4 fresh basil leaves, torn into shreds
- 60 g/2 oz Mozzarella cheese, sliced thinly
- salt and pepper
- fresh basil leaves, to garnish
- mixed salad leaves, to serve

1 Place the onion, garlic and the olive oil in a bowl. Cover and cook on HIGH power for 2 minutes.

2 Meanwhile, skin the tomatoes by cutting a cross in the base of the tomatoes and placing them in a small bowl. Pour on boiling water and leave for about 45 seconds. Drain and then plunge into cold water. The skins will slide off without too much difficulty.

3 Arrange the avocado halves on a plate with the narrow ends pointed towards the centre. Spoon the onions into the hollow of each half.

4 Cut and slice the tomatoes in half. Divide the tomatoes, basil and thin slices of Mozzarella between the avocado halves. Season with salt and pepper to taste.

5 Cook on MEDIUM power for 5 minutes or until the avocados are heated through and the cheese has melted. Transfer the avocados to serving plates, garnish with basil leaves and serve with mixed salad leaves.

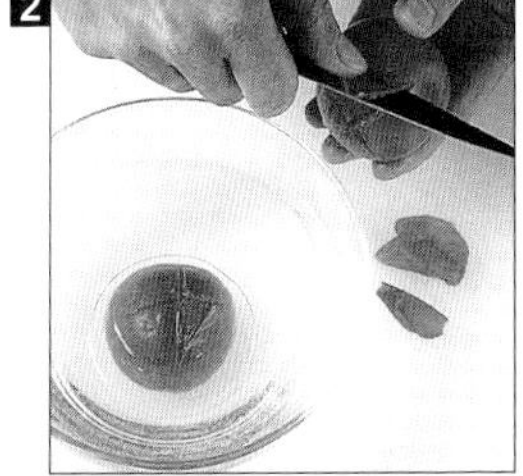

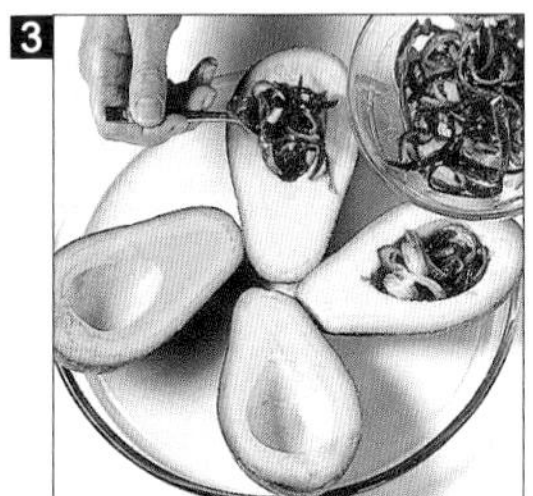

VARIATION

If you are using a combination microwave oven with grill (broiler) – arrange the avocados on the low rack of the grill (broiler), or on the glass turntable. Cook on combination grill (broiler) 1 and LOW power for 8 minutes until browned and bubbling.

Crispy-Fried Vegetables

A hot and sweet dipping sauce makes the perfect accompaniment to fresh vegetables coated in a light batter and deep-fried.

NUTRITIONAL INFORMATION

Calories	258	Sugars	11g
Protein	6g	Fat	9g
Carbohydrate	39g	Saturates	11g

 40 MINS  10 MINS

SERVES 4

INGREDIENTS

- vegetable oil for deep-frying
- 500 g/1 lb 2 oz selection of vegetables, such as cauliflower, broccoli, mushrooms, courgettes (zucchini), (bell) peppers and baby sweetcorn, cut into even-sized pieces

BATTER

- 125 g/4½ oz/1 cup plain (all-purpose) flour
- ½ tsp salt
- 1 tsp caster (superfine) sugar
- 1 tsp baking powder
- 3 tbsp vegetable oil
- 200 ml/7 fl oz/scant 1 cup warm water

SAUCE

- 6 tbsp light malt vinegar
- 2 tbsp fish sauce or light soy sauce
- 2 tbsp water
- 1 tbsp soft brown sugar
- pinch of salt
- 2 garlic cloves, crushed
- 2 tsp grated ginger root
- 2 red chillies, deseeded and chopped finely
- 2 tbsp chopped fresh coriander (cilantro)

1 To make the batter, sift the flour, salt, sugar and baking powder into a bowl. Add the oil and most of the water. Whisk together to make a smooth batter, adding extra water to give it the consistency of single cream. Chill for 20–30 minutes.

2 Meanwhile, make the sauce. Heat the vinegar, fish sauce or soy sauce, water, sugar and salt until boiling. Remove from the heat and leave to cool.

3 Mix together the garlic, ginger, chillies and coriander (cilantro). Add the cooled vinegar mixture and stir well to combine.

4 Heat the oil for deep-frying in a wok. Dip the vegetables in the batter and fry, in batches, until crisp and golden – about 2 minutes. Drain on kitchen paper (paper towels). Serve the vegetables accompanied by the dipping sauce.

Butterfly Prawns (Shrimp)

These prawns (shrimp) look stunning when presented on the skewers, and they will certainly be an impressive prelude to the main meal.

NUTRITIONAL INFORMATION

Calories	183	Sugars	0g
Protein	28g	Fat	8g
Carbohydrate	0g	Saturates	1g

 4½ HOURS  10 MINS

SERVES 2–4

INGREDIENTS

- 500 g/1 lb 2 oz or 16 raw tiger prawns (shrimp), shelled, leaving tails intact
- juice of 2 limes
- 1 tsp cardamom seeds
- 2 tsp cumin seeds, ground
- 2 tsp coriander seeds, ground
- ½ tsp ground cinnamon
- 1 tsp ground turmeric
- 1 garlic clove, crushed
- 1 tsp cayenne pepper
- 2 tbsp oil
- cucumber slices, to garnish

1 Soak 8 wooden skewers in water for 20 minutes. Cut the prawns (shrimp) lengthways in half down to the taiand flatten out to a symmetrical shape.

2 Thread a prawn (shrimp) on to 2 wooden skewers, with the tail between them, so that, when laid flat, the skewers hold the prawn (shrimp) in shape. Thread another 3 prawns (shrimp) on to these 2 skewers in the same way.

3 Repeat until you have 4 sets of 4 prawns (shrimp) each.

4 Lay the skewered prawns (shrimp) in a non-porous, non-metallic dish, and sprinkle over the lime juice.

5 Combine the spices and the oil, and coat the prawns (shrimp) well in the mixture. Cover the prawns (shrimp) and chill for 4 hours.

6 Cook over a hot barbecue (grill) or in a grill (broiler) pan lined with foil under a preheated grill (broiler) for 6 minutes, turning once.

7 Serve immediately, garnished with cucumber and accompanied by a sweet chutney – walnut chutney is ideal.

1

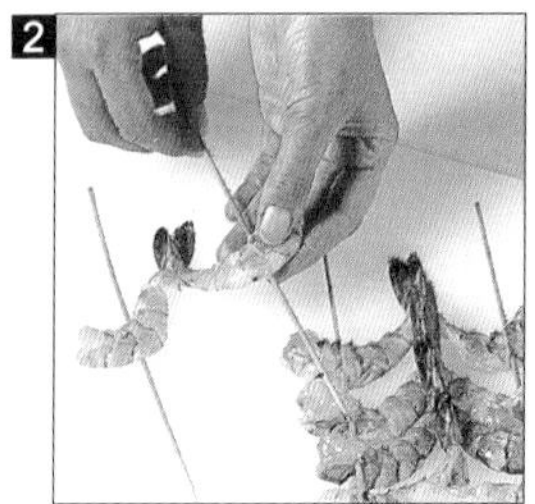
2

4

Tofu Sandwiches

Slices of tofu (beancurd) are sandwiched together with a cucumber and cream cheese filling and coated in batter.

NUTRITIONAL INFORMATION

Calories	398	Sugars	8g
Protein	13g	Fat	24g
Carbohydrate	35g	Saturates	7g

 40 MINS  15 MINS

MAKES 28

INGREDIENTS

- 4 Chinese dried mushrooms (if unavailable, use thinly sliced open-cup mushrooms)
- 275 g/9½ oz tofu (bean curd)
- ½ cucumber, grated
- 1 cm/½ inch piece ginger root, grated
- 60 g/2 oz/¼ cup cream cheese
- salt and pepper

BATTER

- 125 g/4½ oz/1 cup plain (all-purpose) flour
- 1 egg, beaten
- 125 ml/4 fl oz/½ cup water
- ½ tsp salt
- 2 tbsp sesame seeds
- vegetable oil for deep-frying

SAUCE

- 150 ml/¼ pint/⅔ cup natural (unsweetened) yogurt
- 2 tsp honey
- 2 tbsp chopped fresh mint

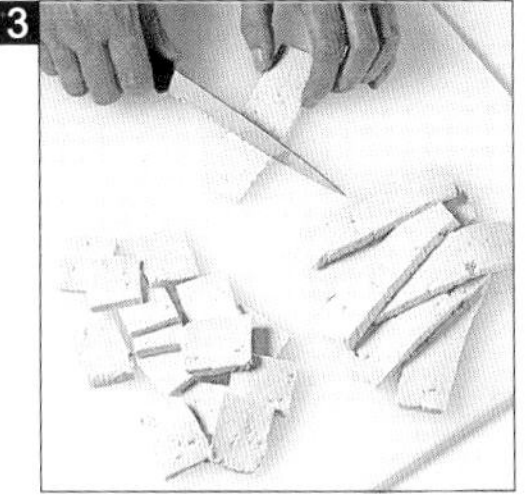

3

4

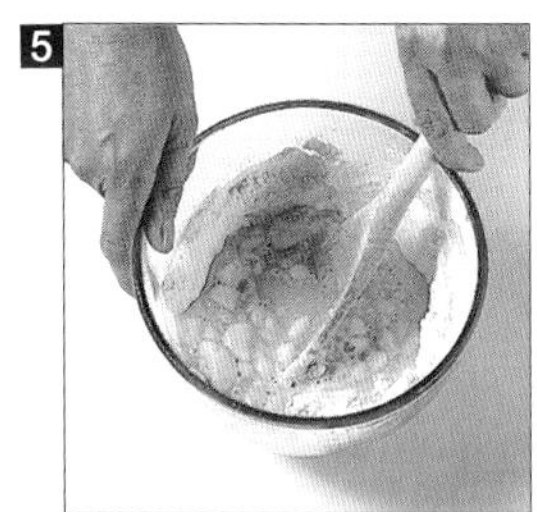

5

1 Place the dried mushrooms in a small bowl and cover with warm water. Leave to soak for 20–25 minutes.

2 Drain the mushrooms, squeezing out the excess water. Remove the tough centres and chop the mushrooms.

3 Drain the tofu (bean curd) and slice thinly. Then cut each slice to make 2.5 cm/1 inch squares.

4 Squeeze the excess liquid from the cucumber and mix the cucumber with the mushrooms, grated ginger and cream cheese. Season well with salt and pepper. Use as a filling to sandwich slices of tofu (bean curd) together to make about 28 sandwiches.

5 To make the batter, sift the flour into a bowl. Beat in the egg, water and salt to make a thick batter. Stir in the sesame seeds. Heat the oil in a wok. Coat the sandwiches in the batter and deep-fry in batches until golden. Remove and drain on kitchen paper (paper towels).

6 To make the dipping sauce, combine the yogurt, honey and mint. Serve with the tofu (bean curd) sandwiches.

Root Croustades

This colourful combination of grated root vegetables and mixed (bell) peppers would make a stunning dinner-party dish.

NUTRITIONAL INFORMATION

Calories	304	Sugars	17g
Protein	6g	Fat	19g
Carbohydrate	28g	Saturates	3g

2½ HOURS 1¼ HOURS

SERVES 4

INGREDIENTS

1 orange (bell) pepper
1 red (bell) pepper
1 yellow (bell) pepper
3 tbsp olive oil
2 tbsp red wine vinegar
1 tsp French mustard
1 tsp clear honey
salt and pepper
flat leaf parsley sprigs, to garnish
green vegetables, to serve

CROUSTADES

225 g/8 oz potatoes, coarsely grated
225 g/8 oz carrots, coarsely grated
350 g/12 oz celeriac (celery root), coarsely grated
1 garlic clove, crushed
1 tbsp lemon juice
25 g/1 oz/2 tbsp butter or margarine, melted
1 egg, beaten
1 tbsp vegetable oil

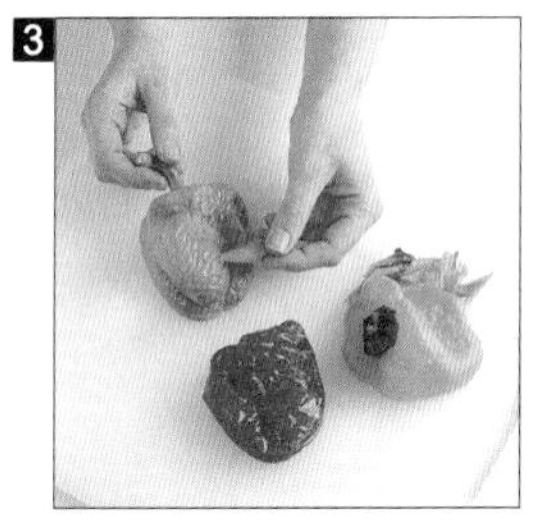
3

5

6

1 Place the (bell) peppers on a baking tray (cookie sheet) and bake in a preheated oven, 190°C/375°F/Gas Mark 5, for 35 minutes, turning after 20 minutes.

2 Cover with a tea towel (dish cloth) and leave to cool for 10 minutes.

3 Peel the skin from the cooked (bell) peppers; cut in half and discard the seeds. Thinly slice the flesh into strips and place in a shallow dish.

4 Put the oil, vinegar, mustard, honey and seasoning in a small screw-top jar and shake well to mix. Pour over the (bell) pepper strips, mix well and set aside to marinate for 2 hours.

5 To make the croustades, put the potatoes, carrots and celeriac (celery root) in a mixing bowl and toss in the garlic and lemon juice.

6 Mix in the melted butter or margarine and the egg. Season to taste with salt and pepper. Divide the mixture into 8 and pile on to 2 baking trays (cookie sheets) lined with baking parchment, forming each into a 10 cm/4 inch round. Brush with oil.

7 Bake in a preheated oven, 220°C/425°F/Gas Mark 7, for 30–35 minutes, until the croustades are crisp around the edges and golden. Carefully transfer to a warmed serving dish. Heat the (bell) peppers and the marinade for 2–3 minutes until warmed through. Spoon the (bell) peppers over the croustades, garnish with flat leaf parsley and serve immediately with green vegetables.

Tofu (Bean Curd) Tempura

Crispy coated vegetables and tofu (bean curd) accompanied by a sweet, spicy dip give a real taste of the Orient in this Japanese-style dish.

NUTRITIONAL INFORMATION

Calories	582	Sugars	10g
Protein	16g	Fat	27g
Carbohydrate	65g	Saturates	4g

 15 MINS  20 MINS

SERVES 4

INGREDIENTS

- 125 g/4½ oz baby courgettes (zucchini)
- 125 g/4½ oz baby carrots
- 125 g/4½ oz baby corn cobs
- 125 g/4½ oz baby leeks
- 2 baby aubergines (eggplants)
- 225 g/8 oz tofu (bean curd)
- vegetable oil, for deep-frying
- julienne strips of carrot, root ginger and baby leek to garnish
- noodles, to serve

BATTER

- 2 egg yolks
- 300 ml/½ pint/1¼ cups water
- 225 g/8 oz/2 cups plain (all-purpose) flour

DIPPING SAUCE

- 5 tbsp mirin or dry sherry
- 5 tbsp Japanese soy sauce
- 2 tsp clear honey
- 1 garlic clove, crushed
- 1 tsp grated root ginger

1 Slice the courgettes (zucchini) and carrots in half lengthways. Trim the corn. Trim the leeks at both ends. Quarter the aubergines (eggplants). Cut the tofu (bean curd) into 2.5 cm/1 inch cubes.

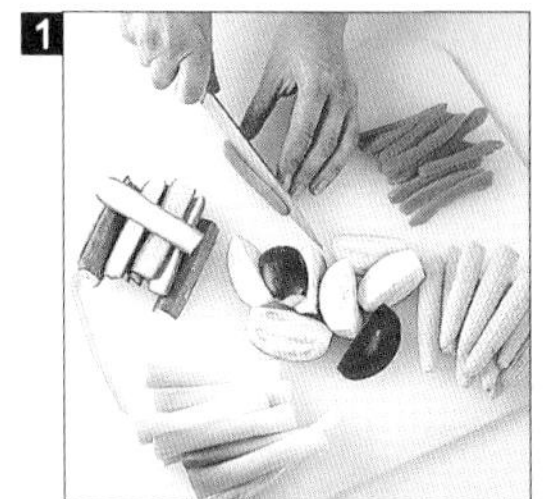

2 To make the batter, mix the egg yolks with the water. Sift in 175 g/6 oz/1½ cups of the flour and beat with a balloon whisk to form a thick batter. Don't worry if there are any lumps. Heat the oil for deep-frying to 180°C/350°F or until a cube of bread browns in 30 seconds.

3 Place the remaining flour on a large plate and toss the vegetables and tofu (bean curd) until lightly coated.

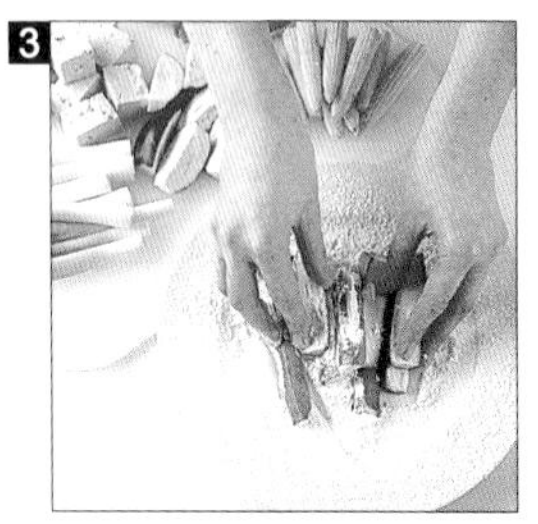

4 Dip the tofu (bean curd) in the batter and deep-fry for 2–3 minutes, until lightly golden. Drain on kitchen paper (paper towels) and keep warm.

5 Dip the vegetables in the batter and deep-fry, a few at a time, for 3–4 minutes, until golden. Drain and place on a warmed serving plate.

6 To make the dipping sauce, mix all the ingredients together. Serve with the vegetables and tofu (bean curd), accompanied with noodles and garnished with julienne strips of vegetables.

Spring Rolls

This classic Chinese dish is very popular in the West. Serve hot or chilled with a soy sauce or hoisin dip.

NUTRITIONAL INFORMATION

Calories	442	Sugars	4g
Protein	23g	Fat	21g
Carbohydrate	42g	Saturates	3g

 45 MINS  45 MINS

SERVES 4

INGREDIENTS

- 175 g/6 oz cooked pork, chopped
- 75 g/2¾ oz cooked chicken, chopped
- 1 tsp light soy sauce
- 1 tsp light brown sugar
- 1 tsp sesame oil
- 1 tsp vegetable oil
- 225 g/8 oz bean sprouts
- 25 g/1 oz canned bamboo shoots, drained, rinsed and chopped
- 1 green (bell) pepper, seeded and chopped
- 2 spring onions (scallions), sliced
- 1 tsp cornflour (cornstarch)
- 2 tsp water
- vegetable oil, for deep-frying

SKINS

- 125 g/4½ oz/1⅛ cups plain (all-purpose) flour
- 5 tbsp cornflour (cornstarch)
- 450 ml/16 fl oz/2 cups water
- 3 tbsp vegetable oil

1 Mix the pork, chicken, soy sauce, sugar and sesame oil. Cover and marinate for 30 minutes.

2 Heat the vegetable oil in a preheated wok. Add the bean sprouts, bamboo shoots, (bell) pepper and spring onions (scallions) to the wok and stir-fry for 2–3 minutes. Add the meat and the marinade to the wok and stir-fry for 2–3 minutes.

3 Blend the cornflour (cornstarch) with the water and stir the mixture into the wok. Set aside to cool completely.

4 To make the skins, mix the flour and cornflour (cornstarch) and gradually stir in the water, to make a smooth batter.

5 Heat a small, oiled frying pan (skillet). Swirl one-eighth of the batter over the base and cook for 2–3 minutes. Repeat with the remaining batter. Cover the skins with a damp tea towel (dish cloth) while frying the remaining skins.

6 Spread out the skins and spoon one-eighth of the filling along the centre of each. Brush the edges with water and fold in the sides, then roll up.

7 Heat the oil for deep-frying in a wok to 180°C/350°F. Cook the spring rolls, in batches, for 2–3 minutes, or until golden and crisp. Remove from the oil with a slotted spoon, drain and serve immediately.

5

6

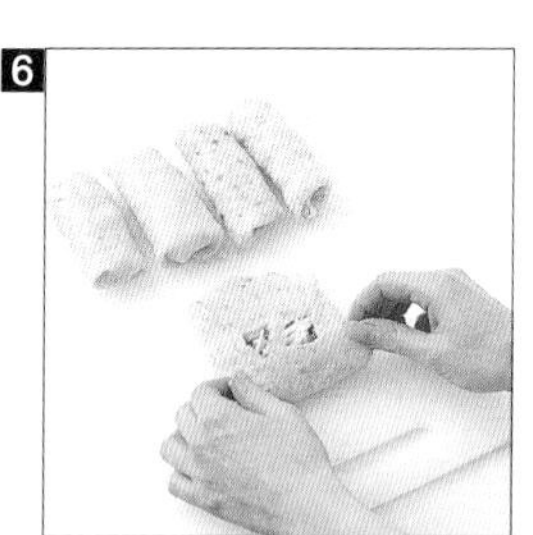

6

Barbecue Pork (Char Siu)

Also called honey-roasted pork, these are the strips of reddish meat sometimes seen hanging in the windows of Cantonese restaurants.

NUTRITIONAL INFORMATION

Calories	250	Sugar	8g
Protein	27g	Fat	10g
Carbohydrate	9g	Saturates	3g

 4¼ HOURS  30 MINS

SERVES 4

INGREDIENTS

- 500 g/1 lb 2 oz pork fillet
- 150 ml/¼ pint/⅔ cup boiling water
- 1 tbsp honey, dissolved with a little hot water

MARINADE

- 1 tbsp sugar
- 1 tbsp crushed yellow bean sauce
- 1 tbsp light soy sauce
- 1 tbsp hoisin sauce
- 1 tbsp oyster sauce
- ½ tsp chilli sauce
- 1 tbsp brandy or rum
- 1 tsp sesame oil
- shredded lettuce, to serve

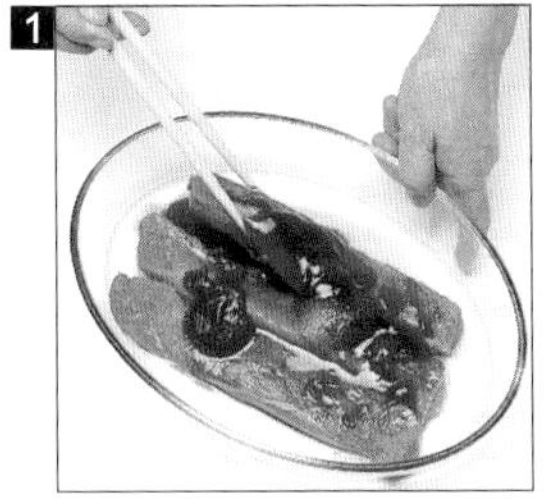

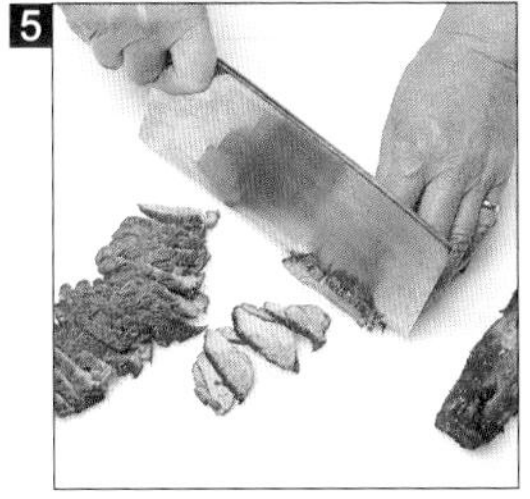

1 Using a sharp knife or meat cleaver, cut the pork into strips about 2.5 cm/1 inch thick and 18-20 cm/7-8 inches long and place in a large shallow dish. Mix the marinade ingredients together and pour over the pork, turning until well coated. Cover, and leave to marinate for at least 3-4 hours, turning occasionally.

2 Remove the pork strips from the dish with a slotted spoon, reserving the marinade. Arrange the pork strips on a rack over a baking tin (pan). Place the tin (pan) in a preheated oven and pour in the boiling water. Roast the pork for about 10-15 minutes.

3 Lower the oven temperature. Baste the pork strips with the reserved marinade and turn over using metal tongs. Roast for a further 10 minutes.

4 Remove the pork from the oven, brush with the honey syrup, and lightly brown under a medium hot grill (broiler) for about 3-4 minutes, turning once or twice.

5 To serve, allow the pork to cool slightly before cutting it. Cut across the grain into thin slices and arrange neatly on a bed of shredded lettuce. Make a sauce by boiling the marinade and the drippings in the baking tin (pan) for a few minutes, strain and pour over the pork.

Chick-peas & Parma Ham

Prosciutto is used in this recipe. It is a cured ham, which is air- and salt-dried for up to 1 year. There are many different varieties available.

NUTRITIONAL INFORMATION

Calories	180	Sugars	2g
Protein	12g	Fat	7g
Carbohydrate	18g	Saturates	1g

 10 MINS  15 MINS

SERVES 4

INGREDIENTS

- 1 tbsp olive oil
- 1 medium onion, thinly sliced
- 1 garlic clove, chopped
- 1 small red (bell) pepper, deseeded and cut into thin strips
- 200 g/7 oz Parma ham (prosciutto), cut into cubes
- 400g/14 oz can chick-peas (garbanzo beans), drained and rinsed
- 1 tbsp chopped parsley, to garnish
- crusty bread, to serve

1

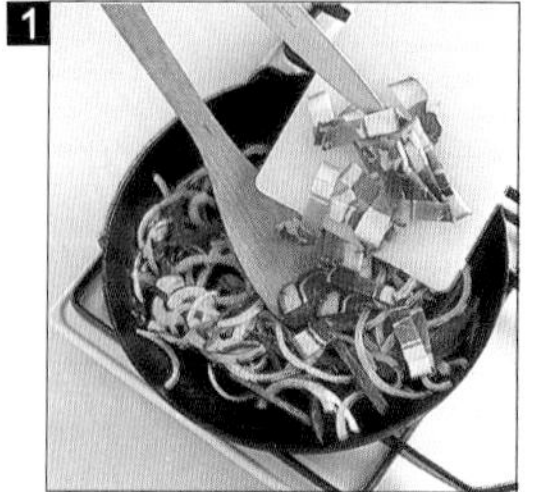

1

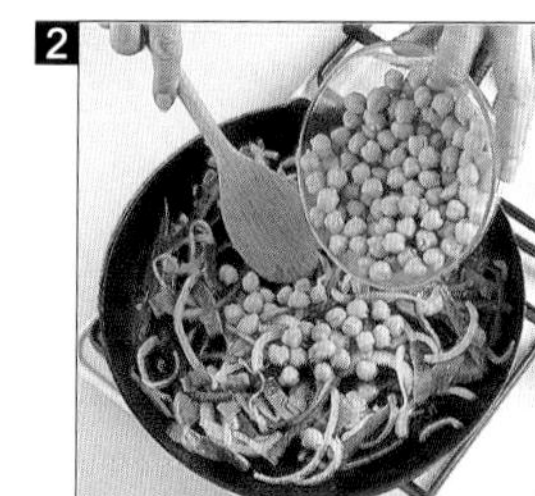

2

1 Heat the oil in a frying pan (skillet). Add the onion, garlic and (bell) pepper and cook for 3–4 minutes or until the vegetables have softened. Add the Parma ham (prosciutto) to the pan (skillet) and fry for 5 minutes or until the ham (prosciutto) is just beginning to brown.

2 Add the chick-peas (garbanzo beans) to the pan (skillet) and cook, stirring, for 2–3 minutes until warmed through.

3 Sprinkle with chopped parsley and transfer to warm serving plates. Serve with lots of fresh crusty bread.

COOK'S TIP

Whenever possible, use fresh herbs when cooking. They are becoming more readily available, especially since the introduction of 'growing' herbs, small pots of herbs which you can buy from the supermarket or greengrocer and grow at home. This ensures the herbs are fresh and also provides a continuous supply.

Cured Meats, Olives & Tomatoes

This is a typical *antipasto* dish with the cold cured meats, stuffed olives and fresh tomatoes, basil and balsamic vinegar.

NUTRITIONAL INFORMATION

Calories	312	Sugars	1g
Protein	12g	Fat	28g
Carbohydrate	2g	Saturates	1g

 10 MINS  5 MINS

SERVES 4

INGREDIENTS

- 4 plum tomatoes
- 1 tbsp balsamic vinegar
- 6 canned anchovy fillets, drained and rinsed
- 2 tbsp capers, drained and rinsed
- 125 g/4½ oz green olives, pitted
- 175 g/6 oz mixed, cured meats, sliced
- 8 fresh basil leaves
- 1 tbsp extra virgin olive oil
- salt and pepper
- crusty bread, to serve

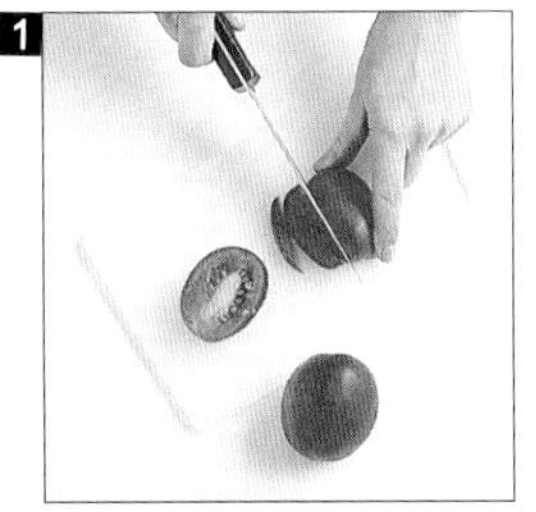
1

2

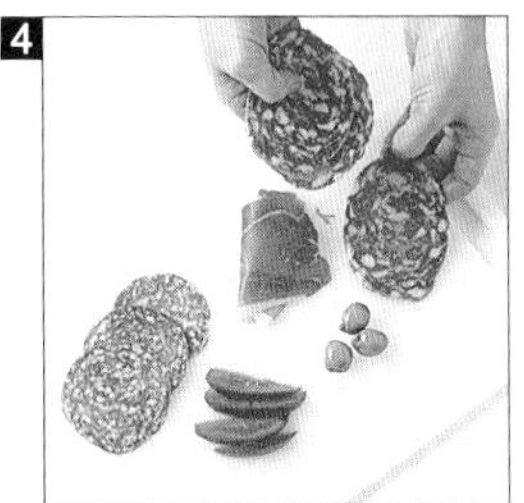
4

1 Using a sharp knife, cut the tomatoes into evenly-sized slices. Sprinkle the tomato slices with the balsamic vinegar and a little salt and pepper to taste, and set aside.

2 Chop the anchovy fillets into pieces measuring about the same length as the olives.

3 Push a piece of anchovy and a caper into each olive.

4 Arrange the sliced meat on 4 individual serving plates together with the tomatoes, filled olives and basil leaves.

5 Lightly drizzle the olive oil over the sliced meat, tomatoes and olives.

6 Serve the cured meats, olives and tomatoes with plenty of fresh crusty bread.

COOK'S TIP

The cured meats for this recipe are up to your individual taste. They can include a selection of Parma ham (prosciutto), pancetta, bresaola (dried salt beef) and salame di Milano (pork and beef sausage).

Deep-fried Vegetables

Choose a selection of your favourite seasonal vegetables, coat them in a light batter and deep-fry them until crispy to make this delightful dish.

NUTRITIONAL INFORMATION

Calories	333	Sugars	9g
Protein	7g	Fat	16g
Carbohydrate	38g	Saturates	2g

 40 MINS ⏲ 15 MINS

SERVES 4

INGREDIENTS

- 500 g/1 lb 2 oz selection of fresh vegetables, such as red and green (bell) peppers, courgettes (zucchini), carrots, spring onions (scallions), cauliflower, broccoli and mushrooms
- oil, for deep-frying

BATTER

- 125 g/4½ oz/1 cup plain (all-purpose) flour
- ½ tsp salt
- 1 tsp caster (superfine) sugar
- 1 tsp baking powder
- 3 tbsp vegetable oil
- 200 ml/7 fl oz/scant 1 cup tepid water

SAUCE

- 1 tbsp light muscovado sugar
- 2 tbsp soy sauce
- 4 tbsp cider vinegar
- 4 tbsp medium sherry
- 1 tbsp cornflour (cornstarch)
- 1 tsp finely grated fresh ginger root

TO GARNISH

- spring onion (scallion) brushes (see page 515)
- chopped spring onions (scallions)

1 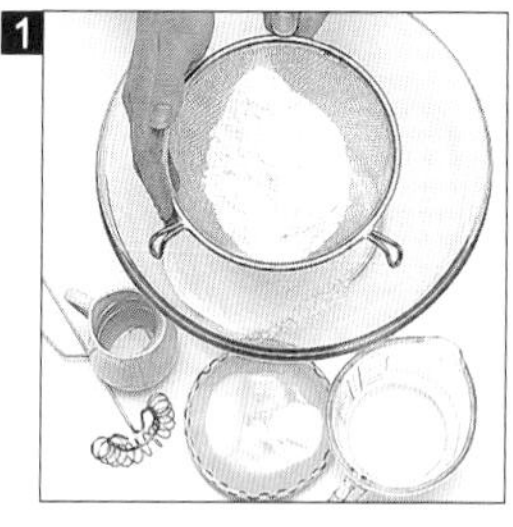

2 

3 

1 To make the batter, sift the flour, salt, sugar and baking powder into a large bowl. Add the oil and most of the water. Whisk together to make a smooth batter, adding extra water to give it the consistency of single (light) cream. Chill for 20–30 minutes.

2 To make the sauce, put all the ingredients into a small saucepan. Heat, stirring, until thickened and smooth.

3 Cut all the vegetables into even, bite-sized pieces. Heat the oil in a wok or deep fat fryer. Dip the vegetables into the batter and fry them in the hot oil, a few at a time, until golden brown and crispy, about 2 minutes. Drain on kitchen paper (paper towels).

4 Garnish and serve the vegetables on a warmed platter accompanied by the dipping sauce.

Mint & Cannellini Bean Dip

This dip is ideal for pre-dinner drinks or for handing around at a party. The cannellini beans require soaking overnight, so prepare in advance.

NUTRITIONAL INFORMATION

Calories	208	Sugars	1g
Protein	10g	Fat	12g
Carbohydrate	16g	Saturates	2g

 40 MINS  30 MINS

SERVES 6

INGREDIENTS

- 175 g/6 oz/1 cup dried cannellini beans
- 1 small garlic clove, crushed
- 1 bunch spring onions (scallions), roughly chopped
- handful of mint leaves
- 2 tbsp tahini (sesame seed paste)
- 2 tbsp olive oil
- 1 tsp ground cumin
- 1 tsp ground coriander
- lemon juice
- salt and pepper
- sprigs of mint, to garnish

TO SERVE

- fresh vegetable crudités, such as cauliflower florets, carrots, cucumber, radishes and (bell) peppers

1 Soak the cannellini beans overnight in plenty of cold water.

2 Rinse and drain the beans, put them into a large saucepan and cover them with cold water. Bring to the boil and boil rapidly for 10 minutes. Reduce the heat, cover and simmer until tender.

3 Drain the beans and transfer them to a bowl or food processor. Add the garlic, spring onions (scallions), mint, tahini (sesame seed paste) and olive oil.

4 Process the mixture for about 15 seconds or mash well by hand, until smooth.

5 Transfer the mixture to a bowl, stir in the cumin, coriander and lemon juice and season to taste with salt and pepper. Mix thoroughly, cover and leave in a cool place for 30 minutes to allow the flavours to develop fully.

6 Spoon the dip into serving bowls, garnish with sprigs of fresh mint and surround with vegetable crudités. Serve at room temperature.

Olive & Anchovy Pâté

The flavour of olives is accentuated by the anchovies. Serve the pâté as an appetizer on thin pieces of toast with a very dry white wine.

NUTRITIONAL INFORMATION

Calories	214	Sugars	1g
Protein	2g	Fat	22g
Carbohydrate	1g	Saturates	8g

 5-10 MINS 35 MINS

SERVES 4

INGREDIENTS

- 175 g/6 oz black olives, pitted and chopped
- finely grated rind and juice of 1 lemon
- 50 g/1½ oz unsalted butter
- 4 canned anchovy fillets, drained and rinsed
- 2 tbsp extra virgin olive oil
- 15 g/½ oz ground almonds
- fresh herbs, to garnish

1 If you are making the pâté by hand, chop the olives very finely and then mash them along with the lemon rind, juice and butter, using a fork or potato masher. Alternatively, place the roughly chopped olives, lemon rind, juice and butter in a food processor and blend until all of the ingredients are finely chopped.

2 Chop the drained anchovies and add them to the olive and lemon mixture. Mash the pâté by hand or blend in a food processor for 20 seconds.

3 Gradually whisk in the olive oil and stir in the ground almonds. Place the black olive pâté in a serving bowl. Leave the pâté to chill in the refrigerator for about 30 minutes. Serve the pâté accompanied by thin pieces of toast, if wished.

COOK'S TIP

This pâté will keep for up to 5 days in a serving bowl in the refrigerator if you pour a thin layer of extra-virgin olive oil over the top of the pâté to seal it. Then use the oil to brush on the toast before spreading the pâté.

Feta Cheese Tartlets

These crisp-baked bread cases, filled with sliced tomatoes, feta cheese, black olives and quail's eggs, are quick to make and taste delicious.

NUTRITIONAL INFORMATION

Calories	570	Sugars	3g
Protein	14g	Fat	42g
Carbohydrate	36g	Saturates	23g

30 MINS

10 MINS

SERVES 4

INGREDIENTS

- 8 slices bread from a medium-cut large loaf
- 125 g/4½ oz/½ cup butter, melted
- 125 g/4½ oz feta cheese, cut into small cubes
- 4 cherry tomatoes, cut into wedges
- 8 pitted black or green olives, halved
- 8 quail's eggs, hard-boiled (hard-cooked)
- 2 tbsp olive oil
- 1 tbsp wine vinegar
- 1 tsp wholegrain mustard
- pinch of caster (superfine) sugar
- salt and pepper
- parsley sprigs, to garnish

1 Remove the crusts from the bread. Trim the bread into squares and flatten each piece with a rolling pin.

2 Brush the bread with melted butter, and then arrange them in bun or muffin tins (pans). Press a piece of crumpled foil into each bread case to secure in place. Bake in a preheated oven, 190°C/375°F/Gas Mark 5, for about 10 minutes, or until crisp and browned.

3 Meanwhile, mix together the feta cheese, tomatoes and olives. Shell the eggs and quarter them. Mix together the olive oil, vinegar, mustard and sugar. Season to taste with salt and pepper.

4 Remove the bread cases from the oven and discard the foil. Leave to cool.

5 Just before serving, fill the bread cases with the cheese and tomato mixture. Arrange the eggs on top and spoon over the dressing. Garnish with parsley sprigs.

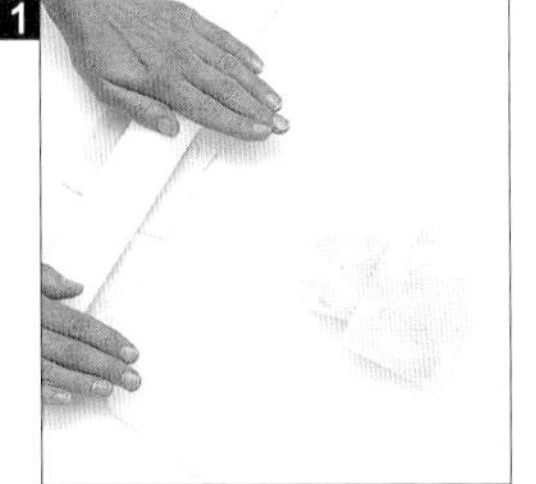

1

2

5

Potato Skins with Guacamole

Although avocados do contain fat, if they are used in small quantities you can still enjoy their creamy texture.

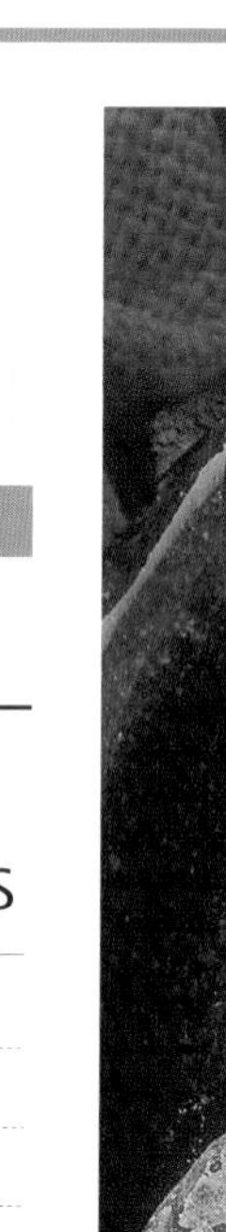

NUTRITIONAL INFORMATION

Calories	399	Sugars	4g
Protein	10g	Fat	15g
Carbohydrate	59g	Saturates	4g

 45 MINS  1¾ HOURS

SERVES 4

INGREDIENTS

- 4 x 225g/8 oz baking potatoes
- 2 tsp olive oil
- coarse sea salt and pepper
- chopped fresh chives, to garnish

GUACAMOLE DIP

- 175 g/6 oz ripe avocado
- 1 tbsp lemon juice
- 2 ripe, firm tomatoes, chopped finely
- 1 tsp grated lemon rind
- 100 g/3½ oz/½ cup low-fat soft cheese with herbs and garlic
- 4 spring onions (scallions), chopped finely
- a few drops of Tabasco sauce
- salt and pepper

2

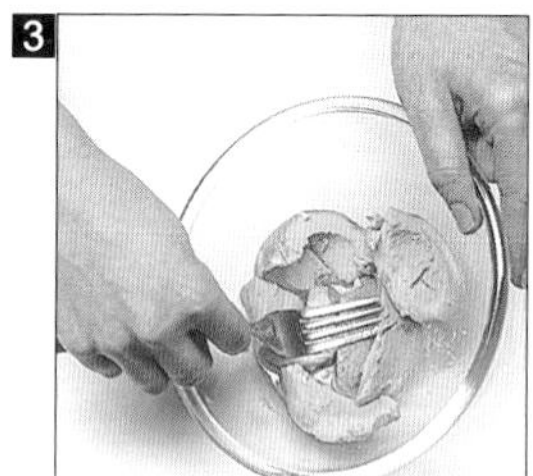
3

3

1 Bake the potatoes in a preheated oven at 200°C/400°F/Gas Mark 6 for 1¼ hours. Remove from the oven and allow to cool for 30 minutes. Reset the oven to 220°C/425°F/Gas Mark 7.

2 Halve the potatoes lengthwise and scoop out 2 tablespoons of the flesh. Slice in half again. Place on a baking tray (cookie) sheet and brush the flesh side lightly with oil. Sprinkle with salt and pepper. Bake for a further 25 minutes until golden and crisp.

3 To make the guacamole dip, mash the avocado with the lemon juice. Add the remaining ingredients and mix.

4 Drain the potato skins on paper towels and transfer to a warmed serving platter. Garnish with chives. Pile the avocado mixture into a serving bowl.

COOK'S TIP

Mash the leftover potato flesh with natural yogurt and seasoning, and serve as an accompaniment to meat, fish and vegetarian dishes.

Spicy Fried Tofu Triangles

Marinated tofu (bean curd) is ideal in this recipe for added flavour, although the spicy coating is very tasty with plain tofu (bean curd).

NUTRITIONAL INFORMATION

Calories	224	Sugars	17g
Protein	10g	Fat	13g
Carbohydrate	18g	Saturates	2g

 1¼ HOURS  10 MINS

SERVES 4

INGREDIENTS

- 1 tbsp sea salt
- 4½ tsp Chinese five-spice powder
- 3 tbsp light brown sugar
- 2 garlic cloves, crushed
- 1 tsp grated fresh root ginger
- 2 x 225 g/8 oz cakes tofu (bean curd)
- vegetable oil, for deep-frying
- 2 leeks, shredded and halved
- shredded leek, to garnish

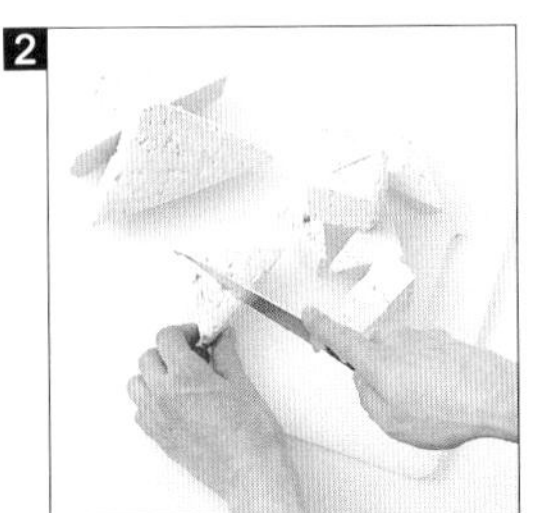

2

3

5

1 Mix together the salt, Chinese five-spice powder, sugar, garlic and ginger in a bowl and transfer to a plate.

2 Cut the tofu (bean curd) cakes in half diagonally to form two triangles. Cut each triangle in half and then in half again to form 16 triangles.

3 Roll the tofu (bean curd) triangles in the spice mixture, turning to coat thoroughly. Set aside for 1 hour.

4 Heat the vegetable oil for deep-frying in a wok until it is almost smoking.

5 Reduce the heat slightly, add the tofu (bean curd) triangles and fry for 5 minutes, until golden brown. Remove the tofu (bean curd) from the wok with a slotted spoon, set aside and keep warm until required.

6 Add the leeks to the wok and stir-fry for 1 minute. Remove from the wok and drain on kitchen paper (paper towels).

7 Arrange the leeks on a warm serving plate and place the fried tofu (bean curd) on top. Garnish with the fresh shredded leek and serve immediately.

COOK'S TIP

Fry the tofu (bean curd) in batches and keep each batch warm until all of the tofu (bean curd) has been fried and is ready to serve.

Pancake Rolls

This classic *dim sum* dish is adaptable to almost any filling of your choice. Here the traditional mixture of pork and pak choi is used.

NUTRITIONAL INFORMATION

Calories	488	Sugars	19g
Protein	16g	Fat	24g
Carbohydrate	55g	Saturates	4g

20 MINS | 20 MINS

SERVES 4

INGREDIENTS

- 4 tsp vegetable oil
- 1-2 garlic cloves, crushed
- 225 g/8 oz minced (ground) pork
- 225/8 oz pak choi, shredded
- 4½ tsp light soy sauce
- ½ tsp sesame oil
- 8 spring roll skins, 25 cm/10 inches square, thawed if frozen
- oil, for deep-frying

CHILLI SAUCE

- 60 g/2 oz/¼ cup caster (superfine) sugar
- 50 ml/2 fl oz/¼ cup rice vinegar
- 2 tbsp water
- 2 red chillies, finely chopped

2

3

3

1 Heat the oil in a preheated wok. Add the garlic and stir-fry for 30 seconds. Add the pork and stir-fry for 2–3 minutes, until lightly coloured.

2 Add the pak choi, soy sauce and sesame oil to the wok and stir-fry for 2–3 minutes. Remove from the heat and set aside to cool.

3 Spread out the spring roll skins on a work surface (counter) and spoon 2 tablespoons of the pork mixture along one edge of each. Roll the skin over once and fold in the sides. Roll up completely to make a sausage shape, brushing the edges with a little water to seal. Set the pancake rolls aside for 10 minutes to seal firmly.

4 To make the chilli sauce, heat the sugar, vinegar and water in a small saucepan, stirring until the sugar dissolves. Bring the mixture to the boil and boil rapidly until a light syrup forms. Remove from the heat and stir in the chopped red chillies. Leave the sauce to cool before serving.

5 Heat the oil for deep-frying in a wok until almost smoking. Reduce the heat slightly and fry the pancake rolls, in batches if necessary, for 3–4 minutes, until golden brown. Remove from the oil with a slotted spoon and drain on absorbent kitchen paper (paper towels). Serve with the chilli sauce.

Deep-Fried Spare Ribs

The spare ribs should be chopped into small bite-sized pieces before or after cooking.

NUTRITIONAL INFORMATION

Calories	177	Sugars	0.2g
Protein	6g	Fat	14g
Carbohydrate	6g	Saturates	4g

 5 MINS  $2^1/_4$ HOURS

SERVES 4

INGREDIENTS

- 8-10 finger spare ribs
- 1 tsp five-spice powder or 1 tbsp mild curry powder
- 1 tbsp rice wine or dry sherry
- 1 egg
- 2 tbsp flour
- vegetable oil, for deep-frying
- 1 tsp finely shredded spring onions (scallions)
- 1 tsp finely shredded fresh green or red hot chillies, seeded
- salt and pepper
- Spicy Salt and Pepper (see page 80), to serve

1 Chop the ribs into 3-4 small pieces. Place the ribs in a bowl with salt, pepper, five-spice or curry powder and the wine. Turn to coat the ribs in the spices and leave to marinate for 1-2 hours.

2 Mix the egg and flour together to make a batter. Dip the ribs in the batter one by one to coat well.

3 Heat the oil in a preheated wok until smoking. Deep-fry the ribs for 4-5 minutes, then remove with chopsticks or a slotted spoon and drain on kitchen paper (paper towels).

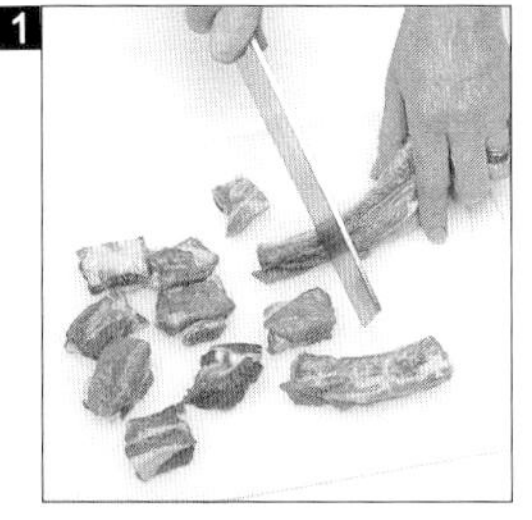

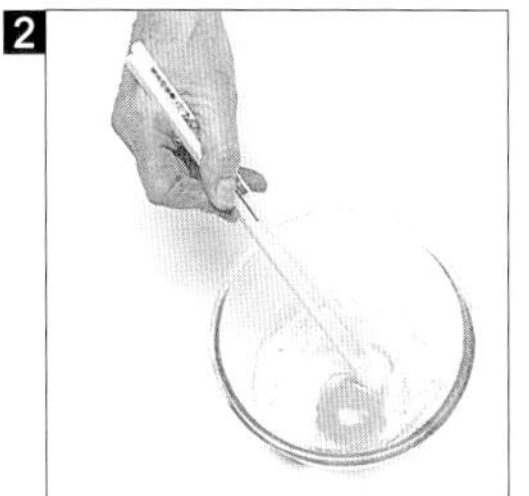

4 Reheat the oil over a high heat and deep-fry the ribs once more for another minute. Remove and drain again on kitchen paper (paper towels).

5 Pour 1 tablespoon of the hot oil over the spring onions (scallions) and chillies and leave for 30-40 seconds. Serve the ribs with Spicy Salt and Pepper, garnished with the shredded spring onions (scallions) and chillies.

COOK'S TIP

To make finger ribs, cut the sheet of spare ribs into individual ribs down each side of the bones. These ribs are then chopped into bite-sized pieces for deep-frying.

Roasted Seafood

Vegetables become deliciously sweet and juicy when they are roasted, and they go particularly well with fish and seafood.

NUTRITIONAL INFORMATION

Calories	280	Sugars	5g
Protein	15g	Fat	12g
Carbohydrate	28g	Saturates	2g

 15 MINS  50 MINS

SERVES 4

INGREDIENTS

- 600 g/1 lb 5 oz new potatoes
- 3 red onions, cut into wedges
- 2 courgettes (zucchini), sliced into chunks
- 8 garlic cloves, peeled
- 2 lemons, cut into wedges
- 4 sprigs rosemary
- 4 tbsp olive oil
- 350 g/12 oz shell-on prawns (shrimp), preferably uncooked
- 2 small squid, chopped into rings
- 4 tomatoes, quartered

1 Scrub the potatoes to remove any excess dirt. Cut any large potatoes in half. Place the potatoes in a large roasting tin (pan), together with the onions, courgettes (zucchini), garlic, lemon and rosemary sprigs.

2 Pour over the oil and toss to coat all of the vegetables in the oil. Cook in a preheated oven, at 200°C/400°F/Gas Mark 6, for 40 minutes, turning occasionally, until the potatoes are tender.

3 Once the potatoes are tender, add the prawns (shrimp), squid and tomatoes, tossing to coat them in the oil, and roast for 10 minutes. All of the vegetables should be cooked through and slightly charred for full flavour.

4 Transfer the roasted seafood and vegetables to warm serving plates and serve hot.

1

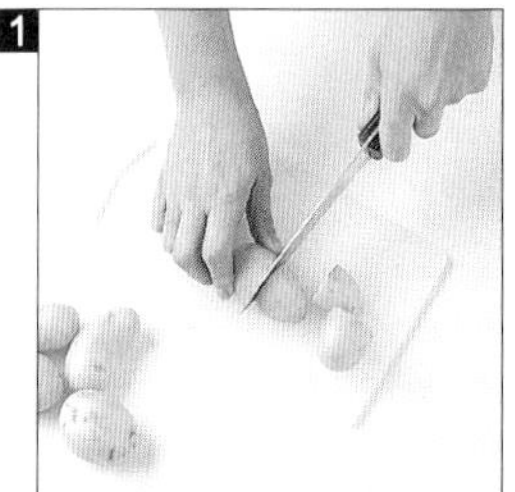

1

2

VARIATION

Most vegetables are suitable for roasting in the oven. Try adding 450 g/1 lb pumpkin, squash or aubergine (eggplant), if you prefer.

Tuna Stuffed Tomatoes

Deliciously sweet roasted tomatoes are filled with home-made lemon mayonnaise and tuna.

NUTRITIONAL INFORMATION

Calories	196	Sugars	2g
Protein	9g	Fat	17g
Carbohydrate	2g	Saturates	3g

5-10 MINS 25 MINS

SERVES 4

INGREDIENTS

- 4 plum tomatoes
- 2 tbsp sun-dried tomato paste
- 2 egg yolks
- 2 tsp lemon juice
- finely grated rind of 1 lemon
- 4 tbsp olive oil
- 115g/4 oz can tuna, drained
- 2 tbsp capers, rinsed
- salt and pepper

TO GARNISH

- 2 sun-dried tomatoes, cut into strips
- fresh basil leaves

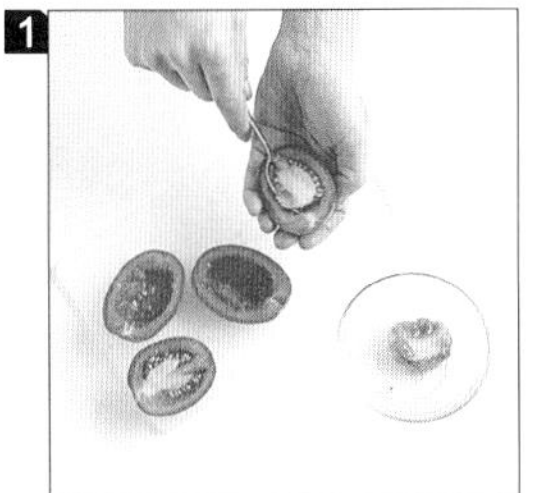

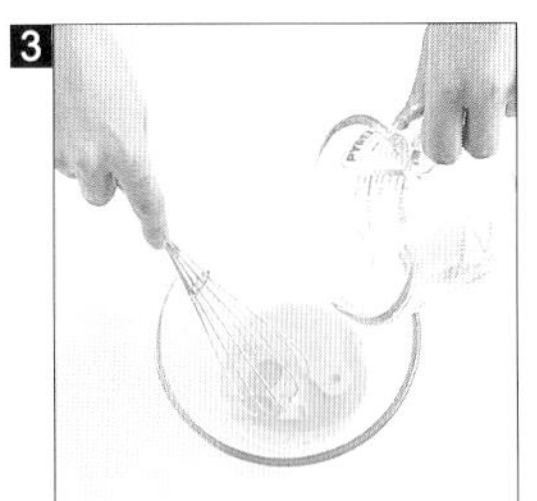

1 Halve the tomatoes and scoop out the seeds. Divide the sun-dried tomato paste among the tomato halves and spread around the inside of the skin.

2 Place on a baking tray (cookie sheet) and roast in a preheated oven at 200°C/400°F/Gas Mark 6 for 12–15 minutes. Leave to cool slightly.

3 Meanwhile, make the mayonnaise. In a food processor, blend the egg yolks and lemon juice with the lemon rind until smooth. Once mixed and with the motor still running slowly, add the olive oil. Stop the processor as soon as the mayonnaise has thickened. Alternatively, use a hand whisk, beating the mixture continuously until it thickens.

4 Add the tuna and capers to the mayonnaise and season.

5 Spoon the tuna mayonnaise mixture into the tomato shells and garnish with sun-dried tomato strips and basil leaves. Return to the oven for a few minutes or serve chilled.

COOK'S TIP

For a picnic, do not roast the tomatoes, just scoop out the seeds, drain, cut-side down on absorbent kitchen paper for 1 hour, and fill with the mayonnaise mixture. They are firmer and easier to handle this way. If you prefer, shop-bought mayonnaise may be used instead – just stir in the lemon rind.

Crab Ravioli

These small parcels are made from won ton wrappers, filled with mixed vegetables and crabmeat for a melt-in-the-mouth starter.

NUTRITIONAL INFORMATION

Calories	292	Sugars	1g
Protein	25g	Fat	17g
Carbohydrate	11g	Saturates	5g

 20 MINS

25 MINS

SERVES 4

INGREDIENTS

- 450 g/1 lb crabmeat (fresh or canned and drained)
- ½ red (bell) pepper, seeded and finely diced
- 125 g/4½ oz Chinese leaves (cabbage), shredded
- 25 g/1 oz bean sprouts, roughly chopped
- 1 tbsp light soy sauce
- 1 tsp lime juice
- 16 wonton wrappers
- 1 small egg, beaten
- 2 tbsp peanut oil
- 1 tsp sesame oil
- salt and pepper

1. Mix together the crabmeat, (bell) pepper, Chinese leaves (cabbage), bean sprouts, soy sauce and lime juice. Season and leave to stand for 15 minutes.

2. Spread out the wonton wrappers on a work surface (counter). Spoon a little of the crabmeat mixture into the centre of each wrapper. Brush the edges with egg and fold in half, pushing out any air. Press the edges together to seal.

3. Heat the peanut oil in a preheated wok or frying pan (skillet). Fry the ravioli, in batches, for 3–4 minutes, turning, until browned. Remove with a slotted spoon and drain on kitchen paper (paper towels).

4. Heat any remaining filling in the wok or frying pan (skillet) over a gentle heat until hot. Serve the ravioli with the hot filling and sprinkled with sesame oil.

COOK'S TIP

Make sure that the edges of the ravioli are sealed well and that all of the air is pressed out to prevent them from opening during cooking.

2

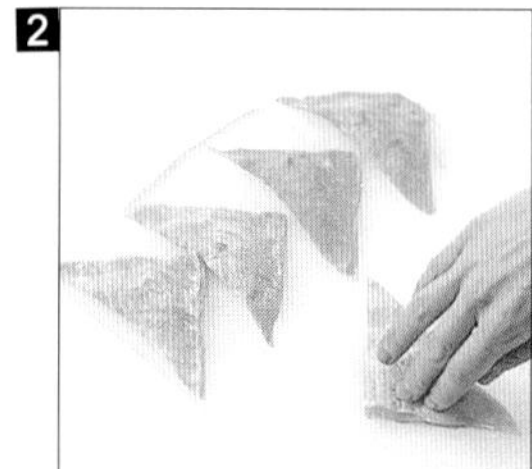

2

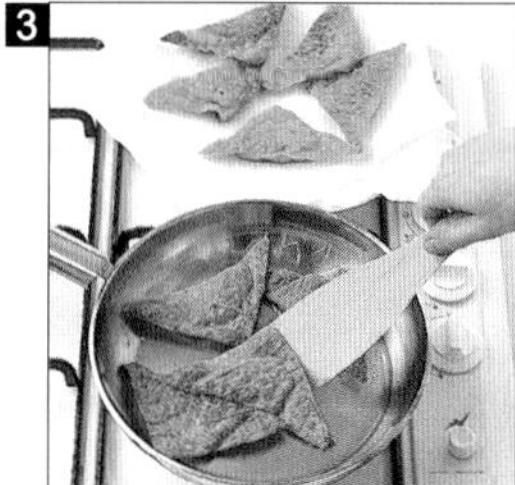

3

Smoked Fish & Potato Pâté

This smoked fish pâté is given a tart fruity flavour by the gooseberries, which complement the fish perfectly.

NUTRITIONAL INFORMATION

Calories	418	Sugars	4g
Protein	18g	Fat	25g
Carbohydrate	32g	Saturates	6g

 20 MINS  10 MINS

SERVES 4

INGREDIENTS

- 650 g/1 lb 7 oz floury (mealy) potatoes, diced
- 300 g/10½ oz smoked mackerel, skinned and flaked
- 75 g/2¾ oz cooked gooseberries
- 2 tsp lemon juice
- 2 tbsp low-fat crème fraîche
- 1 tbsp capers
- 1 gherkin, chopped
- 1 tbsp chopped dill pickle
- 1 tbsp chopped fresh dill
- salt and pepper
- lemon wedges, to garnish
- toast or warm crusty bread, to serve

3

4

5

1 Cook the diced potatoes in a saucepan of boiling water for 10 minutes until tender, then drain well.

2 Place the cooked potatoes in a food processor or blender.

3 Add the skinned and flaked smoked mackerel and process for 30 seconds until fairly smooth. Alternatively, place the ingredients in a bowl and mash with a fork.

4 Add the cooked gooseberries, lemon juice and crème fraîche to the fish and potato mixture. Blend for a further 10 seconds or mash well.

5 Stir in the capers, chopped gherkin and dill pickle, and chopped fresh dill. Season well with salt and pepper.

6 Turn the fish pâté into a serving dish, garnish with lemon wedges and serve with slices of toast or warm crusty bread cut into chunks or slices.

COOK'S TIP

Use stewed, canned or bottled cooked gooseberries for convenience and to save time, or when fresh gooseberries are out of season.

Shrimp Rolls

This variation of a spring roll is made with shrimps, stir-fried with shallots, carrot, cucumber, bamboo shoots and rice.

NUTRITIONAL INFORMATION

Calories	388	Sugars	2g
Protein	9g	Fat	25g
Carbohydrate	33g	Saturates	6g

 10 MINS  15 MINS

SERVES 4

INGREDIENTS

- 2 tbsp vegetable oil
- 3 shallots, chopped very finely
- 1 carrot, cut into matchstick pieces
- 7 cm/3 inch piece of cucumber, cut into matchstick pieces
- 60 g/2 oz/½ cup bamboo shoots, shredded finely
- 125 g/4½ oz/½ cup peeled (small) shrimps
- 90 g/3 oz/½ cup cooked long-grain rice
- 1 tbsp fish sauce or light soy sauce
- 1 tsp sugar
- 2 tsp cornflour (cornstarch), blended in 2 tbsp cold water
- 8 × 25 cm/10 inch spring roll wrappers
- oil for deep-frying
- salt and pepper
- plum sauce, to serve

TO GARNISH

- spring onion (scallion) brushes (see page 515)
- sprigs of fresh coriander (cilantro)

1 Heat the oil in a wok and add the shallots, carrot, cucumber and bamboo shoots. Stir-fry briskly for 2–3 minutes. Add the shrimps and cooked rice, and cook for a further 2 minutes. Season.

2 Mix together the fish sauce or soy sauce, sugar and blended cornflour (cornstarch). Add to the stir-fry and cook, stirring constantly, for about 1 minute, until thickened. Leave to cool slightly.

3 Place spoonfuls of the shrimp and vegetable mixture on the spring roll wrappers. Dampen the edges and roll them up to enclose the filling completely.

4 Heat the oil for deep-frying and fry the spring rolls until crisp and golden brown. Drain on paper towels. Serve the rolls garnished with spring onion (scallion) brushes and fresh coriander (cilantro) and accompanied by the plum sauce.

2

3

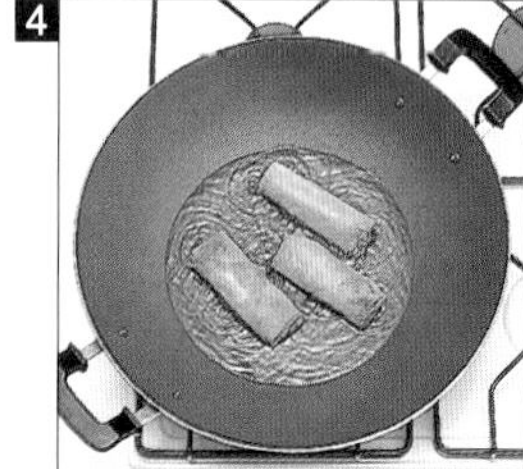
4

Vegetable Fritters

These mixed vegetable fritters are coated in a light batter and deep-fried until golden. They are ideal with the sweet and sour dipping sauce.

NUTRITIONAL INFORMATION

Calories	479	Sugars	18g
Protein	8g	Fat	32g
Carbohydrate	42g	Saturates	5g

 20 MINS  20 MINS

SERVES 4

INGREDIENTS

- 100 g/3½ oz/¾ cup wholemeal (whole wheat) flour
- pinch of caycnnc pepper
- 4 tsp olive oil
- 12 tbsp cold water
- 100 g/3½ oz broccoli florets
- 100 g/3½ oz cauliflower florets
- 50 g/1¾ oz mangetout (snow peas)
- 1 large carrot, cut into batons
- 1 red (bell) pepper, seeded and sliced
- 2 egg whites, beaten
- oil, for deep-frying
- salt

SAUCE

- 150 ml/¼ pint/⅔ cup pineapple juice
- 150 ml/¼ pint/⅔ cup vegetable stock
- 2 tbsp white wine vinegar
- 2 tbsp light brown sugar
- 2 tsp cornflour (cornstarch)
- 2 spring onions (scallions), chopped

1

4

4

1 Sift the flour and a pinch of salt into a mixing bowl and add the cayenne pepper. Make a well in the centre and gradually beat in the oil and cold water to make a smooth batter.

2 Cook the vegetables in boiling water for 5 minutes and drain well.

3 Whisk the egg whites until they form peaks and gently fold them into the flour batter.

4 Dip the vegetables into the batter, turning to coat well. Drain off any excess batter. Heat the oil for deep-frying in a deep-fryer to 180°C/350°F or until a cube of bread browns in 30 seconds. Fry the coated vegetables, in batches, for 1–2 minutes, until golden. Remove from the oil with a slotted spoon and drain on kitchen paper (paper towels).

5 Place all of the sauce ingredients in a pan and bring to the boil, stirring, until thickened and clear. Serve with the fritters.

Tzatziki & Black Olive Dip

Tzatziki is a Greek dish, made with yogurt, mint and cucumber. It tastes superb with warm pitta (pocket) bread.

NUTRITIONAL INFORMATION

Calories	381	Sugars	8g
Protein	11g	Fat	15g
Carbohydrate	52g	Saturates	2g

 1 HOUR  3 MINS

SERVES 4

INGREDIENTS

- ½ cucumber
- 225 g/8 oz/1 cup thick natural (unsweetened) yogurt
- 1 tbsp chopped mint
- salt and pepper
- 4 pitta (pocket) breads

DIP

- 2 garlic cloves, crushed
- 125 g/4½ oz/1 cup pitted black olives
- 4 tbsp olive oil
- 2 tbsp lemon juice
- 1 tbsp chopped parsley

TO GARNISH

- mint sprigs
- parsley sprigs

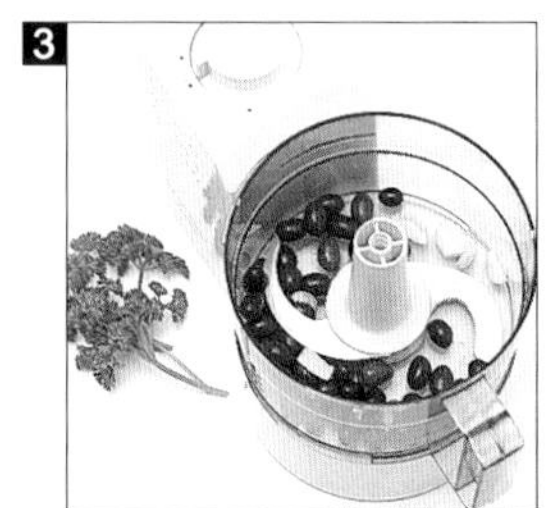

1 To make the tzatziki, peel the cucumber and chop roughly. Sprinkle it with salt and leave to stand for 15–20 minutes. Rinse with cold water and drain well.

2 Mix the cucumber, yogurt and mint together. Season to taste with salt and pepper and transfer to a serving bowl. Cover and chill for 20–30 minutes.

3 To make the black olive dip, put the crushed garlic and olives into a blender or food processor and process for 15–20 seconds. Alternatively, chop them very finely.

4 Add the olive oil, lemon juice and parsley to the blender or food processor and process for a few more seconds. Alternatively, mix with the chopped garlic and olives and mash together. Season with salt and pepper.

5 Wrap the pitta (pocket) breads in foil and place over a barbecue for 2–3 minutes, turning once to warm through. Alternatively, heat in the oven or under the grill (broiler). Cut into pieces and serve with the tzatziki and black olive dip, garnished with sprigs of fresh mint and parsley.

COOK'S TIP

Sprinkling the cucumber with salt draws out some of its moisture, making it crisper. If you are in a hurry, you can omit this procedure. Use green olives instead of black ones if you prefer.

Spinach Roulade

A delicious savoury roll, stuffed with mozzarella and broccoli. Serve as a main course or as an appetizer, in which case it would easily serve six.

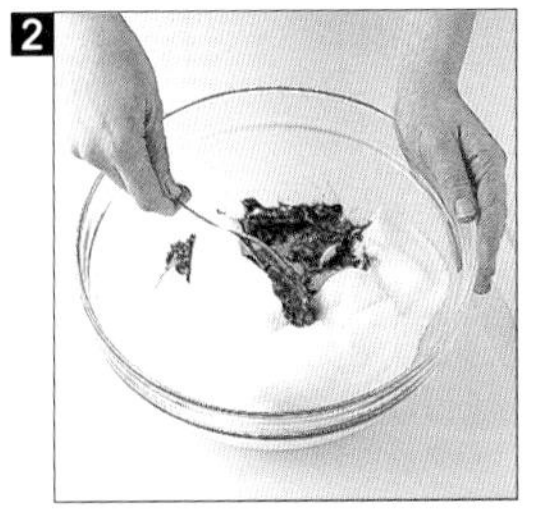

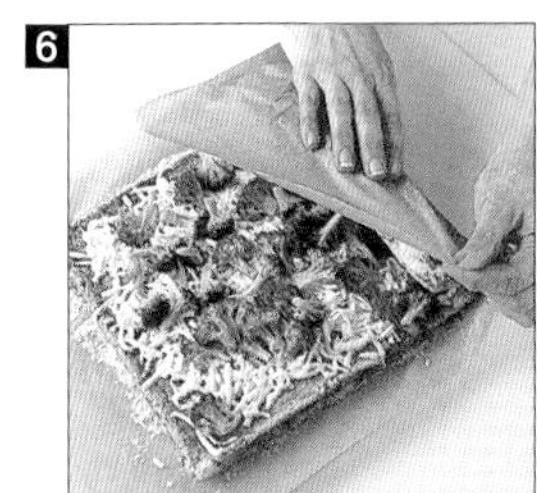

NUTRITIONAL INFORMATION

Calories	287	Sugars	8g
Protein	23g	Fat	12g
Carbohydrate	8g	Saturates	6g

 15 MINS  25 MINS

SERVES 4

INGREDIENTS

- 500 g/1 lb 2 oz small spinach leaves
- 2 tbsp water
- 4 eggs, separated
- ½ tsp ground nutmeg
- salt and pepper
- 300 ml/½ pint/1¼ cups sugocasa, to serve

FILLING

- 175 g/6 oz small broccoli florets
- 25 g/1 oz/¼ cup freshly grated Parmesan cheese
- 175 g/6 oz/1½ cups grated mozzarella cheese

1 Wash the spinach and pack, still wet, into a large saucepan. Add the water. Cover with a tight-fitting lid and cook over a high heat for 4–5 minutes, until reduced and soft. Drain thoroughly, squeezing out excess water. Chop finely and pat dry.

2 Mix the spinach with the egg yolks, seasoning and nutmeg. Whisk the egg whites until very frothy but not too stiff, and fold into the spinach mixture.

3 Grease and line a 32 x 23 cm/ 13 x 9 inch Swiss roll tin (jelly roll pan). Spread the mixture in the tin (pan) and smooth the surface. Bake in a preheated oven, 220°C/425°F/Gas Mark 7, for about 12–15 minutes, until firm to the touch and golden.

4 Meanwhile, cook the broccoli florets in lightly salted boiling water for 4–5 minutes, until just tender. Drain and keep warm.

5 Sprinkle Parmesan on a sheet of baking parchment. Turn the base on to it and peel away the lining paper. Sprinkle with mozzarella and top with broccoli.

6 Hold one end of the paper and roll up the spinach base like a Swiss (jelly) roll. Heat the sugocasa and spoon on to warmed serving plates. Slice the roulade and place on top of the sugocasa.

Poultry, Meat & Game

This chapter features exciting ways of cooking poultry, meat and game to offer a variety of satisfying meals. Dishes range from easy, economical mid-week suppers to sophisticated and elegant meals for special occasions. There are also tempting recipes to liven up a summer barbecue. The dishes bring together a wide range of flavours and ingredients from around the world, from classics such as Spaghetti Bolognese to less well-known but equally delicious dishes such as Kung Po Chicken with Cashews and Lamb Do Pyaza. There are also variations on old favourites, for example Pheasant Lasagne or Mediterranean-style Sunday Roast. Experiment with the ever increasing range of ingredients that are now available from a supermarket near you!

Jerk Chicken

This is perhaps one of the best known Caribbean dishes. The 'jerk' in the name refers to the hot spicy coating.

NUTRITIONAL INFORMATION

Calories	158	Sugars	0.4g
Protein	29g	Fat	4g
Carbohydrate	2g	Saturates	1g

24 HOURS 30 MINS

SERVES 4

INGREDIENTS

- 4 lean chicken portions
- 1 bunch spring onions (scallions), trimmed
- 1–2 Scotch Bonnet chillies, deseeded
- 1 garlic clove
- 5 cm/2 inch piece root (fresh) ginger, peeled and roughly chopped
- ½ tsp dried thyme
- ½ tsp paprika
- ¼ tsp ground allspice
- pinch ground cinnamon
- pinch ground cloves
- 4 tbsp white wine vinegar
- 3 tbsp light soy sauce
- pepper

1 Rinse the chicken portions and pat them dry on absorbent kitchen paper. Place them in a shallow dish.

2 Place the spring onions (scallions), chillies, garlic, ginger, thyme, paprika, allspice, cinnamon, cloves, wine vinegar, soy sauce and pepper to taste in a food processor and process until smooth.

3 Pour the spicy mixture over the chicken. Turn the chicken portions over so that they are well coated in the marinade.

2

3

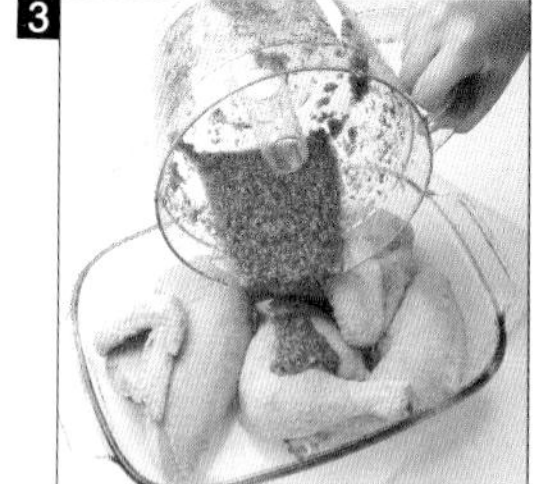

5

4 Transfer the chicken portions to the refrigerator and leave to marinate for up to 24 hours.

5 Remove the chicken from the marinade and barbecue (grill) over medium hot coals for about 30 minutes, turning the chicken over and basting occasionally with any remaining marinade, until the chicken is browned and cooked through.

6 Transfer the chicken portions to individual serving plates and serve at once.

Chicken Marengo

Napoleon's chef was ordered to cook a sumptuous meal on the eve of the battle of Marengo – this feast of flavours was the result.

NUTRITIONAL INFORMATION

Calories	521	Sugars	6g
Protein	47g	Fat	19g
Carbohydrate	34g	Saturates	8g

20 MINS 50 MINS

SERVES 4

INGREDIENTS

- 1 tbsp olive oil
- 8 chicken pieces
- 300 g/10½ oz passata (tomato paste)
- 200 ml/7 fl oz/¾ cup white wine
- 2 tsp dried mixed herbs
- 8 slices white bread
- 40 g/1½ oz butter, melted
- 2 garlic cloves, crushed
- 100 g/3½ oz mixed mushrooms (such as button, oyster and ceps)
- 40 g/1½ oz black olives, chopped
- 1 tsp sugar
- fresh basil, to garnish

1 Using a sharp knife, remove the bone from each of the chicken pieces.

2 Heat the oil in a large frying pan (skillet). Add the chicken pieces and cook for 4–5 minutes, turning occassionally, or until browned all over.

3 Add the passata (tomato paste), wine and mixed herbs to the frying pan (skillet). Bring to the boil and then leave to simmer for 30 minutes or until the chicken is tender and the juices run clear when a skewer is inserted into the thickest part of the meat.

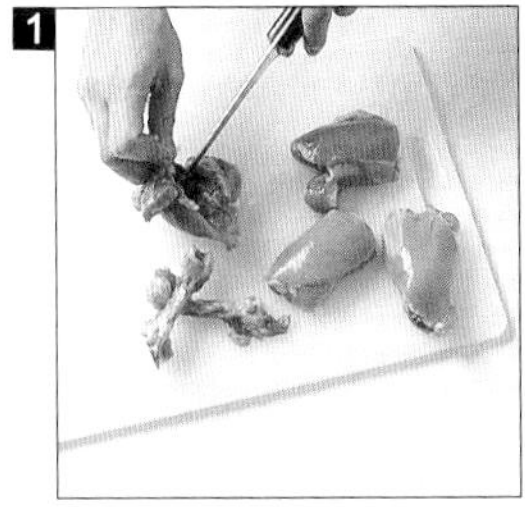
1

3

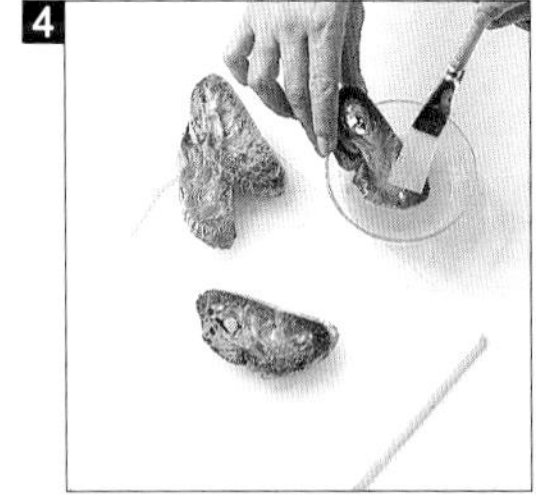
4

4 Mix the melted butter and crushed garlic together. Lightly toast the slices of bread and brush with the garlic butter.

5 Add the remaining oil to a separate frying pan (skillet) and cook the mushrooms for 2–3 minutes or until just browned.

6 Add the olives and sugar to the chicken mixture and warm through.

7 Transfer the chicken and sauce to serving plates. Serve with the bruschetta (fried bread) and fried mushrooms.

Chicken Lasagne

This variation of the traditional beef dish has layers of pasta and chicken or turkey baked in red wine, tomatoes and a delicious cheese sauce.

NUTRITIONAL INFORMATION

Calories	550	Sugars	11g
Protein	35g	Fat	29g
Carbohydrate	34g	Saturates	12g

 20 MINS  1¼ HOURS

SERVES 4

INGREDIENTS

- 350 g/12 oz fresh lasagne (about 9 sheets) or 150 g/5½ oz dried lasagne (about 9 sheets)
- 1 tbsp olive oil
- 1 red onion, finely chopped
- 1 garlic clove, crushed
- 100 g/3½ oz mushrooms, wiped and sliced
- 350 g/12 oz chicken or turkey breast, cut into chunks
- 150 ml/¼ pint/⅔ cup red wine, diluted with 100 ml/3½ fl oz/scant ⅓ cup water
- 250 g/9 oz passata (sieved tomatoes)
- 1 tsp sugar

BECHAMEL SAUCE

- 75 g/2¾ oz/5 tbsp butter
- 50 g/1¾ oz plain (all-purpose) flour
- 600 ml/1 pint/2½ cups milk
- 1 egg, beaten
- 75 g/2¾ oz Parmesan cheese, grated
- salt and pepper

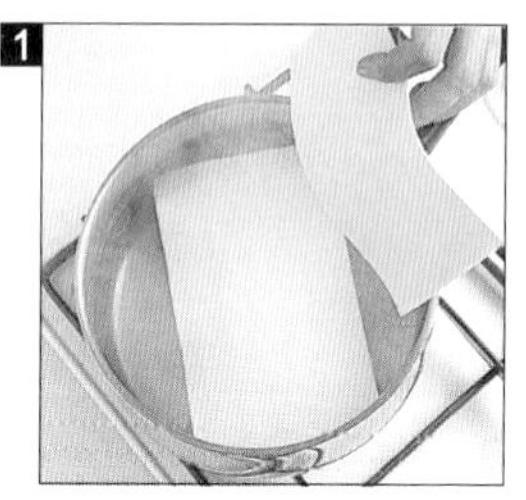

1 Cook the lasagne in a pan of boiling water according to the instructions on the packet. Lightly grease a deep ovenproof dish.

2 Heat the oil in a pan. Add the onion and garlic and cook for 3–4 minutes. Add the mushrooms and chicken and stir-fry for 4 minutes or until the meat browns.

3 Add the wine, bring to the boil, then simmer for 5 minutes. Stir in the passata (sieved tomatoes) and sugar and cook for 3–5 minutes until the meat is tender and cooked through. The sauce should have thickened, but still be quite runny.

4 To make the Béchamel Sauce, melt the butter in a pan, stir in the flour and cook for 2 minutes. Remove the pan from the heat and gradually add the milk, mixing to form a smooth sauce. Return the pan to the heat and bring to the boil, stirring until thickened. Leave to cool slightly, then beat in the egg and half of the cheese. Season to taste.

5 Place 3 sheets of lasagne in the base of the dish and spread with half of the chicken mixture. Repeat the layers. Top with the last 3 sheets of lasagne, pour over the Béchamel Sauce and sprinkle with the Parmesan. Bake in a preheated oven, at 190°C/375°F/Gas Mark 5, for 30 minutes until golden and the pasta is cooked.

Jamaican Hot Pot

A tasty way to make chicken joints go a long way, this hearty casserole is spiced with the warm, subtle flavour of ginger.

NUTRITIONAL INFORMATION

Calories	277	Sugars	6g
Protein	33g	Fat	7g
Carbohydrate	22g	Saturates	1g

5 MINS 1¼ HOURS

SERVES 4

INGREDIENTS

- 2 tsp sunflower oil
- 4 chicken drumsticks
- 4 chicken thighs
- 1 medium onion
- 750 g/1 lb 10 oz piece squash or pumpkin, peeled
- 1 green (bell) pepper
- 2.5 cm/1 inch fresh ginger root, chopped finely
- 425 g/15 oz can chopped tomatoes
- 300ml/½ pint/1¼ cups chicken stock
- 60 g/2 oz/¼ cup split lentils
- garlic salt and cayenne pepper
- 350 g/12 oz can sweetcorn (corn-on-the-cob)

2

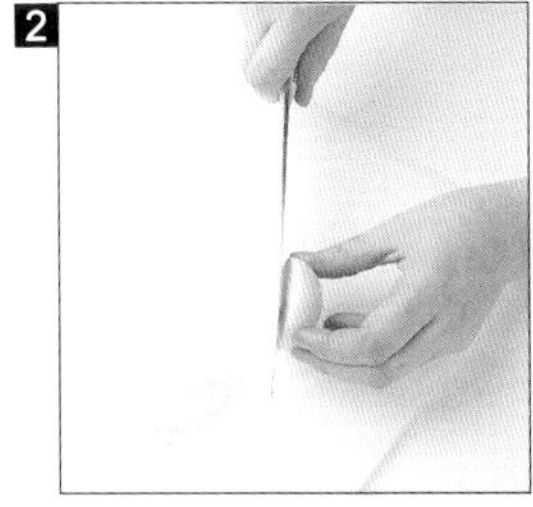

3

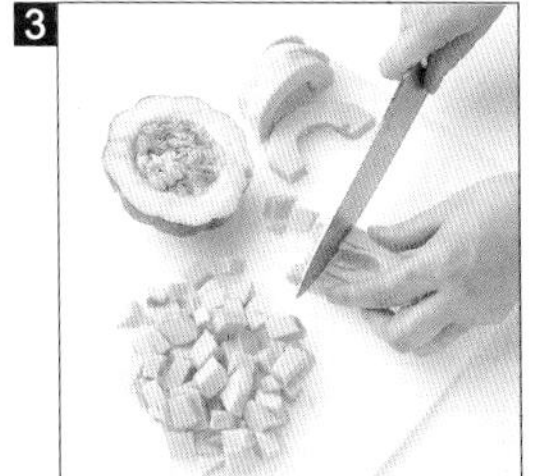

4

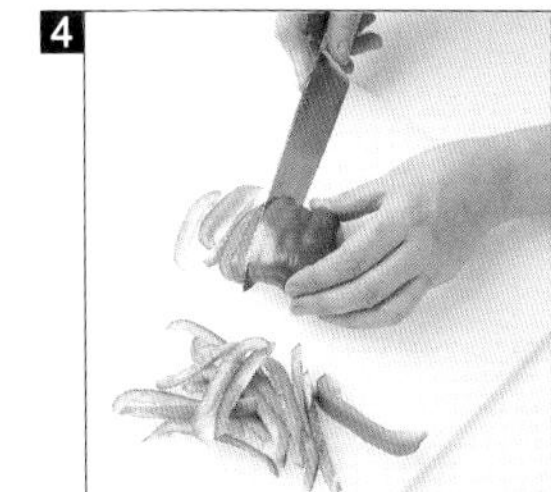

1 Heat the oil in a large flameproof casserole and fry the chicken joints, turning frequently, until they are golden all over.

2 Peel and slice the onion.

3 Using a sharp knife, cut the squash or pumpkin into dice.

4 Deseed and slice the green (bell) pepper.

5 Drain any excess fat from the pan and add the onion, pumpkin and pepper. Gently fry for a few minutes. Add the ginger, tomatoes, stock and lentils. Season with garlic salt and cayenne.

6 Cover and place in a preheated oven, 190°C/375°F/Gas Mark 5, for about 1 hour, until the vegetables are tender and the juices from the chicken run clear.

7 Add the drained corn and cook for a further 5 minutes. Season to taste and serve with crusty bread.

Italian Chicken Spirals

These little foil parcels retain all the natural juices of the chicken while cooking conveniently over the pasta while it boils.

NUTRITIONAL INFORMATION

Calories	367	Sugars	1g
Protein	33g	Fat	12g
Carbohydrate	35g	Saturates	2g

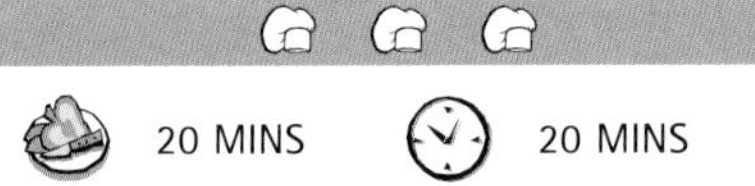

20 MINS 20 MINS

SERVES 4

INGREDIENTS

- 4 skinless, boneless chicken breasts
- 25 g/1 oz/1 cup fresh basil leaves
- 15 g/½ oz/2 tbsp hazelnuts
- 1 garlic clove, crushed
- 250 g/9 oz/2 cups wholemeal (whole wheat) pasta spirals
- 2 sun-dried tomatoes or fresh tomatoes
- 1 tbsp lemon juice
- 1 tbsp olive oil
- 1 tbsp capers
- 60 g/2 oz/½ cup black olives

1 Beat the chicken breasts with a rolling pin to flatten evenly.

2 Place the basil and hazelnuts in a food processor and process until finely chopped. Mix with the garlic and salt and pepper to taste.

3 Spread the basil mixture over the chicken breasts and roll up from one short end to enclose the filling. Wrap the chicken roll tightly in foil so that they hold their shape, then seal the ends well.

4 Bring a pan of lightly salted water to the boil and cook the pasta for 8–10 minutes or until tender, but still firm to the bite. Meanwhile, place the chicken parcels in a steamer or colander set over the pan, cover tightly, and steam for 10 minutes.

5 Using a sharp knife, dice the tomatoes.

6 Drain the pasta and return to the pan with the lemon juice, olive oil, tomatoes, capers and olives. Heat through.

7 Pierce the chicken with a skewer to make sure that the juices run clear and not pink (this shows that the chicken is cooked through). Slice the chicken, arrange over the pasta and serve.

2

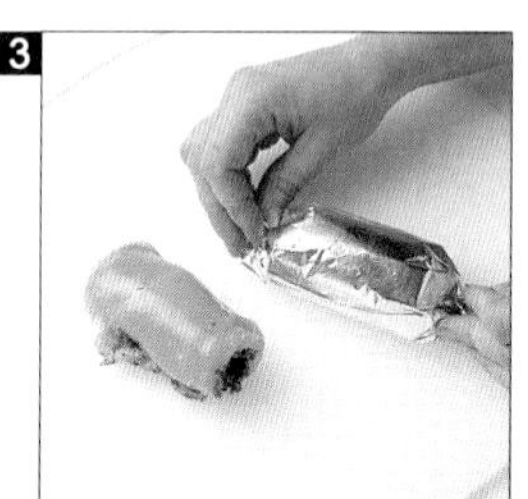

3

6

COOK'S TIP

Sun-dried tomatoes have a wonderful, rich flavour but if they're unavailable, use fresh tomatoes instead.

Thai Red Chicken

This is a really colourful dish, the red of the tomatoes perfectly complementing the orange of the sweet potato.

NUTRITIONAL INFORMATION

Calories	249	Sugars	14g
Protein	26g	Fat	7g
Carbohydrate	22g	Saturates	2g

10 MINS

35 MINS

SERVES 4

INGREDIENTS

- 1 tbsp sunflower oil
- 450 g/1 lb lean boneless, skinless chicken
- 2 cloves garlic, crushed
- 2 tbsp Thai red curry paste
- 2 tbsp fresh grated galangal or root ginger
- 1 tbsp tamarind paste
- 4 lime leaves
- 225 g/8 oz sweet potato
- 600 ml/1 pint/2½ cups coconut milk
- 225 g/8 oz cherry tomatoes, halved
- 3 tbsp chopped fresh coriander (cilantro)
- cooked jasmine or Thai fragrant rice, to serve

3

4

4

1 Heat the sunflower oil in a large preheated wok.

2 Thinly slice the chicken. Add the chicken to the wok and stir-fry for 5 minutes.

3 Add the garlic, curry paste, galangal or root ginger, tamarind and lime leaves to the wok and stir-fry for about 1 minute.

4 Using a sharp knife, peel and dice the sweet potato. Add the coconut milk and sweet potato to the mixture in the wok and bring to the boil. Allow to bubble over a medium heat for 20 minutes, or until the juices start to thicken and reduce.

5 Add the cherry tomatoes and coriander (cilantro) to the curry and cook for a further 5 minutes, stirring occasionally. Transfer to serving plates and serve hot with cooked jasmine or Thai fragrant rice.

COOK'S TIP

Galangal is a spice very similar to ginger and is used to replace the latter in Thai cuisine. It can be bought fresh from Oriental food stores but is also available dried and as a powder. The fresh root, which is not as pungent as ginger, needs to be peeled before slicing to use.

Lemon Chicken

This is on everyone's list of favourite Chinese dishes, and it is so simple to make. Serve with stir-fried vegetables for a truly delicious meal.

NUTRITIONAL INFORMATION

Calories	272	Sugars	1g
Protein	36g	Fat	11g
Carbohydrate	5g	Saturates	2g

 5 MINS

 15 MINS

SERVES 4

INGREDIENTS

- vegetable oil, for deep-frying
- 650 g/1 lb 7 oz skinless, boneless chicken, cut into strips
- lemon slices and shredded spring onion (scallion), to garnish

SAUCE

- 1 tbsp cornflour (cornstarch)
- 6 tbsp cold water
- 3 tbsp fresh lemon juice
- 2 tbsp sweet sherry
- ½ tsp caster (superfine) sugar

1 Heat the oil for deep-frying in a preheated wok or frying pan (skillet) to 180°C/350°F or until a cube of bread browns in 30 seconds

2 Reduce the heat and stir-fry the chicken strips for 3–4 minutes, until cooked through.

3 Remove the chicken with a slotted spoon, set aside and keep warm. Drain the oil from the wok.

4 To make the sauce, mix the cornflour (cornstarch) with 2 tablespoons of the water to form a paste.

5 Pour the lemon juice and remaining water into the mixture in the wok.

6 Add the sweet sherry and caster (superfine) sugar and bring to the boil, stirring until the sugar has completely dissolved.

7 Stir in the cornflour mixture and return to the boil. Reduce the heat and simmer, stirring constantly, for 2-3 minutes, until the sauce is thickened and clear.

8 Transfer the chicken to a warm serving plate and pour the sauce over the top.

9 Garnish the chicken with the lemon slices and shredded spring onion (scallion) and serve immediately.

COOK'S TIP

If you would prefer to use chicken portions rather than strips, cook them in the oil, covered, over a low heat for about 30 minutes, or until cooked through.

Chicken Cacciatora

This is a popular Italian classic in which browned chicken quarters are cooked in a tomato and (bell) pepper sauce.

NUTRITIONAL INFORMATION

Calories	397	Sugars	4g
Protein	37g	Fat	17g
Carbohydrate	22g	Saturates	4g

 20 MINS  1 HOUR

SERVES 4

INGREDIENTS

- 1 roasting chicken, about 1.5 kg/ 3 lb 5 oz, cut into 6 or 8 serving pieces
- 125 g/4½ oz/1 cup plain (all-purpose) flour
- 3 tbsp olive oil
- 150 ml/¼ pint/⅔ cup dry white wine
- 1 green (bell) pepper, deseeded and sliced
- 1 red (bell) pepper, deseeded and sliced
- 1 carrot, chopped finely
- 1 celery stalk, chopped finely
- 1 garlic clove, crushed
- 200 g/7 oz can of chopped tomatoes
- salt and pepper

1

2

4

1 Rinse and pat dry the chicken pieces with paper towels. Lightly dust them with seasoned flour.

2 Heat the oil in a large frying pan (skillet). Add the chicken and fry over a medium heat until browned all over. Remove from the pan and set aside.

3 Drain off all but 2 tablespoons of the fat in the pan. Add the wine and stir for a few minutes. Then add the (bell) peppers, carrots, celery and garlic, season with salt and pepper to taste and simmer together for about 15 minutes.

4 Add the chopped tomatoes to the pan. Cover and simmer for 30 minutes, stirring often, until the chicken is completely cooked through.

5 Check the seasoning before serving piping hot.

Chicken with a Yogurt Crust

A spicy, Indian-style coating is baked around lean chicken to give a full flavour. Serve with a tomato, cucumber and coriander (cilantro) relish.

NUTRITIONAL INFORMATION

Calories	176	Sugars	5g
Protein	30g	Fat	4g
Carbohydrate	5g	Saturates	1g

 10 MINS  35 MINS

SERVES 4

INGREDIENTS

- 1 garlic clove, crushed
- 2.5 cm/1 inch piece root (fresh) ginger, finely chopped
- 1 fresh green chilli, deseeded and finely chopped
- 6 tbsp low-fat natural (unsweetened) yogurt
- 1 tbsp tomato purée (paste)
- 1 tsp ground turmeric
- 1 tsp garam masala
- 1 tbsp lime juice
- 4 boneless, skinless chicken breasts, each 125 g/4½ oz
- salt and pepper
- wedges of lime or lemon, to serve

RELISH

- 4 medium tomatoes
- ¼ cucumber
- 1 small red onion
- 2 tbsp fresh coriander (cilantro), chopped

2

4

5

1 Preheat the oven to 190°C/375°F/Gas Mark 5.

2 Place the garlic, ginger, chilli, yogurt, tomato purée (paste), spices, lime juice and seasoning in a bowl and mix to combine all the ingredients.

3 Wash and pat dry the chicken breasts with absorbent kitchen paper (paper towels) and place them on a baking sheet.

4 Brush or spread the spicy yogurt mix over the chicken and bake in the oven for 30–35 minutes until the meat is tender and cooked through.

5 Meanwhile, make the relish. Finely chop the tomatoes, cucumber and onion and mix together with the coriander (cilantro). Season with salt and pepper to taste, cover and chill in the refrigerator until required.

6 Drain the cooked chicken on absorbent kitchen paper (paper towels) and serve hot with the relish and lemon or lime wedges. Alternatively, allow to cool, chill for at least 1 hour and serve sliced as part of a salad.

Chicken in Spicy Yogurt

Make sure the barbecue (grill) is really hot before you start cooking. The coals should be white and glow red when fanned.

NUTRITIONAL INFORMATION

Calories	74	Sugars	2g
Protein	9g	Fat	4g
Carbohydrate	2g	Saturates	1g

 4¾ HOURS  25 MINS

SERVES 6

INGREDIENTS

3 dried red chillies

2 tbsp coriander seeds

2 tsp turmeric

2 tsp garam masala

4 garlic cloves, crushed

½ onion, chopped

2.5cm/1 inch piece fresh ginger root, grated

2 tbsp lime juice

1 tsp salt

125 ml/4 fl oz/½ cup low-fat natural (unsweetened) yogurt

1 tbsp oil

2 kg/4 lb 8 oz lean chicken, cut into 6 pieces, or 6 chicken portions

TO SERVE

chopped tomatoes

diced cucumber

sliced red onion

cucumber and yogurt

1 Grind together the chillies, coriander seed, turmeric, garam masala, garlic, onion, ginger, lime juice and salt with a pestle and mortar or grinder.

2 Gently heat a frying pan (skillet) and add the spice mixture. Stir until fragrant, about 2 minutes, and turn into a shallow non-porous dish.

3 Add the natural (unsweetened) yogurt and the oil to the spice paste and mix well to combine.

4 Remove the skin from the chicken portions and make three slashes in the flesh of each piece. Add the chicken to the dish containing the yogurt and spice mixture and coat the pieces completely in the marinade. Cover with cling film (plastic wrap) and chill for at least 4 hours. Remove the dish from the refrigerator and leave covered at room temperature for 30 minutes before cooking.

5 Wrap the chicken pieces in foil, sealing well so the juices cannot escape.

6 Cook the chicken pieces over a very hot barbecue (grill) for about 15 minutes, turning once.

7 Remove the foil, with tongs, and brown the chicken on the barbecue (grill) for 5 minutes.

8 Serve the chicken with the chopped tomatoes, diced cucumber, sliced red onion and the yogurt and cucumber mixture.

2

2

5

Spanish Chicken Casserole

Tomatoes, olives, peppers and potatoes, with a splash of Spanish red wine, make this a marvellous peasant-style dish.

NUTRITIONAL INFORMATION

Calories	293	Sugar	6g
Protein	15g	Fats	12g
Carbohydrates	26g	Saturates	2g

 10 MINS  1¼ HOURS

SERVES 4

INGREDIENTS

- 25 g/1 oz/¼ cup plain (all-purpose) flour
- 1 tsp salt
- pepper
- 1 tbsp paprika
- 4 chicken portions
- 3 tbsp olive oil
- 1 large onion, chopped
- 2 garlic cloves, crushed
- 6 tomatoes, chopped, or 425 g/15 oz can chopped tomatoes
- 1 green (bell) pepper, cored, deseeded and chopped
- 150 ml/¼ pint/⅔ cup Spanish red wine
- 300 ml/½ pint/1¼ cups chicken stock
- 3 medium potatoes, peeled and quartered
- 12 pitted black olives
- 1 bay leaf
- crusty bread, to serve

1 Put the plain (all-purpose) flour, salt, pepper and paprika into a large polythene bag.

2 Rinse the chicken portions and pat dry with kitchen paper (paper towels). Put them into the bag and shake to coat in the seasoned flour.

3 Heat the oil in a large flameproof casserole dish. Add the chicken portions and cook over a medium-high heat for 5–8 minutes until well-browned on each side. Lift out of the casserole with a perforated spoon and set aside.

4 Add the onion and garlic to the casserole and cook for a few minutes until browned. Add the tomatoes and (bell) pepper and cook for 2–3 minutes.

5 Return the chicken to the casserole. Add the wine, stock and potatoes, and then the olives and bay leaf. Cover and bake in a preheated oven at 190°C/375°F/Gas Mark 5 for 1 hour until the chicken is tender.

6 Check the seasoning, adding more salt and pepper if necessary. Serve the chicken casserole hot with chunks of crusty bread.

3

4

5

Stir-Fried Ginger Chicken

The oranges add colour and piquancy to this refreshing dish, which complements the chicken well.

NUTRITIONAL INFORMATION

Calories	289	Sugars	15g
Protein	20g	Fat	9g
Carbohydrate	17g	Saturates	2g

 5 MINS  20 MINS

SERVES 4

INGREDIENTS

- 2 tbsp sunflower oil
- 1 onion, sliced
- 175 g/6 oz carrots, cut into thin sticks
- 1 clove garlic, crushed
- 350 g/12 oz boneless skinless chicken breasts
- 2 tbsp fresh ginger, peeled and grated
- 1 tsp ground ginger
- 4 tbsp sweet sherry
- 1 tbsp tomato purée (tomato paste)
- 1 tbsp demerara sugar
- 100 ml/3½ fl oz/⅓ cup orange juice
- 1 tsp cornflour (cornstarch)
- 1 orange, peeled and segmented
- fresh snipped chives, to garnish

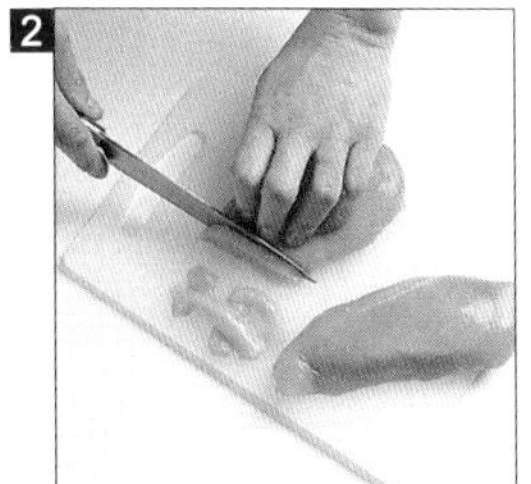

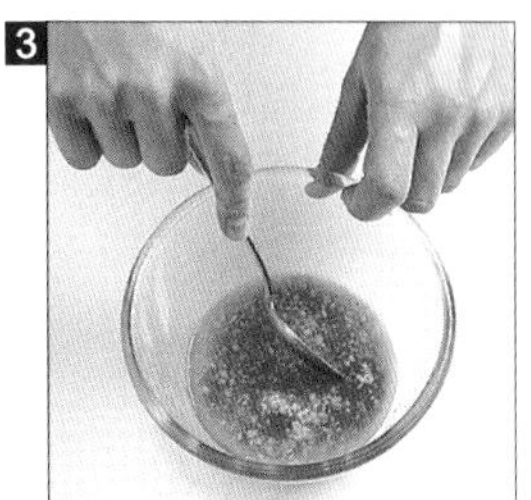

1 Heat the oil in a large preheated wok. Add the onion, carrots and garlic and stir-fry over a high heat for 3 minutes or until the vegetables begin to soften.

2 Slice the chicken into thin strips. Add to the wok with the fresh and ground ginger. Stir-fry for a further 10 minutes, or until the chicken is well cooked through and golden in colour.

3 Mix together the sherry, tomato purée (tomato paste), sugar, orange juice and cornflour (cornstarch) in a bowl. Stir the mixture into the wok and heat through until the mixture bubbles and the juices start to thicken.

4 Add the orange segments and carefully toss to mix.

5 Transfer the stir-fried chicken to warm serving bowls and garnish with freshly snipped chives. Serve immediately.

COOK'S TIP

Make sure that you do not continue cooking the dish once the orange segments have been added in step 4, otherwise they will break up.

Chicken Chop Suey

Chop suey is a well known and popular dish based on bean sprouts and soy sauce with a meat or vegetable flavouring.

NUTRITIONAL INFORMATION

Calories	337	Sugars	7g
Protein	32g	Fat	18g
Carbohydrate	14g	Saturates	3g

 25 MINS  15 MINS

SERVES 4

INGREDIENTS

- 4 tbsp light soy sauce
- 2 tsp light brown sugar
- 500 g/1 lb 2 oz skinless, boneless chicken breasts
- 3 tbsp vegetable oil
- 2 onions, quartered
- 2 garlic cloves, crushed
- 350 g/12 oz bean sprouts
- 3 tsp sesame oil
- 1 tbsp cornflour (cornstarch)
- 3 tbsp water
- 425 ml/¾ pint/2 cups chicken stock
- shredded leek, to garnish

2

3

3

1 Mix the soy sauce and sugar together, stirring until the sugar has dissolved.

2 Trim any fat from the chicken and cut into thin strips. Place the meat in a shallow dish and spoon the soy mixture over them, turning to coat. Marinate in the refrigerator for 20 minutes.

3 Heat the oil in a wok and stir-fry the chicken for 2–3 minutes, until golden brown. Add the onions and garlic and cook for a further 2 minutes. Add the bean sprouts, cook for 4–5 minutes, then add the sesame oil.

4 Mix the cornflour (cornstarch) and water to form a smooth paste. Pour the stock into the wok, add the cornflour (cornstarch) paste and bring to the boil, stirring until the sauce is thickened and clear. Serve, garnished with shredded leek.

VARIATION

This recipe may be made with strips of lean steak, pork or with mixed vegetables. Change the type of stock accordingly.

Chicken with Rice & Peas

The secret of a this dish is that it must be brown in colour, which is achieved by caramelizing the chicken first.

NUTRITIONAL INFORMATION

Calories	335	Sugars	11g
Protein	20g	Fat	12g
Carbohydrate	38g	Saturates	6g

 10 MINS  1 HOUR

SERVES 6

INGREDIENTS

- 1 onion, chopped
- 2 garlic cloves
- 1 tbsp chopped fresh chives
- 1 tbsp chopped fresh thyme
- 2 celery stalks with leaves, chopped
- 350 ml/12 fl oz/1½ cups water
- ½ fresh coconut, chopped
- liquid from 1 fresh coconut
- 500 g/1 lb 2 oz can pigeon peas or kidney beans, drained
- 1 red chilli, deseeded and sliced thinly
- 2 tbsp groundnut oil
- 2 tbsp caster (superfine) sugar
- 1.5 kg/3 lb 5 oz chicken pieces
- 250 g/9 oz/1¼ cups white long-grain rice, rinsed and drained
- salt and pepper
- celery leaves, to garnish

1 Put the onion, garlic, chives, thyme, celery and 4 tablespoons of the water into a food processor. Blend until smooth.

2 Alternatively, chop the onion and celery very finely, then grind with the garlic and herbs in a pestle and mortar, gradually mixing in the water. Pour into a saucepan and set aside.

3 Put the chopped coconut and liquid into the food processor and mix to a thick milk, adding water if necessary. Alternatively, finely grate the coconut and mix with the liquid. Add to the onion and celery mixture. Stir in the drained pigeon peas or kidney beans and chilli. Cook over a low heat for 15 minutes, then season.

4 Put the oil and sugar in a heavy-based casserole and cook over a moderate heat until the sugar begins to caramelize. Add the chicken and cook for 15–20 minutes, turning frequently, until browned all over.

5 Stir in the coconut mixture, the rice and remaining water. Bring to the boil, then reduce the heat, cover and simmer for 20 minutes until the chicken and rice are tender and the liquid has been absorbed. Garnish with celery leaves.

Yellow Bean Chicken

Ready-made yellow bean sauce is available from large supermarkets and Chinese food stores.It is made from yellow soya beans and is quite salty.

NUTRITIONAL INFORMATION

Calories	234	Sugars	1g
Protein	26g	Fat	12g
Carbohydrate	6g	Saturates	2g

 25 MINS  10 MINS

SERVES 4

INGREDIENTS

- 450 g/1 lb skinless, boneless chicken breasts
- 1 egg white, beaten
- 1 tbsp cornflour (cornstarch)
- 1 tbsp rice wine vinegar
- 1 tbsp light soy sauce
- 1 tsp caster (superfine) sugar
- 3 tbsp vegetable oil
- 1 garlic clove, crushed
- 1-cm/½-inch piece fresh root ginger, grated
- 1 green (bell) pepper, seeded and diced
- 2 large mushrooms, sliced
- 3 tbsp yellow bean sauce
- yellow or green (bell) pepper strips, to garnish

1 Trim any fat from the chicken and cut the meat into 2.5-cm/1-inch cubes.

2 Mix the egg white and cornflour (cornstarch) in a shallow bowl. Add the chicken and turn in the mixture to coat. Set aside for 20 minutes.

3 Mix the rice wine vinegar, soy sauce and caster (superfine) sugar in a bowl.

4 Remove the chicken from the egg white mixture.

5 Heat the oil in a preheated wok, add the chicken and stir-fry for 3–4 minutes, until golden brown. Remove the chicken from the wok with a slotted spoon, set aside and keep warm.

6 Add the garlic, ginger, (bell) pepper and mushrooms to the wok and stir-fry for 1–2 minutes.

7 Add the yellow bean sauce and cook for 1 minute. Stir in the vinegar mixture and return the chicken to the wok. Cook for 1–2 minutes and serve hot, garnished with (bell) pepper strips.

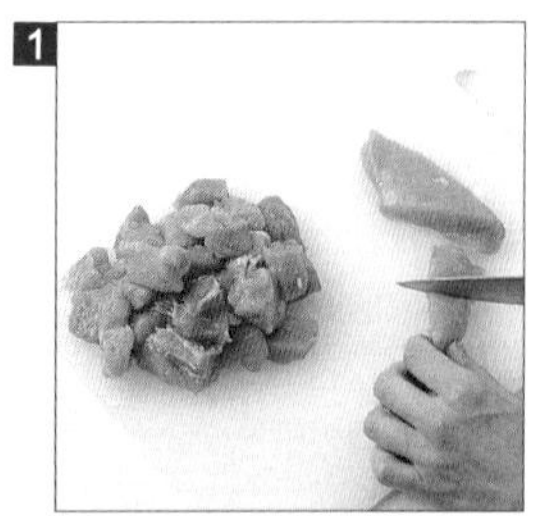
1

6

7

VARIATION

Black bean sauce would work equally well with this recipe. Although this would affect the appearance of the dish, as it is much darker in colour, the flavours would be compatible.

Pan-Cooked Chicken

Artichokes are a familiar ingredient in Italian cookery. In this dish, they are used to delicately flavour chicken.

NUTRITIONAL INFORMATION

Calories	296	Sugars	2g
Protein	27g	Fat	15g
Carbohydrate	7g	Saturates	6g

 15 MINS  55 MINS

SERVES 4

INGREDIENTS

- 4 chicken breasts, part boned
- 25 g/1 oz/2 tbsp butter
- 2 tbsp olive oil
- 2 red onions, cut into wedges
- 2 tbsp lemon juice
- 150 ml/¼ pt/⅔ cup dry white wine
- 150 ml/¼ pt/⅔ cup chicken stock
- 2 tsp plain (all-purpose) flour
- 400 g/14 oz can artichoke halves, drained and halved
- salt and pepper
- chopped fresh parsley, to garnish

1 Season the chicken with salt and pepper to taste. Heat the oil and 15 g/½ oz/1 tablespoon of the butter in a large frying pan (skillet). Add the chicken and fry for 4–5 minutes on each side until lightly golden. Remove from the pan using a slotted spoon.

2 Toss the onion in the lemon juice, and add to the frying pan (skillet). Gently fry, stirring, for 3–4 minutes until just beginning to soften.

3 Return the chicken to the pan. Pour in the wine and stock, bring to the boil, cover and simmer gently for 30 minutes.

4 Remove the chicken from the pan, reserving the cooking juices, and keep warm. Bring the juices to the boil, and boil rapidly for 5 minutes.

5 Blend the remaining butter with the flour to form a paste. Reduce the juices to a simmer and spoon the paste into the frying pan (skillet), stirring until thickened.

6 Adjust the seasoning according to taste, stir in the artichoke hearts and cook for a further 2 minutes. Pour the mixture over the chicken and garnish with chopped parsley.

1

3

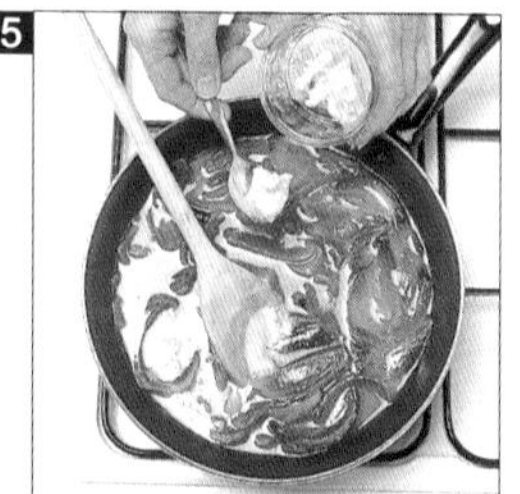

5

Grilled (Broiled) Chicken

This Italian-style dish is richly flavoured with pesto, which is a mixture of basil, olive oil, pine nuts and Parmesan cheese.

NUTRITIONAL INFORMATION

Calories	787	Sugars	6g
Protein	45g	Fat	38g
Carbohydrate	70g	Saturates	9g

10 MINS 25 MINS

SERVES 4

INGREDIENTS

- 8 part-boned chicken thighs
- olive oil, for brushing
- 400 ml/14 fl oz/1⅔ cups passata (sieved tomatoes)
- 125 ml/4 fl oz/½ cup green or red pesto sauce
- 12 slices French bread
- 90 g/3 oz/1 cup freshly grated Parmesan cheese
- 60 g/2 oz/½ cup pine nuts or flaked (slivered) almonds
- salad leaves, to serve

1 Arrange the chicken in a single layer in a wide flameproof dish and brush lightly with oil. Place under a preheated grill (broiler) for about 15 minutes, turning occasionally, until golden brown.

COOK'S TIP

Although leaving the skin on the chicken means that it will have a higher fat content, many people like the rich taste and crispy skin especially when it is blackened by the barbecue (grill). The skin also keeps in the cooking juices.

1

2

4

2 Pierce the chicken with a skewer to test if it is cooked through – the juices will run clear, not pink, when it is ready.

3 Pour off any excess fat. Warm the passata (sieved tomatoes) and half the pesto sauce in a small pan and pour over the chicken. Grill (broil) for a few more minutes, turning until coated.

4 Meanwhile, spread the remaining pesto on to the slices of bread. Arrange the bread over the chicken and sprinkle with the Parmesan cheese. Scatter the pine nuts over the cheese. Grill (broil) for 2–3 minutes, or until browned and bubbling. Serve with salad leaves.

Chilli Coconut Chicken

This tasty dish combines the flavours of lime, peanut, coconut and chilli. You'll find coconut cream in most supermarkets or delicatessens.

NUTRITIONAL INFORMATION

Calories	348	Sugars	2g
Protein	36g	Fat	21g
Carbohydrate	3g	Saturates	8g

 5 MINS  15 MINS

SERVES 4

INGREDIENTS

- 150 ml/¼ pint/⅔ cup hot chicken stock
- 25 g/1 oz/⅓ cup coconut cream
- 1 tbsp sunflower oil
- 8 skinless, boneless chicken thighs, cut into long, thin strips
- 1 small red chilli, sliced thinly
- 4 spring onions (scallions), sliced thinly
- 4 tbsp smooth or crunchy peanut butter
- finely grated rind and juice of 1 lime
- 1 fresh red chilli and spring onion (scallion) tassel, to garnish
- boiled rice, to serve

1 Pour the chicken stock into a measuring jug or small bowl. Crumble the coconut cream into the chicken stock and stir the mixture until the coconut cream dissolves.

2 Heat the oil in a preheated wok or large heavy pan.

3 Add the chicken strips and cook, stirring, until the chicken turns a golden colour.

4 Stir in the chopped red chilli and spring onions (scallions) and cook gently for a few minutes.

5 Add the peanut butter, coconut cream and chicken stock mixture, lime rind, lime juice and simmer, uncovered, for about 5 minutes, stirring frequently to prevent the mixture sticking to the base of the wok or pan.

6 Transfer the chilli coconut chicken to a warm serving dish, garnish with the red chilli and spring onion (scallion) tassel and serve with boiled rice.

COOK'S TIP

Serve jasmine rice with this spicy dish. It has a fragrant aroma that is well-suited to the flavours in this dish.

Garlic & Lime Chicken

Garlic and coriander (cilantro) flavour the chicken breasts which are served with a caramelised sauce, sharpened with lime juice.

NUTRITIONAL INFORMATION

Calories	280	Sugars	7g
Protein	26g	Fat	17g
Carbohydrate	7g	Saturates	8g

10 MINS 25 MINS

SERVES 4

INGREDIENTS

- 4 large skinless, boneless chicken breasts
- 50 g/1¾ oz/3 tbsp garlic butter, softened
- 3 tbsp chopped fresh coriander (cilantro)
- 1 tbsp sunflower oil
- finely grated zest and juice of 2 limes, plus extra zest, to garnish
- 25 g/1 oz/4 tbsp palm sugar or demerara (brown crystal) sugar

TO SERVE

- boiled rice
- lemon wedges

1 Place each chicken breast between 2 sheets of cling film (plastic wrap) and pound with a rolling pin until flattened to about 1 cm/½ inch thick.

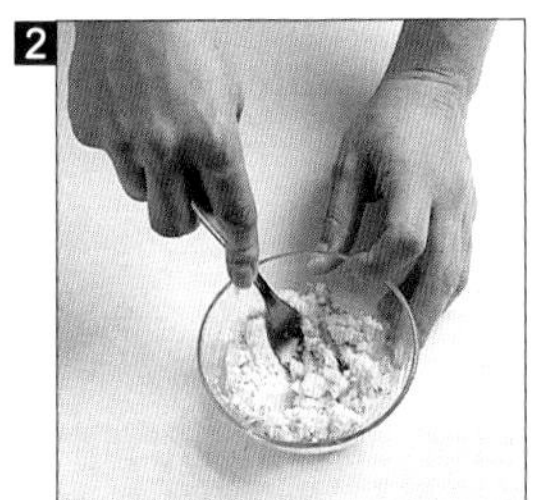

2 Mix together the garlic butter and coriander (cilantro) and spread over each flattened chicken breast. Roll up like a Swiss roll and secure with a cocktail stick (toothpick).

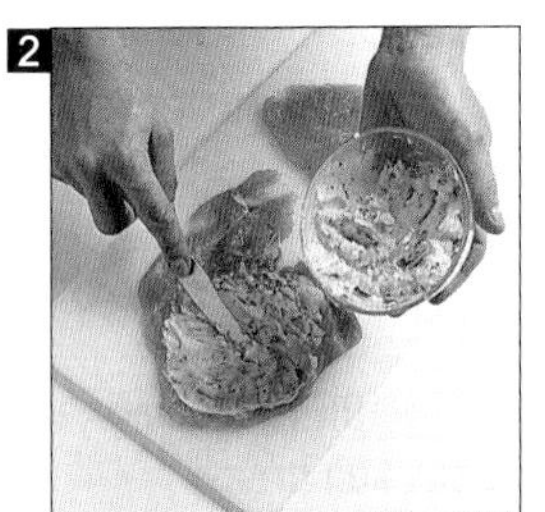

3 Heat the sunflower oil in a preheated wok or heavy-based frying pan (skillet).

4 Add the chicken rolls to the wok or pan and cook, turning, for 15–20 minutes or until cooked through.

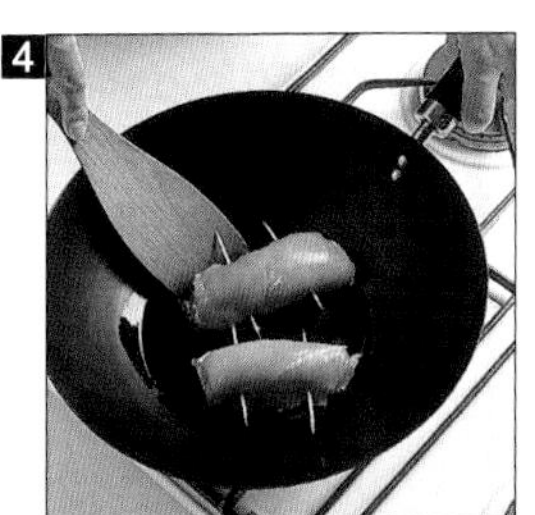

5 Remove the chicken from the wok and transfer to a board. Cut each chicken roll into slices.

6 Add the lime zest, juice and sugar to the wok and heat gently, stirring, until the sugar has dissolved. Raise the heat and allow to bubble for 2 minutes.

7 Arrange the chicken on warmed serving plates and spoon the pan juices over to serve.

8 Garnish the garlic and lime chicken with extra lime zest, if desired

COOK'S TIP

Be sure to check that the chicken is cooked through before slicing and serving. Cook over a gentle heat so as not to overcook the outside, while the inside remains raw.

Chicken Scallops

Served in scallop shells, this makes a stylish presentation for a starter or a light lunch.

NUTRITIONAL INFORMATION

Calories	532	Sugars	3g
Protein	25g	Fat	34g
Carbohydrate	33g	Saturates	14g

 20 MINS  25 MINS

SERVES 4

INGREDIENTS

- 175 g/6 oz short-cut macaroni, or other short pasta shapes
- 3 tbsp vegetable oil, plus extra for brushing
- 1 onion, chopped finely
- 3 rashers unsmoked collar or back bacon, rind removed, chopped
- 125 g/4½ oz button mushrooms, sliced thinly or chopped
- 175 g/6 oz/¾ cup cooked chicken, diced
- 175 ml/6 fl oz/¾ cup crème fraîche
- 4 tbsp dry breadcrumbs
- 60 g/2 oz/½ cup mature (sharp) Cheddar, grated
- salt and pepper
- flat-leaf parsley sprigs, to garnish

1 Cook the pasta in a large pan of boiling salted water, to which you have added 1 tablespoon of the oil, for 8–10 minutes or until tender. Drain the pasta, return to the pan and cover.

2 Heat the grill (broiler) to medium. Heat the remaining oil in a pan over medium heat and fry the onion until it is translucent. Add the chopped bacon and mushrooms and cook for 3–4 minutes, stirring once or twice.

3 Stir in the pasta, chicken and crème fraîche and season to taste with salt and pepper.

4 Brush four large scallop shells with oil. Spoon in the chicken mixture and smooth to make neat mounds.

5 Mix together the breadcrumbs and cheese, and sprinkle over the top of the shells. Press the topping lightly into the chicken mixture, and grill (broil) for 4–5 minutes, until golden brown and bubbling. Garnish with sprigs of flat-leaf parsley, and serve hot.

Chicken with Bean Sprouts

This is the basic Chicken Chop Suey to be found in almost every Chinese restaurant and takeaway all over the world.

NUTRITIONAL INFORMATION

Calories	153	Sugars	4g
Protein	9g	Fat	10g
Carbohydrate	8g	Saturates	1g

 3½ HOURS  10 MINS

SERVES 4

INGREDIENTS

- 125 g/4½ oz chicken breast fillet, skinned
- 1 tsp salt
- ¼ egg white, lightly beaten
- 2 tsp cornflour (cornstarch) paste (see page 6)
- about 300 ml/½ pint/1¼ cups vegetable oil
- 1 small onion, thinly shredded
- 1 small green (bell) pepper, cored, seeded and thinly shredded
- 1 small carrot, thinly shredded
- 125 g/4½ oz fresh beansprouts
- ½ tsp sugar
- 1 tbsp light soy sauce
- 1 tsp rice wine or dry sherry
- 2-3 tbsp Chinese Stock (see page 8)
- a few drops of sesame oil
- chilli sauce, to serve

1. Using a sharp knife or meat cleaver, cut the chicken into thin shreds and place in a bowl.
2. Add a pinch of the salt, the egg white and cornflour (cornstarch) paste to the chicken and mix well.
3. Heat the vegetable oil in a preheated wok or large frying pan (skillet).
4. Add the chicken and stir-fry for about 1 minute, stirring to separate the shreds. Remove with a slotted spoon and drain on kitchen paper (paper towels).
5. Pour off the oil, leaving about 2 tablespoons in the wok. Add the onion, green (bell) pepper and carrot and stir-fry for about 2 minutes.
6. Add the bean sprouts and stir-fry for a few seconds.
7. Add the chicken with the remaining salt, sugar, soy sauce and rice wine or dry sherry, blend well and add the Chinese stock or water.
8. Sprinkle the stir-fry with the sesame oil and serve with the chilli sauce.

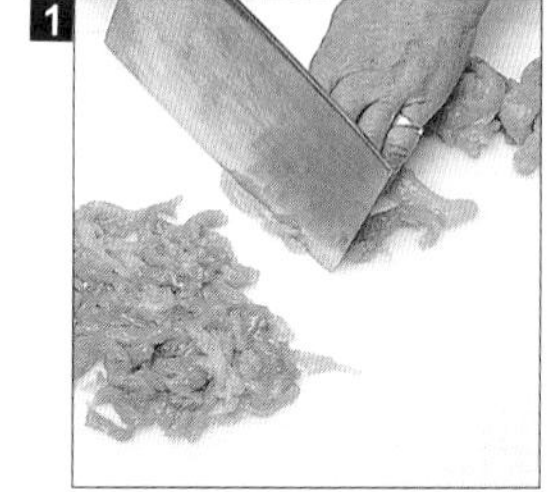
1

4

6

COOK'S TIP

Chop Suey actually originated in San Francisco at the turn of the century when Chinese immigrants were first settling there, and was first devised as a handy dish for using up leftovers.

Orange Chicken Stir-Fry

Chicken thighs are inexpensive, meaty portions which are readily available. Although not as tender as breast, it is perfect for stir-frying.

NUTRITIONAL INFORMATION

Calories	267	Sugars	11g
Protein	23g	Fat	11g
Carbohydrate	15g	Saturates	2g

 10 MINS  15 MINS

SERVES 4

INGREDIENTS

- 3 tbsp sunflower oil
- 350 g/12 oz boneless chicken thighs, skinned and cut into thin strips
- 1 onion, sliced
- 1 clove garlic, crushed
- 1 red (bell) pepper, deseeded and sliced
- 75 g/2¾ oz/1¼ cups mangetout (snow peas)
- 4 tbsp light soy sauce
- 4 tbsp sherry
- 1 tbsp tomato purée (tomato paste)
- finely grated rind and juice of 1 orange
- 1 tsp cornflour (cornstarch)
- 2 oranges
- 100 g/3½ oz/1 cup bean sprouts
- cooked rice or noodles, to serve

1

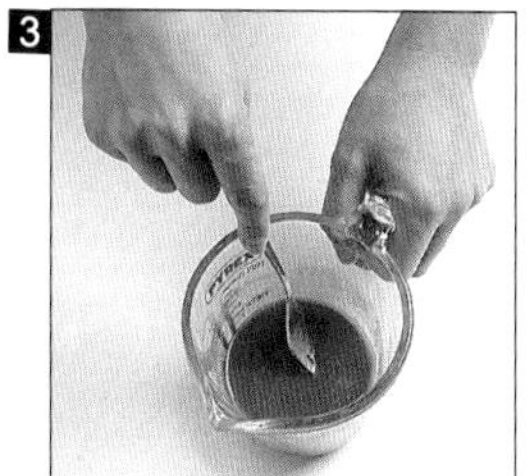

3

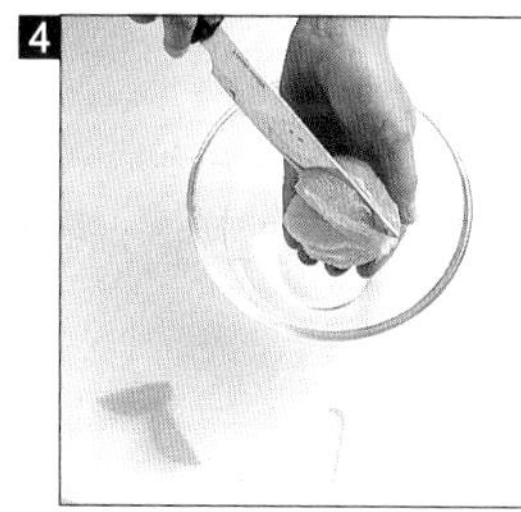

4

1 Heat the oil in a large preheated wok. Add the chicken and stir-fry for 2–3 minutes or until sealed on all sides.

2 Add the onion, garlic, (bell) pepper and mangetout (snow peas) to the wok. Stir-fry for a further 5 minutes, or until the vegetables are just tender and the chicken is completely cooked through.

3 Mix together the soy sauce, sherry, tomato purée (tomato paste), orange rind and juice and the cornflour (cornstarch). Add to the wok and cook, stirring, until the juices start to thicken.

4 Using a sharp knife, peel and segment the oranges. Add the segments to the mixture in the wok with the bean sprouts and heat through for a further 2 minutes.

5 Transfer the stir-fry to serving plates and serve at once with cooked rice or noodles.

COOK'S TIP

Bean sprouts are sprouting mung beans and are a regular ingredient in Chinese cooking. They require very little cooking and may even be eaten raw, if wished.

Poussin with Dried Fruits

Baby chickens are ideal for a one or two portion meal, and cook very easily and quickly for a special dinner – either in the oven or microwave.

NUTRITIONAL INFORMATION

Calories	316	Sugars	23g
Protein	23g	Fat	15g
Carbohydrate	23g	Saturates	2g

 35 MINS  30 MINS

SERVES 2

INGREDIENTS

- 125 g/4½ oz/¾ cup dried apples, peaches and prunes
- 125 ml/4 floz/½ cup boiling water
- 2 baby chickens
- 25 g/1 oz/⅓ cup walnut halves
- 1 tbsp honey
- 1 tsp ground allspice
- 1 tbsp walnut oil
- salt and pepper
- vegetables and new potatoes, to serve

1 Place the fruits in a bowl, cover with the water and leave to stand for about 30 minutes.

2 Cut the chickens in half down the breastbone using a sharp knife, or leave whole.

3 Mix the fruit and any juices with the walnuts, honey and allspice and divide between two small roasting bags or squares of foil.

4 Brush the chickens with walnut oil and sprinkle with salt and pepper then place on top of the fruits.

5 Close the roasting bags or fold the foil over to enclose the chickens and bake on a baking sheet in a preheated oven, 190°C/375°F/Gas Mark 5, for 25–30 minutes or until the juices run clear. To cook in a microwave, use microwave roasting bags and cook on high/100% power for 6–7 minutes each, depending on size.

6 Transfer the poussin to a warm plate and serve hot with fresh vegetables and new potatoes.

VARIATION

Alternative dried fruits that can be used in this recipe are cherries, mangoes or paw-paws (papayas).

1

3

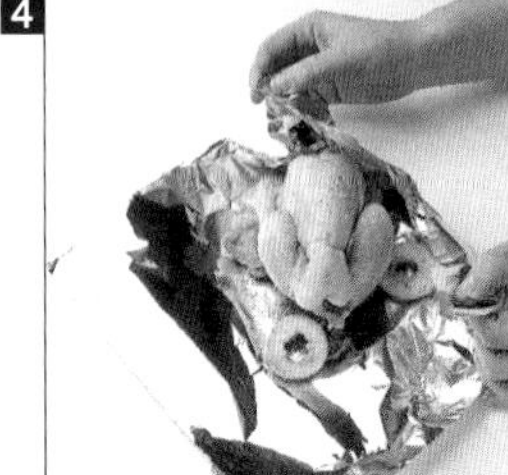

4

Chicken & Potato Bake

Make this when new potatoes are in season. A medium onion or a few shallots can be substituted for the spring onions (scallions).

NUTRITIONAL INFORMATION

Calories	323	Sugars	9g
Protein	30g	Fat	10g
Carbohydrate	29g	Saturates	2g

10 MINS

1¼ HOURS

SERVES 4

INGREDIENTS

- 2 tbsp olive oil
- 4 lean chicken breasts
- 1 bunch spring onions (scallions), trimmed and chopped
- 350 g/12 oz young spring carrots, scrubbed and sliced
- 125 g/4½ oz dwarf green beans, trimmed and sliced
- 600 ml/1 pint/2½ cups chicken stock
- 350 g/12 oz small new potatoes, scrubbed
- 1 small bunch mixed fresh herbs, such as thyme, rosemary, bay and parsley
- salt and pepper
- 2 tbsp cornflour (cornstarch)
- 2–3 tbsp cold water
- sprigs of fresh mixed herbs, to garnish

2

3

4

1 Heat the oil in a large flameproof casserole and add the chicken breasts. Gently fry for 5–8 minutes until browned on both sides. Lift from the casserole with a perforated spoon and set aside.

2 Add the spring onions (scallions), carrots and green beans and gently fry for 3–4 minutes.

3 Return the chicken to the casserole and pour in the stock. Add the potatoes and herbs. Season, bring to the boil, then cover the casserole and transfer to the oven. Bake in a preheated oven at 190°C/375°F/Gas Mark 5 for 40–50 minutes until the potatoes are tender.

4 Blend the cornflour (cornstarch) with the cold water. Add to the casserole, stirring until blended and thickened. Cover and cook for a further 5 minutes. Garnish with fresh herbs and serve.

COOK'S TIP

Use your favourite combination of herbs for this dish. If fresh herbs are unavailable, use half the quantity of dried mixed herbs. Alternatively, use a bouquet garni sachet which is usually a combination of bay, thyme and parsley.

Szechuan Chilli Chicken

In China, the chicken pieces are chopped through the bone for this dish, but if you do not possess a cleaver, use filleted chicken meat.

NUTRITIONAL INFORMATION

Calories	218	Sugars	4g
Protein	23g	Fat	9g
Carbohydrate	8g	Saturates	2g

4 HOURS 15 MINS

SERVES 4

INGREDIENTS

- 500 g/1 lb 2 oz chicken thighs
- ¼ tsp pepper
- 1 tbsp sugar
- 2 tsp light soy sauce
- 1 tsp dark soy sauce
- 1 tbsp rice wine or dry sherry
- 2 tsp cornflour (cornstarch)
- 2-3 tbsp vegetable oil
- 1-2 garlic cloves, crushed
- 2 spring onions (scallions), cut into short sections, with the green and white parts separated
- 4-6 small dried red chillies, soaked and seeded
- 2 tbsp crushed yellow bean sauce
- about 150 ml/¼ pint/⅔ cup Chinese Stock (see page 8) or water

1 Cut or chop the chicken thighs into bite-sized pieces and marinate with the pepper, sugar, soy sauce, wine and cornflour (cornstarch) for 25-30 minutes.

2 Heat the oil in a pre-heated wok and stir-fry the chicken for about 1–2 minutes until lightly brown. Remove with a slotted spoon, transfer to a warm dish and reserve. Add the garlic, the white parts of the spring onions (scallions), the chillies and yellow bean sauce to the wok and stir-fry for about 30 seconds.

3 Return the chicken to the wok, stirring constantly for about 1-2 minutes, then add the stock or water, bring to the boil and cover. Braise over a medium heat for 5-6 minutes, stirring once or twice. Garnish with the green parts of the spring onions (scallions) and serve immediately.

COOK'S TIP

Onc of the striking features of Szechuan cooking is the quantity of chillies used. Food generally in this region is much hotter than elsewhere in China – people tend to keep a string of dry chillies hanging from the eaves of their houses.

1
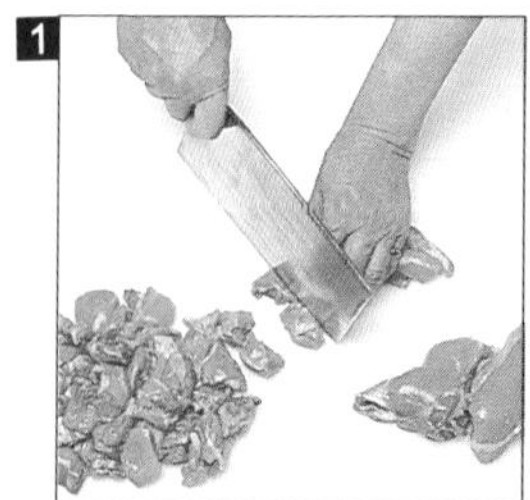

2

2

Chicken & Ginger Stir-fry

The pomegranate seeds add a sharp Chinese flavour to this Indian stir-fry. Serve in the summer with a spicy rice salad or a mixed green salad.

NUTRITIONAL INFORMATION

Calories	291	Sugars	0g
Protein	41g	Fat	14g
Carbohydrate	0g	Saturates	3g

 10 MINS  25 MINS

SERVES 4

INGREDIENTS

- 3 tbsp oil
- 700 g/1 lb 9 oz lean skinless, boneless chicken breasts, cut into 5 cm/2 inch strips
- 3 garlic cloves, crushed
- 3.5 cm/1½ inch piece fresh ginger root, cut into strips
- 1 tsp pomegranate seeds, crushed
- ½ tsp ground turmeric
- 1 tsp garam masala
- 2 fresh green chillies, sliced
- ½ tsp salt
- 4 tbsp lemon juice
- grated rind of 1 lemon
- 6 tbsp chopped fresh coriander (cilantro)
- 125 ml/4 fl oz/½ cup chicken stock
- naan bread, to serve

1

3

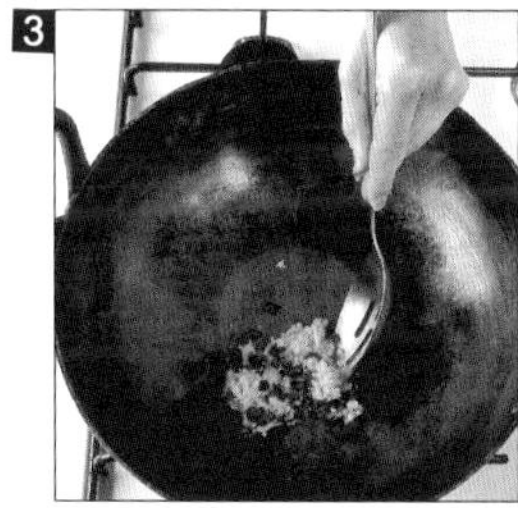

3

1 Heat the oil in a wok or large frying pan (skillet) and stir-fry the chicken until golden brown all over. Remove from the pan and set aside.

2 Add the garlic, ginger and pomegranate seeds to the pan and fry in the oil for 1 minute taking care not to let the garlic burn.

3 Stir in the turmeric, garam masala and chillies, and fry for 30 seconds.

4 Return the chicken to the pan and add the salt, lemon juice, lemon rind, coriander (cilantro) and stock. Stir the chicken well to make sure it is coated in the sauce.

5 Bring the mixture to the boil, then lower the heat and simmer for 10–15 minutes until the chicken is thoroughly cooked. Serve with warm naan bread.

COOK'S TIP

Stir-frying is perfect for low-fat diets as only a little oil is needed. Cooking the food over a high temperature ensures that food is sealed and cooked quickly to hold in the flavour.

Chicken with Orange Sauce

The refreshing combination of chicken and orange sauce makes this a perfect dish for a warm summer evening.

NUTRITIONAL INFORMATION

Calories	797	Sugars	28g
Protein	59g	Fat	25g
Carbohydrate	77g	Saturates	6g

 15 MINS  25 MINS

SERVES 4

INGREDIENTS

- 30 ml/1 fl oz/⅛ cup rapeseed oil
- 3 tbsp olive oil
- 4 x 225 g/8 oz chicken suprêmes
- 150 ml/¼ pint/⅔ cup orange brandy
- 15 g/½ oz/2 tbsp plain (all-purpose) flour
- 150 ml/¼ pint/⅔ cup freshly squeezed orange juice
- 25 g/1 oz courgette (zucchini), cut into matchstick strips
- 25 g/1 oz red (bell) pepper, cut into matchstick strips
- 25 g/1 oz leek, finely shredded
- 400 g/14 oz dried wholemeal (whole-wheat) spaghetti
- 3 large oranges, peeled and cut into segments
- rind of 1 orange, cut into very fine strips
- 2 tbsp chopped fresh tarragon
- 150 ml/¼ pint/⅔ cup fromage frais or ricotta cheese
- salt and pcpper
- fresh tarragon leaves, to garnish

1 Heat the rapeseed oil and 1 tablespoon of the olive oil in a frying pan (skillet). Add the chicken and cook quickly until golden brown. Add the orange brandy and cook for 3 minutes. Sprinkle over the flour and cook for 2 minutes.

2 Lower the heat and add the orange juice, courgette (zucchini), (bell) pepper and leek and season. Simmer for 5 minutes until the sauce has thickened.

3 Meanwhile, bring a pan of salted water to the boil. Add the spaghetti and 1 tablespoon of the olive oil and cook for 10 minutes. Drain the spaghetti, transfer to a serving dish and drizzle over the remaining oil.

4 Add half of the orange segments, half of the orange rind, the tarragon and fromage frais or ricotta cheese to the sauce in the pan and cook for 3 minutes.

5 Place the chicken on top of the pasta, pour over a little sauce, garnish with orange segments, rind and tarragon. Serve immediately.

1

2

4

Green Chicken Stir-Fry

Tender chicken is mixed with a selection of spring greens and flavoured with yellow bean sauce in this crunchy stir-fry.

NUTRITIONAL INFORMATION

Calories	297	Sugars	5g
Protein	30g	Fat	16g
Carbohydrate	8g	Saturates	3g

 5 MINS  15 MINS

SERVES 4

INGREDIENTS

- 2 tbsp sunflower oil
- 450 g/1 lb skinless, boneless chicken breasts
- 2 cloves garlic, crushed
- 1 green (bell) pepper
- 100 g/3½ oz/1½ cups mangetout (snow peas)
- 6 spring onions (scallions), sliced, plus extra to garnish
- 225 g/8 oz spring greens or cabbage, shredded
- 160 g/5¾ oz jar yellow bean sauce
- 50 g/1¾ oz/3 tbsp roasted cashew nuts

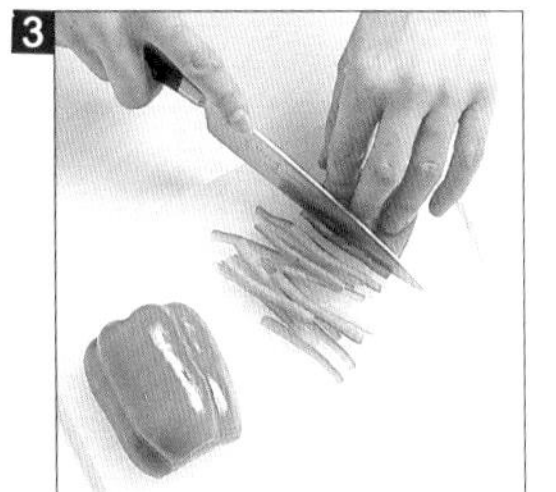

1 Heat the sunflower oil in a large preheated wok.

2 Slice the chicken into thin strips and add to the wok together with the garlic. Stir-fry for about 5 minutes or until the chicken is sealed on all sides and beginning to turn golden.

3 Using a sharp knife, deseed the green (bell) pepper and cut into thin strips.

4 Add the mangetout (snow peas), spring onions (scallions), green (bell) pepper strips and spring greens or cabbage to the wok. Stir-fry for a further 5 minutes or until the vegetables are just tender.

5 Stir in the yellow bean sauce and heat through for about 2 minutes or until the mixture starts to bubble.

6 Scatter the roasted cashew nuts into the wok.

7 Transfer the stir-fry to warm serving plates and garnish with extra spring onions (scallions), if desired. Serve the stir-fry immediately.

COOK'S TIP

Do not add salted cashew nuts to this dish otherwise the dish will be too salty.

Roman Chicken

This classic Roman dish makes an ideal light meal. It is equally good cold and could be taken on a picnic – serve with bread to mop up the juices.

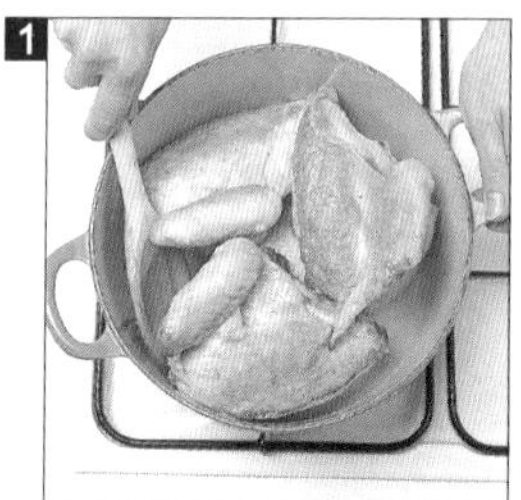

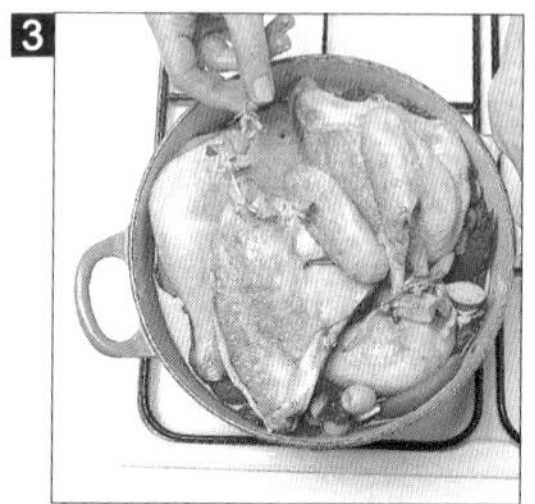

NUTRITIONAL INFORMATION

Calories	317	Sugars	8g
Protein	22g	Fat	22g
Carbohydrate	9g	Saturates	4g

 35 MINS  1 HOUR

SERVES 4

INGREDIENTS

- 4 tbsp olive oil
- 6 chicken pieces
- 2 garlic cloves, crushed with 1 tsp salt
- 1 large red onion, sliced
- 4 large mixed red, green and yellow (bell) peppers, cored, deseeded and cut into strips
- 125 g/4½ oz/⅔ cup pitted green olives
- ½ quantity Basic Tomato Sauce (see page 6)
- 300 ml/½ pint/1¼ cups hot chicken stock
- 2 sprigs fresh marjoram
- salt and pepper

1 Heat half of the oil in a flameproof casserole and brown the chicken pieces on all sides. Remove the chicken and set aside.

2 Add the remaining oil to the casserole and fry the garlic and onion until softened. Stir in the (bell) peppers, olives and tomato sauce.

3 Return the chicken to the casserole with the stock and marjoram. Cover the casserole and simmer for about 45 minutes or until the chicken is tender. Season with salt and pepper to taste and serve with crusty bread.

Honey & Soy Chicken

Clear honey is often added to Chinese recipes for sweetness. It combines well with the saltiness of the soy sauce.

NUTRITIONAL INFORMATION

Calories	279	Sugars	10g
Protein	38g	Fat	8g
Carbohydrate	12g	Saturates	2g

35 MINS 25 MINS

SERVES 4

INGREDIENTS

- 2 tbsp clear honey
- 3 tbsp light soy sauce
- 1 tsp Chinese five-spice powder
- 1 tbsp sweet sherry
- 1 clove garlic, crushed
- 8 chicken thighs
- 1 tbsp sunflower oil
- 1 red chilli
- 100 g/3½ oz/1¼ cups baby corn cobs, halved
- 8 spring onions (scallions), sliced
- 150 g/5½ oz/1½ cups bean sprouts

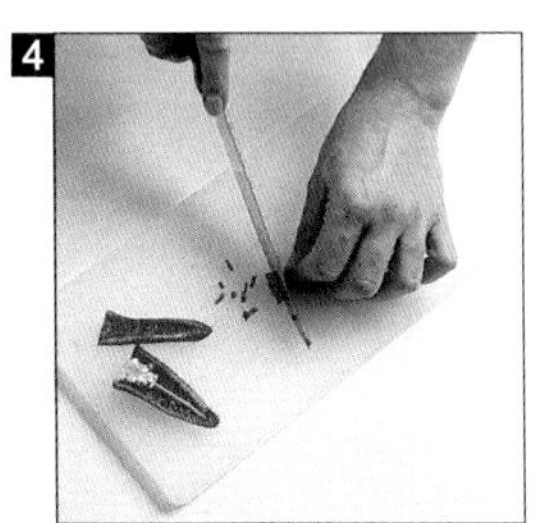

1 Mix together the honey, soy sauce, Chinese five-spice powder, sherry and garlic in a large bowl.

2 Using a sharp knife, make 3 slashes in the skin of each chicken thigh. Brush the honey and soy marinade over the chicken thighs, cover and leave to stand for at least 30 minutes.

3 Heat the oil in a large preheated wok. Add the chicken and cook over a fairly high heat for 12–15 minutes, or until the chicken browns and the skin begins to crispen. Remove the chicken with a slotted spoon and keep warm until required.

4 Using a sharp knife, deseed and very finely chop the chilli.

5 Add the chilli, corn cobs, spring onions (scallions) and bean sprouts to the wok and stir-fry for 5 minutes.

6 Return the chicken to the wok and mix all of the ingredients together until completely heated through. Transfer to serving plates and serve immediately.

COOK'S TIP

Chinese five-spice powder is found in most large supermarkets and is a blend of star anise, fennel seeds, cloves, cinnamon bark and Szechuan pepper.

Rich Chicken Casserole

This casserole is packed with the sunshine flavours of Italy. Sun-dried tomatoes add a wonderful richness.

NUTRITIONAL INFORMATION

Calories	320	Sugars	8g
Protein	34g	Fat	17g
Carbohydrate	8g	Saturates	4g

 15 MINS  1¼ HOURS

SERVES 4

INGREDIENTS

- 8 chicken thighs
- 2 tbsp olive oil
- 1 medium red onion, sliced
- 2 garlic cloves, crushed
- 1 large red (bell) pepper, sliced thickly
- thinly pared rind and juice of 1 small orange
- 125 ml/4 fl oz/½ cup chicken stock
- 400 g/14 oz can chopped tomatoes
- 25 g/1 oz/½ cup sun-dried tomatoes, thinly sliced
- 1 tbsp chopped fresh thyme
- 50 g/1¾ oz/½ cup pitted black olives
- salt and pepper
- thyme sprigs and orange rind, to garnish
- crusty fresh bread, to serve

1 In a heavy or non-stick large frying pan (skillet), fry the chicken without fat over a fairly high heat, turning occasionally until golden brown. Using a slotted spoon, drain off any excess fat from the chicken and transfer to a flameproof casserole.

2 Fry the onion, garlic and (bell) pepper in the pan over a moderate heat for 3–4 minutes. Transfer the vegetables to the casserole.

3 Add the orange rind and juice, chicken stock, canned tomatoes and sun-dried tomatoes and stir to combine.

4 Bring to the boil then cover the casserole with a lid and simmer very gently over a low heat for about 1 hour, stirring occasionally. Add the chopped fresh thyme and pitted black olives, then adjust the seasoning with salt and pepper to taste.

5 Scatter orange rind and thyme over the casserole to garnish, and serve with crusty bread.

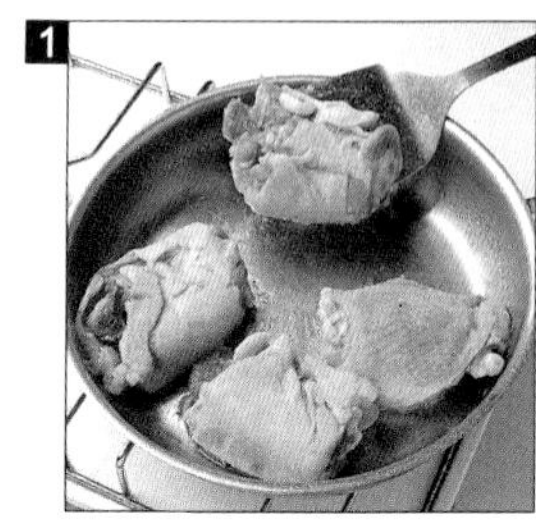

COOK'S TIP

Sun-dried tomatoes have a dense texture and concentrated taste, and add intense flavour to slow-cooking casseroles.

Chicken & Plum Casserole

Full of the flavours of autumn (fall), this combination of lean chicken, shallots, garlic and fresh, juicy plums is a very fruity blend.

NUTRITIONAL INFORMATION

Calories	270	Sugars	9g
Protein	27g	Fat	7g
Carbohydrate	16g	Saturates	2g

2¼ HOURS

35 MINS

SERVES 4

INGREDIENTS

- 2 rashers lean back bacon, rinds removed, trimmed and chopped
- 1 tbsp sunflower oil
- 450 g/1 lb skinless, boneless chicken thighs, cut into 4 equal strips
- 1 garlic clove, crushed
- 175 g/6 oz shallots, halved
- 225 g/8 oz plums, halved or quartered (if large) and stoned
- 1 tbsp light muscovado sugar
- 150 ml/5 fl oz/⅔ cup dry sherry
- 2 tbsp plum sauce
- 450 ml/16 fl oz/2 cups Fresh Chicken Stock (see page 9)
- 2 tsp cornflour (cornstarch) mixed with 4 tsp cold water
- 2 tbsp flat-leaf parsley, chopped, to garnish
- crusty bread, to serve

1

2

3

1 In a large, non-stick frying pan (skillet), dry fry the bacon for 2–3 minutes until the juices run out. Remove the bacon from the pan with a slotted spoon, set aside and keep warm.

2 In the same frying pan (skillet), heat the oil and fry the chicken with the garlic and shallots for 4–5 minutes, stirring occasionally, until well browned .

3 Return the bacon to the pan and stir in the plums, sugar, sherry, plum sauce and stock.

4 Bring to the boil and simmer for 20 minutes until the plums are soft and the chicken is cooked through. Add the cornflour (cornstarch) mixture to the pan and cook, stirring, for a further 2–3 minutes until thickened.

5 Spoon the casserole on to warm serving plates and garnish with chopped parsley. Serve the casserole with chunks of bread.

Barbecued Chicken Wings

These chicken wings are brushed with a simple barbecue (grill) glaze, which can be made in minutes, but will be enjoyed by all.

NUTRITIONAL INFORMATION

Calories	143	Sugars	6g
Protein	14g	Fat	7g
Carbohydrate	6g	Saturates	1g

 5 MINS  20 MINS

SERVES 4

INGREDIENTS

- 8 chicken wings or 1 chicken cut into 8 portions
- 3 tbsp tomato purée (paste)
- 3 tbsp brown fruity sauce
- 1 tbsp white wine vinegar
- 1 tbsp clear honey
- 1 tbsp olive oil
- 1 clove garlic, crushed (optional)
- salad leaves, to serve

1 Remove the skin from the chicken if you want to reduce the fat in the dish.

2 To make the barbecue glaze, place the tomato purée (paste), brown fruity sauce, white wine vinegar, honey, oil and garlic in a small bowl. Stir all of the ingredients together until they are thoroughly blended.

3 Brush the barbecue (grill) glaze over the chicken and barbecue (grill) over hot coals for 15–20 minutes. Turn the chicken portions over occasionally and baste frequently with the barbecue (grill) glaze.

4 If the chicken begins to blacken before it is cooked, raise the rack if possible or move the chicken to a cooler part of the barbecue (grill) to slow down the cooking.

5 Transfer the barbecued (grilled) chicken to warm serving plates and serve with fresh salad leaves.

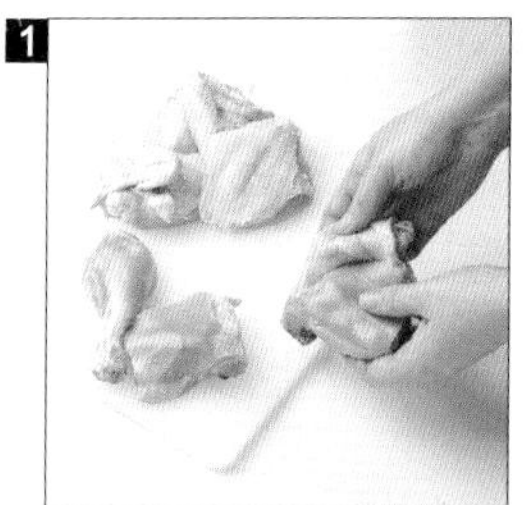
1

2

3

COOK'S TIP

When poultry is cooked over a very hot barbecue (grill) the heat immediately seals in all of the juices, leaving the meat succulent. For this reason make sure that the coals are hot enough before starting to barbecue (grill).

Peppered Chicken

Crushed mixed peppercorns coat tender, thin strips of chicken which are cooked with green and red (bell) peppers for a really colourful dish.

NUTRITIONAL INFORMATION

Calories	219	Sugars	6g
Protein	22g	Fat	10g
Carbohydrate	11g	Saturates	2g

5 MINS 15 MINS

SERVES 4

INGREDIENTS

- 2 tbsp tomato ketchup
- 2 tbsp soy sauce
- 450 g/1 lb boneless, skinless chicken breasts
- 2 tbsp crushed mixed peppercorns
- 2 tbsp sunflower oil
- 1 red (bell) pepper
- 1 green (bell) pepper
- 175 g/6 oz/2½ cups sugar snap peas
- 2 tbsp oyster sauce

1 Mix the tomato ketchup with the soy sauce in a bowl.

2 Using a sharp knife, slice the chicken into thin strips.

3 Toss the chicken in the tomato ketchup and soy sauce mixture until the chicken is well coated.

4 Sprinkle the crushed peppercorns on to a plate. Dip the coated chicken in the peppercorns until evenly coated.

5 Heat the sunflower oil in a preheated wok or large frying pan (skillet), until the oil is smoking.

6 Add the chicken to the wok and stir-fry for 5 minutes.

1

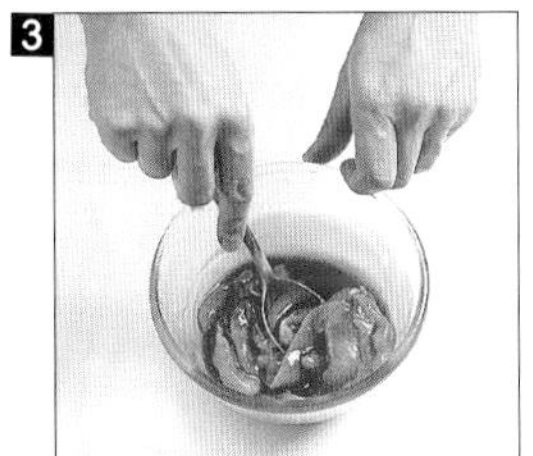

3

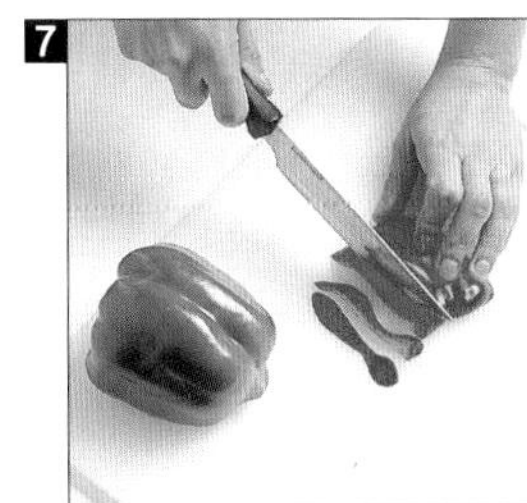

7

7 Using a sharp knife, deseed and slice the (bell) peppers.

8 Add the (bell) peppers to the wok together with the sugar snap peas and stir-fry for a further 5 minutes.

9 Add the oyster sauce and allow to bubble for 2 minutes. Transfer the peppered chicken to serving bowls and serve immediately.

VARIATION

Use mangetout (snow peas) instead of the sugar snap peas, if you prefer.

Chicken with Vegetables

Coconut adds a creamy texture and delicious flavour to this stir-fry, which is spiked with green chilli.

NUTRITIONAL INFORMATION

Calories	330	Sugars	4g
Protein	23g	Fat	24g
Carbohydrate	6g	Saturates	10g

 10 MINS  10 MINS

SERVES 4

INGREDIENTS

- 3 tbsp sesame oil
- 350 g/12 oz chicken breast, sliced thinly
- 8 shallots, sliced
- 2 garlic cloves, finely chopped
- 2.5 cm/1 inch piece fresh root ginger, grated
- 1 green chilli, finely chopped
- 1 each red and green (bell) pepper, sliced thinly
- 3 courgettes (zucchini), thinly sliced
- 2 tbsp ground almonds
- 1 tsp ground cinnamon
- 1 tbsp oyster sauce
- 50 g/1¾ oz/¼ cup creamed coconut, grated
- salt and pepper

1. Heat the sesame oil in a preheated wok or large frying pan (skillet).

2. Add the chicken slices to the wok or frying pan (skillet), season with salt and pepper and stir fry for about 4 minutes.

3. Add the shallots, garlic, ginger and chilli and stir-fry for 2 minutes.

4. Add the red and green (bell) peppers and courgettes (zucchini) and cook for about 1 minute.

5. Finally, add the ground almonds, cinnamon, oyster sauce and coconut. Stir fry for 1 minute.

6. Transfer to a warm serving dish and serve immediately.

VARIATION

You can vary the vegetables in this dish according to seasonal availability or whatever you have at hand. Try broccoli florets or baby sweetcorn cobs.

3

4

5

Mexican Chicken

Chilli, tomatoes and corn are typical ingredients in a Mexican dish. This is a quick and easy meal for unexpected guests.

NUTRITIONAL INFORMATION

Calories	207	Sugars	8g
Protein	18g	Fat	9g
Carbohydrate	13g	Saturates	2g

5 MINS

35 MINS

SERVES 4

INGREDIENTS

- 2 tbsp oil
- 8 chicken drumsticks
- 1 medium onion, finely chopped
- 1 tsp chilli powder
- 1 tsp ground coriander
- 425 g/15 oz can chopped tomatoes
- 2 tbsp tomato purée (paste)
- 125 g/4½ oz/⅔ cup frozen sweetcorn (corn-on-the-cob)
- salt and pepper

TO SERVE

- boiled rice
- mixed (bell) pepper salad

1 Heat the oil in a large frying pan (skillet), add the chicken drumsticks and cook over a medium heat until lightly browned on all sides. Remove from the pan and set aside.

2 Add the onion to the pan and cook for 3–4 minutes until soft, then stir in the chilli powder and coriander and cook for a few seconds.

3 Add the chopped tomatoes with their juice and the tomato purée (paste).

1

3

4

4 Return the chicken to the pan and simmer gently for 20 minutes until the chicken is tender and thoroughly cooked. Add the sweetcorn (corn-on-the-cob) and cook a further 3–4 minutes. Season to taste.

5 Serve with boiled rice and mixed (bell) pepper salad.

COOK'S TIP

If you dislike the heat of the chillies, just leave them out – the chicken will still taste delicious.

Springtime Chicken Cobbler

Fresh spring vegetables are the basis of this colourful casserole, which is topped with hearty wholemeal (whole wheat) dumplings.

NUTRITIONAL INFORMATION

Calories	560	Sugars	10g
Protein	39g	Fat	18g
Carbohydrate	64g	Saturates	4g

 15 MINS  1½ HOURS

SERVES 4

INGREDIENTS

8 skinless chicken drumsticks
1 tbsp oil
1 small onion, sliced
350 g/12 oz/1½ cups baby carrots
2 baby turnips
125 g/4½ oz/1 cup broad beans or peas
1 tsp cornflour
300ml/½ pint/1¼ cups chicken stock
2 bay leaves
salt and pepper

COBBLER TOPPING

250 g/9 oz/2 cups wholemeal (whole wheat) plain flour
2 tsp baking powder
25 g/1 oz/2 tbsp sunflower soft margarine
2 tsp dry wholegrain mustard
60 g/2 oz/½ cup low-fat mature (sharp) Cheddar cheese, grated
skimmed milk, to mix
sesame seeds, to sprinkle

1 Fry the chicken in the oil, turning, until golden brown. Drain well and place in an ovenproof casserole. Sauté the onion for 2–3 minutes to soften.

2 Wash and trim the carrots and turnips and cut into equal-sized pieces. Add to the casserole with the onions and beans or peas.

3 Blend the cornflour with a little of the stock, then stir in the rest and heat gently, stirring until boiling. Pour into the casserole and add the bay leaves, salt and pepper.

4 Cover tightly and bake in a preheated oven, 200°C/400°F/Gas Mark 6, for 50–60 minutes, or until the chicken juices run clear when pierced with a skewer.

5 For the topping, sift the flour and baking powder. Mix in the margarine with a fork. Stir in the mustard, the cheese and enough milk to mix to a fairly soft dough.

6 Roll out and cut 16 rounds with a 4 cm/1½ inch cutter. Uncover the casserole, arrange the scone (biscuit) rounds on top, then brush with milk and sprinkle with sesame seeds. Bake in the oven for 20 minutes or until the topping is golden and firm.

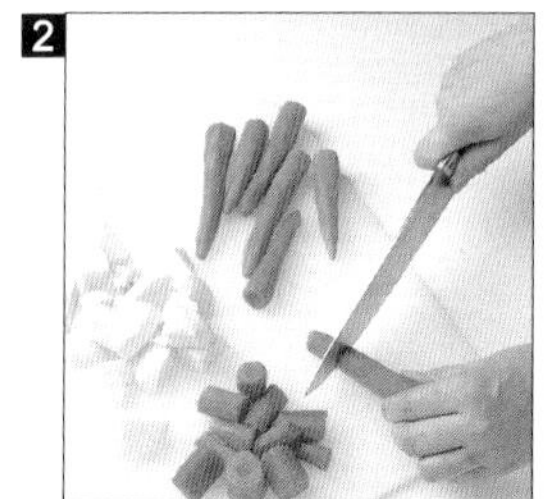
2

5

6

Indian Charred Chicken

An Indian-influenced dish that is delicious served with naan bread and a cucumber raita.

NUTRITIONAL INFORMATION

Calories	228	Sugars	12g
Protein	28g	Fat	8g
Carbohydrate	12g	Saturates	2g

 20 MINS  10 MINS

SERVES 4

INGREDIENTS

- 4 chicken breasts, skinned and boned
- 2 tbsp curry paste
- 1 tbsp sunflower oil
- 1 tbsp light muscovado sugar
- 1 tsp ground ginger
- ½ tsp ground cumin

TO SERVE

- naan bread
- green salad leaves

CUCUMBER RAITA

- ¼ cucumber
- salt
- 150 ml/5 fl oz/⅔ cup low-fat natural yogurt
- ¼ tsp chilli powder

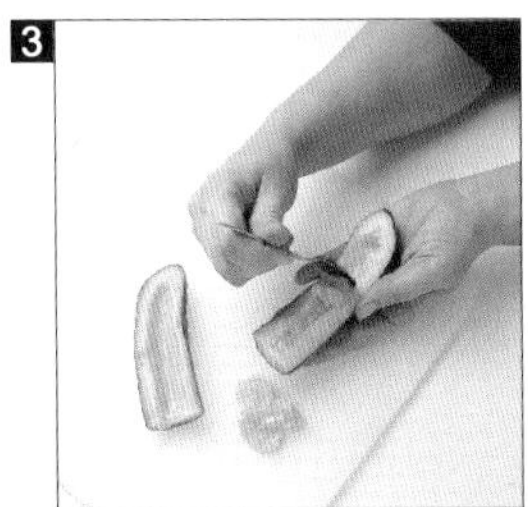

1 Place the chicken breasts between 2 sheets of baking parchment or cling film (plastic wrap). Pound them with the flat side of a meat mallet or rolling pin to flatten them.

2 Mix together the curry paste, oil, sugar, ginger and cumin in a small bowl. Spread the mixture over both sides of the chicken and set aside until required.

3 To make the raita, peel the cucumber and scoop out the seeds with a spoon. Grate the cucumber flesh, sprinkle with salt, place in a sieve and leave to stand for 10 minutes. Rinse off the salt and squeeze out any moisture by pressing the cucumber with the base of a glass or back of a spoon.

4 Mix the cucumber with the yogurt and stir in the chilli powder. Leave to chill until required.

5 Transfer the chicken to an oiled rack and barbecue (grill) over hot coals for 10 minutes, turning once.

6 Warm the naan bread at the side of the barbecue.

7 Serve the chicken with the naan bread and raita and accompanied with fresh green salad leaves.

Springtime Roast Chicken

This combination of baby vegetables and baby chickens with a tangy low-fat sauce makes a healthy meal.

NUTRITIONAL INFORMATION

Calories	280	Sugars	7g
Protein	32g	Fat	7g
Carbohydrate	16g	Saturates	2g

 15 MINS  1 HOUR

SERVES 4

INGREDIENTS

- 5 tbsp fresh brown breadcrumbs
- 200 g/7 oz/½ cup low-fat fromage frais
- 5 tbsp chopped fresh parsley
- 5 tbsp chopped fresh chives
- 4 baby chickens
- 1 tbsp sunflower oil
- 675 g/1½ lb young spring vegetables such as carrots, courgettes (zucchini), sugar snap peas, corn (corn-on-the-cob) and turnips, cut into small chunks
- 125 ml/4 fl oz/½ cup boiling chicken stock
- 2 tsp cornflour (cornstarch)
- 150 ml/¼ pint/⅔ cup dry white wine
- salt and pepper

1 Mix together the breadcrumbs, one-third of the fromage frais and 2 tablespoons each of parsley and chives. Season well then spoon into the neck ends of the baby chickens. Place the chickens on a rack in a roasting tin (pan), brush with oil and season well.

2 Roast in a preheated oven, 220°C/425°F/Gas Mark 7, for 30–35 minutes or until the juices run clear, not pink, when the chickens are pierced with a skewer.

3 Place the vegetables in a shallow ovenproof dish in one layer and add half the remaining herbs with the stock.

4 Cover and bake for 25–30 minutes until tender. Lift the chickens on to a serving plate and skim any fat from the juices in the tin. Add the vegetable juices.

5 Blend the cornflour (cornstarch) with the wine and whisk into the sauce with the remaining fromage frais. Whisk until boiling, then add the remaining herbs. Season to taste. Spoon the sauce over the chickens and serve with the vegetables.

2

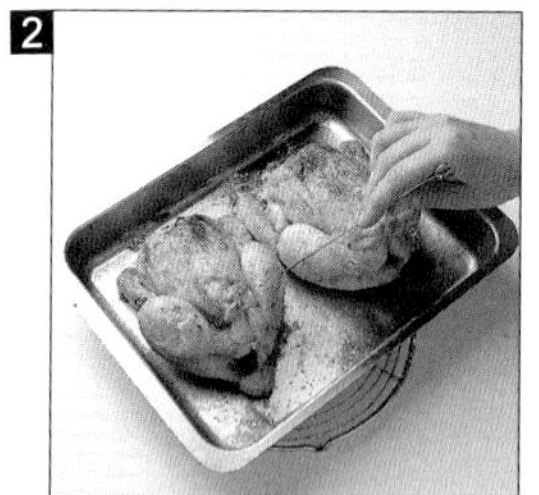

3

5

COOK'S TIP

Baby chickens are simple to prepare, quick to cook and can be easily cut in half lengthways with a knife.

Spiced Apricot Chicken

Spiced chicken legs are partially boned and packed with dried apricot. A golden, spiced, low-fat yogurt coating keeps the chicken moist.

NUTRITIONAL INFORMATION

Calories	305	Sugars	21g
Protein	15g	Fat	8g
Carbohydrate	45g	Saturates	1g

 10 MINS  40 MINS

SERVES 4

INGREDIENTS

- 4 large, lean skinless chicken leg quarters
- finely grated rind of 1 lemon
- 200 g/7 oz/1 cup ready-to-eat dried apricots
- 1 tbsp ground cumin
- 1 tsp ground turmeric
- 125 g/4½ oz/½ cup low-fat natural yogurt
- salt and pepper

TO SERVE

- 250 g/9 oz/1½ cups brown rice
- 2 tbsp flaked hazelnuts, toasted
- 2 tbsp sunflower seeds, toasted

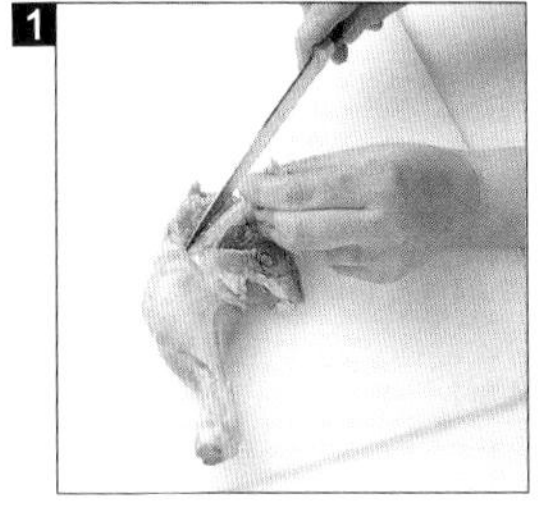

1

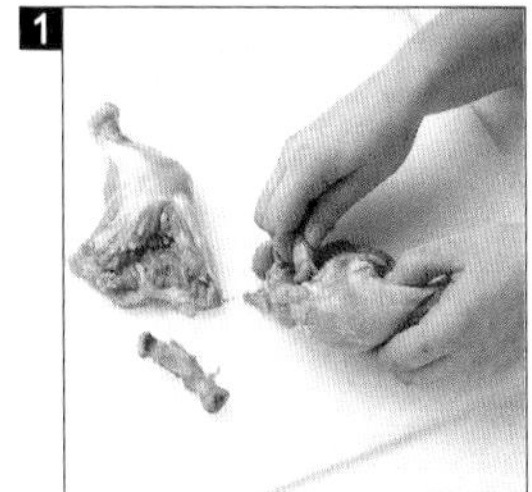

1

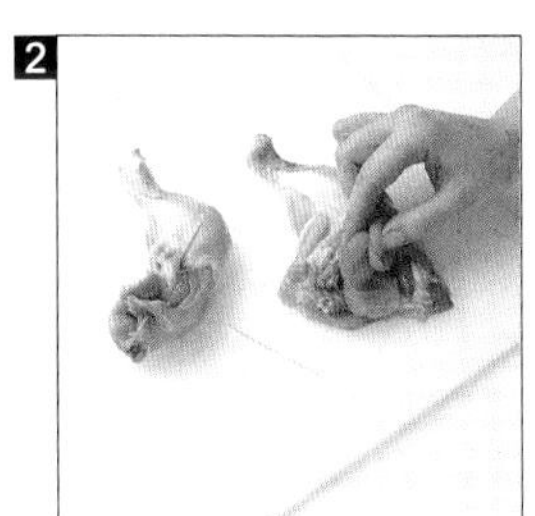

2

1 Remove any excess fat from the chicken legs. Use a small sharp knife to carefully cut the flesh away from the thigh bone. Scrape the meat away down as far as the knuckle. Grasp the thigh bone firmly and twist it to break it away from the drumstick.

2 Open out the boned part of the chicken and sprinkle with lemon rind and pepper. Pack the dried apricots into each piece of chicken.

3 Fold over to enclose, and secure with cocktail sticks. Mix together the cumin, turmeric, yogurt and salt and pepper, then brush this mixture over the chicken to coat evenly. Place the chicken in an ovenproof dish and bake in a preheated oven, 190°C/375°F/Gas Mark 5, for 35–40 minutes, or until the chicken juices run clear, not pink, when pierced through the thickest part with a skewer.

4 Meanwhile, cook the rice in boiling, lightly salted water until just tender, then drain well. Stir the hazelnuts and sunflower seeds into the rice and serve.

VARIATION

For a change use dried herbs instead of spices to flavour the coating. Use dried oregano, tarragon or rosemary – but remember dried herbs are more powerful than fresh, so you will only need a little.

Italian-style Sunday Roast

A mixture of cheese, rosemary and sun-dried tomatoes is stuffed under the chicken skin, then roasted with garlic, potatoes and vegetables.

NUTRITIONAL INFORMATION

Calories	488	Sugars	6g
Protein	37g	Fat	23g
Carbohydrate	34g	Saturates	11g

35 MINS

1½ HOURS

SERVES 6

INGREDIENTS

- 2.5 kg/5 lb 8 oz chicken
- sprigs of fresh rosemary
- 175 g/6 oz/¾ cup feta cheese, coarsely grated
- 2 tbsp sun-dried tomato paste
- 60 g/2 oz/4 tbsp butter, softened
- 1 bulb garlic
- 1 kg/2 lb 4 oz new potatoes, halved if large
- 1 each red, green and yellow (bell) pepper, cut into chunks
- 3 courgettes (zucchini), sliced thinly
- 2 tbsp olive oil
- 2 tbsp plain (all-purpose) flour
- 600 ml/1 pint/2½ cups chicken stock
- salt and pepper

2

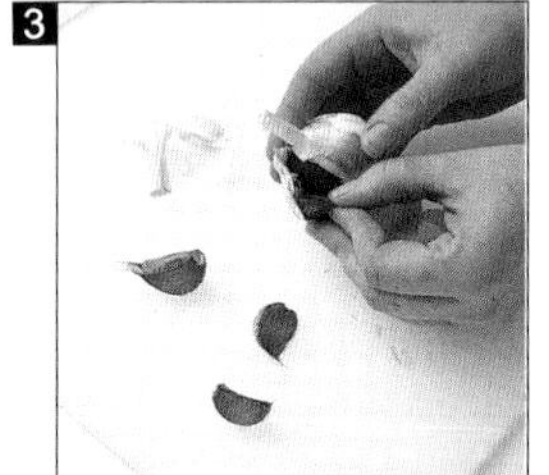

3

4

1 Rinse the chicken inside and out with cold water and drain well. Carefully cut between the skin and the top of the breast meat using a small pointed knife. Slide a finger into the slit and carefully enlarge it to form a pocket. Continue until the skin is completely lifted away from both breasts and the top of the legs.

2 Chop the leaves from 3 rosemary stems. Mix with the feta cheese, sun-dried tomato paste, butter and pepper to taste, then spoon under the skin. Put the chicken in a large roasting tin (pan), cover with foil and cook in a preheated oven, 190°C/375°F/Gas Mark 5, for 20 minutes per 500 g/1 lb 2 oz, plus 20 minutes.

3 Break the garlic bulb into cloves but do not peel. Add the vegetables to the chicken after 40 minutes.

4 Drizzle with oil, tuck in a few stems of rosemary and season with salt and pepper. Cook for the remaining calculated time, removing the foil for the last 40 minutes to brown the chicken.

5 Transfer the chicken to a serving platter. Place some of the vegetables around the chicken and transfer the remainder to a warmed serving dish. Pour the fat out of the roasting tin (pan) and stir the flour into the remaining pan juices. Cook for 2 minutes then gradually stir in the stock. Bring to the boil, stirring until thickened. Strain into a sauce boat and serve with the chicken.

Parma-wrapped Chicken

There is a delicious surprise of creamy herb and garlic soft cheese hidden inside these chicken parcels!

NUTRITIONAL INFORMATION

Calories	272	Sugars	4g
Protein	29g	Fat	13g
Carbohydrate	4g	Saturates	6g

 20 MINS  25 MINS

SERVES 4

INGREDIENTS

- 4 chicken breasts, skin removed
- 100 g/3½ oz full fat soft cheese, flavoured with herbs and garlic
- 8 slices Parma ham (prosciutto)
- 150 ml/¼ pint/⅔ cup red wine
- 150 ml/¼ pint/⅔ cup chicken stock
- 1 tbsp brown sugar

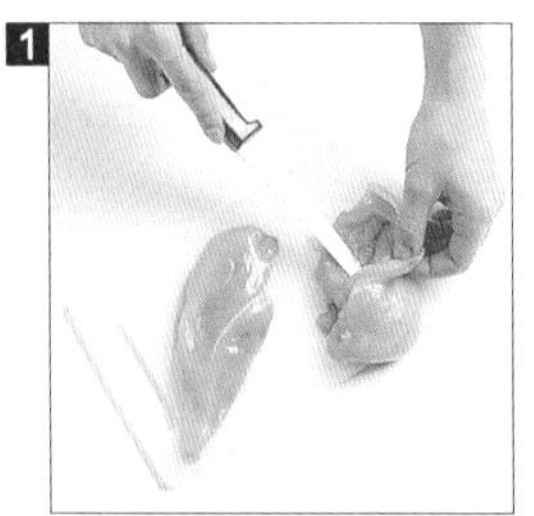

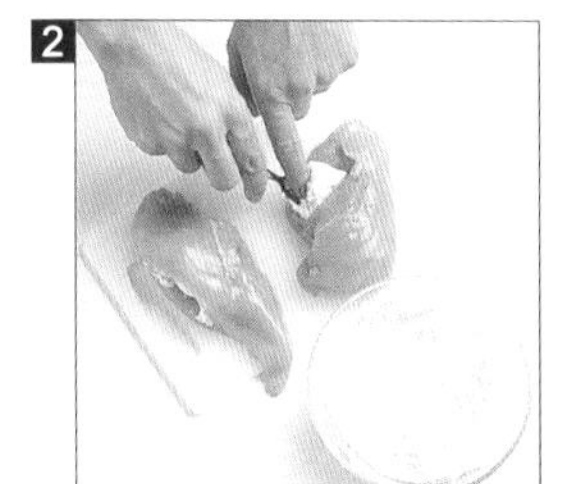

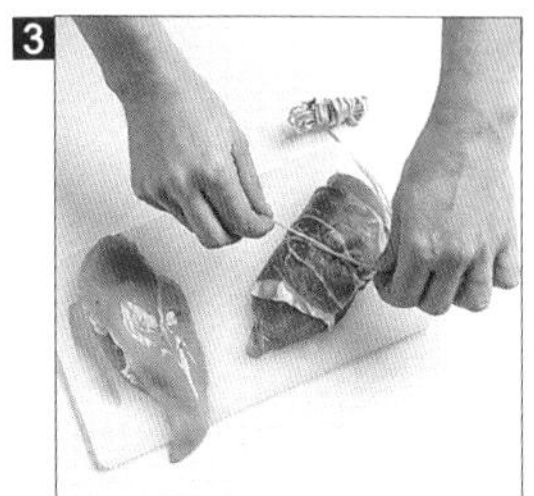

1 Using a sharp knife, make a horizontal slit along the length of each chicken breast to form a pocket.

2 Beat the cheese with a wooden spoon to soften it. Spoon the cheese into the pocket of the chicken breasts.

3 Wrap 2 slices of Parma ham (prosciutto) around each chicken breast and secure firmly in place with a length of string.

4 Pour the wine and chicken stock into a large frying pan (skillet) and bring to the boil. When the mixture is just starting to boil, add the sugar and stir well to dissolve.

5 Add the chicken breasts to the mixture in the frying pan (skillet). Leave to simmer for 12–15 minutes or until the chicken is tender and the juices run clear when a skewer is inserted into the thickest part of the meat.

6 Remove the chicken from the pan, set aside and keep warm.

7 Reheat the sauce and boil until reduced and thickened. Remove the string from the chicken and cut into slices. Pour the sauce over the chicken to serve.

VARIATION

Try adding 2 finely chopped sun-dried tomatoes to the soft cheese in step 2, if you prefer.

Cheesy Baked Chicken

Cheese and mustard, and a simple, crispy coating, make a delicious combination for this healthy dish.

NUTRITIONAL INFORMATION

Calories	225	Sugars	1g
Protein	32g	Fat	7g
Carbohydrate	9g	Saturates	3g

 5 MINS  35 MINS

SERVES 4

INGREDIENTS

- 1 tbsp skimmed milk
- 2 tbsp prepared English mustard
- 60 g/2oz/1 cup grated low-fat mature (sharp) Cheddar cheese
- 3 tbsp plain (all-purpose) flour
- 2 tbsp chopped fresh chives
- 4 skinless, boneless chicken breasts

TO SERVE

- jacket potatoes and fresh vegetables
- crisp salad

1 Mix together the milk and mustard in a bowl. Mix the cheese with the flour and chives on a plate.

2 Dip the chicken into the milk and mustard mixture, brushing with a pastry brush to coat evenly.

3 Dip the chicken breasts into the cheese mixture, pressing to coat them evenly all over.

4 Place on a baking tray (cookie sheet) and spoon any spare cheese coating on top.

5 Bake the chicken in a preheated oven, 200°C/400°F/ Gas Mark 6, for 30–35 minutes, or until golden brown and the juices run clear, not pink, when pierced with a skewer.

6 Serve the chicken hot, with jacket potatoes and fresh vegetables, or serve cold, with a crisp salad.

COOK'S TIP

Part-boned chicken breasts are very suitable for pan-cooking and casseroling, as they stay moist and tender. Try using chicken quarters if part-boned breasts are unavailable.

Karahi Chicken

A karahi is an extremely versatile two-handled metal pan, similar to a wok. Food is always cooked over a high heat in a karahi.

NUTRITIONAL INFORMATION

Calories	270	Sugars	1g
Protein	41g	Fat	11g
Carbohydrate	1g	Saturates	2g

5 MINS — 20 MINS

SERVES 4

INGREDIENTS

- 2 tbsp ghee
- 3 garlic cloves, crushed
- 1 onion, chopped finely
- 2 tbsp garam masala
- 1 tsp coriander seeds, ground
- ½ tsp dried mint
- 1 bay leaf
- 750 g/1 lb 10 oz lean boneless chicken meat, diced
- 200 ml/7 fl oz/scant 1 cup chicken stock
- 1 tbsp fresh coriander (cilantro), chopped
- salt
- warm naan bread or chapatis, to serve

1

3

3

1 Heat the ghee in a karahi, wok or a large, heavy frying pan (skillet). Add the garlic and onion. Stir-fry for about 4 minutes until the onion is golden.

2 Stir in the garam masala, ground coriander, mint and bay leaf.

3 Add the chicken and cook over a high heat, stirring occasionally, for about 5 minutes. Add the stock and simmer for 10 minutes, until the sauce has thickened and the chicken juices run clear when the meat is tested with a sharp knife.

4 Stir in the fresh coriander (cilantro) and mix well, salt to taste and serve immediately with warm naan bread or chapatis.

COOK'S TIP

Always heat a kahari or wok before you add the oil to help maintain the high temperature.

Crispy Stuffed Chicken

An attractive main course of chicken breasts filled with mixed (bell) peppers and set on a sea of red (bell) peppers and tomato sauce.

NUTRITIONAL INFORMATION

Calories	196	Sugars	4g
Protein	29g	Fat	6g
Carbohydrate	6g	Saturates	2g

 20 MINS 50 MINS

SERVES 4

INGREDIENTS

- 4 boneless chicken breasts, about 150 g/5½ oz each, skinned
- 4 sprigs fresh tarragon
- ½ small orange (bell) pepper, deseeded and sliced
- ½ small green (bell) pepper, deseeded and sliced
- 15 g/½ oz wholemeal breadcrumbs
- 1 tbsp sesame seeds
- 4 tbsp lemon juice
- 1 small red (bell) pepper, halved and deseeded
- 200 g/7 oz can chopped tomatoes
- 1 small red chilli, deseeded and chopped
- ¼ tsp celery salt
- salt and pepper
- fresh tarragon, to garnish

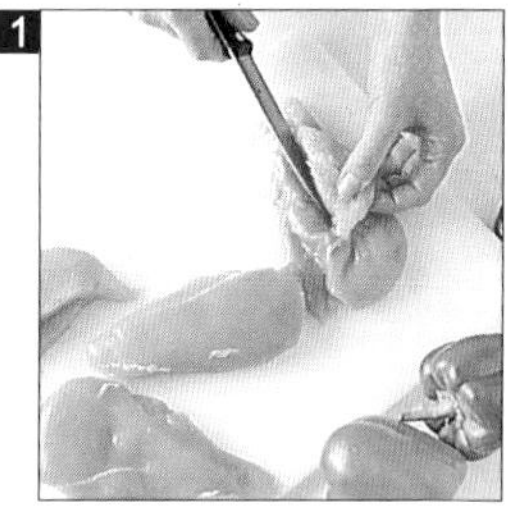

1

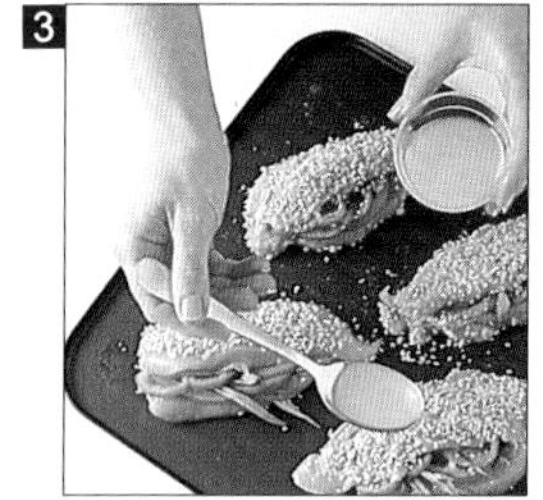

3

5

1 Preheat the oven to 200°C/400°F/Gas Mark 6. Slit the chicken breasts with a small, sharp knife to create a pocket in each. Season inside each pocket.

2 Place a sprig of tarragon and a few slices of orange and green (bell) peppers in each pocket. Place the chicken breasts on a non-stick baking tray (cookie sheet) and sprinkle over the breadcrumbs and sesame seeds.

3 Spoon 1 tablespoon lemon juice over each chicken breast and bake in the oven for 35–40 minutes until the chicken is tender and cooked through.

4 Meanwhile, preheat the grill (broiler) to hot. Arrange the red (bell) pepper halves, skin side up, on the rack and cook for 5–6 minutes until the skin blisters. Leave to cool for 10 minutes, then peel off the skins.

5 Put the red (bell) pepper in a blender, add the tomatoes, chilli and celery salt and process for a few seconds. Season to taste. Alternatively, finely chop the red (bell) pepper and press through a sieve with the tomatoes and chilli.

6 When the chicken is cooked, heat the sauce, spoon a little on to a warm plate and arrange a chicken breast in the centre. Garnish with tarragon and serve.

Chicken with Whisky Sauce

After cooking with stock and vegetables, chicken breasts are served with a velvety sauce made from whisky and low-fat crème fraîche.

NUTRITIONAL INFORMATION

Calories	337	Sugars	6g
Protein	37g	Fat	15g
Carbohydrate	6g	Saturates	8g

5 MINS

30 MINS

SERVES 4

INGREDIENTS

- 25 g/1 oz/2 tbsp butter
- 60 g/2 oz/½ cup shredded leeks
- 60 g/2 oz/⅓ cup diced carrot
- 60 g/2 oz/¼ cup diced celery
- 4 shallots, sliced
- 600 ml/1 pint/2½ cups chicken stock
- 6 chicken breasts
- 50 ml/2 fl oz/¼ cup whisky
- 200 ml/7 fl oz/1 cup low-fat crème fraîche
- 2 tbsp freshly grated horseradish
- 1 tsp honey, warmed
- 1 tsp chopped fresh parsley
- salt and pepper
- parsley, to garnish

TO SERVE

- vegetable patty
- mashed potato
- fresh vegetables

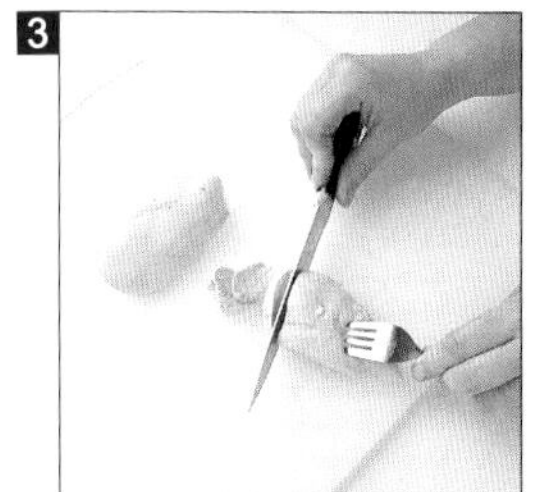

1 Melt the butter in a large saucepan and add the leeks, carrot, celery and shallots. Cook for 3 minutes, add half the chicken stock and cook for about 8 minutes.

2 Add the remaining chicken stock, and bring to the boil. Add the chicken breasts and cook for 10 minutes.

3 Remove the chicken and thinly slice. Place on a large, hot serving dish and keep warm.

4 In another saucepan, heat the whisky until reduced by half. Strain the chicken stock through a fine sieve, add to the pan and reduce the liquid by half.

5 Add the crème fraîche, the horseradish and the honey. Heat gently and add the chopped fresh parsley and salt and pepper to taste.

6 Pour a little of the whisky sauce around the chicken and pour the remaining sauce into a sauceboat to serve.

7 Serve with a vegetable patty made from the leftover vegetables, mashed potato and fresh vegetables. Garnish with parsley.

Chicken Tikka Masala

Try serving the chicken with mango chutney, lime pickle and cucumber raita. Add poppadoms and rice to make a delicious meal.

NUTRITIONAL INFORMATION

Calories	353	Sugars	8g
Protein	44g	Fat	16g
Carbohydrate	8g	Saturates	2g

2¼ HOURS 50 MINS

SERVES 4

INGREDIENTS

½ onion, chopped coarsely
60 g/2 oz/3 tbsp tomato purée (paste)
1 tsp cumin seeds
2.5 cm/1 inch piece ginger root, chopped
3 tbsp lemon juice
2 garlic cloves, crushed
2 tsp chilli powder
750 g/1 lb 10 oz boneless chicken
salt and pepper
fresh mint sprigs, to garnish

MASALA SAUCE

2 tbsp ghee
1 onion, sliced
1 tbsp black onion seeds
3 garlic cloves, crushed
2 fresh green chillies, chopped
200 g/7 oz can tomatoes
125 ml/4 fl oz/½ cup low-fat natural yogurt
125 ml/4 fl oz/½ cup coconut milk
1 tbsp chopped fresh coriander (cilantro)
1 tbsp chopped fresh mint
2 tbsp lemon or lime juice
½ tsp garam masala
sprigs of fresh mint, to garnish

2

2

3

1 Combine the first seven ingredients and seasoning in a food processor or blender and then transfer to a bowl. Cut chicken into 4 cm/1½ inch cubes. Stir into the bowl and leave for 2 hours.

2 Make the masala sauce. Heat the ghee in a saucepan, add the onion and stir over a medium heat for 5 minutes. Add the spices and garlic. Add the tomatoes, yogurt and coconut milk, bring to the boil, then simmer for 20 minutes.

3 Divide the chicken evenly between 8 oiled skewers and cook under a preheated very hot grill (broiler) for 15 minutes, turning frequently. Remove the chicken and add to the sauce. Stir in the herbs, lemon or lime juice, and garam masala. Serve garnished with mint sprigs.

Chicken with Chilli & Basil

Chicken drumsticks are cooked in a delicious sauce and served with deep-fried basil for colour and flavour.

NUTRITIONAL INFORMATION

Calories	196	Sugars	2g
Protein	23g	Fat	10g
Carbohydrate	3g	Saturates	2g

 5 MINS 30 MINS

SERVES 4

INGREDIENTS

- 8 chicken drumsticks
- 2 tbsp soy sauce
- 1 tbsp sunflower oil
- 1 red chilli
- 100 g/3½ oz carrots, cut into thin sticks
- 6 celery stalks, cut into sticks
- 3 tbsp sweet chilli sauce
- oil, for frying
- about 50 fresh basil leaves

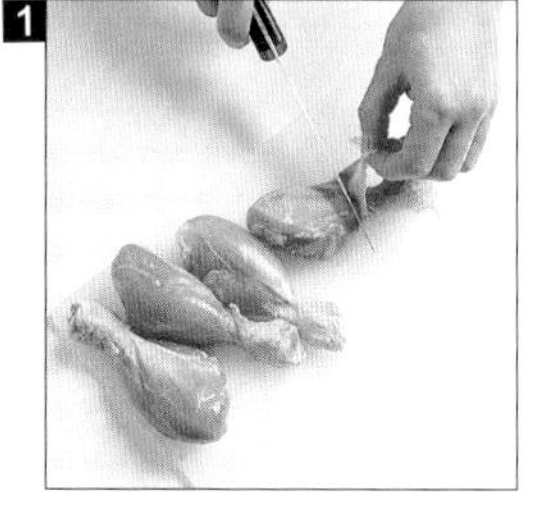

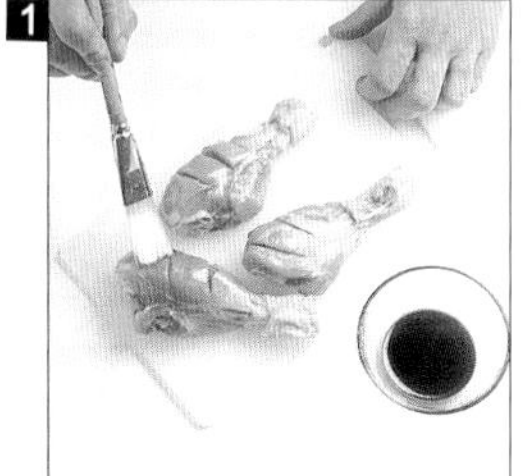

1 Remove the skin from the chicken drumsticks if desired. Make 3 slashes in each drumstick. Brush the drumsticks with the soy sauce.

2 Heat the sunflower oil in a preheated wok and fry the drumsticks for 20 minutes, turning frequently, until they are cooked through.

3 Deseed and finely chop the chilli. Add the chilli, carrots and celery to the wok and cook for a further 5 minutes. Stir in the chilli sauce, cover and allow to bubble gently whilst preparing the basil leaves.

4 Heat a little oil in a heavy based pan. Carefully add the basil leaves – stand well away from the pan and protect your hand with a tea towel (dish cloth) as they may spit a little. Cook the basil leaves for about 30 seconds or until they begin to curl up but not brown. Leave the leaves to drain on absorbent kitchen paper (paper towels).

5 Arrange the cooked chicken, vegetables and pan juices on to a warm serving plate, garnish with the deep-fried crispy basil leaves and serve immediately.

COOK'S TIP

Basil has a very strong flavour which is perfect with chicken and Chinese flavourings. You could use baby spinach instead of the basil, if you prefer.

Chinese Chicken Rice

This is a really colourful main meal or side dish which tastes just as good as it looks.

NUTRITIONAL INFORMATION

Calories	324	Sugars	4g
Protein	24g	Fat	10g
Carbohydrate	37g	Saturates	2g

5 MINS  25 MINS 

SERVES 4

INGREDIENTS

- 350 g/12 oz/1¾ cups long-grain white rice
- 1 tsp turmeric
- 2 tbsp sunflower oil
- 350 g/12 oz skinless, boneless chicken breasts or thighs, sliced
- 1 red (bell) pepper, deseeded and sliced
- 1 green (bell) pepper, deseeded and sliced
- 1 green chilli, deseeded and finely chopped
- 1 medium carrot, coarsely grated
- 150 g/5½ oz/1½ cups bean sprouts
- 6 spring onions (scallions), sliced, plus extra to garnish
- 2 tbsp soy sauce
- salt

1

4

7

1 Place the rice and turmeric in a large saucepan of lightly salted water and cook until the grains of rice are just tender, about 10 minutes. Drain the rice thoroughly and press out any excess water with kitchen paper (paper towels)

2 Heat the sunflower oil in a large preheated wok or frying pan (skillet).

3 Add the strips of chicken to the wok or frying pan (skillet) and stir-fry over a high heat until the chicken is just beginning to turn a golden colour.

4 Add the sliced (bell) peppers and green chilli to the wok and stir-fry for 2–3 minutes.

5 Add the cooked rice to the wok, a little at a time, tossing well after each addition until well combined and the grains of rice are separated.

6 Add the carrot, bean sprouts and spring onions (scallions) to the wok and stir-fry for a further 2 minutes.

7 Drizzle with the soy sauce and toss to combine.

8 Transfer the Chinese chicken rice to a warm serving dish, garnish with extra spring onions (scallions), if wished and serve at once.

Sage Chicken & Rice

Cooking in a single pot means that all of the flavours are retained. This is a substantial meal that needs only a salad and some crusty bread.

NUTRITIONAL INFORMATION

Calories	247	Sugars	5g
Protein	26g	Fat	5g
Carbohydrate	25g	Saturates	2g

 10 MINS  50 MINS

SERVES 4

INGREDIENTS

- 1 large onion, chopped
- 1 garlic clove, crushed
- 2 sticks celery, sliced
- 2 carrots, diced
- 2 sprigs fresh sage
- 300 ml/½ pint/1¼ cups chicken stock
- 350 g/12 oz boneless, skinless chicken breasts
- 225 g/8 oz/1⅓ cups mixed brown and wild rice
- 400 g/14 oz can chopped tomatoes
- dash of Tabasco sauce
- 2 medium courgettes (zucchini), trimmed and thinly sliced
- 100 g/3½ oz lean ham, diced
- salt and pepper
- fresh sage, to garnish

TO SERVE

- salad leaves
- crusty bread

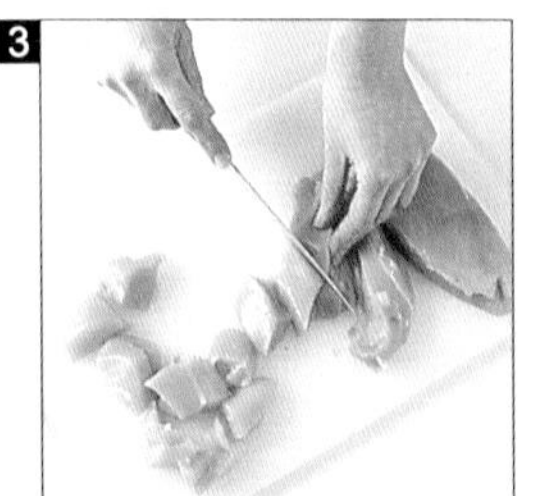

1 Place the pieces of onion, garlic, celery, carrots and sprigs of fresh sage in a large saucepan and pour in the chicken stock.

2 Bring to the boil, cover the pan and simmer for 5 minutes.

3 Cut the chicken into 2.5 cm/1 inch cubes and stir into the pan with the vegetables. Cover the pan and continue to cook for a further 5 minutes.

4 Stir in the mixed brown and wild rice and chopped tomatoes.

5 Add a dash of Tabasco sauce to taste and season well. Bring to the boil, cover and simmer for 25 minutes.

6 Stir in the sliced courgettes (zucchini) and diced ham and continue to cook, uncovered, for a further 10 minutes, stirring occasionally, until the rice is just tender.

7 Remove and discard the sprigs of sage.

8 Garnish with sage leaves and serve with a salad and fresh crusty bread.

Chicken on Crispy Noodles

Blanched noodles are fried in the wok until crisp and brown, and then topped with a shredded chicken sauce for a delightfully tasty dish.

NUTRITIONAL INFORMATION

Calories	376	Sugars	2g
Protein	15g	Fat	27g
Carbohydrate	17g	Saturates	4g

 35 MINS  25 MINS

SERVES 4

INGREDIENTS

- 225 g/8 oz skinless, boneless chicken breasts, shredded
- 1 egg white
- 5 tsp cornflour (cornstarch)
- 225 g/8 oz thin egg noodles
- 300 ml/½ pint/1⅔ cups vegetable oil
- 600 ml/1 pint/2½ cups chicken stock
- 2 tbsp dry sherry
- 2 tbsp oyster sauce
- 1 tbsp light soy sauce
- 1 tbsp hoisin sauce
- 1 red (bell) pepper, seeded and very thinly sliced
- 2 tbsp water
- 3 spring onions (scallions), chopped

1 Mix together the chicken, egg white and 2 teaspoons of the cornflour (cornstarch) in a bowl. Leave to stand for at least 30 minutes.

2 Blanch the noodles in boiling water for 2 minutes, then drain thoroughly.

3 Heat the vegetable oil in a preheated wok. Add the noodles, spreading them to cover the base of the wok. Cook over a low heat for about 5 minutes, until the noodles are browned on the underside. Flip the noodles over and brown on the other side. Remove from the wok when crisp and browned, place on a serving plate and keep warm. Drain the oil from the wok.

4 Add 300 ml/½ pint/1¼ cups of the chicken stock to the wok. Remove from the heat and add the chicken, stirring well so that it does not stick. Return to the heat and cook for 2 minutes. Drain, discarding the stock.

5 Wipe the wok with kitchen paper (paper towels) and return to the heat. Add the sherry, sauces, (bell) pepper and the remaining stock and bring to the boil. Blend the remaining cornflour (cornstarch) with the water and stir it into the mixture.

6 Return the chicken to the wok and cook over a low heat for 2 minutes. Place the chicken on top of the noodles and sprinkle with spring onions (scallions).

3

3

6

Chinese Risotto

Risotto is a creamy Italian dish made with arborio or risotto rice. This Chinese version is simply delicious!

NUTRITIONAL INFORMATION

Calories	436	Sugars	7g
Protein	13g	Fat	14g
Carbohydrate	70g	Saturates	4g

5 MINS 25 MINS

SERVES 4

INGREDIENTS

- 2 tbsp groundnut oil
- 1 onion, sliced
- 2 cloves garlic, crushed
- 1 tsp Chinese five-spice powder
- 225 g/8 oz Chinese sausage, sliced
- 225 g/8 oz carrots, diced
- 1 green (bell) pepper, deseeded and diced
- 275 g/9½ oz/1⅓ cups risotto rice
- 850 ml/1½ pints/1¾ cups vegetable or chicken stock
- 1 tbsp fresh chives

1 Heat the groundnut oil in a large preheated wok or heavy-based frying pan (skillet).

2 Add the onion slices, crushed garlic and Chinese five-spice powder to the wok or frying pan (skillet) and stir-fry for 1 minute.

3 Add the Chinese sausage, carrots and green (bell) pepper to the wok and stir to combine.

4 Stir in the risotto rice and cook for 1 minute.

5 Gradually add the vegetable or chicken stock, a little at a time, stirring constantly until the liquid has been completely absorbed and the rice grains are tender.

6 Snip the chives with a pair of clean kitchen scissors and stir into the wok with the last of the stock.

7 Transfer the Chinese risotto to warm serving bowls and serve immediately.

COOK'S TIP

Chinese sausage is highly flavoured and is made from chopped pork fat, pork meat and spices. Use a spicy Portuguese sausage if Chinese sausage is unavailable.

Spicy Tomato Chicken

These low-fat, spicy skewers are cooked in a matter of minutes – assemble ahead of time and store in the fridge until you need them.

NUTRITIONAL INFORMATION

Calories	195	Sugars	11g
Protein	28g	Fat	4g
Carbohydrate	12g	Saturates	1g

 10 MINS  10 MINS

SERVES 4

INGREDIENTS

- 500 g/1 lb 2 oz skinless, boneless chicken breasts
- 3 tbsp tomato purée (paste)
- 2 tbsp clear honey
- 2 tbsp Worcestershire sauce
- 1 tbsp chopped fresh rosemary
- 250 g/9 oz cherry tomatoes
- sprigs of rosemary, to garnish
- couscous or rice, to serve

1 Cut the chicken into 2.5 cm/1 inch chunks and place in a bowl.

2 Mix together the tomato purée (paste), honey, Worcestershire sauce and rosemary. Add to the chicken, stirring to coat evenly.

3 Alternating the chicken pieces and cherry tomatoes, thread them on to eight wooden skewers.

4 Spoon over any remaining glaze. Cook under a preheated hot grill (broiler) for 8–10 minutes, turning occasionally, until the chicken is thoroughly cooked.

5 Serve on a bed of couscous or rice and garnish with sprigs of rosemary.

COOK'S TIP

Couscous is made from semolina that has been made into separate grains. It usually just needs moistening or steaming before serving.

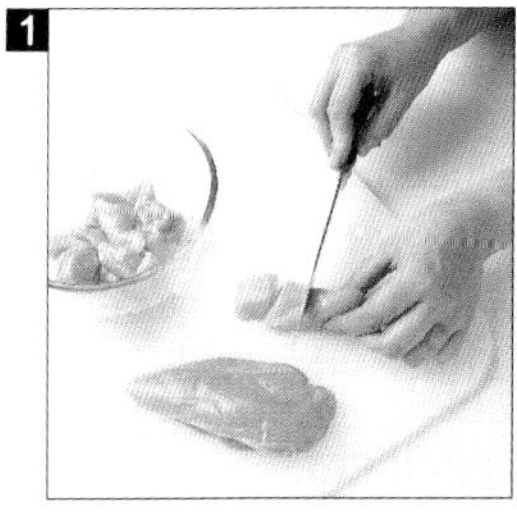

Pot-Roast Orange Chicken

This colourful, nutritious pot-roast could be served for a family meal or for a special dinner. Add more vegetables if you're feeding a crowd.

NUTRITIONAL INFORMATION

Calories	302	Sugar	17g
Protein	29g	Fats	11g
Carbohydrates	22g	Saturates	2g

 10 MINS   2 HOURS

SERVES 4

INGREDIENTS

2 tbsp sunflower oil

1 chicken, weighing about 1.5 kg/3 lb 5 oz

2 large oranges

2 small onions, quartered

500 g/1 lb 2 oz/2 cups small whole carrots or thin carrots, cut into 5 cm/2 inch lengths

150ml/¼ pint/⅔ cup orange juice

2 tbsp brandy

2 tbsp sesame seeds

1 tbsp cornflour (cornstarch)

salt and pepper

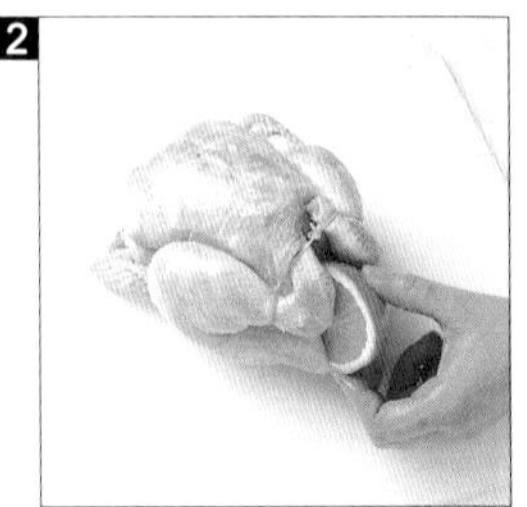
2

3

4

1 Heat the oil in a large flameproof casserole and fry the chicken, turning occasionally until evenly browned.

2 Cut one orange in half and place half inside the cavity of the chicken. Place the chicken in a large, deep casserole. Arrange the onions and carrots around the chicken. Season with salt and pepper and pour over the orange juice.

3 Cut the remaining oranges into thin wedges and tuck around the chicken, among the vegetables.

4 Cover and cook in a preheated oven, 180°C/350°F/Gas Mark 4, for about 1½ hours, or until the chicken juices run clear when pierced, and the vegetables are tender. Remove the lid and sprinkle with the brandy and sesame seeds. Return to the oven for 10 minutes.

5 To serve, lift the chicken on to a large platter and add the vegetables. Skim any excess fat from the juices. Blend the cornflour with 1 tablespoon cold water, then stir into the juices and bring to the boil, stirring all the time. Adjust to taste, then serve the sauce with the chicken.

Roast Baby Chickens

Poussins are stuffed with lemon grass and lime leaves, coated with a spicy marinade, then roasted until crisp and golden.

NUTRITIONAL INFORMATION

Calories	183	Sugars	1g
Protein	30g	Fat	7g
Carbohydrate	1g	Saturates	2g

 10 MINS  55 MINS

SERVES 4

INGREDIENTS

4 small poussins, weighing about 350-500 g/12 oz-1 lb 2 oz each

coriander (cilantro) leaves and lime wedges, to garnish

a mixture of wild rice and Basmati rice, to serve

MARINADE

4 garlic cloves, peeled

2 fresh coriander roots

1 tbsp light soy sauce

salt and pepper

STUFFING

4 blades lemon grass

4 kaffir lime leaves

4 slices ginger root

about 6 tbsp coconut milk, to brush

3

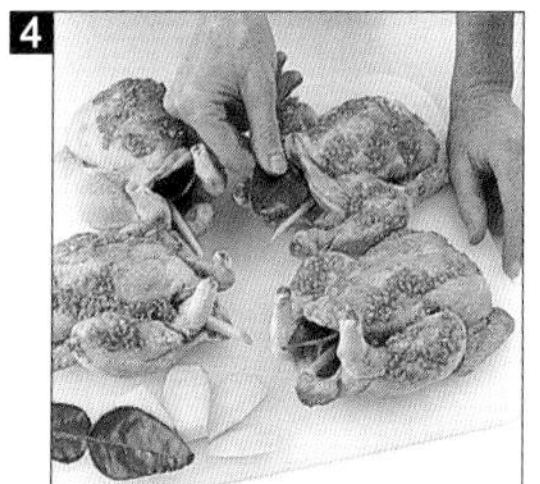

4

5

1 Wash the chickens and dry on kitchen paper (paper towels).

2 Place all the ingredients for the marinade in a small blender and purée until smooth. Alternatively, grind to a paste in a pestle and mortar. Season to taste with salt and pepper.

3 Rub this marinade mixture into the skin of the chickens, using the back of a spoon to spread it evenly over the skins.

4 Place a blade of lemon grass, a lime leaf and a piece of ginger in the cavity of each chicken.

5 Place the chickens in a roasting pan and brush lightly with the coconut milk. Roast for about 30 minutes in a preheated oven.

6 Remove from the oven, brush again with coconut milk, return to the oven and cook for a further 15-25 minutes, until golden and cooked through, depending upon the size of the chickens. The chickens are cooked when the juices from the thigh run clear and are not tinged at all with pink.

7 Serve the baby chickens with the pan juices poured over. Garnish with coriander (cilantro) leaves and lime wedges and serve with rice.

Cashew Chicken

Yellow bean sauce is available from large supermarkets. Try to buy a chunky sauce rather than a smooth sauce for texture.

NUTRITIONAL INFORMATION

Calories	398	Sugars	2g
Protein	31g	Fat	27g
Carbohydrate	8g	Saturates	4g

 10 MINS  15 MINS

SERVES 4

INGREDIENTS

- 450 g/1 lb boneless chicken breasts
- 2 tbsp vegetable oil
- 1 red onion, sliced
- 175 g/6 oz/1½ cups flat mushrooms, sliced
- 100 g/3½ oz/⅓ cup cashew nuts
- 75 g/2¾ oz jar yellow bean sauce
- fresh coriander (cilantro), to garnish
- egg fried rice or plain boiled rice, to serve

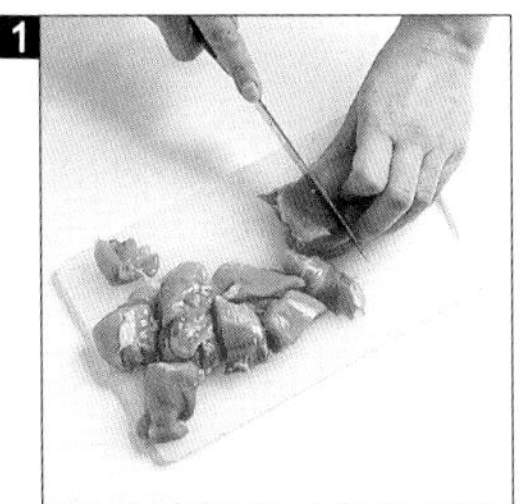

1 Using a sharp knife, remove the excess skin from the chicken breasts, if desired. Cut the chicken into small, bite-sized chunks.

2 Heat the vegetable oil in a preheated wok or frying pan (skillet).

3 Add the chicken to the wok and stir-fry for 5 minutes.

4 Add the red onion and mushrooms to the wok and continue to stir-fry for a further 5 minutes.

5 Place the cashew nuts on a baking tray (cookie sheet) and toast under a preheated medium grill (broiler) until just browning – toasting nuts brings out their flavour.

6 Toss the toasted cashew nuts into the wok together with the yellow bean sauce and heat through.

7 Allow the sauce to bubble for 2–3 minutes.

8 Transfer the chop suey to warm serving bowls and garnish with fresh coriander (cilantro). Serve hot with egg fried rice or plain boiled rice.

VARIATION

Chicken thighs could be used instead of the chicken breasts for a more economical dish.

Garlic Chicken Cassoulet

This is a cassoulet with a twist – it is made with chicken instead of duck and lamb. If you use canned beans, the result will be just as tasty.

NUTRITIONAL INFORMATION

Calories	550	Sugars	2g
Protein	60g	Fat	19g
Carbohydrate	26g	Saturates	4g

 5 MINS  2 1/4 HOURS

SERVES 4

INGREDIENTS

- 4 tbsp sunflower oil
- 900 g/2 lb chicken meat, chopped
- 225 g/8 oz/3 cups mushrooms, sliced
- 16 shallots
- 6 garlic cloves, crushed
- 1 tbsp plain (all-purpose) flour
- 225 ml/8 fl oz/1 cup white wine
- 225 ml/8 fl oz/1 cup chicken stock
- 1 bouquet garni (1 bay leaf, sprig thyme, celery, parsley & sage tied with string)
- 400 g/14 oz can borlotti beans
- salt and pepper

1 Heat the sunflower oil in an ovenproof casserole and fry the chicken until browned all over. Remove from the casserole with a slotted spoon.

2 Add the mushrooms, shallots and garlic to the oil in the casserole and cook for 4 minutes.

3 Return the chicken to the casserole and sprinkle with the flour then cook for a further 2 minutes.

4 Add the wine and stock, stir until boiling then add the bouquet garni. Season well with salt and pepper.

5 Stir in the borlotti beans.

6 Cover and place in the centre of a preheated oven, 150°C/300°F/Gas Mark 2, for 2 hours.

7 Remove the bouquet garni and serve piping hot.

2

3

5

COOK'S TIP

Add chunks of potatoes and other vegetables, such as carrots and celery, for a delicious one-pot meal.

Orange Turkey with Rice

This is a good way to use up left-over rice. Use fresh or canned sweet pink grapefruit for an interesting alternative to the orange.

NUTRITIONAL INFORMATION

Calories	337	Sugars	12g
Protein	32g	Fat	7g
Carbohydrate	40g	Saturates	1g

 30 MINS  40 MINS

SERVES 4

INGREDIENTS

- 1 tbsp olive oil
- 1 medium onion, chopped
- 450 g/1 lb skinless lean turkey (such as fillet), cut into thin strips
- 300 ml/½ pint/1¼ cups unsweetened orange juice
- 1 bay leaf
- 225 g/8 oz small broccoli florets
- 1 large courgette (zucchini), diced
- 1 large orange
- 350 g/12 oz/6 cups cooked brown rice
- salt and pepper
- tomato and onion salad, to serve

TO GARNISH

- 25 g/1 oz pitted black olives in brine, drained and quartered
- shredded basil leaves

2

3

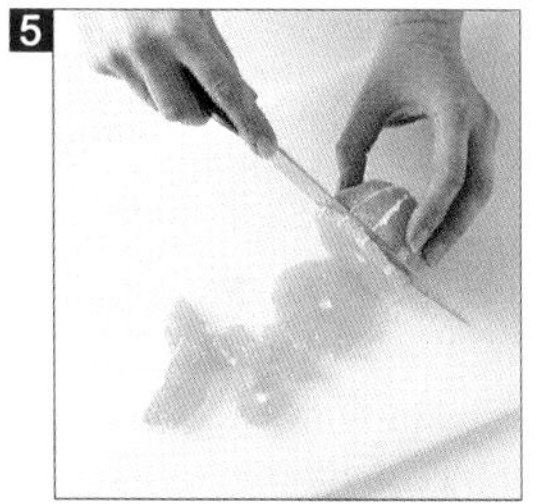

5

1 Heat the oil in a large frying pan (skillet) and fry the onion and turkey, stirring, for 4–5 minutes until lightly browned.

2 Pour in the orange juice and add the bay leaf and seasoning. Bring to the boil and simmer for 10 minutes.

3 Meanwhile, bring a large saucepan of water to the boil and cook the broccoli florets, covered, for 2 minutes. Add the diced courgette (zucchini), bring back to the boil, cover and cook for a further 3 minutes (do not overcook). Drain and set aside.

4 Using a sharp knife, peel off the skin and white pith from the orange.

5 Thinly slice down the orange to make round slices, then halve each slice.

6 Stir the broccoli, courgette (zucchini), rice and orange slices into the turkey mixture. Gently mix together and season, then heat through for a further 3–4 minutes until piping hot.

7 Transfer the turkey rice to warm serving plates and garnish with black olives and shredded basil leaves. Serve the turkey with a fresh tomato and onion salad.

Turkey with Cranberry Glaze

Traditional Christmas ingredients are given a Chinese twist in this stir-fry which containing cranberries, ginger, chestnuts and soy sauce!

NUTRITIONAL INFORMATION

Calories	167	Sugars	11g
Protein	8g	Fat	7g
Carbohydrate	20g	Saturates	1g

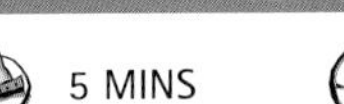 5 MINS  15 MINS

SERVES 4

INGREDIENTS

- 1 turkey breast
- 2 tbsp sunflower oil
- 15 g/½ oz/2 tbsp stem ginger
- 50 g/1¾ oz/½ cup fresh or frozen cranberries
- 100 g/3½ oz/¼ cup canned chestnuts
- 4 tbsp cranberry sauce
- 3 tbsp light soy sauce
- salt and pepper

1 Remove any skin from the turkey breast. Using a sharp knife, thinly slice the turkey breast.

2 Heat the sunflower oil in a large preheated wok or heavy-based frying pan (skillet).

3 Add the turkey to the wok and stir-fry for 5 minutes, or until cooked through.

4 Using a sharp knife, finely chop the stem ginger.

5 Add the ginger and the cranberries to the wok or frying pan (skillet) and stir-fry for 2–3 minutes or until the cranberries have softened.

6 Add the chestnuts, cranberry sauce and soy sauce, season to taste with salt and pepper and allow to bubble for 2–3 minutes.

7 Transfer the turkey stir-fry to warm serving dishes and serve immediately.

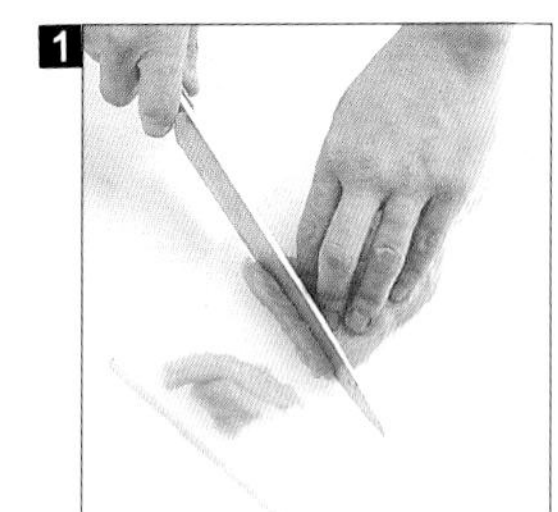

1

3

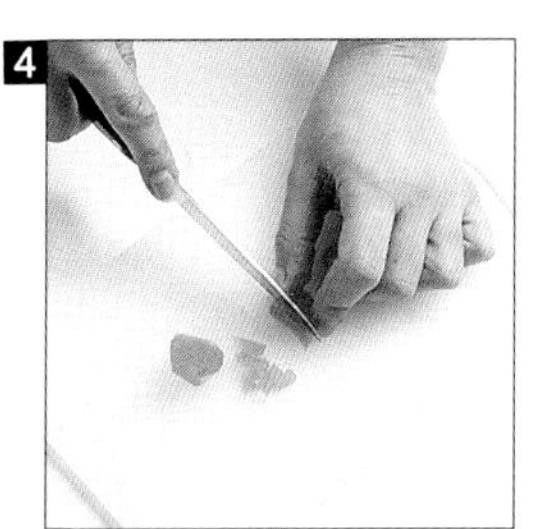

4

COOK'S TIP

It is very important that the wok is very hot before you stir-fry. Test by by holding your hand flat about 7.5 cm/3 inches above the base of the interior – you should be able to feel the heat radiating from it.

Curried Turkey with Apricots

An easy-to-prepare supper dish of lean turkey in a fruit curry sauce served on a bed of spicy rice.

NUTRITIONAL INFORMATION

Calories	377	Sugars	19g
Protein	33g	Fat	6g
Carbohydrate	51g	Saturates	1g

2½ HOURS  30 MINS

SERVES 4

INGREDIENTS

- 1 tbsp vegetable oil
- 1 large onion, chopped
- 450 g/1 lb skinless turkey breast, cut into 2.5 cm/1 inch cubes
- 3 tbsp mild curry paste
- 300 ml/½ pint/1¼ cups Fresh Chicken Stock (see page 9)
- 175 g/6 oz frozen peas
- 400 g/14 oz can apricot halves in natural juice
- 50 g/1¾ oz/⅓ cup sultanas (golden raisins)
- 350 g/12 oz/6 cups Basmati rice, freshly cooked
- 1 tsp ground coriander
- 4 tbsp fresh coriander (cilantro), chopped
- 1 green chilli, deseeded and sliced
- salt and pepper

1 Heat the oil in a large saucepan and gently fry the onion and turkey for 4–5 minutes until the onion has softened but not browned and the turkey is a light golden colour.

2 Stir in the curry paste. Pour in the stock, stirring, and bring to the boil. Cover and simmer for 15 minutes. Stir in the peas and bring back to the boil. Cover and simmer for 5 minutes.

3 Drain the apricots, reserving the juice, and cut into thick slices. Add to the curry, stirring in a little of the juice if the mixture is becoming dry. Add the sultanas and cook for 2 minutes.

4 Mix the rice with the ground and fresh coriander (cilantro), stir in the sliced green chilli and season well. Transfer the rice to warm plates and top with the curry.

VARIATION

Peaches can be used instead of the apricots if you prefer. Cook in exactly the same way.

Duck with Broccoli & Peppers

This is a colourful dish using different coloured (bell) peppers and broccoli to make it both tasty and appealing to the eye.

NUTRITIONAL INFORMATION

Calories	261	Sugars	3g
Protein	26g	Fat	13g
Carbohydrate	11g	Saturates	2g

 35 MINS  15 MINS

SERVES 4

INGREDIENTS

- 1 egg white
- 2 tbsp cornflour (cornstarch)
- 450 g/1 lb skinless, boneless duck meat
- vegetable oil, for deep-frying
- 1 red (bell) pepper, seeded and diced
- 1 yellow (bell) pepper, seeded and diced
- 125 g/4½ oz small broccoli florets
- 1 garlic clove, crushed
- 2 tbsp light soy sauce
- 2 tsp Chinese rice wine or dry sherry
- 1 tsp light brown sugar
- 125 ml/4 fl oz/½ cup chicken stock
- 2 tsp sesame seeds

1 In a mixing bowl, beat together the egg white and cornflour (cornstarch).

2 Using a sharp knife, cut the duck into 2.5-cm/1-inch cubes and stir into the egg white mixture. Leave to stand for 30 minutes.

3 Heat the oil for deep-frying in a preheated wok or heavy-based frying pan (skillet) until almost smoking.

4 Remove the duck from the egg white mixture, add to the wok and fry in the oil for 4–5 minutes, until crisp. Remove the duck from the oil with a slotted spoon and drain on kitchen paper (paper towels).

5 Add the (bell) peppers and broccoli to the wok and fry for 2–3 minutes. Remove with a slotted spoon and drain on kitchen paper (paper towels).

6 Pour all but 2 tablespoons of the oil from the wok and return to the heat. Add the garlic and stir-fry for 30 seconds. Stir in the soy sauce, Chinese rice wine or sherry, sugar and chicken stock and bring to the boil.

7 Stir in the duck and reserved vegetables and cook for 1–2 minutes.

8 Carefully spoon the duck and vegetables on to a warmed serving dish and sprinkle with the sesame seeds. Serve immediately.

2

4

7

Duck with Ginger & Lime

Just the thing for a lazy summer day – roasted duck sliced and served with a dressing made of ginger, lime juice, sesame oil and fish sauce.

NUTRITIONAL INFORMATION

Calories	529	Sugars	3g
Protein	38g	Fat	41g
Carbohydrate	3g	Saturates	6g

20 MINS — 25 MINS

SERVES 4

INGREDIENTS

- 3 boneless Barbary duck breasts, about 250 g/9 oz each
- salt

DRESSING

- 125 ml/4 fl oz/½ cup olive oil
- 2 tsp sesame oil
- 2 tbsp lime juice
- grated rind and juice of 1 orange
- 2 tsp fish sauce
- 1 tbsp grated ginger root
- 1 garlic clove, crushed
- 2 tsp light soy sauce
- 3 spring onions (scallions), finely chopped
- 1 tsp sugar
- about 250 g/9 oz assorted salad leaves
- orange slices, to garnish (optional)

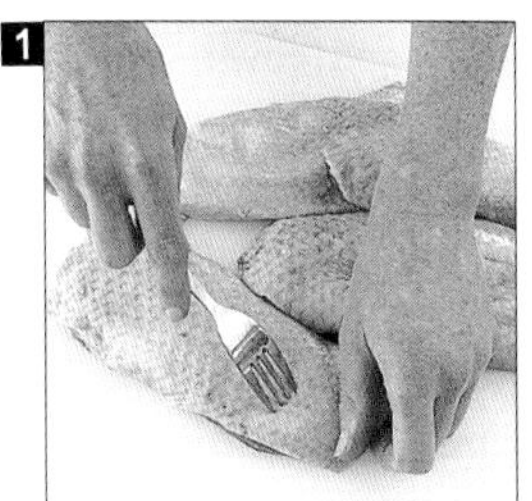

1

3

4

1 Wash the duck breasts, dry on kitchen paper (paper towels), then cut in half. Prick the skin all over with a fork and season well with salt. Place the duck pieces, skin-side down, on a wire rack or trivet over a roasting tin (pan).

2 Cook the duck in a preheated oven for 10 minutes, then turn over and cook for a further 12-15 minutes, or until the duck is cooked, but still pink in the centre, and the skin is crisp.

3 To make the dressing, beat the olive oil and sesame oil with the lime juice, orange rind and juice, fish sauce, grated ginger root, garlic, light soy sauce, spring onions (scallions) and sugar until well blended.

4 Remove the duck from the oven, and allow to cool. Using a sharp knife, cut the duck into thick slices.

5 Add a little of the dressing to moisten and coat the duck.

6 To serve, arrange assorted salad leaves on a serving dish. Top with the sliced duck breasts and drizzle with the remaining salad dressing.

7 Garnish with orange slices, if using, then serve at once.

Roast Duck with Apple

The richness of the duck meat contrasts well with the apricot sauce. If duckling portions are unavailable, use a whole bird cut into joints.

NUTRITIONAL INFORMATION

Calories	316	Sugars	38g
Protein	25g	Fat	6g
Carbohydrate	40g	Saturates	1g

 10 MINS  1 1/2 HOURS

SERVES 4

INGREDIENTS

- 4 duckling portions, 350 g/12 oz each
- 4 tbsp dark soy sauce
- 2 tbsp light muscovado sugar
- 2 red-skinned apples
- 2 green-skinned apples
- juice of 1 lemon
- 2 tbsp clear honey
- few bay leaves
- salt and pepper
- assorted fresh vegetables, to serve

SAUCE

- 400 g/14 oz can apricots, in natural juice
- 4 tbsp sweet sherry

1 Preheat the oven to 190°C/375°F/Gas Mark 5. Wash the duck and trim away any excess fat. Place on a wire rack over a roasting pan and prick all over with a fork.

2 Brush the duck with the soy sauce. Sprinkle over the sugar and season with pepper. Cook in the oven, basting occasionally, for 50–60 minutes until the meat is cooked through – the juices should run clear when a skewer is inserted into the thickest part of the meat.

3 Meanwhile, core the apples and cut each into 6 wedges. Place in a small roasting tin and mix with the lemon juice and honey. Add a few bay leaves and season. Cook alongside the duck, basting occasionally, for 20–25 minutes until tender. Discard the bay leaves.

4 To make the sauce, place the apricots in a blender or food processor together with the juice from the can and the sherry. Process for a few seconds until smooth. Alternatively, mash the apricots with a fork until smooth and mix with the juice and sherry.

5 Just before serving, heat the apricot purée (paste) in a small pan. Remove the skin from the duck and pat the flesh with kitchen paper to absorb any fat. Serve the duck with the apple wedges, apricot sauce and fresh vegetables.

VARIATION

Fruit complements duck perfectly. Use canned pineapple in natural juice for a delicious alternative.

Barbecued (Grilled) Duckling

The sweet, spicy marinade used in this recipe gives the duckling a subtle flavour of the Orient.

NUTRITIONAL INFORMATION

Calories	249	Sugars	20g
Protein	27g	Fat	6g
Carbohydrate	23g	Saturates	2g

 6¼ HOURS  30 MINS

SERVES 4

INGREDIENTS

- 3 cloves garlic, crushed
- 150 ml/5 fl oz/⅔ cup light soy sauce
- 5 tbsp light muscovado sugar
- 2.5 cm/1 inch piece root (fresh) ginger, grated
- 1 tbsp chopped, fresh coriander (cilantro)
- 1 tsp five-spice powder
- 4 duckling breasts
- sprig of fresh coriander (cilantro), to garnish (optional)

1 To make the marinade, mix together the garlic, soy sauce, sugar, grated ginger, chopped coriander (cilantro) and five-spice powder in a small bowl until well combined.

2 Place the duckling breasts in a shallow, non-metallic dish and pour over the marinade. Carefully turn over the duckling so that it is fully coated with the marinade on both sides.

3 Cover the bowl with cling film (plastic wrap) and leave to marinate for 1-6 hours, turning the duckling once or twice so that the marinade is fully absorbed.

4 Remove the duckling from the marinade, reserving the marinade for basting.

1

2

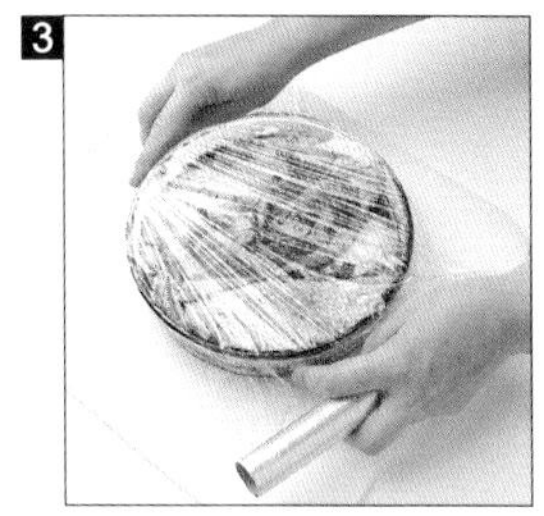
3

5 Barbecue (grill) the duckling breasts over hot coals for about 20–30 minutes, turning and basting frequently with the reserved marinade, using a pastry brush.

6 Cut the duckling into slices and transfer to warm serving plates. Serve the barbecued (grilled) duckling garnished with a sprig of fresh coriander (cilantro), if using.

COOK'S TIP

Duckling is quite a fatty meat so there is no need to add oil to the marinade. However, you must remember to oil the barbecue (grill) rack to prevent the duckling from sticking. Oil the barbecue (grill) rack well away from the barbecue (grill) to avoid any danger of a flare-up.

Ginger Beef with Chilli

Serve these fruity, hot and spicy steaks with noodles. Use a non-stick ridged frying pan (skillet) to cook with a minimum of fat.

NUTRITIONAL INFORMATION

Calories	179	Sugars	8g
Protein	21g	Fat	6g
Carbohydrate	8g	Saturates	2g

 40 MINS  10 MINS

SERVES 4

INGREDIENTS

- 4 lean beef steaks (such as rump, sirloin or fillet), 100 g/3½ oz each
- 2 tbsp ginger wine
- 2.5 cm/1 inch piece root (fresh) ginger, finely chopped
- 1 garlic clove, crushed
- 1 tsp ground chilli
- 1 tsp vegetable oil
- salt and pepper
- red chilli strips, to garnish

TO SERVE

- freshly cooked noodles
- 2 spring onions (scallions), shredded

RELISH

- 225 g/8 oz fresh pineapple
- 1 small red (bell) pepper
- 1 red chilli
- 2 tbsp light soy sauce
- 1 piece stem ginger in syrup, drained and chopped

1 Trim any excess fat from the beef if necessary. Using a meat mallet or covered rolling pin, pound the steaks until 1 cm/½ inch thick. Season on both sides and place in a shallow dish.

2 Mix the ginger wine, root (fresh) ginger, garlic and chilli and pour over the meat. Cover and chill for 30 minutes.

3 Meanwhile, make the relish. Peel and finely chop the pineapple and place it in a bowl. Halve, deseed and finely chop the (bell) pepper and chilli. Stir into the pineapple together with the soy sauce and stem ginger. Cover and chill until required.

4 Brush a grill (broiler) pan with the oil and heat until very hot. Drain the beef and add to the pan, pressing down to seal. Lower the heat and cook for 5 minutes. Turn the steaks over and cook for a further 5 minutes.

5 Drain the steaks on kitchen paper and transfer to serving plates. Garnish with chilli strips, and serve with noodles, spring onions (scallions) and the relish.

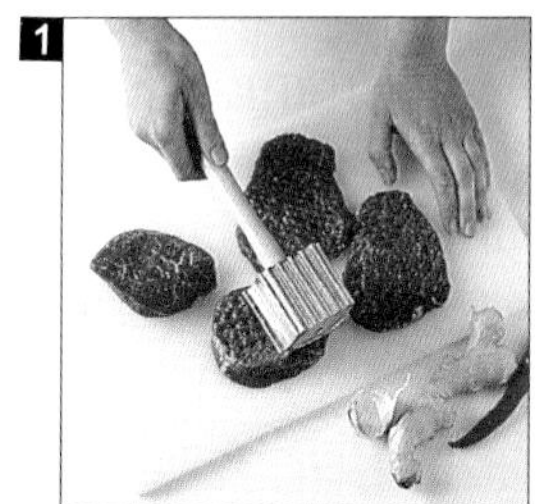
1

3

4

Spaghetti Bolognese

The original recipe takes about 4 hours to cook and should be left over night to allow the flavours to mingle. This version is much quicker.

NUTRITIONAL INFORMATION

Calories	591	Sugars	7g
Protein	29g	Fat	24g
Carbohydrate	64g	Saturates	9g

20 MINS

1 HR 5 MINS

SERVES 4

INGREDIENTS

- 1 tbsp olive oil
- 1 onion, finely chopped
- 2 garlic cloves, chopped
- 1 carrot, scraped and chopped
- 1 stick celery, chopped
- 50 g/1¾ oz pancetta or streaky bacon, diced
- 350 g/12 oz lean minced beef
- 400 g/14 oz can chopped tomatoes
- 2 tsp dried oregano
- 125 ml/4 fl oz/scant ½ cup red wine
- 2 tbsp tomato purée (paste)
- salt and pepper
- 675 g/1½ lb fresh spaghetti or 350 g/12 oz dried spaghetti

2

3

4

1 Heat the oil in a large frying pan (skillet). Add the onions and cook for 3 minutes.

2 Add the garlic, carrot, celery and pancetta or bacon and sauté for 3–4 minutes or until just beginning to brown.

3 Add the beef and cook over a high heat for another 3 minutes or until all of the meat is brown.

4 Stir in the tomatoes, oregano and red wine and bring to the boil. Reduce the heat and leave to simmer for about 45 minutes.

5 Stir in the tomato purée (paste) and season with salt and pepper.

6 Cook the spaghetti in a pan of boiling water for 8–10 minutes until tender, but still has 'bite'. Drain thoroughly.

7 Transfer the spaghetti to a serving plate and pour over the bolognese sauce. Toss to mix well and serve hot.

VARIATION

Try adding 25 g/1 oz dried porcini, soaked for 10 minutes in 2 tablespoons of warm water, to the bolognese sauce in step 4, if you wish.

Beef Goulash

Slow, gentle cooking is the secret to this superb goulash – it really brings out the flavour of the ingredients.

NUTRITIONAL INFORMATION

Calories	386	Sugars	10g
Protein	44g	Fat	16g
Carbohydrate	17g	Saturates	5g

 10 MINS  2¼ HOURS

SERVES 4

INGREDIENTS

- 2 tbsp vegetable oil
- 1 large onion, chopped
- 1 garlic clove, crushed
- 750 g/1 lb 10 oz lean stewing steak
- 2 tbsp paprika
- 425 g/15 oz can chopped tomatoes
- 2 tbsp tomato purée (paste)
- 1 large red (bell) pepper, deseeded and chopped
- 175 g/6 oz mushrooms, sliced
- 600 ml/1 pint/2½ cups beef stock
- 1 tbsp cornflour (cornstarch)
- 1 tbsp water
- 4 tbsp low-fat natural yogurt
- salt and pepper
- paprika for sprinkling
- chopped fresh parsley, to garnish
- long grain rice and wild rice, to serve

1 Heat the vegetable oil in a large frying pan (skillet) and cook the onion and garlic for 3–4 minutes.

2 Cut the stewing steak into chunks and cook over a high heat for 3 minutes until browned all over. Add the paprika and stir well, then add the chopped tomatoes, tomato purée (paste), (bell) pepper and mushrooms. Cook for 2 minutes, stirring frequently.

3 Pour in the beef stock. Bring to the boil, then reduce the heat. Cover and simmer for 1½–2 hours until the meat is tender.

4 Blend the cornflour (cornstarch) with the water, then add to the saucepan, stirring until thickened and smooth. Cook for 1 minute, then season with salt and pepper to taste.

5 Put the natural yogurt in a serving bowl and sprinkle with a little paprika.

6 Transfer the beef goulash to a warm serving dish, garnish with chopped fresh parsley and serve with rice and yogurt.

1

2

3

Crispy Shredded Beef

A very popular Szechuan dish served in most Chinese restaurants all over the world.

NUTRITIONAL INFORMATION

Calories	341	Sugars	17g
Protein	20g	Fat	17g
Carbohydrate	29g	Saturates	4g

3½ HOURS

15 MINS

SERVES 4

INGREDIENTS

- 300-350 g/10½-12 oz beef steak (such as topside or rump)
- 2 eggs
- ¼ tsp salt
- 4-5 tbsp plain (all-purpose) flour
- vegetable oil, for deep-frying
- 2 medium carrots, finely shredded
- 2 spring onions (scallions), thinly shredded
- 1 garlic clove, finely chopped
- 2-3 small fresh green or red chillies, seeded and thinly shredded
- 4 tbsp sugar
- 3 tbsp rice vinegar
- 1 tbsp light soy sauce
- 2-3 tbsp Chinese Stock (see page 8) or water
- 1 tsp cornflour (cornstarch) paste (see page 6)

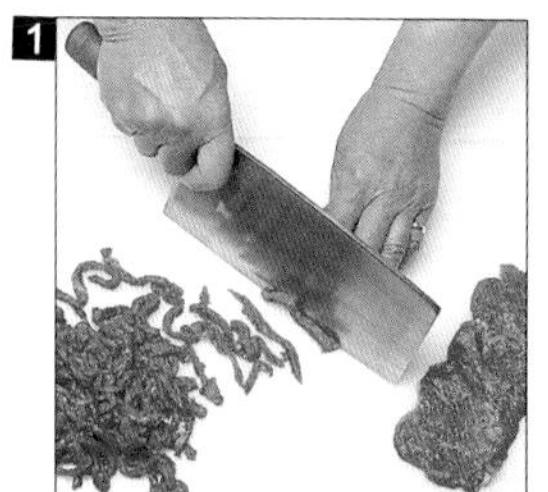

1 Cut the steak across the grain into thin strips. Beat the eggs in a bowl with the salt and flour, adding a little water if necessary. Add the beef strips to the batter and mix well until coated.

2 Heat the oil in a preheated wok until smoking. Add the beef strips and deep-fry for 4-5 minutes, stirring to separate the shreds. Remove with a slotted spoon and drain on absorbent kitchen paper (paper towels).

3 Add the carrots to the wok and deep-fry for about 1-1½ minutes, then remove with a slotted spoon and drain.

4 Pour off the excess oil, leaving about 1 tablespoon in the wok. Add the spring onions (scallions), garlic, chillies and carrots and stir-fry for 1 minute.

5 Add the sugar, rice vinegar, light soy sauce and Chinese stock or water to the wok, blend well and bring to the boil.

6 Stir in the cornflour (cornstarch) paste and simmer for a few minutes to thicken the sauce.

7 Return the beef to the wok and stir until the shreds of meat are well coated with the sauce. Serve hot.

Peppered Beef Cashew

A simple but stunning dish of tender strips of beef mixed with crunchy cashew nuts, coated in a hot sauce. Serve with rice noodles.

NUTRITIONAL INFORMATION

Calories	403	Sugars	7g
Protein	26g	Fat	29g
Carbohydrate	11g	Saturates	9g

10 MINS 10 MINS

SERVES 4

INGREDIENTS

- 1 tbsp groundnut or sunflower oil
- 1 tbsp sesame oil
- 1 onion, sliced
- 1 garlic clove, crushed
- 1 tbsp grated ginger root
- 500 g/1 lb 2 oz fillet or rump steak, cut into thin strips
- 2 tsp palm sugar
- 2 tbsp light soy sauce
- 1 small yellow (bell) pepper, cored, seeded and sliced
- 1 red (bell) pepper, cored, seeded and sliced
- 4 spring onions (scallions), chopped
- 2 celery sticks, chopped
- 4 large open-cap mushrooms, sliced
- 4 tbsp roasted cashew nuts
- 3 tbsp stock or white wine

1 Heat the oils in a large, heavy-based frying pan (skillet) or wok. Add the onion, garlic and ginger and stir-fry for about 2 minutes until softened.

2 Add the steak strips and stir-fry for a further 2-3 minutes, until the meat has browned.

3 Add the sugar and soy sauce, stirring to mix well.

4 Add the (bell) peppers, spring onions (scallions), celery, mushrooms and cashews, mixing well.

5 Add the stock or white wine and stir-fry for 2-3 minutes until the beef is cooked through and the vegetables are tender-crisp.

6 Serve the stir-fry immediately with rice noodles.

COOK'S TIP

Palm sugar is a thick brown sugar with a slightly caramel taste. It is sold in cakes, or in small containers. If not available, use soft dark brown or demerara (brown crystal) sugar.

1

2

4

Ma-po Tofu

Ma-Po was the wife of a Szechuan chef who created this popular dish in the middle of the 19th century.

NUTRITIONAL INFORMATION

Calories	235	Sugars	1g
Protein	16g	Fat	18g
Carbohydrate	3g	Saturates	4g

 $3^1/_2$ HOURS  15 MINS

SERVES 4

INGREDIENTS

- 3 cakes tofu (bean curd)
- 3 tbsp vegetable oil
- 125 g/4½ oz coarsely minced (ground) beef
- ½ tsp finely chopped garlic
- 1 leek, cut into short sections
- ½ tsp salt
- 1 tbsp black bean sauce
- 1 tbsp light soy sauce
- 1 tsp chilli bean sauce
- 3-4 tbsp Chinese Stock (see page 8) or water
- 2 tsp cornflour (cornstarch) paste (see page 6)
- a few drops sesame oil
- black pepper
- finely chopped spring onions (scallions), to garnish

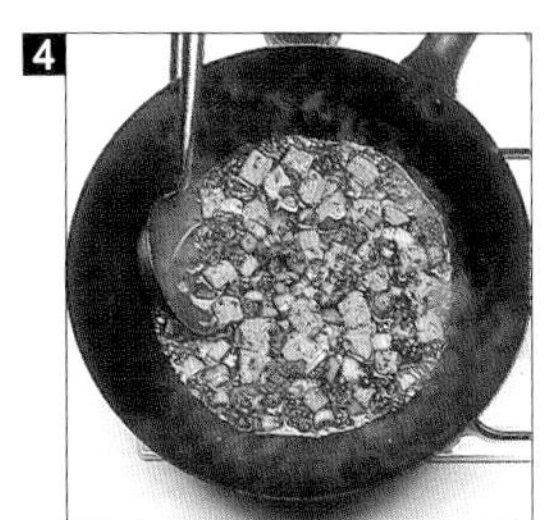

1 Cut the tofu (bean curd) into 1 cm/½ inch cubes, handling it carefully.

2 Bring some water to the boil in a small pan or a wok, add the tofu (bean curd) and blanch for 2-3 minutes to harden. Remove and drain well.

3 Heat the oil in a preheated wok. Add the minced (ground) beef and garlic and stir-fry for about 1 minute, or until the colour of the beef changes. Add the leek, salt and sauces and blend well.

4 Add the stock or water followed by the tofu (bean curd). Bring to the boil and braise gently for 2-3 minutes.

5 Add the cornflour (cornstarch) paste, and stir until the sauce has thickened. Sprinkle with sesame oil and black pepper, garnish and serve hot.

COOK'S TIP

Tofu has been an important element in Chinese cooking for more than 1000 years. It is made of yellow soya beans, which are soaked, ground and mixed with water. Tofu is highly nutritious, being rich in protein and low in fat.

Beef & Tomato Gratin

A satisfying bake of lean minced beef, courgettes (zucchini) and tomatoes cooked in a low-fat 'custard' with a cheesy crust.

NUTRITIONAL INFORMATION

Calories	278	Sugars	10g
Protein	29g	Fat	10g
Carbohydrate	20g	Saturates	5g

10 MINS

1¼ HOURS

SERVES 4

INGREDIENTS

- 350 g/12 oz lean beef, minced (ground)
- 1 large onion, finely chopped
- 1 tsp dried mixed herbs
- 1 tbsp plain (all-purpose) flour
- 300 ml/½ pint/1¼ cups beef stock
- 1 tbsp tomato purée (paste)
- 2 large tomatoes, thinly sliced
- 4 medium courgettes (zucchini), thinly sliced
- 2 tbsp cornflour (cornstarch)
- 300 ml/½ pint/1¼ cups skimmed milk
- 150 ml/5 fl oz/⅔ cup low-fat natural fromage frais (unsweetened yogurt)
- 1 medium egg yolk
- 4 tbsp Parmesan cheese, freshly grated
- salt and pepper

TO SERVE

- crusty bread
- steamed vegetables

1 Preheat the oven to 190°C/375°F/Gas Mark 5. In a large frying pan (skillet), dry-fry the beef and onion for 4–5 minutes until browned.

2 Stir in the dried mixed herbs, flour, beef stock and tomato purée (paste), and season. Bring to the boil and simmer for 30 minutes until the mixture has thickened.

3 Transfer the beef mixture to an ovenproof gratin dish. Cover with a layer of the sliced tomatoes and then add a layer of sliced courgettes (zucchini). Blend the cornflour (cornstarch) with a little milk. Pour the remaining milk into a saucepan and bring to the boil. Add the cornflour (cornstarch) mixture and cook, stirring, for 1–2 minutes until thickened. Remove from the heat and beat in the fromage frais (yogurt) and egg yolk. Season well.

4 Spread the white sauce over the layer of courgettes (zucchini). Place the dish on to a baking sheet and sprinkle with grated Parmesan. Bake in the oven for 25–30 minutes until golden-brown. Serve with crusty bread and vegetables.

1

3

4

Beef & Orange Curry

A citrusy, spicy blend of tender chunks of tender beef with the tang of orange and the warmth of Indian spices.

NUTRITIONAL INFORMATION

Calories	345	Sugars	24g
Protein	28g	Fat	13g
Carbohydrate	31g	Saturates	3g

5¼ HOURS — 1¼ HOURS

SERVES 4

INGREDIENTS

- 1 tbsp vegetable oil
- 225 g/8 oz shallots, halved
- 2 garlic cloves, crushed
- 450 g/1 lb lean rump or sirloin beef, trimmed and cut into 2 cm/¾ inch cubes
- 3 tbsp curry paste
- 450 ml/16 fl oz/2 cups Fresh Beef Stock (see page 9)
- 4 medium oranges
- 2 tsp cornflour (cornstarch)
- salt and pepper
- 2 tbsp fresh coriander (cilantro), chopped, to garnish
- basmati rice, freshly boiled, to serve

RAITA

- ½ cucumber, finely diced
- 3 tbsp chopped fresh mint
- 150 ml/5 fl oz/⅔ cup low-fat natural yogurt

1

3

4

1 Heat the oil in a large saucepan. Gently fry the shallots, garlic and the cubes of beef for 5 minutes, stirring occasionally, until the beef is evenly browned all over.

2 Blend together the curry paste and stock. Add the mixture to the beef and stir to mix thoroughly. Bring to the boil, cover and simmer for about 1 hour.

3 Grate the rind of one orange. Extract the juice from the orange and from one other. Peel the other two oranges, removing the pith. Slice between each segment and remove the flesh.

4 Blend the cornflour (cornstarch) with the orange juice. At the end of the cooking time, stir the orange rind into the beef along with the orange and cornflour (cornstarch) mixture. Bring to the boil and simmer, stirring, for 3–4 minutes until the sauce thickens. Season to taste and stir in the orange segments.

5 To make the raita, mix the cucumber with the mint and stir in the yogurt. Season with salt and pepper to taste.

6 Serve the curry with rice and the cucumber raita, garnished with the chopped coriander (cilantro).

Beef & Black Bean Sauce

It is not necessary to use the expensive cuts of beef steak for this recipe: the meat will be tender as it is cut into small thin slices and marinated.

NUTRITIONAL INFORMATION

Calories	392	Sugars	2g
Protein	13g	Fat	36g
Carbohydrate	3g	Saturates	7g

 3¼ HOURS  10 MINS

SERVES 4

INGREDIENTS

- 250-300 g/9-10½ oz beef steak (such as rump)
- 1 small onion
- 1 small green (bell) pepper, cored and seeded
- about 300 ml/½ pint/1¼ cups vegetable oil
- 1 spring onion (scallion), cut into short sections
- a few small slices of ginger root
- 1-2 small green or red chillies, seeded and sliced
- 2 tbsp crushed black bean sauce

MARINADE

- ½ tsp bicarbonate of soda (baking soda) or baking powder
- ½ tsp sugar
- 1 tbsp light soy sauce
- 2 tsp rice wine or dry sherry
- 2 tsp cornflour (cornstarch) paste (see page 6)
- 2 tsp sesame oil

1 Using a sharp knife or meat cleaver, cut the beef into small thin strips.

2 To make the marinade, mix together all the ingredients in a shallow dish. Add the beef strips, turn to coat and leave to marinate for at least 2-3 hours.

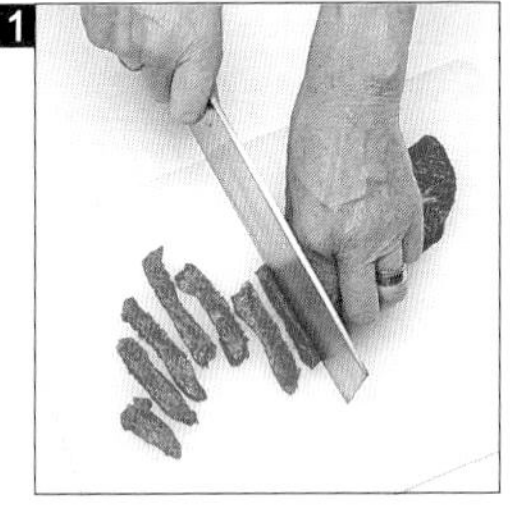

1

3

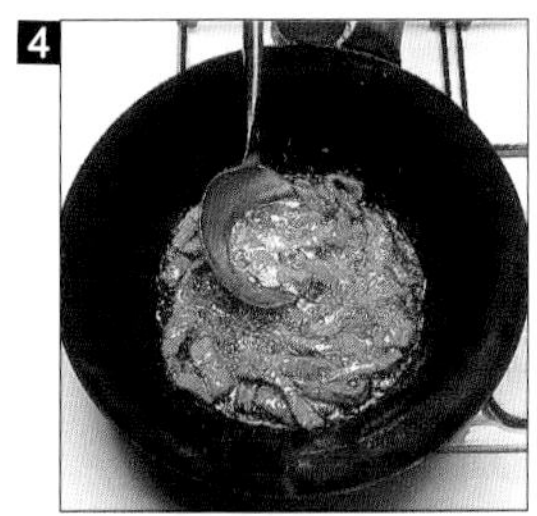

4

3 Cut the onion and green (bell) pepper into small cubes.

4 Heat the vegetable oil in a pre-heated wok or large frying pan (skillet). Add the beef strips and stir-fry for about 1 minute, or until the colour changes. Remove the beef strips with a slotted spoon and drain on absorbent kitchen paper (paper towels). Keep warm and set aside until required.

5 Pour off the excess oil, leaving about 1 tablespoon in the wok. Add the spring onion (scallion), ginger, chillies, onion and green (bell) pepper and stir-fry for about 1 minute.

6 Add the black bean sauce and stir until smooth. Return the beef strips to the wok, blend well and stir-fry for another minute. Transfer the stir-fry to a warm serving dish and serve hot.

Rich Beef Stew

This slow-cooked beef stew is flavoured with oranges, red wine and porcini mushrooms.

NUTRITIONAL INFORMATION

Calories	388	Sugars	15g
Protein	30g	Fat	21g
Carbohydrate	16g	Saturates	9g

45 MINS — 1¾ HOURS

SERVES 4

INGREDIENTS

- 1 tbsp oil
- 15 g/½ oz/1 tbsp butter
- 225 g/8 oz baby onions, peeled and halved
- 600 g/1 lb 5 oz stewing steak, diced into 4 cm/1½ inch chunks
- 300 ml/½ pint/1¼ cup beef stock
- 150 ml/¼ pint/⅔ cup red wine
- 4 tbsp chopped oregano
- 1 tbsp sugar
- 1 orange
- 25 g/1 oz porcini or other dried mushrooms
- 225 g/8 oz fresh plum tomatoes
- cooked rice or potatoes, to serve

1 Heat the oil and butter in a large frying pan (skillet). Add the onions and sauté for 5 minutes or until golden. Remove the onions with a perforated spoon, set aside and keep warm.

2 Add the beef to the pan and cook, stirring, for 5 minutes or until browned all over.

3 Return the onions to the frying pan (skillet) and add the stock, wine, oregano and sugar, stirring to mix well. Transfer the mixture to an ovenproof casserole dish.

4 Pare the rind from the orange and cut it into strips. Slice the orange flesh into rings. Add the orange rings and the rind to the casserole. Cook in a preheated oven, at 180°C/350°F/Gas Mark 4, for 1¼ hours.

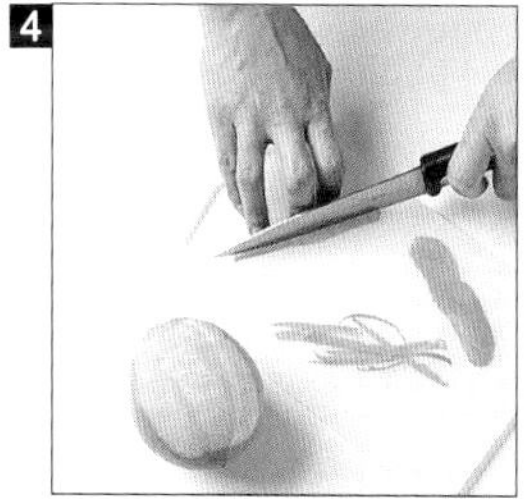

5 Soak the porcini mushrooms for 30 minutes in a small bowl containing 4 tablespoons of warm water.

6 Peel and halve the tomatoes. Add the tomatoes, porcini mushrooms and their soaking liquid to the casserole. Cook for a further 20 minutes until the beef is tender and the juices thickened. Serve with cooked rice or potatoes.

Tamarind Beef Balti

Tamarind has been used in Asian cooking for centuries and gives a sour fruity flavour to the sauce.

NUTRITIONAL INFORMATION

Calories	280	Sugars	7g
Protein	35g	Fat	12g
Carbohydrate	7g	Saturates	4g

 12 HOURS  35 MINS

SERVES 4

INGREDIENTS

- 125 g/4½ oz tamarind block, broken into pieces
- 150 ml/¼ pint/⅔ cup water
- 2 tbsp tomato purée (paste)
- 1 tbsp granulated sugar
- 2.5 cm/1 inch piece ginger root, chopped
- 1 garlic clove, chopped
- ½ tsp salt
- 1 onion, chopped
- 2 tbsp oil
- 1 tsp cumin seeds
- 1 tsp coriander seeds
- 1 tsp brown mustard seeds
- 4 curry leaves
- 750 g/1 lb 10 oz lean braising steak, cut into 2.5 cm/1 inch cubes and par-cooked
- 1 red (bell) pepper, cut in half, sliced
- 2 fresh green chillies, deseeded and sliced
- 1 tsp garam masala
- 1 tbsp chopped fresh coriander (cilantro), to garnish

1 Soak the tamarind overnight in the water. Strain the soaked tamarind, keeping the liquid.

2 Put the tamarind, tomato purée (paste), sugar, ginger, garlic, salt and onion into a food processor or blender and mix to a smooth purée. Alternatively, mash the ingredients together in a bowl.

3 Heat the oil in a Balti pan or wok, add the cumin, coriander seeds, mustard seeds and curry leaves, and cook until the spices start popping.

4 Stir the beef into the spices and stir-fry for 2–4 minutes until the meat is browned.

5 Add the red (bell) pepper, chillies, garam masala, tamarind mixture and reserved tamarind liquid and cook for 20–25 minutes.

6 Serve the beef garnished with fresh coriander (cilantro).

2

4

5

Beef Teriyaki

This Japanese-style teriyaki sauce complements barbecued (grilled) beef, but it can also be used to accompany chicken or salmon.

NUTRITIONAL INFORMATION

Calories	184	Sugars	6g
Protein	24g	Fat	5g
Carbohydrate	8g	Saturates	2g

 2¼ HOURS  15 MINS

SERVES 4

INGREDIENTS

- 450 g/1 lb extra thin lean beef steaks
- 8 spring onions (scallions), trimmed and cut into short lengths
- 1 yellow (bell) pepper, deseeded and cut into chunks
- green salad, to serve

SAUCE

- 1 tsp cornflour (cornstarch)
- 2 tbsp dry sherry
- 2 tbsp white wine vinegar
- 3 tbsp soy sauce
- 1 tbsp dark muscovado sugar
- 1 clove garlic, crushed
- ½ tsp ground cinnamon
- ½ tsp ground ginger

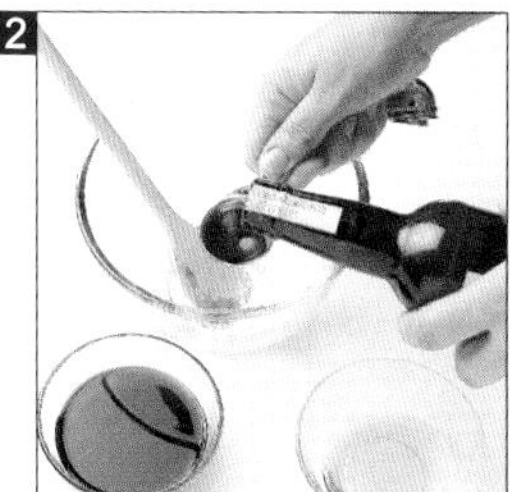
2

3

4

1 Place the meat in a shallow, non-metallic dish.

2 To make the sauce, combine the cornflour (cornstarch) with the sherry, then stir in the remaining sauce ingredients. Pour the sauce over the meat and leave to marinate for at least 2 hours.

3 Remove the meat from the sauce. Pour the sauce into a small saucepan.

4 Cut the meat into thin strips and thread these, concertina-style, on to pre-soaked wooden skewers, alternating each strip of meat with the prepared pieces of spring onion (scallion) and (bell) pepper.

5 Gently heat the sauce until it is just simmering, stirring occasionally.

6 Barbecue (grill) the kebabs over hot coals for 5–8 minutes, turning and basting the beef and vegetables occasionally with the reserved teriyaki sauce.

7 Arrange the skewers on serving plates and pour the remaining sauce over the kebabs. Serve with a green salad.

Mexican Beef

Strips of beef cooked with (bell) peppers and onion and carrot in a tomato and chilli sauce are prepared quickly in the microwave.

NUTRITIONAL INFORMATION

Calories	513	Sugars	7g
Protein	33g	Fat	23g
Carbohydrate	46g	Saturates	8g

 30 MINS  35 MINS

SERVES 4

INGREDIENTS

- 225 g/8 oz/1 generous cup brown rice
- 700 ml/1¼ pints/3 cups boiling water
- ½ tsp salt
- 2 tbsp oil
- 1 onion, sliced into rings
- 1 carrot, cut into thin matchsticks
- ½ each red, green and yellow (bell) peppers
- ½–1 fresh green chilli, deseeded and chopped
- 1 garlic clove, crushed
- 500 g/1 lb 2 oz rump steak, cut into strips
- 225 g/8 oz/scant 1 cup canned tomatoes
- 1 tbsp tomato purée (paste)
- 2 tsp cornflour (cornstarch)
- sprigs of fresh coriander (cilantro), to garnish
- salt and pepper

SALSA

- tomatoes, skinned and chopped
- 2 spring onions (scallions), chopped
- 1 small fresh green chilli, deseeded and chopped
- 2 tbsp lime juice
- 1 tbsp chopped fresh coriander (cilantro)
- 8 flour tortillas

1. Place the rice in a large bowl. Add the boiling water and salt. Cover and cook on HIGH power for 15 minutes. Leave to stand, covered, for 5 minutes before draining.

2. Place the oil, onion and carrot in a large bowl. Cover and cook on HIGH power for 2 minutes. Slice the (bell) peppers, and add with the chilli, garlic and steak to the bowl. Cover and cook on HIGH power for 4 minutes, stirring once.

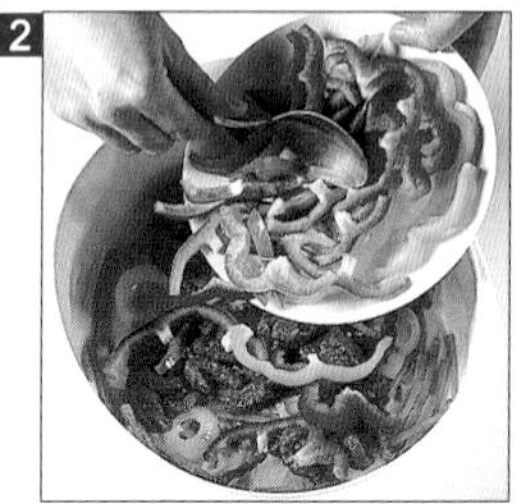

3. Add the canned tomatoes, tomato purée (paste) and seasoning. Mix the cornflour (cornstarch) with a little water, then stir into the bowl. Cover and cook on MEDIUM power for 10 minutes.

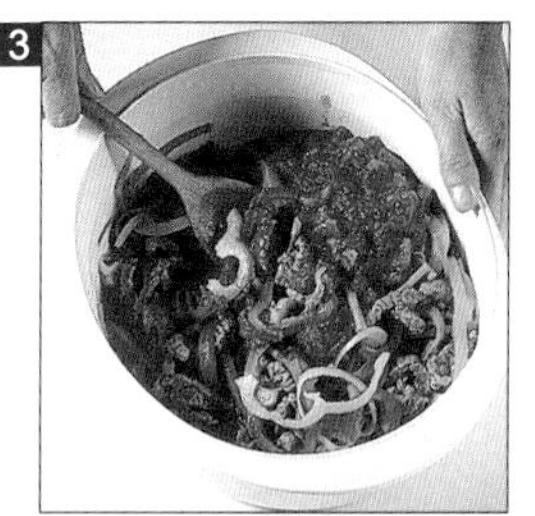

4. To make the salsa, mix together the tomatoes, spring onions (scallions), chilli, lime juice and coriander (cilantro). Season and leave to stand for 10 minutes.

5. Heat the tortillas on HIGH power for 40 seconds, covered, or according to the packet instructions.

6. Garnish the beef with fresh coriander (cilantro) sprigs and serve with the tortillas, rice and salsa.

Beef & Beans

The green of the beans complements the dark colour of the beef, served in a rich sauce.

NUTRITIONAL INFORMATION

Calories	381	Sugars	3g
Protein	25g	Fat	27g
Carbohydrate	10g	Saturates	8g

 35 MINS ⏱ 15 MINS

SERVES 4

INGREDIENTS

- 450 g/1 lb rump or fillet steak, cut into 2.5-cm/1-inch pieces

MARINADE

- 2 tsp cornflour (cornstarch)
- 2 tbsp dark soy sauce
- 2 tsp peanut oil

SAUCE

- 2 tbsp vegetable oil
- 3 garlic cloves, crushed
- 1 small onion, cut into 8
- 225 g/8 oz thin green beans, halved
- 25 g/1 oz/¼ cup unsalted cashews
- 25 g/1 oz canned bamboo shoots, drained and rinsed
- 2 tsp dark soy sauce
- 2 tsp Chinese rice wine or dry sherry
- 125 ml/4 fl oz/½ cup beef stock
- 2 tsp cornflour (cornstarch)
- 4 tsp water
- salt and pepper

2

3

6

1 To make the marinade, mix together the cornflour (cornstarch), soy sauce and peanut oil.

2 Place the steak in a shallow glass bowl. Pour the marinade over the steak, turn to coat thoroughly, cover and leave to marinate in the refrigerator for at least 30 minutes.

3 To make the sauce, heat the oil in a preheated wok. Add the garlic, onion, beans, cashews and bamboo shoots and stir-fry for 2–3 minutes.

4 Remove the steak from the marinade, drain, add to the wok and stir-fry for 3–4 minutes.

5 Mix the soy sauce, Chinese rice wine or sherry and beef stock together. Blend the cornflour (cornstarch) with the water and add to the soy sauce mixture, mixing to combine.

6 Stir the mixture into the wok and bring the sauce to the boil, stirring until thickened and clear. Reduce the heat and leave to simmer for 2–3 minutes. Season to taste and serve immediately.

Carrot-Topped Beef Pie

This is a variation of an old favourite, where a creamy mashed potato and carrot topping is piled thickly on to a delicious beef pie filling.

NUTRITIONAL INFORMATION

Calories	352	Sugars	6g
Protein	28g	Fat	11g
Carbohydrate	38g	Saturates	6g

 10 MINS  1¼ HOURS

SERVES 4

INGREDIENTS

- 450 g/1 lb lean ground beef
- 1 onion, chopped
- 1 garlic clove, crushed
- 1 tbsp plain (all-purpose) flour
- 300 ml/½ pint/1¼ cups beef stock
- 2 tbsp tomato purée (paste)
- 1 celery stick, chopped
- 3 tbsp chopped fresh parsley
- 1 tbsp Worcestershire sauce
- 675 g/1½ lb floury (mealy) potatoes, diced
- 2 large carrots, diced
- 25 g/1 oz/2 tbsp butter
- 3 tbsp skimmed milk
- salt and pepper

1 Dry fry the beef in a large pan set over a high heat for 3-4 minutes or until sealed. Add the onion and garlic and cook for a further 5 minutes, stirring.

2 Add the flour and cook for 1 minute. Gradually blend in the beef stock and tomato purée (paste). Stir in the celery, 1 tbsp of the parsley and the Worcestershire sauce. Season to taste.

3 Bring the mixture to the boil, then reduce the heat and simmer for 20-25 minutes. Spoon the beef mixture into a 1.1 litre/2 pint/5 cup pie dish.

4 Meanwhile, cook the potatoes and carrots in a saucepan of boiling water for 10 minutes. Drain and mash them together.

5 Stir the butter, milk and the remaining parsley into the potato and carrot mixture and season with salt and pepper to taste. Spoon the potato on top of the beef mixture to cover it completely; alternatively, pipe the potato with a piping (pastry) bag.

6 Cook the corrot-topped beef pie in a preheated oven, 190°C/375°F/Gas Mark 5, for 45 minutes or until cooked through. Serve piping hot.

1

2

5

Beef, Tomato & Olive Kebabs

These kebabs (kabobs) have a Mediterranean flavour. The sweetness of the tomatoes and the sharpness of the olives makes them rather more-ish.

NUTRITIONAL INFORMATION

Calories	166	Sugars	1g
Protein	12g	Fat	12g
Carbohydrate	1g	Saturates	3g

 45 MINS  15 MINS

SERVES 8

INGREDIENTS

- 450 g/1 lb rump or sirloin steak
- 16 cherry tomatoes
- 16 large green olives, pitted
- focaccia bread, to serve

BASTE

- 4 tbsp olive oil
- 1 tbsp sherry vinegar
- 1 clove garlic, crushed
- salt and pepper

FRESH TOMATO RELISH

- 1 tbsp olive oil
- ½ red onion, chopped finely
- 1 clove garlic, chopped
- 6 plum tomatoes, deseeded, skinned and chopped
- 2 pitted green olives, sliced
- 1 tbsp chopped, fresh parsley
- 1 tbsp lemon juice

1 Using a sharp knife, trim any fat from the beef and cut the meat into about 24 evenly-sized pieces.

2 Thread the pieces of beef on to 8 wooden skewers, alternating the meat with the cherry tomatoes and the green olives.

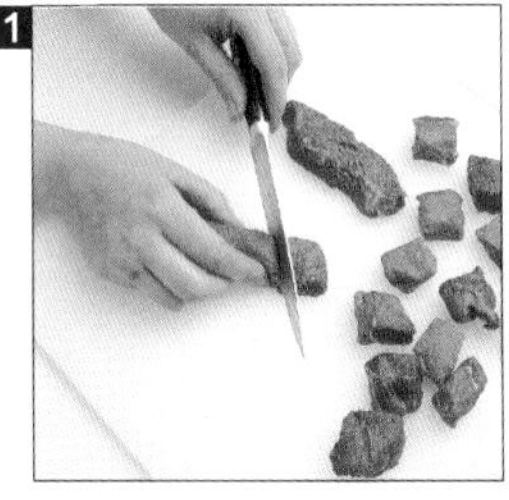
1

3

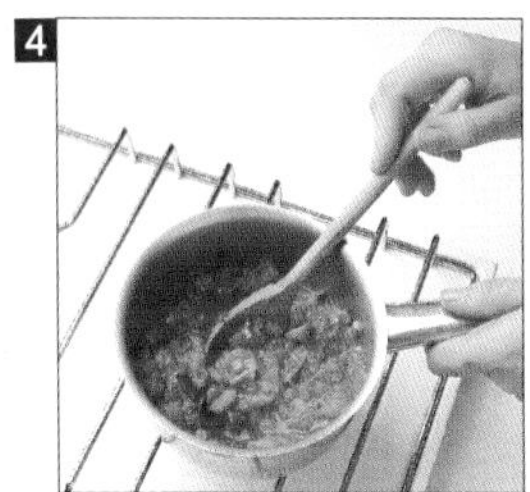
4

3 To make the baste, combine the oil, vinegar, garlic and salt and pepper to taste in a bowl.

4 To make the relish, heat the oil in a small pan and fry the onion and garlic for 3–4 minutes until softened. Add the tomatoes and olives and cook for 2–3 minutes until the tomatoes have softened slightly. Stir in the parsley and lemon juice and season with salt and pepper to taste. Set aside and keep warm or leave to chill.

5 Barbecue (grill) the kebabs (kabobs) on an oiled rack over hot coals for 5–10 minutes, basting and turning frequently. Serve with the tomato relish and slices of focaccia.

COOK'S TIP

The kebabs (kabobs), baste and relish can be prepared several hours in advance, avoiding the need for any last minute rush. For a simple meal, serve with crusty fresh bread and a mixed salad.

Beef & Bok Choy

In this recipe, a colourful selection of vegetables is stir-fried with tender strips of steak.

NUTRITIONAL INFORMATION

Calories	369	Sugars	9g
Protein	29g	Fat	23g
Carbohydrate	12g	Saturates	8g

 15 MINS  5 MINS

SERVES 4

INGREDIENTS

- 1 large head of bok choy, about 250-275 g/9-9½ oz, torn into large pieces
- 2 tbsp vegetable oil
- 2 garlic cloves, crushed
- 500 g/1 lb 2 oz rump or fillet steak, cut into thin strips
- 150 g/5½ oz mangetout (snow peas), trimmed
- 150 g/5½ oz baby or dwarf corn
- 6 spring onions (scallions), chopped
- 2 red (bell) peppers, cored, seeded and thinly sliced
- 2 tbsp oyster sauce
- 1 tbsp fish sauce
- 1 tbsp sugar
- rice or noodles, to serve

1 Steam the bok choy over boiling water until just tender. Keep warm.

2 Heat the oil in a large, heavy-based frying pan (skillet) or wok, add the garlic and steak strips and stir-fry until just browned, about 1-2 minutes.

3 Add the mangetout (snow peas), baby corn, spring onions (scallions), red (bell) pepper, oyster sauce, fish sauce and sugar to the pan, mixing well. Stir-fry for a further 2-3 minutes until the vegetables are just tender, but still crisp.

4 Arrange the bok choy leaves in the base of a heated serving dish and spoon the beef and vegetable mixture into the centre.

5 Serve the stir-fry immediately, with rice or noodles.

COOK'S TIP

Bok choy is one of the most important ingredients in this dish. If unavailable, use Chinese leaves (cabbage), kai choy (mustard leaves) or pak choy.

1

2

3

Rogan Josh

This is one of the best-known curries. Rogan Josh means 'red curry', and is so-called because of the red chillies in the recipe.

NUTRITIONAL INFORMATION

Calories	248	Sugars	2g
Protein	35g	Fat	11g
Carbohydrate	2g	Saturates	5g

 10 MINS  1¾ HOURS

SERVES 6

INGREDIENTS

- 2 tbsp ghee
- 1 kg/2 lb 4 oz lean braising steak, cut into 2.5 cm/1 inch cubes
- 1 onion, chopped finely
- 3 garlic cloves
- 2.5 cm/1 inch piece ginger root, grated
- 4 fresh red chillies, chopped
- 4 green cardamom pods
- 4 cloves
- 2 tsp coriander seeds
- 2 tsp cumin seeds
- 1 tsp paprika
- 1 tsp salt
- 1 bay leaf
- 125 ml/4 fl oz/¼ cup low-fat yogurt
- 2.5 cm/1 inch piece cinnamon stick
- 150 ml/¼ pint/⅔ cup hot water
- ¼ tsp garam masala
- pepper

2

3

5

1 Heat the ghee in a large flameproof casserole and brown the meat in batches. Remove the meat from the casserole and set aside in a bowl.

2 Add the chopped onion to the ghee and stir over a high heat for 3–4 minutes.

3 Grind together the garlic, ginger, chillies, cardamom, cloves, coriander, cumin, paprika and salt. Add the spice paste and bay leaf to the casserole and stir until fragrant.

4 Return the meat and any juices in the bowl to the casserole and simmer for 2–3 minutes. Gradually stir the yogurt into the casserole keeping the sauce simmering.

5 Stir in the cinnamon stick and hot water, and pepper to taste.

6 Cover the casserole and cook in a preheated oven, 180°C/350°F/Gas Mark 4, for 1¼ hours until the meat is very tender and the sauce is slightly reduced. Discard the cinnamon stick and stir in the garam masala. Remove surplus oil from the surface of the casserole before serving.

Fresh Spaghetti & Meatballs

This well-loved Italian dish is famous across the world. Make the most of it by using high-quality steak for the meatballs.

NUTRITIONAL INFORMATION

Calories	665	Sugars	9g
Protein	39g	Fat	24g
Carbohydrate	77g	Saturates	8g

 45 MINS  $1^1/_4$ HOURS

SERVES 4

INGREDIENTS

- 150 g/5½ oz/2½ cups brown breadcrumbs
- 150 ml/¼ pint/⅔ cup milk
- 25 g/1 oz/2 tbsp butter
- 25 g/1 oz/¼ cup wholemeal (whole-wheat) flour
- 200 ml/7 fl oz/⅞ cup beef stock
- 400 g/14 oz can chopped tomatoes
- 2 tbsp tomato purée (paste)
- 1 tsp sugar
- 1 tbsp finely chopped fresh tarragon
- 1 large onion, chopped
- 450 g/1 lb/4 cups minced steak
- 1 tsp paprika
- 4 tbsp olive oil
- 450 g/1 lb fresh spaghetti
- salt and pepper
- fresh tarragon sprigs, to garnish

1 Place the breadcrumbs in a bowl, add the milk and set aside to soak for about 30 minutes.

2 Melt half of the butter in a pan. Add the flour and cook, stirring constantly, for 2 minutes. Gradually stir in the beef stock and cook, stirring constantly, for a further 5 minutes. Add the tomatoes, tomato purée (paste), sugar and tarragon. Season well and simmer for 25 minutes.

3 Mix the onion, steak and paprika into the breadcrumbs and season to taste. Shape the mixture into 14 meatballs.

4 Heat the oil and remaining butter in a frying pan (skillet) and fry the meatballs, turning, until brown all over. Place in a deep casserole, pour over the tomato sauce, cover and bake in a preheated oven, at 180°C/350°F/Gas Mark 4, for 25 minutes.

5 Bring a large saucepan of lightly salted water to the boil. Add the fresh spaghetti, bring back to the boil and cook for about 2–3 minutes or until tender, but still firm to the bite.

6 Meanwhile, remove the meatballs from the oven and allow them to cool for 3 minutes. Serve the meatballs and their sauce with the spaghetti, garnished with tarragon sprigs.

Pathan Beef Stir-Fry

Although the meat can be left in the marinade overnight, this is a quick and tasty dish to make.

NUTRITIONAL INFORMATION			
Calories	325	Sugars	6g
Protein	41g	Fat	15g
Carbohydrate	7g	Saturates	5g

 2¼ HOURS  15 MINS

SERVES 4

INGREDIENTS

- 750 g/1 lb 10 oz fillet of lean beef, cut into 2.5 cm/1 inch strips
- 2 tbsp vegetable oil
- 1 onion
- 2.5 cm/1 inch piece ginger root, cut into strips
- 1 fresh red chilli, deseeded and sliced
- 2 carrots, cut into strips
- 1 green (bell) pepper, cut into strips
- 1 tsp garam masala
- 1 tbsp toasted sesame seeds

MARINADE

- 1 tsp dried fenugreek
- 1 tsp brown mustard seeds, ground
- 1 tsp ground cinnamon
- 1 tsp ground cumin
- 1 garlic clove, crushed
- 150 ml/¼ pint/⅔ cup low-fat natural yogurt

2

4

6

1 To make the marinade, mix the ingredients together in a bowl.

2 Mix the beef with the marinade, then cover and leave to marinate for 1–2 hours, or overnight in the refrigerator.

3 Heat the oil in a Balti pan or wok, add the onion and stir-fry until softened.

4 Stir in the ginger, chilli, carrots and green (bell) pepper and stir-fry for 1 minute.

5 Add the garam masala and beef with its marinade to the vegetables, and stir-fry for 8–10 minutes until the beef is tender; it is best if it is still pinkish inside.

6 Stir in the toasted sesame seeds and serve the stir-fry immediately.

VARIATION

Any selection of vegetables can be added to the stir-fry, which is a good way to use up any vegetables left over in the refrigerator, but add them to the beef for just long enough to heat through.

Creamed Strips of Sirloin

This quick and easy dish tastes superb and would make a delicious treat for a special occasion.

NUTRITIONAL INFORMATION

Calories	796	Sugars	2g
Protein	29g	Fat	63g
Carbohydrate	26g	Saturates	39g

 15 MINS  30 MINS

SERVES 4

INGREDIENTS

- 75 g/3 oz/6 tbsp butter
- 450 g/1 lb sirloin steak, trimmed and cut into thin strips
- 175 g/6 oz button mushrooms, sliced
- 1 tsp mustard
- pinch of freshly grated root ginger
- 2 tbsp dry sherry
- 150 ml/¼ pint/⅔ cup double (heavy) cream
- salt and pepper
- 4 slices hot toast, cut into triangles, to serve

PASTA

- 450 g/1 lb dried rigatoni
- 2 tbsp olive oil
- 2 fresh basil sprigs
- 115 g/4 oz/8 tbsp butter

1 Melt the butter in a large frying pan (skillet) and gently fry the steak over a low heat, stirring frequently, for 6 minutes. Using a slotted spoon, transfer the steak to an ovenproof dish and keep warm.

1

2 Add the sliced mushrooms to the frying pan (skillet) and cook for 2–3 minutes in the juices remaining in the pan. Add the mustard, ginger, salt and pepper. Cook for 2 minutes, then add the sherry and cream. Cook for a further 3 minutes, then pour the cream sauce over the steak.

2

3 Bake the steak and cream mixture in a preheated oven, at 90°C/375°F/Gas Mark 5, for 10 minutes.

4 Meanwhile, cook the pasta. Bring a large saucepan of lightly salted water to the boil. Add the rigatoni, olive oil and 1 of the basil sprigs and boil rapidly for 10 minutes, until tender but still firm to the bite. Drain the pasta and transfer to a warm serving plate. Toss the pasta with the butter and garnish with a sprig of basil.

2

5 Serve the creamed steak strips with the pasta and triangles of warm toast.

COOK'S TIP

Dried pasta will keep for up to 6 months. Keep it in the packet and reseal it once you have opened it, or transfer the pasta to an airtight jar.

Beef Daube

This dish is very French but also very, very New Orleans, especially when the beef is perked up with Tabasco and Cajun spices.

NUTRITIONAL INFORMATION

Calories	251	Sugars	2g
Protein	31g	Fat	10g
Carbohydrate	8g	Saturates	3g

10 MINS

3¼ HOURS

SERVES 6–8

INGREDIENTS

- 2 tbsp olive oil
- 1 large onion, cut into wedges
- 2 celery sticks, chopped
- 1 green (bell) pepper, cored, seeded and chopped
- 1 kg/2¼ lb lean braising steak, cubed
- 60 g/2 oz/½ cup plain flour, seasoned with salt and pepper
- 600 ml/1 pint/2½ cups beef stock
- 2 garlic cloves, crushed
- 150 ml/¼ pint/⅔ cup red wine
- 2 tbsp red wine vinegar
- 2 tbsp tomato purée (paste)
- ½ tsp Tabasco
- 1 tsp chopped fresh thyme
- 2 bay leaves
- ½ tsp Cajun spice mix
- French bread, to serve

1 Heat the oil in a large heavy-based, flameproof casserole. Add the onion wedges and cook until browned on all sides. Remove with a slotted spoon and set aside.

2 Add the celery and (bell) pepper to the pan and cook until softened. Remove the vegetables with a slotted spoon and set aside.

3 Coat the meat in the seasoned flour, add to the pan and sauté until browned on all sides.

4 Add the stock, garlic, wine, vinegar, tomato purée (paste), Tabasco and thyme and heat gently.

5 Return the onions, celery and peppers to the pan. Tuck in the bay leaves and sprinkle with the Cajun seasoning.

6 Bring to the boil, transfer to the oven and cook for 2½–3 hours, or until the meat and vegetables are tender.

7 Serve the beef daube with French bread.

Beef Chow Mein

Chow Mein must be the best-known and most popular noodle dish on any Chinese menu. You can use any meat or vegetables instead of beef.

NUTRITIONAL INFORMATION

Calories	341	Sugars	3g
Protein	27g	Fat	17g
Carbohydrate	20g	Saturates	4g

 10 MINS  20 MINS

SERVES 4

INGREDIENTS

- 450 g/1 lb egg noodles
- 4 tbsp peanut oil
- 450 g/1 lb lean beef steak, cut into thin strips
- 2 garlic cloves, crushed
- 1 tsp grated fresh root ginger
- 1 green (bell) pepper, thinly sliced
- 1 carrot, thinly sliced
- 2 celery sticks, sliced
- 8 spring onions (scallions)
- 1 tsp dark brown sugar
- 1 tbsp dry sherry
- 2 tbsp dark soy sauce
- few drops of chilli sauce

1 Cook the noodles in a saucepan of boiling salted water for 4-5 minutes. Drain well, rinse under cold running water and drain again thoroughly.

2 Toss the noodles in 1 tablespoon of the peanut oil.

3 Heat the remaining oil in a preheated wok. Add the beef and stir-fry for 3-4 minutes, stirring constantly.

4 Add the crushed garlic and grated fresh root ginger to the wok and stir-fry for 30 seconds.

5 Add the (bell) pepper, carrot, celery and spring onions (scallions) and stir-fry for about 2 minutes.

6 Add the dark brown sugar, dry sherry, dark soy sauce and chilli sauce to the mixture in the wok and cook, stirring, for 1 minute.

7 Stir in the noodles, mixing well, and cook until completely warmed through.

8 Transfer the noodles to warm serving bowls and serve immediately.

2

5

7

VARIATION

A variety of different vegetables may be used in this recipe for colour and flavour – try broccoli, red (bell) peppers, green beans or baby sweetcorn cobs.

Spicy Beef

In this recipe beef is marinated in a five-spice and chilli marinade for a spicy flavour.

NUTRITIONAL INFORMATION

Calories	246	Sugars	2g
Protein	21g	Fat	13g
Carbohydrate	10g	Saturates	3g

1¼ HOURS 10 MINS

SERVES 4

INGREDIENTS

225 g/8 oz fillet steak
2 garlic cloves, crushed
1 tsp powdered star anise
1 tbsp dark soy sauce
spring onion (scallion) tassels, to garnish

SAUCE

2 tbsp vegetable oil
1 bunch spring onions (scallions), halved lengthways
1 tbsp dark soy sauce
1 tbsp dry sherry
¼ tsp chilli sauce
150 ml/¼ pint/⅔ cup water
2 tsp cornflour (cornstarch)
4 tsp water

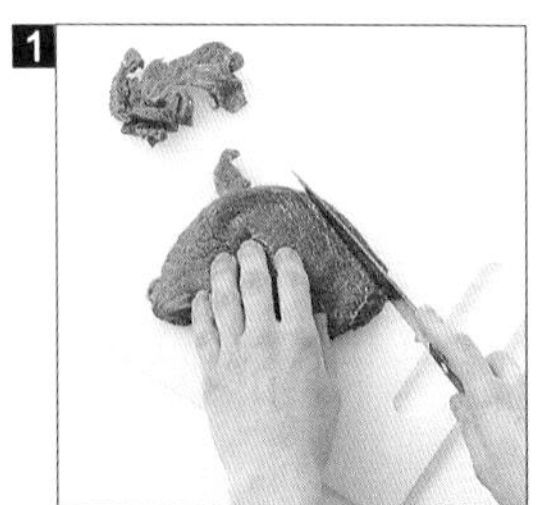

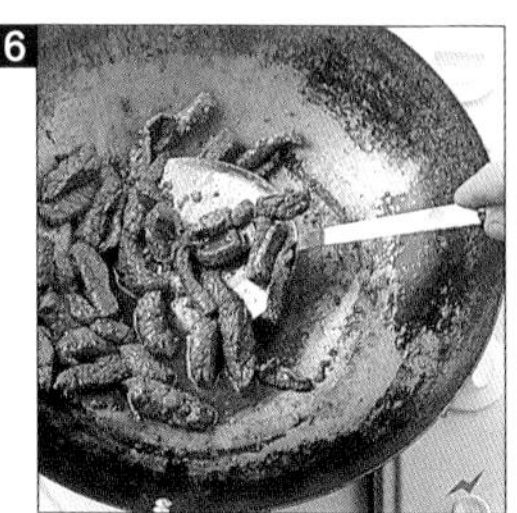

1 Cut the steak into thin strips and place in a shallow dish.

2 Mix together the garlic, star anise and dark soy sauce in a bowl.

3 Pour the sauce mixture over the steak strips, turning them to coat thoroughly. Cover and leave to marinate in the refrigerator for at least 1 hour.

4 To make the sauce, heat the oil in a preheated wok or large frying pan (skillet). Reduce the heat and stir-fry the spring onions (scallions) for 1-2 minutes.

5 Remove the spring onions (scallions) from the wok with a slotted spoon, drain on absorbent kitchen paper (paper towels) and set aside until required.

6 Add the beef to the wok, together with the marinade, and stir-fry for 3-4 minutes. Return the spring onions (scallions) to the wok and add the soy sauce, sherry, chilli sauce and two thirds of the water.

7 Blend the cornflour (cornstarch) with the remaining water and stir into the wok. Bring to the boil, stirring until the sauce thickens and clears.

8 Transfer to a warm serving dish, garnish and serve immediately.

Beef & Broccoli Stir-fry

This is a great combination of ingredients in terms of colour and flavour, and it is so simple and quick to prepare.

NUTRITIONAL INFORMATION

Calories	232	Sugars	1g
Protein	12g	Fat	19g
Carbohydrate	4g	Saturates	6g

4¼ HOURS 15 MINS

SERVES 4

INGREDIENTS

- 225 g/8 oz lean steak, trimmed
- 2 garlic cloves, crushed
- dash of chilli oil
- 1-cm/½-inch piece fresh root ginger, grated
- ½ tsp Chinese five-spice powder
- 2 tbsp dark soy sauce
- 2 tbsp vegetable oil
- 150 g/5½ oz broccoli florets
- 1 tbsp light soy sauce
- 150 ml/¼ pint/⅔ cup beef stock
- 2 tsp cornflour (cornstarch)
- 4 tsp water
- carrot strips, to garnish

1 Using a sharp knife, cut the steak into thin strips and place in a shallow glass dish.

2 Mix together the garlic, chilli oil, grated ginger, Chinese five-spice powder and dark soy sauce in a small bowl and pour over the beef, tossing to coat the strips evenly.

3 Cover the bowl and leave the meat to marinate in the refrigerator for several hours to allow the flavours to develop fully.

4 Heat 1 tablespoon of the vegetable oil in a preheated wok or large frying pan (skillet). Add the broccoli and stir-fry over a medium heat for 4–5 minutes. Remove from the wok with a slotted spoon and set aside until required.

5 Heat the remaining oil in the wok. Add the steak together with the marinade, and stir-fry for 2-3 minutes, until the steak is browned and sealed.

6 Return the broccoli to the wok and stir in the light soy sauce and stock.

7 Blend the cornflour (cornstarch) with the water to form a smooth paste and stir into the wok. Bring to the boil, stirring, until thickened and clear. Cook for 1 minute. Transfer the beef & broccoli stir-fry to a warm serving dish, arrange the carrot strips in a lattice on top and serve immediately.

2

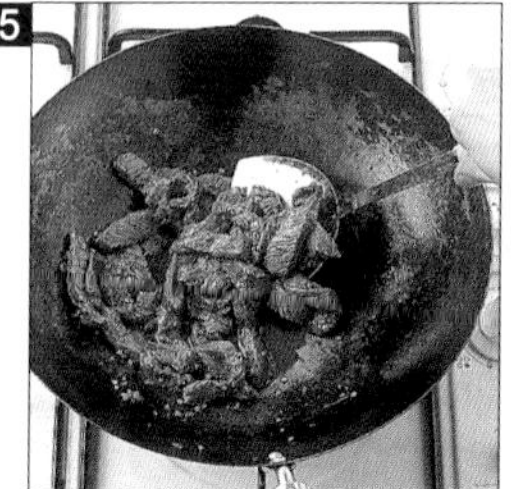

5

6

Roman Pan-fried Lamb

Chunks of tender lamb, pan-fried with garlic and stewed in red wine are a real Roman dish.

NUTRITIONAL INFORMATION

Calories	299	Sugars	1g
Protein	31g	Fat	16g
Carbohydrate	1g	Saturates	7g

 15 MINS  50 MINS

SERVES 4

INGREDIENTS

- 1 tbsp oil
- 15 g/½ oz/1 tbsp butter
- 600 g/1 lb 5 oz lamb (shoulder or leg), cut into 2.5 cm/1 inch chunks
- 4 garlic cloves, peeled
- 3 sprigs thyme, stalks removed
- 6 canned anchovy fillets
- 150 ml/¼ pint/⅔ cup red wine
- 150 ml/¼ pint/⅔ cup lamb or vegetable stock
- 1 tsp sugar
- 50 g/1¾ oz black olives, pitted and halved
- 2 tbsp chopped parsley, to garnish
- mashed potato, to serve

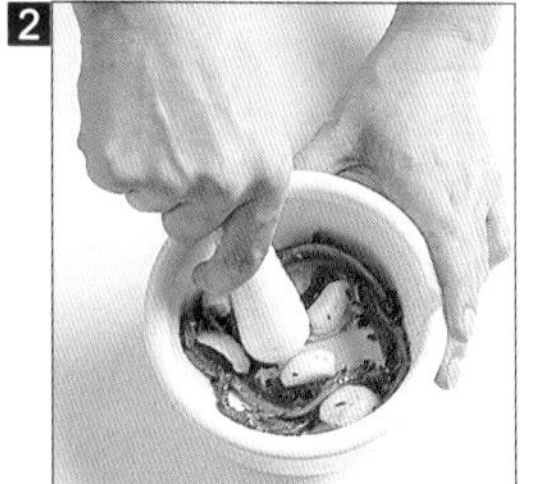

1 Heat the oil and butter in a large frying pan (skillet). Add the lamb and cook for 4–5 minutes, stirring, until the meat is browned all over.

2 Using a pestle and mortar, grind together the garlic, thyme and anchovies to make a smooth paste.

3 Add the wine and lamb or vegetable stock to the frying pan (skillet). Stir in the garlic and anchovy paste together with the sugar.

4 Bring the mixture to the boil, reduce the heat, cover and simmer for 30–40 minutes or until the lamb is tender. For the last 10 minutes of the cooking time, remove the lid to allow the sauce to reduce slightly.

5 Stir the olives into the sauce and mix to combine.

6 Transfer the lamb and the sauce to a serving bowl and garnish. Serve with creamy mashed potatoes.

COOK'S TIP

Rome is the capital of both the region of Lazio and Italy and thus has become a focal point for specialities from all over Italy. Food from this region tends to be fairly simple and quick to prepare, all with plenty of herbs and seasonings giving really robust flavours.

Turkish Lamb Stew

A delicious blend of flavours with lamb, onions and tomatoes, complete with potatoes to make the perfect one-pot dish for two.

NUTRITIONAL INFORMATION

Calories	442	Sugars	5g
Protein	41g	Fat	17g
Carbohydrate	35g	Saturates	7g

 10 MINS  1¼ HOURS

SERVES 2

INGREDIENTS

- 350 g/12 oz lean boneless lamb
- 1 large or 2 small onions
- 1 garlic clove, crushed
- ½ red, yellow or green (bell) pepper, diced roughly
- 300 ml/½ pint/1¼ cups stock
- 1 tbsp balsamic vinegar
- 2 tomatoes, peeled and chopped roughly
- 1½ tsp tomato purée (paste)
- 1 bay leaf
- ½ tsp dried sage
- ½ tsp dried dillweed
- 350 g/12 oz potatoes
- 6–8 black olives, halved and pitted
- salt and pepper

1. Cut the piece of lamb into cubes of about 2 cm/¾ inch, discarding any excess fat or gristle.

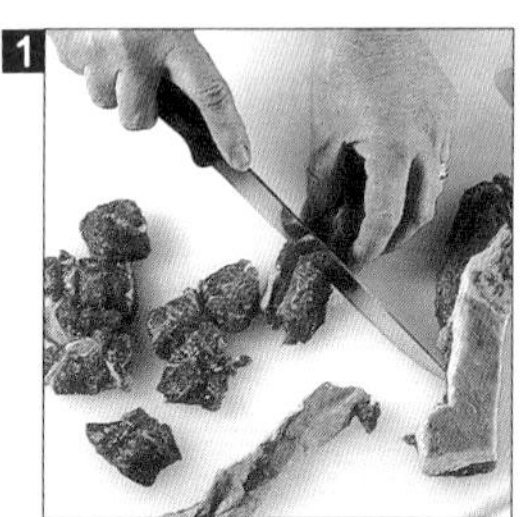

2. Place in a non-stick saucepan with no extra fat and heat gently until the fat runs and the meat begins to seal.

3. Cut the onion into 8 wedges. Add to the lamb with the garlic and fry for a further 3–4 minutes.

4. Add the (bell) pepper, stock, vinegar, tomatoes, tomato purée (paste), bay leaf, sage, dillweed and seasoning. Cover and simmer gently for 30 minutes.

5. Peel the potatoes and cut into 2 cm/¾ inch cubes. Add to the stew and stir well. If necessary, add a little more boiling stock or water if it seems a little dry. Cover the pan again and simmer for a further 25–30 minutes, or until tender.

6. Add the olives and adjust the seasoning. Simmer for a further 5 minutes and serve with vegetables or a salad and crusty bread.

COOK'S TIP

A good accompaniment would be a salad made of shredded white cabbage, Little Gem lettuce, coarsely grated carrot, diced avocado or cucumber and spring onions (scallions).

Lamb with Garlic Sauce

This dish contains Szechuan pepper which is quite hot and may be replaced with black pepper, if preferred.

NUTRITIONAL INFORMATION

Calories	320	Sugars	2g
Protein	25g	Fat	21g
Carbohydrate	4g	Saturates	6g

 35 MINS  10 MINS

SERVES 4

INGREDIENTS

- 450 g/1 lb lamb fillet or loin
- 2 tbsp dark soy sauce
- 2 tsp sesame oil
- 2 tbsp Chinese rice wine or dry sherry
- ½ tsp Szechuan pepper
- 4 tbsp vegetable oil
- 4 garlic cloves, crushed
- 60 g/2 oz water chestnuts, quartered
- 1 green (bell) pepper, seeded and sliced
- 1 tbsp wine vinegar
- 1 tbsp sesame oil
- rice or noodles, to serve

1 Cut the lamb into 2.5-cm/1-inch pieces and place in a shallow dish.

2 Mix together 1 tablespoon of the soy sauce, the sesame oil, Chinese rice wine or sherry and Szechuan pepper. Pour the mixture over the lamb, turning to coat, and leave to marinate for 30 minutes.

3 Heat the vegetable oil in a preheated wok. Remove the lamb from the marinade and add to the wok, together with the garlic. Stir-fry for 2–3 minutes.

4 Add the water chestnuts and (bell) pepper and stir-fry for 1 minute.

5 Add the remaining soy sauce and the wine vinegar, mixing together well.

6 Add the sesame oil and cook, stirring constantly, for 1–2 minutes, or until the lamb is cooked through.

7 Transfer the lamb and garlic sauce to a warm serving dish and serve immediately with rice or noodles.

COOK'S TIP

Chinese chives, also known as garlic chives, would make an appropriate garnish.

Sesame oil is used as a flavouring, rather than for frying, as it burns readily, hence it is added at the end of cooking.

Masala Kebabs

Indian kebab dishes are not necessarily cooked on a skewer; they can also be served in a dish and are always dry dishes with no sauce.

NUTRITIONAL INFORMATION

Calories	294	Sugars	0g
Protein	35g	Fat	17g
Carbohydrate	0g	Saturates	7g

1¼ HOURS 20 MINS

SERVES 4

INGREDIENTS

1 dried bay leaf

2.5 cm/1 inch piece ginger root, chopped

2.5 cm/1 inch cinnamon stick

1 tsp coriander seeds

½ tsp salt

1 tsp fennel seeds

1 tsp chilli powder

1 tsp garam masala

1 tsp lemon juice

1 tsp ground turmeric

1 tbsp oil

750 g/1 lb 10 oz lamb neck fillet

TO GARNISH

sprigs of fresh coriander (cilantro)

lemon wedges

TO SERVE

bread

chutney

1

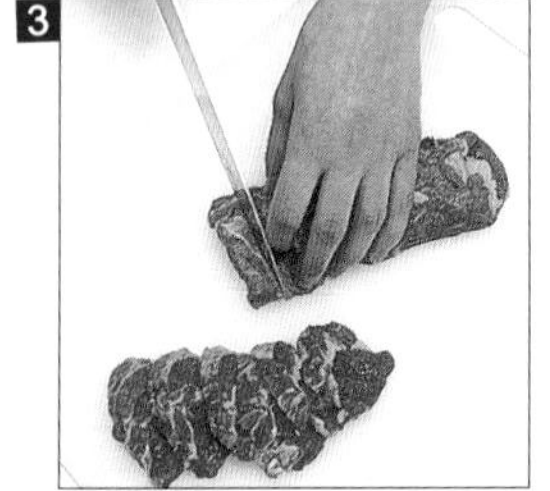

3

4

1 Use a food processor, blender or pestle and mortar to grind together the bay leaf, ginger, cinnamon, coriander seeds, salt, fennel seeds and chilli powder.

2 Combine this spice mix with the garam masala, lemon juice, turmeric and oil in a large bowl.

3 Cut the lamb into 5 mm/¼ inch slices. Add to the spice mix and leave to marinate at room temperature for about 1 hour, or in the refrigerator for 3 hours or overnight.

4 Spread out the pieces of lamb on a baking sheet and cook in a preheated oven, 200°C/400°F/Gas Mark 6, for 20 minutes until well done. Transfer the pices of lamb to paper towels to drain any excess fat.

5 Thread 3 or 4 pieces of meat on to each skewer and garnish with sprigs of fresh coriander (cilantro) and lemon wedges.

6 Serve the masala kebabs hot with bread and chutney.

Lamb with Olives

This is a very simple dish, and the chilli adds a bit of spiciness. It is quick to prepare and makes an ideal supper dish.

NUTRITIONAL INFORMATION

Calories	577	Sugars	1g
Protein	62g	Fat	33g
Carbohydrate	1g	Saturates	10g

15 MINS

1½ HOURS

SERVES 4

INGREDIENTS

- 1.25 kg/2 lb 12 oz boned leg of lamb
- 90 ml/3 fl oz/⅓ cup olive oil
- 2 garlic cloves, crushed
- 1 onion, sliced
- 1 small red chilli, cored, deseeded and chopped finely
- 175 ml/6 fl oz/¾ cup dry white wine
- 175 g/6 oz/1 cup pitted black olives
- salt
- chopped fresh parsley, to garnish

1 Using a sharp knife, cut the lamb into 2.5 cm/1 inch cubes.

2 Heat the oil in a frying pan (skillet) and fry the garlic, onion and chilli for 5 minutes.

3 Add the meat and wine and cook for a further 5 minutes.

4 Stir in the olives, then transfer the mixture to a casserole. Place in a preheated oven, 180°C/350°F/Gas Mark 4, and cook for 1 hour 20 minutes or until the meat is tender. Season with salt to taste, and serve garnished with chopped fresh parsley.

Lamb & Potato Masala

To create delicious Indian dishes at home – simply open a can of curry sauce, add a few interesting ingredients and you have a splendid meal.

NUTRITIONAL INFORMATION

Calories	513	Sugars	6g
Protein	40g	Fat	27g
Carbohydrate	30g	Saturates	8g

15 MINS

1½ HOURS

SERVES 4

INGREDIENTS

- 750 g/1 lb 10 oz lean lamb (from the leg)
- 3 tbsp ghee or vegetable oil
- 500 g/1 lb 2 oz potatoes, peeled and cut in large 2.5 cm/1 inch pieces
- 1 large onion, peeled, quartered and sliced
- 2 garlic cloves, peeled and crushed
- 175 g/6 oz mushrooms, thickly sliced
- 1 x 283 g/10 oz can Tikka Masala Curry Sauce
- 300 ml/½ pint/1¼ cups water
- salt
- 3 tomatoes, halved and cut into thin slices
- 125g/4½ oz spinach, washed and stalks trimmed
- sprigs of mint, to garnish

1 Cut the lamb into 2.5 cm/1 inch cubes. Heat the ghee or oil in a large pan, add the lamb and fry over moderate heat for 3 minutes or until sealed all over. Removethe lamb from the pan.

2 Add the potatoes, onion, garlic and mushrooms and fry for 3-4 minutes, stirring frequently.

3 Stir the curry sauce and water into the pan, add the lamb, mix well and season with salt to taste. Cover and cook very gently for 1 hour or until the lamb is tender and cooked through, stirring occasionally.

4 Add the sliced tomatoes and the spinach to the pan, pushing the leaves well down into the mixture, then cover and cook for a further 10 minutes until the spinach is cooked and tender.

5 Garnish with mint sprigs and serve hot.

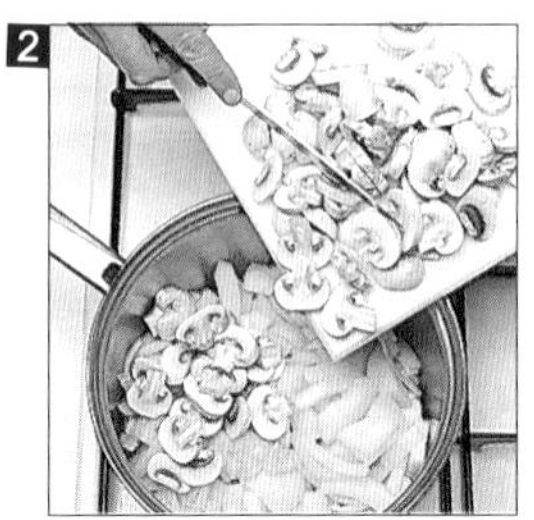

COOK'S TIP

Spinach leaves wilt quickly during cooking, so if the leaves are young and tender add them whole to the mixture; larger leaves may be coarsely shredded, if wished, before adding to the pan.

Lamb Cutlets with Rosemary

A classic combination of flavours, this dish would make a perfect Sunday lunch. Serve with tomato and onion salad and jacket potatoes.

NUTRITIONAL INFORMATION

Calories	560	Sugars	1g
Protein	48g	Fat	40g
Carbohydrate	1g	Saturates	13g

 $1^1/_4$ HOURS  15 MINS

SERVES 4

INGREDIENTS

- 8 lamb cutlets
- 5 tbsp olive oil
- 2 tbsp lemon juice
- 1 clove garlic, crushed
- ½ tsp lemon pepper
- salt
- 8 sprigs rosemary
- jacket potatoes, to serve

SALAD

- 4 tomatoes, sliced
- 4 spring onions (scallion), sliced diagonally

DRESSING

- 2 tbsp olive oil
- 1 tbsp lemon juice
- 1 clove garlic, chopped
- ¼ tsp fresh rosemary, chopped finely

1

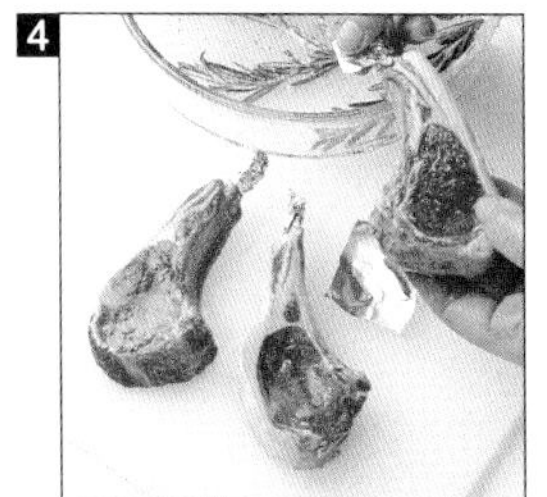
4

5

1 Trim the lamb chops by cutting away the flesh with a sharp knife to expose the tips of the bones.

2 Place the oil, lemon juice, garlic, lemon pepper and salt in a shallow, non-metallic dish and whisk with a fork to combine.

3 Lay the sprigs of rosemary in the dish and place the lamb on top. Leave to marinate for at least 1 hour, turning the lamb cutlets once.

4 Remove the chops from the marinade and wrap a little kitchen foil around the bones to stop them from burning.

5 Place the rosemary sprigs on the rack and place the lamb on top. Barbecue (grill) for 10–15 minutes, turning once.

6 Meanwhile make the salad and dressing. Arrange the tomatoes on a serving dish and scatter the spring onions (scallions) on top. Place all the ingredients for the dressing in a screw-top jar, shake well and pour over the salad. Serve with the lamb cutlets and jacket potatoes.

COOK'S TIP

Choose medium to small baking potatoes if you want to cook jacket potatoes on the barbecue (grill). Scrub them well, prick with a fork and wrap in buttered kitchen foil. Bury them in the hot coals and barbecue (grill) for 50–60 minutes.

Hot Lamb

This is quite a spicy dish, using 2 chillies in the sauce. Halve the number of chillies to reduce the heat or seed the chillies before using if desired.

NUTRITIONAL INFORMATION

Calories	323	Sugars	4g
Protein	26g	Fat	22g
Carbohydrate	5g	Saturates	7g

25 MINS 15 MINS

SERVES 4

INGREDIENTS

- 450 g/1 lb lean, boneless lamb
- 2 tbsp hoisin sauce
- 1 tbsp dark soy sauce
- 1 garlic clove, crushed
- 2 tsp grated fresh root ginger
- 2 tbsp vegetable oil
- 2 onions, sliced
- 1 fennel bulb, sliced
- 4 tbsp water

SAUCE

- 1 large fresh red chilli, cut into thin strips
- 1 fresh green chilli, cut into thin strips
- 2 tbsp rice wine vinegar
- 2 tsp light brown sugar
- 2 tbsp peanut oil
- 1 tsp sesame oil

1 Cut the lamb into 2.5-cm/1-inch cubes and place in a glass dish.

2 Mix together the hoisin sauce, soy sauce, garlic and ginger and pour over the lamb, turning to coat well. Leave to marinate for 20 minutes.

3 Heat the oil in a preheated wok and stir-fry the lamb for 1–2 minutes. Add the onions and fennel and cook for a further 2 minutes, or until they are just beginning to brown. Stir in the water, cover and cook for 2–3 minutes.

4 To make the sauce, place all the ingredients in a pan and cook over a low heat for 3-4 minutes, stirring.

5 Transfer the lamb and onions to a serving dish, toss lightly in the sauce and serve immediately.

VARIATION

Use beef, pork or duck instead of the lamb and vary the vegetables, using leeks or celery instead of the onion and fennel.

Irish Stew with Dumplings

This traditional recipe makes a hearty stew with fluffy parsley dumplings. Cubes of lean lamb shoulder could be used in place of the cutlets.

NUTRITIONAL INFORMATION

Calories	576	Sugars	4g
Protein	27g	Fat	28g
Carbohydrate	55g	Saturates	12g

 10 MINS

 1¼ HOURS

SERVES 4

INGREDIENTS

- 2 tbsp vegetable oil
- 2 large onions, sliced
- 1 leek, sliced
- 1 large carrot, sliced
- 2 celery sticks, sliced
- 850 ml/1½ pints/3¾ cups lamb stock
- 750 g/1 lb 10 oz lean lamb cutlets, trimmed
- 60 g/2 oz/⅓ cup pearl barley
- 2 large potatoes, peeled and cut into large chunks
- salt and pepper
- chopped fresh parsley, to garnish

DUMPLINGS

- 90 g/3 oz self-raising flour
- 25 g/1 oz/¼ cup porridge oats
- 2 tbsp chopped fresh parsley
- pinch of salt
- 60 g/2 oz vegetable suet
- chilled water, to mix

1 First make the dumplings. Put the flour, oats, parsley and salt into a large mixing bowl. Stir in the suet. Add sufficient chilled water to make a soft, but not sticky, dough. Shape into 8 dumplings, cover with a tea towel and set aside.

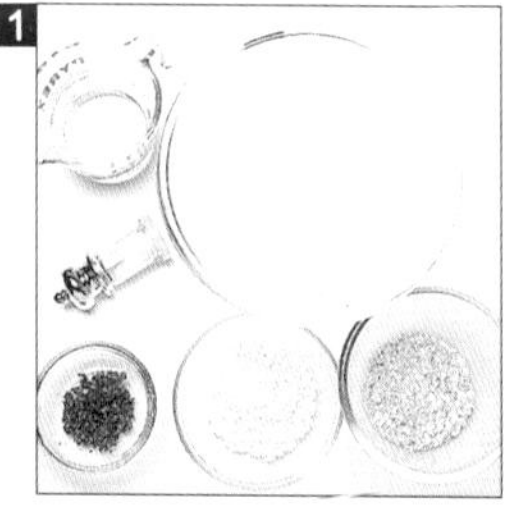

1

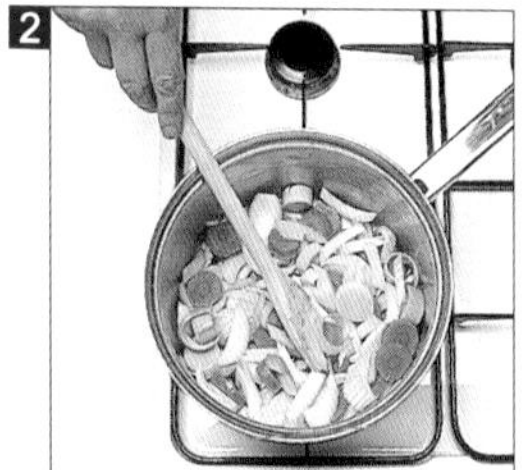

2

2 Heat the vegetable oil in a large saucepan and gently fry the onions, leek, carrot and celery for 5 minutes, without browning.

3 Add the stock, lamb and pearl barley to the saucepan. Bring to the boil and then reduce the heat. Cover and simmer for 20 minutes.

4

4 Add the potatoes and cook for a further 20 minutes. Add the dumplings to the saucepan. Cover and simmer for 15–20 minutes until the dumplings are light and fluffy.

5 Season the stew with salt and pepper, garnish with parsley and serve immediately while still hot.

Five-spice Lamb

Chinese five-spice powder is a blend of cinnamon, fennel, star anise, ginger and cloves, all finely ground together.

NUTRITIONAL INFORMATION

Calories	361	Sugars	3g
Protein	35g	Fat	22g
Carbohydrate	5g	Saturates	8g

 1¼ HOURS  10 MINS

SERVES 4

INGREDIENTS

- 625 g/1 lb 6 oz lean boneless lamb (leg or fillet)
- 2 tsp Chinese five-spice powder
- 3 tbsp sunflower oil
- 1 red (bell) pepper, cored, seeded and thinly sliced
- 1 green (bell) pepper, cored, seeded and thinly sliced
- 1 yellow or orange (bell) pepper, cored, seeded and thinly sliced
- 4-6 spring onions (scallions), thinly sliced diagonally
- 175 g/6 oz French (green) or fine beans, cut into 4 cm/1½ inch lengths
- 2 tbsp soy sauce
- 4 tbsp sherry
- salt and pepper
- Chinese noodles, to serve

TO GARNISH

- strips of red and yellow (bell) pepper
- fresh coriander (cilantro) leaves

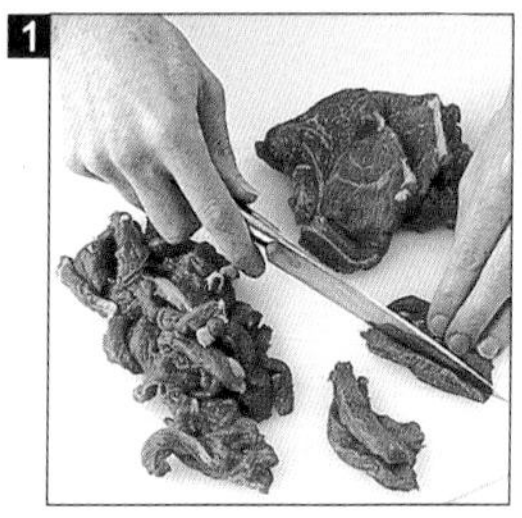

1 Cut the lamb into narrow strips, about 4 cm/1½ inches long, across the grain. Place in a bowl, add the five-spice powder and ¼ teaspoon salt, mix well and leave to marinate, covered, in a cool place for at least an hour and up to 24 hours.

2 Heat half the oil in the wok, swirling it around until really hot. Add the lamb and stir-fry briskly for 3-4 minutes until almost cooked through. Remove from the pan and set aside.

3 Add the remaining oil to the wok and when hot add the (bell) peppers and spring onions (scallions). Stir-fry for 2-3 minutes, then add the beans and stir for a minute or so.

4 Add the soy sauce and sherry to the wok and when hot return the lamb and any juices to the wok. Stir-fry for 1-2 minutes until the lamb is really hot again and thoroughly coated in the sauce. Season to taste.

5 Serve the Five-spice Lamb with Chinese noodles, garnished with strips of red and green (bell) pepper and fresh coriander (cilantro).

Sesame Lamb Stir-Fry

This is a very simple, but delicious dish, in which lean pieces of lamb are cooked in sugar and soy sauce and then sprinkled with sesame seeds.

NUTRITIONAL INFORMATION

Calories	276	Sugars	4g
Protein	25g	Fat	18g
Carbohydrate	5g	Saturates	6g

 5 MINS  10 MINS

SERVES 4

INGREDIENTS

- 450 g/1 lb boneless lean lamb
- 2 tbsp peanut oil
- 2 leeks, sliced
- 1 carrot, cut into matchsticks
- 2 garlic cloves, crushed
- 85 ml/3 fl oz/⅓ cup lamb or vegetable stock
- 2 tsp light brown sugar
- 1 tbsp dark soy sauce
- 4½ tsp sesame seeds

1 Using a sharp knife, cut the lamb into thin strips.

2 Heat the peanut oil in a preheated wok or large frying pan (skillet) until it is really hot.

3 Add the lamb and stir-fry for 2–3 minutes. Remove the lamb from the wok with a slotted spoon and set aside until required.

4 Add the leeks, carrot and garlic to the wok or frying pan (skillet) and stir-fry in the remaining oil for 1–2 minutes.

5 Remove the vegetables from the wok with a slotted spoon and set aside.

6 Drain any remaining oil from the wok. Place the lamb or vegetable stock, light brown sugar and dark soy sauce in the wok and add the lamb. Cook, stirring constantly to coat the lamb, for 2–3 minutes.

3

4

6

7 Sprinkle the sesame seeds over the top, turning the lamb to coat.

8 Spoon the leek, carrot and garlic mixture on to a warm serving dish and top with the lamb. Serve immediately.

COOK'S TIP

Be careful not to burn the sugar in the wok when heating and coating the meat, otherwise the flavour of the dish will be spoiled.

Fruity Lamb Casserole

The sweet spicy blend of cinnamon, coriander and cumin is the perfect foil for the tender lamb and apricots in this warming casserole.

NUTRITIONAL INFORMATION

Calories	384	Sugars	16g
Protein	32g	Fat	22g
Carbohydrate	17g	Saturates	9g

 5 MINS  1¼ HOURS

SERVES 4

INGREDIENTS

- 450 g/1 lb lean lamb, trimmed and cut into 2.5 cm/1 inch cubes
- 1 tsp ground cinnamon
- 1 tsp ground coriander
- 1 tsp ground cumin
- 2 tsp olive oil
- 1 medium red onion, finely chopped
- 1 garlic clove, crushed
- 400 g/14 oz can chopped tomatoes
- 2 tbsp tomato purée (paste)
- 125 g/4½ oz no-soak dried apricots
- 1 tsp caster (superfine) sugar
- 300 ml/½ pint/1¼ cups vegetable stock
- salt and pepper
- 1 small bunch fresh coriander (cilantro), to garnish
- brown rice, steamed couscous or bulgar wheat, to serve

1 Preheat the oven to 180°C/350°F/Gas Mark 4. Place the meat in a mixing bowl and add the spices and oil. Mix thoroughly so that the lamb is well coated in the spices.

2 Heat a non-stick frying pan (skillet) for a few seconds until it is hot, then add the spiced lamb. Reduce the heat and cook for 4–5 minutes, stirring, until browned all over. Using a slotted spoon, remove the lamb and transfer to a large ovenproof casserole.

3 In the same frying pan (skillet), cook the onion, garlic, tomatoes and tomato purée (paste) for 5 minutes. Season to taste. Stir in the apricots and sugar, add the stock and bring to the boil.

4 Spoon the sauce over the lamb and mix well. Cover and cook in the oven for 1 hour, removing the lid for the last 10 minutes.

5 Roughly chop the coriander (cilantro) and sprinkle over the casserole to garnish. Serve with brown rice, steamed couscous or bulgar wheat.

1

2

3

Minty Lamb Kebabs

These spicy lamb kebabs go well with the cool cucumber and yogurt dip. In the summer you can barbecue (grill) the kebabs outside.

NUTRITIONAL INFORMATION

Calories	295	Sugars	4g
Protein	29g	Fat	18g
Carbohydrate	4g	Saturates	9g

 5 MINS  20 MINS

SERVES 4

INGREDIENTS

- 2 tsp coriander seeds
- 2 tsp cumin seeds
- 3 cloves
- 3 green cardamom pods
- 6 black peppercorns
- 1 cm/½ inch piece ginger root
- 2 garlic cloves
- 2 tbsp chopped fresh mint
- 1 small onion, chopped
- 400 g/14 oz/1¾ cups minced (ground) lamb
- ½ tsp salt
- lime slices to serve

DIP

- 150 ml/5 fl oz/⅔ cup low-fat natural yogurt
- 2 tbsp chopped fresh mint
- 7 cm/3 inch piece of cucumber, grated
- 1 tsp mango chutney

2

3

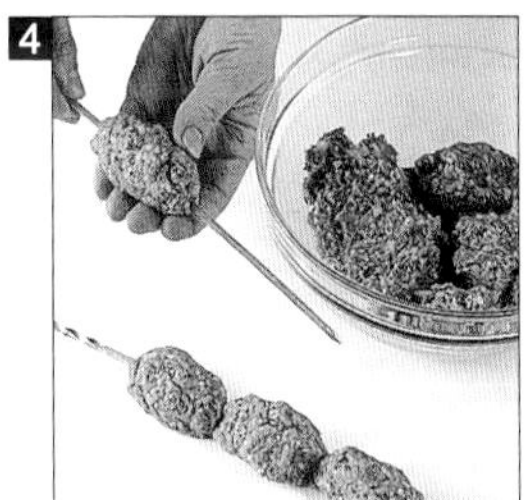

4

1 Heat a frying pan (skillet) and dry-fry the coriander, cumin, cloves, cardamom pods and peppercorns until they turn a shade darker and release a roasted aroma.

2 Grind the spices in a coffee grinder, spice mill or a pestle and mortar.

3 Put the ginger and garlic into a food processor or blender and process to a purée. Add the ground spices, mint, onion, lamb and salt and process until chopped finely. Alternatively, finely chop the garlic and ginger and mix with the ground spices and remaining kebab ingredients.

4 Mould the kebab mixture into small sausage shapes on 4 kebab skewers. Cook under a preheated hot grill (broiler) for 10–15 minutes, turning the skewers occasionally.

5 To make the dip, mix together the yogurt, mint, cucumber and mango chutney.

6 Serve the kebabs with lime slices and the dip.

Lamb & Ginger Stir-fry

Slices of lamb cooked with garlic, ginger and shiitake mushrooms make a quick and easy supper. It is best served with Chinese egg noodles.

NUTRITIONAL INFORMATION

Calories	347	Sugars	2g
Protein	31g	Fat	21g
Carbohydrate	7g	Saturates	7g

 10 MINS  5 MINS

SERVES 4

INGREDIENTS

- 500 g/1 lb 2 oz lamb fillet (tenderloin)
- 2 tbsp sunflower oil
- 1 tbsp chopped ginger root
- 2 garlic cloves, chopped
- 6 spring onions (scallions), white and green parts diagonally sliced
- 175 g/6 oz shiitake mushrooms, sliced
- 175 g/6 oz sugar snap peas
- 1 tsp cornflour (cornstarch)
- 2 tbsp dry sherry
- 1 tbsp light soy sauce
- 1 tsp sesame oil
- 1 tbsp sesame seeds, toasted
- Chinese egg noodles to serve

1 Using a sharp knife or meat cleaver, cut the lamb into 5 mm/$^1/_2$ inch slices.

2 Heat the sunflower oil in a large preheated wok or frying pan (skillet).

3 Add the lamb to the wok or frying pan (skillet) and stir-fry for 2 minutes.

4 Add the chopped ginger root, chopped garlic cloves, sliced spring onions (scallions), mushrooms and sugar snap peas and stir-fry for 2 minutes.

5 Blend the cornflour (cornstarch) with the sherry and stir into the wok.

6 Add the light soy sauce and sesame oil and cook, stirring, for 1 minute until thickened.

7 Sprinkle over the sesame seeds, transfer the lamb and ginger stir-fry to a warm serving dish and serve the stir-fry with Chinese egg noodles.

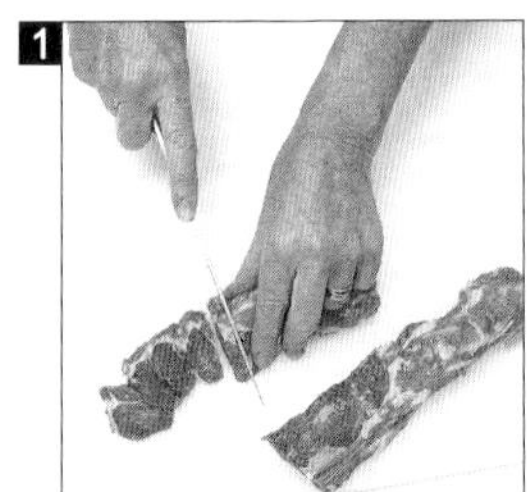
1

3

4

COOK'S TIP

Shiitake mushrooms are much used in Chinese cooking. They have a slightly meaty flavour and can be bought both fresh and dried. Their powerful flavour will permeate more bland mushrooms. Cook them briefly or they begin to toughen.

Sweet Lamb Fillet

Lamb fillet, enhanced by a sweet and spicy glaze, is cooked on the barbecue (grill) in a kitchen foil parcel for deliciously moist results.

NUTRITIONAL INFORMATION

Calories	258	Sugars	13g
Protein	24g	Fat	13g
Carbohydrate	13g	Saturates	5g

5 MINS

1 HOUR

SERVES 4

INGREDIENTS

- 2 fillets of neck of lean lamb, each 225 g/8 oz
- 1 tbsp olive oil
- ½ onion, chopped finely
- 1 clove garlic, crushed
- 2.5 cm/1 inch piece root (fresh) ginger, grated
- 5 tbsp apple juice
- 3 tbsp smooth apple sauce
- 1 tbsp light muscovado sugar
- 1 tbsp tomato ketchup (catsup)
- ½ tsp mild mustard
- salt and pepper
- green salad leaves, croûtons and fresh crusty bread, to serve

3

4

5

1 Place the lamb fillet on a large piece of double thickness kitchen foil. Season with salt and pepper to taste.

2 Heat the oil in a small pan and fry the onion and garlic for 2–3 minutes until softened but not browned. Stir in the grated ginger and cook for 1 minute, stirring occasionally.

3 Stir in the apple juice, apple sauce, sugar, ketchup (catsup) and mustard and bring to the boil. Boil rapidly for about 10 minutes until reduced by half. Stir the mixture occasionally so that it does not burn and stick to the base of the pan.

4 Brush half of the sauce over the lamb, then wrap up the lamb in the kitchen foil to completely enclose it. Barbecue (grill)the lamb parcels over hot coals for about 25 minutes, turning the parcel over occasionally.

5 Open out the kitchen foil and brush the lamb with some of the sauce. Continue to barbecue (grill) for a further 15–20 minutes or until cooked through.

6 Place the lamb on a chopping board, remove the foil and cut into thick slices. Transfer to serving plates and spoon over the remaining sauce. Serve with green salad leaves, croûtons and fresh crusty bread.

Twice-cooked Lamb

Here lamb is first boiled and then fried with soy sauce, oyster sauce and spinach and finally tossed with noodles for a richly flavoured dish.

NUTRITIONAL INFORMATION

Calories	315	Sugars	5g
Protein	27g	Fat	16g
Carbohydrate	16g	Saturates	6g

5 MINS 30 MINS

SERVES 4

INGREDIENTS

250 g/9 oz packet egg noodles
450 g/1 lb lamb loin fillet, thinly sliced
2 tbsp soy sauce
2 tbsp sunflower oil
2 cloves garlic, crushed
1 tbsp caster (superfine) sugar
2 tbsp oyster sauce
175 g/6 oz baby spinach

1 Place the egg noodles in a large bowl and cover with boiling water. Leave to soak for about 10 minutes.

2 Bring a large saucepan of water to the boil. Add the lamb and cook for 5 minutes. Drain thoroughly.

3 Place the slices of lamb in a bowl and mix with the soy sauce and 1 tablespoon of the sunflower oil.

4 Heat the remaining sunflower oil in a large preheated wok, swirling the oil around until it is really hot.

5 Add the marinated lamb and crushed garlic to the wok and stir-fry for about 5 minutes or until the meat is just beginning to brown.

6 Add the caster (superfine) sugar and oyster sauce to the wok and stir well to combine.

7 Drain the noodles thoroughly. Add the noodles to the wok and stir-fry for a further 5 minutes.

8 Add the spinach to the wok and cook for 1 minute or until the leaves just wilt. Transfer the lamb and noodles to serving bowls and serve hot.

COOK'S TIP

If using dried noodles, follow the instructions on the packet as they require less soaking.

2

3
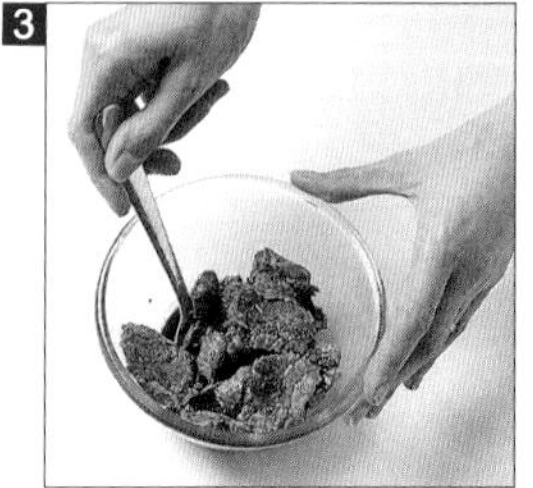

7

Lamb Couscous

Couscous is a dish that originated among the Berbers of North Africa. When steamed, it is a delicious plump grain, ideal for serving with stews.

NUTRITIONAL INFORMATION

Calories	537	Sugars	11g
Protein	32g	Fat	14g
Carbohydrate	73g	Saturates	4g

 15 MINS  35 MINS

SERVES 4

INGREDIENTS

- 2 medium red onions, sliced
- juice of 1 lemon
- 1 large red (bell) pepper, deseeded and thickly sliced
- 1 large green (bell) pepper, deseeded and thickly sliced
- 1 large orange (bell) pepper, deseeded and thickly sliced
- pinch of saffron strands
- cinnamon stick, broken
- 1 tbsp clear honey
- 300 ml/½ pint/1¼ cups vegetable stock
- 2 tsp olive oil
- 350 g/12 oz lean lamb fillet, trimmed and sliced
- 1 tsp Harissa paste
- 200 g/7 oz can chopped tomatoes
- 425 g/15 oz can chick-peas (garbanzo beans), drained
- 350 g/12 oz precooked couscous
- 2 tsp ground cinnamon
- salt and pepper

1

3

4

1 Toss the onions in the lemon juice and transfer to a saucepan. Mix in the (bell) peppers, saffron, cinnamon stick and honey. Pour in the stock, bring to the boil, cover and simmer for 5 minutes.

2 Meanwhile, heat the oil in a frying pan (skillet) and gently fry the lamb for 3–4 minutes until browned all over.

3 Using a slotted spoon, drain the lamb and transfer it to the pan with the onions and peppers. Season and stir in the Harissa paste, tomatoes and chick-peas (garbanzo beans). Mix well, bring back to the boil and simmer, uncovered, for 20 minutes.

4 Soak the couscous, following the packet instructions. Bring a saucepan of water to the boil. Put the couscous in a steamer or sieve (strainer) lined with muslin (cheese-cloth) over the pan of boiling water. Cover and steam.

5 Transfer the couscous to a serving platter and dust with ground cinnamon. Discard the cinnamon stick and spoon the stew over the couscous.

Lamb Meatballs

These small meatballs are made with minced (ground) lamb and flavoured with chilli, garlic, parsley and Chinese curry powder.

NUTRITIONAL INFORMATION

Calories	320	Sugars	1g
Protein	28g	Fat	20g
Carbohydrate	8g	Saturates	6g

 5 MINS  20 MINS

SERVES 4

INGREDIENTS

- 450 g/1 lb minced (ground) lamb
- 3 garlic cloves, crushed
- 2 spring onions (scallions), finely chopped
- ½ tsp chilli powder
- 1 tsp Chinese curry powder
- 1 tbsp chopped fresh parsley
- 25 g/1 oz/½ cup fresh white breadcrumbs
- 1 egg, beaten
- 3 tbsp vegetable oil
- 125 g/4½ oz Chinese leaves (cabbage), shredded
- 1 leek, sliced
- 1 tbsp cornflour (cornstarch)
- 2 tbsp water
- 300 ml/½ pint/1¼ cups lamb stock
- 1 tbsp dark soy sauce
- shredded leek, to garnish

1 Mix the lamb, garlic, spring onions (scallions), chilli powder, Chinese curry powder, parsley and breadcrumbs together in a bowl. Work the egg into the mixture, bringing it together to form a firm mixture. Roll into 16 small, even-sized balls.

2 Heat the oil in a preheated wok. Add the Chinese leaves (cabbage) and leek and stir-fry for 1 minute. Remove from the wok with a slotted spoon and set aside.

3 Add the meatballs to the wok and fry in batches, turning gently, for 3-4 minutes, or until golden brown all over.

4 Mix the cornflour (cornstarch) and water together to form a smooth paste and set aside. Pour the lamb stock and soy sauce into the wok and cook for 2–3 minutes. Stir in the cornflour (cornstarch) paste. Bring to the boil and cook, stirring constantly, until the sauce is thickened and clear.

5 Return the Chinese leaves (cabbage) and leek to the wok and cook for 1 minute, until heated through. Arrange the Chinese leaves (cabbage) and leek on a warm serving dish, top with the meatballs, garnish with shredded leek and serve immediately.

VARIATION

Use minced (ground) pork or beef instead of the lamb as an alternative.

Liver with (Bell) Peppers

This is a richly flavoured dish which is great served with plain rice or noodles to soak up the delicious juices.

NUTRITIONAL INFORMATION

Calories	331	Sugars	5g
Protein	25g	Fat	17g
Carbohydrate	15g	Saturates	4g

 5 MINS  10 MINS

SERVES 4

INGREDIENTS

- 450 g/1 lb lamb's liver
- 2 tbsp cornflour (cornstarch)
- 2 tbsp groundnut oil
- 1 onion, sliced
- 2 cloves garlic, crushed
- 2 green (bell) peppers, deseeded and sliced
- 2 tbsp tomato purée (paste)
- 3 tbsp dry sherry
- 1 tbsp cornflour (cornstarch)
- 2 tbsp soy sauce

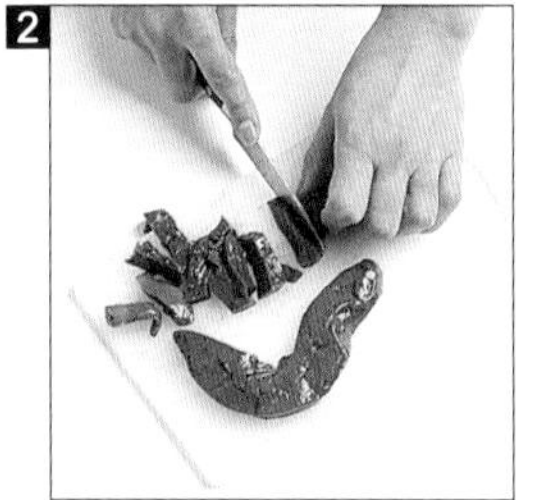
2

3

4

1 Using a sharp knife, trim any excess fat from the lamb's liver. Slice the lamb's liver into thin strips.

2 Place the cornflour (cornstarch) in a large bowl.

3 Add the strips of lamb's liver to the cornflour (cornstarch) and toss well until coated evenly all over.

4 Heat the groundnut oil in a large preheated wok or heavy-based frying pan (skillet).

5 Add the lamb's liver, sliced onion, crushed garlic and sliced green (bell) peppers to the wok or frying pan (skillet) and stir-fry for 6–7 minutes, or until the lamb's liver is just cooked through and the vegetables are tender.

6 Mix together the tomato purée (paste), sherry, cornflour (cornstarch) and soy sauce. Stir the mixture into the wok and cook for a further 2 minutes or until the juices have thickened.

7 Transfer to warm serving bowls and serve immediately.

COOK'S TIP

Use rice wine instead of the sherry for a really authentic Oriental flavour. Chinese rice wine is made from glutinous rice and is also known as 'yellow wine' because of its golden colour. The best variety, from south-east China, is called Shao Hsing or Shaoxing.

Pork with Fennel & Aniseed

Lean pork chops, stuffed with an aniseed and orange filling, are pan-cooked with fennel in an aniseed-flavoured sweet sauce.

NUTRITIONAL INFORMATION

Calories	298	Sugars	10g
Protein	30g	Fat	10g
Carbohydrate	18g	Saturates	3g

 20 MINS  35 MINS

SERVES 4

INGREDIENTS

- 4 lean pork chops, 125 g/4½ oz each
- 60 g/2 oz/⅓ cup brown rice, cooked
- 1 tsp orange rind, grated
- 4 spring onions (scallions), trimmed and finely chopped
- ½ tsp aniseed
- 1 tbsp olive oil
- 1 fennel bulb, trimmed and thinly sliced
- 450 ml/16 fl oz/2 cups unsweetened orange juice
- 1 tbsp cornflour (cornstarch)
- 2 tbsp Pernod
- salt and pepper
- fennel fronds, to garnish
- cooked vegetables, to serve

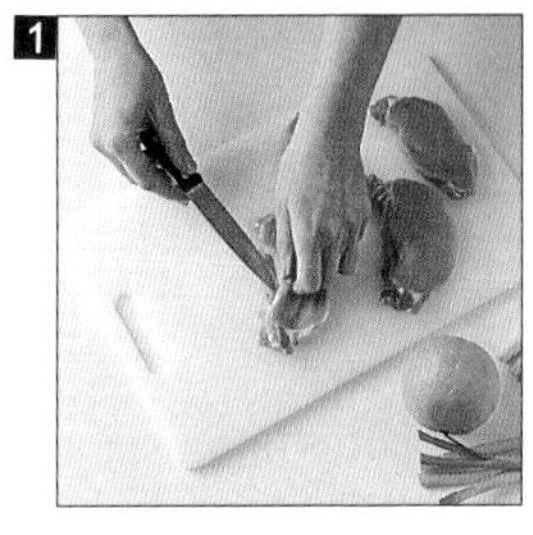

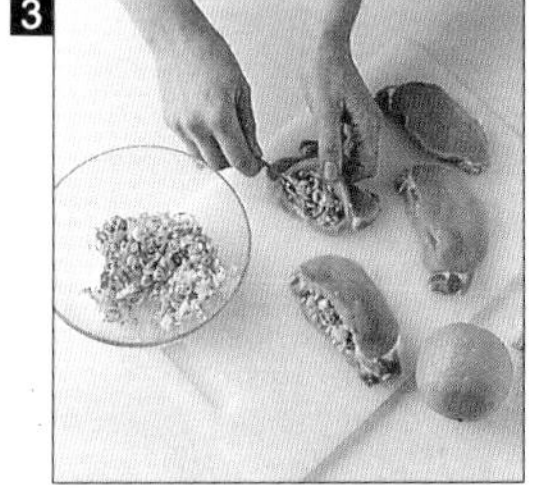

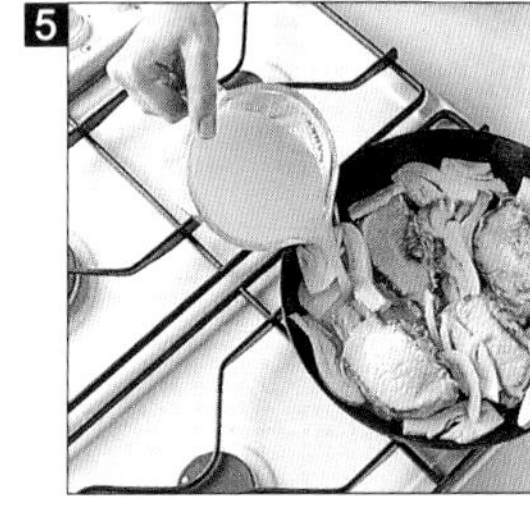

1 Trim away any excess fat from the pork chops. Using a small, sharp knife, make a slit in the centre of each chop to create a pocket.

2 Mix the rice, orange rind, spring onions (scallions), seasoning and aniseed together in a bowl.

3 Push the rice mixture into the pocket of each chop, then press gently to seal.

4 Heat the oil in a frying pan (skillet) and fry the pork chops on each side for 2–3 minutes until lightly browned.

5 Add the sliced fennel and orange juice to the pan, bring to the boil and simmer for 15–20 minutes until the meat is tender and cooked through. Remove the pork and fennel with a slotted spoon and transfer to a serving plate.

6 Blend the cornflour (cornstarch) and Pernod together in a small bowl. Add the cornflour (cornstarch) mixture to the pan and stir into the pan juices. Cook for 2–3 minutes, stirring, until the sauce thickens.

7 Pour the Pernod sauce over the pork chops, garnish with fennel fronds and serve with some cooked vegetables.

Pork Chow Mein

This is a basic recipe – the meat and/or vegetables can be varied as much as you like.

NUTRITIONAL INFORMATION

Calories	239	Sugars	1g
Protein	17g	Fat	14g
Carbohydrate	12g	Saturates	2g

 15 MINS  15 MINS

SERVES 4

INGREDIENTS

- 250 g/9 oz egg noodles
- 4-5 tbsp vegetable oil
- 250 g/9 oz pork fillet, cooked
- 125g/4½ oz French (green) beans
- 2 tbsp light soy sauce
- 1 tsp salt
- ½ tsp sugar
- 1 tbsp Chinese rice wine or dry sherry
- 2 spring onions (scallions), finely shredded
- a few drops sesame oil
- chilli sauce, to serve (optional)

1 Cook the noodles in boiling water according to the instructions on the packet, then drain and rinse under cold water. Drain again then toss with 1 tablespoon of the oil.

2 Slice the pork into thin shreds and top and tail the beans.

3 Heat 3 tablespoons of oil in a preheated wok until hot. Add the noodles and stir-fry for 2-3 minutes with 1 tablespoon soy sauce, then remove to a serving dish. Keep warm.

4 Heat the remaining oil and stir-fry the beans and meat for 2 minutes. Add the salt, sugar, wine or sherry, the remaining soy sauce and about half the spring onions (scallions) to the wok.

5 Stir the mixture in the wok, adding a little stock if necessary, then pour on top of the noodles, and sprinkle with sesame oil and the remaining spring onions (scallions).

6 Serve the chow mein hot or cold with chilli sauce, if desired.

COOK'S TIP

Chow Mein literally means 'stir-fried noodles' and is highly popular in the West as well as in China. Almost any ingredient can be added, such as fish, meat, poultry or vegetables. It is very popular for lunch and makes a tasty salad served cold.

Neapolitan Pork Steaks

An Italian version of grilled pork steaks, this dish is easy to make and delicious to eat.

NUTRITIONAL INFORMATION

Calories	353	Sugars	3g
Protein	39g	Fat	20g
Carbohydrate	4g	Saturates	5g

 10 MINS  25 MINS

SERVES 4

INGREDIENTS

2 tbsp olive oil

1 garlic clove, chopped

1 large onion, sliced

400 g/14 oz can tomatoes

2 tsp yeast extract

4 pork loin steaks, each about 125 g/4½ oz

75 g/2¾ oz black olives, pitted

2 tbsp fresh basil, shredded

freshly grated Parmesan cheese, to serve

1 Heat the oil in a large frying pan (skillet). Add the onions and garlic and cook, stirring, for 3–4 minutes or until they just begin to soften.

2 Add the tomatoes and yeast extract to the frying pan (skillet) and leave to simmer for about 5 minutes or until the sauce starts to thicken.

1

2

4

3 Cook the pork steaks, under a preheated grill (broiler), for 5 minutes on both sides, until the the meat is cooked through. Set the pork aside and keep warm.

4 Add the olives and fresh shredded basil to the sauce in the frying pan (skillet) and stir quickly to combine.

5 Transfer the steaks to warm serving plates. Top the steaks with the sauce, sprinkle with freshly grated Parmesan cheese and serve immediately.

COOK'S TIP

Parmesan is a mature and exceptionally hard cheese produced in Italy. You only need to add a little as it has a very strong flavour.

Pork with Lemon & Garlic

This is a simplified version of a traditional dish from the Marche region of Italy. Pork fillet pockets are stuffed with ham (prosciutto) and herbs.

NUTRITIONAL INFORMATION

Calories	428	Sugars	2g
Protein	31g	Fat	32g
Carbohydrate	4g	Saturates	4g

25 MINS

1 HOUR

SERVES 4

INGREDIENTS

- 450 g/1 lb pork fillet
- 50 g/1¾ oz chopped almonds
- 2 tbsp olive oil
- 100 g/3½ oz raw Parma ham (prosciutto), finely chopped
- 2 garlic cloves, chopped
- 1 tbsp fresh oregano, chopped
- finely grated rind of 2 lemons
- 4 shallots, finely chopped
- 200 ml/7 fl oz/¾ cup ham or chicken stock
- 1 tsp sugar

1 Using a sharp knife, cut the pork fillet into 4 equal pieces. Place the pork between sheets of greaseproof paper and pound each piece with a meat mallet or the end of a rolling pin to flatten it.

2 Cut a horizontal slit in each piece of pork to make a pocket.

3 Place the almonds on a baking tray (cookie sheet). Lightly toast the almonds under a medium-hot grill (broiler) for 2–3 minutes or until golden.

4 Mix the almonds with 1 tbsp oil, ham (prosciutto), garlic, oregano and the finely grated rind from 1 lemon. Spoon the mixture into the pockets of the pork.

5 Heat the remaining oil in a large frying pan (skillet). Add the shallots and cook for 2 minutes.

6 Add the pork to the frying pan (skillet) and cook for 2 minutes on each side or until browned all over.

7 Add the ham or chicken stock to the pan, bring to the boil, cover and leave to simmer for 45 minutes or until the pork is tender. Remove the meat from the pan, set aside and keep warm.

8 Using a zester, pare the remaining lemon. Add the lemon rind and sugar to the pan, boil for 3–4 minutes or until reduced and syrupy. Pour the lemon sauce over the pork fillets and serve immediately.

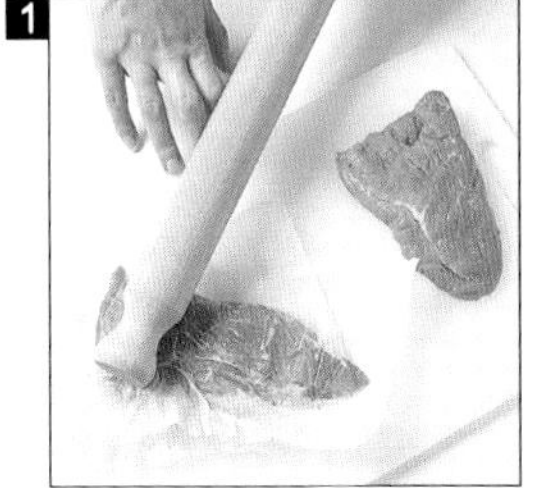
1

4

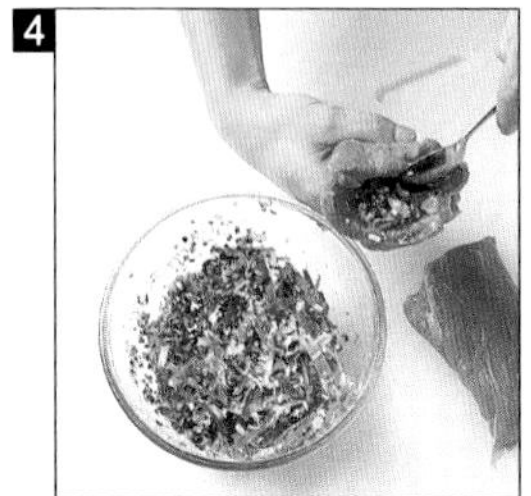
4

Sweet & Sour Pork

In this classic Chinese dish, tender pork pieces are fried and served in a crunchy sauce. This dish is perfect served with plain rice.

NUTRITIONAL INFORMATION

Calories	357	Sugars	25g
Protein	28g	Fat	14g
Carbohydrate	30g	Saturates	4g

10 MINS 20 MINS

SERVES 4

INGREDIENTS

- 450 g/1 lb pork tenderloin
- 2 tbsp sunflower oil
- 225 g/8 oz courgettes (zucchini)
- 1 red onion, cut into thin wedges
- 2 cloves garlic, crushed
- 225 g/8 oz carrots, cut into thin sticks
- 1 red (bell) pepper, deseeded and sliced
- 100 g/3½ oz/1 cup baby corn corbs
- 100 g/3½ oz button mushrooms, halved
- 175 g/6 oz/1¼ cups fresh pineapple, cubed
- 100 g/3½ oz/1 cup bean sprouts
- 150 ml/¼ pint/⅔ cup pineapple juice
- 1 tbsp cornflour (cornstarch)
- 2 tbsp soy sauce
- 3 tbsp tomato ketchup
- 1 tbsp white wine vinegar
- 1 tbsp clear honey

1. Using a sharp knife, thinly slice the pork tenderloin into even-size pieces.

2. Heat the sunflower oil in a large preheated wok. Add the pork to the wok and stir-fry for 10 minutes, or until the pork is completely cooked through and beginning to turn crispy at the edges.

3. Meanwhile, cut the courgettes (zucchini) into thin sticks.

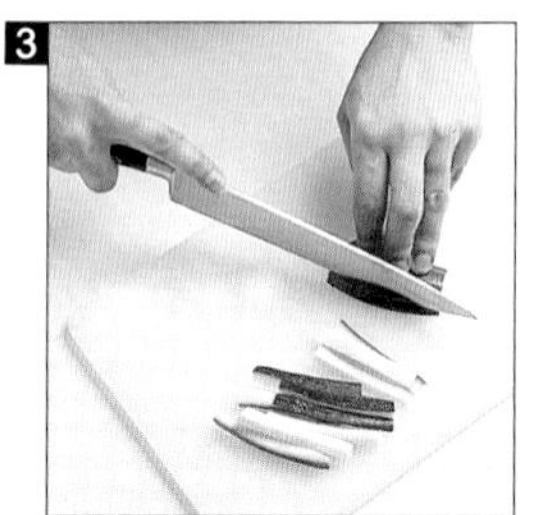

4. Add the onion, garlic, carrots, courgettes (zucchini), (bell) pepper, corn cobs and mushrooms to the wok and stir-fry for a further 5 minutes.

5. Add the pineapple cubes and bean sprouts to the wok and stir-fry for 2 minutes.

6. Mix together the pineapple juice, cornflour (cornstarch), soy sauce, tomato ketchup, white wine vinegar and honey.

7. Pour the sweet and sour mixture into the wok and cook over a high heat, tossing frequently, until the juices thicken. Transfer the sweet and sour pork to serving bowls and serve hot.

COOK'S TIP

If you prefer a crisper coating, toss the pork in a mixture of cornflour (cornstarch) and egg white and deep fry in the wok in step 2.

Pork Chops with Sage

The fresh taste of sage is the perfect ingredient to counteract the richness of pork.

NUTRITIONAL INFORMATION

Calories	364	Sugars	5g
Protein	34g	Fat	19g
Carbohydrate	14g	Saturates	7g

10 MINS 15 MINS

SERVES 4

INGREDIENTS

- 2 tbsp flour
- 1 tbsp chopped fresh sage or 1 tsp dried
- 4 lean boneless pork chops, trimmed of excess fat
- 2 tbsp olive oil
- 15 g/½ oz/1 tbsp butter
- 2 red onions, sliced into rings
- 1 tbsp lemon juice
- 2 tsp caster (superfine) sugar
- 4 plum tomatoes, quartered
- salt and pepper

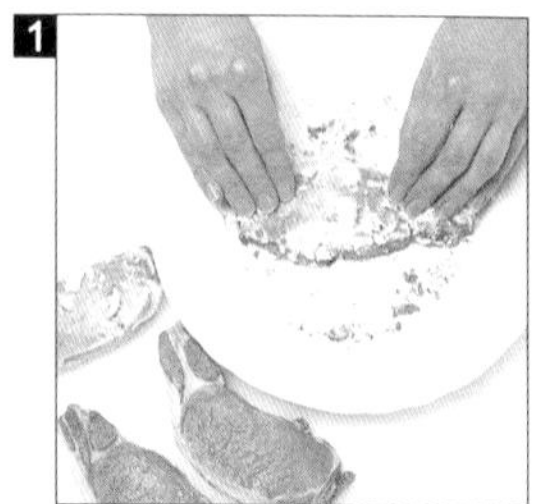

1 Mix the flour, sage and salt and pepper to taste on a plate. Lightly dust the pork chops on both sides with the seasoned flour.

2 Heat the oil and butter in a frying pan (skillet), add the chops and cook them for 6–7 minutes on each side until cooked through. Drain the chops, reserving the pan juices, and keep warm.

3 Toss the onion in the lemon juice and fry along with the sugar and tomatoes for 5 minutes until tender.

4 Serve the pork with the tomato and onion mixture and a green salad.

Fish-flavoured Pork

'Fish-flavoured' is a Szechuan cookery term meaning that the dish is prepared with seasonings normally used in fish dishes.

NUTRITIONAL INFORMATION

Calories	183	Sugars	0.2g
Protein	14g	Fat	13g
Carbohydrate	3g	Saturates	3g

 25 MINS 10 MINS

SERVES 4

INGREDIENTS

- about 2 tbsp dried wood ears
- 250-300 g/9-10½ oz pork fillet
- 1 tsp salt
- 2 tsp cornflour (cornstarch) paste (see page 6)
- 3 tbsp vegetable oil
- 1 garlic clove, finely chopped
- ½ tsp finely chopped ginger root
- 2 spring onions (scallions), finely chopped, with the white and green parts separated
- 2 celery stalks, thinly sliced
- ½ tsp sugar
- 1 tbsp light soy sauce
- 1 tbsp chilli bean sauce
- 2 tsp rice vinegar
- 1 tsp rice wine or dry sherry
- a few drops of sesame oil

1 Soak the wood ears in warm water for about 20 minutes, then rinse in cold water until the water is clear. Drain well, then cut into thin shreds.

2 Cut the pork into thin shreds, then mix in a bowl with a pinch of salt and about half the cornflour (cornstarch) paste until well coated.

3 Heat 1 tablespoon of vegetable oil in a preheated wok. Add the pork strips and stir-fry for about 1 minute, or until the colour changes, then remove with a slotted spoon and set aside until required.

4 Heat the remaining oil to the wok. Add the garlic, ginger, the white parts of the spring onions (scallions), the wood ears and celery and stir-fry for about 1 minute.

5 Return the pork strips together with the salt, sugar, soy sauce, chili bean sauce, vinegar and wine or sherry. Blend well and continue stirring for another minute.

6 Finally add the green parts of the spring onions (scallions) and blend in the remaining cornflour (cornstarch) paste and sesame oil. Stir until the sauce has thickened. Transfer the fish-flavoured pork to a warm serving dish and serve immediately.

1

1

3

COOK'S TIP

Also known as cloud ears, this is a dried grey-black fungus widely used in Szechuan cooking. It is always soaked in warm water before using. Wood ears have a crunchy texture and a mild flavour.

Pork with (Bell) Peppers

This is a really simple yet colourful dish, the trio of (bell) peppers offsetting the pork and sauce wonderfully.

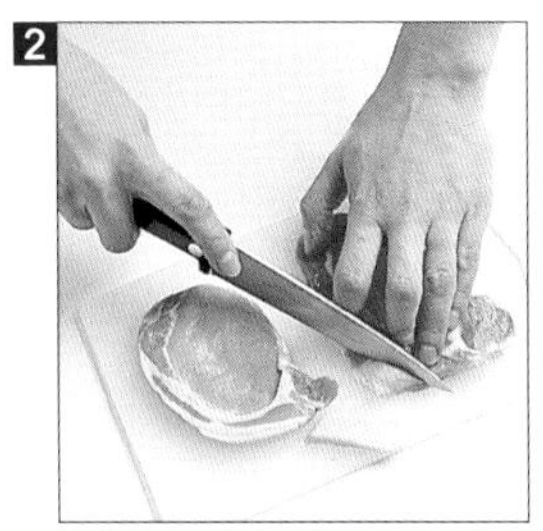

NUTRITIONAL INFORMATION

Calories	459	Sugars	5g
Protein	19g	Fat	39g
Carbohydrate	8g	Saturates	13g

 30 MINS  25 MINS

SERVES 4

INGREDIENTS

- 15 g/½ oz Chinese dried mushrooms
- 450 g/1 lb pork leg steaks
- 2 tbsp vegetable oil
- 1 onion, sliced
- 1 red (bell) pepper, deseeded and diced
- 1 green (bell) pepper, deseeded and diced
- 1 yellow (bell) pepper, deseeded and diced
- 4 tbsp oyster sauce

1 Place the mushrooms in a large bowl. Pour over enough boiling water to cover and leave to stand for 20 minutes.

2 Using a sharp knife, trim any excess fat from the pork steaks. Cut the pork into thin strips.

3 Bring a large saucepan of water to the boil. Add the pork to the boiling water and cook for 5 minutes.

4 Remove the pork from the pan with a slotted spoon and leave to drain thoroughly.

5 Heat the oil in a large preheated wok. Add the pork to the wok and stir-fry for about 5 minutes.

6 Remove the mushrooms from the water and leave to drain thoroughly. Roughly chop the mushrooms.

7 Add the mushrooms, onion and the (bell) peppers to the wok and stir-fry for 5 minutes.

8 Stir in the oyster sauce and cook for 2-3 minutes. Serve immediately.

COOK'S TIP

Use open-cap mushrooms, sliced, instead of Chinese mushrooms, if you prefer.

Pork with Plums

Plum sauce is often used in Chinese cooking with duck or rich, fattier meat to counteract the flavour

NUTRITIONAL INFORMATION

Calories	281	Sugars	6g
Protein	25g	Fat	14g
Carbohydrate	10g	Saturates	4g

 35 MINS  25 MINS

SERVES 4

INGREDIENTS

- 450 g/1 lb pork fillet (tenderloin)
- 1 tbsp cornflour (cornstarch)
- 2 tbsp light soy sauce
- 2 tbsp Chinese rice wine
- 4 tsp light brown sugar
- pinch of ground cinnamon
- 5 tsp vegetable oil
- 2 garlic cloves, crushed
- 2 spring onions (scallions), chopped
- 4 tbsp plum sauce
- 1 tbsp hoisin sauce
- 150 ml/¼ pint/⅔ cup water
- dash of chilli sauce
- fried plum quarters and spring onions (scallions), to garnish

1 Cut the pork fillet (tenderloin) into thin slices.

2 Combine the cornflour (cornstarch), soy sauce, rice wine, sugar and cinnamon in a small bowl.

3 Place the pork in a shallow dish and pour the cornflour (cornstarch) mixture over it. Toss the meat in the marinade until it is completely coated. Cover and leave to marinate for at least 30 minutes.

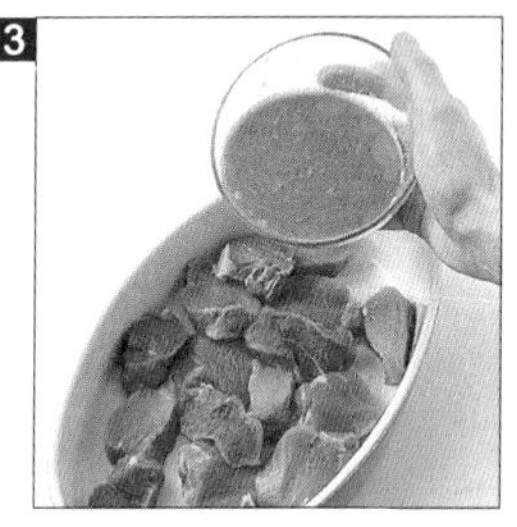
3

6

7

4 Remove the pork from the dish, reserving the marinade.

5 Heat the oil in a preheated wok or large frying pan (skillet). Add the pork and stir-fry for 3–4 minutes, until a light golden colour.

6 Stir in the garlic, spring onions (scallions), plum sauce, hoisin sauce, water and chilli sauce. Bring the sauce to the boil. Reduce the heat, cover and leave to simmer for 8–10 minutes, or until the pork is cooked through and tender.

7 Stir in the reserved marinade and cook, stirring, for about 5 minutes.

8 Transfer the pork stir-fry to a warm serving dish and garnish with fried plum quarters and spring onions (scallions). Serve immediately.

Tangy Pork Fillet

Barbecued (grilled) in a parcel of kitchen foil, these tasty pork fillets are served with a tangy orange sauce.

NUTRITIONAL INFORMATION

Calories	230	Sugars	16g
Protein	19g	Fat	9g
Carbohydrate	20g	Saturates	3g

 10 MINS  55 MINS

SERVES 4

INGREDIENTS

400 g/14 oz lean pork fillet

3 tbsp orange marmalade

grated rind and juice of 1 orange

1 tbsp white wine vinegar

dash of Tabasco sauce

salt and pepper

SAUCE

1 tbsp olive oil

1 small onion, chopped

1 small green (bell) pepper, deseeded and thinly sliced

1 tbsp cornflour (cornstarch)

150 ml/5 fl oz/⅔ cup orange juice

TO SERVE

cooked rice

mixed salad leaves

1 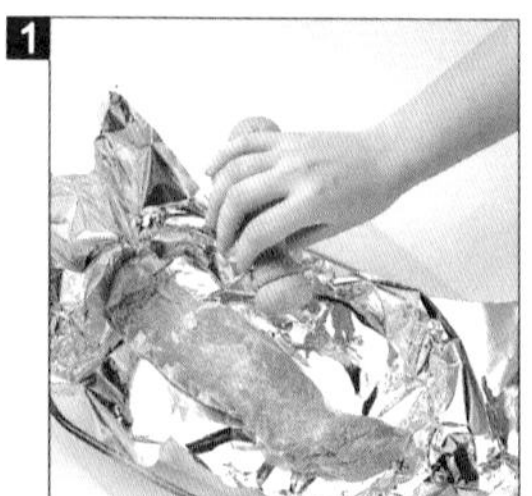

2 

6 

1 Place a large piece of double thickness foil in a shallow dish. Put the pork fillet in the centre of the foil and season.

2 Heat the marmalade, orange rind and juice, vinegar and Tabasco sauce in a small pan, stirring until the marmalade melts and the ingredients combine. Pour the mixture over the pork and wrap the meat in foil, making sure that the parcel is well sealed so that the juices cannot run out. Place over hot coals and barbecue (grill) for about 25 minutes, turning the parcel occasionally.

3 For the sauce, heat the oil and cook the onion for 2–3 minutes. Add the (bell) pepper and cook for 3–4 minutes.

4 Remove the pork from the kitchen foil and place on to the rack. Pour the juices into the pan with the sauce.

5 Barbecue (grill) the pork for a further 10–20 minutes, turning, until cooked through and golden on the outside.

6 In a small bowl, mix the cornflour (cornstarch) with a little orange juice to form a paste. Add to the sauce with the remaining cooking juices. Cook, stirring, until the sauce thickens. Slice the pork, spoon over the sauce and serve with rice and mixed salad leaves.

Pork Chops & Spicy Beans

A tasty and substantial dish, and the spicy bean mixture, served on its own, also makes a good accompaniment to other meat or chicken dishes.

NUTRITIONAL INFORMATION

Calories	388	Sugars	5g
Protein	20g	Fat	27g
Carbohydrate	17g	Saturates	8g

 5 MINS  50 MINS

SERVES 4

INGREDIENTS

- 3 tbsp vegetable oil
- 4 lean pork chops, rind removed
- 2 onions, peeled and thinly sliced
- 2 garlic cloves, peeled and crushed
- 2 fresh green chillies, seeded and chopped or use 1-2 tsp minced chilli (from a jar)
- 2.5 cm/1 in piece ginger root, peeled and chopped
- 1½ tsp cumin seeds
- 1½ tsp ground coriander
- 600 ml/1 pint/2½ cups stock or water
- 2 tbsp tomato purée (paste)
- ½ aubergine (eggplant), trimmed and cut into 1 cm/½ inch dice
- salt
- 1 x 400 g/14 oz can red kidney beans, drained
- 4 tbsp double (heavy) cream
- sprigs of coriander (cilantro), to garnish

1. Heat the ghee or vegetable oil in a large frying pan (skillet), add the pork chops and fry until sealed and browned on both sides. Remove from the pan and set aside until required.

2. Add the sliced onions, garlic, chillies, ginger and spices and fry gently for 2 minutes. Stir in the stock or water, tomato purée (paste), diced aubergine (eggplant) and season with salt and pepper.

3. Bring the mixture to the boil, place the pork chops on top, then cover and simmer gently over medium heat for 30 minutes .

4. Remove the chops for a moment and stir the red kidney beans and double (heavy) cream into the mixture. Return the chops to the pan, cover and heat through gently for 5 minutes.

5. Taste and adjust the seasoning, if necessary. Serve hot, garnished with coriander (cilantro) sprigs.

Pork Fry with Vegetables

This is a very simple dish which lends itself to almost any combination of vegetables that you have to hand.

NUTRITIONAL INFORMATION

Calories	216	Sugars	3g
Protein	19g	Fat	12g
Carbohydrate	5g	Saturates	3g

 5 MINS

 15 MINS

SERVES 4

INGREDIENTS

- 350 g/12 oz lean pork fillet (tenderloin)
- 2 tbsp vegetable oil
- 2 garlic cloves, crushed
- 1-cm/½-inch piece fresh root ginger, cut into slivers
- 1 carrot, cut into thin strips
- 1 red (bell) pepper, seeded and diced
- 1 fennel bulb, sliced
- 25 g/1 oz water chestnuts, halved
- 75 g/2 ¾ oz bean sprouts
- 2 tbsp Chinese rice wine
- 300 ml/½ pint/1¼ cups pork or chicken stock
- pinch of dark brown sugar
- 1 tsp cornflour (cornstarch)
- 2 tsp water

1 Cut the pork into thin slices. Heat the oil in a preheated wok. Add the garlic, ginger and pork and stir-fry for 1–2 minutes, until the meat is sealed.

2 Add the carrot, (bell) pepper, fennel and water chestnuts to the wok and stir-fry for about 2-3 minutes.

3 Add the bean sprouts and stir-fry for 1 minute. Remove the pork and vegetables from the wok and keep warm.

2

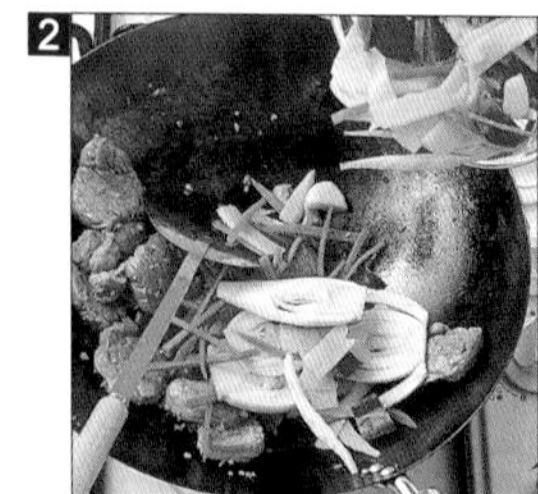
2

4

4 Add the Chinese rice wine, pork or chicken stock and sugar to the wok. Blend the cornflour (cornstarch) to a smooth paste with the water and stir it into the sauce. Bring to the boil, stirring constantly until thickened and clear.

5 Return the meat and vegetables to the wok and cook for 1–2 minutes, until heated through and coated with the sauce. Serve immediately.

VARIATION

Use dry sherry instead of the Chinese rice wine if you have difficulty obtaining it.

Red Roast Pork in Soy Sauce

In this traditional Chinese dish the pork turns 'red' during cooking because it is basted in dark soy sauce.

NUTRITIONAL INFORMATION

Calories	268	Sugars	20g
Protein	26g	Fat	8g
Carbohydrate	22g	Saturates	3g

 1¼ HOURS  1¼ HOURS

SERVES 4

INGREDIENTS

- 450 g/1 lb lean pork fillets
- 6 tbsp dark soy sauce
- 2 tbsp dry sherry
- 1 tsp five-spice powder
- 2 garlic cloves, crushed
- 2.5 cm/1 inch piece root (fresh) ginger, finely chopped
- 1 large red (bell) pepper
- 1 large yellow (bell) pepper
- 1 large orange (bell) pepper
- 4 tbsp caster (superfine) sugar
- 2 tbsp red wine vinegar

TO GARNISH

- spring onions (scallions), shredded
- fresh chives, snipped

2

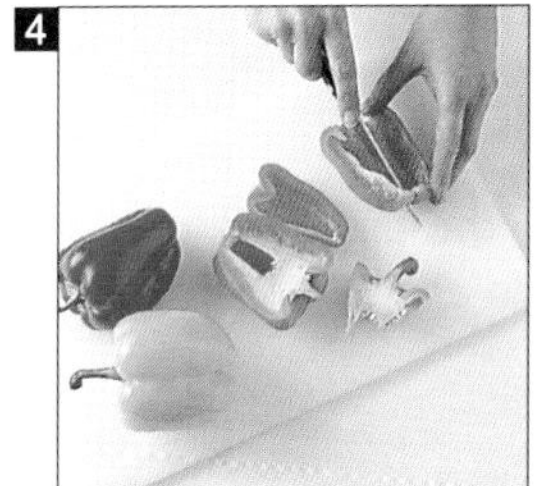
4

6

1 Trim away any excess fat and silver skin from the pork and place in a shallow dish.

2 Mix together the soy sauce, sherry, five-spice powder, garlic and ginger. Spoon over the pork, cover and marinate in the refrigerator for at least 1 hour or until required.

3 Preheat the oven to 190°C/375°F/Gas Mark 5. Drain the pork, reserving the marinade.

4 Place the pork on a roasting rack over a roasting pan. Cook in the oven, occasionally basting with the marinade, for 1 hour or until cooked through.

5 Meanwhile, halve and deseed the (bell) peppers. Cut each (bell) pepper half into 3 equal portions. Arrange them on a baking sheet (cookie sheet) and bake alongside the pork for the last 30 minutes of cooking time.

6 Place the caster (superfine) sugar and vinegar in a saucepan and heat gently until the sugar dissolves. Bring to the boil and simmer for 3–4 minutes, until syrupy.

7 When the pork is cooked, remove it from the oven and brush with the sugar syrup. Leave for about 5 minutes, then slice and arrange on a serving platter with the (bell) peppers, garnished with the spring onions (scallions) and chives.

8 Serve garnished with the spring onions (scallions) and freshly snipped chives.

Twice-cooked Pork

Twice-cooked is a popular way of cooking meat in China. The meat is first boiled to tenderize it, then cut into strips or slices and stir-fried.

NUTRITIONAL INFORMATION

Calories	199	Sugars	3g
Protein	15g	Fat	13g
Carbohydrate	4g	Saturates	3g

3¼ HOURS 30 MINS

SERVES 4

INGREDIENTS

- 250-300 g/9-10½ oz shoulder or leg of pork, in one piece
- 1 small green (bell) pepper, cored and seeded
- 1 small red (bell) pepper, cored and seeded
- 125 g/4½ oz canned sliced bamboo shoots, rinsed and drained
- 3 tbsp vegetable oil
- 1 spring onion (scallion), cut into short sections
- 1 tsp salt
- ½ tsp sugar
- 1 tbsp light soy sauce
- 1 tsp chilli bean sauce or freshly minced chilli
- 1 tsp rice wine or dry sherry
- a few drops of sesame oil

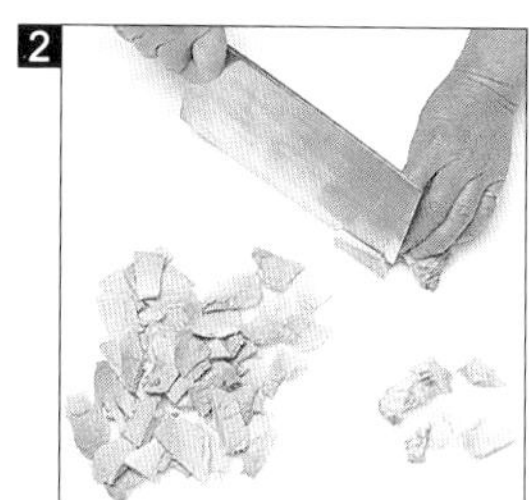

1 Immerse the pork in a pot of boiling water to cover. Return to the boil and skim the surface. Reduce the heat, cover and simmer for 15-20 minutes. Turn off the heat and leave the pork in the water to cool for at least 2-3 hours.

2 Remove the pork and drain well. Trim off any excess fat, then cut into small, thin slices. Cut the (bell) peppers into pieces about the same size as the pork and the sliced bamboo shoots.

3 Heat the vegetable oil in a preheated wok and add the vegetables together with the spring onion (scallion). Stir-fry for about 1 minute.

4 Add the pork, followed by the salt, sugar, light soy sauce, chilli bean sauce and wine or sherry. Blend well and continue stirring for another minute. Transfer the stir-fry to a warm serving dish, sprinkle with sesame oil and serve.

COOK'S TIP

For ease of handling, buy a boned piece of meat, and roll into a compact shape. Tie securely with string before placing in the boiling water.

Spicy Pork Balls

These small meatballs are packed with flavour and cooked in a crunchy tomato sauce for a very quick dish.

NUTRITIONAL INFORMATION

Calories	299	Sugars	3g
Protein	28g	Fat	15g
Carbohydrate	14g	Saturates	4g

10 MINS 40 MINS

SERVES 4

INGREDIENTS

- 450 g/1 lb minced (ground) pork
- 2 shallots, finely chopped
- 2 cloves garlic, crushed
- 1 tsp cumin seeds
- ½ tsp chilli powder
- 25 g/1 oz/½ cup wholemeal breadcrumbs
- 1 egg, beaten
- 2 tbsp sunflower oil
- 400 g/14 oz can chopped tomatoes, flavoured with chilli
- 2 tbsp soy sauce
- 200 g/7 oz can water chestnuts, drained
- 3 tbsp chopped fresh coriander (cilantro)

1

2

3

1 Place the minced (ground) pork in a large mixing bowl. Add the shallots, garlic, cumin seeds, chilli powder, breadcrumbs and beaten egg and mix together well.

2 Form the mixture into balls between the palms of your hands.

3 Heat the oil in a large preheated wok. Add the pork balls and stir-fry, in batches, over a high heat for about 5 minutes or until sealed on all sides.

4 Add the tomatoes, soy sauce and water chestnuts and bring to the boil. Return the pork balls to the wok, reduce the heat and leave to simmer for 15 minutes.

5 Scatter with chopped fresh coriander (cilantro) and serve hot.

COOK'S TIP

Add a few teaspoons of chilli sauce to a tin of chopped tomatoes, if you can't find the flavoured variety.

Pork Ribs with Plum Sauce

Pork ribs are always very popular at barbecues (grills), and you can flavour them with a number of spicy bastes.

NUTRITIONAL INFORMATION

Calories	590	Sugars	1g
Protein	26g	Fat	51g
Carbohydrate	3g	Saturates	17g

 35 MINS  45 MINS

SERVES 4

INGREDIENTS

- 900 g/2 lb pork spare ribs
- 2 tbsp sunflower oil
- 1 tsp sesame oil
- 2 cloves garlic, crushed
- 2.5 cm/1 inch piece root (fresh) ginger, grated
- 150 ml/¼ pint/⅔ cup plum sauce
- 2 tbsp dry sherry
- 2 tbsp hoisin sauce
- 2 tbsp soy sauce
- 4–6 spring onions (scallions), to garnish (optional)

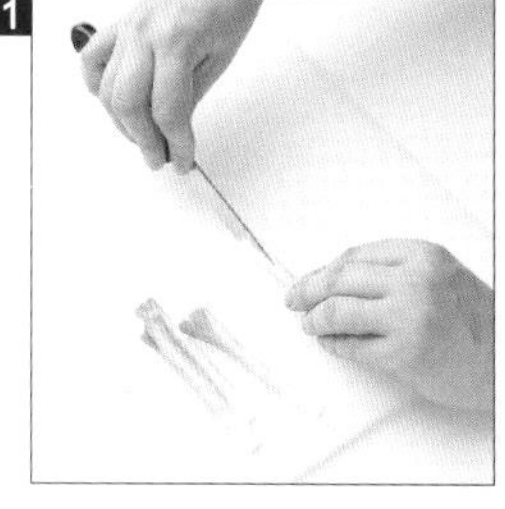

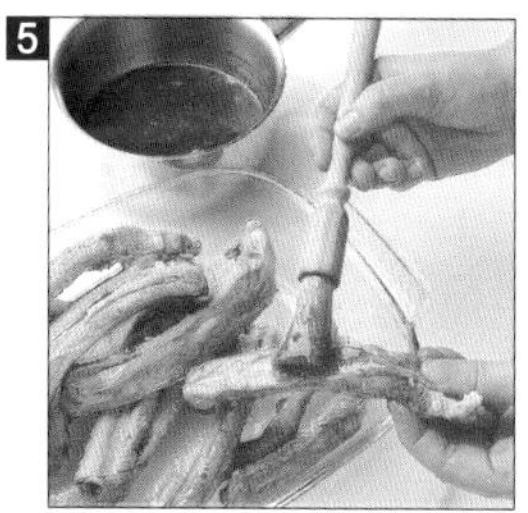

1 To prepare the garnish, trim the spring onions (scallions) to about 7.5 cm/ 3 inches long. Slice both ends into thin strips, leaving the onion intact in the centre.

2 Put the spring onions (scallions) into a bowl of iced water for at least 30 minutes until the ends start to curl up. Leave them in the water and set aside until required.

3 If you buy the spare ribs in a single piece, cut them into individual ribs. Bring a large pan of water to the boil and add the ribs. Cook for 5 minutes, then drain thoroughly.

4 Heat the oils in a pan, add the garlic and ginger and cook gently for 1–2 minutes. Stir in the plum sauce, sherry, hoisin and soy sauce and heat through.

5 Brush the sauce over the pork ribs. Barbecue (grill) over hot coals for 5–10 minutes, then move to a cooler part of the barbecue (grill) for a further 15–20 minutes, basting with the remaining sauce. Garnish and serve hot.

COOK'S TIP

Par-cooking the ribs in boiling water removes excess fat, which helps prevent the ribs from spitting during cooking. Do not be put off by the large quantity – there is only a little meat on each, but they are quite cheap to buy.

Artichoke & Ham Salad

This elegant starter would make a good first course. Serve it with a little fresh bread for mopping up the juices.

NUTRITIONAL INFORMATION

Calories	124	Sugars	2g
Protein	2g	Fat	11g
Carbohydrate	4g	Saturates	1g

 25 MINS  0 MINS

SERVES 4

INGREDIENTS

- 275 g/9 ½ oz can artichoke hearts in oil, drained
- 4 small tomatoes
- 25 g/1 oz sun-dried tomatoes in oil
- 40 g/1 ½ oz Parma ham (prosciutto)
- 25 g/1 oz pitted black olives, halved
- a few basil leaves

DRESSING

- 3 tbsp olive oil
- 1 tbsp white wine vinegar
- 1 clove garlic, crushed
- ½ tsp mild mustard
- 1 tsp clear honey
- salt and pepper

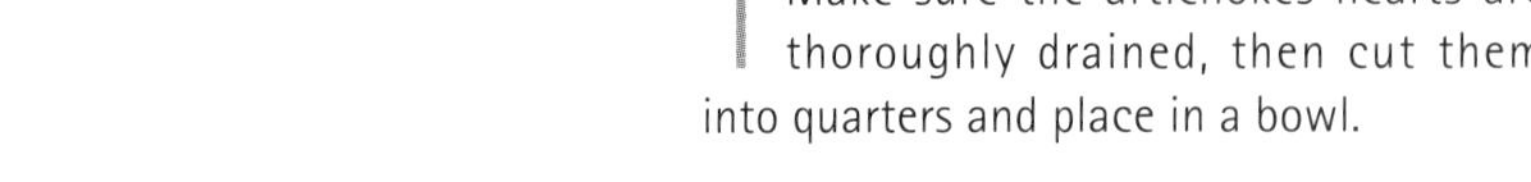

1 Make sure the artichokes hearts are thoroughly drained, then cut them into quarters and place in a bowl.

2 Cut each fresh tomato into wedges. Slice the sun-dried tomatoes into thin strips. Cut the Parma ham (prosciutto) into thin strips and add to the bowl with the tomatoes and olive halves.

3 Keeping a few basil leaves whole for garnishing, tear the remainder of the leaves into small pieces and add to the bowl containing the other salad ingredients.

4 To make the dressing, put the oil, wine vinegar, garlic, mustard, honey and salt and pepper to taste in a screw-top jar and shake vigorously until the ingredients are well blended.

5 Pour the dressing over the salad and toss together.

6 Serve the salad garnished with a few whole basil leaves.

COOK'S TIP

Use bottled artichokes in oil if you can find them as they have a better flavour. If only canned artichokes are available, rinse them carefully to remove the salty liquid.

Fruity Stuffed Bacon Chops

This combination of green lentils, celery and apricots stuffed into bacon chops, served with a sweet sauce is a speedy dish for the microwave.

NUTRITIONAL INFORMATION

Calories	148	Sugars	5g
Protein	15g	Fat	6g
Carbohydrate	9g	Saturates	3g

20 MINS

30 MINS

SERVES 4

INGREDIENTS

- 60 g/2 oz/¼ cup green lentils, washed
- 1 celery stick, sliced
- 2 spring onions (scallions), chopped
- 4 thick cut tendersweet lean bacon chops
- 1 tbsp chopped fresh sage
- 4 apricot halves canned in natural juice, drained and chopped
- 1 tsp cornflour (cornstarch)
- 4 tbsp natural juice from can of apricots
- 2 tbsp fresh orange juice
- 1 tsp grated orange rind
- 1 tbsp low-fat crème fraîche
- salt and pepper

TO GARNISH

- orange slices
- sprigs of fresh sage

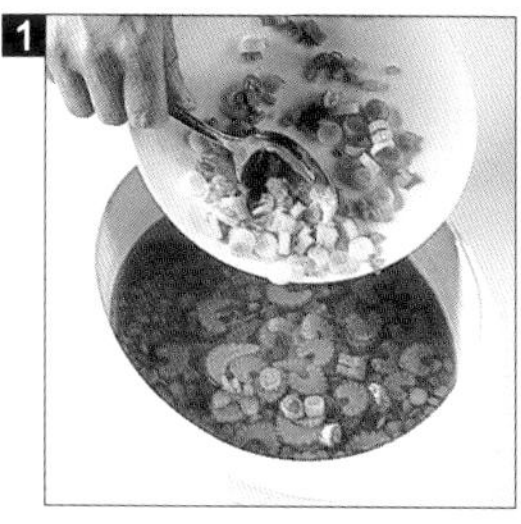
1

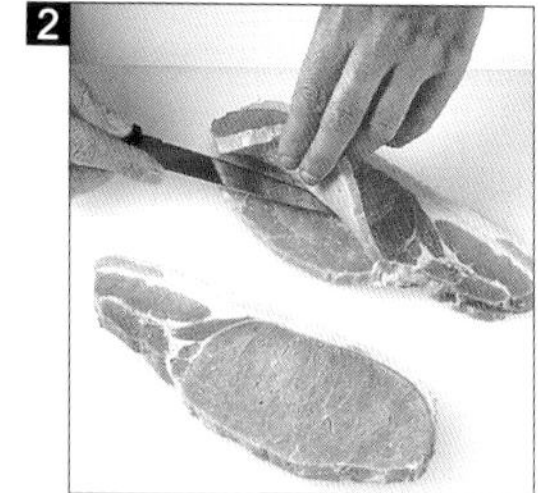
2

3

1 Place the lentils and celery in a bowl. Pour on boiling water to cover them. Cover and cook on HIGH power for 18–20 minutes until tender, adding extra water if necessary. Add the spring onions (scallions) for the last minute of cooking. Leave to stand, covered, for 10 minutes.

2 Using a sharp knife, slit the meaty end of each chop nearly through to the fat side, to form a pocket.

3 Drain the lentils and mix with half of the sage and the apricots. Season to taste.

4 Spoon the lentil stuffing into the pockets in the bacon chops. Arrange 2 on a plate. Cover with a paper towel. Cook on HIGH power for 4 minutes until cooked through. Transfer to warmed plates, cover and keep warm while cooking the remaining stuffed chops.

5 Mix the cornflour (cornstarch) with a little water in a bowl, then stir in the juice from the apricots, and the orange juice and rind. Cover and cook on HIGH power for 2 minutes, stirring every 30 seconds. Stir in the crème fraîche and remaining sage. Season and reheat on HIGH power for 30 seconds.

6 Serve the chops with the sauce. Garnish with orange slices and sage.

Sausage & Bean Casserole

In this traditional Tuscan dish, Italian sausages are cooked with cannellini beans and tomatoes.

NUTRITIONAL INFORMATION

Calories	609	Sugars	7g
Protein	27g	Fat	47g
Carbohydrate	20g	Saturates	16g

 15 MINS  35 MINS

SERVES 4

INGREDIENTS

- 8 Italian sausages
- 1 tbsp olive oil
- 1 large onion, chopped
- 2 garlic cloves, chopped
- 1 green (bell) pepper
- 225g/8 oz fresh tomatoes, skinned and chopped or 400 g/14 oz can tomatoes, chopped
- 2 tbsp sun-dried tomato paste
- 400 g/14 oz can cannellini beans
- mashed potato or rice, to serve

1 Using a sharp knife, deseed the (bell) pepper and cut it into thin strips.

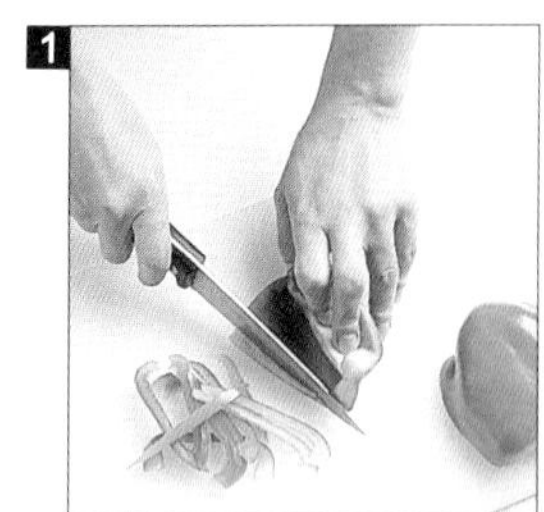

2 Prick the Italian sausages all over with a fork. Cook the sausages, under a preheated grill (broiler), for 10–12 minutes, turning occasionally, until brown all over. Set aside and keep warm.

3 Heat the oil in a large frying pan (skillet). Add the onion, garlic and (bell) pepper to the frying pan (skillet) and cook for 5 minutes, stirring occasionally, or until softened.

4 Add the tomatoes to the frying pan (skillet) and leave the mixture to simmer for about 5 minutes, stirring occasionally, or until slightly reduced and thickened.

5 Stir the sun-dried tomato paste, cannellini beans and Italian sausages into the mixture in the frying pan (skillet). Cook for 4–5 minutes or until the mixture is piping hot. Add 4–5 tablespoons of water, if the mixture becomes too dry during cooking.

6 Transfer the Italian sausage and bean casserole to serving plates and serve with mashed potato or cooked rice.

COOK'S TIP

Italian sausages are coarse in texture and have quite a strong flavour. They can be bought in specialist sausage shops, Italian delicatessens and some larger supermarkets. They are replaceable in this recipe only by game sausages.

Escalopes & Italian Sausage

Anchovies are often used to enhance flavour, particularly in meat dishes. Either veal or turkey escalopes can be used for this pan-fried dish.

NUTRITIONAL INFORMATION

Calories	233	Sugars	1g
Protein	28g	Fat	13g
Carbohydrate	1g	Saturates	1g

 10 MINS  20 MINS

SERVES 4

INGREDIENTS

- 1 tbsp olive oil
- 6 canned anchovy fillets, drained
- 1 tbsp capers, drained
- 1 tbsp fresh rosemary, stalks removed
- finely grated rind and juice of 1 orange
- 75 g/2¾ oz Italian sausage, diced
- 3 tomatoes, skinned and chopped
- 4 turkey or veal escalopes, each about 125 g/4½ oz
- salt and pepper
- crusty bread or cooked polenta, to serve

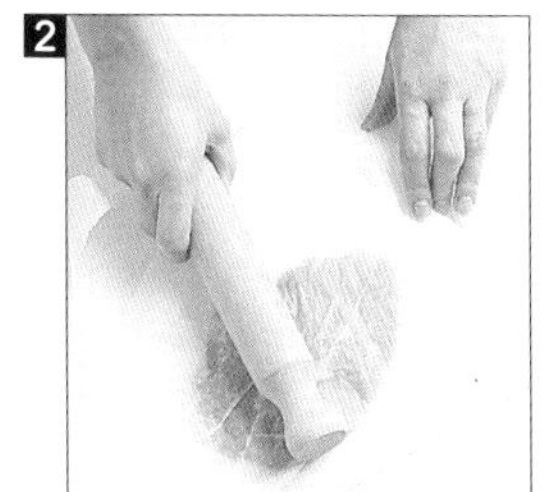

1 Heat the oil in a large frying pan (skillet). Add the anchovies, capers, fresh rosemary, orange rind and juice, Italian sausage and tomatoes to the pan and cook for 5–6 minutes, stirring occasionally.

2 Meanwhile, place the turkey or veal escalopes between sheets of greasproof paper. Pound the meat with a meat mallet or the end of a rolling pin to flatten it.

3 Add the meat to the mixture in the frying pan (skillet). Season to taste with salt and pepper, cover and cook for 3–5 minutes on each side, slightly longer if the meat is thicker.

4 Transfer to serving plates and serve with fresh crusty bread or cooked polenta, if you prefer.

VARIATION

Try using 4-minute steaks, slightly flattened, instead of the turkey or veal. Cook them for 4–5 minutes on top of the sauce in the pan.

Vitello Tonnato

Veal dishes are the speciality of Lombardy, with this dish being one of the more sophisticated. Serve cold with seasonal salads.

NUTRITIONAL INFORMATION

Calories	654	Sugars	1g
Protein	49g	Fat	47g
Carbohydrate	1g	Saturates	8g

 30 MINS  1 1/4 HOURS

SERVES 4

INGREDIENTS

- 750 g/1 lb 10 oz boned leg of veal, rolled
- 2 bay leaves
- 10 black peppercorns
- 2–3 cloves
- ½ tsp salt
- 2 carrots, sliced
- 1 onion, sliced
- 2 celery stalks, sliced
- about 700 ml/1¼ pints/3 cups stock or water
- 150 ml/¼ pint/⅔ cup dry white wine (optional)
- 90 g/3 oz canned tuna fish, well drained
- 50 g/1½ oz can anchovy fillets, drained
- 150 ml/¼ pint/⅔ cup olive oil
- 2 tsp bottled capers, drained
- 2 egg yolks
- 1 tbsp lemon juice
- salt and pepper

TO GARNISH

- capers
- lemon wedges
- fresh herbs

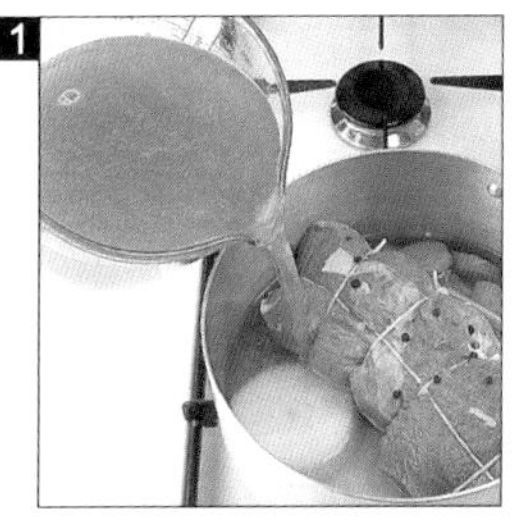

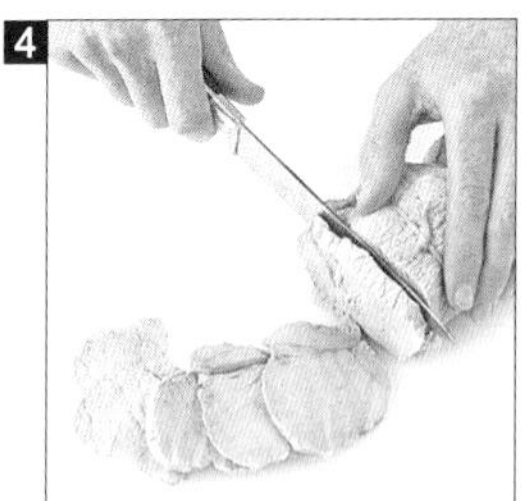

1 Put the veal in a saucepan with the bay leaves, peppercorns, cloves, salt and vegetables. Add sufficient stock or water and the wine (if using) to barely cover the veal. Bring to the boil, remove any scum from the surface, then cover the pan and simmer gently for about 1 hour or until tender. Leave in the water until cold, then drain thoroughly. If time allows, chill the veal to make it easier to carve.

2 For the tuna sauce: thoroughly mash the tuna with 4 anchovy fillets, 1 tablespoon of oil and the capers. Add the egg yolks and press through a sieve (strainer) or purée in a food processor or liquidizer until smooth.

3 Stir in the lemon juice then gradually whisk in the rest of the oil a few drops at a time until the sauce is smooth and has the consistency of thick cream. Season with salt and pepper to taste.

4 Slice the veal thinly and arrange on a platter in overlapping slices. Spoon the sauce over the veal to cover. Then cover the dish and chill overnight.

5 Before serving, uncover the veal carefully. Arrange the remaining anchovy fillets and the capers in a decorative pattern on top, and then garnish with lemon wedges and sprigs of fresh herbs.

Neapolitan Veal Cutlets

The delicious combination of apple, onion and mushroom perfectly complements the delicate flavour of veal.

NUTRITIONAL INFORMATION

Calories	1071	Sugars	13g
Protein	74g	Fat	59g
Carbohydrate	66g	Saturates	16g

20 MINS

45 MINS

SERVES 4

INGREDIENTS

- 200 g/7 oz/⅞ cup butter
- 4 x 250 g/9 oz veal cutlets, trimmed
- 1 large onion, sliced
- 2 apples, peeled, cored and sliced
- 175 g/6 oz button mushrooms
- 1 tbsp chopped fresh tarragon
- 8 black peppercorns
- 1 tbsp sesame seeds
- 400 g/14 oz dried marille
- 100 ml/3½fl oz/scant ½ cup extra virgin olive oil
- 175 g/6 oz/¾ cup mascarpone cheese, broken into small pieces
- 2 large beef tomatoes, cut in half
- leaves of 1 fresh basil sprig
- salt and pepper
- fresh basil leaves, to garnish

1 Melt 60 g/2 oz/4 tbsp of the butter in a frying pan (skillet). Fry the veal over a low heat for 5 minutes on each side. Transfer to a dish and keep warm.

2 Fry the onion and apples in the pan until lightly browned. Transfer to a dish, place the veal on top and keep warm.

3 Melt the remaining butter in the frying pan (skillet). Gently fry the mushrooms, tarragon and peppercorns over a low heat for 3 minutes. Sprinkle over the sesame seeds.

4 Bring a pan of salted water to the boil. Add the pasta and 1 tbsp of oil. Cook for 8–10 minutes or until tender, but still firm to the bite. Drain; transfer to a plate.

5 Grill (broil) or fry the tomatoes and basil for 2–3 minutes.

6 Top the pasta with the mascarpone cheese and sprinkle over the remaining olive oil. Place the onions, apples and veal cutlets on top of the pasta. Spoon the mushrooms, peppercorns and pan juices on to the cutlets, place the tomatoes and basil leaves around the edge and place in a preheated oven at 150°C/300°F/Gas Mark 2 for 5 minutes.

7 Season to taste with salt and pepper, garnish with fresh basil leaves and serve immediately.

1

2

3

Saltimbocca

The Italian name for this dish, *saltimbocca*, means 'jump into the mouth'. The stuffed rolls are quick and easy to make and taste delicious.

NUTRITIONAL INFORMATION

Calories	303	Sugars	0.3g
Protein	29g	Fat	17g
Carbohydrate	1g	Saturates	1g

 15 MINS  20 MINS

SERVES 4

INGREDIENTS

- 4 turkey fillets or 4 veal escalopes, about 450 g/1 lb in total
- 100 g/3½ oz Parma ham (prosciutto)
- 8 sage leaves
- 1 tbsp olive oil
- 1 onion, finely chopped
- 200 ml/7 fl oz/¾ cup white wine
- 200 ml/7 fl oz/¾ cup chicken stock

1 Place the turkey or veal between sheets of greaseproof paper. Pound the meat with a meat mallet or the end of a rolling pin to flatten it slightly. Cut each escalope in half.

2 Trim the Parma ham (prosciutto) to fit each piece of turkey or veal and place over the meat. Lay a sage leaf on top. Roll up the escalopes and secure with a cocktail stick (toothpick).

3 Heat the oil in a frying pan (skillet) and cook the onion for 3–4 minutes. Add the turkey or veal rolls to the pan and cook for 5 minutes until browned all over.

4 Pour the white wine and chicken stock into the pan and leave to simmer for 15 minutes if using turkey, and 20 minutes if using veal, or until tender. Serve immediately.

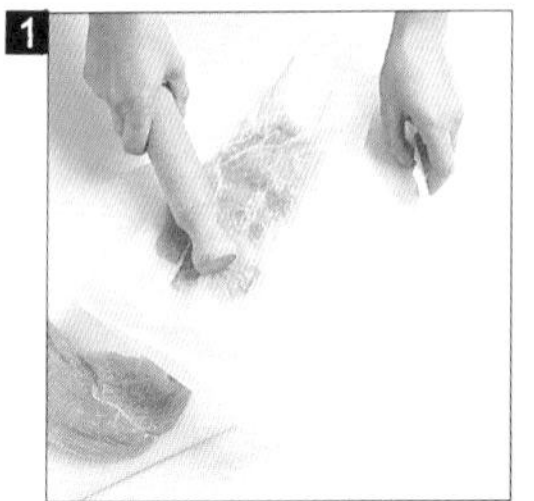
1

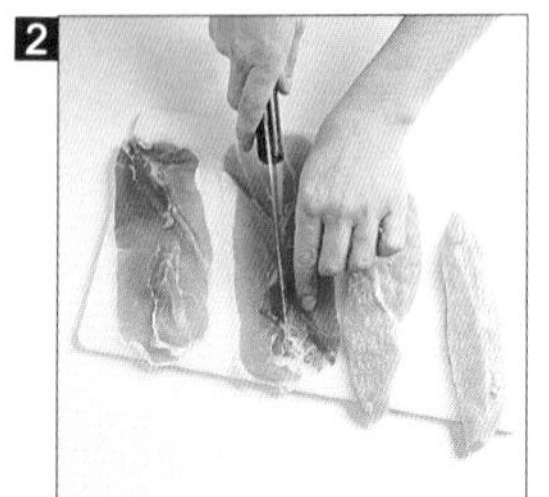
2

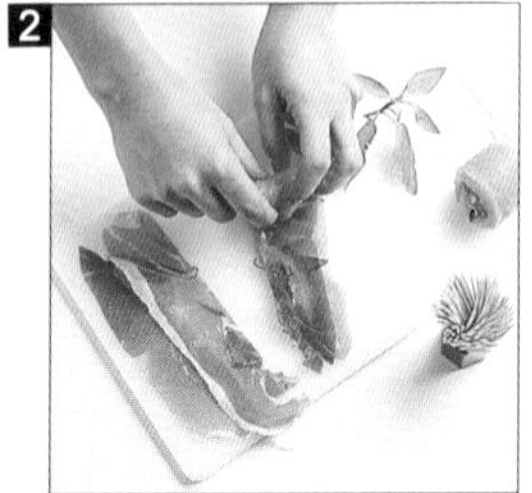
2

VARIATION

Try a similar recipe called *bocconcini*, meaning 'little mouthfuls'. Follow the same method as given here, but replace the sage leaf with a piece of Gruyère cheese.

Veal in a Rose Petal Sauce

This truly spectacular dish is equally delicious whether you use veal or pork fillet. Make sure the roses are free of blemishes and pesticides.

NUTRITIONAL INFORMATION

Calories	810	Sugars	2g
Protein	31g	Fat	56g
Carbohydrate	49g	Saturates	28g

 10 MINS  35 MINS

SERVES 4

INGREDIENTS

- 450 g/1 lb dried fettuccine
- 7 tbsp olive oil
- 1 tsp chopped fresh oregano
- 1 tsp chopped fresh marjoram
- 175 g/6 oz/¾ cup butter
- 450 g/1 lb veal fillet, thinly sliced
- 150 ml/¼ pint/⅔ cup rose petal vinegar (see Cook's Tip)
- 150 ml/¼ pint/⅔ cup fish stock
- 50 ml/2 fl oz/¼ cup grapefruit juice
- 50 ml/2 fl oz/¼ cup double (heavy) cream
- salt

TO GARNISH

- 12 pink grapefruit segments
- 12 pink peppercorns
- rose petals
- fresh herb leaves

2

3

3

1 Bring a large saucepan of lightly salted water to the boil. Add the fettuccine and 1 tablespoon of the oil and cook for 8–10 minutes or until tender, but still firm to the bite. Drain and transfer to a warm serving dish, sprinkle over 2 tablespoons of the olive oil, the oregano and marjoram.

2 Heat 50 g/2 oz/4 tbsp of the butter with the remaining oil in a large frying pan (skillet). Add the veal and cook over a low heat for 6 minutes. Remove the veal from the pan and place on top of the pasta.

3 Add the vinegar and fish stock to the pan and bring to the boil. Boil vigorously until reduced by two thirds. Add the grapefruit juice and cream and simmer over a low heat for 4 minutes. Dice the remaining butter and add to the pan, one piece at a time, whisking constantly until it has been completely incorporated.

4 Pour the sauce around the veal, garnish with grapefruit segments, pink peppercorns, the rose petals (washed) and your favourite herb leaves.

COOK'S TIP

To make rose petal vinegar, infuse the petals of 8 pesticide-free roses in 150 ml/¼ pint/⅔ cup white wine vinegar for 48 hours. Prepare well in advance to reduce the preparation time.

Venison Meatballs

The sharp, citrusy flavour of kumqats is the perfect complement to these tasty steamed meatballs. Serve simply on a bed of pasta or noodles.

NUTRITIONAL INFORMATION

Calories	309	Sugars	5g
Protein	40g	Fat	7g
Carbohydrate	15g	Saturates	0g

 10 MINS  20 MINS

SERVES 4

INGREDIENTS

- 450 g/1 lb lean venison, minced (ground)
- 1 small leek, finely chopped
- 1 medium carrot, finely grated
- ½ tsp ground nutmeg
- 1 medium egg white, lightly beaten
- salt and pepper

TO SERVE

- freshly cooked pasta or noodles
- freshly cooked vegetables

SAUCE

- 100 g/3½ oz kumquats
- 15 g/½ oz caster (superfine) sugar
- 150 ml/5 fl oz/⅔ cup water
- 4 tbsp dry sherry
- 1 tsp cornflour (cornstarch)

2

3

5

1 Place the venison in a mixing bowl together with the leek, carrot, seasoning and nutmeg. Add the egg white and bind the ingredients together with your hands until the mixture is well moulded and firm.

2 Divide the venison mixture into 16 equal portions. Wirh your hands and fingers, form each portion into a small round ball.

3 Bring a large saucepan of water to the boil. Arrange the meatballs on a layer of baking parchment in a steamer or large sieve (strainer) and place over the pan. Cover and steam for 10 minutes.

4 To make the sauce. Wash and thinly slice the kumquats. Place them in a saucepan with the sugar and water and bring to the boil. Simmer for 2–3 minutes.

5 Blend the sherry and cornflour (cornstarch) together and add to the pan. Heat through, stirring, until the sauce thickens. Season to taste with the salt and pepper.

6 Drain the meatballs and transfer to a serving plate. Spoon over the sauce and serve the meatballs with pasta or noodles and vegetables.

Char-Grilled Venison Steaks

Venison has a good strong flavour, which makes it an ideal meat to barbecue (grill). Marinate overnight to tenderize the meat.

NUTRITIONAL INFORMATION

Calories	233	Sugars	2g
Protein	35g	Fat	6g
Carbohydrate	3g	Saturates	0g

 12 HOURS  25 MINS

SERVES 4

INGREDIENTS

4 venison steaks
150 ml/5 fl oz/⅔ cup red wine
2 tbsp sunflower oil
1 tbsp red wine vinegar
1 onion, chopped
few sprigs fresh parsley
2 sprigs fresh thyme
1 bay leaf
1 tsp caster (superfine) sugar
½ tsp mild mustard
salt and pepper

TO SERVE

jacket potatoes
salad leaves and cherry tomatoes

1 

2 

3 

1 Place the venison steaks in a shallow, non-metallic dish.

2 Combine the wine, oil, wine vinegar, onion, fresh parsley, thyme, bay leaf, sugar, mustard and salt and pepper to taste in a screw-top jar and shake vigorously until well combined. Alternatively, using a fork, whisk the ingredients together in a bowl.

3 Pour the marinade mixture over the venison, cover and leave to marinate in the refrigerator overnight. Turn the steaks over in the mixture occasionally so that the meat is well coated.

4 Barbecue (grill) the venison over hot coals, searing the meat over the hottest part of the barbecue (grill) for about 2 minutes on each side.

5 Move the meat to an area with slightly less intense heat and barbecue (grill) for a further 4–10 minutes on each side, depending on how well done you like your steaks.

6 Test if the meat is cooked by inserting the tip of a knife into the meat – the juices will run from red when the meat is still rare to clear as the meat becomes well cooked.

7 Serve with jacket potatoes, salad leaves and tomatoes.

Venison with Plums

The rich, slightly gamey flavour of venison is complemented by the sharpness of the plums. Add port and brandy for a delectable sauce.

NUTRITIONAL INFORMATION

Calories	311	Sugars	4g
Protein	35g	Fat	12g
Carbohydrate	8g	Saturates	1g

5 MINS 10 MINS

SERVES 4

INGREDIENTS

- 500 g/1 lb 2 oz venison fillet (tenderloin)
- 2 tbsp olive oil
- 4 plums, halved, pitted and sliced
- 1 tsp chopped fresh sage
- 6 spring onions (scallions), white and green parts, cut into 2.5 cm/ 1 inch lengths
- 1 tbsp cornflour (cornstarch)
- 2 tbsp orange juice
- 150 ml/¼ pint/⅔ cup stock
- 4 tbsp port
- 1 tbsp redcurrant jelly
- 1 tbsp brandy
- salt and pepper
- fresh purple sage sprigs, to garnish
- creamed potatoes, to serve

1 Cut the venison into 1 cm/½ inch strips. Heat the oil in a heavy-based frying pan (skillet) and fry the venison over a high heat for about 2 minutes until browned. Remove from the pan with a perforated spoon.

2 Add the plums, sage and spring onions (scallions) to the pan and cook for 2 minutes, stirring occasionally.

3 Mix the cornflour (cornstarch) with the orange juice and add to the pan.

4 Add the stock, port and redcurrant jelly and heat, stirring, until thickened.

5 Return the venison to the pan, season to taste and pour in the brandy or port. Heat gently to warm through.

6 Garnish with purple sage and serve with creamed potatoes.

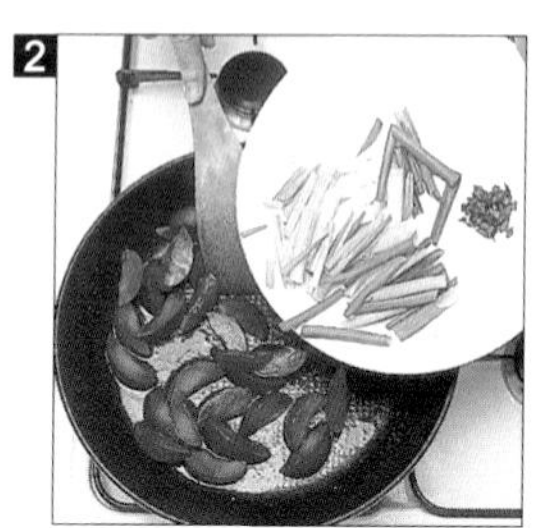

COOK'S TIP

If venison is eaten young it is very tender, and better cuts such as saddle or loin can be roasted, but do not overcook them – they should still be fairly pink inside.

Venison & Garlic Mash

Rich game is best served with a sweet fruit sauce. Here the venison steaks are cooked with sweet, juicy prunes and redcurrant jelly.

NUTRITIONAL INFORMATION

Calories	602	Sugars	18g
Protein	51g	Fat	14g
Carbohydrate	62g	Saturates	1g

10 MINS 35 MINS

SERVES 4

INGREDIENTS

8 medallions of venison, 75 g/2¾ oz each

1 tbsp vegetable oil

1 red onion, chopped

150 ml/5 fl oz/⅔ cup Fresh Beef Stock (see page 9)

150 ml/5 fl oz/⅔ cup red wine

3 tbsp redcurrant jelly

100 g/3½ oz no-need-to-soak dried, pitted prunes

2 tsp cornflour (cornstarch)

2 tbsp brandy

salt and pepper

patty pans, to serve (optional)

GARLIC MASH

900 g/2 lb potatoes, peeled and diced

½ tsp garlic purée (paste)

2 tbsp low-fat natural fromage frais (unsweetened yogurt)

4 tbsp fresh parsley, chopped

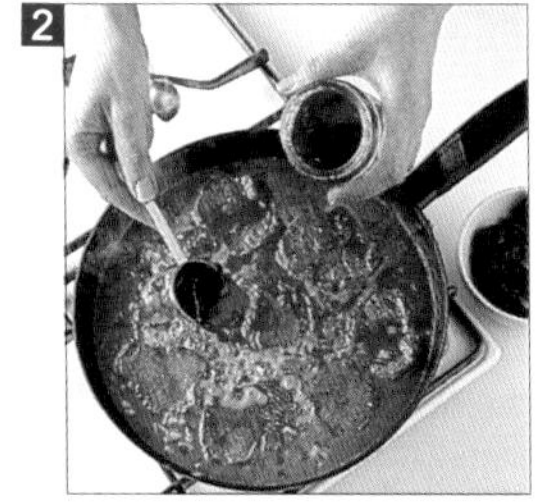

1 Trim off any excess fat from the meat and season with salt and pepper on both sides. Heat the oil in a frying pan (skillet) and fry the lamb with the onions for 2 minutes on each side until brown.

2 Lower the heat and pour in the stock and wine. Add the redcurrant jelly and prunes and stir until the jelly melts. Cover and simmer for 10 minutes.

3 Meanwhile, make the garlic mash. Place the potatoes in a saucepan and cover with water. Bring to the boil and cook for 8–10 minutes. Drain well and mash until smooth. Add the garlic purée (paste), fromage frais (yogurt) and parsley and blend thoroughly. Season, set aside and keep warm.

4 Remove the medallions from the frying pan (skillet) with a slotted spoon and keep warm.

5 Blend the cornflour (cornstarch) with the brandy in a small bowl and add to the pan juices. Heat, stirring, until thickened. Season with salt and pepper to taste. Serve the venison with the redcurrant and prune sauce, garlic mash and patty pans (if using).

WILKENS

Fish & Seafood

Naturally low in fat, yet rich in minerals and proteins, white fish and shellfish are important ingredients in a low-fat diet. The different varieties of fish vary enormously in texture and flavour and therefore lend themselves to assorted cooking methods. Grilling (broiling) and steaming, two of the most popular methods for cooking fish, are also low in fat, thereby providing a mouthwatering yet also healthy meal. Whenever you serve fish, remember that it must always be fresh – try to cook it within 24 hours, and always store it in the refrigerator. As well as fish, this chapter also includes an exciting selection of seafood dishes from around the world, including Provençale-style Mussels, Seared Scallops with Butter Sauce and Squid & Macaroni Stew. Whatever the occasion, you are sure to find a dish to tempt your guests.

Stir-fried Salmon with Leeks

Salmon is marinated in a deliciously rich, sweet sauce, stir-fried and served on a bed of crispy leeks.

NUTRITIONAL INFORMATION

Calories	360	Sugars	9g
Protein	24g	Fat	25
Carbohydrate	11g	Saturates	4g

 35 MINS  15 MINS

SERVES 4

INGREDIENTS

- 450 g/1 lb salmon fillet, skinned
- 2 tbsp sweet soy sauce
- 2 tbsp tomato ketchup
- 1 tsp rice wine vinegar
- 1 tbsp demerara (brown crystal) sugar
- 1 clove garlic, crushed
- 4 tbsp corn oil
- 450 g/1 lb leeks, thinly shredded
- finely chopped red chillies, to garnish

1 Using a sharp knife, cut the salmon into slices. Place the slices of salmon in a shallow non-metallic dish.

2 Mix together the soy sauce, tomato ketchup, rice wine vinegar, sugar and garlic.

3 Pour the mixture over the salmon, toss well and leave to marinate for about 30 minutes.

4 Meanwhile, heat 3 tablespoons of the corn oil in a large preheated wok.

5 Add the leeks to the wok and stir-fry over a medium-high heat for about 10 minutes, or until the leeks become crispy and tender.

6 Using a slotted spoon, carefully remove the leeks from the wok and transfer to warmed serving plates.

7 Add the remaining oil to the wok. Add the salmon and the marinade to the wok and cook for 2 minutes.

8 Remove the salmon from the wok and spoon over the leeks, garnish with finely chopped red chillies and serve immediately.

VARIATION

You can use a fillet of beef instead of the salmon, if you prefer.

Grilled (Broiled) Stuffed Sole

A delicious stuffing of sun-dried tomatoes and fresh lemon thyme are used to stuff whole sole.

NUTRITIONAL INFORMATION

Calories	207	Sugars	0.2g
Protein	24g	Fat	10g
Carbohydrate	8g	Saturates	4g

 25 MINS  20 MINS

SERVES 4

INGREDIENTS

1 tbsp olive oil
25 g/1 oz/2 tbsp butter
1 small onion, finely chopped
1 garlic clove, chopped
3 sun-dried tomatoes, chopped
2 tbsp lemon thyme
50 g/1¾ oz breadcrumbs
1 tbsp lemon juice
4 small whole sole, gutted and cleaned
salt and pepper
lemon wedges, to garnish
fresh green salad leaves, to serve

1 Heat the oil and butter in a frying pan (skillet) until it just begins to froth.

2 Add the onion and garlic to the frying pan (skillet) and cook, stirring, for 5 minutes until just softened.

3 To make the stuffing, mix the tomatoes, thyme, breadcrumbs and lemon juice in a bowl, and season.

4 Add the stuffing mixture to the pan, and stir to mix.

5 Using a sharp knife, pare the skin from the bone inside the gut hole of the fish to make a pocket. Spoon the tomato and herb stuffing into the pocket.

6 Cook the fish, under a preheated grill (broiler), for 6 minutes on each side or until golden brown.

7 Transfer the stuffed fish to serving plates and garnish with lemon wedges. Serve immediately with fresh green salad leaves.

COOK'S TIP

Lemon thyme (*Thymus* x *citriodorus*) has a delicate lemon scent and flavour. Ordinary thyme can be used instead, but mix it with 1 teaspoon of lemon rind to add extra flavour.

Salt Cod Fritters

These tasty little fried fish cakes make an excellent snack or main course. Prepare in advance as the salt cod needs to be soaked overnight.

NUTRITIONAL INFORMATION

Calories	142	Sugars	2g
Protein	10g	Fat	5g
Carbohydrate	14g	Saturates	1g

 30 MINS  45 MINS

SERVES 6

INGREDIENTS

- 100 g/3½ oz self-raising flour
- 1 egg, beaten
- 150 ml/¼ pint/⅔ cup milk
- 250 g/9 oz salt cod, soaked overnight
- 1 small red onion, finely chopped
- 1 small fennel bulb, finely chopped
- 1 red chilli, finely chopped
- 2 tbsp oil

TO SERVE

- crisp salad and chilli relish, or cooked rice and fresh vegetables

1. Sift the flour into a large bowl. Make a well in the centre of the flour and add the egg.

2. Using a wooden spoon, gradually draw in the flour, slowly adding the milk, and mix to form a smooth batter. Leave to stand for 10 minutes.

3. Drain the salt cod and rinse it under cold running water. Drain again thoroughly.

4. Remove and discard the skin and any bones from the fish, then mash the flesh with a fork.

5. Place the fish in a large bowl and combine with the onion, fennel and chilli. Add the mixture to the batter and blend together.

6. Heat the oil in a large frying pan (skillet) and, taking about 1 tablespoon of the mixture at a time, spoon it into the hot oil. Cook the fritters, in batches, for 3–4 minutes on each side until golden and slightly puffed. Keep warm while cooking the remaining mixture.

7. Serve with salad and a chilli relish for a light meal or with vegetables and rice.

2

5

5

COOK'S TIP

If you prefer larger fritters, use 2 tablespoons per fritter and cook for slightly longer.

Crispy Fish

This is a very hot dish – not for the faint hearted! It may be made without the chilli flavourings, if preferred.

NUTRITIONAL INFORMATION

Calories	281	Sugars	3g
Protein	25g	Fat	12g
Carbohydrate	15g	Saturates	2g

 30 MINS  40 MINS

SERVES 4

INGREDIENTS

450 g/1 lb white fish fillets

BATTER

60 g/2 oz/½ cup plain (all-purpose) flour

1 egg, separated

1 tbsp peanut oil

4 tbsp milk

vegetable oil, for deep-frying

SAUCE

1 fresh red chilli, chopped

2 garlic cloves, crushed

pinch of chilli powder

3 tbsp tomato purée (paste)

1 tbsp rice wine vinegar

2 tbsp dark soy sauce

2 tbsp Chinese rice wine

2 tbsp water

pinch of caster (superfine) sugar

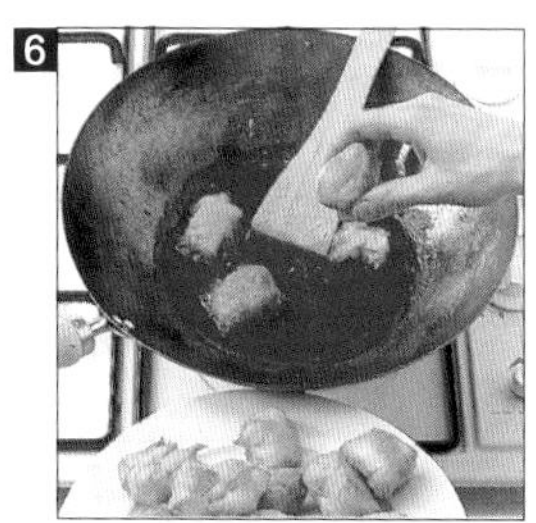

1 Cut the fish into 2.5-cm/1-inch cubes and set aside.

2 Sift the plain (all-purpose) flour into a mixing bowl and make a well in the centre. Add the egg yolk and peanut oil to the mixing bowl and gradually stir in the milk, incorporating the flour to form a smooth batter. Leave to stand for about 20 minutes.

3 Whisk the egg white until it forms peaks and fold into the batter until thoroughly incorporated.

4 Heat the vegetable oil in a preheated wok or large frying pan (skillet). Dip the fish into the batter and fry, in batches, for 8–10 minutes, until cooked through. Remove the fish from the wok with a slotted spoon, set aside and keep warm until required.

5 Pour off all but 1 tablespoon of oil from the wok and return to the heat. Add the chilli, garlic, chilli powder, tomato purée (paste), rice wine vinegar, soy sauce, Chinese rice wine, water and sugar and cook, stirring, for 3–4 minutes.

6 Return the fish to the wok and stir gently to coat it in the sauce. Cook for 2-3 minutes, until hot. Transfer to a serving dish and serve immediately.

Sardinian Red Mullet

Red mullet has a beautiful pink skin, which is enhanced in this dish by being cooked in red wine and orange juice.

NUTRITIONAL INFORMATION

Calories	287	Sugars	15g
Protein	31g	Fat	9g
Carbohydrate	15g	Saturates	1g

 2½ HOURS 25 MINS

SERVES 4

INGREDIENTS

50 g/1¾ oz sultanas

150 ml/¼ pint/⅔ cup red wine

2 tbsp olive oil

2 medium onions, sliced

1 courgette (zucchini), cut into 5 cm/2 inch sticks

2 oranges

2 tsp coriander seeds, lightly crushed

4 red mullet, boned and filleted

50g/1¾ oz can anchovy fillets, drained

2 tbsp chopped, fresh oregano

1 Place the sultanas in a bowl. Pour over the red wine and leave to soak for about 10 minutes.

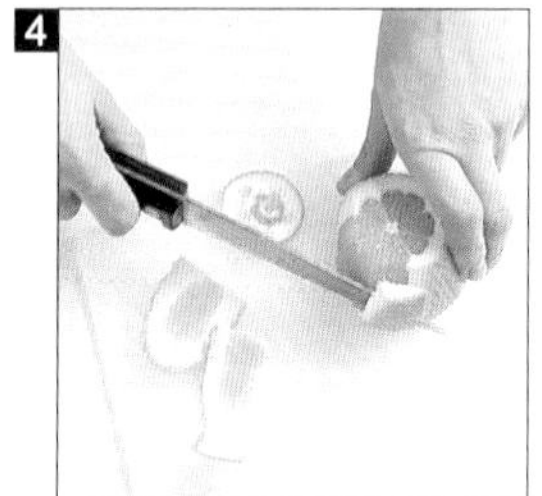

2 Heat the oil in a large frying pan (skillet). Add the onions and sauté for 2 minutes.

3 Add the courgettes (zucchini) to the pan and fry for a further 3 minutes or until tender.

4 Using a zester, pare long, thin strips from one of the oranges. Using a sharp knife, remove the skin from both of the oranges, then segment the oranges by slicing between the lines of pith.

5 Add the orange zest to the frying pan (skillet). Add the red wine, sultanas, red mullet and anchovies to the pan and leave to simmer for 10–15 minutes or until the fish is cooked through.

6 Stir in the oregano, set aside and leave to cool. Place the mixture in a large bowl and leave to chill, covered, in the refrigerator for at least 2 hours to allow the flavours to mingle. Transfer to serving plates and serve.

COOK'S TIP

Red mullet is usually available all year round – frozen, if not fresh – from your fishmonger or supermarket. If you cannot get hold of it try using Tilapia. This dish can also be served warm, if you prefer.

Fish with Saffron Sauce

White fish cooked in a bamboo steamer over the wok and served with a light creamy saffron sauce with a real bite to it.

NUTRITIONAL INFORMATION

Calories	254	Sugars	0.5g
Protein	30g	Fat	14g
Carbohydrate	2g	Saturates	5g

5 MINS  30 MINS

SERVES 4

INGREDIENTS

- 625-750 g/1 lb 6 oz-1 lb 10 oz white fish fillets (cod, haddock, whiting etc)
- pinch of Chinese five-spice powder
- 4 sprigs fresh thyme
- large pinch saffron threads
- 250 ml/9 fl oz/1 cup boiling fish or vegetable stock
- 2 tbsp sunflower oil
- 125 g/4½ oz button mushrooms, thinly sliced
- grated rind of ½ lemon
- 1 tbsp lemon juice
- ½ tsp freshly chopped thyme or ¼ tsp dried thyme
- ½ bunch watercress, chopped
- 1½ tsp cornflour (cornstarch)
- 3 tbsp single or double (heavy) cream
- salt and pepper

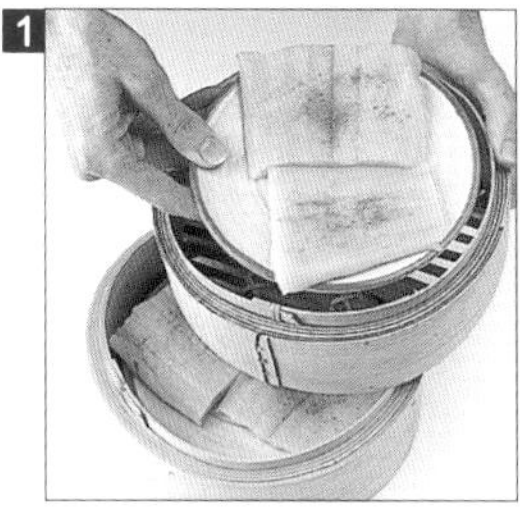
1

2

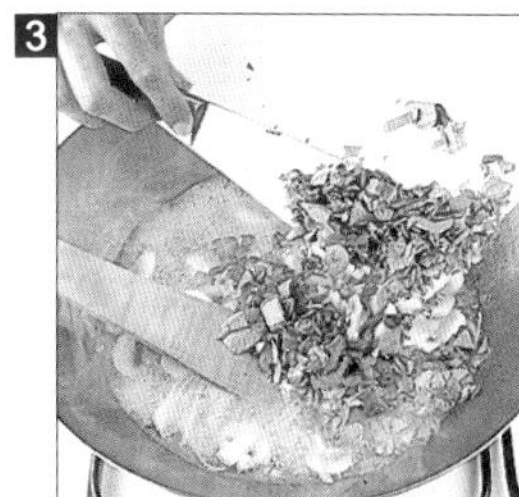
3

1 Skin the fish and cut into 4 even-sized portions. Season with salt and pepper and five-spice powder. Arrange the fish on a plate and place in the bottom of a bamboo steamer, laying a sprig of thyme on each piece of fish.

2 Stand a low metal trivet in a wok and add water to come almost to the top of it. Bring to the boil, stand the bamboo steamer on the trivet and cover with the bamboo lid and then the lid of the wok or a piece of foil. Simmer for 20 minutes until the fish is tender, adding more boiling water to the wok if necessary. Meanwhile, soak the saffron threads in the boiling stock.

3 When the fish is tender, remove and keep warm. Empty the wok and wipe dry. Heat the oil in the wok and stir-fry the mushrooms for about 2 minutes. Add the saffron stock, lemon rind and juice and chopped thyme and bring to the boil. Add the watercress and simmer for 1-2 minutes.

4 Blend the cornflour (cornstarch) with the cream, add a little of the sauce from the wok, then return to the wok and heat gently until thickened. Serve the fish surrounded by the sauce.

Sesame Salmon with Cream

Salmon fillet holds its shape when tossed in sesame seeds and stir-fried. It is served in a creamy sauce of diced courgettes (zucchini).

NUTRITIONAL INFORMATION

Calories	550	Sugars	1g
Protein	35g	Fat	45g
Carbohydrate	2g	Saturates	12g

 5 MINS  10 MINS

SERVES 4

INGREDIENTS

- 625-750 g/1 lb 6 oz– 1 lb 10 oz salmon or pink trout fillets
- 2 tbsp light soy sauce
- 3 tbsp sesame seeds
- 3 tbsp sunflower oil
- 4 spring onions (scallions), thinly sliced diagonally
- 2 large courgettes (zucchini), diced, or 2.5-cm/5-inch piece cucumber, diced
- grated rind of ½ lemon
- 1 tbsp lemon juice
- ½ tsp turmeric
- 6 tbsp fish stock or water
- 3 tbsp double (heavy) cream or fromage frais
- salt and pepper
- curly endive, to garnish

1. Skin the fish and cut into strips about 4 x 2 cm/1½ x ¾ inch. Pat dry on kitchen paper (paper towels). Season lightly, then brush with soy sauce and sprinkle all over with sesame seeds.

2. Heat 2 tablespoons of oil in the wok. Add the pieces of fish and stir-fry for 3-4 minutes until lightly browned all over. Remove with a fish slice, drain on kitchen paper (paper towels) and keep warm.

3. Heat the remaining oil to the wok and add the spring onions (scallions) and courgettes (zucchini) or cucumber and stir-fry for 1-2 minutes. Add the lemon rind and juice, turmeric, stock and seasoning and bring to the boil for 1 minute. Stir in the cream or fromage frais.

4. Return the fish pieces to the wok and toss gently in the sauce until they are really hot. Garnish and serve.

COOK'S TIP

Lay the fillet skin-side down. Insert a sharp, flexible knife at one end between the flesh and the skin. Hold the skin tightly at the end and push the knife along, keeping the knife blade as flat as possible against the skin.

1

2

3

Fish with Ginger Butter

Whole mackerel or trout are stuffed with herbs, wrapped in foil, baked and then drizzled with a fresh ginger butter.

NUTRITIONAL INFORMATION

Calories	328	Sugar	0g
Protein	24g	Fat	25g
Carbohydrate	1g	Saturates	13g

 10 MINS 30 MINS

SERVES 4

INGREDIENTS

- 4 x 250 g/9 oz whole trout or mackerel, gutted
- 4 tbsp chopped fresh coriander (cilantro)
- 5 garlic cloves, crushed
- 2 tsp grated lemon or lime zest
- 2 tsp vegetable oil
- banana leaves, for wrapping (optional)
- 90 g/3 oz/6 tbsp butter
- 1 tbsp grated ginger root
- 1 tbsp light soy sauce
- salt and pepper
- coriander (cilantro) sprigs and lemon or lime wedges, to garnish

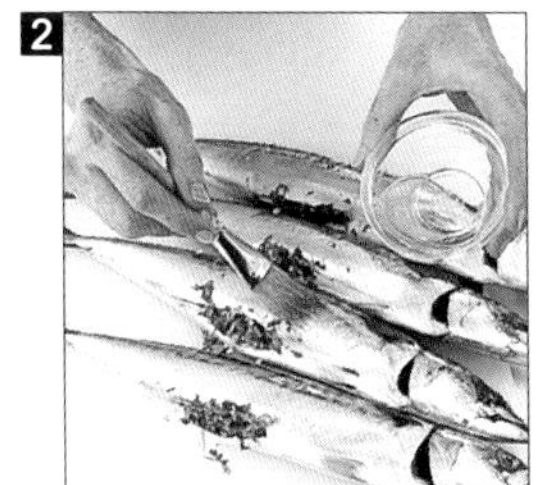
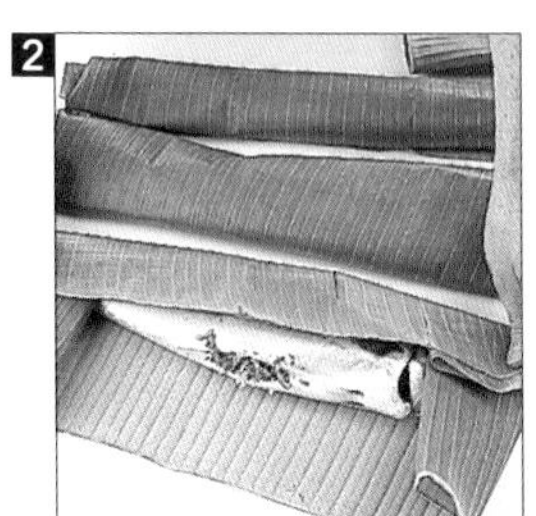

1 Wash and dry the fish. Mix the coriander (cilantro) with the garlic, lemon or lime zest and salt and pepper to taste. Spoon into the fish cavities.

2 Brush the fish with a little oil, season well and place each fish on a double thickness sheet of baking parchment or foil and wrap up well to enclose. Alternatively, wrap in banana leaves (see right).

3 Place on a baking tray (cookie sheet) and bake in a preheated oven for about 25 minutes or until the flesh will flake easily.

4 Meanwhile, melt the butter in a small pan. Add the ginger and mix well.

5 Stir the light soy sauce into the saucepan.

6 To serve, unwrap the fish parcels, drizzle over the ginger butter and garnish with coriander (cilantro) and lemon or lime wedges.

COOK'S TIP

For a really authentic touch, wrap the fish in banana leaves, which can be ordered from specialist oriental supermarkets. They are not edible, but impart a delicate flavour to the fish.

Poached Salmon

Salmon steaks, poached in a well-flavoured stock and served with a piquant sauce, make a delicious summer lunch or supper dish.

NUTRITIONAL INFORMATION

Calories	712	Sugars	5g
Protein	66g	Fat	47g
Carbohydrate	6g	Saturates	9g

 10 MINS  30 MINS

SERVES 4

INGREDIENTS

- 1 small onion, sliced
- 1 small carrot, sliced
- 1 stick celery, sliced
- 1 bay leaf
- pared rind and juice of ½ orange
- a few stalks of parsley
- salt
- 5-6 black peppercorns
- 700 ml/1¼ pints/3 cups water
- 4 salmon steaks, about 350 g/12 oz each
- salad leaves, to serve
- lemon twists, to garnish

SAUCE

- 1 large avocado, peeled, halved and stoned
- 125 ml/4 fl oz/½ cup low-fat natural yogurt
- grated zest and juice of ½ orange
- black pepper
- a few drops of hot red pepper sauce

1 Put the onion, carrot, celery, bay leaf, orange rind, orange juice, parsley stalks, salt and peppercorns in a pan just large enough to take the salmon steaks in a single layer. Pour on the water, cover the pan and bring to the boil. Simmer the stock for 20 minutes.

2 Arrange the salmon steaks in the pan, return the stock to the boil and simmer for 3 minutes. Cover the pan, remove from the heat and leave the salmon to cool in the stock.

3 Roughly chop the avocado and place it in a blender or food processor with the yogurt, orange zest and orange juice. Process until smooth, then season to taste with salt, pepper and hot pepper sauce.

4 Remove the salmon steaks from the stock (reserve it to make fish soup or a sauce), skin them and pat dry with kitchen paper (paper towels).

5 Cover the serving dish with salad leaves, arrange the salmon steaks on top and spoon a little of the sauce into the centre of each one. Garnish the fish with lemon twists, and serve the remaining sauce separately.

1

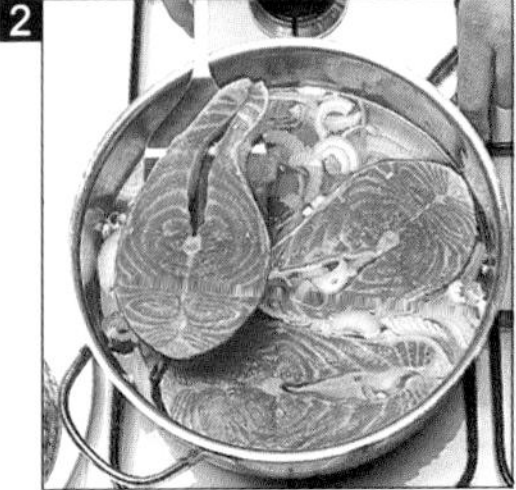

2

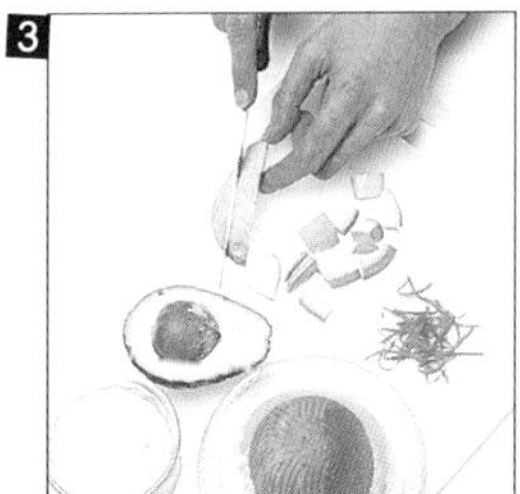

3

Steamed Stuffed Snapper

Red mullet may be used instead of the snapper, although they are a little more difficult to stuff because of their size. Use one mullet per person.

NUTRITIONAL INFORMATION

Calories	406	Sugar	4g
Protein	68g	Fat	9g
Carbohydrate	9g	Saturates	0g

20 MINS 10 MINS

SERVES 4

INGREDIENTS

- 1.4 kg/3 lb whole snapper, cleaned and scaled
- 175 g/6 oz spinach
- orange slices and shredded spring onion (scallion), to garnish

STUFFING

- 60 g/2 oz/2 cups cooked long-grain rice
- 1 tsp grated fresh root ginger
- 2 spring onions (scallions), finely chopped
- 2 tsp light soy sauce
- 1 tsp sesame oil
- ½ tsp ground star anise
- 1 orange, segmented and chopped

1 Rinse the fish inside and out under cold running water and pat dry with kitchen paper (paper towels).

2 Blanch the spinach for 40 seconds, rinse in cold water and drain well, pressing out as much moisture as possible.

3 Arrange the spinach on a heatproof plate and place the fish on top.

4 To make the stuffing, mix together the cooked rice, grated ginger, spring onions (scallions), soy sauce, sesame oil, star anise and orange in a bowl.

5 Spoon the stuffing into the body cavity of the fish, pressing it in well with a spoon.

6 Cover the plate and cook in a steamer for 10 minutes, or until the fish is cooked through.

7 Transfer the fish to a warmed serving dish, garnish with orange slices and shredded spring onion (scallion) and serve.

COOK'S TIP

The name snapper covers a family of tropical and subtropical fish that vary in colour. They may be red, orange, pink, grey or blue-green. Some are striped or spotted and they range in size from about 15 cm/ 6 inches to 90 cm/3 ft.

Yucatan Fish

Herbs, onion, green (bell) pepper and pumpkin seeds are used to flavour this baked fish dish, which is first marinated in lime juice.

NUTRITIONAL INFORMATION

Calories	248	Sugars	2g
Protein	33g	Fat	11g
Carbohydrate	3g	Saturates	1g

 40 MINS  35 MINS

SERVES 4

INGREDIENTS

- 4 cod cutlets or steaks or hake cutlets (about 175 g/6 oz each)
- 2 tbsp lime juice
- salt and pepper
- 1 green (bell) pepper
- 1 tbsp olive oil
- 1 onion, chopped finely
- 1–2 garlic cloves, crushed
- 40 g/1½ oz green pumpkin seeds
- grated rind of ½ lime
- 1 tbsp chopped fresh coriander (cilantro) or parsley
- 1 tbsp chopped fresh mixed herbs
- 60 g/2 oz button mushrooms, sliced thinly
- 2–3 tbsp fresh orange juice or white wine

TO GARNISH

- lime wedges
- fresh mixed herbs

1 Wipe the fish, place in a shallow ovenproof dish and pour the lime juice over. Turn the fish in the juice, season with salt and pepper, cover and leave in a cool place for 15–30 minutes.

2 Halve the (bell) pepper, remove the seeds and place under a preheated moderate grill, skin-side upwards, until the skin burns and splits. Leave to cool slightly, then peel off the skin and chop the flesh.

3 Heat the oil in a pan and fry the onion, garlic, (bell) pepper and pumpkin seeds gently for a few minutes until the onion is soft.

4 Stir in the lime rind, coriander (cilantro) or parsley, mixed herbs, mushrooms and seasoning, and spoon over the fish.

5 Spoon or pour the orange juice or wine over the fish, cover with foil or a lid and place in a preheated oven at 180°C/350°F/Gas Mark 4 for about 30 minutes, or until the fish is just tender.

6 Garnish the fish with lime wedges and fresh herbs and serve.

1

2
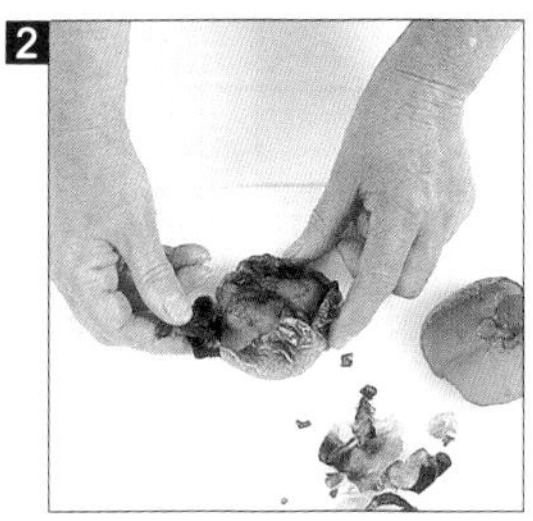

3

Herrings with Lemon

Cook these fish in foil parcels for a wonderfully moist texture. Serve with lots of fresh bread to soak up the delicious juices.

NUTRITIONAL INFORMATION

Calories	355	Sugars	0g
Protein	19g	Fat	31g
Carbohydrate	0g	Saturates	13g

 10 MINS  20 MINS

SERVES 4

INGREDIENTS

- 4 herrings, cleaned
- salt
- 4 bay leaves
- 1 lemon, sliced
- 50 g/1¾ oz unsalted butter
- 2 tbsp chopped fresh parsley
- ½ tsp lemon pepper
- fresh crusty bread, to serve

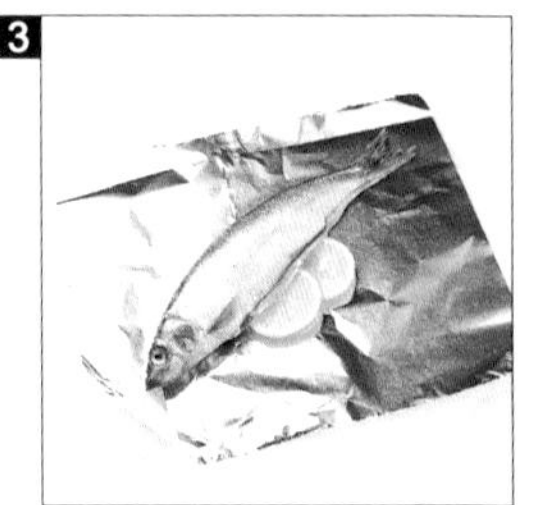

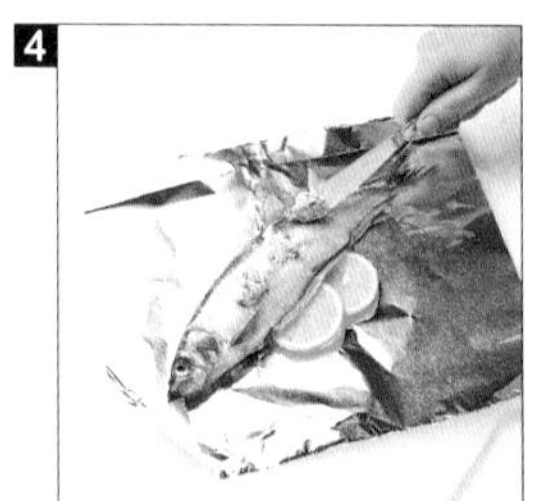

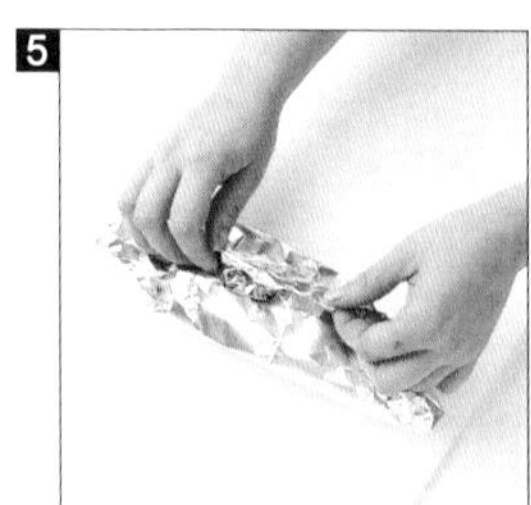

1 Season the prepared herrings inside and out with freshly ground salt to taste.

2 Place a bay leaf inside the cavity of each fish.

3 Place 4 squares of kitchen foil on the work surface and divide the lemon slices evenly among them. Place a fish on top of the lemon slices.

4 Beat the butter until softened, then mix in the parsley and lemon pepper. Dot the flavoured butter liberally all over the fish.

5 Wrap the fish tightly in the kitchen foil and barbecue (grill) over medium hot coals for 15-20 minutes or until the fish is cooked through – the flesh should be white in colour and firm to the touch (unwrap the foil to check, then wrap up the fish again).

6 Transfer the wrapped fish parcels to individual, warm serving plates.

7 Unwrap the foil parcels before serving.

8 Serve the fish with fresh, crusty bread to mop up the cooking juices.

COOK'S TIP

For a main course use trout instead of herring. Cook for 20–30 minutes until the flesh is firm to the touch and opaque in colour.

Lemon Sole & Haddock Ravioli

This delicate-tasting dish is surprisingly satisfying for even the hungriest appetites. Prepare the Italian Red Wine Sauce well in advance.

NUTRITIONAL INFORMATION

Calories	977	Sugars	7g
Protein	67g	Fat	40g
Carbohydrate	93g	Saturates	17g

 9¾ HOURS  25 MINS

SERVES 4

INGREDIENTS

- 450 g/1 lb lemon sole fillets, skinned
- 450 g/1 lb haddock fillets, skinned
- 3 eggs beaten
- 450 g/1 lb cooked potato gnocchi
- 175 g/6 oz/3 cups fresh breadcrumbs
- 50 ml/2 fl oz/¼ cup double (heavy) cream
- 450 g/1 lb Basic Pasta Dough (see page 6)
- 300 ml/½ pint/1¼ cups Italian Red Wine Sauce (see page 7)
- 60 g/2 oz/⅔ cup freshly grated Parmesan cheese
- salt and pepper

1 Flake the lemon sole and haddock fillets with a fork and transfer the flesh to a large mixing bowl.

2 Mix the eggs, cooked potato gnocchi, breadcrumbs and cream in a bowl until thoroughly combined. Add the fish to the bowl containing the gnocchi and season the mixture with salt and pepper to taste.

3 Roll out the pasta dough on to a lightly floured surface and cut out 7.5 cm/3 inch rounds using a plain cutter.

4 Place a spoonful of the fish stuffing on each round. Dampen the edges slightly and fold the pasta rounds over, pressing together to seal.

5 Bring a large saucepan of lightly salted water to the boil. Add the ravioli and cook for 15 minutes.

6 Drain the ravioli, using a slotted spoon, and transfer to a large serving dish. Pour over the Italian Red Wine Sauce, sprinkle over the Parmesan cheese and serve immediately.

2

3
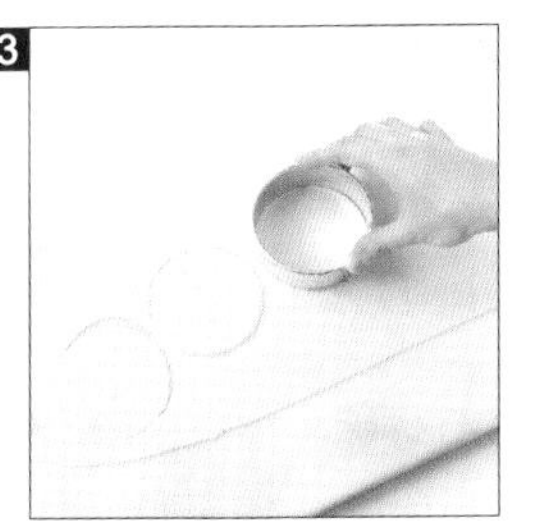

4
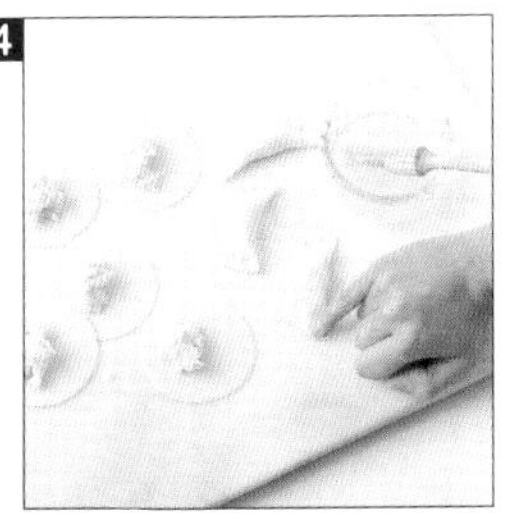

COOK'S TIP

For square ravioli, divide the dough in two. Wrap half in cling film; thinly roll out the other half. Cover; roll out the remaining dough. Pipe the filling at regular intervals and brush the spaces in between with water or beaten egg. Lift the second sheet of dough into position with a rolling pin and press between the filling to seal. Cut with a ravioli cutter or a knife.

Fillets of Red Mullet & Pasta

This simple recipe perfectly complements the sweet flavour and delicate texture of the fish.

NUTRITIONAL INFORMATION

Calories	457	Sugars	3g
Protein	39g	Fat	12g
Carbohydrate	44g	Saturates	5g

 15 MINS  1 HOUR

SERVES 4

INGREDIENTS

- 1 kg/2 lb 4 oz red mullet fillets
- 300 ml/½ pint/1¼ cups dry white wine
- 4 shallots, finely chopped
- 1 garlic clove, crushed
- 3 tbsp finely chopped mixed fresh herbs
- finely grated rind and juice of 1 lemon
- pinch of freshly grated nutmeg
- 3 anchovy fillets, roughly chopped
- 2 tbsp double (heavy) cream
- 1 tsp cornflour (cornstarch)
- 450 g/1 lb dried vermicelli
- 1 tbsp olive oil
- salt and pepper

TO GARNISH

- 1 fresh mint sprig
- lemon slices
- lemon rind

1 Put the red mullet fillets in a large casserole. Pour over the wine and add the shallots, garlic, herbs, lemon rind and juice, nutmeg and anchovies. Season. Cover and bake in a preheated oven at 180°C/350°F/Gas Mark 4 for 35 minutes.

2 Transfer the mullet to a warm dish. Set aside and keep warm.

3 Pour the cooking liquid into a pan and bring to the boil. Simmer for 25 minutes, until reduced by half. Mix the cream and cornflour (cornstarch) and stir into the sauce to thicken.

4 Meanwhile, bring a pan of lightly salted water to the boil. Add the vermicelli and oil and cook for 8–10 minutes, until tender but still firm to the bite. Drain the pasta and transfer to a warm serving dish.

5 Arrange the red mullet fillets on top of the vermicelli and pour over the sauce. Garnish with a fresh mint sprig, slices of lemon and strips of lemon rind and serve immediately.

Pasta Pudding

A tasty mixture of creamy fish and pasta cooked in a bowl, unmoulded and drizzled with tomato sauce presents macaroni in a new guise.

NUTRITIONAL INFORMATION

Calories	536	Sugars	4g
Protein	35g	Fat	35g
Carbohydrate	21g	Saturates	17g

 35 MINS  2 HOURS

SERVES 4

INGREDIENTS

- 125 g/4½ oz short-cut macaroni
- 1 tbsp olive oil
- 15 g/½ oz/1 tbsp butter, plus extra for greasing
- 500 g/1 lb 2 oz white fish fillets, such as cod or coley, or for luxury, monkfish
- a few parsley stalks
- 6 black peppercorns
- 125 ml/4 fl oz/½ cup double (heavy) cream
- 2 eggs, separated
- 2 tbsp chopped parsley
- pinch of grated nutmeg
- 60 g/2 oz/½ cup Parmesan, grated
- Basic Tomato Sauce (see page 6), to serve
- pepper
- parsley sprigs, to garnish

1 Cook the pasta in a pan of salted boiling water, adding the oil, for 8–10 minutes. Drain, return to the pan, add the butter and cover. Keep warm.

2 Place the fish in a frying pan (skillet) with the parsley stalks and peppercorns and pour on just enough water to cover. Bring to the boil, cover, and simmer for 10 minutes. Lift out the fish with a fish slice, reserving the liquor. When the fish is cool enough to handle, skin and remove any bones. Cut into bite-sized pieces.

3 Transfer the pasta to a large bowl and stir in the cream, egg yolks and dill. Stir in the fish, taking care not to break it up, and enough liquor to make a moist but firm mixture. It should fall easily from a spoon, but not be too runny. Whisk the egg whites until stiff but not dry, then fold into the mixture.

4 Grease a heatproof bowl or pudding basin and spoon in the mixture to within 4 cm/1½ inch of the rim. Cover the top with greased greaseproof paper and a cloth, or with foil, and tie firmly around the rim. Do not use foil if you cook the pudding in a microwave.

5 Stand the pudding on a trivet in a large pan of boiling water to come halfway up the sides. Cover and steam for 1½ hours, topping up the boiling water as needed, or cook in a microwave on maximum power for 7 minutes.

6 Run a knife around the inside of the bowl and invert on to a warm serving dish. Pour some tomato sauce over the top; serve the rest separately. Garnish and serve.

2

3

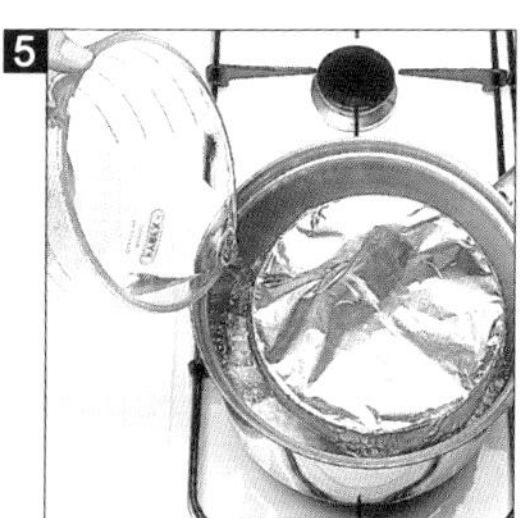
5

Japanese Plaice (Flounder)

The marinade for this dish has a distinctly Japanese flavour. Its subtle flavour goes well with any white fish.

NUTRITIONAL INFORMATION

Calories	207	Sugars	9g
Protein	22g	Fat	8g
Carbohydrate	10g	Saturates	1g

 6 HOURS 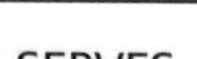 10 MINS

SERVES 4

INGREDIENTS

- 4 small plaice (flounders)
- 6 tbsp soy sauce
- 2 tbsp sake or dry white wine
- 2 tbsp sesame oil
- 1 tbsp lemon juice
- 2 tbsp light muscovado sugar
- 1 tsp root (fresh) ginger, grated
- 1 clove garlic, crushed

TO GARNISH

- 1 small carrot
- 4 spring onions (scallion)

2
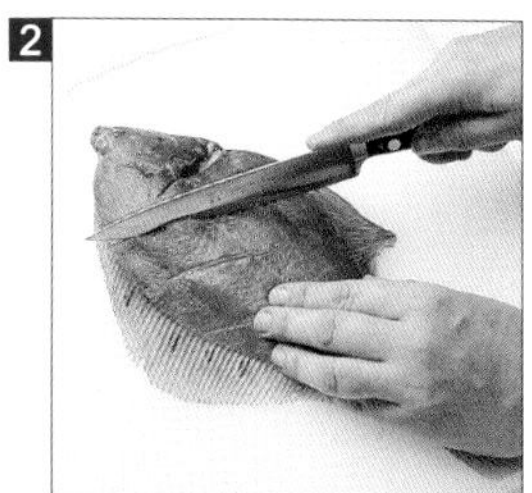

4
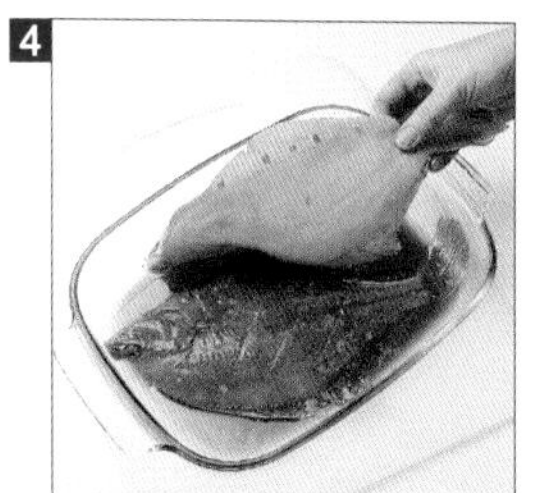

5
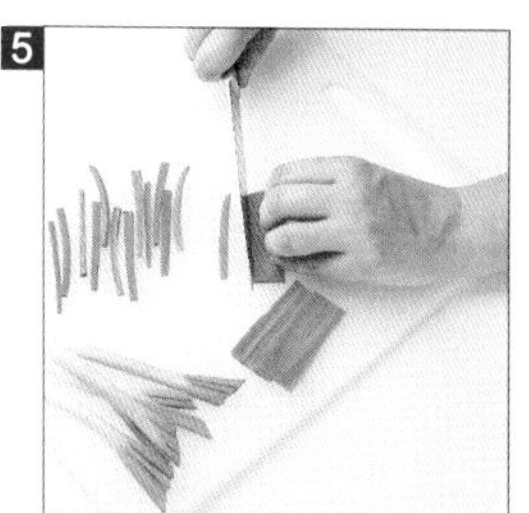

1 Rinse the fish and pat them dry on kitchen paper (paper towels).

2 Cut a few slashes into the sides of the fish so that they absorb the marinade.

3 Mix together the soy sauce, sake or wine, oil, lemon juice, sugar, ginger and garlic in a large, shallow dish.

4 Place the fish in the marinade and turn them over so that they are well coated on both sides. Leave to stand in the refrigerator for 1–6 hours.

5 Meanwhile, prepare the garnish. Cut the carrot into evenly-sized thin sticks and clean and shred the spring onions (scallions).

6 Barbecue (grill) the fish over hot coals for about 10 minutes, turning once.

7 Scatter the chopped spring onions (scallions) and carrot over the fish and transfer the fish to a serving dish. Serve immediately.

VARIATION

Use sole instead of the plaice (flounders) and scatter over some toasted sesame seeds instead of the carrot and spring onions (scallions), if you prefer.

Sole & Smoked Salmon Rolls

In this elegant dish, the delicate flavour of sole and salmon blend together perfectly with a light, citrus filling.

NUTRITIONAL INFORMATION

Calories	....	Sugars	....
Protein	....	Fat	....
Carbohydrate	......	Saturates	....

 1 HOUR  20 MINS

SERVES 4

INGREDIENTS

- 60 g/2 oz/1 cup fresh wholemeal (whole wheat) breadcrumbs
- ½ tsp grated lime rind
- 1 tbsp lime juice
- 60 g/2 oz/¼ cup low-fat soft cheese
- 4 × 125 g/4½ oz sole fillets
- 60 g/2 oz smoked salmon
- 150 ml/¼ pint/⅔ cup Fresh Fish Stock (see page 8)
- 150 ml/¼ pint/⅔ cup low-fat natural yogurt
- 1 tbsp chopped fresh chervil
- salt and pepper
- fresh chervil, to garnish

TO SERVE

- selection of freshly steamed vegetables
- lime wedges

1 In a mixing bowl, combine the breadcrumbs, lime rind and juice, soft cheese and seasoning, to form a soft stuffing mixture.

2 Skin the sole fillets by inserting a sharp knife in between the skin and flesh at the tail end. Holding the skin in your fingers and keeping it taut, strip the flesh away from the skin.

3 Halve the sole fillets lengthways. Place strips of smoked salmon over the skinned side of each fillet, trimming the salmon as necessary.

4 Spoon one-eighth of the stuffing on to each fish fillet and press down along the fish with the back of a spoon. Carefully roll up from the head to the tail end. Place, seam-side down, in an ovenproof dish and pour in the stock. Bake in a preheated oven at 190°C/ 375°F/Gas Mark 5 for 15 minutes.

5 Using a fish slice, transfer the fish to a warm serving plate, cover and keep warm. Pour the cooking juices into a saucepan and add the yogurt and chopped chervil. Season to taste and heat gently without boiling. Garnish the fish rolls with chervil and serve with the yogurt sauce, and the steamed vegetables and lime wedges.

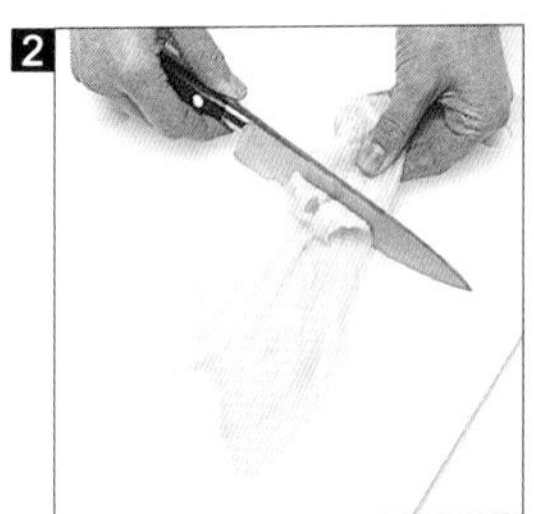

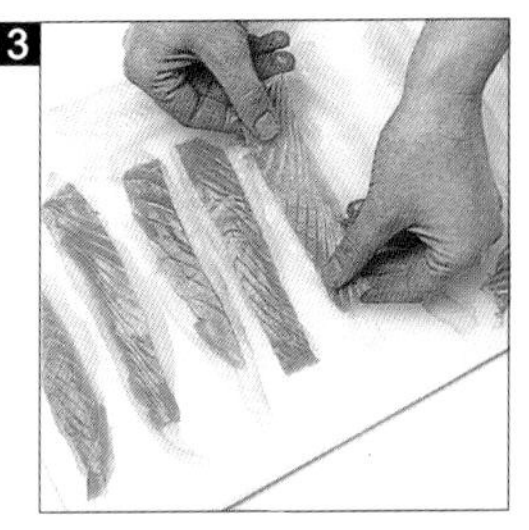

COOK'S TIP

When buying fresh fish, choose fish with a bright eye and red gills. The fish should be firm to the touch, with just a slight 'fishy' smell.

Herrings with Tarragon

The fish are filled with an orange-flavoured stuffing and are wrapped in kitchen foil before being baked on the barbecue (grill).

NUTRITIONAL INFORMATION

Calories	332	Sugars	4g
Protein	21g	Fat	24g
Carbohydrate	9g	Saturates	6g

 15 MINS

 35 MINS

SERVES 4

INGREDIENTS

- 1 orange
- 4 spring onions (scallions)
- 50 g/1¾ oz fresh wholemeal breadcrumbs
- 1 tbsp fresh tarragon, chopped
- 4 herrings, cleaned and gutted
- salt and pepper
- green salad, to serve

TO GARNISH

- 2 oranges
- 1 tbsp light brown sugar
- 1 tbsp olive oil
- sprigs of fresh tarragon

1 To make the stuffing, grate the rind from half of the orange, using a zester.

2 Peel and chop all of the orange flesh on a plate in order to catch all of the juice.

3 Mix together the orange flesh, juice, rind, spring onions (scallions), breadcrumbs and tarragon in a bowl. Season with salt and pepper to taste.

4 Divide the stuffing into 4 equal portions and use it to fill the body cavities of the fish.

1

2

3

5 Place each fish on to a square of lightly greased kitchen foil and wrap the foil around the fish so that it is completely enclosed. Barbecue (grill) over hot coals for 20–30 minutes until the fish are cooked through – the flesh should be white and firm to the touch.

6 Meanwhile make the garnish. Peel and thickly slice the 2 oranges and sprinkle over the sugar.

7 Just before the fish is cooked, drizzle a little oil over the orange slices and place them on the barbecue for about 5 minutes to heat through.

8 Transfer the fish to serving plates and garnish with the barbecued (grilled) orange slices and sprigs of fresh tarragon.

9 Serve the fish with fresh green salad leaves.

Mediterranean Fish Stew

Popular in fishing ports around Europe, gentle stewing is an excellent way to maintain the flavour and succulent texture of fish and shellfish.

NUTRITIONAL INFORMATION

Calories	533	Sugars	11g
Protein	71g	Fat	10g
Carbohydrate	30g	Saturates	2g

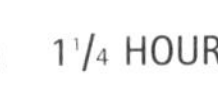 1¼ HOURS 25 MINS

SERVES 4

INGREDIENTS

- 2 tsp olive oil
- 2 red onions, sliced
- 2 garlic cloves, crushed
- 2 tbsp red wine vinegar
- 2 tsp caster (superfine) sugar
- 300 ml/½ pint/1¼ cups Fresh Fish Stock (see page 78)
- 300 ml/½ pint/1¼ cups dry red wine
- 2 × 400 g/14 oz cans chopped tomatoes
- 225 g/8 oz baby aubergines (eggplant), quartered
- 225 g/8 oz yellow courgettes (zucchini), quartered or sliced
- 1 green (bell) pepper, sliced
- 1 tbsp chopped fresh rosemary
- 500 g/1 lb 2 oz halibut fillet, skinned and cut into 2.5 cm/1 inch cubes
- 750 g/1 lb 10 oz fresh mussels, prepared
- 225 g/8 oz baby squid, cleaned, trimmed and sliced into rings
- 225 g/8 oz fresh tiger prawns (shrimp), peeled and deveined
- salt and pepper
- 4 slices toasted French bread rubbed with a cut garlic clove
- lemon wedges, to serve

1 Heat the oil in a large non-stick saucepan and fry the onions and garlic gently for 3 minutes.

2 Stir in the vinegar and sugar and cook for a further 2 minutes.

3 Stir in the stock, wine, canned tomatoes, aubergines (eggplant) courgettes (zucchini), (bell) pepper and rosemary. Bring to the boil and simmer, uncovered, for 10 minutes.

4 Add the halibut, mussels and squid. Mix well and simmer, covered, for 5 minutes until the fish is opaque.

5 Stir in the prawns (shrimp) and continue to simmer, covered, for a further 2–3 minutes until the prawns (shrimp) are pink and cooked through.

6 Discard any mussels which haven't opened and season to taste.

7 To serve, put a slice of the prepared garlic bread in the base of each warmed serving bowl and ladle the stew over the top. Serve with lemon wedges.

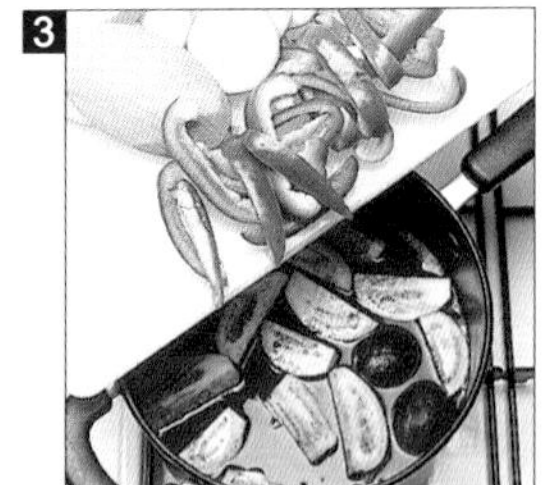
3

4

5

Monkfish with Caper Sauce

Monkfish is a very meaty-textured fish. It cooks very well as it doesn't flake like most other fish.

NUTRITIONAL INFORMATION

Calories	405	Sugars	0g
Protein	36g	Fat	29g
Carbohydrate	0g	Saturates	4g

 25 MINS 10 MINS

SERVES 4

INGREDIENTS

- 750 g/1 lb 10 oz monkfish tail
- finely grated rind and juice 1 small lemon
- 2 tbsp olive oil
- a small bunch of fresh bay leaves
- 1 small lemon, cut into wedges

SAUCE

- 6 tbsp olive oil
- 1 garlic clove, chopped finely
- finely grated rind and juice 1 small lemon
- 1 tbsp chopped fresh parsley
- 2 tbsp capers, drained and chopped
- 3 anchovy fillets, chopped finely
- pepper

1 Wash and pat dry the monkfish using paper towels. Carefully trim away the pinky grey membrane and slice either side of the central bone to give 2 thick fillets.

2 Cut the monkfish into 2.5 cm/1 inch cubes and place in a shallow dish. Toss in the lemon rind and juice and the olive oil.

3 Drain the fish, reserving the juices, and thread on to four bamboo skewers, threading a few bay leaves and wedges of lemon in between the fish cubes.

4 Preheat a grill (broiler) to medium. Place the skewers on a rack and cover the ends of the skewers with foil to prevent burning. Brush with some of the reserved juices and cook for 3 minutes. Turn over, brush again and cook for a further 3–4 minutes until tender and cooked through.

5 Meanwhile, mix together all the ingredients for the caper sauce and set aside.

6 Drain the skewers and transfer to warmed serving plates. Serve with the sauce and a green salad.

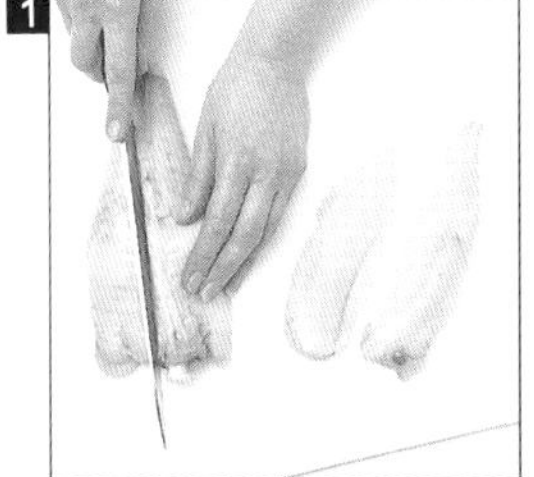
1

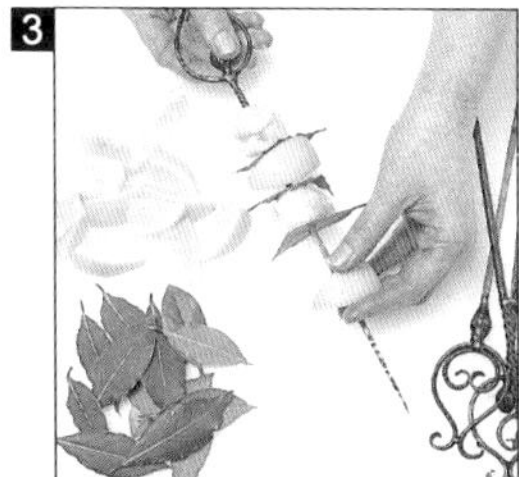
3

5

Pasta & Fish Pudding

This is a great recipe to cook mid-week when you want something satisfying and delicious, yet not too heavy.

NUTRITIONAL INFORMATION

Calories	454	Sugars	1g
Protein	30g	Fat	30g
Carbohydrate	17g	Saturates	16g

 10 MINS  2 HOURS

SERVES 4

INGREDIENTS

- 115 g/4 oz/1 cup dried short-cut macaroni or penne
- 1 tbsp olive oil
- 15 g/½ oz/1 tbsp butter, plus extra for greasing
- 450 g/1 lb haddock fillets
- 2–3 fresh parsley sprigs
- 6 black peppercorns
- 125 ml/4 fl oz/½ cup double (heavy) cream
- 2 eggs, separated
- 2 tbsp chopped fresh dill
- pinch of freshly grated nutmeg
- 60 g/2 oz/⅔ cup freshly grated Peccorino cheese
- salt and pepper
- fresh dill sprigs, to garnish

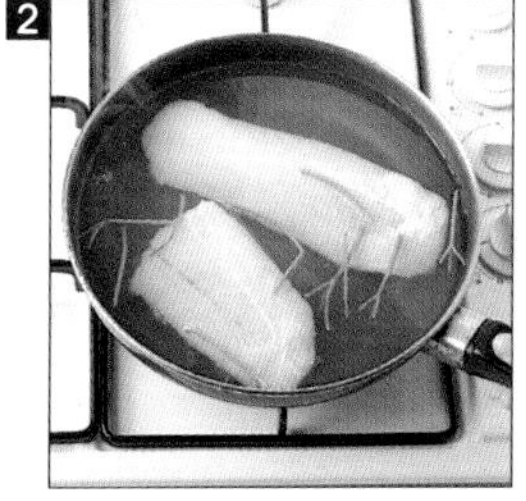
2

3

3

1 Bring a pan of salted water to the boil. Add the pasta and oil and cook for 8 10 minutes until tender, but still firm to the bite. Drain the pasta and return to the pan. Add the butter, cover and keep warm.

2 Place the fish in a frying pan (skillet). Add the parsley sprigs, peppercorns and enough water to cover. Bring to the boil, cover and simmer for 10 minutes. Lift out the fish and set aside to cool. Reserve the cooking liquid.

3 Skin the fish carefully and then cut into bite-size pieces. Put the pasta in a bowl. Mix the cream, egg yolks, chopped dill, nutmeg and Peccorino cheese together. Pour this mixture into the pasta and mix. Spoon in the fish without breaking it. Add enough of the reserved cooking liquid to make a moist, but firm mixture. Whisk the egg whites until stiff, then fold them into the mixture.

4 Grease a heatproof bowl and spoon in the fish mixture to within 4 cm/1½ inches of the rim. Cover with greased greaseproof (baking) paper and foil and tie securely with string.

5 Stand the bowl on a trivet in a saucepan. Add boiling water to reach halfway up the sides. Cover and steam for 1½ hours.

6 Invert the pudding carefully onto a serving plate. Garnish and serve immediately with a tomato relish or tartare sauce.

Ocean Pie

A tasty fish pie combining a mixture of fish and shellfish. You can use a wide variety of fish – whatever is available.

NUTRITIONAL INFORMATION

Calories	599	Sugars	8g
Protein	45g	Fat	21g
Carbohydrate	58g	Saturates	4g

15 MINS 1 HOUR

SERVES 4

INGREDIENTS

- 500 g/1 lb 2 oz cod or haddock fillet, skinned
- 225 g/8 oz salmon steak
- 425 ml/¾ pint/scant 2 cups skimmed milk
- 1 bay leaf
- 1 kg/2 lb potatoes
- 60 g/2 oz/⅓ cup peeled prawns (shrimp), thawed if frozen
- 60 g/2 oz/¼ cup margarine
- 25 g/1 oz/4 tbsp plain (all-purpose) flour
- 2–4 tbsp white wine
- 1 tsp chopped fresh dill or ½ tsp dried dill
- 2 tbsp drained capers
- salt and pepper
- few whole prawns (shrimp) in their shells, to garnish

1 Put the fish into a saucepan with 300 ml/½ pint/1¼ cups of the milk, the bay leaf and seasoning. Bring to the boil, cover and simmer gently for 10–15 minutes until tender.

2 Coarsely chop the potatoes and cook in boiling salted water until tender.

3 Drain the fish, reserving 300 ml/½ pint/1¼ cups of the cooking liquid (make up with more milk if necessary). Flake the fish, discarding any bones and place in a shallow ovenproof dish. Add the prawns (shrimp).

4 Melt half the margarine in a saucepan, add the flour and cook, stirring, for a minute or so. Gradually stir in the reserved stock and the wine and bring to the boil. Add the dill, capers and seasoning to taste and simmer until thickened. Pour over the fish and mix well.

5 Drain the potatoes and mash, adding the remaining margarine, seasoning and sufficient milk to give a piping consistency.

6 Put the mashed potato into a piping bag. Use a large star nozzle (tip) and pipe over the fish. Cook in a preheated oven at 200°C/400°F/Gas Mark 6 for about 25 minutes until piping hot and browned. Serve garnished with prawns (shrimp).

Smoked Haddock Casserole

This quick, easy and inexpensive dish would be ideal for a mid-week family supper.

NUTRITIONAL INFORMATION

Calories	525	Sugars	8g
Protein	41g	Fat	18g
Carbohydrate	53g	Saturates	10g

 20 MINS   45 MINS

SERVES 4

INGREDIENTS

- 25 g/1 oz/2 tbsp butter, plus extra for greasing
- 450 g/1 lb smoked haddock fillets, cut into 4 slices
- 600 ml/1 pint/2½ cups milk
- 25 g/1 oz/¼ cup plain (all purpose) flour
- pinch of freshly grated nutmeg
- 3 tbsp double (heavy) cream
- 1 tbsp chopped fresh parsley
- 2 eggs, hard boiled (hard cooked) and mashed to a pulp
- 450 g/1 lb/4 cups dried fusilli
- 1 tbsp lemon juice
- salt and pepper
- boiled new potatoes and beetroot (beet), to serve

1 Thoroughly grease a casserole with butter. Put the haddock in the casserole and pour over the milk. Bake in a preheated oven at 200°C/400°F/Gas Mark 6 for about 15 minutes. Carefully pour the cooking liquid into a jug (pitcher) without breaking up the fish.

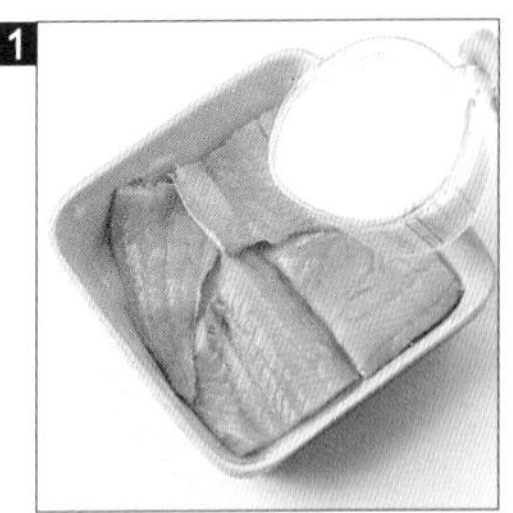
1

2 Melt the butter in a saucepan and stir in the flour. Gradually whisk in the reserved cooking liquid. Season to taste with salt, pepper and nutmeg. Stir in the cream, parsley and mashed egg and cook, stirring constantly, for 2 minutes.

2

3 Meanwhile, bring a large saucepan of lightly salted water to the boil. Add the fusilli and lemon juice and cook for 8–10 minutes until tender, but still firm to the bite.

4 Drain the pasta and spoon or tip it over the fish. Top with the egg sauce and return the casserole to the oven for 10 minutes.

4

5 Serve the casserole with boiled new potatoes and beetroot (beet).

VARIATION

You can use any type of dried pasta for this casserole. Try penne, conchiglie or rigatoni.

Sardine & Potato Bake

Fresh sardines are now readily available, so this traditional dish from Liguria can be enjoyed by all.

NUTRITIONAL INFORMATION

Calories	626	Sugars	6g
Protein	45g	Fat	29g
Carbohydrate	43g	Saturates	8g

 20 MINS 1 HOUR

SERVES 4

INGREDIENTS

- 1 kg/2 lb 4 oz potatoes
- 1 kg/2 lb 4 oz sardines, defrosted if frozen
- 1 tbsp olive oil, plus extra for oiling
- 1 onion, chopped
- 2–3 garlic cloves, crushed
- 2 tbsp chopped fresh parsley
- 350 g/12 oz ripe tomatoes, peeled and sliced or 400 g/14 oz can peeled tomatoes, partly drained and chopped
- 1–2 tbsp chopped fresh Italian herbs, such as oregano, thyme, rosemary, marjoram
- 150 ml/¼ pint/⅔ cup dry white wine
- salt and pepper

1 Put the potatoes in a pan of salted water, bring to the boil, cover and simmer for 10 minutes, then drain. When cool enough to handle, cut into slices about 5 mm/¼ inch thick.

2 Gut and clean the sardines: cut off their heads and tails and then slit open the length of the belly. Turn the fish over so the skin is facing upwards and press firmly along the backbone to loosen the bones. Turn over again and carefully remove the backbone. Wash the fish in cold water, drain well and dry them on paper towels.

3 Heat the oil in a pan and fry the onion and garlic until soft, but not coloured.

4 Arrange the potatoes in a well-oiled ovenproof dish and sprinkle with the onions, parsley and plenty of salt and pepper to taste.

5 Lay the open sardines over the potatoes, skin-side down, then cover with the tomatoes and the rest of the herbs. Pour on the wine and season with salt and pepper.

6 Cook uncovered in a preheated oven, 190°C/180°F/Gas Mark 5, for about 40 minutes until the fish is tender. If the casserole seems to be drying out, add another couple of tablespoons of wine. Serve hot.

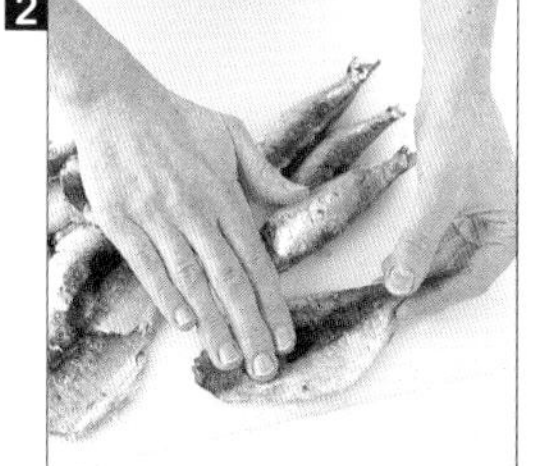
2

4

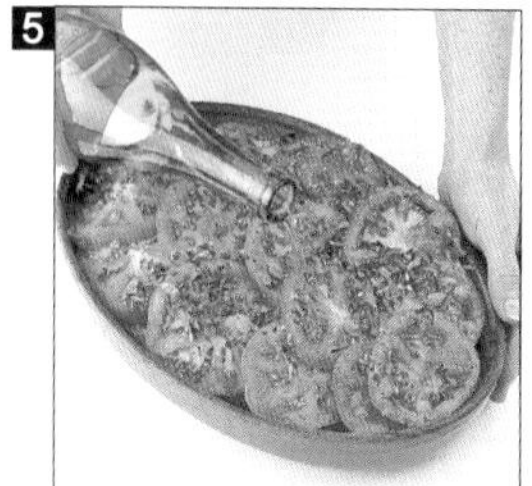
5

Pasta Vongole

Fresh clams are available from most good fishmongers. If you prefer, used canned clams, which are less messy to eat but not as attractive.

NUTRITIONAL INFORMATION

Calories	410	Sugars	1g
Protein	39g	Fat	9g
Carbohydrate	39g	Saturates	1g

 20 MINS  20 MINS

SERVES 4

INGREDIENTS

- 675 g/1½ lb fresh clams or 1 x 290 g/10 oz can clams, drained
- 400 g/14 oz mixed seafood, such as prawns (shrimps), squid and mussels, defrosted if frozen
- 2 tbsp olive oil
- 2 cloves garlic, finely chopped
- 150 ml/¼ pint/⅔ cup white wine
- 150 ml/¼ pint/⅔ cup fish stock
- 2 tbsp chopped tarragon
- salt and pepper
- 675 g/1½ lb fresh pasta or 350 g/12 oz dried pasta

1. If you are using fresh clams, scrub them clean and discard any that are already open.

2. Heat the oil in a large frying pan (skillet). Add the garlic and the clams to the pan and cook for 2 minutes, shaking the pan to ensure that all of the clams are coated in the oil.

3. Add the remaining seafood mixture to the pan and cook for a further 2 minutes.

4. Pour the wine and stock over the mixed seafood and garlic and bring to the boil. Cover the pan, reduce the heat and leave to simmer for 8–10 minutes or until the shells open. Discard any clams or mussels that do not open.

5. Meanwhile, cook the pasta in a saucepan of boiling water for 8–10 minutes or until it is cooked through, but still has 'bite'. Drain the pasta thoroughly.

6. Stir the tarragon into the sauce and season with salt and pepper to taste.

7. Transfer the pasta to a serving plate and pour over the sauce. Serve immediately.

VARIATION

Red clam sauce can be made by adding 8 tablespoons of passata (sieved tomatoes) to the sauce along with the stock in step 4. Follow the same cooking method.

Sardines, Olives & Tomatoes

Tomatoes flavoured with basil and olives make sardines into a very tasty meal.

NUTRITIONAL INFORMATION

Calories	741	Sugars	1g
Protein	77g	Fat	48g
Carbohydrate	1g	Saturates	10g

 25 MINS · 25 MINS

SERVES 4

INGREDIENTS

- 12 fresh sardines, gutted and cleaned
- fresh basil leaves
- 4 plum tomatoes
- 8 pitted black olives
- 15 g/½ oz butter
- 1 tbsp olive oil
- 2 tbsp lemon juice
- salt and pepper

TO GARNISH

- plum tomatoes, sliced
- olives, sliced
- 1 fresh basil sprig

1 Season the sardines inside and out with salt and pepper to taste. Insert 1-2 basil leaves inside the cavity of each fish. Using a sharp knife, make a few slashes in the body of each fish.

2 Cut the tomatoes and olives into slices and transfer to a large bowl. Tear 4 basil leaves into small pieces and toss them together with the tomatoes and olives.

3 Divide the tomato and olive mixture among 4 large sheets of kitchen foil, and place 3 sardines on top of each individual portion.

2

4

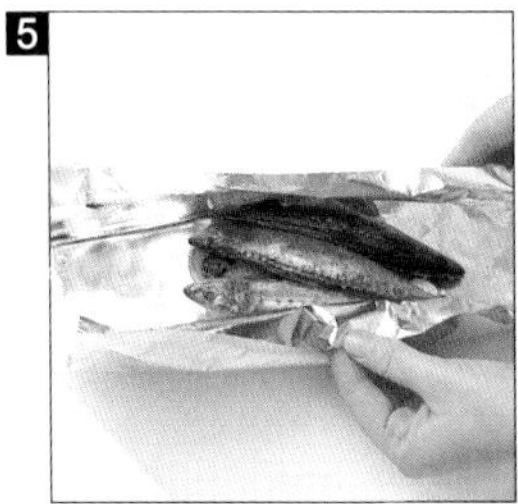
5

4 Melt the butter and oil together in a small pan. Stir in the lemon juice and pour the mixture over the fish.

5 Wrap up the fish in the foil. Barbecue (grill) the fish over medium hot coals for 15–20 minutes until the fish is firm and cooked through.

6 Transfer the fish to serving plates and remove the kitchen foil. Garnish the fish with slices of tomato and olive, and with a fresh sprig of basil. Serve at once.

COOK'S TIP

Slashing the body of the fish helps the flesh to absorb the flavours. It is particularly important if you do not have time to marinate the fish before cooking.

Fresh Baked Sardines

Here, fresh sardines are baked with eggs, herbs and vegetables to form a dish similar to an omelette.

NUTRITIONAL INFORMATION

Calories	679	Sugars	5g
Protein	60g	Fat	47g
Carbohydrate	6g	Saturates	15g

 15 MINS   40 MINS

SERVES 4

INGREDIENTS

- 2 tbsp olive oil
- 2 large onions, sliced into rings
- 3 garlic cloves, chopped
- 2 large courgettes (zucchini), cut into sticks
- 3 tbsp fresh thyme, stalks removed
- 8 sardine fillets or about 1 kg/2 lb 4 oz whole sardines, filleted
- 75 g/2¾ oz Parmesan cheese, grated
- 4 eggs, beaten
- 150 ml/¼ pint/⅔ pint milk
- salt and pepper

1 Heat 1 tablespoon of the oil in a frying pan (skillet). Add the onions and garlic and sauté for 2–3 minutes.

2 Add the courgettes (zucchini) to the frying pan (skillet) and cook for about 5 minutes or until golden.

2

4

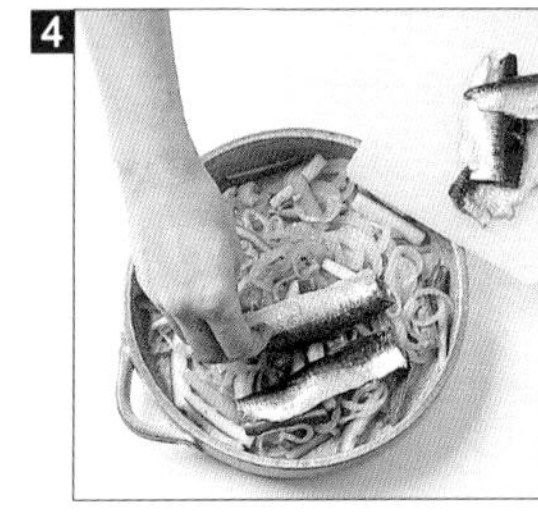

4

3 Stir 2 tablespoons of the thyme into the mixture.

4 Place half of the onions and courgettes (zucchini) in the base of a large ovenproof dish. Top with the sardine fillets and half of the Parmesan cheese.

5 Place the remaining onions and courgettes (zucchini) on top and sprinkle with the remaining thyme.

6 Mix the eggs and milk together in a bowl and season to taste with salt and pepper. Pour the mixture over the vegetables and sardines in the dish. Sprinkle the remaining Parmesan cheese over the top.

7 Bake in a preheated oven at 180°C/350°F/Gas Mark 4 for 20–25 minutes or until golden and set. Serve hot, straight from the oven.

VARIATION

If you cannot find sardines that are large enough to fillet, use small mackerel instead.

Plaice with Mushrooms

The moist texture of grilled (broiled) fish is complemented by the texture of the mushrooms.

NUTRITIONAL INFORMATION

Calories	243	Sugars	2g
Protein	30g	Fat	13g
Carbohydrate	2g	Saturates	3g

10 MINS 20 MINS

SERVES 4

INGREDIENTS

- 4 × 150 g/5½ oz white-skinned plaice fillets
- 2 tbsp lime juice
- celery salt and pepper
- 90 g/3 oz/⅓ cup low-fat spread
- 300 g/10½ oz/2½ cups mixed small mushrooms such as button, oyster, shiitake, chanterelle or morel, sliced or quartered
- 4 tomatoes, skinned, seeded and chopped
- basil leaves, to garnish
- mixed salad, to serve

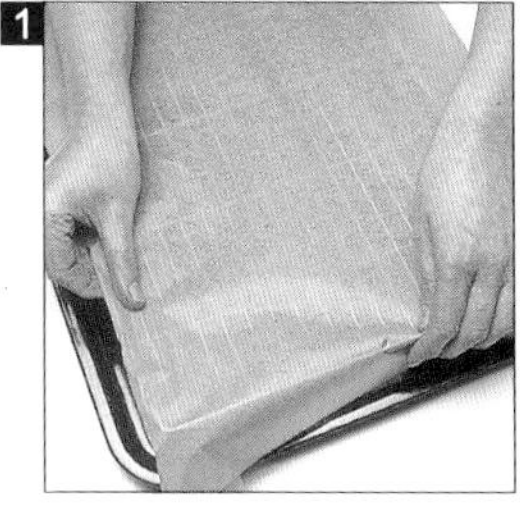

1 Line a grill (broiler) rack with baking parchment and place the fish on top.

2 Sprinkle over the lime juice and season with celery salt and pepper.

3 Place under a preheated moderate grill (broiler) and cook for 7–8 minutes without turning, until just cooked. Keep warm.

4 Meanwhile, gently melt the low fat spread in a non-stick frying pan (skillet), add the mushrooms and fry for 4–5 minutes over a low heat until cooked through.

5 Gently heat the tomatoes in a small saucepan.

6 Spoon the mushrooms, with any pan juices, and the tomatoes over the plaice.

7 Garnish the grilled plaice with the basil leaves and serve with a mixed salad, if wished.

COOK'S TIP

Mushrooms are ideal in a low-fat diet, as they are packed full of flavour and contain no fat. More 'meaty' types of mushroom, such as chestnut (crimini), will take slightly longer to cook.

Indian Cod with Tomatoes

Quick and easy – cod steaks are cooked in a rich tomato and coconut sauce to produce tender, succulent results.

NUTRITIONAL INFORMATION

Calories	194	Sugars	6g
Protein	21g	Fat	9g
Carbohydrate	7g	Saturates	1g

 5 MINS  25 MINS

SERVES 4

INGREDIENTS

- 3 tbsp vegetable oil
- 4 cod steaks, about 2.5 cm/1 inch thick
- salt and freshly ground black pepper
- 1 onion, peeled and finely chopped
- 2 garlic cloves, peeled and crushed
- 1 red (bell) pepper, seeded and chopped
- 1 tsp ground coriander
- 1 tsp ground cumin
- 1 tsp ground turmeric
- ½ tsp garam masala
- 1 x 400 g/14 oz can chopped tomatoes
- 150 ml/¼ pint/⅔ cup coconut milk
- 1-2 tbsp chopped fresh coriander (cilantro) or parsley

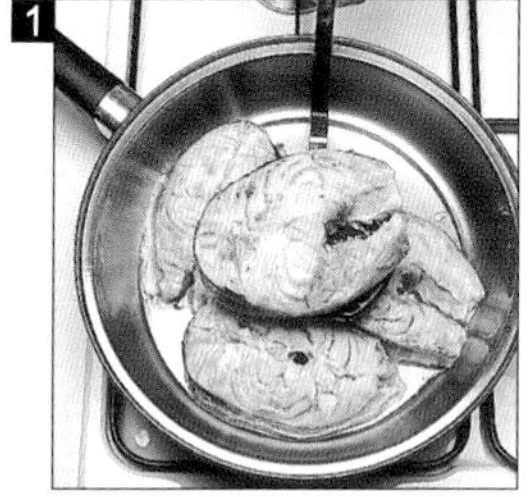

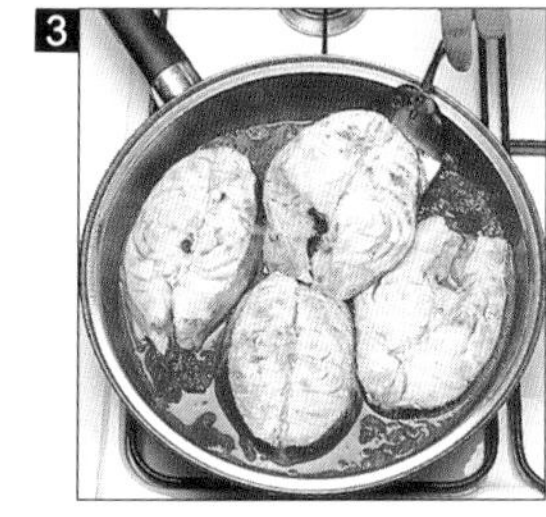

1 Heat the oil in a frying pan, add the fish steaks, season with salt and pepper and fry until browned on both sides (but not cooked through). Remove from the pan and reserve.

2 Add the onion, garlic, red (bell) pepper and spices and cook very gently for 2 minutes, stirring frequently. Add the tomatoes, bring to the boil and simmer for 5 minutes.

3 Add the fish steaks to the pan and simmer gently for 8 minutes or until the fish is cooked through.

4 Remove from the pan and keep warm on a serving dish. Add the coconut milk and coriander (cilantro) or parsley to the pan and reheat gently.

5 Spoon the sauce over the cod steaks and serve immediately.

VARIATION

The mixture may be flavoured with a tablespoonful of curry powder or curry paste (mild, medium or hot, according to personal preference) instead of the mixture of spices at step 2, if wished.

Herrings with Hot Pesto

By omitting the cheese when making a simple pesto sauce, it is possible to heat the paste without it becoming stringy, so it can be used hot.

NUTRITIONAL INFORMATION

Calories	546	Sugars	2g
Protein	32g	Fat	46g
Carbohydrate	2g	Saturates	9g

15 MINS   20 MINS

SERVES 4

INGREDIENTS

- 4 whole herrings or small mackerel, cleaned and gutted
- 2 tbsp olive oil
- 225 g/8 oz tomatoes, peeled, deseeded and chopped
- 8 canned anchovy fillets, chopped
- about 30 fresh basil leaves
- 50 g/1¾ oz pine nuts
- 2 garlic cloves, crushed

1 Cook the herrings under a preheated grill (broiler) for about 8-10 minutes on each side, or until the skin is slightly charred on both sides.

2 Meanwhile, heat 1 tablespoon of the olive oil in a large saucepan.

3 Add the tomatoes and anchovies to the saucepan and cook over a medium heat for 5 minutes.

4 Meanwhile, place the basil, pine nuts, garlic and remaining oil into a food processor and blend to form a smooth paste. Alternatively, pound the ingredients by hand in a mortar and pestle until a smooth paste is formed.

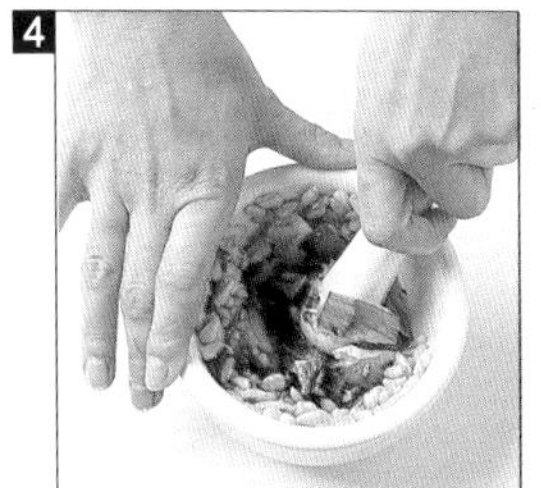

5 Add the pesto mixture to the saucepan containing the tomato and anchovy mixture, and stir to heat through.

6 Spoon some of the pesto sauce on to warm individual serving plates. Place the fish on top and pour the rest of the pesto sauce over the fish. Serve immediately.

COOK'S TIP

Try barbecuing (grilling) the fish for an extra char-grilled flavour, if you prefer.

Red Mullet & Coconut Loaf

This fish and coconut loaf is ideal to take along on picnics, as it can be served cold as well as hot.

NUTRITIONAL INFORMATION

Calories	138	Sugars	12g
Protein	11g	Fat	1g
Carbohydrate	23g	Saturates	0g

15 MINS

$1^1/_4$ HOURS

SERVES 4–6

INGREDIENTS

225 g/8 oz red mullet fillets, skinned

2 small tomatoes, deseeded and chopped finely

2 green (bell) peppers, chopped finely

1 onion, chopped finely

1 fresh red chilli, chopped finely

150 g/5½ oz/2½ cups breadcrumbs

600 ml/1 pint/2½ cups coconut liquid

salt and pepper

HOT PEPPER SAUCE

125 ml/4 fl oz/½ cup tomato ketchup

1 tsp West Indian hot pepper sauce

¼ tsp hot mustard

TO GARNISH

lemon twists

sprigs of fresh chervil

1 Finely chop the fish and mix with the tomatoes, (bell) peppers, onion and chilli.

2 Stir in the breadcrumbs, coconut liquid and seasoning. If using fresh coconut, use a hammer and screwdriver or the tip of a sturdy knife to poke out the three 'eyes' in the top of the coconut and pour out the liquid.

3 Grease and base-line a 500 g/1 lb 2 oz loaf tin (pan) and add the fish.

4 Bake in a preheated oven at 200°C/400°F/Gas Mark 6 for 1–1¼ hours until set.

5 To make the hot pepper sauce, mix together the tomato ketchup, hot pepper sauce and mustard until smooth and creamy.

6 To serve, cut the loaf into slices, garnish with lemon twists and chervil and serve hot or cold with the hot pepper sauce.

COOK'S TIP

Be careful when preparing chillies because the juices can irritate the skin, especially the face. Wash your hands after handling them or wear clean rubber gloves to prepare them if preferred.

Poached Salmon with Penne

Fresh salmon and pasta in a mouth-watering lemon and watercress sauce – a wonderful summer evening treat.

NUTRITIONAL INFORMATION

Calories	968	Sugars	3g
Protein	59g	Fat	58g
Carbohydrate	49g	Saturates	19g

 10 MINS  30 MINS

SERVES 4

INGREDIENTS

- 4 x 275 g/9½ oz fresh salmon steaks
- 60 g/2 oz/4 tbsp butter
- 175 ml/6 fl oz/¾ cup dry white wine
- sea salt
- 8 peppercorns
- fresh dill sprig
- fresh tarragon sprig
- 1 lemon, sliced
- 450 g/1 lb dried penne
- 2 tbsp olive oil
- lemon slices and fresh watercress, to garnish

LEMON & WATERCRESS SAUCE

- 25 g/1 oz/2 tbsp butter
- 25 g/1 oz/¼ cup plain (all-purpose) flour
- 150 ml/¼ pint/⅝ cup warm milk
- juice and finely grated rind of 2 lemons
- 60 g/2 oz watercress, chopped
- salt and pepper

1. Put the salmon in a large, non-stick pan. Add the butter, wine, a pinch of sea salt, the peppercorns, dill, tarragon and lemon. Cover, bring to the boil, and simmer for 10 minutes.

2. Using a fish slice, carefully remove the salmon. Strain and reserve the cooking liquid. Remove and discard the salmon skin and centre bones. Place on a warm dish, cover and keep warm.

3. Meanwhile, bring a saucepan of salted water to the boil. Add the penne and 1 tbsp of the oil and cook for 8–10 minutes, until tender but still firm to the bite. Drain and sprinkle over the remaining olive oil. Place on a warm serving dish, top with the salmon steaks and keep warm.

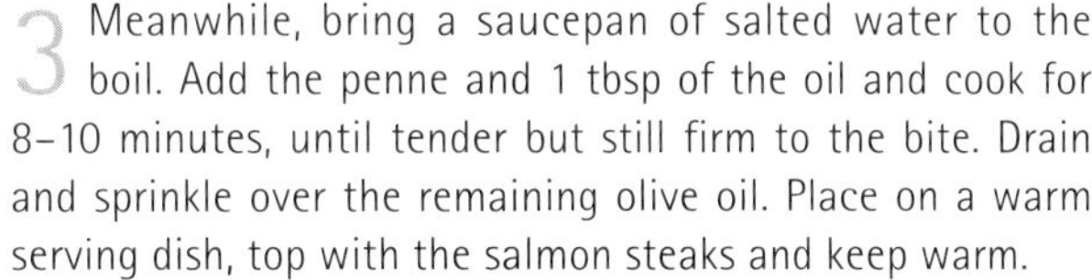

4. To make the sauce, melt the butter and stir in the flour for 2 minutes. Stir in the milk and about 7 tablespoons of the reserved cooking liquid. Add the lemon juice and rind and cook, stirring, for a further 10 minutes.

5. Add the watercress to the sauce, stir gently and season to taste with salt and pepper.

6. Pour the sauce over the salmon and penne, garnish with slices of lemon and fresh watercress and serve.

Plaice Fillets with Grapes

Fish is ideal for a quick meal, especially when cut into strips as in this recipe – it takes only minutes to cook.

NUTRITIONAL INFORMATION

Calories	226	Sugars	6g
Protein	23g	Fat	9g
Carbohydrate	9g	Saturates	4g

5 MINS 10 MINS

SERVES 4

INGREDIENTS

- 500 g/1 lb 2 oz plaice fillets, skinned
- 4 spring onions (scallions), white and green parts, sliced diagonally
- 125 ml/4 fl oz/½ cup dry white wine
- 1 tbsp cornflour (cornstarch)
- 2 tbsp skimmed milk
- 2 tbsp chopped fresh dill
- 50 ml/2 fl oz/¼ cup double (heavy) cream
- 125 g/4½ oz seedless white (green) grapes
- 1 tsp lemon juice
- salt and pepper
- fresh dill sprigs, to garnish

TO SERVE

- basmati rice
- courgette ribbons

1 Cut the fish into strips about 4 cm/1¾ inches long and put into a frying pan (skillet) with the spring onions (scallions), wine and seasoning.

2 Bring to the boil, cover and simmer for 4 minutes. Carefully transfer the fish to a warm serving dish. Cover and keep warm.

3 Mix the cornflour (cornstarch) and milk then add to the pan with the dill and cream. Bring to the boil, and boil, stirring, for 2 minutes until thickened.

4 Add the grapes and lemon juice and heat through gently for 1–2 minutes, then pour over the fish. Garnish with dill and serve with rice and courgette ribbons.

COOK'S TIP

Dill has a fairly strong aniseed flavour that goes very well with fish. The feathery leaves are particularly attractive when used as a garnish.

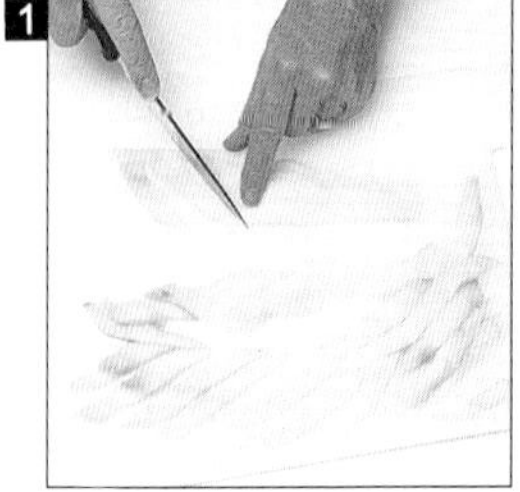

1

2

3

Spicy Fish & Potato Fritters

You need nice, floury-textured old (main crop) potatoes for making these tasty fritters. Any white fish of your choice may be used.

NUTRITIONAL INFORMATION

Calories	349	Sugars	4g
Protein	31g	Fat	8g
Carbohydrate	41g	Saturates	1g

15 MINS
25 MINS

SERVES 4

INGREDIENTS

- 500 g/1 lb 2 oz potatoes, peeled and cut into even-sized pieces
- 500g/1 lb 2 oz white fish fillets, such as cod or haddock, skinned and boned
- 6 spring onions (scallions), sliced
- 1 fresh green chilli, seeded
- 2 garlic cloves, peeled
- 1 tsp salt
- 1 tbsp medium or hot curry paste
- 2 eggs, beaten
- 150 g/5½ oz/2½ cups fresh white breadcrumbs
- vegetable oil, for shallow frying
- mango chutney, to serve
- lime wedges and coriander sprigs, to garnish

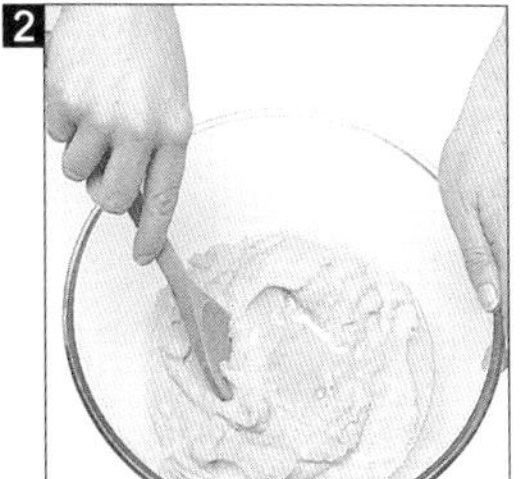

1 Cook the potatoes in a pan of boiling, salted water until tender. Drain well, return the potatoes to the pan and place over a moderate heat for a few moments to dry off. Cool slightly, then place in a food processor with the fish, onions, chilli, garlic, salt and curry paste. Process until the ingredients are very finely chopped and blended.

2 Turn the potato mixture into a bowl and mix in 2 tablespoons of beaten egg and 60 g/2 oz/1 cup of breadcrumbs. Place the remaining beaten egg and breadcrumbs in separate dishes.

3 Divide the fish mixture into 8 and, using a spoon to help you (the mixture is quite soft), dip first in the beaten egg and then coat in the breadcrumbs, and carefully shape the mixture into ovals.

4 Heat enough oil in a large frying pan for shallow frying and fry the fritters over moderate heat for 3-4 minutes, turning frequently, until golden brown and cooked through.

5 Drain on absorbent kitchen paper (paper towels) and garnish with lime wedges and coriander sprigs. Serve hot, with mango chutney.

Salmon with Caper Sauce

The richness of salmon is beautifully balanced by the tangy capers in this creamy herb sauce.

NUTRITIONAL INFORMATION

Calories	302	Sugars	0g
Protein	21g	Fat	24g
Carbohydrate	1g	Saturates	9g

 5 MINS  25 MINS

SERVES 4

INGREDIENTS

- 4 salmon fillets, skinned
- 1 fresh bay leaf
- few black peppercorns
- 1 tsp white wine vinegar
- 150 ml/¼ pint/⅔ cup fish stock
- 3 tbsp double (heavy) cream
- 1 tbsp capers
- 1 tbsp chopped fresh dill
- 1 tbsp chopped fresh chives
- 1 tsp cornflour (cornstarch)
- 2 tbsp skimmed milk
- salt and pepper
- new potatoes, to serve

TO GARNISH

- fresh dill sprigs
- chive flowers

1 Lay the salmon fillets in a shallow ovenproof dish. Add the bay leaf, peppercorns, vinegar and stock.

2 Cover with foil and bake in a preheated oven at 180°C/350°F/ Gas Mark 4 for 15–20 minutes until the flesh is opaque and flakes easily when tested with a fork.

3 Transfer the fish to warmed serving plates, cover and keep warm.

4 Strain the cooking liquid into a saucepan. Stir in the cream, capers, dill and chives and seasoning to taste.

5 Blend the cornflour (cornstarch) with the milk. Add to the saucepan and heat, stirring, until thickened slightly. Boil for 1 minute.

6 Spoon the sauce over the salmon, garnish with dill sprigs and chive flowers.

7 Serve with new potatoes.

1

2

4

COOK'S TIP

Ask the fishmonger to skin the fillets for you. The cooking time for the salmon will depend on the thickness of the fish: the thin tail end of the salmon takes the least time to cook.

Soused Trout

In this recipe, fillets of trout are gently poached in a spiced vinegar, left to marinate for 24 hours and served cold with a potato salad.

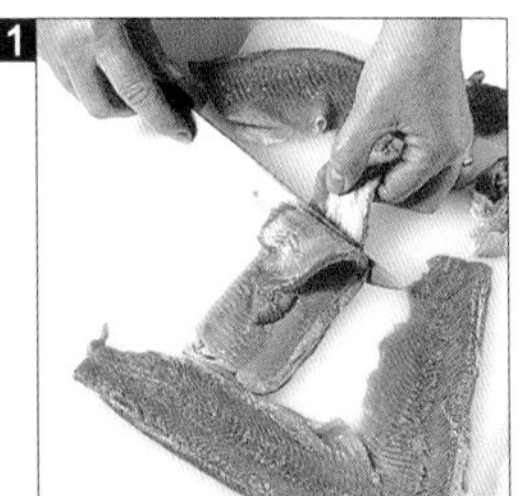

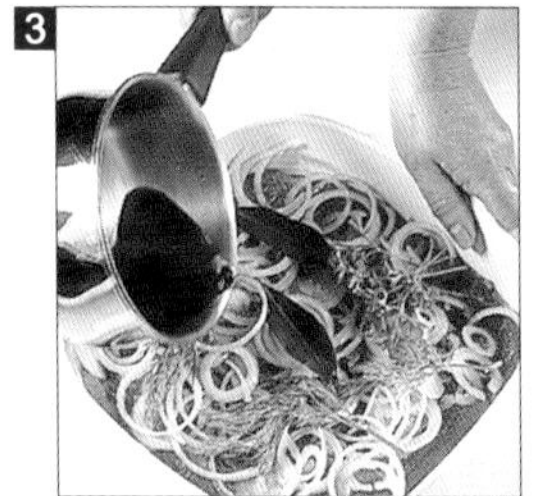

NUTRITIONAL INFORMATION

Calories	521	Sugars	3g
Protein	61g	Fat	20g
Carbohydrate	27g	Saturates	4g

 5 HOURS  35 MINS

SERVES 4

INGREDIENTS

- 4 trout, about 225–350 g/8–12 oz each, filleted
- 1 onion, sliced very thinly
- 2 bay leaves, preferably fresh
- sprigs of fresh parsley and dill, or other fresh herbs
- 10–12 black peppercorns
- 4–6 cloves
- good pinch of salt
- 150 ml/¼ pint/⅔ cup red wine vinegar
- salad leaves, to garnish

POTATO SALAD

- 500 g/1 lb 2 oz small new potatoes
- 2 tbsp French dressing
- 4 tbsp thick low-fat mayonnaise
- 3–4 spring onions (scallions), sliced

1 Trim the trout fillets, cutting off any pieces of fin. If preferred, remove the skin – use a sharp knife and, beginning at the tail end, carefully cut the flesh from the skin, pressing the knife down firmly as you go.

2 Lightly grease a shallow ovenproof dish and lay the fillets in it, packing them fairly tightly together but keeping them in a single layer. Arrange the sliced onion, bay leaves and herbs over the fish.

3 Put the peppercorns, cloves, salt and vinegar into a saucepan and bring almost to the boil. Remove from the heat and pour evenly over the fish. Cover with foil and cook in a preheated oven at 160°C/325°F/ Gas Mark 3 for 15 minutes. Leave until cold, and then chill thoroughly.

4 Cook the potatoes in boiling salted water for 10–15 minutes until just tender. Drain. While still warm, cut into large dice and place in a bowl. Combine the French dressing and mayonnaise, add to the potatoes while warm and toss evenly. Leave until cold, then sprinkle the potato salad with chopped spring onions (scallions).

5 Pour a little of the juices over each portion of fish. Garnish with salad leaves and serve with the potato salad.

Smoky Fish Skewers

The combination of fresh and smoked fish gives these kebabs a special flavour. Choose thick fish fillets to get good-sized pieces.

NUTRITIONAL INFORMATION

Calories	221	Sugars	0g
Protein	33g	Fat	10g
Carbohydrate	0g	Saturates	1g

4 HOURS 10 MINS

SERVES 4

INGREDIENTS

- 350 g/12 oz smoked cod fillet
- 350 g/12 oz cod fillet
- 8 large raw prawns (shrimp)
- 8 bay leaves
- fresh dill, to garnish (optional)

MARINADE

- 4 tbsp sunflower oil, plus a little for brushing
- 2 tbsp lemon or lime juice
- rind of ½ lemon or lime, grated
- ¼ tsp dried dill
- salt and pepper

1 Skin both types of cod and cut the flesh into bite-size pieces. Peel the prawns (shrimp), leaving just the tail.

2 To make the marinade, combine the oil, lemon or lime juice and rind, dill and salt and pepper to taste in a shallow, non-metallic dish.

3 Place the prepared fish in the marinade and stir together until the fish is well coated on all sides. Leave the fish to marinate for 1–4 hours.

4 Thread the fish on to 4 skewers, alternating the 2 types of cod with the prawns (shrimp) and bay leaves.

5 Cover the rack with lightly oiled kitchen foil and place the fish skewers on top of the foil.

6 Barbecue (grill) the fish skewers over hot coals for 5-10 minutes, basting with any remaining marinade, turning once.

7 Garnish the skewers with fresh dill (if using) and serve immediately.

COOK'S TIP

Cod fillet can be rather flaky, so choose the thicker end which is easier to cut into chunky pieces. Cook the fish on kitchen foil rather directly on the rack, so that if the fish breaks away from the skewer, it is not wasted.

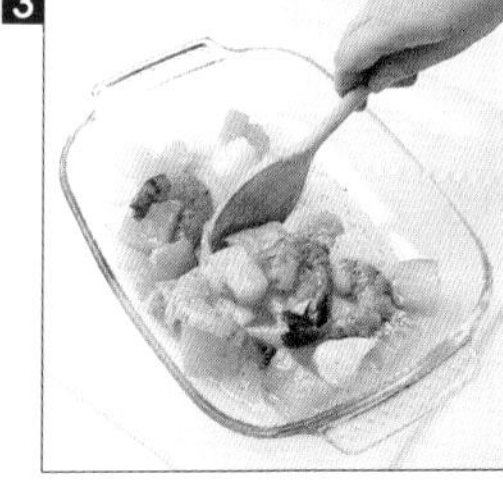
3

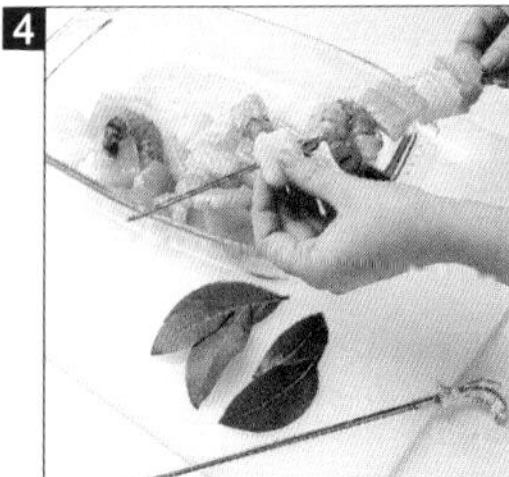
4

6

Citrus Fish Kebabs

Use your favourite fish for this dish as long as it is firm enough to thread on to skewer. The tang of orange makes this a refreshing meal.

NUTRITIONAL INFORMATION

Calories	333	Sugars	10g
Protein	41g	Fat	14g
Carbohydrate	10g	Saturates	3g

 2½ HOURS 10 MINS

SERVES 4

INGREDIENTS

450 g/1 lb firm white fish fillets (such as cod or monkfish)

450 g/1 lb thick salmon fillet

2 large oranges

1 pink grapefruit

1 bunch fresh bay leaves

1 tsp finely grated lemon rind

3 tbsp lemon juice

2 tsp clear honey

2 garlic cloves, crushed

salt and pepper

TO SERVE

crusty bread

mixed salad

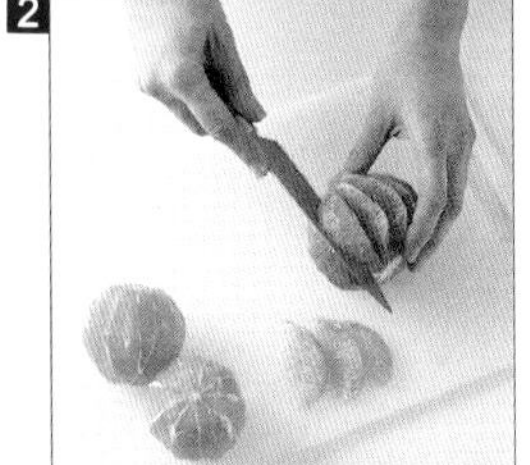

1 Skin the white fish and the salmon, rinse and pat dry on kitchen paper (paper towels). Cut each fillet into 16 pieces.

2 Using a sharp knife, remove the skin and pith from the oranges and grapefruit. Cut out the segments of flesh, removing all remaining traces of the pith and dividing membrane.

3 Thread the pieces of fish alternately with the orange and grapefruit segments and the bay leaves onto 8 skewers. Place the kebabs in a shallow dish.

4 In a small bowl, mix together the lemon rind and juice, the honey and garlic.

5 Pour over the fish kebabs and then season well. Cover and chill for 2 hours, turning occasionally.

6 Preheat the grill (broiler) to medium. Remove the fish kebabs from the marinade and place on the rack.

7 Cook for 7–8 minutes, turning once, until cooked through.

8 Drain, transfer to serving plates and serve with crusty bread and a fresh mixed salad.

Char-grilled Mackerel

The sharpness of the apricot glaze complements the oiliness of the fish and has a delicious hint of ginger.

NUTRITIONAL INFORMATION

Calories	343	Sugars	21g
Protein	23g	Fat	18g
Carbohydrate	22g	Saturates	4g

 5 MINS  10 MINS

SERVES 4

INGREDIENTS

- 4 mackerel, about 225 g/8 oz each
- 400 g/14 oz can apricots in natural juice
- 3 tbsp dark muscovado sugar
- 3 tbsp Worcestershire sauce
- 3 tbsp soy sauce
- 2 tbsp tomato purée (paste)
- 1 tsp ground ginger
- dash Tabasco sauce
- 1 clove garlic, crushed (optional)
- salt and pepper

1 Clean and gut the mackerel, removing the heads if preferred. Place the fish in a shallow dish.

2 Drain the apricots, reserving the juice. Roughly chop half of the apricots and set aside. Place the remaining apricots in a food processor with the sugar, Worcestershire sauce, soy sauce, tomato purée (paste), ginger, Tabasco sauce and garlic (if using) and process until smooth. Alternatively, chop the apricots and mix with the other ingredients. Season to taste.

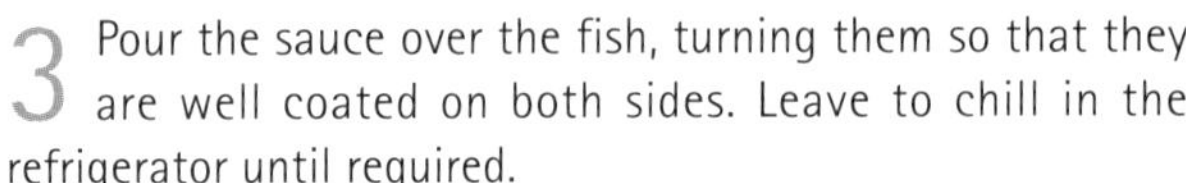

3 Pour the sauce over the fish, turning them so that they are well coated on both sides. Leave to chill in the refrigerator until required.

4 Transfer the mackerel to the barbecue (grill) either directly on the rack or on a piece of greased kitchen foil. Barbecue (grill) the mackerel over hot coals for 5–7 minutes, turning once.

5 Spoon any remaining marinade into a saucepan. Add the reserved chopped apricots and about half of the reserved apricot juice and bring to the boil. Reduce the heat and simmer for 2 minutes. Transfer the mackerel to a serving plate and serve with the apricot sauce.

2

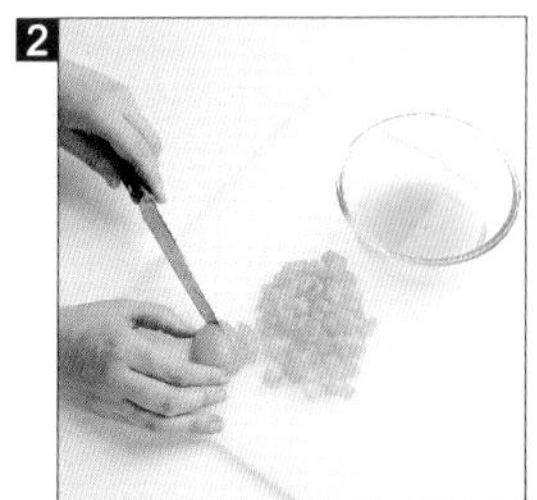

2

5

COOK'S TIP

Use a hinged rack if you have one as it will make it much easier to turn the fish during barbecueing (grilling).

Fish with Black Bean Sauce

Any firm and delicate fish steaks such as salmon or salmon trout can be cooked by the same method.

NUTRITIONAL INFORMATION

Calories	194	Sugars	0.2g
Protein	27g	Fat	9g
Carbohydrate	1g	Saturates	2g

5 MINS  20 MINS

SERVES 6

INGREDIENTS

- 1 sea bass, trout or turbot, weighing about 700g/1 lb 9 oz, cleaned
- 1 tsp salt
- 1 tbsp sesame oil
- 2-3 spring onions (scallions), cut in half lengthways
- 1 tbsp light soy sauce
- 1 tbsp Chinese rice wine or dry sherry
- 1 tbsp finely shredded ginger root
- 1 tbsp oil
- 2 tbsp crushed black bean sauce
- 2 finely shredded spring onions (scallions)
- fresh coriander leaves, to garnish (optional)
- lemon slices, to garnish

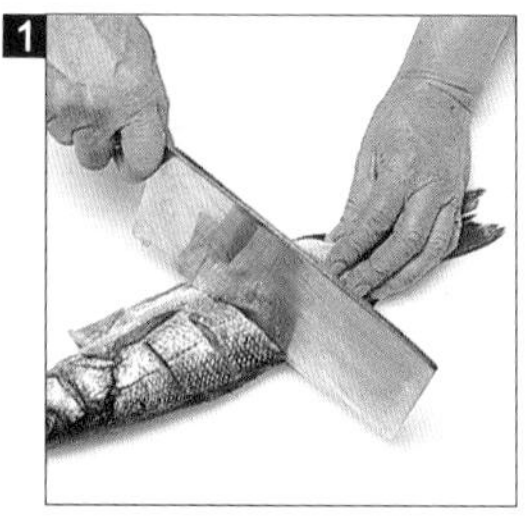

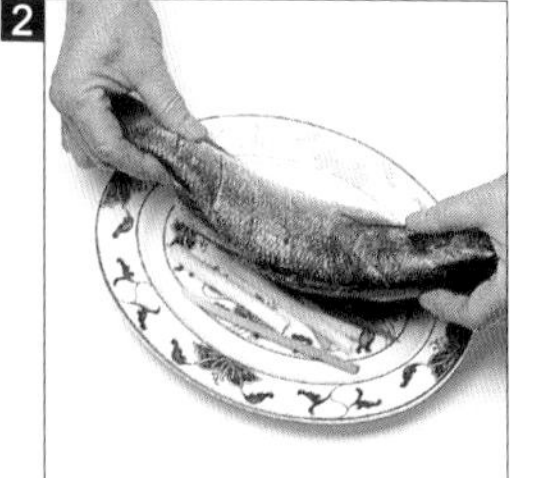

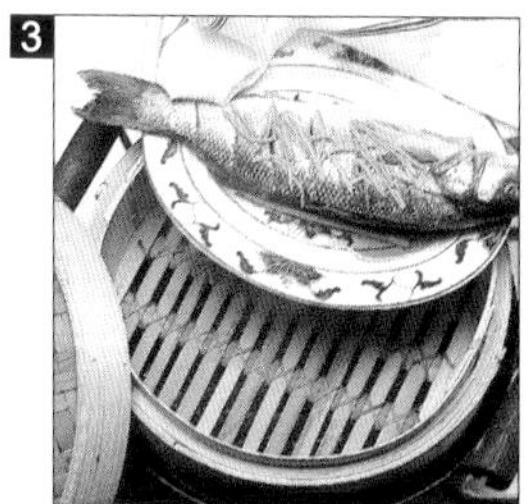

1 Score both sides of the fish with diagonal cuts at 2.5 cm (1 inch) intervals. Rub both the inside and outside of the fish with salt and sesame oil.

2 Place the fish on top of the spring onions (scallions) on a heat-proof platter. Blend the soy sauce and wine with the ginger shreds and pour evenly all over the fish.

3 Place the fish on the platter in a very hot steamer (or inside a wok on a rack), cover and steam vigorously for 12-15 minutes.

4 Heat the oil until hot, then blend in the black bean sauce. Remove the fish from the steamer and place on a serving dish.

5 Pour the hot black bean sauce over the whole length of the fish and place the shredded spring onions (scallions) on top. Place the fish on a platter and serve garnished with coriander leaves (if using) and lemon slices.

COOK'S TIP

If using fish steaks, rub them with the salt and sesame oil, but do not score with a knife. The fish may require less cooking, depending on the thickness of the steaks – test with a skewer after about 8 minutes to check whether they are done.

Spaghetti al Tonno

The classic Italian combination of pasta and tuna is enhanced in this recipe with a delicious parsley sauce.

NUTRITIONAL INFORMATION

Calories	1065	Sugars	3g
Protein	27g	Fat	85g
Carbohydrate	52g	Saturates	18g

 10 MINS  15 MINS

SERVES 4

INGREDIENTS

- 200 g/7 oz can tuna, drained
- 60 g/2 oz can anchovies, drained
- 250 ml/9 fl oz/1⅛ cups olive oil
- 60 g/2 oz/1 cup roughly chopped flat leaf parsley
- 150 ml/¼ pint/⅔ cup crème fraîche
- 450 g/1 lb dried spaghetti
- 25 g/1 oz/2 tbsp butter
- salt and pepper
- black olives, to garnish
- crusty bread, to serve

1 Remove any bones from the tuna. Put the tuna into a food processor or blender, together with the anchovies, 225 ml/8 fl oz/1 cup of the olive oil and the flat leaf parsley. Process until the sauce is very smooth.

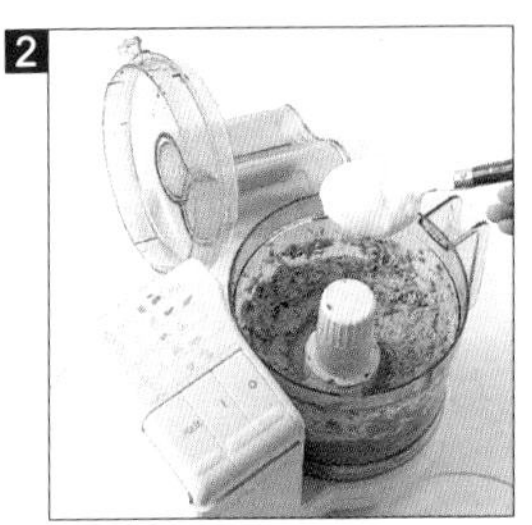

2 Spoon the crème fraîche into the food processor or blender and process again for a few seconds to blend thoroughly. Season with salt and pepper to taste.

3 Bring a large pan of lightly salted water to the boil. Add the spaghetti and the remaining olive oil and cook for 8–10 minutes until tender, but still firm to the bite.

4 Drain the spaghetti, return to the pan and place over a medium heat. Add the butter and toss well to coat. Spoon in the sauce and quickly toss into the spaghetti, using 2 forks.

5 Remove the pan from the heat and divide the spaghetti between 4 warm individual serving plates. Garnish with the olives and serve immediately with warm, crusty bread.

VARIATION

If liked, you could add 1–2 garlic cloves to the sauce, substitute 25 g/1 oz/½ cup chopped fresh basil for half the parsley and garnish with capers instead of black olives.

Spaghetti & Smoked Salmon

Made in moments, this is a luxurious dish to astonish and delight unexpected guests.

NUTRITIONAL INFORMATION

Calories	803	Sugars	3g
Protein	21g	Fat	49g
Carbohydrate	52g	Saturates	27g

 10 MINS  20 MINS

SERVES 4

INGREDIENTS

450 g/1 lb dried buckwheat spaghetti
2 tbsp olive oil
90 g/3 oz/½ cup crumbled Feta cheese
salt
fresh coriander (cilantro) or parsley leaves, to garnish

SAUCE

300 ml/½ pint/1¼ cups double (heavy) cream
150 ml/¼ pint/⅝ cup whisky or brandy
125 g/4½ oz smoked salmon
pinch of cayenne pepper
pepper
2 tbsp chopped fresh coriander (cilantro) or parsley

2

3

3

1 Bring a large pan of lightly salted water to the boil. Add the spaghetti and 1 tablespoon of the olive oil and cook for 8–10 minutes until tender, but still firm to the bite. Drain the spaghetti, return to the pan and sprinkle over the remaining olive oil. Cover, shake the pan, set aside and keep warm.

2 Pour the cream into a small saucepan and bring to simmering point, but do not let it boil. Pour the whisky or brandy into another small saucepan and bring to simmering point, but do not allow it to boil. Remove both saucepans from the heat and mix together the cream and whisky or brandy.

3 Cut the smoked salmon into thin strips and add to the cream mixture. Season to taste with cayenne and pepper. Just before serving, stir in the fresh coriander (cilantro) or parsley.

4 Transfer the spaghetti to a warm serving dish, pour over the sauce and toss thoroughly with 2 large forks. Scatter over the crumbled Feta cheese, garnish with the coriander (cilantro) or parsley leaves and serve immediately.

Pan-Seared Halibut

Liven up firm steaks of white fish with a spicy, colourful relish. Use red onions for a slightly sweeter flavour.

NUTRITIONAL INFORMATION

Calories	197	Sugars	1g
Protein	31g	Fat	7g
Carbohydrate	2g	Saturates	1g

 55 MINS  30 MINS

SERVES 4

INGREDIENTS

- 1 tsp olive oil
- 4 halibut steaks, skinned, 175 g/6 oz each
- ½ tsp cornflour (cornstarch) mixed with 2 tsp cold water
- salt and pepper
- 2 tbsp fresh chives, snipped, to garnish

RED ONION RELISH

- 2 tsp olive oil
- 2 medium red onions
- 6 shallots
- 1 tbsp lemon juice
- 2 tbsp red wine vinegar
- 2 tsp caster (superfine) sugar
- 150 ml/5 fl oz/⅔ cup Fresh Fish Stock (see page 8)

1 To make the relish, peel and thinly shred the onions and shallots. Place in a small bowl and toss in the lemon juice.

2 Heat the oil in a pan and fry the onions and shallots for 3–4 minutes until just softened.

3 Add the vinegar and sugar and continue to cook for a further 2 minutes over a high heat. Pour in the stock and season well. Bring to the boil and simmer gently for a further 8–9 minutes until the sauce has thickened and is slightly reduced.

4 Brush a non-stick, ridged frying pan (skillet) with oil and heat until hot. Press the fish steaks into the pan to seal, lower the heat and cook for 4 minutes. Turn the fish over and cook for 4–5 minutes until cooked through. Drain on kitchen paper (paper towels) and keep warm.

5 Stir the cornflour (cornstarch) paste into the onion sauce and heat through, stirring, until thickened. Season to taste.

6 Pile the relish on to 4 warm serving plates and place a halibut steak on top of each. Garnish with chives.

1

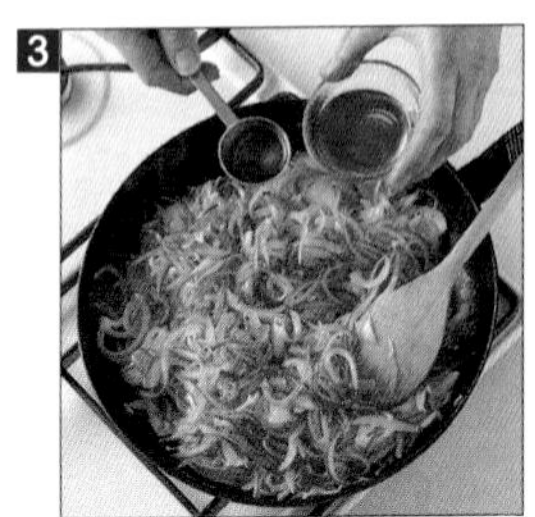
3

4

COOK'S TIP

If raw onions make your eyes water, try peeling them under a tap of cold, running water. Alternatively, stand or sit well back from the onion so that your face isn't hanging over it.

Tuna with Roast (Bell) Peppers

Fresh tuna will be either a small bonito fish or steaks from a skipjack. The more delicately flavoured fish have a paler flesh.

NUTRITIONAL INFORMATION

Calories	428	Sugars	5g
Protein	60g	Fat	19g
Carbohydrate	5g	Saturates	3g

 20 MINS ◷ 30 MINS

SERVES 4

INGREDIENTS

- 4 tuna steaks, about 250 g/9 oz each
- 3 tbsp lemon juice
- 1 litre/1¾ pints/4 cups water
- 6 tbsp olive oil
- 2 orange (bell) peppers
- 2 red (bell) peppers
- 12 black olives
- 1 tsp balsamic vinegar
- salt and pepper

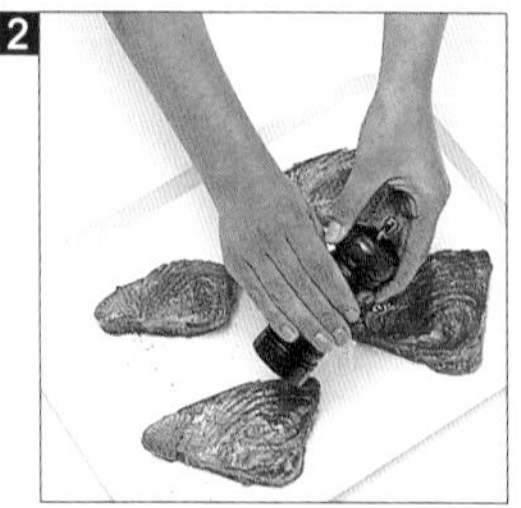

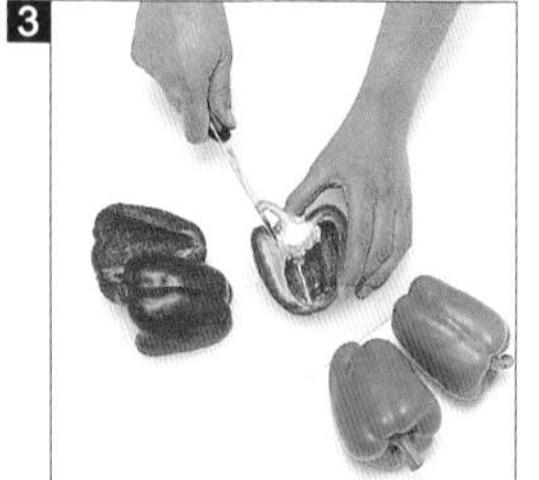

1 Put the tuna steaks into a bowl with the lemon juice and water. Leave for 15 minutes.

2 Drain and brush the steaks all over with olive oil and season well with salt and pepper.

3 Halve, core and deseed the (bell) peppers. Put them over a hot barbecue (grill) and cook for 12 minutes until they are charred all over. Put them into a plastic bag and seal it.

4 Meanwhile, cook the tuna over a hot barbecue (grill) for 12–15 minutes, turning once.

5 When the (bell) peppers are cool enough to handle, peel them and cut each piece into 4 strips. Toss them with the remaining olive oil, olives and balsamic vinegar.

6 Serve the tuna steaks piping hot, with the roasted (bell) pepper salad.

COOK'S TIP

Red, orange and yellow (bell) peppers can also be peeled by cooking them in a hot oven for 30 minutes, turning them frequently, or roasting them straight over a naked gas flame, again turning them frequently. In both methods, deseed the (bell) peppers after peeling.

Balti Cod & Red Lentils

The aniseed in this recipe gives a very delicate aroma to the fish and really enhances the flavour. Serve with wholemeal (wholewheat) bread.

NUTRITIONAL INFORMATION

Calories	236	Sugars	3g
Protein	29g	Fat	7g
Carbohydrate	15g	Saturates	1g

5 MINS — 1 HOUR

SERVES 4

INGREDIENTS

- 2 tbsp oil
- ¼ tsp ground asafoetida (optional)
- 1 tbsp crushed aniseed
- 1 tsp ground ginger
- 1 tsp chilli powder
- ¼ tsp ground turmeric
- 225 g/8 oz/1 cup split red lentils, washed
- 1 tsp salt
- 500 g/1 lb 2 oz cod, skinned, filleted and cut into 2.5 cm/1 inch cubes
- 1 fresh red chilli, chopped
- 3 tbsp low-fat natural yogurt
- 2 tbsp chopped fresh coriander (cilantro)
- wholemeal (wholewheat) bread, to serve

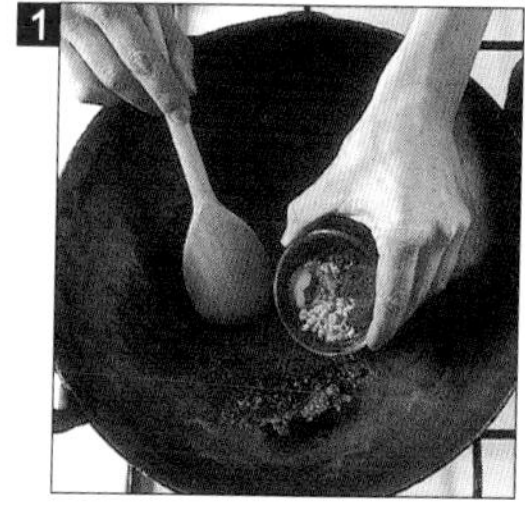
1

3

5

1 Heat the oil in a Balti pan or wok, add the asafoetida (if using), and fry for about 10 seconds to burn off the smell of the asafoetida.

2 Add the aniseed, ginger, chilli powder and turmeric and fry for 30 seconds.

3 Wash the lentils thoroughly then add to the pan with the salt and enough water to cover.

4 Bring to the boil, then simmer gently for 45 minutes, until the lentils are soft but not mushy.

5 Add the cod and red chilli, bring to the boil and simmer for a further 10 minutes.

6 Stir in the yogurt and fresh coriander (cilantro) into the fish mixture and serve with warm bread.

COOK'S TIP

Ground asafoetida is easier to use than the type that comes on a block. It should only be used in small quantities. Do not be put off by the smell, which is very pungent.

Baked Tuna & Ricotta Rigatoni

Ribbed tubes of pasta are filled with tuna and ricotta cheese and then baked in a creamy sauce.

NUTRITIONAL INFORMATION

Calories	949	Sugars	5g
Protein	51g	Fat	48g
Carbohydrate	85g	Saturates	26g

10 MINS 45 MINS

SERVES 4

INGREDIENTS

- butter, for greasing
- 450 g/1 lb dried rigatoni
- 1 tbsp olive oil
- 200 g /7 oz can flaked tuna, drained
- 225 g/ 8 oz ricotta cheese
- 125 ml/4 fl oz/ ½ cup double (heavy) cream
- 225 g/8 oz/2 ⅔ cups grated Parmesan cheese
- 125 g/4 oz sun-dried tomatoes, drained and sliced
- salt and pepper

1 Lightly grease a large ovenproof dish with butter.

2 Bring a large saucepan of lightly salted water to the boil. Add the rigatoni and olive oil and cook for 8–10 minutes until just tender, but still firm to the bite. Drain the pasta and set aside until cool enough to handle.

3 Meanwhile, in a bowl, mix together the tuna and ricotta cheese to form a soft paste. Spoon the mixture into a piping bag and use to fill the rigatoni. Arrange the filled pasta tubes side by side in the prepared ovenproof dish.

3

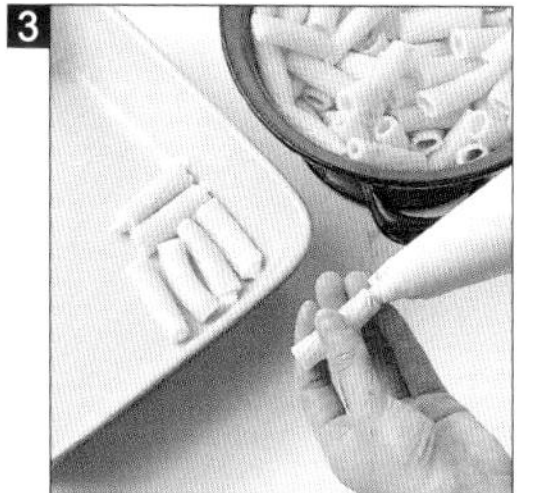

3

4

4 To make the sauce, mix the cream and Parmesan cheese and season with salt and pepper to taste. Spoon the sauce over the rigatoni and top with the sun-dried tomatoes, arranged in a criss-cross pattern. Bake in a preheated oven at 200°C/400°F/Gas Mark 6 for 20 minutes. Serve hot straight from the dish.

VARIATION

For a vegetarian alternative of this recipe, simply substitute a mixture of stoned (pitted) and chopped black olives and chopped walnuts for the tuna. Follow exactly the same cooking method.

Noodles with Cod & Mango

Fish and fruit are tossed with a trio of (bell) peppers in this spicy dish served with noodles for a quick, healthy meal.

NUTRITIONAL INFORMATION

Calories	274	Sugars	11g
Protein	25g	Fat	8g
Carbohydrate	26g	Saturates	1g

 10 MINS  25 MINS

SERVES 4

INGREDIENTS

- 250 g/9 oz packet egg noodles
- 450 g/1 lb skinless cod fillet
- 1 tbsp paprika
- 2 tbsp sunflower oil
- 1 red onion, sliced
- 1 orange (bell) pepper, deseeded and sliced
- 1 green (bell) pepper, deseeded and sliced
- 100 g/3½ oz baby corn cobs, halved
- 1 mango, sliced
- 100 g/3½ oz/1 cup bean sprouts
- 2 tbsp tomato ketchup
- 2 tbsp soy sauce
- 2 tbsp medium sherry
- 1 tsp cornflour (cornstarch)

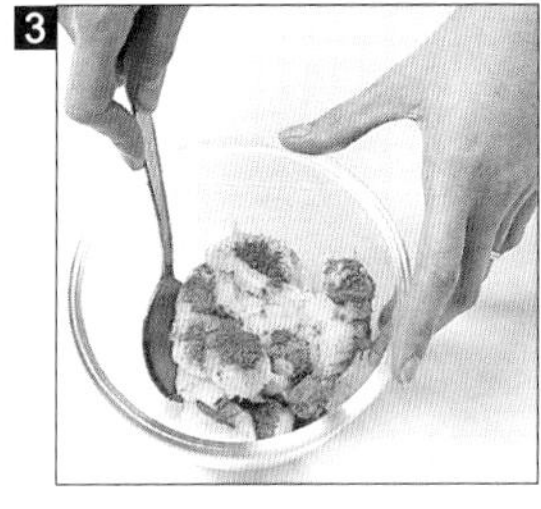
3

5

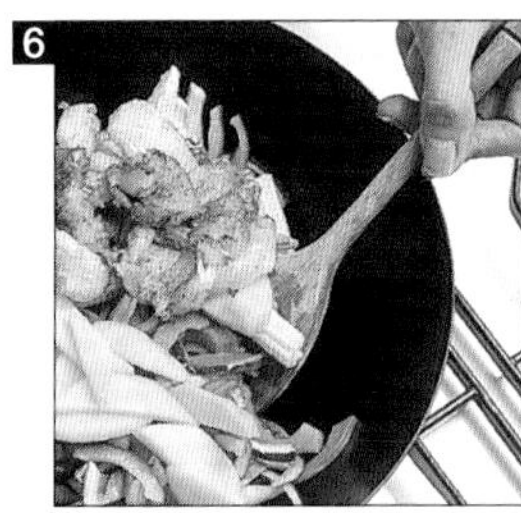
6

1 Place the egg noodles in a large bowl and cover with boiling water. Leave to stand for about 10 minutes.

2 Rinse the cod fillet and pat dry with absorbent kitchen paper (paper towels). Cut the cod flesh into thin strips.

3 Place the cod strips in a large bowl. Add the paprika and toss well to coat the fish.

4 Heat the sunflower oil in a large preheated wok.

5 Add the onion, (bell) peppers and baby corn cobs to the wok and stir-fry for about 5 minutes.

6 Add the cod to the wok together with the sliced mango and stir-fry for a further 2–3 minutes or until the fish is tender.

7 Add the bean sprouts to the wok and toss well to combine.

8 Mix together the tomato ketchup, soy sauce, sherry and cornflour (cornstarch). Add the mixture to the wok and cook, stirring occasionally, until the juices thicken.

9 Drain the noodles thoroughly and transfer to warm serving bowls. Transfer the cod and mango stir-fry to separate serving bowls and serve immediately.

Smoked Cod Polenta

Using polenta as a crust for a gratin dish gives a lovely crispy outer texture and a smooth inside. It works well with smoked fish and chicken.

NUTRITIONAL INFORMATION

Calories	616	Sugars	3g
Protein	41g	Fat	24g
Carbohydrate	58g	Saturates	12g

30 MINS  1¼ HOURS

SERVES 4

INGREDIENTS

- 350 g/12 oz instant polenta
- 1.5 litres/2¾ pints/6½ cups water
- 200 g/7 oz chopped frozen spinach, defrosted
- 50 g/1¾ oz/3 tbsp butter
- 50 g/1¾ oz pecorino cheese, grated
- 200 ml/7 fl oz/¾ cup milk
- 450 g/1 lb smoked cod fillet, skinned and boned
- 4 eggs, beaten
- salt and pepper

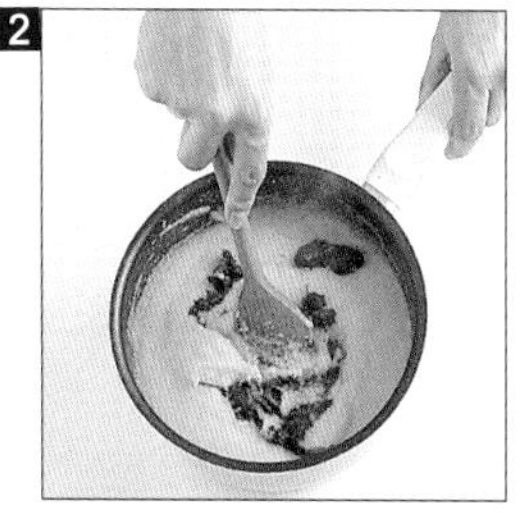
2

4

5

1 Cook the polenta, using 1.5 litres/2¾ pints/6½ cups of water to 350 g/12 oz polenta, stirring, for 30–35 minutes.

2 Stir the spinach, butter and half of the pecorino cheese into the polenta. Season to taste with salt and pepper.

3 Divide the polenta among 4 individual ovenproof dishes, spreading the polenta evenly across the bottom and up the sides of the dishes.

4 In a frying pan (skillet), bring the milk to the boil. Add the fish and cook for 8–10 minutes, turning once, or until tender. Remove the fish with a perforated spoon.

5 Remove the pan from the heat. Pour the eggs into the milk in the pan and mix together.

6 Using a fork, flake the fish into smaller pieces and place it in the centre of the dishes.

7 Pour the milk and egg mixture over the fish.

8 Sprinkle with the remaining cheese and bake in a preheated oven, at 190°C/375°F/ Gas Mark 5, for 25–30 minutes or until set and golden. Serve hot.

VARIATION

Try using 350 g/12 oz cooked chicken breast with 2 tablespoons of chopped tarragon, instead of the smoked cod, if you prefer.

Spinach & Anchovy Pasta

This colourful light meal can be made with a variety of different pasta, including spaghetti and linguine.

NUTRITIONAL INFORMATION

Calories	619	Sugars	5g
Protein	21g	Fat	31g
Carbohydrate	67g	Saturates	3g

10 MINS 25 MINS

SERVES 4

INGREDIENTS

- 900 g/2 lb fresh, young spinach leaves
- 400 g/14 oz dried fettuccine
- 6 tbsp olive oil
- 3 tbsp pine nuts (kernels)
- 3 garlic cloves, crushed
- 8 canned anchovy fillets, drained and chopped
- salt

1 Trim off any tough spinach stalks. Rinse the spinach leaves and place them in a large saucepan with only the water that is clinging to them after washing. Cover and cook over a high heat, shaking the pan from time, until the spinach has wilted, but retains its colour. Drain well, set aside and keep warm.

2 Bring a large saucepan of lightly salted water to the boil. Add the fettuccine and 1 tablespoon of the oil and cook for 8–10 minutes until it is just tender, but still firm to the bite.

3 Heat 4 tablespoons of the remaining oil in a saucepan. Add the pine kernels (nuts) and fry until golden. Remove the pine kernels (nuts) from the pan and set aside until required.

4 Add the garlic to the pan and fry until golden. Add the anchovies and stir in the spinach. Cook, stirring, for 2-3 minutes, until heated through. Return the pine nuts (kernels) to the pan.

5 Drain the fettuccine, toss in the remaining olive oil and transfer to a warm serving dish. Spoon the anchovy and spinach sauce over the fettucine, toss lightly and serve immediately.

COOK'S TIP

If you are in a hurry, you can use frozen spinach. Thaw and drain it thoroughly, pressing out as much moisture as possible. Cut the leaves into strips and add to the dish with the anchovies in step 4.

Charred Tuna Steaks

Tuna has a firm flesh, which is ideal for barbecuing (grilling), but it can be a little dry unless it is marinated first.

NUTRITIONAL INFORMATION

Calories	153	Sugars	1g
Protein	29g	Fat	3g
Carbohydrate	1g	Saturates	1g

2 HOURS 15 MINS

SERVES 4

INGREDIENTS

- 4 tuna steaks
- 3 tbsp soy sauce
- 1 tbsp Worcestershire sauce
- 1 tsp wholegrain mustard
- 1 tsp caster (superfine) sugar
- 1 tbsp sunflower oil
- green salad, to serve

TO GARNISH

- flat-leaf parsley
- lemon wedges

1 Place the tuna steaks in a shallow dish.

2 Mix together the soy sauce, Worcestershire sauce, mustard, sugar and oil in a small bowl.

3 Pour the marinade over the tuna steaks.

4 Gently turn over the tuna steaks, using your fingers or a fork. Make sure that the fish steaks are well coated with the marinade.

5 Cover and place the tuna steaks in the refrigerator.Leave to chill for between 30 minutes and 2 hours.

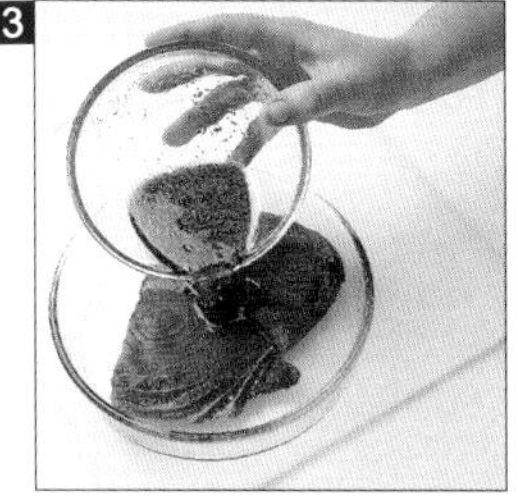

3

4

6

6 Barbecue (grill) the marinated fish over hot coals for 10–15 minutes, turning once.

7 Baste frequently with any of the marinade that is left in the dish.

8 Garnish with flat-leaf parsley and lemon wedges. Serve with a fresh green salad.

COOK'S TIP

If a marinade contains soy sauce, the marinating time should be limited, usually to 2 hours. If allowed to marinate for too long, the fish will dry out and become tough.

Orange Mackerel

Mackerel can be quite rich, but when it is stuffed with oranges and toasted ground almonds it is tangy and light.

NUTRITIONAL INFORMATION

Calories	623	Sugars	7g
Protein	42g	Fat	47g
Carbohydrate	8g	Saturates	8g

 15 MINS 35 MINS

SERVES 4

INGREDIENTS

- 2 tbsp oil
- 4 spring onions (scallions), chopped
- 2 oranges
- 50 g/1¾ oz ground almonds
- 1 tbsp oats
- 50 g/1¾ oz mixed green and black olives, pitted and chopped
- 8 mackerel fillets
- salt and pepper
- crisp salad, to serve

1 Heat the oil in a frying pan (skillet). Add the spring onions (scallions) and cook for 2 minutes.

2 Finely grate the rind of the oranges, then, using a sharp knife, cut away the remaining skin and white pith.

3 Using a sharp knife, segment the oranges by cutting down either side of the lines of pith to loosen each segment. Do this over a plate so that you can reserve any juices. Cut each orange segment in half.

4 Lightly toast the almonds, under a preheated grill (broiler), for 2–3 minutes or until golden; watch them carefully as they brown very quickly.

1

5

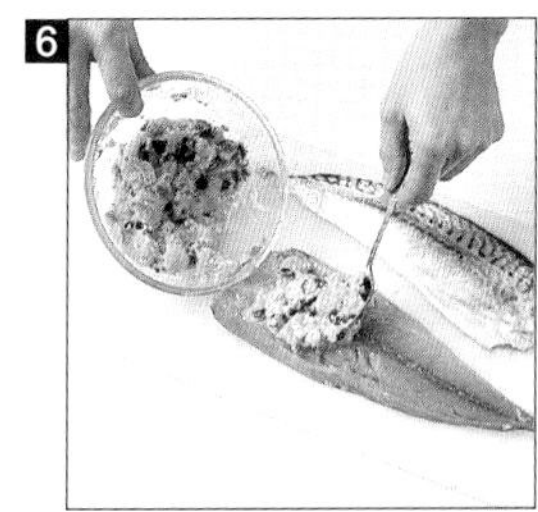
6

5 Mix the spring onions (scallions), oranges, ground almonds, oats and olives together in a bowl and season to taste with salt and pepper.

6 Spoon the orange mixture along the centre of each fillet. Roll up each fillet, securing it in place with a cocktail stick (toothpick) or skewer.

7 Bake in a preheated oven at 190°C/375°F/Gas Mark 5 for 25 minutes until the fish is tender.

8 Transfer to serving plates and serve warm with a salad.

Delicately Spiced Trout

The firm, sweet flesh of the trout is enhanced by the sweet-spicy flavour of the marinade and cooking juices.

NUTRITIONAL INFORMATION

Calories	374	Sugars	13g
Protein	38g	Fat	19g
Carbohydrate	14g	Saturates	3g

 45 MINS  20 MINS

SERVES 4

INGREDIENTS

- 4 trout, each weighing 175–250 g/ 6–9 oz, cleaned
- 3 tbsp oil
- 1 tsp fennel seeds
- 1tsp onion seeds
- 1 garlic clove, crushed
- 150 ml/¼ pint/⅔ cup coconut milk or fish stock
- 3 tbsp tomato purée (paste)
- 60 g/2 oz/⅓ cup sultanas (golden raisins)
- ½ tsp garam masala

TO GARNISH

- 25 g/1 oz/¼ cup chopped cashew nuts
- lemon wedges
- sprigs of fresh coriander (cilantro)

MARINADE

- 4 tbsp lemon juice
- 2 tbsp chopped fresh coriander (cilantro)
- 1 tsp ground cumin
- ½ tsp salt
- ½ tsp ground black pepper

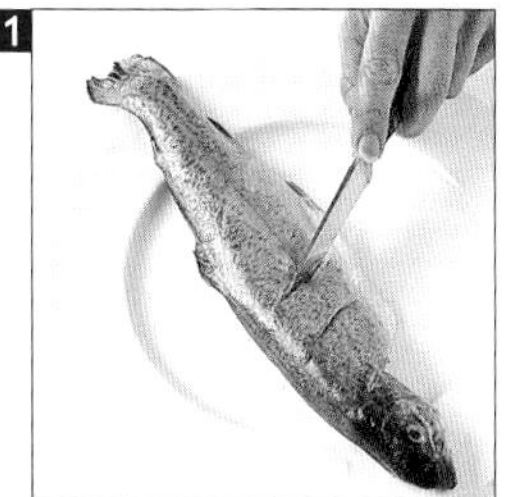
1

3

4

1 Slash the trout skin in several places on both sides with a sharp knife.

2 To make the marinade, mix all the ingredients together in a bowl.

3 Put the trout in a shallow dish and pour over the marinade. Leave to marinate for 30–40 minutes; turn the fish over during the marinating time.

4 Heat the oil in a Balti pan or wok and fry the fennel seeds and onion seeds until they start popping.

5 Add the crushed garlic, coconut milk or fish stock, and tomato purée (paste) and bring the mixture in the wok to the boil.

6 Add the sultanas (golden raisins), garam masala and trout with the juices from the marinade. Cover and simmer for 5 minutes. Turn the trout over and simmer for a further 10 minutes.

7 Serve garnished with the nuts, lemon and coriander (cilantro) sprigs.

Seafood in Red Curry Sauce

For something very quick and simple that sets your tastebuds alight, try this inspired dish of prawns (shrimp) in a wonderfully spicy sauce.

NUTRITIONAL INFORMATION

Calories	175	Sugars	3g
Protein	29g	Fat	5g
Carbohydrate	3g	Saturates	1g

 10 MINS  10 MINS

SERVES 4

INGREDIENTS

- 1 tbsp vegetable oil
- 6 spring onions (scallions), trimmed and sliced
- 1 stalk lemon grass
- 1 cm/½ inch piece of fresh ginger root
- 250 ml/9 fl oz/1 cup coconut milk
- 2 tbsp Thai red curry paste
- 1 tbsp fish sauce
- 500 g/1 lb 2 oz/3 cups uncooked king prawns (jumbo shrimp)
- 1 tbsp chopped fresh coriander (cilantro)
- fresh chillies, to garnish

1

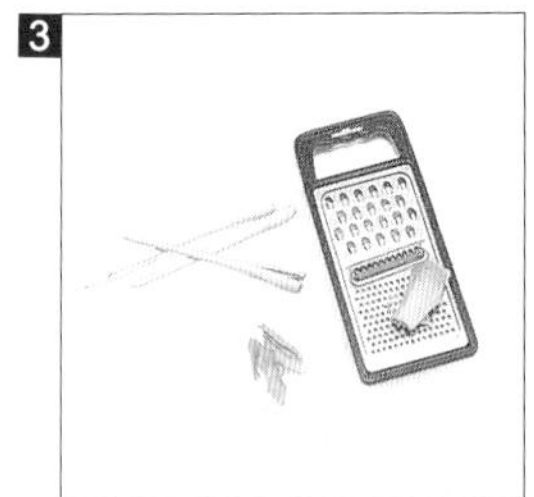
3

4

1 Heat the vegetable oil in a wok or large frying pan (skillet) and fry the spring onions (scallions) gently until softened, about 2 minutes.

2 Bruise the stalk of lemon grass using a meat mallet or rolling pin.

3 Peel and finely grate the piece of fresh ginger root.

4 Add the bruised lemon grass and grated ginger root to the wok or frying pan (skillet) with the coconut milk, Thai red curry paste and fish sauce. Heat the coconut milk until almost boiling.

5 Peel the prawns (shrimp), leaving the tails intact. Remove the black vein along the back of each prawn (shrimp).

6 Add the prawns (shrimp) to the wok or frying pan (skillet) with the chopped coriander (cilantro) and cook gently for 5 minutes.

7 Serve the prawns (shrimp) with the sauce, garnished with fresh chillies.

VARIATION

Try this recipe using Thai green curry sauce instead of red. Both varieties are obtainable from many supermarkets – look for them in the oriental foods section.

Caribbean Prawns (Shrimp)

This is an ideal recipe for cooks who have difficulty in finding raw prawns (shrimp).

NUTRITIONAL INFORMATION

Calories	110	Sugars	15g
Protein	5g	Fat	4g
Carbohydrate	15g	Saturates	3g

40 MINS 15 MINS

SERVES 4

INGREDIENTS

- 16 cooked king (tiger) prawns (shrimp)
- 1 small pineapple
- flaked coconut, to garnish (optional)

MARINADE

- 150 ml/5 fl oz/⅔ cup pineapple juice
- 2 tbsp white wine vinegar
- 2 tbsp dark muscovado sugar
- 2 tbsp desiccated (shredded) coconut

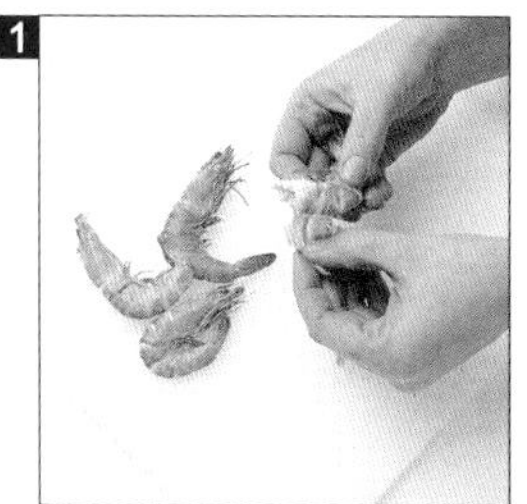

1

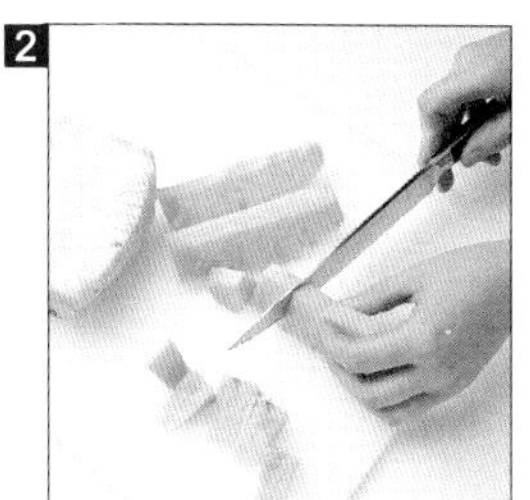

2

5

1 If they are unpeeled, peel the prawns (shrimp), leaving the tails attached if preferred.

2 Peel the pineapple and cut it in half lengthways. Cut one pineapple half into wedges then into chunks.

3 To make the marinade, mix together half of the pineapple juice and the vinegar, sugar and coconut in a shallow, non-metallic dish. Add the peeled prawns (shrimp) and pineapple chunks and toss until well coated. Leave the prawns and pineapple to marinate for at least 30 minutes.

4 Remove the pineapple and prawns (shrimp) from the marinade and thread them on to skewers. Reserve the marinade.

5 Strain the marinade and place in a food processor. Roughly chop the remaining pineapple and add to the processor with the remaining pineapple juice. Process the pineapple for a few seconds to produce a thick sauce.

6 Pour the sauce into a small saucepan. Bring to the boil then simmer for about 5 minutes. If you prefer, you can heat up the sauce by the side of the barbecue (grill).

7 Transfer the kebabs to the barbecue (grill) and brush with some of the sauce. Barbecue (grill) for about 5 minutes until the kebabs are piping hot. Turn the kebabs, brushing occasionally with the sauce. Serve the kebabs with extra sauce, sprinkled with flaked coconut (if using).

Prawn (Shrimp) Omelette

This really is a meal in minutes, combining many Chinese ingredients for a truly tasty dish.

NUTRITIONAL INFORMATION

Calories	270	Sugars	1g
Protein	30g	Fat	15g
Carbohydrate	3g	Saturates	3g

 5 MINS  10 MINS

SERVES 4

INGREDIENTS

- 2 tbsp sunflower oil
- 4 spring onions (scallions)
- 350 g/12 oz peeled prawns (shrimp)
- 100 g/3½ oz/1 cup bean sprouts
- 1 tsp cornflour (cornstarch)
- 1 tbsp light soy sauce
- 6 eggs
- 3 tbsp cold water

1 Heat the sunflower oil in a large preheated wok or frying pan (skillet).

2 Using a sharp knife, trim the spring onions (scallions) and cut into slices.

3 Add the prawns (shrimp), spring onions (scallions) and bean sprouts to the wok and stir-fry for 2 minutes.

4 In a small bowl, mix together the cornflour (cornstarch) and soy sauce until well combined.

5 In a separate bowl, beat the eggs with the water, using a metal fork, and then blend with the cornflour (cornstarch) and soy mixture.

6 Add the egg mixture to the wok and cook for 5–6 minutes, or until the mixture sets.

7 Transfer the omelette to a warm serving plate and cut into quarters to serve.

COOK'S TIP

It is important to use fresh bean sprouts for this dish as the canned ones don't have the crunchy texture necessary.

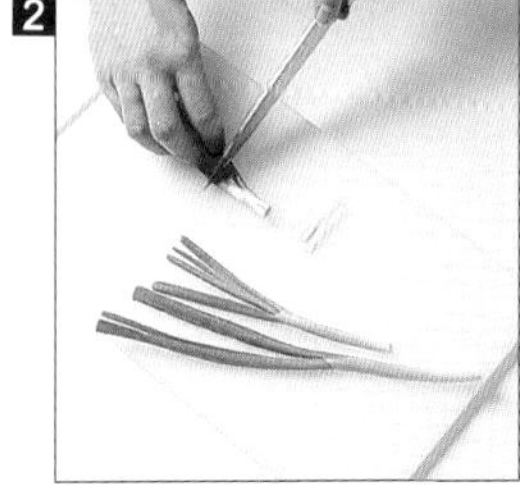

Prawn (Shrimp) Biryani

The flavours in this recipe are quite subtle, so it is a lighter dish and therefore suitable for every day.

NUTRITIONAL INFORMATION

Calories	177	Sugars	6g
Protein	15g	Fat	6g
Carbohydrate	18g	Saturates	0.5g

2½ HOURS 45 MINS

SERVES 8

INGREDIENTS

- 1 tsp saffron strands
- 50 ml/2 fl oz/4 tbsp tepid water
- 2 shallots, chopped coarsely
- 3 garlic cloves, crushed
- 1 tsp chopped ginger root
- 2 tsp coriander seeds
- ½ tsp black peppercorns
- 2 cloves
- 2 green cardamom pods
- 2.5 cm/1 inch piece cinnamon stick
- 1 tsp ground turmeric
- 1 fresh green chilli, chopped
- ½ tsp salt
- 2 tbsp ghee
- 1 tsp whole black mustard seeds
- 500 g/1 lb 2 oz uncooked tiger prawns (shrimp) in their shells, or 400 g/14 oz uncooked and peeled
- 300 ml/½ pint/1¼ cups coconut milk
- 300 ml/½ pint/1¼ cups low-fat natural yogurt
- 225 g/8 oz/generous 1 cup basmati rice, soaked for 2 hours and drained
- 1 tbsp sultanas (golden raisins)
- flaked (slivered) almonds, toasted and 1 spring onion (scallion), sliced, to garnish

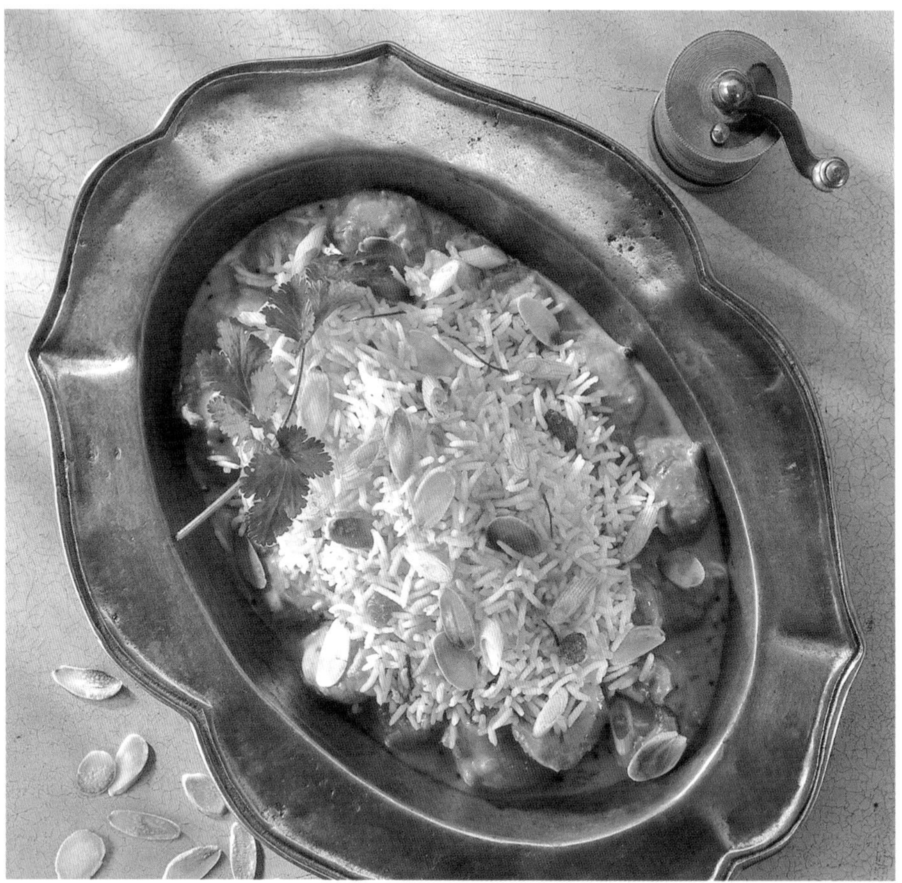

2

2

3

1 Soak the saffron in the tepid water for 10 minutes. Put the shallots, garlic, spices and salt into a spice grinder or pestle and mortar and grind to a paste.

2 Heat the ghee in a saucepan and add the mustard seeds. When they start to pop, add the prawns (shrimp) and stir over a high heat for 1 minute. Stir in the spice mix, then the coconut milk and yogurt. Simmer for 20 minutes.

3 Bring a large saucepan of salted water to the boil. Add the rice to the pan. Boil for 12 minutes. Drain. Pile the rice on the prawns. Spoon over the sultanas (golden raisins) and trickle the saffron water over the rice in lines. Cover the pan with a clean cloth and put the lid on tightly. Remove the pan from heat and leave to stand for 5 minutes. Serve, garnished with the almonds and spring onion (scallion).

Stir-fried Prawns (Shrimp)

The (bell) peppers in this dish can be replaced by either mangetout (snow peas), or broccoli to maintain the attractive pink-green contrast.

NUTRITIONAL INFORMATION

Calories	116	Sugars	1g
Protein	10g	Fat	6g
Carbohydrate	4g	Saturates	1g

 5 MINS  10 MINS

SERVES 4

INGREDIENTS

- 170 g/6 oz raw prawns (shrimp), peeled
- 1 tsp salt
- ¼ tsp egg white
- 2 tsp cornflour (cornstarch) paste (see page 6)
- 300 ml/½ pint/1¼ cups vegetable oil
- 1 spring onion (scallion), cut into short sections
- 2.5-cm/1-inch piece ginger root, thinly sliced
- 1 small green (bell) pepper, cored, seeded and cubed
- ½ tsp sugar
- 1 tbsp light soy sauce
- 1 tsp rice wine or dry sherry
- a few drops sesame oil

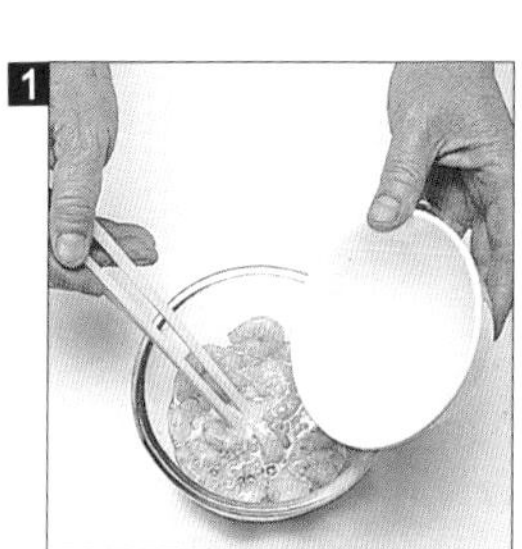

1

2

3

1 Mix the prawns (shrimp) with a pinch of the salt, the egg white and cornflour (cornstarch) paste until well coated.

2 Heat the oil in a preheated wok and stir-fry the prawns (shrimp) for 30-40 seconds only. Remove and drain on kitchen paper (paper towels).

3 Pour off the oil, leaving about 1 tablespoon in the wok. Add the spring onion (scallion) and ginger to flavour the oil for a few seconds, then add the green (bell) pepper and stir-fry for about 1 minute.

4 Add the remaining salt and the sugar followed by the prawns (shrimp). Continue stirring for another minute or so, then add the soy sauce and wine and blend well. Sprinkle with sesame oil and serve immediately.

VARIATION

1-2 small green or red hot chillies, sliced, can be added with the green (bell) pepper to create a more spicy dish. Leave the chillies unseeded for a very hot dish.

Sweet & Sour Prawns

Use raw prawns (shrimp) if possible. Omit steps 1 and 2 if ready-cooked ones are used.

NUTRITIONAL INFORMATION

Calories	373	Sugars	11g
Protein	13g	Fat	26g
Carbohydrate	19g	Saturates	3g

3½ HOURS 10 MINS

SERVES 4

INGREDIENTS

- 175-250 g/6-9 oz peeled raw tiger prawns
- pinch of salt
- 1 tsp egg white
- 1 tsp cornflour (cornstarch) paste (see page 6)
- 300 ml/½ pint/1¼ cups vegetable oil

SAUCE

- 1 tbsp vegetable oil
- ½ small green (bell) pepper, cored, seeded and thinly sliced
- ½ small carrot, thinly sliced
- 125 g/4½ oz canned water chestnuts, drained and sliced
- ½ tsp salt
- 1 tbsp light soy sauce
- 2 tbsp sugar
- 3 tbsp rice or sherry vinegar
- 1 tsp rice wine or dry sherry
- 1 tbsp tomato sauce
- ½ tsp chilli sauce
- 3-4 tbsp Chinese Stock (see page 8) or water
- 2 tsp cornflour (cornstarch) paste (see page 6)
- a few drops sesame oil

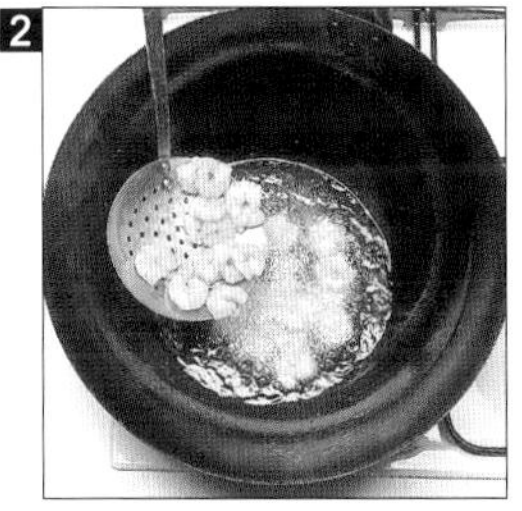

2

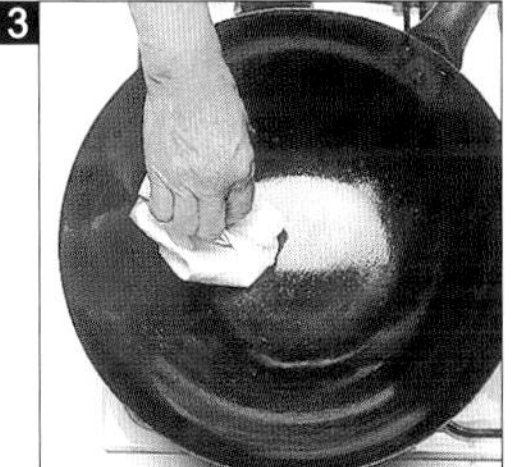

3

3

1 Mix together the prawns (shrimp) with the salt, egg white and cornflour (cornstarch) paste.

2 Heat the oil in a preheated wok and stir-fry the prawns (shrimp) for 30-40 seconds only. Remove and drain on kitchen paper (paper towels).

3 Pour off the oil and wipe the wok clean with kitchen paper (paper towels). To make the sauce, first heat the tablespoon of oil. Add the vegetables and stir-fry for about 1 minute, then add the seasonings with the stock or water and bring to the boil.

4 Add the prawns (shrimp) and stir until blended well. Thicken the sauce with the cornflour (cornstarch) paste and stir until smooth. Sprinkle with sesame oil and serve hot.

Vegetable & Egg Prawns

In this recipe, a light Chinese omelette is shredded and tossed back into the dish before serving.

NUTRITIONAL INFORMATION

Calories	258	Sugars	7g
Protein	21g	Fat	15g
Carbohydrate	10g	Saturates	3g

 10 MINS  15 MINS

SERVES 4

INGREDIENTS

- 225 g/8 oz courgettes (zucchini)
- 3 tbsp vegetable oil
- 2 eggs
- 2 tbsp cold water
- 225 g/8 oz carrots, grated
- 1 onion, sliced
- 150 g/5½ oz/1½ cups bean sprouts
- 225 g/8 oz peeled prawns (shrimp)
- 2 tbsp soy sauce
- pinch of Chinese five-spice powder
- 25 g/1 oz/¼ cup peanuts, chopped
- 2 tbsp fresh chopped coriander (cilantro)

1 Finely grate the courgettes (zucchini).

2 Heat 1 tablespoon of the vegetable oil in a large preheated wok.

3 Beat the eggs with the water and pour the mixture into the wok and cook for 2–3 minutes or until the egg sets.

4 Remove the omelette from the wok and transfer to a clean board. Fold the omelette, cut it into thin strips and set aside until required.

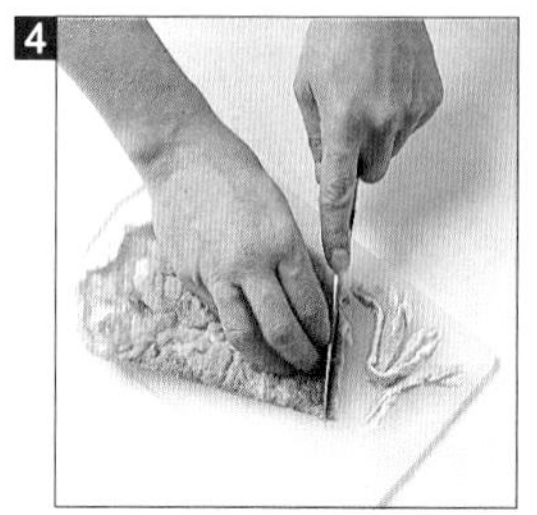

5 Add the remaining oil to the wok. Add the carrots, onion and courgettes (zucchini) and stir-fry for 5 minutes.

6 Add the bean sprouts and prawns (shrimp) to the wok and cook for a further 2 minutes, or until the prawns (shrimp) are heated through.

7 Add the soy sauce, Chinese five-spice powder and peanuts to the wok, together with the strips of omelette and heat through. Garnish with chopped fresh coriander (cilantro) and serve.

COOK'S TIP

The water is mixed with the egg in step 3 for a lighter, less rubbery omelette.

Pork Sesame Toasts

This classic Chinese appetizer is also a great nibble for serving at parties – but be sure to make plenty!

NUTRITIONAL INFORMATION

Calories	674	Sugars	2g
Protein	33g	Fat	46g
Carbohydrate	33g	Saturates	7g

5 MINS  35 MINS

SERVES 4

INGREDIENTS

- 250 g/9 oz lean pork
- 250 g/9 oz/⅔ cup uncooked peeled prawns (shrimp), deveined
- 4 spring onions (scallions), trimmed
- 1 garlic clove, crushed
- 1 tbsp chopped fresh coriander (cilantro) leaves and stems
- 1 tbsp fish sauce
- 1 egg
- 8–10 slices of thick-cut white bread
- 3 tbsp sesame seeds
- 150 ml/¼ pint/⅔ cup vegetable oil
- salt and pepper

TO GARNISH

- sprigs of fresh coriander (cilantro)
- red (bell) pepper, sliced finely

1 Put the pork, prawns (shrimp), spring onions (scallions), garlic, coriander (cilantro), fish sauce, egg and seasoning into a food processor or blender. Process for a few seconds until the ingredients are finely chopped. Transfer the mixture to a bowl. Alternatively, chop the pork, prawns (shrimp) and spring onions (scallions) very finely, and mix with the garlic, coriander (cilantro), fish sauce, beaten egg and seasoning until all the ingredients are well combined.

2 Spread the pork and prawn (shrimp) mixture thickly over the bread so that it reaches right up to the edges. Cut off the crusts and slice each piece of bread into 4 squares or triangles.

3 Sprinkle the topping liberally with sesame seeds.

4 Heat the oil in a wok or frying pan (skillet). Fry a few pieces of the bread, topping side down first so that it sets the egg, for about 2 minutes or until golden brown. Turn the pieces over to cook on the other side, about 1 minute.

5 Drain the pork and prawn (shrimp) toasts and place them on kitchen paper (paper towels). Fry the remaining pieces. Serve garnished with sprigs of fresh coriander (cilantro) and strips of red (bell) pepper.

Hot & Sweet Prawns (Shrimp)

Uncooked prawns (shrimp) are speared on skewers, brushed with a sesame oil, lime juice and coriander (cilantro) baste and then grilled.

NUTRITIONAL INFORMATION

Calories	239	Sugars	8g
Protein	28g	Fat	11g
Carbohydrate	8g	Saturates	2g

 1 HOUR

10 MINS

SERVES 4

INGREDIENTS

- wooden skewers soaked in warm water for 20 minutes
- 500 g/1 lb 2 oz/2½ cups uncooked prawns (shrimp)
- 3 tbsp sesame oil
- 2 tbsp lime juice
- 1 tbsp chopped fresh coriander (cilantro)

SAUCE

- 4 tbsp light malt vinegar
- 2 tbsp fish sauce or light soy sauce
- 2 tbsp water
- 2 tbsp light muscovado sugar
- 2 garlic cloves, crushed
- 2 tsp grated fresh ginger root
- 1 red chilli, deseeded and chopped finely
- 2 tbsp chopped fresh coriander (cilantro)
- salt

1

2

3

1 Peel the prawns (shrimp), leaving the tails intact. Remove the black vein that runs along the back of each one, then skewer the prawns (shrimp) on to the wooden skewers.

2 Mix together the sesame oil, lime juice and chopped coriander (cilantro) in a shallow bowl. Lay the skewered prawns (shrimp) in this mixture. Cover and chill in the refrigerator for 30 minutes, turning once, so that the prawns (shrimp) absorb the marinade.

3 Meanwhile, make the sauce. Heat the vinegar, fish sauce or soy sauce, water, sugar and salt to taste until boiling. Remove from the heat and leave to cool.

4 Mix together the crushed garlic, grated ginger, red chilli and coriander (cilantro) in a small serving bowl. Add the cooled vinegar mixture and stir until well combined.

5 Place the prawns (shrimp) on a foil-lined grill (broiler) pan under a preheated grill (broiler) for about 6 minutes, turning once and basting often with the marinade, until cooked.

6 Transfer to a warmed serving platter and serve with the dipping sauce.

Shrimp & Sweetcorn Patties

Chopped (small) shrimps and sweetcorn are combined in a light batter, which is dropped in spoonfuls into hot fat to make these tasty patties.

NUTRITIONAL INFORMATION

Calories	250	Sugars	1g
Protein	17g	Fat	9g
Carbohydrate	26g	Saturates	2g

 35 MINS   20 MINS

SERVES 4

INGREDIENTS

- 125 g/4½ oz/1 cup plain (all-purpose) flour
- 1½ tsp baking powder
- 2 eggs
- about 250 ml/9 fl oz/1 cup cold water
- 1 garlic clove, very finely chopped
- 3 spring onions (scallions), trimmed and very finely chopped
- 250 g/9 oz/1 cup peeled (small) shrimps, chopped
- 125 g/4½ oz/½ cup canned sweetcorn, drained
- vegetable oil for frying
- salt and pepper

TO GARNISH

- spring onion (scallion) brushes (see Cook's Tip, right)
- lime slices
- 1 chilli flower

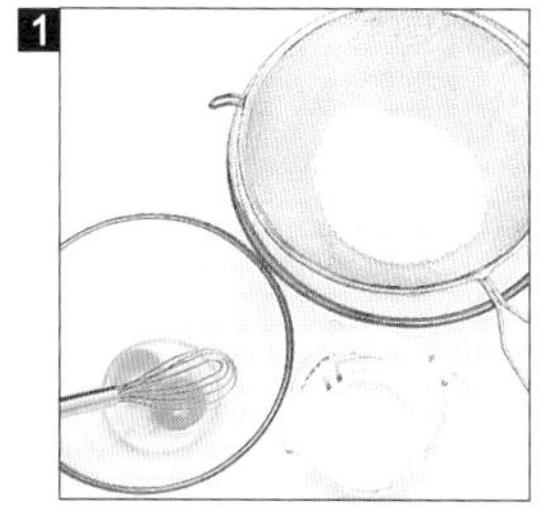

1

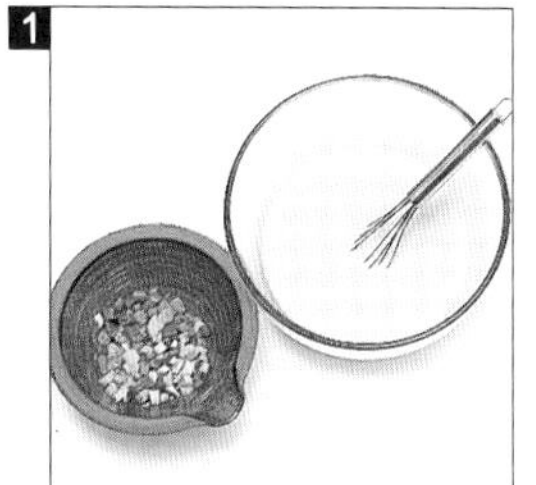

1

2

1 Sift the flour, baking powder and ½ tsp salt into a bowl. Add the eggs and half the water and beat to make a smooth batter, adding extra water to give the consistency of double (heavy) cream. Add the garlic and spring onions (scallions). Cover and leave for 30 minutes.

2 Stir the (small) shrimps and corn into the batter. Season with pepper.

3 Heat 2–3 tablespoons of oil in a wok. Drop tablespoonfuls of the batter into the wok and cook over a medium heat until bubbles rise and the surface just sets. Flip the patties over and cook the other side until golden brown. Drain on kitchen paper (paper towels).

4 Cook the remaining batter in the same way, adding more oil to the wok if required. Garnish and serve at once.

COOK'S TIP

Make a spring onion (scallion) brush by trimming off the tips of the leaves and making several fine cuts from the leaf tips to the top of the bulb. Place in iced water to make the leaves curl.

Shrimp Curry & Fruit Sauce

Serve this lightly-spiced dish as part of a buffet meal, or as a refreshingly different lunch dish, with a bowl of rice.

NUTRITIONAL INFORMATION

Calories	538	Sugars	28g
Protein	40g	Fat	28g
Carbohydrate	33g	Saturates	15g

 30 MINS  20 MINS

SERVES 4

INGREDIENTS

- 2 tbsp vegetable oil
- 25 g/1 oz/2 tbsp butter
- 2 onions, finely chopped
- 2 garlic cloves, finely chopped
- 1 tsp cumin seeds, lightly crushed
- 1 tsp ground turmeric
- 1 tsp paprika
- ½ tsp chilli powder, or to taste
- 60 g/2 oz creamed coconut
- 1 x 400g/14 oz can chopped tomatoes
- 1 tbsp tomato purée (paste)
- 500 g/1 lb 2 oz frozen cooked shrimps, defrosted
- ½ cucumber, thinly diced
- 150 ml/¼ pint/⅔ cup low-fat yogurt
- 2 hard-boiled eggs, quartered
- salt
- coriander and onion rings, to garnish

FRUIT SAUCE

- 300 ml/½ pint/1¼ cups low-fat natural yogurt
- ¼ tsp salt
- 1 garlic clove, crushed
- 2 tbsp chopped mint
- 4 tbsp seedless raisins
- 1 small pomegranate

1 Heat the oil and butter in a frying pan. Add the chopped onions and fry until translucent. Add the garlic and fry for a further minute, until softened but not browned.

2 Stir in the spices and cook for 2 minutes, stirring. Stir in the creamed coconut, chopped tomatoes and tomato purée (paste) and bring to the boil. Simmer for 10 minutes, or until the sauce has thickened slightly. It should not be at all runny.

3 Remove the pan from the heat and set aside to cool. Stir in the shrimps, cucumber and yogurt. Taste the sauce and adjust the seasoning if necessary. Cover and chill until ready to serve.

4 To make the fruit sauce, place everything except the pomegrantes into a bowl. Cut the pomegranate in half, scoop out the seeds, discarding the white membrane, and stir into the fruit mixture, reserving a few for garnish.

5 Transfer the curry to a serving dish and arrange the hard-boiled egg, coriander and onion rings on top. Serve the sauce separately, sprinkled with the reserved pomegranate seeds.

Prawns (Shrimp) with Ginger

Crispy ginger is a wonderful garnish which offsets the spicy prawns (shrimp) both visually and in flavour.

NUTRITIONAL INFORMATION

Calories	229	Sugars	7g
Protein	29g	Fat	8g
Carbohydrate	10g	Saturates	1g

 10 MINS  15 MINS

SERVES 4

INGREDIENTS

- 5 cm/2 inch piece fresh root ginger
- oil, for frying
- 1 onion, diced
- 225 g/8 oz carrots, diced
- 100 g/3½ oz/½ cup frozen peas
- 100 g/3½ oz/1 cup bean sprouts
- 450 g/1 lb peeled king prawns (shrimp)
- 1 tsp Chinese five-spice powder
- 1 tbsp tomato purée (paste)
- 1 tbsp soy sauce

1 Using a sharp knife, peel the ginger and slice it into very thin sticks.

2 Heat about 2.5 cm/1 inch of oil in a large preheated wok. Add the ginger and stir-fry for 1 minute or until the ginger is crispy. Remove the ginger with a slotted spoon and leave to drain on absorbent kitchen paper (paper towels).

3 Drain all of the oil from the wok except for about 2 tablespoons. Add the onions and carrots to the wok and stir-fry for 5 minutes. Add the peas and bean sprouts and stir-fry for 2 minutes.

4 Rinse the prawns (shrimp) under cold running water and pat dry with absorbent kitchen paper (paper towels).

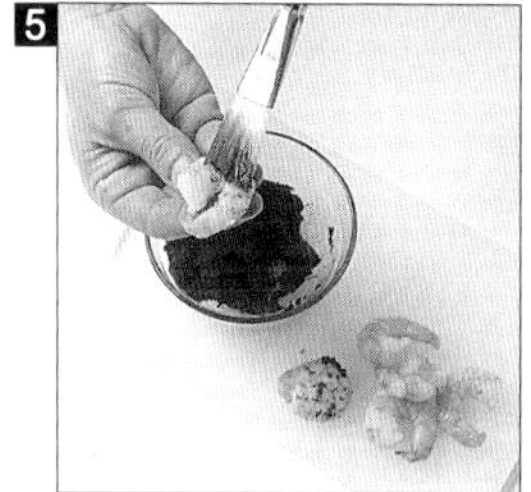

5 Combine the five-spice, tomato purée (paste) and soy sauce. Brush the mixture over the prawns (shrimp).

6 Add the prawns (shrimp) to the wok and stir-fry for a further 2 minutes, or until the prawns (shrimp) are completely cooked through. Transfer the prawn (shrimp) mixture to a warm serving bowl and top with the reserved crispy ginger. Serve immediately.

VARIATION

Use slices of white fish instead of the prawns (shrimp) as an alternative, if you wish.

Pan-Fried Prawns (Shrimp)

A luxurious dish which makes an impressive starter or light meal. Prawns (shrimp) and garlic are a winning combination.

NUTRITIONAL INFORMATION

Calories	455	Sugars	0g
Protein	6g	Fat	37g
Carbohydrate	0g	Saturates	18g

 10 MINS  5 MINS

SERVES 4

INGREDIENTS

- 4 garlic cloves
- 20–24 unshelled large raw prawns (shrimp)
- 125 g/4½ oz/8 tbsp butter
- 4 tbsp olive oil
- 6 tbsp brandy
- salt and pepper
- 2 tbsp chopped fresh parsley

TO SERVE

- lemon wedges
- ciabatta bread

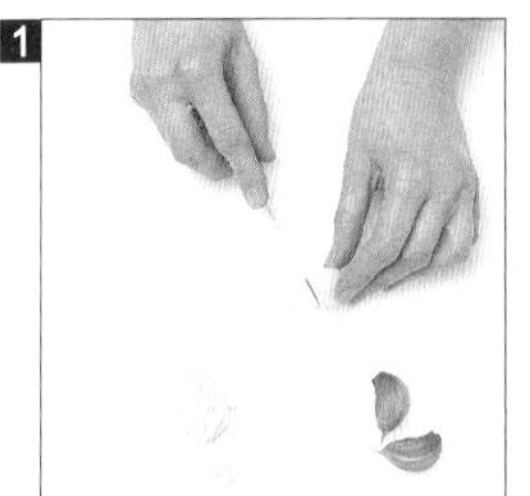

1 Using a sharp knife, peel and slice the garlic.

2 Wash the prawns (shrimp) and pat dry using paper towels.

3 Melt the butter with the oil in a large frying pan (skillet), add the garlic and prawns (shrimp), and fry over a high heat, stirring, for 3–4 minutes until the prawns (shrimp) are pink.

4 Sprinkle with brandy and season with salt and pepper to taste. Sprinkle with parsley and serve immediately with lemon wedges and ciabatta bread, if liked.

Cantonese Prawns (Shrimp)

This prawn (shrimp) dish is very simple and is ideal for supper or lunch when time is short.

NUTRITIONAL INFORMATION

Calories	460	Sugar	3g
Protein	53g	Fat	24
Carbohydrate	6g	Saturates	5g

 10 MINS 20 MINS

SERVES 4

INGREDIENTS

- 5 tbsp vegetable oil
- 4 garlic cloves, crushed
- 675 g/1½ lb raw prawns (shrimp), shelled and deveined
- 5-cm/2-inch piece fresh root ginger, chopped
- 175 g/6 oz lean pork, diced
- 1 leek, sliced
- 3 eggs, beaten
- shredded leek and red (bell) pepper matchsticks, to garnish
- rice, to serve

SAUCE

- 2 tbsp Chinese rice wine or dry sherry
- 2 tbsp light soy sauce
- 2 tsp caster (superfine) sugar
- 150 ml/¼ pint/⅔ cup fish stock
- 4½ tsp cornflour (cornstarch)
- 3 tbsp water

1 Heat 2 tablespoons of the vegetable oil in a preheated wok.

2 Add the garlic to the wok and stir-fry for 30 seconds.

3 Add the prawns (shrimp) to the wok and stir-fry for 5 minutes, or until they change colour. Remove the prawns (shrimp) from the wok or frying pan (skillet) with a slotted spoon, set aside and keep warm.

4 Add the remaining oil to the wok and heat, swirling the oil around the base of the wok until it is really hot.

5 Add the ginger, diced pork and leek to the wok and stir-fry over a medium heat for 4-5 minutes, or until the pork is lightly coloured and sealed.

6 To make the sauce, add the rice wine or sherry, soy sauce, caster (superfine) sugar and fish stock to the wok and stir to blend.

7 In a small bowl, blend the cornflour (cornstarch) with the water to form a smooth paste and stir it into the wok. Cook, stirring, until the sauce thickens and clears.

8 Return the prawns (shrimp) to the wok and add the beaten eggs. Cook for 5–6 minutes, gently stirring occasionally, until the eggs set.

9 Transfer to a warm serving dish, garnish with shredded leek and (bell) pepper matchsticks and serve immediately with rice.

3

5

5

Prawns with Vegetables

This colourful and delicious dish is cooked with vegetables: vary them according to seasonal availability.

NUTRITIONAL INFORMATION

Calories	298	Sugars	1g
Protein	13g	Fat	26g
Carbohydrate	3g	Saturates	3g

 5 MINS  10 MINS

SERVES 4

INGREDIENTS

- 60 g/2 oz mangetout (snow peas)
- ½ small carrot
- 60 g/2 oz baby sweetcorn
- 60 g/2 oz straw mushrooms
- 175-250 g/6-9 oz raw tiger prawns (jumbo shrimp), peeled
- 1 tsp salt
- ½ egg white, lightly beaten
- 1 tsp cornflour (cornstarch) paste (see page 6)
- about 300 ml/½ pint/1¼ cups vegetable oil
- 1 spring onion (scallion), cut into short sections
- 4 slices ginger root, peeled and finely chopped
- ½ tsp sugar
- 1 tbsp light soy sauce
- 1 tsp Chinese rice wine or dry sherry
- a few drops sesame oil
- lemon slices and chopped fresh chives, to garnish

1. Using a sharp knife, top and tail the mangetout (snow peas); cut the carrot into the same size as the mangetout (snow peas); halve the baby sweetcorn and straw mushrooms.

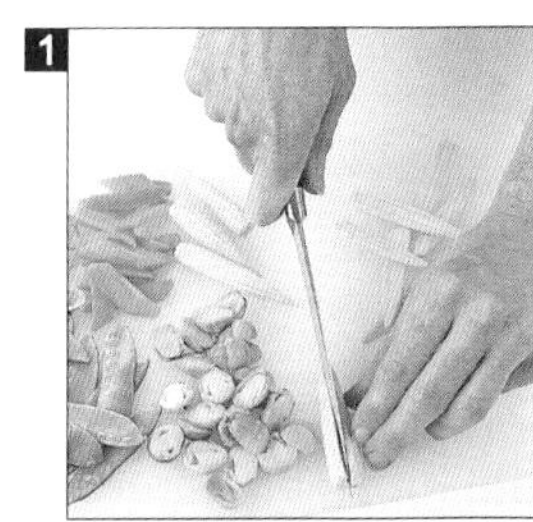

2. Mix the prawns (shrimp) with a pinch of the salt, the egg white and cornflour (cornstarch) paste until the prawns (shrimp) are evenly coated.

3. Preheat a wok over a high heat for 2-3 minutes, then add the vegetable oil and heat to medium-hot.

4. Add the prawns (shrimp) to the wok, stirring to separate them. Remove the prawns (shrimp) with a slotted spoon as soon as the colour changes.

5. Pour off the oil, leaving about 1 tablespoon in the wok. Add the mangetout (snow peas), carrot, sweetcorn, mushrooms and spring onions (scallions).

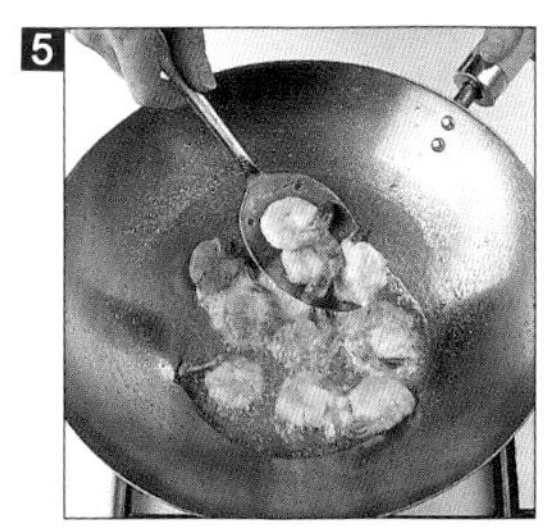

6. Add the prawns (shrimp) together with the ginger, sugar, soy sauce and wine or sherry, blending well.

7. Sprinkle with the sesame oil and serve hot, garnished with lemon slices and chopped fresh chives.

COOK'S TIP

The water is mixed with the egg in step 3 for a lighter, less rubbery omelete.

Fried Rice with Prawns

Use either large peeled prawns (shrimp) or tiger prawns (jumbo shrimp) for this rice dish.

NUTRITIONAL INFORMATION

Calories	599	Sugars	0g
Protein	26g	Fat	16g
Carbohydrate	94g	Saturates	3g

 5 MINS  35 MINS

SERVES 4

INGREDIENTS

300 g/10½ oz/1½ cups long-grain rice

2 eggs

4 tsp cold water

salt and pepper

3 tbsp sunflower oil

4 spring onions (scallions), thinly sliced diagonally

1 garlic clove, crushed

125 g/4½ oz closed-cup or button mushrooms, thinly sliced

2 tbsp oyster or anchovy sauce

1 x 200 g/7 oz can water chestnuts, drained and sliced

250 g/9 oz peeled prawns (shrimp), defrosted if frozen

½ bunch watercress, roughly chopped

watercress sprigs, to garnish (optional)

3

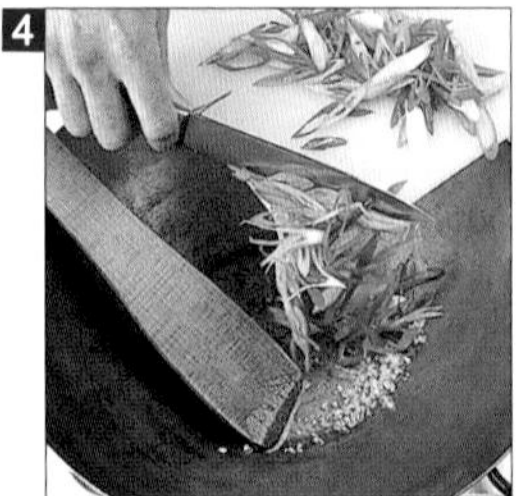
4

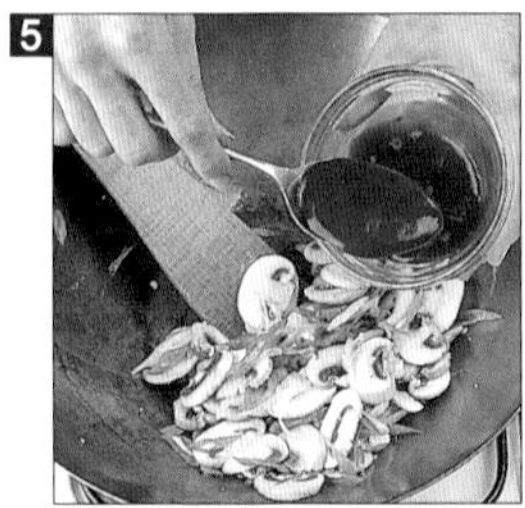
5

1 Cook the rice in boiling salted water and keep warm.

2 Beat each egg separately with 2 teaspoons of cold water and salt and pepper.

3 Heat 2 teaspoons of sunflower oil in a wok or large frying pan (skillet), swirling it around until really hot. Pour in the first egg, swirl it around and leave to cook undisturbed until set. Remove to a plate or board and repeat with the second egg. Cut the omelettes into 2.5 cm/1 inch squares.

4 Heat the remaining oil in the wok and when really hot add the spring onions (scallions) and garlic and stir-fry for 1 minute. Add the mushrooms and continue to cook for a further 2 minutes.

5 Stir in the oyster or anchovy sauce and seasoning and add the water chestnuts and prawns (shrimp); stir-fry for 2 minutes.

6 Stir in the cooked rice and stir-fry for 1 minute, then add the watercress and omelette squares and stir-fry for a further 1-2 minutes until piping hot. Serve at once garnished with sprigs of watercress, if liked.

Crispy Fried Squid

Squid tubes are classically used in Chinese cooking and are most attractive when presented as in the following recipe.

NUTRITIONAL INFORMATION

Calories	156	Sugars	0g
Protein	17g	Fat	6g
Carbohydrate	7g	Saturates	8g

 10 MINS  10 MINS

SERVES 4

INGREDIENTS

- 450 g/1 lb squid, cleaned
- 25 g/1 oz/4 tbsp cornflour (cornstarch)
- 1 tsp salt
- 1 tsp freshly ground black pepper
- 1 tsp chilli flakes
- groundnut oil, for frying
- dipping sauce, to serve

1 Using a sharp knife, remove the tentacles from the squid and trim. Slice the bodies down one side and open out to give a flat piece.

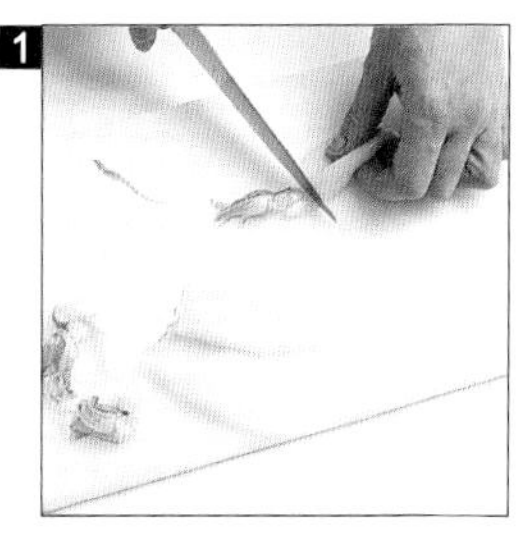

2 Score the flat pieces with a criss-cross pattern then cut each piece into 4.

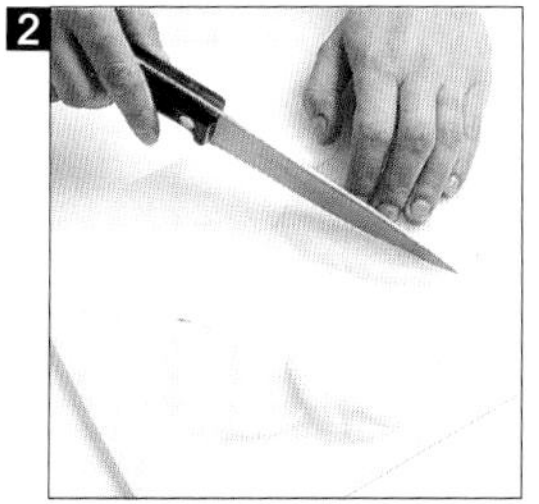

3 Mix together the cornflour (cornstarch), salt, pepper and chilli flakes.

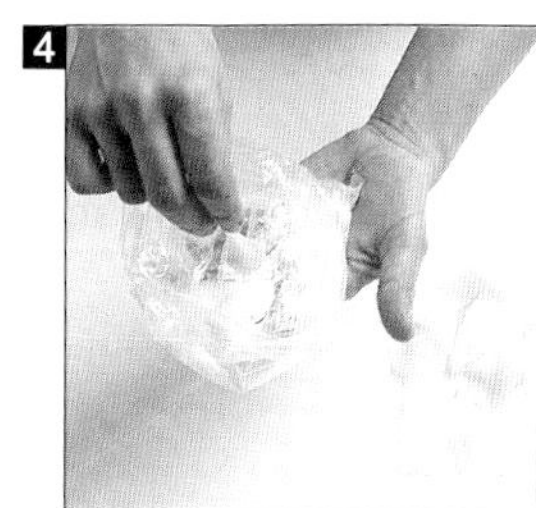

4 Place the salt and pepper mixture in a large polythene bag. Add the squid pieces and shake the bag thoroughly to coat the squid in the flour mixture.

5 Heat about 5 cm/2 inches of groundnut oil in a large preheated wok.

6 Add the squid pieces to the wok and stir-fry, in batches, for about 2 minutes, or until the squid pieces start to curl up. Do not overcook or the squid will become tough.

7 Remove the squid pieces with a slotted spoon, transfer to absorbent kitchen paper (paper towels) and leave to drain thoroughly.

8 Transfer the fried squid pieces to serving plates and serve immediately with a dipping sauce.

COOK'S TIP

Squid tubes may be purchased frozen if they are not available fresh. They are usually ready-cleaned and are easy to use. Ensure that they are completely defrosted before cooking.

Stuffed Squid

Whole squid are stuffed with a mixture of fresh herbs and sun-dried tomatoes and then cooked in a wine sauce.

NUTRITIONAL INFORMATION

Calories	276	Sugars	1g
Protein	23g	Fat	8g
Carbohydrate	20g	Saturates	1g

 25 MINS  35 MINS

SERVES 4

INGREDIENTS

- 8 squid, cleaned and gutted but left whole (ask your fishmonger to do this)
- 6 canned anchovies, chopped
- 2 garlic cloves, chopped
- 2 tbsp rosemary, stalks removed and leaves chopped
- 2 sun-dried tomatoes, chopped
- 150 g/5½ oz breadcrumbs
- 1 tbsp olive oil
- 1 onion, finely chopped
- 200 ml/7 fl oz/¾ cup white wine
- 200 ml/7 fl oz/¾ cup fish stock
- cooked rice, to serve

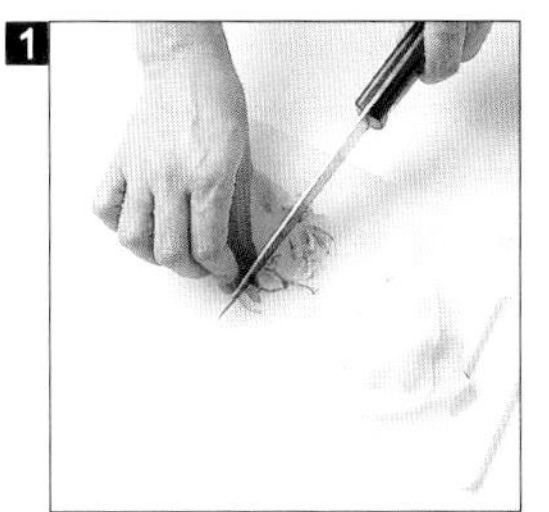

1 Remove the tentacles from the body of the squid and chop the flesh finely.

2 Grind the anchovies, garlic, rosemary and tomatoes to a paste in a mortar and pestle.

3 Add the breadcrumbs and the chopped squid tentacles and mix. If the mixture is too dry to form a thick paste at this point, add 1 teaspoon of water.

4 Spoon the paste into the body sacs of the squid then tie a length of cotton around the end of each sac to fasten them. Do not overfill the sacs, because they will expand during cooking.

5 Heat the oil in a frying pan (skillet). Add the onion and cook, stirring, for 3–4 minutes or until golden.

6 Add the stuffed squid to the pan and cook for 3–4 minutes or until brown all over.

7 Add the wine and stock and bring to the boil. Reduce the heat, cover and then leave to simmer for 15 minutes.

8 Remove the lid and cook for a further 5 minutes or until the squid is tender and the juices reduced. Serve with plenty of cooked rice.

Octopus & Squid with Chilli

Try to buy cleaned squid tubes for this dish; if they are not available, see page 536 for instructions on preparing squid.

NUTRITIONAL INFORMATION

Calories	319	Sugars	2g
Protein	40g	Fat	13g
Carbohydrate	4g	Saturates	1g

8½ HOURS 10 MINS

SERVES 6

INGREDIENTS

- 150 ml/¼ pint/⅔ cup rice vinegar
- 50 ml/2 fl oz/¼ cup dry sherry
- 2 red chillies, chopped
- 1 tsp sugar
- 4 tbsp oil
- 12 baby octopus
- 12 small squid tubes, cleaned
- 2 spring onions (scallions), sliced
- 1 garlic clove, crushed
- 2.5 cm/1 inch piece ginger, grated
- 4 tbsp sweet chilli sauce
- salt

1 Combine the vinegar, dry sherry, red chillies, sugar, 2 tablespoon of the oil and a pinch of salt in a large bowl.

2 Wash each octopus under cold running water and drain. Lay each on its side on a chopping board. Find the 'neck' and cut through. The 'beak' of the octopus should be left in the head; if it is not, make a cut nearer the tentacles and check again. Discard the head and beak, and put the tentacles, which should all be in one piece, into the vinegar mixture.

3 Put the squid tubes into the vinegar mixture and turn to coat well. Cover and chill for 8 hours or overnight.

4 Heat the remaining oil in a wok and stir-fry the spring onions (scallions), garlic and ginger for 1 minute over a very hot barbecue. Remove from the heat and add the chilli sauce. Set aside.

5 Drain the fish from the marinade. Cut the pointed bottom end off each squid tube, so the tubes are of even width. Open out the squid so that it is flat. Score the squid to create a lattice pattern.

6 Cook the octopus and squid over the hottest part of the barbecue for 4–5 minutes, turning them constantly. The octopus tentacles will curl up, and are cooked when the flesh is no longer translucent. The squid tubes will curl back on themselves, revealing the lattice cuts.

7 When cooked, toss them into the pan with the chilli sauce to coat completely and serve immediately.

1

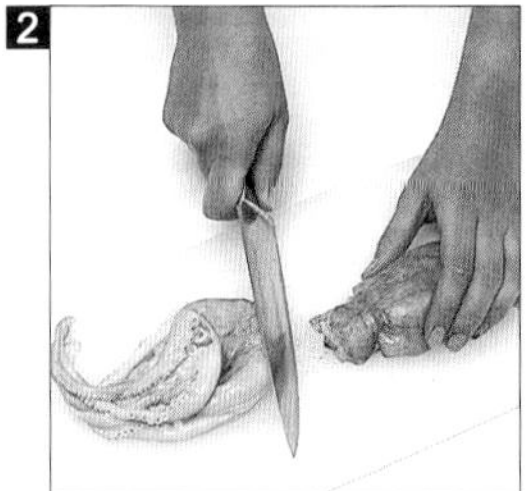
2

3

Squid with Black Bean Sauce

Squid really is wonderful if quickly cooked as in this recipe, and contrary to popular belief it is not tough and rubbery unless it is overcooked.

NUTRITIONAL INFORMATION

Calories	180	Sugars	2g
Protein	19g	Fat	7g
Carbohydrate	10g	Saturates	1g

 5 MINS   20 MINS

SERVES 4

INGREDIENTS

- 450 g/1 lb squid rings
- 2 tbsp plain (all-purpose) flour
- ½ tsp salt
- 1 green (bell) pepper
- 2 tbsp groundnut oil
- 1 red onion, sliced
- 160 g/5¾ oz jar black bean sauce

1 Rinse the squid rings under cold running water and pat dry thoroughly with absorbent kitchen paper (paper towels).

2 Place the plain (all-purpose) flour and salt in a bowl and mix together. Add the squid rings and toss until they are evenly coated.

3 Using a sharp knife, deseed the (bell) pepper. Slice the (bell) pepper into thin strips.

4 Heat the groundnut oil in a large preheated wok or heavy-based frying pan (skillet), swirling the oil around the base of the wok until it is really hot.

5 Add the (bell) pepper slices and red onion to the wok or frying pan (skillet) and stir-fry for about 2 minutes, or until the vegetables are just beginning to soften.

2

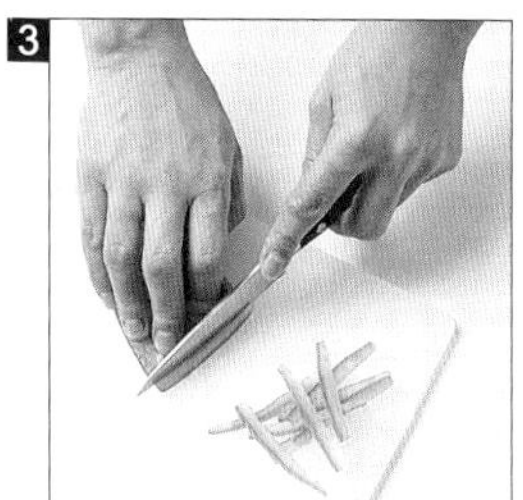
3

5

6 Add the squid rings to the wok or frying pan (skillet) and cook for a further 5 minutes, or until the squid is cooked through. Be careful not to overcook the squid.

7 Add the black bean sauce to the wok and heat through until the juices are bubbling. Transfer the squid stir-fry to warm serving bowls and serve immediately.

COOK'S TIP

Serve this recipe with fried rice or noodles tossed in soy sauce, if you wish.

Oysters with Tofu

Oysters are often eaten raw, but are delicious when quickly cooked as in this recipe, and mixed with salt and citrus flavours.

NUTRITIONAL INFORMATION

Calories	175	Sugars	2g
Protein	18g	Fat	10g
Carbohydrate	3g	Saturates	1g

 5 MINS  10 MINS

SERVES 4

INGREDIENTS

- 225 g/8 oz leeks
- 350 g/12 oz tofu (bean curd)
- 2 tbsp sunflower oil
- 350 g/12 oz shelled oysters
- 2 tbsp fresh lemon juice
- 1 tsp cornflour (cornstarch)
- 2 tbsp light soy sauce
- 100 ml/3½ fl oz/⅓ cup fish stock
- 2 tbsp chopped fresh coriander (cilantro)
- 1 tsp finely grated lemon zest

1 Using a sharp knife, trim and slice the leeks.

2 Cut the tofu (bean curd) into bite-sized pieces.

3 Heat the sunflower oil in a large preheated wok or frying pan (skillet).

4 Add the leeks to the wok and stir-fry for about 2 minutes.

5 Add the tofu (bean curd) and oysters and stir-fry for 1–2 minutes.

6 Mix together the lemon juice, cornflour (cornstarch), light soy sauce and fish stock in a small bowl, stirring until well blended.

7 Pour the cornflour (cornstarch) mixture into the wok and cook, stirring occasionally, until the juices start to thicken.

8 Transfer to serving bowls and scatter the coriander (cilantro) and lemon zest on top. Serve immediately.

1

2

5

VARIATION

Shelled clams or mussels could be used instead of the oysters, if you prefer.

Mussels with Lettuce

Mussels require careful preparation but very little cooking. They are available fresh or in vacuum packs when out of season.

NUTRITIONAL INFORMATION

Calories	205	Sugars	0.3g
Protein	31g	Fat	9g
Carbohydrate	1g	Saturates	4g

 15 MINS  5 MINS

SERVES 4

INGREDIENTS

- 1 kg/2 lb 4 oz mussels in their shells, scrubbed
- 2 stalks lemon grass
- 1 Iceberg lettuce
- 2 tbsp lemon juice
- 100 ml/3½ fl oz/⅓ cup water
- 25 g/1 oz/2 tbsp butter
- finely grated zest of 1 lemon
- 2 tbsp oyster sauce

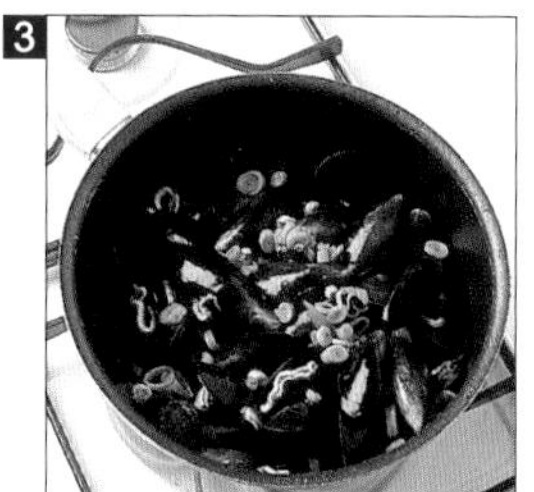
3

4

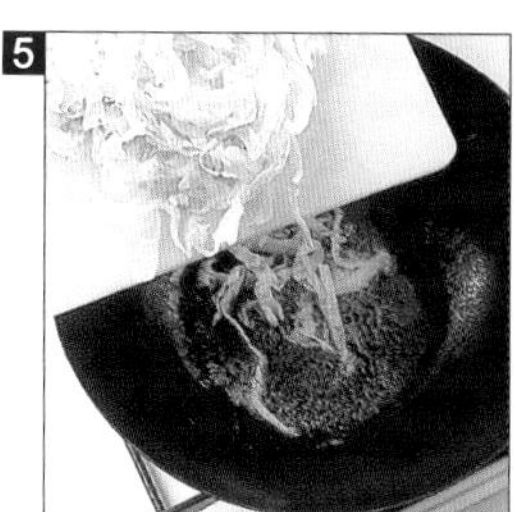
5

1 Place the scrubbed mussels in a large saucepan.

2 Using a sharp knife, thinly slice the lemon grass and shred the lettuce.

3 Add the lemon grass, lemon juice and water to the pan of mussels, cover with a tight-fitting lid and cook for 5 minutes or until the mussels have opened. Discard any mussels that do not open.

4 Carefully remove the cooked mussels from their shells, using a fork and set aside until required.

5 Heat the butter in a large preheated wok or frying pan (skillet). Add the lettuce and finely grated lemon zest to the wok or fying pan (skillet) and stir-fry for 2 minutes, or until the lettuce begins to wilt.

6 Add the oyster sauce to the mixture in the wok and heat through, stirring well until the sauce is thoroughly incorporated in the mixture.

7 Transfer the mixture in the wok to a warm serving dish and serve immediately.

COOK'S TIP

When using fresh mussels, be sure to discard any opened mussels before scrubbing and any unopened mussels after cooking.

Mussels in Black Bean Sauce

This dish looks so impressive, the combination of colours making it look almost too good to eat!

NUTRITIONAL INFORMATION

Calories	174	Sugars	4g
Protein	19g	Fat	8g
Carbohydrate	6g	Saturates	1g

 5 MINS  10 MINS

SERVES 4

INGREDIENTS

- 350 g/12 oz leeks
- 350 g/12 oz cooked green-lipped mussels (shelled)
- 1 tsp cumin seeds
- 2 tbsp vegetable oil
- 2 cloves garlic, crushed
- 1 red (bell) pepper, deseeded and sliced
- 50 g/1¾ oz/¾ cup canned bamboo shoots, drained
- 175 g/6 oz baby spinach
- 160 g/5¾ oz jar black bean sauce

1 Using a sharp knife, trim the leeks and shred them.

2 Place the cooked green-lipped mussels in a large bowl, sprinkle with the cumin seeds and toss well to coat all over. Set aside until required.

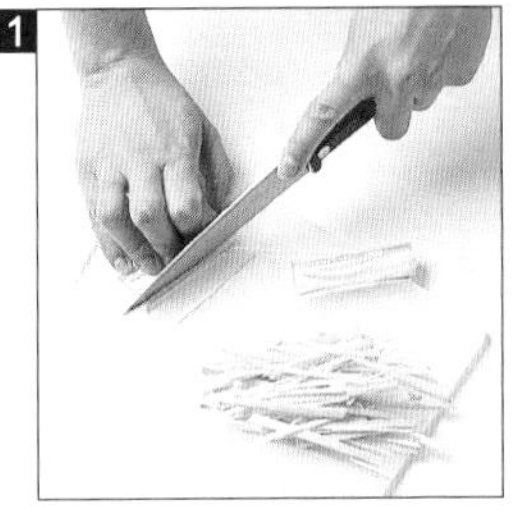

1

4

5

3 Heat the vegetable oil in a preheated wok, swirling the oil around the base of the wok until it is really hot.

4 Add the shredded leeks, garlic and sliced red (bell) pepper to the wok and stir-fry for 5 minutes, or until the vegetables are tender.

5 Add the bamboo shoots, baby spinach leaves and cooked green-lipped mussels to the wok and stir-fry for about 2 minutes.

6 Pour the black bean sauce over the ingredients in the wok, toss well to coat all the ingredients in the sauce and leave to simmer for a few seconds, stirring occasionally.

7 Transfer the stir-fry to warm serving bowls and serve immediately.

COOK'S TIP

If the green-lipped mussels are not available they can be bought shelled in cans and jars from most large supermarkets.

Pasta Shells with Mussels

Serve this aromatic seafood dish with plenty of fresh, crusty bread to soak up the delicious sauce.

NUTRITIONAL INFORMATION

Calories	735	Sugars	3g
Protein	37g	Fat	46g
Carbohydrate	41g	Saturates	26g

 25 MINS  25 MINS

SERVES 6

INGREDIENTS

400 g/14 oz pasta shells

1 tbsp olive oil

SAUCE

3.5 litres/6 pints mussels, scrubbed

250 ml/9 fl oz/1 cup dry white wine

2 large onions, chopped

125 g/4½ oz/½ cup unsalted butter

6 large garlic cloves, chopped finely

5 tbsp chopped fresh parsley

300 ml/½ pint/1¼ cups double (heavy) cream

salt and pepper

crusty bread, to serve

1 Pull off the 'beards' from the mussels and rinse well in several changes of water. Discard any mussels that refuse to close when tapped. Put the mussels in a large pan with the white wine and half of the onions. Cover the pan, shake and cook over a medium heat for 2–3 minutes until the mussels open.

2 Remove the pan from the heat, lift out the mussels with a slotted spoon, reserving the liquor, and set aside until they are cool enough to handle. Discard any mussels that have not opened.

3 Melt the butter in a pan over medium heat and fry the remaining onion for 3–4 minutes or until translucent. Stir in the garlic and cook for 1 minute. Gradually pour on the reserved cooking liquor, stirring to blend thoroughly. Stir in the parsley and cream. Season to taste and bring to simmering point. Taste and adjust the seasoning if necessary.

4 Cook the pasta in a large pan of salted boiling water, adding the oil, for 8–10 minutes or until tender. Drain the pasta in a colander, return to the pan, cover and keep warm.

5 Remove the mussels from their shells, reserving a few shells for garnish. Stir the mussels into the cream sauce. Tip the pasta into a warmed serving dish, pour on the sauce and, using 2 large spoons, toss it together well. Garnish with a few of the reserved mussel shells. Serve hot, with warm, crusty bread.

Mussel & Scallop Spaghetti

Juicy mussels and scallops poached gently in white wine are the perfect accompaniment to pasta to make a sophisticated meal.

NUTRITIONAL INFORMATION

Calories	301	Sugars	1g
Protein	42g	Fat	5g
Carbohydrate	17g	Saturates	1g

 55 MINS  30 MINS

SERVES 4

INGREDIENTS

- 225 g/8 oz dried wholemeal (wholewheat) spaghetti
- 60 g/2 oz/2 slices rindless lean back bacon, chopped
- 2 shallots, chopped finely
- 2 celery stick, chopped finely
- 150 ml/¼ pint/⅔ cup dry white wine
- 150 ml/¼ pint/⅔ cup Fresh Fish Stock (see page 8)
- 500 g/1 lb 2 oz fresh mussels, prepared
- 225 g/8 oz shelled queen or China bay scallops
- 1 tbsp chopped fresh parsley
- salt and pepper

1 Cook the spaghetti in a saucepan of boiling water according to the packet instructions, until the pasta is cooked but 'al dente', firm to the bite – about 10 minutes.

2 Meanwhile, gently dry-fry the bacon in a large non-stick frying pan (skillet) for 2–3 minutes. Stir in the shallots, celery and wine. Simmer gently, uncovered, for 5 minutes until softened.

3 Add the stock, mussels and scallops, cover and cook for a further 6–7 minutes. Discard any mussels that remain unopened.

4 Drain the spaghetti and add to the frying pan (skillet). Add the parsley, season to taste and toss together. Continue to cook for 1–2 minutes to heat through. Pile on to warmed serving plates, spooning over the cooking juices.

1

2

3

COOK'S TIP

Wholemeal (wholewheat) pasta doesn't have any egg added to the dough, so it is low in fat, and higher in fibre than other pastas.

Mussels with Lemon Grass

Give fresh mussels a Far Eastern flavour by using some Kaffir lime leaves, garlic and lemon grass in the stock used for steaming them.

NUTRITIONAL INFORMATION

Calories	194	Sugar	0g
Protein	33g	Fat	7g
Carbohydrate	1g	Saturates	1g

 10 MINS  10 MINS

SERVES 4

INGREDIENTS

- 750 g/1 lb 10 oz live mussels
- 1 tbsp sesame oil
- 3 shallots, chopped finely
- 2 garlic cloves, chopped finely
- 1 stalk lemon grass
- 2 Kaffir lime leaves
- 2 tbsp chopped fresh coriander (cilantro)
- finely grated rind of 1 lime
- 2 tbsp lime juice
- 300 ml/½ pint/1¼ cups hot vegetable stock
- crusty bread, to serve
- fresh coriander (cilantro), to garnish

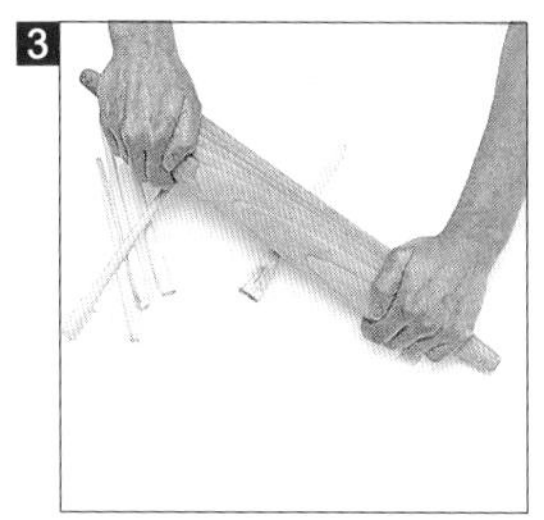

1 Using a small sharp knife, scrape the beards off the mussels under cold running water. Scrub them well, discarding any that are damaged or remain open when tapped. Keep rinsing until there is no trace of sand.

2 Heat the sesame oil in a large saucepan and fry the shallots and garlic gently until softened, about 2 minutes.

3 Bruise the lemon grass, using a meat mallet or rolling pin, and add to the pan with the Kaffir lime leaves, coriander (cilantro), lime rind and juice, mussels and stock. Put the lid on the saucepan and cook over a moderate heat for 3–5 minutes. Shake the pan from time to time.

4 Lift the mussels out into 4 warmed soup plates, discarding any that remain shut. Boil the remaining liquid rapidly to reduce slightly. Remove the lemon grass and lime leaves, then pour the liquid over the mussels.

5 Garnish with coriander (cilantro) and lime wedges, and serve at once.

COOK'S TIP

Mussels are now farmed, so they should be available from good fishmongers throughout the year.

Baked Scallops & Pasta

This is another tempting seafood dish where the eye is delighted as much as the tastebuds.

NUTRITIONAL INFORMATION

Calories	725	Sugars	2g
Protein	38g	Fat	48g
Carbohydrate	38g	Saturates	25g

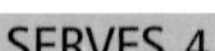

20 MINS 30 MINS

SERVES 4

INGREDIENTS

- 12 scallops
- 3 tbsp olive oil
- 350 g/12 oz/3 cups small, dried wholemeal (whole-wheat) pasta shells
- 150 ml/¼ pint/⅔ cup fish stock
- 1 onion, chopped
- juice and finely grated rind of 2 lemons
- 150 ml/¼ pint/⅔ cup double (heavy) cream
- 225 g/8 oz/2 cups grated Cheddar cheese
- salt and pepper
- crusty brown bread, to serve

1 Remove the scallops from their shells. Scrape off the skirt and the black intestinal thread. Reserve the white part (the flesh) and the orange part (the coral or roe). Very carefully ease the flesh and coral from the shell with a short, but very strong knife.

2 Wash the shells thoroughly and dry them well. Put the shells on a baking tray (cookie sheet), sprinkle lightly with two thirds of the olive oil and set aside.

3 Meanwhile, bring a large saucepan of lightly salted water to the boil. Add the pasta shells and remaining olive oil and cook for 8–10 minutes or until tender, but still firm to the bite. Drain well and spoon about 25 g/1 oz of pasta into each scallop shell.

4 Put the scallops, fish stock and onion in an ovenproof dish and season to taste with pepper. Cover with foil and bake in a preheated oven at 180°C/350°F/Gas Mark 4 for 8 minutes.

5 Remove the dish from the oven. Remove the foil and, using a slotted spoon, transfer the scallops to the shells. Add 1 tablespoon of the cooking liquid to each shell, together with a drizzle of lemon juice and a little cream, and top with the grated cheese.

6 Increase the oven temperature to 230°C/450°F/Gas Mark 8 and return the scallops to the oven for a further 4 minutes.

7 Serve the scallops in their shells with crusty brown bread and butter.

Mussels with Tomato Sauce

This recipe for Mediterranean-style baked mussels, topped with a fresh tomato sauce and breadcrumbs, has been adapted for the microwave.

NUTRITIONAL INFORMATION

Calories	254	Sugars	1g
Protein	37g	Fat	10g
Carbohydrate	4g	Saturates	3g

 20 MINS  15 MINS

SERVES 4

INGREDIENTS

- ½ small onion, chopped
- 1 garlic clove, crushed
- 1 tbsp olive oil
- 3 tomatoes
- 1 tbsp chopped fresh parsley
- 900 g/2 lb live mussels
- 1 tbsp freshly grated Parmesan cheese
- 1 tbsp fresh white breadcrumbs
- salt and pepper
- chopped fresh parsley, to garnish

1 Place the onion, garlic and oil in a bowl. Cover and cook on HIGH power for 3 minutes.

2 Cut a cross in the base of each tomato and place them in a small bowl. Pour on boiling water and leave for about 45 seconds. Drain and then plunge into cold water. The skins will slide off easily. Chop the tomatoes, removing any hard cores.

3 Add the tomatoes to the onion mixture, cover and cook on HIGH power for 3 minutes. Stir in the parsley and season to taste.

4 Scrub the mussels well in several changes of cold water. Remove the beards and discard any open mussels and those which do not close when tapped sharply with the back of a knife.

5 Place the mussels in a large bowl. Add enough boiling water to cover them. Cover and cook on HIGH power for 2 minutes, stirring halfway through, until the mussels open. Drain well and remove the empty half of each shell. Arrange the mussels in 1 layer on a plate.

6 Spoon the tomato sauce over each mussel. Mix the Parmesan cheese with the breadcrumbs and sprinkle on top. Cook, uncovered, on HIGH power for 2 minutes. Garnish with parsley and serve.

COOK'S TIP

Dry out the breadcrumbs in the microwave for an extra crunchy topping. Spread them on a plate and cook on HIGH power for 2 minutes, stirring once. Leave to stand, uncovered.

Saffron Mussel Tagliatelle

Saffron is the most expensive spice in the world, but you only ever need a small quantity. Saffron threads or powdered saffron may be used.

NUTRITIONAL INFORMATION

Calories	854	Sugars	3g
Protein	43g	Fat	49g
Carbohydrate	57g	Saturates	28g

 15 MINS  35 MINS

SERVES 4

INGREDIENTS

- 1 kg/2 lb 4 oz mussels
- 150 ml/¼ pint/⅔ cup white wine
- 1 medium onion, finely chopped
- 25 g/1 oz/2 tbsp butter
- 2 garlic cloves, crushed
- 2 tsp cornflour (cornstarch)
- 300 ml/½ pint/1¼ cups double (heavy) cream
- pinch of saffron threads or saffron powder
- juice of ½ lemon
- 1 egg yolk
- 450 g/1 lb dried tagliatelle
- 1 tbsp olive oil
- salt and pepper
- 3 tbsp chopped fresh parsley, to garnish

4

4

5

1 Scrub and debeard the mussels under cold running water. Discard any that do not close when sharply tapped. Put the mussels in a pan with the wine and onion. Cover and cook over a high heat, shaking the pan, for 5–8 minutes, until the shells open.

2 Drain and reserve the cooking liquid. Discard any mussels that are still closed. Reserve a few mussels for the garnish and remove the remainder from their shells.

3 Strain the cooking liquid into a pan. Bring to the boil and reduce by about half. Remove the pan from the heat.

4 Melt the butter in a saucepan. Add the garlic and cook, stirring frequently, for 2 minutes, until golden brown. Stir in the cornflour (cornstarch) and cook, stirring, for 1 minute. Gradually stir in the cooking liquid and the cream. Crush the saffron threads and add to the pan. Season with salt and pepper to taste and simmer over a low heat for 2–3 minutes, until thickened.

5 Stir in the egg yolk, lemon juice and shelled mussels. Do not allow the mixture to boil.

6 Meanwhile, bring a pan of salted water to the boil. Add the pasta and oil and cook for 8–10 minutes until tender, but still firm to the bite. Drain and transfer to a serving dish. Add the mussel sauce and toss. Garnish with the parsley and reserved mussels and serve.

Penne with Fried Mussels

This is quick and simple, but one of the nicest of Italian fried fish dishes, served with penne.

NUTRITIONAL INFORMATION

Calories	537	Sugars	2g
Protein	22g	Fat	24g
Carbohydrate	62g	Saturates	3g

 10 MINS  25 MINS

SERVES 6

INGREDIENTS

- 400 g/14 oz/3½ cups dried penne
- 125 ml/4 fl oz/½ cup olive oil
- 450 g/1 lb mussels, cooked and shelled
- 1 tsp sea salt
- 90 g/3 oz/⅔ cup flour
- 100 g/3½ oz sun-dried tomatoes, sliced
- 2 tbsp chopped fresh basil leaves
- salt and pepper
- 1 lemon, thinly sliced, to garnish

1

3

4

1 Bring a large saucepan of lightly salted water to the boil. Add the penne and 1 tablespoon of the olive oil and cook for 8–10 minutes or until the pasta is just tender, but still firm to the bite.

2 Drain the pasta thoroughly and place in a large, warm serving dish. Set aside and keep warm while you cook the mussels.

3 Lightly sprinkle the mussels with the sea salt. Season the flour with salt and pepper to taste, sprinkle into a bowl and toss the mussels in the flour until well coated.

4 Heat the remaining oil in a large frying pan (skillet). Add the mussels and fry, stirring frequently, until a golden brown colour.

5 Toss the mussels with the penne and sprinkle with the sun-dried tomatoes and basil leaves. Garnish with slices of lemon and serve immediately.

COOK'S TIP

Sun-dried tomatoes, used in Italy for a long time, have become popular elsewhere only quite recently. They are dried and then preserved in oil. They have a concentrated, roasted flavour and a dense texture. They should be drained and chopped or sliced before using.

Thai Potato Crab Cakes

These small crab cakes are based on a traditional Thai recipe. They make a delicious snack when served with this sweet and sour cucumber sauce.

NUTRITIONAL INFORMATION

Calories	254	Sugars	9g
Protein	12g	Fat	6g
Carbohydrate	40g	Saturates	1g

 10 MINS  30 MINS

SERVES 4

INGREDIENTS

- 450 g/1 lb floury (mealy) potatoes, diced
- 175 g/6 oz white crab meat, drained if canned
- 4 spring onions (scallions), chopped
- 1 tsp light soy sauce
- ½ tsp sesame oil
- 1 tsp chopped lemon grass
- 1 tsp lime juice
- 3 tbsp plain (all-purpose) flour
- 2 tbsp vegetable oil
- salt and pepper

SAUCE

- 4 tbsp finely chopped cucumber
- 2 tbsp clear honey
- 1 tbsp garlic wine vinegar
- ½ tsp light soy sauce
- 1 chopped red chilli

TO GARNISH

- 1 red chilli, sliced
- cucumber slices

2

3

5

1 Cook the diced potatoes in a saucepan of boiling water for 10 minutes until cooked through. Drain well and mash.

2 Mix the crab meat into the potato with the spring onions (scallions), soy sauce, sesame oil, lemon grass, lime juice and flour. Season with salt and pepper.

3 Divide the potato mixture into 8 portions of equal size and shape them into small rounds, using floured hands.

4 Heat the oil in a wok or frying pan (skillet) and cook the cakes, 4 at a time, for 5-7 minutes, turning once. Keep warm and repeat with the remaining crab cakes.

5 Meanwhile, make the sauce. In a small serving bowl, mix the cucumber, honey, vinegar, soy sauce and chopped red chilli.

6 Garnish the cakes with the sliced red chilli and cucumber slices and serve with the sauce.

Spiced Scallops

Scallops are available both fresh and frozen. Make sure they are completely defrosted before cooking.

NUTRITIONAL INFORMATION

Calories	276	Sugar	6g
Protein	25g	Fat	15g
Carbohydrate	8g	Saturates	2g

 10 MINS  10 MINS

SERVES 4

INGREDIENTS

- 12 large scallops with coral attached, defrosted if frozen, or 350 g/12 oz small scallops without coral, defrosted
- 4 tbsp sunflower oil
- 4-6 spring onions (scallions), thinly sliced diagonally
- 1 garlic clove, crushed
- 2.5 cm/1 inch ginger root, finely chopped
- 250 g/9 oz mangetout (snow peas)
- 125 g/4½ oz button or closed cup mushrooms, sliced
- 2 tbsp sherry
- 2 tbsp soy sauce
- 1 tbsp clear honey
- ¼ tsp ground allspice
- salt and pepper
- 1 tbsp sesame seeds, toasted

1 Wash and dry the scallops, discarding any black pieces and detach the corals, if using.

2 Slice each scallop into 3-4 pieces and if the corals are large halve them.

3 Heat 2 tablespoons of the sunflower oil in a preheated wok or large, heavy-based frying pan (skillet), swirling it around until really hot.

4 Add the spring onions (scallions), garlic and ginger to the wok or frying pan (skillet) and stir-fry for about 1 minute.

5 Add the mangetout (snow peas) to the wok and continue to cook for a further 2-3 minutes, stirring continuously. Remove to a bowl and set aside.

6 Add the remaining sunflower oil to the wok and when really hot add the scallops and corals and stir-fry for a couple of minutes.

7 Add the mushrooms and continue to cook for a further minute or so.

8 Add the sherry, soy sauce, honey and allspice to the wok, with salt and pepper to taste. Mix thoroughly, then return the mangetout (snow peas) mixture to the wok.

9 Season well with salt and pepper and toss together over a high heat for a minute or so until piping hot. Serve the scallops and vegetables immediately, sprinkled with sesame seeds.

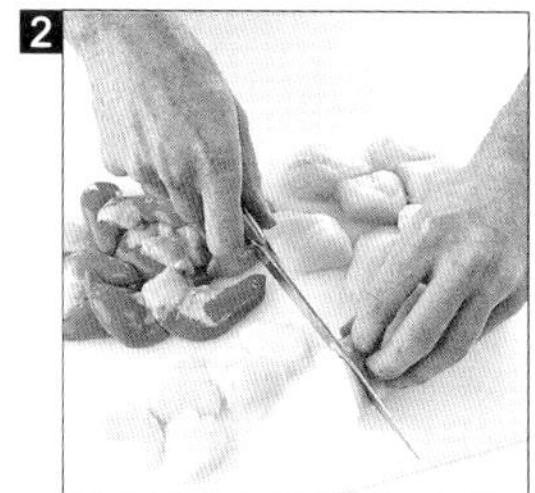

2

6

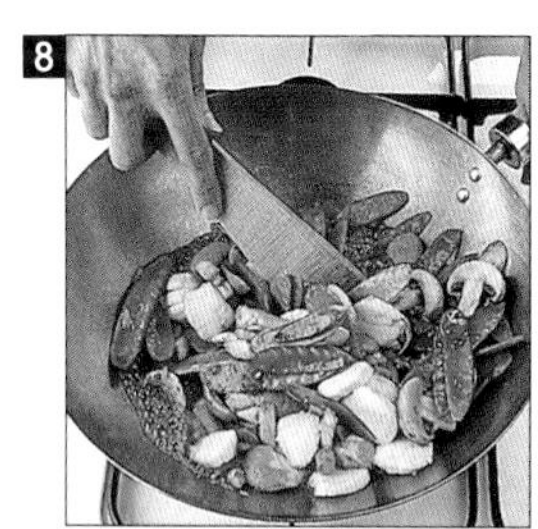

8

Seared Scallops

Scallops have a terrific, subtle flavour which is complemented in this dish by the buttery sauce.

NUTRITIONAL INFORMATION

Calories	272	Sugars	0g
Protein	28g	Fat	17g
Carbohydrate	2g	Saturates	8g

 5 MINS  10 MINS

SERVES 4

INGREDIENTS

- 450 g/1 lb fresh scallops, without roe, or the same amount of frozen scallops, defrosted thoroughly
- 6 spring onions (scallions)
- 2 tbsp vegetable oil
- 1 green chilli, deseeded and sliced
- 3 tbsp sweet soy sauce
- 50 g/1¾ oz/1½ tbsp butter, cubed

1 Rinse the scallops thoroughly under cold running water, drain and pat the scallops dry with absorbent kitchen paper (paper towels).

2 Using a sharp knife, slice each scallop in half horizontally.

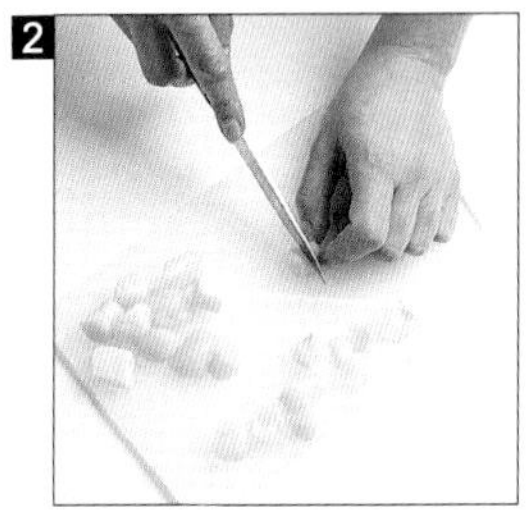

3 Using a sharp knife, trim and slice the spring onions (scallions).

4 Heat the vegetable oil in a large preheated wok or heavy-based frying pan (skillet), swirling the oil around the base of the wok until it is really hot.

5 Add the sliced green chilli, spring onions (scallions) and scallops to the wok and stir-fry over a high heat for 4–5 minutes, or until the scallops are just cooked through. If using frozen scallops, be sure not to overcook them as they will easily disintegrate.

6 Add the soy sauce and butter to the scallop stir-fry and heat through until the butter melts.

7 Transfer to warm serving bowls and serve hot.

COOK'S TIP

If you buy scallops on the shell, slide a knife underneath the membrane to loosen it and cut off the tough muscle that holds the scallop to the shell. Discard the black stomach sac and intestinal vein.

Scallops with Mushrooms

Scallops have a rich but delicate flavour. When sautéed with mushrooms and bathed in brandy and cream, they make a really special meal.

NUTRITIONAL INFORMATION

Calories	390	Sugars	1g
Protein	31g	Fat	28g
Carbohydrate	1g	Saturates	4g

 5 MINS  10 MINS

SERVES 2

INGREDIENTS

- 15 g/½ oz/1 tbsp butter
- 225 g/8 oz shelled queen scallops
- 1 tbsp olive oil
- 50 g/1¾ oz oyster mushrooms, sliced
- 50 g/1¾ oz shiitake mushrooms, sliced
- 1 garlic clove, chopped
- 4 spring onions (scallions), white and green parts sliced
- 3 tbsp double (heavy) cream
- 1 tbsp brandy
- salt and pepper
- sprigs of fresh dill, to garnish
- basmati rice to serve

1 Heat the butter in a heavy-based frying pan (skillet) and fry the scallops for about 1 minute, turning occasionally.

2 Remove the scallops from the frying pan (skillet) with a perforated spoon and keep warm.

3 Add the olive oil to the pan and heat. Add the mushrooms, garlic and spring onions (scallions) and cook for 2 minutes, stirring constantly.

4 Return the scallops to the pan. Add the double (heavy) cream and brandy, stirring well to mix.

5 Season with salt and pepper to taste and heat to warm through.

6 Garnish with fresh dill sprigs and serve with rice.

COOK'S TIP

Scallops, which consist of a large, round white muscle with bright orange roe, are the most delicious seafood in the prettiest of shells. The rounded half of the shell can be used as a dish in which to serve the scallops.

Scallop Pancakes

Scallops, like most shellfish require very little cooking, and this original dish is a perfect example of how to use shellfish to its full potential.

NUTRITIONAL INFORMATION

Calories	240	Sugars	1g
Protein	29g	Fat	9g
Carbohydrate	11g	Saturates	1g

 5 MINS 30 MINS

SERVES 4

INGREDIENTS

- 100 g/3½ oz fine green beans
- 1 red chilli
- 450 g/1 lb scallops, without roe
- 1 egg
- 3 spring onions (scallions), sliced
- 50 g/1¾ oz/½ cup rice flour
- 1 tbsp fish sauce
- oil, for frying
- salt
- sweet chilli dip, to serve

1 Using a sharp knife, trim the green beans and slice them very thinly.

2 Using a sharp knife, deseed and very finely chop the red chilli.

3 Bring a small saucepan of lightly salted water to the boil. Add the green beans to the pan and cook for 3–4 minutes or until just softened.

4 Roughly chop the scallops and place them in a large bowl. Add the cooked beans to the scallops.

5 Mix the egg with the spring onions (scallions), rice flour, fish sauce and chilli until well combined. Add to the scallops and mix well.

6 Heat about 2.5 cm/1 inch of oil in a large preheated wok. Add a ladleful of the mixture to the wok and cook for 5 minutes until golden and set.

7 Remove the pancake from the wok and leave to drain on absorbent kitchen paper (paper towels). Keep warm while cooking the remaining pancake mixture. Serve the pancakes hot with a sweet chilli dip.

1

2

5

VARIATION

You could use prawns (shrimp) or shelled clams instead of the scallops, if you prefer.

Scallop Skewers

As the scallops are marinated, it is not essential that they are fresh; frozen shellfish are fine for a barbecue (grill).

NUTRITIONAL INFORMATION

Calories	182	Sugars	0g
Protein	29g	Fat	7g
Carbohydrate	0g	Saturates	1g

 30 MINS  10 MINS

SERVES 4

INGREDIENTS

- grated zest and juice of 2 limes
- 2 tbsp finely chopped lemon grass or 1 tbsp lemon juice
- 2 garlic cloves, crushed
- 1 green chilli, deseeded and chopped
- 16 scallops, with corals
- 2 limes, each cut into 8 segments
- 2 tbsp sunflower oil
- 1 tbsp lemon juice
- salt and pepper

TO SERVE

- 60 g/2 oz/1 cup rocket (arugula) salad
- 200 g/7 oz/3 cups mixed salad leaves (greens)

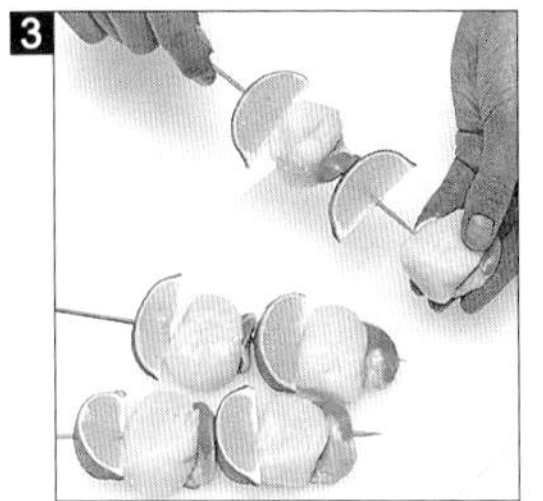

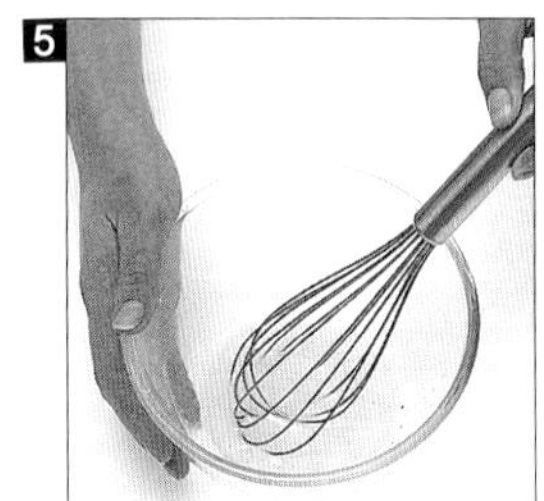

1 Soak 8 skewers in warm water for at least 10 minutes before you use them to prevent the food from sticking.

2 Combine the lime juice and zest, lemon grass, garlic and chilli together in a pestle and mortar or spice grinder to make a paste.

3 Thread 2 scallops on to each of the soaked skewers. Cover the ends with foil to prevent them from burning.

4 Alternate the scallops with the lime segments.

5 Whisk together the oil, lemon juice, salt and pepper to make thedressing.

6 Coat the scallops with the spice paste and place over a medium barbecue, basting occasionally.

7 Cook for 10 minutes, turning once.

8 Toss the rocket (arugula), mixed salad leaves (greens) and dressing together well. Put into a serving bowl.

9 Serve the scallops piping hot, 2 skewers on each plate, with the salad.

Curried Crab

If you can buy fresh crab, clean the shell and brush lightly with oil and use as a container for the crab meat.

NUTRITIONAL INFORMATION

Calories	272	Sugars	5g
Protein	27g	Fat	16g
Carbohydrate	5g	Saturates	2g

 5 MINS  15 MINS

SERVES 4

INGREDIENTS

- 2 tbsp mustard oil
- 1 tbsp ghee
- 1 onion, chopped finely
- 5 cm/2 inch piece ginger root, grated
- 2 garlic cloves, peeled but left whole
- 1 tsp ground turmeric
- 1 tsp salt
- 1 tsp chilli powder
- 2 fresh green chillies, chopped
- 1 tsp paprika
- 125 g/4½ oz/½ cup brown crab meat
- 350 g/12 oz/1½ cups white crab meat
- 250 ml/9 fl oz /1 cup low-fat natural yogurt
- 1 tsp garam masala
- basmati rice, to serve
- fresh coriander (cilantro), to garnish

1 Heat the mustard oil in a large, preferably non-stick, frying pan (skillet), wok or saucepan.

2 When it starts to smoke, add the ghee and onion. Stir for 3 minutes over a medium heat until the onion is soft.

3 Stir in the ginger and whole garlic cloves.

4 Add the turmeric, salt, chilli powder, chillies and paprika. Mix thoroughly.

5 Increase the heat and add the crab meat and yogurt. Simmer, stirring occasionally, for 10 minutes until the sauce is thickened slightly.

6 Add garam masala to taste.

7 Serve hot, over plain basmati rice, with the fresh coriander (cilantro) either chopped or in sprigs.

2

3

4

COOK'S TIP

For an unusual combination of flavours, mix the crab meat with segments of grapefruit in a mayonnaise. Sprinkle with slivers of almonds.

Crab with Chinese Leaves

The delicate flavour of Chinese leaves (cabbage) and crab meat are enhanced by the coconut milk in this recipe.

NUTRITIONAL INFORMATION

Calories	109	Sugars	1g
Protein	11g	Fat	6g
Carbohydrate	2g	Saturates	1g

5 MINS 10 MINS

SERVES 4

INGREDIENTS

- 225 g/8 oz shiitake mushrooms
- 2 tbsp vegetable oil
- 2 cloves garlic, crushed
- 6 spring onions (scallions), sliced
- 1 head Chinese leaves (cabbage), shredded
- 1 tbsp mild curry paste
- 6 tbsp coconut milk
- 200 g/7 oz can white crab meat, drained
- 1 tsp chilli flakes

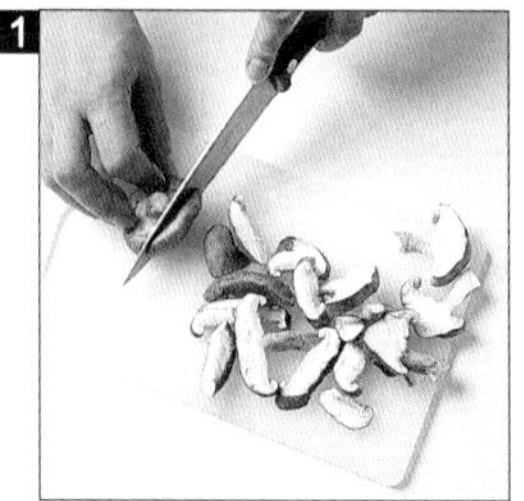
1

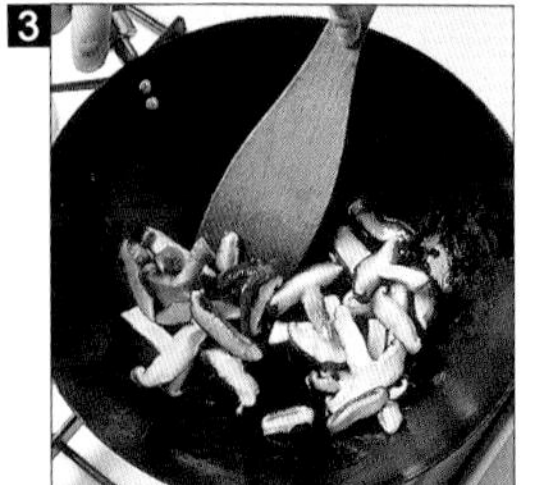
3

4

1 Using a sharp knife, cut the the mushrooms into slices.

2 Heat the vegetable oil in a large preheated wok or heavy-based frying pan (skillet).

3 Add the mushrooms and garlic to the wok or frying pan (skillet) and stir-fry for 3 minutes or until the mushrooms have softened.

4 Add the spring onions (scallions) and shredded Chinese leaves (cabbage) to the wok and stir-fry until the leaves have wilted.

5 Mix together the mild curry paste and coconut milk in a small bowl.

6 Add the curry paste and coconut milk mixture to the wok, together with the crab meat and chilli flakes. Mix together until well combined.

7 Heat the mixture in the wok until the juices start to bubble.

8 Transfer the crab and vegetable stir-fry to warm serving bowls and serve immediately.

COOK'S TIP

Shiitake mushrooms are now readily available in the fresh vegetable section of most large supermarkets.

Seafood Stir Fry

This combination of assorted seafood and tender vegetables flavoured with ginger makes an ideal light meal served with thread noodles.

NUTRITIONAL INFORMATION

Calories	226	Sugars	5g
Protein	35g	Fat	7g
Carbohydrate	6g	Saturates	1g

 5 MINS  15 MINS

SERVES 4

INGREDIENTS

- 100 g/3½ oz small, thin asparagus spears, trimmed
- 1 tbsp sunflower oil
- 2.5 cm/1 inch piece root (fresh) ginger, cut into thin strips
- 1 medium leek, shredded
- 2 medium carrots, julienned
- 100 g/3½ oz baby sweetcorn cobs, quartered lengthwise
- 2 tbsp light soy sauce
- 1 tbsp oyster sauce
- 1 tsp clear honey
- 450 g/1 lb cooked, assorted shellfish, thawed if frozen
- freshly cooked egg noodles, to serve

TO GARNISH

- 4 large cooked prawns
- small bunch fresh chives, freshly snipped

1

3

5

1 Bring a small saucepan of water to the boil and blanch the asparagus for 1–2 minutes.

2 Drain the asparagus, set aside and keep warm.

3 Heat the oil in a wok or large frying pan (skillet) and stir-fry the ginger, leek, carrot and sweetcorn for about 3 minutes. Do not allow the vegetables to brown.

4 Add the soy sauce, oyster sauce and honey to the wok or frying pan (skillet).

5 Stir in the cooked shellfish and continue to stir-fry for 2–3 minutes until the vegetables are just tender and the shellfish are thoroughly heated through. Add the blanched asparagus and stir-fry for about 2 minutes.

6 To serve, pile the cooked noodles on to 4 warm serving plates and spoon the seafood and vegetable stir fry over them.

7 Garnish with the cooked prawns and freshly snipped chives and serve immediately. Serve garnished with a large prawn and freshly snipped chives.

Crab Meat Cakes

Make these tasty crab-meat cakes to serve as a snack or starter, or as an accompaniment to a main meal.

NUTRITIONAL INFORMATION

Calories	262	Sugars	4g
Protein	13g	Fat	17g
Carbohydrate	14g	Saturates	3g

 20 MINS 55 MINS

SERVES 4

INGREDIENTS

- 90 g/3 oz/generous 1 cup long-grain rice
- 1 tbsp sesame oil
- 1 small onion, chopped finely
- 1 large garlic clove, crushed
- 2 tbsp chopped fresh coriander (cilantro)
- 200 g/7 oz can of crab meat, drained
- 1 tbsp fish sauce or light soy sauce
- 250 ml/9 fl oz/1 cup coconut milk
- 2 eggs
- 4 tbsp vegetable oil
- salt and pepper
- sliced spring onions (scallions), to garnish

2

3

3

1 Cook the rice in plenty of boiling, lightly salted water until just tender, about 12 minutes. Rinse with cold water and drain well.

2 Heat the sesame oil in a small frying pan (skillet) and fry the onion and garlic gently for about 5 minutes, until softened and golden brown.

3 Combine the rice, onion, garlic, coriander (cilantro), crab meat, fish sauce or soy sauce and coconut milk. Season. Beat the eggs and add to the mixture. Divide the mixture between 8 greased ramekin dishes or teacups and place them in a baking dish or roasting tin (pan) with enough warm water to come halfway up their sides. Place in a preheated oven at 180°C/ 350°F/Gas Mark 4 for 25 minutes, until set. Leave to cool.

4 Turn the crab cakes out of the ramekin dishes . Heat the oil in a wok or frying pan (skillet) and fry the crab cakes in the oil until golden brown. Drain on kitchen paper (paper towels), garnish and serve.

COOK'S TIP

If you want, you can prepare these crab cakes up to the point where they have been baked. Cool them, then cover and chill, ready for frying when needed.

Vermicelli with Clams

A quickly-cooked recipe that transforms store-cupboard ingredients into a dish with style.

NUTRITIONAL INFORMATION

Calories	520	Sugars	2g
Protein	26g	Fat	13g
Carbohydrate	71g	Saturates	4g

 10 MINS  25 MINS

SERVES 4

INGREDIENTS

- 400 g/14 oz dried vermicelli, spaghetti or other long pasta
- 2 tbsp olive oil
- 25 g/1 oz/2 tbsp butter
- 2 onions, chopped
- 2 garlic cloves, chopped
- 2 x 200 g/7 oz jars clams in brine
- 125 ml/4 fl oz/½ cup white wine
- 4 tbsp chopped fresh parsley
- ½ tsp dried oregano
- pinch of freshly grated nutmeg
- salt and pepper

TO GARNISH

- 2 tbsp Parmesan cheese shavings
- fresh basil sprigs

COOK'S TIP

There are many different types of clams found along almost every coast in the world. Those traditionally used in this dish are the tiny ones – only 2.5-5 cm/1-2 inches across – known in Italy as vongole.

1 Bring a large pan of lightly salted water to the boil. Add the pasta and half of the olive oil and cook for 8–10 minutes until tender, but still firm to the bite. Drain, return to the pan and add the butter. Cover the pan, shake well and keep warm.

2 Heat the remaining oil in a pan over a medium heat. Add the onions and fry until they are translucent. Stir in the garlic and cook for 1 minute.

3 Strain the liquid from 1 jar of clams and add the liquid to the pan, with the wine. Stir, bring to simmering point and simmer for 3 minutes. Drain the second jar of clams and discard the liquid.

4 Add the clams, parsley and oregano to the pan and season with pepper and nutmeg. Lower the heat and cook until the sauce is heated through.

5 Transfer the pasta to a warm serving dish and pour over the sauce. Sprinkle with the Parmesan cheese, garnish with the basil and serve immediately.

2

3

4

Farfallini Buttered Lobster

This is one of those dishes that looks almost too lovely to eat – but you should!

NUTRITIONAL INFORMATION

Calories	686	Sugars	1g
Protein	45g	Fat	36g
Carbohydrate	44g	Saturates	19g

 30 MINS  25 MINS

SERVES 4

INGREDIENTS

- 2 x 700 g/1 lb 9 oz lobsters, split into halves
- juice and grated rind of 1 lemon
- 115 g/4 oz/½ cup butter
- 4 tbsp fresh white breadcrumbs
- 2 tbsp brandy
- 5 tbsp double (heavy) cream or crème fraîche
- 450 g/1 lb dried farfallini
- 1 tbsp olive oil
- 60 g/2 oz/⅔ cup freshly grated Parmesan cheese
- salt and pepper

TO GARNISH

- 1 kiwi fruit, sliced
- 4 unpeeled, cooked king prawns (shrimp)
- fresh dill sprigs

1 Carefully discard the stomach sac, vein and gills from each lobster. Remove all the meat from the tail and chop. Crack the claws and legs, remove the meat and chop. Transfer the meat to a bowl and add the lemon juice and grated lemon rind.

2 Clean the shells thoroughly and place in a warm oven at 170°C/325°/Gas Mark 3 to dry out.

3 Melt 25 g/1 oz/2 tbsp of the butter in a frying pan (skillet). Add the breadcrumbs and fry for about 3 minutes, until crisp and golden brown.

4 Melt the remaining butter in a saucepan. Add the lobster meat and heat through gently. Add the brandy and cook for a further 3 minutes, then add the cream or crème fraîche and season to taste with salt and pepper.

5 Meanwhile, bring a large pan of lightly salted water to the boil. Add the farfallini and olive oil and cook for 8–10 minutes, until tender but still firm to the bite. Drain and spoon the pasta into the clean lobster shells.

6 Top with the buttered lobster and sprinkle with a little grated Parmesan cheese and the breadcrumbs. Grill (broil) for 2–3 minutes, until golden brown.

7 Transfer the lobster shells to a warm serving dish, garnish with the lemon slices, kiwi fruit, king prawns (shrimp) and dill sprigs and serve immediately.

1

3

6

Seafood Medley

Use any combination of fish and seafood in this delicious dish of coated fish served in a wine sauce.

NUTRITIONAL INFORMATION

Calories	168	Sugars	2g
Protein	29g	Fat	3g
Carbohydrate	4g	Saturates	1g

 5 MINS  15 MINS

SERVES 4

INGREDIENTS

- 2 tbsp dry white wine
- 1 egg white, lightly beaten
- ½ tsp Chinese five-spice powder
- 1 tsp cornflour (cornstarch)
- 300 g/10½ oz raw prawns (shrimp), peeled and deveined
- 125 g/4½ oz prepared squid, cut into rings
- 125 g/4½ oz white fish fillets, cut into strips
- vegetable oil, for deep-frying
- 1 green (bell) pepper, seeded and cut into thin strips
- 1 carrot, cut into thin strips
- 4 baby corn cobs, halved lengthways

1 Mix the wine, egg white, five-spice powder and cornflour (cornstarch) in a large bowl. Add the prawns (shrimp), squid rings and fish fillets and stir to coat evenly. Remove the fish and seafood with a slotted spoon, reserving any leftover cornflour (cornstarch) mixture.

2 Heat the oil in a preheated wok and deep-fry the prawns (shrimp), squid and fish for 2–3 minutes. Remove the seafood mixture from the wok with a slotted spoon and set aside.

3 Pour off all but 1 tablespoon of oil from the wok and return to the heat. Add the (bell) pepper, carrot and corn cobs and stir-fry for 4–5 minutes.

4 Return the seafood to the wok with any remaining cornflour (cornstarch) mixture. Heat through, stirring, and serve.

1

2

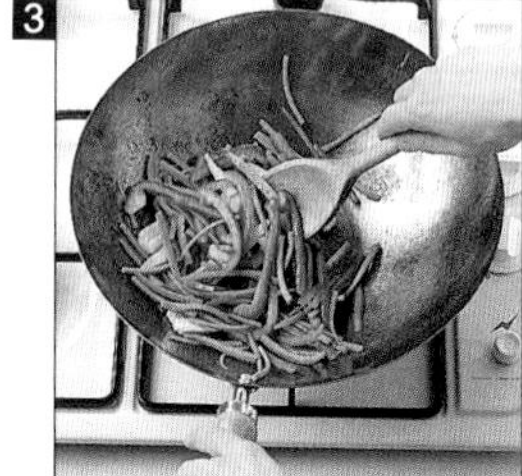

3

COOK'S TIP

Open up the squid rings and using a sharp knife, score a lattice pattern on the flesh to make them look attractive.

Seafood Pizza

Make a change from the standard pizza toppings – this dish is piled high with seafood baked with a red (bell) pepper and tomato sauce.

NUTRITIONAL INFORMATION

Calories	248	Sugars	7g
Protein	27g	Fat	6g
Carbohydrate	22g	Saturates	2g

 25 MINS  55 MINS

SERVES 4

INGREDIENTS

- 145 g/5 oz standard pizza base mix
- 4 tbsp chopped fresh dill or 2 tbsp dried dill
- fresh dill, to garnish

SAUCE

- 1 large red (bell) pepper
- 400 g/14 oz can chopped tomatoes with onion and herbs
- 3 tbsp tomato purée (paste)
- salt and pepper

TOPPING

- 350 g/12 oz assorted cooked seafood, thawed if frozen
- 1 tbsp capers in brine, drained
- 25 g/1 oz pitted black olives in brine, drained
- 25 g/1 oz low-fat Mozzarella cheese, grated
- 1 tbsp grated, fresh Parmesan cheese

2

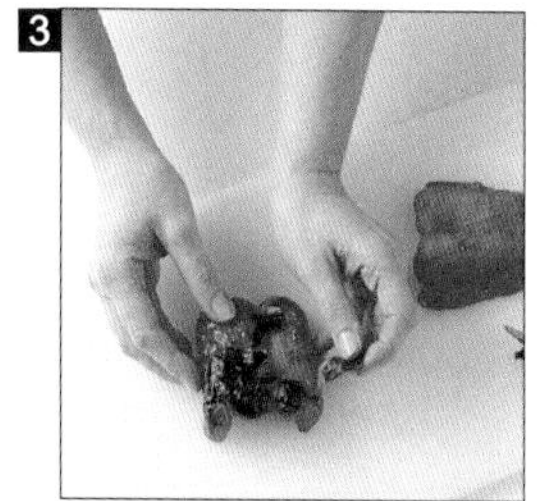
3

5

1 Preheat the oven to 200°C/400°F/Gas Mark 6. Place the pizza base mix in a bowl and stir in the dill. Make the dough according to the instructions on the packet.

2 Press the dough into a round measuring 25.5 cm/10 inches across on a baking sheet lined with baking parchment. Set aside to prove (rise).

3 Preheat the grill (broiler) to hot. To make the sauce, halve and deseed the (bell) pepper and arrange on a grill (broiler) rack. Cook for 8–10 minutes until softened and charred. Leave to cool slightly, peel off the skin and chop the flesh.

4 Place the tomatoes and (bell) pepper in a saucepan. Bring to the boil and simmer for 10 minutes. Stir in the tomato purée (paste) and season to taste.

5 Spread the sauce over the pizza base and top with the seafood. Sprinkle over the capers and olives, top with the cheeses and bake for 25–30 minutes.

6 Garnish with sprigs of dill and serve hot.

Seafood Chow Mein

Use whatever seafood is available for this delicious noodle dish – mussels or crab would also be suitable.

NUTRITIONAL INFORMATION

Calories	281	Sugars	1g
Protein	15g	Fat	18g
Carbohydrate	16g	Saturates	2g

15 MINS 15 MINS

SERVES 4

INGREDIENTS

- 90 g/3 oz squid, cleaned
- 3-4 fresh scallops
- 90 g/3 oz raw prawns (shrimp), shelled
- ½ egg white, lightly beaten
- 1 tbsp cornflour (cornstarch) paste (see page 6)
- 275 g/9½ oz egg noodles
- 5-6 tbsp vegetable oil
- 2 tbsp light soy sauce
- 60 g/2 oz mangetout (snow peas)
- ½ tsp salt
- ½ tsp sugar
- 1 tsp Chinese rice wine
- 2 spring onions (scallions), finely shredded
- a few drops of sesame oil

1 Open up the squid and score the inside in a criss-cross pattern, then cut into pieces about the size of a postage stamp. Soak the squid in a bowl of boiling water until all the pieces curl up. Rinse in cold water and drain.

2 Cut each scallop into 3-4 slices. Cut the prawns (shrimp) in half lengthways if large. Mix the scallops and prawns (shrimp) with the egg white and cornflour (cornstarch) paste.

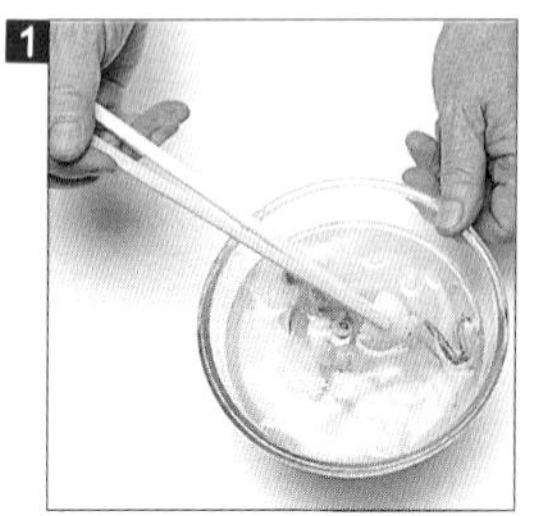

3 Cook the noodles in boiling water according to the packet instructions, then drain and rinse under cold water. Drain well, then toss with about 1 tablespoon of oil.

4 Heat 3 tablespoons of oil in a preheated wok. Add the noodles and 1 tablespoon of the soy sauce and stir-fry for 2-3 minutes. Remove to a large serving dish.

5 Heat the remaining oil in the wok and add the mangetout (snow peas) and seafood. Stir-fry for about 2 minutes, then add the salt, sugar, wine, remaining soy sauce and about half the spring onions (scallions). Blend well and add a little stock or water if necessary. Pour the seafood mixture on top of the noodles and sprinkle with sesame oil. Garnish with the remaining spring onions (scallions) and serve.

COOK'S TIP

Chinese rice wine, made from glutinous rice, is also known as 'Yellow wine' because of its golden amber colour. If it is unavailable, a good dry or medium sherry is an acceptable substitute.

Seafood Lasagne

You can use any fish and any sauce you like in this recipe: try smoked finnan haddock and whisky sauce or cod with cheese sauce.

NUTRITIONAL INFORMATION

Calories	790	Sugars	23g
Protein	55g	Fat	32g
Carbohydrate	74g	Saturates	19g

 30 MINS  45 MINS

SERVES 4

INGREDIENTS

- 450 g/1 lb finnan haddock, filleted, skin removed and flesh flaked
- 115 g/ 4 oz prawns (shrimp)
- 115 g/4 oz sole fillet, skin removed and flesh sliced
- juice of 1 lemon
- 60 g/2 oz/4 tbsp butter
- 3 leeks, very thinly sliced
- 60 g/2 oz/½ cup plain (all purpose) flour
- about 600 ml/1 pint/2⅓ cups milk
- 2 tbsp clear honey
- 200g/7 oz /1¾ cups grated Mozzarella cheese
- 450g/1 lb pre-cooked lasagne
- 60 g/2 oz/⅔ cup freshly grated Parmesan cheese
- pepper

1

3

3

1 Put the haddock fillet, prawns (shrimp) and sole fillet into a large bowl and season with pepper and lemon juice according to taste. Set aside while you make the sauce.

2 Melt the butter in a large saucepan. Add the leeks and cook, stirring occasionally, for 8 minutes. Add the flour and cook, stirring constantly, for 1 minute. Gradually stir in enough milk to make a thick, creamy sauce.

3 Blend in the honey and Mozzarella cheese and cook for a further 3 minutes. Remove the pan from the heat and mix in the fish and prawns (shrimp).

4 Make alternate layers of fish sauce and lasagne in an ovenproof dish, finishing with a layer of fish sauce on top. Generously sprinkle over the grated Parmesan cheese and bake in a preheated oven at 180°C/350°F/Gas Mark 4 for 30 minutes. Serve immediately.

VARIATION

For a cider sauce, substitute 1 finely chopped shallot for the leeks, 300 ml/½ pint/1½ cups cider and 300 ml/½ pint/1½ cups double (heavy) cream for the milk and 1 tsp mustard for the honey. For a Tuscan sauce, substitute 1 chopped fennel bulb for the leeks; omit the honey.

Marinara

This pizza is topped with a cocktail of mixed seafood, such as prawns (shrimp), mussels, cockles and squid rings.

NUTRITIONAL INFORMATION

Calories	359	Sugars	9g
Protein	19g	Fat	14g
Carbohydrate	42g	Saturates	4g

 3¼ HOURS  20 MINS

SERVES 4

INGREDIENTS

- Basic Pizza Dough (see page 861)
- Basic Tomato Sauce (see page 6)
- 200 g/7 oz frozen seafood cocktail, defrosted
- 1 tbsp capers
- 1 small yellow (bell) pepper, chopped
- 1 tbsp chopped fresh marjoram
- ½ tsp dried oregano
- 60 g/2 oz Mozzarella, grated
- 15 g/½ oz Parmesan, grated
- 12 black olives
- olive oil, for drizzling
- salt and pepper
- sprig of fresh marjoram or oregano, to garnish

1 Roll out or press out the pizza dough, using a rolling pin or your hands, into a 25 cm/10 inch circle on a lightly floured work surface.

2 Place the dough on a large greased baking tray (cookie sheet) or pizza pan and push up the edge a little with your fingers to form a rim.

3 Spread the tomato sauce evenly over the base almost to the edge.

3

4

5

4 Arrange the seafood cocktail, capers and yellow (bell) pepper on top of the tomato sauce.

5 Sprinkle over the herbs and cheeses. Arrange the olives on top. Drizzle over a little olive oil and season with salt and pepper to taste.

6 Bake in a preheated oven, at 200°C/ 400°F/Gas Mark 6, for 18–20 minutes or until the edge of the pizza is crisp and golden brown.

7 Transfer to a warmed serving plate, garnish with a sprig of marjoram or oregano and serve immediately.

Genoese Seafood Risotto

This is cooked in a different way from any of the other risottos. First, you cook the rice, then you prepare a sauce, then you mix the two together.

NUTRITIONAL INFORMATION

Calories	424	Sugars	0g
Protein	23g	Fat	17g
Carbohydrate	46g	Saturates	10g

 10 MINS 25 MINS

SERVES 4

INGREDIENTS

- 1.2 litres/2 pints/5 cups hot fish or chicken stock
- 350 g/12 oz arborio (risotto) rice, washed
- 50 g/1¾ oz/3 tbsp butter
- 2 garlic cloves, chopped
- 250 g/9 oz mixed seafood, preferably raw, such as prawns (shrimp), squid, mussels, clams and (small) shrimps
- 2 tbsp chopped oregano, plus extra for garnishing
- 50 g/1¾ oz pecorino or Parmesan cheese, grated

1 In a large saucepan, bring the stock to the boil. Add the rice and cook for about 12 minutes, stirring, or until the rice is tender. Drain thoroughly, reserving any excess liquid.

2 Heat the butter in a large frying pan (skillet) and add the garlic, stirring.

3 Add the raw mixed seafood to the pan (skillet) and cook for 5 minutes. If you are using cooked seafood, fry for 2–3 minutes.

4 Stir the oregano into the seafood mixture in the frying pan (skillet).

5 Add the cooked rice to the pan and cook for 2–3 minutes, stirring, or until hot. Add the reserved stock if the mixture gets too sticky.

6 Add the pecorino or Parmesan cheese and mix well.

7 Transfer the risotto to warm serving dishes and serve immediately.

COOK'S TIP

The Genoese are excellent cooks, and they make particularly delicious fish dishes flavoured with the local olive oil.

Seafood Omelette

This delicious omelette is filled with a mixture of fresh vegetables, sliced squid and prawns (shrimp).

NUTRITIONAL INFORMATION

Calories	216	Sugars	2g
Protein	20g	Fat	13g
Carbohydrate	4g	Saturates	4g

 5 MINS  10 MINS

SERVES 4

INGREDIENTS

- 4 eggs
- 3 tbsp milk
- 1 tbsp fish sauce or light soy sauce
- 1 tbsp sesame oil
- 3 shallots, sliced finely
- 1 small red (bell) pepper, cored, deseeded and sliced very finely
- 1 small leek, trimmed and cut into matchstick pieces
- 125 g/4½ oz squid rings
- 125 g/4½ oz/⅔ cup cooked peeled prawns (shrimp)
- 1 tbsp chopped fresh basil
- 15 g/½ oz/1 tbsp butter
- salt and pepper
- sprigs of fresh basil, to garnish

1 Beat the eggs, milk and fish sauce or soy sauce together.

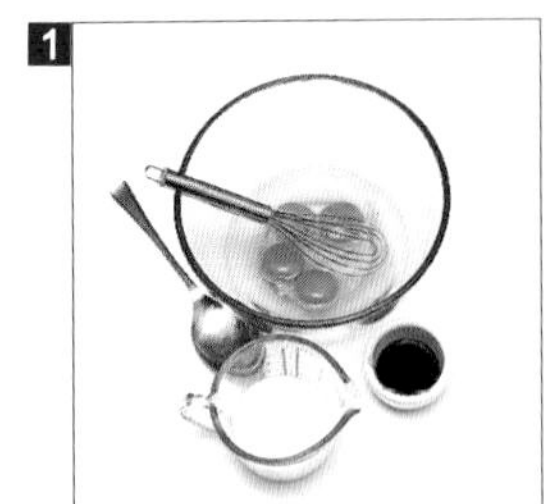

2 Heat the sesame oil in a wok or large frying pan (skillet) and add the shallots, (bell) pepper and leek. Stir-fry briskly for 2–3 minutes.

3 Add the squid rings, prawns (shrimp) and chopped basil to the wok or frying pan (skillet). Stir-fry for a further 2–3 minutes, until the squid looks opaque.

4 Season the mixture in the wok with salt and pepper to taste. Transfer to a warmed plate and keep warm until required.

5 Melt the butter in a large omelette pan or frying pan (skillet) and add the beaten egg mixture. Cook over a medium-high heat until just set.

6 Spoon the vegetable and seafood mixture in a line down the middle of the omelette, then fold each side of the omelette over.

7 Transfer the omelette to a warmed serving dish and cut into 4 portions. Garnish with sprigs of fresh basil and serve at once.

VARIATION

Chopped, cooked chicken makes a delicious alternative to the squid.

Use fresh coriander (cilantro) instead of the basil, if desired.

Prawn (Shrimp) Stir-fry

A very quick and tasty stir-fry using prawns (shrimp) and cucumber, cooked with lemon grass, chilli and ginger.

NUTRITIONAL INFORMATION

Calories	178	Sugars	1g
Protein	22g	Fat	7g
Carbohydrate	3g	Saturates	1g

 5 MINS  5 MINS

SERVES 4

INGREDIENTS

- ½ cucumber
- 2 tbsp sunflower oil
- 6 spring onions (scallions), halved lengthways and cut into 4 cm/ 1½ inch lengths
- 1 stalk lemon grass, sliced thinly
- 1 garlic clove, chopped
- 1 tsp chopped fresh red chilli
- 125 g/4½ oz oyster mushrooms
- 1 tsp chopped ginger root
- 350 g/12 oz cooked peeled prawns (shrimp)
- 2 tsp cornflour (cornstarch)
- 2 tbsp water
- 1 tbsp dark soy sauce
- ½ tsp fish sauce
- 2 tbsp dry sherry or rice wine
- boiled rice, to serve

1

3

4

1 Cut the cucumber into strips about 5 mm x 4 cm/¼ x 1¾ inches.

2 Heat the sunflower oil in a wok or large frying pan (skillet).

3 Add the spring onions (scallions), cucumber, lemon grass, garlic, chilli, oyster mushrooms and ginger to the wok or frying pan (skillet) and stir-fry for 2 minutes.

4 Add the prawns (shrimp) and stir-fry for a further minute.

5 Mix together the cornflour (cornstarch), water, soy sauce and fish sauce until smooth.

6 Stir the cornflour (cornstarch) mixture and sherry or wine into the wok and heat through, stirring, until the sauce has thickened. Serve with rice.

COOK'S TIP

The white part of the lemon grass stem can be thinly sliced and left in the cooked dish. If using the whole stem, remove it before serving. You can buy lemon grass chopped and dried, or preserved in jars, but neither has the fragrance or delicacy of the fresh variety.

A Seafood Medley

You can use almost any kind of sea fish in this recipe. Red sea bream is an especially good choice.

NUTRITIONAL INFORMATION

Calories	699	Sugars	4g
Protein	56g	Fat	35g
Carbohydrate	35g	Saturates	20g

 20 MINS  30 MINS

SERVES 4

INGREDIENTS

- 12 raw tiger prawns (shrimp)
- 12 raw (small) shrimp
- 450 g/1 lb fillet of sea bream
- 60 g/2 oz/4 tbsp butter
- 12 scallops, shelled
- 125 g/4½ oz freshwater prawns (shrimp)
- juice and finely grated rind of 1 lemon
- pinch of saffron powder or threads
- 1 litre/1¾ pints/4 cups vegetable stock
- 150 ml/¼ pint/⅔ cup rose petal vinegar
- 450 g/1 lb dried farfalle
- 1 tbsp olive oil
- 150 ml/¼ pint/⅔ cup white wine
- 1 tbsp pink peppercorns
- 115 g/4 oz baby carrots
- 150 ml/¼ pint/⅔ cup double (heavy) cream or fromage frais
- salt and pepper

1 Peel and devein the prawns (shrimp) and (small) shrimp. Thinly slice the sea bream. Melt the butter in a frying pan (skillet), add the sea bream, scallops, prawns (shrimp) and (small) shrimp and cook for 1–2 minutes.

2 Season with pepper to taste. Add the lemon juice and grated rind. Very carefully add a pinch of saffron powder or a few strands of saffron to the cooking juices (not to the seafood).

3 Remove the seafood from the pan, set aside and keep warm.

4 Return the pan to the heat and add the stock. Bring to the boil and reduce by one third. Add the rose petal vinegar and cook for 4 minutes, until reduced.

5 Bring a pan of salted water to the boil. Add the farfalle and oil and cook for 8–10 minutes until tender, but still firm to the bite. Drain the pasta, transfer to a serving plate and top with the seafood.

6 Add the wine, peppercorns, and carrots to the pan and reduce the sauce for 6 minutes. Add the cream or fromage frais and simmer for 2 minutes.

7 Pour the sauce over the seafood and pasta and serve immediately.

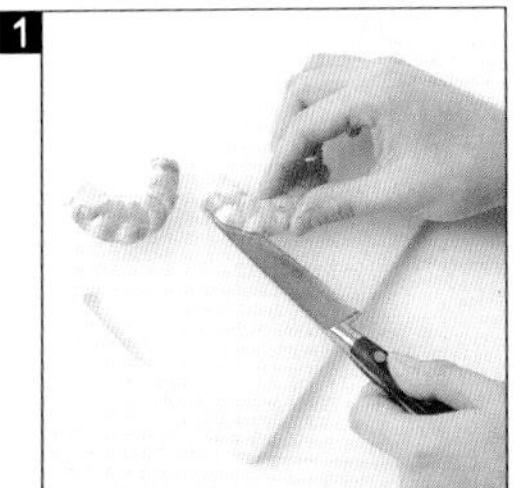
1

1

4

Seafood Pasta

This attractive seafood salad platter is full of different flavours, textures and colours.

NUTRITIONAL INFORMATION

Calories	188	Sugars	2g
Protein	16g	Fat	7g
Carbohydrate	13g	Saturates	1g

 30 MINS  30 MINS

SERVES 8

INGREDIENTS

- 175 g/6 oz/1½ cups dried pasta shapes
- 1 tbsp oil
- 4 tbsp Italian dressing
- 2 garlic cloves, crushed
- 6 tbsp white wine
- 125 g/4½ oz baby button mushrooms, trimmed
- 3 carrots
- 600 ml/1 pint/2½ cups fresh mussels in shells
- 125–175 g/4½–6 oz frozen squid or octopus rings, thawed
- 175 g/6 oz/1 cup peeled tiger prawns (shrimp), thawed if frozen
- 6 sun-dried tomatoes, drained and sliced
- 3 tbsp chives, cut into 2.5 cm/1 inch pieces
- salt and pepper

TO GARNISH

- 24 mangetout (snow peas), trimmed
- 12 baby corn
- 12 prawns (shrimp) in shells

1 Cook the pasta in a pan of boiling salted water, with the oil added, for 8–10 minutes or until just tender. Drain the pasta thoroughly.

2 Combine the dressing, garlic and 2 tablespoons of wine. Mix in the mushrooms and leave to marinate.

3 Slice the carrots about 1 cm/½ inch thick and using a cocktail cutter, cut each slice into shapes. Blanch for 3–4 minutes, drain and add to the mushrooms.

4 Scrub the mussels, discarding any that are open or do not close when sharply tapped. Put into a saucepan with 150 ml/¼ pint/⅔ cup water and the remaining wine. Bring to the boil, cover and simmer for 3–4 minutes or until they open. Drain, discarding any that are still closed. Reserve 12 mussels for garnish, leaving them on the half shell; remove the other mussels from the shells and add to the mushroom mixture with the squid or octopus rings and prawns (shrimp).

5 Add the sun-dried tomatoes, pasta and chives to the salad. Toss to mix and turn on to a large platter.

6 Blanch the mangetout (snow peas) for 1 minute and baby corn for 3 minutes, rinse under cold water and drain. Arrange around the edge of the salad, alternating with the mussels on shells and whole prawns (shrimp). Cover with cling film (plastic wrap) and leave to chill until ready to serve.

4

5

6

Aromatic Seafood Rice

One of those easy, delicious meals where the rice and fish are cooked together in one pan. Remove the whole spices before serving

NUTRITIONAL INFORMATION

Calories	380	Sugar	2g
Protein	40g	Fats	13g
Carbohydrates	26g	Saturates	5g

 20 MINS  25 MINS

SERVES 4

INGREDIENTS

- 225 g/8 oz/1¼ cups basmati rice
- 2 tbsp ghee or vegetable oil
- 1 onion, peeled and chopped
- 1 garlic clove, peeled and crushed
- 1 tsp cumin seeds
- ½-1 tsp chilli powder
- 4 cloves
- 1 cinnamon stick or a piece of cassia bark
- 2 tsp curry paste
- 225 g/8 oz peeled prawns (shrimp)
- 500g/1 lb 2 oz white fish fillets (such as monkfish, cod or haddock), skinned and boned and cut into bite-sized pieces
- salt and freshly ground black pepper
- 600 ml/1 pint/2½ cups boiling water
- 60 g/2 oz/⅓ cup frozen peas
- 60 g/2 oz/⅓ cup frozen sweetcorn kernels
- 1-2 tbsp lime juice
- 2 tbsp toasted desiccated (shredded) coconut
- coriander (cilantro) sprigs and lime slices, to garnish

1 Place the rice in a sieve and wash well under cold running water until the water runs clear, then drain well.

2 Heat the ghee or oil in a saucepan, add the onion, garlic, spices and curry paste and fry very gently for 1 minute.

3 Stir in the rice and mix well until coated in the spiced oil. Add the prawns (shrimp) and white fish and season well with salt and pepper. Stir lightly, then pour in the boiling water.

4 Cover and cook gently for 10 minutes, without uncovering the pan. Add the peas and corn, cover and continue cooking for a further 8 minutes. Remove from the heat and allow to stand for 10 minutes.

5 Uncover the pan, fluff up the rice with a fork and transfer to a warm serving platter.

6 Sprinkle the dish with the lime juice and toasted coconut, and serve garnished with coriander (cilantro) sprigs and lime slices.

Spaghetti & Seafood Sauce

Peeled prawns (shrimp) from the freezer can become the star ingredient in this colourful and tasty dish.

NUTRITIONAL INFORMATION

Calories	498	Sugars	5g
Protein	32g	Fat	23g
Carbohydrate	43g	Saturates	11g

 30 MINS 35 MINS

SERVES 4

INGREDIENTS

- 225 g/8 oz dried spaghetti, broken into 15 cm/6 inch lengths
- 2 tbsp olive oil
- 300 ml/½ pint/1¼ cups chicken stock
- 1 tsp lemon juice
- 1 small cauliflower, cut into florets
- 2 carrots, thinly sliced
- 115 g/4 oz mangetout (snow peas)
- 60 g/2 oz/4 tbsp butter
- 1 onion, sliced
- 225 g/8 oz courgettes (zucchini), sliced
- 1 garlic clove, chopped
- 350 g/12 oz frozen, cooked, peeled prawns (shrimp), defrosted
- 2 tbsp chopped fresh parsley
- 25 g/1 oz/⅓ cup freshly grated Parmesan cheese
- ½ tsp paprika
- salt and pepper
- 4 unpeeled, cooked prawns (shrimp), to garnish

1 Bring a pan of lightly salted water to the boil. Add the spaghetti and 1 tbsp of the olive oil and cook for 8–10 minutes until tender, but still firm to the bite. Drain the spaghetti and return to the pan. Toss with the remaining olive oil, cover and keep warm.

2 Bring the chicken stock and lemon juice to the boil. Add the cauliflower and carrots and cook for 3–4 minutes. Remove from the pan and set aside. Add the mangetout (snow peas) to the pan and cook for 1–2 minutes. Set aside with the other vegetables.

3 Melt half of the butter in a frying pan (skillet) over a medium heat. Add the onion and courgettes (zucchini) and fry for about 3 minutes. Add the garlic and prawns (shrimp) and cook for a further 2–3 minutes, until thoroughly heated through.

4 Stir in the reserved vegetables and heat through. Season to taste and stir in the remaining butter.

5 Transfer the spaghetti to a warm serving dish. Pour over the sauce and add the chopped parsley. Toss well with 2 forks until coated. Sprinkle over the Parmesan cheese and paprika, garnish with the unpeeled prawns (shrimp) and serve immediately.

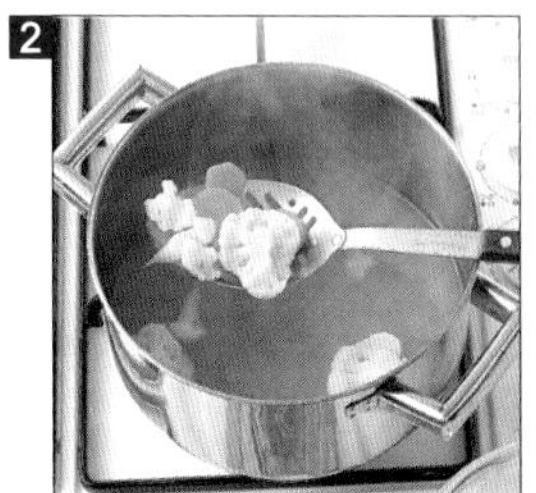

2

3

4

Vegetables & Salads

Anyone with more than a passing interest in their health can be unaware of the importance of fresh fruit and vegetables in the diet. We should, according to recent studies, be eating at least five portions a day. Elsewhere in the world, particularly China and India, vegetables play a larger role in the diet. This is due to both economic and religious reasons. The recipes in this chapter offer a sumptuous range of vegetable and vegetarian dishes, as well as salads, from India, China, Italy, Turkey, France, and many other countries to show you how easy it is to incorporate fruit and vegetables into your diet. Original and inventive ways to cook vegetables so that you do not even miss the meat include Vegetable Lasagne, Mexican Chilli Corn Pie, or Broccoli, (Bell) Pepper & Almond Salad.

Potato & Cheese Soufflé

This soufflé is very simple to make, yet it has a delicious flavour and melts in the mouth. Choose three alternative cheeses, if preferred.

NUTRITIONAL INFORMATION

Calories	447	Sugars	1g
Protein	22g	Fat	23g
Carbohydrate	41g	Saturates	11g

10 MINS 55 MINS

SERVES 4

INGREDIENTS

- 25 g/1 oz/2 tbsp butter
- 2 tsp plain (all-purpose) flour
- 900 g/2 lb floury (mealy) potatoes
- 8 eggs, separated
- 25 g/1 oz/¼ cup grated Gruyère (Swiss) cheese
- 25 g/1 oz/¼ cup crumbled blue cheese
- 25 g/1 oz/¼ cup grated mature (sharp) Cheddar cheese
- salt and pepper

1 Butter a 2.4 litre/4 pint/10 cup soufflé dish and dust with the flour. Set aside.

2 Cook the potatoes in a saucepan of boiling water until tender. Mash until very smooth and then transfer to a mixing bowl to cool.

3 Beat the egg yolks into the potato and stir in the Gruyère (Swiss) cheese, blue cheese and Cheddar, mixing well. Season to taste with salt and pepper.

4 Whisk the egg whites until standing in peaks, then gently fold them into the potato mixture with a metal spoon until fully incorporated.

5 Spoon the potato mixture into the prepared soufflé dish.

6 Cook in a preheated oven, 220°C/425°F/Gas Mark 7, for 35–40 minutes, until risen and set. Serve immediately.

1

3

4

COOK'S TIP

Insert a fine skewer into the centre of the soufflé; it should come out clean when the soufflé is fully cooked through.

Kidney Bean Kiev

This is a vegetarian version of chicken Kiev – the bean patties are topped with garlic and herb butter and coated in breadcrumbs.

NUTRITIONAL INFORMATION

Calories	688	Sugars	8g
Protein	17g	Fat	49g
Carbohydrate	49g	Saturates	20g

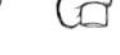

 25 MINS  20 MINS

SERVES 4

INGREDIENTS

GARLIC BUTTER

- 100 g/3½ oz/ 7 tbsp butter
- 3 garlic cloves, crushed
- 1 tbsp chopped parsley

BEAN PATTIES

- 675 g/1½ lb canned red kidney beans
- 150 g/5½ oz/1¼ cups fresh white breadcrumbs
- 25 g/1 oz/2 tbsp butter
- 1 leek, chopped
- 1 celery stick, chopped
- 1 tbsp chopped parsley
- 1 egg, beaten
- salt and pepper
- vegetable oil, for shallow frying

1 To make the garlic butter, put the butter, garlic and parsley in a bowl and blend together with a wooden spoon. Place the garlic butter on to a sheet of baking parchment, roll into a cigar shape and wrap in the baking parchment. Chill in the refrigerator until required.

2 Using a potato masher, mash the red kidney beans in a mixing bowl and stir in 75 g/ 2¾ oz/¾ cup of the breadcrumbs until thoroughly blended.

3 Melt the butter in a heavy-based frying pan (skillet). Add the leek and celery and sauté over a low heat, stirring constantly,for 3–4 minutes.

4 Add the bean mixture to the pan, together with the parsley, season with salt and pepper to taste and mix thoroughly. Remove the pan from the heat and set aside to cool slightly.

5 Divide the kidney bean mixture into 4 equal portions and shape them into ovals.

6 Slice the garlic butter into 4 pieces and place a slice in the centre of each bean patty. With your hands, mould the bean mixture around the garlic butter to encase it completely.

7 Dip each bean patty into the beaten egg to coat and then roll in the remaining breadcrumbs.

8 Heat a little oil in a frying pan (skillet) and fry the patties, turning once, for 7–10 minutes. or until golden brown. Serve immediately.

Red Bean Stew & Dumplings

There's nothing better on a cold day than a hearty dish topped with dumplings. This recipe is quick and easy to prepare.

NUTRITIONAL INFORMATION

Calories	508	Sugars	15g
Protein	22g	Fat	12g
Carbohydrate	83g	Saturates	4g

 1¼ HOURS  35 MINS

SERVES 4

INGREDIENTS

- 1 tbsp vegetable oil
- 1 red onion, sliced
- 2 celery stalks, chopped
- 850 ml/1½ pints/3½ cups Fresh Vegetable Stock (see page 8)
- 225 g/8 oz carrots, diced
- 225 g/8 oz potatoes, diced
- 225 g/8 oz courgettes (zucchini), diced
- 4 tomatoes, peeled and chopped
- 125 g/4½ oz/½ cup red lentils
- 400 g/14 oz can kidney beans, rinsed and drained
- 1 tsp paprika
- salt and pepper

DUMPLINGS

- 125 g/4½ oz/1 cup plain (all-purpose) flour
- ½ tsp salt
- 2 tsp baking powder
- 1 tsp paprika
- 1 tsp dried mixed herbs
- 25 g/1 oz/2 tbsp vegetable suet
- 7 tbsp water
- sprigs of fresh flat-leaf parsley, to garnish

1. Heat the oil in a flameproof casserole or a large saucepan and gently fry the onion and celery for 3–4 minutes until just softened. Pour in the stock and stir in the carrots and potatoes. Bring to the boil, cover and cook for 5 minutes.

2. Stir in the courgettes (zucchini), tomatoes, lentils, kidney beans, paprika and seasoning. Bring to the boil, cover and cook for 5 minutes.

3. To make the dumplings, sift the flour, salt, baking powder and paprika into a bowl. Stir in the herbs and suet. Bind together with the water to form a soft dough. Divide into eight and roll into balls.

4. Add the dumplings to the stew, pushing them slightly into the stew. Cover and simmer for 15 minutes until the dumplings have risen and are cooked through. Garnish with flat-leaf parsley.

1

3

4

Butternut Squash Stir-fry

Butternut squash is as its name suggests, deliciously buttery and nutty in flavour. If the squash is not in season, use sweet potatoes instead.

NUTRITIONAL INFORMATION

Calories	301	Sugars	4g
Protein	9g	Fat	22g
Carbohydrate	19g	Saturates	4g

5 MINS 25 MINS

SERVES 4

INGREDIENTS

- 1 kg/2 lb 4 oz butternut squash, peeled
- 3 tbsp groundnut oil
- 1 onion, sliced
- 2 cloves garlic, crushed
- 1 tsp coriander seeds
- 1 tsp cumin seeds
- 2 tbsp chopped coriander (cilantro)
- 150 ml/¼ pint/⅔ cup coconut milk
- 100 ml/3½ fl oz/½ cup water
- 100 g/3½ oz/⅓ cup salted cashew nuts

TO GARNISH

- freshly grated lime zest
- fresh coriander (cilantro)
- lime wedges

1 Using a sharp knife, slice the butternut squash into small, bite-sized cubes.

2 Heat the groundnut oil in a large preheated wok.

3 Add the butternut squash, onion and garlic to the wok and stir-fry for 5 minutes.

4 Stir in the coriander seeds, cumin seeds and fresh coriander (cilantro) and stir-fry for 1 minute.

5 Add the coconut milk and water to the wok and bring to the boil. Cover the wok and leave to simmer for 10–15 minutes, or until the squash is tender.

6 Add the cashew nuts and stir to combine.

7 Transfer to warm serving dishes and garnish with freshly grated lime zest, fresh coriander (cilantro) and lime wedges. Serve hot.

COOK'S TIP

If you do not have coconut milk, grate some creamed coconut into the dish with the water in step 5.

Penne & Butternut Squash

The creamy, nutty flavour of squash complements the 'al dente' texture of the pasta perfectly. This recipe has been adapted for the microwave.

NUTRITIONAL INFORMATION

Calories	499	Sugars	4g
Protein	20g	Fat	26g
Carbohydrate	49g	Saturates	13g

 15 MINS  30 MINS

SERVES 4

INGREDIENTS

- 2 tbsp olive oil
- 1 garlic clove, crushed
- 60 g/2 oz/1 cup fresh white breadcrumbs
- 500 g/1 lb 2 oz peeled and deseeded butternut squash
- 8 tbsp water
- 500 g/1 lb 2 oz fresh penne, or other pasta shape
- 15 g/½ oz/1 tbsp butter
- 1 onion, sliced
- 125 g/4½ oz/½ cup ham, cut into strips
- 200 ml/7 fl oz/scant cup single (light) cream
- 60 g/2 oz/½ cup Cheddar cheese, grated
- 2 tbsp chopped fresh parsley
- salt and pepper

1 Mix together the oil, garlic and breadcrumbs and spread out on a large plate. Cook on HIGH power for 4–5 minutes, stirring every minute, until crisp and beginning to brown. Set aside.

2 Dice the squash. Place in a large bowl with half of the water. Cover and cook on HIGH power for 8–9 minutes, stirring occasionally. Leave to stand for 2 minutes.

3 Place the pasta in a large bowl, add a little salt and pour over boiling water to cover by 2.5 cm/1 inch. Cover and cook on HIGH power for 5 minutes, stirring once, until the pasta is just tender but still firm to the bite. Leave to stand, covered, for 1 minute before draining.

4 Place the butter and onion in a large bowl. Cover and cook on HIGH power for 3 minutes.

5 Coarsely mash the squash, using a fork. Add to the onion with the pasta, ham, cream, cheese, parsley and remaining water. Season generously and mix well. Cover and cook on HIGH power for 4 minutes until heated through.

6 Serve the pasta sprinkled with the crisp garlic crumbs.

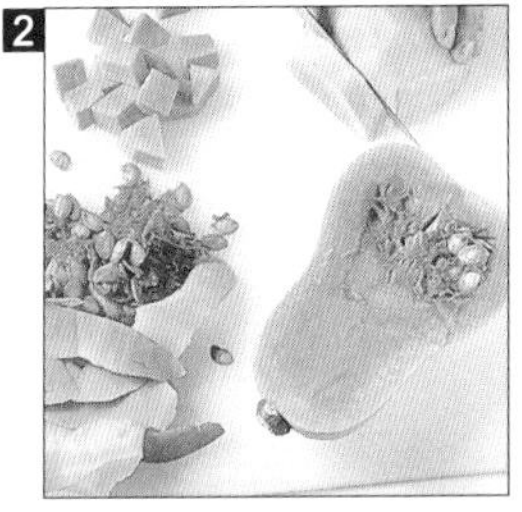
2

3

5

COOK'S TIP

If the squash weighs more than is needed for this recipe, blanch the excess for 3–4 minutes on HIGH power in a covered bowl with a little water. Drain, cool and place in a freezer bag. Store in the freezer for up to 3 months.

Tofu with Mushrooms & Peas

Chinese mushrooms are available from Chinese supermarkets and health food shops and add a unique flavour to Oriental dishes.

NUTRITIONAL INFORMATION

Calories	218	Sugars	1g
Protein	12g	Fat	14g
Carbohydrate	13g	Saturates	2g

 15 MINS ⏱ 15 MINS

SERVES 4

INGREDIENTS

- 25 g/1 oz dried Chinese mushrooms
- 450 g/1 lb tofu (bean curd)
- 25 g/1 oz/4 tbsp cornflour (cornstarch)
- oil, for deep-frying
- 2 cloves garlic, finely chopped
- 2.5 cm/1 inch piece root ginger, grated
- 100 g/3½ oz/¾ cup frozen or fresh peas

1

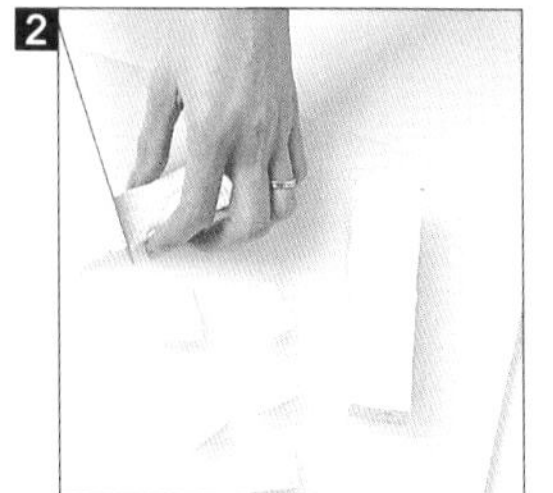
2

6

1 Place the Chinese mushrooms in a large bowl. Pour in enough boiling water to cover and leave to stand for about 10 minutes.

2 Meanwhile, cut the tofu (bean curd) into bite-sized cubes, using a sharp knife.

3 Place the cornflour (cornstarch) in a large bowl.

4 Add the tofu (bean curd) to the bowl and toss in the cornflour (cornstarch) until evenly coated.

5 Heat the oil for deep-frying in a large preheated wok.

6 Add the cubes of tofu (bean curd) to the wok and deep-fry, in batches, for 2–3 minutes or until golden and crispy. Remove the tofu (bean curd) with a slotted spoon and leave to drain on absorbent kitchen paper (paper towels).

7 Drain off all but 2 tablespoons of oil from the wok. Add the garlic, ginger and Chinese mushrooms to the wok and stir-fry for 2–3 minutes.

8 Return the cooked tofu (bean curd) to the wok and add the peas. Heat through for 1 minute then serve hot.

COOK'S TIP

Chinese dried mushrooms add flavour and a distinctive aroma. Sold dried in packets, they can be expensive but only a few are needed per dish and they store indefinitely. If they are unavailable, use open-cap mushrooms instead.

Braised Vegetables with Tofu

Also known Buddha's Delight, the original recipe calls for 18 different vegetables to represent the 18 Buddhas – but 6-8 are quite acceptable!

NUTRITIONAL INFORMATION

Calories	300	Sugars	2g
Protein	8g	Fat	28g
Carbohydrate	6g	Saturates	3g

3¾ HOURS 10 MINS

SERVES 4

INGREDIENTS

- 5 g/¼ oz dried wood ears
- 1 cake tofu (bean curd)
- 60 g/2 oz mangetout (snow peas)
- 125 g/4½ oz Chinese leaves (cabbage)
- 1 small carrot
- 90 g/3 oz canned baby sweetcorn, drained
- 90 g/3 oz canned straw mushrooms, drained
- 60 g/2 oz canned water chestnuts, drained
- 300 ml/½ pint/1¼ cups vegetable oil
- 1 tsp salt
- ½ tsp sugar
- 1 tbsp light soy sauce or oyster sauce
- 2-3 tbsp Chinese Stock (see page 8) or water
- a few drops sesame oil

1

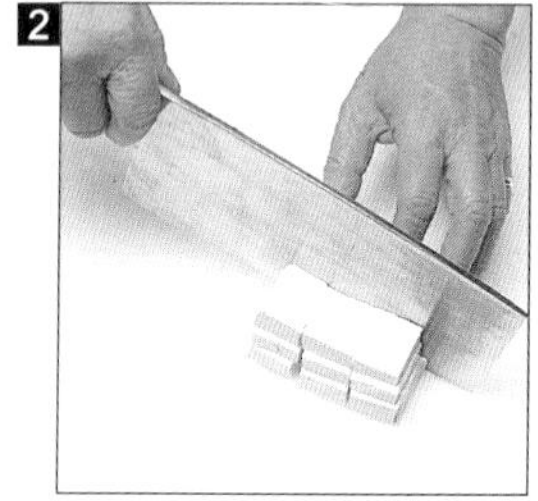

2

4

1 Soak the wood ears in warm water for 15-20 minutes, then rinse and drain, discarding any hard bits, and dry on kitchen paper (paper towels).

2 Cut the cake of tofu into about 18 small pieces.

3 Top and tail the mangetout (snow peas). Cut the Chinese leaves (cabbage) and the carrot into slices roughly the same size and shape as the mangetout (snow peas). Cut the baby sweetcorn, the straw mushrooms and the water chestnuts in half.

4 Heat the oil in a preheated wok. Add the tofu (bean curd) and deep-fry for about 2 minutes until it turns slightly golden. Remove and drain.

5 Pour off the oil, leaving about 2 tablespoons in the wok. Add the carrot, Chinese leaves (cabbage) and mangetout (snow peas) and stir-fry for about 1 minute.

6 Add the sweetcorn, mushrooms and water chestnuts. Stir gently for 2 more minutes, then add the salt, sugar, soy sauce or oyster sauce and Chinese stock or water. Bring to the boil and stir-fry for 1 more minute. Sprinkle with sesame oil and serve hot or cold.

Green Curry with Tempeh

Green curry paste will keep for up to three weeks in the refrigerator. Serve the curry over rice or noodles.

NUTRITIONAL INFORMATION

Calories	237	Sugars	4g
Protein	16g	Fat	17g
Carbohydrate	5g	Saturates	3g

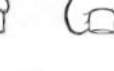

20 MINS 15-20 MINS

SERVES 4

INGREDIENTS

- 1 tbsp sunflower oil
- 175 g/6 oz marinated or plain tempeh, cut into diamonds
- 6 spring onions (scallions), cut into 2.5 cm/1 inch pieces
- 150 ml/¼ pint/⅔ cup coconut milk
- grated rind of 1 lime
- 15 g/½ oz/¼ cup fresh basil leaves
- ¼ tsp liquid seasoning, such as Maggi

GREEN CURRY PASTE

- 2 tsp coriander seeds
- 1 tsp cumin seeds
- 1 tsp black peppercorns
- 4 large green chillies, seeded
- 2 shallots, quartered
- 2 garlic cloves,
- 2 tbsp chopped coriander (cilantro)
- grated rind of 1 lime
- 1 tbsp roughly chopped galangal
- 1 tsp ground turmeric
- salt
- 2 tbsp oil

TO GARNISH

- coriander (cilantro) leaves
- 2 green chillies, thinly sliced

1 To make the green curry paste, grind together the coriander and cumin seeds and the peppercorns in a food processor or in a mortar with a pestle.

2 Blend the remaining ingredients together and add the ground spice mixture. Store in a clean, dry jar for up to 3 weeks in the refrigerator, or freeze in a suitable container.

3 Heat the oil in a wok or large, heavy frying pan (skillet). Add the tempeh and stir over a high heat for about 2 minutes until sealed on all sides. Add the spring onions (scallions) and stir-fry for 1 minute. Remove the tempeh and spring onions (scallions) and reserve.

4 Put half the coconut milk into the wok or pan (skillet) and bring to the boil. Add 6 tablespoons of the curry paste and the lime rind, and cook for 1 minute, until fragrant. Add the reserved tempeh and spring onions (scallions).

5 Add the remaining coconut milk and simmer for 7–8 minutes. Stir in the basil leaves and liquid seasoning. Leave to simmer for 1 minute before serving, garnished with coriander (cilantro) leaves and chillies.

3

4

5

Tagliatelle with Pumpkin

This unusual pasta dish comes from the Emilia Romagna region of Italy.

NUTRITIONAL INFORMATION

Calories	454	Sugars	4g
Protein	9g	Fat	33g
Carbohydrate	33g	Saturates	12g

15 MINS 35 MINS

SERVES 4

INGREDIENTS

500 g/1 lb 2 oz pumpkin or butternut squash

2 tbsp olive oil

1 onion, chopped finely

2 garlic cloves, crushed

4–6 tbsp chopped fresh parsley

good pinch of ground or freshly grated nutmeg

about 250 ml/9 fl oz/1 cup chicken or vegetable stock

125 g/4½ oz Parma ham (prosciutto), cut into narrow strips

275 g/9 oz tagliatelle, green or white (fresh or dried)

150 ml/¼ pint/⅔ cup double (heavy) cream

salt and pepper

freshly grated Parmesan, to serve

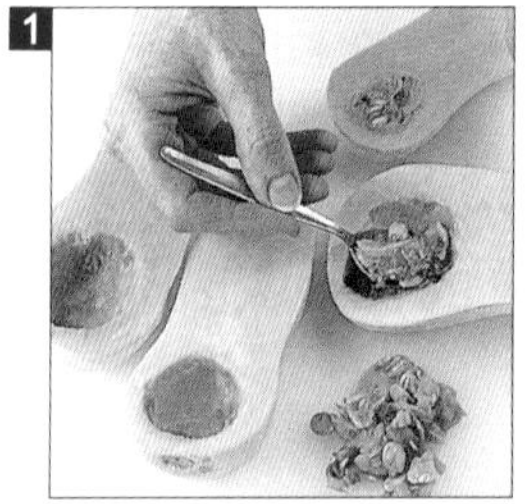

1 Peel the pumpkin or squash and scoop out the seeds and membrane. Cut the flesh into 1 cm/½ inch dice.

2 Heat the olive oil in a pan and gently fry the onion and garlic until softened. Add half of the parsley and fry for 1–2 minutes.

3 Add the pumpkin or squash and continue to cook for 2–3 minutes. Season well with salt, pepper and nutmeg.

4 Add half of the stock, bring to the boil, cover and simmer for about 10 minutes or until the pumpkin is tender, adding more stock as necessary. Add the Parma ham (prosciutto) and continue to cook for 2 minutes, stirring frequently.

5 Meanwhile, cook the tagliatelle in a large saucepan of boiling salted water, allowing 3–4 minutes for fresh pasta or 8–10 minutes for dried. Drain thoroughly and turn into a warmed dish.

6 Add the cream to the ham mixture and heat gently. Season and spoon over the pasta. Sprinkle with the remaining parsley and grated Parmesan separately.

Tofu (Bean Curd), Corn & Peas

Chunks of tofu (bean curd) marinated in ginger and soy sauce impart something of an oriental flavour to this pizza.

NUTRITIONAL INFORMATION

Calories	596	Sugars	17g
Protein	33g	Fat	23g
Carbohydrate	66g	Saturates	9g

 1 HOUR  35 MINS

SERVES 4

INGREDIENTS

- 1 litre/1¾ pints milk
- 1 tsp salt
- 225 g/8 oz semolina
- 1 tbsp soy sauce
- 1 tbsp dry sherry
- ½ tsp grated fresh ginger root
- 250 g/9 oz tofu (bean curd), cut into chunks
- 2 eggs
- 60 g/2 oz Parmesan, grated
- Basic Tomato Sauce (see page 6)
- 25 g/1 oz baby sweetcorn, cut into 4
- 25 g/1 oz mangetout (snow peas), trimmed and cut into 4
- 4 spring onions (scallions), trimmed and cut into 2.5 cm/1 inch strips
- 60 g/2 oz Mozzarella, sliced thinly
- 2 tsp sesame oil
- salt and pepper

1 Bring the milk to the boil with the salt. Sprinkle the semolina over the surface, stirring all the time. Cook for 10 minutes over a low heat, stirring occasionally, taking care not to let it burn. Remove from the heat and leave to cool until tepid.

2 Mix the soy sauce, sherry and ginger together in a bowl, add the tofu (bean curd) and stir gently to coat. Leave to marinate in a cool place for 20 minutes.

3 Beat the eggs with a little pepper. Add to the semolina with the Parmesan and mix well. Place on a large greased baking tray (cookie sheet) or pizza pan and pat into a 25 cm/10 inch round, using the back of a metal spoon. Spread the tomato sauce almost to the edge.

4 Blanch the sweetcorn and mangetout (snow peas) in a saucepan of boiling water for 1 minute, drain and place on the pizza with the drained tofu (bean curd). Top with the spring onions (scallions) and slices of cheese. Drizzle over the sesame oil and season with salt and pepper.

5 Bake in a preheated oven, at 200°C/400°F/Gas Mark 6, for 18–20 minutes, or until the edge is crisp and golden. Serve immediately.

1

2

4

Black Bean Casserole

This colourful Chinese-style casserole is made with tofu (bean curd), vegetables and black bean sauce.

NUTRITIONAL INFORMATION

Calories	513	Sugars	5g
Protein	19g	Fat	25g
Carbohydrate	56g	Saturates	4g

 30 MINS  30 MINS

SERVES 4

INGREDIENTS

- 6 Chinese dried mushrooms
- 275 g/9½ oz tofu (bean curd)
- 3 tbsp vegetable oil
- 1 carrot, cut into thin strips
- 125 g/4½ oz mangetout (snow peas)
- 125 g/4½ oz/8 baby corn, halved lengthways
- 225 g/8 oz can sliced bamboo shoots, drained
- 1 red (bell) pepper, cut into chunks
- 125 g/4½ oz Chinese leaves (cabbage), shredded
- 1 tbsp soy sauce
- 1 tbsp black bean sauce
- 1 tsp sugar
- 1 tsp cornflour (cornstarch)
- vegetable oil for deep-frying
- 250 g/9 oz Chinese rice noodles
- salt

1 Soak the dried mushrooms in a bowl of warm water for 20–25 minutes. Drain and squeeze out the excess water, reserving the liquid. Remove the tough centres and slice the mushrooms thinly.

2 Cut the tofu (bean curd) into cubes. Boil in a pan of lightly salted water for 2–3 minutes to firm up and then drain.

3 Heat half the oil in a saucepan. Add the tofu (bean curd) and fry until lightly browned. Remove and drain on kitchen paper (paper towels).

4 Add the remaining oil and stir-fry the mushrooms, carrot, mangetout (snow peas), baby corn, bamboo shoots and (bell) pepper for 2–3 minutes. Add the Chinese leaves (cabbage) and tofu (bean curd), and stir-fry for a further 2 minutes.

5 Stir in the sauces and sugar, and season with salt. Add 6 tbsp of the reserved mushroom liquid mixed with the cornflour (cornstarch). Bring to the boil, reduce the heat, cover and braise for 2–3 minutes until the sauce thickens slightly.

6 Heat the oil for deep-frying in a large pan. Deep-fry the noodles, in batches, until puffed up and lightly golden. Drain and serve with the casserole.

Italian Spaghetti

Delicious Mediterranean vegetables, cooked in a rich tomato sauce, make an ideal topping for nutty wholewheat pasta.

NUTRITIONAL INFORMATION

Calories	393	Sugars	11g
Protein	14g	Fat	11g
Carbohydrate	63g	Saturates	2g

20 MINS 35 MINS

SERVES 4

INGREDIENTS

- 2 tbsp olive oil
- 1 large red onion, chopped
- 2 garlic cloves, crushed
- 1 tbsp lemon juice
- 4 baby aubergines (eggplant), quartered
- 600 ml/1 pint/2½ cups passata (sieved tomatoes)
- 2 tsp caster (superfine) sugar
- 2 tbsp tomato purée (paste)
- 400 g/14 oz can artichoke hearts, drained and halved
- 125 g/4½ oz/¾ cup pitted black olives
- 350 g/12 oz wholewheat dried spaghetti
- salt and pepper
- sprigs of fresh basil, to garnish
- olive bread, to serve

1 Heat 1 tablespoon of the oil in a large frying pan (skillet) and gently fry the onion, garlic, lemon juice and aubergines (eggplant) for 4–5 minutes or until lightly browned.

2 Pour in the passata (sieved tomatoes), season with salt and pepper to taste and add the sugar and tomato purée (paste). Bring to the boil, reduce the heat and simmer for 20 minutes.

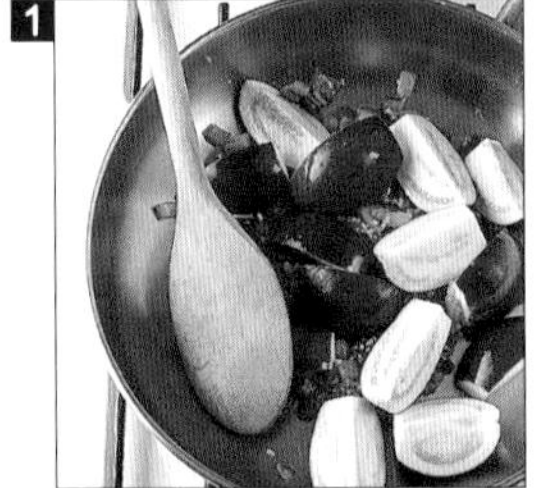

1

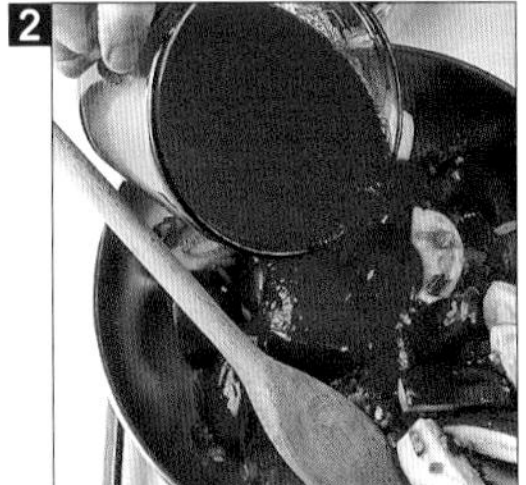

2

3

3 Gently stir in the artichoke halves and olives and cook for 5 minutes.

4 Meanwhile, bring a large saucepan of lightly salted water to the boil, and cook the spaghetti for 8–10 minutes or until just tender. Drain well, toss in the remaining olive oil and season with salt and pepper to taste.

5 Transfer the spaghetti to a warmed serving bowl and top with the vegetable sauce. Garnish with basil sprigs and serve with olive bread.

Tagliatelle & Broccoli

Some of the simplest and most satisfying dishes are made with pasta, such as this delicious combination of tagliatelle with two-cheese sauce.

NUTRITIONAL INFORMATION

Calories	624	Sugars	2g
Protein	22g	Fat	45g
Carbohydrate	34g	Saturates	28g

5 MINS

15 MINS

SERVES 4

INGREDIENTS

300 g/10½ oz dried tagliatelle tricolore (plain, spinach- and tomato-flavoured noodles)

225 g/8 oz/2½ cups broccoli, broken into small florets

350g/12 oz/1½ cups Mascarpone cheese

125 g/4½ oz/1 cup blue cheese, chopped

1 tbsp chopped fresh oregano

25 g/1 oz/2 tbsp butter

salt and pepper

sprigs of fresh oregano, to garnish

freshly grated Parmesan, to serve

1 Cook the tagliatelle in plenty of boiling salted water for 8–10 minutes or until just tender.

2 Meanwhile, cook the broccoli florets in a small amount of lightly salted, boiling water. Avoid overcooking the broccoli, so that it retains much of its colour and texture.

3 Heat the Mascarpone and blue cheeses together gently in a large saucepan until they are melted. Stir in the oregano and season with salt and pepper to taste.

4 Drain the pasta thoroughly. Return it to the saucepan and add the butter, tossing the tagliatelle to coat it. Drain the broccoli well and add to the pasta with the sauce, tossing gently to mix.

5 Divide the pasta between 4 warmed serving plates. Garnish with sprigs of fresh oregano and serve with freshly grated Parmesan.

1

3

4

Gorgonzola & Pumpkin Pizza

A combination of blue Gorgonzola cheese and pears combine to give a colourful pizza. The wholemeal base adds a nutty flavour and texture.

NUTRITIONAL INFORMATION

Calories	470	Sugars	5g
Protein	17g	Fat	15g
Carbohydrate	72g	Saturates	6g

 1¼ HOURS  35 MINS

SERVES 4

INGREDIENTS

PIZZA DOUGH

- 7 g/¼ oz dried yeast
- 1 tsp sugar
- 250 ml/9 fl oz/1 cup hand-hot water
- 175 g/6 oz wholemeal flour
- 175 g/6 oz strong white flour
- 1 tsp salt
- 1 tbsp olive oil

TOPPING

- 400 g/14 oz pumpkin or squash, peeled and cubed
- 1 tbsp olive oil
- 1 pear, cored, peeled and sliced
- 100 g 3½ oz Gorgonzola cheese
- 1 sprig fresh rosemary, to garnish

1 Place the yeast and sugar in a measuring jug and mix with 50 ml/2 fl oz/4 tbsp of the water. Leave the yeast mixture in a warm place for 15 minutes or until frothy.

2 Mix both of the flours with the salt and make a well in the centre. Add the oil, the yeast mixture and the remaining water. Using a wooden spoon, mix to form a dough.

3 Turn the dough out on to a floured surface and knead for 4–5 minutes or until smooth.

4 Return the dough to the bowl, cover with an oiled sheet of cling film (plastic wrap) and leave to rise for 30 minutes or until doubled in size.

5 Remove the dough from the bowl. Knead the dough for 2 minutes. Using a rolling pin, roll out the dough to form a long oval shape, then place it on an oiled baking tray (cookie sheet), pushing out the edges until even. The dough should be no more than 6 mm/¼ inch thick because it will rise during cooking.

6 To make the topping, place the pumpkin in a shallow roasting tin (pan). Drizzle with the olive oil and cook under a preheated grill (broiler) for 20 minutes or until soft and lightly golden.

7 Top the dough with the pear and the pumpkin, brushing with the oil from the tin (pan). Sprinkle over the Gorgonzola. Bake in a preheated oven, at 200°C/400°F/ Gas Mark 6 for 15 minutes or until the base is golden. Garnish with rosemary.

5

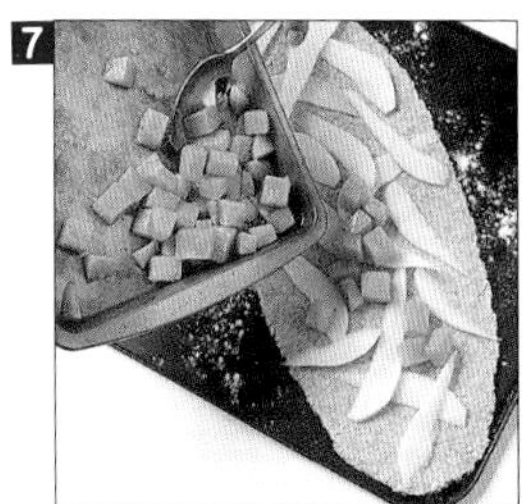
7

7

Ratatouille & Lentil Pizza

Ratatouille and lentils on a wholemeal bread base are topped with cheese and sunflower seeds. The lentils need to be soaked so prepare in advance.

NUTRITIONAL INFORMATION

Calories	377	Sugars	6g
Protein	11g	Fat	19g
Carbohydrate	44g	Saturates	5g

 2½ HOURS  55 MINS

SERVES 4

INGREDIENTS

- 60 g/2 oz green lentils
- ½ small aubergine (eggplant), diced
- 1 small onion, sliced
- 1 garlic clove, crushed
- 3 tbsp olive oil
- ½ courgette (zucchini), sliced
- ½ red (bell) pepper, sliced
- ½ green (bell) pepper, sliced
- 200 g/7 oz can chopped tomatoes
- 1 tbsp chopped fresh oregano or 1 tsp dried
- Basic Pizza Dough (see page 861), made with wholemeal flour
- 60 g/2 oz Cheddar, sliced thinly
- 1 tbsp sunflower seeds
- olive oil, for drizzling
- salt and pepper

1 Soak the lentils in hot water for 30 minutes. Drain and rinse; then cover with fresh water and simmer over a low heat for 10 minutes.

2 Place the aubergine (eggplant) in a colander, sprinkle with a little salt and leave the bitter juices to drain for about 20 minutes. Rinse well and pat dry with paper towels.

3 Fry the onion and garlic gently in the oil for 3 minutes. Add the courgette (zucchini), (bell) peppers and aubergine (eggplant). Cover and leave to cook over a low heat for about 5 minutes.

4 Add the tomatoes, drained lentils, oregano, 2 tablespoons of water and seasoning. Cover and simmer for 15 minutes, stirring occasionally, adding more water if necessary.

5 Roll out or press the dough, using a rolling pin or your hands, into a 25 cm/10 inch circle on a lightly floured work surface. Place on a large greased baking tray (cookie sheet) or pizza pan and push up the edge slightly. Cover and leave the dough to rise slightly for 10 minutes in a warm place.

6 Spread the ratatouille over the dough base almost to the edge. Arrange the cheese slices on top and sprinkle over the sunflower seeds. Drizzle with a little olive oil and season with a little salt and pepper to taste.

7 Bake in a preheated oven, at 200°C/400°F/Gas Mark 6, for 18–20 minutes, or until the edge is crisp and golden brown. Serve immediately.

1

3

6

Creamy Baked Fennel

Fennel tastes fabulous in this creamy sauce, flavoured with caraway seeds. A crunchy breadcrumb topping gives an interesting texture.

NUTRITIONAL INFORMATION

Calories	292	Sugars	5g
Protein	10g	Fat	23g
Carbohydrate	12g	Saturates	14g

 10 MINS  45 MINS

SERVES 4

INGREDIENTS

- 2 tbsp lemon juice
- 2 fennel bulbs, thinly sliced
- 60 g/2 oz/¼ cup butter, plus extra for greasing
- 125 g/4½ oz/¼ cup low-fat soft cheese
- 150 ml/¼ pint/⅔ cup single (light) cream
- 150 ml/¼ pint/⅔ cup milk
- 1 egg, beaten
- 2 tsp caraway seeds
- 60 g/2 oz/1 cup fresh white breadcrumbs
- salt and pepper
- parsley sprigs, to garnish

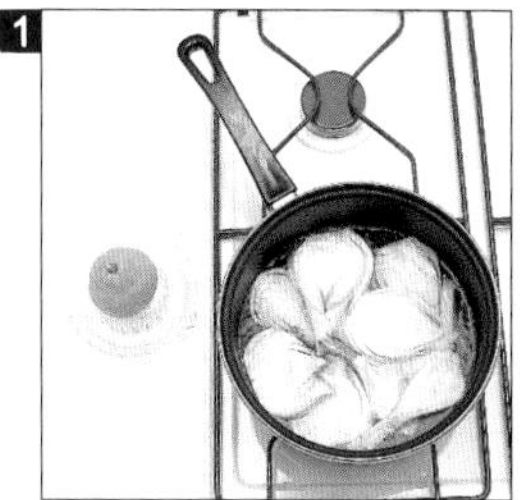

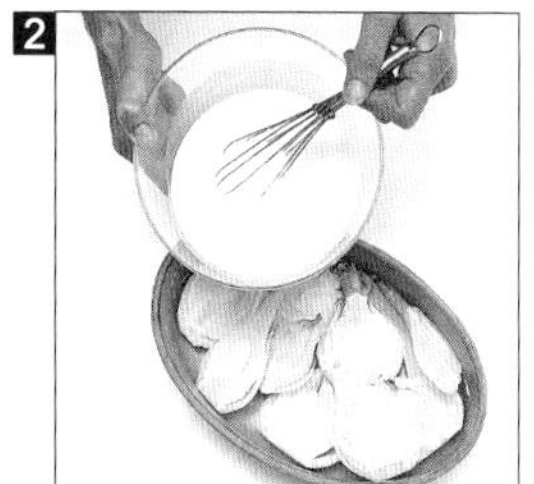

1 Bring a saucepan of water to the boil and add the lemon juice and fennel. Cook for 2–3 minutes to blanch, drain and place in a greased ovenproof dish.

2 Beat the soft cheese in a bowl until smooth. Add the cream, milk and beaten egg, and whisk together until combined. Season with salt and pepper and pour the mixture over the fennel.

3 Melt 15 g/½ oz/1 tbsp of the butter in a small frying pan (skillet) and fry the caraway seeds gently for 1–2 minutes, until they release their aroma. Sprinkle them over the fennel.

4 Melt the remaining butter in a frying pan (skillet). Add the breadcrumbs and fry over a low heat, stirring frequently, until lightly browned. Sprinkle them evenly over the surface of the fennel.

5 Place in a preheated oven, 180°C/350°F/Gas Mark 4, and bake for 25–30 minutes, or until the fennel is tender. Serve immediately, garnished with sprigs of parsley.

Chilli & (Bell) Pepper Pasta

This roasted (bell) pepper and chilli sauce is sweet and spicy – the perfect combination!

NUTRITIONAL INFORMATION

Calories	423	Sugars	5g
Protein	9g	Fat	27g
Carbohydrate	38g	Saturates	4g

 25 MINS  30 MINS

SERVES 4

INGREDIENTS

- 2 red (bell) peppers, halved and deseeded
- 1 small red chilli
- 4 tomatoes, halved
- 2 garlic cloves
- 50 g/1¾ oz ground almonds
- 7 tbsp olive oil
- 675 g/1½ lb fresh pasta or 350 g/12 oz dried pasta
- fresh oregano leaves, to garnish

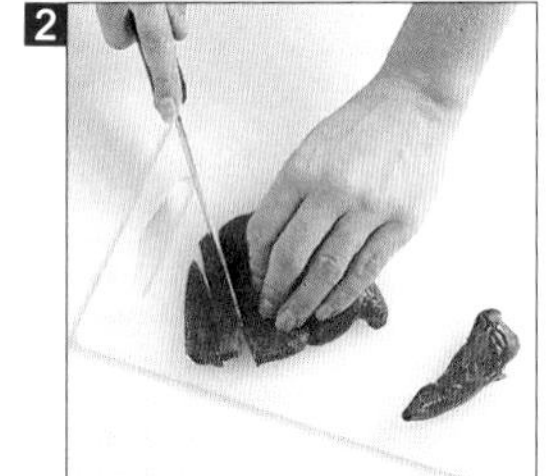

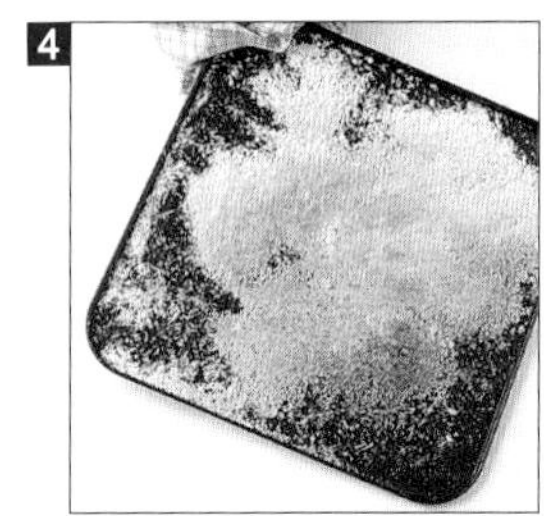

1 Place the (bell) peppers, skin-side up, on a baking tray (cookie sheet) with the chilli and tomatoes. Cook under a preheated grill (broiler) for 15 minutes or until charred. After 10 minutes turn the tomatoes skin-side up. Place the (bell) peppers and chillies in a polythene bag and leave to sweat for 10 minutes.

2 Remove the skin from the (bell) peppers and chillies and slice the flesh into strips, using a sharp knife.

3 Peel the garlic, and peel and deseed the tomatoes.

4 Place the almonds on a baking tray (cookie sheet) and place under the grill (broiler) for 2–3 minutes until golden.

5 Using a food processor, blend the (bell) pepper, chilli, garlic and tomatoes to make a purée. Keep the motor running and slowly add the olive oil to form a thick sauce. Alternatively, mash the mixture with a fork and beat in the olive oil, drop by drop.

6 Stir the toasted ground almonds into the mixture.

7 Warm the sauce in a saucepan until it is heated through.

8 Cook the pasta in a saucepan of boiling water for 8–10 minutes if using dried, or 3–5 minutes if using fresh. Drain the pasta thoroughly and transfer to a serving dish. Pour over the sauce and toss to mix. Garnish with the fresh oregano leaves.

VARIATION

Add 2 tablespoons of red wine vinegar to the sauce and use as a dressing for a cold pasta salad, if you wish.

Red Curry with Cashews

This is a wonderfully quick dish to prepare. If you don't time to prepare the curry paste, it can be bought ready-made.

NUTRITIONAL INFORMATION

Calories	274	Sugars	5g
Protein	10g	Fat	10g
Carbohydrate	38g	Saturates	3g

25 MINS — 15 MINS

SERVES 4

INGREDIENTS

- 250 ml/9 fl oz/1 cup coconut milk
- 1 kaffir lime leaf
- ¼ tsp light soy sauce
- 60 g/2 oz/4 baby corn cobs, halved lengthways
- 125 g/4½ oz/1¼ cups broccoli florets
- 125 g/4½ oz French (green) beans, cut into 5 cm/2 inch pieces
- 25 g/1 oz/¼ cup cashew nuts
- 15 fresh basil leaves
- 1 tbsp chopped coriander (cilantro)
- 1 tbsp chopped roast peanuts, to garnish

RED CURRY PASTE

- 7 fresh red chillies, halved, seeded and blanched
- 2 tsp cumin seeds
- 2 tsp coriander seeds
- 2.5 cm/1 inch piece galangal, chopped
- ½ stalk lemon grass, chopped
- 1 tsp salt
- grated rind of 1 lime
- 4 garlic cloves, chopped
- 3 shallots, chopped
- 2 kaffir lime leaves, shredded
- 1 tbsp vegetable oil

1 To make the curry paste, grind all the ingredients together in a large mortar with a pestle or a grinder. Alternatively, process briefly in a food processor. The quantity of red curry paste is more than required for this recipe. However, it will keep for up to 3 weeks in a sealed container in the refrigerator.

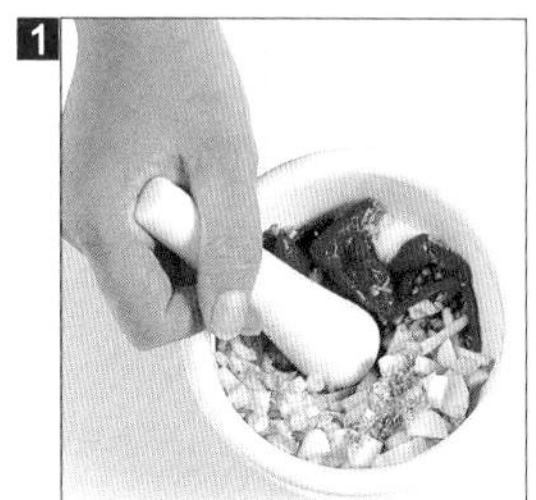
1

2 Put a wok or large, heavy-based frying pan (skillet) over a high heat, add 3 tablespoons of the red curry paste and stir until it gives off its aroma. Reduce the heat to medium.

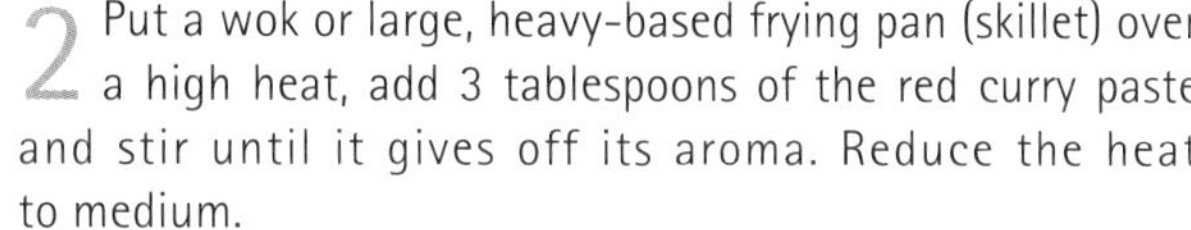

3 Add the coconut milk, kaffir lime leaf, light soy sauce, baby corn cobs, broccoli florets, French (green) beans and cashew nuts. Bring to the boil and simmer for about 10 minutes, until the vegetables are cooked, but still firm and crunchy.

3

4 Remove and discard the lime leaf and stir in the basil leaves and coriander (cilantro). Transfer to a warmed serving dish, garnish with peanuts and serve immediately.

4

Lentil & Vegetable Shells

These stuffed aubergines (eggplants) are delicious served hot or cold, topped with natural (unsweetened) yogurt or cucumber raita.

NUTRITIONAL INFORMATION

Calories	386	Sugars	9g
Protein	14g	Fat	24g
Carbohydrate	30g	Saturates	3g

 25 MINS  1 HOUR

SERVES 6

INGREDIENTS

- 225 g/8 oz/1⅓ cup continental lentils
- 850 ml/1½ pints/3¾ cups water
- 2 garlic cloves, crushed
- 3 well-shaped aubergines (eggplants)
- 150 ml/¼ pint/⅔ cup vegetable oil, plus extra for brushing
- 2 onions, chopped
- 4 tomatoes, chopped
- 2 tsp cumin seeds
- 1 tsp ground cinnamon
- 2 tbsp mild curry paste
- 1 tsp minced chilli
- 2 tbsp chopped mint
- salt and pepper
- natural (unsweetened) yogurt and mint sprigs, to serve

1. Rinse the lentils under cold running water. Drain and place in a saucepan with the water and garlic. Cover and simmer for 30 minutes.

1

2. Cook the aubergines (eggplants) in a saucepan of boiling water for 5 minutes. Drain, then plunge into cold water for 5 minutes. Drain again, then cut the aubergines (eggplants) in half lengthways and scoop out most of the flesh and reserve, leaving a 1 cm/½ inch thick border to form a shell.

3. Place the aubergine (eggplant) shells in a shallow greased ovenproof dish, brush with a little oil and sprinkle with salt and pepper. Cook in a preheated oven, 190°C/375°F/Gas Mark 5, for 10 minutes. Meanwhile, heat half the remaining oil in a frying pan, add the onions and tomatoes and fry gently for 5 minutes. Chop the reserved aubergine (eggplant) flesh, add to the pan with the spices and cook gently for 5 minutes. Season with salt.

3

4. Stir in the lentils, most of the remaining oil, reserving a little for later, and the mint. Spoon the mixture into the shells. Drizzle with remaining oil and bake for 15 minutes. Serve hot or cold, topped with a spoonful of natural (unsweetened) yogurt and mint sprigs.

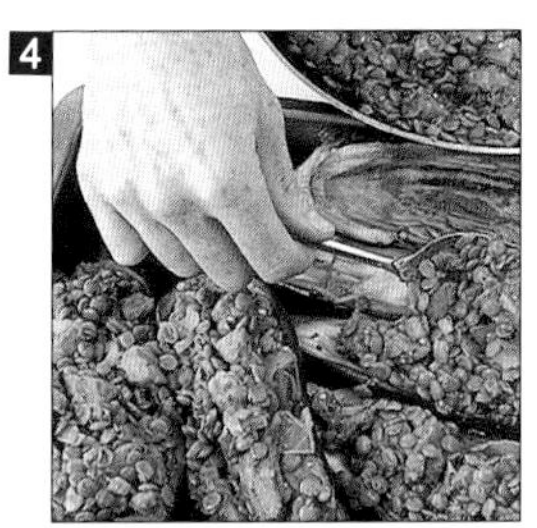

4

COOK'S TIP

Choose nice plump aubergines (eggplants), rather than thin tapering ones, as they retain their shape better when filled and baked with a stuffing.

Vegetable Stir-Fry

A range of delicious flavours are captured in this simple recipe which is ideal if you are in a hurry.

NUTRITIONAL INFORMATION

Calories	127	Sugars	7g
Protein	4g	Fat	9g
Carbohydrate	8g	Saturates	1g

 5 MINS  25 MINS

SERVES 4

INGREDIENTS

- 3 tbsp vegetable oil
- 8 baby onions, halved
- 1 aubergine (eggplant), cubed
- 225 g/8 oz courgettes (zucchini), sliced
- 225 g/8 oz open-cap mushrooms, halved
- 2 cloves garlic, crushed
- 400 g/14 oz can chopped tomatoes
- 2 tbsp sundried tomato purée (paste)
- 2 tbsp soy sauce
- 1 tsp sesame oil
- 1 tbsp Chinese rice wine or dry sherry
- freshly ground black pepper
- fresh basil leaves, to garnish

2

3

5

1 Heat the vegetable oil in a large preheated wok or frying pan (skillet).

2 Add the baby onions and aubergine (eggplant) to the wok or frying pan (skillet) and stir-fry for 5 minutes, or until the vegetables are golden and just beginning to soften.

3 Add the sliced courgettes (zucchini), mushrooms, garlic, chopped tomatoes and tomato purée (paste) to the wok and stir-fry for about 5 minutes. Reduce the heat and leave to simmer for 10 minutes, or until the vegetables are tender.

4 Add the soy sauce, sesame oil and rice wine or sherry to the wok, bring back to the boil and cook for 1 minute.

5 Season the vegetable stir-fry with freshly ground black pepper and scatter with fresh basil leaves. Serve immediately.

COOK'S TIP

Basil has a very strong flavour which is perfect with vegetables and Chinese flavourings. Instead of using basil simply as a garnish in this dish, try adding a handful of fresh basil leaves to the stir-fry in step 4.

Deep South Rice & Beans

Cajun spices add a flavour of the American Deep South to this colourful rice and red kidney bean salad.

NUTRITIONAL INFORMATION

Calories	336	Sugars	8g
Protein	7g	Fat	13g
Carbohydrate	51g	Saturates	2g

 10 MINS  15 MINS

SERVES 4

INGREDIENTS

175 g/6 oz/scant 1 cup long grain rice

4 tbsp olive oil

1 small green (bell) pepper, seeded and chopped

1 small red (bell) pepper, seeded and chopped

1 onion, finely chopped

1 small red or green chilli, seeded and finely chopped

2 tomatoes, chopped

125 g/4½ oz/½ cup canned red kidney beans, rinsed and drained

1 tbsp chopped fresh basil

2 tsp chopped fresh thyme

1 tsp Cajun spice

salt and pepper

fresh basil leaves, to garnish

2

4

5

1 Cook the rice in plenty of boiling, lightly salted water for about 12 minutes, until just tender. Rinse with cold water and drain well.

2 Meanwhile, heat the olive oil in a frying pan (skillet) and fry the green and red (bell) peppers and onion gently for about 5 minutes, until softened.

3 Add the chilli and tomatoes, and cook for a further 2 minutes.

4 Add the vegetable mixture and red kidney beans to the rice. Stir well to combine thoroughly.

5 Stir the chopped herbs and Cajun spice into the rice mixture. Season to taste with salt and pepper, and serve, garnished with basil leaves.

Eight Jewel Vegetables

This recipe, as the title suggests, is a colourful mixture of eight vegetables, cooked in a black bean and soy sauce.

NUTRITIONAL INFORMATION

Calories	110	Sugars	3g
Protein	4g	Fat	8g
Carbohydrate	7g	Saturates	1g

 5 MINS  10 MINS

SERVES 4

INGREDIENTS

- 2 tbsp peanut oil
- 6 spring onions (scallions), sliced
- 3 garlic cloves, crushed
- 1 green (bell) pepper, seeded and diced
- 1 red (bell) pepper, seeded and diced
- 1 fresh red chilli, sliced
- 2 tbsp chopped water chestnuts
- 1 courgette (zucchini), chopped
- 125 g/4½ oz oyster mushrooms
- 3 tbsp black bean sauce
- 2 tsp Chinese rice wine or dry sherry
- 4 tbsp dark soy sauce
- 1 tsp dark brown sugar
- 2 tbsp water
- 1 tsp sesame oil

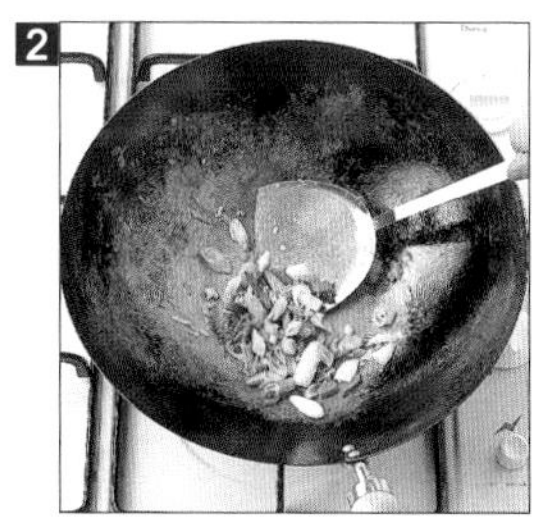

2

3

4

1 Heat the peanut oil in a preheated wok or large frying pan (skillet) until it is almost smoking.

2 Lower the heat slightly, add the spring onions (scallions) and garlic and stir-fry for about 30 seconds.

3 Add the red and green (bell) peppers, fresh red chilli, water chestnuts and courgette (zucchini) to the wok or frying pan (skillet) and stir-fry for 2–3 minutes, or until the vegetables are just beginning to soften.

4 Add the oyster mushrooms, black bean sauce, Chinese rice wine or dry sherry, dark soy sauce, dark brown sugar and water to the wok and stir-fry for a further 4 minutes.

5 Sprinkle the stir-fry with sesame oil and serve immediately.

COOK'S TIP

Eight jewels or treasures form a traditional part of the Chinese New Year celebrations, which start in the last week of the old year. The Kitchen God, an important figure, is sent to give a report to heaven, returning on New Year's Eve in time for the feasting.

Stuffed Vegetables

You can fill your favourite vegetables with this nutty-tasting combination of cracked wheat, tomatoes and cucumber.

NUTRITIONAL INFORMATION

Calories	194	Sugars	7g
Protein	5g	Fat	4g
Carbohydrate	36g	Saturates	0.5g

 40 MINS  25 MINS

SERVES 4

INGREDIENTS

- 4 large beefsteak tomatoes
- 4 medium courgettes (zucchini)
- 2 orange (bell) peppers
- salt and pepper

FILLING

- 225 g/8 oz/1¼ cups cracked wheat
- ¼ cucumber
- 1 medium red onion
- 2 tbsp lemon juice
- 2 tbsp chopped fresh coriander (cilantro)
- 2 tbsp chopped fresh mint
- 1 tbsp olive oil
- 2 tsp cumin seeds

TO SERVE

- warm pitta bread and low-fat hummus

1 Preheat the oven to 200°C/400°F/Gas Mark 6. Cut off the tops of the tomatoes and reserve. Using a teaspoon, scoop out the tomato pulp, chop and place in a bowl. Season the tomato shells, then turn them upside down on absorbent kitchen paper.

1

2 Trim the courgettes (zucchini) and cut a V-shaped groove lengthwise down each one. Finely chop the cut-out courgette (zucchini) flesh and add to the tomato pulp. Season the courgettes (zucchini) shells and set aside. Halve the (bell) peppers. Leaving the stalks intact, cut out the seeds and discard. Season the (bell) pepper shells and set aside.

2

3 To make the filling, soak the cracked wheat according to the instructions on the packet. Finely chop the cucumber and add to the reserved tomato pulp and courgette (zucchini) mixture. Finely chop the red onion, and add to the vegetable mixture with the lemon juice, herbs, olive oil, cumin and seasoning and mix together well.

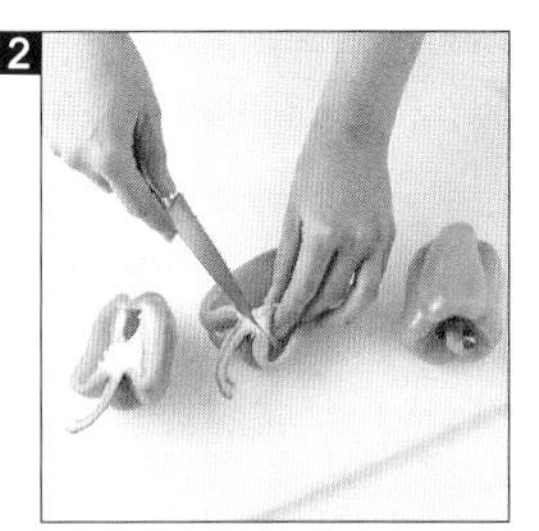
2

4 When the wheat has soaked, mix with the vegetables and stuff into the tomato, courgette (zucchini) and (bell) pepper shells. Place the tops on the tomatoes, transfer to a roasting tin (pan) and bake for 20–25 minutes until cooked through. Drain and serve pitta bread and hummus.

COOK'S TIP

It is a good idea to blanch vegetables (except for tomatoes) before stuffing. Blanch (bell) peppers, courgettes (zucchini) and aubergine (eggplant) for 5 minutes.

Italian Stuffed (Bell) Peppers

Halved (bell) peppers are stuffed with the flavours of Italy in this sunshine-bright dish.

NUTRITIONAL INFORMATION

Calories	193	Sugars	8g
Protein	2g	Fat	17g
Carbohydrate	9g	Saturates	2g

 20 MINS 25 MINS

SERVES 4

INGREDIENTS

- 1 red (bell) pepper
- 1 green (bell) pepper
- 1 yellow (bell) pepper
- 1 orange (bell) pepper
- 6 tbsp olive oil
- 1 small red onion, sliced
- 1 small aubergine (eggplant), chopped roughly
- 125 g/4½ oz button mushrooms, wiped
- 125 g/4½ oz/1 cup cherry tomatoes, halved
- few drops of mushroom ketchup
- handful of fresh basil leaves, torn into pieces
- 2 tbsp lemon juice
- salt and pepper
- sprigs of fresh basil, to garnish
- lemon wedges, to serve

1 Halve the (bell) peppers, remove the cores and deseed them. Sprinkle over a few drops of olive oil and season.

2 Heat the remaining olive oil in a frying pan (skillet). Add the onion, aubergine (eggplant) and mushrooms, and fry for 3–4 minutes, stirring frequently. Remove from the heat and transfer to a mixing bowl.

3 Add the cherry tomatoes, mushroom ketchup, basil leaves and lemon juice to the aubergine (eggplant) mixture. Season well with salt and pepper.

4 Spoon the aubergine (eggplant) mixture into the (bell) pepper halves. Enclose in foil parcels (packages) and barbecue (grill) over the hot coals for about 15–20 minutes, turning once.

5 Unwrap carefully and serve garnished with sprigs of fresh basil. Serve with lemon wedges.

VARIATION

Dried herbs can be used instead of fresh ones if they are unavailable. Substitute 1 tsp dried basil or use mixed dried Italian herbs as an alternative. If you wish, top these stuffed (bell) peppers with grated Mozzarella or Cheddar cheese – 75 g/3 oz/¼ cup will be sufficient.

Ratatouille Vegetable Grill

Ratatouille is a classic dish of vegetables cooked in a tomato and herb sauce. Here it is topped with diced potatoes and cheese.

NUTRITIONAL INFORMATION

Calories	287	Sugars	13g
Protein	14g	Fat	4g
Carbohydrate	53g	Saturates	2g

 15 MINS 45 MINS

SERVES 4

INGREDIENTS

- 2 medium onions
- 1 garlic clove
- 1 medium red (bell) pepper
- 1 medium green (bell) pepper
- 1 medium aubergine (eggplant)
- 2 medium courgettes (zucchini)
- 2 x 400 g/14 oz cans chopped tomatoes
- 1 bouquet garni
- 2 tbsp tomato purée (paste)
- 900 g/2 lb potatoes
- 75 g/2¾ oz reduced-fat mature (sharp) Cheddar cheese, grated
- salt and pepper
- 2 tbsp snipped fresh chives, to garnish

1 Peel and finely chop the onions and garlic. Rinse, deseed and slice the (bell) peppers. Rinse, trim and cut the aubergine (eggplant) into small dice. Rinse, trim and thinly slice the courgettes (zucchini).

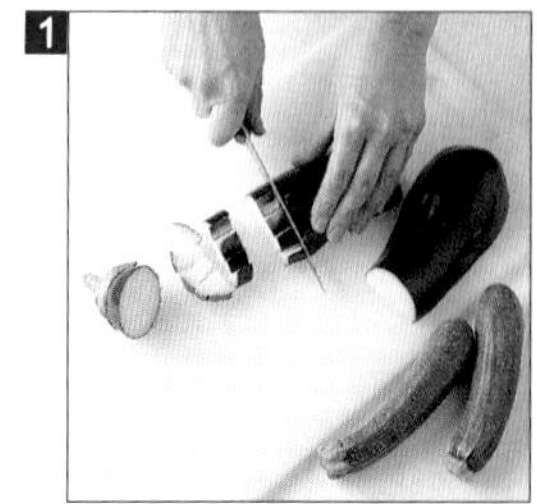

2 Place the onion, garlic and (bell) peppers into a large saucepan. Add the tomatoes, and stir in the bouquet garni, tomato purée (paste) and salt and pepper to taste. Bring to the boil, cover and simmer for 10 minutes, stirring half-way through. Stir in the prepared aubergine (eggplant) and courgettes (zucchini) and cook, uncovered, for a further 10 minutes, stirring occasionally.

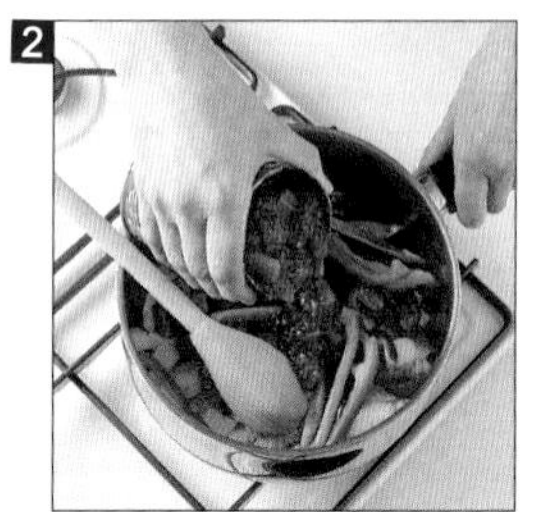

3 Meanwhile, peel the potatoes and cut into 2.5 cm/1 inch cubes. Place the potatoes into another saucepan and cover with water. Bring to the boil and cook for 10–12 minutes until tender. Drain and set aside.

4 Transfer the vegetables to a heatproof gratin dish. Arrange the cooked potatoevenly over the vegetables.

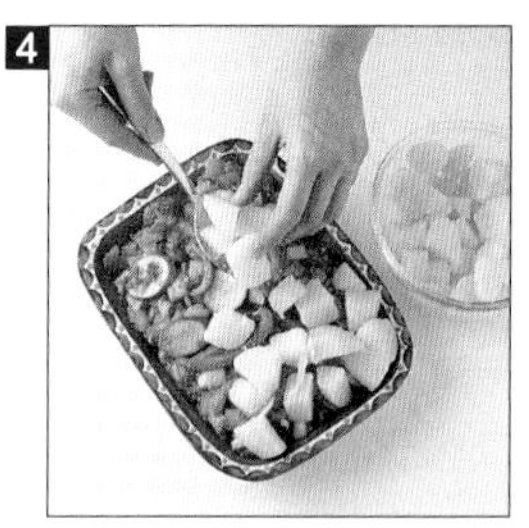

5 Preheat the grill (broiler) to medium. Sprinkle grated cheese over the potatoes and place under the grill for 5 minutes until golden, bubbling and hot. Serve garnished with snipped chives.

VARIATION

You can vary the vegetables in this dish depending on seasonal availability and personal preference. Try broccoli, carrots or sweetcorn, if you prefer.

Char-Grilled Kebabs

This medley of (bell) peppers, courgettes (zucchini), aubergine (eggplant) and red onion can be served on its own or as an unusual side dish.

NUTRITIONAL INFORMATION

Calories	66	Sugars	7g
Protein	2g	Fat	3g
Carbohydrate	7g	Saturates	0.5g

 15 MINS — 15 MINS

SERVES 4

INGREDIENTS

- 1 large red (bell) pepper
- 1 large green (bell) pepper
- 1 large orange (bell) pepper
- 1 large courgette (zucchini)
- 4 baby aubergines (eggplant)
- 2 medium red onions
- 2 tbsp lemon juice
- 1 tbsp olive oil
- 1 garlic clove, crushed
- 1 tbsp chopped, fresh rosemary or 1 tsp dried rosemary
- salt and pepper

TO SERVE

- cracked wheat, cooked
- tomato and olive relish

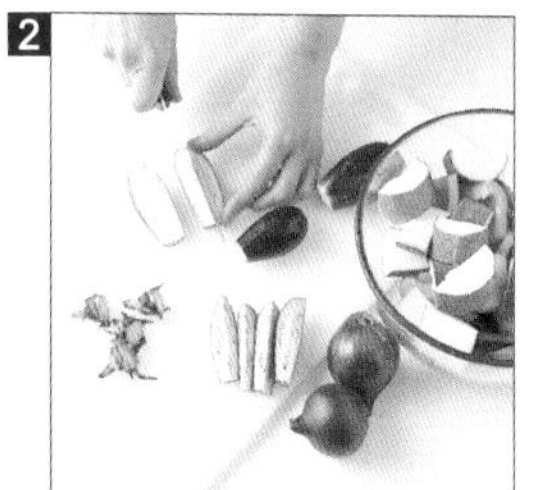

1 Halve and deseed the (bell) peppers and cut into even sized pieces, about 2.5 cm/1 inch wide.

2 Trim the courgettes (zucchini), cut in half lengthways and slice into 2.5 cm/1 inch pieces. Place the (bell) peppers and courgettes (zucchini) in a large bowl.

3 Trim the aubergines (eggplant) and quarter them lengthways. Peel both the onions, then cut each one into 8 even-sized wedges.

4 Add the pieces of aubergine (eggplant) and onions to the bowl containing the wedges of (bell) peppers and courgettes (zucchini).

5 In a small bowl, whisk together the lemon juice, olive oil, garlic, rosemary and seasoning.

6 Pour the mixture over the vegetables and stir to coat evenly.

7 Preheat the grill (broiler) to medium. Thread the vegetables on to 8 metal or pre-soaked wooden skewers. Arrange the kebabs on the rack and cook for 10–12 minutes, turning frequently until the vegetables are lightly charred and just softened.

8 Drain the vegetable kebabs and serve on a bed of cracked wheat accompanied with a tomato and olive relish.

Homemade Noodles

These noodles are simple to make; you do not need a pasta-making machine as they are rolled out by hand.

NUTRITIONAL INFORMATION

Calories	294	Sugars	3g
Protein	7g	Fat	15g
Carbohydrate	35g	Saturates	2g

 20 MINS  15 MINS

SERVES 2–4

INGREDIENTS

NOODLES

- 125 g/4½ oz/1 cup plain (all-purpose) flour
- 2 tbsp cornflour (cornstarch)
- ½ tsp salt
- 125 ml/4 fl oz/½ cup boiling water
- 5 tbsp vegetable oil

STIR-FRY

- 1 courgette (zucchini), cut into thin sticks
- 1 celery stick, cut into thin sticks
- 1 carrot, cut into thin sticks
- 125 g/4½ oz open-cup mushrooms, sliced
- 125 g/4½ oz broccoli florets and stalks, peeled and thinly sliced
- 1 leek, sliced
- 125 g/4½ oz/2 cups bean sprouts
- 1 tbsp soy sauce
- 2 tsp rice wine vinegar
- ½ tsp sugar

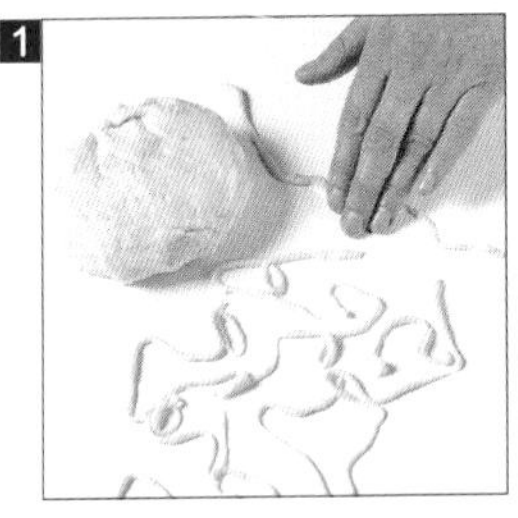
1

2

3

1 To prepare the noodles, sift the flour, cornflour (cornstarch) and salt into a bowl. Make a well in the centre and pour in the boiling water and 1 teaspoon of oil. Mix quickly to make a soft dough. Cover and leave for 5–6 minutes.

2 Make the noodles by breaking off small pieces of dough and rolling into balls. Roll each ball across a very lightly oiled work surface (counter) with the palm of your hand to form thin noodles. Do not worry if some of the noodles break into shorter lengths. Set the noodles aside.

3 Heat 3 tablespoons of oil in a wok. Add the noodles in batches and fry over a high heat for 1 minute. Reduce the heat and cook for a further 2 minutes. Remove and drain on kitchen paper (paper towels). Set aside.

4 Heat the remaining oil in the pan. Add the courgette (zucchini), celery and carrot, and stir-fry for 1 minute. Add the mushrooms, broccoli and leek, and stir-fry for a further minute. Stir in the remaining ingredients and mix well until thoroughly heated.

5 Add the noodles and cook over a high heat, tossing to mix the ingredients. Serve immediately.

Layered Vegetable Gratin

In this tasty recipe an assortment of vegetables are cooked in a light nutmeg sauce with a potato and cheese topping.

NUTRITIONAL INFORMATION

Calories	236	Sugars	9g
Protein	9g	Fat	9g
Carbohydrate	31g	Saturates	3g

 25 MINS  1½ HOURS

SERVES 6

INGREDIENTS

- 225 g/8 oz/2 large carrots
- 225 g/8 oz baby parsnips
- 1 fennel bulb
- 500 g/1 lb 2 oz/3 potatoes
- 90 g/3 oz/⅓ cup low-fat spread
- 25 g/1 oz/¼ cup plain (all-purpose) flour
- 300 ml/½ pint/1¼ cups skimmed milk
- ½ tsp ground nutmeg
- 1 egg, beaten
- 25 g/1 oz/¼ cup freshly grated Parmesan cheese
- salt and pepper

TO SERVE

- crusty bread
- tomato salad

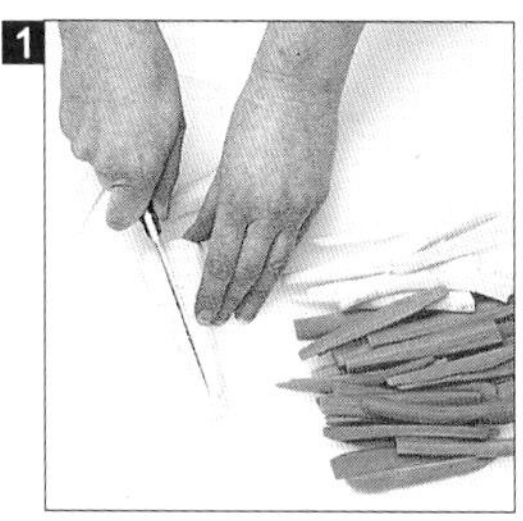

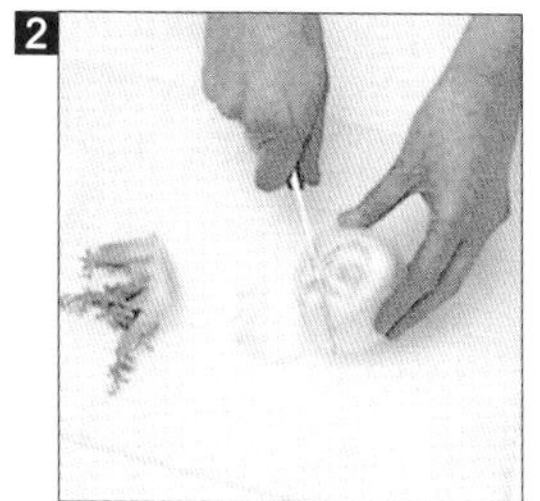

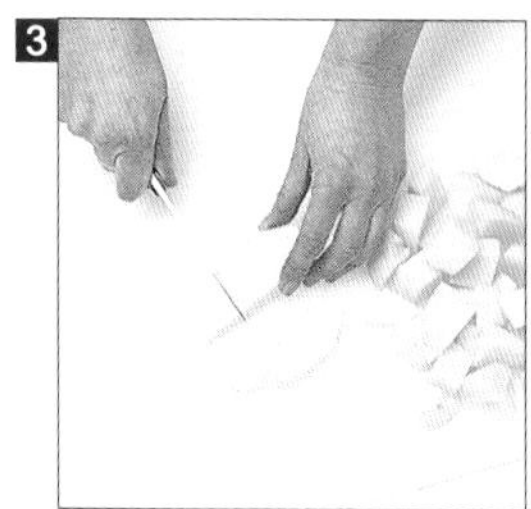

1 Cut the carrots and parsnips into thin strips lengthways. Cook in boiling water for 5 minutes. Drain well and transfer to an ovenproof baking dish.

2 Thinly slice the fennel and cook in boiling water for 2–3 minutes. Drain well and add to the carrots and parsnips. Season.

3 Peel and dice the potatoes into 2 cm/¾ inch cubes. Cook in boiling water for 6 minutes. Drain well.

4 Gently melt half the low-fat spread and stir in the flour. Remove from the heat and gradually mix in the milk.

5 Return to the heat and stir until thickened. Season and stir in the nutmeg. Cool for 10 minutes.

6 Beat in the egg and spoon over the vegetables. Arrange the potatoes on top and sprinkle over the cheese.

7 Dot the potatoes with the remaining low-fat spread. Bake in a preheated oven at 180°C/350°F/Gas Mark 4 for 1 hour until the vegetables are tender.

8 Serve the vegetable gratin as a light meal with wedges of crusty bread and a tomato salad, or as an accompaniment to a light main course.

Stuffed Globe Artichokes

This imaginative and attractive recipe for artichokes stuffed with nuts, tomatoes, olives and mushrooms, has been adapted for the microwave.

NUTRITIONAL INFORMATION

Calories	248	Sugars	8g
Protein	5g	Fat	19g
Carbohydrate	16g	Saturates	2g

 30 MINS 25 MINS

SERVES 4

INGREDIENTS

- 4 globe artichokes
- 8 tbsp water
- 4 tbsp lemon juice
- 1 onion, chopped
- 1 garlic clove, crushed
- 2 tbsp olive oil
- 225 g/8 oz/2 cups button mushrooms, chopped
- 40 g/1½ oz/½ cup pitted black olives, sliced
- 60 g/2 oz/¼ cup sun-dried tomatoes in oil, drained and chopped
- 1 tbsp chopped fresh basil
- 60 g/2 oz/1 cup fresh white breadcrumbs
- 25 g/1 oz/¼ cup pine nuts, toasted
- oil from the jar of sun-dried tomatoes for drizzling
- salt and pepper

1 Cut the stalks and lower leaves off the artichokes. Snip off the leaf tips with scissors. Place 2 artichokes in a large bowl with half the water and half the lemon juice. Cover and cook on HIGH power for 10 minutes, turning the artichokes over halfway through, until a leaf pulls away easily from the base. Leave to stand, covered, for 3 minutes before draining. Turn the artichokes upside down and leave to cool. Repeat to cook the remaining artichokes.

2 Place the onion, garlic and oil in a bowl. Cover and cook on HIGH power for 2 minutes, stirring once. Add the mushrooms, olives and sun-dried tomatoes. Cover and cook on HIGH power for 2 minutes.

3 Stir in the basil, breadcrumbs and pine nuts. Season to taste with salt and pepper.

4 Turn the artichokes the right way up and carefully pull the leaves apart. Remove the purple-tipped central leaves. Using a teaspoon, scrape out the hairy choke and discard.

5 Divide the stuffing into 4 equal portions and spoon into the centre of each artichoke. Push the leaves back around the stuffing.

6 Arrange in a shallow dish and drizzle over a little oil from the jar of sun-dried tomatoes. Cook on HIGH power for 7–8 minutes to reheat, turning the artichokes around halfway through.

1

4

5

Potato Hash

This is a variation of the American dish, beef hash, which was made with salt beef and leftovers, and served to seagoing New Englanders.

NUTRITIONAL INFORMATION

Calories	302	Sugars	05g
Protein	15g	Fat	10g
Carbohydrate	40g	Saturates	4g

5 MINS 30 MINS

SERVES 4

INGREDIENTS

- 25 g/1 oz/2 tbsp butter
- 1 red onion, halved and sliced
- 1 carrot, diced
- 25 g/1 oz French (green) beans, halved
- 3 large waxy potatoes, diced
- 2 tbsp plain (all purpose) flour
- 600 ml/1 pint/1¼ cups vegetable stock
- 225 g/8 oz tofu (bean curd), diced
- salt and pepper
- chopped fresh parsley, to garnish

1 Melt the butter in a frying pan (skillet).

2 Add the onion, carrot, French (green) beans and potatoes and fry gently, stirring, for 5-7 minutes or until the vegetables begin to brown.

3 Add the flour to the frying pan (skillet) and cook for 1 minute, stirring constantly.

4 Gradually pour in the stock.

5 Reduce the heat and leave the mixture to simmer for 15 minutes or until the potatoes are tender.

6 Add the diced tofu (bean curd) to the mixture and cook for a further 5 minutes.

7 Season to taste with salt and pepper.

8 Sprinkle the chopped parsley over the top of the potato hash to garnish, then serve hot from the pan (skillet).

COOK'S TIP

Hash is an American term meaning to chop food into small pieces. Therefore a traditional hash dish is made from chopped fresh ingredients, such as roast beef or corned beef, (bell) peppers, onion and celery, often served with gravy.

Basil & Tomato Pasta

Roasting the tomatoes gives a sweeter flavour to this sauce. Buy Italian tomatoes, such as plum or flavia, as these have a better flavour and colour.

NUTRITIONAL INFORMATION

Calories	177	Sugars	4g
Protein	5g	Fat	4g
Carbohydrate	31g	Saturates	1g

 15 MINS  35 MINS

SERVES 4

INGREDIENTS

- 1 tbsp olive oil
- 2 sprigs rosemary
- 2 cloves garlic
- 450 g/1 lb tomatoes, halved
- 1 tbsp sun-dried tomato paste
- 12 fresh basil leaves, plus extra to garnish
- salt and pepper
- 675 g/1½ lb fresh farfalle or 350 g/12 oz dried farfalle

2

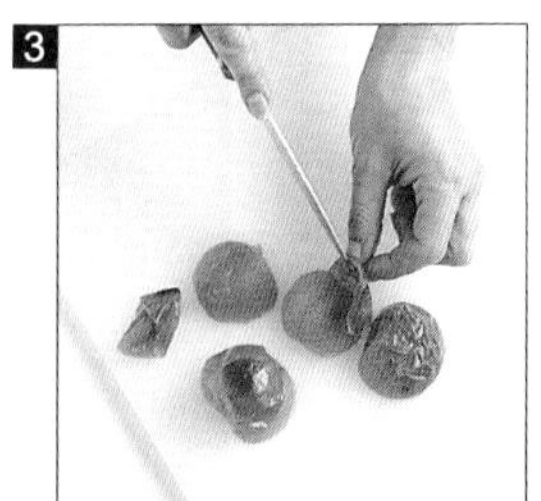
3

4

1 Place the oil, rosemary, garlic and tomatoes, skin side up, in a shallow roasting tin (pan).

2 Drizzle with a little oil and cook under a preheated grill (broiler) for 20 minutes or until the tomato skins are slightly charred.

3 Peel the skin from the tomatoes. Roughly chop the tomato flesh and place in a pan.

4 Squeeze the pulp from the garlic cloves and mix with the tomato flesh and sun-dried tomato paste.

5 Roughly tear the fresh basil leaves into smaller pieces and then stir them into the sauce. Season with a little salt and pepper to taste. Set aside.

6 Cook the farfalle in a saucepan of boiling water for 8–10 minutes or until it is cooked through, but still has 'bite'. Drain well.

7 Gently re-heat the tomato and basil sauce, stirring.

8 Transfer the farfalle to serving plates and pour over the basil and tomato sauce. Serve at once.

COOK'S TIP

This sauce tastes just as good when served cold in a pasta salad.

Pasta Provençale

A Mediterranean mixture of red (bell) peppers, garlic and courgettes (zucchini) cooked in olive oil and tossed with pasta.

NUTRITIONAL INFORMATION

Calories	487	Sugars	14g
Protein	17g	Fat	24g
Carbohydrate	53g	Saturates	8g

5 MINS 20 MINS

SERVES 4

INGREDIENTS

- 3 tbsp olive oil
- 1 onion, sliced
- 2 garlic cloves, chopped
- 3 red (bell) peppers, seeded and cut into strips
- 3 courgettes (zucchini), sliced
- 400 g/14 oz can chopped tomatoes
- 3 tbsp sun-dried tomato paste
- 2 tbsp chopped fresh basil
- 225 g/8 oz fresh pasta spirals
- 125 g/4½ oz/1 cup grated Gruyère cheese
- salt and pepper
- fresh basil sprigs, to garnish

1 Heat the oil in a heavy-based saucepan or flameproof casserole. Add the onion and garlic and cook, stirring occasionally, until softened. Add the (bell) peppers and courgettes (zucchini) and fry, stirring occasionally, for 5 minutes.

2 Add the tomatoes, sun-dried tomato paste and basil and season to taste with salt and pepper. Cover and cook for a further 5 minutes.

3 Meanwhile, bring a large saucepan of salted water to the boil and add the pasta. Stir and bring back to the boil. Reduce the heat slightly and cook, uncovered, for 3 minutes, until just tender. Drain thoroughly and add to the vegetables. Toss gently to mix well.

4 Transfer to a shallow flameproof dish and sprinkle with the cheese.

5 Cook under a preheated grill (broiler) for 5 minutes, until the cheese is golden brown and bubbling. Garnish with basil sprigs and serve immediately.

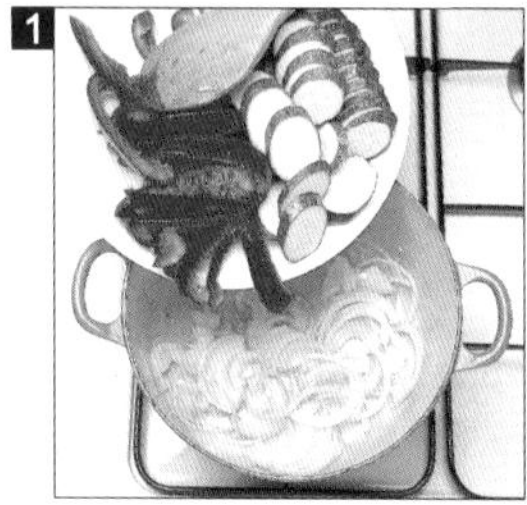

Tomato Sauce & (Bell) Peppers

This pizza is made with a pastry base flavoured with cheese and topped with a delicious tomato sauce and roasted (bell) peppers.

NUTRITIONAL INFORMATION

Calories	611	Sugars	8g
Protein	14g	Fat	38g
Carbohydrate	56g	Saturates	21g

 1½ HOURS  55 MINS

SERVES 4

INGREDIENTS

- 225 g/8 oz plain (all-purpose) flour
- 125 g/4½ oz butter, diced
- ½ tsp salt
- 2 tbsp dried Parmesan cheese
- 1 egg, beaten
- 2 tbsp cold water
- 2 tbsp olive oil
- 1 large onion, finely chopped
- 1 garlic clove, chopped
- 400 g/14 oz can chopped tomatoes
- 4 tbsp concentrated tomato purée (paste)
- 1 red (bell) pepper, halved
- 5 sprigs of thyme, stalks removed
- 6 black olives, pitted and halved
- 25 g/1 oz Parmesan cheese, grated

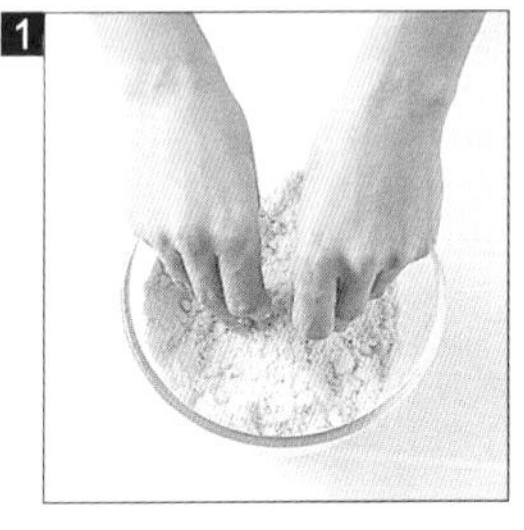
1

1

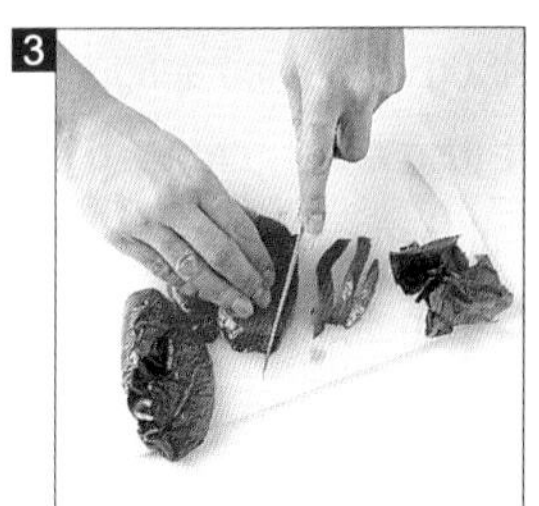
3

1 Sift the flour and rub in the butter to make breadcrumbs. Stir in the salt and dried Parmesan. Add the egg and 1 tablespoon of the water and mix with a round-bladed knife. Add more water if necessary to make a soft dough. Cover with cling film (plastic wrap) and chill for 30 minutes.

2 Meanwhile, heat the oil in a frying pan (skillet) and cook the onions and garlic for about 5 minutes or until golden. Add the tomatoes and cook for 8–10 minutes. Stir in the tomato purée (paste).

3 Place the (bell) peppers, skin-side up, on a baking tray (cookie sheet) and cook under a preheated grill (broiler) for 15 minutes until charred. Place in a plastic bag and leave to sweat for 10 minutes. Peel off the skin and slice the flesh into thin strips.

4 Roll out the dough to fit a 23 cm/9 inch loose base fluted flan tin (pan). Line with foil and bake in a preheated oven, at 200°C/400°F/Gas Mark 6, for 10 minutes or until just set. Remove the foil and bake for a further 5 minutes until lightly golden. Leave to cool slightly.

5 Spoon the tomato sauce over the pastry base and top with the (bell) peppers, thyme, olives and fresh Parmesan. Return to the oven for 15 minutes or until the pastry is crisp. Serve warm or cold.

Spinach & Ricotta Pie

This puff pastry pie looks impressive, but it is actually fairly easy and quite quick to make. Serve it hot or cold.

NUTRITIONAL INFORMATION

Calories	545	Sugars	3g
Protein	19g	Fat	42g
Carbohydrate	25g	Saturates	13g

 25 mins  50 mins

SERVES 4

INGREDIENTS

- 225 g/8 oz spinach
- 25 g/1 oz pine kernels
- 100 g/3½ oz ricotta cheese
- 2 large eggs, beaten
- 50 g/1¾ oz ground almonds
- 40 g/1½ oz Parmesan cheese, freshly grated
- 250 g/9 oz puff pastry, defrosted if frozen
- 1 small egg, beaten

1

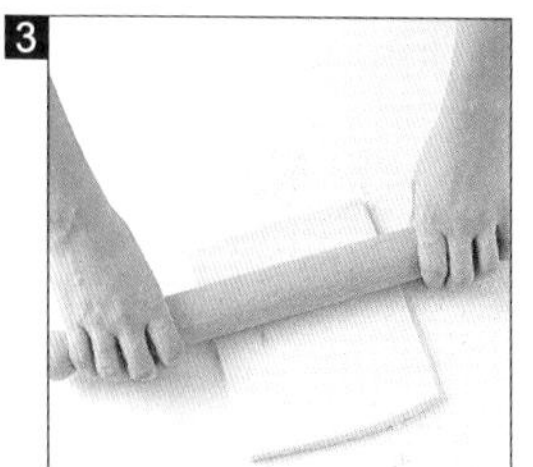
3

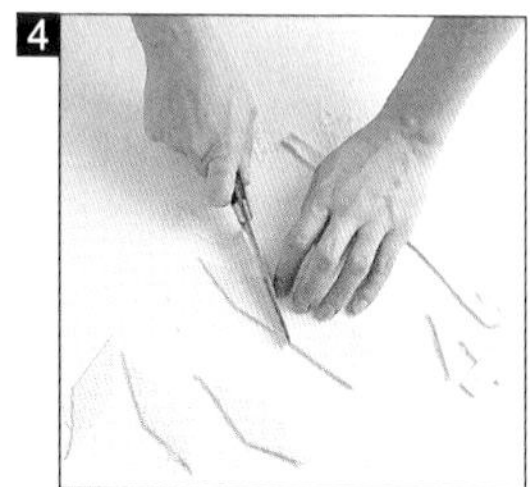
4

1 Rinse the spinach, place in a large pan and cook with just the water clinging to the leaves for 4–5 minutes until wilted. Drain thoroughly. When the spinach is cool enough to handle, squeeze out the excess liquid.

2 Place the pine kernels on a baking tray and lightly toast under a preheated grill for 2–3 minutes or until golden brown.

3 Place the ricotta, spinach and eggs in a bowl and mix together. Add the pine kernels, beat well, then stir in the ground almonds and Parmesan cheese.

4 Roll out the puff pastry and make 2 squares, 20 cm/8 inches wide. Trim the edges, reserving the pastry trimmings.

5 Place 1 pastry square on a baking tray. Spoon over the spinach mixture to within 1 cm/½ inch of the edge of the pastry. Brush the edges with beaten egg and place the second square over the top.

6 Using a round-bladed knife, press the pastry edges together by tapping along the sealed edge. Use the pastry trimmings to make a few leaves to decorate the pie.

7 Brush the pie with the beaten egg and bake in a preheated oven, 220°C/425°F/Gas Mark 8, for 10 minutes. Reduce the oven temperature to 190°C/375°F/Gas Mark 5 and bake for a further 25–30 minutes. Serve hot.

COOK'S TIP

Spinach must be washed very thoroughly in several changes of water to get rid of the grit and soil that can be trapped in it. Cut off any thick central ribs.

Carrot & Poppy Seed Bake

The poppy seeds add texture and flavour to this recipe, and counteract the slightly sweet flavour of the carrots.

NUTRITIONAL INFORMATION

Calories	138	Sugars	31g
Protein	2g	Fat	1g
Carbohydrate	32g	Saturates	0.2g

 10 MINS  40 MINS

SERVES 4

INGREDIENTS

- 675 g/1½ lb carrots, cut into thin strips
- 1 leek, sliced
- 300 ml/½ pint/1¼ cups fresh orange juice
- 2 tbsp clear honey
- 1 garlic clove, crushed
- 1 tsp mixed spice
- 2 tsp chopped thyme
- 1 tbsp poppy seeds
- salt and pepper
- fresh thyme sprigs and orange rind, to garnish

1 Cook the carrots and leek in a saucepan of boiling salted water for 5–6 minutes. Drain well and transfer to a shallow baking dish until required.

2 Mix together the orange juice, honey, garlic, mixed spice and thyme and pour the mixture over the vegetables. Add salt and pepper to taste.

3 Cover the baking dish and cook in a preheated oven, 180°C/350°F/Gas Mark 4, for 30 minutes or until the vegetables are tender.

4 Remove the lid and sprinkle with poppy seeds. Garnish with fresh thyme sprigs and orange rind and serve immediately.

VARIATION

If you prefer, use 2 tsp cumin instead of the mixed spice and omit the thyme, as cumin works particularly well with carrots.

1

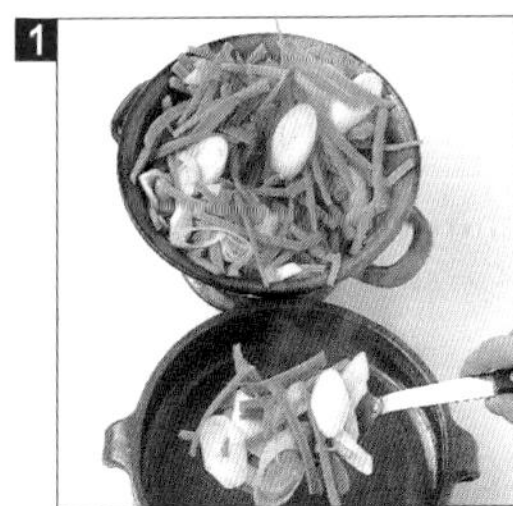

2

4

Spicy Black Eye Beans

A hearty casscrole of black eye beans in a rich, sweet tomato sauce flavoured with treacle (molasses) and mustard.

NUTRITIONAL INFORMATION

Calories	233	Sugars	21g
Protein	11g	Fat	4g
Carbohydrate	42g	Saturates	1g

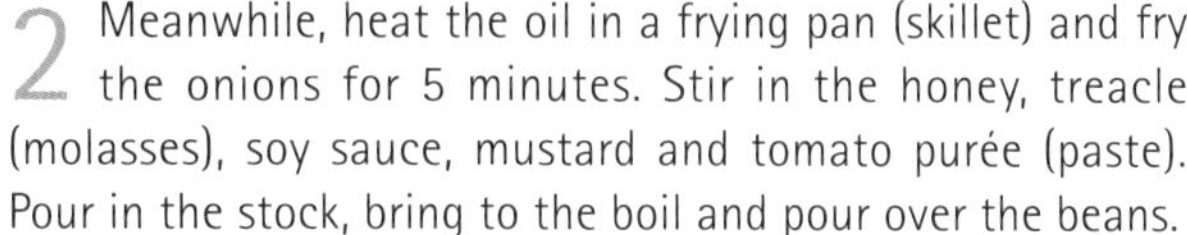

 12 HOURS  2½ HOURS

SERVES 4

INGREDIENTS

- 350 g/12 oz/2 cups black eye beans, soaked overnight in cold water
- 1 tbsp vegetable oil
- 2 medium onions, chopped
- 1 tbsp clear honey
- 2 tbsp treacle (molasses)
- 4 tbsp dark soy sauce
- 1 tsp dry mustard powder
- 4 tbsp tomato purée (paste)
- 450 ml/16 fl oz/2 cups Fresh Vegetable Stock (see page 8)
- 1 bay leaf
- 1 sprig each of rosemary, thyme and sage
- 1 small orange
- pepper
- 1 tbsp cornflour (cornstarch)
- 2 medium red (bell) peppers, deseeded and diced
- 2 tbsp chopped fresh flat-leaf parsley, to garnish
- crusty bread, to serve

1 Preheat the oven to 150°C/300°F/Gas Mark 2. Rinse the beans and place in a saucepan. Cover with water, bring to the boil and boil rapidly for 10 minutes. Drain and place in an ovenproof casserole dish.

2 Meanwhile, heat the oil in a frying pan (skillet) and fry the onions for 5 minutes. Stir in the honey, treacle (molasses), soy sauce, mustard and tomato purée (paste). Pour in the stock, bring to the boil and pour over the beans.

3 Tie the bay leaf and herbs together with a clean piece of string and add to the pan containing the beans. Using a vegetable peeler, pare off 3 pieces of orange rind and mix into the beans, along with plenty of pepper. Cover and cook for 1 hour.

4 Extract the juice from the orange and blend with the cornflour (cornstarch) to form a paste. Stir into the beans along with the red (bell) peppers. Cover and cook for 1 hour, until the sauce is rich and thick and the beans are tender. Discard the herbs and orange rind.

5 Garnish with chopped parsley and serve with crusty bread.

1

2

3

Egg & Chick-pea Curry

This quick and easy vegetarian curry is a great favourite. Double the quantities if you're cooking for a crowd.

NUTRITIONAL INFORMATION

Calories	403	Sugars	19g
Protein	19g	Fat	15g
Carbohydrate	31g	Saturates	3g

 1¼ HOURS  45 MINS

SERVES 4

INGREDIENTS

- 2 tbsp vegetable oil
- 2 garlic cloves, crushed
- 1 large onion, chopped
- 1 large carrot, sliced
- 1 apple, cored and chopped
- 2 tbsp medium-hot curry powder
- 1 tsp finely grated ginger root
- 2 tsp paprika
- 850 ml/1½ pints/3½ cups Fresh Vegetable Stock (see page 8)
- 2 tbsp tomato purée (paste)
- ½ small cauliflower, broken into florets
- 425 g/15 oz can chick-peas (garbanzo beans), rinsed and drained
- 25 g/1 oz/2 tbsp sultanas (golden raisins) 2 tbsp cornflour (cornstarch)
- 2 tbsp water
- 4 hard-boiled (hard-cooked) eggs, quartered
- salt and pepper
- paprika, to garnish

CUCUMBER DIP

- 7.5 cm/3 inch piece cucumber, chopped
- 1 tbsp chopped fresh mint
- 150 ml/¼ pint/⅔ cup low-fat natural yogurt
- sprigs of fresh mint, to garnish

1

1

2

1 Heat the oil in a large saucepan and fry the garlic, onion, carrot and apple for 4–5 minutes. Add the curry powder, ginger and paprika and fry for 1 minute. Stir in the stock and tomato purée (paste).

2 Add the cauliflower, chick-peas (garbanzo beans) and sultanas (golden raisins). Bring to the boil, then reduce the heat and simmer, covered, for 25–30 minutes until tender.

3 Blend the cornflour (cornstarch) with the water and add to the curry, stirring until thickened. Cook gently for 2 minutes. Season to taste.

4 Mix together the cucumber, mint and yogurt in a small serving bowl. Ladle the curry on to serving plates and arrange the eggs on top. Sprinkle with a little paprika. Garnish the cucumber and mint dip with mint and serve with the curry.

Fish Aubergine (Eggplant)

There is no fish involved in this dish and the meat can be omitted without affecting the flavour if you prefer a vegetarian diet.

NUTRITIONAL INFORMATION

Calories	130	Sugars	3g
Protein	8g	Fat	8g
Carbohydrate	6g	Saturates	2g

 35 MINS  15 MINS

SERVES 4

INGREDIENTS

- 500 g/1 lb 2 oz aubergine (eggplant)
- vegetable oil, for deep-frying
- 1 garlic clove, finely chopped
- ½ tsp finely chopped ginger root
- 2 spring onions (scallions), finely chopped, with the white and green parts separated
- 125 g/4½ oz pork, thinly shredded (optional)
- 1 tbsp light soy sauce
- 2 tsp rice wine or dry sherry
- 1 tbsp chilli bean sauce
- ½ tsp sugar
- 1 tbsp rice vinegar
- 2 tsp cornflour (cornstarch) paste (see page 6)
- a few drops sesame oil
- salt

1 Using a sharp knife, cut the aubergine (eggplant) into rounds and then into thin strips about the size of potato chips – the skin can either be peeled or left on. Place the aubergine (eggplant) strips into a colander, sprinkle with salt and leave to stand for 30 minutes. Rinse thoroughly and pat dry on kitchen paper (paper towels). This process removes the bitter juices from the aubergine (eggplant).

2 Heat the vegetable oil in a preheated wok or large frying pan (skillet) until smoking.

3 Add the aubergine (eggplant) chips and deep-fry for about 3-4 minutes, or until soft. Remove and drain on absorbent kitchen paper (paper towels).

4 Pour off the hot oil, leaving about 1 tablespoon in the wok. Add the garlic, ginger and the white parts of the spring onions (scallions), followed by the pork (if using). Stir-fry for about 1 minute or until the colour of the meat changes, then add the light soy sauce, rice wine or dry sherry and chilli bean sauce, blending well.

5 Return the aubergine (eggplant) chips to the wok or frying pan (skillet) together with the sugar, ½ teaspoon salt and the rice vinegar.

6 Continue stirring the mixture in the wok for another minute or so, then add the cornflour (cornstarch) paste and stir until the sauce has thickened.

7 Add the green parts of the spring onions (scallions) to the wok and toss to combine. Sprinkle on the sesame oil and serve immediately.

1
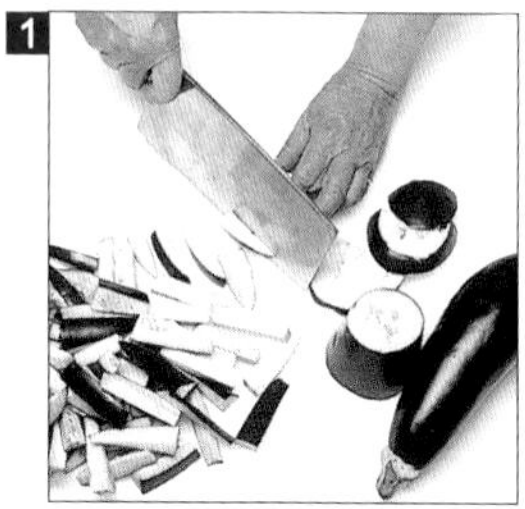

3

4

Mexican Chilli Corn Pie

This bake of sweetcorn (corn) and kidney beans, flavoured with chilli and fresh coriander (cilantro), is topped with crispy cheese cornbread.

NUTRITIONAL INFORMATION

Calories	519	Sugars	17g
Protein	22g	Fat	22g
Carbohydrate	61g	Saturates	9g

 25 MINS  20 MINS

SERVES 4

INGREDIENTS

- 1 tbsp corn oil
- 2 garlic cloves, crushed
- 1 red (bell) pepper, seeded and diced
- 1 green (bell) pepper, seeded and diced
- 1 celery stick, diced
- 1 tsp hot chilli powder
- 400 g/14 oz can chopped tomatoes
- 325 g/11½ oz can sweetcorn (corn), drained
- 215 g/7½ oz can kidney beans, drained and rinsed
- 2 tbsp chopped coriander (cilantro)
- salt and pepper
- coriander (cilantro) sprigs, to garnish
- tomato and avocado salad, to serve

TOPPING

- 125 g/4½ oz/⅔ cup cornmeal
- 1 tbsp plain (all-purpose) flour
- ½ tsp salt
- 2 tsp baking powder
- 1 egg, beaten
- 6 tbsp milk
- 1 tbsp corn oil
- 125 g/4½ oz/1 cup grated mature (sharp) Cheddar cheese

1 Heat the oil in a large frying pan (skillet) and gently fry the garlic (bell) peppers and celery for 5–6 minutes until just softened.

2 Stir in the chilli powder, tomatoes, sweetcorn, beans and seasoning. Bring to the boil and simmer for 10 minutes. Stir in the coriander (cilantro) and spoon into an ovenproof dish.

3 To make the topping, mix together the cornmeal, flour, salt and baking powder. Make a well in the centre, add the egg, milk and oil and beat until a smooth batter is formed.

4 Spoon over the (bell) pepper and sweetcorn mixture and sprinkle with the cheese. Bake in a preheated oven, at 220°C/425°F/Gas Mark 7, for 25–30 minutes until golden and firm.

5 Garnish with coriander (cilantro) sprigs and serve immediately with a tomato and avocado salad.

2

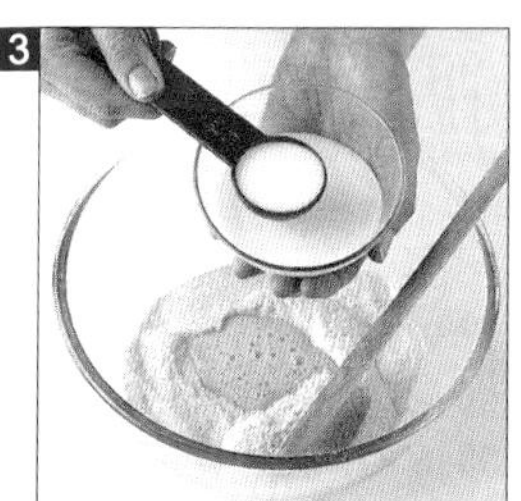
3

4

Leek & Herb Soufflé

Hot soufflés look very impressive if served as soon as they come out of the oven, otherwise they will sink quite quickly.

NUTRITIONAL INFORMATION

Calories	182	Sugars	4g
Protein	8g	Fat	15g
Carbohydrate	5g	Saturates	2g

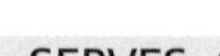

15 MINS   50 MINS

SERVES 4

INGREDIENTS

- 350 g/12 oz baby leeks
- 1 tbsp olive oil
- 125 ml/4 fl oz/½ cup vegetable stock
- 50 g/1¾ oz/½ cup walnuts
- 2 eggs, separated
- 2 tbsp chopped mixed herbs
- 2 tbsp natural (unsweetened) yogurt
- salt and pepper

1 Using a sharp knife, chop the leeks finely. Heat the oil in a frying pan (skillet). Add the leeks and sauté over a medium heat, stirring occasionally, for 2–3 minutes.

2 Add the vegetable stock to the pan, lower the heat and simmer gently for a further 5 minutes.

3 Place the walnuts in a food processor and process until finely chopped. Add the leek mixture to the nuts and process briefly to form a purée. Transfer to a mixing bowl.

4 Mix together the egg yolks, herbs and yogurt until thoroughly combined. Pour the egg mixture into the leek purée. Season with salt and pepper to taste and mix well.

5 In a separate mixing bowl, whisk the egg whites until firm peaks form.

6 Fold the egg whites into the leek mixture. Spoon the mixture into a lightly greased 900 ml/1½ pint/3¾ cup soufflé dish and place on a warmed baking tray (cookie sheet).

7 Cook in a preheated oven, 180°C/350°F/Gas Mark 4, for 35–40 minutes, or until risen and set. Serve the soufflé immediately.

COOK'S TIP

Placing the soufflé dish on a warm baking tray (cookie sheet) helps to cook the soufflé from the bottom, thus aiding its cooking and lightness.

Chow Mein

Egg noodles are cooked and then fried with a colourful variety of vegetables to make this well-known and ever-popular dish.

NUTRITIONAL INFORMATION			
Calories	669	Sugars	9g
Protein	19g	Fat	23g
Carbohydrate	100g	Saturates	4g

 15 MINS  10 MINS

SERVES 4

INGREDIENTS

- 500 g/1 lb 2 oz egg noodles
- 4 tbsp vegetable oil
- 1 onion, thinly sliced
- 2 carrots, cut into thin sticks
- 125 g/4½ oz/1⅓ cups button mushrooms, quartered
- 125 g/4½ oz mangetout (snow peas)
- ½ cucumber, cut into sticks
- 125 g/4½ oz/2 cups spinach, shredded
- 125 g/4½ oz/2 cups beansprouts
- 2 tbsp dark soy sauce
- 1 tbsp sherry
- 1 tsp salt
- 1 tsp sugar
- 1 tsp cornflour (cornstarch)
- 1 tsp sesame oil

2

4

5

1 Cook the noodles according to the instructions on the packet. Drain and rinse under cold running water until cool. Set aside.

2 Heat 3 tablespoons of the vegetable oil in a preheated wok or frying pan (skillet). Add the onion and carrots, and stir-fry for 1 minute. Add the mushrooms, mangetout (snow peas) and cucumber and stir-fry for 1 minute.

3 Stir in the remaining vegetable oil and add the drained noodles, together with the spinach and beansprouts.

4 Blend together all the remaining ingredients and pour over the noodles and vegetables.

5 Stir-fry until the noodle mixture is thoroughly heated through, transfer to a warm serving dish and serve.

COOK'S TIP

For a spicy hot chow mein, add 1 tablespoon chilli sauce or substitute chilli oil for the sesame oil.

Spicy Japanese Noodles

These noodles are highly spiced with chilli and flavoured with sesame seeds for a nutty taste that is a true delight.

NUTRITIONAL INFORMATION

Calories	381	Sugars	12g
Protein	11g	Fat	13g
Carbohydrate	59g	Saturates	2g

 5 MINS  15 MINS

SERVES 4

INGREDIENTS

- 500 g/1 lb 2 oz fresh Japanese noodles
- 1 tbsp sesame oil
- 1 tbsp sesame seeds
- 1 tbsp sunflower oil
- 1 red onion, sliced
- 100 g/3½ oz mangetout, (snow peas)
- 175 g/6 oz carrots, thinly sliced
- 350 g/12 oz white cabbage, shredded
- 3 tbsp sweet chilli sauce
- 2 spring onions (scallions), sliced, to garnish

1 Bring a large saucepan of water to the boil. Add the Japanese noodles to the pan and cook for 2–3 minutes. Drain the noodles thoroughly.

2 Toss the noodles with the sesame oil and sesame seeds.

3 Heat the sunflower oil in a large preheated wok.

4 Add the onion slices, mangetout (snow peas), carrot slices and shredded cabbage to the wok and stir-fry for about 5 minutes.

5 Add the sweet chilli sauce to the wok and cook, stirring occasionally, for a further 2 minutes.

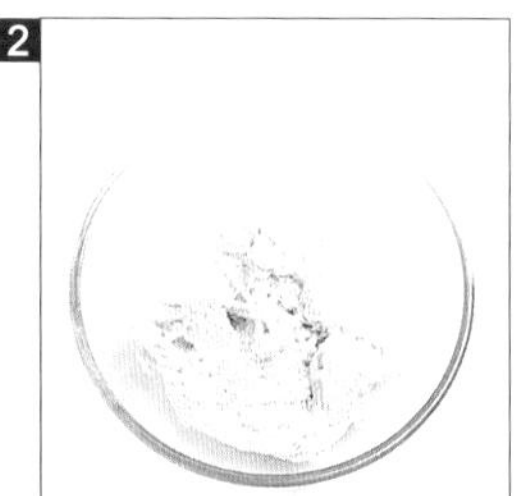
2

4

5

6 Add the sesame noodles to the wok, toss thoroughly to combine and heat through for a further 2–3 minutes. (You may wish to serve the noodles separately, so transfer them to the serving bowls.)

7 Transfer the Japanese noodles and spicy vegetables to warm individual serving bowls, scatter over the sliced spring onions (scallions) to garnish and serve immediately.

COOK'S TIP

If fresh Japanese noodles are difficult to get hold of, use dried rice noodles or thin egg noodles instead.

Cauliflower & Broccoli Flan

This really is a tasty flan, the pastry case for which may be made in advance and frozen until required.

NUTRITIONAL INFORMATION

Calories	252	Sugars	3g
Protein	7g	Fat	16g
Carbohydrate	22g	Saturates	5g

 15 MINS  50 MINS

SERVES 8

INGREDIENTS

PASTRY

- 175 g/6 oz/1½ cups plain (all-purpose) flour
- pinch of salt
- ½ tsp paprika
- 1 tsp dried thyme
- 75 g/2¾ oz/6 tbsp margarine
- 3 tbsp water

FILLING

- 100 g/3½ oz cauliflower florets
- 100 g/3½ oz broccoli florets
- 1 onion, cut into eight
- 25 g/1 oz/2 tbsp butter or margarine
- 1 tbsp plain (all-purpose) flour
- 6 tbsp vegetable stock
- 125 ml/4 fl oz/½ cup milk
- 75 g/2¾ oz/¾ cup grated Cheddar cheese,
- salt and pepper
- paprika, to garnish

1 To make the pastry, sift the flour and salt into a bowl. Add the paprika and thyme and rub in the margarine. Stir in the water and bind to form a dough.

2 Roll out the pastry on a floured surface and use to line an 18 cm/7 inch loose-based flan tin (pan). Prick the base with a fork and line with baking parchment. Fill with baking beans and bake in a preheated oven, 190°C/375°F/Gas Mark 5, for 15 minutes. Remove the parchment and beans and return the pastry case to the oven for 5 minutes.

3 To make the filling, cook the vegetables in a pan of lightly salted boiling water for 10–12 minutes, until tender. Drain and reserve.

4 Melt the butter in a pan. Add the flour and cook, stirring constantly, for 1 minute. Remove from the heat, stir in the stock and milk and return to the heat. Bring to the boil, stirring, and add 50 g/1¾ oz/½ cup of the cheese. Season to taste with salt and pepper.

5 Spoon the cauliflower, broccoli and onion into the pastry case. Pour over the sauce and sprinkle with the cheese. Return to the oven for 10 minutes, until the cheese is bubbling. Dust with paprika, garnish and serve.

2

4

5

Mushroom & Nut Crumble

A filling, tasty dish that is ideal for a warming family supper. The crunchy topping is flavoured with three different types of nuts.

NUTRITIONAL INFORMATION

Calories	779	Sugars	5g
Protein	16g	Fat	59g
Carbohydrate	48g	Saturates	14g

 20 MINS  55 MINS

SERVES 4

INGREDIENTS

- 350 g/12 oz/5 cups sliced open-cup mushrooms
- 350 g/12 oz/5 cups sliced chestnut (crimini) mushrooms, sliced
- 400 ml/14 fl oz/1¾ cups vegetable stock
- 60 g/2 oz/¼ cup butter or margarine
- 1 large onion, finely chopped
- 1 garlic clove, crushed
- 60 g/2 oz/½ cup plain (all-purpose) flour
- 4 tbsp double (heavy) cream
- 2 tbsp chopped parsley
- salt and pepper
- herbs, to garnish

CRUMBLE TOPPING

- 90 g/3 oz/¾ cup medium oatmeal
- 90 g/3 oz/¾ cup wholemeal (whole wheat) flour
- 25 g/1 oz/¼ cup ground almonds
- 25 g/1 oz/¼ cup finely chopped walnuts
- 60 g/2 oz/½ cup finely chopped unsalted shelled pistachio nuts
- 1 tsp dried thyme
- 90 g/3 oz/⅓ cup butter or margarine, softened
- 1 tbsp fennel seeds

1 Put the mushrooms and stock in a large saucepan, bring to the boil, cover and simmer for 15 minutes, until tender. Drain, reserving the stock.

2 In another saucepan, melt the butter or margarine and fry the onion and garlic for 2–3 minutes, until just soft. Stir in the flour and cook for 1 minute.

3 Remove from the heat and gradually stir in the reserved mushroom stock. Return to the heat and cook, stirring, until thickened. Stir in the mushrooms, seasoning, cream and parsley and spoon into a shallow ovenproof dish.

4 To make the topping, in a bowl, mix together the oatmeal, flour, nuts, thyme and plenty of salt and pepper to taste.

5 Using a fork, mix in the butter or margarine until the topping resembles coarse breadcrumbs.

6 Sprinkle the topping mixture evenly over the mushrooms and then sprinkle with the fennel seeds. Bake in a preheated oven, at 190°C/375°F/Gas Mark 5, for about 25–30 minutes, or until the topping is golden and crisp. Garnish with fresh herbs and serve immediately.

Wild Mushroom Risotto

This creamy risotto is flavoured with a mixture of wild and cultivated mushrooms and thyme.

NUTRITIONAL INFORMATION

Calories	364	Sugars	1g
Protein	15g	Fat	16g
Carbohydrate	44g	Saturates	6g

 15 MINS 25 MINS

SERVES 4

INGREDIENTS

- 2 tbsp olive oil
- 1 large onion, finely chopped
- 1 garlic clove, crushed
- 200 g /7 oz mixed wild and cultivated mushrooms, such as ceps, oyster, porcini and button, wiped and sliced if large
- 250 g/9 oz arborio (risotto) rice, washed
- pinch saffron threads
- 700 ml/1¼ pints/scant 3 cups hot vegetable stock
- 100 g/3½ oz Parmesan cheese, grated, plus extra for serving
- 2 tbsp chopped thyme
- salt and pepper

1. Heat the oil in a large frying pan (skillet). Add the onions and garlic and sauté for 3–4 minutes or until just softened.

2. Add the mushrooms to the pan and cook for 3 minutes or until they are just beginning to brown.

3. Add the rice and saffron to the pan and stir to coat the rice in the oil.

4. Mix together the stock and the wine and add to the pan, a ladleful at a time. Stir the rice mixture and allow the liquid to be fully absorbed before adding more liquid, a ladleful at a time.

5. When all of the wine and stock is incorporated, the rice should be cooked. Test by tasting a grain – if it is still crunchy, add a little more water and continue cooking. It should take at least 15 minutes to cook.

6. Stir in the cheese and thyme, and season with pepper to taste.

7. Transfer the risotto to serving dishes and serve sprinkled with extra Parmesan cheese.

1

2

4

COOK'S TIP

Wild mushrooms each have their own distinctive flavours and make a change from button mushrooms. However, they can be quite expensive, so you can always use a mixture with chestnut (crimini) or button mushrooms instead.

Potatoes & Peas

This quick and easy-to-prepare Indian dish can be served either as an accompaniment or on its own with chapatis.

NUTRITIONAL INFORMATION

Calories	434	Sugars	6g
Protein	5g	Fat	35g
Carbohydrate	28g	Saturates	4g

 15 MINS  25 MINS

SERVES 4

INGREDIENTS

- 150 ml/¼ pint/⅔ cup oil
- 3 medium onions, sliced
- 1 tsp crushed garlic
- 1 tsp finely chopped root ginger
- 1 tsp chilli powder
- ½ tsp turmeric
- 1 tsp salt
- 2 fresh green chillies, finely chopped
- 300 ml/½ pint/1¼ cups water
- 3 medium potatoes
- 100 g/3½ oz/1 cup peas
- coriander (cilantro) leaves and chopped red chillies, to garnish

1 Heat the oil in a large, heavy-based frying pan (skillet).

2 Add the onions to the frying pan (skillet) and fry, stirring occasionally, until the onions are golden brown.

3 Mix together the garlic, ginger, chilli powder, turmeric, salt and fresh green chillies. Add the spice mixture to the onions in the pan.

4 Stir in 150 ml/¼ pint/⅔ cup of the water, cover and cook until the onions are cooked through.

5 Meanwhile, cut the potatoes into six slices each, using a sharp knife.

6 Add the potato slices to the mixture in the pan and stir-fry for 5 minutes.

7 Add the peas and the remaining 150 ml/¼ pint/⅔ cup of the water to the pan, cover and cook for 7–10 minutes.

8 Transfer the potatoes and peas to serving plates and serve, garnished with fresh coriander (cilantro) leaves.

COOK'S TIP

Turmeric is an aromatic root which is dried and ground to produce the distinctive bright yellow-orange powder used in many Indian dishes. It has a warm, aromatic smell and a full, somewhat musty taste.

Vegetable Couscous

Couscous is a semolina grain which is very quick and easy to cook, and it makes a pleasant change from rice or pasta.

NUTRITIONAL INFORMATION

Calories	280	Sugars	13g
Protein	10g	Fat	7g
Carbohydrate	47g	Saturates	1g

 20 MINS  40 MINS

SERVES 4

INGREDIENTS

- 2 tbsp vegetable oil
- 1 large onion, coarsely chopped
- 1 carrot, chopped
- 1 turnip, chopped
- 600 ml/1 pint/2½ cups vegetable stock
- 175 g/6 oz/1 cup couscous
- 2 tomatoes, peeled and quartered
- 2 courgettes (zucchini), chopped
- 1 red (bell) pepper, seeded and chopped
- 125 g/4½ oz French (green) beans, chopped
- grated rind of 1 lemon
- pinch of ground turmeric (optional)
- 1 tbsp finely chopped fresh coriander (cilantro) or parsley
- salt and pepper
- fresh flat leaf parsley sprigs, to garnish

1

2

3

1 Heat the oil in a large saucepan and fry the onion, carrot and turnip for 3–4 minutes. Add the stock, bring to the boil, cover and simmer for 20 minutes.

2 Meanwhile, put the couscous in a bowl and moisten with a little boiling water, stirring, until the grains have swollen and separated.

3 Add the tomatoes, courgettes (zucchini), (bell) pepper and French (green) beans to the saucepan.

4 Stir the lemon rind into the couscous and add the turmeric, if using, the and mix thoroughly. Put the couscous in a steamer and position it over the saucepan of vegetables. Simmer the vegetables so that the couscous steams for about 8–10 minutes.

5 Pile the couscous on to warmed serving plates. Ladle the vegetables and some of the liquid over the top. Scatter with the coriander (cilantro) or parsley and serve at once, garnished with parsley sprigs.

Risotto-stuffed (Bell) Peppers

Sweet roasted (bell) peppers are delightful containers for a creamy risotto and especially good topped with Mozzarella cheese.

NUTRITIONAL INFORMATION

Calories	613	Sugars	7g
Protein	17g	Fat	32g
Carbohydrate	61g	Saturates	15g

 15 MINS  35 MINS

SERVES 4

INGREDIENTS

- 4 red or orange (bell) peppers
- 1 tbsp olive oil
- 1 large onion, finely chopped
- 350 g/12 oz arborio (risotto) rice, washed
- about 15 strands of saffron
- 150 ml/¼ pint/⅔ cup white wine
- 850 ml/1½ pints hot vegetable or chicken stock
- 50 g/1¾ oz/3 tbsp butter
- 50 g/1¾ oz pecorino cheese, grated
- 50 g/1¾ oz Italian sausage, such as felino salame or other coarse Italian salame, chopped
- 200 g/7 oz Mozzarella cheese, sliced

2

5

6

1 Cut the (bell) peppers in half, retaining some of the stalk. Remove the seeds.

2 Place the (bell) peppers, cut side up, under a preheated grill (broiler) for 12–15 minutes or until softened and charred.

3 Meanwhile, heat the oil in a large frying pan (skillet). Add the onion and cook for 3–4 minutes or until softened. Add the rice and saffron, stirring to coat in the oil, and cook for 1 minute.

4 Add the wine and stock slowly, a ladleful at a time, making sure that all of the liquid is absorbed before adding the next ladleful of liquid. When all of the liquid is absorbed, the rice should be cooked. Test by tasting a grain – if it is still crunchy add a little more water and continue cooking. It should take at least 15 minutes to cook.

5 Stir in the butter, pecorino cheese and the chopped Italian sausage.

6 Spoon the risotto into the (bell) peppers. Top with a slice of Mozzarella and grill (broil) for 4–5 minutes or until the cheese is bubbling. Serve hot.

VARIATION

Use tomatoes instead of the (bell) peppers, if you prefer. Halve 4 large tomatoes and scoop out the seeds. Follow steps 3–6 as there is no need to roast them.

Tofu with Mushrooms

Chunks of cucumber and smoked tofu (beancurd) stir-fried with straw mushrooms, mangetout (snow peas) and corn in a yellow bean sauce.

NUTRITIONAL INFORMATION

Calories	130	Sugars	2g
Protein	9g	Fat	9g
Carbohydrate	3g	Saturates	1g

15 MINS 10 MINS

SERVES 4

INGREDIENTS

- 1 large cucumber
- 1 tsp salt
- 225 g/8 oz smoked tofu (bean curd)
- 2 tbsp vegetable oil
- 60 g/2 oz mangetout (snow peas)
- 125 g/4½ oz/8 baby corn
- 1 celery stick, sliced diagonally
- 425 g/15 oz can straw mushrooms, drained
- 2 spring onions (scallions), cut into strips
- 1 cm/½ inch piece ginger root, chopped
- 1 tbsp yellow bean sauce
- 1 tbsp light soy sauce
- 1 tbsp dry sherry

1 Halve the cucumber lengthways and remove the seeds, using a teaspoon or melon baller.

2 Cut the cucumber into cubes, place in a colander and sprinkle over the salt. Leave to drain for 10 minutes. Rinse thoroughly in cold water to remove the salt and drain thoroughly on absorbent kitchen paper (paper towels).

2

3 Cut the tofu (bean curd) into cubes.

4 Heat the vegetable oil in a wok or large frying pan (skillet) until smoking.

5 Add the tofu (bean curd), mangetout (snow peas), baby corn and celery to the wok. Stir until the tofu (bean curd) is lightly browned.

5

6 Add the straw mushrooms, spring onions (scallions) and ginger, and stir-fry for a further minute.

7 Stir in the cucumber, yellow bean sauce, light soy sauce, dry sherry and 2 tablespoons of water. Stir-fry for 1 minute and ensure that all the vegetables are coated in the sauces before serving.

7

COOK'S TIP

Straw mushrooms are available in cans from oriental suppliers and some supermarkets. If unavailable, substitute 250 g/ 9 oz baby button mushrooms.

Vegetable Fried Rice

This dish can be served as part of a substantial meal for a number of people or as a vegetarian meal in itself for four.

NUTRITIONAL INFORMATION

Calories	175	Sugars	3g
Protein	3g	Fat	10g
Carbohydrate	20g	Saturates	2g

10 MINS 20 MINS

SERVES 4

INGREDIENTS

- 125 g/4½ oz/⅔ cup long-grain white rice
- 3 tbsp peanut oil
- 2 garlic cloves, crushed
- ½ tsp Chinese five-spice powder
- 60 g/2 oz/⅓ cup green beans
- 1 green (bell) pepper, seeded and chopped
- 4 baby corn cobs, sliced
- 25 g/1 oz bamboo shoots, chopped
- 3 tomatoes, skinned, seeded and chopped
- 60 g/2 oz/½ cup cooked peas
- 1 tsp sesame oil

1 Bring a large saucepan of water to the boil.

2 Add the long-grain white rice to the saucepan and cook for about 15 minutes. Drain the rice well, rinse under cold running water and drain thoroughly again.

3 Heat the peanut oil in a preheated wok or large frying pan (skillet). Add the garlic and Chinese five-spice and stir-fry for 30 seconds.

4 Add the green beans, chopped green (bell) pepper and sliced corn cobs and stir-fry the ingredients in the wok for 2 minutes.

5 Stir the bamboo shoots, tomatoes, peas and rice into the mixture in the wok and stir-fry for 1 further minute.

6 Sprinkle with sesame oil and transfer to serving dishes. Serve immediately.

VARIATION

Use a selection of vegetables of in this recipe, cutting them to a similar size to ensure that they cook in the same amount of time.

Tofu Casserole

Tofu (bean curd) is ideal for absorbing all the other flavours in this dish. If marinated tofu (bean curd) is used, it will add a flavour of its own.

NUTRITIONAL INFORMATION

Calories	228	Sugars	3g
Protein	16g	Fat	15g
Carbohydrate	7g	Saturates	2g

 5 MINS  15 MINS

SERVES 4

INGREDIENTS

- 450 g/1 lb tofu (bean curd)
- 2 tbsp peanut oil
- 8 spring onions (scallions), cut into batons
- 2 celery sticks, sliced
- 125 g/4½ oz broccoli florets
- 125 g/4½ oz courgettes (zucchini), sliced
- 2 garlic cloves, thinly sliced
- 450 g/1 lb baby spinach
- rice, to serve

SAUCE

- 425 ml/¾ pint/2 cups vegetable stock
- 2 tbsp light soy sauce
- 3 tbsp hoisin sauce
- ½ tsp chilli powder
- 1 tbsp sesame oil

1. Cut the tofu (bean curd) into 2.5-cm/1-inch cubes and set aside until required.

2. Heat the peanut oil in a preheated wok or large frying pan (skillet).

3. Add the spring onions (scallions), celery, broccoli, courgettes (zucchini), garlic, spinach and tofu (bean curd) to the wok or frying pan (skillet) and stir-fry for 3–4 minutes.

4. To make the sauce, mix together the vegetable stock, soy sauce, hoisin sauce, chilli powder and sesame oil in a flameproof casserole and bring to the boil.

5. Add the stir-fried vegetables and tofu (bean curd) to the saucepan, reduce the heat, cover and simmer for 10 minutes.

6. Transfer the tofu (bean curd) and vegetables to a warm serving dish and serve with rice.

3

4

5

VARIATION

This recipe has a green vegetable theme, but alter the colour and flavour by adding your favourite vegetables. Add 75 g/2¾ oz fresh or canned and drained straw mushrooms with the vegetables in step 2.

Satay Noodles

Rice noodles and vegetables are tossed in a crunchy peanut and chilli sauce for a quick satay-flavoured recipe.

NUTRITIONAL INFORMATION

Calories	281	Sugars	7g
Protein	9g	Fat	20g
Carbohydrate	18g	Saturates	4g

5 MINS

20 MINS

SERVES 4

INGREDIENTS

- 275 g/9½ oz rice sticks (wide, flat rice noodles)
- 3 tbsp groundnut oil
- 2 cloves garlic, crushed
- 2 shallots, sliced
- 225 g/8 oz green beans, sliced
- 100 g/3¾ oz cherry tomatoes, halved
- 1 tsp chilli flakes
- 4 tbsp crunchy peanut butter
- 150 ml/¼ pint/⅔ cup coconut milk
- 1 tbsp tomato purée (paste)
- sliced spring onions (scallions), to garnish

4

5

7

1 Place the rice sticks (wide, flat rice noodles) in a large bowl and pour over enough boiling water to cover. Leave to stand for 10 minutes.

2 Heat the groundnut oil in a large preheated wok or heavy-based frying pan (skillet).

3 Add the crushed garlic and sliced shallots to the wok or frying pan (skillet) and stir-fry for 1 minute.

4 Drain the rice sticks (wide, flat rice noodles) thoroughly. Add the green beans and drained noodles to the wok or frying pan (skillet) and stir-fry for about 5 minutes.

5 Add the cherry tomatoes to the wok and mix well.

6 Mix together the chilli flakes, peanut butter, coconut milk and tomato purée (paste).

7 Pour the chilli mixture over the noodles, toss well until all the ingredients are thoroughly combined and heat through.

8 Transfer the satay noodles to warm serving dishes and garnish with spring onion (scallion) slices and serve immediately.

Fried Vegetable Noodles

In this recipe, noodles are first boiled and then deep-fried for a crisply textured dish, and tossed with fried vegetables.

NUTRITIONAL INFORMATION

Calories	229	Sugars	4g
Protein	5g	Fat	15g
Carbohydrate	20g	Saturates	2g

5 MINS 25 MINS

SERVES 4

INGREDIENTS

- 350 g/12 oz/3 cups dried egg noodles
- 2 tbsp peanut oil
- 2 garlic cloves, crushed
- ½ tsp ground star anise
- 1 carrot, cut into matchsticks
- 1 green (bell) pepper, cut into matchsticks
- 1 onion, quartered and sliced
- 125 g/4½ oz broccoli florets
- 75 g/2¾ oz bamboo shoots
- 1 celery stick, sliced
- 1 tbsp light soy sauce
- 150 ml/¼ pint/⅔ cup vegetable stock
- oil, for deep-frying
- 1 tsp cornflour (cornstarch)
- 2 tsp water

1 Cook the noodles in a saucepan of boiling water for 1-2 minutes. Drain well and rinse under cold running water. Leave the noodles to drain thoroughly in a colander until required.

2 Heat the peanut oil in a preheated wok until smoking. Reduce the heat, add the crushed garlic and ground star anise and stir-fry for 30 seconds. Add the remaining vegetables and stir-fry for 1-2 minutes.

3 Add the soy sauce and vegetable stock to the wok and cook over a low heat for 5 minutes.

4 Heat the oil for deep-frying to 180°C/350°F, or until a cube of bread browns in 30 seconds.

5 Using a fork, twist the drained noodles and form them into rounds. Deep-fry them in batches until crisp, turning once. Leave to drain on kitchen paper (paper towels).

6 Blend the cornflour (cornstarch) with the water to form a paste and stir into the wok. Bring to the boil, stirring until the sauce is thickened and clear.

7 Arrange the noodles on a warm serving plate, spoon the vegetables on top and serve immediately.

2

3

5

Mushroom Pizza

Juicy mushrooms and stringy Mozzarella top this tomato-based pizza. Use wild mushrooms or a combination of wild and cultivated mushrooms.

NUTRITIONAL INFORMATION

Calories	302	Sugars	7g
Protein	10g	Fat	12g
Carbohydrate	41g	Saturates	4g

1¼ HOURS 45 MINS

SERVES 4

INGREDIENTS

1 portion Basic Pizza Dough (see page 861)

TOPPING

400g/14 oz can chopped tomatoes

2 garlic cloves, crushed

1 tsp dried basil

1 tbsp olive oil

2 tbsp tomato purée (paste)

200 g/7 oz mushrooms

150 g/5½ oz Mozzarella cheese, grated

salt and pepper

basil leaves, to garnish

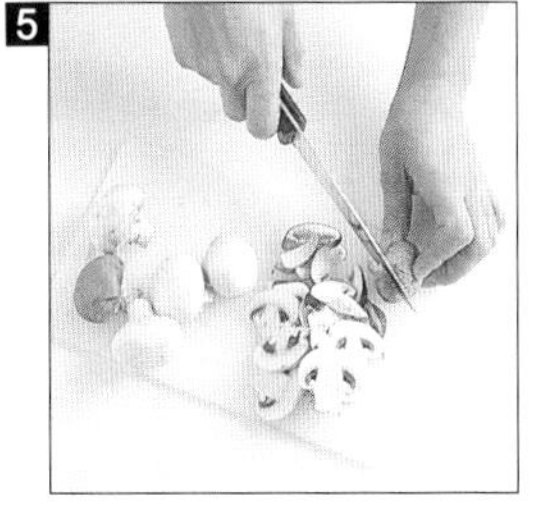

5

6

6

1 Place the yeast and sugar in a measuring jug and mix with 50 ml/2 fl oz/4 tbsp of the water. Leave the yeast mixture in a warm place for 15 minutes or until frothy.

2 Mix the flour with the salt and make a well in the centre. Add the oil, the yeast mixture and the remaining water. Using a wooden spoon, mix to form a smooth dough.

3 Turn the dough out on to a floured surface and knead for 4–5 minutes or until smooth. Return the dough to the bowl, cover with an oiled sheet of cling film (plastic wrap) and leave to rise for 30 minutes or until doubled in size.

4 Remove the dough from the bowl. Knead the dough for 2 minutes. Using a rolling pin, roll out the dough to form an oval or a circular shape, then place it on an oiled baking tray (cookie sheet), pushing out the edges until even. The dough should be no more than 6 mm/¼ inch thick because it will rise during cooking.

5 Using a sharp knife, chop the mushrooms into slices.

6 To make the topping, place the tomatoes, garlic, dried basil, olive oil and salt and pepper in a large pan and simmer for 20 minutes or until the sauce has thickened. Stir in the tomato purée (paste) and leave to cool slightly.

7 Spread the sauce over the base of the pizza, top with the mushrooms and scatter over the Mozzarella. Bake in a preheated oven, at 200°C/400°F/Gas Mark 6, for 25 minutes. Garnish with basil leaves.

Baked Potatoes with Pesto

This is an easy, but very filling meal. The potatoes are baked until fluffy, then they are mixed with a tasty pesto filling and baked again.

NUTRITIONAL INFORMATION

Calories	444	Sugars	3g
Protein	10g	Fat	28g
Carbohydrate	40g	Saturates	13g

 10 MINS  1½ HOURS

SERVES 4

INGREDIENTS

4 baking potatoes, about 225 g/8 oz each

150 ml/¼ pint/⅔ cup double (heavy) cream

75 ml/3 fl oz/⅓ cup vegetable stock

1 tbsp lemon juice

2 garlic cloves, crushed

3 tbsp chopped basil

2 tbsp pine nuts

2 tbsp grated Parmesan cheese

salt and pepper

1 Scrub the potatoes well and prick the skins with a fork. Rub a little salt into the skins and place on a baking tray (cookie sheet).

2 Cook in a preheated oven, 190°C/375°F/Gas Mark 5, for 1 hour, or until the potatoes are cooked through and the skins are crisp.

3 Remove the potatoes from the oven and cut them in half lengthways. Using a spoon, scoop the potato flesh into a mixing bowl, leaving a thin shell of potato inside the skins. Mash the potato flesh with a fork.

4 Meanwhile, mix the cream and stock in a saucepan and simmer over a low heat for about 8-10 minutes, or until reduced by half.

5 Stir in the lemon juice, garlic and chopped basil and season to taste with salt and pepper. Stir the mixture into the mashed potato flesh, together with the pine nuts.

6 Spoon the mixture back into the potato shells and sprinkle the Parmesan cheese on top. Return the potatoes to the oven for 10 minutes, or until the cheese has browned. Serve.

3

4

6

VARIATION

Add full-fat soft cheese or thinly sliced mushrooms to the mashed potato flesh in step 5, if you prefer.

Cabbage & Walnut Stir-Fry

This is a really quick, one-pan dish using white and red cabbage for both colour and flavour.

NUTRITIONAL INFORMATION

Calories	422	Sugars	9g
Protein	13g	Fat	37g
Carbohydrate	10g	Saturates	5g

 10 MINS  10 MINS

SERVES 4

INGREDIENTS

- 350 g/12 oz white cabbage
- 350 g/12 oz red cabbage
- 4 tbsp peanut oil
- 1 tbsp walnut oil
- 2 garlic cloves, crushed
- 8 spring onions (scallions)
- 225 g/8 oz firm tofu (bean curd), cubed
- 2 tbsp lemon juice
- 100 g/3½ oz walnut halves
- 2 tsp Dijon mustard
- 2 tsp poppy seeds
- salt and pepper

1 Using a sharp knife, shred the white and red cabbages thinly and set aside until required.

2 Heat the peanut and walnut oils in a preheated wok or heavy-based frying pan (skillet). Add the garlic, cabbage, spring onions (scallions) and tofu (bean curd) and cook, stirring constantly, for 5 minutes.

3 Add the lemon juice, walnuts and Dijon mustard, season to taste with salt and pepper and cook for a further 5 minutes, or until the cabbage is tender.

1 

2 

3 

4 Transfer the stir-fry to a warm serving bowl, sprinkle with poppy seeds and serve immediately.

COOK'S TIP

As well as adding protein, vitamins and useful fats to the diet, nuts and seeds add flavour and texture to vegetarian meals. Keep a good supply of them in your store-cupboard as they can be used in a great variety of dishes – salads, bakes, stir-fries to name but a few.

Sauté of Summer Vegetables

The freshness of lightly cooked summer vegetables is enhanced by the aromatic flavour of a tarragon and white wine dressing.

NUTRITIONAL INFORMATION

Calories	217	Sugars	8g
Protein	2g	Fat	18g
Carbohydrate	9g	Saturates	9g

 10 MINS  10–15 MINS

SERVES 4

INGREDIENTS

- 225 g/8 oz baby carrots, scrubbed
- 125 g/4½ oz runner (string) beans
- 2 courgettes (zucchini), trimmed
- 1 bunch large spring onions (scallions)
- 1 bunch radishes
- 60 g/2 oz/½ cup butter
- 2 tbsp light olive oil
- 2 tbsp white wine vinegar
- 4 tbsp dry white wine
- 1 tsp caster (superfine) sugar
- 1 tbsp chopped tarragon
- salt and pepper
- tarragon sprigs, to garnish

1 Cut the carrots in half lengthways, slice the beans and courgettes (zucchini), and halve the spring onions (scallions) and radishes, so that all the vegetables are cut to even-size pieces.

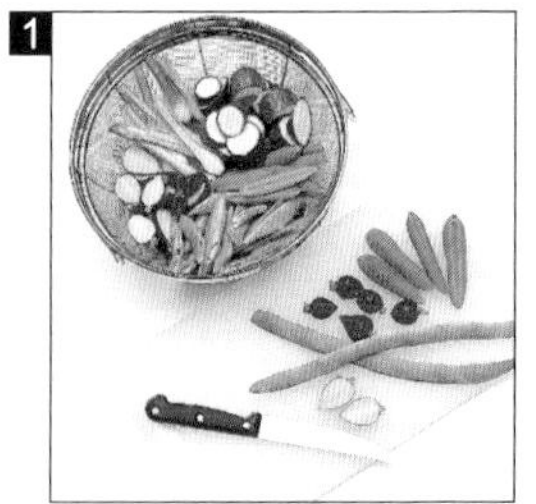

2 Melt the butter in a large, heavy-based frying pan (skillet) or wok. Add all the vegetables and fry them over a medium heat, stirring frequently, until they are tender, but still crisp and firm to the bite.

3 Heat the olive oil, vinegar, white wine and sugar in a small saucepan over a low heat, stirring until the sugar has dissolved. Remove from the heat and add the chopped tarragon.

4 When the vegetables are just cooked, pour over the 'dressing'. Stir through, tossing the vegetables well to coat, and then transfer to a warmed serving dish. Garnish with sprigs of fresh tarragon and serve at once.

Carrots with Coconut

Sliced carrots and chunks of parsnip are cooked in a creamy coconut sauce with ground almonds and served on a bed of spinach.

NUTRITIONAL INFORMATION

Calories	386	Sugars	14g
Protein	6g	Fat	32g
Carbohydrate	20g	Saturates	15g

 10 MINS 35 MINS

SERVES 4

INGREDIENTS

- 90 g/3 oz/⅓ cup creamed coconut
- 300 ml/½ pint/1¼ cups hot water
- 15 g/½ oz/2 tbsp flaked (slivered) almonds
- 4 tbsp vegetable oil
- 5 cardamom pods
- 4 thin slices ginger root
- 350 g/12 oz/2½ cups carrots, sliced
- 350 g/12 oz/2½ cups parsnips, cut into small chunks
- ¼ tsp five-spice powder
- 15 g/½ oz/2 tbsp ground almonds
- 200 g/7 oz/4 cups young spinach leaves
- ½ red onion, sliced thinly
- 1 garlic clove, sliced
- salt

1

3

4

1 Crumble the creamed coconut into a bowl or jug, add the hot water and stir until dissolved.

2 Heat a saucepan and dry-fry the flaked (slivered) almonds until golden. Remove from the pan and set aside until required.

3 Heat half the oil in the saucepan. Lightly crush the cardamom pods (this helps to release their flavour) and add to the saucepan with the ginger root. Fry for 30 seconds to flavour the oil. Add the chopped carrots and parsnips. Stir-fry for 2–3 minutes.

4 Stir in the five-spice powder and ground almonds, and pour in the coconut liquid. Bring to the boil and season with salt to taste. Cover and simmer for 12–15 minutes until the vegetables are tender. Stir occasionally, adding extra water if necessary.

5 Wash and drain the spinach. Remove any stalks. Heat the remaining oil in a wok and stir-fry the onion and garlic for 2 minutes. Add the spinach and stir-fry until it has just wilted. Drain off any excess liquid and season with salt.

6 Remove the cardamom pods and ginger from the carrots and parsnips, and adjust the seasoning. Serve on a bed of the spinach sprinkled with the almonds.

Giardiniera

As the name implies, this colourful pizza should be topped with fresh vegetables from the garden, especially in the summer months.

NUTRITIONAL INFORMATION

Calories	362	Sugars	10g
Protein	13g	Fat	15g
Carbohydrate	48g	Saturates	5g

 3½ HOURS  20 MINS

SERVES 4

INGREDIENTS

- 6 spinach leaves
- Basic Pizza Dough (see page 861)
- Basic Tomato Sauce (see page 6)
- 1 tomato, sliced
- 1 celery stalk, sliced thinly
- ½ green (bell) pepper, sliced thinly
- 1 baby courgette (zucchini), sliced
- 25 g/1 oz asparagus tips
- 25 g/1 oz sweetcorn, defrosted if frozen
- 25 g/1 oz peas, defrosted if frozen
- 4 spring onions (scallions), trimmed and chopped
- 1 tbsp chopped fresh mixed herbs
- 60 g/2 oz Mozzarella, grated
- 2 tbsp freshly grated Parmesan
- 1 artichoke heart
- olive oil, for drizzling
- salt and pepper

1 Remove any tough stalks from the spinach and wash the leaves in cold water. Pat dry with paper towels.

2 Roll out or press the pizza dough, using a rolling pin or your hands, into a large 25 cm/10 inch circle on a lightly floured work surface. Place the round on a large greased baking tray (cookie sheet) or pizza pan and push up the edge a little. Spread with the tomato sauce.

3 Arrange the spinach leaves on the sauce, followed by the tomato slices. Top with the remaining vegetables and the herbs.

4 Mix together the cheeses and sprinkle over. Place the artichoke heart in the centre. Drizzle the pizza with a little olive oil and season.

5 Bake in a preheated oven, at 200°C/400°F/Gas Mark 6, for 18–20 minutes, or until the edges are crisp and golden brown. Serve immediately.

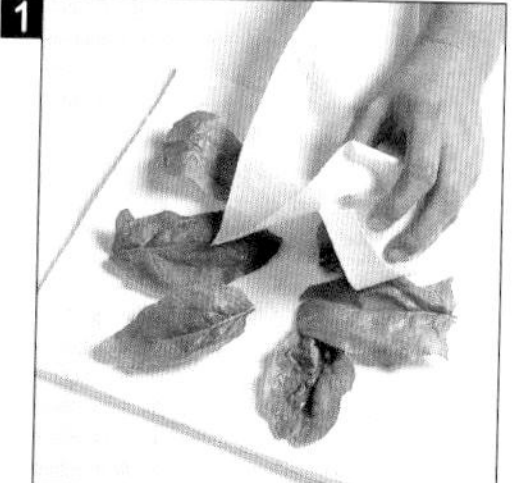
1

3

4

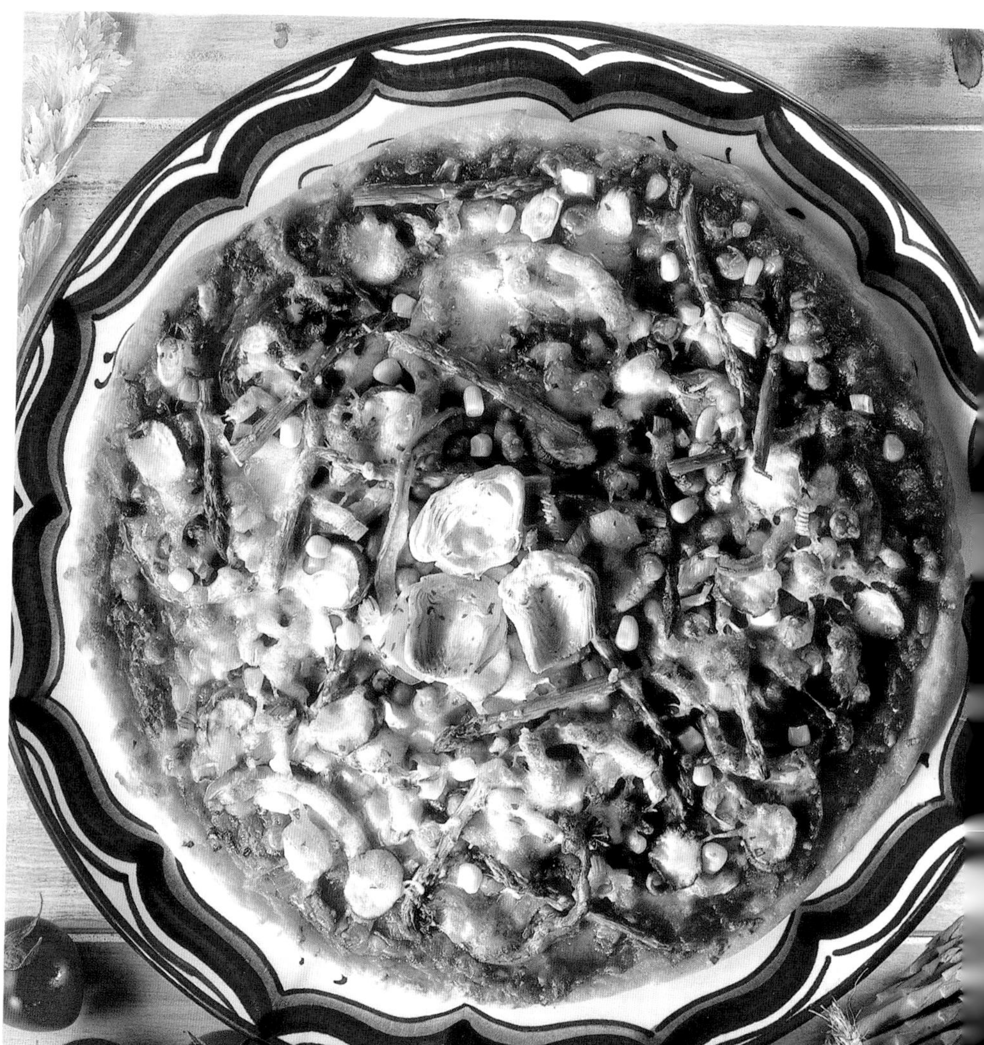

Couscous Royale

Serve this stunning dish as a centrepiece for a North African-style feast; it will prove to be a truly memorable meal.

NUTRITIONAL INFORMATION

Calories	329	Sugars	31g
Protein	6g	Fat	13g
Carbohydrate	50g	Saturates	6g

25 MINS 45 MINS

SERVES 6

INGREDIENTS

- 3 carrots
- 3 courgettes (zucchini)
- 350 g/12 oz pumpkin or squash
- 1.25 litres/2¼ pints/5 cups vegetable stock
- 2 cinnamon sticks, broken in half
- 2 tsp ground cumin
- 1 tsp ground coriander
- pinch of saffron strands
- 2 tbsp olive oil
- pared rind and juice of 1 lemon
- 2 tbsp clear honey
- 500 g/1 lb 2 oz/2¾ cups pre-cooked couscous
- 60 g/2 oz/¼ cup butter or, softened
- 175 g/6 oz/1 cup large seedless raisins
- salt and pepper
- coriander (cilantro), to garnish

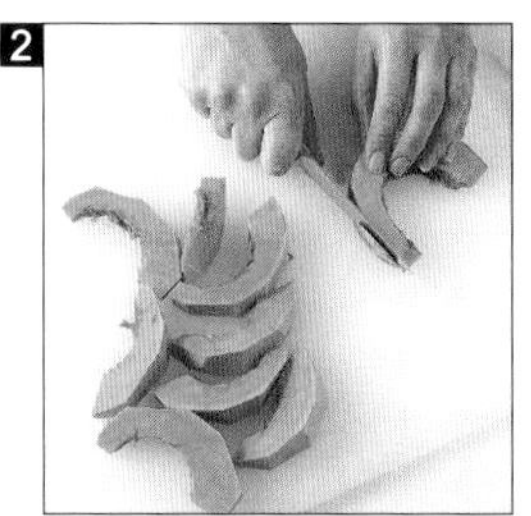

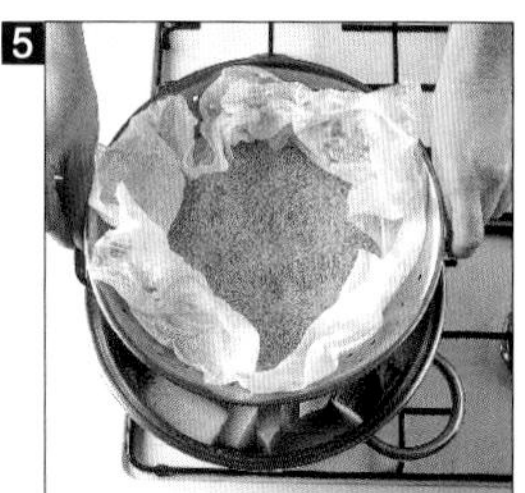

1 Cut the carrots and courgettes (zucchini) into 7 cm/3 inch pieces and cut in half lengthways.

2 Trim the pumpkin or squash and discard the seeds. Peel and cut into pieces the same size as the carrots and courgettes (zucchini).

3 Put the stock, spices, saffron and carrots in a large saucepan. Bring to the boil, skim off any scum and add the olive oil. Simmer for 15 minutes.

4 Add the lemon rind and juice to the pan, together with the honey, courgettes (zucchini) and pumpkin or squash. Season well. Bring back to the boil and simmer for a further 10 minutes.

5 Meanwhile, soak the couscous according to the packet instructions. Transfer to a steamer or large strainer lined with muslin (cheesecloth) and place over the vegetable pan. Cover and steam as directed. Stir in the butter.

6 Pile the couscous on to a warmed serving plate. Drain the vegetables, reserving the stock, lemon rind and cinnamon. Arrange the vegetables on top of the couscous. Put the raisins on top and spoon over 6 tablespoons of the reserved stock. Keep warm.

7 Return the remaining stock to the heat and boil for 5 minutes to reduce slightly. Discard the lemon rind and cinnamon. Garnish with sprigs of coriander (cilantro) and serve immediately, handing the sauce separately.

Chatuchak Fried Rice

An excellent way to use up leftover rice. Pop it in the freezer as soon as it is cool, and it will be ready to reheat at any time.

NUTRITIONAL INFORMATION

Calories	241	Sugars	5g
Protein	7g	Fat	5g
Carbohydrate	46g	Saturates	1g

 25 MINS 15 MINS

SERVES 4

INGREDIENTS

- 1 tbsp sunflower oil
- 3 shallots, chopped finely
- 2 garlic cloves, crushed
- 1 red chilli, deseeded and chopped finely
- 2.5-cm/1-inch piece ginger root, shredded finely
- ½ green (bell) pepper, deseeded and sliced finely
- 150 g/5½ oz/2-3 baby aubergines (eggplants), quartered
- 90 g/3 oz sugar snap peas or mangetout (snow peas), trimmed and blanched
- 90 g/3 oz/6 baby sweetcorn, halved lengthways and blanched
- 1 tomato, cut into 8 pieces
- 90 g/3 oz/1½ cups bean sprouts
- 500 g/1 lb 2 oz/3 cups cooked jasmine rice
- 2 tbsp tomato ketchup
- 2 tbsp light soy sauce

TO GARNISH

- fresh coriander (cilantro) leaves
- lime wedges

1 Heat the sunflower oil in a wok or large, heavy frying pan (skillet) over a high heat.

2 Add the shallots, garlic, chilli and ginger to the wok or frying pan (skillet). Stir until the shallots have softened.

3 Add the green (bell) pepper and baby aubergines (eggplants) and stir well.

4 Add the sugar snap peas or mangetout (snow peas), baby sweetcorn, tomato and bean sprouts. Stir-fry for 3 minutes.

5 Add the cooked jasmine rice to the wok, and lift and stir with two spoons for 4–5 minutes, until no more steam is released.

6 Stir the tomato ketchup and soy sauce into the mixture in the wok.

7 Serve the Chatuchak fried rice immediately, garnished with coriander (cilantro) leaves and lime wedges to squeeze over.

2

4

5

Chilled Noodles & Peppers

This is a convenient dish to serve when you are arriving home just before family or friends. Quick to prepare and assemble, it is ready in minutes.

NUTRITIONAL INFORMATION

Calories	260	Sugars	4g
Protein	4g	Fat	21g
Carbohydrate	15g	Saturates	4g

 5 MINS  15 MINS

SERVES 4–6

INGREDIENTS

250 g/9 oz ribbon noodles, or Chinese egg noodles

1 tbsp sesame oil

1 red (bell) pepper

1 yellow (bell) pepper

1 green (bell) pepper

6 spring onions (scallions), cut into matchstick strips

salt

DRESSING

5 tbsp sesame oil

2 tbsp light soy sauce

1 tbsp tahini (sesame seed paste)

4-5 drops hot pepper sauce

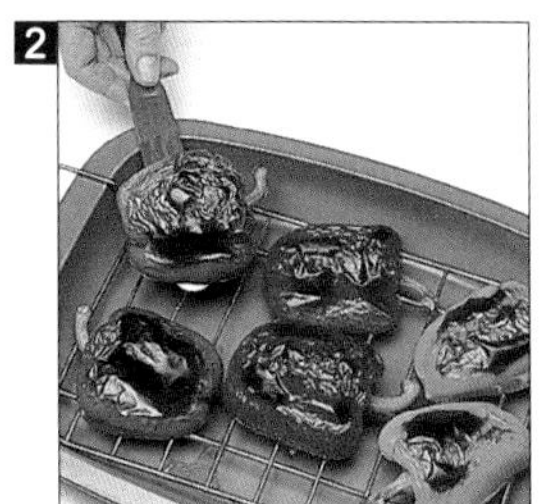

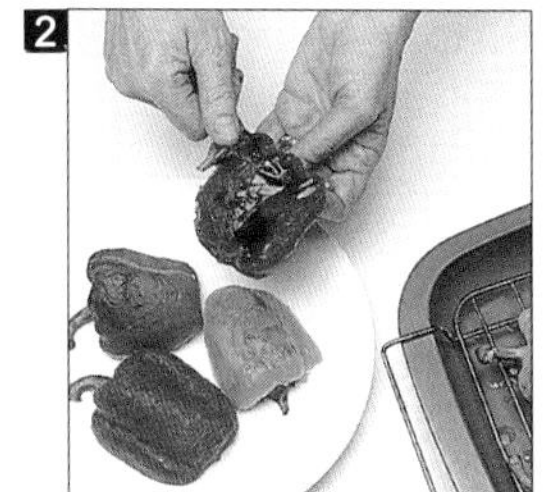

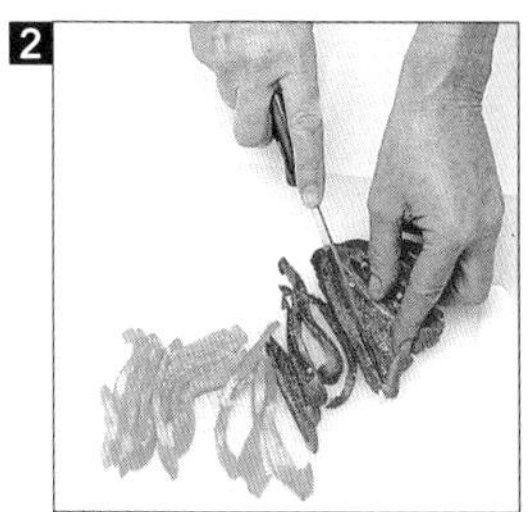

1 Preheat the grill (broiler) to medium. Cook the noodles in a large pan of boiling, salted water until they are almost tender. Drain them in a colander, run cold water through them and drain thoroughly. Tip the noodles into a bowl, stir in the sesame oil, cover and chill.

2 Cook the (bell) peppers under the grill (broiler), turning them frequently, until they are blackened on all sides. Plunge into cold water, then skin them. Cut in half, remove the core and seeds and cut the flesh into thick strips. Set aside in a covered container.

3 To make the dressing, mix together the sesame oil, light soy sauce, tahini (sesame seed paste) and hot pepper sauce until well combined.

4 Pour the dressing on the noodles, reserving 1 tablespoon, and toss well. Turn the noodles into a serving dish, arrange the grilled (bell) peppers over the noodles and spoon on the reserved dressing. Scatter on the spring onion (scallion) strips.

COOK'S TIP

If you have time, another way of skinning (bell) peppers is to first grill (broil) them, then place in a plastic bag, seal and leave for about 20 minutes. The skin will then peel off easily.

Green Rice

Based on the Mexican dish *Arroz Verde*, this recipe is perfect for (bell) pepper and chilli lovers. Serve with iced lemonade to quell the fire!

NUTRITIONAL INFORMATION

Calories	445	Sugars	6g
Protein	13g	Fat	12g
Carbohydrate	76g	Saturates	2g

 25 MINS  30 MINS

SERVES 4

INGREDIENTS

- 2 large green (bell) peppers
- 2 fresh green chillies
- 2 tbsp, plus 1 tsp vegetable oil
- 1 large onion, finely chopped
- 1 garlic clove, crushed
- 1 tbsp ground coriander
- 300 g/10½ oz/1½ cups long grain rice
- 700 ml/1¼ pints/3 cups Vegetable stock
- 225 g/8 oz/2 cups frozen peas
- 6 tbsp chopped coriander (cilantro)
- 1 egg, beaten
- salt and pepper
- coriander (cilantro), to garnish

TO SERVE

- tortilla chips
- lime wedges

COOK'S TIP

There are hundreds of varieties of chillies, many of them very similar in appearance, so it is not always easy to tell how hot they are. As a general rule, small, pointed chillies are hotter than larger, more rounded ones, but this is not invariable.

2

3

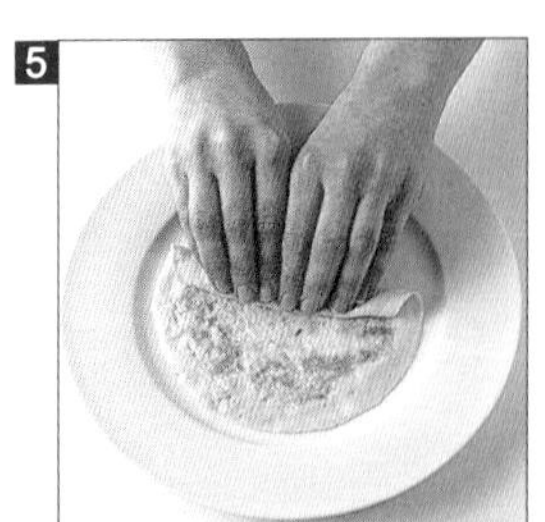
5

1 Halve, core and seed the (bell) peppers. Cut the flesh into small cubes. Seed and finely chop the chillies.

2 Heat 2 tablespoons of the oil in a saucepan and fry the onion, garlic, (bell) peppers and chillies for 5–6 minutes, until softened, but not browned.

3 Stir in the ground coriander, rice, and stock. Bring to the boil, cover and simmer for 10 minutes. Add the peas, bring back to the boil, cover and simmer for a further 5 minutes, until the rice is tender. Remove from the heat and leave to stand, covered, for 10 minutes.

4 Season to taste with salt and pepper and mix in the fresh coriander (cilantro). Pile into a warmed serving dish and keep warm.

5 Heat the remaining oil in a small omelette pan. Pour in the egg and cook over a medium heat for 1–2 minutes on each side, until set. Slide the omelette on to a plate, roll up loosely and slice into thin rounds.

6 Arrange the omelette strips on top of the rice. Garnish with coriander (cilantro) and serve immediately with tortilla chips and lime wedges.

Vegetable & Lentil Koftas

A mixture of vegetables, nuts and lentils is shaped into small balls and baked in the oven with a sprinkling of aromatic garam masala.

NUTRITIONAL INFORMATION

Calories	679	Sugars	20g
Protein	29g	Fat	33g
Carbohydrate	73g	Saturates	5g

30 MINS 50 MINS

SERVES 4

INGREDIENTS

- 6 tbsp vegetable ghee or oil
- 1 onion, finely chopped
- 2 carrots, finely chopped
- 2 celery sticks, finely chopped
- 2 garlic cloves, crushed
- 1 fresh green chilli, seeded and finely chopped
- 4½ tsp curry powder or paste
- 225 g/8 oz/1¼ cups split red lentils
- 600 ml/1 pint/2½ cups vegetable stock
- 2 tbsp tomato purée (paste)
- 125 g/4½ oz/2 cups fresh wholemeal (whole wheat) breadcrumbs
- 90 g/3 oz/¾ cup unsalted cashews, finely chopped
- 2 tbsp chopped coriander (cilantro)
- 1 egg, beaten
- salt and pepper
- garam masala, for sprinkling

YOGURT DRESSING

- 250 ml/9 fl oz/1 cup natural (unsweetened) yogurt
- 1-2 tbsp chopped coriander
- 1-2 tbsp mango chutney, chopped if necessary

1 Heat 4 tablespoons of ghee or oil in a large saucepan and gently fry the onion, carrots, celery, garlic and chilli, stirring frequently, for 5 minutes. Add the curry powder or paste and the lentils and cook, stirring constantly, for 1 minute.

2 Add the stock and tomato purée (paste) and bring to the boil. Reduce the heat, cover and simmer for 20 minutes, or until the lentils are tender and all the liquid is absorbed.

3 Remove from the heat and cool slightly. Add the breadcrumbs, nuts, coriander (cilantro), egg and seasoning to taste. Mix well and leave to cool. Shape into rounds about the size of golf balls (use 2 spoons to help shape the rounds).

4 Place the balls on a greased baking tray (cookie sheet), drizzle with the remaining oil and sprinkle with a little garam masala, to taste. Cook in a preheated oven, at 180°C/350°F/Gas Mark 4, for 15-20 minutes, or until piping hot and lightly golden in colour.

5 Meanwhile, make the yogurt dressing. Mix all the ingredients together in a bowl. Serve the koftas hot with the yogurt dressing.

3

4

5

Stir-Fried Japanese Noodles

This quick dish is an ideal lunchtime meal, packed with whatever mixture of mushrooms you like in a sweet sauce.

NUTRITIONAL INFORMATION

Calories	379	Sugars	8g
Protein	12g	Fat	13g
Carbohydrate	53g	Saturates	3g

 15 MINS  15 MINS

SERVES 4

INGREDIENTS

- 225 g/8 oz Japanese egg noodles
- 2 tbsp sunflower oil
- 1 red onion, sliced
- 1 garlic clove, crushed
- 500 g/1 lb 2 oz mixed mushrooms, such as shiitake, oyster, brown cap
- 350 g/12 oz pak choi
- 2 tbsp sweet sherry
- 6 tbsp soy sauce
- 4 spring onions (scallions), sliced
- 1 tbsp toasted sesame seeds

1 Place the egg noodles in a large bowl. Pour over enough boiling water to cover and leave to soak for 10 minutes.

2 Heat the sunflower oil in a large preheated wok.

3 Add the red onion and garlic to the wok and stir-fry for 2–3 minutes, or until softened.

4 Add the mushrooms to the wok and stir-fry for about 5 minutes, or until the mushrooms have softened.

5 Drain the Japanese egg noodles thoroughly and set aside.

6 Add the the pak choi, noodles, sweet sherry and soy sauce to the wok. Toss all of the ingredients together to mix well and stir-fry for 2–3 minutes, or until the liquid is just bubbling.

7 Transfer the mushroom noodles to warm serving bowls and scatter with sliced spring onions (scallions) and toasted sesame seeds. Serve immediately.

3

4

6

COOK'S TIP

The variety of mushrooms in supermarkets has greatly improved and a good mixture should be easily obtainable. If not, use the more common button and flat mushrooms.

Bean & Tomato Casserole

This quick and easy casserole can be eaten as a healthy supper dish or as a side dish to accompany sausages or grilled fish.

NUTRITIONAL INFORMATION

Calories	273	Sugars	8g
Protein	15g	Fat	7g
Carbohydrate	40g	Saturates	1g

 10 MINS  15 MINS

SERVES 4

INGREDIENTS

400g/14 oz can cannellini beans

400g/14 oz can borlotti beans

2 tbsp olive oil

1 stick celery

2 garlic cloves, chopped

175 g/6 oz baby onions, halved

450 g/1 lb tomatoes

75 g/2¾ oz rocket (arugula)

1 Drain both cans of beans and reserve 6 tablespoons of the liquid.

2 Heat the oil in a large pan. Add the celery, garlic and onions and sauté for 5 minutes or until the onions are golden.

3 Cut a cross in the base of each tomato and plunge them into a bowl of boiling water for 30 seconds until the skins split. Remove the tomatoes with a perforated spoon and leave until cool enough to handle. Peel off the skin and chop the flesh.

4 Add the tomato flesh and the reserved bean liquid to the pan and cook for 5 minutes.

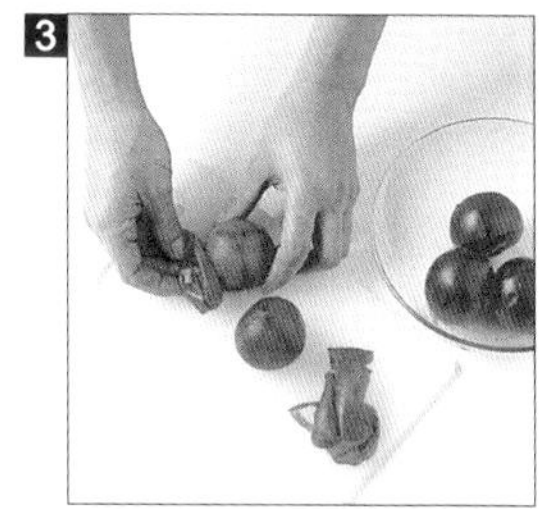

5 Add the beans to the pan and cook for a further 3–4 minutes or until the beans are hot.

6 Stir in the rocket (arugula) and allow to wilt slightly before serving. Serve hot.

VARIATION

For a spicier tasting dish, add 1–2 teaspoons of hot pepper sauce with the cannellini and borlotti beans in step 5.

Stuffed Rice Pancakes

Dosas (pancakes) are widely eaten in southern India. The rice and urid dhal need to soak and ferment, so prepare well in advance.

NUTRITIONAL INFORMATION

Calories	748	Sugars	1g
Protein	10g	Fat	47g
Carbohydrate	76g	Saturates	5g

 6¼ HOURS  40–45 MINS

SERVES 4

INGREDIENTS

- 200 g/7 oz/1 cup rice and 50 g/1¾ oz/¼ cup urid dhal, or 200 g/7 oz/1¾ cups ground rice and 50 g/1¾ oz/7 tbsp urid dhal flour (ata)
- 425–600 ml/¾–1 pint/2–2½ cups water
- 1 tsp salt
- 4 tbsp vegetable oil

FILLING

- 4 medium potatoes, diced
- 3 fresh green chillies, chopped
- ½ tsp turmeric
- 1 tsp salt
- 150 ml/¼ pint/⅔ cup oil
- 1 tsp mixed mustard and onion seeds
- 3 dried chillies
- 4 curry leaves
- 2 tbsp lemon juice

1 To make the dosas (pancakes), soak the rice and urid dhal for 3 hours. Grind the rice and urid dhal to a smooth consistency, adding water if necessary. Set aside for a further 3 hours to ferment. Alternatively, if you are using ground rice and urid dhal flour (ata), mix together in a bowl. Add the water and salt and stir until a batter is formed.

2 Heat about 1 tablespoon of oil in a large, non-stick, frying-pan (skillet). Using a ladle, spoon the batter into the frying-pan (skillet). Tilt the frying-pan (skillet) to spread the mixture over the base. Cover and cook over a medium heat for about 2 minutes. Remove the lid and turn the dosa over very carefully. Pour a little oil around the edge, cover and cook for a further 2 minutes. Repeat with the remaining batter.

3 To make the filling, cook the potatoes in a pan of boiling water. Add the chillies, turmeric and salt and cook until the potatoes are just soft. Drain and mash lightly with a fork.

4 Heat the oil in a saucepan and fry the mustard and onion seeds, dried red chillies and curry leaves, stirring constantly, for about 1 minute. Pour the spice mixture over the mashed potatoes, then sprinkle over the lemon juice and mix well. Spoon the potato filling on one half of each of the dosas (pancakes) and fold the other half over it. Transfer to a warmed serving dish and serve hot.

1

1

2

Vegetable & Goat's Cheese

Wonderfully colourful vegetables are roasted in olive oil with thyme and garlic. The goat's cheese adds a nutty, piquant flavour.

NUTRITIONAL INFORMATION

Calories	387	Sugars	9g
Protein	10g	Fat	21g
Carbohydrate	42g	Saturates	5g

 2½ HOURS  40 MINS

SERVES 4

INGREDIENTS

- 2 baby courgettes (zucchini), halved lengthways
- 2 baby aubergines (eggplant), quartered lengthways
- ½ red (bell) pepper, cut into 4 strips
- ½ yellow (bell) pepper, cut into 4 strips
- 1 small red onion, cut into wedges
- 2 garlic cloves, unpeeled
- 4 tbsp olive oil
- 1 tbsp red wine vinegar
- 1 tbsp chopped fresh thyme
- Basic Pizza Dough (see page 861)
- Basic Tomato Sauce (see page 6)
- 90 g/3 oz goat's cheese
- salt and pepper
- fresh basil leaves, to garnish

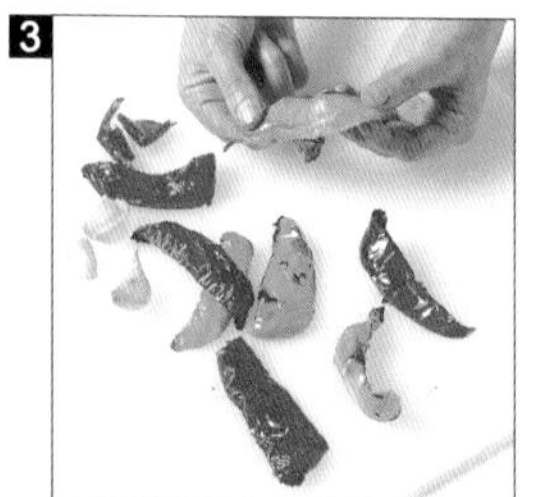

1 Place all of the prepared vegetables in a large roasting tin (pan). Mix together the olive oil, vinegar, thyme and plenty of seasoning and pour over, coating well.

2 Roast the vegetables in a preheated oven, at 200°C/400°F/Gas Mark 6, for 15–20 minutes or until the skins have started to blacken in places, turning half-way through. Leave to rest for 5 minutes after roasting.

3 Carefully peel off the skins from the roast (bell) peppers and the garlic cloves. Slice the garlic.

4 Roll out or press the dough, using a rolling pin or your hands, into a 25 cm/10 inch circle on a lightly floured work surface. Place on a large greased baking tray (cookie sheet) or pizza pan and raise the edge a little. Cover and leave for 10 minutes to rise slightly in a warm place. Spread with the tomato sauce almost to the edge.

5 Arrange the roasted vegetables on top and dot with the cheese. Drizzle the oil and juices from the roasting tin (pan) over the pizza and season.

6 Bake in a preheated oven, at 200°C/400°F/Gas Mark 6, for 18–20 minutes, or until the edge is crisp and golden. Serve immediately, garnished with basil leaves.

Filled Jacket Potatoes

Cook these potatoes conventionally, wrap them in foil and keep warm at the edge of the barbecue (grill), ready to fill with inspired mixtures.

NUTRITIONAL INFORMATION

Calories	564	Sugars	14g
Protein	21g	Fat	29g
Carbohydrate	58g	Saturates	18g

 15 MINS  1 HR 5 MINS

SERVES 4

INGREDIENTS

- 4 large or 8 medium baking potatoes
- paprika or chilli powder, or chopped herbs, to garnish

MEXICAN RELISH

- 225 g/8 oz can sweetcorn (corn), drained
- ½ red (bell) pepper, seeded and chopped
- 5 cm/2 inch piece of cucumber, finely chopped
- ½ tsp chilli powder
- salt and pepper

CHEESE & CHIVES

- 125 g/4½ oz/½ cup full-fat soft cheese
- 125 g/4½ oz/½ cup natural fromage frais
- 125 g/4½ oz blue cheese, cut into cubes
- 1 celery stick, finely chopped
- 2 tsp snipped chives
- celery salt and pepper

SPICY MUSHROOMS

- 25 g/1 oz/2 tbsp butter or margarine
- 225 g/8 oz button mushrooms
- 150 g/5½ oz/⅔ cup natural (unsweetened) yogurt
- 1 tbsp tomato purée (paste)
- 2 tsp mild curry powder
- salt and pepper

2 

3 

4 

1 Scrub the potatoes and prick them with a fork. Bake in a preheated oven, 200°C/400°F/Gas Mark 6, for about 1 hour, until just tender.

2 To make the Mexican Relish, put half the sweetcorn (corn) into a bowl. Process the remainder into a blender or food processor for 10–15 seconds, or chop and mash roughly by hand. Add the puréed corn to the corn kernels with the (bell) pepper, cucumber and chilli powder. Season to taste with salt and pepper.

3 To make the Cheese & Chives filling, mix the soft cheese and fromage frais together until smooth. Add the blue cheese, celery and chives. Season with celery salt and pepper.

4 To make the Spicy Mushrooms, melt the butter or margarine in a small frying pan (skillet). Add the mushrooms and cook gently for 3–4 minutes. Remove from the heat and stir in the yogurt, tomato purée (paste) and curry powder. Season to taste with salt and pepper.

5 Wrap the cooked potatoes in foil and keep warm at the edge of the barbecue. Serve the fillings sprinkled with paprika or chilli powder or herbs.

Spicy Fried Noodles

This is a simple idea to add an extra kick to noodles, which accompany many main course dishes in Thailand.

NUTRITIONAL INFORMATION

Calories	568	Sugars	3g
Protein	16g	Fat	19g
Carbohydrate	90g	Saturates	4g

 15 MINS 3-5 MINS

SERVES 4

INGREDIENTS

- 500 g/1 lb 2 oz medium egg noodles
- 60 g/2 oz/1 cup bean sprouts
- 15 g/½ oz chives
- 3 tbsp sunflower oil
- 1 garlic clove, crushed
- 4 fresh green chillies, seeded, sliced and soaked in 2 tbsp rice vinegar
- salt

1 Place the noodles in a bowl, cover with boiling water and soak for 10 minutes. Drain and set aside.

2 Pick over the bean sprouts and soak in cold water while you cut the chives into 2.5 cm/1 inch pieces. Set a few chives aside for the garnish. Drain the bean sprouts thoroughly.

3 Heat the oil in a preheated wok or large, heavy-based frying pan (skillet). Add the crushed garlic and stir; then add the chillies and stir-fry for about 1 minute, until fragrant.

4 Add the bean sprouts, stir and then add the noodles. Stir in salt to taste and add the chives. Using 2 spoons or a wok scoop, lift and toss the noodles for 1 minute.

1

3

4

5 Transfer the noodles to a warm serving dish, garnish the with the reserved chives and serve immediately.

COOK'S TIP

Soaking a chilli in rice vinegar has the effect of distributing the hot chilli flavour throughout the dish. To reduce the heat, you can slice the chilli more thickly before soaking.

Roast (Bell) Pepper Tart

This tastes truly delicious, the flavour of roasted vegetables being entirely different from that of boiled or fried.

NUTRITIONAL INFORMATION

Calories	237	Sugars	3g
Protein	6g	Fat	15g
Carbohydrate	20g	Saturates	4g

25 MINS — 40 MINS

SERVES 8

INGREDIENTS

PASTRY

- 175 g/6 oz/1½ cups plain (all-purpose) flour
- pinch of salt
- 75 g/2¾ oz/6 tbsp butter or margarine
- 2 tbsp green pitted olives, finely chopped
- 3 tbsp cold water

FILLING

- 1 red (bell) pepper
- 1 green (bell) pepper
- 1 yellow (bell) pepper
- 2 garlic cloves, crushed
- 2 tbsp olive oil
- 100 g/3½ oz/1 cup grated mozzarella cheese
- 2 eggs
- 150 ml/¼ pint/⅔ cup milk
- 1 tbsp chopped basil
- salt and pepper

1 To make the pastry, sift the flour and salt into a bowl. Rub in the butter or margarine until the mixture resembles breadcrumbs. Add the olives and cold water, bringing the mixture together to form a dough.

2 Roll the dough out on a floured surface and use to line a 20 cm/8 inch loose-based flan tin (pan). Prick the base with a fork and leave to chill.

3 Cut all the (bell) peppers in half lengthways, seed and place them, skin side uppermost, on a baking tray (cookie sheet). Mix the garlic and oil and brush over the (bell) peppers. Cook in a preheated oven, 200°C/400°F/Gas Mark 6, for 20 minutes, or until beginning to char slightly. Let the (bell) peppers cool slightly and thinly slice. Arrange in the base of the pastry case, layering with the mozzarella.

4 Beat the egg and milk and add the basil. Season and pour over the (bell) peppers. Put the tart on a baking tray (cookie sheet) and return to the oven for 20 minutes, or until set. Serve hot or cold.

3

3

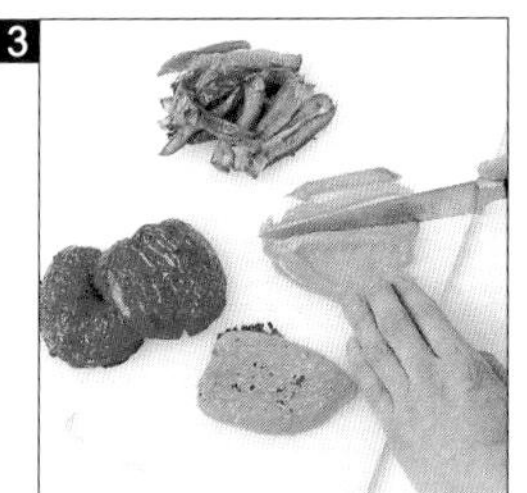

4

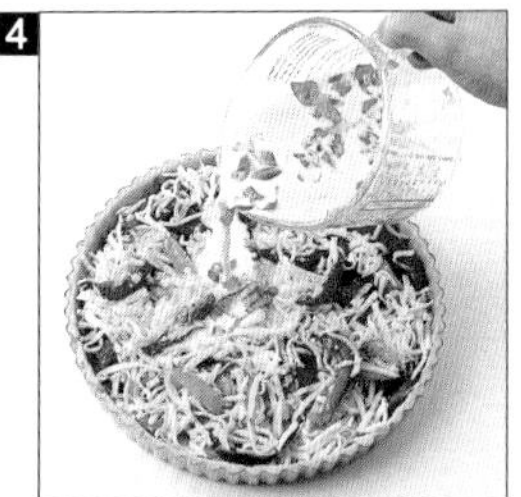

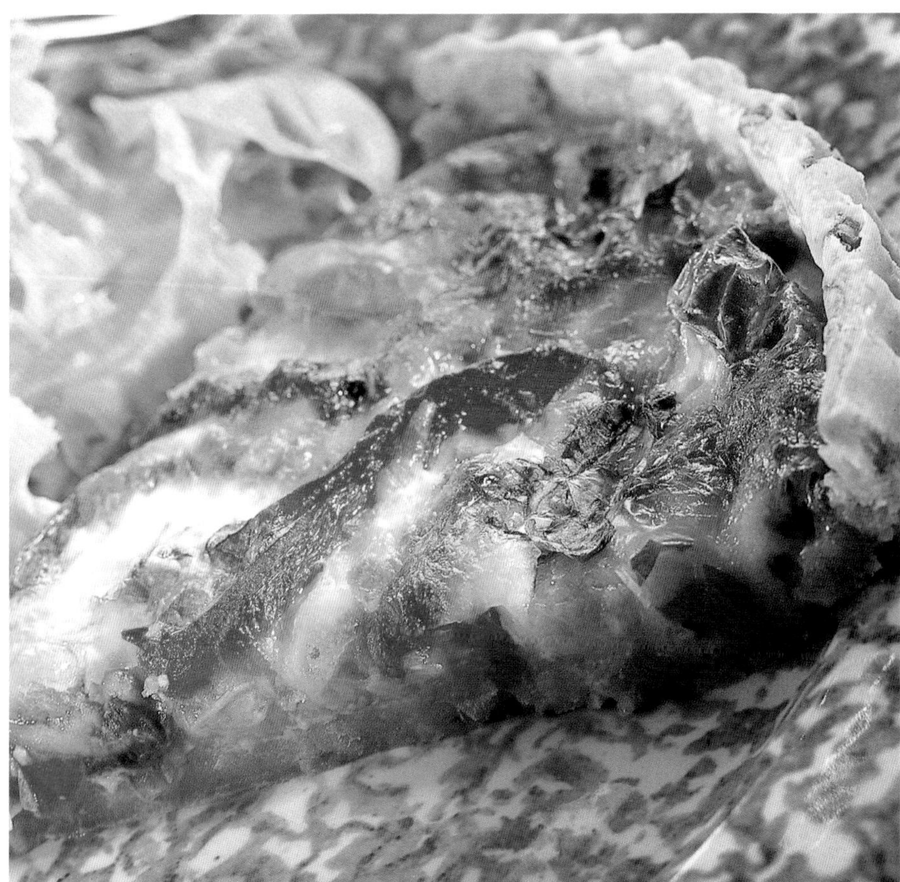

Potato & Spinach Gnocchi

These small potato dumplings are flavoured with spinach, cooked in boiling water and served with a simple tomato sauce.

NUTRITIONAL INFORMATION

Calories	315	Sugars	7g
Protein	8g	Fat	8g
Carbohydrate	56g	Saturates	1g

20 MINS  30 MINS

SERVES 4

INGREDIENTS

- 300 g/10½ oz floury (mealy) potatoes, diced
- 175 g/6 oz spinach
- 1 egg yolk
- 1 tsp olive oil
- 125 g/4½ oz/1 cup plain (all-purpose) flour
- salt and pepper
- spinach leaves, to garnish

SAUCE

- 1 tbsp olive oil
- 2 shallots, chopped
- 1 garlic clove, crushed
- 300 ml/½ pint/1¼ cups passata (sieved tomatoes)
- 2 tsp soft light brown sugar

3

3

6

1 Cook the diced potatoes in a saucepan of boiling water for 10 minutes or until cooked through. Drain and mash the potatoes.

2 Meanwhile, in a separate pan, blanch the spinach in a little boiling water for 1-2 minutes. Drain the spinach and shred the leaves.

3 Transfer the mashed potato to a lightly floured chopping board and make a well in the centre. Add the egg yolk, olive oil, spinach and a little of the flour and quickly mix the ingredients into the potato, adding more flour as you go, until you have a firm dough. Divide the mixture into very small dumplings.

4 Cook the gnocchi, in batches, in a saucepan of boiling salted water for about 5 minutes or until they rise to the surface.

5 Meanwhile, make the sauce. Put the oil, shallots, garlic, passata (sieved tomatoes) and sugar into a saucepan and cook over a low heat for 10-15 minutes or until the sauce has thickened.

6 Drain the gnocchi using a perforated spoon and transfer to warm serving dishes. Spoon the sauce over the gnocchi and garnish with the fresh spinach leaves.

VARIATION

Add chopped fresh herbs and cheese to the gnocchi dough instead of the spinach, if you prefer.

Vegetable Crêpes

Crêpes or pancakes are ideal for filling with your favourite ingredients. In this recipe they are packed with a spicy vegetable filling.

2

4

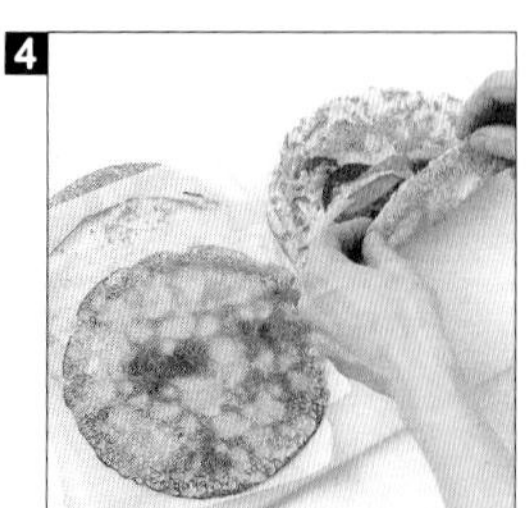
4

NUTRITIONAL INFORMATION

Calories	509	Sugars	10g
Protein	17g	Fat	34g
Carbohydrate	36g	Saturates	9g

15 MINS 45 MINS

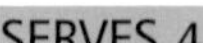

SERVES 4

INGREDIENTS

CREPES

100 g/3½ oz/¾ cup plain (all-purpose) flour
pinch of salt
1 egg, beaten
300 ml/½ pint/1¼ cups milk
vegetable oil, for frying

FILLING

2 tbsp vegetable oil
1 leek, shredded
½ tsp chilli powder
½ tsp ground cumin
50 g/1¾ oz mangetout (snow peas)
100 g/3½ oz button mushrooms,
1 red (bell) pepper, sliced
25 g/1 oz/¼ cup cashew nuts, chopped

SAUCE

25 g/1 oz/2 tbsp margarine
25 g/1 oz/3 tbsp plain (all-purpose) flour
150 ml/¼ pint/⅔ cup vegetable stock
150 ml/¼ pint/⅔ cup milk
1 tsp Dijon mustard
75 g/2¾ oz/¾ cup grated Cheddar cheese
2 tbsp chopped coriander (cilantro)

1 For the crêpes, sift the flour and salt into a bowl. Beat in the egg and milk to make a batter.

2 For the filling, heat the oil and sauté the leek for 2–3 minutes. Add the remaining ingredients and cook, stirring, for 5 minutes.

3 For the sauce, melt the margarine in a pan and add the flour. Cook, stirring, for 1 minute. Remove from the heat, stir in the stock and milk and return to the heat. Bring to the boil, stirring until thick. Add the mustard, half the cheese and the coriander (cilantro); cook for 1 minute.

4 Heat 1 tablespoon of oil in a small frying pan (skillet). Pour off the oil and add an eighth of the batter. Tilt to cover the base. Cook for 2 minutes, turn and cook the other side for 1 minute. Repeat with the remaining batter. Spoon a little of the filling along the centre of each crêpe and roll up. Place in a flameproof dish and pour the sauce on top. Top with cheese and heat under a hot grill (broiler) for 3–5 minutes or until the cheese melts.

Stuffed Mushrooms

Large mushrooms have more flavour than the smaller button mushrooms. Serve these mushrooms as a side vegetable or appetizer.

NUTRITIONAL INFORMATION

Calories	148	Sugars	1g
Protein	11g	Fat	7g
Carbohydrate	11g	Saturates	3g

 10 MINS  15 MINS

SERVES 4

INGREDIENTS

- 12 open-cap mushrooms
- 4 spring onions (scallions), chopped
- 4 tsp olive oil
- 100 g/3½ oz fresh brown breadcrumbs
- 1 tsp fresh oregano, chopped
- 100 g/3½ oz low-fat mature (sharp) Cheddar cheese

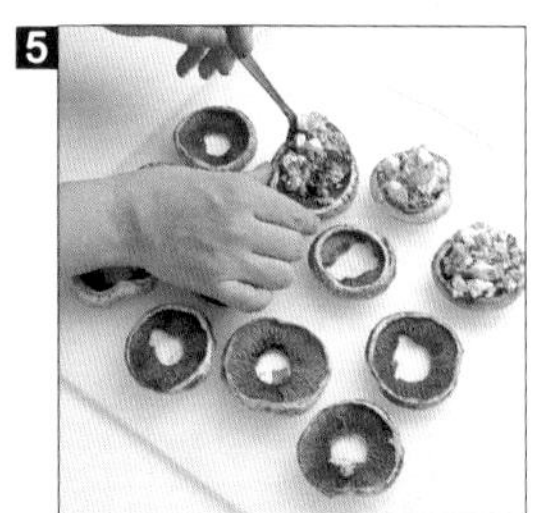

1 Wash the mushrooms and pat dry with kitchen paper (paper towels). Remove the stalks and chop the stalks finely.

2 Sauté the mushroom stalks and spring onions (scallions) in half of the oil.

3 In a large bowl, mix together the mushroom stalks and spring onions (scallions).

4 Add the breadcrumbs and oregano to the mushrooms and spring onions (scallions), mix and set aside.

5 Crumble the cheese into small pieces in a small bowl. Add the cheese to the breadcrumb mixture and mix well. Spoon the stuffing mixture into the mushroom caps.

6 Drizzle the remaining oil over the mushrooms. Barbecue (grill) on an oiled rack over medium hot coals for 10 minutes or until cooked through.

7 Transfer the mushrooms to serving plates and serve hot.

VARIATION

For a change replace the cheese with finely-chopped chorizo sausage (remove the skin first), chopped hard-boiled eggs, chopped olives or chopped anchovy fillets. Mop up the juices with some crusty bread.

Baked Potatoes with Salsa

This is a great way to eat a baked potato! Once cooked, the flesh is flavoured with avocado and served with a hot tomato salsa.

NUTRITIONAL INFORMATION

Calories	274	Sugars	4g
Protein	110	Fat	8g
Carbohydrate	43g	Saturates	2g

 15 MINS

 1 HOUR

SERVES 4

INGREDIENTS

- 4 baking potatoes, about 225 g/8 oz each
- 1 large ripe avocado
- 1 tsp lemon juice
- 175 g/6 oz smoked tofu (bean curd), diced
- 2 garlic cloves, crushed
- 1 onion, chopped finely
- 1 tomato, chopped finely
- 125 g/4½ oz mixed salad leaves
- fresh coriander (cilantro) sprigs, to garnish

SALSA

- 2 ripe tomatoes, seeded and diced
- 1 tbsp chopped coriander (cilantro)
- 1 shallot, diced finely
- 1 green chilli, diced
- 1 tbsp lemon juice
- salt and pepper

1 Scrub the potatoes and prick the skins with a fork. Rub a little salt into the skins and place them on a baking tray (cookie sheet).

2 Cook in a preheated oven, 190°C/375°F/Gas Mark 5, for 1 hour or until cooked through and the skins are crisp.

3 Cut the potatoes in half lengthways and scoop the flesh into a bowl, leaving a thin layer of potato inside the shells.

4 Halve and stone the avocado. Using a spoon, scoop out the avocado flesh and add to the bowl containing the potato. Stir in the lemon juice and mash the mixture together with a fork. Mix in the tofu (bean curd), garlic, onion and tomato. Spoon the mixture into one half of the potato shells.

5 Arrange the mixed salad leaves on top of the guacamole mixture and place the other half of the potato shell on top.

4

4

6

Cheese & Artichoke Pizza

Sliced artichokes combined with mature (sharp) Cheddar, Parmesan and blue cheese give a really delicious topping to this pizza.

NUTRITIONAL INFORMATION

Calories	424	Sugars	9g
Protein	16g	Fat	20g
Carbohydrate	47g	Saturates	8g

 1¾ HOURS  20 MINS

SERVES 4

INGREDIENTS

- Basic Pizza Dough (see page 861)
- Basic Tomato Sauce (see page 6)
- 60 g/2 oz blue cheese, sliced
- 125 g/4½ oz artichoke hearts in oil, sliced
- ½ small red onion, chopped
- 45 g/1½ oz mature (sharp) cheese, grated
- 2 tbsp freshly grated Parmesan
- 1 tbsp chopped fresh thyme
- oil from artichokes for drizzling
- salt and pepper

TO SERVE

- salad leaves
- cherry tomatoes, halved

3

4

6

1 Roll out or press the dough, using a rolling pin or your hands, to form a 25 cm/10 inch circle on a lightly floured work surface.

2 Place the pizza base on a large greased baking tray (cookie sheet) or pizza pan and push up the edge slightly. Cover and leave to rise for 10 minutes in a warm place.

3 Spread the tomato sauce almost to the edge of the base. Arrange the blue cheese on top of the tomato sauce, followed by the artichoke hearts and red onion.

4 Mix the Cheddar and Parmesan cheeses together with the thyme and sprinkle the mixture over the pizza. Drizzle a little of the oil from the jar of artichokes over the pizza and season to taste.

5 Bake in a preheated oven, at 200°C/400°F/Gas Mark 6, for 18–20 minutes, or until the edge is crisp and golden and the cheese is bubbling.

6 Mix the fresh salad leaves and cherry tomato halves together and serve with the pizza, cut into slices.

Neapolitan Seafood Salad

This delicious mix of seafood, salad leaves (greens) and ripe tomatoes conjures up all the warmth and sunshine of Naples.

NUTRITIONAL INFORMATION

Calories	1152	Sugars	3g
Protein	67g	Fat	81g
Carbohydrate	35g	Saturates	12g

6½ HOURS

25 MINS

SERVES 4

INGREDIENTS

- 450 g/1 lb prepared squid, cut into strips
- 750 g/1 lb 10 oz cooked mussels
- 450 g/1 lb cooked cockles in brine
- 150 ml/¼ pint/⅔ cup white wine
- 300 ml/½ pint/1¼ cups olive oil
- 225 g/8 oz/2 cups dried campanelle or other small pasta shapes
- juice of 1 lemon
- 1 bunch chives, snipped
- 1 bunch fresh parsley, finely chopped
- 4 large tomatoes
- mixed salad leaves (greens)
- salt and pepper
- sprig of fresh basil, to garnish

1. Put all of the seafood into a large bowl, pour over the wine and half of the olive oil, and set aside for 6 hours.

2. Put the seafood mixture into a saucepan and simmer over a low heat for 10 minutes. Set aside to cool.

3. Bring a large saucepan of lightly salted water to the boil. Add the pasta and 1 tablespoon of the remaining olive oil and cook for 8–10 minutes or until tender, but still firm to the bite. Drain thoroughly and refresh in cold water.

4. Strain off about half of the cooking liquid from the seafood and discard the rest. Mix in the lemon juice, chives, parsley and the remaining olive oil. Season to taste with salt and pepper. Drain the pasta and add to the seafood.

5. Cut the tomatoes into quarters. Shred the salad leaves (greens) and arrange them at the base of a salad bowl. Spoon in the seafood salad and garnish with the tomatoes and a sprig of basil. Serve.

1

4

5

VARIATION

You can substitute cooked scallops for the mussels and clams in brine for the cockles, if you prefer. The seafood needs to be marinated for 6 hours, so prepare well in advance.

Tabbouleh Salad

This kind of salad is eaten widely throughout the Middle East. The flavour improves as it is kept, so it tastes even better on the second day.

NUTRITIONAL INFORMATION

Calories	637	Sugars	8g
Protein	20g	Fat	41g
Carbohydrate	50g	Saturates	11g

 1½ HOURS  5-10 MINS

SERVES 2

INGREDIENTS

- 125 g/4½ oz/1 cup bulgar wheat
- 600 ml/1 pint/2½ cups boiling water
- 1 red (bell) pepper, seeded and halved
- 3 tbsp olive oil
- 1 garlic clove, crushed
- grated rind of ½ lime
- about 1 tbsp lime juice
- 1 tbsp chopped mint
- 1 tbsp chopped parsley
- 3–4 spring onions (scallions), trimmed and thinly sliced
- 8 pitted black olives, halved
- 40 g/1½ oz/½ cup large salted peanuts or cashew nuts
- 1–2 tsp lemon juice
- 60–90 g/2–3 oz Gruyère cheese
- salt and pepper
- mint sprigs, to garnish
- warm pitta (pocket) bread or crusty rolls, to serve

1 Put the bulgar wheat into a bowl and cover with the boiling water to reach about 2.5 cm/1 inch above the bulgar. Set aside to soak for up to 1 hour, until most of the water is absorbed and is cold.

2 Meanwhile, put the halved red (bell) pepper, skin side upwards, on a grill (broiler) rack and cook under a preheated moderate grill (broiler) until the skin is thoroughly charred and blistered. Leave to cool slightly.

3 When cool enough to handle, peel off the skin and discard the seeds. Cut the (bell) pepper flesh into narrow strips.

4 Whisk together the oil, garlic and lime rind and juice. Season to taste and whisk until thoroughly blended. Add 4½ teaspoons of the dressing to the (bell) peppers and mix lightly.

5 Drain the soaked bulgar wheat thoroughly, squeezing it in a dry cloth to make it even drier, then place in a bowl.

6 Add the chopped herbs, spring onions (scallions), olives and peanuts or cashew nuts to the bulgar and toss . Add the lemon juice to the remaining dressing, and stir through the salad. Spoon the salad on to 2 serving plates.

7 Cut the cheese into narrow strips and mix with the (bell) pepper strips. Spoon alongside the bulgar salad. Garnish with mint sprigs and serve with warm pitta (pocket) bread or crusty rolls.

1

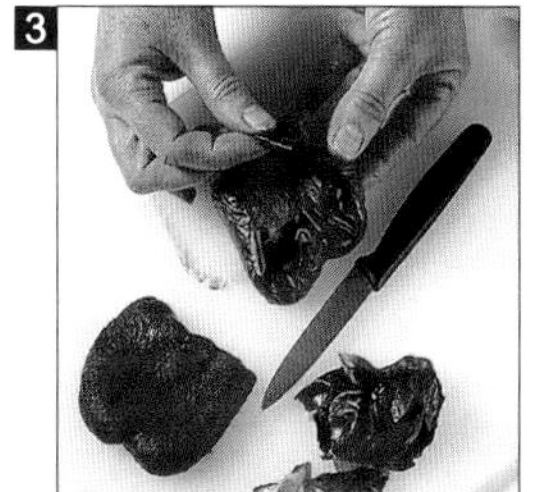
3

7

Mixed Bean Salad

Use a mixture of any canned beans in this crunchy, very filling salad.

NUTRITIONAL INFORMATION

Calories	198	Sugars	6g
Protein	10g	Fat	6g
Carbohydrate	26g	Saturates	1g

 30 MINS 15-20 MINS

SERVES 8

INGREDIENTS

- 400 g/14 oz can flageolet (small navy) beans, drained
- 400 g/14 oz can red kidney beans, drained
- 400 g/14 oz can butter beans, drained
- 1 small red onion, thinly sliced
- 175 g/6 oz dwarf green beans, topped and tailed
- 1 red (bell) pepper, halved and deseeded

DRESSING

- 4 tbsp olive oil
- 2 tbsp sherry vinegar
- 2 tbsp lemon juice
- 1 tsp light muscovado sugar
- 1 tsp chilli sauce (optional)

1 Put the canned beans in a large mixing bowl. Add the sliced onion and mix together.

2 Cut the dwarf green beans in half and cook in lightly salted boiling water for about 8 minutes until just tender. Refresh under cold water and drain again. Add to the mixed beans and onions.

3 Place the (bell) pepper halves, cut side down, on a grill (broiler) rack and cook until the skin blackens and chars. Leave to cool slightly then pop them into a plastic bag for about 10 minutes. Peel away the skin from the (bell) peppers and discard. Roughly chop the (bell) pepper flesh and add it to the beans.

4 To make the dressing, place the oil, sherry vinegar, lemon juice, sugar and chilli sauce (if using) in a screw-top jar and shake vigorously.

5 Pour the dressing over the mixed bean salad and toss well. Leave to chill in the refrigerator until required.

1

2

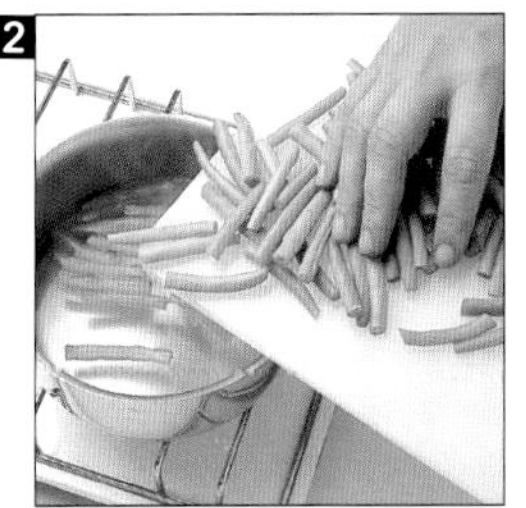

5

COOK'S TIP

You can use any combination of beans in this salad. For a distinctive flavour, add 1 teaspoon of curry paste instead of the chilli sauce.

Hot & Sour Duck Salad

This is a lovely tangy salad, drizzled with a lime juice and fish sauce dressing. It makes a splendid starter or light main course dish.

NUTRITIONAL INFORMATION

Calories	236	Sugars	3g
Protein	27g	Fat	10g
Carbohydrate	10g	Saturates	3g

 40 MINS  5 MINS

SERVES 4

INGREDIENTS

- 2 heads crisp salad lettuce, washed and separated into leaves
- 2 shallots, thinly sliced
- 4 spring onions (scallions), chopped
- 1 celery stick, finely sliced into julienne strips
- 5 cm/2 in piece cucumber, cut into julienne strips
- 125 g/4½ oz bean sprouts
- 1 x 200 g/7 oz can water chestnuts, drained and sliced
- 4 duck breast fillets, roasted and sliced
- orange slices, to serve

DRESSING

- 3 tbsp fish sauce
- 1½ tbsp lime juice
- 2 garlic cloves, crushed
- 1 red chilli pepper, seeded and very finely chopped
- 1 green chilli pepper, seeded and very finely chopped
- 1 tsp palm or demerara (brown crystal) sugar

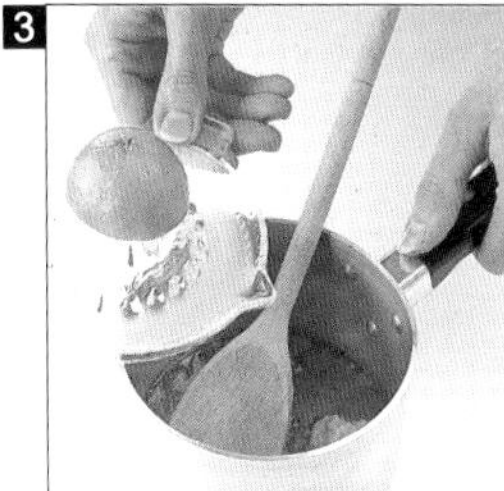

1 Place the lettuce leaves into a large mixing bowl. Add the sliced shallots, chopped spring onions (scallions), celery strips, cucumber strips, bean sprouts and sliced water chestnuts. Toss well to mix. Place the mixture on a large serving platter.

2 Arrange the duck breast slices on top of the salad in an attractive overlapping pattern.

3 To make the dressing, put the fish sauce, lime juice, garlic, chillies and sugar into a small saucepan. Heat gently, stirring constantly. Taste and adjust the piquancy if liked by adding more lime juice, or add more fish sauce to reduce the sharpness.

4 Drizzle the warm salad dressing over the duck salad and serve immediately with orange slices.

Coleslaw

Home-made coleslaw tastes far superior to any that you can buy. If you make it in advance, add the sunflower seeds just before serving.

NUTRITIONAL INFORMATION

Calories	224	Sugars	8g
Protein	3g	Fat	20g
Carbohydrate	8g	Saturates	3g

10 MINS

5 MINS

SERVES 4

INGREDIENTS

- 150 ml/5 fl oz/⅔ cup low-fat mayonnaise
- 150 ml/5 fl oz/⅔ cup low-fat natural yogurt
- dash of Tabasco sauce
- 1 medium head white cabbage
- 4 carrots
- 1 green (bell) pepper
- 2 tbsp sunflower seeds
- salt and pepper

1 To make the dressing, combine the mayonnaise, yogurt, Tabasco sauce and salt and pepper to taste in a small bowl. Leave to chill until required.

2 Cut the cabbage in half and then into quarters. Remove and discard the tough centre stalk. Shred the cabbage leaves finely. Wash the leaves and dry them thoroughly.

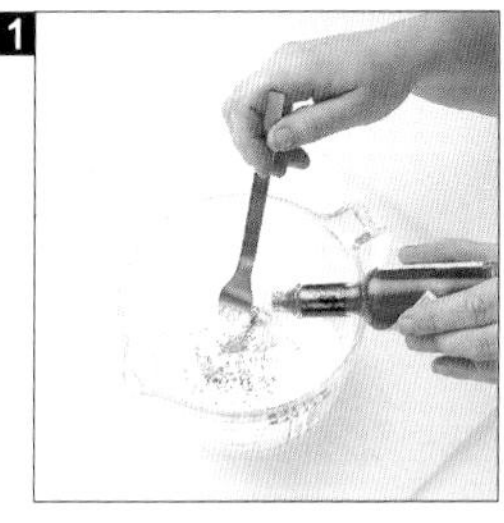
1

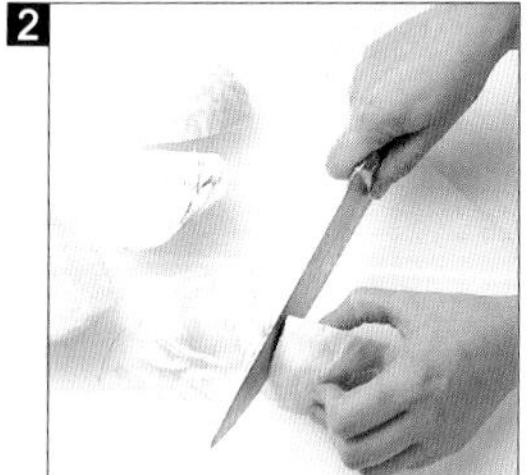
2

5

3 Peel the carrots and shred using a food processor or mandolin. Alternatively, coarsely grate the carrot.

4 Quarter and deseed the (bell) pepper and cut the flesh into thin strips.

5 Combine the vegetables in a large mixing bowl and toss to mix. Pour over the dressing and toss until the vegetables are well coated. Leave to chill in the refrigerator until required.

6 Just before serving, place the sunflower seeds on a baking tray (cookie sheet) and toast them in the oven or under the grill (broiler) until golden brown. Transfer the salad to a large serving dish, scatter with sunflower seeds and serve.

VARIATION

For a slightly different taste, add one or more of the following ingredients to the coleslaw: raisins, grapes, grated apple, chopped walnuts, cubes of cheese or roasted peanuts.

Coconut Couscous Salad

The nutty taste of toasted coconut really stands out in this delicious dish. Serve it hot, without the dressing, to accompany a rich lamb stew.

NUTRITIONAL INFORMATION

Calories	330	Sugars	18g
Protein	7g	Fat	7g
Carbohydrate	63g	Saturates	3g

 $1\frac{1}{2}$ HOURS  15 MINS

SERVES 4

INGREDIENTS

- 350 g/12 oz precooked couscous
- 175 g/6 oz no-need-to-soak dried apricots
- 1 small bunch fresh chives
- 2 tbsp unsweetened desiccated (shredded) coconut
- 1 tsp ground cinnamon
- salt and pepper
- shredded mint leaves, to garnish

DRESSING

- 1 tbsp olive oil
- 2 tbsp unsweetened orange juice
- ½ tsp finely grated orange rind
- 1 tsp wholegrain mustard
- 1 tsp clear honey
- 2 tbsp chopped fresh mint leaves

1 Soak the couscous according to the instructions on the packet. Bring a large saucepan of water to the boil. Transfer the couscous to a steamer or large sieve (strainer) lined with muslin (cheesecloth) and place over the water. Cover and steam as directed. Remove from the heat, place in heatproof bowl and set aside to cool.

2 Slice the apricots into thin strips and place in a small bowl. Using scissors, snip the chives over the apricots.

3 When the couscous is cool, mix in the apricots, chives, coconut and cinnamon. Season well.

4 To make the dressing, mix all the ingredients together and season. Pour over the couscous and mix until well combined. Cover and leave to chill for 1 hour to allow the flavours to develop. Serve the salad garnished with shredded mint leaves.

VARIATION

To serve this salad hot, when the couscous has been steamed, mix in the apricots, chives, coconut, cinnamon and seasoning along with 1 tbsp olive oil. Transfer to a warmed serving bowl and serve.

Provençale Pasta Salad

A combination of Italian vegetables tossed in a tomato dressing, served on a bed of assorted salad leaves, makes an appetizing meal.

NUTRITIONAL INFORMATION

Calories	197	Sugars	5g
Protein	10g	Fat	5g
Carbohydrate	30g	Saturates	1g

 10 MINS 15 MINS

SERVES 4

INGREDIENTS

- 225 g/8 oz penne (quills)
- 1 tbsp olive oil
- 25 g/1 oz pitted black olives, drained and chopped
- 25 g/1 oz dry-pack sun-dried tomatoes, soaked, drained and chopped
- 400 g/14 oz can artichoke hearts, drained and halved
- 115 g/4 oz baby courgettes (zucchini), trimmed and sliced
- 115 g/4 oz baby plum tomatoes, halved
- 100 g/3½ oz assorted baby salad leaves
- salt and pepper
- shredded basil leaves, to garnish

DRESSING

- 4 tbsp passata (sieved tomatoes)
- 2 tbsp low-fat natural fromage frais (unsweetened yogurt)
- 1 tbsp unsweetened orange juice
- 1 small bunch fresh basil, shredded

1

3

4

1 Cook the penne (quills) according to the instructions on the packet. Do not overcook the pasta – it should still have 'bite'. Drain well and return to the pan.

2 Stir in the olive oil, salt and pepper, olives and sun-dried tomatoes. Leave to cool.

3 Gently mix the artichokes, courgettes (zucchini) and plum tomatoes into the cooked pasta. Arrange the salad leaves in a serving bowl.

4 To make the dressing, mix all the ingredients together and toss into the vegetables and pasta.

5 Spoon the mixture on top of the salad leaves and garnish with shredded basil leaves.

Moroccan Salad

Couscous is a type of semolina made from durum wheat. It is wonderful in salads, as it readily takes up the flavour of the dressing.

NUTRITIONAL INFORMATION

Calories	195	Sugars	15g
Protein	8g	Fat	2g
Carbohydrate	40g	Saturates	0.3g

 30-35 MINS  0 MINS

SERVES 6

INGREDIENTS

175 g/6 oz/2 cups couscous

1 bunch spring onions (scallions), finely chopped

1 small green (bell) pepper, seeded and chopped

10 cm/4 inch piece of cucumber, chopped

175 g/6 oz can chickpeas (garbanzo beans), rinsed and drained

60 g/2 oz/⅔ cup sultanas (golden raisins) or raisins

2 oranges

salt and pepper

mint sprigs, to garnish

lettuce leaves, to serve

DRESSING

finely grated rind of 1 orange

1 tbsp chopped fresh mint

150 ml/¼ pint/⅔ cup natural yogurt

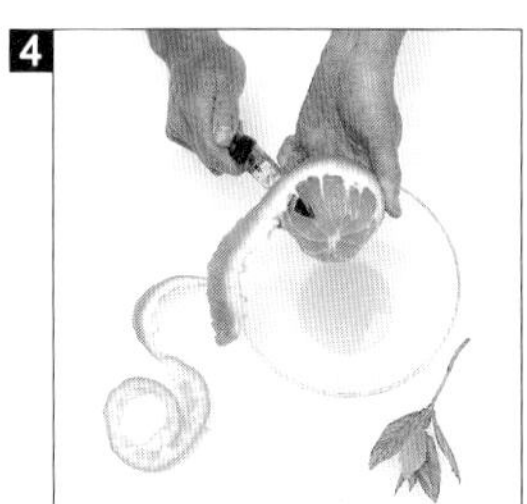

1 Put the couscous into a bowl and cover with boiling water. Leave it to soak for about 15 minutes to swell the grains, then stir gently with a fork to separate them.

2 Add the spring onions (scallions), green (bell) pepper, cucumber, chickpeas (garbanzo beans) and sultanas (golden raisins) or raisins to the couscous, stirring to combine. Season well with salt and pepper.

3 To make the dressing, place the orange rind, mint and yogurt in a bowl and mix together until well combined. Pour over the couscous mixture and stir to mix well.

4 Using a sharp serrated knife, remove the peel and pith from the oranges. Cut the flesh into segments, removing all the membrane.

5 Arrange the lettuce leaves on 4 serving plates. Divide the couscous mixture between the plates and arrange the orange segments on top. Garnish with sprigs of fresh mint and serve.

Three-Way Potato Salad

Small new potatoes, served warm in a delicious dressing. The nutritional information is for the potato salad with the curry dressing only.

NUTRITIONAL INFORMATION

Calories	310	Sugars	12g
Protein	6g	Fat	19g
Carbohydrate	31g	Saturates	4g

 15-20 MINS  20 MINS

SERVES 4

INGREDIENTS

- 500 g/1 lb 2 oz new potatoes (for each dressing)
- herbs, to garnish

LIGHT CURRY DRESSING

- 1 tbsp vegetable oil
- 1 tbsp medium curry paste
- 1 small onion, chopped
- 1 tbsp mango chutney, chopped
- 6 tbsp natural (unsweetened) yogurt
- 3 tbsp single (light) cream
- 2 tbsp mayonnaise
- salt and pepper
- 1 tbsp single (light) cream, to garnish

VINAIGRETTE DRESSING

- 6 tbsp hazelnut oil
- 3 tbsp cider vinegar
- 1 tsp wholegrain mustard
- 1 tsp caster (superfine) sugar
- few basil leaves, torn

PARSLEY CREAM

- 150 ml/¼ pint/⅔ cup soured cream
- 3 tbsp light mayonnaise
- 4 spring onions (scallions), finely chopped
- 1 tbsp chopped fresh parsley

1

2

4

1 To make the Light Curry Dressing, heat the vegetable oil in a saucepan, add the curry paste and onion and fry, stirring frequently, until the onion is soft. Remove from the heat and set aside to cool slightly.

2 Mix together the mango chutney, yogurt, cream and mayonnaise. Add the curry mixture and blend together. Season with salt and pepper.

3 To make the Vinaigrette Dressing, whisk the oil, vinegar, mustard, sugar and basil together in a small jug or bowl. Season with salt and pepper.

4 To make the Parsley Cream, combine the mayonnaise, soured cream, spring onions (scallions) and parsley, mixing well. Season with salt and pepper.

5 Cook the potatoes in lightly salted boiling water until just tender. Drain well and set aside to cool for 5 minutes, then add the chosen dressing, tossing to coat. Serve, garnished with fresh herbs, spooning a little single (light) cream on to the potatoes if you have used the curry dressing.

Italian Potato Salad

Potato salad is always a favourite, but it is even more delicious with the addition of sun-dried tomatoes and fresh parsley.

NUTRITIONAL INFORMATION

Calories	425	Sugars	6g
Protein	6g	Fat	27g
Carbohydrate	43g	Saturates	5g

 40 MINS  15 MINS

SERVES 4

INGREDIENTS

- 450 g/1 lb baby potatoes, unpeeled, or larger potatoes, halved
- 4 tbsp natural yogurt
- 4 tbsp mayonnaise
- 8 sun-dried tomatoes
- 2 tbsp flat leaf parsley, chopped
- salt and pepper

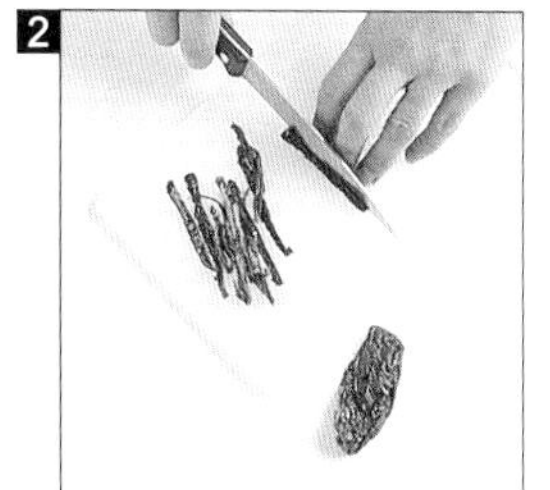

1 Rinse and clean the potatoes and place them in a large pan of water. Bring to the boil and cook for 8–12 minutes or until just tender. (The cooking time will vary according to the size of the potatoes.)

2 Using a sharp knife, cut the sun-dried tomatoes into thin slices.

3 To make the dressing, mix together the yogurt and mayonnaise in a bowl and season to taste with a little salt and pepper. Stir in the sun-dried tomato slices and the chopped flat leaf parsley.

4 Remove the potatoes with a perforated spoon, drain them thoroughly and then set them aside to cool. If you are using larger potatoes, cut them into 5 cm/2 inch chunks.

5 Pour the dressing over the potatoes and toss to mix.

6 Leave the potato salad to chill in the refrigerator for about 20 minutes, then serve as a starter or as an accompaniment.

COOK'S TIP

It is easier to cut the larger potatoes once they are cooked. Although smaller pieces of potato will cook more quickly, they tend to disintegrate and become mushy.

Potato & Beetroot Salad

The beetroot adds a rich colour to this dish. The dill dressing with the potato salad is a classic combination.

NUTRITIONAL INFORMATION

Calories	174	Sugars	8g
Protein	4g	Fat	6g
Carbohydrate	27g	Saturates	1g

 25 MINS  15 MINS

SERVES 4

INGREDIENTS

- 450 g/1 lb waxy potatoes, diced
- 4 small cooked beetroot, sliced
- ½ small cucumber, sliced thinly
- 2 large dill pickles, sliced
- 1 red onion, halved and sliced
- dill sprigs, to garnish

DRESSING

- 1 garlic clove, crushed
- 2 tbsp olive oil
- 2 tbsp red wine vinegar
- 2 tbsp chopped fresh dill
- salt and pepper

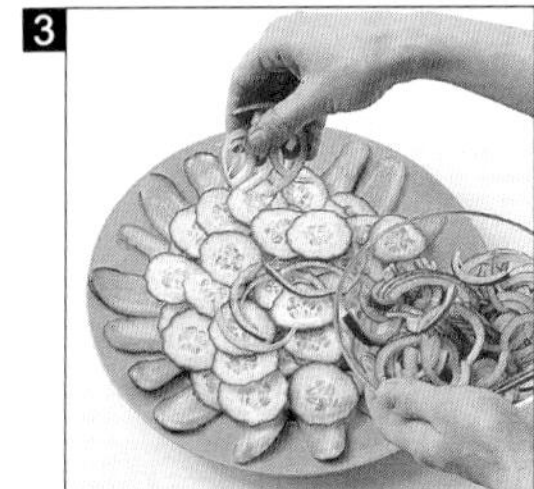

1 Cook the potatoes in a saucepan of boiling water for 15 minutes or until tender. Drain and leave to cool.

2 When cool, mix the potato and beetroot together in a bowl and set aside.

3 Line a salad platter with the slices of cucumber, dill pickles and red onion.

4 Spoon the potato and beetroot mixture into the centre of the platter.

5 In a small bowl, whisk all the dressing ingredients together, then pour it over the salad.

6 Serve the potato and beetroot salad immediately, (see Cook's Tip, left), garnished with dill sprigs.

COOK'S TIP

If making the salad in advance, do not mix the beetroot and potatoes until just before serving, as the beetroot will bleed its colour.

Sweet Potato & Nut Salad

Pecan nuts with their slightly bitter flavour are mixed with sweet potatoes to make a sweet and sour salad with an interesting texture.

NUTRITIONAL INFORMATION

Calories	330	Sugars	5g
Protein	4g	Fat	20g
Carbohydrate	36g	Saturates	2g

 25 MINS  10 MINS

SERVES 4

INGREDIENTS

- 500 g/1 lb 2 oz sweet potatoes, diced
- 2 celery sticks, sliced
- 125 g/4½ oz celeriac (celery root), grated
- 2 spring onions (scallions), sliced
- 50 g/1¾ oz/½ cup pecan nuts, chopped
- 2 heads chicory (endive), separated
- 1 tsp lemon juice
- thyme sprigs, to garnish

DRESSING

- 4 tbsp vegetable oil
- 1 tbsp garlic wine vinegar
- 1 tsp soft light brown sugar
- 2 tsp chopped thyme

1 Cook the sweet potatoes in a large saucepan of boiling water for 5 minutes, until tender. Drain thoroughly and set aside to cool.

2 When cooled, stir in the celery, celeriac (celery root), spring onions (scallions) and pecan nuts.

3 Line a salad plate with the chicory (endive) leaves and sprinkle with lemon juice.

4 Spoon the sweet potato mixture into the centre of the leaves.

2

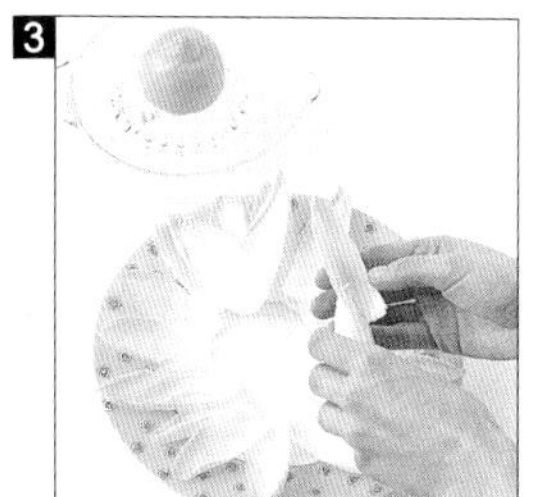

3

6

5 In a small bowl, whisk the dressing ingredients together.

6 Pour the dressing over the salad and serve at once, garnished with fresh thyme sprigs.

COOK'S TIP

Sweet potatoes do not store as well as ordinary potatoes. It is best to store them in a cool, dark place (not the refrigerator) and use within 1 week of purchase.

Potato & Banana Salad

This hot fruity salad combines sweet potato and fried bananas with colourful mixed (bell) peppers, tossed in a honey-based dressing.

NUTRITIONAL INFORMATION

Calories	424	Sugars	29g
Protein	5g	Fat	17g
Carbohydrate	68g	Saturates	8g

15 MINS

20 MINS

SERVES 4

INGREDIENTS

- 500 g/1 lb 2 oz sweet potatoes, diced
- 50 g/1¾ oz/4 tbsp butter
- 1 tbsp lemon juice
- 1 garlic clove, crushed
- 1 red (bell) pepper, seeded and diced
- 1 green (bell) pepper, seeded and diced
- 2 bananas, thickly sliced
- 2 thick slices white bread, crusts removed, diced
- salt and pepper

DRESSING

- 2 tbsp clear honey
- 2 tbsp chopped chives
- 2 tbsp lemon juice
- 2 tbsp olive oil

1 Cook the sweet potatoes in a saucepan of boiling water for 10–15 minutes, until tender. Drain thoroughly and reserve.

2 Meanwhile, melt the butter in a frying pan (skillet). Add the lemon juice, garlic and (bell) peppers and cook, stirring constantly for 3 minutes.

3 Add the banana slices to the pan and cook for 1 minute. Remove the bananas from the pan with a slotted spoon and stir into the potatoes.

4 Add the bread cubes to the frying pan (skillet) and cook, stirring frequently, for 2 minutes, until they are golden brown on all sides.

5 Mix the dressing ingredients together in a small saucepan and heat until the honey is runny.

6 Spoon the potato mixture into a serving dish and season to taste with salt and pepper. Pour the dressing over the potatoes and sprinkle the croûtons over the top. Serve immediately.

1

3

4

COOK'S TIP

Use firm, slightly underripe bananas in this recipe as they won't turn soft and mushy when they are fried.

Indian Potato Salad

There are many hot Indian-flavoured potato dishes which are served with curry but this fruity salad is delicious chilled.

NUTRITIONAL INFORMATION

Calories	175	Sugars	8g
Protein	6g	Fat	1g
Carbohydrate	38g	Saturates	0.3g

 25 MINS  20 MINS

SERVES 4

INGREDIENTS

4 medium floury (mealy) potatoes, diced

75 g/2¾ oz small broccoli florets

1 small mango, diced

4 spring onions (scallions), sliced

salt and pepper

small cooked spiced poppadoms, to serve

DRESSING

½ tsp ground cumin

½ tsp ground coriander

1 tbsp mango chutney

150 ml/¼ pint/⅔ cup low-fat natural yogurt

1 tsp ginger root, chopped

2 tbsp chopped fresh coriander (cilantro)

2

3

5

1 Cook the potatoes in a saucepan of boiling water for 10 minutes or until tender. Drain and place in a mixing bowl.

2 Meanwhile, blanch the broccoli florets in a separate saucepan of boiling water for 2 minutes. Drain the broccoli well and add to the potatoes in the bowl.

3 When the potatoes and broccoli have cooled, add the diced mango and sliced spring onions (scallions). Season to taste with salt and pepper and mix well to combine.

4 In a small bowl, stir all of the dressing ingredients together.

5 Spoon the dressing over the potato mixture and mix together carefully, taking care not to break up the potatoes and broccoli.

6 Serve the salad immediately, accompanied by small cooked spiced poppadoms.

COOK'S TIP

Mix the dressing ingredients together in advance and leave to chill in the refrigerator for a few hours in order for a stronger flavour to develop.

Potato, Apple & Bean Salad

Use any mixture of beans you have to hand in this recipe, but the wider the variety, the more colourful the salad.

NUTRITIONAL INFORMATION

Calories	183	Sugars	8g
Protein	6g	Fat	7g
Carbohydrate	26g	Saturates	1g

 10 MINS  15 MINS

SERVES 4

INGREDIENTS

- 225 g/8 oz new potatoes, scrubbed and quartered
- 225 g/8 oz mixed canned beans, such as red kidney beans, flageolet and borlotti beans, drained and rinsed
- 1 red dessert apple, diced and tossed in 1 tbsp lemon juice
- 1 small yellow (bell) pepper, diced
- 1 shallot, sliced
- ½ head fennel, sliced
- oak leaf lettuce leaves

DRESSING

- 1 tbsp red wine vinegar
- 2 tbsp olive oil
- ½ tbsp American mustard
- 1 garlic clove, crushed
- 2 tsp chopped fresh thyme

1 Cook the quartered potatoes in a saucepan of boiling water for 15 minutes until tender. Drain and transfer to a mixing bowl.

2 Add the potatoes to the mixed beans with the diced apple and yellow (bell) pepper, and the sliced shallots and fennel. Mix well, taking care not to break up the cooked potatoes.

3 In a bowl, whisk all the dressing ingredients together.

4 Pour the dressing over the potato salad.

5 Line a plate or salad bowl with the oak leaf and spoon the potato mixture into the centre. Serve the salad immediately.

COOK'S TIP

Canned beans are used here for convenience, but dried beans may be used instead. Soak for 8 hours or overnight, drain and place in a saucepan. Cover with water, bring to the boil and boil for 10 minutes, then simmer until tender.

2

3

4

Potato & Radish Salad

The radishes and the herb and mustard dressing give this colourful salad a mild mustard flavour which complements the potatoes perfectly.

NUTRITIONAL INFORMATION

Calories	140	Sugars	3g
Protein	3g	Fat	6g
Carbohydrate	20g	Saturates	1g

 1 3/4 HOURS  20 MINS

SERVES 4

INGREDIENTS

- 450 g/1 lb new potatoes, scrubbed and halved
- ½ cucumber, sliced thinly
- 2 tsp salt
- 1 bunch radishes, sliced thinly

DRESSING

- 1 tbsp Dijon mustard
- 2 tbsp olive oil
- 1 tbsp white wine vinegar
- 2 tbsp mixed chopped herbs

1. Cook the potatoes in a saucepan of boiling water for 10-15 minutes or until tender. Drain and leave to cool.

2. Spread out the cucumber slices on a plate and sprinkle with the salt. Leave to stand for 30 minutes, then rinse under cold running water and pat dry with kitchen paper (paper towels).

3. Arrange the cucumber and radish slices on a serving plate in a decorative pattern

4. Pile the cooked potatoes in the centre of the cucumber and radish slices.

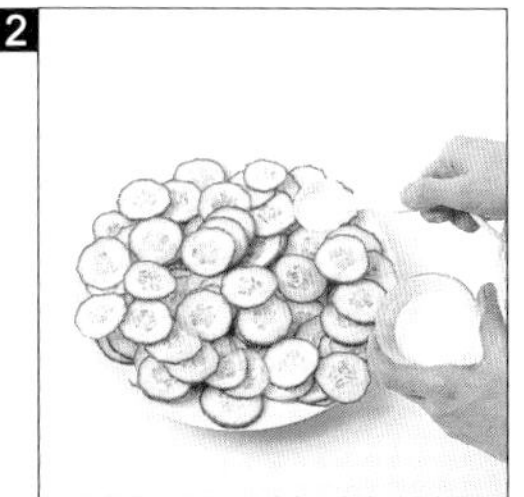
2

2

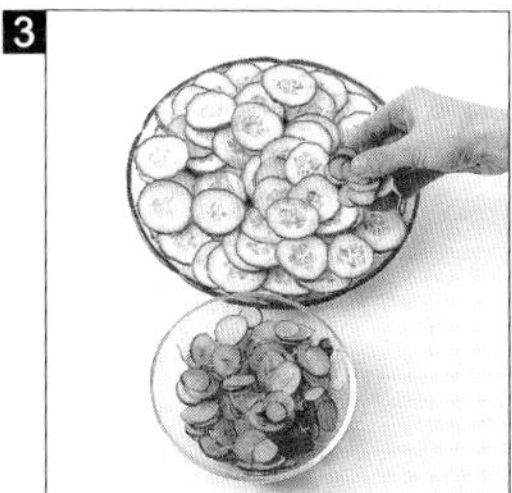
3

5. Pour all the dressing ingredients in a screw-top jar and shake vigorously to combine all the ingredients. Pour the dressing over the salad, tossing well to coat all of the salad ingredients.

6. Leave the salad to chill in the refrigerator before serving.

COOK'S TIP

Dijon mustard has a mild clean taste which is perfect for this salad as it does not overpower the other flavours. If unavailable, use another mild mustard – English mustard is too strong for this salad.

Green & White Salad

This potato, rocket (arugula) and apple salad is flavoured with creamy, salty goat's cheese – perfect with salad leaves (greens).

NUTRITIONAL INFORMATION

Calories	282	Sugars	10g
Protein	8g	Fat	17g
Carbohydrate	26g	Saturates	5g

15 MINS 20 MINS

SERVES 4

INGREDIENTS

- 2 large potatoes, unpeeled and sliced
- 2 green eating apples, diced
- 1 tsp lemon juice
- 25 g/1 oz/¼ cup walnut pieces
- 125 g/4½ oz goat's cheese, cubed
- 150 g/5½ oz/2–3 bunches rocket (arugula) leaves
- salt and pepper

DRESSING

- 2 tbsp olive oil
- 1 tbsp red wine vinegar
- 1 tsp clear honey
- 1 tsp fennel seeds

COOK'S TIP

Serve this salad immediately to prevent the apple from discolouring. Alternatively, prepare all of the other ingredients in advance and add the apple at the last minute.

1 Cook the potatoes in a pan of boiling water for 15 minutes, until tender. Drain and set aside to cool. Transfer the cooled potatoes to a serving bowl.

2 Toss the diced apples in the lemon juice, drain and stir them into the cold potatoes.

3 Add the walnut pieces, cheese cubes and rocket (arugula) leaves, then toss the salad to mix.

4 In a small bowl, whisk the dressing ingredients together until well combined and pour the dressing over the salad. Serve immediately.

Chinese Salad Nests

Crisp fried potato nests are perfect as an edible salad bowl and delicious when filled with a colourful Chinese-style salad of vegetables and fruit.

NUTRITIONAL INFORMATION

Calories	272	Sugars	11g
Protein	4g	Fat	4g
Carbohydrate	59g	Saturates	0.4g

 15 MINS  15 MINS

SERVES 4

INGREDIENTS

POTATO NESTS

450 g/1 lb floury (mealy) potatoes, grated

125 g/4½ oz/1 cup cornflour (cornstarch)

vegetable oil, for frying

fresh chives, to garnish

SALAD

125 g/4½ oz pineapple, cubed

1 green (bell) pepper, cut into strips

1 carrot, cut into thin strips

50 g/1¾ oz mangetout (snowpeas), sliced thickly

4 baby sweetcorn cobs, halved lengthways

25 g/1 oz beansprouts

2 spring onions (scallions), sliced

DRESSING

1 tbsp clear honey

1 tsp light soy sauce

1 garlic clove, crushed

1 tsp lemon juice

1

2
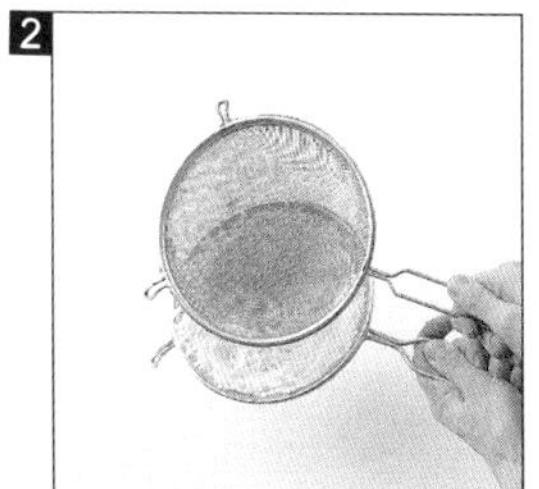

3

1 To make the nests, rinse the potatoes several times in cold water. Drain well on kitchen paper (paper towels) so they are completely dry. This is to prevent the potatoes spitting when they are cooked in the fat. Place the potatoes in a mixing bowl. Add the cornflour (cornstarch), mixing well to coat the potatoes.

2 Half fill a wok with vegetable oil and heat until smoking. Line a 15 cm/ 6 inch diameter wire sieve with a quarter of the potato mixture and press another sieve of the same size on top.

3 Lower the sieves into the oil and cook for 2 minutes until the potato nest is golden brown and crisp. Remove from the wok, allowing the excess oil to drain off.

4 Repeat 3 more times to use up all of the mixture and make a total of 4 nests. Leave to cool.

5 Mix the salad ingredients together then spoon into the potato baskets.

6 Mix the dressing ingredients together in a bowl. Pour the dressing over the salad, garnish with chives and serve immediately.

Potato & Tuna Salad

This colourful dish is a variation of the classic Salade Niçoise. Packed with tuna and vegetables, it is both filling and delicious.

NUTRITIONAL INFORMATION

Calories	225	Sugars	5g
Protein	21g	Fat	5g
Carbohydrate	27g	Saturates	2g

 40 MINS  20 MINS

SERVES 4

INGREDIENTS

- 450 g/1 lb new potatoes, scrubbed and quartered
- 1 green (bell) pepper, sliced
- 50 g/1¾ oz canned sweetcorn, drained
- 1 red onion, sliced
- 300 g/10½ oz canned tuna in brine, drained and flaked
- 2 tbsp chopped stoned (pitted) black olives
- salt and pepper
- lime wedges, to garnish

DRESSING

- 2 tbsp low-fat mayonnaise
- 2 tbsp soured cream
- 1 tbsp lime juice
- 2 garlic cloves, crushed
- finely grated rind of 1 lime

1 Cook the potatoes in a saucepan of boiling water for 15 minutes until tender. Drain and leave to cool in a mixing bowl.

2 Gently stir in the sliced green (bell) pepper, sweetcorn and sliced red onion.

3 Spoon the potato mixture into a large serving bowl and arrange the flaked tuna and chopped black olives over the top.

4 Season the salad generously with salt and pepper.

5 To make the dressing, mix together the mayonnaise, soured cream, lime juice, garlic and lime rind in a bowl.

6 Spoon the dressing over the tuna and olives, garnish with lime wedges and serve.

2

3

4

COOK'S TIP

Green beans and hard-boiled (hard-cooked) egg slices can be added to the salad for a more traditional Salade Niçoise.

Waldorf Chicken Salad

This colourful and healthy dish is a variation of a classic salad. You can use a selection of mixed salad leaves, if preferred.

NUTRITIONAL INFORMATION

Calories	471	Sugars	19g
Protein	38g	Fat	27g
Carbohydrate	20g	Saturates	4g

 30 MINS  0 MINS

SERVES 4

INGREDIENTS

- 500 g/1 lb 2 oz red apples, diced
- 3 tbsp fresh lemon juice
- 150 ml/¼ pint/⅔ cup low-fat mayonnaise
- 1 head of celery
- 4 shallots, sliced
- 1 garlic clove, crushed
- 90 g/3 oz/¾ cup walnuts, chopped
- 500 g/1 lb 2 oz lean cooked chicken, cubed
- 1 cos (romaine) lettuce
- pepper
- sliced apple and walnuts, to garnish

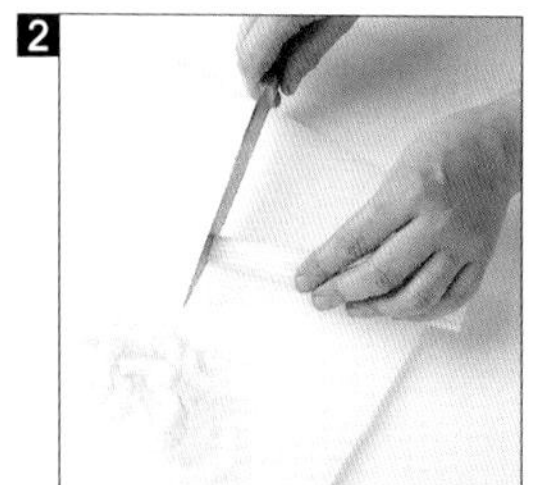

1 Place the apples in a bowl with the lemon juice and 1 tablespoon of mayonnaise. Leave for 40 minutes or until required.

2 Slice the celery very thinly. Add the celery with the shallots, garlic and walnuts to the apple, mix and then add the remaining mayonnaise and blend thoroughly.

3 Add the chicken and mix with the other ingredients.

4 Lline a glass salad bowl or serving dish with the lettuce.

5 Pile the chicken salad into the centre, sprinkle with pepper and garnish with apple slices and walnuts.

VARIATION

Instead of the shallots, use spring onions (scallions) for a milder flavour. Trim the spring onions (scallions) and slice finely.

Potato & Sausage Salad

Sliced Italian sausage blends well with the other Mediterranean flavours of sun-dried tomato and basil in this salad.

NUTRITIONAL INFORMATION

Calories	450	Sugars	6g
Protein	13g	Fat	28g
Carbohydrate	38g	Saturates	1g

 25 MINS  25 MINS

SERVES 4

INGREDIENTS

- 450 g/1 lb waxy potatoes
- 1 raddichio or lollo rosso lettuce
- 1 green (bell) pepper, sliced
- 175 g/6 oz Italian sausage, sliced
- 1 red onion, halved and sliced
- 125 g/4½ oz sun-dried tomatoes, sliced
- 2 tbsp shredded fresh basil

DRESSING

- 1 tbsp balsamic vinegar
- 1 tsp tomato purée (paste)
- 2 tbsp olive oil
- salt and pepper

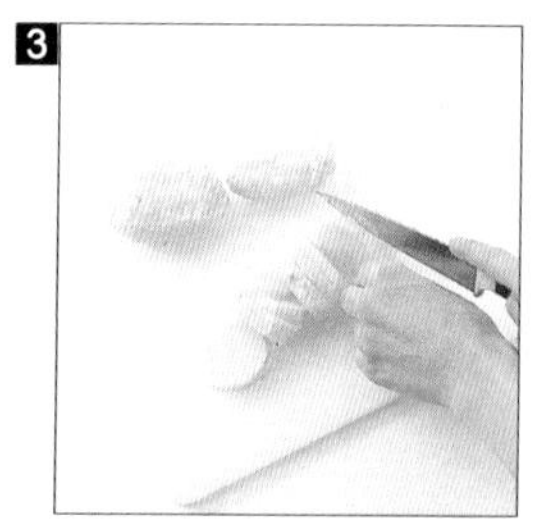
3

3

4

COOK'S TIP

Any sliced Italian sausage or salami can be used in this salad. Italy is home of the salami and there are numerous varieties to choose from – those from the south tend to be more highly spiced than those from the north of the country.

1 Cook the potatoes in a saucepan of boiling water for 20 minutes or until cooked through. Drain and leave to cool.

2 Line a large serving platter with the radicchio or lollo rosso lettuce leaves.

3 Slice the cooled potatoes and arrange them in layers on the lettuce-lined serving platter together with the sliced green (bell) pepper, sliced Italian sausage, red onion, sun-dried tomatoes and shredded fresh basil.

4 In a small bowl, whisk the balsamic vinegar, tomato purée (paste) and olive oil together and season to taste with salt and pepper. Pour the dressing over the potato salad and serve immediately.

Mexican Potato Salad

The flavours of Mexico are echoed in this dish where potato slices are topped with tomatoes, chillies and ham, and served with guacamole.

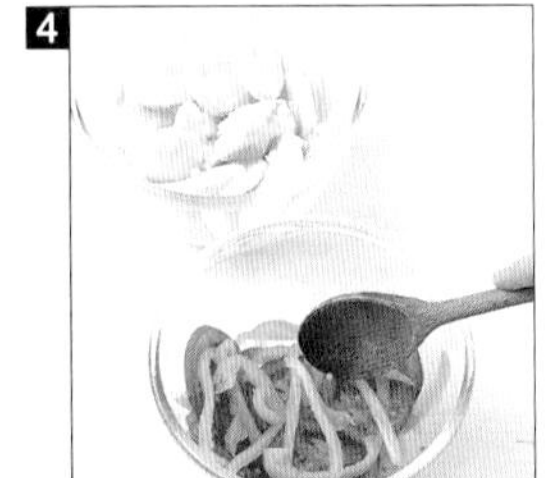

NUTRITIONAL INFORMATION

Calories	260	Sugars	6g
Protein	6g	Fat	9g
Carbohydrate	41g	Saturates	2g

 20 MINS  20 MINS

SERVES 4

INGREDIENTS

- 4 large waxy potatoes, sliced
- 1 ripe avocado
- 1 tsp olive oil
- 1 tsp lemon juice
- 1 garlic clove, crushed
- 1 onion, chopped
- 2 large tomatoes, sliced
- 1 green chilli, chopped
- 1 yellow (bell) pepper, seeded and sliced
- 2 tbsp chopped coriander (cilantro)
- salt and pepper
- lemon wedges, to garnish

1 Cook the potato slices in a saucepan of boiling water for 10–15 minutes, or until tender. Drain and set aside to cool.

2 Meanwhile, cut the avocado in half and remove the stone (pit). Mash the avocado flesh with a fork (you could also scoop the avocado flesh from the 2 halves using a spoon and then mash it).

3 Add the olive oil, lemon juice, garlic and chopped onion to the avocado flesh and stir to mix. Cover the bowl with clear film (plastic wrap), to minimize discolouration, and set aside.

4 Mix the tomatoes, chilli and yellow (bell) pepper together and transfer to a salad bowl with the potato slices.

5 Arrange the avocado mixture on top of the salad and sprinkle with the coriander (cilantro). Season to taste with salt and pepper and serve garnished with lemon wedges.

VARIATION

You can omit the green chilli from this salad if you do not like hot dishes.

Chicory (Endive) Salad

The contrast of the pink grapefruit, creamy chicory (endive) and bright green lamb's lettuce (corn salad) make this a stunning accompaniment.

NUTRITIONAL INFORMATION

Calories	137	Sugars	4g
Protein	1g	Fat	13g
Carbohydrate	4g	Saturates	2g

 10 MINS   0 MINS

SERVES 4

INGREDIENTS

- 1 pink grapefruit
- 1 avocado
- 1 packet lamb's lettuce (corn salad), washed thoroughly
- 2 heads chicory (endive), sliced diagonally
- 1 tbsp chopped fresh mint

FRENCH DRESSING

- 3 tbsp olive oil
- 1 tbsp wine vinegar
- 1 small garlic clove, crushed
- ½ tsp Dijon or Meaux mustard
- 1 tsp clear honey
- salt and pepper

1 Peel the grapefruit with a serrated-edge knife.

2 Cut the grapefruit into segments by cutting between the membranes.

3 To make the French dressing, put all the ingredients into a screw-top jar and shake vigorously.

4 Halve the avocado and remove the stone (pit) by stabbing the stone (pit) with a sharp knife and twisting to loosen. Remove the skin.

5 Cut the avocado into small slices, put into a bowl and toss in the French dressing.

6 Remove any stalks from the lamb's lettuce (corn salad) and put into a bowl with the grapefruit, chicory (endive) and mint.

7 Add the avocado and 2 tablespoons of the French dressing. Toss well and transfer to serving plates.

1
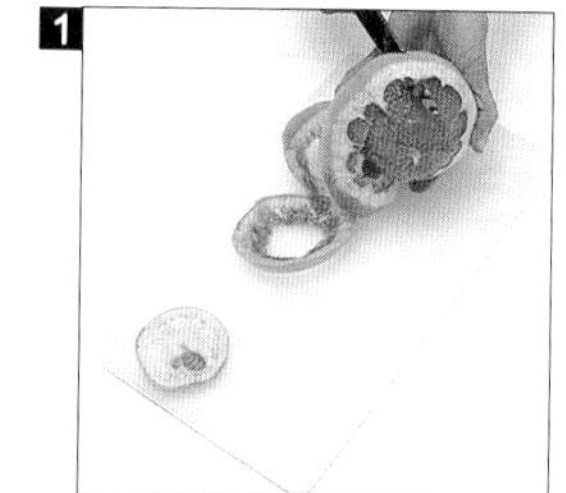

2
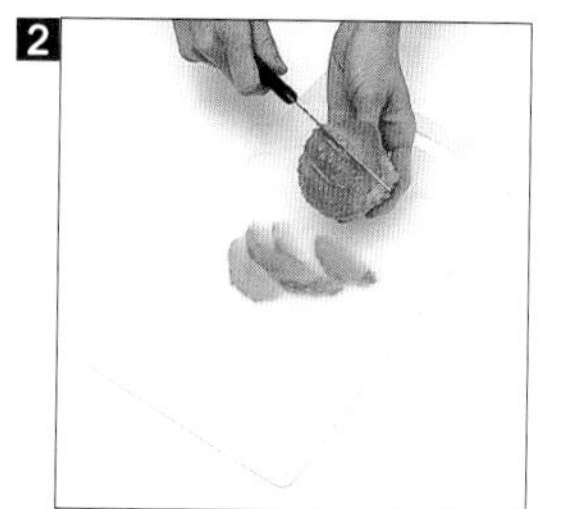

5

COOK'S TIP

Lamb's lettuce is so called because the shape of its dark green leaves resembles a lamb's tongue. It is also known as corn salad and the French call it mâche. It is easy to grow in the garden and will withstand the frost.

Paw-paw (Papaya) Salad

Choose firm paw-paws – or papayas as they are sometimes called – for this delicious salad.

NUTRITIONAL INFORMATION

Calories	193	Sugars	11g
Protein	3g	Fat	15g
Carbohydrate	12g	Saturates	2g

 10 MINS  0 MINS

SERVES 4

INGREDIENTS

DRESSING

- 4 tbsp olive oil
- 1 tbsp fish sauce or light soy sauce
- 2 tbsp lime or lemon juice
- 1 tbsp dark muscovado sugar
- 1 tsp finely chopped fresh red or green chilli

SALAD

- 1 crisp lettuce
- ¼ small white cabbage
- 2 paw-paws (papayas)
- 2 tomatoes
- 25 g/1 oz/¼ cup roasted peanuts, chopped roughly
- 4 spring onions (scallions), trimmed and sliced thinly
- basil leaves, to garnish

1

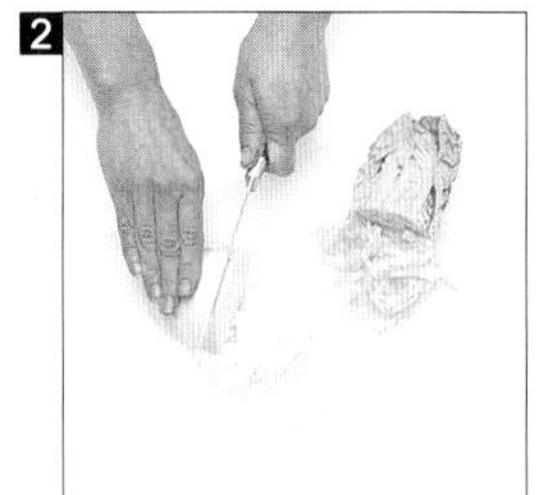

2

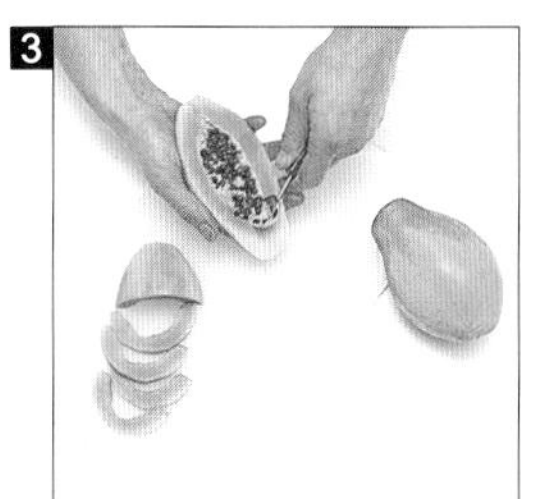

3

1 To make the dressing, whisk together the oil, fish sauce or soy sauce, lime or lemon juice, sugar and chilli. Set aside, stirring occasionally to dissolve the sugar.

2 Shred the lettuce and white cabbage, then toss together and arrange on a large serving plate.

3 Peel the paw-paws (papayas) and slice them in half. Scoop out the seeds, then slice the flesh thinly. Arrange on top of the lettuce and cabbage.

4 Soak the tomatoes in a bowl of boiling water for 1 minute, then lift out and peel. Remove the seeds and chop the flesh. Arrange on the salad leaves.

5 Scatter the peanuts and spring onions (scallions) over the top. Whisk the dressing and pour over the salad. Garnish with basil leaves and serve at once.

COOK'S TIP

Choose plain, unsalted peanuts and toast them under the grill (broiler) until golden to get the best flavour. Take care not to burn them, as they brown very quickly.

Grapefruit & Coconut Salad

This salad is quite deceptive – it is, in fact, surprisingly filling, even though it looks very light.

NUTRITIONAL INFORMATION

Calories	201	Sugars	13g
Protein	3g	Fat	15g
Carbohydrate	14g	Saturates	9g

 10 MINS

10 MINS

SERVES 4

INGREDIENTS

- 125 g/4½ oz/1 cup grated coconut
- 2 tsp light soy sauce
- 2 tbsp lime juice
- 2 tbsp water
- 2 tsp sunflower oil
- 1 garlic clove, halved
- 1 onion, finely chopped
- 2 large ruby grapefruits, peeled and segmented
- 90 g/3 oz/1½ cups alfalfa sprouts

1. Toast the coconut in a dry frying pan (skillet) over a low heat, stirring constantly, for about 3 minutes, or until golden brown. Transfer the toasted coconut to a bowl.

2. Add the light soy sauce, lime juice and water to the toasted coconut and mix together well.

3. Heat the oil in a saucepan and fry the garlic and onion until soft. Stir the onion into the coconut mixture. Remove and discard the garlic.

4. Divide the grapefruit segments between 4 plates. Sprinkle each with a quarter of the alfalfa sprouts and spoon over a quarter of the coconut mixture.

1

2

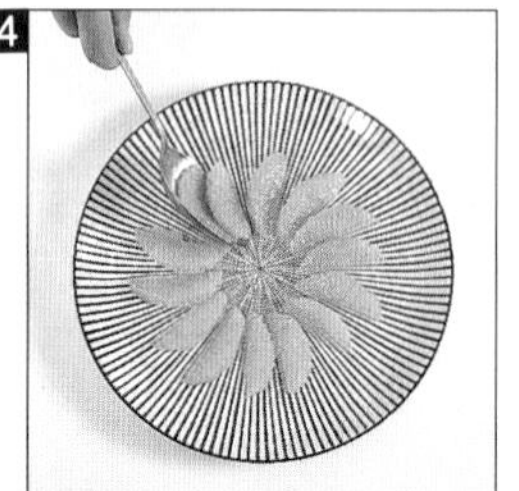
4

COOK'S TIP

Alfalfa sprouts can be bought in trays or packets from most supermarkets, but you can easily grow your own, if you like to have a constant and cheap supply.

Pear & Roquefort Salad

The sweetness of the pear is a perfect partner to the 'bite' of the radicchio.

NUTRITIONAL INFORMATION

Calories	94	Sugars	10g
Protein	5g	Fat	4g
Carbohydrate	10g	Saturates	3g

 10 MINS  0 MINS

SERVES 4

INGREDIENTS

- 50 g/1¾ oz Roquefort cheese
- 150 ml/5 fl oz/⅔ cup low-fat natural yogurt
- 2 tbsp snipped chives
- few leaves of lollo rosso
- few leaves of radicchio
- few leaves of lamb's lettuce (corn salad)
- 2 ripe pears
- pepper
- whole chives, to garnish

1 Place the cheese in a bowl and mash with a fork. Gradually blend the yogurt into the cheese to make a smooth dressing Add the chives and season with pepper to taste.

2 Tear the lollo rosso, radicchio and lamb's lettuce leaves into manageable pieces. Arrange the salad leaves on a serving platter or on individual serving plates.

3 Quarter and core the pears and then cut them into slices.

4 Arrange the pear slices over the salad leaves.

5 Drizzle the dressing over the pears and garnish with a few whole chives.

COOK'S TIP

Look out for bags of mixed salad leaves as these are generally more economical than buying lots of different leaves separately.

Noodle & Mango Salad

Fruit combines well with the peanut dressing, (bell) peppers and chilli in this delicous hot salad.

NUTRITIONAL INFORMATION

Calories	368	Sugars	11g
Protein	11g	Fat	26g
Carbohydrate	24g	Saturates	5g

 15 MINS  5 MINS

SERVES 4

INGREDIENTS

- 250 g/9 oz thread egg noodles
- 2 tbsp groundnut oil
- 4 shallots, sliced
- 2 cloves garlic, crushed
- 1 red chilli, deseeded and sliced
- 1 red (bell) pepper, deseeded and sliced
- 1 green (bell) pepper, deseeded and sliced
- 1 ripe mango, sliced into thin strips
- 25 g/1 oz/¼ cup salted peanuts, chopped

DRESSING

- 4 tbsp peanut butter
- 100 ml/3½ fl oz/⅓ cup coconut milk
- 1 tbsp tomato purée (tomato paste)

1

3

4

1 Place the egg noodles in a large dish or bowl. Pour over enough boiling water to cover the noodles and leave to stand for 10 minutes.

2 Heat the groundnut oil in a large preheated wok or frying pan (skillet).

3 Add the shallots, crushed garlic, chilli and (bell) pepper slices to the wok or frying pan (skillet) and stir-fry for 2–3 minutes.

4 Drain the egg noodles thoroughly in a colander. Add the drained noodles and mango slices to the wok or frying pan (skillet) and heat through for about 2 minutes.

5 Transfer the noodle and mango salad to warmed serving dishes and scatter with chopped peanuts.

6 To make the dressing, mix together the peanut butter, coconut milk and tomato purée (tomato paste) then spoon over the noodle salad. Serve immediately.

COOK'S TIP

If preferred, gently heat the peanut dressing before pouring over the noodle salad.

Minted Fennel Salad

This is a very refreshing salad. The subtle liquorice flavour of fennel combines well with the cucumber and mint.

NUTRITIONAL INFORMATION

Calories	90	Sugars	7g
Protein	4g	Fat	5g
Carbohydrate	7g	Saturates	1g

 25 MINS  0 MINS

SERVES 4

INGREDIENTS

- 1 bulb fennel
- 2 small oranges
- 1 small or ½ a large cucumber
- 1 tbsp chopped mint
- 1 tbsp virgin olive oil
- 2 eggs, hard boiled (cooked)

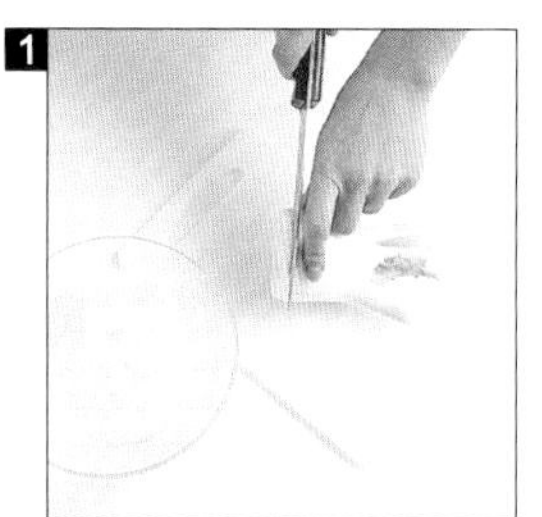

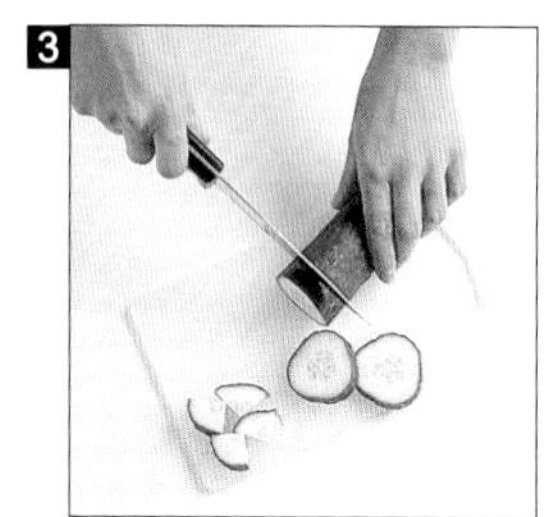

1 Using a sharp knife, trim the outer leaves from the fennel. Slice the fennel bulb thinly into a bowl of water and sprinkle with lemon juice (see Cook's Tip).

2 Grate the rind of the oranges over a bowl. Using a sharp knife, pare away the orange peel, then segment the orange by carefully slicing between each line of pith. Do this over the bowl in order to retain the juice.

3 Using a sharp knife, cut the cucumber into 12 mm/½ inch rounds and then cut each round into quarters.

4 Add the cucumber to the fennel and orange mixture together with the mint.

5 Pour the olive oil over the fennel and cucumber salad and toss well.

6 Peel and quarter the eggs and use these to decorate the top of the salad. Serve at once.

COOK'S TIP

Fennel will discolour if it is left for any length of time without a dressing. To prevent any discoloration, place it in a bowl of water and sprinkle with lemon juice.

Cucumber Salad

This is a very refreshing accompaniment to any main dish and is an excellent 'cooler' for curries.

NUTRITIONAL INFORMATION

Calories	33	Sugars	8g
Protein	0.2g	Fat	0g
Carbohydrate	9g	Saturates	0g

10 MINS 0 MINS

SERVES 4

INGREDIENTS

½ cucumber

1 tbsp rice vinegar

2 tbsp sugar

½ tsp salt

2 tbsp hot water

1 small shallot

1 Wash the cucumber thoroughly and pat dry with absorbent kitchen paper (paper towels).

2 Peel the cucumber, halve it lengthways, and deseed it, using a teaspoon or a melon baller.

3 Using a sharp knife, slice the cucumber thinly.

4 Arrange the cucumber slices in an attractive pattern on a serving plate.

5 To make the dressing, mix together the rice vinegar, sugar and salt in a bowl. Pour on the hot water and stir until the sugar has dissolved. Leave the dressing to cool slightly.

6 Pour the dressing evenly over the cucumber slices.

7 Using a sharp knife, thinly slice the shallot and sprinkle over the cucumber.

8 Cover the cucumber salad with cling film (plastic wrap) and leave to chill in the refrigerator before serving. Serve as a cooling accompaniment to curries.

COOK'S TIP

Some people dislike the bitter taste that cucumbers can have – I find that peeling off the skin and deseeding the cucumber often eliminates this problem. Using a melon baller is the neatest method of deseeding a cucumber.

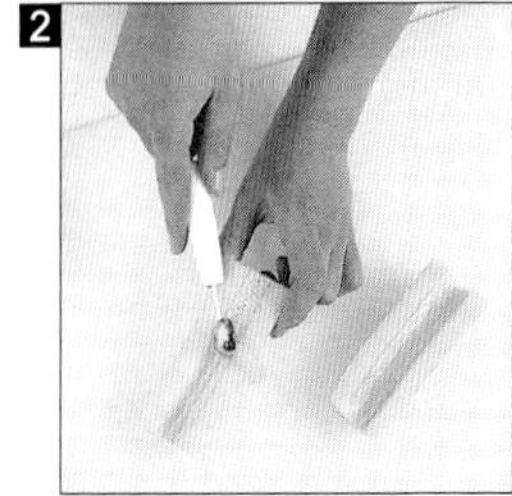

2

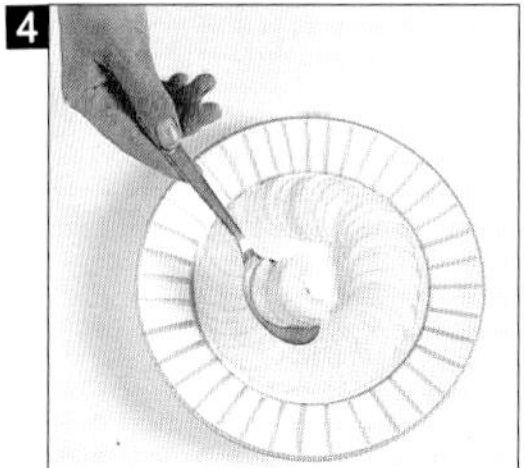

4

5

Italian Mozzarella Salad

This colourful salad is packed full of delicious flavours but is easy to make.

NUTRITIONAL INFORMATION

Calories	79	Sugars	2g
Protein	4g	Fat	6g
Carbohydrate	2g	Saturates	2g

 20 MINS  0 MINS

SERVES 6

INGREDIENTS

- 200 g/7 oz baby spinach
- 125 g/4 ½ oz watercress
- 125 g/4 ½ oz Mozzarella cheese
- 225 g/8 oz cherry tomatoes
- 2 tsp balsamic vinegar
- 1 ½ tbsp extra virgin olive oil
- salt and pepper

1 Wash the spinach and watercress and drain thoroughly on absorbent kitchen paper. Remove any tough stalks. Place the spinach and watercress leaves in a large serving dish.

2 Cut the Mozzarella into small pieces and scatter them over the spinach and watercress leaves.

3 Cut the cherry tomatoes in half and scatter them over the salad.

4 Sprinkle over the balsamic vinegar and oil, and season with salt and pepper to taste. Toss the mixture together to coat the leaves. Serve at once or leave to chill in the refrigerator until required.

1

2

3

Chicken & Noodle Salad

Strips of chicken are coated in a delicious spicy mixture, then stir-fried with noodles and served on a bed of salad.

NUTRITIONAL INFORMATION

Calories	217	Sugars	1g
Protein	21g	Fat	11g
Carbohydrate	9g	Saturates	2g

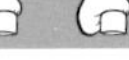

 10 MINS  10 MINS

SERVES 4

INGREDIENTS

- 1 tsp finely grated fresh ginger root
- ½ tsp Chinese five-spice powder
- 1 tbsp plain (all-purpose) flour
- ½ tsp chilli powder
- 350 g/12 oz boned chicken breast, skinned and sliced thinly
- 60 g/2 oz rice noodles
- 125 g/4½ oz/1½ cups Chinese leaves (cabbage) or hard white cabbage, shredded finely
- 7 cm/3 inch piece of cucumber, sliced finely
- 1 large carrot, pared thinly
- 1 tbsp olive oil
- 2 tbsp lime or lemon juice
- 2 tbsp sesame oil
- salt and pepper

TO GARNISH

- lemon or lime slices
- fresh coriander (cilantro) leaves

1 Mix together the ginger, five-spice powder, flour and chilli powder in a shallow mixing bowl. Season with salt and pepper. Add the strips of chicken and roll in the mixture until well coated.

2 Put the noodles into a large bowl and cover with warm water. Leave to soak for about 5 minutes, then drain them well.

3 Mix together the Chinese leaves (cabbage) or white cabbage, cucumber and carrot, and arrange in a salad bowl. Whisk together the olive oil and lime or lemon juice, season with a salt and pepper, and use to dress the salad.

4 Heat the sesame oil in a wok or frying pan (skillet) and add the chicken. Stir-fry for 5–6 minutes until well-browned and crispy on the outside. Remove from the wok or frying pan (skillet) with a perforated spoon and drain on absorbent kitchen paper (paper towels).

5 Add the noodles to the wok or frying pan (skillet) and stir-fry for 3–4 minutes until heated through. Remove from the wok, mix with the chicken and pile the mixture on top of the salad. Serve garnished with lime or lemon slices and coriander (cilantro) leaves.

1

2

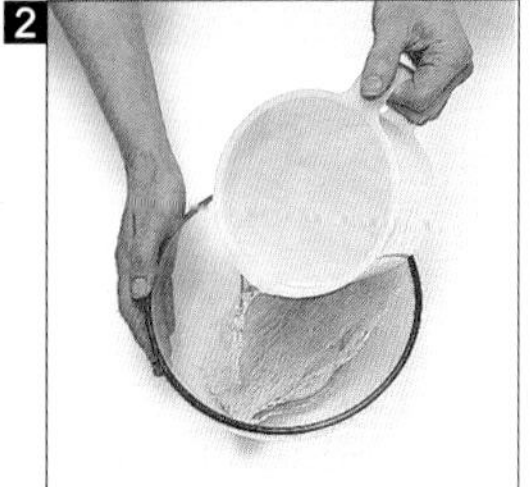

3

Roast (Bell) Pepper Salad

Serve chilled as an antipasto with cold meats, or warm as a side dish. Garlic bread makes a delicious accompaniment.

NUTRITIONAL INFORMATION

Calories	141	Sugars	8g
Protein	1g	Fat	11g
Carbohydrate	9g	Saturates	2g

 20 MINS  20 MINS

SERVES

INGREDIENTS

4 large mixed red, green and yellow (bell) peppers

4 tbsp olive oil

1 large red onion, sliced

2 garlic cloves, crushed

4 tomatoes, peeled and chopped

pinch of sugar

1 tsp lemon juice

salt and pepper

1 Trim and halve the (bell) peppers and remove the seeds.

2 Place the (bell) peppers, skin-side up, under a preheated hot grill (broiler). Cook until the skins char. Rinse under cold water and remove the skins.

3 Trim off any thick membranes and slice thinly.

4 Heat the oil and fry the onion and garlic until softened. Then add the (bell) peppers and tomatoes and fry over a low heat for 10 minutes.

5 Remove from the heat, add the sugar and lemon juice, and season to taste. Serve immediately or leave to cool (the flavours will develop as the salad cools).

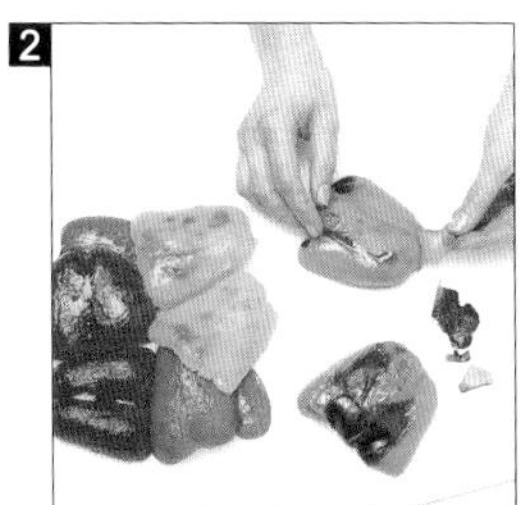

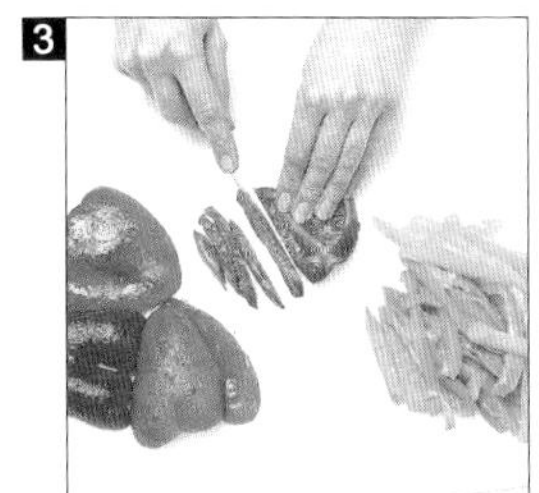

Carrot & Nut Coleslaw

This simple salad has a dressing made from poppy seeds pan-fried in sesame oil to bring out their flavour and aroma.

NUTRITIONAL INFORMATION

Calories	220	Sugars	7g
Protein	4g	Fat	19g
Carbohydrate	10g	Saturates	3g

 15 MINS  5–10 MINS

SERVES 4

INGREDIENTS

- 1 large carrot, grated
- 1 small onion, finely chopped
- 2 celery sticks, chopped
- ¼ small hard white cabbage, shredded
- 1 tbsp chopped parsley
- 4 tbsp sesame oil
- ½ tsp poppy seeds
- 60 g/2 oz/½ cup cashew nuts
- 2 tbsp white wine vinegar or cider vinegar
- salt and pepper
- parsley sprigs, to garnish

1 In a large salad bowl, mix together the carrot, onion, celery and cabbage. Stir in the chopped parsley and season to taste with salt and pepper.

2 Heat the sesame oil in a saucepan with a lid. Add the poppy seeds and cover the pan. Cook over a medium-high heat until the seeds start to make a popping sound. Remove from the heat and set aside to cool.

3 Spread out the cashew nuts on a baking tray (cookie sheet). Place them under a medium-hot grill (broiler) and toast until lightly browned, being careful not to burn them. Leave to cool.

2

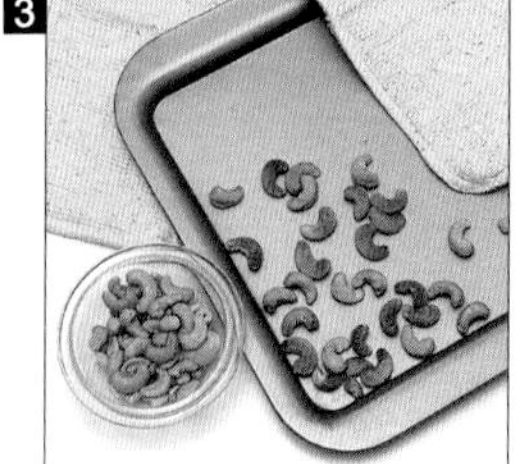
3

4

4 Add the vinegar to the oil and poppy seeds, then pour the dressing over the carrot mixture. Add the cooled cashew nuts. Toss together to coat well.

5 Garnish the salad with sprigs of fresh parsley and serve immediately.

Coronation Salad

This dish is based on Coronation Chicken which was invented to celebrate Queen Victoria's coronation as a symbol of Anglo-Indian links.

NUTRITIONAL INFORMATION

Calories	236	Sugars	24g
Protein	7g	Fat	5g
Carbohydrate	43g	Saturates	1g

 25 MINS  0 MINS

SERVES 4

INGREDIENTS

- 1 red (bell) pepper
- 60 g/2 oz/⅓ cup sultanas (golden raisins)
- 1 celery stick, sliced
- 125 g/4½ oz/¾ cup sweetcorn
- 1 Granny Smith apple, diced
- 125 g/4½ oz/1 cup white seedless grapes, washed and halved
- 250 g/9 oz/1½ cups cooked basmati rice
- 60 g/2 oz/½ cup cooked, peeled prawns (shrimp) (optional)
- 1 cos (romaine) lettuce, washed and drained
- 1 tsp paprika to garnish

DRESSING

- 4 tbsp low-fat mayonnaise
- 2 tsp mild curry powder
- 1 tsp lemon juice
- 1 tsp paprika
- pinch of salt

1 Deseed and chop the red (bell) pepper.

2 Combine the sultanas (golden raisins), red (bell) pepper, celery, sweetcorn, apple and grapes in a large bowl. Stir in the rice, and prawns (shrimp), if using.

3 For the dressing, put the mayonnaise, curry powder, lemon juice, paprika and salt into a small bowl and mix well.

4 Pour the dressing over the salad and gently mix until evenly coated.

5 Line the serving plate with cos (romaine) lettuce leaves and spoon on the salad. Sprinkle over the paprika and serve.

COOK'S TIP

Mayonnaise can be bought in varying thicknesses, from the type that you spoon out of the jar to the pouring variety. If you need to thin down mayonnaise for a dressing, simply add water little by little until the desired consistency is reached.

Beef & Peanut Salad

Although peanuts are very high in fat, they do have a strong flavour, so you can make a little go a long way.

NUTRITIONAL INFORMATION

Calories	194	Sugars	3g
Protein	21g	Fat	10g
Carbohydrate	5g	Saturates	3g

 10 MINS 10 MINS

SERVES 4

INGREDIENTS

- ½ head Chinese leaves (cabbage)
- 1 large carrot
- 125 g/4½ oz radishes
- 100 g/3½ oz baby corn
- 1 tbsp groundnut oil
- 1 red chilli, deseeded and chopped finely
- 1 clove garlic, chopped finely
- 350 g/12 oz lean beef
- 1 tbsp dark soy sauce
- 25 g/1 oz fresh peanuts (optional)
- red chilli, sliced, to garnish

DRESSING

- 1 tbsp smooth peanut butter
- 1 tsp caster (superfine) sugar
- 2 tbsp light soy sauce
- 1 tbsp sherry vinegar
- salt and pepper

1 Finely shred the Chinese leaves (cabbage) and arrange on a platter. Peel the carrot and cut into thin, matchstick-like strips.

2 Wash, trim and quarter the radishes, and halve the baby corn lengthwise. Arrange these ingredients around the edge of the dish and set aside.

3 Trim the beef and slice into fine strips. Heat the oil in a non-stick wok or large frying pan (skillet) and stir-fry the chilli, garlic and beef for 5 minutes. Add the dark soy sauce and stir-fry for a further 1–2 minutes until tender and cooked through.

4 Meanwhile, make the dressing. Place all of the ingredients in a small bowl and blend them together until smooth.

5 Place the hot cooked beef in the centre of the salad ingredients. Spoon over the dressing and sprinkle with a few peanuts (if using).

6 Garnish the salad with slices of red chilli and serve immediately.

VARIATION

If preferred, use chicken, turkey, lean pork or even strips of venison instead of beef in this recipe. Cut off all visible fat before you begin.

Potatoes in Italian Dressing

The warm potatoes quickly absorb the wonderful flavours of olives, tomatoes and olive oil. This salad is good warm, and cold.

NUTRITIONAL INFORMATION

Calories	239	Sugars	2g
Protein	4g	Fat	10g
Carbohydrate	36g	Saturates	1g

 15 MINS  15 MINS

SERVES 4

INGREDIENTS

- 750 g/1 lb 10 oz waxy potatoes
- 1 shallot
- 2 tomatoes
- 1 tbsp chopped fresh basil
- salt

ITALIAN DRESSING

- 1 tomato, skinned and chopped finely
- 4 black olives, pitted and chopped finely
- 4 tbsp olive oil
- 1 tbsp wine vinegar
- 1 garlic clove, crushed
- salt and pepper

1 Cook the potatoes in a saucepan of boiling salted water for 15 minutes or until they are tender.

2 Drain the potatoes well, chop roughly and put into a bowl.

3 Chop the shallot. Cut the tomatoes into wedges and add the shallot and tomatoes to the potatoes.

4 To make the dressing, put all the ingredients into a screw-top jar and mix together thoroughly.

3

4

5

5 Pour the dressing over the potato mixture and toss thoroughly.

6 Transfer the salad to a serving dish and sprinkle with the basil.

COOK'S TIP

This recipe works well with floury (mealy) potatoes. It doesn't look so attractive, as the potatoes break up when they are cooked, but they absorb the dressing wonderfully. Be sure to use an extra virgin olive oil for the dressing to give a really fruity flavour to the potatoes.

Tomato Salsa

This salad is used extensively in Mexican cooking and served as a dip or a relish, and is eaten as an accompaniment to almost any dish.

NUTRITIONAL INFORMATION

Calories	10	Sugars	2g
Protein	0.4g	Fat	0.1g
Carbohydrate	2g	Saturates	0g

 10 MINS  0 MINS

SERVES 4

INGREDIENTS

- 4 ripe red tomatoes
- 1 medium red onion or 6 spring onions (scallions)
- 1–2 garlic cloves, crushed (optional)
- 2 tbsp chopped fresh coriander (cilantro)
- ½ red or green chilli (optional)
- finely grated rind of ½–1 lemon or lime
- 1–2 tbsp lemon or lime juice
- pepper

1 Chop the tomatoes fairly finely and evenly, and put into a bowl. They must be firm and a good strong red colour for the best results, but if preferred, they may be peeled by placing them in boiling water for about 20 seconds and then plunging into cold water. The skins should then slip off easily when they are nicked with a knife.

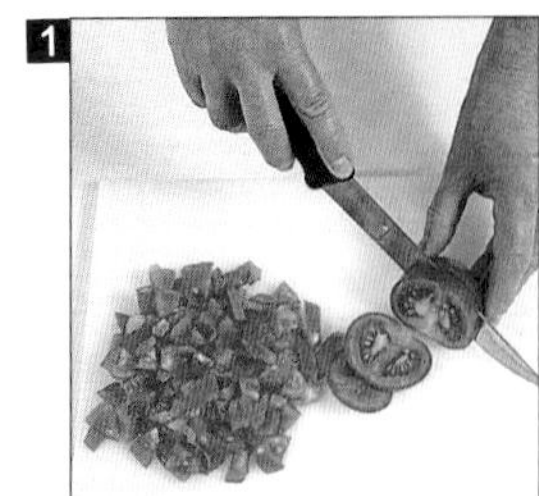

2 Peel and slice the red onion thinly, or trim the spring onions (scallions) and cut into thin slanting slices; add to the tomatoes with the garlic and coriander (cilantro) and mix lightly.

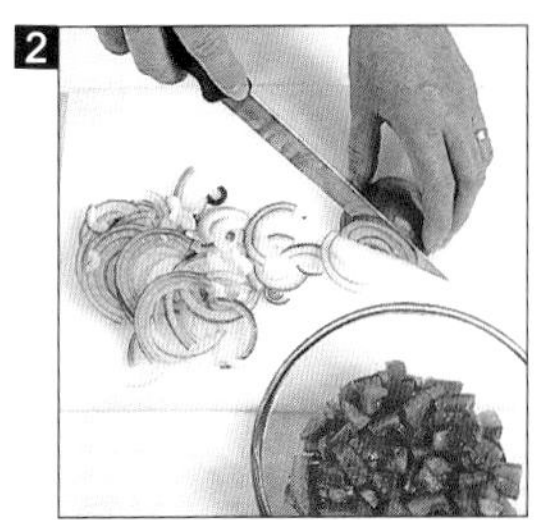

3 Remove the seeds from the red or green chilli (if using) chop the flesh very finely and add to the salad. Treat the chillies with care; do not touch your eyes or face after handling them until you have washed your hands thoroughly. Chilli juices can burn.

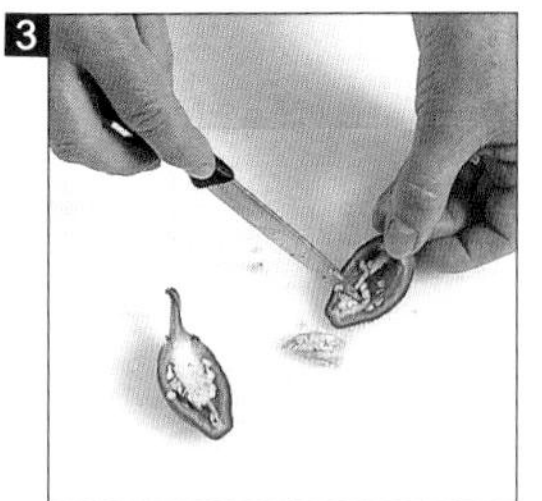

4 Add the lemon or lime rind and juice to the salsa, and mix well. Transfer to a serving bowl and sprinkle with pepper.

COOK'S TIP

If you don't like the distinctive flavour of fresh coriander (cilantro), you can replace it with flat-leaf parsley instead.

Green Salad

Herb-flavoured croûtons are topped with peppery rocket (arugula), red chard, green olives and pistachios to make an elegant combination.

NUTRITIONAL INFORMATION

Calories	256	Sugars	3g
Protein	4g	Fat	17g
Carbohydrate	23g	Saturates	3g

 25 MINS  10 MINS

SERVES 4

INGREDIENTS

- 25 g/1 oz pistachio nuts
- 5 tbsp extra virgin olive oil
- 1 tbsp rosemary, chopped
- 2 garlic cloves, chopped
- 4 slices rustic bread
- 1 tbsp red wine vinegar
- 1 tsp wholegrain mustard
- 1 tsp sugar
- 25 g/1 oz rocket (arugula)
- 25 g/1 oz red chard
- 50 g/1¾ oz green olives, pitted
- 2 tbsp fresh basil, shredded

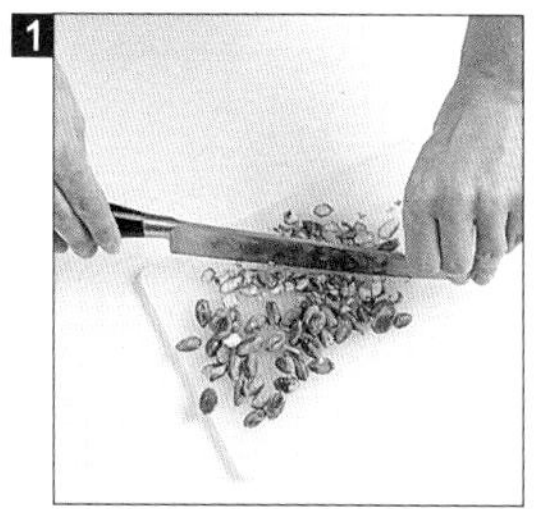

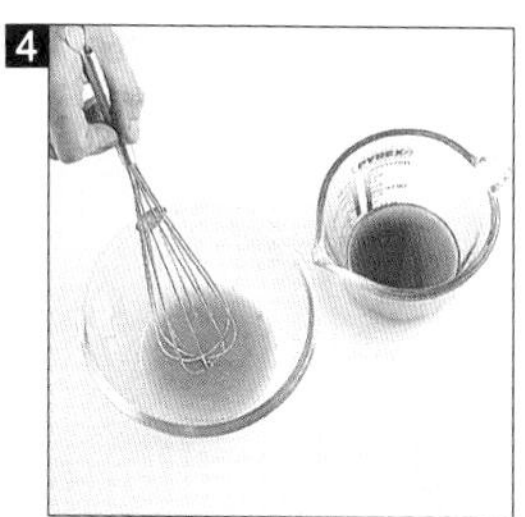

1 Shell the pistachios and roughly chop them, using a sharp knife.

2 Place 2 tablespoons of the extra virgin olive oil in a frying pan (skillet). Add the rosemary and garlic and cook for 2 minutes.

3 Add the slices of bread to the pan and fry for 2–3 minutes on both sides until golden. Remove the bread from the pan and drain on absorbent kitchen paper.

4 To make the dressing, mix together the remaining olive oil with the red wine vinegar, mustard and sugar.

5 Place a slice of bread on to a serving plate and top with the rocket (arugula) and red chard. Sprinkle with the olives.

6 Drizzle the dressing over the top of the salad leaves. Sprinkle with the chopped pistachios and shredded basil leaves and serve the salad immediately.

COOK'S TIP

If you cannot find red chard, try slicing a tomato into very thin wedges to add a splash of vibrant red colour to the salad.

Potato & Chicken Salad

The spicy peanut dressing served with this salad may be prepared in advance and left to chill a day before required.

NUTRITIONAL INFORMATION

Calories	802	Sugars	15g
Protein	35g	Fat	55g
Carbohydrate	45g	Saturates	10g

 5 MINS

 15 MINS

SERVES 4

INGREDIENTS

- 4 large waxy potatoes
- 300 g/10½ oz fresh pineapple, diced
- 2 carrots, grated
- 175 g/6 oz bean sprouts
- 1 bunch spring onions (scallions), sliced
- 1 large courgette (zucchini), cut into matchsticks
- 3 celery sticks, cut into matchsticks
- 175 g/6 oz unsalted peanuts
- 2 cooked chicken breast fillets, about 125 g/4½ oz each, sliced

DRESSING

- 6 tbsp crunchy peanut butter
- 6 tbsp olive oil
- 2 tbsp light soy sauce
- 1 red chilli, chopped
- 2 tsp sesame oil
- 4 tsp lime juice

1 Using a sharp knife, cut the potatoes into small dice. Bring a saucepan of water to the boil.

2 Cook the diced potatoes in a saucepan of boiling water for 10 minutes or until tender. Drain and leave to cool until required.

3 Transfer the cooled potatoes to a salad bowl.

4 Add the pineapple, carrots, bean sprouts, spring onions (scallions), courgette (zucchini), celery, peanuts and sliced chicken to the potatoes. Toss well to mix all the salad ingredients together.

5 To make the dressing, put the peanut butter in a small mixing bowl and gradually whisk in the olive oil and light soy sauce.

6 Stir in the chopped red chilli, sesame oil and lime juice. Mix until well combined.

7 Pour the spicy dressing over the salad and toss lightly to coat all of the ingredients. Serve the potato and chicken salad immediately.

4

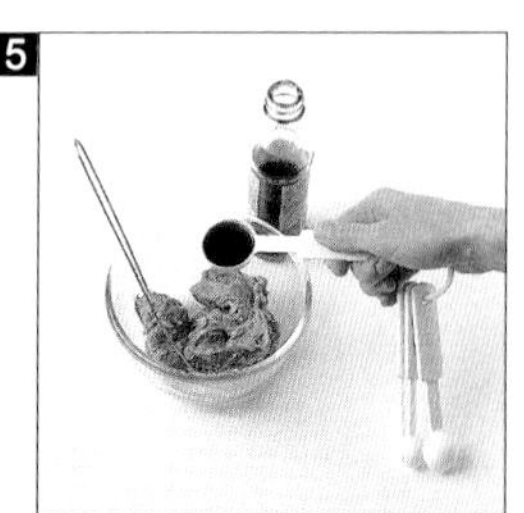

5

6

COOK'S TIP

Unsweetened canned pineapple may be used in place of the fresh pineapple for convenience. If only sweetened canned pineapple is available, drain it and rinse under cold running water before using.

Pasta & Garlic Mayo Salad

This crisp salad would make an excellent accompaniment to grilled (broiled) meat and is ideal for summer barbecues (grills).

NUTRITIONAL INFORMATION

Calories	858	Sugars	35g
Protein	11g	Fat	64g
Carbohydrate	64g	Saturates	8g

1½ HOURS — 10 MINS

SERVES 4

INGREDIENTS

- 2 large lettuces
- 260 g/9 oz dried penne
- 1 tbsp olive oil
- 8 red eating apples
- juice of 4 lemons
- 1 head of celery, sliced
- 115 g/4 oz/¾ cup shelled, halved walnuts
- 250 ml/9 fl oz/1⅛ cups fresh garlic mayonnaise (see Cook's Tip)
- salt

1 Wash, drain and pat dry the lettuce leaves with kitchen paper. Transfer them to the refrigerator for 1 hour or until crisp.

2 Meanwhile, bring a large saucepan of lightly salted water to the boil. Add the pasta and olive oil and cook for 8–10 minutes or until tender, but still firm to the bite. Drain the pasta and refresh under cold running water. Drain thoroughly again and set aside.

3 Core and dice the apples, place them in a small bowl and sprinkle with the lemon juice.

1

3

4

4 Mix together the pasta, celery, apples and walnuts and toss the mixture in the garlic mayonnaise (see Cook's Tip, right). Add more mayonnaise, if liked.

5 Line a salad bowl with the lettuce leaves and spoon the pasta salad into the lined bowl. Serve when required.

COOK'S TIP

To make garlic mayo, beat 2 egg yolks with a pinch of salt and 6 crushed garlic cloves. Start beating in 350ml/12 fl oz/1½ cups oil, 1–2 tsp at a time. When ¼ of the oil has been incorporated, beat in 1–2 tbsp white wine vinegar. Continue beating in the oil. Stir in 1 tsp Dijon mustard and season.

Mango Salad

This is an unusual combination but works well as long as the mango is very unripe. Paw-paw (papaya) can be used instead, if you prefer.

NUTRITIONAL INFORMATION

Calories	26	Sugars	3g
Protein	1g	Fat	0.2g
Carbohydrate	6g	Saturates	0g

 10 MINS  0 MINS

SERVES 4

INGREDIENTS

- 1 large unripe mango, peeled and cut into long thin shreds
- 1 small red chilli, deseeded and chopped finely
- 2 shallots, chopped finely
- 2 tbsp lemon juice
- 1 tbsp light soy sauce
- 6 roasted canned chestnuts, quartered
- 1 melon, to serve
- 1 lollo biondo lettuce, or any crunchy lettuce
- 15 g/½ oz coriander (cilantro) leaves

1 Soak the mango briefly in cold water, in order to remove any syrup. Meanwhile, combine the chilli, shallots, lemon juice and soy sauce. Drain the mango and combine with the chestnuts.

2 To make the melon basket, stand the watermelon on one end on a level surface. Holding a knife level and in one place, turn the watermelon on its axis so that the knife marks an even line all around the middle. Mark a 2.5 cm/ 1 inch wide handle across the top and through the centre stem, joining the middle line at either end. (If you prefer a zigzag finish, mark the shape to be cut at this point before any cuts are made, to ensure even zigzags.)

3 Take a sharp knife and, following the marks made for the handle, make the first vertical cut. Then cut down the other side of the handle. Now follow the middle line and make your straight or zigzag cut, taking care that the knife is always pointing towards the centre of the watermelon, and is level with the work surface (counter), as this ensures that when you reach the handle cuts, the cut out piece of melon will pull away cleanly.

4 Hollow out the flesh with a spoon, leaving a clean edge and line with the lettuce and coriander (cilantro). Fill with the salad, pour over the dressing and serve.

1

1

4

COOK'S TIP

A relative of the onion, though less pungent, shallots come in round and elongated varieties. When buying shallots, choose firm, dry-skinned ones which show no signs of wrinkling. Fresh shallots can be stored in the refrigerator for up to a week.

Quick Bean Salad

This attractive-looking salad served with meat from the barbecue (grill) makes a delicious light meal in summer.

NUTRITIONAL INFORMATION

Calories	139	Sugars	5g
Protein	8g	Fat	3g
Carbohydrate	21g	Saturates	0.4g

 10 MINS  0 MINS

SERVES 4

INGREDIENTS

- 400 g/14 oz can chick-peas (garbanzo beans)
- 4 carrots
- 1 bunch spring onions (scallions)
- 1 medium cucumber
- ½ tsp salt
- ½ tsp pepper
- 3 tbsp lemon juice
- 1 red (bell) pepper

1 Drain the chick-peas (garbanzo beans) and place in a salad bowl.

2 Using a sharp knife, peel and slice the carrots.

3 Cut the spring onions (scallions) into small pieces.

4 Cut the cucumber into thick quarters.

5 Add the carrots, spring onions (scallions) and cucumber to the chick-peas (garbanzo beans) and mix. Season with the salt and pepper and sprinkle with the lemon juice.

6 Toss the salad ingredients together gently using 2 serving spoons.

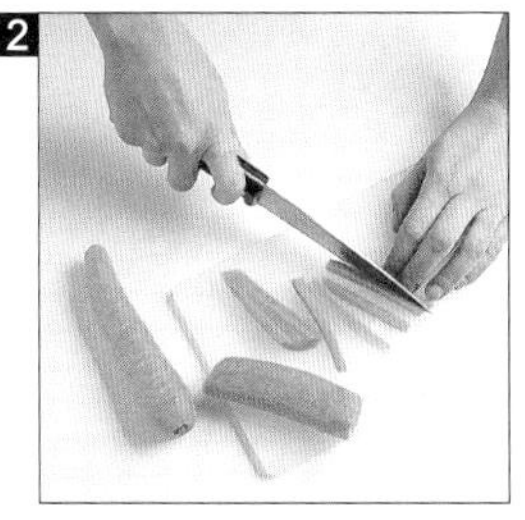
2

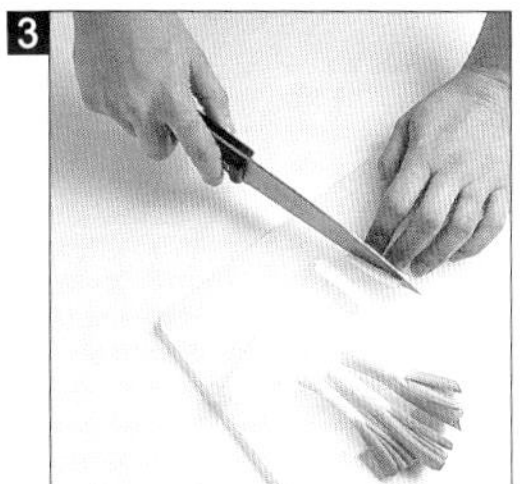
3

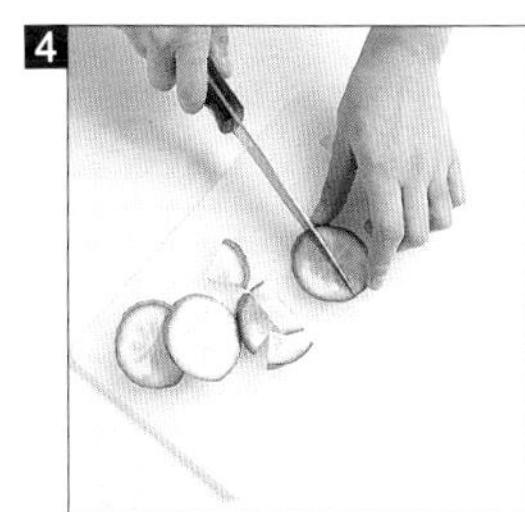
4

7 Using a sharp knife, slice the red (bell) pepper thinly.

8 Arrange the slices of red (bell) pepper on top of the chick-pea (garbanzo bean) salad.

9 Serve the salad immediately or leave to chill in the refrigerator and serve when required.

COOK'S TIP

Using canned chick-peas (garbanzo beans) rather than the dried ones speeds up the cooking time.

Sweet & Sour Fish Salad

This refreshing blend of pink and white fish mixed with fresh pineapple and (bell) peppers makesan interesting starter or a light meal.

NUTRITIONAL INFORMATION

Calories	168	Sugars	5g
Protein	24g	Fat	6g
Carbohydrate	5g	Saturates	1g

 35 MINS 10 MINS

SERVES 4

INGREDIENTS

- 225 g/8 oz trout fillets
- 225 g/8 oz white fish fillets (such as haddock or cod)
- 300 ml/½ pint/1¼ cups water
- 1 stalk lemon grass
- 2 lime leaves
- 1 large red chilli
- 1 bunch spring onions (scallions), trimmed and shredded
- 115 g/4 oz fresh pineapple flesh, diced
- 1 small red (bell) pepper, deseeded and diced
- 1 bunch watercress, washed and trimmed
- fresh snipped chives, to garnish

DRESSING

- 1 tbsp sunflower oil
- 1 tbsp rice wine vinegar
- pinch of chilli powder
- 1 tsp clear honey
- salt and pepper

1 Rinse the fish, place in a frying pan (skillet) and pour over the water. Bend the lemon grass in half to bruise it and add to the pan with the lime leaves. Prick the chilli with a fork and add to the pan. Bring to the boil and simmer for 7–8 minutes. Let cool.

2 Drain the fish fillet thoroughly, flake the flesh away from the skin and place in a bowl. Gently stir in the spring onions (scallions), pineapple and (bell) pepper.

3 Arrange the washed watercress on 4 serving plates and spoon the cooked fish mixture on top.

4 To make the dressing, mix all the ingredients together and season well. Spoon over the fish and serve garnished

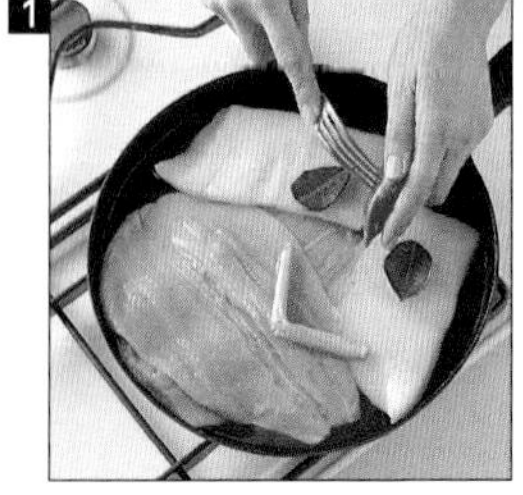

1

2

3

Pasta & Chicken Medley

Strips of cooked chicken are tossed with coloured pasta, grapes and carrot sticks in a pesto-flavoured dressing.

NUTRITIONAL INFORMATION

Calories	609	Sugars	11g
Protein	26g	Fat	38g
Carbohydrate	45g	Saturates	6g

 30 MINS  10 MINS

SERVES 2

INGREDIENTS

- 125–150 g/4½–5½ oz dried pasta shapes, such as twists or bows
- 1 tbsp oil
- 2 tbsp mayonnaise
- 2 tsp bottled pesto sauce
- 1 tbsp soured cream or natural fromage frais
- 175 g/6 oz cooked skinless, boneless chicken meat
- 1–2 celery stalks
- 125 g/4½ oz/1 cup black grapes (preferably seedless)
- 1 large carrot, trimmed
- salt and pepper
- celery leaves, to garnish

FRENCH DRESSING

- 1 tbsp wine vinegar
- 3 tbsp extra-virgin olive oil
- salt and pepper

1 To make the French dressing, whisk all the ingredients together until smooth.

2 Cook the pasta with the oil for 8–10 minutes in plenty of boiling salted water until just tender. Drain thoroughly, rinse and drain again. Transfer to a bowl and mix in 1 tablespoon of the French dressing while hot; set aside until cold.

3 Combine the mayonnaise, pesto sauce and soured cream or fromage frais in a bowl, and season to taste.

4 Cut the chicken into narrow strips. Cut the celery diagonally into narrow slices. Reserve a few grapes for garnish, halve the rest and remove any pips (seeds). Cut the carrot into narrow julienne strips.

5 Add the chicken, the celery, the halved grapes, the carrot and the mayonnaise mixture to the pasta, and toss thoroughly. Check the seasoning, adding more salt and pepper if necessary.

6 Arrange the pasta mixture on two plates and garnish with the reserved black grapes and the celery leaves.

2

4

5

Hot Rice Salad

Nutty brown rice combines well with peanuts and a sweet and sour mixture of fruit and vegetables in this tangy combination.

NUTRITIONAL INFORMATION

Calories	464	Sugars	17g
Protein	15g	Fat	24g
Carbohydrate	52g	Saturates	4g

5 MINS 30 MINS

SERVES 4

INGREDIENTS

- 300 g/10½ oz/1½ cups brown rice
- 1 bunch spring onions (scallions)
- 1 red (bell) pepper
- 125 g/4½ oz radishes
- 425 g/15 oz can pineapple pieces in natural juice, drained
- 125 g/4½ oz/2 cups bean sprouts
- 90 g/3 oz/¾ cup dry-roasted peanuts

DRESSING

- 2 tbsp crunchy peanut butter
- 1 tbsp groundnut oil
- 2 tbsp light soy sauce
- 2 tbsp white wine vinegar
- 2 tsp clear honey
- 1 tsp chilli powder
- ½ tsp garlic salt
- pepper

1

3

6

1 Put the rice in a pan and cover with water. Bring to the boil, then cover and simmer for 30 minutes until tender.

2 Meanwhile, chop the spring onions (scallions), using a sharp knife. Deseed and chop the red (bell) pepper and thinly slice the radishes.

3 To make the dressing. Place the crunchy peanut butter, groundnut oil, light soy sauce, white wine vinegar, honey, chilli powder, garlic salt and pepper in a small bowl and whisk for a few seconds until well combined.

4 Drain the rice thoroughly and place in a heatproof bowl.

5 Heat the dressing in a small saucepan for 1 minute and then toss into the rice and mix well.

6 Working quickly, stir the pineapple pieces, spring onions (scallions), (bell) pepper, bean sprouts and peanuts into the mixture in the bowl.

7 Pile the hot rice salad into a warmed serving dish.

8 Arrange the radish slices around the outside of the salad and serve immediately.

(Bell) Pepper Salad

Colourful marinated Mediterranean vegetables make a tasty starter. Serve with fresh bread or Tomato Toasts (see below).

NUTRITIONAL INFORMATION

Calories	234	Sugars	4g
Protein	6g	Fat	17g
Carbohydrate	15g	Saturates	2g

 5-10 MINS  35 MINS

SERVES 4

INGREDIENTS

- 1 onion
- 2 red (bell) peppers
- 2 yellow (bell) peppers
- 3 tbsp olive oil
- 2 large courgettes (zucchini), sliced
- 2 garlic cloves, sliced
- 1 tbsp balsamic vinegar
- 50 g/1¾ oz anchovy fillets, chopped
- 25 g/1 oz/¼ cup black olives, halved and pitted
- 1 tbsp chopped fresh basil
- salt and pepper

TOMATO TOASTS

- small stick of French bread
- 1 garlic clove, crushed
- 1 tomato, peeled and chopped
- 2 tbsp olive oil

1 Cut the onion into wedges. Core and deseed the (bell) peppers and cut into thick slices.

2 Heat the oil in a large heavy-based frying pan (skillet). Add the onion, (bell) peppers, courgettes (zucchini) and garlic and fry gently for 20 minutes, stirring occasionally.

3 Add the vinegar, anchovies, olives and seasoning to taste, mix thoroughly and leave to cool.

4 Spoon on to individual plates and sprinkle with the basil.

5 To make the tomato toasts, cut the French bread diagonally into 1 cm/½ inch slices.

6 Mix the garlic, tomato, oil and seasoning together, and spread thinly over each slice of bread.

7 Place the bread on a baking tray (cookie sheet), drizzle with the olive oil and bake in a preheated oven, 220°C/425°F/Gas Mark 7, for 5–10 minutes until crisp. Serve the Tomato Toasts with the (Bell) Pepper Salad.

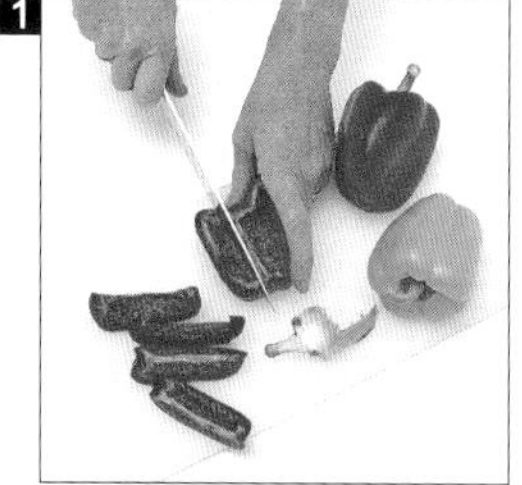

Pasta Niçoise Salad

Based on the classic French salad niçoise, this recipe has a light olive oil dressing with the tang of capers and the fragrance of fresh basil.

NUTRITIONAL INFORMATION

Calories	214	Sugars	2g
Protein	26g	Fat	7g
Carbohydrate	14g	Saturates	1g

 15 MINS  35 MINS

SERVES 4

INGREDIENTS

- 225 g/8 oz farfalle (bows)
- 175 g/6 oz French (green) beans, topped and tailed
- 350 g/12 oz fresh tuna steaks
- 115 g/4 oz baby plum tomatoes, halved
- 8 anchovy fillets, drained on absorbent kitchen paper
- 2 tbsp capers in brine, drained
- 25 g/1 oz pitted black olives in brine, drained
- fresh basil leaves, to garnish
- salt and pepper

DRESSING

- 1 tbsp olive oil
- 1 garlic clove, crushed
- 1 tbsp lemon juice
- ½ tsp finely grated lemon rind
- 1 tbsp shredded fresh basil leaves

1 Cook the pasta in lightly salted boiling water according to the instructions on the packet until just cooked. Drain well, set aside and keep warm.

2 Bring a small saucepan of lightly salted water to the boil and cook the French (green) beans for 5–6 minutes until just tender. Drain well and toss into the pasta. Set aside and keep warm.

3 Preheat the grill (broiler) to medium. Rinse and pat the tuna steaks dry on absorbent kitchen paper (paper towels). Season on both sides with black pepper. Place the tuna steaks on the grill (broiler) rack and cook for 4–5 minutes on each side until cooked through.

4 Drain the tuna on absorbent kitchen paper and flake into bite-sized pieces. Toss the tuna into the pasta along with the tomatoes, anchovies, capers and olives. Set aside and keep warm.

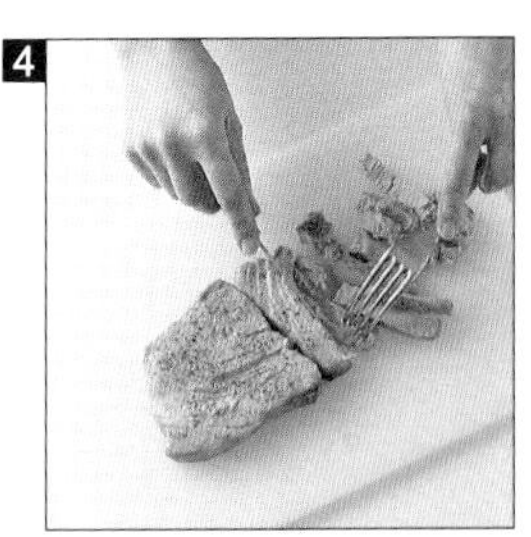

5 Meanwhile, prepare the dressing. Mix all the ingredients together and season well. Pour the dressing over the pasta mixture and mix carefully. Transfer the salad to a warmed serving bowl and serve sprinkled with fresh basil leaves.

VARIATION

Any pasta shape is suitable for this salad – to make it even more colourful, use different pasta.

Salad with Garlic Dressing

This is a very quick and refreshing salad using a whole range of colourful ingredients which make it look as good as it tastes.

NUTRITIONAL INFORMATION

Calories	82	Sugars	5g
Protein	2g	Fat	6g
Carbohydrate	5g	Saturates	1g

 10 MINS  0 MINS

SERVES 4

INGREDIENTS

75 g/2¾ oz cucumber, cut into sticks

6 spring onions (scallions), halved

2 tomatoes, seeded and cut into eight

1 yellow (bell) pepper, cut into strips

2 celery sticks, cut into strips

4 radishes, quartered

75 g/2¾ oz rocket

1 tbsp chopped mint, to serve

DRESSING

2 tbsp lemon juice

1 garlic clove, crushed

150 ml/¼ pint/⅔ cup low-fat natural (unsweetened) yogurt

2 tbsp olive oil

salt and pepper

1

2

3

1 To make the salad, mix the cucumber, spring onions (scallions), tomatoes, (bell) pepper, celery, radishes and rocket together in a large serving bowl.

2 To make the dressing, stir the lemon juice, garlic, natural (unsweetened) yogurt and olive oil together.

3 Season well with salt and pepper.

4 Spoon the dressing over the salad and toss to mix. Sprinkle the salad with chopped mint and serve.

COOK'S TIP

Rocket has a distinct warm, peppery flavour which is ideal in green salads. If rocket is unavailable, lamb's lettuce (corn salad) makes a good substitute.

Light Meals & Side Dishes

In the busy lives we lead today, quick meals are becoming great favourites. But care must be taken to ensure 'food on the move' is properly prepared and cooked, well-balanced and not just 'junk' food. The recipes for light meals offer something for every taste – vegetables, cheese, meat and pasta. Pizza, everyone's favourite snack food, is also seen in many inventive guises, for example, Hawaiian Pizza, Mexican-style Pizzas or American Hot Chilli Beef Pizza. There is also a selection of side dishes in this chapter which are a welcome departure from boiled potatoes and soggy beans. Try Pommes Anna, Fragrant Rice in Lotus Leaves or Greek Green Beans – they all taste delicious.

Teppanyaki

This simple, Japanese style of cooking is ideal for thinly-sliced breast of chicken. You can use thin turkey escalopes, if you prefer.

NUTRITIONAL INFORMATION

Calories	206	Sugars	4g
Protein	30g	Fat	7g
Carbohydrate	6g	Saturates	2g

5 MINS 10 MINS

SERVES 4

INGREDIENTS

- 4 boneless chicken breasts
- 1 red (bell) pepper
- 1 green (bell) pepper
- 4 spring onions (scallions)
- 8 baby corn cobs (corn-on-the-cob)
- 100 g/3½ oz/½ cup bean sprouts
- 1 tbsp sesame or sunflower oil
- 4 tbsp soy sauce
- 4 tbsp mirin
- 1 tbsp grated fresh ginger root

1 Remove the skin from the chicken and slice at a slight angle, to a thickness of about 5 mm/¼ inch.

2 Deseed and thinly slice the (bell) peppers and trim and slice the spring onions (scallions) and corn cobs (corn-on-the-cob).

3 Arrange the (bell) peppers, spring onions (scallions), corn and bean sprouts on a plate with the sliced chicken.

4 Heat a large griddle or heavy frying pan then lightly brush with oil. Add the vegetables and chicken slices in small batches, allowing space between them so that they cook thoroughly.

5 Combine the soy sauce, mirin and ginger and serve as a dip with the chicken and vegetables.

COOK'S TIP

Mirin is a rich, sweet rice wine which you can buy in oriental shops, but if it is not available add one 1 tablespoon of soft light brown sugar to the sauce instead.

1
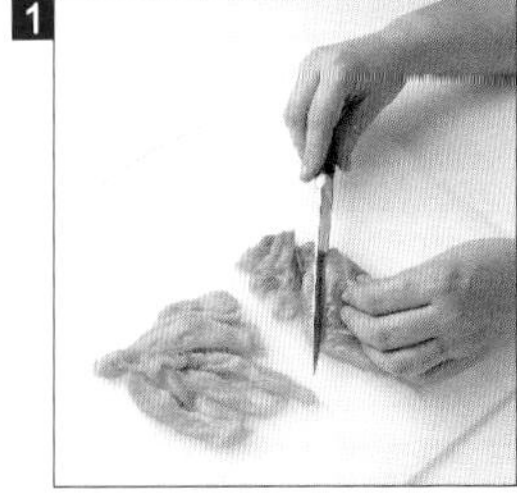

2

5

Steamed Chicken Parcels

A healthy recipe with a delicate oriental flavour. Use large spinach leaves to wrap around the chicken, but make sure they are young leaves.

NUTRITIONAL INFORMATION

Calories	216	Sugars	7g
Protein	31g	Fat	7g
Carbohydrate	7g	Saturates	2g

20 MINS 30 MINS

SERVES 4

INGREDIENTS

- 4 lean boneless, skinless chicken breasts
- 1 tsp ground lemon grass
- 2 spring onions (scallions), chopped finely
- 250 g/9 oz/1 cup young carrots
- 250 g/9 oz/1¾ cups young courgettes (zucchini)
- 2 sticks (stalks) celery
- 1 tsp light soy sauce
- 250 g/9 oz/¾ cup spinach leaves
- 2 tsp sesame oil
- salt and pepper

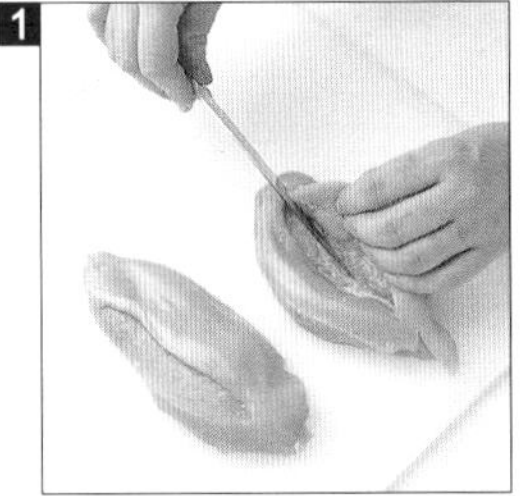
1

3

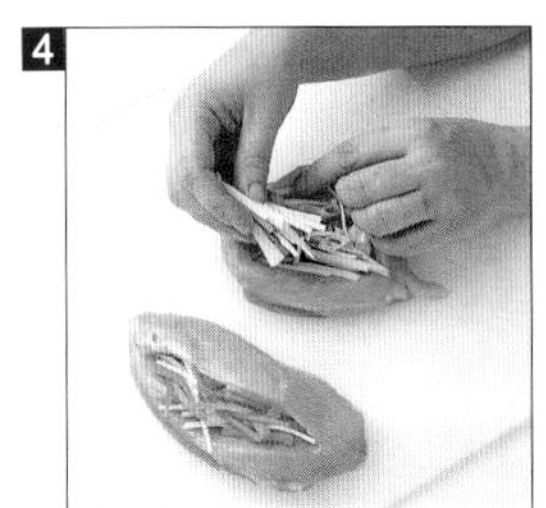
4

1 With a sharp knife, make a slit through one side of each chicken breast, to open out a large pocket.

2 Sprinkle the inside of the pocket with lemon grass, salt and pepper. Tuck the spring onions (scallions) into the chicken pockets.

3 Trim the carrots, courgettes and celery then cut into small matchsticks. Plunge them into a pan of boiling water for 1 minute, then drain and toss in the soy sauce.

4 Pack into the pockets in each chicken breast and fold over firmly to enclose. Reserve the remaining vegetables. Wash and dry the spinach leaves then wrap the chicken breasts firmly in the leaves to enclose completely. If the leaves are too firm, steam them for a few seconds until they are softened and flexible.

5 Place the wrapped chicken in a steamer and steam over rapidly boiling water for 20–25 minutes, depending on size.

6 Stir-fry any leftover vegetable sticks and spinach for 1–2 minutes in the sesame oil and serve with the chicken.

Thai-style Chicken Skewers

The chicken is marinated in an aromatic sauce before being cooked on the barbecue (grill). Use bay leaves if kaffir lime leaves are unavailable.

NUTRITIONAL INFORMATION

Calories	218	Sugars	4g
Protein	28g	Fat	10g
Carbohydrate	5g	Saturates	2g

 2¼ HOURS  20 MINS

SERVES 4

INGREDIENTS

- lean chicken breasts, skinned and boned
- 1 onion, peeled and cut into wedges
- 1 large red (bell) pepper, deseeded
- 1 large yellow (bell) pepper deseeded
- 12 kaffir lime leaves
- 2 tbsp sunflower oil
- 2 tbsp lime juice
- tomato halves, to serve

MARINADE

- 1 tbsp Thai red curry paste
- 150 ml/5 fl oz/⅔ cup canned coconut milk

1 To make the marinade, place the red curry paste in a small pan over medium heat and cook for 1 minute. Add half of the coconut milk to the pan and bring the mixture to the boil. Boil for 2–3 minutes until the liquid has reduced by about two-thirds.

2 Remove the pan from the heat and stir in the remaining coconut milk. Set aside to cool.

3 Cut the chicken into 2.5 cm/1 inch pieces. Stir the chicken into the cold marinade, cover and leave to chill for at least 2 hours.

4 Cut the onion into wedges and the (bell) peppers into 2.5 cm/1 inch pieces.

5 Remove the chicken pieces from the marinade and thread them on to skewers, alternating the chicken with the vegetables and lime leaves.

6 Combine the oil and lime juice in a small bowl and brush the mixture over the kebabs. Barbecue (grill) the skewers over hot coals, turning and basting frequently for 10–15 minutes until the chicken is cooked through. Barbecue (grill) the tomato halves and serve with the chicken skewers.

1

1

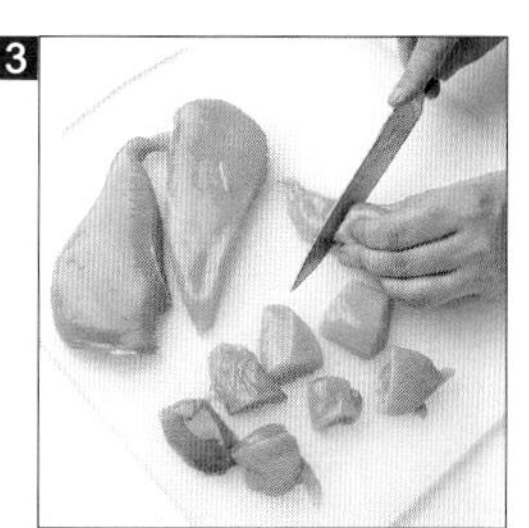
3

COOK'S TIP

Cooking the marinade first intensifies the flavour. It is important to allow the marinade to cool before adding the chicken, or bacteria may breed in the warm temperature.

Basil & Pine Nut Pesto

Delicious stirred into pasta, soups and salad dressings, pesto is available in most supermarkets, but making your own gives a concentrated flavour.

NUTRITIONAL INFORMATION

Calories	321	Sugars	1g
Protein	11g	Fat	17g
Carbohydrate	32g	Saturates	4g

 15 MINS  10 MINS

SERVES 4

INGREDIENTS

about 40 fresh basil leaves, washed and dried
3 garlic cloves, crushed
25 g/1 oz pine nuts
50 g/1¾ oz Parmesan cheese, finely grated
2–3 tbsp extra virgin olive oil
salt and pepper
675 g/1½ lb fresh pasta or 350 g/12 oz dried pasta

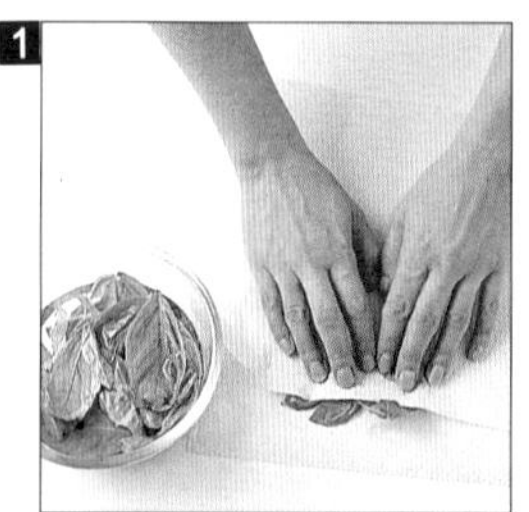

1

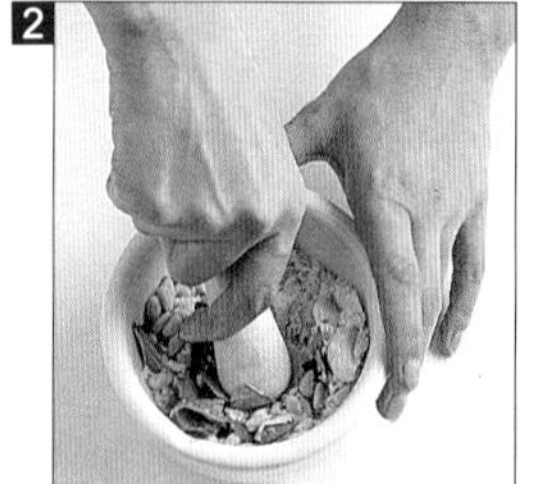

2

3

1 Rinse the basil leaves and pat them dry with paper towels.

2 Put the basil leaves, garlic, pine nuts and grated Parmesan into a food processor and blend for about 30 seconds or until smooth. Alternatively, pound all of the ingredients by hand, using a mortar and pestle.

3 If you are using a food processor, keep the motor running and slowly add the olive oil. Alternatively, add the oil drop by drop while stirring briskly. Season with salt and pepper to taste.

4 Cook the pasta in a saucepan of boiling water allowing 3–4 minutes for fresh pasta or 8–10 minutes for dried, or until it is cooked through, but still has 'bite'. Drain the pasta thoroughly in a colander.

5 Transfer the pasta to a serving plate and serve with the pesto. Toss to mix well and serve hot.

COOK'S TIP

You can store pesto in the refrigerator for about 4 weeks. Cover the surface of the pesto with olive oil before sealing the container or bottle, to prevent the basil from oxidizing and turning black.

Italian Chicken Parcels

This cooking method makes the chicken aromatic and succulent, and reduces the oil needed as the chicken and vegetables cook in their own juices.

NUTRITIONAL INFORMATION

Calories	234	Sugars	5g
Protein	28g	Fat	12g
Carbohydrate	5g	Saturates	5g

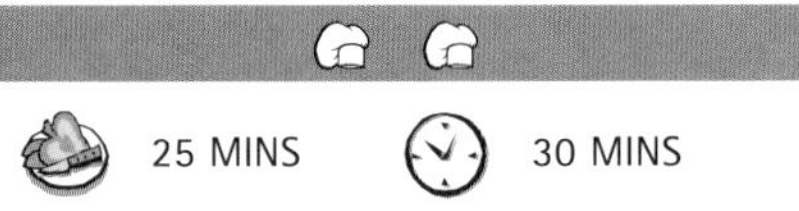

25 MINS 30 MINS

SERVES 6

INGREDIENTS

- 1 tbsp olive oil
- 6 skinless chicken breast fillets
- 250 g/9 oz/2 cups Mozzarella cheese
- 500 g/1 lb 2 oz/3½ cups courgettes (zucchini), sliced
- 6 large tomatoes, sliced
- 1 small bunch fresh basil or oregano
- pepper
- rice or pasta, to serve

1 Cut 6 pieces of foil, each measuring about 25 cm/10 inches square. Brush the foil squares lightly with oil and set aside until required.

2 With a sharp knife, slash each chicken breast at regular intervals. Slice the Mozzarella cheese and place between the cuts in the chicken.

COOK'S TIP

To aid cooking, place the vegetables and chicken on the shiny side of the foil so that once the parcel is wrapped up the dull surface of the foil is facing outwards. This ensures that the heat is absorbed into the parcel and not reflected away from it.

3 Divide the courgettes (zucchini) and tomatoes between the pieces of foil and sprinkle with pepper to taste. Tear or roughly chop the basil or oregano and scatter over the vegetables in each parcel.

4 Place the chicken on top of each pile of vegetables then wrap in the foil to enclose the chicken and vegetables, tucking in the ends.

5 Place on a baking tray (cookie sheet) and bake in a preheated oven, 200°C/400°C/Gas Mark 6, for about 30 minutes.

6 To serve, unwrap each foil parcel and serve with rice or pasta.

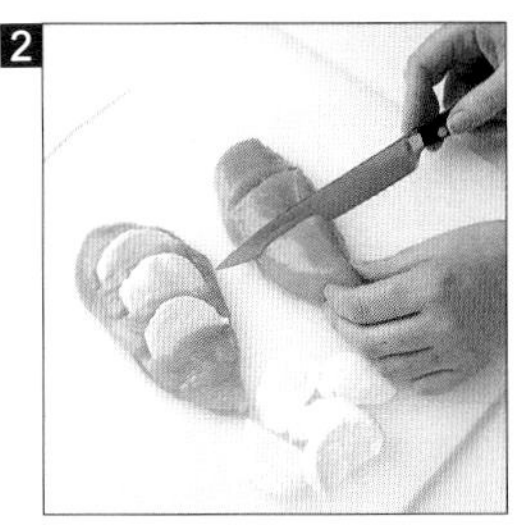

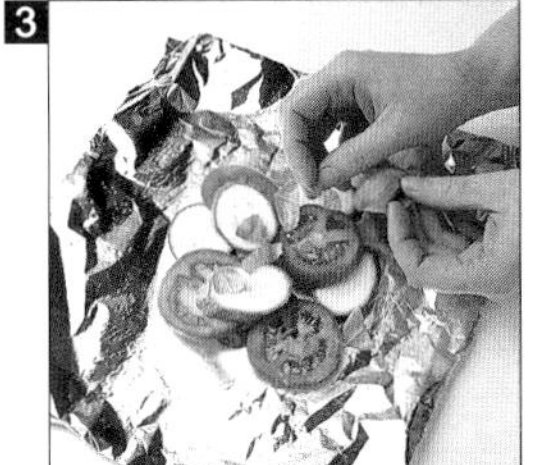

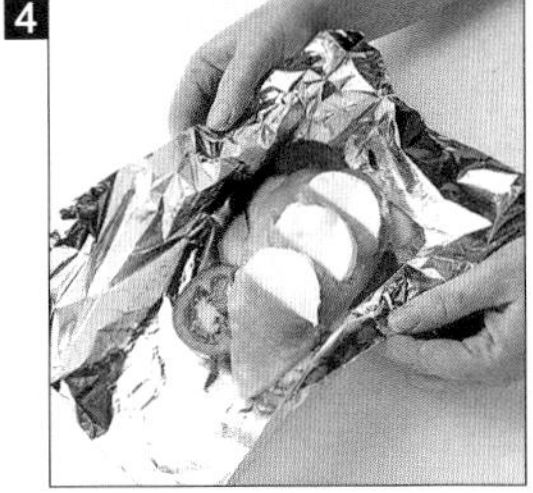

Potato Stir-Fry

In this sweet and sour dish, tender vegetables are simply stir-fried with spices and coconut milk, and flavoured with lime.

NUTRITIONAL INFORMATION

Calories	138	Sugars	5g
Protein	2g	Fat	6g
Carbohydrate	20g	Saturates	1g

 10 MINS 20 MINS

SERVES 4

INGREDIENTS

- 4 waxy potatoes
- 2 tbsp vegetable oil
- 1 yellow (bell) pepper, diced
- 1 red (bell) pepper, diced
- 1 carrot, cut into matchstick strips
- 1 courgette (zucchini), cut into matchstick strips
- 2 garlic cloves, crushed
- 1 red chilli, sliced
- 1 bunch spring onions (scallions), halved lengthways
- 8 tbsp coconut milk
- 1 tsp chopped lemon grass
- 2 tsp lime juice
- finely grated rind of 1 lime
- 1 tbsp chopped fresh coriander (cilantro)

1 Using a sharp knife, cut the potatoes into small dice.

2 Bring a large saucepan of water to the boil and cook the diced potatoes for 5 minutes. Drain thoroughly.

3 Heat the vegetable oil in a wok or large frying pan (skillet), swirling the oil around the base of the wok until it is really hot.

4

5

6

4 Add the potatoes, diced (bell) peppers, carrot, courgette (zucchini), garlic and chilli to the wok and stir-fry the vegetables for 2-3 minutes.

5 Stir in the spring onions, (scallions), coconut milk, chopped lemon grass and lime juice and stir-fry the mixture for a further 5 minutes.

6 Add the lime rind and coriander (cilantro) and stir-fry for 1 minute. Serve hot.

COOK'S TIP

Check that the potatoes are not overcooked in step 2, otherwise the potato pieces will disintegrate when they are stir-fried in the wok.

Vine (Grape) Leaf Parcels

A wonderful combination of soft cheese, chopped dates, ground almonds and lightly fried nuts is encased in vine (grape) leaves.

NUTRITIONAL INFORMATION

Calories	459	Sugars	8g
Protein	12g	Fat	42g
Carbohydrate	9g	Saturates	20g

25 MINS 15 MINS

SERVES 4

INGREDIENTS

- 300 g/10½ oz/1¼ cups full-fat soft cheese
- 60 g/2 oz/¼ cup ground almonds
- 25 g/1 oz/2 tbsp dates, pitted and chopped
- 25 g/1 oz/2 tbsp butter
- 25 g/1 oz/¼ cup flaked (slivered) almonds
- 12–16 vine (grape) leaves
- salt and pepper
- barbecued (grilled) baby corn, to serve

TO GARNISH

- rosemary sprigs
- tomato wedges

1 Beat the soft cheese in a large bowl until smooth. Add the ground almonds and chopped dates, and mix together thoroughly. Season to taste with salt and pepper.

2 Melt the butter in a small frying pan (skillet). Add the flaked (slivered) almonds and fry over a very low heat, stirring constantly, for 2–3 minutes, until golden brown. Remove from the heat and set aside to cool for a few minutes.

3 Mix the fried almonds into the soft cheese mixture, stirring well to combine thoroughly.

1

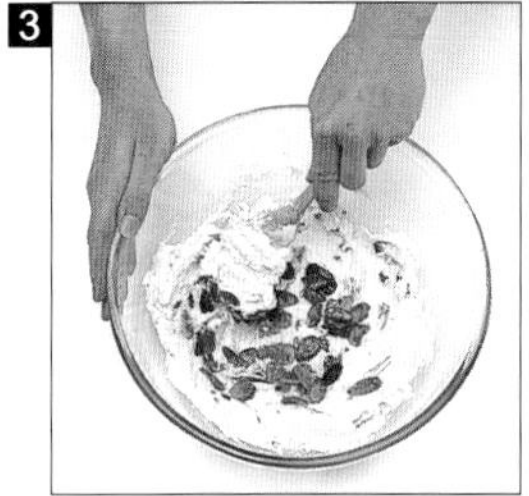

3

4

4 Soak the vine (grape) leaves in water to remove some of the saltiness, if specified on the packet. Drain them, lay them out on a work surface (counter) and spoon an equal amount of the soft cheese mixture on to each one. Fold over the leaves to enclose the filling.

5 Wrap the vine (grape) leaf parcels in foil, 1 or 2 per foil package. Place over the barbecue (grill) to heat through for about 8–10 minutes, turning once. Serve with barbecued (grilled) baby corn and garnish with sprigs of rosemary and tomato wedges.

Fragrant Curry

There are many different ways of cooking chickpeas (garbanzo beans), but this version is probably one of the most delicious and popular.

NUTRITIONAL INFORMATION

Calories	313	Sugars	5g
Protein	8g	Fat	19g
Carbohydrate	29g	Saturates	2g

10 MINS 20 MINS

SERVES 4

INGREDIENTS

- 6 tbsp vegetable oil
- 2 medium onions, sliced
- 1 tsp finely chopped root ginger
- 1 tsp ground cumin
- 1 tsp ground coriander
- 1 tsp crushed garlic
- 1 tsp chilli powder
- 2 fresh green chillies
- coriander (cilantro) leaves
- 150 ml/¼ pint/⅔ cup water
- 1 large potato
- 400 g/14 oz can chickpeas (garbanzo beans), drained
- 1 tbsp lemon juice

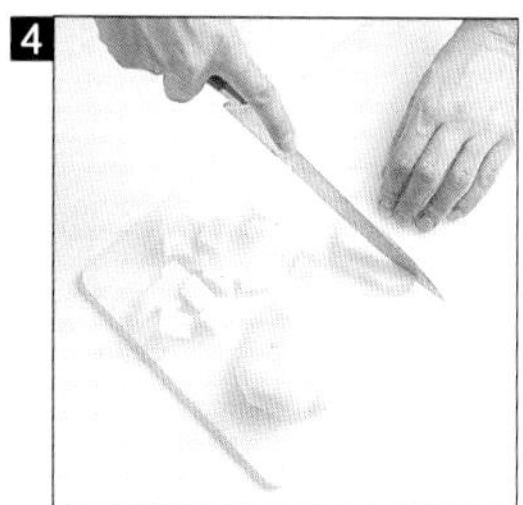

1 Heat the oil in a large saucepan. Add the onions to the and fry over a medium heat, stirring occasionally, for 5–8 minutes, until golden brown.

2 Reduce the heat, add the ginger, ground cumin, ground coriander, garlic, chilli powder, fresh green chillies and coriander (cilantro) leaves to the pan and stir-fry for 2 minutes.

3 Add the water to the mixture in the pan and stir well to mix.

4 Using a sharp knife, cut the potato into small dice. Add the potato and the drained chickpeas (garbanzo beans) to the mixture in the pan. Lower the heat, cover and simmer, stirring occasionally, for 5-7 minutes.

5 Sprinkle the lemon juice over the curry and stir.

6 Transfer the chickpea (garbanzo bean) curry to warmed individual serving dishes and serve immediately.

COOK'S TIP

Using canned chickpeas (garbanzo beans) saves time, but you can use dried chickpeas (garbanzo beans) if you prefer. Soak them overnight, then boil them for 15-20 minutes, or until soft.

Two-in-One Chicken

Cook four chicken pieces and serve two hot, topped with a crunchy herb mixture. Serve the remainder as a salad in a delicious curry sauce.

NUTRITIONAL INFORMATION

Calories	421	Sugars	20g
Protein	31g	Fat	18g
Carbohydrate	34g	Saturates	4g

2½ HOURS 45 MINS

SERVES 2

INGREDIENTS

- 4 lean chicken thighs
- oil for brushing
- garlic powder
- ½ dessert (eating) apple, grated coarsely
- 1½ tbsp dry parsley and thyme stuffing mix
- salt and pepper
- pasta shapes, to serve

SAUCE

- 15 g/½ oz/1 tbsp butter or margarine
- 2 tsp plain (all-purpose) flour
- 5 tbsp skimmed milk
- 2 tbsp dry white wine or stock
- ½ tsp dried mustard powder
- 1 tsp capers or chopped gherkins

SPICED CHICKEN SALAD

- ½ small onion, chopped finely
- 1 tbsp oil
- 1 tsp tomato purée (paste)
- ½ tsp curry powder
- 1 tsp apricot jam
- 1 tsp lemon juice
- 2 tbsp low-fat mayonnaise
- 1 tbsp low-fat natural fromage frais
- 90 g/3 oz/¾ cup seedless grapes, halved
- 60 g/2 oz ¼ cup white long-grain rice, cooked, to serve

1 Place the chicken in a shallow ovenproof dish. Brush with oil, sprinkle with garlic powder and season with salt and pepper. Place in a preheated oven, 200°C/400°F/Gas Mark 6, for 25 minutes, or until almost cooked through. Combine the apple with the stuffing mix. Baste the chicken, then spoon the mixture over two of the pieces. Return all the chicken pieces to the oven for about 10 minutes until the chicken is cooked.

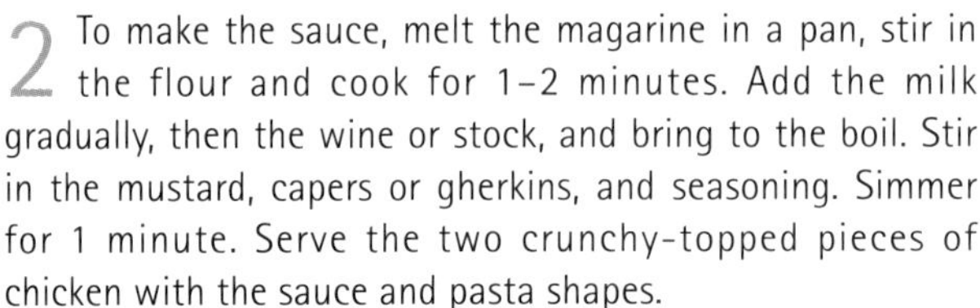

2 To make the sauce, melt the magarine in a pan, stir in the flour and cook for 1–2 minutes. Add the milk gradually, then the wine or stock, and bring to the boil. Stir in the mustard, capers or gherkins, and seasoning. Simmer for 1 minute. Serve the two crunchy-topped pieces of chicken with the sauce and pasta shapes.

3 For the salad, fry the onion gently in the oil until barely coloured. Add the tomato purée (paste), curry powder and jam, and cook for 1 minute. Leave the mixture to cool. Blend the mixture in a food processor, or press through a sieve (strainer). Beat in the lemon juice, mayonnaise and fromage frais. Season to taste with salt and pepper.

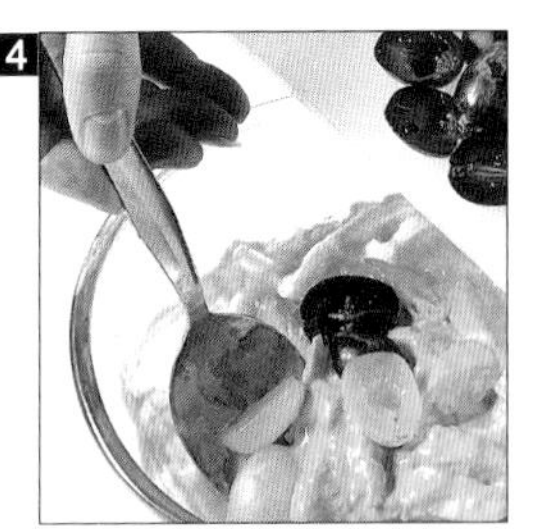

4 Cut the chicken into strips and add to the sauce with the grapes. Mix well, and chill. Serve with the rice.

Pasta with Bacon & Tomatoes

As this dish cooks, the mouth-watering aroma of bacon, sweet tomatoes and oregano is a feast in itself.

NUTRITIONAL INFORMATION

Calories	431	Sugars	8g
Protein	10g	Fat	29g
Carbohydrate	34g	Saturates	14g

 10 MINS 35 MINS

SERVES 4

INGREDIENTS

- 900 g/2 lb small, sweet tomatoes
- 6 slices rindless smoked bacon
- 60 g/2 oz/4 tbsp butter
- 1 onion, chopped
- 1 garlic clove, crushed
- 4 fresh oregano sprigs, finely chopped
- 450 g/1 lb/4 cups dried orecchiette
- 1 tbsp olive oil
- salt and pepper
- freshly grated Pecorino cheese, to serve

1 Blanch the tomatoes in boiling water. Drain, skin and seed the tomatoes, then roughly chop the flesh.

2 Using a sharp knife, chop the bacon into small dice.

3 Melt the butter in a saucepan. Add the bacon and fry until it is golden.

4 Add the onion and garlic and fry over a medium heat for 5-7 minutes, until just softened.

5 Add the tomatoes and oregano to the pan and then season to taste with salt and pepper. Lower the heat and simmer for 10-12 minutes.

1
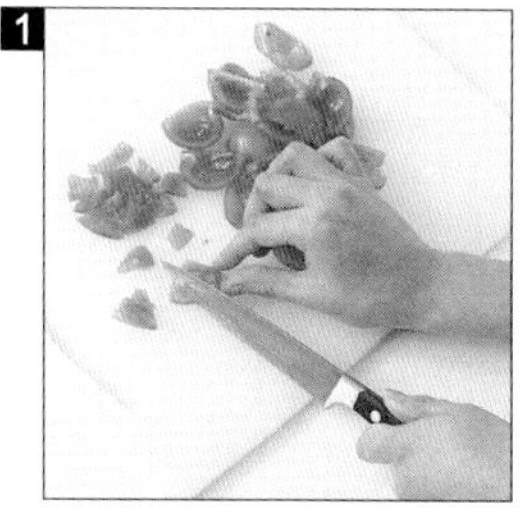

3

5

6 Bring a large pan of lightly salted water to the boil. Add the orecchiette and oil and cook for 12 minutes, until just tender, but still firm to the bite. Drain the pasta and transfer to a warm serving dish or bowl.

7 Spoon the bacon and tomato sauce over the pasta, toss to coat and serve with the cheese.

COOK'S TIP

For an authentic Italian flavour use pancetta, rather than ordinary bacon. This kind of bacon is streaked with fat and adds rich undertones of flavour to many traditional dishes. It is available both smoked and unsmoked from large supermarkets and Italian delicatessens.

Potato & Tuna Quiche

The base for this quiche is made from mashed potato instead of pastry, giving a softer textured case (shell) for the tasty tuna filling.

NUTRITIONAL INFORMATION

Calories	383	Sugars	5g
Protein	25g	Fat	15g
Carbohydrate	40g	Saturates	6g

 20 MINS  1 HOUR

SERVES 4

INGREDIENTS

- 450 g/1 lb floury (mealy) potatoes, diced
- 25 g/1 oz/2 tbsp butter
- 6 tbsp plain (all-purpose) flour

FILLING

- 1 tbsp vegetable oil
- 1 shallot, chopped
- 1 garlic clove, crushed
- 1 red (bell) pepper, diced
- 175g/6 oz can tuna in brine, drained
- 50 g/1¾ oz canned sweetcorn, drained
- 150 ml/¼ pint/⅔ cup skimmed milk
- 3 eggs, beaten
- 1 tbsp chopped fresh dill
- 50 g/1¾ oz mature (sharp) low-fat cheese, grated
- salt and pepper

TO GARNISH

- fresh dill sprigs
- lemon wedges

2

3

5

1 Cook the potatoes in a pan of boiling water for 10 minutes or until tender. Drain and mash the potatoes. Add the butter and flour and mix to form a dough.

2 Knead the potato dough on a floured surface and press the mixture into a 20 cm/8 inch flan tin (pan). Prick the base with a fork. Line with baking parchment and baking beans and bake blind in a preheated oven, 200°C/400°F/Gas Mark 6, for 20 minutes.

3 Heat the oil in a frying pan (skillet), add the shallot, garlic and (bell) pepper and fry gently for 5 minutes. Drain well and spoon the mixture into the flan case (shell). Flake the tuna and arrange it over the top with the sweetcorn.

4 In a bowl, mix the milk, eggs and chopped dill and season.

5 Pour the egg and dill mixture into the flan case (shell) and sprinkle the grated cheese on top.

6 Bake in the oven for 20 minutes or until the filling has set. Garnish the quiche with fresh dill and lemon wedges. Serve with mixed vegetables or salad.

Chicken Tortellini

Tortellini were said to have been created in the image of the goddess Venus's navel. Whatever the story, they are a delicious blend of Italian flavours.

NUTRITIONAL INFORMATION

Calories	635	Sugars	4g
Protein	31g	Fat	36g
Carbohydrate	50g	Saturates	16g

 1 HOUR  35 MINS

SERVES 4

INGREDIENTS

115 g/4 oz boned chicken breast, skinned
60 g/2 oz Parma ham (prosciutto)
40 g/1½ oz cooked spinach, well drained
1 tbsp finely chopped onion
2 tbsp freshly grated Parmesan cheese
pinch of ground allspice
1 egg, beaten
450 g/1 lb Basic Pasta Dough (see page 6)
salt and pepper
2 tbsp chopped fresh parsley, to garnish

SAUCE

300 ml/½ pint/1¼ cups single (light) cream
2 garlic cloves, crushed
115 g/4 oz button mushrooms, thinly sliced
4 tbsp freshly grated Parmesan cheese

1

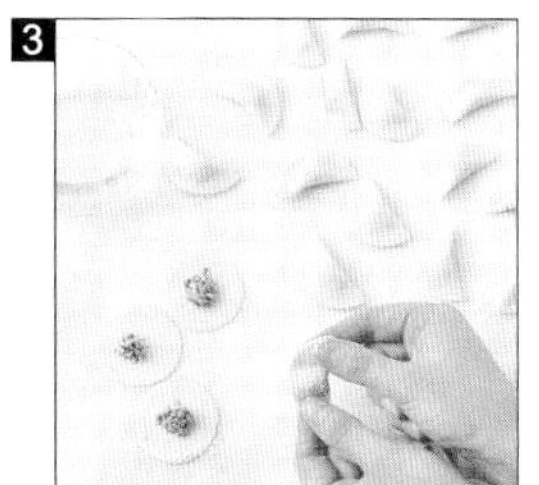
3

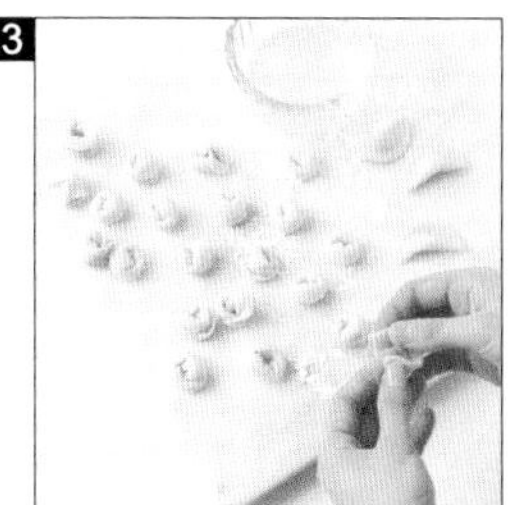
3

1 Bring a saucepan of seasoned water to the boil. Add the chicken and poach for about 10 minutes. Leave to cool slightly, then put in a food processor with the Parma ham (prosciutto), spinach and onion and process until finely chopped. Stir in the Parmesan cheese, allspice and egg and season with salt and pepper to taste.

2 Thinly roll out the pasta dough and cut into 4–5 cm/1½–2 inch rounds.

3 Place ½ teaspoon of the filling in the centre of each round. Fold the pieces in half and press the edges to seal. Then wrap each piece around your index finger, cross over the ends and curl the rest of the dough backwards to make a navel shape. Re-roll the trimmings and repeat until all of the dough is used up.

4 Bring a saucepan of salted water to the boil. Add the tortellini, in batches, bring back to the boil and cook for 5 minutes. Drain well and transfer to a serving dish.

5 To make the sauce, bring the cream and garlic to the boil in a small pan, then simmer for 3 minutes. Add the mushrooms and half of the cheese, season with salt and pepper to taste and simmer for 2–3 minutes. Pour the sauce over the chicken tortellini. Sprinkle over the remaining Parmesan cheese, garnish with the parsley and serve.

Buck Rarebit

This substantial version of cheese on toast – a creamy cheese sauce topped with a poached egg – makes a tasty, filling snack.

NUTRITIONAL INFORMATION

Calories	478	Sugars	2g
Protein	29g	Fat	34g
Carbohydrate	14g	Saturates	20g

 X MINS   X MINS

SERVES 4

INGREDIENTS

- 350 g/12 oz mature (sharp) Cheddar
- 125 g/4 oz Gouda (Dutch), Gruyère or Emmenthal (Swiss) cheese
- 1 tsp mustard powder
- 1 tsp wholegrain mustard
- 2-4 tbsp brown ale, cider or milk
- ½ tsp Worcestershire sauce
- 4 thick slices white or brown bread
- 4 eggs
- salt and pepper

TO GARNISH

- tomato wedges
- watercress sprigs

1 Grate the cheeses and place in a non-stick saucepan.

2 Add the mustards, seasoning, brown ale, cider or milk and Worcestershire sauce and mix well.

VARIATION

For a change, you can use part or all Stilton or other blue cheese; the appearance is not so attractive but the flavour is very good.

3

4

6

3 Heat the cheese mixture gently, stirring until it has melted and is completely thick and creamy. Remove from the heat and leave to cool a little.

4 Toast the slices of bread on each side under a preheated grill (broiler) then spread the rarebit mixture evenly over each piece. Put under a moderate grill (broiler) until golden brown and bubbling.

5 Meanwhile, poach the eggs. If using a poacher, grease the cups, heat the water in the pan and, when just boiling, break the eggs into the cups. Cover and simmer for 4-5 minutes until just set. Alternatively, bring about 4cm/1½ inches of water to the boil in a frying pan (skillet) or large saucepan and for each egg quickly swirl the water with a knife and drop the egg into the "hole" created. Cook for about 4 minutes until just set.

6 Top the rarebits with a poached egg and serve garnished with tomato wedges and sprigs of watercress.

Tagliatelle with Garlic Butter

Pasta is not difficult to make yourself, just a little time consuming. The resulting pasta only takes a couplc of minutes to cook and tastes wonderful.

NUTRITIONAL INFORMATION

Calories	642	Sugars	2g
Protein	16g	Fat	29g
Carbohydrate	84g	Saturates	13g

 45 MINS  5 MINS

SERVES 4

INGREDIENTS

450 g/1 lb strong white flour, plus extra for dredging

2 tsp salt

4 eggs, beaten

3 tbsp olive oil

75 g/2¾ oz/5 tbsp butter, melted

3 garlic cloves, finely chopped

2 tbsp chopped, fresh parsley

pepper

2

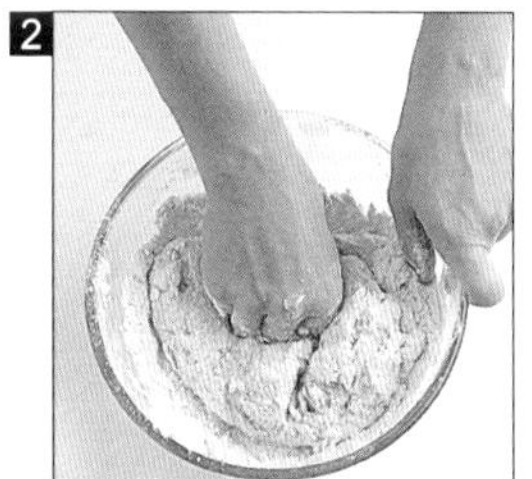
2

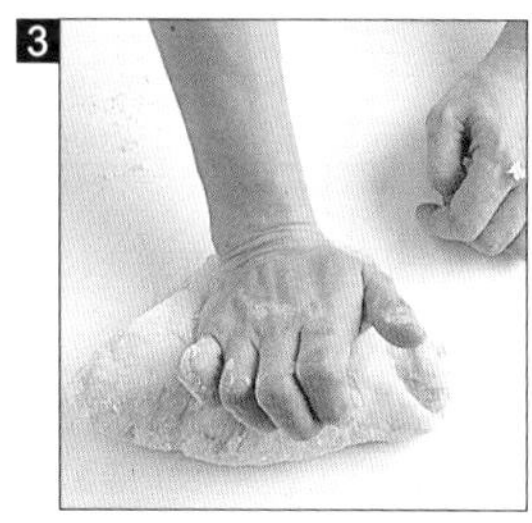
3

1 Sift the flour into a large bowl and stir in the salt.

2 Make a well in the middle of the dry ingredients and add the eggs and 2 tablespoons of oil. Using a wooden spoon, stir in the eggs, gradually drawing in the flour. After a few minutes the dough will be too stiff to use a spoon and you will need to use your fingers.

3 Once all of the flour has been incorporated, turn the dough out on to a floured surface and knead for about 5 minutes, or until smooth and elastic. If you find the dough is too wet, add a little more flour and continue kneading. Cover with cling film (plastic wrap) and leave to rest for at least 15 minutes.

4 The basic dough is now ready; roll out the pasta thinly and create the pasta shapes required. This can be done by hand or using a pasta machine. Results from a machine are usually neater and thinner, but not necessarily better.

5 To make the tagliatelle by hand, fold the thinly rolled pasta sheets into 3 and cut out long, thin stips, about 1 cm/½ inch wide.

6 To cook, bring a pan of water to the boil, add 1 tbsp of oil and the pasta. It will take 2–3 minutes to cook, and the texture should have a slight bite to it. Drain.

7 Mix together the butter, garlic and parsley. Stir into the pasta, season with a little pepper to taste and serve immediately.

COOK'S TIP

Generally allow about 150 g/5½ oz fresh pasta or about 100 g/3½ oz dried pasta per person.

Sticky Chicken Wings

These need to be eaten with your fingers so serve them at an informal supper.

NUTRITIONAL INFORMATION

Calories	165	Sugars	12g
Protein	14g	Fat	7g
Carbohydrate	12g	Saturates	1g

 3¼ HOURS  1 HOUR

SERVES 4–6

INGREDIENTS

- 2 tbsp olive oil
- 1 small onion, finely chopped
- 2 garlic cloves, crushed
- 425 ml/¾ pint passata (sieved tomatoes)
- 2 tsp dried thyme
- 1 tsp dried oregano
- pinch fennel seeds
- 3 tbsp red wine vinegar
- 2 tbsp Dijon mustard
- pinch ground cinnamon
- 2 tbsp brown sugar
- 1 tsp chilli flakes
- 2 tbsp black treacle
- 16 chicken wings
- salt and pepper

TO GARNISH

- celery stalks
- cherry tomatoes

1 Heat the olive oil in a large frying pan (skillet) and fry the onion and garlic for about 10 minutes.

2 Add the passata (sieved tomatoes), dried herbs, fennel, red wine vinegar, mustard and cinnamon to the frying pan (skillet) along with the sugar, chilli flakes, treacle, and salt and pepper. Bring to the boil, then reduce the heat and simmer gently for about 15 minutes, until the sauce is slightly reduced.

3 Put the chicken wings in a large dish, and coat liberally with the sauce. Leave to marinate for 3 hours or as long as possible, turning the wings over often in the marinade.

4 Transfer the wings to a clean baking sheet (cookie sheet), and roast in a preheated oven, 220°C/425°F/ Gas Mark 7, for 10 minutes. Reduce the heat to 190°C/375°F/Gas Mark 5 and cook for 20 minutes, basting often.

5 Serve the wings piping hot, garnished with celery stalks and cherry tomatoes.

1

2

3

Stuffed Tomatoes

These barbecued (grilled) tomato cups are filled with a delicious Greek-style combination of herbs, nuts and raisins.

NUTRITIONAL INFORMATION

Calories	156	Sugars	10g
Protein	3g	Fat	7g
Carbohydrate	22g	Saturates	0.7g

 25 MINS  10 MINS

SERVES 4

INGREDIENTS

4 beefsteak tomatoes

300 g/10½ oz/4½ cups cooked rice

8 spring onions (scallions), chopped

3 tbsp chopped, fresh mint

2 tbsp chopped, fresh parsley

3 tbsp pine nuts

3 tbsp raisins

2 tsp olive oil

salt and pepper

1 Cut the tomatoes in half, then scoop out the seeds and discard.

2 Stand the tomatoes upside down on absorbent kitchen paper (paper towels) for a few moments in order for the juices to drain out.

3 Turn the tomatoes the right way up and sprinkle the insides with salt and pepper.

4 Mix together the rice, spring onions (scallions), mint, parsley, pine nuts and raisins.

5 Spoon the mixture into the tomato cups.

6 Drizzle over a little olive oil, then barbecue (grill) the tomatoes on an oiled rack over medium hot coals for about 10 minutes until they are tender and cooked through.

7 Transfer the tomatoes to serving plates and serve immediately while still hot.

COOK'S TIP

Tomatoes are a popular barbecue (grill) vegetable. Try grilling (broiling) slices of beefsteak tomato and slices of onion, brushed with a little oil and topped with sprigs of fresh herbs. Or thread cherry tomatoes on to skewers and barbecue (grill) for 5–10 minutes.

Vegballs with Chilli Sauce

These tasty, nutty morsels are delicious served with a fiery, tangy sauce that counteracts the richness of the peanuts.

NUTRITIONAL INFORMATION

Calories	615	Sugars	13g
Protein	23g	Fat	43g
Carbohydrate	37g	Saturates	8g

25 MINS 30 MINS

SERVES 4

INGREDIENTS

- 3 tbsp groundnut oil
- 1 onion, finely chopped
- 1 celery stalk, chopped
- 1 tsp dried mixed herbs
- 225 g/8 oz/2 cups roasted unsalted peanuts, ground
- 175 g/6 oz/1 cup canned chickpeas (garbanzo beans), drained and mashed
- 1 tsp yeast extract
- 60 g/2 oz/1 cup fresh wholemeal (whole wheat) breadcrumbs
- 1 egg yolk
- 25 g/1 oz/¼ cup plain (all-purpose) flour
- strips of fresh red chilli, to garnish

HOT CHILLI SAUCE

- 2 tsp groundnut oil
- 1 large red chilli, seeded and finely chopped
- 2 spring onions (scallions), finely chopped
- 2 tbsp red wine vinegar
- 200 g/7 oz can chopped tomatoes
- 2 tbsp tomato purée (paste)
- 2 tsp caster (superfine) sugar
- salt and pepper
- rice and green salad (salad greens), to serve

1 Heat 1 tablespoon of the oil in a frying pan (skillet) and gently fry the onion and celery for 3–4 minutes, until softened, but not browned.

2 Place all the other ingredients, except the remaining oil and the flour, in a mixing bowl and add the onion and celery. Mix well.

3 Divide the mixture into 12 portions and roll into small balls. Coat all over with the flour.

4 Heat the remaining oil in a frying pan (skillet). Add the chickpea (garbanzo bean) balls and cook over a medium heat, turning frequently, for 15 minutes, until cooked through and golden. Drain on kitchen paper (paper towels).

5 Meanwhile, make the hot chilli sauce. Heat the oil in a small frying pan (skillet) and gently fry the chilli and spring onions (scallions) for 2–3 minutes. Stir in the remaining ingredients and season. Bring to the boil and simmer for 5 minutes.

6 Serve the chickpea (garbanzo bean) and peanut balls with the hot chilli sauce, rice and a salad.

2

3

4

Egg & Lentil Curry

A nutritious meal that is easy and relatively quick to make. The curried lentil sauce would also be delicious served with cooked vegetables.

NUTRITIONAL INFORMATION

Calories	298	Sugars	6g
Protein	17g	Fat	17g
Carbohydrate	20g	Saturates	4g

 10 MINS  35 MINS

SERVES 4

INGREDIENTS

- 3 tbsp vegetable ghee or oil
- 1 large onion, chopped
- 2 garlic cloves, chopped
- 2.5 cm/1 inch piece of root, ginger chopped
- ½ tsp minced chilli or chilli powder
- 1 tsp ground coriander
- 1 tsp ground cumin
- 1 tsp paprika
- 90 g/3 oz/⅓ cup split red lentils
- 425 ml/¾ pint/1¾ cups vegetable stock
- 225 g/8 oz can chopped tomatoes
- 6 eggs
- 50 ml/2 fl oz/¼ cup coconut milk
- salt
- 2 tomatoes, cut into wedges, and coriander (cilantro) sprigs, to garnish
- parathas, chapatis or naan bread, to serve

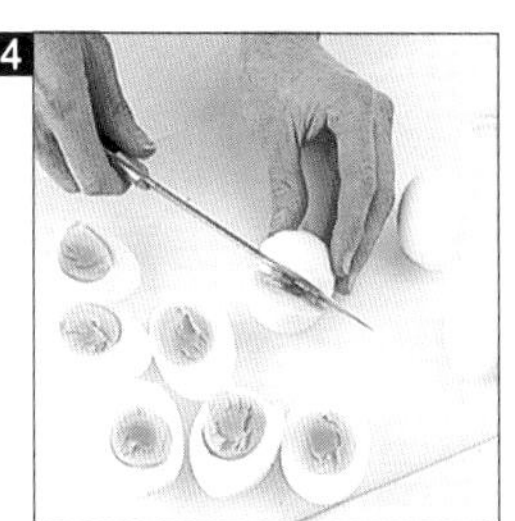

1 Heat the ghee or oil in a saucepan, add the onion and fry gently for 3 minutes. Stir in the garlic, ginger, chilli and spices and cook gently, stirring frequently, for 1 minute. Stir in the lentils, stock and chopped tomatoes and bring to the boil. Reduce the heat, cover and simmer, stirring occasionally, for 30 minutes, until the lentils are tender.

2 Meanwhile, place the eggs in a saucepan of cold water and bring to the boil. Reduce the heat and simmer for 10 minutes. Drain and cover immediately with cold water.

3 Stir the coconut milk into the lentil mixture and season well with salt to taste. Process the mixture in a blender or food processor until smooth. Return to the pan and heat through.

4 Shell the hard-boiled (hard-cooked) eggs and cut in half lengthways. Arrange 3 halves, in a petal design, on each serving plate. Spoon the hot lentil sauce over the eggs, adding enough to flood the plate. Arrange a tomato wedge and a coriander (cilantro) sprig between each halved egg. Serve hot with parathas, chapatis or naan bread.

Spinach & Ricotta Shells

This is a classic combination in which the smooth, creamy cheese balances the sharper taste of the spinach.

NUTRITIONAL INFORMATION

Calories	672	Sugars	10g
Protein	23g	Fat	26g
Carbohydrate	93g	Saturates	8g

5 MINS 40 MINS

SERVES 4

INGREDIENTS

- 400 g/14 oz dried lumache rigate grande
- 5 tbsp olive oil
- 60 g/2 oz/1 cup fresh white breadcrumbs
- 125 ml/4 fl oz/½ cup milk
- 300 g/10½ oz frozen spinach, thawed and drained
- 225 g/8 oz/1 cup ricotta cheese
- pinch of freshly grated nutmeg
- 400 g/14 oz can chopped tomatoes, drained
- 1 garlic clove, crushed
- salt and pepper

1 Bring a large saucepan of lightly salted water to the boil. Add the lumache and 1 tbsp of the olive oil and cook for 8–10 minutes until just tender, but still firm to the bite. Drain the pasta, refresh under cold water and set aside until required.

2 Put the breadcrumbs, milk and 3 tbsp of the remaining olive oil in a food processor and work to combine.

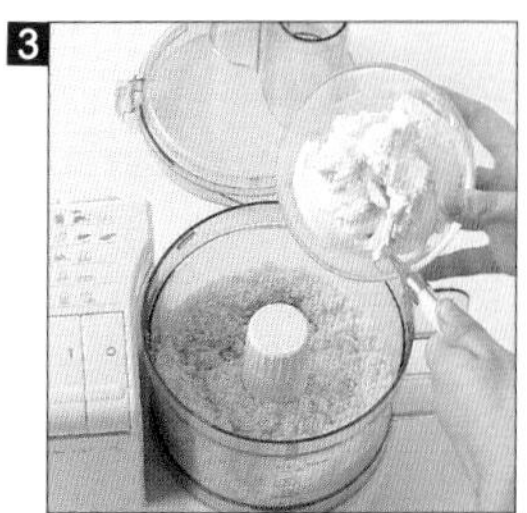

3 Add the spinach and ricotta cheese to the food processor and work to a smooth mixture. Transfer to a bowl, stir in the nutmeg, and season with salt and pepper to taste.

4 Mix together the tomatoes, garlic and remaining oil and spoon the mixture into the base of a large ovenproof dish.

5 Using a teaspoon, fill the lumache with the spinach and ricotta mixture and arrange on top of the tomato mixture in the dish. Cover and bake in a preheated oven at 180°C/350°F/Gas 4 for 20 minutes. Serve hot.

COOK'S TIP

Ricotta is a creamy Italian cheese traditionally made from ewes' milk whey. It is soft and white, with a smooth texture and a slightly sweet flavour. It should be used within 2–3 days of purchase.

Baked Stuffed Onions

Spanish onions are ideal for this recipe, as they have a milder, sweeter flavour that is not too overpowering.

NUTRITIONAL INFORMATION

Calories	182	Sugars	6g
Protein	10g	Fat	9g
Carbohydrate	18g	Saturates	5g

 15 MINS  2¼ HOURS

SERVES 4

INGREDIENTS

- 4 large Spanish onions
- 2 slices streaky bacon, diced
- ½ red (bell) pepper, deseeded and diced
- 125 g/4½ oz lean minced (ground) beef
- 1 tbsp chopped mixed fresh herbs such as parsley, thyme and rosemary or 1 tsp dried mixed herbs
- 25 g/1 oz/½ cup fresh white breadcrumbs
- 300 ml/½ pint/1¼ cups beef stock
- salt and pepper
- chopped fresh parsley to garnish
- long grain rice to serve

GRAVY

- 25 g/1 oz/2 tbsp butter
- 125 g/4½ oz mushrooms, chopped finely
- 300 ml/½ pint/1¼ cups beef stock
- 2 tbsp cornflour (cornstarch)
- 2 tbsp water

1 Put the onions in a saucepan of lightly salted water. Bring to the boil, then simmer for 15 minutes until tender.

2 Remove the onions from the pan, drain and cool slightly, then hollow out the centres and finely chop.

3 Heat a frying pan (skillet) and cook the bacon until the fat runs. Add the chopped onion and (bell) pepper and cook for 5–7 minutes, stirring frequently.

4 Add the beef to the frying pan (skillet) and cook, stirring, for 3 minutes, until browned. Remove from the heat and stir in the herbs, breadcrumbs and seasoning.

5 Grease an ovenproof dish and stand the whole onions in it. Pack the beef mixture into the centres and pour the stock around them.

6 Bake the stuffed onions in a preheated oven at 180°C/350°F/Gas Mark 4 for 1–1½ hours or until tender.

7 To make the gravy, heat the butter in a small saucepan and fry the mushrooms for 3–4 minutes. Strain the liquid from the onions and add to the pan with the stock. Cook for 2–3 minutes.

8 Mix the cornflour (cornstarch) with the water then stir into the gravy and heat, stirring, until thickened and smooth. Season with salt and pepper to taste. Serve the onions with the gravy and rice, garnished with chopped fresh parsley.

1

4

5

Vegetable Calzone

These pizza base parcels are great for making in advance and freezing – they can be defrosted when required for a quick snack.

NUTRITIONAL INFORMATION

Calories	499	Sugars	7g
Protein	16g	Fat	9g
Carbohydrate	95g	Saturates	2g

 1½ HOURS  40 MINS

SERVES 4

INGREDIENTS

DOUGH

- 450 g/1 lb/3½ cups strong white flour
- 2 tsp easy-blend dried yeast
- 1 tsp caster (superfine) sugar
- 150 ml/¼ pint/¾ cup vegetable stock
- 150 ml/¼ pint/¾ cup passata (sieved tomatoes)
- beaten egg

FILLING

- 1 tbsp vegetable oil
- 1 onion, chopped
- 1 garlic clove, crushed
- 2 tbsp chopped sun-dried tomatoes
- 100 g/3½ oz spinach, chopped
- 3 tbsp canned and drained sweetcorn
- 25 g/1 oz/¼ cup French (green) beans, cut into 3
- 1 tbsp tomato purée (paste)
- 1 tbsp chopped oregano
- 50 g/1¾ oz Mozzarella cheese, sliced
- salt and pepper

1 Sieve the flour into a bowl. Add the yeast and sugar and beat in the stock and passata (sieved tomatoes) to make a smooth dough.

2 Knead the dough on a lightly floured surface for 10 minutes, then place in a clean, lightly oiled bowl and leave to rise in a warm place for 1 hour.

3 Heat the oil in a frying pan (skillet) and sauté the onion for 2–3 minutes.

4 Stir in the garlic, tomatoes, spinach, corn and beans and cook for 3–4 minutes. Add the tomato purée (paste) and oregano and season with salt and pepper to taste.

5 Divide the risen dough into 4 equal portions and roll each on to a floured surface to form an 18 cm/7 inch circle.

6 Spoon a quarter of the filling on to one half of each circle and top with cheese. Fold the dough over to encase the filling, sealing the edge with a fork. Glaze with beaten egg. Put the calzone on a lightly greased baking tray (cookie sheet) and cook in a preheated oven, at 220°C/425°F/Gas Mark 7, for 25–30 minutes until risen and golden. Serve warm.

2

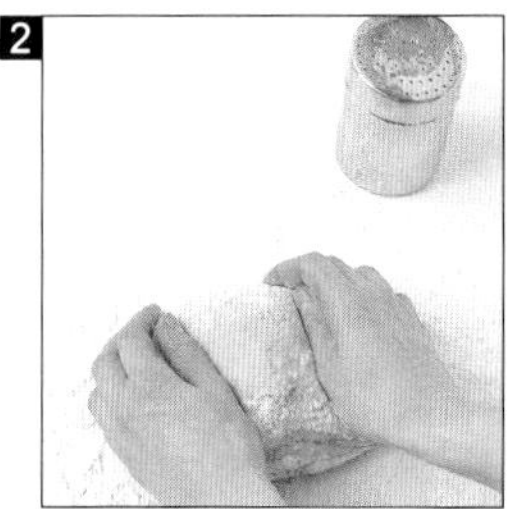

5

6

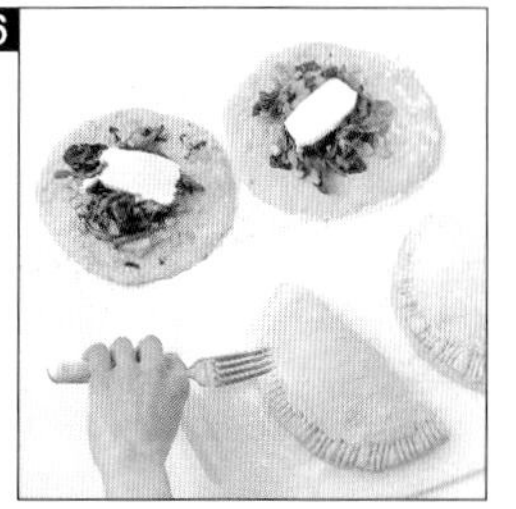

Kofta Kebabs (Kabobs)

Traditionally, koftas are made from a spicy meat mixture, but this bean and wheat version makes a tasty vegetarian alternative.

NUTRITIONAL INFORMATION

Calories	598	Sugars	7g
Protein	26g	Fat	17g
Carbohydrate	90g	Saturates	3g

 1 HR 20 MINS  1½ HOURS

SERVES 4

INGREDIENTS

- 175 g/6 oz/1 cup aduki beans
- 175 g/6 oz/1 cup bulgur wheat
- 450 ml/16 fl oz/scant 2 cups vegetable stock
- 3 tbsp olive oil
- 1 onion, finely chopped
- 2 garlic cloves, crushed
- 1 tsp ground coriander
- 1 tsp ground cumin
- 2 tbsp chopped fresh coriander (cilantro)
- 3 eggs, beaten
- 125 g/4½ oz/¾ cup dried breadcrumbs
- salt and pepper

TABBOULEH

- 175 g/6 oz/1 cup bulgur wheat
- 2 tbsp lemon juice
- 1 tbsp olive oil
- 6 tbsp chopped parsley
- 4 spring onions (scallions), finely chopped
- 60 g/2 oz cucumber, finely chopped
- 3 tbsp chopped mint
- 1 extra-large tomato, finely chopped

TO SERVE

- black olives
- pitta (pocket bread)

4  5  6 

1 Cook the aduki beans in boiling water for 40 minutes, until tender. Drain, rinse and leave to cool. Cook the bulgur wheat in the stock for 10 minutes, until the stock is absorbed. Set aside.

2 Heat 1 tablespoon of the oil in a frying pan (skillet) and fry the onion, garlic and spices for 4–5 minutes.

3 Transfer to a bowl, together with the beans, coriander (cilantro), seasoning and eggs and mash with a potato masher or fork. Add the breadcrumbs and bulgur wheat and stir well. Cover and chill for 1 hour, until firm.

4 To make the tabbouleh, soak the bulgur wheat in 450 ml/¾ pint/scant 2 cups of boiling water for 15 minutes. Combine with the remaining ingredients. Cover and chill.

5 With wet hands, mould the kofta mixture into 32 oval shapes.

6 Press on to skewers, brush with oil and grill (broil) for 5–6 minutes. until golden. Turn, brush with oil again and cook for 5–6 minutes. Drain on kitchen paper (paper towels). Garnish and serve with the tabbouleh, black olives and pitta (pocket) bread.

Chicken Fajitas

This spicy chicken filling, made up of mixed peppers, chillies and mushrooms, is put into folded tortillas and topped with soured cream.

NUTRITIONAL INFORMATION

Calories	303	Sugars	8g
Protein	23g	Fat	18g
Carbohydrate	13g	Saturates	7g

15 MINS   25 MINS

SERVES 4

INGREDIENTS

- 2 red (bell) peppers
- 2 green (bell) peppers
- 2 tbsp olive oil
- 2 onions, chopped
- 3 garlic cloves, crushed
- 1 chilli, deseeded and chopped finely
- 2 boneless chicken breasts (about 350 g/ 12 oz)
- 60 g/2 oz button mushrooms, sliced
- 2 tsp freshly chopped coriander (cilantro)
- grated rind of ½ lime
- 2 tbsp lime juice
- salt and pepper
- 4 wheat or corn tortillas
- 4–6 tbsp soured cream

TO GARNISH

- Tomato Salsa (see page 756)
- lime wedges

1 Halve the (bell) peppers, remove the seeds and place skin-side upwards under a preheated moderate grill until well charred. Leave to cool slightly and then peel off the skin; cut the flesh into thin slices.

2 Heat the oil in a pan, add the onions, garlic and chilli, and fry them for a few minutes just until the onion has softened.

3 Cut the chicken into narrow strips, add to the vegetable mixture in the pan and fry for 4–5 minutes until almost cooked through, stirring occasionally.

4 Add the peppers, mushrooms, coriander, lime rind and juice, and continue to cook for 2–3 minutes. Season to taste.

5 Heat the tortillas, wrapped in foil, in a preheated oven at 180°C/350°F/Gas Mark 4 for a few minutes. Bend them in half and divide the chicken mixture between them.

6 Top the chicken filling in each tortilla with a spoonful of soured cream and serve garnished with tomato salsa and lime wedges.

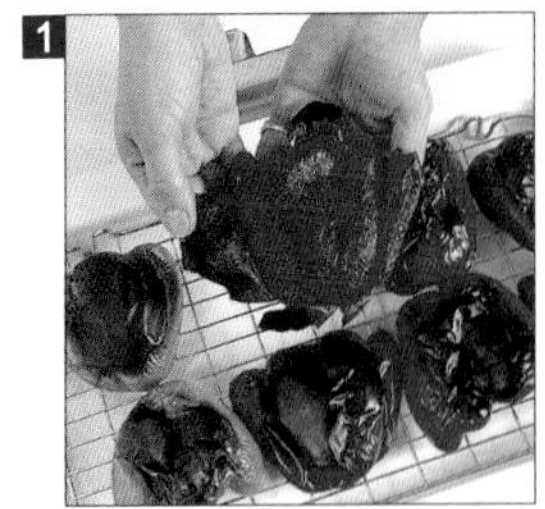
1

2

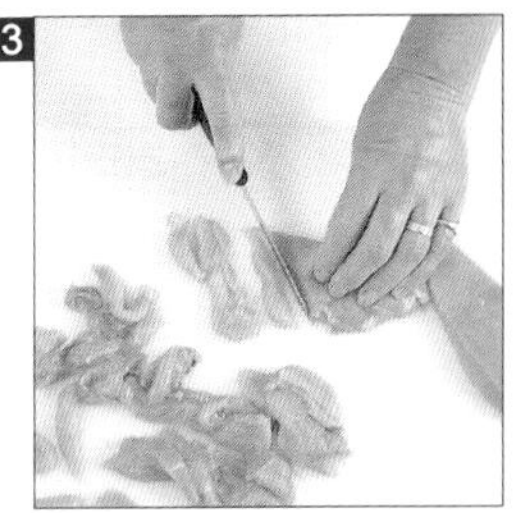
3

Chicken Pepperonata

All the sunshine colours and flavours of Italy are combined in this easy dish.

NUTRITIONAL INFORMATION

Calories	328	Sugars	7g
Protein	35g	Fat	15g
Carbohydrate	13g	Saturates	4g

 15 MINS 40 MINS

SERVES 4

INGREDIENTS

- 8 skinless chicken thighs
- 2 tbsp wholemeal (whole wheat) flour
- 2 tbsp olive oil
- 1 small onion, sliced thinly
- 1 garlic clove, crushed
- 1 each large red, yellow and green (bell) peppers, sliced thinly
- 400 g/14 oz can chopped tomatoes
- 1 tbsp chopped oregano
- salt and pepper
- fresh oregano, to garnish
- crusty wholemeal (whole wheat) bread, to serve

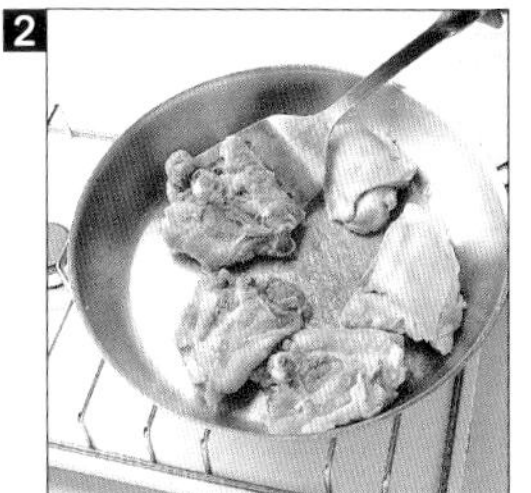

1 Remove the skin from the chicken thighs and toss in the flour.

2 Heat the oil in a wide frying pan (skillet) and fry the chicken quickly until sealed and lightly browned, then remove from the pan.

3 Add the onion to the pan and gently fry until soft. Add the garlic, (bell) peppers, tomatoes and oregano, then bring to the boil, stirring.

4 Arrange the chicken over the vegetables, season well with salt and pepper, then cover the pan tightly and simmer for 20–25 minutes or until the chicken is completely cooked and tender.

5 Season with salt and pepper to taste, garnish with oregano and serve with crusty wholemeal (whole wheat) bread.

COOK'S TIP

For extra flavour, halve the (bell) peppers and grill (broil) under a preheated grill (broiler) until the skins are charred. Leave to cool then remove the skins and seeds. Slice the (bell) peppers thinly and use in the recipe.

Pancakes with Smoked Fish

These are delicious as a starter or light supper dish and you can vary the filling with whichever fish you prefer.

NUTRITIONAL INFORMATION

Calories	399	Sugars	6g
Protein	36g	Fat	18g
Carbohydrate	25g	Saturates	10g

15 MINS 1 HR 20 MINS

Makes 12 pancakes

INGREDIENTS

PANCAKES

100 g/3 ½ oz flour

½ tsp salt

1 egg, beaten

300 ml/ ½ pint/1 ¼ cups milk

1 tbsp oil, for frying

SAUCE

450 g/1 lb smoked haddock, skinned

300 ml/ ½ pint/1 ¼ cups milk

40 g/1 ½ oz/3 tbsp butter or margarine

40 g/1 ½ oz flour

300 ml/ ½ pint/1 ¼ cups fish stock

75 g/2 ¾ oz Parmesan cheese, grated

100 g/3 ½ oz frozen peas, defrosted

100 g/3 ½ oz prawns (shrimp), cooked and peeled

50 g/1 ¾ oz Gruyère cheese, grated

salt and pepper

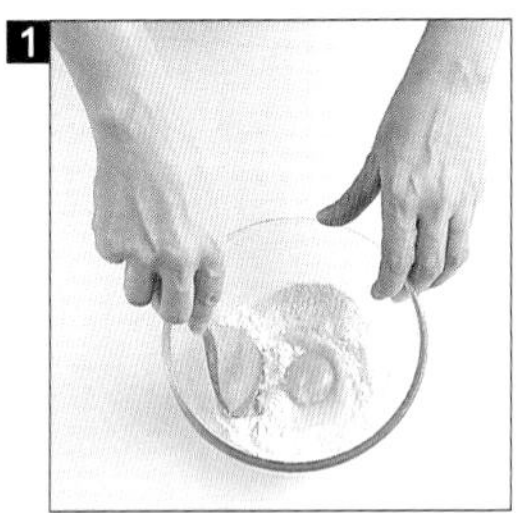
1

2

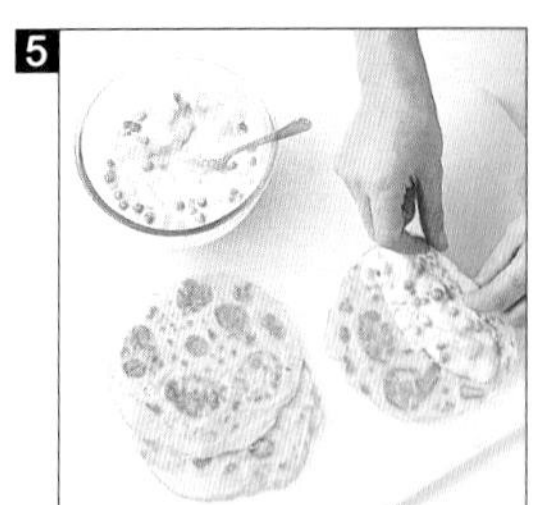
5

1 To make the pancake batter, sift the flour and salt into a large bowl and make a well in the centre. Add the egg and, using a wooden spoon, begin to draw in the flour. Slowly add the milk and beat together to form a smooth batter. Set aside until required.

2 Place the fish in a large frying pan (skillet), add the milk and bring to the boil. Simmer for 10 minutes or until the fish begins to flake. Drain thoroughly, reserving the milk.

3 Melt the butter in a saucepan. Add the flour, mix to a paste and cook for 2–3 minutes. Remove the pan from the heat and add the reserved milk a little at a time, stirring to make a smooth sauce. Repeat with the fish stock. Return to the heat and bring to the boil, stirring. Stir in the Parmesan and season with salt and pepper to taste.

4 Grease a frying pan (skillet) with oil. Add 2 tablespoons of the pancake batter, swirling it around the pan and cook for 2–3 minutes. Loosen the sides with a palette knife (spatula) and flip over the pancake. Cook for 2–3 minutes until golden; repeat. Stack the pancakes with sheets of baking parchment between them and keep warm in the oven.

5 Stir the flaked fish, peas and prawns (shrimp) into half of the sauce and use to fill each pancake. Pour over the remaining sauce, top with the Gruyère and bake for 20 minutes until golden.

Potato Fritters

Chunks of cooked potato are coated first in Parmesan cheese, then in a light batter before being fried until golden for a delicious hot snack.

NUTRITIONAL INFORMATION

Calories	599	Sugars	9g
Protein	22g	Fat	39g
Carbohydrate	42g	Saturates	13g

 20 MINS

20-25 MINS

SERVES 4

INGREDIENTS

- 500 g/1 lb 2 oz waxy potatoes, cut into large cubes
- 125 g/4½ oz/1¼ cups grated Parmesan cheese
- oil, for deep-frying

SAUCE

- 25 g/1 oz/2 tbsp butter
- 1 onion, halved and sliced
- 2 garlic cloves, crushed
- 25 g/1 oz/¼ cup plain (all-purpose) flour
- 300 ml/½ pint/1¼ cups milk
- 1 tbsp chopped parsley

BATTER

- 50 g/1¾ oz/½ cup plain (all-purpose) flour
- 1 small egg
- 150 ml/¼ pint/⅔ cup milk

4

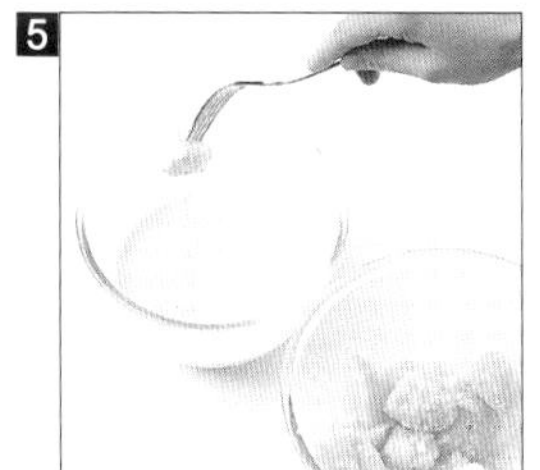

5

7

1 To make the sauce, melt the butter in a saucepan and cook the sliced onion and garlic over a low heat, stirring frequently, for 2-3 minutes. Add the flour and cook, stirring constantly, for 1 minute.

2 Remove from the heat and stir in the milk and parsley. Return to the heat and bring to the boil. Keep warm.

3 Meanwhile, cook the cubed potatoes in a saucepan of boiling water for 5–10 minutes, until just firm. Do not overcook or they will fall apart.

4 Drain the potatoes and toss them in the Parmesan cheese. If the potatoes are still slightly wet, the cheese sticks to them and coats them well.

5 To make the batter, place the flour in a mixing bowl and gradually beat in the egg and milk until smooth. Dip the potato cubes into the batter to coat them.

6 In a large saucepan or deep-fryer, heat the oil to 180°C/350°F or until a cube of bread browns in 30 seconds. Add the fritters and cook for 3–4 minutes, or until golden.

7 Remove the fritters with a slotted spoon and drain well. Transfer them to a warm serving bowl and serve immediately with the garlic sauce.

Polenta Kebabs (Kabobs)

Here, skewers of thyme-flavoured polenta, wrapped in Parma ham (prosciutto), are grilled (broiled) or barbecued (grilled).

NUTRITIONAL INFORMATION

Calories	212	Sugars	0g
Protein	8g	Fat	6g
Carbohydrate	32g	Saturates	1g

20 MINS 45 MINS

SERVES 4

INGREDIENTS

- 175 g/6 oz instant polenta
- 750 ml/1 pint/scant 3¾ cups water
- 2 tbsp fresh thyme, stalks removed
- 8 slices Parma ham (prosciutto) (about 75 g/2¾ oz)
- 1 tbsp olive oil
- salt and pepper
- fresh green salad, to serve

1 Cook the polenta, using 750 ml/1 pint 7 fl oz/3¼ cups of water to 175 g/6 oz polenta, stirring occasionally, for 30–35 minutes. Alternatively, follow the instructions on the packet.

2 Add the fresh thyme to the polenta mixture and season to taste with salt and pepper.

4

5

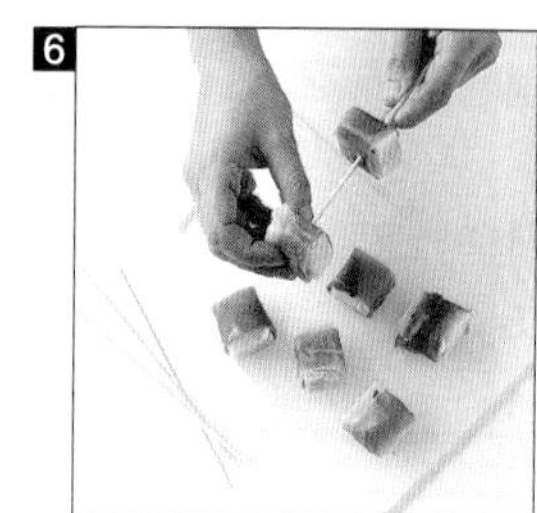
6

3 Spread out the polenta, about 2.5 cm/1 inch thick, on to a board. Set aside to cool.

4 Using a sharp knife, cut the cooled polenta into 2.5 cm/1 inch cubes.

5 Cut the Parma ham (prosciutto) slices into 2 pieces lengthways. Wrap the Parma ham (prosciutto) around the polenta cubes.

6 Thread the Parma ham (prosciutto) wrapped polenta cubes on to skewers.

7 Brush the kebabs (kabobs) with a little oil and cook under a preheated grill (broiler), turning frequently, for 7–8 minutes. Alternatively, barbecue (grill) the kebabs (kabobs) until golden. Transfer to serving plates and serve with a salad.

COOK'S TIP

Try flavouring the polenta with chopped oregano, basil or marjoram instead of the thyme, if you prefer. You should use 3 tablespoons of chopped herbs to every 350 g/12 oz instant polenta.

Kibbeh

This Lebanese barbeque dish is similar to the Turkish kofte and the Indian kofta, but the spices used to flavour the meat are quite different.

NUTRITIONAL INFORMATION

Calories	232	Sugars	3g
Protein	19g	Fat	13g
Carbohydrate	9g	Saturates	4g

1 HOUR 15 MINS

SERVES 4

INGREDIENTS

- 75 g/2¾ oz couscous
- 1 small onion
- 350 g/12 oz lean minced lamb
- ½ tsp ground cinnamon
- ¼ tsp cayenne
- 4 tsp ground allspice
- green salad and onion rings, to serve

BASTE

- 2 tbsp tomato ketchup (catsup)
- 2 tbsp sunflower oil

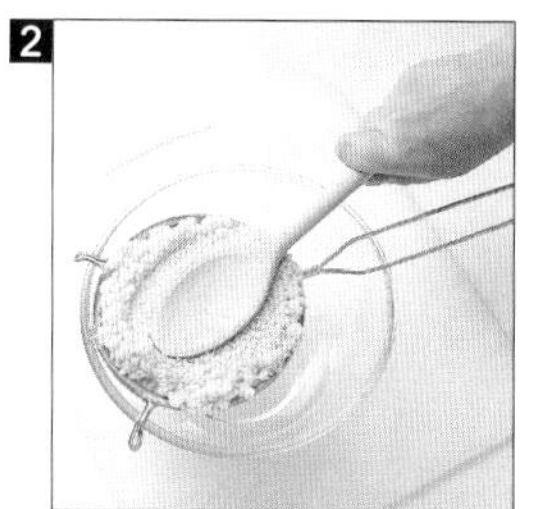

1 Place the couscous in a large bowl, cover with cold water and leave to stand for 30 minutes or until the couscous has swelled and softened. Alternatively, soak the couscous according to the instructions on the packet.

2 Drain the couscous through a sieve and squeeze out as much moisture as you can.

3 If you have a food processor, add the onion and chop finely. Add the lamb and process briefly to chop the mince further. If you do not have a processor, grate the onion then add to the lamb.

4 Combine the couscous, lamb and spices and mix well together. Divide the mixture into 8 equal sized portions. Press and shape the mixture around 8 skewers, pressing the mixture together firmly so that it holds it shape. Leave to chill for at least 30 minutes or until required.

5 To make the baste, combine the oil and ketchup (catsup).

6 Barbecue (grill) the kibbeh over hot coals for 10–15 minutes, turning and basting frequently. Serve with barbecued (grilled) onion rings and green salad leaves, if wished.

Spinach & Ricotta Gnocchi

Try not to handle the mixture too much when making gnocchi, as this will make the dough a little heavy.

NUTRITIONAL INFORMATION

Calories	712	Sugars	15g
Protein	29g	Fat	59g
Carbohydrate	16g	Saturates	33g

 20 MINS  15 MINS

SERVES 4

INGREDIENTS

1 kg/2 lb 4 oz spinach

350 g/12 oz/1½ cups Ricotta

125 g/4½ oz/1 cup Pecorino, grated

3 eggs, beaten

¼ tsp freshly grated nutmeg

plain (all-purpose) flour, to mix

125 g/4½ oz/½ cup unsalted butter

25 g/1 oz/¼ cup pine kernels (nuts)

50 g/2 oz/⅓ cup raisins

salt and pepper

1 Wash and drain the spinach well and cook in a covered saucepan without any extra liquid until softened, about 8 minutes. Place the spinach in a colander and press well to remove as much juice as possible. Either rub the spinach through a sieve (strainer) or purée in a blender.

2 Combine the spinach purée with the Ricotta, half of the Pecorino, the eggs, nutmeg and seasoning to taste, mixing lightly but thoroughly. Work in enough flour, lightly and quickly, to make the mixture easy to handle.

3 Shape the dough quickly into small lozenge shapes, and dust lightly with a little flour.

4 Add a dash of oil to a large saucepan of salted water and bring to the boil. Add the gnocchi carefully and boil for about 2 minutes or until they float to the surface. Using a perforated spoon, transfer the gnocchi to a buttered ovenproof dish. Keep warm.

5 Melt the butter in a frying pan (skillet). Add the pine kernels (nuts) and raisins and fry until the nuts start to brown slightly, but do not allow the butter to burn. Pour the mixture over the gnocchi and serve sprinkled with the remaining grated Pecorino.

2

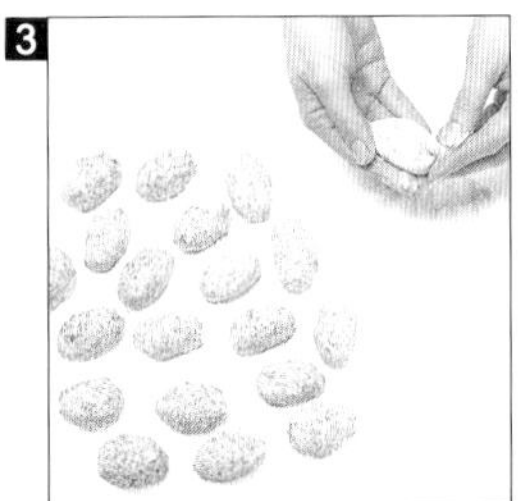
3

5

Potato Noodles

Potatoes are used to make a 'pasta' dough which is cut into thin noodlcs and boiled. The noodles are served with a bacon and mushroom sauce.

NUTRITIONAL INFORMATION

Calories	810	Sugars	5g
Protein	21g	Fat	47g
Carbohydrate	81g	Saturates	26g

30 MINS 25 MINS

SERVES 4

INGREDIENTS

- 450 g/1 lb floury (mealy) potatoes, diced
- 225 g/8 oz/2 cups plain (all-purpose) flour
- 1 egg, beaten
- 1 tbsp milk
- salt and pepper
- parsley sprig, to garnish

SAUCE

- 1 tbsp vegetable oil
- 1 onion, chopped
- 1 garlic clove, crushed
- 125 g/4½ oz open-capped mushrooms, sliced
- 3 smoked bacon slices, chopped
- 50 g/1¾ oz Parmesan cheese, grated
- 300 ml/½ pint/1¼ cups double (heavy) cream
- 2 tbsp chopped fresh parsley

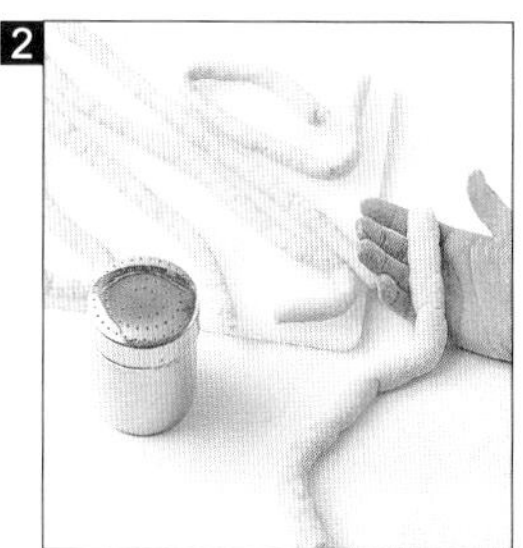
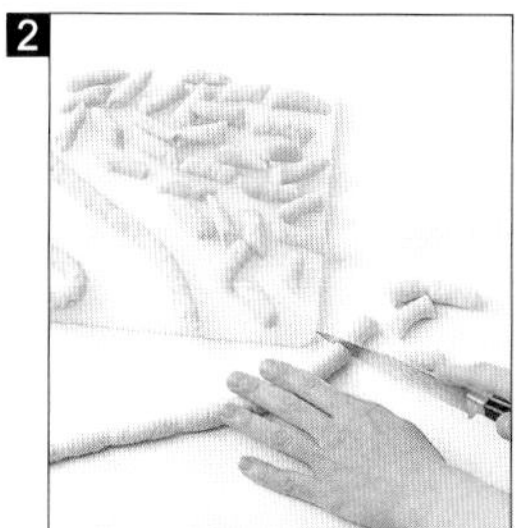

1 Cook the diced potatoes in a saucepan of boiling water for 10 minutes or until cooked through. Drain well. Mash the potatoes until smooth, then beat in the flour, egg and milk. Season with salt and pepper to taste and bring together to form a stiff paste.

2 On a lightly floured surface, roll out the paste to form a thin sausage shape. Cut the sausage into 2.5 cm/1 inch lengths. Bring a large pan of salted water to the boil, drop in the dough pieces and cook for 3-4 minutes. They will rise to the surface when cooked.

3 To make the sauce, heat the oil in a pan and sauté the onion and garlic for 2 minutes. Add the mushrooms and bacon and cook for 5 minutes. Stir in the cheese, cream and parsley, and season.

4 Drain the noodles and transfer to a warm pasta bowl. Spoon the sauce over the top and toss to mix. Garnish with a parsley sprig and serve.

COOK'S TIP

Make the dough in advance, then wrap and store the noodles in the refrigerator for up to 24 hours.

Pan Bagna

This is a deliciously moist picnic dish, lunch dish or snack. It is of Italian origin, designed for workers to take to the fields in a box.

NUTRITIONAL INFORMATION

Calories	377	Sugars	3g
Protein	20g	Fat	25g
Carbohydrate	19g	Saturates	6g

10 MINS 2½ HOURS

SERVES 4

INGREDIENTS

- 1 red (bell) pepper, halved, cored and deseeded
- 225 g/8 oz sirloin steak, 2.5 cm/1 inch thick
- 1 small white bloomer loaf or French stick
- 4 tbsp olive oil
- 2 extra-large tomatoes, sliced
- 10 black olives, halved
- ½ cucumber, peeled and sliced
- 6 anchovies, chopped
- salt and pepper

3

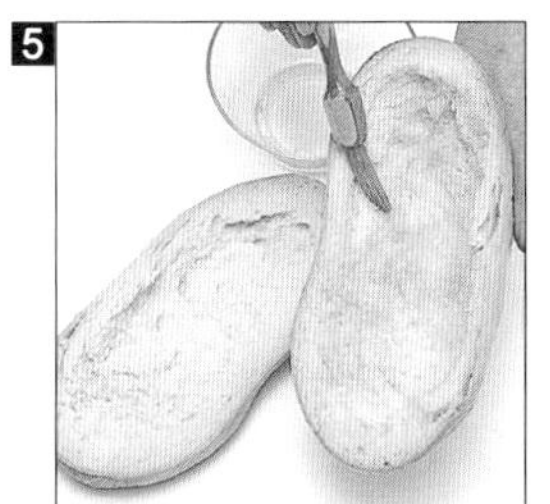

5

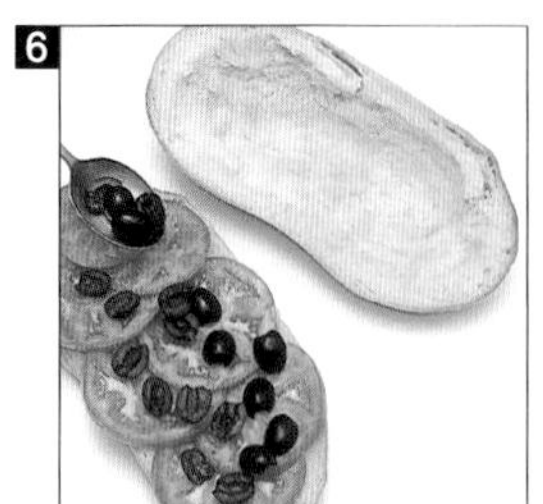

6

1 Cook the (bell) pepper over a hot barbecue (grill) for 15 minutes, turning once. Put the (bell) pepper into a plastic bag and seal.

2 Meanwhile, sear both sides of the steak first and then grill for 8 minutes, turning once.

3 When the (bell) pepper is cool enough to handle, peel and slice it.

4 Using a sharp knife, cut the steak into thin strips.

5 Cut the loaf of bread lengthways and hollow out each half, leaving a 2.5 cm/1 inch crust. Brush both halves very liberally with olive oil.

6 Lay the tomatoes, olives, cucumber, steak strips, anchovies and red (bell) pepper strips on the bottom half. Season with salt and pepper to taste and cover with the top half.

7 Put the Pan Bagna on top of a piece of greaseproof paper (baking parchment). Squash the whole loaf and its filling down well and wrap tightly in cling film (plastic wrap). Secure with adhesive tape if necessary. Chill for at least 2 hours. If made in the morning, by lunchtime it will be ready to eat and all the flavours will have combined.

VARIATIONS

Different fillings, such as pâtés, sausages and other salad items, can be used according to appetite and taste. Mozzarella cheese is good, as it is so moist. Onions give a bit of a zing to the other ingredients.

Chorizo & Mushroom Pasta

Simple and quick to make, this spicy dish is sure to set thc taste buds tingling.

NUTRITIONAL INFORMATION

Calories	495	Sugars	1g
Protein	15g	Fat	35g
Carbohydrate	33g	Saturates	5g

 5 MINS  20 MINS

SERVES 6

INGREDIENTS

- 680 g/1½ lb dried vermicelli
- 125 ml/4 fl oz/½ cup olive oil
- 2 garlic cloves
- 125 g/4½ oz chorizo, sliced
- 225 g/8 oz wild mushrooms
- 3 fresh red chillies, chopped
- 2 tbsp freshly grated Parmesan cheese
- salt and pepper
- 10 anchovy fillets, to garnish

1 Bring a large saucepan of lightly salted water to the boil. Add the vermicelli and 1 tablespoon of the oil and cook for 8–10 minutes or until just tender, but still firm to the bite.

2 Drain the pasta thoroughly, place on a large, warm serving plate and keep warm.

3 Meanwhile, heat the remaining oil in a large frying pan (skillet). Add the garlic and fry for 1 minute.

4 Add the chorizo and wild mushrooms and cook for 4 minutes,

5 Add the chopped chillies and cook for 1 further minute.

2

4

5

6 Pour the chorizo and wild mushroom mixture over the vermicelli and season with a little salt and pepper.

7 Sprinkle with freshly grated Parmesan cheese, garnish with a lattice of anchovy fillcts and serve immediately.

COOK'S TIP

Many varieties of mushrooms are now cultivated and most are indistinguishable from the wild varieties. Mixed colour oyster mushrooms have been used here, but you could also use chanterelles. Remember that chanterelles shrink during cooking, so you may need more.

Tagliarini with Gorgonzola

This simple, creamy pasta sauce is a classic Italian recipe. You could use Danish blue cheese instead of the Gorgonzola, if you prefer.

NUTRITIONAL INFORMATION

Calories	904	Sugars	4g
Protein	27g	Fat	53g
Carbohydrate	83g	Saturates	36g

 5 MINS  20 MINS

SERVES 4

INGREDIENTS

- 25 g/1 oz/2 tbsp butter
- 225 g/8 oz Gorgonzola cheese, roughly crumbled
- 150 ml/¼ pint/⅝ cup double (heavy) cream
- 30 ml/2 tbsp dry white wine
- 1 tsp cornflour (cornstarch)
- 4 fresh sage sprigs, finely chopped
- 400 g/14 oz dried tagliarini
- 2 tbsp olive oil
- salt and white pepper

1 Melt the butter in a heavy-based pan. Stir in 175 g/6 oz of the cheese and melt, over a low heat, for about 2 minutes.

2 Add the cream, wine and cornflour (cornstarch) and beat with a whisk until fully incorporated.

3 Stir in the sage and season to taste with salt and white pepper. Bring to the boil over a low heat, whisking constantly, until the sauce thickens. Remove from the heat and set aside while you cook the pasta.

4 Bring a large saucepan of lightly salted water to the boil. Add the tagliarini and 1 tbsp of the olive oil. Cook the pasta for 8–10 minutes or until just tender, drain thoroughly and toss in the remaining olive oil. Transfer the pasta to a serving dish and keep warm.

5 Reheat the sauce over a low heat, whisking constantly. Spoon the Gorgonzola sauce over the tagliarini, generously sprinkle over the remaining cheese and serve immediately.

COOK'S TIP

Gorgonzola is one of the world's oldest veined cheeses and, arguably, its finest. When buying, always check that it is creamy yellow with delicate green veining. Avoid hard or discoloured cheese. It should have a rich, piquant aroma, not a bitter smell.

White Nut Filo Parcels

These crisp, buttery parcels, filled with nuts and pesto, would make an interesting break with tradition for Sunday lunch.

NUTRITIONAL INFORMATION

Calories	1100	Sugars	9g
Protein	29g	Fat	80g
Carbohydrate	73g	Saturates	15g

 15 MINS 25 MINS

SERVES 4

INGREDIENTS

- 40 g/1½ oz/3 tbsp butter or margarine
- 1 large onion, finely chopped
- 275 g/9½ oz/2¼ cups mixed white nuts, such as pine nuts, unsalted cashew nuts, blanched almonds, unsalted peanuts, finely chopped
- 90 g/3 oz/1½ cups fresh white breadcrumbs
- ½ tsp ground mace
- 1 egg, beaten
- 1 egg yolk
- 3 tbsp pesto sauce
- 2 tbsp chopped basil
- 125 g/4½ oz/½ cup butter or margarine, melted
- 16 sheets filo pastry
- salt and pepper
- basil sprigs to garnish

TO SERVE

- cranberry sauce
- steamed vegetables

2

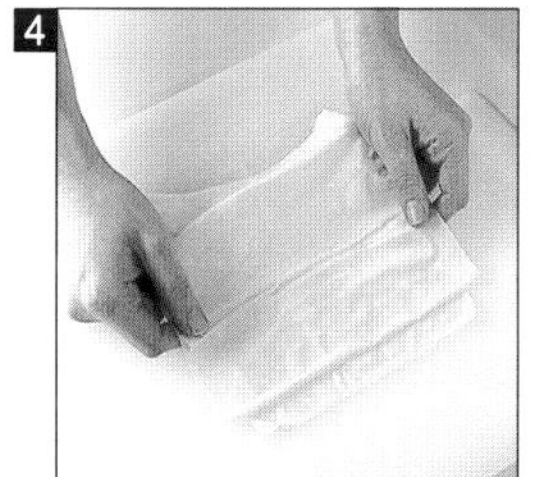
4

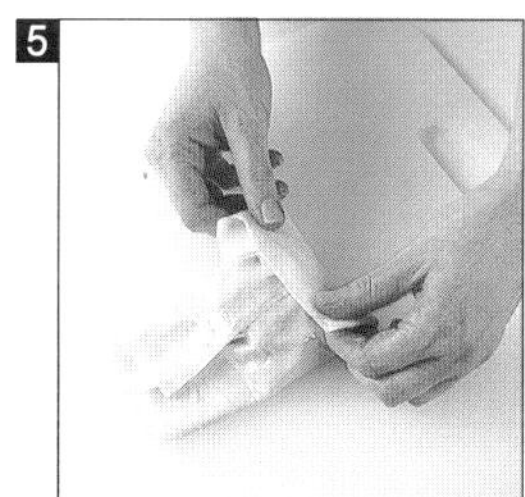
5

1 Melt the butter or margarine in a frying pan (skillet) and gently fry the onion for 2–3 minutes, until just softened but not browned.

2 Remove from the heat and stir in the nuts, two-thirds of the breadcrumbs, the mace and beaten egg. Season to taste with salt and pepper. Set aside.

3 Place the remaining breadcrumbs in a bowl and stir in the egg yolk, pesto sauce, basil, and 1 tablespoon of the melted butter or margarine. Mix well.

4 Brush 1 sheet of filo with melted butter or margarine. Fold in half and brush again. Repeat with a second sheet and lay it on top of the first one so that it forms a cross.

5 Put one-eighth of the nut mixture in the centre of the pastry. Top with one-eighth of the pesto mixture. Fold over the edges, brushing with more butter or margarine, to form a parcel. Brush the top with butter or margarine and transfer to a baking tray (cookie sheet). Make eight parcels in the same way and brush with the remaining butter or margarine..

6 Bake in a preheated oven at 220°C/425°F/Gas Mark 7 for 15–20 minutes, until golden. Transfer to serving plates, garnish with basil sprigs and serve with cranberry sauce and steamed vegetables.

Three-Cheese Fondue

A hot cheese dip made from three different cheeses can be prepared easily and with guaranteed success in the microwave oven.

NUTRITIONAL INFORMATION

Calories	565	Sugars	1g
Protein	29g	Fat	38g
Carbohydrate	15g	Saturates	24g

 15 MINS  10 MINS

SERVES 4

INGREDIENTS

- 1 garlic clove
- 300 ml/½ pint/1¼ cups dry white wine
- 250 g/8 oz/2 cups grated mild Cheddar cheese
- 125 g/4½ oz/1 cup grated Gruyère (Swiss) cheese
- 125 g/4½ oz/1 cup grated mozzarella cheese
- 2 tbsp cornflour (cornstarch)
- pepper

TO SERVE

- French bread
- vegetables, such as courgettes (zucchini), mushrooms, baby corn cobs and cauliflower

1 Bruise the garlic by placing the flat side of a knife on top and pressing down with the heel of your hand.

2 Rub the garlic around the inside of a large bowl. Discard the garlic.

3 Pour the wine into the bowl and heat, uncovered, on HIGH power for 3–4 minutes, until hot but not boiling.

4 Gradually add the Cheddar and Gruyère (Swiss) cheeses, stirring well after each addition, then add the mozzarella. Stir until completely melted.

5 Mix the cornflour (cornstarch) with a little water to a smooth paste and stir into the cheese mixture. Season to taste with pepper.

6 Cover and cook on MEDIUM power for 6 minutes, stirring twice during cooking, until the sauce is smooth.

7 Cut the French bread into cubes and the vegetables into batons, slices or florets. To serve, keep the fondue warm over a spirit lamp or reheat as necessary in the microwave oven. Dip in cubes of French bread and batons, slices or florets of vegetables.

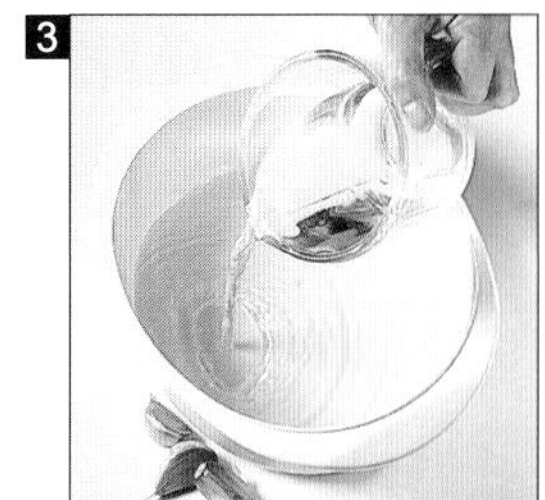
3

4

5

COOK'S TIP

Make sure you add the cheese to the wine gradually, mixing well in between each addition, otherwise the mixture might curdle.

Falafel

These are a very tasty, well-known Middle Eastern dish of small chickpea (garbanzo bean) based balls, spiced and deep-fried.

NUTRITIONAL INFORMATION

Calories	491	Sugars	3g
Protein	15g	Fat	30g
Carbohydrate	43g	Saturates	3g

 25 MINS  10–15 MINS

SERVES 4

INGREDIENTS

- 675 g/1½ lb/6 cups canned chickpeas (garbanzo beans), drained
- 1 red onion, chopped
- 3 garlic cloves, crushed
- 100 g/3½ oz wholemeal (whole wheat) bread
- 2 small fresh red chillies
- 1 tsp ground cumin
- 1 tsp ground coriander
- ½ tsp turmeric
- 1 tbsp chopped coriander (cilantro), plus extra to garnish
- 1 egg, beaten
- 100 g/3½ oz/1 cup wholemeal (whole wheat) breadcrumbs
- vegetable oil, for deep-frying
- salt and pepper
- tomato and cucumber salad and lemon wedges, to serve

2

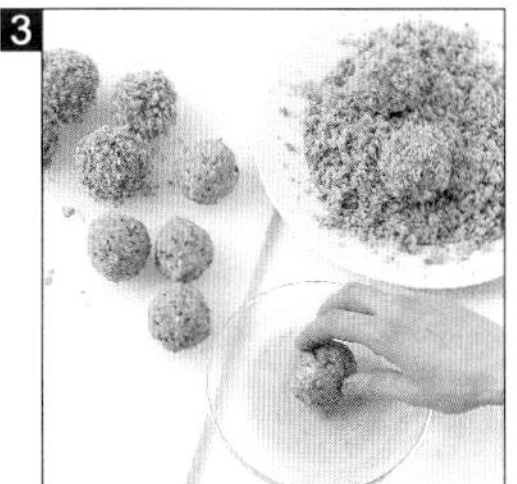

3

4

1 Put the chickpeas (garbanzo beans), onion, garlic, bread, chillies, spices and coriander (cilantro) in a food processor and process for 30 seconds. Stir and season to taste with salt and pepper.

2 Remove the mixture from the food processor and shape into walnut-sized balls.

3 Place the beaten egg in a shallow bowl and place the wholemeal (whole wheat) breadcrumbs on a plate. Dip the balls first into the egg to coat and then roll them in the breadcrumbs, shaking off any excess.

4 Heat the oil for deep-frying to 180°C/350°F or until a cube of bread browns in 30 seconds. Fry the falafel, in batches if necessary, for 2–3 minutes, until crisp and browned. Remove from the oil with a slotted spoon and dry on absorbent kitchen paper (paper towels). Garnish with coriander (cilantro) and serve with a tomato and cucumber salad and lemon wedges.

Potatoes Lyonnaise

In this classic French recipe, sliced potatoes are cooked with onions to make a delicious accompaniment to a main meal.

NUTRITIONAL INFORMATION

Calories	277	Sugars	4g
Protein	5g	Fat	12g
Carbohydrate	40g	Saturates	4g

10 MINS

25 MINS

SERVES 6

INGREDIENTS

- 1.25 kg/2 lb 12 oz potatoes
- 4 tbsp olive oil
- 25 g/1 oz/2 tbsp butter
- 2 onions, sliced
- 2–3 garlic cloves, crushed (optional)
- salt and pepper
- chopped parsley, to garnish

1 Slice the potatoes into 5 mm/¼ inch slices. Put in a large saucepan of lightly salted water and bring to the boil. Cover and simmer gently for about 10–12 minutes, until just tender. Avoid boiling too rapidly or the potatoes will break up and lose their shape. When cooked, drain well.

2

3

4

2 While the potatoes are cooking, heat the oil and butter in a very large frying pan (skillet). Add the onions and garlic, if using, and fry over a medium heat, stirring frequently, until the onions are softened.

3 Add the cooked potato slices to the frying pan (skillet) and cook with the onions, carefully stirring occasionally, for about 5–8 minutes until the potatoes are well browned.

4 Season to taste with salt and pepper. Sprinkle over the chopped parsley to serve. If wished, transfer the potatoes and onions to a large ovenproof dish and keep warm in a low oven until ready to serve.

COOK'S TIP

If the potatoes blacken slightly as they are boiling, add a spoonful of lemon juice to the cooking water.

Spicy Chicken Tortillas

The chicken filling for these easy-to-prepare tortillas has a mild, mellow spicy heat and a fresh salad makes a perfect accompaniment.

NUTRITIONAL INFORMATION	
Calories 650	Sugars 15g
Protein 48g	Fat 31g
Carbohydrate ...47g	Saturates 10g

 10 MINS  35 MINS

SERVES 4

INGREDIENTS

- 2 tbsp oil
- 8 skinless, boneless chicken thighs, sliced
- 1 onion, chopped
- 2 garlic cloves, chopped
- 1 tsp cumin seeds, roughly crushed
- 2 large dried chillies, sliced
- 400 g/14 oz can tomatoes
- 400 g/14 oz can red kidney beans, drained
- 150 ml/¼ pint/⅔ cup chicken stock
- 2 tsp sugar
- salt and pepper
- lime wedges, to garnish

TO SERVE

- 1 large ripe avocado
- 1 lime
- 8 soft tortillas
- 225 ml/8 fl oz/1 cup thick yogurt

1

4

5

1 Heat the oil in a large frying pan or wok, add the chicken and fry for 3 minutes.

2 Add the chopped onion and fry for 5 minutes, stirring until browned.

3 Add the chopped garlic, cumin and chillies, with their seeds, and cook for about 1 minute.

4 Add the tomatoes, kidney beans, stock, sugar and salt and pepper. Bring to the boil, breaking up the tomatoes. Cover and simmer for 15 minutes. Remove the lid and cook for 5 minutes, stirring occasionally until the sauce has thickened.

5 Halve the avocado, discard the stone and scoop out the flesh onto a plate. Mash the avocado with a fork.

6 Cut half of the lime into 8 thin wedges. Now squeeze the juice from the remaining lime over the mashed avocado.

7 Warm the tortillas according to the directions on the pack. Put two tortillas on each serving plate, fill with the chicken mixture and top with spoonfuls of avocado and yogurt. Garnish the tortillas with lime wedges.

Curry Pasties

These pasties, which are suitable for vegans, are a delicious combination of vegetables and spices. They can be eaten either hot or cold.

NUTRITIONAL INFORMATION

Calories	455	Sugars	5g
Protein	8g	Fat	27g
Carbohydrate	48g	Saturates	5g

 1 HOUR  1 HOUR

SERVES 4

INGREDIENTS

225 g/8 oz/2 cups plain (all-purpose) wholemeal (whole wheat) flour

100 g/3½ oz/ ⅓ cup margarine, cut into small pieces

4 tbsp water

2 tbsp oil

225 g/8 oz diced root vegetables, such as potatoes, carrots and parsnips

1 small onion, chopped

2 garlic cloves, finely chopped

½ tsp curry powder

½ tsp ground turmeric

½ tsp ground cumin

½ tsp wholegrain mustard

5 tbsp vegetable stock

soya milk, to glaze

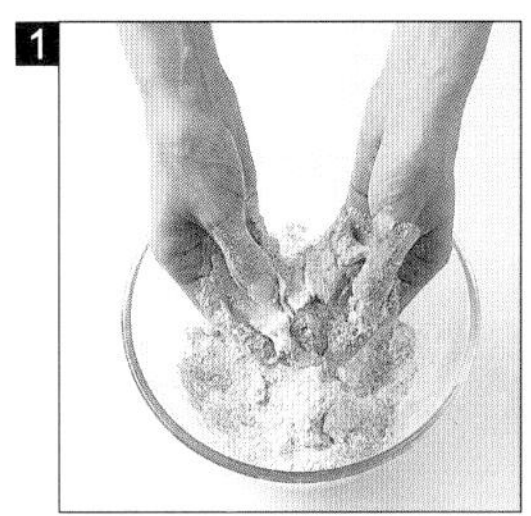

1

2

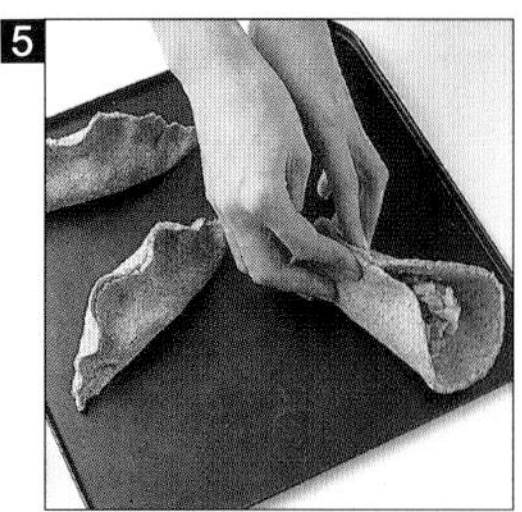

5

1 Place the flour in a mixing bowl and rub in the margarine with your fingertips until the mixture resembles breadcrumbs. Stir in the water and bring together to form a soft dough. Wrap and set aside to chill in the refrigerator for 30 minutes.

2 To make the filling, heat the oil in a large saucepan. Add the diced root vegetables, chopped onion and garlic and fry, stirring occasionally, for 2 minutes. Stir in all of the spices, turning the vegetables to coat them thoroughly. Fry the vegetables, stirring constantly, for a further 1 minute.

3 Add the stock to the pan and bring to the boil. Cover and simmer, stirring occasionally, for about 20 minutes, until the vegetables are tender and the liquid has been absorbed. Leave to cool.

4 Divide the pastry (pie dough) into 4 portions. Roll each portion into a 15 cm/6 inch round. Place the filling on one half of each round.

5 Brush the edges of each round with soya milk, then fold over and press the edges together to seal. Place on a baking tray (cookie sheet). Bake in a preheated oven, 200°C/ 400°F/Gas Mark 6, for 25–30 minutes until golden brown.

Chilli Tofu (Bean Curd)

A tasty Mexican-style dish with a melt-in-the-mouth combination of tofu (bean curd) and avocado served with a tangy tomato sauce.

NUTRITIONAL INFORMATION

Calories	806	Sugars	20g
Protein	37g	Fat	54g
Carbohydrate	45g	Saturates	19g

 30 MINS  35 MINS

SERVES 4

INGREDIENTS

- ½ tsp chilli powder
- 1 tsp paprika
- 2 tbsp plain (all-purpose) flour
- 225 g/8 oz tofu (bean curd), cut into 1 cm/½ inch pieces
- 2 tbsp vegetable oil
- 1 onion, finely chopped
- 1 garlic clove, crushed
- 1 large red (bell) pepper, seeded and finely chopped
- 1 large ripe avocado
- 1 tbsp lime juice
- 4 tomatoes, peeled, seeded and chopped
- 125 g/4½ oz/1 cup grated Cheddar cheese
- 8 soft flour tortillas
- 150 ml/¼ pint/⅔ cup soured cream
- salt and pepper
- coriander (cilantro) sprigs to garnish
- pickled green jalapeño chillies, to serve

SAUCE

- 850 ml/1½ pints/3¾ cups sugocasa
- 3 tbsp chopped parsley
- 3 tbsp chopped coriander (cilantro)

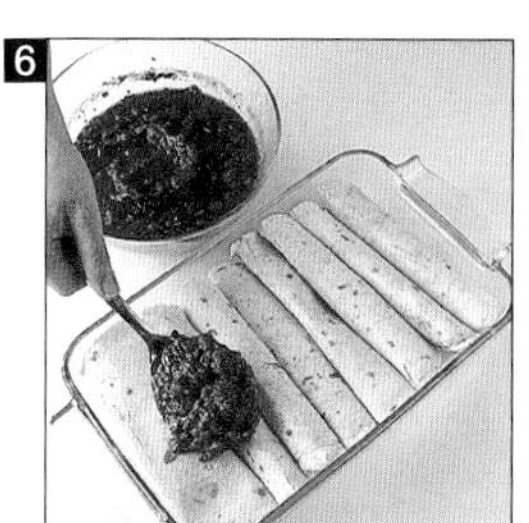

1 Mix the chilli powder, paprika, flour and salt and pepper on a plate and coat the tofu (bean curd) pieces.

2 Heat the oil in a frying pan (skillet) and gently fry the tofu (bean curd) for 3–4 minutes, until golden. Remove with a slotted spoon, drain on kitchen paper (paper towels) and set aside.

3 Add the onion, garlic and (bell) pepper to the oil and fry for 2–3 minutes, until just softened. Drain and set aside.

4 Halve the avocado, peel and remove the stone (pit). Slice lengthways, put in a bowl with the lime juice and toss to coat.

5 Add the tofu (bean curd) and onion mixture and gently stir in the tomatoes and half the cheese. Spoon one-eighth of the filling down the centre of each tortilla, top with soured cream and roll up. Arrange the tortillas in a shallow ovenproof dish in a single layer.

6 To make the sauce, mix together all the ingredients. Spoon the sauce over the tortillas, sprinkle with the remaining grated cheese and bake in a preheated oven, 190°C/375°F/Gas Mark 5, for 25 minutes, until golden and bubbling. Garnish with coriander (cilantro) sprigs and serve immediately with pickled jalapeño chillies.

Calabrian Pizza

Traditionally, this pizza has a double layer of dough to make it robust and filling. Alternatively, it can be made as a single pizza (as shown here).

NUTRITIONAL INFORMATION

Calories	574	Sugars	6g
Protein	20g	Fat	30g
Carbohydrate	60g	Saturates	7g

 2½ HOURS 55 MINS

SERVES 6

INGREDIENTS

- 400 g/14 oz/3½ cups plain (all-purpose) flour
- ½ tsp salt
- 1 sachet easy-blend yeast
- 2 tbsp olive oil
- about 275 ml/9 fl oz/generous 1 cup warm water

FILLING

- 2 tbsp olive oil
- 2 garlic cloves, crushed
- 1 red (bell) pepper, cored, deseeded and sliced
- 1 yellow (bell) pepper, cored, deseeded and sliced
- 125 g/4½ oz Ricotta
- 175 g/6 oz jar sun-dried tomatoes, drained
- 3 hard-boiled (hard-cooked) eggs, sliced thinly
- 1 tbsp chopped fresh mixed herbs
- 125 g/4½ oz salami, cut into strips
- 150–175 g/5½–6 oz Mozzarella, grated
- a little milk, to glaze
- salt and pepper

1 Sift the flour and salt into a bowl and mix in the easy-blend yeast.

2 Add the olive oil and enough warm water to mix to a smooth, pliable dough. Knead for 10–15 minutes by hand, or process for 5 minutes in a mixer.

3 Shape the dough into a ball, place in a lightly oiled polythene bag and put in a warm place for 1–1½ hours or until doubled in size.

4 To make the filling, heat the oil in a frying pan (skillet) and fry the garlic and (bell) peppers slowly in the oil until softened.

5 Knock back the dough and roll out half to fit the base of a 30 x 25 cm/12 x 10 inch oiled roasting tin (pan).

6 Season the dough and spread with the Ricotta, then cover with sun-dried tomatoes, hard-boiled (hard-cooked) eggs, herbs and the (bell) pepper mixture. Arrange the salami strips on top and sprinkle with the grated cheese.

7 Roll out the remaining dough and place over the filling, sealing the edges well, or use to make a second pizza. Leave to rise for 1 hour in a warm place. An uncovered pizza will only take about 30–40 minutes to rise.

8 Prick the double pizza with a fork about 20 times, brush the top with milk and cook in a preheated oven, at 180°C/350°F/Gas Mark 4, for about 50 minutes or until lightly browned. The uncovered pizza will take only 35–40 minutes. Serve hot.

2

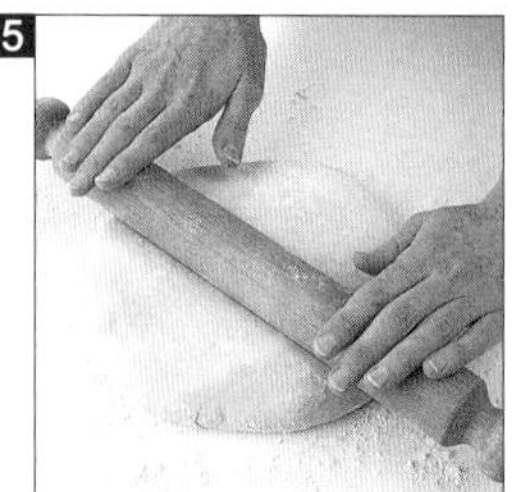
5

6

Muffin Pizzas

Toasted muffins are topped with pineapple and Parma ham (prosciutto). Plain, wholemeal or cheese muffins will all make great pizza bases.

NUTRITIONAL INFORMATION

Calories	259	Sugars	7g
Protein	9g	Fat	15g
Carbohydrate	24g	Saturates	3g

 45 MINS  5 MINS

SERVES 4

INGREDIENTS

- 4 muffins
- 1 quantity Basic Tomato Sauce (see page 6)
- 2 sun-dried tomatoes in oil, chopped
- 60 g/2 oz Parma ham (prosciutto)
- 2 rings canned pineapple, chopped
- ½ green (bell) pepper, chopped
- 125 g/4½ oz Mozzarella cheese, sliced thinly
- olive oil, for drizzling
- salt and pepper
- fresh basil leaves, to garnish

1 Cut the muffins in half and toast the cut side lightly.

2 Spread the tomato sauce evenly over the muffins.

3 Sprinkle the sun-dried tomatoes on top of the tomato sauce.

4 Cut the ham into thin strips and place on the muffins with the pineapple and green (bell) pepper.

5 Carefully arrange the Mozzarella slices on top.

6 Drizzle a little olive oil over each pizza, and season.

7 Place under a preheated medium grill (broiler) and cook until the cheese melts and bubbles.

8 Serve immediately garnished with small basil leaves.

COOK'S TIP

You don't have to use plain muffins for your base; wholemeal or cheese muffins will also make ideal pizza bases. Muffins freeze well, so always keep some in the freezer for an instant pizza.

Spicy Tomato Tagliatelle

A deliciously fresh and slightly spicy tomato sauce which is excellent for lunch or a light supper.

NUTRITIONAL INFORMATION

Calories	306	Sugars	7g
Protein	8g	Fat	12g
Carbohydrate	45g	Saturates	7g

 15 MINS

 35 MINS

SERVES 4

INGREDIENTS

- 50 g/1¾ oz/3 tbsp butter
- 1 onion, finely chopped
- 1 garlic clove, crushed
- 2 small red chillies, deseeded and diced
- 450 g/1 lb fresh tomatoes, skinned, deseeded and diced
- 200 ml/7 fl oz/¾ cup vegetable stock
- 2 tbsp tomato purée (paste)
- 1 tsp sugar
- salt and pepper
- 675 g/1½ lb fresh green and white tagliatelle, or 350 g/12 oz dried

1 Melt the butter in a large saucepan. Add the onion and garlic and cook for 3–4 minutes or until softened.

2 Add the chillies to the pan and continue cooking for about 2 minutes.

3 Add the tomatoes and stock, reduce the heat and leave to simmer for 10 minutes, stirring.

4 Pour the sauce into a food processor and blend for 1 minute until smooth. Alternatively, push the sauce through a sieve.

5 Return the sauce to the pan and add the tomato purée (paste) sugar, and salt and pepper to taste. Gently reheat over a low heat, until piping hot.

6 Cook the tagliatelle in a pan of boiling water for 8–10 minutes or until it is tender, but still has 'bite'. Drain the tagliatelle, transfer to serving plates and serve with the tomato sauce.

VARIATION

Try topping your pasta dish with 50 g/1¾ oz pancetta or unsmoked bacon, diced and dry-fried for 5 minutes until crispy.

Four Seasons Pizza

This is a traditional pizza on which the toppings are divided into four sections, each of which is supposed to depict a season of the year.

NUTRITIONAL INFORMATION

Calories	313	Sugars	8g
Protein	8g	Fat	13g
Carbohydrate	44g	Saturates	3g

 2¾ HOURS 20 MINS

SERVES 4

INGREDIENTS

- Basic Pizza Dough (see page 861)
- Basic Tomato Sauce (see page 6)
- 25 g/1 oz chorizo sausage, sliced thinly
- 25 g/1 oz button mushrooms, wiped and sliced thinly
- 45 g/1½ oz artichoke hearts, sliced thinly
- 25 g/1 oz Mozzarella, sliced thinly
- 3 anchovies, halved lengthways
- 2 tsp capers
- 4 pitted black olives, sliced
- 4 fresh basil leaves, shredded
- olive oil, for drizzling
- salt and pepper

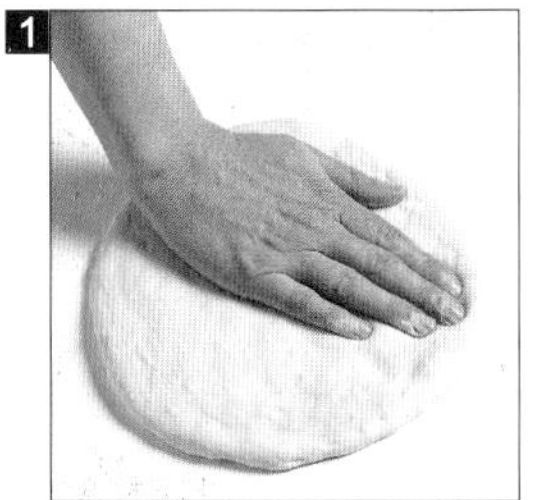
1

3

4

1 Roll out or press the dough, using a rolling pin or your hands, into a 25 cm/10 inch circle on a lightly floured surface. Place on a large greased baking tray (cookie sheet) or pizza pan and push up the edge a little.

2 Cover and leave to rise slightly for 10 minutes in a warm place. Spread the tomato sauce over the pizza base, almost to the edge.

3 Put the sliced chorizo on to one quarter of the pizza, the sliced mushrooms on another, the artichoke hearts on a third, and the Mozzarella and anchovies on the fourth.

4 Dot with the capers, olives and basil leaves. Drizzle with a little olive oil and season. Do not put any salt on the anchovy section as the fish are very salty.

5 Bake in a preheated oven, at 200°C/400°F/Gas Mark 6, for 18–20 minutes, or until the crust is golden and crisp. Serve immediately.

Spicy Mushrooms

A mixture of mushrooms, common in Western cooking, have been used in this recipe for a richly flavoured dish.

NUTRITIONAL INFORMATION

Calories	103	Sugars	4g
Protein	3g	Fat	8g
Carbohydrate	5g	Saturates	2g

5 MINS

10 MINS

SERVES 4

INGREDIENTS

- 2 tbsp peanut oil
- 2 garlic cloves, crushed
- 3 spring onions (scallions), chopped
- 300 g/10½ oz button mushrooms
- 2 large open-cap mushrooms, sliced
- 125 g/4½ oz oyster mushrooms
- 1 tsp chilli sauce
- 1 tbsp dark soy sauce
- 1 tbsp hoisin sauce
- 1 tbsp wine vinegar
- ½ tsp ground Szechuan pepper
- 1 tbsp dark brown sugar
- 1 tsp sesame oil
- chopped parsley, to garnish

1 Heat the peanut oil in a preheated wok or large frying pan (skillet) until almost smoking.

2 Reduce the heat slightly, add the garlic and spring onions (scallions) to the wok or frying pan (skillet) and stir-fry for 30 seconds.

3 Add all the mushrooms to the wok, together with the chilli sauce, dark soy sauce, hoisin sauce, wine vinegar, ground Szechuan pepper and dark brown sugar and stir-fry for 4–5 minutes, or until the mushrooms are cooked through. Stir constantly to prevent the mixture sticking to the base of the wok.

4 Sprinkle the sesame oil on top of the mixture in the wok. Transfer to a warm serving dish, garnish with parsley and serve immediately.

COOK'S TIP

If Chinese dried mushrooms are available, add a small quantity to this dish for texture. Wood (tree) ears are widely used and are available dried from Chinese food stores. They should be rinsed, soaked in warm water for 20 minutes and rinsed again before use.

Onion & Anchovy Pizza

This tasty onion pizza is topped with a lattice pattern of anchovies and black olives. Cut the pizza into squares to serve.

NUTRITIONAL INFORMATION

Calories	373	Sugars	5g
Protein	12g	Fat	20g
Carbohydrate	39g	Saturates	4g

 $1\frac{3}{4}$ HOURS  30 MINS

MAKES 6

INGREDIENTS

- 4 tbsp olive oil
- 3 onions, sliced thinly
- 1 garlic clove, crushed
- 1 tsp soft brown sugar
- ½ tsp crushed fresh rosemary
- 200 g/7 oz can chopped tomatoes
- Basic Pizza Dough (see page 861)
- 2 tbsp freshly grated Parmesan
- 50 g/1¾ oz can anchovies
- 12–14 black olives
- salt and pepper

1 Heat 3 tablespoons of the oil in a large saucepan and add the onions, garlic, sugar and rosemary. Cover and fry gently, stirring occasionally, for 10 minutes or until the onions are soft but not brown.

2 Add the tomatoes to the pan, stir and season with salt and pepper to taste. Leave to cool slightly.

3 Roll out or press the dough, using a rolling pin or your hands, on a lightly floured work surface to fit a 30 x 18 cm/ 12 x 7 inch greased Swiss roll tin (pan). Place in the tin (pan) and push up the edges slightly to form a rim.

4 Brush the remaining oil over the dough and sprinkle with the cheese. Cover and leave to rise slightly in a warm place for about 10 minutes.

5 Spread the onion and tomato topping over the base. Drain the anchovies, reserving the oil. Split each anchovy in half lengthways and arrange on the pizza in a lattice pattern. Place the olives in between the anchovies and drizzle over a little of the reserved oil. Season to taste.

6 Bake in a preheated oven, at 200°C/ 400°F/Gas Mark 6, for 18–20 minutes, or until the edges are crisp and golden. Cut the pizza into 6 squares and serve immediately.

1

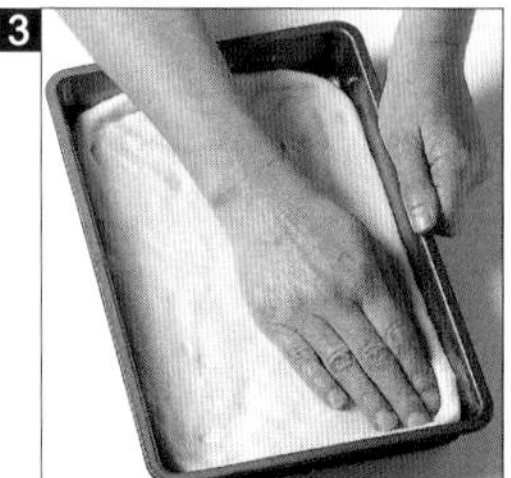
3

5

Greek Green Beans

This dish contains many Greek flavours such as lemon, garlic, oregano and olives, for a really flavourful recipe.

NUTRITIONAL INFORMATION

Calories	115	Sugars	4g
Protein	6g	Fat	4g
Carbohydrate	15g	Saturates	0.6g

 5 MINS  1 HOUR

SERVES 4

INGREDIENTS

- 400 g/14 oz can haricot (navy) beans, drained
- 1 tbsp olive oil
- 3 garlic cloves, crushed
- 425 ml/¾ pint/2 cups vegetable stock
- 1 bay leaf
- 2 sprigs oregano
- 1 tbsp tomato purée (paste)
- juice of 1 lemon
- 1 small red onion, chopped
- 25 g/1 oz pitted black olives, halved
- salt and pepper

1 Put the haricot (navy) beans in a flameproof casserole dish.

2 Add the olive oil and crushed garlic and cook over a gentle heat, stirring occasionally, for 4–5 minutes.

3 Add the stock, bay leaf, oregano, tomato purée (paste), lemon juice and red onion, cover and simmer for about 1 hour or until the sauce has thickened.

4 Stir in the olives, season with salt and pepper to taste and serve warm or cold.

VARIATION

You can substitute other canned beans for the haricot (navy) beans – try cannellini or black-eyed beans (peas), or chick-peas (garbanzo beans) instead. Drain and rinse them before use as canned beans often have sugar or salt added.

2

3

4

Stuffed Courgettes (Zucchini)

Hollow out some courgettes (zucchini), fill them with a spicy beef mixture and bake them in the oven for a delicious side dish.

NUTRITIONAL INFORMATION

Calories	208	Sugars	3g
Protein	12g	Fat	9g
Carbohydrate	20g	Saturates	4g

 45 MINS  35 MINS

SERVES 4

INGREDIENTS

- 8 medium courgettes (zucchini)
- 1 tbsp sesame or vegetable oil
- 1 garlic clove, crushed
- 2 shallots, chopped finely
- 1 small red chilli, deseeded and chopped finely
- 250 g/9 oz/1 cup lean minced (ground) beef
- 1 tbsp fish sauce or mushroom ketchup
- 1 tbsp chopped fresh coriander (cilantro) or basil
- 2 tsp cornflour (cornstarch), blended with a little cold water
- 90 g/3 oz/½ cup cooked long-grain rice
- salt and pepper

TO GARNISH

- sprigs of fresh coriander (cilantro) or basil
- carrot slices

2 

3 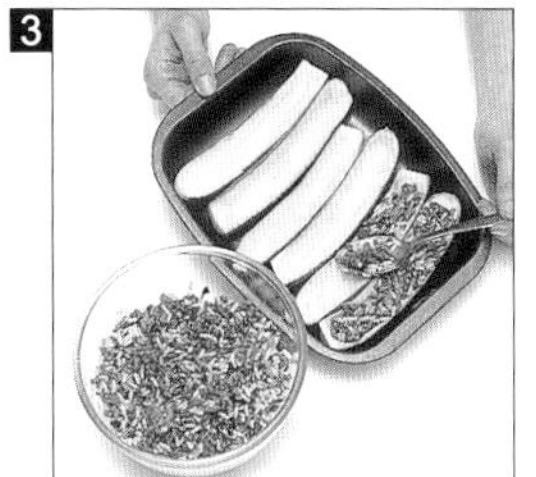

4 

1 Slice the courgettes (zucchini) in half horizontally and scoop out a channel down the middle, discarding all the seeds. Sprinkle with salt and set aside for 15 minutes.

2 Heat the oil in a wok or frying pan (skillet) and add the garlic, shallots and chilli. Stir-fry for 2 minutes, until golden. Add the minced (ground) beef and stir-fry briskly for about 5 minutes. Stir in the fish sauce or mushroom ketchup, the chopped coriander (cilantro) or basil and the blended cornflour (cornstarch), and cook for 2 minutes, stirring until thickened. Season with salt and pepper, then remove from the heat.

3 Rinse the courgettes (zucchini) in cold water and arrange them in a greased shallow ovenproof dish, cut side uppermost. Mix the cooked rice into the minced (ground) beef, then use this mixture to stuff the courgettes (zucchini).

4 Cover with foil and bake in a preheated oven at 190°C/375°F/ Gas Mark 5 for 20–25 minutes, removing the foil for the last 5 minutes of cooking time.

5 Serve at once, garnished with sprigs of fresh coriander (cilantro) or basil, and carrot slices.

Lemon Beans

Use a variety of beans if possible, although this recipe is perfectly acceptable with just one type of bean.

NUTRITIONAL INFORMATION

Calories	285	Sugars	6g
Protein	9g	Fat	19g
Carbohydrate	18g	Saturates	6g

 5 MINS  20 MINS

SERVES 4

INGREDIENTS

- 900 g/2 lb mixed green beans, such as broad (fava) beans, French (green) beans, runner (string) beans
- 65 g/2½ oz/5 tbsp butter or margarine
- 4 tsp plain (all-purpose) flour
- 300 ml/½ pint/1¼ cups vegetable stock
- 5 tbsp dry white wine
- 6 tbsp single (light) cream
- 3 tbsp chopped mixed herbs
- 2 tbsp lemon juice
- grated rind of 1 lemon
- salt and pepper

1 Cook the beans in a saucepan of boiling salted water for 10 minutes, or until tender. Drain and place in a warmed serving dish.

2 Meanwhile, melt the butter in a saucepan. Add the flour and cook, stirring constantly, for 1 minute. Remove the pan from the heat and gradually stir in the stock and wine. Return the pan to the heat and bring to the boil, stirring.

3 Remove the pan from the heat once again and stir in the single (light) cream, mixed herbs, lemon juice and rind. Season with salt and pepper to taste. Pour the sauce over the beans, mixing well. Serve immediately.

VARIATION

Use lime rind and juice instead of lemon for an alternative citrus flavour. Replace the single (light) cream with natural (unsweetened) yogurt for a healthier version of this dish.

Potatoes with Almonds

This oven-cooked dish has a subtle creamy, almond flavour and a pale yellow colour as a result of being cooked with turmeric.

NUTRITIONAL INFORMATION

Calories	531	Sugars	6g
Protein	7g	Fat	46g
Carbohydrate	24g	Saturates	23g

 5 MINS  40–45 MINS

SERVES 4

INGREDIENTS

- 2 large potatoes, unpeeled and sliced
- 1 tbsp vegetable oil
- 1 red onion, halved and sliced
- 1 garlic clove, crushed
- 50 g/1¾ oz/½ cup almond flakes
- ½ tsp turmeric
- 300ml/½ pint/1¼ cups double (heavy) cream
- 125 g/4½ oz/2 bunches rocket (arugula)
- salt and pepper

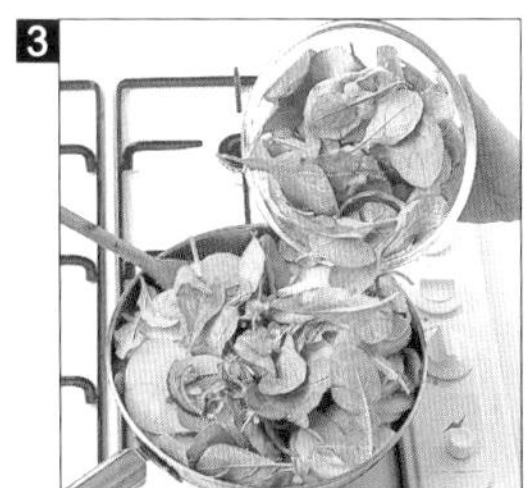

1 Cook the sliced potatoes in a saucepan of boiling water for 10 minutes. Drain thoroughly.

2 Heat the vegetable oil in a heavy-based frying pan (skillet. Add the onion and garlic and fry over a medium heat, stirring frequently, for 3-4 minutes.

3 Add the almonds, turmeric and potato slices to the frying pan (skillet) and cook, stirring constantly, for 2-3 minutes. Stir in the rocket (arugula).

4 Transfer the potato and almond mixture to a shallow ovenproof dish. Pour the double (heavy) cream over the top and season with salt and pepper.

5 Cook in a preheated oven, 190°C/375°F/Gas Mark 5, for 20 minutes, or until the potatoes are cooked through. Transfer to a warmed serving dish and serve immediately.

Lemon Chinese Leaves

These stir-fried Chinese leaves (cabbage) are served with a tangy sauce made of grated lemon rind, lemon juice and ginger.

NUTRITIONAL INFORMATION

Calories	120	Sugars	0g
Protein	5g	Fat	8g
Carbohydrate	8g	Saturates	1g

5 MINS   10 MINS

SERVES 4

INGREDIENTS

- 500 g/1 lb 2 oz Chinese leaves (cabbage)
- 3 tbsp vegetable oil
- 1 cm/½ inch piece ginger root, grated
- 1 tsp salt
- 1 tsp sugar
- 125 ml/4 fl oz/½ cup water or vegetable stock
- 1 tsp grated lemon rind
- 1 tbsp cornflour (cornstarch)
- 1 tbsp lemon juice

1 Separate the Chinese leaves (cabbage), wash and drain thoroughly. Pat dry with absorbent kitchen paper (paper towels).

2 Cut the Chinese leaves (cabbage) into 5 cm/2 inch wide slices.

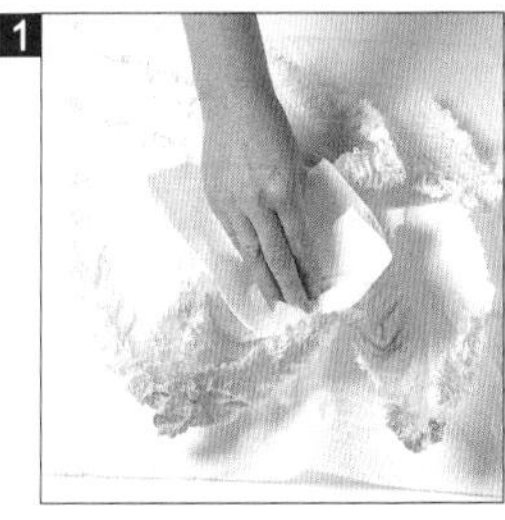

3 Heat the oil in a wok and add the grated ginger root followed by the Chinese leaves (cabbage), stir-fry for 2–3 minutes or until the leaves begin to wilt.

4 Add the salt and sugar, and mix well until the leaves soften. Remove the leaves with a slotted spoon and set aside.

5 Add the water or stock to the wok with the lemon rind. Bring to the boil.

6 Meanwhile, mix the cornflour (cornstarch) to a smooth paste with the lemon juice, then add to the wok. Simmer, stirring constantly, for about 1 minute to make a smooth sauce.

7 Return the cooked Chinese leaves (cabbage) to the pan and mix thoroughly to coat the leaves in the sauce. Arrange on a serving plate and serve immediately.

COOK'S TIP

If Chinese leaves (cabbage) are unavailable, substitute slices of savoy cabbage. Cook for 1 extra minute to soften the leaves.

Spiced Potatoes & Spinach

This is a classic Indian accompaniment for many different curries or plainer main vegetable dishes. It is very quick to cook.

NUTRITIONAL INFORMATION

Calories	176	Sugars	4g
Protein	6g	Fat	9g
Carbohydrate	18g	Saturates	1g

 10 MINS  20–25 MINS

SERVES 4

INGREDIENTS

- 3 tbsp vegetable oil
- 1 red onion, sliced
- 2 garlic cloves, crushed
- ½ tsp chilli powder
- 2 tsp ground coriander
- 1 tsp ground cumin
- 150 ml/¼ pint/⅔ cup vegetable stock
- 300 g/10½ oz potatoes, diced
- 500 g/1 lb 2 oz baby spinach
- 1 red chilli, sliced
- salt and pepper

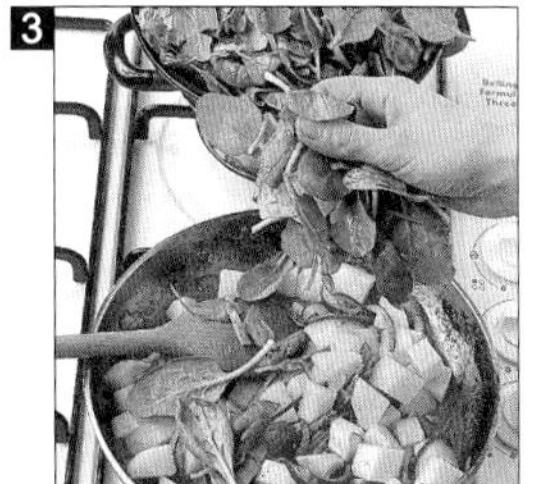

1 Heat the oil in a heavy-based frying pan (skillet). Add the onion and garlic and sauté over a medium heat, stirring occasionally, for 2–3 minutes.

2 Stir in the chilli powder, ground coriander and cumin and cook, stirring constantly, for a further 30 seconds.

3 Add the vegetable stock, diced potatoes and spinach and bring to the boil. Reduce the heat, cover the frying pan (skillet) and simmer for about 10 minutes, or until the potatoes are cooked through and tender.

4 Uncover, season to taste with salt and pepper, add the chilli and cook for a further 2–3 minutes. Transfer to a warmed serving dish and serve immediately.

COOK'S TIP

Besides adding extra colour to a dish, red onions have a sweeter, less pungent flavour than other varieties.

Broccoli in Oyster Sauce

Some Cantonese restaurants use only the stalks of the broccoli for this dish, for the crunchy texture.

NUTRITIONAL INFORMATION

Calories	100	Sugars	1g
Protein	3g	Fat	9g
Carbohydrate	2g	Saturates	1g

 3½ HOURS  5 MINS

SERVES 4

INGREDIENTS

- 250-300 g/9-10½ oz broccoli
- 3 tbsp vegetable oil
- 3-4 small slices ginger root
- ½ tsp salt
- ½ tsp sugar
- 3-4 tbsp Chinese Stock (see page 8) or water
- 1 tbsp oyster sauce

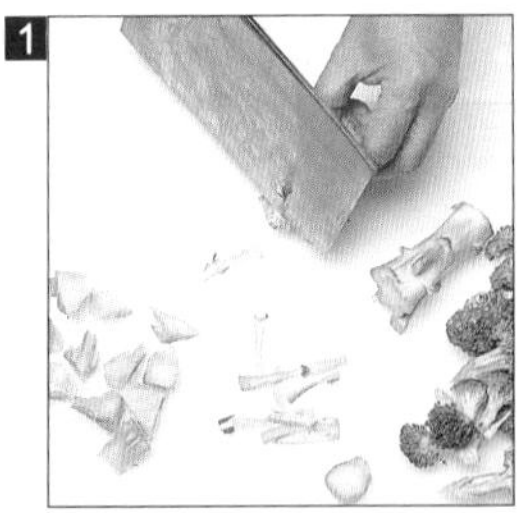

1 Using a sharp knife, cut the broccoli spears into small florets. Trim the stalks, peel off the rough skin, and cut the stalks diagonally into diamond-shaped chunks.

2 Heat the vegetable oil in a preheated wok until really hot.

3 Add the pieces of broccoli stalk and the slices of ginger root to the wok and stir-fry for half a minute, then add the florets and continue to stir-fry for another 2 minutes.

4 Add the salt, sugar and Chinese stock or water, and continue stirring for another minute or so.

5 Blend in the oyster sauce. Transfer the broccoli to a serving dish and serve hot or cold.

COOK'S TIP

The broccoli stalks have to be peeled and cut diagonally to ensure that they will cook evenly. If they are thin stalks, the pieces can be added to the wok at the same time as the florets, but otherwise add the stalks first, to ensure that they will be tender.

Curried Roast Potatoes

This is the kind of Indian-inspired dish that would fit easily into any Western menu or how about serving with a curry in place of rice?

NUTRITIONAL INFORMATION

Calories	297	Sugars	2g
Protein	3g	Fat	19g
Carbohydrate	30g	Saturates	12g

5 MINS

30–35 MINS

SERVES 4

INGREDIENTS

- 2 tsp cumin seeds
- 2 tsp coriander seeds
- 90 g/3 oz/6 tbsp butter
- 1 tsp ground turmeric
- 1 tsp black mustard seeds
- 2 garlic cloves, crushed
- 2 dried red chillies
- 750 g/1 lb 10 oz baby new potatoes

1 Grind the cumin and coriander seeds together in a mortar with a pestle or spice grinder. Grinding them fresh like this captures all of the flavour before it has a chance to dry out.

2 Melt the butter gently in a roasting tin (pan) and add the turmeric, mustard seeds, garlic and chillies and the ground cumin and coriander seeds. Stir well to combine evenly. Place in a preheated oven at 200°C/400°F/Gas Mark 6 for 5 minutes.

3 Remove the tin (pan) from the oven – the spices should be very fragrant at this stage – and add the potatoes. Stir well so that the butter and spice mix coats the potatoes completely.

1

2

4

4 Return to the oven and bake for 20–25 minutes. Stir occasionally to ensure that the potatoes are coated evenly. Test the potatoes with a skewer – if they drop off the end of the skewer when lifted, they are done. Transfer to a serving dish and serve immediately.

COOK'S TIP

Baby new potatoes are now available all year round from supermarkets. However, they are not essential for this recipe. Red or white old potatoes can be substituted, cut into 2.5 cm/1 inch cubes. You can also try substituting parsnips, carrots or turnips, cut into 2.5 cm/1 inch cubes.

Fried Spiced Potatoes

Deliciously good and a super accompaniment to almost any main course dish, although rather high in calories!

NUTRITIONAL INFORMATION

Calories	430	Sugars	7g
Protein	4g	Fat	35g
Carbohydrate	26g	Saturates	11g

 15 MINS  30 MINS

SERVES 6

INGREDIENTS

- 2 onions, quartered
- 5 cm/2 inch piece of root ginger, finely chopped
- 2 garlic cloves
- 2–3 tbsp mild or medium curry paste
- 4 tbsp water
- 750 g/1 lb 10 oz new potatoes
- vegetable oil, for deep frying
- 3 tbsp vegetable ghee or oil
- 150 ml/¼ pint/⅔ cup strained Greek yogurt
- 150 ml/¼ pint/⅔ cup double (heavy) cream
- 3 tbsp chopped mint
- salt and pepper
- ½ bunch spring onions (scallions), chopped, to garnish

1 Place the onions, ginger, garlic, curry paste and water in a blender or food processor and process until smooth, scraping down the sides of the machine and processing again, if necessary.

2 Cut the potatoes into quarters – the pieces need to be about 2.5 cm/1 inch in size – and pat dry with absorbent kitchen paper (paper towels). Heat the oil in a deep fryer to 180°C/350°F/Gas 4 or until a cube of bread browns in 30 seconds and fry the potatoes, in batches, for about 5 minutes or until golden brown, turning frequently. Remove from the pan and drain on kitchen paper (paper towels).

3 Heat the ghee or oil in a large frying pan (skillet), add the curry and onion mixture and fry gently, stirring constantly, for 2 minutes. Add the yogurt, cream and 2 tablespoons of mint and mix well.

4 Add the fried potatoes and stir until coated in the sauce. Cook, stirring frequently, for a further 5–7 minutes, or until heated through and sauce has thickened. Season with salt and pepper to taste and sprinkle with the remaining mint and sliced spring onions (scallions). Serve immediately.

COOK'S TIP

When buying new potatoes, look for the freshest you can find. The skin should be beginning to rub off. Cook them as soon as after purchase as possible, but if you have to store them, keep them in a cool, dark well-ventilated place.

Gnocchi & Tomato Sauce

Freshly made potato gnocchi are delicious, especially when they are topped with a fragrant tomato sauce.

NUTRITIONAL INFORMATION

Calories	216	Sugars	5g
Protein	5g	Fat	6g
Carbohydrate	39g	Saturates	1g

 30 MINS  45 MINS

SERVES 4

INGREDIENTS

- 350 g/12 oz floury (mealy) potatoes (those suitable for baking or mashing), halved
- 75 g/2¾ oz self-raising flour, plus extra for rolling out
- 2 tsp dried oregano
- 2 tbsp oil
- 1 large onion, chopped
- 2 garlic cloves, chopped
- 400 g/14 oz can chopped tomatoes
- ½ vegetable stock cube dissolved in 100 ml/3½ fl oz/⅓ cup boiling water
- 2 tbsp basil, shredded, plus whole leaves to garnish
- salt and pepper
- Parmesan cheese, grated, to serve

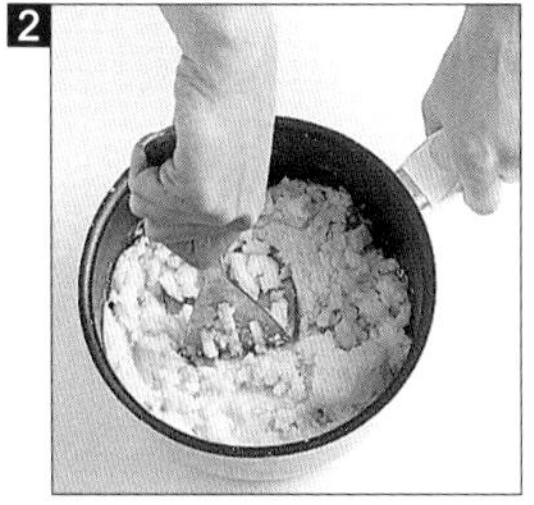

2

3

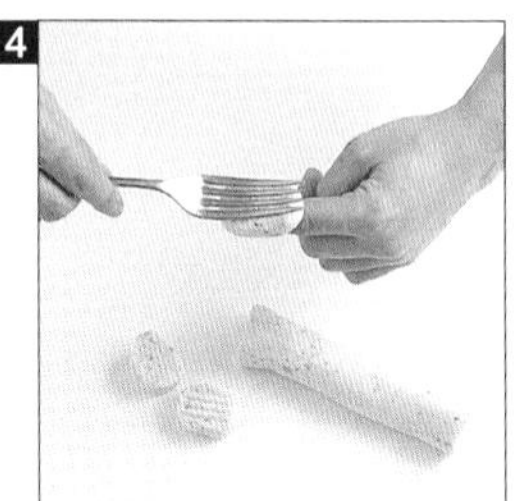

4

1 Bring a large saucepan of water to the boil. Add the potatoes and cook for 12–15 minutes or until tender. Drain and leave to cool.

2 Peel and then mash the potatoes with the salt and pepper, sifted flour and oregano. Mix together with your hands to form a dough.

3 Heat the oil in a pan. Add the onions and garlic and cook for 3–4 minutes. Add the tomatoes and stock and cook, uncovered, for 10 minutes. Season with salt and pepper to taste.

4 Roll the potato dough into a sausage about 2.5 cm/1 inch in diameter. Cut the sausage into 2.5 cm/1 inch lengths. Flour your hands, then press a fork into each piece to create a series of ridges on one side and the indent of your index finger on the other.

5 Bring a large saucepan of water to the boil and cook the gnocchi, in batches, for 2–3 minutes. They should rise to the surface when cooked. Drain well and keep warm.

6 Stir the basil into the tomato sauce and pour over the gnocchi. Garnish with basil leaves and season with pepper to taste. Sprinkle with Parmesan and serve at once.

VARIATION

Try serving the gnocchi with pesto for a change.

Dry Moong Dhal

This dhal has a baghaar (seasoned oil dressing) of butter, dried red chillies and white cumin seeds. It is simple to cook and tastes very good.

NUTRITIONAL INFORMATION

Calories	304	Sugars	1g
Protein	9g	Fat	21g
Carbohydrate	21g	Saturates	14g

 5 MINS  30–35 MINS

SERVES 4

INGREDIENTS

- 150 g/5½ oz/1 cup moong dhal
- 1 tsp finely chopped root ginger
- ½ tsp ground cumin
- ½ tsp ground coriander
- 1 tsp fresh garlic, crushed
- ½ tsp chilli powder
- 600 ml/1 pint/2½ cups water
- 1 tsp salt

BAGHAAR

- 100 g/3½ oz/8 tbsp unsalted (sweet) butter
- 5 dried red chillies
- 1 tsp white cumin seeds

TO SERVE

- chapati
- vegetable curry

2

3

4

1 Rinse the lentils under cold running water and place them in a large saucepan. Add the ginger, ground cumin, ground coriander, garlic and chilli powder, and stir to mix well.

2 Pour in enough of the water to cover the lentil mixture. Cook over a medium heat, stirring frequently, until the lentils are soft but not mushy.

3 Stir in the salt, transfer to a serving dish and keep warm.

4 Meanwhile, make the baghaar. Melt the butter in a heavy-based saucepan over a fairly low heat. Add the dried red chillies and white cumin seeds and fry, stirring constantly, until they begin to pop.

5 Pour the baghaar over the lentils and serve immediately with chapati and a vegetable curry.

COOK'S TIP

Moong dhal are tear-drop-shaped yellow split lentils, more popular in northern India than in the south. Dried red chillies are the quickest way to add heat to a dish.

Gingered Potatoes

This is a simple spicy dish which is ideal with a plain main course. The cashew nuts and celery add extra crunch.

NUTRITIONAL INFORMATION

Calories	325	Sugars	1g
Protein	5g	Fat	21g
Carbohydrate	30g	Saturates	9g

 20 MINS  30 MINS

SERVES 4

INGREDIENTS

- 675 g/1½ lb waxy potatoes, cubed
- 2 tbsp vegetable oil
- 5 cm/2 inch piece of root ginger, grated
- 1 fresh green chilli, chopped
- 1 celery stick, chopped
- 25 g/1 oz/¼ cup cashew nuts
- few strands of saffron
- 3 tbsp boiling water
- 60 g/2 oz/¼ cup butter
- celery leaves, to garnish

1 Cook the potatoes in a saucepan of boiling water for 10 minutes, then drain thoroughly.

2 Heat the oil in a heavy-based frying pan (skillet) and add the potatoes. Cook over a medium heat, stirring constantly, for 3-4 minutes.

3 Add the grated ginger, chilli, celery and cashew nuts and cook for 1 minute.

4 Meanwhile, place the saffron strands in a small bowl. Add the boiling water and set aside to soak for 5 minutes.

5 Add the butter to the pan, lower the heat and stir in the saffron mixture. Cook over a low heat for 10 minutes, or until the potatoes are tender.

6 Transfer to a warm serving dish, garnish the gingered potatoes with the celery leaves and serve at once.

COOK'S TIP

Use a non-stick, heavy-based frying pan (skillet) as the potato mixture is fairly dry and may stick to an ordinary pan.

Green Bean Stir-fry

These beans are simply cooked in a spicy, hot sauce for a tasty and very easy recipe.

NUTRITIONAL INFORMATION

Calories	86	Sugars	4g
Protein	2g	Fat	6g
Carbohydrates	6g	Saturates	1g

5 MINS 5 MINS

SERVES 4

INGREDIENTS

- 450 g/1 lb thin green beans
- 2 fresh red chillies
- 2 tbsp peanut oil
- ½ tsp ground star anise
- 1 garlic clove, crushed
- 2 tbsp light soy sauce
- 2 tsp clear honey
- ½ tsp sesame oil

1 Using a sharp knife, cut the green beans in half.

2 Slice the fresh chillies, removing the seeds first if you prefer a milder dish.

3 Heat the oil in a preheated wok or large frying pan (skillet) until the oil is almost smoking.

4 Lower the heat slightly, add the halved green beans to the wok and stir-fry for 1 minute.

5 Add the sliced red chillies, star anise and garlic to the wok and stir-fry for a further 30 seconds.

6 Mix together the soy sauce, honey and sesame oil in a small bowl.

7 Stir the sauce mixture into the wok. Cook for 2 minutes, tossing the beans to ensure that they are thoroughly coated in the sauce.

8 Transfer the mixture in the wok or pan to a warm serving dish and serve immediately.

VARIATION

This recipe is surprisingly delicious made with Brussels sprouts instead of green beans. Trim the sprouts, then shred them finely. Stir-fry the sprouts in hot oil for 2 minutes, then proceed with the recipe from step 4.

4

5

7

Ginger & Orange Broccoli

Thinly sliced broccoli florets are lightly stir-fried and served in a ginger and orange sauce.

NUTRITIONAL INFORMATION

Calories	133	Sugars	6g
Protein	9g	Fat	7g
Carbohydrate	10g	Saturates	1g

 5 MINS — 10 MINS

SERVES 4

INGREDIENTS

- 750 g/1 lb 10 oz broccoli
- 2 thin slices ginger root
- 2 garlic cloves
- 1 orange
- 2 tsp cornflour (cornstarch)
- 1 tbsp light soy sauce
- ½ tsp sugar
- 2 tbsp vegetable oil

1 Divide the broccoli into small florets. Peel the stems, using a vegetable peeler, and then cut the stems into thin slices, using a sharp knife.

2 Cut the ginger root into matchsticks and slice the garlic.

3 Peel 2 long strips of zest from the orange and cut into thin strips. Place the strips in a bowl, cover with cold water and set aside.

4 Squeeze the juice from the orange and mix with the cornflour (cornstarch), light soy sauce, sugar and 4 tablespoons water.

5 Heat the vegetable oil in a wok or large frying pan (skillet). Add the broccoli stem slices and stir-fry for 2 minutes.

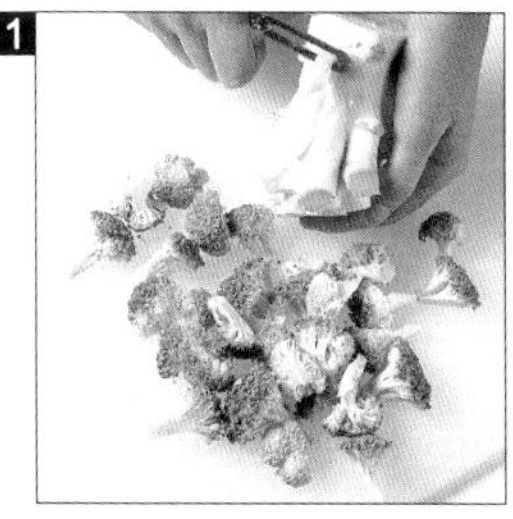

1

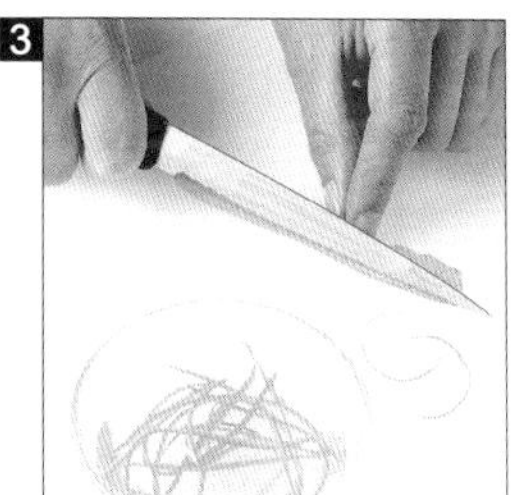

3

6

6 Add the ginger root slices, garlic and broccoli florets, and stir-fry for a further 3 minutes.

7 Stir the orange sauce mixture into the wok and cook, stirring constantly, until the sauce has thickened and coated the broccoli.

8 Drain the reserved orange rind and stir into the wok before serving.

VARIATION

This dish could be made with cauliflower, if you prefer, or a mixture of cauliflower and broccoli.

Bombay Potatoes

Although virtually unknown in India, this dish is a very popular item on Indian restaurant menus in other parts of the world.

NUTRITIONAL INFORMATION

Calories	307	Sugars	9g
Protein	9g	Fat	9g
Carbohydrate	51g	Saturates	5g

 5 MINS  1 HR 10 MINS

SERVES 4

INGREDIENTS

- 1 kg/2 lb 4 oz waxy potatoes
- 2 tbsp vegetable ghee
- 1 tsp panch poran spice mix
- 3 tsp ground turmeric
- 2 tbsp tomato purée (paste)
- 300 ml/½ pint/1¼ cups natural (unsweetened) yogurt
- salt
- chopped coriander (cilantro), to garnish

1 Put the whole potatoes into a large saucepan of salted cold water, bring to the boil, then simmer until the potatoes are just cooked, but not tender; the time depends on the size of the potato, but an average-sized one should take about 15 minutes.

2

2

3

2 Heat the ghee in a saucepan over a medium heat and add the panch poran, turmeric, tomato purée (paste), yogurt and salt. Bring to the boil, and simmer, uncovered, for 5 minutes.

3 Drain the potatoes and cut each one into 4 pieces. Add the potatoes to the pan, cover and cook briefly. Transfer to an ovenproof casserole, cover and cook in a preheated oven, 180°C/350°F/Gas Mark 4, for about 40 minutes, or until the potatoes are tender and the sauce has thickened a little.

4 Sprinkle with chopped coriander (cilantro) and serve immediately.

COOK'S TIP

Panch poran spice mix can be bought from Asian or Indian grocery stores, or make your own from equal quantities of cumin seeds, fennel seeds, mustard seeds, nigella seeds and fenugreek seeds.

Pizza Margherita

Pizza means 'pie' in Italian. The fresh bread dough is not difficult to make but it does take a little time.

NUTRITIONAL INFORMATION

Calories	456	Sugars	7g
Protein	16g	Fat	13g
Carbohydrate	74g	Saturates	5g

 1 HOUR  45 MINS

SERVES 4

INGREDIENTS

BASIC PIZZA DOUGH

7 g/½ oz dried yeast
1 tsp sugar
250 ml/9 fl oz/1 cup hand-hot water
350 g/12 oz strong flour
1 tsp salt
1 tbsp olive oil

TOPPING

400 g/14 oz can tomatoes, chopped
2 garlic cloves, crushed
2 tsp dried basil
1 tbsp olive oil
2 tbsp tomato purée
100 g/3½ oz Mozzarella cheese, chopped
2 tbsp freshly grated Parmesan cheese
salt and pepper

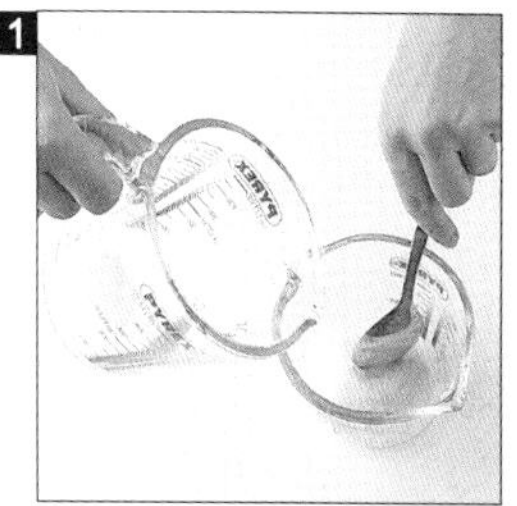

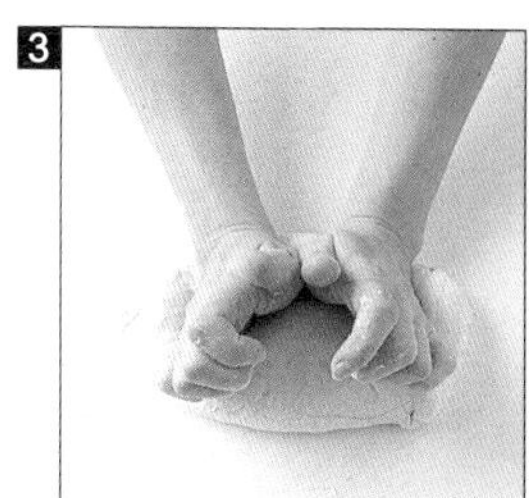
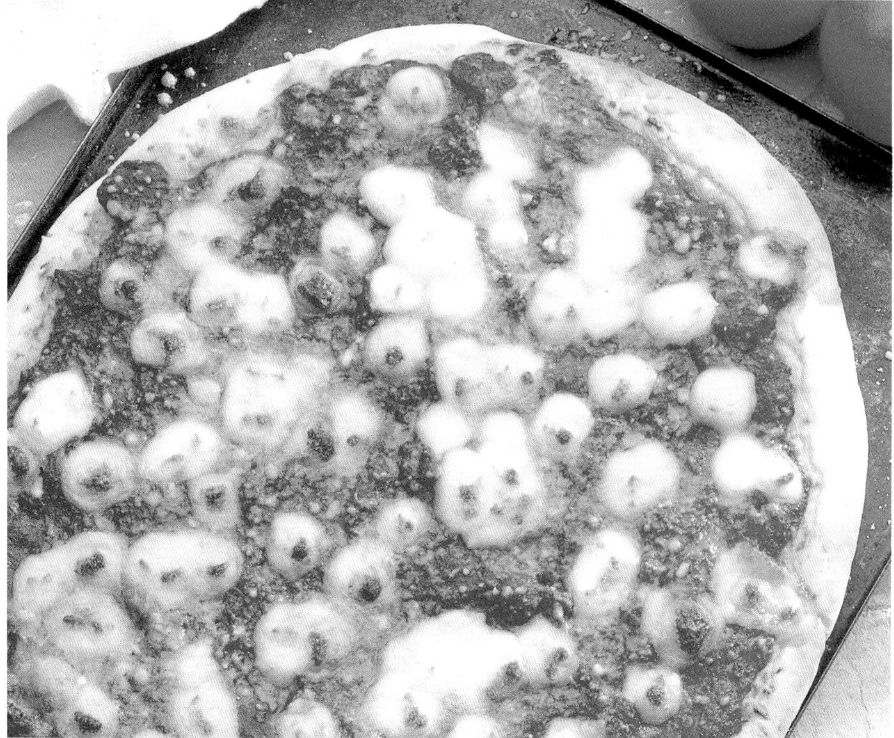

1 Place the yeast and sugar in a measuring jug and mix with 50 ml/2 fl oz/4 tbsp of the water. Leave the yeast mixture in a warm place for 15 minutes or until frothy.

2 Mix the flour with the salt and make a well in the centre. Add the oil, the yeast mixture and the remaining water. Using a wooden spoon, mix to form a smooth dough.

3 Turn the dough out on to a floured surface and knead for 4–5 minutes or until smooth.

4 Return the dough to the bowl, cover with an oiled sheet of cling film (plastic wrap) and leave to rise for 30 minutes or until doubled in size.

5 Knead the dough for 2 minutes. Stretch the dough with your hands, then place it on an oiled baking tray (cookie sheet), pushing out the edges until even. The dough should be no more than 6 mm/¼ inch thick because it will rise during cooking.

6 To make the topping, place the tomatoes, garlic, dried basil, olive oil and salt and pepper to taste in a large frying pan (skillet) and leave to simmer for 20 minutes or until the sauce has thickened. Stir in the tomato purée and leave to cool slightly.

7 Spread the topping evenly over the pizza base. Top with the Mozzarella and Parmesan cheeses and bake in a preheated oven, at 200°C/400°F/Gas Mark 6, for 20–25 minutes. Serve hot.

Spicy Potatoes & Onions

Masala aloo are potatoes cooked in spices and onions. Semi-dry when cooked, they make an excellent accompaniment to almost any curry.

NUTRITIONAL INFORMATION

Calories	313	Sugars	5g
Protein	2g	Fat	25g
Carbohydrate	21g	Saturates	3g

 10-15 MINS  10 MINS

SERVES 4

INGREDIENTS

6 tbsp vegetable oil
2 medium-sized onions, finely chopped
1 tsp finely chopped root ginger
1 tsp crushed garlic
1 tsp chilli powder
1½ tsp ground cumin
1½ tsp ground coriander
1 tsp salt
400 g/14 oz can new potatoes
1 tbsp lemon juice

BAGHAAR

3 tbsp oil
3 dried red chillies
½ tsp onion seeds
½ tsp mustard seeds
½ tsp fenugreek seeds

TO GARNISH

fresh coriander (cilantro) leaves
1 green chilli, finely chopped

1 Heat the oil in a large, heavy-based saucepan. Add the onions and fry, stirring, until golden brown. Reduce the heat, add the ginger, garlic, chilli powder, ground cumin, ground coriander and salt and stir-fry for about 1 minute. Remove the pan from the heat and set aside until required.

2 Drain the water from the potatoes. Add the potatoes to the onion mixture and spice mixture and heat through. Sprinkle over the lemon juice and mix well.

3 To make the baghaar, heat the oil in a separate pan. Add the red chillies, onion seeds, mustard seeds and fenugreek seeds and fry until the seeds turn a shade darker. Remove the pan from the heat and pour the baghaar over the potatoes.

4 Garnish with coriander (cilantro) leaves and chillies, then serve.

Potatoes en Papillotes

New potatoes are perfect for this recipe. The potatoes and vegetables are wrapped in greaseproof (waxed) paper, sealed and steamed in the oven.

NUTRITIONAL INFORMATION

Calories	85	Sugars	4g
Protein	2g	Fat	0.5g
Carbohydrate	15g	Saturates	0.1g

 10 MINS

35 MINS

SERVES 4

INGREDIENTS

- 16 small new potatoes
- 1 carrot, cut into matchstick strips
- 1 fennel bulb, sliced
- 75 g/2¾ oz French (green) beans
- 1 yellow (bell) pepper, cut into strips
- 16 tbsp dry white wine
- 4 rosemary sprigs
- salt and pepper
- rosemary sprigs, to garnish

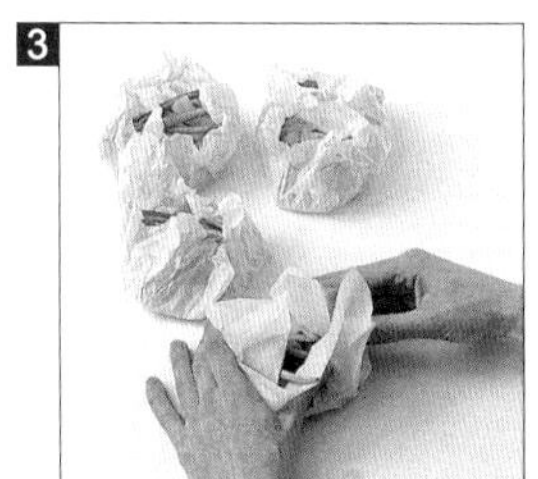

1 Cut 4 squares of greaseproof (waxed) paper measuring about 25 cm/10 inches in size.

2 Divide the vegetables equally between the 4 paper squares, placing them in the centre.

3 Bring the edges of the paper together and scrunch them together to encase the vegetables, leaving the top open.

4 Place the parcels in a shallow roasting tin (pan) and spoon 4 tablespoons of white wine into each parcel. Add a rosemary sprig and season.

5 Fold the top of each parcel over to seal it. Cook in a preheated oven, 190°C/375°F/Gas Mark 5, for 30-35 minutes or until the vegetables are tender.

6 Transfer the sealed parcels to 4 individual serving plates and garnish with rosemary sprigs.

7 Open the parcels at the table in order for the full aroma of the vegetables to be appreciated.

COOK'S TIP

If small new potatoes are unavailable, use larger potatoes which have been halved or quartered to ensure that they cook through in the specified cooking time.

Colcannon

This is an old Irish recipe, usually served with a piece of bacon, but it is equally delicious with a vegetarian main course dish.

NUTRITIONAL INFORMATION

Calories	102	Sugars	4g
Protein	4g	Fat	4g
Carbohydrate	14g	Saturates	2g

 20 MINS

20 MINS

SERVES 4

INGREDIENTS

- 225 g/8 oz green cabbage, shredded
- 5 tbsp milk
- 225 g/8 oz floury (mealy) potatoes, diced
- 1 large leek, chopped
- pinch of grated nutmeg
- 15 g/½ oz/1 tbsp butter, melted
- salt and pepper

1 Cook the shredded cabbage in a saucepan of boiling salted water for 7–10 minutes. Drain thoroughly and set aside.

2 Meanwhile, in a separate saucepan, bring the milk to the boil and add the potatoes and leek. Reduce the heat and simmer for 15–20 minutes, or until they are cooked through.

3 Stir in the grated nutmeg and thoroughly mash the potatoes and leek together.

4 Add the drained cabbage to the mashed potato and leek mixture and mix well.

5 Spoon the mixture into a warmed serving dish, making a hollow in the centre with the back of a spoon.

6 Pour the melted butter into the hollow and serve the colcannon immediately.

2

4

5

COOK'S TIP

There are many different varieties of cabbage, which produce hearts at varying times of year, so you can be sure of being able to make this delicious cabbage dish all year round.

Corn Cobs & Parsley Butter

There are a number of ways of cooking corn-on-the-cob on the barbecue. Leaving on the husks protects the tender corn niblets.

NUTRITIONAL INFORMATION

Calories	178	Sugars	7g
Protein	2g	Fat	11g
Carbohydrate	19g	Saturates	7g

 10 MINS  30 MINS

SERVES 4

INGREDIENTS

- 4 corn cobs, with husks
- 100 g/3½ oz/½ cup butter
- 1 tbsp chopped parsley
- 1 tsp chopped chives
- 1 tsp chopped thyme
- grated rind of 1 lemon
- salt and pepper

1

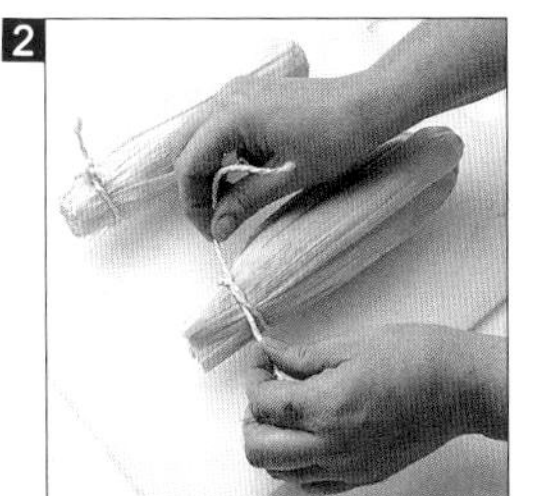

2

5

1 To prepare the corn cobs, peel back the husks and remove the silken hairs.

2 Fold back the husks and secure them in place with string, if necessary.

3 Blanch the corn cobs in a large saucepan of boiling water for about 5 minutes. Remove the cobs with a slotted spoon and drain thoroughly.

4 Barbecue (grill) the cobs over medium hot coals for about 20–30 minutes, turning frequently.

5 Meanwhile, soften the butter and beat in the parsley, chives, thyme, and lemon rind and season with salt and pepper to taste.

6 Transfer the corn cobs to serving plates, remove the string, if used, and pull back the husks. Serve with a generous portion of herb butter. Eat with two forks or corn cob holders and provide plenty of paper napkins.

COOK'S TIP

If you are unable to get fresh cobs, cook frozen corn cobs on the barbecue (grill). Spread some of the herb butter on to a double thickness of kitchen foil. Wrap the cobs in the foil and barbecue (grill) among the coals for 20–30 minutes.

Pommes Anna

This is a classic potato dish, which may be left to cook unattended while the remainder of the meal is being prepared, so it is ideal with stews.

NUTRITIONAL INFORMATION

Calories	237	Sugars	1g
Protein	4g	Fat	13g
Carbohydrate	29g	Saturates	8g

 15 MINS

 2 HOURS

SERVES 4

INGREDIENTS

- 60 g/2 oz/¼ cup butter, melted
- 675 g/1½ lb waxy potatoes
- 4 tbsp chopped mixed herbs
- salt and pepper
- chopped fresh herbs, to garnish

1 Brush a shallow 1 litre/1¾ pint/4 cup ovenproof dish with a little of the melted butter.

2 Slice the potatoes thinly and pat dry with kitchen paper (paper towels).

3 Arrange a layer of potato slices in the prepared dish until the base is covered. Brush with a little butter and sprinkle with a quarter of the chopped mixed herbs. Season to taste.

4 Continue layering the potato slices, brushing each layer with melted butter and sprinkling with herbs, until they are all used up.

5 Brush the top layer of potato slices with butter, cover the dish and cook in a preheated oven, 190°C/375°F/Gas Mark 5, for 1½ hours.

6 Turn out on to a warm ovenproof platter and return to the oven for a further 25–30 minutes, until golden brown. Serve at once, garnished with fresh herbs.

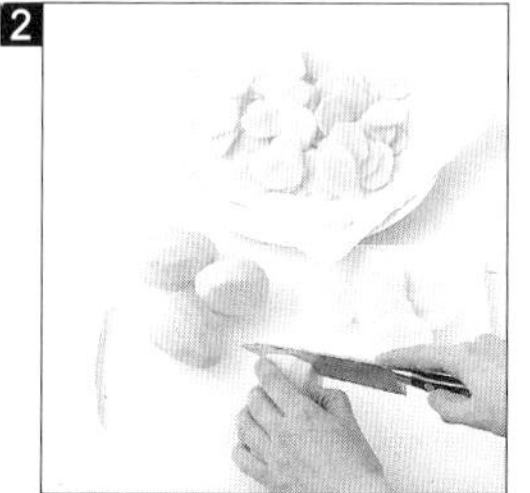

2

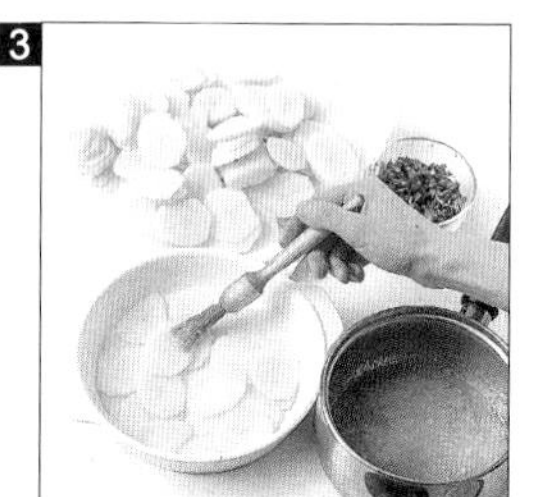

3

6

COOK'S TIP

Make sure that the potatoes are sliced very thinly so that they are almost transparent. This will ensure that they cook thoroughly.

Smoky Bacon & Pepperoni

This more traditional kind of pizza is topped with peperoni, smoked bacon and (bell) peppers covered in a smoked cheese.

NUTRITIONAL INFORMATION

Calories	450	Sugars	6g
Protein	19g	Fat	24g
Carbohydrate	41g	Saturates	6g

 $1^1/_2$ HOURS  20 MINS

SERVES 4

INGREDIENTS

Basic Pizza Dough (see page 861)

1 tbsp olive oil

1 tbsp freshly grated Parmesan

Basic Tomato Sauce (see page 6)

125 g/4½ oz lightly smoked bacon, diced

½ green (bell) pepper, sliced thinly

½ yellow (bell) pepper, sliced thinly

60 g/2 oz pepperoni-style sliced spicy sausage

60 g/2 oz smoked Bavarian cheese, grated

½ tsp dried oregano

olive oil, for drizzling

salt and pepper

1 Roll out or press the dough, using a rolling pin or your hands, into a 25 cm/10 inch circle on a lightly floured work surface.

2 Place the dough base on a large greased baking tray (cookie sheet) or pizza pan and push up the edge a little with your fingers, to form a rim.

3 Brush the base with the olive oil and sprinkle with the Parmesan. Cover and leave to rise slightly in a warm place for about 10 minutes.

4 Spread the tomato sauce over the base almost to the edge. Top with the bacon and (bell) peppers. Arrange the pepperoni on top and sprinkle with the smoked cheese.

5 Sprinkle over the oregano and drizzle with a little olive oil. Season well.

6 Bake in a preheated oven, at 200°C/400°F/Gas Mark 6, for 18–20 minutes, or until the crust is golden and crisp around the edge. Cut the pizza into wedges and serve immediately.

3

4

5

Aloo Chat

Aloo Chat is one of a variety of Indian foods served at any time of the day. The chickpeas (garbanzo beans) need to be soaked overnight.

NUTRITIONAL INFORMATION

Calories	262	Sugars	6g
Protein	13g	Fat	4g
Carbohydrate	46g	Saturates	0.5g

35 MINS

1 HR 5 MINS

SERVES 4

INGREDIENTS

- 125 g/4½ oz/generous ½ cup chickpeas (garbanzo beans), soaked overnight in cold water and drained
- 1 dried red chilli
- 500 g/1 lb 2 oz waxy potatoes, boiled in their skins and peeled
- 1 tsp cumin seeds
- 2 tsp salt
- 1 tsp black peppercorns
- ½ tsp dried mint
- ½ tsp chilli powder
- ½ tsp ground ginger
- 2 tsp mango powder
- 125 ml/4 fl oz/½ cup natural (unsweetened) yogurt
- oil, for deep frying
- 4 poppadoms

VARIATION

Instead of chickpeas (garbanzo beans), diced tropical fruits can be stirred into the potatoes and spice mix; add a little lemon juice to balance the sweetness.

1 Boil the chickpeas (garbanzo beans) with the chilli in plenty of water for about 1 hour, until tender. Drain.

2 Cut the potatoes into 2.5 cm/1 inch dice and mix into the chickpeas (garbanzo beans) while they are still warm. Set aside.

3 Grind together the cumin, salt and peppercorns in a spice grinder or with a pestle and mortar. Stir in the mint, chilli powder, ginger and mango powder.

4 Put a small saucepan or frying pan (skillet) over a low heat and add the spice mix. Stir until the spices give off their aroma and then immediately remove the pan from the heat.

5 Stir half of the spice mix into the chickpea (garbanzo bean) and potato mixture and stir the other half into the yogurt.

6 Cook the poppadoms according to the instructions on the packet. Drain on plenty of kitchen paper (paper towels). Break into bite-size pieces and stir into the potatoes and chickpeas (garbanzo beans), spoon over the spiced yogurt and serve immediately.

2

3

4

Pumpkin Parcels with Chilli

This spicy side dish is perfect for a Hallowe'en or Bonfire Night barbecue (grill) party, although it is equally delicious on a summer evening, too.

NUTRITIONAL INFORMATION

Energy	118	Sugar	3g
Protein	1g	Fat	11g
Carbohydrates	4g	Saturates	4g

10 MINS

25–30 MINS

SERVES 4

INGREDIENTS

700 g/1 lb 9 oz pumpkin or squash

2 tbsp sunflower oil

25 g/1 oz/2 tbsp butter

½ tsp chilli sauce

grated rind of 1 lime

2 tsp lime juice

1 Halve the pumpkin or squash and scoop out the seeds. Rinse the seeds and reserve. Cut the pumpkin into thin wedges and peel.

2 Heat the oil and butter together in a large saucepan, stirring constantly, until melted. Stir in the chilli sauce, lime rind and juice.

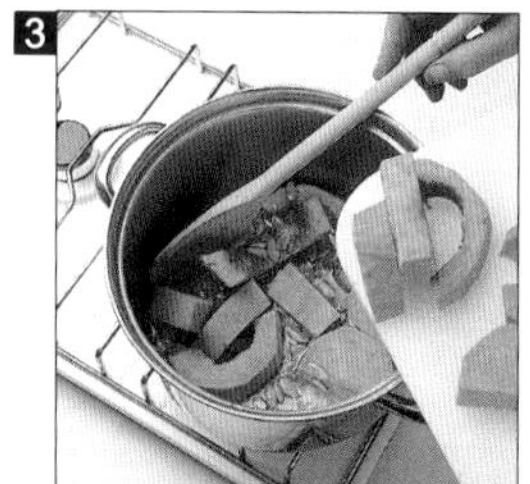

3 Add the pumpkin or squash and seeds to the pan and toss to coat all over in the flavoured butter.

4 Divide the mixture between 4 double thickness sheets of kitchen foil. Fold over the kitchen foil to enclose the pumpkin or squash mixture completely.

5 Barbecue (grill) the foil parcels over hot coals for 15–25 minutes, or until the pumpkin or squash is tender.

6 Transfer the foil parcels to warm serving plates. Open the parcels at the table and serve at once.

VARIATION

Add 2 teaspoons of curry paste to the oil instead of the lime and chilli. Use butternut squash when pumpkin is not available.

Herby Potatoes & Onion

Fried potatoes are a classic favourite; here they are given extra flavour by frying them in butter with onion, garlic and herbs.

NUTRITIONAL INFORMATION

Calories	413	Sugars	4g
Protein	5g	Fat	26g
Carbohydrate	42g	Saturates	17g

 10 MINS  50 MINS

SERVES 4

INGREDIENTS

- 900 g/2 lb waxy potatoes, cut into cubes
- 125 g/4½ oz/½ cup butter
- 1 red onion, cut into 8
- 2 garlic cloves, crushed
- 1 tsp lemon juice
- 2 tbsp chopped thyme
- salt and pepper

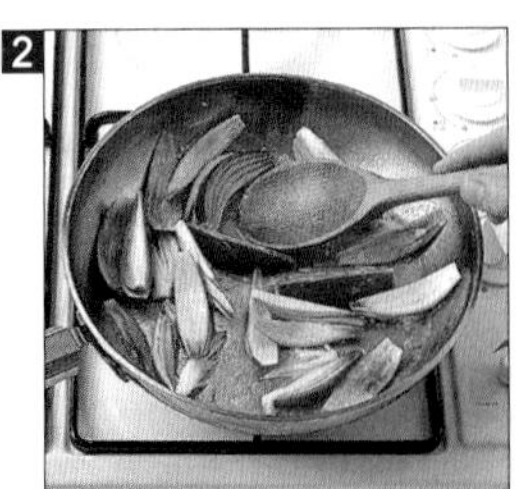

1 Cook the cubed potatoes in a saucepan of boiling water for 10 minutes. Drain thoroughly.

2 Melt the butter in a large, heavy-based frying pan (skillet) and add the red onion wedges, garlic and lemon juice. Cook, stirring constantly for 2–3 minutes.

3 Add the potatoes to the pan and mix well to coat in the butter mixture.

4 Reduce the heat, cover and cook for 25–30 minutes, or until the potatoes are golden brown and tender.

5 Sprinkle the chopped thyme over the top of the potatoes and season.

6 Transfer to a warm serving dish and serve immediately.

COOK'S TIP

Keep checking the potatoes and stirring throughout the cooking time to ensure that they do not burn or stick to the base of the frying pan (skillet).

Saffron-flavoured Potatoes

Saffron is made from the dried stigma of the crocus and is native to Greece. It is very expensive, but only a very small amount is needed.

NUTRITIONAL INFORMATION

Calories	197	Sugars	4g
Protein	4g	Fat	6g
Carbohydrate	30g	Saturates	1g

 25 MINS  40 MINS

SERVES 4

INGREDIENTS

- 1 tsp saffron strands
- 6 tbsp boiling water
- 675 g/1½ lb waxy potatoes, unpeeled and cut into wedges
- 1 red onion, cut into 8 wedges
- 2 garlic cloves, crushed
- 1 tbsp white wine vinegar
- 2 tbsp olive oil
- 1 tbsp wholegrain mustard
- 5 tbsp vegetable stock
- 5 tbsp dry white wine
- 2 tsp chopped rosemary
- salt and pepper

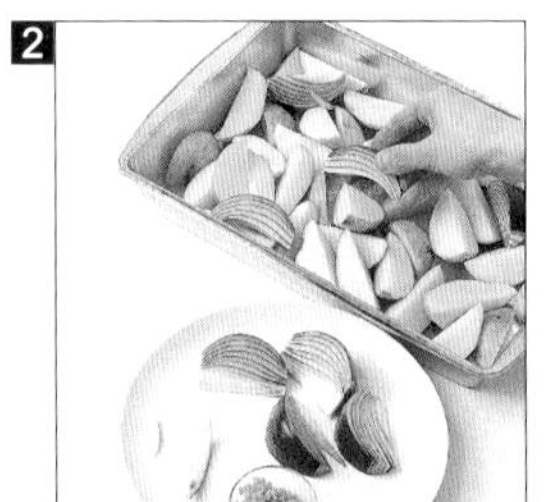

1 Place the saffron strands in a small bowl and pour over the boiling water. Set aside to soak for about 10 minutes.

2 Place the potatoes in a roasting tin (pan), together with the red onion wedges and crushed garlic.

3 Add the vinegar, oil, mustard, vegetable stock, white wine, rosemary and saffron water to the potatoes and onion in the tin (pan). Season to taste with salt and pepper.

4 Cover the roasting tin (pan) with kitchen foil and bake in a preheated oven, 200°C/400°F/Gas Mark 6, for 30 minutes.

5 Remove the foil and cook the potatoes for a further 10 minutes until crisp, browned and cooked through. Serve hot.

COOK'S TIP

Turmeric may be used instead of saffron to provide the yellow colour in this recipe. However, it is worth using saffron, if possible, for the lovely nutty flavour it gives a dish.

Potato Crumble

This is a delicious way to liven up mashed potato by topping it with a crumble mixture flavoured with herbs, mustard and onion.

NUTRITIONAL INFORMATION

Calories	451	Sugars	5g
Protein	13g	Fat	19g
Carbohydrate	60g	Saturates	12g

 25 MINS  30 MINS

SERVES 4

INGREDIENTS

900 g/2 lb floury (mealy) potatoes, diced
25 g/1 oz/2 tbsp butter
2 tbsp milk
50 g/1¾ oz/½ cup grated mature (sharp) cheese or blue cheese

CRUMBLE TOPPING

40 g/1½ oz/3 tbsp butter
1 onion, cut into chunks
1 garlic clove, crushed
1 tbsp wholegrain mustard
175 g/6 oz/3 cups fresh wholemeal (whole wheat) breadcrumbs
2 tbsp chopped parsley
salt and pepper

1 Cook the potatoes in a pan of lightly salted boiling water for 10 minutes, or until cooked through.

2 Meanwhile, make the crumble topping. Melt the butter in a frying pan (skillet). Add the onion, garlic and mustard and fry over a medium heat, stirring constantly, for 5 minutes, until the onion has softened.

3 Put the breadcrumbs in a mixing bowl and stir in the fried onion. Season to taste with salt and pepper.

4 Drain the potatoes thoroughly and place them in another mixing bowl. Add the butter and milk, then mash until smooth. Stir in the grated cheese while the potato is still hot.

5 Spoon the mashed potato into a shallow ovenproof dish and sprinkle with the crumble topping.

6 Cook in a preheated oven, 200°C/400°F/Gas Mark 6, for 10-15 minutes, until the crumble topping is golden brown and crunchy. Serve immediately.

COOK'S TIP

For extra crunch, add freshly cooked vegetables, such as celery and (bell) peppers, to the mashed potato in step 4.

Creamy Green Vegetables

This dish is very quick to make. A dash of cream is added to the sauce, but this may be omitted, if preferred.

NUTRITIONAL INFORMATION

Calories	111	Sugars	2g
Protein	5g	Fat	8g
Carbohydrate	7g	Saturates	2g

 5 MINS  20 MINS

SERVES 4

INGREDIENTS

- 450 g/1 lb Chinese leaves (cabbage), shredded
- 2 tbsp peanut oil
- 2 leeks, shredded
- 4 garlic cloves, crushed
- 300 ml/½ pint/1¼ cups vegetable stock
- 1 tbsp light soy sauce
- 2 tsp cornflour (cornstarch)
- 4 tsp water
- 2 tbsp single (light) cream or natural (unsweetened) yogurt
- 1 tbsp chopped coriander (cilantro)

1

3

5

1 Blanch the Chinese leaves (cabbage) in boiling water for 30 seconds. Drain, rinse under cold running water, then drain thoroughly again.

2 Heat the oil in a preheated wok and add the Chinese leaves (cabbage), leeks and garlic. Stir-fry for 2–3 minutes.

3 Add the stock and soy sauce to the wok, reduce the heat to low, cover and simmer for 10 minutes.

4 Remove the vegetables from the wok with a slotted spoon and set aside. Bring the stock to the boil and boil vigorously until reduced by about half.

5 Blend the cornflour (cornstarch) with the water and stir into the wok. Bring to the boil, and cook, stirring constantly, until thickened and clear.

6 Reduce the heat and stir in the vegetables and cream or yogurt. Cook over a low heat for 1 minute.

7 Transfer to a serving dish, sprinkle over the chopped coriander (cilantro) and serve.

COOK'S TIP

Do not boil the sauce once the cream or yogurt has been added, as it will separate.

Steamed Vegetables

Serve these vegetables in their paper parcels to retain the juices. The result is truly delicious.

NUTRITIONAL INFORMATION

Calories	64	Sugars	9g
Protein	2g	Fat	0.5g
Carbohydrate	12g	Saturates	0.1g

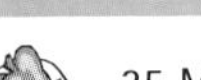 25 MINS  20 MINS

SERVES 4

INGREDIENTS

- 1 carrot, cut into batons
- 1 fennel bulb, sliced
- 100 g/3½ oz courgettes (zucchini), sliced
- 1 red (bell) pepper, seeded and sliced
- 4 small onions, halved
- 8 tbsp vermouth
- 4 tbsp lime juice
- grated rind of 1 lime
- pinch of paprika
- 4 sprigs tarragon
- salt and pepper
- tarragon sprigs, to garnish

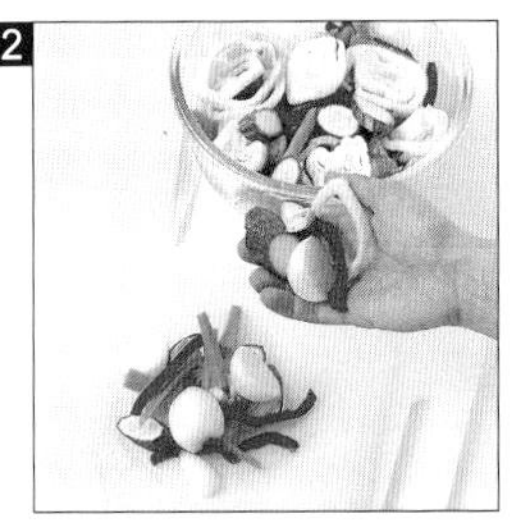
2

2

3

1 Place all of the vegetables in a large bowl and mix well.

2 Cut 4 large squares of baking parchment and place a quarter of the vegetables in the centre of each. Bring the sides of the paper up and pinch together to make an open parcel.

3 Mix together the vermouth, lime juice, grated lime rind and paprika and pour a quarter of the mixture into each parcel. Season to taste with salt and pepper and add a tarragon sprig to each. Fold and pinch the tops of the parcels firmly together to seal, enclosing the vegetables completely.

4 Place the parcels in a steamer, cover and cook for 15–20 minutes, or until the vegetables are tender. Garnish and serve immediately.

COOK'S TIP

Vermouth is a fortified white wine flavoured with various herbs and spices. It its available in both sweet and dry forms.

Chilli Polenta Chips

Polenta is used in Italy in the same way as potatoes and rice. It has little flavour, but combined with butter, garlic and herbs, it is transformed.

NUTRITIONAL INFORMATION

Calories	365	Sugars	1g
Protein	8g	Fat	12g
Carbohydrate	54g	Saturates	5g

5 MINS 20 MINS

SERVES 4

INGREDIENTS

- 350 g/12 oz instant polenta
- 2 tsp chilli powder
- 1 tbsp olive oil
- 150 ml/¼ pint/⅔ cup soured cream
- 1 tbsp chopped parsley
- salt and pepper

1 Place 1.5 litres/2¾ pints/6¼ cups of water in a saucepan and bring to the boil. Add 2 teaspoons of salt and then add the polenta in a steady stream, stirring constantly.

2 Reduce the heat slightly and continue stirring for about 5 minutes. It is essential to stir the polenta, otherwise it will stick and burn. The polenta should have a thick consistency at this point and should be stiff enough to hold the spoon upright in the pan.

3 Add the chilli powder to the polenta mixture and stir well. Season to taste with a little salt and pepper.

4 Spread the polenta out on to a board or baking tray (cookie sheet) to about 4 cm/1½ inch thick. Leave to cool and set.

5 Cut the cooled polenta mixture into thin wedges.

6 Heat 1 tablespoon of oil in a pan. Add the polenta wedges and fry for 3–4 minutes on each side or until golden and crispy. Alternatively, brush with melted butter and grill (broil) for 6–7 minutes until golden. Drain the cooked polenta on paper towels.

7 Mix the soured cream with parsley and place in a bowl.

8 Serve the polenta with the soured cream and parsley dip.

COOK'S TIP

Easy-cook instant polenta is widely available in supermarkets and is quick to make. It will keep for up to 1 week in the refrigerator. The polenta can also be baked in a preheated oven, at 200°C/400°F/Gas Mark 6, for 20 minutes.

Onion Dhal

This dhal is semi-dry when cooked, so it is best to serve it with a curry which has a sauce. Ordinary onions can be used as a substitute.

NUTRITIONAL INFORMATION

Calories	232	Sugars	1g
Protein	6g	Fat	17g
Carbohydrate	15g	Saturates	2g

 5 MINS  30 MINS

SERVES 4

INGREDIENTS

- 100 g/3½ oz/½ cup masoor dhal
- 6 tbsp vegetable oil
- 1 small bunch spring onions (scallions), chopped
- 1 tsp finely chopped root ginger
- 1 tsp crushed garlic
- ½ tsp chilli powder
- ½ tsp turmeric
- 300 ml/½ pint/1¼ cups water
- 1 tsp salt
- 1 fresh green chilli, finely chopped
- fresh coriander (cilantro) leaves

1 Rinse the lentils thoroughly and set aside until required.

2 Heat the oil in a heavy-based saucepan. Add the spring onions (scallions) to the pan and fry over a medium heat, stirring frequently, until lightly browned.

3 Reduce the heat and add the ginger, garlic, chilli powder and turmeric. Briefly stir-fry the spring onions (scallions) with the spices. Add the lentils and mix to blend together.

4 Add the water to the lentil mixture, reduce the heat to low and cook for 20–25 minutes.

5 When the lentils are cooked thoroughly, add the salt and stir gently to mix well.

6 Transfer the onion lentils to a serving dish. Garnish with the chopped green chillies and fresh coriander (cilantro) leaves and serve immediately.

COOK'S TIP

Masoor dhal are small, round, pale orange split lentils. They turn a pale yellow colour when cooked.

Spanish Potatoes

This type of dish is usually served as part of a Spanish *tapas*, and is delicious with salad or or a simply cooked main course dish.

NUTRITIONAL INFORMATION

Calories	176	Sugars	9g
Protein	5g	Fat	6g
Carbohydrate	27g	Saturates	1g

 20 MINS  35 MINS

SERVES 4

INGREDIENTS

- 2 tbsp olive oil
- 500 g/1 lb 2 oz small new potatoes, halved
- 1 onion, halved and sliced
- 1 green (bell) pepper, seeded and cut into strips
- 1 tsp chilli powder
- 1 tsp prepared mustard
- 300 ml/½ pint/1¼ cups passata (sieved tomatoes)
- 300 ml/½ pint/1¼ cups vegetable stock
- salt and pepper
- chopped parsley, to garnish

1 Heat the olive oil in a large heavy-based frying pan (skillet). Add the halved new potatoes and the sliced onion and cook, stirring frequently, for 4–5 minutes, until the onion slices are soft and translucent.

2 Add the green (bell) pepper strips, chilli powder and mustard to the pan and cook for a further 2–3 minutes.

3 Stir the passata (sieved tomatoes) and the vegetable stock into the pan and bring to the boil. Reduce the heat and simmer for about 25 minutes, or until the potatoes are tender.

1

2

3

4 Transfer the potatoes to a warmed serving dish. Sprinkle the parsley over the top and serve immediately. Alternatively, leave the Spanish potatoes to cool completely and serve cold, at room temperature.

COOK'S TIP

In Spain, tapas are traditionally served with a glass of chilled sherry or some other aperitif.

Crispy Cabbage & Almonds

This dish is better known as crispy seaweed. It does not actually contain seaweed, but consists of spring greens (collard greens) or pak choi.

NUTRITIONAL INFORMATION

Calories	431	Sugars	17g
Protein	9g	Fat	37g
Carbohydrate	17g	Saturates	4g

 10 MINS  10 MINS

SERVES 4

INGREDIENTS

- 1.25 kg/2 lb 12 oz pak choi or spring greens (collard greens)
- 700 ml/1¼ pints/3 cups vegetable oil
- 75 g/2¾ oz/¾ cup blanched almonds
- 1 tsp salt
- 1 tbsp light brown sugar
- pinch of ground cinnamon

1 Separate the leaves from the pak choi or spring greens (collard greens) and rinse them well. Drain thoroughly and pat dry with absorbent kitchen paper (paper towels).

2 Shred the greens (collard greens) into thin strips, using a sharp knife.

3 Heat the vegetable oil in a preheated wok or large, heavy-based frying pan (skillet) until the oil is almost smoking.

4 Reduce the heat and add the pak choi or spring greens (collard greens). Cook for 2–3 minutes, or until the greens begin to float in the oil and are crisp.

5 Remove the greens from the oil with a slotted spoon and leave to drain thoroughly on absorbent kitchen paper (paper towels).

6 Add the blanched almonds to the oil in the wok and cook for 30 seconds. Remove the almonds from the oil with a slotted spoon and drain thoroughly on absorbent kitchen paper (paper towels).

7 Mix together the salt, light brown sugar and ground cinnamon and sprinkle on to the greens.

8 Toss the almonds into the greens.

9 Transfer the greens and almonds to a warm serving dish and serve immediately.

2

4

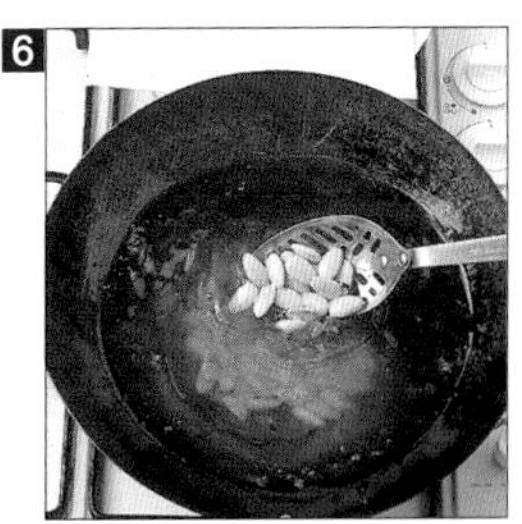

6

COOK'S TIP

Ensure that the greens are completely dry before adding them to the oil, otherwise it will spit. The greens will not become crisp if they are wet when placed in the oil.

Murkha Dhal

In this dhal recipe, the garlic is intended to burn in the base of the pan, and this flavour permeates the dish.

NUTRITIONAL INFORMATION

Calories	372	Sugars	7g
Protein	18g	Fat	16g
Carbohydrate	42g	Saturates	10g

 5 MINS  55 MINS

SERVES 4

INGREDIENTS

- 60 g/2 oz/¼ cup butter
- 2 tsp black mustard seeds
- 1 onion, finely chopped
- 2 garlic cloves, finely chopped
- 1 tbsp grated root ginger
- 1 tsp turmeric
- 2 green chillies, seeded and finely chopped
- 225 g/8 oz/1 cup red lentils
- 1 litre/1¾ pints/4 cups water
- 300 ml/½ pint/1¼ cups coconut milk
- 1 tsp salt

1 Melt the butter in a large heavy-based saucepan over a moderate heat. Add the mustard seeds and cover the pan. When you can hear the seeds popping, add the onion, garlic and grated ginger. Cook, uncovered, for about 7–8 minutes, until the onion is soft and the garlic is brown.

2 Stir in the turmeric and green chillies and cook for 1–2 minutes, until the chillies soften a little.

3 Add the lentils and cook, stirring frequently, for 2 minutes, until the lentils begin to turn translucent.

2

3

4

4 Stir in the water, coconut milk and salt. Bring to the boil, then reduce the heat and simmer for 40 minutes, or until the desired consistency is reached. However, if you intend to reheat the dhal later rather than eat it straight away, cook it for only 30 minutes to allow for reheating time.

5 Transfer the dhal to a warmed serving dish and serve immediately, while piping hot.

COOK'S TIP

There are many types of lentils used in India, but the two most common are red lentils and green or beige lentils. The red lentils are very useful, as they cook in a relatively short time to form a homogeneous mass. Green and beige lentils stay more separate when cooked.

Steamed Rice in Lotus Leaves

The fragrance of the leaves penetrates the rice, giving it a unique taste. Lotus leaves can be bought from specialist Chinese shops.

NUTRITIONAL INFORMATION

Calories	163	Sugars	0.1g
Protein	5g	Fat	6g
Carbohydrate	2.1g	Saturates	1g

 1 HOUR   40 MINS

SERVES 4

INGREDIENTS

- 2 lotus leaves
- 4 Chinese dried mushrooms (if unavailable, use thinly sliced open-cup mushrooms)
- 175 g/6 oz/generous ¾ cup long-grain rice
- 1 cinnamon stick
- 6 cardamom pods
- 4 cloves
- 1 tsp salt
- 2 eggs
- 1 tbsp vegetable oil
- 2 spring onions (scallions), chopped
- 1 tbsp soy sauce
- 2 tbsp sherry
- 1 tsp sugar
- 1 tsp sesame oil

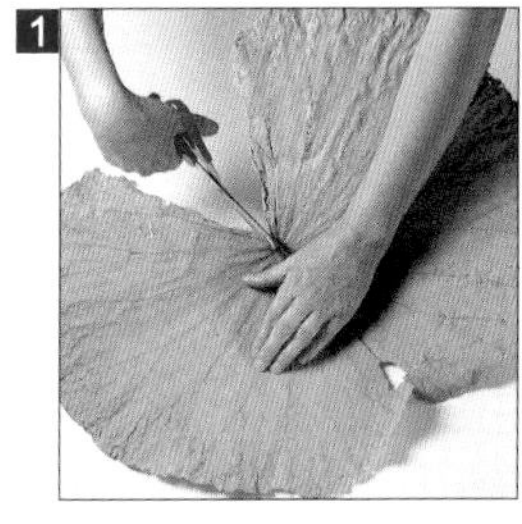

1 Unfold the lotus leaves carefully and cut along the fold to divide each leaf in half. Lay on a large baking sheet and pour over enough hot water to cover. Soak for about 30 minutes until softened.

2 Place the dried mushrooms in a small bowl and cover with warm water. Leave to soak for 20–25 minutes.

3 Cook the rice in a saucepan of boiling water with the cinnamon stick, cardamom pods, cloves and salt for about 10 minutes – the rice should be partially cooked. Drain thoroughly and remove the cinnamon stick. Place the rice in a bowl

4 Beat the eggs lightly. Heat the oil in a wok and cook the eggs quickly, stirring until set. Remove and set aside.

5 Drain the mushrooms, squeezing out the excess water. Remove the tough centres and chop the mushrooms. Stir into the rice with the cooked egg, spring onions (scallions), soy sauce, sherry, sugar and sesame oil.

6 Drain the lotus leaves and divide the rice into four portions. Place a portion in the centre of each leaf and fold up to form a parcel (packet). Place in a steamer, cover and steam over simmering water for 20 minutes. To serve, cut the tops of the lotus leaves open to expose the rice inside.

Kashmiri Spinach

This is an imaginative way to serve spinach, which adds a little zip to it. It is a very simple dish, which will complement almost any curry.

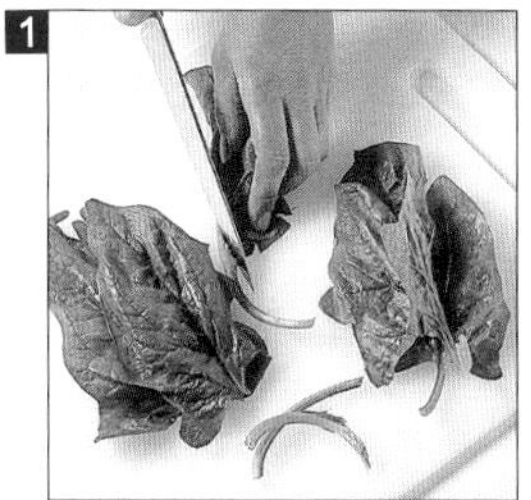

NUTRITIONAL INFORMATION

Calories	81	Sugars	2g
Protein	4g	Fat	7g
Carbohydrate	2g	Saturates	1g

 5 MINS  25 MINS

SERVES 4

INGREDIENTS

- 500 g/1 lb 2 oz spinach or Swiss chard or baby leaf spinach
- 2 tbsp mustard oil
- ¼ tsp garam masala
- 1 tsp yellow mustard seeds
- 2 spring onions (scallions), sliced

1 Remove the tough stalks from the spinach.

2 Heat the mustard oil in a preheated wok or large heavy-based frying pan (skillet) until it smokes. Add the garam masala and mustard seeds. Cover the pan quickly – you will hear the mustard seeds popping inside.

3 When the popping has ceased, remove the cover, add the spring onions (scallions) and spinach. Cook, stirring constantly, until the spinach has wilted.

4 Continue cooking the spinach, uncovered, over a medium heat for 10–15 minutes, until most of the water has evaporated. If using frozen spinach, it will not need to cook for so long – cook it until most of the water has evaporated.

5 Remove the spinach and spring onions (scallions) with a slotted spoon, draining off any remaining liquid. (This dish is pleasanter to eat when it is served as dry as possible.)

6 Transfer to a warmed serving dish and serve immediately, while it is still piping hot.

COOK'S TIP

Mustard oil is made from mustard seeds and is very fiery when raw. However, when it is heated to this smoking stage, it loses a lot of the fire and takes on a delightful sweet quality.

Chilli Fried Rice

Not so much a side dish as a meal in itself, this delicious fried rice can be served on its own or as an accompaniment to many Chinese dishes.

NUTRITIONAL INFORMATION

Calories	290	Sugars	2g
Protein	11g	Fat	14g
Carbohydrate	26g	Saturates	2g

 20 MINS  15 MINS

SERVES 4

INGREDIENTS

- 250 g/9 oz/generous 1 cup long-grain rice
- 4 tbsp vegetable oil
- 2 garlic cloves, chopped finely
- 1 small red chilli, deseeded and chopped finely
- 8 spring onions (scallions), trimmed and sliced finely
- 1 tbsp red curry paste or 2 tsp chilli sauce
- 1 red (bell) pepper, cored, deseeded and chopped
- 90 g/3 oz/¾ cup dwarf green beans, chopped
- 250 g/9 oz/1½ cups cooked peeled prawns (shrimp) or chopped cooked chicken
- 2 tbsp fish sauce

TO GARNISH

- cucumber slices
- shredded spring onion (scallion)

1 Cook the rice in plenty of boiling, lightly salted water until tender, about 12 minutes. Drain, rinse with cold water and drain thoroughly.

1

2 Heat the vegetable oil in a wok or large frying pan (skillet) until the oil is really hot.

3 Add the garlic to the wok and fry gently for 2 minutes until golden.

4 Add the chilli and spring onions (scallions) and cook, stirring, for 3–4 minutes.

4

5 Add the red curry paste or chilli sauce to the wok or frying pan (skillet) and fry for 1 minute, then add the red (bell) pepper and dwarf green beans. Stir-fry briskly for 2 minutes.

6 Tip the cooked rice into the wok or frying pan (skillet) and add the prawns (shrimp) or chicken and the fish sauce. Stir-fry over a medium-high heat for about 4–5 minutes, until the rice is hot:

5

7 Transfer the chilli fried rice to warm serving dishes, garnish with cucumber slices and shredded spring onion (scallion) and serve.

COOK'S TIP

Cook the rice the day before if you can remember – it will give an even better result. Alternatively, use rice left over from another dish to make this recipe.

Kabli Channa Sag

Pulses such as chickpeas (garbanzo beans) are widely used in India. They need to be soaked overnight so prepare well in advance.

NUTRITIONAL INFORMATION

Calories	217	Sugars	5g
Protein	12g	Fat	9g
Carbohydrate	25g	Saturates	1g

10 MINS

1 HOUR

SERVES 6

INGREDIENTS

- 225 g/8 oz/generous cup chickpeas (garbanzo beans), soaked overnight and drained
- 5 cloves
- 2.5 cm/1 inch piece of cinnamon stick
- 2 garlic cloves
- 3 tbsp sunflower oil
- 1 small onion, sliced
- 3 tbsp lemon juice
- 1 tsp coriander seeds
- 2 tomatoes, peeled, seeded and chopped
- 500 g/1 lb 2 oz spinach, rinsed and any tough stems removed
- 1 tbsp chopped coriander (cilantro)

TO GARNISH

- coriander (cilantro) sprigs
- lemon slices

1 Put the chickpeas (garbanzo beans) into a saucepan with enough water to cover. Add the cloves, cinnamon and 1 whole unpeeled garlic clove that has been lightly crushed with the back of a knife to release the juices. Bring to the boil, reduce the heat and simmer for 40–50 minutes, or until the chickpeas (garbanzo beans) are tender when tested with a skewer. Skim off any foam that comes to the surface.

2 Meanwhile, heat 1 tablespoon of the oil in a saucepan. Crush the remaining garlic clove. Put this into the pan with the oil and the onion, and cook over a moderate heat for about 5 minutes.

3 Remove the cloves, cinnamon and garlic from the pan of chickpeas (garbanzo beans). Drain the chickpeas (garbanzo beans). Using a food processor or a fork, blend 90 g/3 oz/½ cup of the chickpeas (garbanzo beans) with the onion and garlic, the lemon juice and 1 tablespoon of the oil until smooth. Stir this purée into the remaining chickpeas (garbanzo beans).

4 Heat the remaining oil in a large frying pan (skillet), add the coriander seeds and stir for 1 minute. Add the tomatoes, stir and add the spinach. Cover and cook for 1 minute over a moderate heat. The spinach should be wilted, but not soggy. Stir in the chopped coriander (cilantro) and remove from the heat.

5 Transfer the chickpeas (garbanzo beans) to a warm serving dish and spoon over the spinach. Garnish with the coriander (cilantro) and slices of lemon and serve immediately.

Deep-fried Courgettes

These courgette (zucchini) fritters are irresistible and could be served as a starter or snack with a chilli dip.

NUTRITIONAL INFORMATION

Calories	117	Sugars	2g
Protein	3g	Fat	6g
Carbohydrate	14g	Saturates	1g

 5 MINS  20 MINS

SERVES 4

INGREDIENTS

- 450 g/1 lb courgettes (zucchini)
- 1 egg white
- 50 g/1¾ oz/⅓ cup cornflour (cornstarch)
- 1 tsp salt
- 1 tsp Chinese five-spice powder
- oil, for deep-frying
- chilli dip, to serve

1 Using a sharp knife, slice the courgettes (zucchini) into rings or chunky sticks.

2 Place the egg white in a small mixing bowl. Lightly whip the egg white until foamy, using a fork.

3 Mix the cornflour (cornstarch), salt and Chinese five-spice powder together and sprinkle on to a large plate.

4 Heat the oil for deep-frying in a large preheated wok or heavy-based frying pan (skillet).

5 Dip each piece of courgette (zucchini) into the beaten egg white then coat in the cornflour (cornstarch) and five-spice mixture.

6 Deep-fry the courgettes (zucchini), in batches, for about 5 minutes or until pale golden and crispy. Repeat with the remaining courgettes (zucchini).

7 Remove the courgettes (zucchini) with a slotted spoon and leave to drain on absorbent kitchen paper (paper towels) while deep-frying the remainder.

8 Transfer the courgettes (zucchini) to serving plates and serve immediately with a chilli dip.

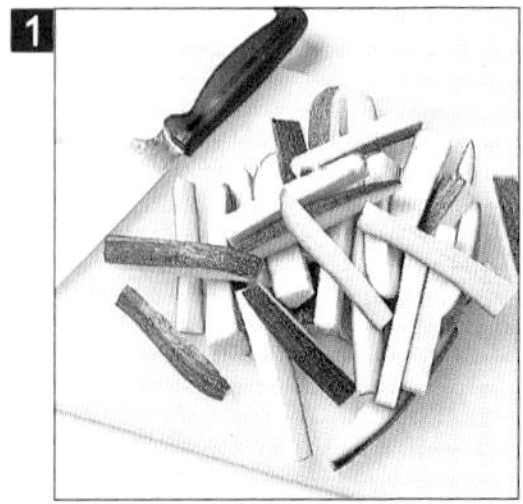

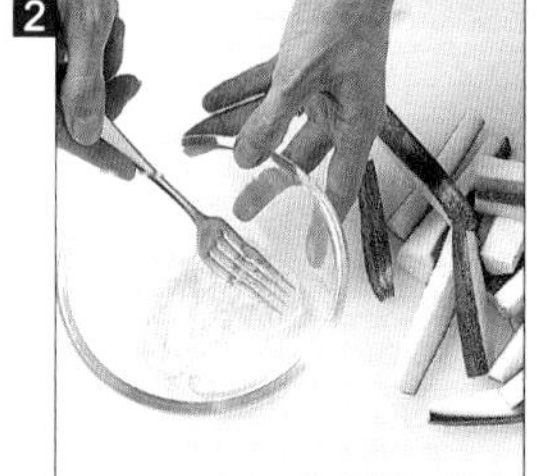

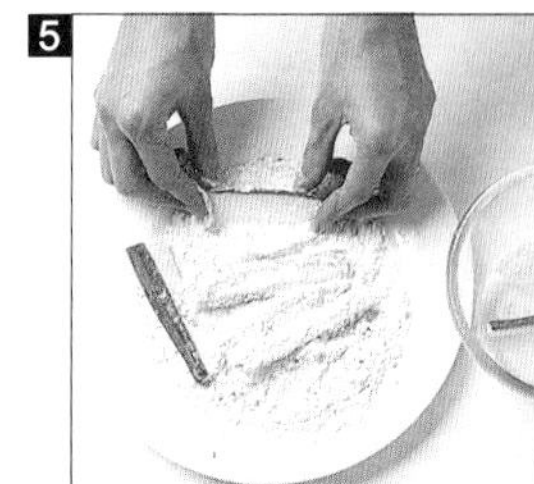

VARIATION

Alter the seasoning by using chilli powder or curry powder instead of the Chinese five-spice powder, if you prefer.

Candied Sweet Potatoes

A taste of the Caribbean is introduced in this recipe, where sweet potatoes are cooked with sugar and lime with a dash of brandy.

NUTRITIONAL INFORMATION

Calories	348	Sugars	21g
Protein	3g	Fat	9g
Carbohydrate	67g	Saturates	6g

 15 MINS  25 MINS

SERVES 4

INGREDIENTS

- 675 g/1½ lb sweet potatoes, sliced
- 40 g/1½ oz/3 tbsp butter
- 1 tbsp lime juice
- 75 g/2¾ oz/½ cup soft dark brown sugar
- 1 tbsp brandy
- grated rind of 1 lime
- lime wedges, to garnish

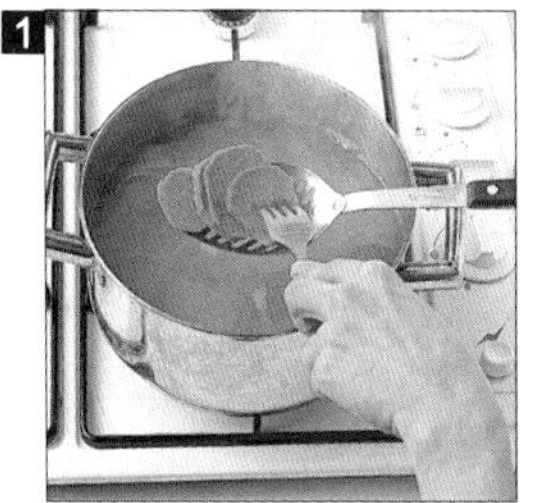

1 Cook the sweet potatoes in a saucepan of boiling water for about 5 minutes. Test the potatoes have softened by pricking with a fork. Remove the sweet potatoes with a perforated spoon and drain thoroughly.

2 Melt the butter in a large frying pan (skillet). Add the lime juice and brown sugar and heat gently, stirring, to dissolve the sugar.

3 Stir the sweet potatoes and the brandy into the sugar and lime juice mixture. Cook over a low heat for about 10 minutes or until the potato slices are cooked through.

4 Sprinkle the lime rind over the top of the sweet potatoes and mix well.

5 Transfer the candied sweet potatoes to a serving plate. Garnish with lime wedges and serve at once.

COOK'S TIP

Sweet potatoes have a pinkish skin and either white, yellow or orange flesh. It doesn't matter which type is used for this dish.

Baked Celery with Cream

This dish is topped with breadcrumbs for a crunchy topping, underneath which is hidden a creamy celery and pecan mixture.

NUTRITIONAL INFORMATION

Calories	237	Sugars	5g
Protein	7g	Fat	19g
Carbohydrate	11g	Saturates	7g

15 MINS 40 MINS

SERVES 4

INGREDIENTS

- 1 head of celery
- ½ tsp ground cumin
- ½ tsp ground coriander
- 1 garlic clove, crushed
- 1 red onion, thinly sliced
- 50 g/1¾ oz/½ cup pecan nut halves
- 150 ml/¼ pint/⅔ cup vegetable stock
- 150 ml/¼ pint/⅔ cup single (light) cream
- 50 g/1¾ oz/1 cup fresh wholemeal (whole wheat) breadcrumbs
- 25 g/1 oz/⅓ cup grated Parmesan cheese
- salt and pepper
- celery leaves, to garnish

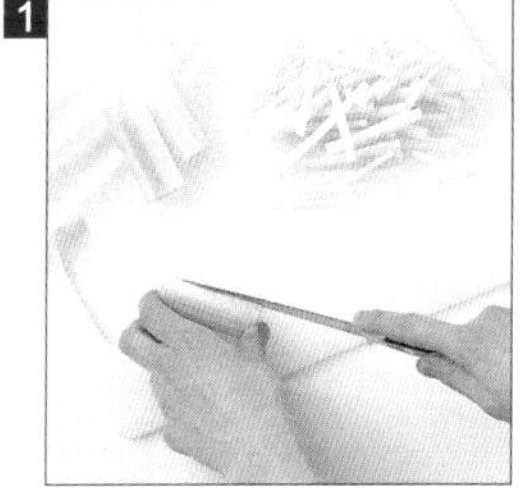
1

2

3

1 Trim the celery and cut into matchsticks. Place the celery in an ovenproof dish, together with the ground cumin, coriander, garlic, red onion and pecan nuts.

2 Mix the stock and cream together and pour over the vegetables. Season with salt and pepper to taste.

3 Mix the breadcrumbs and cheese together and sprinkle over the top to cover the vegetables.

4 Cook in a preheated oven, 200°C/400°F/Gas Mark 6, for 40 minutes, or until the vegetables are tender and the top crispy. Garnish with celery leaves and serve at once.

COOK'S TIP

Once grated, Parmesan cheese quickly loses its 'bite' so it is best to grate only the amount you need for the recipe. Wrap the rest tightly in foil and it will keep for several months in the refrigerator.

Thai-Style Stir-Fried Noodles

This dish is considered the Thai national dish, as it is made and eaten everywhere – a one-dish, fast food for eating on the move.

NUTRITIONAL INFORMATION

Calories	407	Sugars	11g
Protein	14g	Fat	16g
Carbohydrate	56g	Saturates	3g

 15 MINS  5 MINS

SERVES 4

INGREDIENTS

- 225 g/8 oz dried rice noodles
- 2 red chillies, seeded and finely chopped
- 2 shallots, finely chopped
- 2 tbsp sugar
- 2 tbsp tamarind water
- 1 tbsp lime juice
- 2 tbsp light soy sauce
- 1 tbsp sunflower oil
- 1 tsp sesame oil
- 175 g/6 oz/¾ cup diced smoked tofu (bean curd)
- pepper
- 2 tbsp chopped roasted peanuts, to garnish

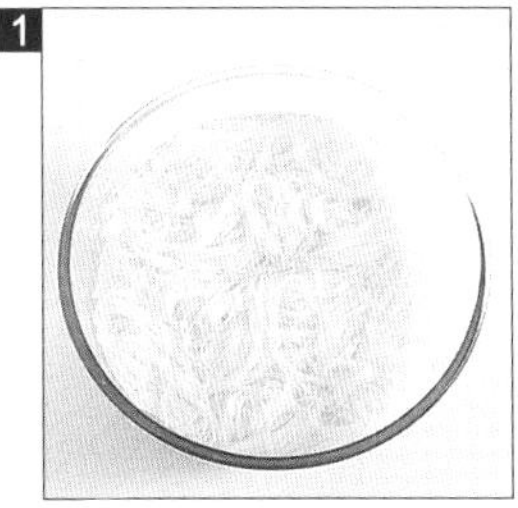

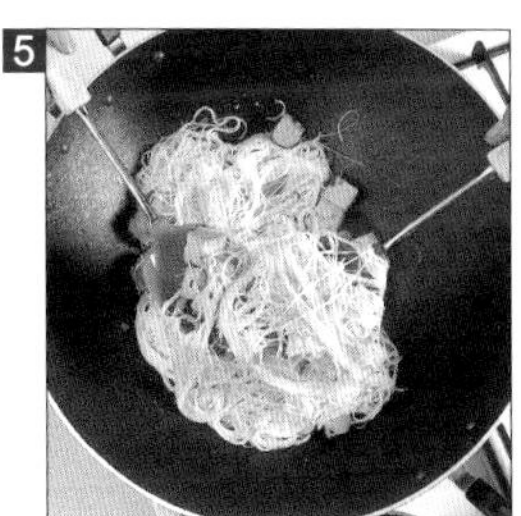

1 Cook the rice noodles as directed on the pack, or soak them in boiling water for 5 minutes.

2 Grind together the chillies, shallots, sugar, tamarind water, lime juice, light soy sauce and pepper to taste.

3 Heat both the oils together in a preheated wok or large, heavy frying pan (skillet) over a high heat. Add the tofu (bean curd) and stir for 1 minute.

4 Add the chilli mixture, bring to the boil, and cook, stirring constantly, for about 2 minutes, until thickened.

5 Drain the rice noodles and add them to the chilli mixture. Use 2 spoons to lift and stir them until they are no longer steaming. Serve immediately, garnished with the peanuts.

COOK'S TIP

This is a quick one-dish meal that is very useful if you are catering for a single vegetarian in the family.

Sweet Chilli Pork Fried Rice

This is a variation of egg fried rice which may be served as an accompaniment to a main meal dish.

NUTRITIONAL INFORMATION

Calories	366	Sugars	5g
Protein	29g	Fat	16g
Carbohydrate	28g	Saturates	4g

25 MINS  20 MINS

SERVES 4

INGREDIENTS

- 450 g/1 lb pork tenderloin
- 2 tbsp sunflower oil
- 2 tbsp sweet chilli sauce, plus extra to serve
- 1 onion, sliced
- 175 g/6 oz carrots, cut into thin sticks
- 175 g/6 oz courgettes (zucchini), cut into sticks
- 100 g/3½ oz/1 cup canned bamboo shoots, drained
- 275 g/9½ oz/4¾ cups cooked long-grain rice
- 1 egg, beaten
- 1 tbsp chopped fresh parsley

1 Using a sharp knife, cut the pork tenderloin into thin slices.

2 Heat the sunflower oil in a large preheated wok or frying pan (skillet).

3 Add the pork to the wok and stir-fry for 5 minutes.

4 Add the chilli sauce to the wok and allow to bubble, stirring, for 2–3 minutes or until syrupy.

5 Add the onion, carrots, courgettes (zucchini) and bamboo shoots to the wok and stir-fry for a further 3 minutes.

6 Add the cooked rice and stir-fry for 2–3 minutes, or until the rice is heated through.

7 Drizzle the beaten egg over the top of the fried rice and cook, tossing the ingredients in the wok with two spoons, until the egg sets.

8 Scatter with chopped fresh parsley and serve immediately, with extra sweet chilli sauce, if desired.

COOK'S TIP

For a really quick dish, add frozen mixed vegetables to the rice instead of the freshly prepared vegetables.

Sesame Hot Noodles

Plain egg noodles are tossed in a dressing made with sesame oil, soy sauce, peanut butter, coriander (cilantro), lime, chilli and sesame seeds.

NUTRITIONAL INFORMATION

Calories	300	Sugars	1g
Protein	7g	Fat	21g
Carbohydrate	21g	Saturates	3g

 5 MINS  10 MINS

SERVES 4

INGREDIENTS

- 2 x 250 g/9 oz packets medium egg noodles
- 3 tbsp sunflower oil
- 2 tbsp sesame oil
- 1 garlic clove, crushed
- 1 tbsp smooth peanut butter
- 1 small green chilli, seeded and very finely chopped
- 3 tbsp toasted sesame seeds
- 4 tbsp light soy sauce
- ½ tbsp lime juice
- salt and pepper
- 4 tbsp chopped fresh coriander (cilantro)

1

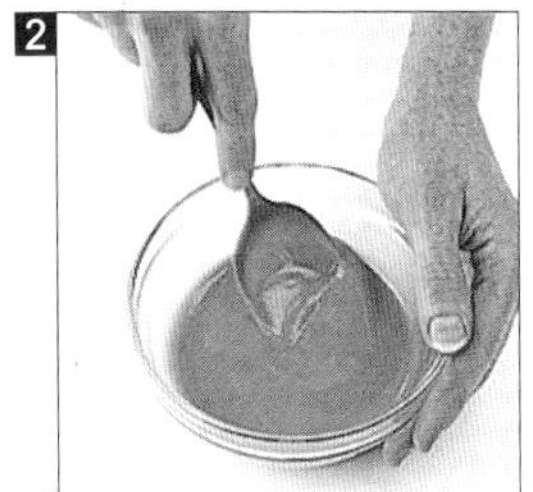

2

3

1 Place the noodles in a large pan of boiling water, then immediately remove from the heat. Cover and leave to stand for 6 minutes, stirring once halfway through the time. At the end of 6 minutes the noodles will be perfectly cooked. Alternatively, cook the noodles following the packet instructions.

2 Meanwhile, make the dressing. Mix together the sunflower oil, sesame oil, crushed garlic and peanut butter in a mixing bowl until smooth.

3 Add the chopped green chilli, sesame seeds and light soy sauce to the other dressing ingredients. Add the lime juice, according to taste, and mix well. Season with salt and pepper.

4 Drain the noodles thoroughly then place in a heated serving bowl.

5 Add the dressing and chopped fresh coriander (cilantro) to the noodles and toss well to mix. Serve hot as a main meal accompaniment.

COOK'S TIP

If you are cooking the noodles ahead of time, toss the cooked, drained noodles in 2 teaspoons of sesame oil, then turn into a bowl. Cover and keep warm until required.

Fried Noodles (Chow Mein)

This is a basic recipe for Chow Mein. Additional ingredients such as chicken or pork can be added if liked.

NUTRITIONAL INFORMATION

Calories	716	Sugars	2g
Protein	4g	Fat	12g
Carbohydrate	14g	Saturates	1g

 5 MINS  15 MINS

SERVES 4

INGREDIENTS

- 275 g/9½ oz egg noodles
- 3-4 tbsp vegetable oil
- 1 small onion, finely shredded
- 125 g/4½ oz fresh bean sprouts
- 1 spring onion (scallion), finely shredded
- 2 tbsp light soy sauce
- a few drops of sesame oil
- salt

1 Bring a wok or saucepan of salted water to the boil.

2 Add the egg noodles to the saucepan or wok and cook according to the instructions on the packet (usually no more than 4-5 minutes).

3 Drain the noodles well and rinse in cold water; drain thoroughly again, then transfer to a large mixing bowl and toss with a little vegetable oil.

4 Heat the remaining vegetable oil in a preheated wok or large frying pan (skillet) until really hot.

5 Add the shredded onion to the wok and stir-fry for about 30-40 seconds.

6 Add the bean sprouts and drained noodles to the wok, stir and toss for 1 more minute.

7 Add the shredded spring onion (scallion) and light soy sauce and blend well.

8 Transfer the noodles to a warm serving dish, sprinkle with the sesame oil and serve immediately.

COOK'S TIP

Noodles, a symbol of longevity, are made from wheat or rice flour, water and egg. Handmade noodles are made by an elaborate process of kneading, pulling and twisting the dough, and it takes years to learn the art.

Crispy Deep-fried Noodles

This dish requires a certain amount of care and attention to get the crispy noodles properly cooked, but it is well worth the effort.

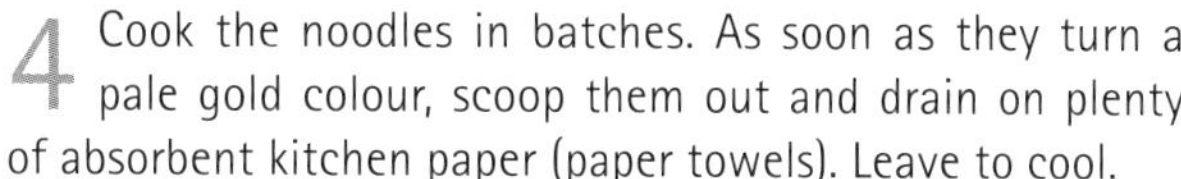

NUTRITIONAL INFORMATION

Calories	242	Sugars	2g
Protein	13g	Fat	17g
Carbohydrate	10g	Saturates	3g

 35 MINS  25 MINS

SERVES 4

INGREDIENTS

- 175 g/6 oz thread egg noodles
- 600 ml/1 pint/2½ cups sunflower oil, for deep-frying
- 2 tsp grated lemon peel
- 1 tbsp light soy sauce
- 1 tbsp rice vinegar
- 1 tbsp lemon juice
- 1½ tbsp sugar
- 250 g/9 oz/1 cup marinated tofu (bean curd), diced
- 2 garlic cloves, crushed
- 1 red chilli, sliced finely
- 1 red (bell) pepper, diced
- 4 eggs, beaten
- red chilli flower, to garnish)

1 Blanch the egg noodles briefly in hot water, to which a little of the oil has been added. Drain the noodles and spread out to dry for at least 30 minutes. Cut into threads about 7 cm/3 inches long.

2 Combine the lemon peel, light soy sauce, rice vinegar, lemon juice and sugar in a small bowl. Set the mixture aside until required.

3 Heat the sunflower oil in a wok or large, heavy frying pan (skillet), and test the temperature with a few strands of noodles. They should swell to many times their size, but if they do not, wait until the oil is hot enough; otherwise they will be tough and stringy, not puffy and light.

4 Cook the noodles in batches. As soon as they turn a pale gold colour, scoop them out and drain on plenty of absorbent kitchen paper (paper towels). Leave to cool.

5 Reserve 2 tablespoons of the oil and drain off the rest. Heat the reserved oil in the wok or pan (skillet).

6 Add the marinated tofu (bean curd) to the wok or frying pan (skillet) and cook quickly over a high heat to seal.

7 Add the crushed garlic cloves, sliced red chilli and diced red (bell) pepper to the wok. Stir-fry for 1–2 minutes.

8 Add the reserved vinegar mixture to the wok, stir to mix well and add the beaten eggs, stirring until they are set.

9 Serve the tofu (bean curd) mixture with the crispy fried noodles, garnished with a red chilli flower.

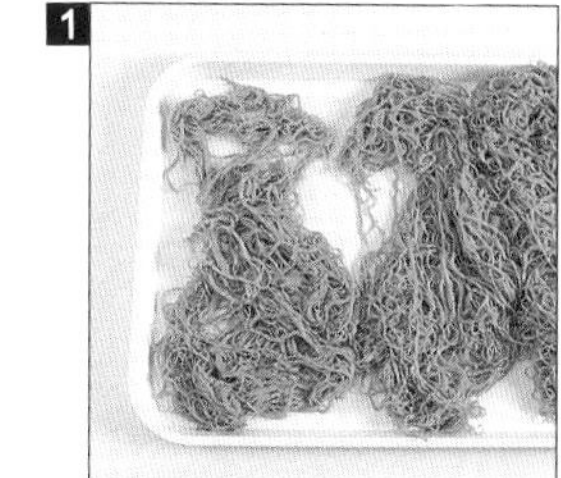
1

2

3

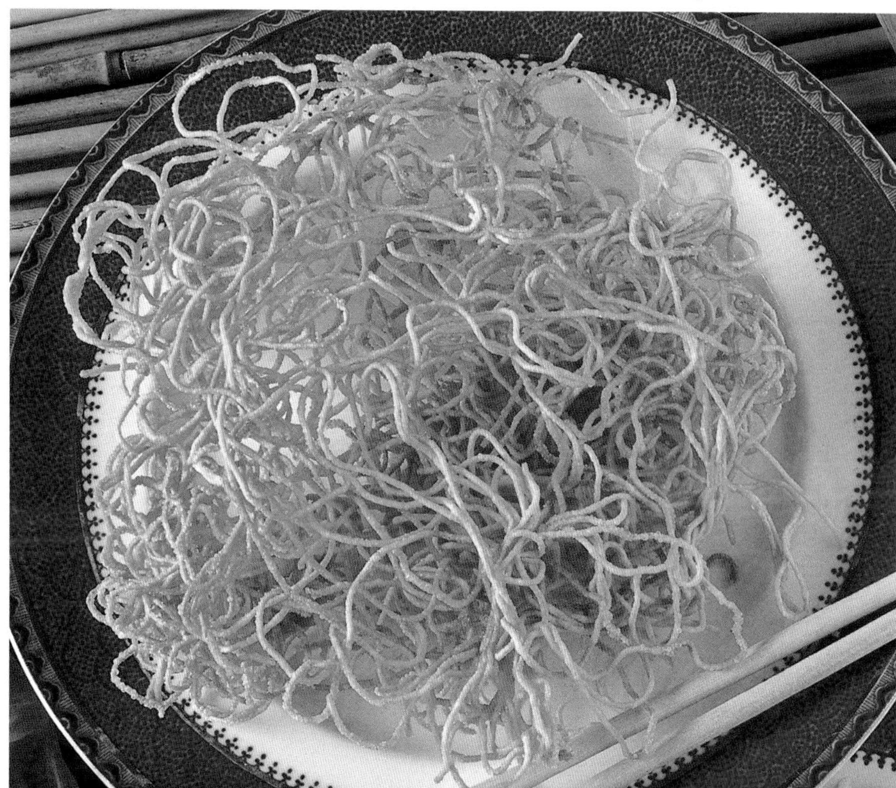

Chilli Roast Potatoes

Small new potatoes are scrubbed and boiled in their skins, before being coated in a chilli mixture and roasted to perfection in the oven.

NUTRITIONAL INFORMATION

Calories	178	Sugars	2g
Protein	2g	Fat	11g
Carbohydrate	18g	Saturates	1g

5-10 MINS 30 MINS

SERVES 4

INGREDIENTS

- 500 g/1 lb 2 oz small new potatoes, scrubbed
- 150 ml/¼ pint/⅔ cup vegetable oil
- 1 tsp chilli powder
- ½ tsp caraway seeds
- 1 tsp salt
- 1 tbsp chopped basil

1 Cook the potatoes in a saucepan of boiling water for 10 minutes, then drain thoroughly.

2 Pour a little of the oil into a shallow roasting tin (pan) to coat the base. Heat the oil in a preheated oven, 200°C/400°F/Gas Mark 6, for 10 minutes. Add the potatoes to the tin (pan) and brush them with the hot oil.

3 In a small bowl, mix together the chilli powder, caraway seeds and salt. Sprinkle the mixture over the potatoes, turning to coat them all over.

4 Add the remaining oil to the tin (pan) and roast in the oven for about 15 minutes, or until the potatoes are cooked through.

5 Using a slotted spoon, remove the potatoes from the the oil, draining them well and transfer them to a warmed serving dish. Sprinkle the chopped basil over the top and serve immediately.

2

3

5

VARIATION

Use any other spice of your choice, such as curry powder or paprika, for a variation in flavour.

Sun-dried Tomato Risotto

A Milanese risotto can be cooked in a variety of ways – but always with saffron. This version with sun-dried tomatoes has a lovely tangy flavour.

NUTRITIONAL INFORMATION

Calories	558	Sugars	2g
Protein	16g	Fat	19g
Carbohydrate	80g	Saturates	9g

 10 MINS  30 MINS

SERVES 4

INGREDIENTS

- 1 tbsp olive oil
- 25 g/1 oz/2 tbsp butter
- 1 large onion, finely chopped
- 350 g/12 oz arborio (risotto) rice, washed
- about 15 strands of saffron
- 150 ml/¼ pint/⅔ cup white wine
- 850 ml/1½ pints/3¾ cups hot vegetable or chicken stock
- 8 sun-dried tomatoes, cut into strips
- 100 g/3½ oz frozen peas, defrosted
- 50 g/1¾ oz Parma ham (prosciutto), shredded
- 75 g/2¾ oz Parmesan cheese, grated

2

4

6

1 Heat the oil and butter in a large frying pan (skillet). Add the onion and cook for 4–5 minutes or until softened.

2 Add the rice and saffron to the frying pan (skillet), stirring well to coat the rice in the oil, and cook for 1 minute.

3 Add the wine and stock slowly to the rice mixture in the pan, a ladleful at a time, stirring and making sure that all the liquid is absorbed before adding the next ladleful of liquid.

4 About half-way through adding the stock, stir in the sun-dried tomatoes.

5 When all of the wine and stock has been absorbed, the rice should be cooked. Test by tasting a grain – if it is still crunchy, add a little more water and continue cooking. It should take 15–20 minutes to cook.

6 Stir in the peas, Parma ham (prosciutto) and cheese. Cook for 2–3 minutes, stirring, until hot. Serve with extra Parmesan.

COOK'S TIP

The finished risotto should have moist but separate grains. This is achieved by adding the hot stock a little at a time, only adding more when the last addition has been absorbed. Don't leave the risotto to cook by itself: it needs constant checking to see when more liquid is required.

Spiced Rice & Lentils

This is a lovely combination of rice and masoor dhal and is simple to cook. You can add a knob of unsalted butter before serving, if liked.

NUTRITIONAL INFORMATION

Calories	394	Sugars	3g
Protein	14g	Fat	8g
Carbohydrate	70g	Saturates	1g

 5 MINS  30 MINS

SERVES 4

INGREDIENTS

- 200 g/7 oz/1 cup basmati rice
- 175 g/6 oz/¾ cup masoor dhal
- 2 tbsp vegetable ghee
- 1 small onion, sliced
- 1 tsp finely chopped root ginger
- 1 tsp crushed garlic
- ½ tsp turmeric
- 600 ml/1 pint/2½ cups water
- 1 tsp salt

1 Combine the rice and dhal and rinse thoroughly in cold running water. Set aside until required.

2 Heat the ghee in a large saucepan. Add the onion and fry, stirring occasionally, for about 2 minutes.

3 Reduce the heat, add the ginger, garlic, and turmeric and stir-fry for 1 minute.

4 Add the rice and dhal to the mixture in the pan and blend together, mixing gently, but thoroughly.

5 Add the water to the mixture in the pan and bring to the boil over a medium heat. Reduce the heat, cover and cook for 20–25 minutes, until the rice is tender and the liquid is absorbed.

6 Just before serving, add the salt and mix to combine.

7 Transfer the spiced rice and lentils to a large warmed serving dish and serve immediately.

COOK'S TIP

Many Indian recipes specify using ghee as the cooking fat. This is because it is similar to clarified butter in that it can be heated to a very high temperature without burning. Ghee adds a nutty flavour to dishes and a glossy shine to sauces.

Fruity Coconut Rice

A pale yellow rice flavoured with coconut and spices to serve as an accompaniment – or as a main dish with added diced chicken or pork.

NUTRITIONAL INFORMATION

Calories	578	Sugars	17g
Protein	8g	Fat	31g
Carbohydrate	71g	Saturates	15g

5 MINS  35 MINS

SERVES 4

INGREDIENTS

- 90 g/3 oz creamed coconut
- 700 ml/1¼ pints/3 cups boiling water
- 1 tbsp sunflower oil (or olive oil for a stronger flavour)
- 1 onion, thinly sliced or chopped
- 250 g/9 oz/generous 1 cup long-grain rice
- ¼ tsp turmeric
- 6 whole cloves
- 1 cinnamon stick
- ½ tsp salt
- 60-90 g/2-3 oz/½ cup raisins or sultanas
- 60 g/2 oz/½ cup walnut or pecan halves, roughly chopped
- 2 tbsp pumpkin seeds (optional)

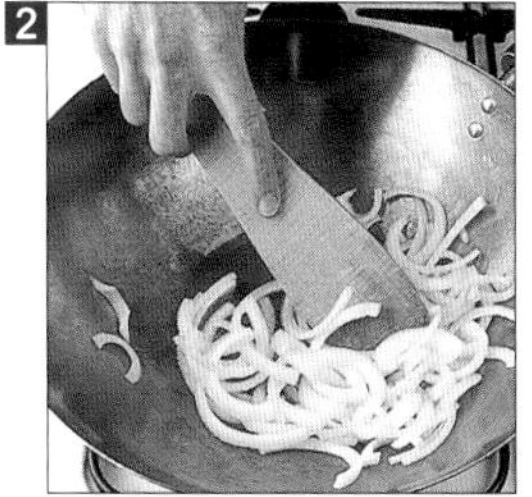

2

3

4

1 Blend the creamed coconut with half the boiling water until smooth, then stir in the remainder until well blended.

2 Heat the oil in a preheated wok, add the onion and stir-fry gently for 3-4 minutes until the onion begins to soften.

3 Rinse the rice thoroughly under cold running water, drain well and add to the wok with the turmeric. Cook for 1-2 minutes, stirring all the time.

4 Add the coconut milk, cloves, cinnamon stick and salt and bring to the boil. Cover and simmer very gently for 10 minutes.

5 Add the raisins, nuts and pumpkin seeds, if using, and mix well. Cover the wok again and continue to cook for a further 5-8 minutes or until all the liquid has been absorbed and the rice is tender. Remove from the heat and leave to stand, still tightly covered, for 5 minutes. Remove the cinnamon stick and serve.

COOK'S TIP

250g/9 oz/1 cup cooked chicken or pork cut into dice or thin slivers may be added with the raisins to turn this into a main dish. The addition of coconut milk makes the cooked rice slightly sticky.

Saffron Rice

This is the classic way to serve rice, paired with saffron, so that each brings out the best in the other.

NUTRITIONAL INFORMATION

Calories	63	Sugars	0.1g
Protein	1.4g	Fat	2g
Carbohydrate	11g	Saturates	0.2g

 15 MINS  25 MINS

SERVES 8

INGREDIENTS

- 12 saffron threads, crushed lightly
- 2 tbsp warm water
- 400 ml/14 fl oz/1¾ cups water
- 225 g/8 oz basmati rice
- 1 tbsp toasted, flaked (slivered) almonds

1 Put the saffron threads into a bowl with the warm water and leave for 10 minutes. They need to be crushed before soaking to ensure that the maximum flavour and colour is extracted at this stage.

2 Put the water and rice into a medium saucepan and set it over the heat to boil. Add the saffron and saffron water and stir.

3 Bring back to a gentle boil, stir again and let the rice simmer, uncovered, for about 10 minutes, until all the water has been absorbed.

4 Cover tightly, reduce the heat as much as possible and leave for 10 minutes. Do not remove the lid. This ensures that the grains separate and that the rice is not soggy.

5 Alternatively, you can soak the rice overnight and drain before cooking. Cook as before but reduce the cooking time by 3–4 minutes to compensate for the presoaking.

6 Remove the rice from the heat and transfer to a serving dish. Fork through the rice gently and sprinkle on the toasted almonds before serving.

COOK'S TIP

Saffron, grown in Europe and the Middle East, is the most ancient of spices and continues to be the most expensive – literally worth its weight in gold. It is still harvested and sorted by hand and is a treasured commodity.

Lemony & Herby Potatoes

Choose from these two divine recipes for new potatoes. To check if new potatoes are fresh, rub the skin; the skin will come off easily if fresh.

NUTRITIONAL INFORMATION

Calories	226	Sugars	2g
Protein	5g	Fat	5g
Carbohydrate	42g	Saturates	3g

 20 MINS  35 MINS

SERVES 4

INGREDIENTS

LEMONY NEW POTATOES

- 1 kg/2 lb 4 oz new potatoes
- 25 g/1 oz/2 tbsp butter
- 1 tbsp finely grated lemon rind
- 2 tbsp lemon juice
- 1 tbsp chopped fresh dill or chives
- salt and pepper
- extra chopped fresh dill or chives, to garnishes

HERBY NEW POTATOES

- 1 kg/2 lb 4 oz new potatoes
- 3 tbsp light olive oil
- 1h tbsp white wine vinegar
- pinch of dry mustard
- pinch of caster (superfine) sugar
- salt and pepper
- 2 tbsp chopped mixed fresh herbs, such as parsley, chives, marjoram, basil and rosemary
- extra chopped fresh mixed herbs, to garnish

1 For the lemony potatoes, either scrub the potatoes well or remove skins by scraping off with a sharp knife. Cook the potatoes in plenty of lightly salted boiling water for about 15 minutes until just tender.

1

2

4

2 While the potatoes are cooking, melt the butter over a low heat. Add the lemon rind, juice and herbs. Season with salt and pepper.

3 Drain the cooked potatoes and transfer to a serving bowl.

4 Pour over the lemony butter mixture and stir gently to mix. Garnish with extra herbs and serve hot or warm.

5 For the herby potatoes prepare and cook the potatoes as described in step 1 above. Whisk the oil, vinegar, mustard, caster (superfine) sugar and seasoning together in a small bowl. Add the chopped herbs and mix well.

6 Drain the potatoes and pour over the oil and vinegar mixture, stirring to coat evenly. Garnish with extra fresh herbs and serve warm or cold.

Egg Fried Rice

In this classic Chinese dish, boiled rice is fried with peas, spring onions (scallions) and egg and flavoured with soy sauce.

NUTRITIONAL INFORMATION

Calories	203	Sugars	1g
Protein	9g	Fat	11g
Carbohydrate	19g	Saturates	2g

20 MINS 10 MINS

SERVES 4

INGREDIENTS

- 150 g/5½ oz/⅔ cup long-grain rice
- 3 eggs, beaten
- 2 tbsp vegetable oil
- 2 garlic cloves, crushed
- 4 spring onions (scallions), chopped
- 125 g/4½ oz/1 cup cooked peas
- 1 tbsp light soy sauce
- pinch of salt
- shredded spring onion (scallion), to garnish

1 Cook the rice in a pan of boiling water for 10-12 minutes, until almost cooked, but not soft. Drain well, rinse under cold water and drain again.

2 Place the beaten eggs in a saucepan and cook over a gentle heat, stirring until softly scrambled.

3 Heat the vegetable oil in a preheated wok or large frying pan (skillet), swirling the oil around the base of the wok until it is really hot.

4 Add the crushed garlic, spring onions (scallions) and peas and sauté, stirring occasionally, for 1-2 minutes. Stir the rice into the wok, mixing to combine.

5 Add the eggs, light soy sauce and a pinch of salt to the wok or frying pan (skillet) and stir to mix the egg in thoroughly.

6 Transfer the egg fried rice to serving dishes and serve garnished with the shredded spring onion (scallion).

COOK'S TIP

The rice is rinsed under cold water to wash out the tarch and prevent it from sticking together.

Pesto Rice with Garlic Bread

Try this combination of two types of rice with the richness of pine kernels (nuts), basil, and freshly grated Parmesan.

NUTRITIONAL INFORMATION

Calories	918	Sugars	2g
Protein	18g	Fat	64g
Carbohydrate	73g	Saturates	19g

20 MINS  40 MINS

SERVES 4

INGREDIENTS

300 g/10½ oz/1½ cups mixed long-grain and wild rice

fresh basil sprigs, to garnish

tomato and orange salad, to serve

PESTO DRESSING

15 g/½ oz fresh basil

125 g/4½ oz/1 cup pine kernels (nuts)

2 garlic cloves, crushed

6 tbsp olive oil

60 g/2 oz/½ cup freshly grated Parmesan

salt and pepper

GARLIC BREAD

2 small granary or whole wheat French bread sticks

90 g/3 oz/½ cup butter or margarine, softened

2 garlic cloves, crushed

1 tsp dried mixed herbs

1 Place the rice in a saucepan and cover with water. Bring to the boil and cook for 15–20 minutes. Drain well and keep warm.

2 Meanwhile, make the pesto dressing. Remove the basil leaves from the stalks and finely chop the leaves. Reserve 25 g/1 oz/¼ cup of the pine kernels (nuts) and finely chop the remainder. Mix with the chopped basil and dressing ingredients. Alternatively, put all the ingredients in a food processor or blender and blend for a few seconds until smooth. Set aside.

3 To make the garlic bread, slice the bread at 2.5 cm/1 inch intervals, taking care not to slice all the way through. Mix the butter or margarine with the garlic, herbs and seasoning. Spread thickly between each slice.

4 Wrap the bread in foil and bake in a preheated oven, 200°C/400°F/Gas Mark 6, for 10–15 minutes.

5 To serve, toast the reserved pine kernels (nuts) under a preheated medium grill (broiler) for 2–3 minutes until golden. Toss the pesto dressing into the hot rice and pile into a warmed serving dish. Sprinkle with toasted pine kernels (nuts) and garnish with basil sprigs. Serve with the garlic bread and a tomato and orange salad.

2

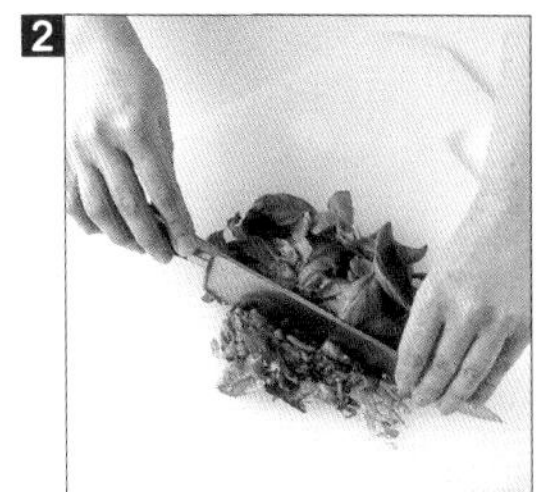

3

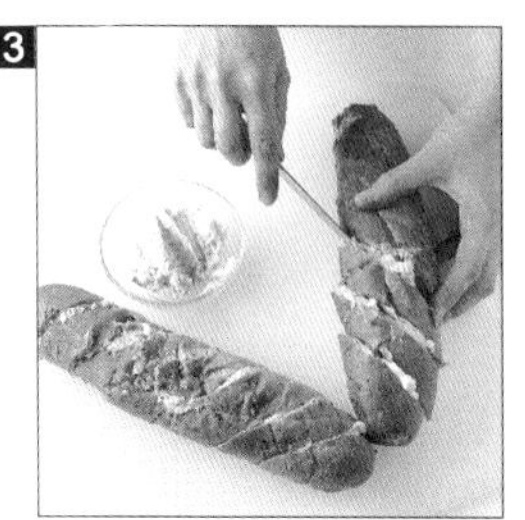

5

Coconut Rice with Lentils

Rice and green lentils are cooked with coconut, lemon grass and curry leaves. It will serve 2 people as a main course or 4 as a side dish.

NUTRITIONAL INFORMATION

Calories	511	Sugars	3g
Protein	12g	Fat	24g
Carbohydrate	67g	Saturates	15g

 5 MINS  50 MINS

SERVES 4

INGREDIENTS

- 90 g/3 oz/⅓ cup green lentils
- 250 g/9 oz/generous 1 cup long-grain rice
- 2 tbsp vegetable oil
- 1 onion, sliced
- 2 garlic cloves, crushed
- 3 curry leaves
- 1 stalk lemon grass, chopped (if unavailable, use grated rind of ½ lemon)
- 1 green chilli, deseeded and chopped
- ½ tsp cumin seeds
- 1½ tsp salt
- 90 g/3 oz/⅓ cup creamed coconut
- 600 ml/1 pint/2½ cups hot water
- 2 tbsp chopped fresh coriander (cilantro)

TO GARNISH

- shredded radishes
- shredded cucumber

1 Wash the lentils and place in a saucepan. Cover with cold water, bring to the boil and boil rapidly for 10 minutes.

2 Wash the rice thoroughly and drain well. Set aside until required.

3 Heat the vegetable oil in a large saucepan which has a tight-fitting lid and fry the onion for 3–4 minutes. Add the garlic, curry leaves, lemon grass, chilli, cumin seeds and salt, and stir well.

4 Drain the lentils and rinse. Add to the onion and spices with the rice and mix well.

5 Add the creamed coconut to the hot water and stir until dissolved. Stir the coconut liquid into the rice mixture and bring to the boil. Turn down the heat to low, put the lid on tightly and leave to cook undisturbed for 15 minutes.

6 Without removing the lid, remove the pan from the heat and leave to rest for 10 minutes to allow the rice and lentils to finish cooking in their own steam.

7 Stir in the coriander (cilantro) and remove the curry leaves. Serve garnished with the radishes and cucumber.

Special Fried Rice

This dish is a popular choice in Chinese restaurants. Ham and prawns (shrimp) are mixed with vegetables in a soy-flavoured rice.

NUTRITIONAL INFORMATION

Calories	301	Sugars	1g
Protein	26g	Fat	13g
Carbohydrate	21g	Saturates	3g

 5 MINS  30 MINS

SERVES 4

INGREDIENTS

- 150 g/5½ oz/⅔ cup long-grain rice
- 2 tbsp vegetable oil
- 2 eggs, beaten
- 2 garlic cloves, crushed
- 1 tsp grated fresh root ginger
- 3 spring onions (scallions), sliced
- 75 g/2¾ oz/¾ cup cooked peas
- 150 g/5½ oz/⅔ cup bean sprouts
- 225 g/8 oz/1⅓ cups shredded ham
- 150 g/5½ oz peeled, cooked prawns (shrimp)
- 2 tbsp light soy sauce

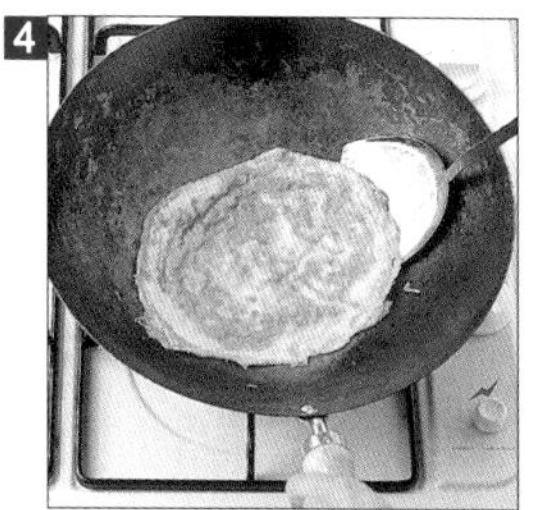

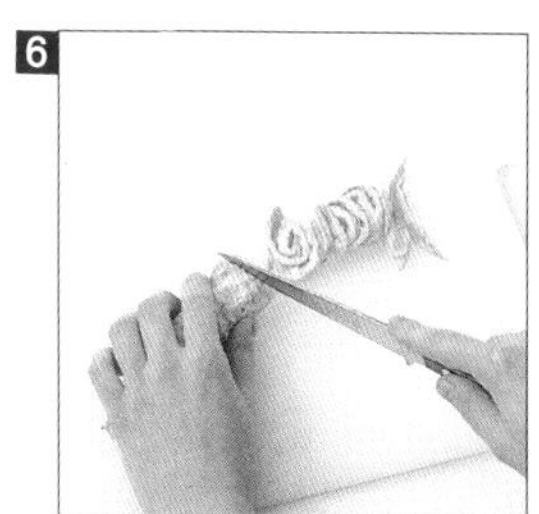

1 Cook the rice in a saucepan of boiling water for about 15 minutes. Drain well, rinse under cold water and drain thoroughly again.

2 Heat 1 tablespoon of the vegetable oil in a preheated wok.

3 Add the beaten eggs and a further 1 teaspoon of oil. Tilt the wok so that the egg covers the base to make a thin pancake.

4 Cook until lightly browned on the underside, then flip the pancake over and cook on the other side for 1 minute. Remove from the wok and leave to cool.

5 Heat the remaining oil in the wok and stir-fry the garlic and ginger for 30 seconds. Add the spring onions (scallions), peas, bean sprouts, ham and prawns (shrimp). Stir-fry for 2 minutes.

6 Stir in the soy sauce and rice and cook for a further 2 minutes. Transfer the rice to serving dishes. Roll up the pancake, slice it very thinly and use to garnish the rice. Serve immediately.

COOK'S TIP

As this recipe contains meat and fish, it is ideal served with simpler vegetable dishes.

Thai Jasmine Rice

Every Thai meal has as its centrepiece a big bowl of steaming, fluffy Thai jasmine rice, to which salt should not be added.

NUTRITIONAL INFORMATION

Calories	239	Sugars	0g
Protein	5g	Fat	2g
Carbohydrate	54g	Saturates	0.6g

 5 MINS  10–15 MINS

SERVES 4

INGREDIENTS

OPEN PAN METHOD

- 225 g/8 oz/generous 1 cup Thai jasmine rice
- 1 litre/1¾ pints/4 cups water

ABSORPTION METHOD

- 225 g/8 oz/generous 1 cup Thai jasmine rice
- 450 ml/16 fl oz/scant 2 cups water

2

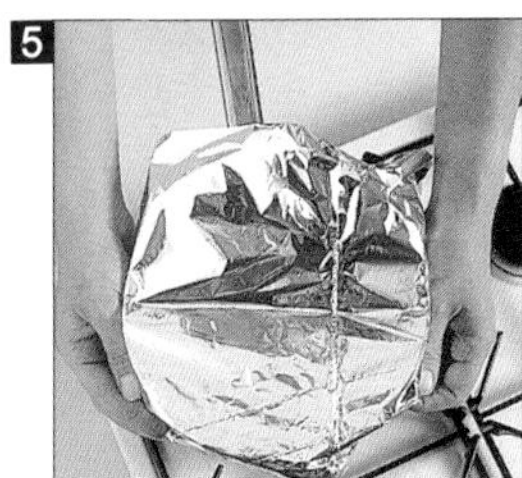

5

6

1 For the open pan method, rinse the rice in a strainer under cold running water and leave to drain.

2 Bring the water to the boil. Add the rice, stir once and return to a medium boil. Cook, uncovered, for 8–10 minutes, until tender.

3 Drain thoroughly and fork through lightly before serving.

4 For the absorption method, rinse the rice under cold running water.

5 Put the rice and water into a saucepan and bring to the boil. Stir once and then cover the pan tightly. Lower the heat as much as possible. Cook for 10 minutes. Leave to rest for 5 minutes.

6 Fork through lightly and serve the rice immediately.

COOK'S TIP

Thai jasmine rice can be frozen. Freeze in a plastic sealed container. Frozen rice is ideal for stir-fry dishes, as the process seems to separate the grains.

Fried Rice in Pineapple

This looks very impressive on a party buffet. Mix the remaining pineapple flesh with paw-paw (papaya) and mango for an exotic fruit salad.

NUTRITIONAL INFORMATION

Calories	197	Sugars	8g
Protein	5g	Fat	8g
Carbohydrate	29g	Saturates	1g

 20 MINS  10 MINS

SERVES 4

INGREDIENTS

- 1 large pineapple
- 1 tbsp sunflower oil
- 1 garlic clove, crushed
- 1 small onion, diced
- ½ celery stick, sliced
- 1 tsp coriander seeds, ground
- 1 tsp cumin seeds, ground
- 150 g/5½ oz/1½ cups button mushrooms, sliced
- 250 g/9 oz/1⅓ cups cooked rice
- 2 tbsp light soy sauce
- ½ tsp sugar
- ½ tsp salt
- 25 g/1 oz/¼ cup cashew nuts

TO GARNISH

- 1 spring onion (scallion), sliced finely
- fresh coriander (cilantro) leaves
- mint sprig

1 Using a sharp knife, halve the pineapple lengthways and cut out the flesh to make 2 boat-shaped shells.

2 Cut the flesh into cubes and reserve 125 g/4½ oz/1 cup to use in this recipe. (Any remaining pineapple cubes can be served separately.)

3 Heat the sunflower oil in a wok or large, heavy frying pan (skillet).

4 Cook the garlic, onion and celery over a high heat, stirring constantly, for 2 minutes. Stir in the coriander and cumin seeds, and the mushrooms.

5 Add the reserved pineapple cubes and cooked rice to the wok or frying pan (skillet) and stir well.

6 Stir in the soy sauce, sugar, salt and cashew nuts.

7 Using 2 spoons, lift and stir the rice for about 4 minutes until it is thoroughly heated.

8 Spoon the rice mixture into the pineapple boats. Garnish with sliced spring onion (scallion), coriander (cilantro) leaves and a mint sprig.

Pulao Rice

Plain boiled rice is eaten by most people in India every day, but for entertaining, a more interesting rice dish, such as this, is served.

NUTRITIONAL INFORMATION

Calories	265	Sugars	0g
Protein	4g	Fat	10g
Carbohydrate	43g	Saturates	6g

 5 MINS  25 MINS

SERVES 4

INGREDIENTS

- 200 g/7 oz/1 cup basmati rice
- 2 tbsp vegetable ghee
- 3 green cardamoms
- 2 cloves
- 3 peppercorns
- ½ tsp salt
- ½ tsp saffron
- 400 ml/14 fl oz/scant 2 cups water

1 Rinse the rice twice under running water and set aside until required.

2 Heat the ghee in a saucepan. Add the cardamoms, cloves and peppercorns to the pan and fry, stirring constantly, for about 1 minute.

3 Add the rice and stir-fry over a medium heat for a further 2 minutes.

4 Add the salt, saffron and water to the rice mixture and reduce the heat. Cover the pan and simmer over a low heat until the water has been absorbed.

5 Transfer the pulao rice to a serving dish and serve hot.

3

4

4

COOK'S TIP

The most expensive of all spices, saffron strands are the stamens of a type of crocus. They give dishes a rich, golden colour, as well as adding a distinctive, slightly bitter taste. Saffron is sold as a powder or in the more expensive strands.

Oriental-Style Millet Pilau

Millet makes an interesting alternative to rice, which is the more traditional ingredient for a pilau. Serve with a crisp oriental salad.

NUTRITIONAL INFORMATION

Calories	660	Sugars	28g
Protein	15g	Fat	27g
Carbohydrate	94g	Saturates	5g

20 MINS 30 MINS

SERVES 4

INGREDIENTS

- 300 g/10½ oz/1½ cups millet grains
- 1 tbsp vegetable oil
- 1 bunch spring onions (scallions), white and green parts, chopped
- 1 garlic clove, crushed
- 1 tsp grated root ginger
- 1 orange (bell) pepper, seeded and diced
- 600 ml/1 pint/2½ cups water
- 1 orange
- 125 g/4½ oz/¾ cup chopped pitted dates
- 2 tsp sesame oil
- 125 g/4½ oz/1 cup roasted cashew nuts
- 2 tbsp pumpkin seeds
- salt and pepper
- oriental salad vegetables, to serve

1

3

4

1 Place the millet in a large saucepan and toast over a medium heat, shaking the pan occasionally, for 4–5 minutes, until the grains begin to crack and pop.

2 Heat the oil in another saucepan. Add the spring onions (scallions), garlic, ginger and (bell) pepper and fry, stirring frequently, for 2–3 minutes, until just softened, but not browned. Add the millet and pour in the water.

3 Using a vegetable peeler, pare the rind from the orange and add the rind to the pan. Squeeze the juice from the orange into the pan. Season to taste with salt and pepper.

4 Bring to the boil, reduce the heat, cover and cook gently for 20 minutes, until all the liquid has been absorbed. Remove from the heat, stir in the dates and sesame oil and leave to stand for 10 minutes.

5 Discard the orange rind and stir in the cashew nuts. Pile into a warmed serving dish, sprinkle with pumpkin seeds and serve with oriental salad vegetables.

Spiced Basmati Pilau

The whole spices are not meant to be eaten and may be removed before serving. Omit the broccoli and mushrooms for a plain, spiced pilau.

NUTRITIONAL INFORMATION

Calories	450	Sugars	3g
Protein	9g	Fat	15g
Carbohydrate	76g	Saturates	2g

 20 MINS  25 MINS

SERVES 6

INGREDIENTS

- 500 g/1 lb 2 oz/2½ cups basmati rice
- 175 g/6 oz broccoli, trimmed
- 6 tbsp vegetable oil
- 2 large onions, chopped
- 225 g/8 oz/3 cups sliced mushrooms
- 2 garlic cloves, crushed
- 6 cardamom pods, split
- 6 whole cloves
- 8 black peppercorns
- 1 cinnamon stick or piece of cassia bark
- 1 tsp ground turmeric
- 1.2 litres/2 pints/5 cups boiling vegetable stock or water
- salt and pepper
- 60 g/2 oz/⅓ cup seedless raisins
- 60 g/2 oz/½ cup unsalted pistachios, coarsely chopped

VARIATION

For added richness, you could stir a spoonful of vegetable ghee through the rice mixture just before serving. A little diced red (bell) pepper and a few cooked peas forked through at step 4 add a colourful touch.

1 Place the rice in a strainer and wash well under cold running water. Drain. Trim off most of the broccoli stalk and cut into small florets, then quarter the stalk lengthways and cut diagonally into 1 cm/½ inch pieces.

2 Heat the oil in a large saucepan. Add the onions and broccoli stalks and cook over a low heat, stirring frequently, for 3 minutes. Add the mushrooms, rice, garlic and spices and cook for 1 minute, stirring, until the rice is coated in oil.

3 Add the boiling stock and season to taste with salt and pepper. Stir in the broccoli florets and return the mixture to the boil. Cover, reduce the heat and cook over a low heat for 15 minutes without uncovering the pan.

4 Remove from the heat and leave to stand for 5 minutes without uncovering. Add the raisins and pistachios and gently fork through to fluff up the grains. Serve hot.

1

3

4

Curried Rice with Tofu

Cooked rice is combined with marinated tofu (bean curd), vegetables and peanuts to make this deliciously rich curry.

NUTRITIONAL INFORMATION

Calories	598	Sugars	2g
Protein	16g	Fat	25
Carbohydrate	81g	Saturates	4g

 15 MINS  15 MINS

SERVES 4

INGREDIENTS

- 1 tsp coriander seeds
- 1 tsp cumin seeds
- 1 tsp ground cinnamon
- 1 tsp cloves
- 1 whole star anise
- 1 tsp cardamom pods
- 1 tsp white peppercorns
- 1 tbsp oil
- 6 shallots, chopped very roughly
- 6 garlic cloves, chopped very roughly
- 5-cm/2-inch piece lemon grass, sliced
- 4 fresh red chillies, deseeded and chopped
- grated rind of 1 lime
- 1 tsp salt
- 3 tbsp sunflower oil
- 250 g/9 oz/1 cup marinated tofu (bean curd), cut into 2.5 cm/1 inch cubes
- 125 g/4½ oz green beans, cut into 2.5cm/1 inch lengths
- 1 kg/2 lb 4 oz/6 cups cooked rice (300 g/10½ oz/1½ cups raw weight)
- 3 shallots, diced finely and deep-fried
- 1 spring onion (scallion), chopped finely
- 2 tbsp chopped roast peanuts
- 1 tbsp lime juice

1 

2 

3 

1 To make the curry paste, grind together the seeds and spices in a pestle and mortar or spice grinder.

2 Heat the sunflower oil in a preheated wok until it is really hot. Add the shallots, garlic and lemon grass and cook over a low heat until soft, about 5 minutes. Add the chillies and grind together with the dry spices. Stir in the lime rind and salt.

3 To make the curry, heat the oil in a wok or large, heavy frying pan (skillet). Cook the tofu (bean curd) over a high heat for 2 minutes to seal. Stir in the curry paste and beans. Add the rice and, stir over a high heat for about 3 minutes.

4 Transfer to a warmed serving dish. Sprinkle with the deep-fried shallots, spring onion (scallion) and peanuts. Squeeze over the lime juice.

Savoury (Bell) Pepper Bread

This flavoursome bread contains only the minimum amount of fat. Serve with a bowl of hot soup for a filling and nutritious light meal.

NUTRITIONAL INFORMATION

Calories	468	Sugars	11g
Protein	16g	Fat	5g
Carbohydrate	97g	Saturates	1g

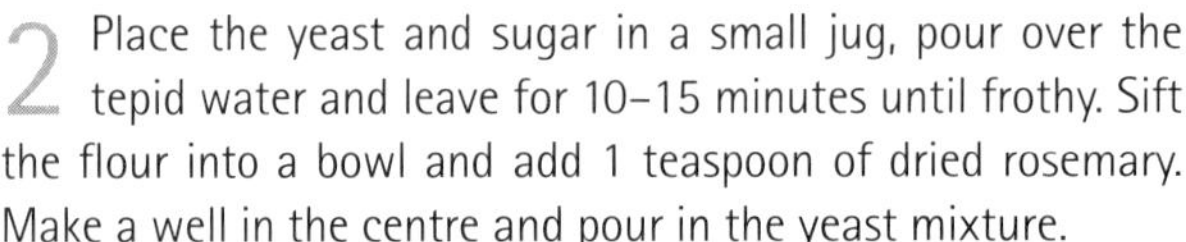

 2 HOURS  50 MINS

SERVES 4

INGREDIENTS

- 1 small red (bell) pepper
- 1 small green (bell) pepper
- 1 small yellow (bell) pepper
- 60 g/2 oz dry-pack sun-dried tomatoes
- 50 ml/2 fl oz/¼ cup boiling water
- 2 tsp dried yeast
- 1 tsp caster (superfine) sugar
- 150 ml/5 fl oz/⅔ cup tepid water
- 450 g/1 lb/4 cups strong white bread flour
- 2 tsp dried rosemary
- 2 tbsp tomato purée (paste)
- 150 ml/5 fl oz/⅔ cup low-fat natural fromage frais (unsweetened yogurt)
- 1 tbsp coarse salt
- 1 tbsp olive oil

1 Preheat the oven to 220°C/425°F/Gas Mark 7 and the grill (broiler) to hot. Halve and deseed the (bell) peppers, arrange on the grill (broiler) rack and cook until the skin is charred. Leave to cool for 10 minutes, peel off the skin and chop the flesh. Slice the tomatoes into strips, place in a bowl and pour over the boiling water. Leave to soak.

2 Place the yeast and sugar in a small jug, pour over the tepid water and leave for 10–15 minutes until frothy. Sift the flour into a bowl and add 1 teaspoon of dried rosemary. Make a well in the centre and pour in the yeast mixture.

3 Add the tomato purée (paste), tomatoes and soaking liquid, (bell) peppers, fromage frais (yogurt) and half the salt. Mix to form a soft dough. Turn out on to a lightly floured surface and knead for 3–4 minutes until smooth and elastic. Place in a lightly floured bowl, cover and leave in a warm room for 40 minutes until doubled in size.

4 Knead the dough again and place in a lightly greased 23 cm/9 inch round spring-clip cake tin. Using a wooden spoon, form 'dimples' in the surface. Cover and leave for 30 minutes. Brush with oil and sprinkle with rosemary and salt. Bake for 35–40 minutes, cool for 10 minutes and release from the tin. Leave to cool on a rack and serve.

2

3

4

COOK'S TIP

For a quick, filling snack serve the bread with a bowl of hot soup in winter, or a crisp leaf salad in summer.

Roasted (Bell) Pepper Bread

(Bell) peppers become sweet and mild when they are roasted and make this bread delicious.

NUTRITIONAL INFORMATION

Calories	426	Sugars	4g
Protein	12g	Fat	4g
Carbohydrate	90g	Saturates	1g

 1¾ HOURS  1 HR 5 MINS

SERVES 4

INGREDIENTS

- 1 red (bell) pepper, halved and deseeded
- 1 yellow (bell) pepper, halved and deseeded
- 2 sprigs of rosemary
- 1 tbsp olive oil
- 7 g/¼ oz dried yeast
- 1 tsp sugar
- 300 ml/½ pint/1¼ cups hand-hot water
- 450 g/1 lb strong white flour
- 1 tsp salt

1 Grease a 23 cm/9 inch deep round cake tin (pan).

2 Place the (bell) peppers and rosemary in a shallow roasting tin (pan). Pour over the oil and roast in a preheated oven, at 200°C/400°F/Gas Mark 6, for 20 minutes or until slightly charred. Remove the skin from the (bell) peppers and cut the flesh into slices.

3 Place the yeast and sugar in a small bowl and mix with 100 ml/3½ fl oz/8 tablespoons of hand-hot water. Leave to ferment in a warm place for 15 minutes.

4 Mix the flour and salt together in a large bowl. Stir in the yeast mixture and the remaining water and mix to form a smooth dough.

5 Knead the dough for about 5 minutes until smooth. Cover with oiled cling film (plastic wrap) and leave to rise for about 30 minutes or until doubled in size.

6 Cut the dough into 3 equal portions. Roll the portions into rounds slightly larger than the cake tin (pan).

7 Place 1 round in the base of the tin (pan) so that it reaches up the sides of the tin (pan) by about 2 cm/¾ inch. Top with half of the (bell) pepper mixture.

8 Place the second round of dough on top, followed by the remaining (bell) pepper mixture. Place the last round of dough on top, pushing the edges of the dough down the sides of the tin (pan).

9 Cover the dough with oiled cling film (plastic wrap) and leave to rise for 30–40 minutes. Return to the oven and bake for 45 minutes until golden or the base sounds hollow when lightly tapped. Serve warm.

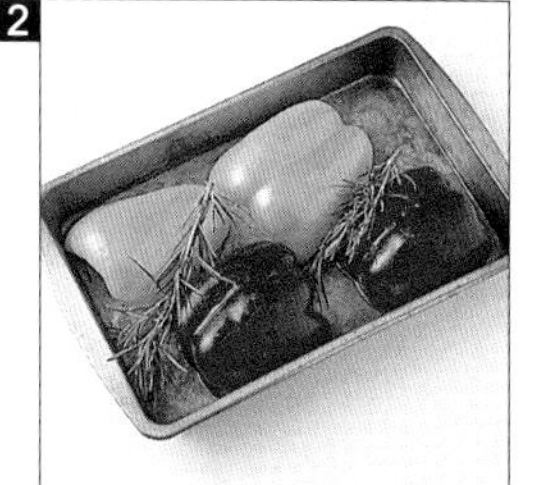
2

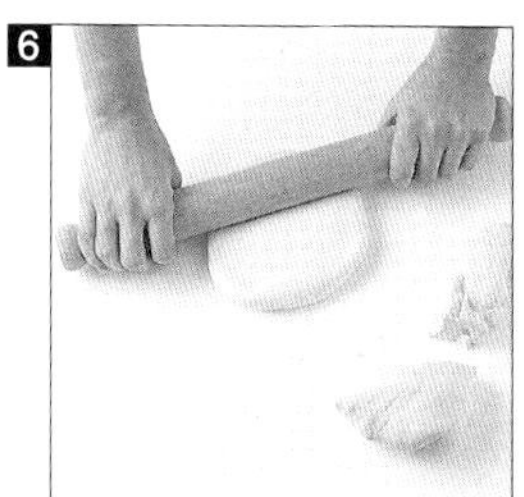
6

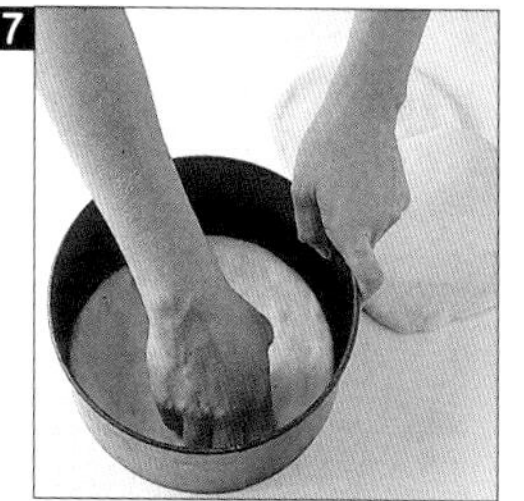
7

Garlic Potato Wedges

This is a great recipe for the barbecue (grill). Serve this tasty potato dish with grilled (broiled) meat or fish.

NUTRITIONAL INFORMATION

Calories	259	Sugars	1g
Protein	3g	Fat	17g
Carbohydrate	26g	Saturates	5g

 10 MINS  35 MINS

SERVES 4

INGREDIENTS

- 3 large baking potatoes, scrubbed
- 4 tbsp olive oil
- 25 g/1 oz butter
- 2 garlic cloves, chopped
- 1 tbsp chopped, fresh rosemary
- 1 tbsp chopped, fresh parsley
- 1 tbsp chopped, fresh thyme
- salt and pepper

1 Bring a large saucepan of water to the boil, add the potatoes and par-boil them for 10 minutes. Drain the potatoes, refresh under cold water and drain them again thoroughly.

2 Transfer the potatoes to a chopping board. When the potatoes are cold enough to handle, cut them into thick wedges, but do not remove the skins.

2

3

4

3 Heat the oil and butter in a small pan together with the garlic. Cook gently until the garlic begins to brown, then remove the pan from the heat.

4 Stir the herbs and salt and pepper to taste into the mixture in the pan.

5 Brush the herb mixture all over the potatoes.

6 Barbecue (grill) the potatoes over hot coals for 10–15 minutes, brushing liberally with any of the remaining herb and butter mixture, or until the potatoes are just tender.

7 Transfer the barbecued (grilled) garlic potatoes to a warm serving plate and serve as a starter or as a side dish.

COOK'S TIP

You may find it easier to barbecue (grill) these potatoes in a hinged rack or in a specially designed barbecue (grill) roasting tray.

Chapati

This Indian bread contains no fat, but some people like to brush them with a little melted butter before serving.

NUTRITIONAL INFORMATION

Calories	61	Sugars	0.5g
Protein	2g	Fat	0.3g
Carbohydrate	13g	Saturates	0g

 40 MINS  25 MINS

MAKES 10–12

INGREDIENTS

- 225 g/8 oz/1½ cups wholemeal flour (ata or chapati flour)
- ½ tsp salt
- 200 ml/⅓ pint/¾ cup water

1 Place the flour in a large mixing bowl. Add the salt and mix to combine.

2 Make a well in the middle of the flour and gradually pour in the water, mixing well with your fingers to form a supple dough.

3 Knead the dough for about 7-10 minutes. Ideally, set the dough aside and leave to rise for about 15-20 minutes, but if time is short roll out the dough straightaway. Divide the dough into 10-12 equal portions. Roll out each piece to form a round on a well-floured surface.

4 Place a heavy-based frying-pan (skillet) on a high heat. When steam starts to rise from the frying pan (skillet), lower the heat to medium.

5 Place a chapati in the frying pan (skillet) and when the chapati starts to bubble turn it over. Carefully press down on the chapati with a clean tea towel (dishcloth) or a flat spoon and turn the chapati over once again. Remove the chapati from the pan, set aside and keep warm while you make the others.

6 Repeat the process until all of the chapatis are cooked.

1

2

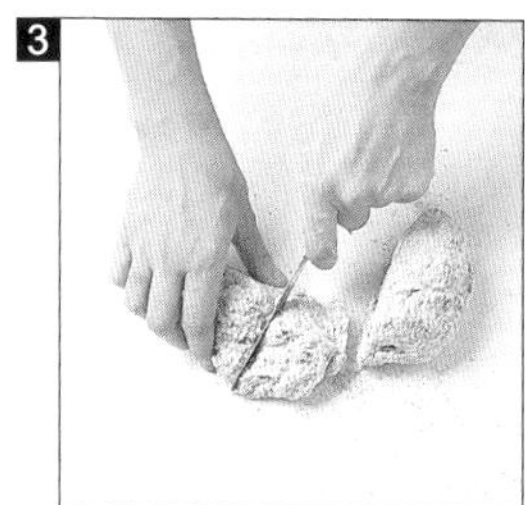
3

COOK'S TIP

Ideally, chapatis should be eaten as they come out of the frying pan (skillet), but if that is not practical keep them warm after cooking by wrapping them up in foil. In India, chapatis are sometimes cooked on a naked flame, which makes them puff up.

Roman Focaccia

Roman focaccia makes a delicious snack on its own or serve it with cured meats and salad for a quick supper.

NUTRITIONAL INFORMATION

Calories	119	Sugars	2g
Protein	3g	Fat	2g
Carbohydrate	24g	Saturates	0.3g

 1 HOUR  45 MINS

Makes 16 squares

INGREDIENTS

- 1 tsp sugar
- 300 ml/½ pint/1¼ cups hand-hot water
- 450 g/1 lb strong white flour
- 2 tsp salt
- 3 tbsp rosemary, chopped
- 2 tbsp olive oil
- 450 g/1 lb mixed red and white onions, sliced into rings
- 4 garlic cloves, sliced

1 Place the yeast and the sugar in a small bowl and mix with 100 ml/3½ fl oz/8 tablespoons of the water. Leave to ferment in a warm place for 15 minutes.

2 Mix the flour with the salt in a large bowl. Add the yeast mixture, half of the rosemary and the remaining water and mix to form a smooth dough. Knead the dough for 4 minutes.

3 Cover the dough with oiled cling film (plastic wrap) and leave to rise for 30 minutes or until doubled in size.

4 Meanwhile, heat the oil in a large pan. Add the onions and garlic and fry for 5 minutes or until softened. Cover the pan and continue to cook for 7–8 minutes or until the onions are lightly caramelized.

5 Remove the dough from the bowl and knead it again for 1–2 minutes.

6 Roll the dough out to form a square shape. The dough should be no more than 6 mm/¼ inch thick because it will rise during cooking. Place the dough on to a large baking tray (cookie sheet), pushing out the edges until even.

7 Spread the onions over the dough, and sprinkle with the remaining rosemary.

8 Bake in a preheated oven, at 200°C/400°F/Gas Mark 6, for 25–30 minutes or until a golden brown colour. Cut the focaccia into 16 squares and serve immediately.

2

4

6

Parathas

These triangular shaped breads are so easy to make and are the perfect addition to most Indian meals. Serve hot, spread with a little butter.

NUTRITIONAL INFORMATION

Calories	127	Sugars	0.5g
Protein	3g	Fat	4g
Carbohydrate	22g	Saturates	0.4g

 50 MINS  10 MINS

SERVES 6

INGREDIENTS

- 90 g/3 oz/¾ cup plain (all-purpose) wholemeal (whole wheat)flour
- 90 g/3 oz/¾ cup plain (all-purpose) flour
- pinch of salt
- 1 tbsp vegetable oil, plus extra for greasing
- 75 ml/3 fl oz/⅓ cup tepid water

1 Place the flours and the salt in a bowl. Drizzle 1 tablespoon of oil over the flour, add the tepid water and mix to form a soft dough, adding a little more water, if necessary. Knead on a lightly floured surface until smooth, then cover and leave for 30 minutes.

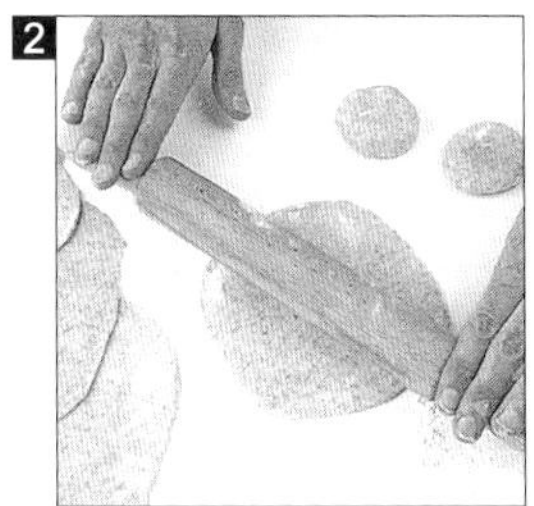

2

2 Knead the dough on a floured surface and divide into 6 equal pieces. Shape each one into a ball. Roll out on a floured surface to a 15 cm/6 inch round and brush very lightly with oil.

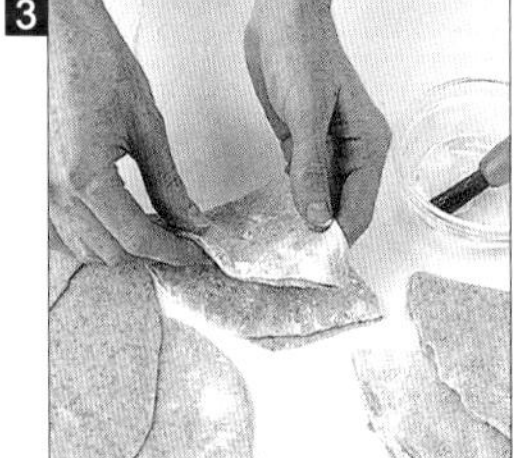

3

3 Fold in half, and then in half again to form a triangle. Roll out to form an 18 cm/7 in triangle (when measured from point to centre top), dusting with extra flour as necessary.

4

4 Brush a large, heavy-based frying pan (skillet) with a little oil and heat until hot, then add one or two parathas and cook for about 1–1½ minutes. Brush the surfaces very lightly with oil, then turn and cook the other sides for 1½ minutes until completely cooked through.

5 Place the cooked parathas on a plate and cover with foil, or place between the folds of a clean tea towel (dish cloth) to keep warm, while you are cooking the remainder in the same way, greasing the pan between cooking each batch.

VARIATION

If the parathas puff up a lot during cooking, press down lightly with a fish slice. Make parathas in advance, if wished: wrap in kitchen foil and reheat in a hot oven for about 15 minutes when required.

Italian Bruschetta

It is important to use a good quality olive oil for this recipe. Serve the bruschetta with kebabs (kabobs) or fish for a really summery taste.

NUTRITIONAL INFORMATION

Calories	415	Sugars	2g
Protein	8g	Fat	24g
Carbohydrate	45g	Saturates	4g

 10 MINS  10 MINS

Makes 1 loaf

INGREDIENTS

- 1 ciabatta loaf or small stick of French bread
- 1 plump clove garlic
- extra virgin olive oil
- fresh Parmesan cheese, grated (optional)

1 Slice the bread in half crossways and again lengthwise to give 4 portions.

2 Do not peel the garlic clove, but cut it in half.

3 Barbecue (grill) the bread over hot coals for 2–3 minutes on both sides or until golden brown.

4 Rub the garlic, cut side down, all over the toasted surface of the bread.

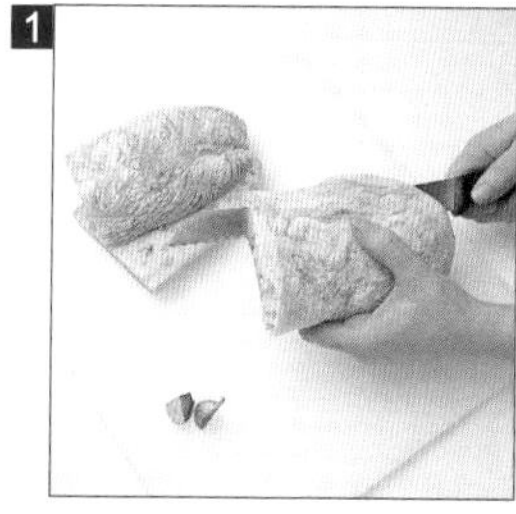
1

3

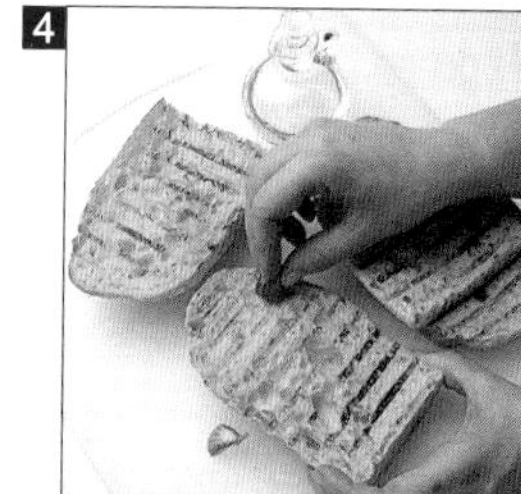
4

5 Drizzle the olive oil over the bread and serve hot as an accompaniment.

6 If using Parmesan cheese, sprinkle the cheese over the bread.

7 Return the bread to the barbecue (grill), cut side up, for 1–2 minutes or until the cheese just begins to melt. Serve hot.

COOK'S TIP

As ready-grated Parmesan quickly loses its pungency and 'bite', it is better to buy small quantities of the cheese in one piece and grate it as needed. Tightly wrapped in cling film (plastic wrap) or foil, it will keep in the refrigerator for several months.

Naan Bread

There are many ways of making naan bread, but this recipe is very easy to follow. Naan bread should be served immediately after cooking.

NUTRITIONAL INFORMATION

Calories	152	Sugars	1g
Protein	3g	Fat	7g
Carbohydrate	20g	Saturates	4g

2¼ HOURS · 10 MINS

SERVES 8

INGREDIENTS

- 1 tsp sugar
- 1 tsp fresh yeast
- 150 ml/¼ pint/⅔ cup warm water
- 200 g/7 oz/1½ cups plain (all-purpose) flour
- 1 tbsp ghee
- 1 tsp salt
- 50 g/1¾ oz/4 tbsp unsalted butter
- 1 tsp poppy seeds

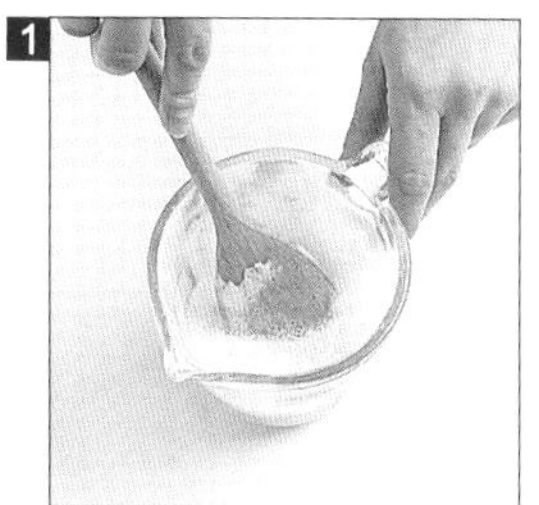

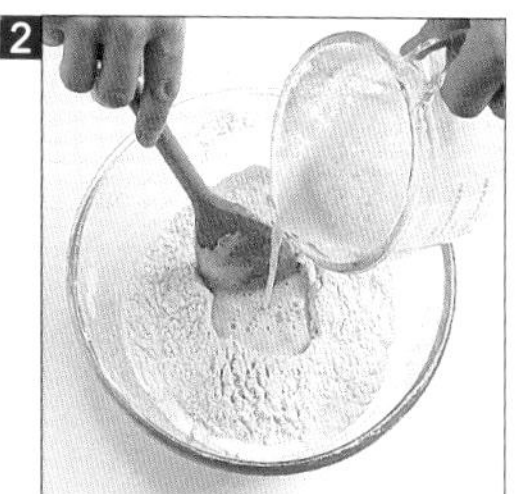

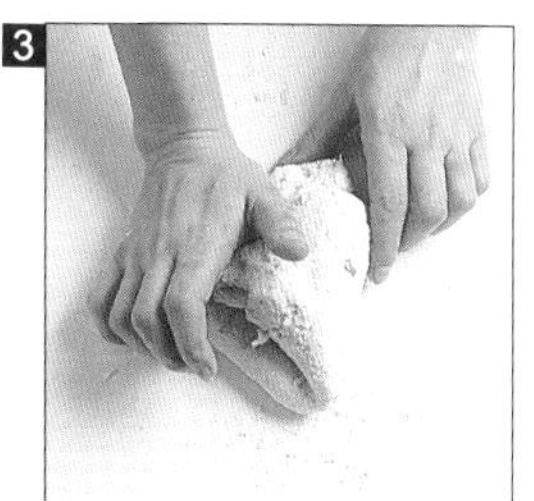

1 Put the sugar and yeast in a small bowl or jug together with the warm water and mix thoroughly until the yeast has completely dissolved. Set aside for about 10 minutes, or until the mixture is frothy.

2 Place the flour in a large mixing bowl. Make a well in the centre of the flour, add the ghee and salt and pour in the yeast mixture. Mix thoroughly to form a dough, using your hands and adding more water if required.

3 Turn the dough out on to a floured work surface (counter) and knead for about 5 minutes, or until smooth.

4 Return the dough to the bowl, cover and set aside to rise in a warm place for 1½ hours, or until doubled in size.

5 Turn the dough out on to a floured surface and knead for a further 2 minutes. Break off small balls with your hand and pat them into rounds about 12 cm/ 5 inches in diameter and 1 cm/ ½ inch thick.

6 Place the dough rounds on a greased sheet of foil and grill (broil) under a very hot preheated grill (broiler) for 7–10 minutes, turning twice and brushing with the butter and sprinkling with the poppy seeds.

7 Serve warm immediately, or keep wrapped in foil until required.

Lightly Fried Bread

This is perfect with egg dishes and vegetable curries. Allow 2 portions of bread per person. The nutritional information is for each portion.

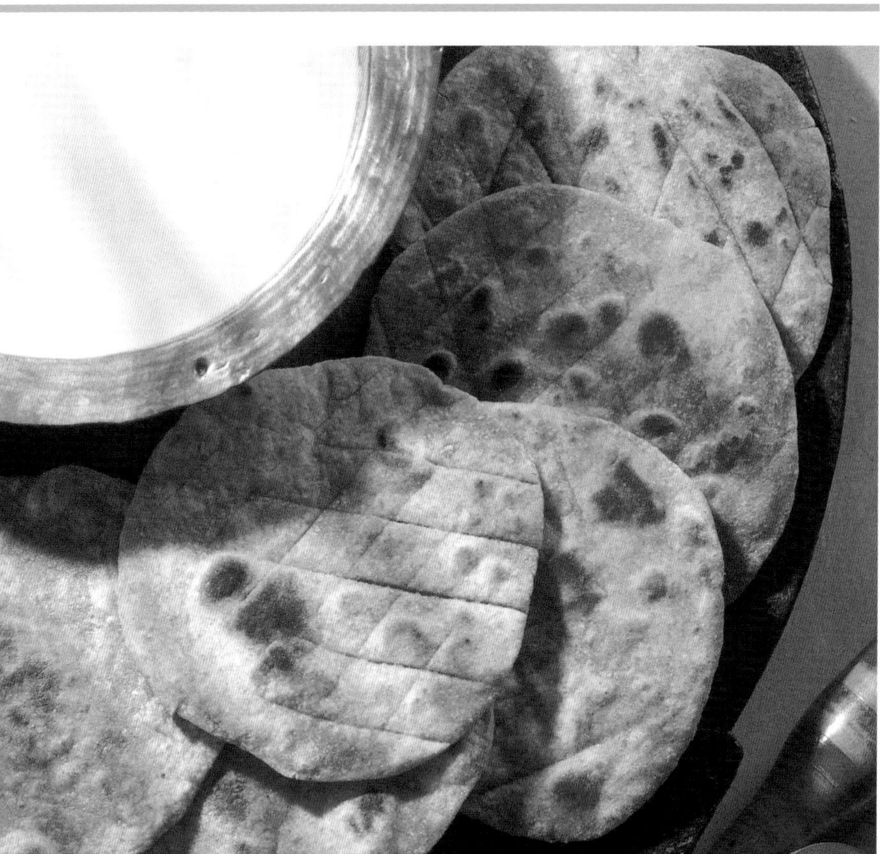

NUTRITIONAL INFORMATION

Calories	133	Sugars	1g
Protein	3g	Fat	7g
Carbohydrate	17g	Saturates	4g

 35 MINS  20–25 MINS

MAKES 10

INGREDIENTS

225 g/8 oz/1½ cups wholemeal (whole wheat) ata or chapati flour

½ tsp salt

1 tbsp ghee

300 ml/½ pint/1¼ cups water

1 Place the flour and the salt in a large mixing bowl and mix to combine.

2 Make a well in the centre of the flour. Add the ghee and rub in well. Gradually pour in the water and work to form a soft dough. Set the dough aside to rise for 10–15 minutes.

3 Carefully knead the dough for about 5–7 minutes. Divide the dough into about 10 equal portions.

2

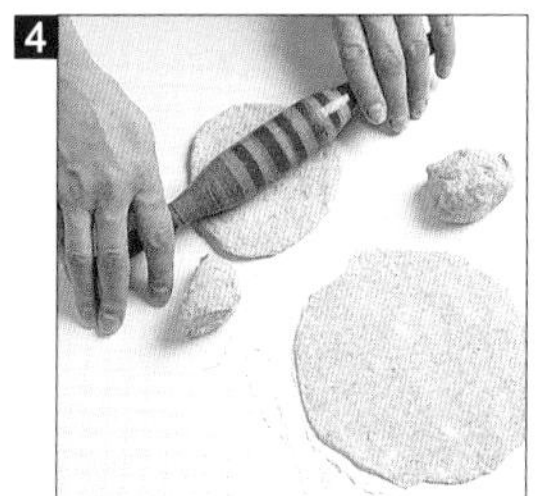

4

6

4 On a lightly floured surface, roll out each dough portion to form a flat pancake shape.

5 Using a sharp knife, lightly draw lines in a criss-cross pattern on each rolled-out dough portion.

6 Heat a heavy-based frying pan (skillet). Gently place the dough portions, one by one, into the pan.

7 Cook the bread for about 1 minute, then turn over and spread with 1 teaspoon of ghee. Turn the bread over again and fry gently, moving it around the pan with a spatula, until golden. Turn the bread over once again, then remove from the pan and keep warm while you cook the remaining batches.

COOK'S TIP

In India, breads are cooked on a tava, a traditional flat griddle. A large frying pan (skillet) makes an adequate substitute.

Sun-dried Tomato Loaf

This delicious tomato bread is great with cheese or soup or to make an unusual sandwich. This recipe makes one loaf.

NUTRITIONAL INFORMATION

Calories	403	Sugars	5g
Protein	12g	Fat	2g
Carbohydrate	91g	Saturates	0.3g

 $1^3/_4$ HOURS  35 MINS

SERVES 4

INGREDIENTS

- 7 g/¼ oz dried yeast
- 1 tsp sugar
- 300 ml/½ pint/1¼ cups hand-hot water
- 1 tsp salt
- 2 tsp dried basil
- 450 g/1 lb strong white flour
- 2 tbsp sun-dried tomato paste or tomato purée (paste)
- 12 sun-dried tomatoes, cut into strips

1 Place the yeast and sugar in a bowl and mix with 100 ml/3½ fl oz/ 8 tablespoons of the water. Leave to ferment in a warm place for 15 minutes.

2 Place the flour in a bowl and stir in the salt. Make a well in the dry ingredients and add the basil, the yeast mixture, tomato paste and half of the remaining water. Using a wooden spoon, draw the flour into the liquid and mix to form a dough, adding the rest of the water gradually.

3 Turn out the dough on to a floured surface and knead for 5 minutes or until smooth. Cover with oiled cling film (plastic wrap) and leave in a warm place to rise for about 30 minutes or until doubled in size.

2

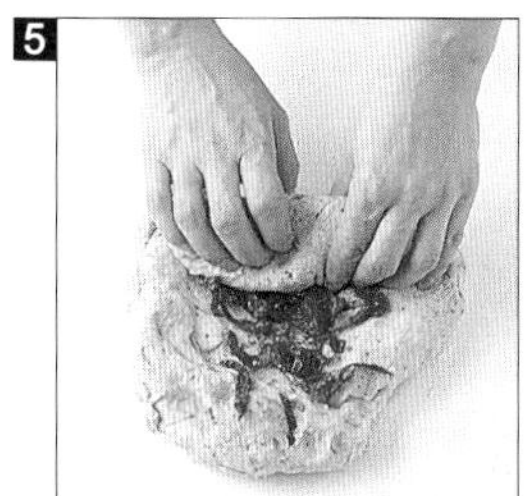

5

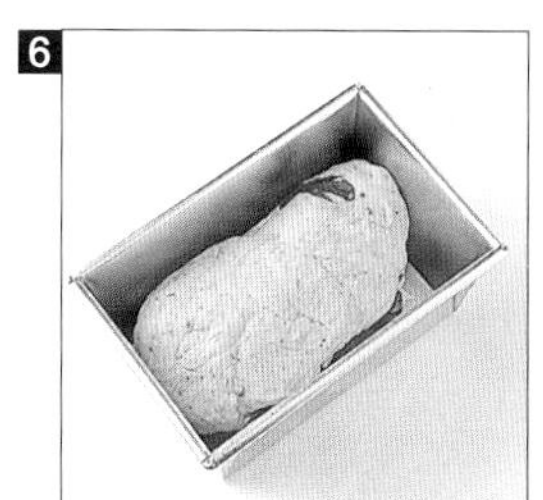

6

4 Lightly grease a 900 g/2 lb loaf tin (pan).

5 Remove the dough from the bowl and knead in the sun-dried tomatoes. Knead again for 2–3 minutes.

6 Place the dough in the tin (pan) and leave to rise for 30–40 minutes.or until it has doubled in size again,. Bake in a preheated oven, at 190°C/375°F/Gas Mark 5, for 30–35 minutes or until golden and the base sounds hollow when tapped.

COOK'S TIP

You could make mini sun-dried tomato loaves for children. Divide the dough into 8 equal portions, leave to rise and bake in mini-loaf tins (pans) for 20 minutes. Alternatively, make 12 small rounds, leave to rise and bake as rolls for 12–15 minutes.

Olive Oil Bread with Cheese

This flat cheese bread is sometimes called *foccacia*. It is delicious served with *antipasto* or simply on its own. This recipe makes one loaf.

NUTRITIONAL INFORMATION

Calories	586	Sugars	3g
Protein	22g	Fat	26g
Carbohydrate	69g	Saturates	12g

 1 HOUR 30 MINS

SERVES 4

INGREDIENTS

- 15 g/½ oz dried yeast
- 1 tsp sugar
- 250 ml/9 fl oz hand-hot water
- 350 g/12 oz strong flour
- 1 tsp salt
- 3 tbsp olive oil
- 200 g/7 oz pecorino cheese, cubed
- ½ tbsp fennel seeds, lightly crushed

1 Mix the yeast with the sugar and 100 ml/3½ fl oz/8 tbsp of the water. Leave to ferment in a warm place for about 15 minutes.

2 Mix the flour with the salt. Add 1 tablespoon of the oil, the yeast mixture and the remaining water to form a smooth dough. Knead the dough for 4 minutes.

3 Divide the dough into 2 equal portions. Roll out each portion to a form a round 6 mm/¼ inch thick. Place 1 round on a baking tray (cookie sheet).

4 Scatter the cheese and half of the fennel seeds evenly over the round.

5 Place the second round on top and squeeze the edges together to seal so that the filling does not leak during the cooking time.

6 Using a sharp knife, make a few slashes in the top of the dough and brush with the remaining olive oil.

7 Sprinkle with the remaining fennel seeds and leave the dough to rise for 20–30 minutes.

8 Bake in a preheated oven, at 200°C/400°F/Gas Mark 6, for 30 minutes or until golden brown. Serve immediately.

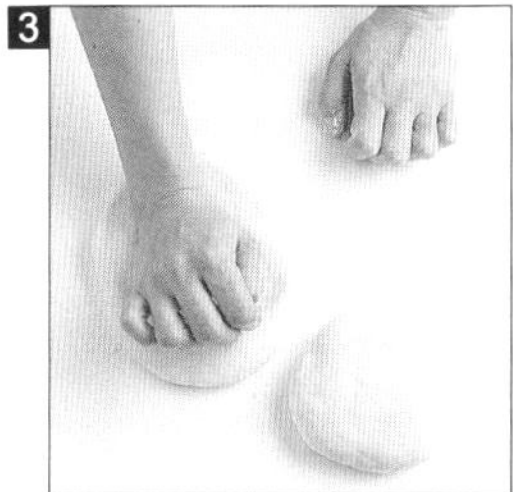
3

4

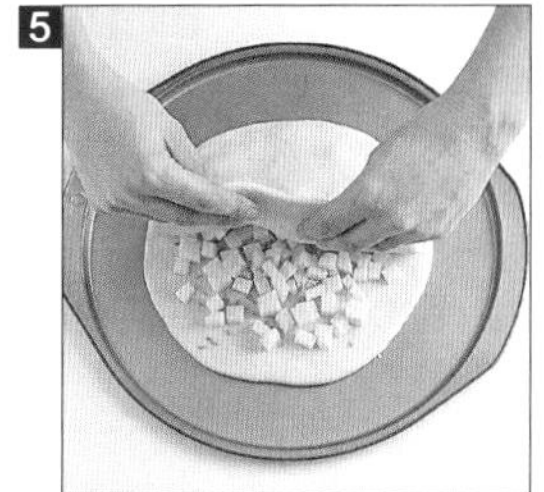
5

COOK'S TIP

Pecorino is a hard, quite salty cheese, which is sold in most large supermarkets and Italian delicatessens. If you cannot obtain pecorino, use strong Cheddar or Parmesan cheese instead.

Garlic Bread

A perennial favourite, garlic bread is perfect with a range of barbecue (grill) meals.

NUTRITIONAL INFORMATION

Calories	261	Sugars	1g
Protein	3g	Fat	22g
Carbohydrate	15g	Saturates	14g

 10 MINS  15 MINS

SERVES 6

INGREDIENTS

- 150 g/5½ oz butter, softened
- 3 cloves garlic, crushed
- 2 tbsp chopped, fresh parsley
- pepper
- 1 large or 2 small sticks of French bread

1 Mix together the butter, garlic and parsley in a bowl until well combined. Season with pepper to taste and mix well.

2 Cut the French bread into thick slices.

3 Spread the flavoured butter over one side of each slice and reassemble the loaf on a large sheet of thick kitchen foil.

4 Wrap the bread well and barbecue (grill) over hot coals for 10–15 minutes until the butter melts and the bread is piping hot.

5 Serve as an accompaniment to a wide range of dishes.

1

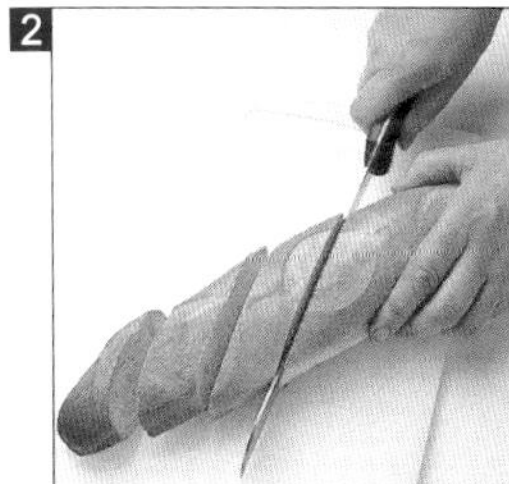
2

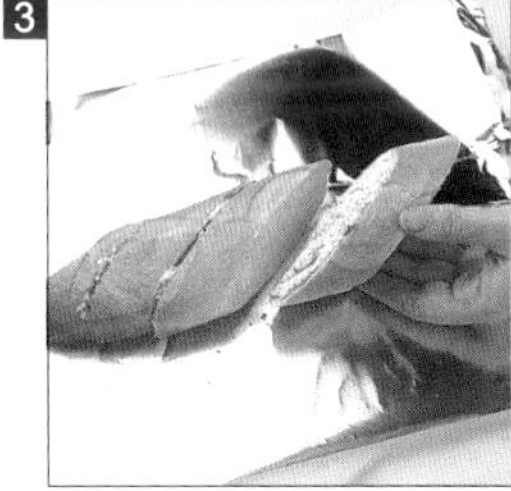
3

Desserts

Not everyone has a sweet tooth or is a great pudding fanatic, but most people will have a longing for some type of sweet from time to time, and a dessert is always a good way to round off a meal. Here is a selection of all-time classic desserts from around the world. Bread & Butter Pudding, Syrup Sponge and Summer Pudding are great British favourites while classics from other countries include Tiramisu and Zabaglione from Italy and Cherry Clafoutis from France. There is also a selection of Indian desserts for those who have a very sweet tooth: Sweet Carrot Halva, Semolina Dessert and Indian Vermicelli Pudding are just a few. Fruit is always a good way to end a meal as it is naturally rich in sugar and this chapter contains various fruit and fruit-based desserts including several variations on fruit salad.

Cherry Clafoutis

This is a hot dessert that is simple and quick to put together. Try the batter with other fruits. Apricots and plums are particularly delicious.

NUTRITIONAL INFORMATION

Calories	261	Sugars	24g
Protein	10g	Fat	6g
Carbohydrate	40g	Saturates	3g

10 MINS 40 MINS

SERVES 6

INGREDIENTS

- 125 g/4½ oz/1 cup plain (all-purpose) flour
- 4 eggs, lightly beaten
- 2 tbsp caster (superfine) sugar
- pinch of salt
- 600 ml/1 pint/2½ cups milk
- butter, for greasing
- 500 g/1 lb 2 oz black cherries, fresh or canned, stoned (pitted)
- 3 tbsp brandy
- 1 tbsp sugar, to decorate

1 Sift the flour into a large mixing bowl. Make a well in the centre and add the eggs, sugar and salt. Gradually, draw in the flour from around the edges and whisk.

2 Pour in the milk and whisk the batter thoroughly until very smooth.

3 Thoroughly grease a 1.75 litre/3 pint/7½ cup ovenproof serving dish with butter and pour in about half of the batter.

4 Spoon over the cherries and pour the remaining batter over the top. Sprinkle the brandy over the batter.

5 Bake in a preheated oven, 180°C/350°F/Gas Mark 4, for 40 minutes, until risen and golden.

6 Remove from the oven and sprinkle over the sugar just before serving. Serve warm.

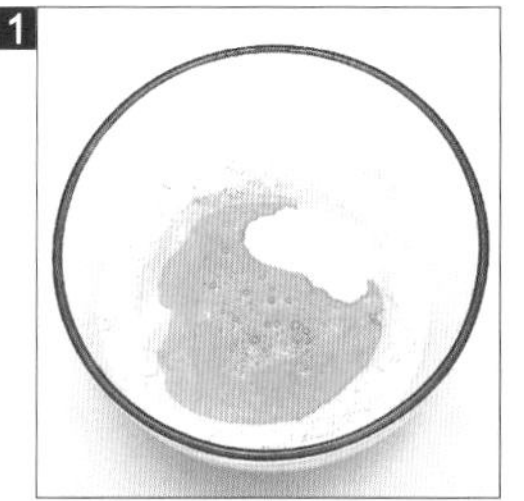

1

2

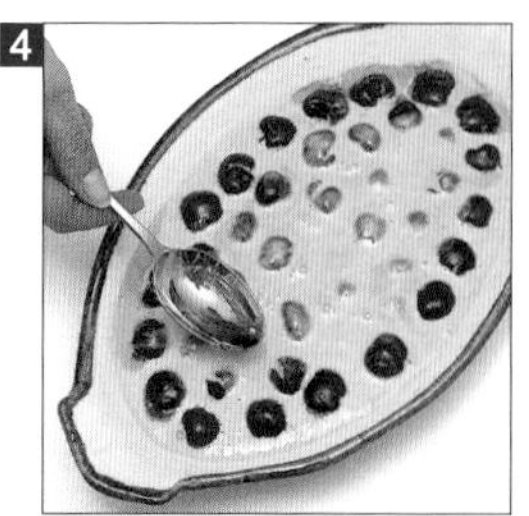

4

Tiramisu Layers

This is a modern version of the well-known and very traditional chocolate dessert from Italy.

NUTRITIONAL INFORMATION

Calories	798	Sugars	60g
Protein	12g	Fat	50g
Carbohydrate	76g	Saturates	25g

1¼ HOURS — 5 MINS

SERVES 6

INGREDIENTS

- 300 g/10½ oz dark chocolate
- 400 g/14 oz mascarpone cheese
- 150 ml/¼ pint/⅔ cup double (heavy) cream, whipped until it just holds its shape
- 400 ml/14 fl oz black coffee with 50 g/1¾ oz caster (superfine) sugar, cooled
- 6 tbsp dark rum or brandy
- 36 sponge fingers (lady-fingers), about 400 g/14 oz
- cocoa powder, to dust

1

1

2

1 Melt the chocolate in a bowl set over a saucepan of simmering water, stirring occasionally. Leave the chocolate to cool slightly, then stir it into the mascarpone and cream.

2 Mix the coffee and rum together in a bowl. Dip the sponge fingers (lady-fingers) into the mixture briefly so that they absorb the coffee and rum liquid but do not become soggy.

3 Place 3 sponge fingers (lady-fingers) on 3 serving plates.

4 Spoon a layer of the mascarpone and chocolate mixture over the sponge fingers (lady-fingers).

5 Place 3 more sponge fingers (lady-fingers) on top of the mascarpone layer. Spread another layer of mascarpone and chocolate mixture and place 3 more sponge fingers (lady-fingers) on top.

6 Leave the tiramisu to chill in the refrigerator for at least 1 hour. Dust all over with a little cocoa powder just before serving.

VARIATION

Try adding 50 g/1¾ oz toasted, chopped hazelnuts to the chocolate cream mixture in step 1, if you prefer.

Coconut Cream Moulds

Smooth, creamy and refreshing – these tempting little custards are made with an unusual combination of coconut milk, cream and eggs.

NUTRITIONAL INFORMATION

Calories	288	Sugar	24g
Protein	4g	Fat	20g
Carbohydrate	25g	Saturates	14g

10 MINS 45 MINS

SERVES 8

INGREDIENTS

CARAMEL

- 125 g/4½ oz/½ cup granulated sugar
- 150 ml/¼ pint/⅔ cup water

CUSTARD

- 300 ml/½ pint/1¼ cups water
- 90g/3 oz creamed coconut, chopped
- 2 eggs
- 2 egg yolks
- 1½ tbsp caster (superfine) sugar
- 300 ml/½ pint/1¼ cups single (light) cream
- sliced banana or slivers of fresh pineapple
- 1-2 tbsp freshly grated or desiccated (shredded) coconut

1 Have ready 8 small ovenproof dishes about 150 ml/¼ pint/⅔ cup capacity. To make the caramel, place the granulated sugar and water in a saucepan and heat gently to dissolve the sugar, then boil rapidly, without stirring, until the mixture turns a rich golden brown.

2 Immediately remove the pan from the heat and dip the base into a bowl of cold water in order to stop it cooking further. Quickly, but carefully, pour the caramel into the ovenproof dishes to coat the bases.

3 To make the custard, place the water in the same saucepan, add the coconut and heat, stirring constantly, until the coconut dissolves. Place the eggs, egg yolks and caster (superfine) sugar in a bowl and beat well with a fork. Add the hot coconut milk and stir well to dissolve the sugar. Stir in the cream and strain the mixture into a jug.

4 Arrange the dishes in a roasting tin (pan) and fill with enough cold water to come halfway up the sides of the dishes. Pour the custard mixture into the caramel-lined dishes, cover with greaseproof paper or foil and cook in a preheated oven, 150°C/300°F/Gas Mark 2, for about 40 minutes, or until set.

5 Remove the dishes, set aside to cool and then chill overnight. To serve, run a knife around the edge of each dish and turn out on to a serving plate. Serve with slices of banana or slivers of fresh pineapple sprinkled with freshly grated or desiccated coconut.

1

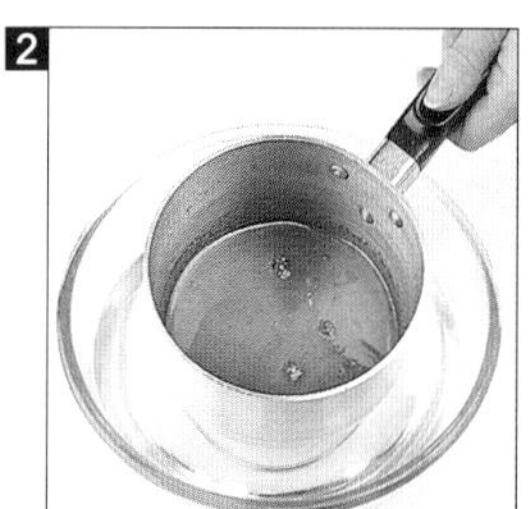
2

3

Exotic Fruit Parcels

Delicious pieces of exotic fruit are warmed through in a deliciously scented sauce to make a fabulous barbecue (grill) dessert.

NUTRITIONAL INFORMATION

Calories	43	Sugars	9g
Protein	2g	Fat	0.3g
Carbohydrate	9g	Saturates	0.1g

 40 MINS  20 MINS

SERVES 4

INGREDIENTS

- 1 paw-paw (papaya)
- 1 mango
- 1 star fruit
- 1 tbsp grenadine
- 3 tbsp orange juice
- single (light) cream or natural yogurt, to serve

1

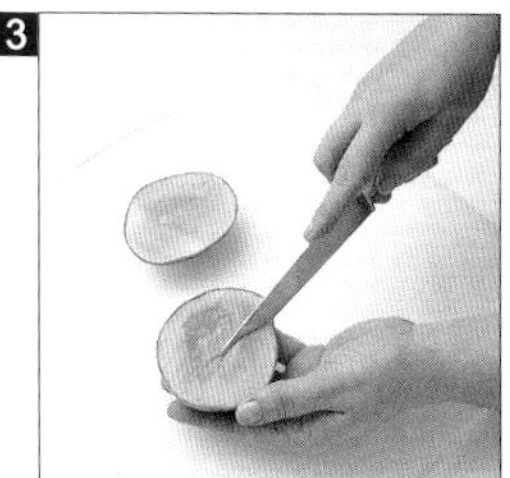
3

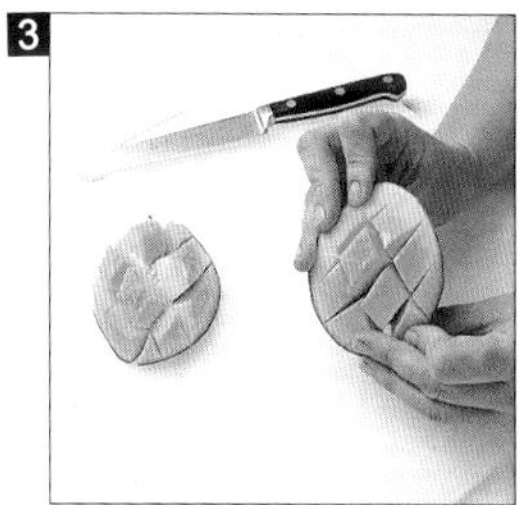
3

1 Cut the paw-paw (papaya) in half, scoop out the seeds and discard them. Peel the paw-paw (papaya) and cut the flesh into thick slices.

2 Prepare the mango by cutting it lengthways in half either side of the central stone.

3 Score each mango half in a criss-cross pattern. Push each mango half inside out to separate the cubes and cut them away from the peel.

4 Using a sharp knife, thickly slice the star fruit.

5 Place all of the fruit in a bowl and mix them together.

6 Mix the grenadine and orange juice together and pour over the fruit. Leave to marinate for at least 30 minutes.

7 Divide the fruit among 4 double thickness squares of kitchen foil and gather up the edges to form a parcel that encloses the fruit.

8 Place the foil parcel on a rack set over warm coals and barbecue (grill) the fruit for 15–20 minutes.

9 Serve the fruit in the parcel, with the low-fat natural yogurt.

COOK'S TIP

Grenadine is a sweet syrup made from pomegranates. If you prefer you could use pomegranate juice instead. To extract the juice, cut the pomegranate in half and squeeze gently with a lemon squeezer – do not press too hard or the juice may become bitter.

Tuscan Pudding

These baked mini-ricotta puddings are delicious served warm or chilled and will keep in the refrigerator for 3–4 days.

NUTRITIONAL INFORMATION

Calories	293	Sugars	28g
Protein	9g	Fat	17g
Carbohydrate	28g	Saturates	9g

 20 MINS  15 MINS

SERVES 4

INGREDIENTS

- 15 g/½ oz/1 tbsp butter
- 75 g/2¾ oz mixed dried fruit
- 250 g/9 oz ricotta cheese
- 3 egg yolks
- 50 g/1¾ oz caster (superfine) sugar
- 1 tsp cinnamon
- finely grated rind of 1 orange, plus extra to decorate
- crème fraîche (soured cream), to serve

1

3

4

1 Lightly grease 4 mini pudding basins or ramekin dishes with the butter.

2 Put the dried fruit in a bowl and cover with warm water. Leave to soak for 10 minutes.

3 Beat the ricotta cheese with the egg yolks in a bowl. Stir in the caster (superfine) sugar, cinnamon and orange rind and mix to combine.

4 Drain the dried fruit in a sieve set over a bowl. Mix the drained fruit with the ricotta cheese mixture.

5 Spoon the mixture into the basins or ramekin dishes.

6 Bake in a preheated oven, at 180°C/350°F/Gas Mark 4, for 15 minutes. The tops should be firm to the touch but not brown.

7 Decorate the puddings with grated orange rind. Serve warm or chilled with a dollop of crème fraîche (soured cream), if liked.

COOK'S TIP

Crème fraîche (soured cream) has a slightly sour, nutty taste and is very thick. It is suitable for cooking, but has the same fat content as double (heavy) cream. It can be made by stirring cultured buttermilk into double (heavy) cream and refrigerating overnight.

Grilled Fruit Platter

This variation of a hot fruit salad includes wedges of tropical fruits, dusted with sugar beforc grilling and served with a lime 'butter'.

NUTRITIONAL INFORMATION

Calories	120	Sugars	20g
Protein	1g	Fat	3g
Carbohydrate	21g	Saturates	1g

40 MINS 5 MINS

SERVES 10

INGREDIENTS

1 baby pineapple

1 ripe paw-paw (papaya)

1 ripe mango

2 kiwi fruit

4 apple (finger) bananas

4 tbsp dark rum

1 tsp ground allspice

2 tbsp lime juice

4 tbsp dark muscovado sugar

LIME 'BUTTER'

60 g/2 oz low-fat spread

½ tsp finely grated lime rind

1 tbsp icing (confectioners') sugar

1

3

5

1 Using a sharp knife, quarter the pineapple, trimming away most of the leaves, and place in a shallow dish. Peel the paw-paw (papaya), cut it in half and scoop out the seeds. Cut the flesh into thick wedges and place in the same dish as the pineapple.

2 Peel the mango, cut either side of the smooth, central flat stone and remove the stone. Slice the flesh into thick wedges. Peel the kiwi fruit and cut in half. Peel the bananas. Add all of these fruits to the dish.

3 Sprinkle over the rum, allspice and lime juice, cover and leave at room temperature for 30 minutes, turning occasionally, to allow the flavours to develop.

4 Meanwhile, make the 'butter'. Place the low-fat spread in a small bowl and beat in the lime rind and sugar until well mixed. Leave to chill until required.

5 Preheat the grill (broiler) to hot. Drain the fruit, reserving the juices, and arrange in the grill (broiler) pan. Sprinkle with the sugar and grill (broil) for 3–4 minutes until hot, bubbling and just beginning to char.

6 Transfer the fruit to a serving plate and spoon over the juices. Serve with the lime 'butter'.

Honey & Walnut Nests

Pistachio nuts and honey are combined with crisp cooked angel hair pasta in this unusual dessert.

NUTRITIONAL INFORMATION

Calories	802	Sugars	53g
Protein	13g	Fat	48g
Carbohydrate	85g	Saturates	16g

10 MINS

1 HOUR

SERVES 4

INGREDIENTS

- 225 g/8 oz angel hair pasta
- 115 g/4 oz/8 tbsp butter
- 175 g/6 oz/1½ cups shelled pistachio nuts, chopped
- 115 g/4 oz/½ cup sugar
- 115 g/4 oz/⅓ cup clear honey
- 150 ml/¼ pint/⅔ cup water
- 2 tsp lemon juice
- salt
- Greek-style yogurt, to serve

1 Bring a large saucepan of lightly salted water to the boil. Add the angel hair pasta and cook for 8–10 minutes or until tender, but still firm to the bite. Drain the pasta and return to the pan. Add the butter and toss to coat the pasta thoroughly. Set aside to cool.

2 Arrange 4 small flan or poaching rings on a baking tray (cookie sheet). Divide the angel hair pasta into 8 equal quantities and spoon 4 of them into the rings. Press down lightly. Top the pasta with half of the nuts, then add the remaining pasta.

3 Bake in a preheated oven, at 180°C/350°F/Gas Mark 4, for 45 minutes, or until golden brown.

4 Meanwhile, put the sugar, honey and water in a saucepan and bring to the boil over a low heat, stirring constantly until the sugar has dissolved completely. Simmer for 10 minutes, add the lemon juice and simmer for 5 minutes.

5 Using a palette knife (spatula), carefully transfer the angel hair nests to a serving dish. Pour over the honey syrup, sprinkle over the remaining nuts and set aside to cool completely before serving. Serve the Greek-style yogurt separately.

2

2

2

COOK'S TIP

Angel hair pasta is also known as *capelli d'Angelo.* Long and very fine, it is usually sold in small bunches that already resemble nests.

Panforte di Siena

This famous Tuscan honey and nut cake is a Christmas speciality. In Italy it is sold in pretty boxes, and served in very thin slices.

NUTRITIONAL INFORMATION

Calories	257	Sugars	29g
Protein	5g	Fat	13g
Carbohydrate	33g	Saturates	1g

10 MINS 1¼ HOURS

SERVES 12

INGREDIENTS

- 125 g/4½ oz/1 cup split whole almonds
- 125 g/4½ oz/¾ cup hazelnuts
- 90 g/3 oz/½ cup cut mixed peel
- 60 g/2 oz/⅓ cup no-soak dried apricots
- 60 g/2 oz glacé or crystallized pineapple
- grated rind of 1 large orange
- 60 g/2 oz/½ cup plain (all-purpose) flour
- 2 tbsp cocoa powder
- 2 tsp ground cinnamon
- 125 g/4½ oz/½ cup caster (superfine) sugar
- 175 g/6 oz/½ cup honey
- icing (confectioners') sugar, for dredging

2

3

6

1 Toast the almonds under the grill (broiler) until lightly browned and place in a bowl.

2 Toast the hazelnuts until the skins split. Place on a dry tea towel (dish cloth) and rub off the skins. Roughly chop the hazelnuts and add to the almonds with the mixed peel.

3 Chop the apricots and pineapple fairly finely, add to the nuts with the orange rind and mix well.

4 Sift the flour with the cocoa and cinnamon, add to the nut mixture; mix.

5 Line a round 20 cm/8 inch cake tin or deep loose-based flan tin (pan) with baking parchment.

6 Put the sugar and honey into a saucepan and heat until the sugar dissolves, then boil gently for about 5 minutes or until the mixture thickens and begins to turn a deeper shade of brown. Quickly add to the nut mixture and mix evenly. Turn into the prepared tin (pan) and level the top using the back of a damp spoon.

7 Cook in a preheated oven, at 150°C/300°F/Gas Mark 2, for 1 hour. Remove from the oven and leave in the tin (pan) until cold. Take out of the tin (pan) and carefully peel off the paper. Before serving, dredge the cake heavily with sifted icing (confectioners') sugar. Serve in very thin slices.

Aromatic Fruit Salad

The fruits in this salad are arranged attractively on serving plates with a spicy syrup spooned over.

NUTRITIONAL INFORMATION	
Calories 125	Sugars 29g
Protein 3g	Fat 1g
Carbohydrate ...29g	Saturates 0.2g

25 MINS 5 MINS

SERVES 6

INGREDIENTS

- 60 g/1½ oz/3 tbsp granulated sugar
- 150 ml/¼ pint/⅔ cup water
- 1 cinnamon stick or large piece of cassia bark
- 4 cardamom pods, crushed
- 1 clove
- juice of 1 orange
- juice of 1 lime
- ½ honeydew melon
- a good-sized wedge of watermelon
- 2 ripe guavas
- 3 ripe nectarines
- about 18 strawberries
- a little toasted, shredded coconut, for sprinkling
- sprigs of mint or rose petals, to decorate
- strained low-fat (unsweetened) yogurt, for serving

1 First prepare the syrup. Put the sugar, water, cinnamon, cardamom pods and cloves into a pan and bring to the boil, stirring to dissolve the sugar. Simmer for 2 minutes, then remove from heat.

2 Add the orange and lime juices to the syrup and leave to cool and infuse while preparing the fruits.

3 Peel and remove the seeds from the melons and cut the flesh into neat slices.

4 Cut the guavas in half, scoop out the seeds, then peel and slice the flesh neatly.

5 Cut the nectarines into slices and hull and slice the strawberries.

6 Arrange the slices of fruit attractively on 6 serving plates.

7 Strain the prepared cooled syrup and spoon over the sliced fruits.

8 Sprinkle the fruit salad with a little toasted coconut. Decorate each serving with sprigs of mint or rose petals and serve with yogurt.

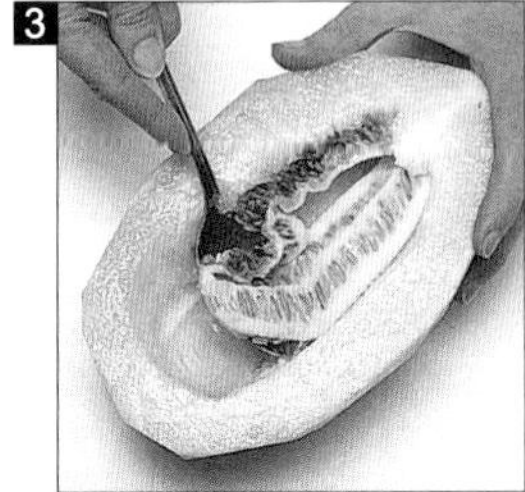

Coconut Bananas

This elaborate dessert is the perfect finale for a Chinese banquet. Bananas are fried in a citrus-flavoured butter and served with coconut.

NUTRITIONAL INFORMATION

Calories	514	Sugars	70g
Protein	4g	Fat	21g
Carbohydrate	75g	Saturates	14g

10 MINS 10 MINS

SERVES 4

INGREDIENTS

- 3 tbsp shredded fresh coconut
- 60 g/2 oz/¼ cup unsalted butter
- 1 tbsp grated ginger root
- grated zest of 1 orange
- 60 g/2 oz/¼ cup caster (superfine) sugar
- 4 tbsp fresh lime juice
- 6 bananas
- 6 tbsp orange liqueur (Cointreau or Grand Marnier, for example)
- 3 tsp toasted sesame seeds
- lime slices, to decorate
- ice-cream, to serve (optional)

1

2

3

1 Heat a small non-stick frying pan (skillet) until hot. Add the coconut and cook, stirring constantly, for 1 minute until lightly coloured. Remove from the pan and allow to cool.

2 Melt the butter in a large frying pan (skillet) and add the ginger, orange zest, sugar and lime juice. Mix well.

3 Peel and slice the bananas lengthways (and halve if they are very large). Place the bananas cut-side down in the butter mixture and cook for 1-2 minutes or until the sauce mixture starts to become sticky. Turn the bananas to coat in the sauce.

4 Remove the bananas and place on heated serving plates. Keep warm.

5 Return the pan to the heat and add the orange liqueur, blending well. Ignite with a taper, allow the flames to die down, then pour over the bananas.

6 Sprinkle with the reserved coconut and sesame seeds and serve at once, decorated with slices of lime.

COOK'S TIP

For a very special treat try serving this with a flavoured ice-cream such as coconut, ginger or praline.

Tropical Fruit Rice Mould

A rice pudding with a twist. Light flakes of rice with a tang of pineapple and lime. You can serve it with any selection of your favourite fruits.

NUTRITIONAL INFORMATION

Calories	145	Sugars	18g
Protein	7g	Fat	1g
Carbohydrate	30g	Saturates	0.3g

4¼ HOURS — 25 MINS

SERVES 8

INGREDIENTS

- 225 g/8 oz/1 cup + 2 tbsp short-grain or pudding rice, rinsed
- 850 ml/1½ pints/3¾ cups skimmed milk
- 1 tbsp caster (superfine) sugar
- 4 tbsp white rum with coconut or unsweetened pineapple juice
- 175 ml/6 fl oz/¾ cup low-fat natural yogurt
- 400 g/14 oz can pineapple pieces in natural juice, drained and chopped
- 1 tsp grated lime rind
- 1 tbsp lime juice
- 1 sachet/1 envelope powdered gelatine dissolved in 3 tbsp boiling water
- lime wedges, to decorate
- mixed tropical fruits such as passion-fruit, baby pineapple, paw-paw (papaya), mango, carambola (star fruit), to serve

1 Place the rice and milk in a saucepan. Bring to the boil, then simmer gently, uncovered, for 20 minutes until the rice is soft and the milk is absorbed.

2 Stir the mixture occasionally and keep the heat low to prevent sticking. Transfer to a mixing bowl and leave to cool.

3 Stir the sugar, white rum with coconut or pineapple juice, yogurt, pineapple pieces, lime rind and juice into the rice. Fold into the gelatine mixture.

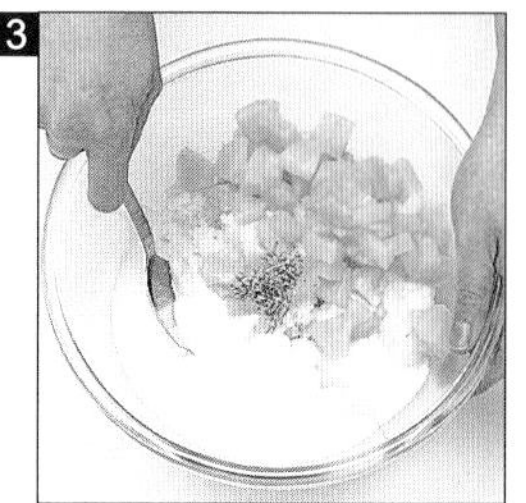

4 Rinse a 1.5 litre/2½ pint/1½ quart non-stick ring mould or ring cake tin (pan) with water and spoon in the rice mixture. Press down well and chill for 2 hours until firm.

5 To serve, loosen the rice from the mould with a small palette knife (spatula) and invert on to a serving plate.

6 Decorate with lime wedges and fill the centre with assorted tropical fruits.

COOK'S TIP

Try serving this dessert with a light sauce made from 300 ml/ ½ pint/1¼ cups tropical fruit or pineapple juice thickened with 2 tsp arrowroot.

Poached Allspice Pears

These pears are moist and delicious after poaching in a sugar and all-spice mixturc. They are wonderful served hot or cold.

NUTRITIONAL INFORMATION

Calories	157	Sugars	17g
Protein	5g	Fat	19g
Carbohydrate	17g	Saturates	12g

 5 MINS  15 MINS

SERVES 4

INGREDIENTS

- 4 large, ripe pears
- 300 ml/½ pint/1¼ cups orange juice
- 2 tsp ground allspice
- 60 g/2 oz/⅓ cup raisins
- 2 tbsp light brown sugar
- grated orange rind, to decorate

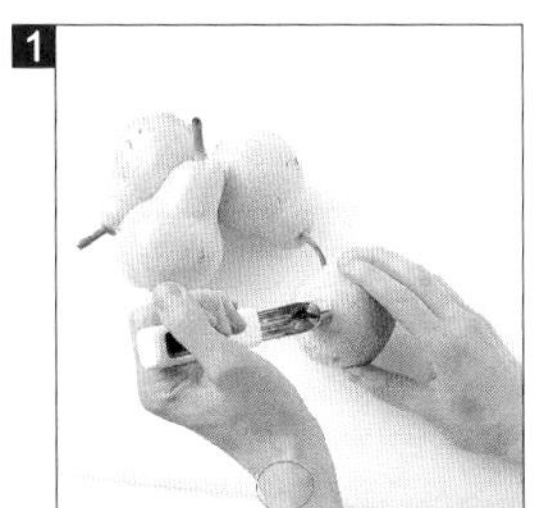

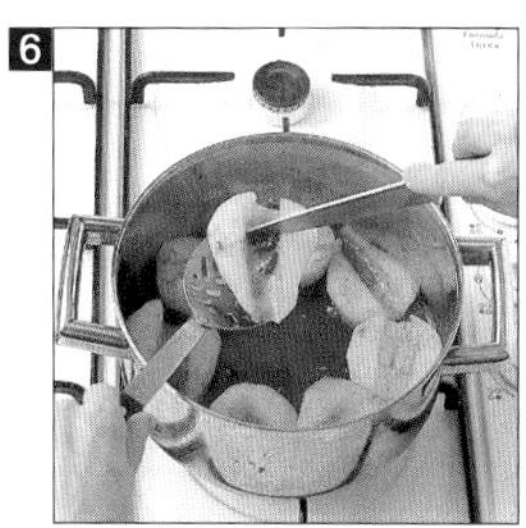

1 Using an apple corer, core the pears.

2 Using a sharp knife, peel the pears and cut them in half.

3 Place the pear halves in a large saucepan.

4 Add the orange juice, ground allspice, raisins and light brown sugar to the saucepan and heat gently, stirring, until the sugar has dissolved.

5 Bring the mixture in the saucepan to the boil and continue to boil for 1 minute.

6 Reduce the heat to low and leave to simmer for about 10 minutes, or until the pears are cooked, but still fairly firm. Test whether the pears are cooked or not by inserting the tip of a sharp knife.

7 Remove the pears from the pan with a slotted spoon and transfer to serving plates.

8 Decorate with grated orange rind and serve hot with the syrup.

COOK'S TIP

The Chinese do not usually have desserts to finish off a meal, except at banquets and special occasions. Sweet dishes are usually served in between main meals as snacks, but fruit is refreshing at the end of a big meal.

Mango Dumplings

Fresh mango and canned lychees fill these small steamed dumplings, making a really colourful and tasty treat.

NUTRITIONAL INFORMATION

Calories	434	Sugars	16g
Protein	12g	Fat	4g
Carbohydrate	93g	Saturates	1g

 1¾ HOURS  25 MINS

SERVES 4

INGREDIENTS

DOUGH

2 tsp baking powder

1 tbsp caster (superfine) sugar

150 ml/¼ pint/⅔ cup water

150 ml/¼ pint/⅔ cup milk

400 g/14 oz/3½ cups plain (all-purpose) flour

FILLING AND SAUCE

1 small mango

100 g/3½ oz can lychees, drained

1 tbsp ground almonds

4 tbsp orange juice

ground cinnamon, for dusting

1 To make the dough, place the baking powder and caster (superfine) sugar in a large mixing bowl.

2 Mix the water and milk together and then stir this mixture into the baking powder and sugar mixture until well combined. Gradually stir in the plain (sll-purpose) flour to make a soft dough. Set the dough aside in a warm place for about 1 hour.

3 To make the filling, peel the mango and cut the flesh from the stone (pit). Roughly chop the mango flesh; reserve half and set aside for the sauce.

4 Chop the lychees and add to half of the chopped mango, together with the ground almonds. Leave to stand for 20 minutes.

5 Meanwhile, make the sauce. Blend the reserved mango and the orange juice in a food processor until smooth. Using the back of a spoon, press the mixture through a sieve to make a smooth sauce.

6 Divide the dough into 16 equal pieces. Roll each piece out on a lightly floured surface into 7.5-cm/3-inch rounds.

7 Spoon a little of the mango and lychee filling on to the centre of each round and fold the dough over the filling to make semi-circles. Pinch the edges together to seal firmly.

8 Place the dumplings on a heatproof plate in a steamer, cover and steam for about 20-25 minutes, or until cooked through.

9 Remove the mango dumplings from the steamer, dust with a little ground cinnamon and serve with the mango sauce.

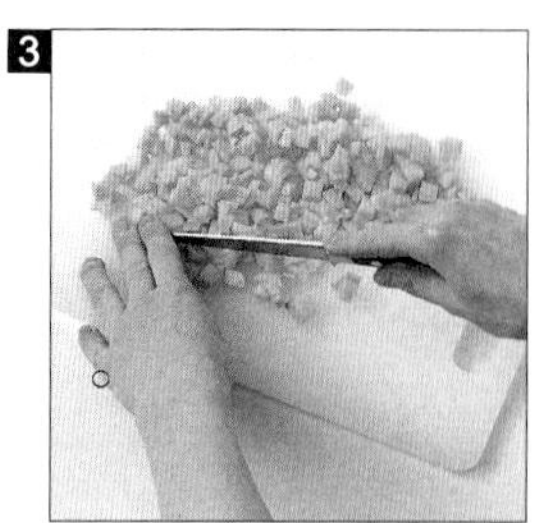
3

5

7

Rosemary Biscuits (Cookies)

Do not be put off by the idea of herbs being used in these crisp biscuits (cookies) – try them and you will be pleasantly surprised.

NUTRITIONAL INFORMATION

Calories	50	Sugars	2g
Protein	1g	Fat	2g
Carbohydrate	8g	Saturates	1g

 45 MINS  15 MINS

MAKES 25

INGREDIENTS

- 50 g/1¾ oz/10 tsp butter, softened
- 4 tbsp caster (superfine) sugar
- grated rind of 1 lemon
- 4 tbsp lemon juice
- 1 egg, separated
- 2 tsp finely chopped fresh rosemary
- 200 g/7 oz/1¾ cups plain (all-purpose) flour, sieved (strained)
- caster (superfine) sugar, for sprinkling (optional)

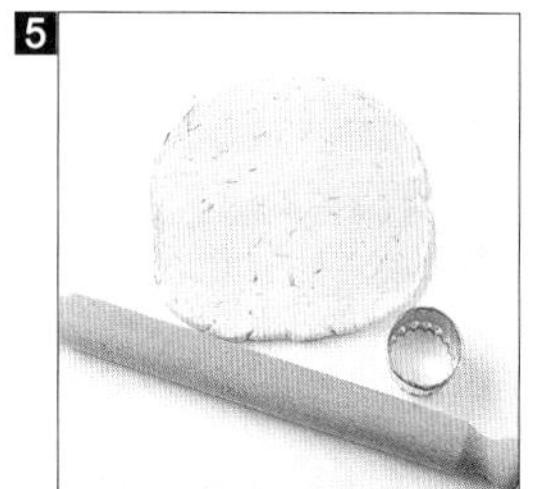

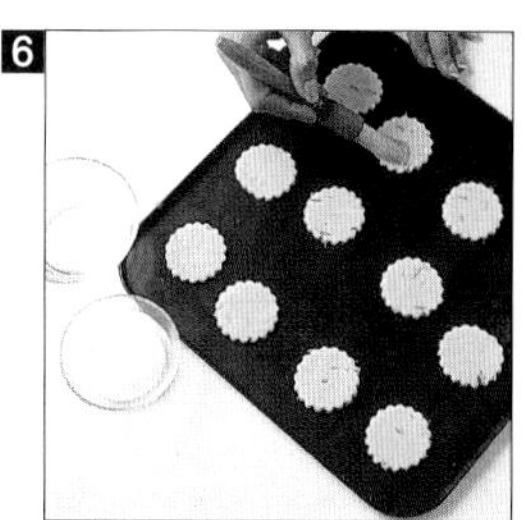

1 Lightly grease 2 baking trays (cookie sheets).

2 In a large mixing bowl, cream together the butter and sugar until pale and fluffy.

3 Add the lemon rind and juice, then the egg yolk and beat until they are thoroughly combined. Stir in the chopped fresh rosemary.

4 Add the sieved (strained) flour, mixing well until a soft dough is formed. Wrap and leave to chill for 30 minutes.

5 On a lightly floured surface, roll out the dough thinly and then stamp out 25 circles with a 6 cm/2½ inch biscuit (cookie) cutter. Arrange the dough circles on the prepared baking trays (cookie sheets).

6 In a bowl, lightly whisk the egg white. Gently brush the egg white over the surface of each biscuit (cookie), then sprinkle with a little caster (superfine) sugar, if liked.

7 Bake in a preheated oven, at 180°C/350°F/Gas Mark 4, for about 15 minutes.

8 Transfer the biscuits (cookies) to a wire rack and leave to cool before serving.

COOK'S TIP

Store the biscuits (cookies) in an airtight container for up to 1 week.

Lemon Granita

A delightful end to a meal or a refreshing way to cleanse the palate, granitas are made from slushy ice, so they need to be served very quickly.

NUTRITIONAL INFORMATION

Calories	102	Sugars	27g
Protein	0.1g	Fat	0g
Carbohydrate	27g	Saturates	0g

5¼ HOURS

6 MINS

SERVES 4

INGREDIENTS

LEMON GRANITA

3 lemons
200 ml/7 fl oz/¾ cup lemon juice
100 g/3½ oz caster (superfine) sugar
500 ml/18 fl oz/2¼ cups cold water

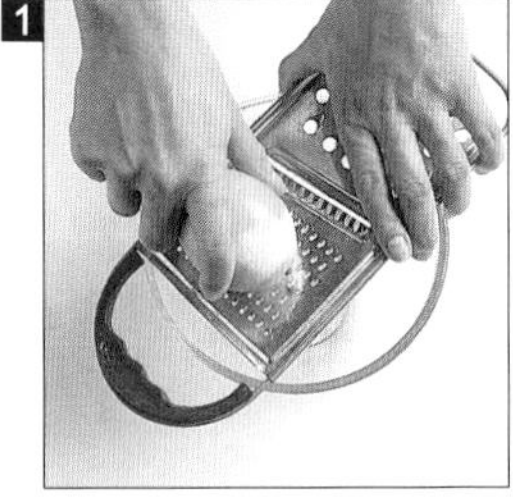

1 To make lemon granita, finely grate the lemon rind.

2 Place the lemon rind, juice and caster (superfine) sugar in a pan. Bring the mixture to the boil and leave to simmer for 5-6 minutes or until thick and syrupy. Leave to cool.

3 Once cooled, stir in the cold water and pour into a shallow freezer container with a lid.

4 Freeze the granita for 4–5 hours, stirring occasionally to break up the ice. Serve as a palate cleanser between dinner courses.

VARIATION

To make coffee granita, place 2 tablespoons of instant coffee and 2 tablespoons of sugar in a bowl and pour over 2 tablespoons of hot water, stirring until dissolved. Stir in 600 ml/1 pint/2½ cups cold water and 2 tablespoons of rum or brandy. Pour into a shallow freezer container with a lid. Freeze for at least 6 hours, stirring occasionally, to create a grainy texture.

Raspberry Fusilli

This is the ultimate in self-indulgence – a truly delicious dessert that tastes every bit as good as it looks.

NUTRITIONAL INFORMATION

Calories	235	Sugars	20g
Protein	7g	Fat	7g
Carbohydrate	36g	Saturates	1g

 5 MINS  20 MINS

SERVES 4

INGREDIENTS

- 175 g/6 oz/½ cup fusilli
- 700 g/1 lb 9 oz/4 cups raspberries
- 2 tbsp caster (superfine) sugar
- 1 tbsp lemon juice
- 4 tbsp flaked (slivered) almonds
- 3 tbsp raspberry liqueur

1 Bring a large saucepan of lightly salted water to the boil. Add the fusilli and cook for 8–10 minutes until tender, but still firm to the bite. Drain the fusilli thoroughly, return to the pan and set aside to cool.

2 Using a spoon, firmly press 225 g/ 8 oz/1⅓ cups of the raspberries through a sieve (strainer) set over a large mixing bowl to form a smooth purée (paste).

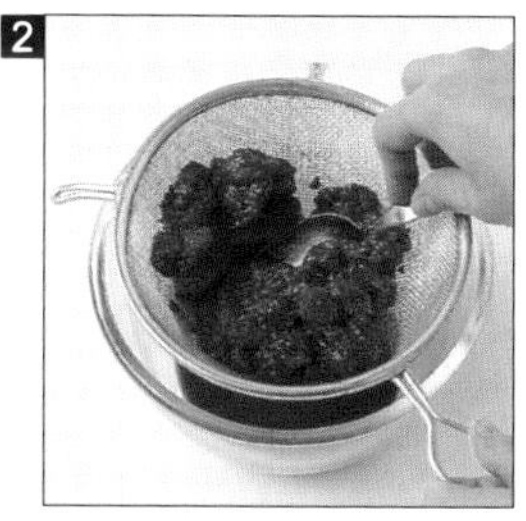

2

3 Put the raspberry purée (paste) and sugar in a small saucepan and simmer over a low heat, stirring occasionally, for 5 minutes.

3

4 Stir in the lemon juice and set the sauce aside until required.

4

5 Add the remaining raspberries to the fusilli in the pan and mix together well. Transfer the raspberry and fusilli mixture to a serving dish.

6 Spread the almonds out on a baking tray (cookie sheet) and toast under the grill (broiler) until golden brown. Remove and set aside to cool slightly.

7 Stir the raspberry liqueur into the reserved raspberry sauce and mix together well until very smooth. Pour the raspberry sauce over the fusilli, sprinkle over the toasted almonds and serve.

VARIATION

You could use any sweet, ripe berry for making this dessert. Strawberries and blackberries are especially suitable, combined with the correspondingly flavoured liqueur. Alternatively, you could use a different berry mixed with the fusilli, but still pour over raspberry sauce.

Chocolate Fudge Pudding

This pudding has a hidden surprise when cooked, as it separates to give a rich chocolate sauce at the bottom of the dish.

NUTRITIONAL INFORMATION

Calories	397	Sugars	27g
Protein	10g	Fat	25g
Carbohydrate	36g	Saturates	5g

 10 MINS  40 MINS

SERVES 4

INGREDIENTS

- 50 g/1¾ oz/4 tbsp margarine, plus extra for greasing
- 75 g/2¾ oz/6 tbsp light brown sugar
- 2 eggs, beaten
- 350 ml/12 fl oz/1¼ cups milk
- 50 g/1¾ oz/½ cup chopped walnuts
- 40 g/1½ oz/¼ cup plain (all-purpose) flour
- 2 tbsp cocoa powder (unsweetened cocoa
- icing (confectioners') sugar and cocoa powder (unsweetened cocoa), to dust

1 Lightly grease a 1 litre/1¾ pint/4 cup ovenproof dish.

2 Cream together the margarine and sugar in a large mixing bowl until fluffy. Beat in the eggs.

2

3

4

3 Gradually stir in the milk and add the walnuts, stirring to mix.

4 Sift the flour and cocoa powder (unsweetened cocoa) into the mixture and fold in gently, with a metal spoon, until well mixed.

5 Spoon the mixture into the dish and cook in a preheated oven, 180°C/350°F/Gas Mark 4, for 35–40 minutes, or until the sponge is cooked.

6 Dust with sugar and cocoa powder (unsweetened cocoa) and serve.

VARIATION

Add 1–2 tbsp brandy or rum to the mixture for a slightly alcoholic pudding, or 1–2 tbsp orange juice for a child-friendly version.

Chinese Fruit Salad

The syrup for this colourful dish is filled with Chinese flavours for a refreshing dessert.

NUTRITIONAL INFORMATION

Calories	405	Sugars	81g
Protein	3g	Fat	6g
Carbohydrate	83g	Saturates	1g

 1¾ HOURS  10 MINS

SERVES 4

INGREDIENTS

- 75 ml/3 fl oz Chinese rice wine or dry sherry
- rind and juice of 1 lemon
- 850 ml/1½ pints water
- 225 g/8 oz caster (superfine) sugar
- 2 cloves
- 2.5-cm/1-inch piece cinnamon stick, bruised
- 1 vanilla pod (bean)
- pinch of mixed (apple pie) spice
- 1 star anise pod
- 2.5-cm/1-inch piece fresh ginger root, sliced
- 50 g/1¾ oz unsalted cashew nuts
- 2 kiwi fruits
- 1 star fruit
- 115 g/4 oz strawberries
- 400 g/14 oz can lychees in syrup, drained
- 1 piece stem (preserved) ginger, drained and sliced
- chopped mint, to decorate

1 Put the Chinese rice wine or sherry, lemon rind and juice and water in a saucepan.

2 Add the caster (superfine) sugar, cloves, cinnamon stick, vanilla pod (bean), mixed (apple pie) spice, star anise and fresh ginger root to the saucepan.

3 Heat the mixture in the pan gently, stirring constantly, until the sugar has dissolved and then bring to the boil. Reduce the heat and simmer for 5 minutes. Set aside to cool completely.

4 Strain the syrup, discarding the flavourings. Stir in the cashew nuts, cover with cling film (plastic wrap) and chill in the refrigerator.

5 Meanwhile, prepare the fruits: halve and slice the kiwi fruit, slice the star fruit, and hull and slice the strawberries.

6 Spoon the prepared fruit into a dish with the lychees and ginger. Stir through gently to mix.

7 Pour the syrup over the fruit, decorate with chopped mint and serve.

2

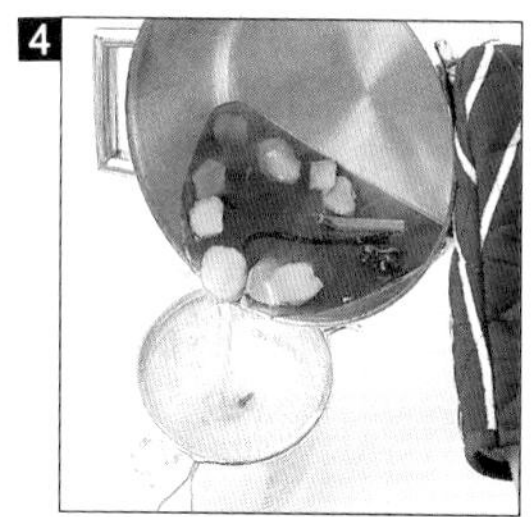
4

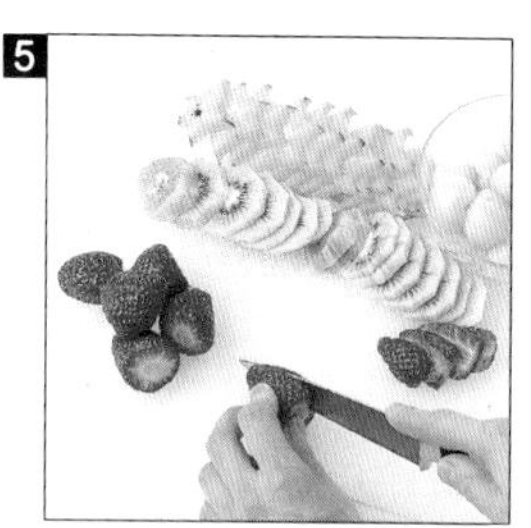
5

Orange Syllabub

A zesty, creamy whip made from yogurt and milk with a hint of orange, served with light and luscious sweet sponge cakes.

NUTRITIONAL INFORMATION

Calories	464	Sugars	74g
Protein	22g	Fat	5g
Carbohydrate	89g	Saturates	2g

 1½ HOURS  10 MINS

SERVES 4

INGREDIENTS

- 4 oranges
- 600 ml/1 pint/2½ cups low-fat natural yogurt
- 6 tbsp low-fat skimmed milk powder
- 4 tbsp caster (superfine) sugar
- 1 tbsp grated orange rind
- 4 tbsp orange juice
- 2 egg whites
- fresh orange zest to decorate

SPONGE HEARTS

- 2 eggs, size 2
- 90 g/3 oz/6 tbsp caster (superfine) sugar
- 40 g/1½ oz/6 tbsp plain (all-purpose) flour
- 40 g/1½ oz/6 tbsp wholemeal (whole wheat) flour
- 1 tbsp hot water
- 1 tsp icing (confectioners') sugar

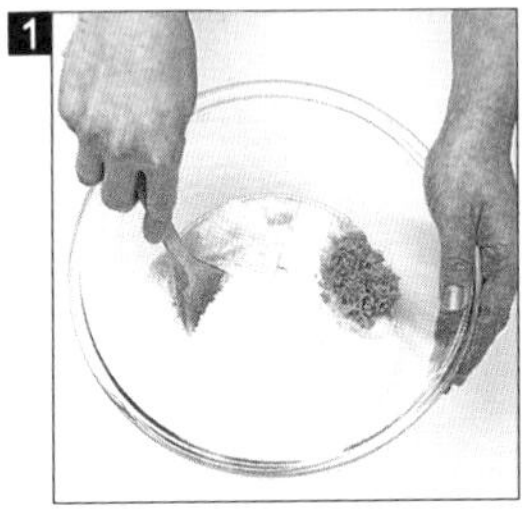

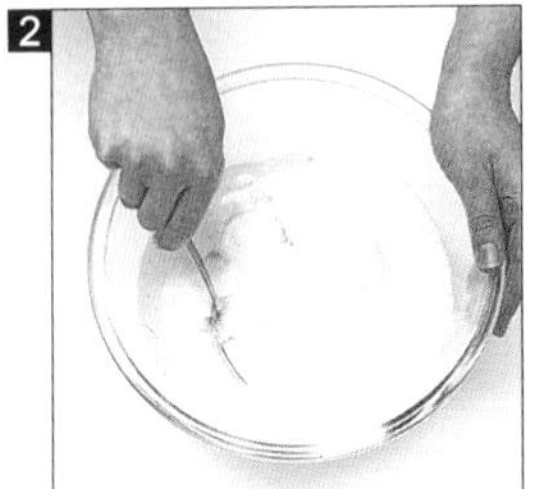

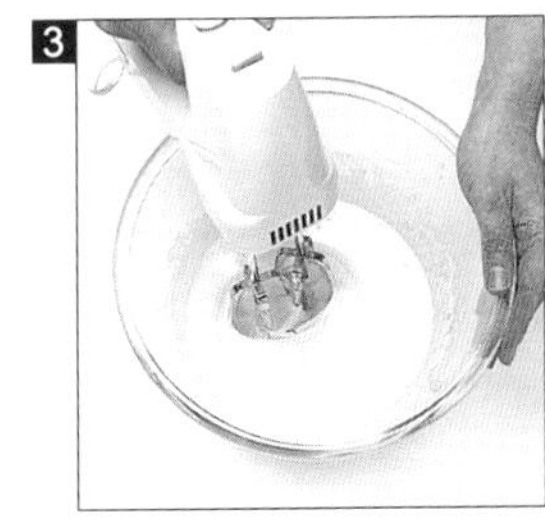

1 Slice off the tops and bottoms of the oranges and the skin. Then cut out the segments, removing the zest and membranes between each one. Divide the orange segments between 4 dessert glasses, then chill.

2 In a mixing bowl, combine the yogurt, milk powder, sugar, orange rind and juice. Cover and chill for 1 hour. Whisk the egg whites until stiff, then fold into the yogurt mixture. Pile on to the orange slices and chill for an hour. Decorate with fresh orange rind and sponge hearts.

3 To make the sponge hearts, line a 15 × 25 cm/6 × 10 inch baking tin (pan) with baking parchment. Whisk the eggs and caster (superfine) sugar until thick and pale. Sieve, then fold in the flours using a large metal spoon, adding the hot water at the same time.

4 Pour into the tin (pan) and bake in a preheated oven at 220°C/425°F/ Gas Mark 7 for 9–10 minutes until golden and firm to the touch.

5 Turn on to a sheet of baking parchment. Using a 5 cm/2 inch heart-shaped cutter, stamp out hearts. Transfer to a wire rack to cool. Lightly dust with icing (confectioners') sugar before serving with the syllabub.

Fruit Salad with Ginger Syrup

This is a very special fruit salad made from the most exotic and colourful fruits that are soaked in a syrup made with fresh ginger and ginger wine.

NUTRITIONAL INFORMATION

Calories	225	Sugars	45g
Protein	2g	Fat	4g
Carbohydrate	45g	Saturates	3g

4½ HOURS 5 MINS

SERVES 4

INGREDIENTS

- 2.5 cm/1 inch ginger root, peeled and chopped
- 60 g/2 oz/¼ cup caster sugar
- 150 ml/¼ pint/⅔ cup water
- grated rind and juice of 1 lime
- 4 tbsp/⅓ cup ginger wine
- 1 fresh pineapple, peeled, cored and cut into bite-sized pieces
- 2 ripe mangoes, peeled, stoned and diced
- 4 kiwi fruit, peeled and sliced
- 1 paw-paw (papaya), peeled, seeded and diced
- 2 passion-fruit, halved and flesh removed
- 350 g/12 oz lychees, peeled and stoned
- ¼ fresh coconut, grated
- 60 g/2 oz Cape gooseberries, to decorate (optional)
- coconut ice-cream, to serve (optional)

1

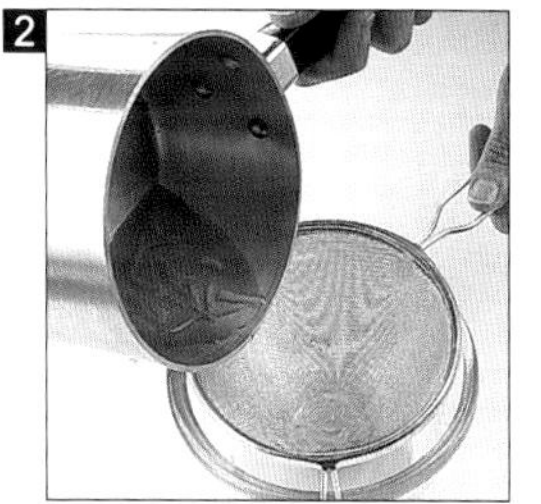

2

2

1 Place the ginger, sugar, water and lime juice in a pan and bring slowly to the boil. Simmer for 1 minute, remove from the heat and allow to cool slightly.

2 Sieve (strain) the syrup, add the ginger wine and mix well. Cool completely.

3 Place the prepared fruit in a serving bowl. Add the cold syrup and mix well. Cover and chill in the refrigerator for 2-4 hours.

4 Just before serving, add half of the grated coconut to the salad and mix well. Sprinkle the remainder on top.

5 If using Cape gooseberries to decorate the salad, peel back each calyx to form a flower. Wipe the berries clean, then arrange them around the side of the fruit salad before serving.

COOK'S TIP

Despite their name, Cape gooseberries are golden in colour and more similar in appearance to ground cherries. They make a delightful decoration to many fruit-based desserts.

Mangoes with Sticky Rice

These delightful rice puddings make a lovely dessert or afternoon snack. You can have fun experimenting with different-shaped rice moulds.

NUTRITIONAL INFORMATION

Calories	202	Sugars	31g
Protein	2g	Fat	2g
Carbohydrate	47g	Saturates	0.3g

12¾ HOURS

50 MINS

SERVES 4

INGREDIENTS

- 125 g/4½ oz/generous ½ cup glutinous (sticky) rice
- 250 ml/9 fl oz/1 cup coconut milk
- 60 g/2 oz/⅓ cup light muscovado sugar
- ½ tsp salt
- 1 tsp sesame seeds, toasted
- 4 ripe mangoes, peeled, halved, stoned (pitted) and sliced

1 Put the glutinous (sticky) rice into a colander and rinse well with plenty of cold water until the water runs clear. Transfer the rice to a large bowl, cover with cold water and leave to soak overnight, or for at least 12 hours. Drain the rice thoroughly.

2 Line a bamboo basket or steamer with muslin (cheesecloth) or finely woven cotton cloth. Add the rice and steam over a pan of gently simmering water until the rice is tender, about 40 minutes.

3 Remove the rice from the heat and transfer to a large mixing bowl.

4 Reserve 4 tablespoons of the coconut milk and put the remainder into a small saucepan with the light muscovado sugar and salt. Heat and simmer gently for about 8 minutes until reduced by about one third.

5 Pour the coconut milk mixture over the rice, fluffing up the rice with a fork so that the mixture is absorbed. Set aside for 10–15 minutes.

6 Pack the rice into individual moulds and then invert them on to serving plates.

7 Pour a little reserved coconut milk over each rice mound and sprinkle with the sesame seeds.

8 Arrange the sliced mango on the plates and serve, decorated with pieces of mango cut into different shapes with tiny cutters.

1

2

4

COOK'S TIP

Glutinous or sticky rice is available from stockists of Thai ingredients, although you can try making this recipe with short-grain pudding rice instead.

Sticky Sesame Bananas

These tasty morsels are a real treat. Pieces of banana are dipped in caramel and then sprinkled with a few sesame seeds.

NUTRITIONAL INFORMATION

Calories	215	Sugars	38g
Protein	6g	Fat	3g
Carbohydrate	41g	Saturates	1g

10 MINS 20 MINS

SERVES 4

INGREDIENTS

- 4 ripe medium bananas
- 3 tbsp lemon juice
- 125 g/4½ oz caster (superfine) sugar
- 4 tbsp cold water
- 2 tbsp sesame seeds
- 150 ml/5 fl oz/⅔ cup low-fat natural fromage frais (unsweetened yogurt)
- 1 tbsp icing (confectioners') sugar
- 1 tsp vanilla essence (extract)
- lemon and lime rind, shredded, to decorate

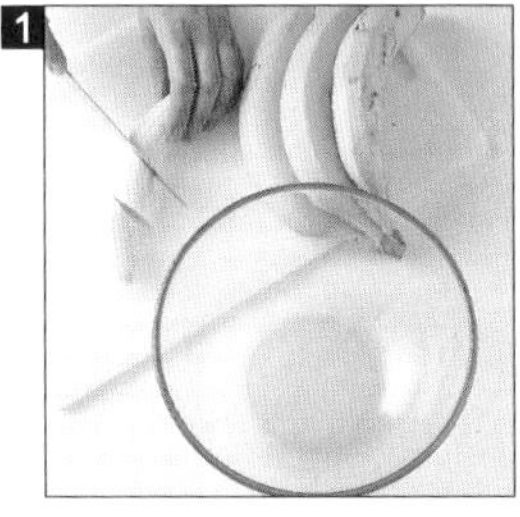

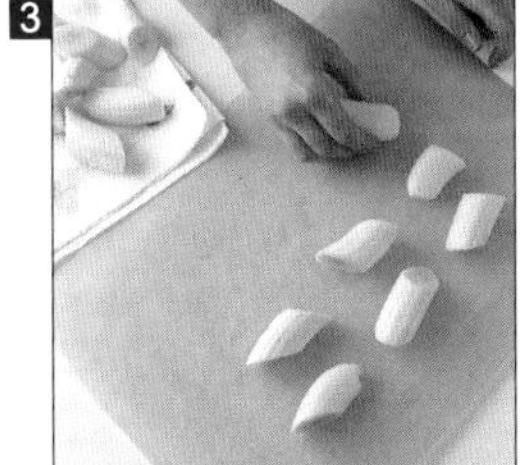

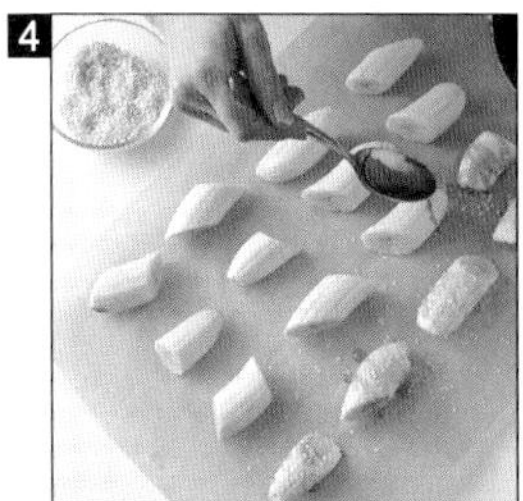

1 Peel the bananas and cut into 5 cm/2 inch pieces. Place the banana pieces in a bowl, spoon over the lemon juice and stir well to coat – this will help prevent the bananas from discoloring.

2 Place the sugar and water in a small saucepan and heat gently, stirring, until the sugar dissolves. Bring to the boil and cook for 5–6 minutes until the mixture turns golden-brown.

3 Meanwhile, drain the bananas and blot with kitchen paper (paper towels) to dry. Line a baking sheet or board with baking parchment and arrange the bananas, well spaced out, on top.

4 When the caramel is ready, drizzle it over the bananas, working quickly because the caramel sets almost instantly. Sprinkle the sesame seedsover the caramelized bananas and leave to cool for 10 minutes.

5 Mix the fromage frais (unsweetened yogurt) together with the icing (confectioner's) sugar and vanilla essence (extract).

6 Peel the bananas away from the paper and arrange on serving plates.

7 Serve the fromage frais (unsweetened yogurt) as a dip, decorated with the shredded lemon and lime rind.

Chocolate Brownies

You really can have a low-fat chocolate treat. These moist bars contain a dried fruit purée, which enables you to bake without adding any fat.

NUTRITIONAL INFORMATION

Calories	271	Sugars	45g
Protein	5g	Fat	4g
Carbohydrate	57g	Saturates	2g

30 MINS 40 MINS

MAKES 12

INGREDIENTS

- 60 g/2 oz unsweetened pitted dates, chopped
- 60 g/2 oz no-need-to-soak dried prunes, chopped
- 6 tbsp unsweetened apple juice
- 4 medium eggs, beaten
- 300 g/10½ oz dark muscovado sugar
- 1 tsp vanilla essence (extract)
- 4 tbsp low-fat drinking chocolate powder, plus extra for dusting
- 2 tbsp cocoa powder
- 175 g/6 oz plain (all-purpose) flour
- 60 g/2 oz dark chocolate chips

ICING

- 125 g/4½ oz icing (confectioners') sugar
- 1–2 tsp water
- 1 tsp vanilla essence (extract)

1 Preheat the oven to 180°C/350°F/Gas Mark 4. Grease and line a 18 x 28 cm/7 x 11 inch cake tin with baking parchment. Place the dates and prunes in a small saucepan and add the apple juice. Bring to the boil, cover and simmer for 10 minutes until soft. Beat to form a smooth paste, then set aside to cool.

2

2 Place the cooled fruit in a mixing bowl and stir in the eggs, sugar and vanilla essence. Sift in 4 tbsp drinking chocolate, the cocoa and the flour, and fold in along with the chocolate chips until well incorporated.

2

3 Spoon the mixture into the prepared tin and smooth over the top. Bake for 25–30 minutes until firm to the touch or until a skewer inserted into the centre comes out clean. Cut into 12 bars and leave to cool in the tin for 10 minutes. Transfer to a wire rack to cool completely.

3

4 To make the icing (frosting), sift the sugar into a bowl and mix with sufficient water and the vanilla essence (extract) to form a soft, but not too runny, icing (frosting).

5 Drizzle the icing (frosting) over the chocolate brownies and allow to set. Dust with the extra chocolate powder before serving.

COOK'S TIP

Make double the amount, cut one of the cakes into bars and open freeze, then store in plastic bags. Take out pieces of cake as and when you need them - they'll take no time at all to defrost.

Zabaglione

This well-known dish is really a light but rich egg mousse flavoured with Marsala.

NUTRITIONAL INFORMATION

Calories	158	Sugars	29g
Protein	1g	Fat	1g
Carbohydrate	29g	Saturates	0.2g

 5 MINS  15 MINS

SERVES 4

INGREDIENTS

5 egg yolks

100 g/3½ oz caster (superfine) sugar

150 ml/¼ pint/⅔ cup Marsala or sweet sherry

amaretti biscuits (cookies), to serve (optional)

2

2

4

1 Place the egg yolks in a large mixing bowl.

2 Add the caster (superfine) sugar to the egg yolks and whisk until the mixture is thick and very pale and has doubled in volume.

3 Place the bowl containing the egg yolk and sugar mixture over a saucepan of gently simmering water.

4 Add the Marsala or sherry to the egg yolk and sugar mixture and continue whisking until the foam mixture becomes warm. This process may take as long as 10 minutes.

5 Pour the mixture, which should be frothy and light, into 4 wine glasses.

6 Serve the zabaglione warm with fresh fruit or amaretti biscuits (cookies), if you wish.

Orange & Almond Cake

This light and tangy citrus cake from Sicily is better eaten as a dessert than as a cake. It is especially good served after a large meal.

NUTRITIONAL INFORMATION

Calories	399	Sugars	20g
Protein	8g	Fat	31g
Carbohydrate	23g	Saturates	13g

30 MINS 40 MINS

SERVES 8

INGREDIENTS

- 4 eggs, separated
- 125 g/4½ oz caster (superfine) sugar, plus 2 tsp for the cream
- finely grated rind and juice of 2 oranges
- finely grated rind and juice of 1 lemon
- 125 g/4½ oz ground almonds
- 25 g/1 oz self-raising flour
- 200 ml/7 fl oz/¾ cup whipping (light) cream
- 1 tsp cinnamon
- 25 g/1 oz flaked (slivered) almonds, toasted
- icing (confectioners') sugar, to dust

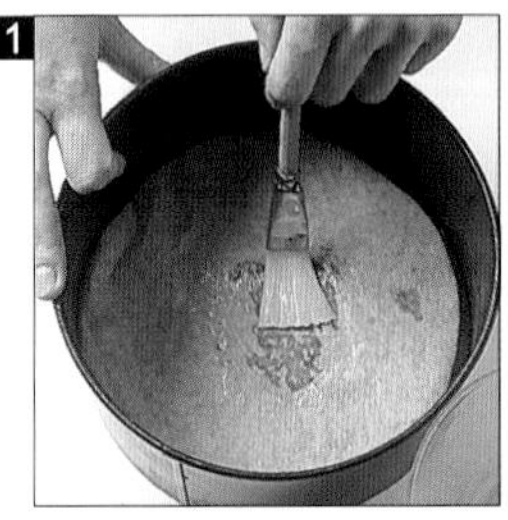

1

2

3

1 Grease and line the base of a 18 cm/7 inch round deep cake tin (pan).

2 Blend the egg yolks with the sugar until the mixture is thick and creamy. Whisk half of the orange rind and all of the lemon rind into the egg yolks.

3 Mix the juice from both oranges and the lemon with the ground almonds and stir into the egg yolks. The mixture will become quite runny at this point. Fold in the flour.

4 Whisk the egg whites until stiff and gently fold into the egg yolk mixture.

5 Pour the mixture into the tin (pan) and bake in a preheated oven, at 180°C/350°F/Gas Mark 4, for 35–40 minutes, or until golden and springy to the touch. Leave to cool in the tin (pan) for 10 minutes and then turn out. It is likely to sink slightly at this stage.

6 Whip the cream to form soft peaks. Stir in the remaining orange rind, cinnamon and sugar.

7 Once the cake is cold, cover with the almonds, dust with icing (confectioners') sugar and serve with the cream.

VARIATION

You could serve this cake with a syrup. Boil the juice and finely grated rind of 2 oranges, 75 g/2¾ oz caster (superfine) sugar and 2 tbsp of water for 5–6 minutes until slightly thickened. Stir in 1 tbsp of orange liqueur just before serving.

Summer Puddings

A wonderful mixture of summer fruits encased in slices of white bread which soak up all the deep red, flavoursome juices.

NUTRITIONAL INFORMATION

Calories	250	Sugars	41g
Protein	4g	Fat	4g
Carbohydrate	53g	Saturates	2g

 10 MINS  10 MINS

SERVES 6

INGREDIENTS

- vegetable oil or butter, for greasing
- 6–8 thin slices white bread, crusts removed
- 175 g/6 oz/¾ cup caster (superfine) sugar
- 300 ml/½ pint/1¼ cups water
- 225 g/8 oz/2 cups strawberries
- 500 g/1 lb 2 oz/2½ cups raspberries
- 175 g/6 oz/1¼ cups black- and/or redcurrants
- 175 g/6 oz/¾ cup blackberries or loganberries
- mint sprigs, to decorate
- pouring cream, to serve

1 Grease six 150 ml/¼ pint/⅔ cup moulds (molds) with butter or oil.

2 Line the moulds (molds) with the bread, cutting it so it fits snugly.

3 Place the sugar in a saucepan with the water and heat gently, stirring frequently until dissolved, then bring to the boil and boil for 2 minutes.

4 Reserve 6 large strawberries for decoration. Add half the raspberries and the rest of the fruits to the syrup, cutting the strawberries in half if large, and simmer gently for a few minutes, until beginning to soften but still retaining their shape.

5 Spoon the fruits and some of the liquid into moulds (molds). Cover with more slices of bread. Spoon a little juice around the sides of the moulds (molds) so the bread is well soaked. Cover with a saucer and a heavy weight, leave to cool, then chill thoroughly, preferably overnight.

6 Process the remaining raspberries in a food processor or blender, or press through a non-metallic strainer. Add enough of the liquid from the fruits to give a coating consistency.

7 Turn on to serving plates and spoon the raspberry sauce over. Decorate with the mint sprigs and reserved strawberries and serve with cream.

Mocha Swirl Mousse

A combination of feather-light yet rich chocolate and coffee mousses, whipped and attractively served in serving glasses.

NUTRITIONAL INFORMATION

Calories	130	Sugars	10g
Protein	5g	Fat	8g
Carbohydrate	11g	Saturates	5g

 1¼ HOURS  0 MINS

SERVES 4

INGREDIENTS

- 1 tbsp coffee and chicory essence (extract)
- 2 tsp cocoa powder, plus extra for dusting
- 1 tsp low-fat drinking chocolate powder
- 150 ml/5 fl oz/⅔ cup low-fat crème fraîche, plus 4 tsp to serve
- 2 tsp powdered gelatine
- 2 tbsp boiling water
- 2 large egg whites
- 2 tbsp caster (superfine) sugar
- 4 chocolate coffee beans, to serve

1 Place the coffee and chicory essence (extract) in one bowl, and 2 teaspoons cocoa powder and the drinking chocolate in another bowl. Divide the crème fraîche between the 2 bowls and mix both well.

2 Dissolve the gelatine in the boiling water and set aside. In a grease-free bowl, whisk the egg whites and sugar until stiff and divide this evenly between the two mixtures.

3 Divide the dissolved gelatine between the 2 mixtures and, using a large metal spoon, gently fold until well mixed.

4 Spoon small amounts of the 2 mousses alternately into 4 serving glasses and swirl together gently. Chill for 1 hour or until set.

5 To serve, top each mousse with a teaspoonful of crème fraîche, a chocolate coffee bean and a light dusting of cocoa powder. Serve immediately.

COOK'S TIP

Vegetarians should not be denied this delicious chocolate dessert. Instead of gelatine use the vegetarian equivalent, gelozone, available from health-food shops. However, be sure to read the instructions on the packet first as it is prepared differently from gelatine.

1

2

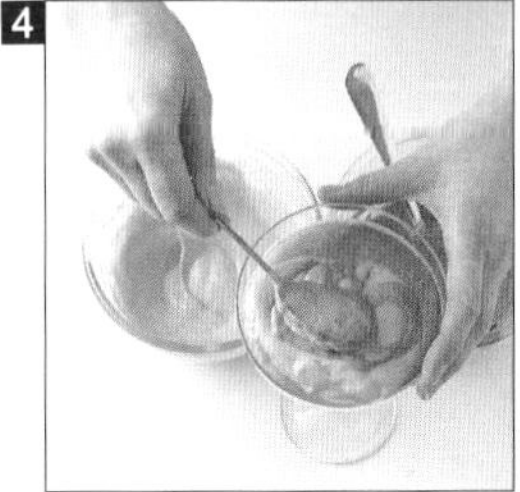
4

Baked Coconut Rice Pudding

A wonderful baked rice pudding cooked with flavoursome coconut milk and a little lime rind. Serve hot or chilled with fresh or stewed fruit.

NUTRITIONAL INFORMATION

Calories	211	Sugars	27g
Protein	5g	Fat	2g
Carbohydrate	46g	Saturates	1g

 5 MINS  2½ HOURS

SERVES 4–6

INGREDIENTS

- 90 g/3 oz/scant ⅓ cup short or round-grain pudding rice
- 600 ml/1 pint/2½ cups coconut milk
- 300 ml/½ pint/1¼ cups milk
- 1 large strip lime rind
- 60 g/2 oz/¼ cup caster (superfine) sugar
- knob of butter
- pinch of ground star anise (optional)
- fresh or stewed fruit, to serve

1 Lightly grease a 1.4 litre/2½ pint shallow ovenproof dish.

2 Mix the pudding rice with the coconut milk, milk, lime rind and caster (superfine) sugar until all the ingredients are well blended.

3 Pour the rice mixture into the greased ovenproof dish and dot the surface with a little butter. Bake in the oven for about 30 minutes.

4 Remove the dish from the oven. Remove and discard the strip of lime from the rice pudding.

5 Stir the pudding well, add the pinch of ground star anise, if using, return to the oven and cook for a further 1-2 hours or until almost all the milk has been absorbed and a golden brown skin has baked on the top of the pudding.

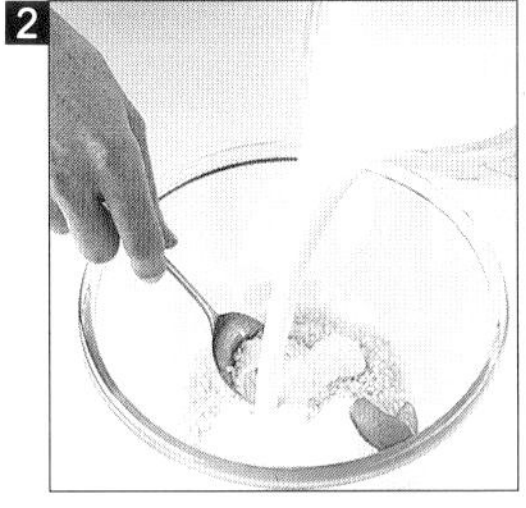

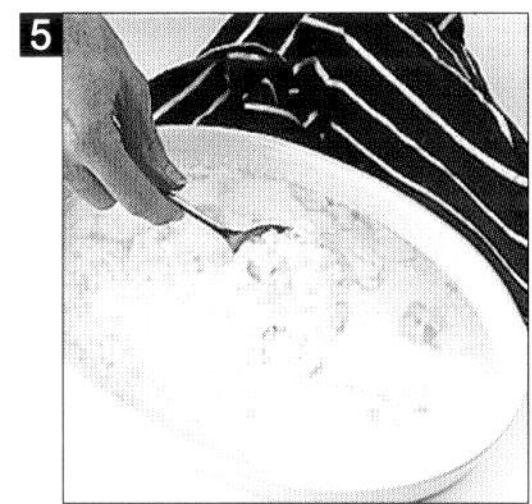

6 Cover the top of the pudding with foil if it starts to brown too much towards the end of the cooking time.

7 Serve the baked coconut rice pudding warm, or chilled if you prefer, with fresh or stewed fruit.

COOK'S TIP

As the mixture cools it thickens. If you plan to serve the rice chilled then fold in about 3 tablespoons cream or extra coconut milk before serving to give a thinner consistency.

Pink Syllabubs

The pretty pink colour of this dessert is achieved by adding blackcurrant liqueur to the wine and cream before whipping.

NUTRITIONAL INFORMATION

Calories	536	Sugars	17g
Protein	2g	Fat	48g
Carbohydrate	17g	Saturates	30g

45 MINS   0 MINS

SERVES 2

INGREDIENTS

- 5 tbsp white wine
- 2–3 tsp blackcurrant liqueur
- finely grated rind of ½ lemon or orange
- 1 tbsp caster (superfine) sugar
- 200 ml/7 fl oz/scant 1 cup double (heavy) cream
- 4 boudoir biscuits (lady-fingers) (optional)

TO DECORATE

- fresh fruit, such as strawberries, raspberries or redcurrants, or pecan or walnut halves
- mint sprigs

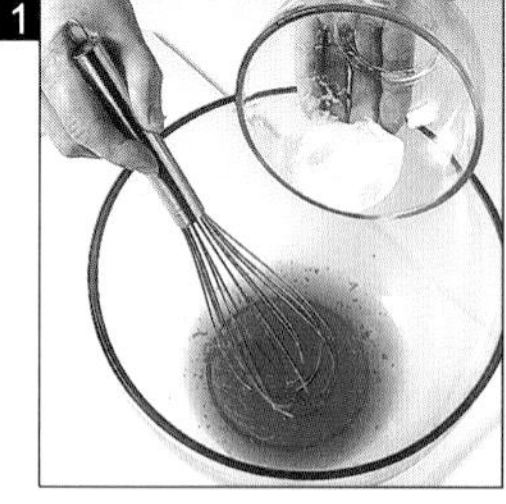

1 Mix together the white wine, blackcurrant liqueur, grated lemon or orange rind and caster (superfine) sugar in a bowl and set aside for at least 30 minutes.

2 Add the cream to the wine mixture and whip until the mixture has thickened enough to stand in soft peaks.

3 If you are using the boudoir biscuits (lady-fingers), break them up roughly and divide them between 2 glasses.

4 Put the mixture into a piping bag fitted with a large star or plain nozzle (tip) and pipe it over the biscuits (lady-fingers). Alternatively, simply pour the syllabub over the biscuits (lady-fingers). Chill until ready to serve.

5 Before serving, decorate each syllabub with slices or small pieces of fresh soft fruit or nuts, and sprigs of mint.

COOK'S TIP

These syllabubs will keep in the refrigerator for 48 hours, so it is worth making more than you need, and keeping the extra for another day.

Pear Tart

Pears are a very popular fruit in Italy. In this recipe from Trentino they are flavoured with almonds, cinnamon, raisins and apricot jam.

NUTRITIONAL INFORMATION

Calories	629	Sugars	70g
Protein	7g	Fat	21g
Carbohydrate	109g	Saturates	13g

1½ HOURS 50 MINS

SERVES 6

INGREDIENTS

- 275 g/9½ oz/2¼ cups plain (all-purpose) flour
- pinch of salt
- 125 g/4½ oz/½ cup caster (superfine) sugar
- 125 g/4½ oz/½ cup butter, diced
- 1 egg
- 1 egg yolk
- few drops of vanilla essence (extract)
- 2–3 tsp water
- sifted icing (confectioners') sugar, for sprinkling

FILLING

- 4 tbsp apricot jam
- 60 g/2 oz amaretti or ratafia biscuits (cookies), crumbled
- 850–1 kg/1¾–2 lb 4 oz pears, peeled and cored
- 1 tsp ground cinnamon
- 90 g/3 oz/½ cup raisins
- 60 g/2 oz/⅓ cup soft brown or demerara sugar

1 Sift the flour and salt on to a flat surface, make a well in the centre and add the sugar, butter, egg, egg yolk, vanilla essence (extract) and most of the water.

2 Using your fingers, gradually work the flour into the other ingredients to give a smooth dough, adding more water if necessary. Wrap in cling film (plastic wrap) and chill for 1 hour or until firm. Alternatively, put all the ingredients into a food processor and work until smooth.

3 Roll out three-quarters of the dough and use to line a shallow 25 cm/10 inch cake tin (pan) or deep flan tin (pan). Spread the jam over the base and sprinkle with the crushed biscuits (cookies).

4 Slice the pears very thinly. Arrange over the biscuits (cookies) in the pastry case. Sprinkle with cinnamon then with raisins, and finally with brown sugar.

5 Roll out a thin sausage shape using one-third of the remaining dough, and place around the edge of the pie. Roll the remainder into thin sausages and arrange in a lattice over the pie, 4 or 5 strips in each direction, attaching them to the strip around the edge.

6 Cook in a preheated oven, at 200°C/400°F/Gas Mark 6, for 50 minutes until golden and cooked through. Leave to cool, then serve warm or chilled, sprinkled with sifted icing (confectioners') sugar.

1

3

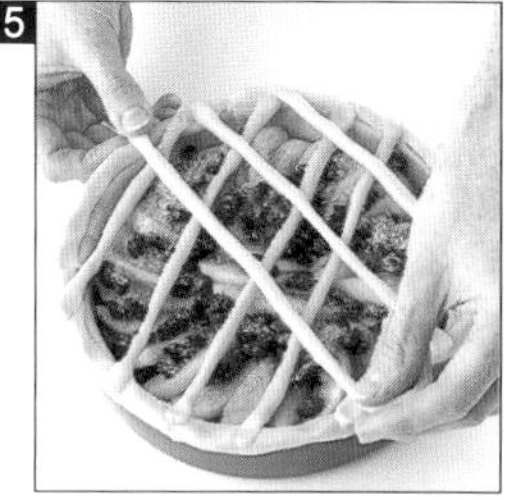

5

New Age Spotted Dick

This is a deliciously moist low-fat pudding. The sauce is in the centre of the pudding, and will spill out when the pudding is cut.

NUTRITIONAL INFORMATION

Calories	529	Sugars	41g
Protein	9g	Fat	31g
Carbohydrate	58g	Saturates	4g

 25 MINS

1¼ HOURS

SERVES 6–8

INGREDIENTS

- 125 g/4½ oz/¾ cup raisins
- 125 ml/4 fl oz/generous ½ cup corn oil, plus a little for brushing
- 125 g/4½ oz/generous ½ cup caster (superfine) sugar
- 25 g/1 oz/¼ cup ground almonds
- 2 eggs, lightly beaten
- 175 g/6 oz/1½ cups self-raising flour

SAUCE

- 60 g/2 oz/½ cup walnuts, chopped
- 60 g/2 oz/½ cup ground almonds
- 300 ml/½ pint/1¼ cups semi-skimmed milk
- 4 tbsp granulated sugar

1 Put the raisins in a saucepan with 125 ml/4 fl oz/½ cup water. Bring to the boil, then remove from the heat. Leave to steep for 10 minutes, then drain.

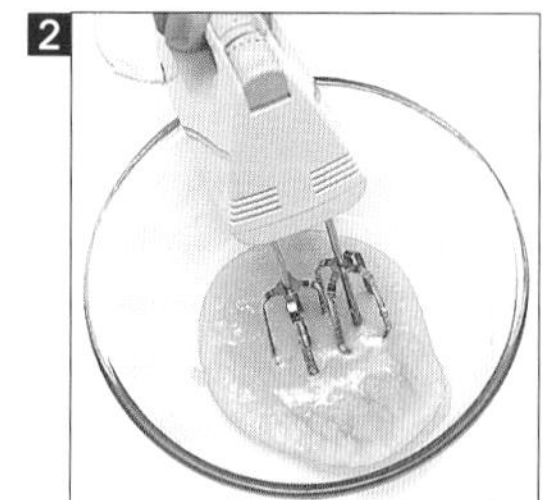
2

2 Whisk together the oil, sugar and ground almonds until thick and syrupy; this will need about 8 minutes of beating (on medium speed if using an electric whisk).

3

3 Add the eggs, one at a time, beating well after each addition. Combine the flour and raisins. Stir into the mixture. Brush a 1 litre/1¾ pint/4 cup pudding basin with oil, or line with baking parchment.

3

4 Put all the sauce ingredients into a saucepan. Bring to the boil, stir and simmer for 10 minutes.

5 Transfer the sponge mixture to the greased basin and pour on the hot sauce. Place on a baking tray (cookie sheet).

6 Bake in a preheated oven at 170°C/340°F/Gas Mark 3½ for about 1 hour. Lay a piece of baking parchment across the top if it starts to brown too fast.

7 Leave to cool for 2–3 minutes in the basin before turning out on to a serving plate.

COOK'S TIP

Always soak raisins before baking them, as they retain their moisture nicely and you taste the flavour of them instead of biting on a dried-out raisin.

Exotic Fruit Pancakes

These pancakes are filled with an exotic array of tropical fruits. Decorate lavishly with tropical flowers or mint sprigs.

NUTRITIONAL INFORMATION

Calories	382	Sugars	24g
Protein	7g	Fat	17g
Carbohydrate	53g	Saturates	3g

40 MINS 35 MINS

SERVES 4

INGREDIENTS

BATTER

- 125 g/4½ oz/1 cup plain flour
- pinch of salt
- 1 egg
- 1 egg yolk
- 300 ml/½ pint/1¼ cups coconut milk
- 4 tsp vegetable oil, plus oil for frying

FILLING

- 1 banana
- 1 paw-paw (papaya)
- juice of 1 lime
- 2 passion fruit
- 1 mango, peeled, stoned and sliced
- 4 lychees, stoned and halved
- 1-2 tbsp honey
- flowers or mint sprigs, to decorate

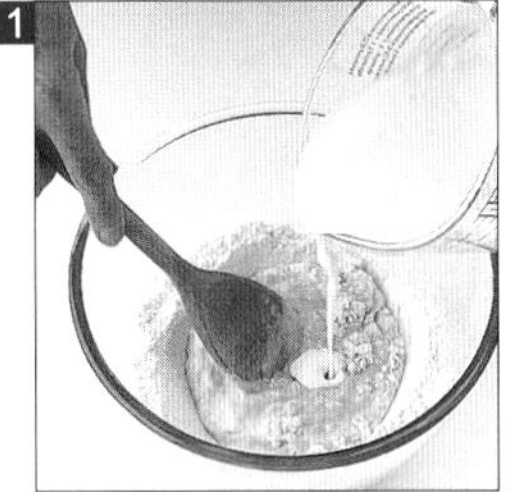

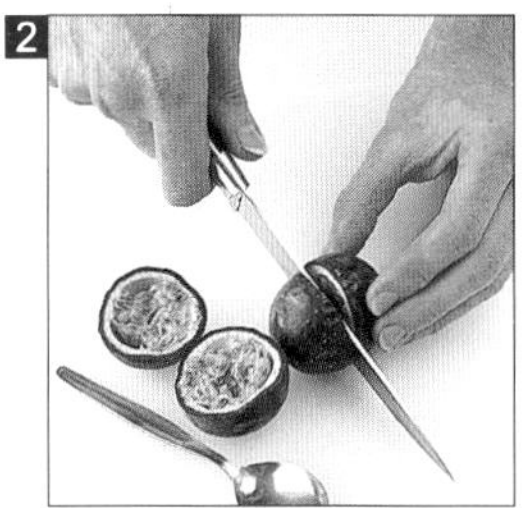

1 Sift the flour and salt into a bowl. Make a well in the centre and add the egg, egg yolk and a little of the coconut milk. Gradually draw the flour into the egg mixture, beating well and slowly adding the remaining coconut milk to make a smooth batter. Stir in the oil. Cover and chill for 30 minutes.

2 Peel and slice the banana and place in a bowl. Peel and slice the paw-paw (papaya), discarding the seeds. Add to the banana with the lime juice and mix well. Cut the passion-fruit in half and scoop out the flesh and seeds into the fruit bowl. Stir in the mango, lychees and honey.

3 Heat a little oil in a 15 cm/6 inch frying pan (skillet). Pour in just enough of the pancake batter to cover the base of the pan and tilt so that it spreads thinly and evenly. Cook until the pancake is just set and the underside is lightly browned, turn and briefly cook the other side. Remove from the pan and keep warm. Repeat with the remaining batter to make a total of 8 pancakes.

4 To serve, place a little of the prepared fruit filling along the centre of each pancake and then roll it into a cone shape. Lay seam-side down on warmed serving plates, decorate with flowers or mint sprigs and serve.

Mascarpone Cheesecake

The mascarpone gives this baked cheesecake a wonderfully tangy flavour. Ricotta cheese could be used as an alternative.

NUTRITIONAL INFORMATION

Calories	327	Sugars	25g
Protein	9g	Fat	18g
Carbohydrate	33g	Saturates	11g

15 MINS 50 MINS

SERVES 8

INGREDIENTS

- 50 g/1¾ oz/1½ tbsp unsalted butter
- 150 g/5½ oz ginger biscuits (cookies), crushed
- 25 g/1 oz stem ginger (candied), chopped
- 500 g/1 lb 2 oz mascarpone cheese
- finely grated rind and juice of 2 lemons
- 100 g/3½ oz caster (superfine) sugar
- 2 large eggs, separated
- fruit coulis (see Cook's Tip), to serve

1 Grease and line the base of a 25 cm/10 inch spring-form cake tin (pan) or loose-bottomed tin (pan).

2 Melt the butter in a pan and stir in the crushed biscuits (cookies) and chopped ginger. Use the mixture to line the tin (pan), pressing the mixture about 6 mm/¼ inch up the sides.

COOK'S TIP

Fruit coulis can be made by cooking 400 g/14 oz fruit, such as blueberries, for 5 minutes with 2 tablespoons of water. Sieve the mixture, then stir in 1 tablespoon (or more to taste) of sifted icing (confectioners') sugar. Leave to cool before serving.

1

2

2

3 Beat together the cheese, lemon rind and juice, sugar and egg yolks until quite smooth.

4 Whisk the egg whites until they are stiff and fold into the cheese and lemon mixture.

5 Pour the mixture into the tin (pan) and bake in a preheated oven, at 180°C/350°F/Gas Mark 4, for 35–45 minutes until just set. Don't worry if it cracks or sinks – this is quite normal.

6 Leave the cheesecake in the tin (pan) to cool. Serve with fruit coulis (see Cook's Tip).

Italian Chocolate Truffles

These are flavoured with almonds and chocolate, and are simplicity itself to make. Served with coffee, they are the perfect end to a meal.

NUTRITIONAL INFORMATION

Calories	82	Sugars	7g
Protein	1g	Fat	5g
Carbohydrate	8g	Saturates	3g

 5 MINS  5 MINS

MAKES 24

INGREDIENTS

- 175 g/6 oz dark chocolate
- 2 tbsp almond-flavoured liqueur (amaretto) or orange-flavoured liqueur
- 40 g/1½ oz/3 tbsp unsalted butter
- 50 g/1¾ oz icing (confectioners') sugar
- 50 g/1¾ oz/½ cup ground almonds
- 50 g/1¾ oz grated milk chocolate

1 Melt the dark chocolate with the liqueur in a bowl set over a saucepan of hot water, stirring until well combined.

2 Add the butter and stir until it has melted. Stir in the icing (confectioners') sugar and the ground almonds.

3 Leave the mixture in a cool place until firm enough to roll into 24 balls.

4 Place the grated chocolate on a plate and roll the truffles in the chocolate to coat them.

5 Place the truffles in paper sweet (candy) cases and chill.

2

2

4

Chinese Custard Tarts

These small tarts are irresistible – a custard is baked in a rich, sweet pastry. The tarts may be served warm or cold.

NUTRITIONAL INFORMATION

Calories	474	Sugars	30g
Protein	9g	Fat	22g
Carbohydrate	64g	Saturates	12g

 20 MINS  30 MINS

SERVES 4

INGREDIENTS

DOUGH

- 175 g/6 oz/1½ cups plain (all-purpose) flour
- 3 tbsp caster (superfine) sugar
- 60 g/2 oz/4 tbsp unsalted butter
- 25 g/1 oz/2 tbsp lard (shortening)
- 2 tbsp water

CUSTARD

- 2 small eggs
- 60 g/2 oz/¼ cup caster (superfine) sugar
- 175 ml/6 fl oz/¾ cup pint milk
- ½ tsp ground nutmeg, plus extra for sprinkling
- cream, to serve

1 To make the dough, sift the plain (all-purpose) flour into a bowl. Add the caster (superfine) sugar and rub in the butter and lard (shortening) until the mixture resembles breadcrumbs. Add the water and mix to form a firm dough.

2 Transfer the dough to a lightly floured surface and knead for 5 minutes, until smooth. Cover with cling film (plastic wrap) and leave to chill in the refrigerator while you prepare the filling.

3 To make the custard, beat the eggs and sugar together. Gradually add the milk and ground nutmeg and beat until well combined.

4 Separate the dough into 15 even-sized pieces. Flatten the dough pieces into rounds and press into shallow patty tins (pans).

5 Spoon the custard into the pastry cases (tart shells) and cook in a preheated oven, at 150°C/300°F/Gas 2, for 25-30 minutes.

6 Transfer the Chinese custard tarts to a wire rack, leave to cool slightly, then sprinkle with nutmeg. Serve hot or cold with cream.

3

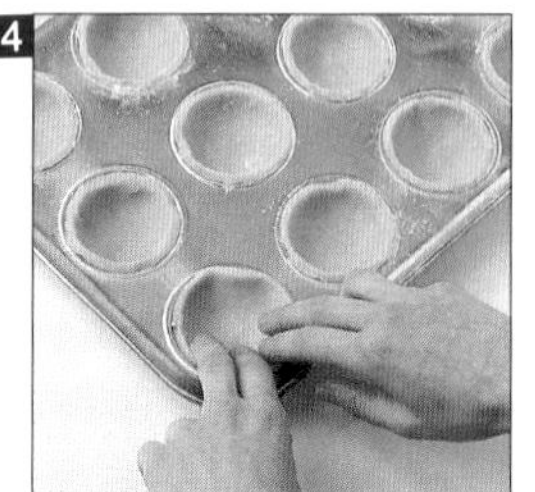

4

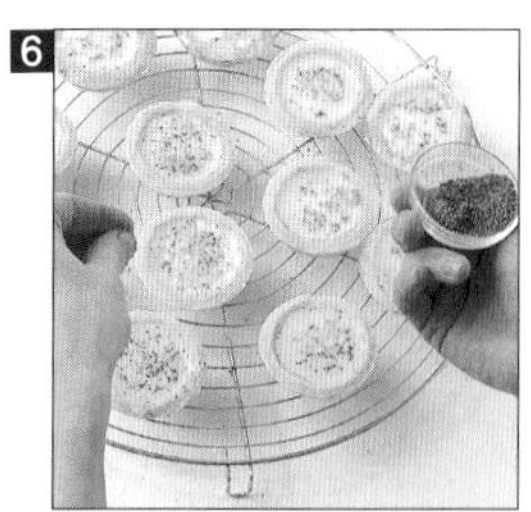

6

COOK'S TIP

For extra convenience, make the dough in advance, cover and leave to chill in the refrigerator until required.

Baked Apples with Berries

This winter dessert is a classic dish. Large, fluffy apples are hollowed out and filled with spices, almonds and blackberries.

NUTRITIONAL INFORMATION

Calories	228	Sugars	31g
Protein	1g	Fat	2g
Carbohydrate	31g	Saturates	0.2g

10 MINS 45 MINS

SERVES 4

INGREDIENTS

- 4 medium-sized cooking apples
- 1 tbsp lemon juice
- 100 g/3½ oz prepared blackberries, thawed if frozen
- 15 g/½ oz flaked (slivered) almonds
- ½ tsp ground allspice
- ½ tsp finely grated lemon rind
- 2 tbsp demerara (brown crystal) sugar
- 300 ml/½ pint/1¼ cups ruby port
- 1 cinnamon stick, broken
- 2 tsp cornflour (cornstarch) blended with 2 tbsp cold water
- low-fat custard, to serve

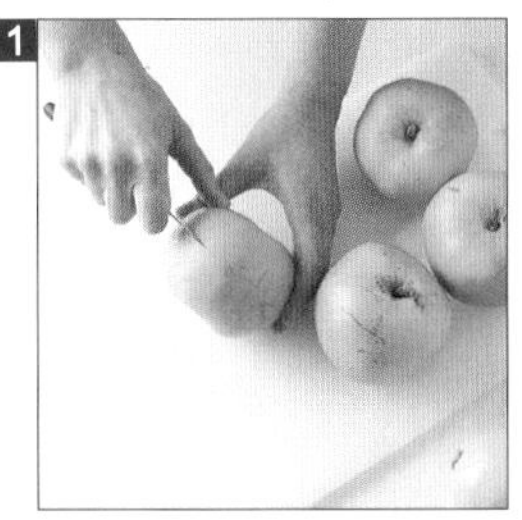

1

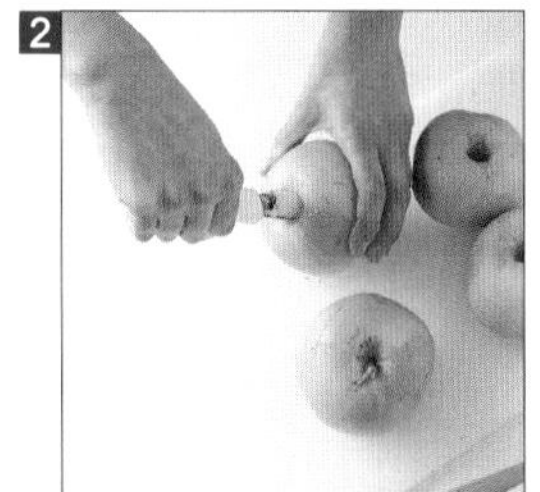

2

3

1 Preheat the oven to 200°C/400°F/Gas Mark 6. Wash and dry the apples. Using a small sharp knife, make a shallow cut through the skin around the middle of each apple – this will help the apples to cook through.

2 Core the apples, brush the centres with the lemon juice to prevent browning and stand in an ovenproof dish.

3 In a bowl, mix together the blackberries, almonds, allspice, lemon rind and sugar. Using a teaspoon, spoon the mixture into the centre of each apple.

4 Pour the port into the dish, add the cinnamon stick and bake the apples in the oven for 35–40 minutes or until tender and soft. Drain the cooking juices into a pan and keep the apples warm.

5 Discard the cinnamon and add the cornflour (cornstarch) mixture to the cooking juices. Heat, stirring, until thickened.

6 Heat the custard until piping hot. Pour the sauce over the apples and serve with the custard.

Indian Bread Pudding

This, the Indian equivalent of the English bread and butter pudding, is rather a special dessert, usually cooked for special occasions.

NUTRITIONAL INFORMATION

Calories	445	Sugars	43g
Protein	10g	Fat	20g
Carbohydrate	60g	Saturates	11g

20 MINS 25 MINS

SERVES 6

INGREDIENTS

- 6 medium slices bread
- 5 tbsp ghee (preferably pure)
- 150 g/5½ oz/¾ cup sugar
- 300 ml/½ pint/1¼ cups water
- 3 green cardamoms, without husks
- 600 ml/1 pint/2½ cups milk
- 175 ml/6 fl oz/¾ cup evaporated milk or khoya (see Cook's Tip)
- ½ tsp saffron strands
- double (heavy) cream, to serve (optional)

TO DECORATE

- 8 pistachio nuts, soaked, peeled and chopped
- chopped almonds
- 2 leaves varq (silver leaf) (optional)

COOK'S TIP

To make khoya, bring 900 ml/1½ pints/3¾ cups milk to the boil in a large, heavy saucepan. Reduce the heat and boil, stirring occasionally, for 35-40 minutes, until reduced to a quarter of its volume and resembling a sticky dough.

1 Cut the bread slices into quarters. Heat the ghee in a large, heavy-based frying-pan (skillet). Add the bread slices and fry, turning once, until a crisp golden brown colour. Place the fried bread in the base of a heatproof dish and set aside.

2 To make a syrup, place the sugar, water and cardamom seeds in a saucepan and bring to the boil over a medium heat, stirring constantly, until the sugar has dissolved. Boil until the syrup thickens. Pour the syrup over the fried bread.

3 Put the milk, evaporated milk or khoya (see Cook's Tip) and the saffron in a separate saucepan and bring to the boil over a low heat. Simmer until the it has halved in volume. Pour the mixture over the syrup-coated bread.

4 Decorate with the pistachios, chopped almonds and varq (if using). Serve the bread pudding with cream, if liked.

1

2

3

Apricot Brûlée

Serve this melt-in-the-mouth dessert with crisp-baked meringues for an extra-special occasion.

NUTRITIONAL INFORMATION

Calories	307	Sugars	38g
Protein	5g	Fat	16g
Carbohydrate	38g	Saturates	9g

 2¼ HOURS  35 MINS

SERVES 6

I N G R E D I E N T S

- 125 g/4½ oz/⅔ cup unsulphured dried apricots
- 150 ml/¼ pint/⅔ cup orange juice
- 4 egg yolks
- 2 tbsp caster (superfine) sugar
- 150 ml/¼ pint/⅔ cup natural (unsweetened) yogurt
- 150 ml/¼ pint/⅔ cup double (heavy) cream
- 1 tsp vanilla essence (extract)
- 90 g/3 oz/½ cup demerara (brown crystal) sugar
- meringues, to serve (optional)

1 Place the apricots and orange juice in a bowl and set aside to soak for at least 1 hour. Pour into a small pan, bring slowly to the boil and simmer for 20 minutes. Process in a blender or food processor or chop very finely and push through a strainer.

2 Beat together the egg yolks and sugar until the mixture is light and fluffy. Place the yogurt in a small pan, add the cream and vanilla and bring to the boil over a low heat.

3 Pour the yogurt mixture over the eggs, beating all the time, then transfer to the top of a double boiler or place the bowl over a pan of simmering water. Stir until the custard thickens. Divide the apricot mixture between 6 ramekins and carefully pour on the custard. Cool, then chill in the refrigerator at least 1 hour.

4 Sprinkle the demerara (brown crystal) sugar evenly over the custard and place under a preheated grill (broiler) until the sugar caramelizes. Set aside to cool. To serve the brûlée, crack the hard caramel topping with the back of a tablespoon.

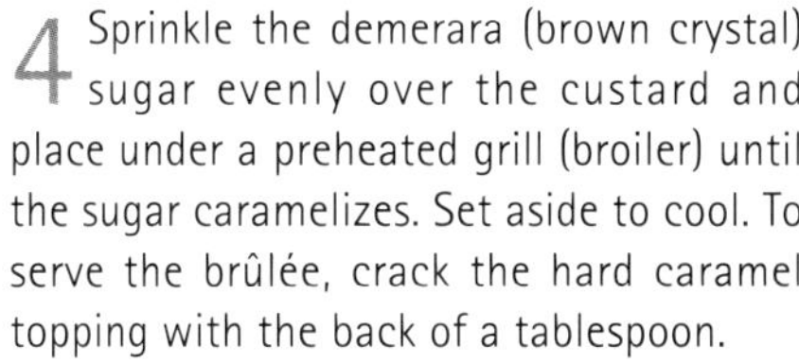

2

3

4

Eggless Sponge

This is a healthy variation of the classic Victoria sponge cake (sponge layer cake) and is suitable for vegans.

NUTRITIONAL INFORMATION

Calories	273	Sugars	27g
Protein	3g	Fat	9g
Carbohydrate	49g	Saturates	1g

 1¼ HOURS  30 MINS

1 x 8" CAKE

INGREDIENTS

- 225 g/8 oz/1¾ cups self-raising wholemeal (whole wheat) flour
- 2 tsp baking powder
- 175 g/6 oz/¾ cup caster (superfine) sugar
- 6 tbsp sunflower oil
- 250 ml/9 fl oz/1 cup water
- 1 tsp vanilla flavouring (extract)
- 4 tbsp strawberry or raspberry reduced-sugar spread
- caster (superfine) sugar, for dusting

1 Grease two 20 cm/8 inch sandwich cake tins (layer pans) and line them with baking parchment.

2 Sieve (strain) the self-raising flour and baking powder into a large mixing bowl, stirring in any bran remaining in the sieve. Stir in the caster (superfine) sugar.

3 Pour in the sunflower oil, water and vanilla flavouring (extract). Mix well with a wooden spoon for about 1 minute until the mixture is smooth, then divide between the prepared tins (pans).

3

3

3

4 Bake in a preheated oven, 180°C/350°F/Gas Mark 4, for about 25-30 minutes until the centre springs back when lightly touched.

5 Leave the sponges to cool in the tins (pans) before turning out and transferring to a wire rack.

6 To serve, remove the baking parchment and place one of the sponges on to a serving plate. Spread with the jam and place the other sponge on top.

7 Dust the eggless sponge cake with a little caster (superfine) sugar before serving.

Caramelized Oranges

The secret of these oranges is to allow them to marinate in the syrup for at least 24 hours, so the flavours amalgamate.

NUTRITIONAL INFORMATION

Calories	235	Sugars	59g
Protein	2g	Fat	0.2g
Carbohydrate	59g	Saturates	0g

 3¼ HOURS  20 MINS

SERVES 6

INGREDIENTS

- 6 large oranges
- 225 g/8 oz/1 cup sugar
- 250 ml/9 fl oz/1 cup water
- 6 whole cloves (optional)
- 2–4 tbsp orange-flavoured liqueur or brandy

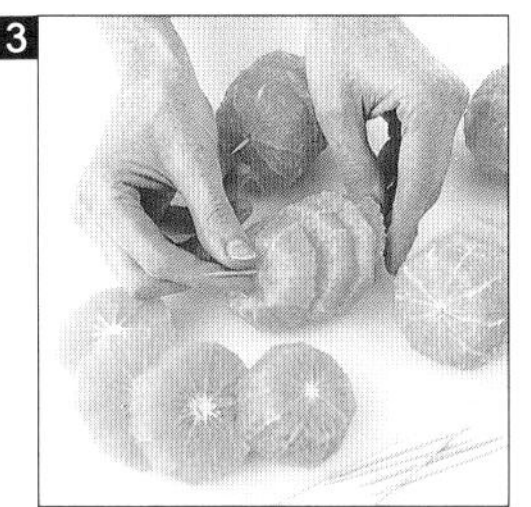

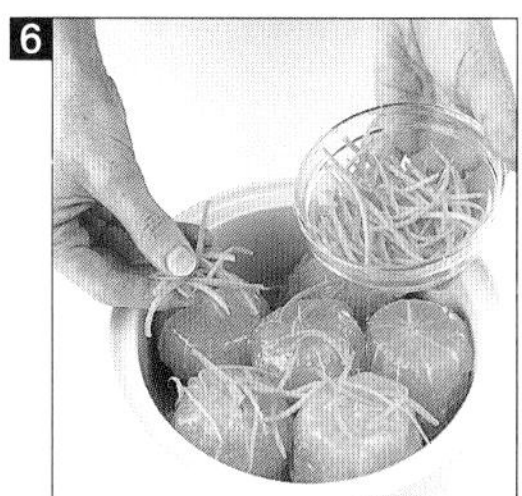

1 Using a citrus zester or potato peeler, pare the rind from 2 of the oranges in narrow strips without any white pith attached. If using a potato peeler, cut the peel into very thin julienne strips.

2 Put the strips into a small saucepan and barely cover with water. Bring to the boil and simmer for 5 minutes. Drain the strips and reserve the water.

3 Cut away all the white pith and peel from the remaining oranges using a very sharp knife. Then cut horizontally into 4 slices. Reassemble the oranges and hold in place with wooden cocktail sticks (toothpick). Stand in a heatproof dish.

4 Put the sugar and water into a heavy-based saucepan with the cloves, if using. Bring to the boil and simmer gently until the sugar has dissolved, then boil hard without stirring until the syrup thickens and begins to colour. Continue to cook until a light golden brown, then quickly remove from the heat and carefully pour in the reserved orange rind liquid.

5 Place over a gentle heat until the caramel has fully dissolved again, then remove from the heat and add the liqueur or brandy. Pour over the oranges.

6 Sprinkle the orange strips over the oranges, cover with cling film (plastic wrap) and leave until cold. Chill for at least 3 hours and preferably for 24–48 hours before serving. If time allows, spoon the syrup over the oranges several times while they are marinating. Discard the cocktail stick (toothpick) before serving.

Vanilla Ice Cream

This home-made version of real vanilla ice cream is absolutely delicious and so easy to make. A tutti-frutti variation is also provided.

NUTRITIONAL INFORMATION

Calories	626	Sugars	33g
Protein	7g	Fat	53g
Carbohydrate	33g	Saturates	31g

 5 MINS  15 MINS

SERVES 6

INGREDIENTS

- 600 ml/1 pint/2½ cups double (heavy) cream
- 1 vanilla pod
- pared rind of 1 lemon
- 4 eggs, beaten
- 2 egg, yolks
- 175 g/6 oz caster (superfine) sugar

1 Place the cream in a heavy-based saucepan and heat gently, whisking.

2 Add the vanilla pod, lemon rind, eggs and egg yolks to the pan and heat until the mixture reaches just below boiling point.

3 Reduce the heat and cook for 8–10 minutes, whisking the mixture continuously, until thickened.

4 Stir the sugar into the cream mixture, set aside and leave to cool.

5 Strain the cream mixture through a sieve.

6 Slit open the vanilla pod, scoop out the tiny black seeds and stir them into the cream.

7 Pour the mixture into a shallow freezing container with a lid and freeze overnight until set. Serve the ice cream when required.

1

4

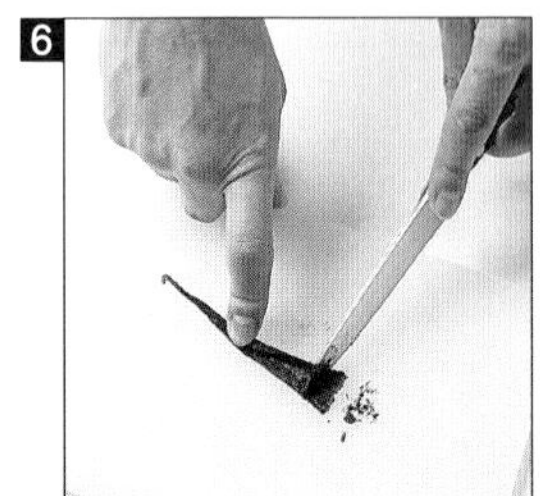
6

VARIATION

For tutti frutti ice cream, soak 100 g/3½ oz mixed dried fruit in 2 tbsp Marsala or sweet sherry for 20 minutes. Follow the method for vanilla ice cream, omitting the vanilla pod, and stir in the Marsala or sherry-soaked fruit in step 5, just before freezing.

Battered Bananas

These bananas are quite irresistible, therefore it may be wise to make double quantities for weak-willed guests!

NUTRITIONAL INFORMATION

Calories	562	Sugars	79g
Protein	6g	Fat	10g
Carbohydrate	118g	Saturates	1g

 10 MINS  20 MINS

SERVES 4

INGREDIENTS

- 8 medium bananas
- 2 tsp lemon juice
- 75 g/2¾ oz/⅔ cup self-raising flour
- 75 g/2¾ oz/⅔ cup rice flour
- 1 tbsp cornflour (cornstarch)
- ½ tsp ground cinnamon
- 250 ml/9 fl oz/1 cup water
- oil, for deep-frying
- 4 tbsp light brown sugar
- cream or ice cream, to serve

1 Cut the bananas into even-sized chunks and place them in a large mixing bowl.

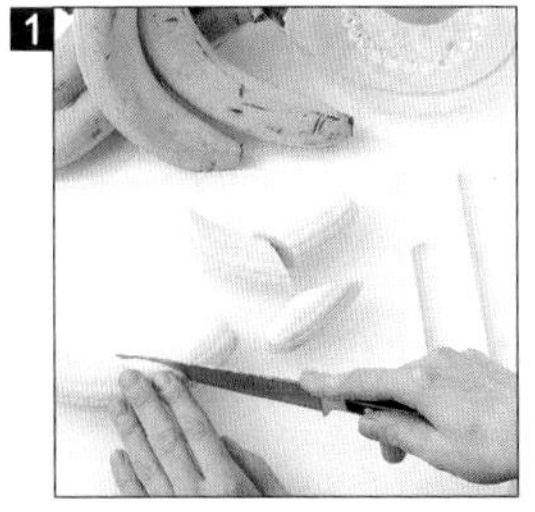
1

2 Sprinkle the lemon juice over the bananas to prevent discoloration.

3 Sift the self-raising flour, rice flour, cornflour (cornstarch) and cinnamon into a mixing bowl. Gradually stir in the water to make a thin batter.

4 Heat the oil in a preheated wok until almost smoking, then reduce the heat slightly.

5 Place a piece of banana on the end of a fork and carefully dip it into the batter, draining off any excess. Repeat with the remaining banana pieces.

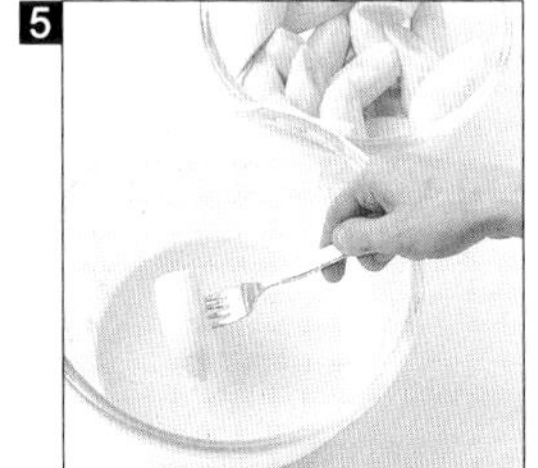
5

6 Sprinkle the light brown sugar on to a large plate.

7 Carefully place the banana pieces in the oil and cook for 2-3 minutes, until golden. Remove the banana pieces from the oil with a slotted spoon and roll them in the sugar.

7

8 Transfer the bananas to serving bowls and serve with cream or ice cream.

COOK'S TIP

Rice flour can be bought from wholefood shops or from Chinese supermarkets.

Christmas Shortbread

Make this wonderful shortbread and then give it the Christmas touch by cutting it into shapes with seasonal biscuit (cookie) cutters.

NUTRITIONAL INFORMATION

Calories	162	Sugars	10g
Protein	1g	Fat	9g
Carbohydrate	21g	Saturates	6g

 45 MINS

 15 MINS

MAKES 24

INGREDIENTS

- 125 g/4½ oz/½ cup caster (superfine) sugar
- 225 g/8 oz/1 cup butter
- 350 g/12 oz/3 cups plain (all-purpose) flour, sifted
- pinch of salt

TO DECORATE

- 60 g/2 oz/½ cup icing (confectioners') sugar
- silver balls
- glacé (candied) cherries
- angelica

1 Beat the sugar and butter together in a large bowl until combined (thorough creaming is not necessary).

2 Sift in the flour and salt and work together to form a stiff dough. Turn out on to a lightly floured surface. Knead lightly for a few moments until smooth, but avoid overhandling. Chill in the refrigerator for 10–15 minutes.

3 Roll out the dough on a lightly floured work surface and cut into shapes with small Christmas cutters, such as bells, stars and angels. Place on greased baking trays (cookie sheets).

4 Bake the biscuits (cookies) in a preheated oven, 180°C/350°F/Gas Mark 4 for 10–15 minutes, until pale golden brown. Leave on the baking trays (cookie sheets) for 10 minutes, then transfer to wire racks to cool completely.

5 Mix the icing (confectioners') sugar with a little water to make a glacé icing (frosting), and use to ice (frost) the biscuits (cookies). Decorate with silver balls, tiny pieces of glacé (candied) cherries and angelica. Store in an airtight container or wrap the biscuits (cookies) individually in cellophane, tie with coloured ribbon or string and then hang them on the Christmas tree as edible decorations.

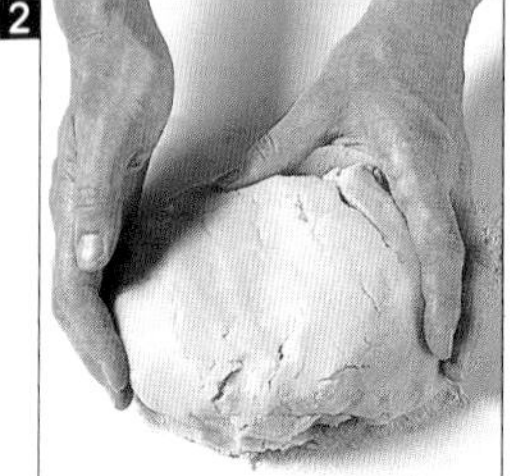
2

3

5

Semolina Dessert

This dish is eaten with pooris and potato curry for breakfast in northern India, but you can serve it with fresh cream for a delicious dessert.

NUTRITIONAL INFORMATION

Calories	676	Sugars	66g
Protein	10g	Fat	31g
Carbohydrate	96g	Saturates	19g

5 MINS 10 MINS

SERVES 4

INGREDIENTS

- 6 tbsp pure ghee
- 3 whole cloves
- 3 whole cardamoms
- 8 tbsp coarse semolina
- ½ tsp saffron
- 50 g/1¾ oz/½ cup sultanas (golden raisins)
- 10 tbsp sugar
- 300 ml/½ pint/1¼ cups water
- 300 ml/½ pint/1¼ cups milk
- cream, to serve

TO DECORATE

- 25 g/1 oz/½ cup desiccated (shredded) coconut, toasted
- 25 g/1 oz/¼ cup chopped almonds
- 25 g/1 oz/¼ cup pistachio nuts, soaked and chopped (optional)

2

3

4

1 Place the ghee in a saucepan and melt over a medium heat.

2 Add the cloves and the whole cardamoms to the melted butter and reduce the heat, stirring to mix.

3 Add the semolina to the mixture in the pan and stir-fry until it turns a little darker.

4 Add the saffron, sultanas (golden raisins) and the sugar to the semolina mixture, stirring to mix well.

5 Pour in the water and milk and stir-fry the mixture continuously until the semolina has softened. Add a little more water if required.

6 Remove the pan from the heat and transfer the semolina to a warmed serving dish.

7 Decorate the semolina dessert with the toasted coconut, flaked almonds and pistachios. Serve with a little cream drizzled over the top.

Banana & Lime Cake

A substantial cake that is ideal served for tea. The mashed bananas help to keep the cake moist, and the lime icing gives it extra zing and zest.

NUTRITIONAL INFORMATION

Calories	235	Sugars	31g
Protein	5g	Fat	1g
Carbohydrate	55g	Saturates	0.3g

35 MINS 45 MINS

SERVES 10

INGREDIENTS

- 300 g/10½ oz plain (all-purpose) flour
- 1 tsp salt
- 1½ tsp baking powder
- 175 g/6 oz light muscovado sugar
- 1 tsp lime rind, grated
- 1 medium egg, beaten
- 1 medium banana, mashed with 1 tbsp lime juice
- 150 ml/5 fl oz/⅔ cup low-fat natural fromage frais (unsweetened yogurt)
- 115 g/4 oz sultanas
- banana chips, to decorate
- lime rind, finely grated, to decorate

TOPPING

- 115 g/4 oz icing (confectioners') sugar
- 1–2 tsp lime juice
- ½ tsp lime rind, finely grated

1 Preheat the oven to 180°C/350°F/Gas Mark 4. Grease and line a deep 18 cm/7 inch round cake tin with baking parchment.

2 Sift the flour, salt and baking powder into a mixing bowl and stir in the sugar and lime rind.

3 Make a well in the centre of the dry ingredients and add the egg, banana, fromage frais (yogurt) and sultanas. Mix well until thoroughly incorporated.

4 Spoon the mixture into the tin and smooth the surface. Bake for 40–45 minutes until firm to the touch or until a skewer inserted in the centre comes out clean. Leave to cool for 10 minutes, then turn out on to a wire rack.

5 To make the topping, sift the icing (confectioners') sugar into a small bowl and mix with the lime juice to form a soft, but not too runny, icing. Stir in the grated lime rind. Drizzle the icing over the cake, letting it run down the sides.

6 Decorate the cake with banana chips and lime rind. Let the cake stand for 15 minutes so that the icing sets.

1

3

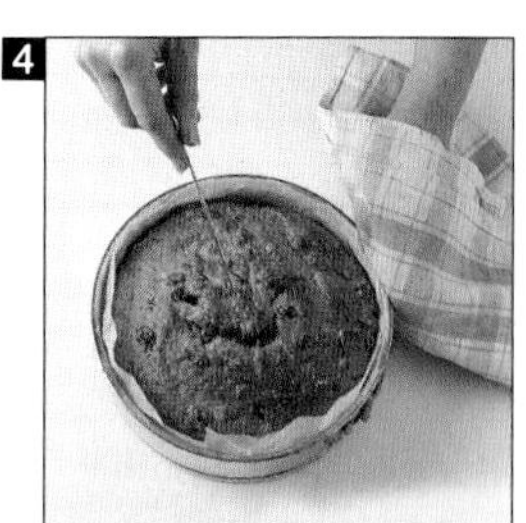

4

VARIATION

For a delicious alternative, replace the lime rind and juice with orange and the sultanas with chopped apricots.

Baked Pears with Cinnamon

This simple recipe is easy to prepare and cook but is deliciously warming. For a treat, serve hot on a pool of low-fat custard.

NUTRITIONAL INFORMATION

Calories	207	Sugars	35g
Protein	3g	Fat	6g
Carbohydrate	37g	Saturates	2g

 10 MINS  25 MINS

SERVES 4

INGREDIENTS

- 4 ripe pears
- 2 tbsp lemon juice
- 4 tbsp light muscovado sugar
- 1 tsp ground cinnamon
- 60 g/2 oz low-fat spread
- low-fat custard, to serve
- lemon rind, finely grated, to decorate

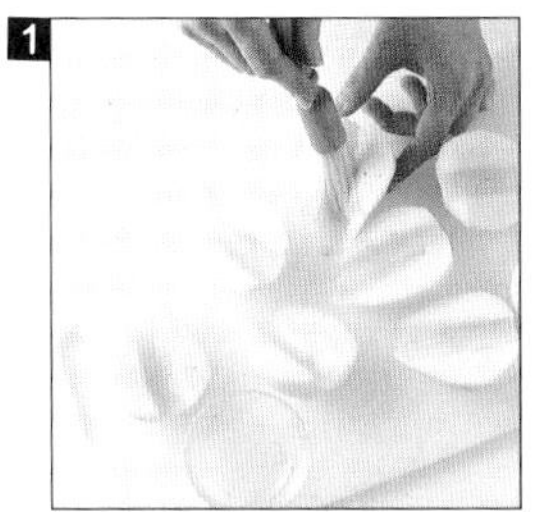

1 Preheat the oven to 200°C/400°F/Gas Mark 6. Core and peel the pears, then slice them in half lengthwise and brush all over with the lemon juice. Place the pears, cored side down, in a small non-stick roasting tin (pan).

2 Place the sugar, cinnamon and low-fat spread in a small saucepan and heat gently, stirring, until the sugar has melted. Keep the heat low to stop too much water evaporating from the low-fat spread as it gets hot. Spoon the mixture over the pears.

3 Bake for 20–25 minutes or until the pears are tender and golden, occasionally spooning the sugar mixture over the fruit during the cooking time.

4 To serve, heat the custard until it is piping hot and spoon over the bases of 4 warm dessert plates. Arrange 2 pear halves on each plate.

5 Decorate with grated lemon rind and serve.

VARIATION

For alternative flavours, replace the cinnamon with ground ginger and serve the pears sprinkled with chopped stem ginger in syrup. Alternatively, use ground allspice and spoon over some warmed dark rum to serve.

Honeyed Rice Puddings

These small rice puddings are quite sweet, but have a wonderful flavour because of the combination of ginger, honey and cinnamon.

NUTRITIONAL INFORMATION

Calories	199	Sugars	15g
Protein	3g	Fat	1g
Carbohydrate	46g	Saturates	0g

10 MINS 50 MINS

SERVES 4

INGREDIENTS

- 300 g/10½ oz/1½ cups pudding rice
- 2 tbsp clear honey, plus extra for drizzling
- large pinch of ground cinnamon
- 15 no-need-to-soak dried apricots, chopped
- 3 pieces stem (preserved) ginger, drained and chopped
- 8 whole no-need-to-soak dried apricots, to decorate

1 Put the rice in a saucepan and just cover with cold water. Bring to the boil, reduce the heat, cover and cook for about 15 minutes, or until the water has been absorbed. Stir the honey and cinnamon into the rice.

2 Grease 4 x 150 ml/¼ pint/⅔ cup ramekin dishes.

3 Blend the chopped dried apricots and ginger in a food processor to make a smooth paste.

4 Divide the paste into 4 equal portions and shape each into a flat round to fit into the base of the ramekin dishes.

5 Divide half of the rice between the ramekin dishes and place the apricot paste on top.

6 Cover the apricot paste with the remaining rice. Cover the ramekins with greaseproof (wax) paper and foil and steam for 30 minutes, or until set.

7 Remove the ramekins from the steamer and let stand for 5 minutes.

8 Turn the puddings out on to warm serving plates and drizzle with honey. Decorate with dried apricots and serve.

COOK'S TIP

The puddings may be left to chill in their ramekin dishes in the refrigerator, then turned out and served with ice cream or cream.

1

4

6

Bread & Butter Pudding

Everyone has their own favourite recipe for this dish. This one has added marmalade and grated apples for a really rich and unique taste.

NUTRITIONAL INFORMATION

Calories	427	Sugars	63g
Protein	9g	Fat	13g
Carbohydrate	74g	Saturates	7g

 45 MINS  1 HOUR

SERVES 6

INGREDIENTS

about 60 g/2 oz/¼ cup butter, softened
4–5 slices white or brown bread
4 tbsp chunky orange marmalade
grated rind of 1 lemon
90–125 g/3–4½ oz/½–¾ cup raisins or sultanas (golden raisins)
40 g/1½ oz/¼ cup chopped mixed (candied) peel
1 tsp ground cinnamon or mixed spice (apple spice)
1 cooking apple, peeled, cored and coarsely grated
90 g/3 oz/scant ½ cup light brown sugar
3 eggs
500 ml/18 fl oz/2 cups milk
2 tbsp demerara (brown crystal) sugar

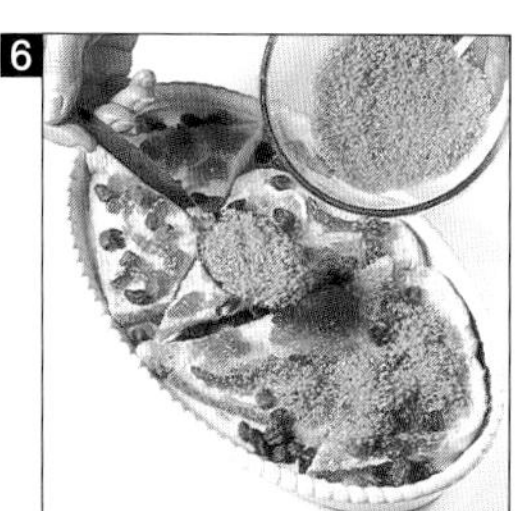

1 Use the butter to grease an ovenproof dish and to spread on the slices of bread, then spread the bread with the marmalade.

2 Place a layer of bread in the base of the dish and sprinkle with the lemon rind, half the raisins or sultanas (golden raisins), half the mixed (candied) peel, half the spice, all of the apple and half the light brown sugar.

3 Add another layer of bread, cutting so it fits the dish.

4 Sprinkle over most of the remaining raisins or sultanas (golden raisins) and the remaining peel, spice and light brown sugar, sprinkling it evenly over the bread. Top with a final layer of bread, again cutting to fit the dish.

5 Lightly beat together the eggs and milk and then carefully strain the mixture over the bread in the dish. If time allows, set aside to stand for 20–30 minutes.

6 Sprinkle the top of the pudding with the demerara (brown crystal) sugar and scatter over the remaining raisins or sultanas (golden raisins) and cook in a preheated oven, 200°C/400°F/Gas Mark 6, for 50–60 minutes, until risen and golden brown. Serve immediately or allow to cool and then serve cold.

Strawberry Roulade

Serve this moist, light sponge rolled up with an almond and strawberry fromage frais (yogurt) filling for a delicious tea-time treat.

NUTRITIONAL INFORMATION

Calories	166	Sugars	19g
Protein	6g	Fat	3g
Carbohydrate	30g	Saturates	1g

30 MINS   10 MINS

SERVES 8

INGREDIENTS

- 3 large eggs
- 125 g/4½ oz caster (superfine) sugar
- 125 g/4½ oz plain (all-purpose) flour
- 1 tbsp hot water

FILLING

- 200 ml/7 fl oz/¾ cup low-fat natural fromage frais (unsweetened yogurt)
- 1 tsp almond essence (extract)
- 225 g/8 oz small strawberries
- 15 g/½ oz toasted almonds, flaked (slivered)
- 1 tsp icing (confectioners') sugar

1 Preheat the oven to 220°C/425°F/Gas Mark 7. Line a 35 x 25 cm/14 x 10 inch Swiss roll tin with baking parchment. Place the eggs in a mixing bowl with the caster (superfine) sugar. Place the bowl over a pan of hot water and whisk until pale and thick.

2 Remove the bowl from the pan. Sift in the flour and fold into the eggs with the hot water. Pour the mixture into the tin and bake for 8–10 minutes, until golden and set.

3 Transfer the mixture to a sheet of baking parchment. Peel off the lining paper and roll up the sponge tightly along with the baking parchment. Wrap in a tea towel (dish towel) and let cool.

4 Mix together the fromage frais (yogurt) and the almond essence (extract). Reserving a few strawberries for decoration, wash, hull and slice the rest. Leave the mixture to chill in the refrigerator until required.

5 Unroll the sponge, spread the fromage frais (yogurt) mixture over the sponge and sprinkle with strawberries. Roll the sponge up again and transfer to a serving plate. Sprinkle with almonds and lightly dust with icing (confectioners') sugar. Decorate with the reserved strawberries.

1

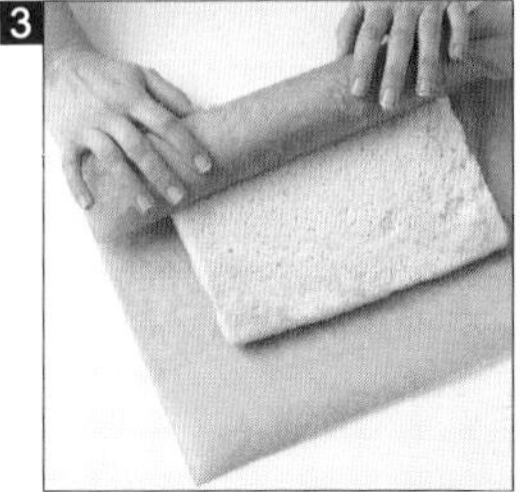

3

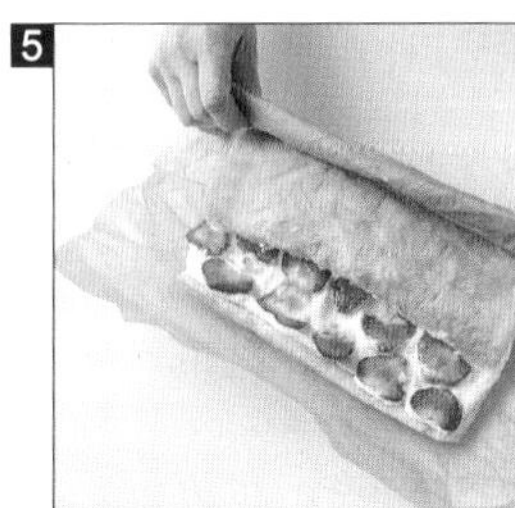

5

Boston Chocolate Pie

This lighter version of the popular chocolate cream pie is made with yogurt and crème fraîche.

NUTRITIONAL INFORMATION

Calories	795	Sugars	73g
Protein	13g	Fat	40g
Carbohydrate	99g	Saturates	21g

25 MINS 35 MINS

SERVES 6

INGREDIENTS

225 g/8 oz shortcrust pastry (see page 988)

CHOCOLATE CARAQUE

225 g/8 oz dark chocolate

FILLING

3 eggs

125 g/4½ oz/½ cup caster sugar

60 g/2 oz/½ cup flour, plus extra for dusting

1 tbsp icing (confectioners') sugar

pinch of salt

1 tsp vanilla essence (extract)

400 ml/14 fl oz/1⅔ cups milk

150 ml/¼ pint/⅔ cup natural (unsweetened) yogurt

150 g/5½ oz dark chocolate, broken into pieces

2 tbsp kirsch

TOPPING

150 ml/¼ pint/⅔ cup crème fraîche

1 Roll out the pastry and use to line a 23 cm/9 inch loose-based flan tin (pan). Prick the base with a fork, line with baking parchment and fill with dried beans. Bake blind for 20 minutes. Remove the beans and paper and return to the oven for 5 minutes. Remove from the oven and place on a wire rack to cool.

2 To make the chocolate caraque, put pieces of chocolate on a plate over a pan of simmering water until melted. Spread on a cool surface with a palette knife (spatula). When cool, scrape it into curls with a sharp knife.

3 To make the filling, beat the eggs and sugar until fluffy. Sift in the flour, icing (confectioners') sugar and salt. Stir in the vanilla essence (extract).

4 Bring the milk and yogurt to the boil in a small pan and strain on to the egg mixture. Pour into a double boiler or set over a pan of simmering water. Stir until it coats the back of a spoon.

5 Gently heat the chocolate and kirsch in a small pan until melted. Stir into the custard. Remove from the heat and stand the double boiler or bowl in cold water. Leave it to cool .

6 Pour the chocolate mixture into the pastry case. Spread the crème fraîche over the chocolate, and arrange the caraque rolls on top.

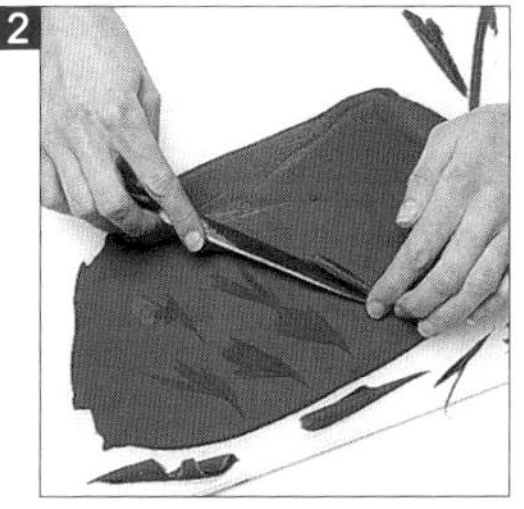
2

4

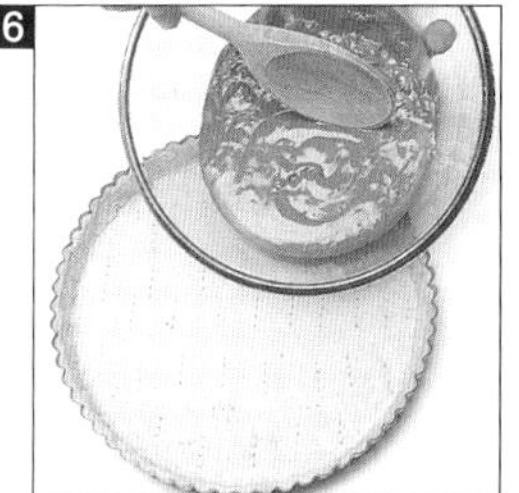
6

Frozen Citrus Soufflés

These delicious desserts are a refreshing way to end a meal. They can be made in advance and kept in the freezer until required.

NUTRITIONAL INFORMATION

Calories	364	Sugars	27g
Protein	11g	Fat	24g
Carbohydrate	27g	Saturates	14g

 35 MINS  0 MINS

SERVES 4

INGREDIENTS

1 tbsp vegetarian gelatine (gelozone)

6 tbsp very hot water

3 eggs, separated

90 g/3 oz/⅓ cup caster (superfine) sugar

finely grated rind and juice of 1 lemon, ½ lime and ½ orange

150 ml/¼ pint/⅔ cup double (heavy) cream

125 g/4½ oz/½ cup plain fromage frais

thin lemon, lime and orange slices to decorate

1 Tie greaseproof paper collars around 4 individual soufflé or ramekin dishes or around 1 large (15 cm/6 inch diameter) soufflé dish.

2 Sprinkle the gelatine (gelozone) into the very hot (not boiling) water, stirring well to disperse. Leave to stand for 2–3 minutes, stirring occasionally, to give a completely clear liquid. Leave to cool for 10–15 minutes.

3 Meanwhile, whisk the egg yolks and sugar, using a hand-held electric mixer or wire whisk until very pale and light in texture. Add the rind and juice from the fruits, mixing well. Stir in the cooled gelatine (gelozone) liquid, making sure that it is thoroughly incorporated.

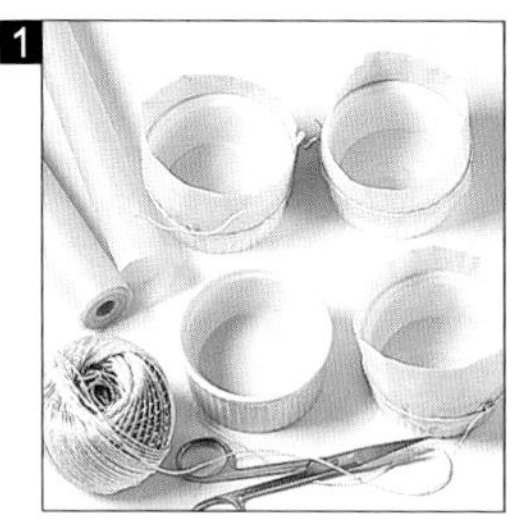

1

4

6

4 Put the cream in a large chilled bowl and whip until it holds its shape. Stir the fromage frais and then add it to the cream, mixing it in gently. Fold the cream mixture into the citrus mixture, using a large metal spoon.

5 Using a clean whisk, beat the egg whites in a clean bowl until stiff and then gently fold them into the citrus mixture, using a metal spoon.

6 Pour the mixture into the prepared dishes, almost to the top of their collars. Allow some room for the mixture to expand on freezing. Transfer the dishes to the freezer and open-freeze for about 2 hours, until frozen.

7 Remove from the freezer 10 minutes before serving. Peel away the paper collars carefully and decorate with the slices of lemon, lime and orange.

Peaches in White Wine

A very simple but incredibly pleasing dessert, which is especially good for a dinner party on a hot summer day.

NUTRITIONAL INFORMATION

Calories	89	Sugars	14g
Protein	1g	Fat	0g
Carbohydrate	14g	Saturates	0g

 1¼ HOURS  0 MINS

SERVES 4

INGREDIENTS

- 4 large ripe peaches
- 2 tbsp icing (confectioners') sugar, sifted
- pared rind and juice of 1 orange
- 200 ml/7 fl oz/¾ cup medium or sweet white wine, chilled

1 Using a sharp knife, halve the peaches, remove the stones and discard them. Peel the peaches, if you prefer. Slice the peaches into thin wedges.

2 Place the peach wedges in a serving bowl and sprinkle over the sugar.

3 Using a sharp knife, pare the rind from the orange. Cut the orange rind into matchsticks, place them in a bowl of cold water and set aside.

4 Squeeze the juice from the orange and pour over the peaches together with the wine.

5 Let the peaches marinate and chill in the refrigerator for at least 1 hour.

6 Remove the orange rind from the cold water and pat dry with paper towels.

7 Garnish the peaches with the strips of orange rind and serve immediately.

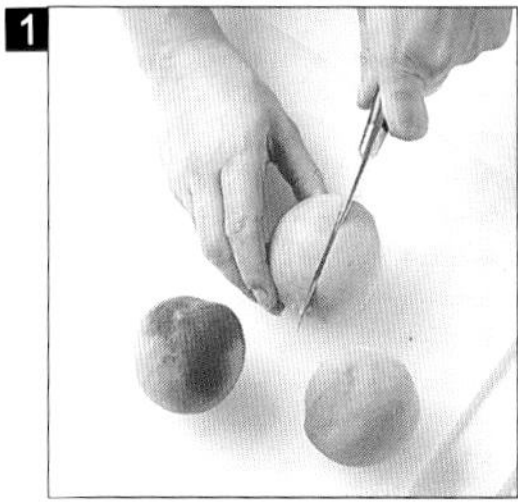
1

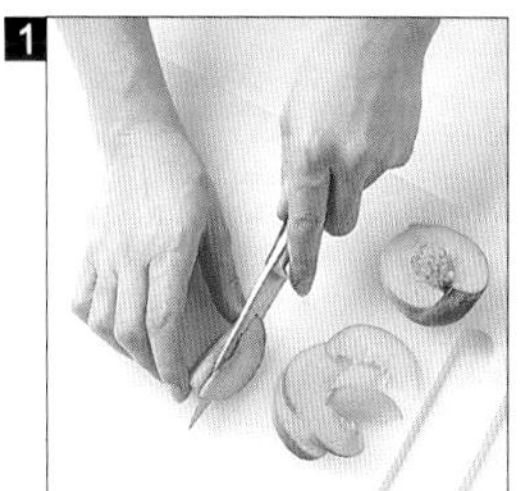
1

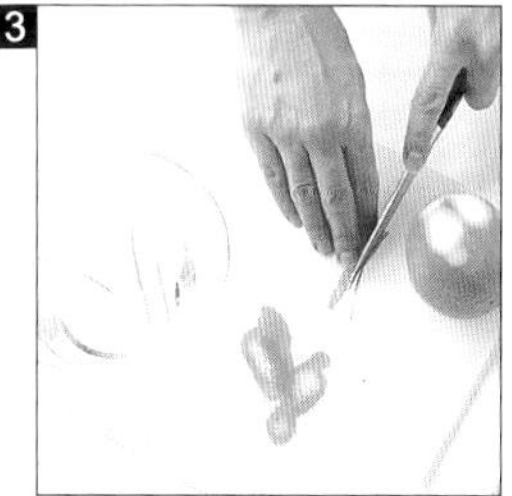
3

Pavlova

This fruit meringue dish was created for Anna Pavlova, and it looks very impressive. Use fruits of your choice to make a colourful display.

NUTRITIONAL INFORMATION

Calories	321	Sugars	37g
Protein	3g	Fat	18g
Carbohydrate	37g	Saturates	11g

1½ HOURS 1½ HOURS

SERVES 8

INGREDIENTS

- 6 egg whites
- ½ tsp cream of tartar
- 225 g/8 oz/1 cup caster (superfine) sugar
- 1 tsp vanilla flavouring (extract)
- 300 ml/½ pint/1¼ cups whipping cream
- 400 g/14 oz/2½ cups strawberries, hulled and halved
- 3 tbsp orange-flavoured liqueur
- fruit of your choice, to decorate

1 Line a baking (cookie) sheet with baking parchment and mark out a circle to fit your serving plate. The recipe makes enough meringue for a 30 cm/12 inch circle.

2 Whisk the egg whites and cream of tartar together until stiff. Gradually beat in the caster (superfine) sugar and vanilla flavouring (extract). Whisk well until glossy and stiff.

3 Either spoon or pipe the meringue mixture into the marked circle, in an even layer, slightly raised at the edges, to form a dip in the centre.

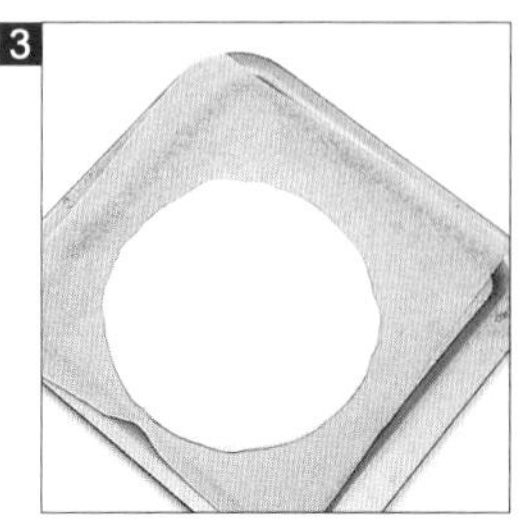

4 Baking the meringue depends on your preference. If you like a soft chewy meringue, bake at 140°C/275°F/ Gas Mark 1 for about 1½ hours until dry but slightly soft in the centre. If you prefer a drier meringue, bake in the oven at 110°C/225°F/Gas Mark ¼ for 3 hours until dry.

5 Before serving, whip the cream to a piping consistency, and either spoon or pipe on to the meringue base, leaving a border of meringue all around the edge.

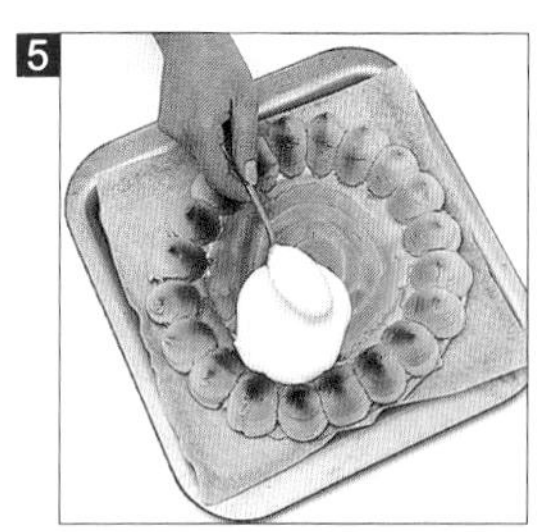

6 Stir the strawberries and liqueur together and spoon on to the cream. Decorate with fruit of your choice.

COOK'S TIP

If you like a dry meringue, you can leave it in the oven on the lowest setting overnight. However, do not use this technique with a gas oven – but in an electric oven or solid fuel cooker it would be fine.

Ginger & Apricot Alaskas

No ice cream in this Alaska but a mixture of apples and apricots poached in orange juice enclosed in meringue.

NUTRITIONAL INFORMATION

Calories	442	Sugars	77g
Protein	7g	Fat	9g
Carbohydrate	83g	Saturates	3g

15 MINS 10 MINS

SERVES 2

INGREDIENTS

- 2 slices rich, dark ginger cake, about 2 cm/¾ inch thick
- 1–2 tbsp ginger wine or rum
- 1 eating apple
- 6 ready-to-eat dried apricots, chopped
- 4 tbsp orange juice or water
- 15 g/½ oz/1 tbsp flaked (slivered) almonds
- 2 small egg whites
- 100 g/3½ oz/⅓ cup caster (superfine) sugar

1 Place each slice of ginger cake on an ovenproof plate and sprinkle with the ginger wine or rum.

2 Quarter, core and slice the apple into a small saucepan. Add the chopped apricots and orange juice or water, and simmer over a low heat for about 5 minutes, or until tender.

3 Stir the almonds into the fruit and spoon the mixture equally over the slices of soaked cake, piling it up in the centre.

4 Whisk the egg whites until very stiff and dry, then whisk in the sugar, a little at a time, making sure the meringue has become stiff again before adding any more sugar.

5 Either pipe or spread the meringue over the fruit and cake, making sure that both are completely covered.

6 Place in a preheated oven, 200°C/400°F/Gas Mark 6, for 4–5 minutes, until golden brown. Serve hot.

VARIATION

A slice of vanilla, coffee or chocolate ice cream can be placed on the fruit before adding the meringue, but this must be done at the last minute and the dessert must be eaten immediately after it is removed from the oven.

Exotic Fruit Salad

This is a sophisticated fruit salad that makes use of some of the exotic fruits that can now be seen in the supermarket.

NUTRITIONAL INFORMATION

Calories	149	Sugars	39g
Protein	1g	Fat	0.1g
Carbohydrate	39g	Saturates	0g

 10 MINS  15 MINS

SERVES 6

INGREDIENTS

- 3 passion-fruit
- 125 g/4 oz/½ cup caster (superfine) sugar
- 150 ml/¼ pint/⅔ cup water
- 1 mango
- 10 lychees, canned or fresh
- 1 star-fruit

1 Halve the passion-fruit and press the flesh through a sieve (strainer) into a saucepan.

2 Add the sugar and water to the saucepan and bring to a gentle boil, stirring frequently.

3 Cut a thick slice from either side of the mango, cutting as near to the stone (pit) as possible. Cut away as much flesh as possible in large chunks from the stone (pit) section.

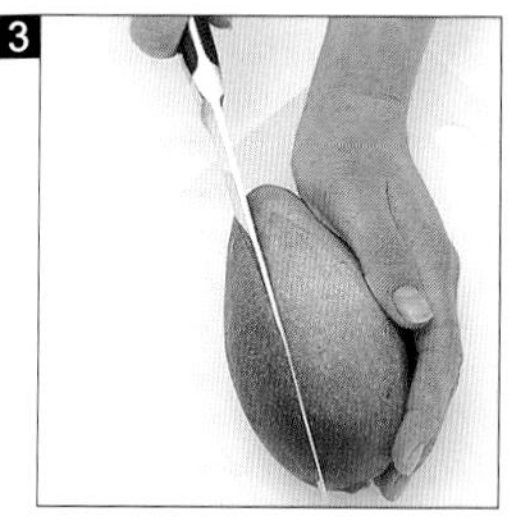
3

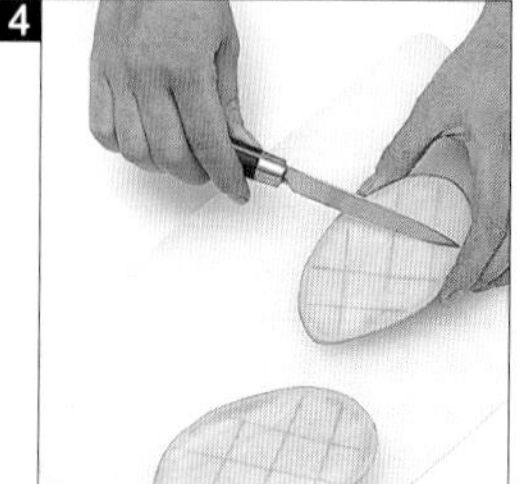
4

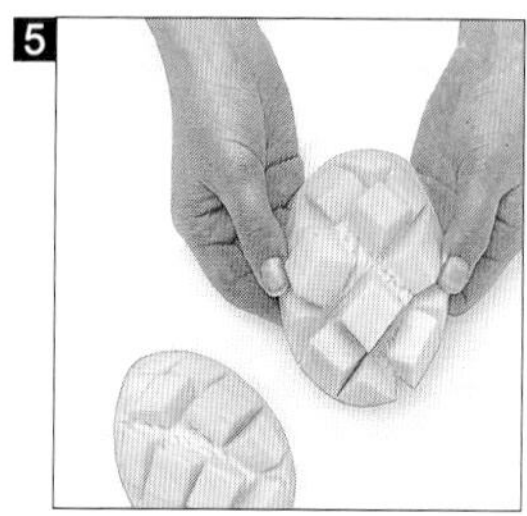
5

4 Take the 2 side slices and make 3 cuts through the flesh but not the skin, and 3 more at right angles to make a lattice pattern.

5 Push inside out so that the cubed flesh is exposed and you can easily cut it off.

6 Peel and stone (pit) the lychees and cut the star-fruit into 12 slices.

7 Add all the mango flesh, the lychees and star-fruit to the passion-fruit syrup and poach gently for 5 minutes. Remove the fruit with a perforated spoon.

8 Bring the syrup to the boil and cook for 5 minutes until it thickens slightly.

9 To serve, transfer all the fruit to individual serving glasses, pour over the sugar syrup and serve warm.

COOK'S TIP

A delicious accompaniment to any exotic fruit dish is cardamom cream. Crush the seeds from 8 cardamom pods, add 300 ml/½ pint/1¼ cups whipping cream and whip until soft peaks form.

Lime Mousse with Mango

Lime-flavoured cream moulds, served with a fresh mango and lime sauce, make a stunning dessert.

NUTRITIONAL INFORMATION

Calories	254	Sugars	17g
Protein	5g	Fat	19g
Carbohydrate	17g	Saturates	12g

 10 MINS  0 MINS

SERVES 4

INGREDIENTS

- 250 g/9 oz/1 cup fromage frais
- grated rind of 1 lime
- 1 tbsp caster (superfine) sugar
- 125 ml/4 fl oz/½ cup double (heavy) cream

MANGO SAUCE

- 1 mango
- juice of 1 lime
- 4 tsp caster (superfine) sugar

TO DECORATE

- 4 Cape gooseberries
- strips of lime rind

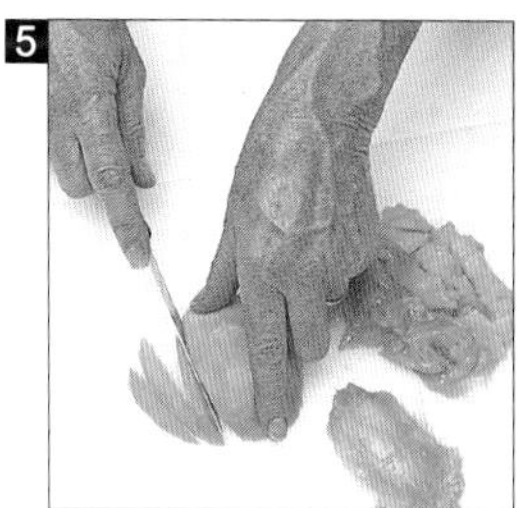

1 Put the fromage frais, lime rind and sugar in a bowl and mix together.

2 Whisk the double (heavy) cream in a separate bowl and fold into the fromage frais.

3 Line 4 decorative moulds or ramekin dishes with muslin (cheesecloth) or cling film (plastic wrap) and divide the mixture evenly between them. Fold the muslin (cheesecloth) over the top and press down firmly.

4 To make the sauce, slice through the mango on each side of the large flat stone, then cut the flesh from the stone. Remove the skin.

5 Cut off 12 thin slices and set aside. Chop the remaining mango, put into a food processor with the lime juice and sugar. Blend until smooth. Alternatively, push the mango through a sieve (strainer) then mix with the lime juice and sugar.

6 Turn out the moulds on to serving plates. Arrange 3 slices of mango on each plate, pour some sauce around, decorate and serve.

COOK'S TIP

Cape gooseberries have a tart and mildly scented flavour and make an excellent decoration for many desserts. Peel back the papery husks to expose the bright orange fruits.

Brown Bread Ice Cream

Although it sounds unusual, this yogurt-based recipe is delicious. It contains no cream and is ideal for a low-fat diet.

NUTRITIONAL INFORMATION

Calories	264	Sugars	25g
Protein	12g	Fat	6g
Carbohydrate	43g	Saturates	1g

2¼ HOURS 5 MINS

SERVES 4

INGREDIENTS

- 175 g/6 oz fresh wholemeal breadcrumbs
- 25 g/1 oz finely chopped walnuts
- 60 g/2 oz caster (superfine) sugar
- ½ tsp ground nutmeg
- 1 tsp finely grated orange rind
- 450 ml/16 fl oz/2 cups low-fat natural (unsweetened) yogurt
- 2 large egg whites

TO DECORATE

- walnut halves
- orange slices
- fresh mint

1 Preheat the grill (broiler) to medium. Mix the breadcrumbs, walnuts and sugar and spread over a sheet of foil in the grill (broiler) pan.

2 Grill (broil), stirring frequently, for 5 minutes until crisp and evenly browned. (Take care that the sugar does not burn.) Remove from the heat and leave to cool.

3 When cool, transfer to a mixing bowl and mix in the nutmeg, orange rind and yogurt. In another bowl, whisk the egg whites until stiff. Gently fold into the breadcrumb mixture, using a metal spoon.

4 Spoon the mixture into 4 mini-basins, smooth over the tops and freeze for 1½–2 hours until firm.

5 To serve, hold the bases of the moulds (molds) in hot water for a few seconds, then turn on to serving plates.

6 Serve immediately, decorated with the walnuts, oranges and fresh mint.

COOK'S TIP

If you don't have mini-basins, use ramekins or teacups or, if you prefer, use one large bowl. Alternatively, spoon the mixture into a large, freezing container to freeze and serve the ice cream in scoops.

1

3

4

Sweet Mascarpone Mousse

A sweet cream cheese dessert that complements the tartness of fresh summer fruits rather well.

NUTRITIONAL INFORMATION

Calories	542	Sugars	31g
Protein	14g	Fat	41g
Carbohydrate	31g	Saturates	24g

 $1^1/_2$ HOURS  0 MINS

SERVES 4

INGREDIENTS

- 450 g/1 lb mascarpone cheese
- 100 g/3½ oz caster (superfine) sugar
- 4 egg yolks
- 400 g/14 oz frozen summer fruits, such as raspberries and redcurrants
- redcurrants, to garnish
- amaretti biscuits (cookies), to serve

1 Place the mascarpone cheese in a large mixing bowl. Using a wooden spoon, beat the mascarpone cheese until quite smooth.

2 Stir the egg yolks and sugar into the mascarpone cheese, mixing well. Leave the mixture to chill in the refrigerator for about 1 hour.

3 Spoon a layer of the mascarpone mixture into the bottom of 4 individual serving dishes. Spoon a layer of the summer fruits on top. Repeat the layers in the same order, reserving some of the mascarpone mixture for the top.

4 Leave the mousses to chill in the refrigerator for about 20 minutes. The fruits should still be slightly frozen.

5 Serve the mascarpone mousses with amaretti biscuits (cookies).

Traditional Apple Pie

This apple pie has a double crust and can be served either hot or cold. The apples can be flavoured with other spices or grated citrus rind.

NUTRITIONAL INFORMATION

Calories	577	Sugars	36g
Protein	6g	Fat	28g
Carbohydrate	80g	Saturates	9g

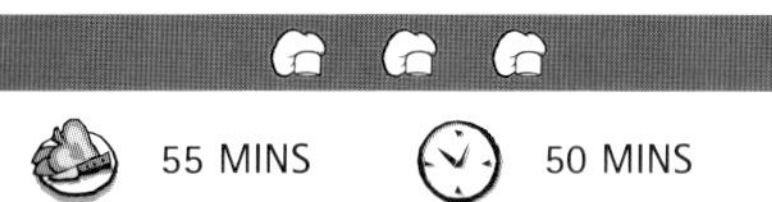

55 MINS 50 MINS

SERVES 6

INGREDIENTS

- 750 g–1 kg/1 lb 10 oz–2 lb 4 oz cooking apples, peeled, cored and sliced
- about 125 g/4½ oz/generous ½ cup brown or white sugar, plus extra for sprinkling
- ½–1 tsp ground cinnamon, mixed spice (apple spice) or ground ginger
- 1–2 tbsp water

SHORTCRUST PASTRY (PIE DOUGH)

- 350 g/12 oz/3 cups plain (all-purpose) flour
- pinch of salt
- 90 g/3 oz/6 tbsp butter or margarine
- 90 g/3 oz/⅓ cup white vegetable fat (shortening)
- about 6 tbsp cold water
- beaten egg or milk, for glazing

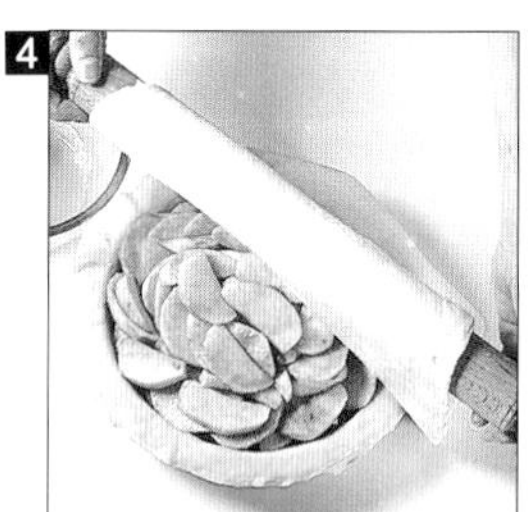

1 To make the pastry (pie dough), sift the flour and salt into a mixing bowl. Add the butter or margarine and shortening and rub in with the fingertips until the mixture resembles fine breadcrumbs. Add the water and gather the mixture together into a dough. Wrap the dough and chill for 30 minutes.

2 Roll out almost two-thirds of the pastry (pie dough) thinly and use to line a 20–23 cm/8–9 inch deep pie plate or shallow pie tin (pan).

3 Mix the apples with the sugar and spice and pack into the pastry case (pie shell); the filling can come up above the rim. Add the water if liked, particularly if the apples are a dry variety.

4 Roll out the remaining pastry (pie dough) to form a lid. Dampen the edges of the pie rim with water and position the lid, pressing the edges firmly together. Trim and crimp the edges.

5 Use the trimmings to cut out leaves or other shapes to decorate the top of the pie, dampen and attach. Glaze the top of the pie with beaten egg or milk, make 1–2 slits in the top and put the pie on a baking sheet (cookie sheet).

6 Bake in a preheated oven, 220°C/425°F/Gas Mark 7, for 20 minutes, then reduce the temperature to 180°C/350°F/Gas Mark 4 and cook for about 30 minutes, until the pastry is a light golden brown. Serve hot or cold, sprinkled with sugar.

Pistachio Dessert

Rather an attractive-looking dessert, especially when decorated with *varq*, this is another dish that can be prepared in advance.

NUTRITIONAL INFORMATION

Calories	676	Sugars	98g
Protein	15g	Fat	27g
Carbohydrate	98g	Saturates	9g

15 MINS

10 MINS

SERVES 6

INGREDIENTS

850 ml/1½ pints/3¾ cups water

225 g/8 oz/2 cups pistachio nuts

225 g/8 oz/1¾ cups full-cream dried milk

500 g/1 lb 2 oz/2⅓ cups sugar

2 cardamoms, with seeds crushed

2 tbsp rosewater

a few strands of saffron

TO DECORATE

25 g/1 oz/¼ cup flaked (slivered) almonds

mint leaves

2

4

4

1 Put about 1 pint/600 ml/2½ cups water in a saucepan and bring to the boil. Remove the pan from the heat and soak the pistachios in this water for about 5 minutes. Drain the pistachios thoroughly and remove the skins.

2 Process the pistachios in a food processor or grind in a mortar with a pestle.

3 Add the dried milk powder to the ground pistachios and mix well.

4 To make the syrup, place the remaining water and the sugar in a pan and heat gently. When the liquid begins to thicken, add the cardamom seeds, rosewater and saffron.

5 Add the syrup to the pistachio mixture and cook, stirring constantly, for about 5 minutes, until the mixture thickens. Set the mixture aside and to cool slightly.

6 Once cool enough to handle, roll the mixture into balls in the palms of your hands. Decorate with the flaked (slivered) almonds and fresh mint leaves and leave to set before serving.

COOK'S TIP

It is best to buy whole pistachio nuts and grind them yourself, rather than using packets of ready-ground nuts. Freshly ground nuts have the best flavour, as grinding releases their natural oils.

Lychees with Orange Sorbet

This dish is truly delicious! The fresh flavour of the sorbet perfectly complements the spicy lychees.

NUTRITIONAL INFORMATION

Calories	313	Sugars	82g
Protein	1g	Fat	0g
Carbohydrate	82g	Saturates	0g

10½ HOURS 5 MINS

SERVES 4

INGREDIENTS

SORBET

- 225 g/8 oz/¼ cups caster (superfine) sugar
- 425 ml/¾ pint/2 cups cold water
- 350 g/12 oz can mandarins, in natural juice
- 2 tbsp lemon juice

STUFFED LYCHEES

- 425 g/15 oz can lychees, drained
- 60 g/2 oz stem (preserved) ginger, drained and finely chopped
- lime zest, cut into diamond shapes, to decorate

1 To make the sorbet, place the sugar and water in a saucepan and stir over a low heat until the sugar has dissolved. Bring the mixture to the boil and boil vigorously for 2-3 minutes.

2 Blend the mandarins in a food processor or blender until smooth. Press the purée through a sieve then stir into the syrup, together with the lemon juice. Set aside to cool. Once cooled, pour the mixture into a rigid, plastic container and freeze until set, stirring occasionally.

3 Meanwhile, drain the lychees on absorbent kitchen paper (paper towels). Spoon the chopped ginger into the centre of the lychees.

4 Arrange the lychees on serving plates and serve with scoops of orange sorbet. Decorate with lime zest.

COOK'S TIP

It is best to leave the sorbet in the refrigerator for 10 minutes, so that it softens slightly, allowing you to scoop it to serve.

2

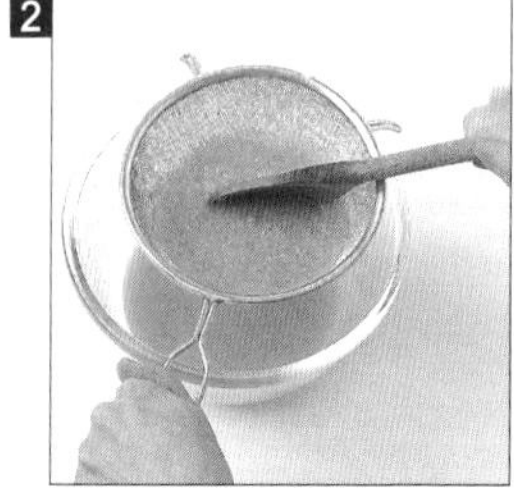

2

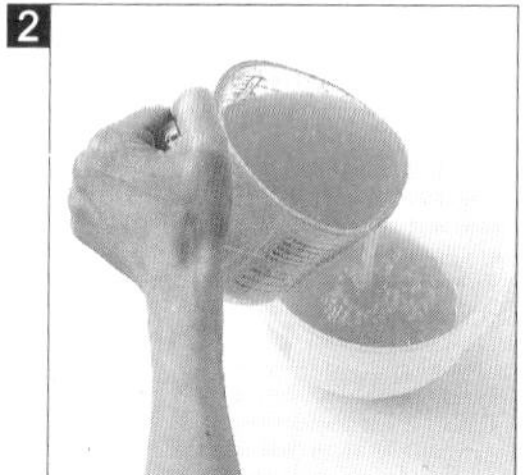

3

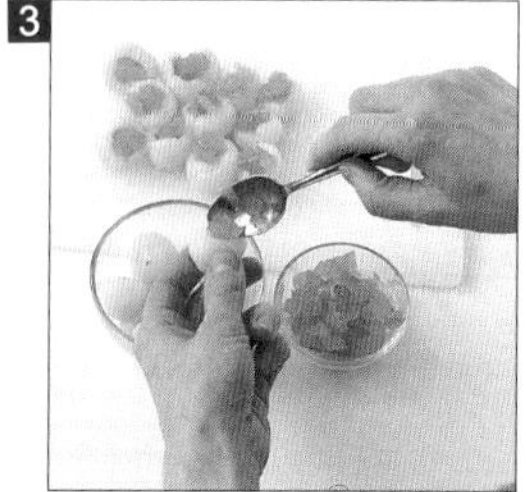

Raspberry Fool

This dish is very easy to make and can be prepared in advance and stored in the refrigerator until required.

NUTRITIONAL INFORMATION

Calories	288	Sugars	19g
Protein	4g	Fat	22g
Carbohydrate	19g	Saturates	14g

1¼ HOURS   0 MINS

SERVES 4

INGREDIENTS

- 300 g/10½ oz/1⅔ cups fresh raspberries
- 50 g/1¾ oz/¼ cup icing (confectioners') sugar
- 300 ml/½ pint/1¼ cups crème fraîche, plus extra to decorate
- ½ tsp vanilla essence (extract)
- 2 egg whites
- raspberries and lemon balm leaves, to decorate

1 Put the raspberries and icing (confectioners') sugar in a food processor or blender and process until smooth. Alternatively, press through a strainer with the back of a spoon.

2 Reserve 1 tablespoon per portion of crème fraîche for decorating.

3 Put the vanilla essence (extract) and remaining crème fraîche in a bowl and stir in the raspberry mixture.

4 Whisk the egg whites in a separate mixing bowl until stiff peaks form. Gently fold the egg whites into the raspberry mixture using a metal spoon, until fully incorporated.

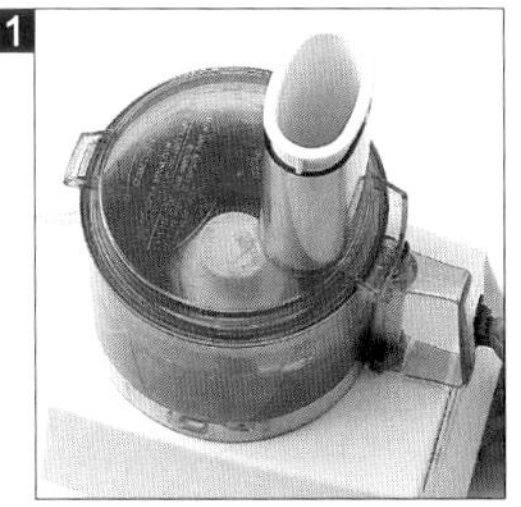

1

3

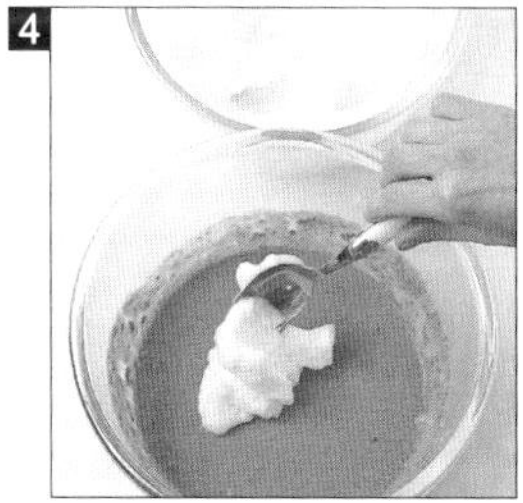

4

5 Spoon the raspberry fool into individual serving dishes and chill for at least 1 hour. Decorate with the reserved crème fraîche, raspberries and lemon balm leaves and serve.

COOK'S TIP

Although this dessert is best made with fresh raspberries in season, an acceptable result can be achieved with frozen raspberries, which are available from most supermarkets.

White Chocolate Florentines

These attractive jewelled biscuits (cookies) are coated with white chocolate to give them a delicious flavour.

NUTRITIONAL INFORMATION

Calories	235	Sugars	20g
Protein	3g	Fat	17g
Carbohydrate	20g	Saturates	7g

 20 MINS  15 MINS

MAKES 24

INGREDIENTS

- 200 g/7 oz butter
- 225 g/8 oz caster sugar
- 125 g/4½ oz walnuts, chopped
- 125 g/4½ oz almonds, chopped
- 60 g/2 oz sultanas, chopped
- 25 g/1 oz glacé cherries, chopped
- 25 g/1 oz mixed candied peel, chopped finely
- 2 tbsp single (thin) cream
- 225 g/8 oz white chocolate

1 Line 3–4 baking trays (cookie sheets) with non-stick baking parchment.

2 Melt the butter over a low heat and then add the sugar, stirring until it has dissolved. Boil the mixture for exactly 1 minute. Remove from the heat.

4 

5 

6 

3 Add the walnuts, almonds, sultanas, glacé cherries, candied peel and cream to the saucepan, stirring well to mix.

4 Drop heaped teaspoonfuls of the mixture on to the baking trays (cookie sheets), allowing plenty of room for them to spread while cooking. Bake in a preheated oven, at 180°C/350°F/Gas Mark 4, for 10 minutes or until golden brown.

5 Remove the biscuits (cookies) from the oven and neaten the edges with a knife while they are still warm. Leave to cool slightly, and then transfer them to a wire rack to cool completely.

6 Melt the chocolate in a bowl placed over a pan of gently simmering water. Spread the underside of the biscuits (cookies) with chocolate and use a fork to make wavy lines across the surface. Leave to cool completely.

7 Store the Florentines in an airtight tin, kept in a cool place.

COOK'S TIP

A combination of white and dark chocolate Florentines looks very attractive, especially if you are making them as gifts. Pack them in pretty boxes, lined with tissue paper and tied with some ribbon.

Cherry Pancakes

This dish can be made with either fresh stoned (pitted) cherries or, if time is short, with canned cherries for extra speed.

NUTRITIONAL INFORMATION

Calories	345	Sugars	25g
Protein	8g	Fat	11g
Carbohydrate	56g	Saturates	2g

 10 MINS  15 MINS

SERVES 4

INGREDIENTS

FILLING

- 400 g/14 oz can stoned (pitted) cherries
- ½ tsp almond essence (extract)
- ½ tsp mixed spice (apple spice)
- 2 tbsp cornflour (cornstarch)

PANCAKES

- 100 g/3½ oz/¾ cup plain (all-purpose) flour
- pinch of salt
- 2 tbsp chopped mint
- 1 egg
- 300 ml/½ pint/1¼ cups milk
- vegetable oil, for frying
- icing (confectioners' sugar) and toasted flaked (slivered) almonds, to decorate

1 Put the cherries and 300 ml/½ pint/1¼ cups of the can juice in a pan with the almond essence (extract) and mixed spice (apple spice). Stir in the cornflour (cornstarch) and bring to the boil, stirring until thickened and clear. Set aside.

2 To make the pancakes, sift the flour into a bowl with the salt. Add the chopped mint and make a well in the centre. Gradually beat in the egg and milk to make a smooth batter.

3 Heat 1 tablespoon of oil in an 18 cm/7 inch frying pan (skillet); pour off the oil when hot. Add just enough batter to coat the base of the frying pan (skillet) and cook for 1–2 minutes, or until the underside is cooked. Flip the pancake over and cook for 1 minute. Remove from the pan and keep warm. Heat 1 tablespoon of the oil in the pan again and repeat to use up all the batter.

4 Spoon a quarter of the cherry filling on to a quarter of each pancake and fold the pancake into a cone shape. Dust with icing (confectioners') sugar and sprinkle the flaked (slivered) almonds over the top. Serve immediately.

Sweet Fruit Wontons

These sweet wontons are very adaptable and may be filled with whole, small fruits or a spicy chopped mixture as here.

NUTRITIONAL INFORMATION

Calories	244	Sugars	25g
Protein	2g	Fat	12g
Carbohydrate	35g	Saturates	3g

 10 MINS  15 MINS

SERVES 4

INGREDIENTS

- 12 wonton wrappers
- 2 tsp cornflour (cornstarch)
- 6 tsp cold water
- oil, for deep-frying
- 2 tbsp clear honey
- selection of fresh fruit (such as kiwi fruit, limes, oranges, mango and apples), sliced, to serve

FILLING

- 175 g/6 oz/1 cup chopped dried, stoned (pitted) dates
- 2 tsp dark brown sugar
- ½ tsp ground cinnamon

1 To make the filling, mix together the dates, sugar and cinnamon in a bowl.

2 Spread out the wonton wrappers on a chopping board and spoon a little of the filling into the centre of each wrapper.

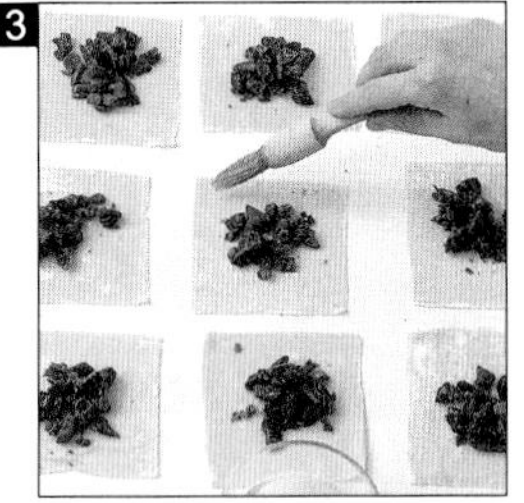

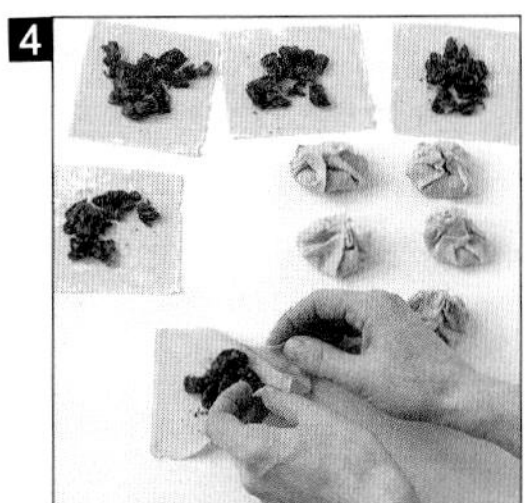

3 Blend the cornflour (cornstarch) and water and brush this mixture around the edges of the wrappers.

4 Fold the wrappers over the filling, bringing the edges together, then bring the two corners together, sealing with the cornflour (cornstarch) mixture.

5 Heat the oil for deep-frying in a wok to 180°C/350°F, or until a cube of bread browns in 30 seconds. Fry the wontons, in batches, for 2-3 minutes, until golden. Remove the wontons from the oil with a slotted spoon and leave to drain on absorbent kitchen paper (paper towels).

6 Place the honey in a bowl and stand it in warm water, to soften it slightly. Drizzle the honey over the sweet fruit wontons and serve with a selection of fresh fruit.

COOK'S TIP

Wonton wrappers may be easily found in Chinese supermarkets.

Sweet Carrot Halva

This nutritious dessert is flavoured with spices, nuts and raisins. The nutritional information does not include serving with cream.

NUTRITIONAL INFORMATION

Calories	284	Sugars	33g
Protein	7g	Fat	14g
Carbohydrate	34g	Saturates	3g

10 MINS 55 MINS

SERVES 6

INGREDIENTS

- 750 g/1 lb 10 oz carrots, grated
- 700 ml/1¼ pints/3 cups milk
- 1 cinnamon stick or piece of cassia bark (optional)
- 4 tbsp vegetable ghee or oil
- 60 g/2 oz/¼ cup granulated sugar
- 25 g/1 oz/¼ cup unsalted pistachio nuts, chopped
- 25-50 g/1-1¾ oz/¼-½ cup blanched almonds, flaked (slivered) or chopped
- 60 g/2 oz/⅓ cup seedless raisins
- 8 cardamom pods, split and seeds removed and crushed
- thick cream, to serve

1 Put the grated carrots, milk and cinnamon or cassia, if using, into a large, heavy-based saucepan and bring to the boil. Reduce the heat to very low and simmer, uncovered, for about 35–40 minutes, or until the mixture is thick (with no milk remaining). Stir the mixture frequently during cooking to prevent it from sticking.

2 Remove and discard the cinnamon or cassia. Heat the ghee or oil in a non-stick frying pan, add the carrot mixture and stir-fry over a medium heat for about 5 minutes, or until the carrots take on a glossy sheen.

3 Add the sugar, pistachios, almonds, raisins and crushed cardamom seeds, mix thoroughly and continue frying for a further 3–4 minutes, stirring frequently. Serve warm or cold with thick cream.

COOK'S TIP

The quickest and easiest way to grate this quantity of carrots is by using a food processor fitted with the appropriate blade. This mixture may be prepared ahead of time and reheated in the microwave when required.

Rhubarb & Orange Crumble

A mixture of rhubarb and apples flavoured with orange rind, brown sugar and spices and topped with a crunchy crumble topping.

NUTRITIONAL INFORMATION

Calories	516	Sugars	45g
Protein	6g	Fat	22g
Carbohydrate	77g	Saturates	4g

 15 MINS  45 MINS

SERVES 6

INGREDIENTS

- 500 g/1 lb 2 oz rhubarb
- 500 g/1 lb 2 oz cooking apples
- grated rind and juice of 1 orange
- ½–1 tsp ground cinnamon
- about 90 g/3 oz/scant ½ cup light soft brown sugar

CRUMBLE

- 225 g/8 oz/2 cups plain (all-purpose) flour
- 125 g/4½ oz/½ cup butter or margarine
- 125 g/4½ oz/generous ½ cup light soft brown sugar
- 40–60 g/1½–2 oz/⅓–½ cup toasted chopped hazelnuts
- 2 tbsp demerara (brown crystal) sugar (optional)

1 Cut the rhubarb into 2.5 cm/1 inch lengths and place in a large saucepan.

2 Peel, core and slice the apples and add to the rhubarb, together with the grated orange rind and juice. Bring to the boil, lower the heat and simmer for 2–3 minutes, until the fruit begins to soften.

3 Add the cinnamon and sugar to taste and turn the mixture into an ovenproof dish, so it is not more than two-thirds full.

4 Sift the flour into a bowl and rub in the butter or margarine until the mixture resembles fine breadcrumbs (this can be done by hand or in a food processor). Stir in the sugar, followed by the nuts.

5 Spoon the crumble mixture evenly over the fruit in the dish and level the top. Sprinkle with demerara (brown crystal) sugar, if liked.

6 Cook in a preheated oven, 200°C/ 400°F/Gas Mark 6, for 30–40 minutes, until the topping is browned. Serve hot or cold.

3

4

5

VARIATION

Other flavourings, such as 60 g/2 oz/ generous ¼ cup chopped stem (preserved) ginger, can be added either to the fruit or the crumb mixture. Any fruit, or mixtures of fruit can be topped with crumble.

Quick Syrup Sponge

You won't bclicvc your eyes when you see just how quickly this light-as-air sponge pudding cooks in the microwave oven!

NUTRITIONAL INFORMATION

Calories	650	Sugars	60g
Protein	10g	Fat	31g
Carbohydrate	89g	Saturates	7g

15 MINS 5 MINS

SERVES 4

INGREDIENTS

- 125 g/4½ oz/½ cup butter or margarine
- 4 tbsp golden (light corn) syrup
- 90 g/3 oz/⅓ cup caster (superfine) sugar
- 2 eggs
- 125 g/4½ oz/1 cup self-raising (self-rising) flour
- 1 tsp baking powder
- about 2 tbsp warm water
- custard, to serve

1 Grease a 1.5 litre/2½ pint/1½ quart pudding basin (heatproof bowl) with a small amount of the butter or margarine. Spoon the syrup into the basin (bowl).

2 Cream the remaining butter or margarine with the sugar until light and fluffy. Gradually add the eggs, beating well between each addition.

3 Sift the flour and baking powder together, then fold into the creamed mixture using a large metal spoon. Add enough water to give a soft, dropping consistency. Spoon into the pudding basin (bowl) and level the surface.

4 Cover with microwave-safe film, leaving a small space to allow air to escape. Microwave on HIGH power for 4 minutes, then remove from the microwave and allow the pudding to stand for 5 minutes, while it continues to cook.

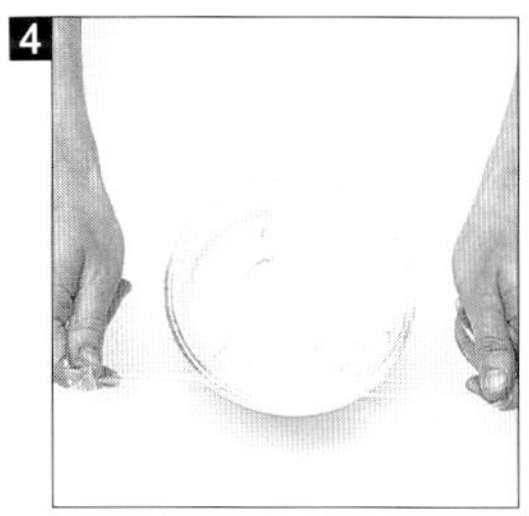

5 Turn the pudding out on to a serving plate. Serve with custard.

COOK'S TIP

If you don't have a microwave, this pudding can be steamed. Cover the with a piece of pleated baking parchment and a piece of pleated foil. Place in a saucepan, add boiling water and steam for 1½ hours.

Almond Cheesecakes

These creamy cheese desserts are so delicious that it's hard to believe that they are low in fat.

NUTRITIONAL INFORMATION

Calories	361	Sugars	29g
Protein	16g	Fat	15g
Carbohydrate	43g	Saturates	4g

 1¼ HOURS  10 MINS

SERVES 4

INGREDIENTS

- 12 Amaretti di Saronno biscuits
- 1 medium egg white, lightly beaten
- 225 g/8 oz skimmed-milk soft cheese
- ½ tsp almond essence (extract)
- ½ tsp finely grated lime rind
- 25 g/1 oz ground almonds
- 25 g/1 oz caster (superfine) sugar
- 60 g/2 oz sultanas (golden raisins)
- 2 tsp powdered gelatine
- 2 tbsp boiling water
- 2 tbsp lime juice

TO DECORATE

- 25 g/1 oz flaked (slivered) toasted almonds
- strips of lime rind

1 Preheat the oven to 180°C/350°F/Gas Mark 4. Place the biscuits in a clean plastic bag, seal the bag and using a rolling pin, crush them into small pieces.

2 Place the crumbs in a bowl and bind together with the egg white.

3 Arrange 4 non-stick pastry rings or poached egg rings, 9 cm/3½ inches across, on a baking tray (cookie sheet) lined with baking parchment. Divide the biscuit mixture into 4 equal portions and spoon it into the rings, pressing down well. Bake for 10 minutes until crisp and leave to cool in the rings.

4 Beat together the soft cheese, almond essence (extract), lime rind, ground almonds, sugar and sultanas until well mixed.

5 Dissolve the gelatine in the boiling water and stir in the lime juice. Fold into the cheese mixture and spoon over the biscuit bases. Smooth over the tops and chill for 1 hour or until set.

6 Loosen the cheesecakes from the tins using a small palette knife or spatula and transfer to serving plates. Decorate with flaked (slivered) toasted almonds and strips of lime rind, and serve.

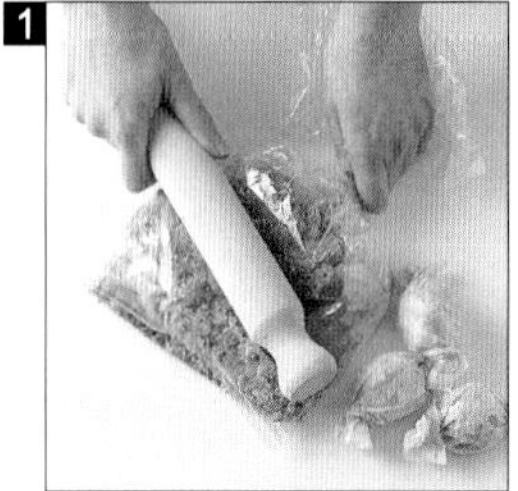
1

3

5

Lemon & Lime Syllabub

This dessert is rich but absolutely delicious. It is not, however, for the calorie conscious as it contains a high proportion of cream.

NUTRITIONAL INFORMATION			
Calories	403	Sugars	16g
Protein	2g	Fat	36g
Carbohydrate	16g	Saturates	22g

 4¼ HOURS  0 MINS

SERVES 4

INGREDIENTS

- 50 g/1¾ oz/¼ cup caster (superfine) sugar
- grated rind and juice of 1 small lemon
- grated rind and juice of 1 small lime
- 50 ml/2 fl oz/¼ cup Marsala or medium sherry
- 300 ml/½ pint/1¼ cups double (heavy) cream
- lime and lemon rind, to decorate

1 Put the sugar, lemon juice and rind, lime juice and rind and sherry in a bowl, mix well and set aside to infuse for 2 hours.

2 Add the cream to the fruit juice mixture and whisk until it just holds its shape.

3 Spoon the mixture into 4 tall serving glasses and chill in the refrigerator for 2 hours.

4 Decorate with lime and lemon rind and serve.

1

2

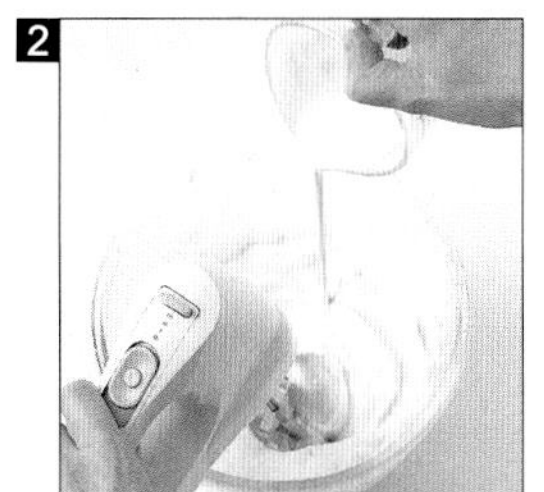

3

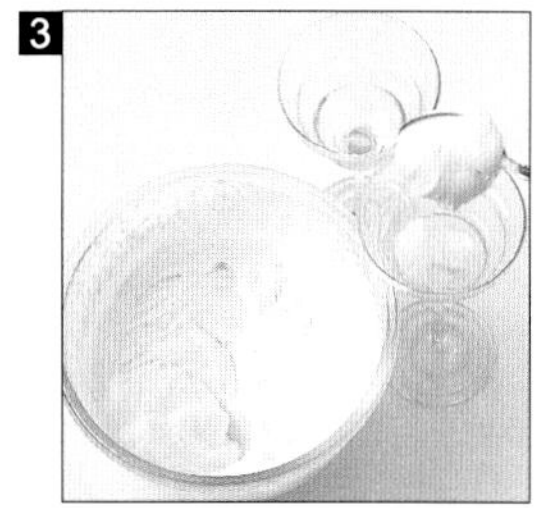

Coconut Sweet

Quick and easy to make, this sweet is very similar to coconut ice. Pink food colouring may be added towards the end if desired.

NUTRITIONAL INFORMATION			
Calories	338	Sugars	5g
Protein	4g	Fat	34g
Carbohydrate	5g	Saturates	26g

 1¼ HOURS  15 MINS

SERVES 6

INGREDIENTS

- 75 g/2¾ oz/6 tbsp butter
- 200 g/7 oz/3 cups desiccated (shredded) coconut
- 175 ml/6 fl oz/¾ cup condensed milk
- a few drops of pink food colouring (optional)

1. Place the butter in a heavy-based saucepan and melt over a low heat, stirring constantly so that the butter doesn't burn on the base of the pan.

2. Add the desiccated (shredded) coconut to the melted butter, stirring to mix.

3. Stir in the condensed milk and the pink food colouring (if using) and mix continuously for 7–10 minutes.

2

3

3

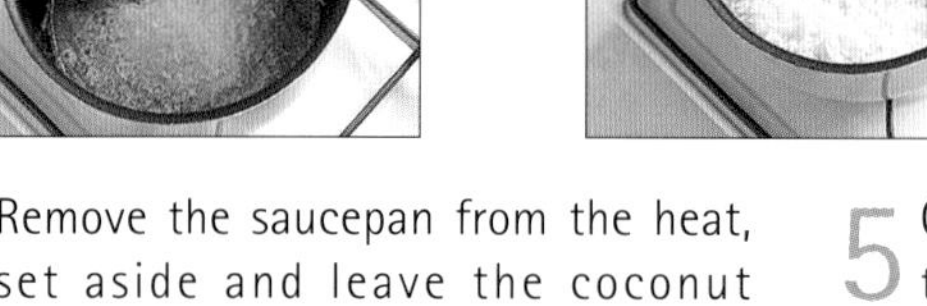

4. Remove the saucepan from the heat, set aside and leave the coconut mixture to cool slightly.

5. Once cool enough to handle, shape the coconut mixture into long blocks and cut into equal-sized rectangles. Leave to set for about 1 hour, then serve.

VARIATION

If you prefer, you could divide the coconut mixture in step 2, and add the pink food colouring to only one half of the mixture. This way, you will have an attractive combination of pink and white coconut sweets.

Ricotta Ice Cream

The ricotta cheese adds a creamy flavour, while the nuts add a crunchy texture. This ice cream needs to be chilled in the freezer overnight.

NUTRITIONAL INFORMATION

Calories	438	Sugars	39g
Protein	13g	Fat	25g
Carbohydrate	40g	Saturates	9g

20 MINS — 0 MINS

SERVES 6

INGREDIENTS

- 25 g/1 oz/¼ cup pistachio nuts
- 25 g/1 oz/¼ cup walnuts or pecan nuts
- 25 g/1 oz/¼ cup toasted chopped hazelnuts
- grated rind of 1 orange
- grated rind of 1 lemon
- 25 g/1 oz/2 tbsp crystallized or stem ginger
- 25 g/1 oz/2 tbsp glacé cherries
- 25 g/1 oz/¼ cup dried apricots
- 25 g/1 oz/3 tbsp raisins
- 500 g/1 lb 2 oz/1½ cups Ricotta
- 2 tbsp Maraschino, Amaretto or brandy
- 1 tsp vanilla essence (extract)
- 4 egg yolks
- 125 g/4½ oz/½ cup caster (superfine) sugar

TO DECORATE

- whipped cream
- a few glacé cherries, pistachio nuts or mint leaves

1

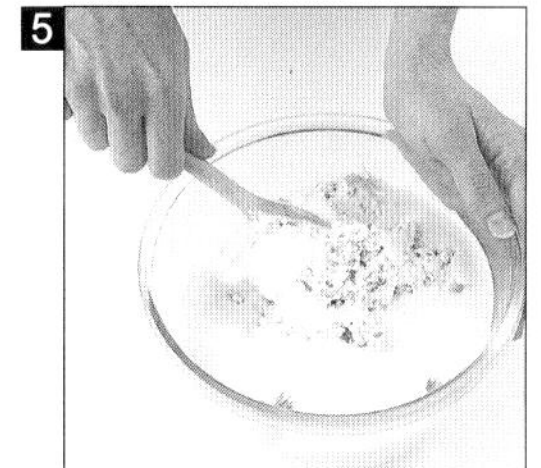

5

6

1 Roughly chop the pistachio nuts and walnuts and mix with the toasted hazelnuts, orange and lemon rind.

2 Finely chop the ginger, cherries, apricots and raisins, and add to the bowl.

3 Stir the Ricotta evenly through the fruit mixture, then beat in the liqueur and vanilla essence (extract).

4 Put the egg yolks and sugar in a bowl and whisk hard until very thick and creamy – they may be whisked over a saucepan of gently simmering water to speed up the process. Leave to cool if necessary.

5 Carefully fold the Ricotta mixture evenly through the beaten eggs and sugar until smooth.

6 Line a 18 x 12 cm/7 x 5 inch loaf tin (pan) with a double layer of cling film (plastic wrap) or baking parchment. Pour in the Ricotta mixture, level the top, cover with more cling film (plastic wrap) or baking parchment and chill in the freezer until firm – at least overnight.

7 To serve, carefully remove the ice-cream from the tin (pan) and peel off the paper. Place on a serving dish and decorate with whipped cream, glacé cherries, pistachio nuts and/or mint leaves. Serve in slices.

Steamed Coffee Sponge

This sponge pudding is very light and is quite delicious served with a sweet chocolate sauce.

NUTRITIONAL INFORMATION

Calories	300	Sugars	21g
Protein	8g	Fat	13g
Carbohydrate	40g	Saturates	4g

10 MINS 1¼ HOURS

SERVES 4

INGREDIENTS

- 25 g/1 oz/2 tbsp margarine
- 2 tbsp soft brown sugar
- 2 eggs
- 50 g/1¾ oz/⅓ cup plain (all-purpose) flour
- ¾ tsp baking powder
- 6 tbsp milk
- 1 tsp coffee flavouring (extract)

SAUCE

- 300 ml/½ pint/1¼ cups milk
- 1 tbsp soft brown sugar
- 1 tsp cocoa powder (unsweetened) cocoa
- 2 tbsp cornflour (cornstarch)

1 Lightly grease a 600 ml/1 pint/2½ cup pudding basin (heatproof bowl). Cream the margarine and sugar until light and fluffy and beat in the eggs.

2 Gradually stir in the flour and baking powder and then the milk and coffee flavouring (extract) to make a smooth batter.

3 Spoon the mixture into the prepared pudding basin (heatproof bowl) and cover with a pleated piece of baking parchment and then a pleated piece of foil, securing around the bowl with string. Place in a steamer or large pan and half fill with boiling water. Cover and steam for 1–1¼ hours, or until cooked through.

4 To make the sauce, put the milk, soft brown sugar and cocoa powder (unsweetened cocoa) in a pan and heat , stirring constantly, until the sugar dissolves. Blend the cornflour (cornstarch) with 4 tablespoons of cold water to make a smooth paste and stir into the pan. Bring to the boil, stirring constantly until thickened. Cook over a gentle heat for 1 minute.

5 Turn the pudding out on to a warmed serving plate and spoon the sauce over the top. Serve immediately.

1

2

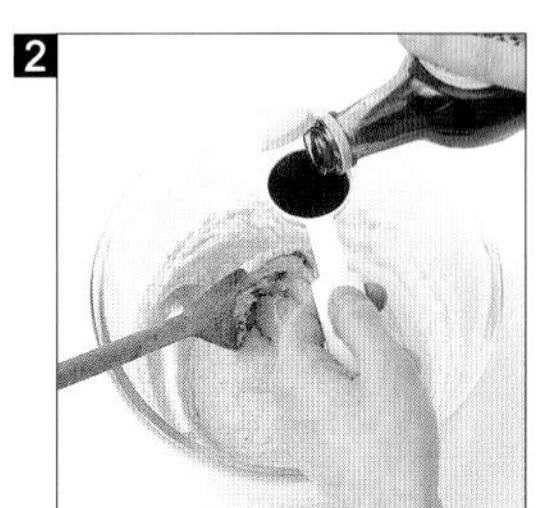

3

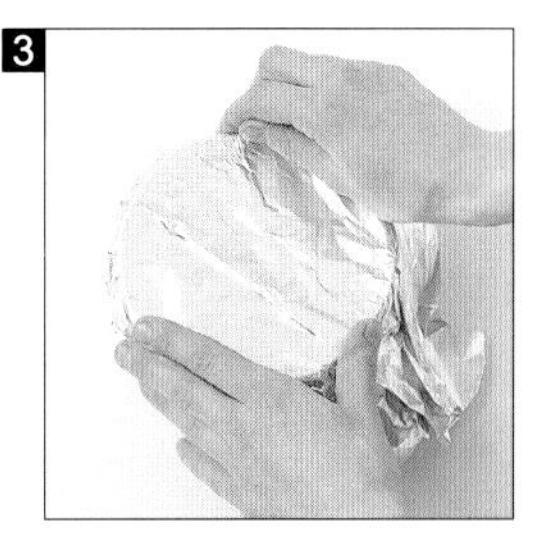

COOK'S TIP

The pudding is covered with pleated paper and foil to allow it to rise. The foil will react with the steam and must therefore not be placed directly against the pudding.

Sweet Saffron Rice

This is a traditional dessert, which is quick and easy to make and looks very impressive, especially decorated with pistachio nuts and *varq*.

NUTRITIONAL INFORMATION

Calories	460	Sugars	57g
Protein	4g	Fat	9g
Carbohydrate	97g	Saturates	5g

5 MINS

35 MINS

SERVES 4

INGREDIENTS

- 200 g/7 oz/1 cup basmati rice
- 200 g/7 oz/1 cup sugar
- 1 pinch saffron strands
- 300 ml/½ pint/1¼ cups water
- 2 tbsp vegetable ghee
- 3 cloves
- 3 cardamoms
- 25 g/1 oz/2 tbsp sultanas (golden raisins)

TO DECORATE

- a few pistachio nuts (optional)
- varq (silver leaf) (optional)

1 Rinse the rice twice and bring to the boil in a saucepan of water, stirring constantly. Remove the pan from the heat when the rice is half-cooked, drain the rice thoroughly and set aside.

2 In a separate saucepan, boil the sugar and saffron in the water, stirring constantly, until the syrup thickens. Set the syrup aside until required.

3 In another saucepan, heat the ghee, cloves and cardamoms, stirring occasionally. Remove the pan from the heat.

4 Return the rice to a low heat and stir in the sultanas (golden raisins).

5 Pour the syrup over the rice mixture and stir to mix.

6 Pour the ghee mixture over the rice and simmer over a low heat for about 10–15 minutes. Check to see whether the rice is cooked. If it is not, add a little boiling water, cover and continue to simmer until tender.

7 Serve warm, decorated with pistachio nuts and varq (silver leaf), if desired.

VARIATION

Basmati rice is the 'prince of rices' and comes from the Himalayan foothills. Its name means fragrant and it has a superb texture and flavour.

Tropical Fruit Fool

Fruit fools are always popular, and this light, tangy version will be no exception. Use your favourite fruits in this recipe if you prefer.

NUTRITIONAL INFORMATION

Calories	149	Sugars	25g
Protein	6g	Fat	0.4g
Carbohydrate	32g	Saturates	0.2g

 35 MINS  0 MINS

SERVES 4

INGREDIENTS

- 1 medium ripe mango
- 2 kiwi fruit
- 1 medium banana
- 2 tbsp lime juice
- ½ tsp finely grated lime rind, plus extra to decorate
- 2 medium egg whites
- 425 g/15 oz can low-fat custard
- ½ tsp vanilla essence (extract)
- 2 passion fruit

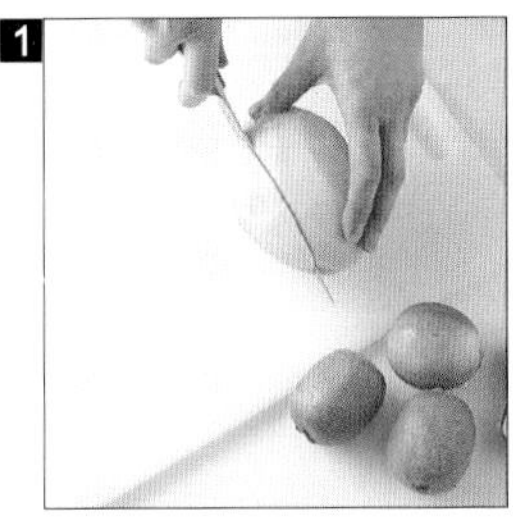

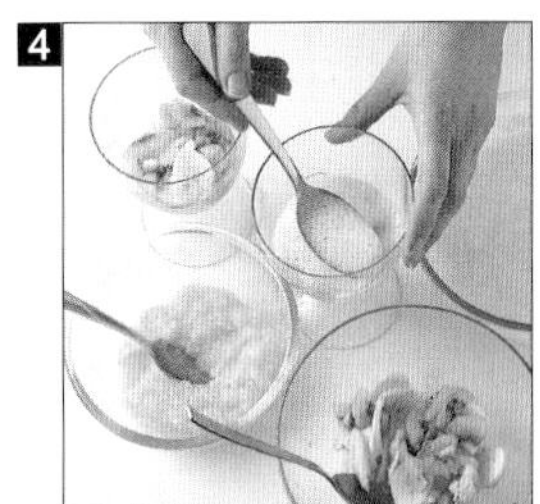

1 To peel the mango, slice either side of the smooth, flat central stone. Roughly chop the flesh and blend the fruit in a food processor or blender until smooth. Alternatively, mash with a fork.

2 Peel the kiwi fruit, chop the flesh into small pieces and place in a bowl. Peel and chop the banana and add to the bowl. Toss all of the fruit in the lime juice and rind and mix well.

3 In a grease-free bowl, whisk the egg whites until stiff and then gently fold in the custard and vanilla essence (extract) until thoroughly mixed.

4 In 4 tall glasses, alternately layer the chopped fruit, mango purée and custard mixture, finishing with the custard on top. Leave to chill in the refrigerator for 20 minutes.

5 Halve the passion fruits, scoop out the seeds and spoon the passion fruit over the fruit fools. Decorate each serving with the extra lime rind and serve.

VARIATION

Other tropical fruits to try include paw-paw (papaya) purée, with chopped pineapple and dates or pomegranate seeds to decorate. Or make a summer fruit fool by using strawberry purée, topped with raspberries and blackberries and cherries.

Florentines

These luxury biscuits (cookies) will be popular at any time of the year, but make a particularly wonderful treat at Christmas.

NUTRITIONAL INFORMATION

Calories	186	Sugars	19g
Protein	2g	Fat	11g
Carbohydrate	22g	Saturates	5g

 20 MINS  15 MINS

MAKES 10

INGREDIENTS

- 50 g/1¾ oz/ 10 tsp butter
- 50 g/1¾ oz/¼ cup caster (superfine) sugar
- 25 g/1 oz/¼ cup plain (all-purpose) flour, sieved (strained)
- 50 g/1¾ oz/⅓ cup almonds, chopped
- 50 g/1¾ oz/⅓ cup chopped mixed peel
- 25 g/1 oz/¼ cup raisins, chopped
- 25 g/1 oz/2 tbsp glacé (candied) cherries, chopped
- finely grated rind of ½ lemon
- 125 g/4½ oz dark chocolate, melted

1 Line 2 large baking trays (cookie sheets) with baking parchment.

2 Heat the butter and caster (superfine) sugar in a small saucepan until the butter has just melted and the sugar dissolved. Remove the pan from the heat.

3 Stir in the flour and mix well. Stir in the chopped almonds, mixed peel, raisins, cherries and lemon rind. Place teaspoonfuls of the mixture well apart on the baking trays (cookie sheets).

4 Bake in a preheated oven, at 180°C/ 350°F/Gas Mark 4, for 10 minutes or until lightly golden.

5 As soon as the florentines are removed from the oven, press the edges into neat shapes while still on the baking trays (cookie sheets), using a biscuit (cookie) cutter. Leave to cool on the baking trays (cookie sheets) until firm, then transfer to a wire rack to cool completely.

6 Spread the melted chocolate over the smooth side of each florentine. As the chocolate begins to set, mark wavy lines in it with a fork. Leave the florentines until set, chocolate side up.

VARIATION

Replace the dark chocolate with white chocolate or, for a dramatic effect, cover half of the florentines in dark chocolate and half in white.

Autumn Fruit Bread Pudding

This is like a summer pudding, but it uses fruits which appear later in the year. This dessert requires chilling overnight so prepare in advance.

NUTRITIONAL INFORMATION

Calories	177	Sugars	29g
Protein	3g	Fat	1g
Carbohydrate	42g	Saturates	0.1g

 10 MINS  15 MINS

SERVES 8

INGREDIENTS

- 900 g/2 lb/4 cups mixed blackberries, chopped apples, chopped pears
- 150 g/5½ oz/¾ cup soft light brown sugar
- 1 tsp cinnamon
- 225 g/8 oz white bread, thinly sliced, crusts removed (about 12 slices)

1 Place the fruit in a large saucepan with the soft light brown sugar, cinnamon and 7 tablespoons of water, stir and bring to the boil. Reduce the heat and simmer for 5–10 minutes so that the fruits soften but still hold their shape.

2 Meanwhile, line the base and sides of a 900 ml/1½ pint/3¾ cup pudding basin (bowl) with the bread slices, ensuring that there are no gaps between the pieces of bread.

3 Spoon the fruit into the centre of the bread-lined bowl and cover the fruit with the remaining bread.

4 Place a saucer on top of the bread and weigh it down. Chill the pudding in the refrigerator overnight.

5 Turn the pudding out on to a serving plate and serve immediately.

2

3

4

COOK'S TIP

This pudding would be delicious served with vanilla ice cream to counteract the tartness of the blackberries. Stand the pudding on a plate when chilling to catch any juices that run down the sides of the basin (bowl).

Green Fruit Salad

This delightfully refreshing fruit salad is the perfect finale for a Chinese meal. It has a lovely light syrup made with fresh mint and honey.

NUTRITIONAL INFORMATION

Calories	157	Sugars	34g
Protein	1g	Fat	0.2g
Carbohydrate	34g	Saturates	0g

30 MINS 15 MINS

SERVES 4

INGREDIENTS

- 1 small Charentais or honeydew melon
- 2 green apples
- 2 kiwi fruit
- 125 g/4½ oz/1 cup seedless white grapes
- fresh mint sprigs, to decorate

SYRUP

- 1 lemon
- 150 ml/¼ pint/⅔ cup white wine
- 150 ml/¼ pint/⅔ cup water
- 4 tbsp clear honey
- few sprigs of fresh mint

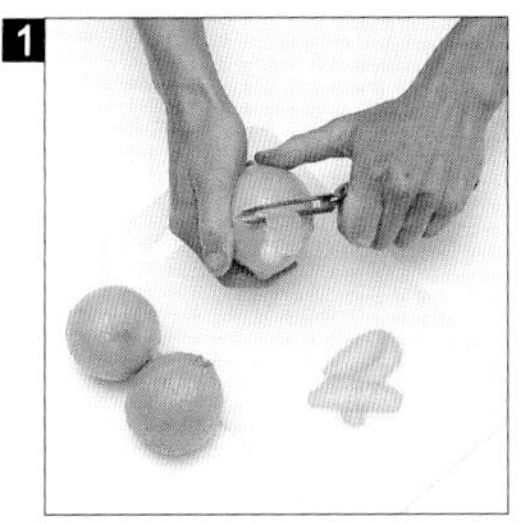

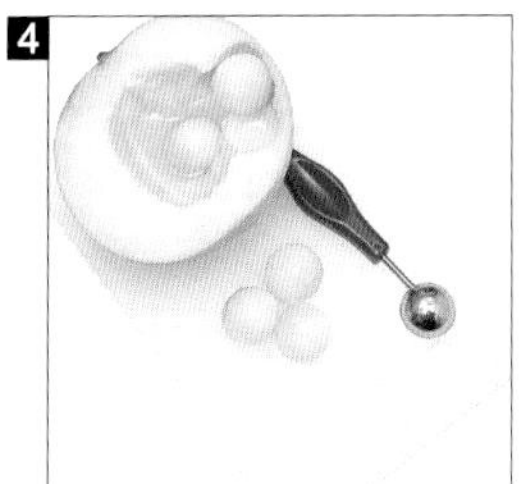

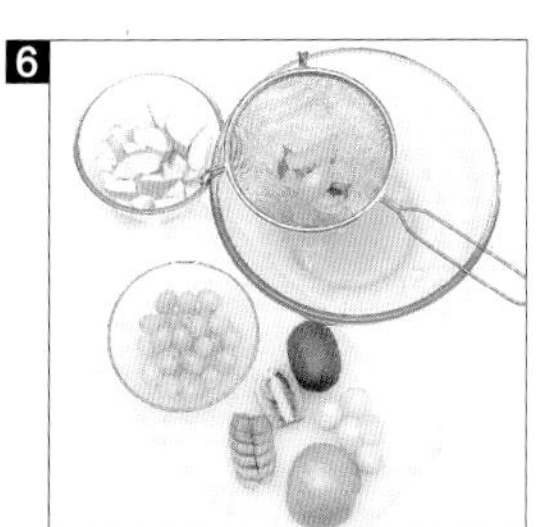

1 To make the syrup, pare the rind from the lemon using a potato peeler.

2 Put the lemon rind in a saucepan with the white wine, water and clear honey. Bring to the boil, then simmer gently for 10 minutes.

3 Remove the syrup from the heat. Add the sprigs of mint and leave to cool.

4 To prepare the fruit, first slice the melon in half and scoop out the seeds. Use a melon baller or a teaspoon to make melon balls.

5 Core and chop the apples. Peel and slice the kiwi fruit.

6 Strain the cooled syrup into a serving bowl, removing and reserving the lemon rind and discarding the mint sprigs.

7 Add the apple, grapes, kiwi fruit and melon to the serving bowl. Stir through gently to mix.

8 Serve the fruit salad, decorated with sprigs of fresh mint and some of the reserved lemon rind.

COOK'S TIP

Single-flower honey has a better, more individual flavour than blended honey. Acacia honey is typically Chinese, but you could also try clove, lemon blossom, lime flower or orange blossom.

Panettone & Strawberries

Panettone is a sweet Italian bread. It is delicious toasted, and when it is topped with marscapone and strawberries it makes a sumptuous dessert.

NUTRITIONAL INFORMATION

Calories	227	Sugars	11g
Protein	5g	Fat	13g
Carbohydrate	19g	Saturates	8g

 35 MINS  2 MINS

SERVES 4

INGREDIENTS

- 225 g/8 oz strawberries
- 25 g/1 oz caster (superfine) sugar
- 6 tbsp Marsala wine
- ½ tsp ground cinnamon
- 4 slices panettone
- 4 tbsp mascarpone cheese

1 Hull and slice the strawberries and place them in a bowl. Add the sugar, Marsala and cinnamon to the strawberries.

2 Toss the strawberries in the sugar and cinnamon mixture until they are well coated. Leave to chill in the refrigerator for at least 30 minutes.

3 When ready to serve, transfer the slices of panettone to a rack set over medium hot coals. Barbecue (grill) the panettone for about 1 minute on each side or until golden brown.

4 Carefully remove the panettone from the barbecue (grill) and transfer to serving plates.

5 Top the panettone with the mascarpone cheese and the marinated strawberries. Serve immediately.

1

3

5

Satsuma & Pecan Pavlova

Make this spectacular dessert for the perfect way to round off a special occasion. You can make the meringue base well in advance.

NUTRITIONAL INFORMATION

Calories	339	Sugars	36g
Protein	3g	Fat	21g
Carbohydrate	37g	Saturates	10g

2½ HOURS 3 HOURS

SERVES 8

INGREDIENTS

- 4 egg whites
- 225 g/8 oz/1 cup light muscovado sugar
- 300 ml/½ pint double (heavy) or whipping cream
- 60 g/2 oz/½ cup pecan nuts
- 4 satsumas, peeled
- 1 passion fruit or pomegranate

1 Line 2 baking sheets (cookie sheets) with non-stick baking parchment or greaseproof paper. Draw a 23 cm/9 inch circle on one of them.

2 Whip the egg whites in a large grease-free bowl until stiff. Add the sugar gradually, continuing to beat until the mixture is very glossy.

3 Pipe or spoon a layer of meringue mixture on to the circle marked on the baking parchment; then pipe large rosettes or place spoonfuls on top of the meringue's outer edge. Pipe any remaining meringue mixture in tiny rosettes on the second baking sheet (cookie sheet).

4 Bake in a preheated oven, 140°C/275°F/Gas Mark 1 for 2–3 hours, making sure that the oven is well-ventilated by using a folded tea towel (dish cloth) to keep the door slightly open. Remove from the oven and leave to cool completely. When cold, peel off the baking parchment carefully.

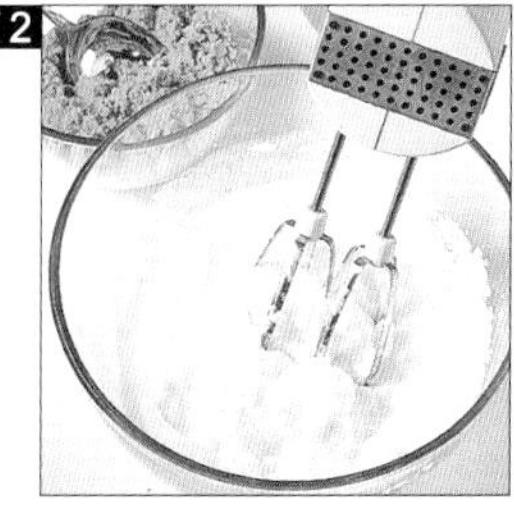

2

3

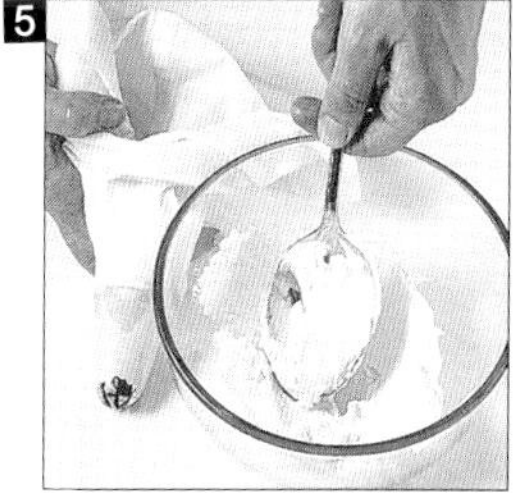

5

5 Whip the double (heavy) or whipping cream in a large chilled bowl until thick. Spoon about one-third into a piping bag, fitted with a star nozzle (tip). Reserve a few pecan nuts and 1 satsuma for decoration. Chop the remaining nuts and fruit, and fold into the remaining cream.

6 Pile on top of the meringue base and decorate with the tiny meringue rosettes, piped cream, segments of satsuma and pecan nuts. Scoop the seeds from the passion fruit or pomegranate with a teaspoon and sprinkle them on top.

Passion-Fruit Rice

This creamy rice pudding, adapted for the microwave, is spiced with cardamom, cinnamon and bay leaf and served with passion-fruit.

NUTRITIONAL INFORMATION

Calories	534	Sugars	42g
Protein	9g	Fat	22g
Carbohydrate	80g	Saturates	13g

1¼ HOURS 30 MINS

SERVES 4

INGREDIENTS

- 175 g/6 oz/scant 1 cup jasmine fragrant rice
- 600 ml/1 pint/2½ cups milk
- 125 g/4½ oz/½ cup caster (superfine) sugar
- 6 cardamom pods, split open
- 1 dried bay leaf
- 1 cinnamon stick
- 150 ml/¼ pint/⅔ cup double (heavy) cream, whipped
- 4 passion-fruit
- soft berry fruits, to decorate

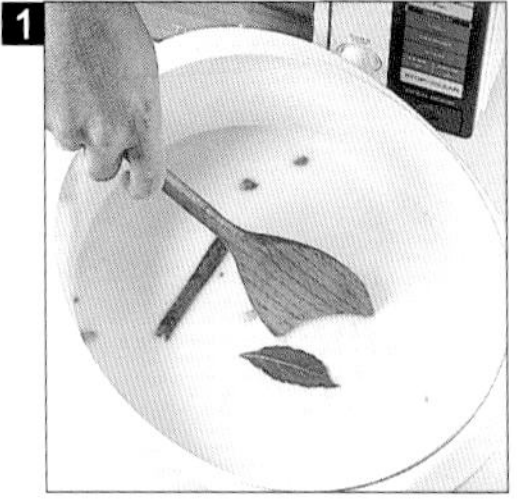

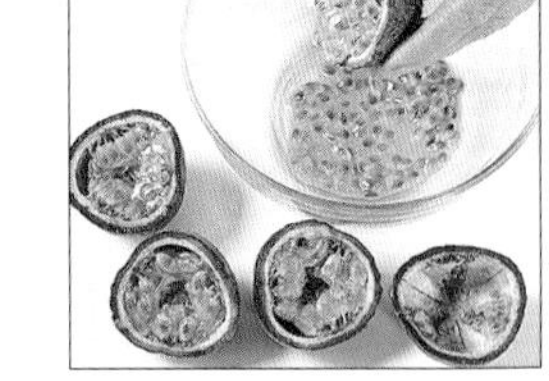

1 Place the jasmine fragrant rice in a large bowl with the milk, caster (superfine) sugar, cardamom pods, bay leaf and cinnamon stick. Cover and cook on medium power for 25–30 minutes, stirring occasionally. The rice should be just tender and have absorbed most of the milk. Add a little extra milk, if necessary.

2 Leave the rice to cool, still covered. Remove the bay leaf, cardamom husks and cinnamon stick.

3 Gently fold the cream into the cooled rice mixture.

4 Halve the passion-fruits and scoop out the centres into a bowl.

5 Layer the rice with the passion-fruit in 4 tall glasses, finishing with a layer of passion-fruit. Leave to chill in the refrigerator for 30 minutes.

6 Decorate the passion-fruit rice with soft berry fruits and serve immediately.

COOK'S TIP

If you are unable to obtain passion-fruit, you can use a purée of another fruit of your choice, such as kiwi fruit, raspberry or strawberry.

Apricot & Orange Jellies

These bright fruity little desserts are easy to make and taste so much better than shop-bought jellies. Serve them with low-fat ice cream.

NUTRITIONAL INFORMATION

Calories	206	Sugars	36g
Protein	8g	Fat	5g
Carbohydrate	36g	Saturates	3g

 4¼ HOURS  25 MINS

SERVES 4

INGREDIENTS

- 225 g/8 oz no-need-to-soak dried apricots
- 300 ml/½ pint/1¼ cups unsweetened orange juice
- 2 tbsp lemon juice
- 2–3 tsp clear honey
- 1 tbsp powdered gelatine
- 4 tbsp boiling water

TO DECORATE

- orange segments
- sprigs of mint

CINNAMON 'CREAM'

- 125 g/4½ oz medium-fat ricotta cheese
- 125 g/4½ oz low-fat natural fromage frais (unsweetened yogurt)
- 1 tsp ground cinnamon
- 1 tbsp clear honey

1 Place the apricots in a saucepan and pour in the orange juice. Bring to the boil, cover and simmer for 15–20 minutes until plump and soft. Cool for 10 minutes.

2 Transfer the mixture to a blender or food processor and blend until smooth. Stir in the lemon juice and add the honey. Pour the mixture into a measuring jug and make up to 600 ml/ 1 pint /2½ cups with cold water.

3 Dissolve the gelatine in the boiling water and stir into the apricot mixture.

4 Pour the mixture into 4 individual moulds (molds), each 150 ml/5 fl oz/⅔ cup, or 1 large mould, 600 ml/ 1 pint/2½ cups. Leave to chill until set.

5 Meanwhile, make the cinnamon 'cream'. Mix all the ingredients together and place in a small bowl. Cover the mixture and leave to chill until

6 To turn out the jellies, dip the moulds (molds) in hot water for a few seconds and invert on to serving plates.

7 Decorate with the orange segments and sprigs of mint. Serve with the cinnamon 'cream' dusted with extra cinnamon.

Orchard Fruits Bristol

An elegant fruit salad of poached pears and apples, oranges and strawberries in a wine and caramel syrup topped with crumbled caramel.

NUTRITIONAL INFORMATION

Calories	395	Sugars	94g
Protein	3g	Fat	0.5g
Carbohydrate	94g	Saturates	0g

30 MINS 20 MINS

SERVES 4

INGREDIENTS

- 4 oranges
- 175 g/6 oz/¾ cup granulated sugar
- 4 tbsp water
- 150 ml/¼ pint/⅔ cup white wine
- 4 firm pears
- 4 dessert (eating) apples
- 125 g/4½ oz/¾ cup strawberries

1 Pare the rind thinly from 1 orange and cut into narrow strips. Cook in the minimum of boiling water for 3–4 minutes until tender. Drain and reserve the liquor. Squeeze the juice from this and 1 other orange.

2 Lay a sheet of non-stick baking parchment on a baking sheet or board.

3 Heat the sugar gently in a pan until it melts, then continue without stirring until it turns a pale golden brown. Pour half the caramel quickly on to the parchment and leave to set.

4 Add the water and squeezed orange juice immediately to the caramel left in the pan with 150 ml/¼ pint/⅔ cup orange rind liquor. Heat until it melts, then add the wine and remove from the heat.

5 Peel, core and slice the pears and apples thickly (you can leave the apple skins on, if you prefer) and add to the caramel syrup. Bring gently to the boil and simmer for 3–4 minutes until just beginning to soften – they should still be firm in the centre. Transfer the fruits to a bowl.

6 Cut away the peel and pith from the remaining oranges and either ease out the segments or cut into slices, discarding any pips (seeds). Add to the other fruits. Hull the strawberries and halve, quarter or slice thickly depending on the size and add to the other fruits.

7 Add the orange strands to the syrup and bring back to the boil for 1 minute, then pour over the fruits. Leave until cold, then break up the caramel and sprinkle over the fruit. Cover and chill until ready to serve.

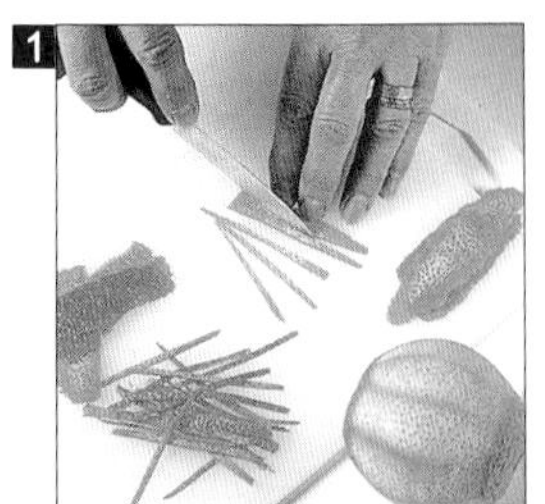
1

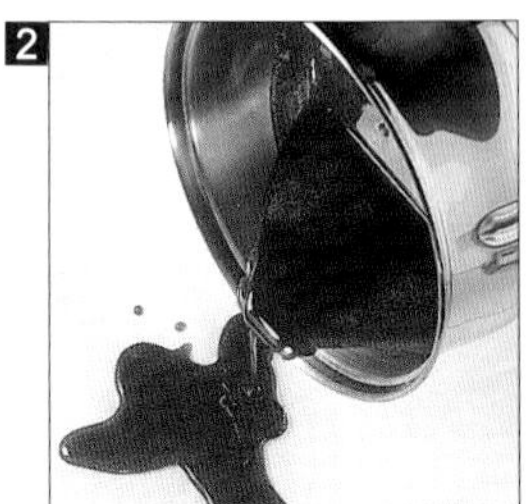
2

5

COOK'S TIP

The caramel will begin to melt when added to the fruit, so do this as near to serving as possible.

Brown Sugar Pavlovas

This simple combination of fudgey meringue topped with fromage frais (yogurt) and raspberries is the perfect finale to any meal.

NUTRITIONAL INFORMATION

Calories	155	Sugars	34g
Protein	5g	Fat	0.2g
Carbohydrate	35g	Saturates	0g

1 HOUR   1 HOUR

SERVES 4

INGREDIENTS

2 large egg whites

1 tsp cornflour (cornstarch)

1 tsp raspberry vinegar

100 g/3½ oz light muscovado sugar, crushed free of lumps

2 tbsp redcurrant jelly

2 tbsp unsweetened orange juice

150 ml/5 fl oz/⅔ cup low-fat natural fromage frais (unsweetened yogurt)

175 g/6 oz raspberries, thawed if frozen

rose-scented geranium leaves, to decorate (optional)

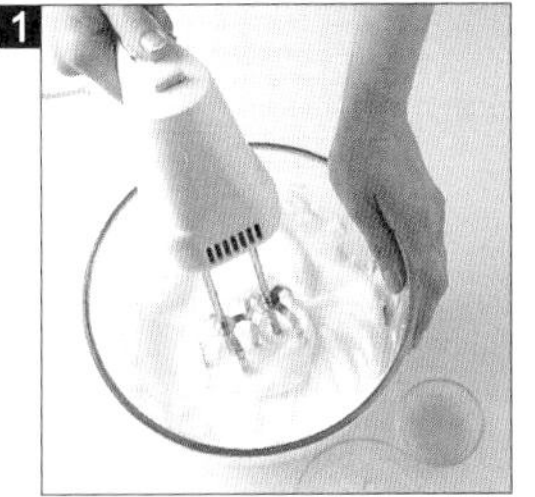

1 Preheat the oven to 150°C/300°F/Gas Mark 2. Line a large baking tray (cookie sheet) with baking parchment. Whisk the egg whites until very stiff and dry. Fold in the cornflour (cornstarch) and vinegar.

2 Gradually whisk in the sugar, a spoonful at a time, until the mixture is thick and glossy.

3 Divide the mixture into 4 and spoon on to the baking sheet, spaced well apart. Smooth each into a round, about 10 cm/4 inches across, and bake in the oven for 40–45 minutes until lightly browned and crisp. Leave to cool on the baking tray (cookie sheet).

4 Place the redcurrant jelly and orange juice in a small pan and heat, stirring, until melted. Leave to cool for 10 minutes.

5 Using a palette knife, carefully remove each pavlova from the baking parchment and transfer to a serving plate. Top with the fromage frais (unsweetened yogurt) and the raspberries. Glaze the fruit with the redcurrant jelly, and decorate with the geranium leaves (if using).

COOK'S TIP

Make a large pavlova by forming the meringue into a round, measuring 18 cm/7 inches across, on a lined baking tray (cookie sheet) and bake for 1 hour.

Upside-down Cake

This recipe shows how a classic favourite can be adapted for vegans by using vegetarian margarine and oil instead of butter and eggs.

NUTRITIONAL INFORMATION

Calories	354	Sugars	31g
Protein	3g	Fat	15g
Carbohydrate	56g	Saturates	2g

 15 MINS  50 MINS

SERVES 6

INGREDIENTS

- 50 g/1¾ oz/¼ cup vegan margarine, cut into small pieces, plus extra for greasing
- 425 g/15 oz can unsweetened pineapple pieces, drained and juice reserved
- 4 tsp cornflour (cornstarch)
- 50 g/1¾ oz/¼ cup soft brown sugar
- 125 ml/4 fl oz/½ cup water
- rind of 1 lemon

SPONGE

- 50 ml/2 fl oz/¼ cup sunflower oil
- 75 g/2¾ oz/⅓ cup soft brown sugar
- 150 ml/¼ pint/⅔ cup water
- 150 g/5½ oz/1¼ cups plain (all-purpose) flour
- 2 tsp baking powder
- 1 tsp ground cinnamon

2

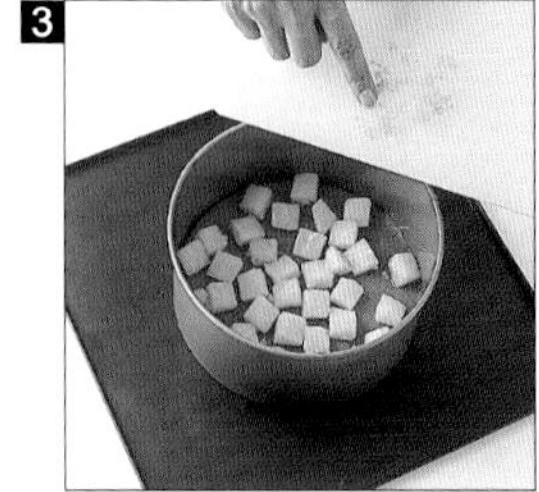
3

3

1 Grease a deep 18 cm/7 inch cake tin (pan). Mix the reserved juice from the pineapple with the cornflour (cornstarch) until it forms a smooth paste. Put the paste in a saucepan with the sugar, margarine and water and stir over a low heat until the sugar has dissolved. Bring to the boil and simmer for 2–3 minutes, until thickened. Set aside to cool slightly.

2 To make the sponge, place the oil, sugar and water in a saucepan. Heat gently until the sugar has dissolved; do not allow it to boil. Remove from the heat and leave to cool. Sift the flour, baking powder and ground cinnamon into a mixing bowl. Pour over the cooled sugar syrup and beat well to form a batter.

3 Place the pineapple pieces and lemon rind on the base of the prepared tin (pan) and pour over 4 tablespoons of the pineapple syrup. Spoon the sponge batter on top.

4 Bake in a preheated oven, 180°C/350°F/Gas Mark 4, for 35–40 minutes, until set and a fine metal skewer inserted into the centre comes out clean. Invert on to a plate, leave to stand for 5 minutes, then remove the tin (pan). Serve with the remaining syrup.

Almond Slices

A mouth-watering dessert that is sure to impress your guests, especially if it is served with whipped cream.

NUTRITIONAL INFORMATION

Calories	416	Sugars	37g
Protein	11g	Fat	26g
Carbohydrate	38g	Saturates	12g

 5 MINS   5 MINS

SERVES 8

INGREDIENTS

- 3 eggs
- 75 g/2¾ oz/½ cup ground almonds
- 200 g/7 oz/1½ cups milk powder
- 200 g/7 oz/1 cup sugar
- ½ tsp saffron strands
- 100 g/3½ oz/½ cup unsalted butter
- 25 g/1 oz/1 tbsp flaked (slivered) almonds

1 Beat the eggs together in a bowl and set aside.

2 Place the ground almonds, milk powder, sugar and saffron in a large mixing bowl and stir to mix well.

2

3 Melt the butter in a small saucepan. Pour the melted butter over the dry ingredients and mix well until thoroughly combined.

3

4 Add the reserved beaten eggs to the mixture and stir to blend well.

4

5 Spread the mixture in a shallow 15–20 cm/7–9 inch ovenproof dish and bake in a preheated oven, 160°C/325°F/Gas Mark 3, for 45 minutes. Test whether the cake is cooked through by piercing with the tip of a sharp knife or a skewer – it will come out clean if it is cooked thoroughly.

6 Cut the almond cake into slices. Decorate the almond slices with flaked (slivered) almonds and transfer to serving plates. Serve hot or cold.

COOK'S TIP

These almond slices are best eaten hot, but they may also be served cold. They can be made a day or even a week in advance and re-heated. They also freeze beautifully.

Fruit & Nut Loaf

This loaf is like a fruit bread which may be served warm or cold, perhaps spread with a little margarine or butter or topped with jam (jelly).

NUTRITIONAL INFORMATION

Calories	354	Sugars	36g
Protein	8g	Fat	9g
Carbohydrate	64g	Saturates	1.2g

35 MINS

40 MINS

SERVES 6

INGREDIENTS

- 225 g/8 oz/1¾ cups white bread flour, plus extra for dusting
- ½ tsp salt
- 1 tbsp margarine, plus extra for greasing
- 2 tbsp light brown sugar
- 100 g/3½ oz/⅔ cup sultanas (golden raisins)
- 50 g/1¾ oz/¼ cup ready-to-eat dried apricots, chopped
- 50 g/1¾ oz/½ cup chopped hazelnuts
- 2 tsp easy-blend dried (active dry) yeast
- 6 tbsp orange juice
- 6 tbsp natural (unsweetened) yogurt
- 2 tbsp strained apricot jam (jelly)

1

3

4

1 Sift the flour and salt into a mixing bowl. Add the margarine and rub in with the fingertips. Stir in the sugar, sultanas (golden raisins), apricots, nuts and yeast.

2 Warm the orange juice in a saucepan, but do not allow to boil.

3 Stir the warm orange juice into the flour mixture, together with the natural (unsweetened) yogurt and bring the mixture together to form a dough.

4 Knead the dough on a lightly floured surface for 5 minutes, until smooth and elastic. Shape into a round and place on a lightly greased baking tray (cookie sheet). Cover with a clean tea towel (dish cloth) and leave to rise in a warm place until doubled in size.

5 Cook the loaf in a preheated oven, 220°C/425°F/Gas Mark 7, for 35–40 minutes, until cooked through. Transfer to a wire rack and brush with the apricot jam. Leave to cool before serving.

VARIATION

You can vary the nuts according to whatever you have at hand – try chopped walnuts or almonds.

Baked Sweet Ravioli

These scrumptious little parcels are the perfect dessert for anyone with a really sweet tooth.

NUTRITIONAL INFORMATION

Calories	765	Sugars	56g
Protein	16g	Fat	30g
Carbohydrate	114g	Saturates	15g

 1½ HOURS  20 MINS

SERVES 4

INGREDIENTS

PASTA

- 425 g/15 oz/3¾ cups plain (all purpose) flour
- 140 g/5 oz/10 tbsp butter, plus extra for greasing
- 140 g/5 oz/¾ cup caster (superfine) sugar
- 4 eggs
- 25 g/1 oz yeast
- 125 ml/4 fl oz warm milk

FILLING

- 175 g/6 oz/⅔ cup chestnut purée (paste)
- 60 g/2 oz/½ cup cocoa powder
- 60 g/2 oz/¼ cup caster (superfine) sugar
- 60 g/2 oz/½ cup chopped almonds
- 60 g/2 oz/1 cup crushed amaretti biscuits (cookies)
- 175 g/6 oz/⅝ cup orange marmalade

1 To make the sweet pasta dough, sift the flour into a mixing bowl, then mix in the butter, sugar and 3 eggs.

2 Mix together the yeast and warm milk in a small bowl and when thoroughly combined, mix into the dough.

3 Knead the dough for 20 minutes, cover with a clean cloth and set aside in a warm place for 1 hour to rise.

4 Mix together the chestnut purée (paste), cocoa powder, sugar, almonds, crushed amaretti biscuits (cookies) and orange marmalade in a separate bowl.

5 Grease a baking tray (cookie sheet) with butter.

6 Lightly flour the work surface (counter). Roll out the pasta dough into a thin sheet and cut into 5 cm/2 inch rounds with a plain pastry cutter.

7 Put a spoonful of filling on to each round and then fold in half, pressing the edges to seal. Arrange on the prepared baking tray (cookie sheet), spacing the ravioli out well.

8 Beat the remaining egg and brush all over the ravioli to glaze. Bake in a preheated oven, at 180°C/350°F/Gas Mark 4, for 20 minutes. Serve hot.

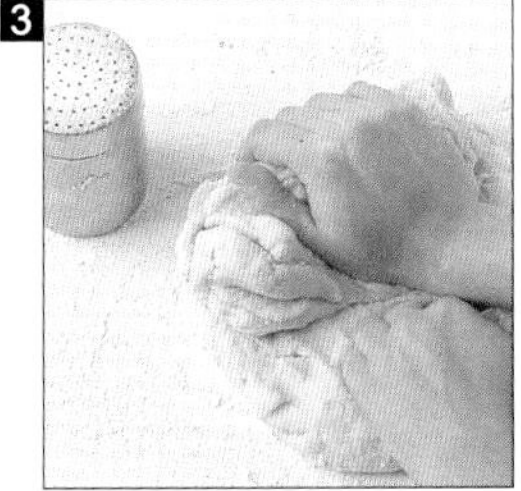
3

4

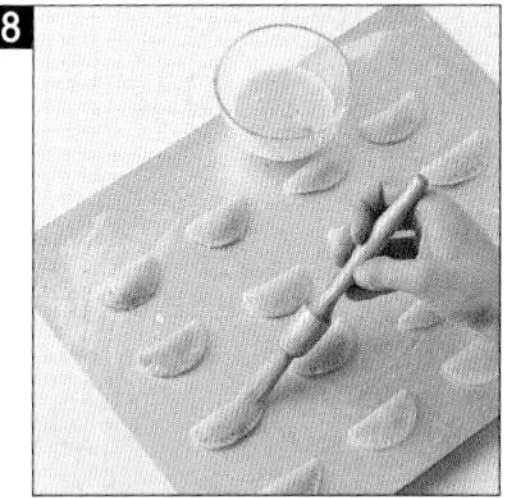
8

Tropical Salad

Paw-paws (papayas) are ready to eat when they yield to gentle pressure. Serve in the shells of baby pineapples for a stunning effect.

NUTRITIONAL INFORMATION			
Calories	69	Sugars	13g
Protein	1g	Fat	0.3g
Carbohydrate	14g	Saturates	0g

 10 MINS  0 MINS

SERVES 8

INGREDIENTS

- 1 paw-paw (papaya)
- 2 tbsp fresh orange juice
- 3 tbsp rum
- 2 bananas
- 2 guavas
- 1 small pineapple or 2 baby pineapples
- 2 passion-fruit
- pineapple leaves to decorate

1 Cut the paw-paw (papaya) in half and remove the seeds. Peel and slice the flesh into a bowl.

1

2 Pour over the orange juice together with the rum.

3 Slice the bananas, peel and slice the guavas, and add both to the bowl.

3

4 Cut the top and base from the pineapple, then cut off the skin.

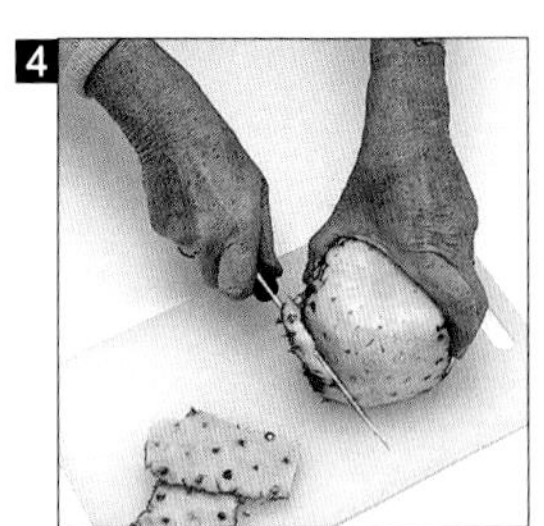
4

5 Slice the pineapple flesh, discard the core, cut into pieces and add to the bowl.

6 Halve the passion-fruit, scoop out the flesh with a teaspoon, add to the bowl and stir well to mix.

7 Spoon the salad into glass bowls and decorate with pineapple leaves.

COOK'S TIP

Guavas have a heavenly smell when ripe – their scent will fill a whole room. They should give to gentle pressure when ripe, and their skins should be yellow. The canned varieties are very good and have a pink tinge to the flesh.

Mixed Fruit Brûlées

Traditionally a rich mixture made with cream, this fruit-based version is just as tempting using natural (unsweetened) yogurt as a topping.

NUTRITIONAL INFORMATION	
Calories 165	Sugars 21g
Protein 5g	Fat 7g
Carbohydrate ...21g	Saturates 5g

 5 MINS  5 MINS

SERVES 4

INGREDIENTS

- 450 g/1 lb prepared assorted summer fruits (such as strawberries, raspberries, blackcurrants, redcurrants and cherries), thawed if frozen
- 150 ml/5 fl oz/¾ cup half-fat double (heavy) cream alternative
- 150 ml/5 fl oz/¾ cup low-fat natural fromage frais (unsweetened yogurt)
- 1 tsp vanilla essence (extract)
- 4 tbsp demerara (brown crystal) sugar

1

2

3

1 Divide the prepared strawberries, raspberries, blackcurrants, redcurrants and cherries evenly among 4 small heatproof ramekin dishes.

2 Mix together the half-fat cream alternative, fromage frais (unsweetened yogurt) and vanilla essence (extract) until well combined.

3 Generously spoon the mixture over the fruit in the ramekin dishes, to cover the fruit completely.

4 Preheat the grill (broiler) to hot.

5 Top each serving with 1 tbsp demerara (brown crystal) sugar and grill (broil) the desserts for 2–3 minutes, until the sugar melts and begins to caramelize. Leave to stand for a couple of minutes before serving.

COOK'S TIP

Look out for half-fat creams, in single and double (light and heavy) varieties. They are good substitutes for occasional use. Alternatively, in this recipe, omit the cream and double the quantity of fromage frais (yogurt) for a lower fat version.

Rich Chocolate Loaf

Another rich chocolate dessert, this loaf is very simple to make and can be served as a tea-time treat as well.

NUTRITIONAL INFORMATION

Calories	180	Sugars	16g
Protein	3g	Fat	11g
Carbohydrate	18g	Saturates	5g

 1¼ HOURS  5 MINS

MAKES 16 SLICES

INGREDIENTS

- 150 g/5½ oz dark chocolate
- 75 g/2¾ oz/6 tbsp butter, unsalted
- 210 g/7¼ oz tin of condensed milk
- 2 tsp cinnamon
- 75 g/2¾ oz almonds
- 75 g/2¾ oz amaretti biscuits (cookies), broken
- 50 g/1¾ oz dried no-need-to-soak apricots, roughly chopped

1 Line a 675 g/1½ lb loaf tin (pan) with a sheet of kitchen foil.

2 Using a sharp knife, roughly chop the almonds.

3 Place the chocolate, butter, milk and cinnamon in a heavy-based saucepan.

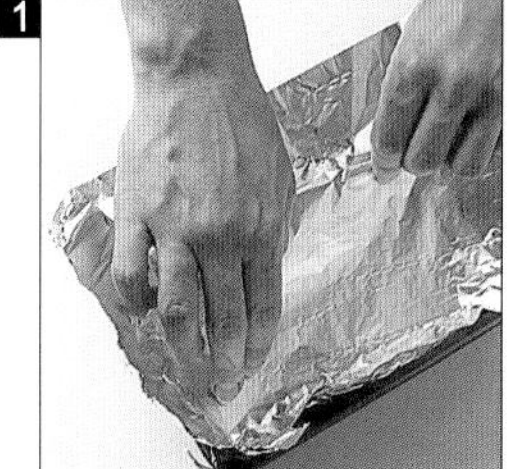
1

2

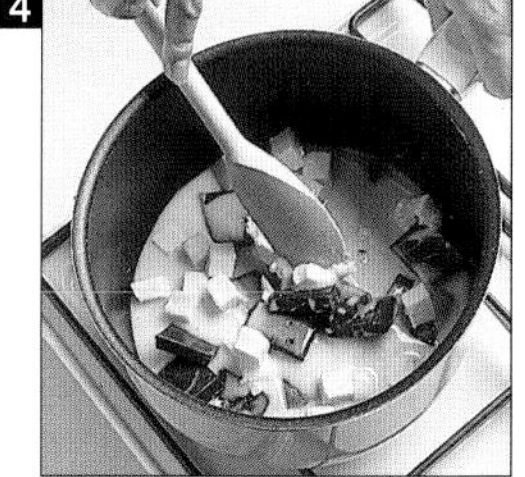
4

4 Heat the chocolate mixture over a low heat for 3–4 minutes, stirring with a wooden spoon, or until the chocolate has melted. Beat the mixture well.

5 Stir the almonds, biscuits and apricots into the chocolate mixture, stirring with a wooden spoon, until well mixed.

6 Pour the mixture into the prepared tin (pan) and leave to chill in the refrigerator for about 1 hour or until set.

7 Cut the rich chocolate loaf into slices to serve.

COOK'S TIP

To melt chocolate, first break it into manageable pieces. The smaller the pieces, the quicker it will melt.

Fresh Fruit Compôte

Elderflower cordial is used in the syrup for this refreshing fruit compôte, giving it a delightfully summery flavour.

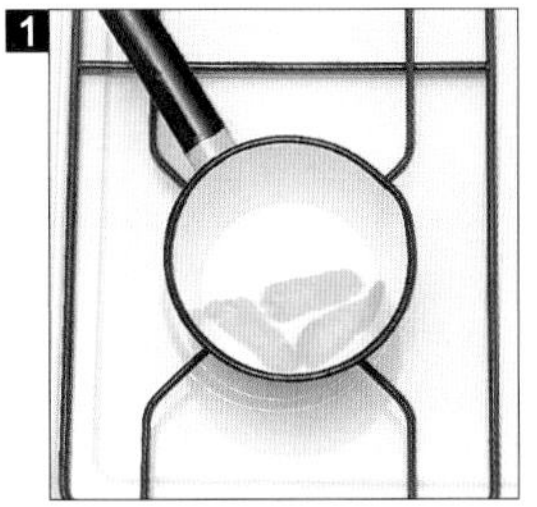

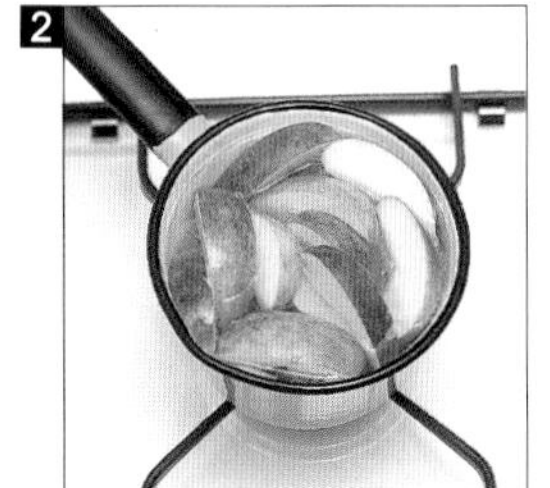

NUTRITIONAL INFORMATION

Calories	255	Sugars	61g
Protein	4g	Fat	1g
Carbohydrate	61g	Saturates	0.2g

20 MINS 15 MINS

SERVES 4

INGREDIENTS

- 1 lemon
- 60 g/2 oz/¼ cup caster (superfine) sugar
- 4 tbsp elderflower cordial
- 300 ml/½ pint/1¼ cups water
- 4 eating apples
- 225 g/8 oz/1 cup blackberries
- 2 fresh figs

TOPPING

- 150 g/5½ oz/⅔ cup thick natural (unsweetened) yogurt
- 2 tbsp clear honey

1 Thinly pare the rind from the lemon using a swivel vegetable peeler. Squeeze the juice. Put the lemon rind and juice into a saucepan, together with the sugar, elderflower cordial and water. Set over a low heat and simmer, uncovered, for 10 minutes.

2 Peel, core and slice the apples. Add the apples to the saucepan. Simmer gently for about 4–5 minutes, until just tender. Remove the pan from the heat and set aside to cool.

3 When cold, transfer the apples and syrup to a serving bowl and add the blackberries. Slice and add the figs. Stir gently to mix. Cover and chill in the refrigerator until ready to serve.

4 Spoon the yogurt into a small serving bowl and drizzle the honey over the top. Cover and chill before serving.

COOK'S TIP

Greek-style yogurt may be made from cow's or ewe's milk. The former is often strained to make it more concentrated and has a high fat content, which perfectly counterbalances the sharpness and acidity of fruit.

Index